Publication of the Max Planck Institute
for Comparative Public Law and International Law
Heidelberg

under the direction of

Jochen Abr. Frowein · Rüdiger Wolfrum

Karin Oellers-Frahm · Andreas Zimmermann (Eds.)

Dispute Settlement
in Public International Law

Texts and Materials

2nd completely revised and updated edition

Springer

Berlin Heidelberg New York Barcelona
Hongkong London
Mailand Paris Singapur Tokio

ISBN 3-540-41743-5 Springer-Verlag Berlin Heidelberg New York

Library of Congress Cataloging-in-Publication Data applied for
Die Deutsche Bibliothek – CIP-Einheitsaufnahme
Dispute settlement in public international law: texts and materials / ed.: Karin Oellers-Frahm; Andreas
Zimmermann. – 2. ed. – Berlin; Heidelberg; New York; Barcelona; Hong Kong; London; Milan; Paris;
Singapore; Tokyo: Springer, 2001
 ISBN 3-540-41743-5

Springer-Verlag Berlin Heidelberg New York
a member of BertelsmannSpringer Science+Business Media GmbH

http://www.springer.de

© by Max-Planck-Gesellschaft zur Förderung der Wissenschaften e.V., to be exercised by Max-Planck-In-
stitut für ausländisches öffentliches Recht und Völkerrecht, Heidelberg 2001
Printed in Germany

Cover design: Erich Kirchner, Heidelberg
SPIN 10797031   64/2202xz-5 4 3 2 1 0 – Printed on acid-free paper

Preface

Increasing awareness for the pacific settlement of disputes throughout the world and covering nearly all fields of international law has led to an impressive multiplication of instruments and institutions for dispute settlement, which accordingly made it necessary to envisage a revised and considerably enlarged second edition of this collection of texts and materials, the first edition of which was published in 1984.

The purpose and concept of the publication has, however, remained largely unchanged, namely to make available to researchers, scholars and practitioners in a reliable and appropriate format a collection of significant documents from this important area of international law, which in part may be rather difficult to find elsewhere.

As in the first edition, the documents reproduced here are designed to give an overview of judicial and arbitral institutions which are available for the settlement of international disputes in a broad sense. Accordingly the documents cover mainly, but not exclusively, disputes between States. In addition, texts related to international criminal law, such as the Statute of the ICTY, or to the protection of human rights, are also included.

As far as possible, the texts are reproduced in English in order to make them accessible to a wide public even if this version is sometimes not an authentic one. However, some documents were not available in English and have therefore been reproduced in another language.

The authors are aware of the obvious fact that not all existing relevant texts and materials will be found in this work. On the one hand, completeness in this field of international law can certainly be only an idealistic aim. On the other hand, a need for restrictions was imposed by the multitude and quantity of materials so that, sometimes, a difficult choice had to be made. In that regard, the main criterion for the selection of relevant institutions was that they should, as a matter of principle, be based upon arrangements already existing or be provided for in a treaty. The collection is, however, not limited to permanent institutions; it also includes those institutions which can be brought into existence unilaterally by one of the parties to a dispute through the selection of judges or arbitrators from a pre-prepared list. Nevertheless, as far as Parts I to V are concerned, one main selection criterion was always a certain degree of institutionalization, which cannot be found in ad hoc procedures. Accordingly, the arbitration clauses and compromissory clauses contained in Part VI have been included as examples to complete the picture of possible arbitral and judicial methods for the settlement of disputes.

Procedures and institutions created within the framework of international organizations have only been taken into account to the extent that they possess a quasi-judicial character. Thus, political and other procedures have been generally excluded. However, reporting systems created in the framework of human rights instruments and in other fields of international law, in particular as far as the protection of the environment is concerned, have been included especially where they may lead in the last resort to a judicial or quasi-judicial procedure. International administrative courts and tribunals with jurisdiction over the relations between international organizations and their respective officials have not been included. The same is true, albeit with some exceptions, as far as international commercial arbitration is concerned.

After intensive consideration, we decided to include all instruments contained in the first edition — unless they were since then superseded by more recent ones — even though some of them have lapsed in the meantime or are of mere historical significance in marking new developments or serving as models for later arrangements.

As to the presentation of the texts, the structure of the first edition is largely followed. The texts included first reproduce the relevant rules on the creation of the court or tribunal and its functions, usually but not exclusively laid down in a formal treaty; in the second place, the statute and rules and, where applicable, additional texts, such as internal rules or rules concerning legal aid are also reproduced. Where certain questions are regulated more than once in various texts governing the same forum or where identical or almost identical provisions exist for different institutions, e.g. as far as the ad hoc international criminal tribunals for Yugoslavia and Rwanda are concerned, a reference is made at the appropriate place.

The introductory notes, preceding the texts reproduced with regard to each court or tribunal, are limited to a general overview of the origins, aims and competence as well as the functioning of the individual institutions. The introductory remarks are followed by a list of the most accessible publications where the reader may find the relevant texts in the authentic and other languages. Where available, reference is also made to case reports. The bibliographical notes represent a selection only. They contain references to the sometimes extensive literature available for further study and in particular are designed to provide access to literature in different languages.

In conclusion, we would like to express our appreciation to Dr. Peter Macalister-Smith for his valuable assistance in the review of the manuscript and Angelika Schmidt for her inestimable engagement in preparing the manuscript and Alice Thomas for her care and attention in preparing the index.

Heidelberg, January 2001

                    Karin Oellers-Frahm   Andreas Zimmermann

Contents

Volume I

---

*   See also Supplement 1.

Volume II

Fourth Part: Subjects of a Technical Nature... 1075

---

*   See also Supplement 2.

Abbreviations

AFDI	Annuaire Français de Droit International
AJCL	American Journal of Comparative Law
AJIL	American Journal of International Law
Ann.IDI	Annuaire de l'Institut de Droit International
AP	Außenpolitik
ArchVR	Archiv des Völkerrechts
AS	Sammlung der eidgenössischen Gesetze. Amtliche Sammlung der Bundesgesetze und Verordnungen
ASIL	American Society of International Law
BayVerwBl.	Bayerische Verwaltungsblätter
BGBl.	Bundesgesetzblatt
BGBl. (Austria)	Österreichisches Bundesgesetzblatt
BYIL	British Yearbook of International Law
CanYIL	Canadian Yearbook of International Law
CDE	Cahiers de droit européen
CIM	Convention internationale concernant le transport des marchandises par chemins de fer (International Convention Concerning the Carriage of Goods by Rail)
CIV	Convention internationale concernant le transport des voyageurs et des bagages par chemins de fer (International Convention Concerning the Carriage of Passengers and Luggage by Rail)
Clunet	Journal de Droit International
Cmnd.	Command Papers
ColJTransL	Columbia Journal of Transnational Law
COTIF	Convention relative aux transports internationaux ferroviaires (Convention on the International Transport by Rail)
CSCE	Conference on Security and Cooperation in Europe
DJZ	Deutsche Juristenzeitung
EA	Europa-Archiv
ECSC	European Coal and Steel Community
EEC	European Economic Community
EJIL	European Journal of International Law
EPIL	Encyclopedia of Public International Law
ESO	European Organization for Astronomical Research in the Southern Hemisphere
EuGRZ	Europäische Grundrechte-Zeitschrift
EuR	Europarecht
Euratom	European Atomic Energy Community

EUROCHEMIC	European Company for the Chemical Processing of Irridiated Fuels
Fontes	Fontes Iuris Gentium
FRG	Federal Republic of Germany
Georgia JICL	Georgia Journal of International and Comparative Law
Harvard ILJ	Harvard International Law Journal
HRLJ	Human Rights Law Journal
ICAO	International Civil Aviation Organization
ICLQ	International and Comparative Law Quarterly
ICSID	International Centre for Settlement of Investment Disputes
IJIL	Indian Journal of International Law
ILA Reports	International Law Association, Reports
ILJ	International Law Journal
ILM	International Legal Materials
IMCO	Intergovernmental Maritime Consultative Organization
INTELSAT	International Telecommunications Satellite Organization
JALC	Journal of Air Law and Commerce
JIR	Jahrbuch für Internationales Recht
J.O.	Journal Officiel de la République Française, Edition Lois et Décrets
JöR	Jahrbuch des öffentlichen Rechts
JW	Juristische Wochenschrift
JWTL	Journal of World Trade Law
JZ	Juristenzeitung
LJ	Law Journal
LNTS	League of Nations Treaty Series
LR	Law Review
MartensR	Martens Recueil de Traités
Martens NRG2	Martens Nouveau Recueil Général de Traités, 2me Série
Martens NRG3	Martens Nouveau Recueil Général de Traités, 3me Série
MB	Moniteur Belge
Misc.	Miscellaneous
NILR	Netherlands International Law Review
NordTIR	Nordisk Tidsskrift for International Ret
NQHR	Netherlands Quarterly of Human Rights
NTIR	Nederlands Tijdschrift voor Internationaal Recht
OAPEC	Arab Organization for the Petroleum Exporting Countries
OAS	Organization of American States
OAU	Organization of African Unity
OECD	Organization for Economic Co-operation and Development
OEEC	Organization for European Economic Cooperation
ÖJZ	Österreichische Juristenzeitung
ÖZöR	Österreichische Zeitschrift für öffentliches Recht
RabelsZ	Rabels Zeitschrift für ausländisches und internationales Privatrecht
RdC	Académie de Droit International, Recueil des Cours
Rev.belge	Revue belge de droit international

Rev.égypt.DI	Revue égyptienne de droit international
Revista IIDH	Revista Instituto Interamericano de Derechos Humanos
RFSP	Revue Française de Science Politique
RGBl.	Reichsgesetzblatt
RGDIP	Revue Générale de Droit International Public
RIAA	Reports of International Arbitral Awards
RIW	Recht der Internationalen Wirtschaft
Schweiz.JIR	Schweizerisches Jahrbuch für internationales Recht
T.B.	Tractatenblad van het Koninkrijk der Nederlanden
Texas ILJ	Texas International Law Journal
TIAS	Treaties and Other International Acts Series
TS	Treaty Series
UNTS	United Nations Treaty Series
UST	United States Treaties and Other International Agreements
VRÜ	Verfassung und Recht in Übersee
Virginia JIL	Virginia Journal of International Law
WTO	World Trade Organization
ZaöRV	Zeitschrift für ausländisches öffentliches Recht und Völkerrecht
ZLW	Zeitschrift für Luft- und Weltraumrecht
ZV	Zeitschrift für Völkerrecht

Selected Bibliography Concerning the Settlement of International Disputes in General

Anand, R. P.: International Courts and Contemporary Conflicts (1974)

Ascher, A.: Wesen und Grenzen der internationalen Schiedsgerichtsbarkeit als Grundlage für das Völkerrecht der Zukunft (1929)

Bardonnet, D. (ed.): Le règlement pacifique des différends internationaux en Europe, Colloque 6–8 sept. 1990 (1991)

Bastid, S.: La fonction juridictionnelle dans les relations internationales (1957)

Bayer, W. F.: Das Wesen der internationalen Schiedsgerichtsbarkeit (1953)

Bernhardt, R. (ed.): Encyclopedia of Public International Law, Instalment 1: Settlement of Disputes (1981) updated and arranged in alphabetical order in Vol. I (1992); Vol. II (1995), Vol. III (1997) and Vol. IV (2001)

Boczek, B. A.: Historical dictionary of international tribunals (1994)

Bos, M.: Les conditions du procès en droit international public (1957)

Boulery, C.: Bibliography on peaceful settlement of international disputes (1990)

Bowett, D. W.: Contemporary developments in legal techniques in the settlement of disputes, RdC Vol. 189 (1983 II), 169–236

Brendt, W.: Das Obligatorium in der internationalen Schiedsgerichtsbarkeit (1928)

Brus, M.: Third party dispute settlement in an interdependent world: developing a theoretical framework (1995)

Bulterman, M. K. (ed.): Compliance with judgments of international courts: proceedings of the symposium organized in honour of Professor Henry G. Schermers by Mordenate College and the Department of International Public Law of Leiden University (1996)

Caflisch, L. (ed.): Règlement pacifique des différends entre Etats: perspectives universelle et européenne (1998)

Carlston, K. S.: The Process of International Arbitration (1946)

Chapal, Ph.: L'arbitrabilité des différends internationaux (1967)

Charney, J. I.: Is international law threatened by multiple international tribunals? RdC Vol. 271 (1998), 101–382

Chaudri, M. A.: The Prospects of International Arbitration (1966)

Chayes, A.: International Legal Process: Materials for an Introductory Course (1968/69)

Clad, C.: Wesen und Grenzen der internationalen Schiedsgerichtsbarkeit als Grundlage für das Völkerrecht der Zukunft (1928)

Collier, J. G.: The settlement of disputes in international law: institutions and procedures (1999)

Compétence obligatoire des instances judiciaires et arbitrales internationales, Ann.IDI Vol. 47 (1957 I), pp. 34–322; Vol. 48 (1959 II), pp.55–177, 358–366

Corten, O.: L'utilisation du "raisonnable" par le juge international: discours juridique, raison et contradictions (1997)

Cory, H. M.: Compulsory Arbitration of International Disputes (1932)

DeVisscher, C.: De l'équité dans le règlement arbitral ou judiciaire des litiges du droit international public (1972)

L'extension de l'arbitrage obligatoire et de la compétence obligatoire de la Cour Permanente de Justice Internationale, Ann.IDI Vol. 33 (1927), pp. 669–833; Vol. 35 (1929 I), pp. 467–504; Vol. 35 (1929 II), pp. 170–183, 303–304

Grieves, F. L.: Supranationalism and International Adjudication (1969)

Handbook on the Peaceful Settlement of Disputes between States, United Nations, Office of Legal Affairs (1992)

Hudson, M. O.: International Tribunals (1944)

Hudson, M. O.: International Tribunals, Past and Future (1944)

Infante Caffe, M. T. (ed.): Solución judicial de controversias: el derecho internacional ante los tribunales internacionales e internos (1995)

International Disputes. The Legal Aspects (1972)

Janis, W. M. (ed.): International Courts for the Twenty-First Century (1992)

Jenks, C. W.: The Prospects of International Adjudication (1964)

Judicial and Arbitral Settlement of International Disputes Involving more than Two States, Ann.IDI Vol. 68 (1999 I), 60–153

Judicial Settlement of International Disputes. International Court of Justice — Other Courts and Tribunals — Arbitration and Conciliation. An International Symposium (Beiträge zum ausländischen öffentlichen Recht und Völkerrecht, Vol. 62) (1974)

Kazazi, M.: Burden of Proof and Related Issues: a Study on Evidence before International Tribunals (1996)

Klecker, S.-M.: Peaceful settlement of disputes in international law: international law bibliography (1985)

La méthode de travail du juge international: actes de la journée d'études du 23 novembre 1996, organisée par M. Kdhir (1997)

Lammasch, H.: Die Lehre von der Schiedsgerichtsbarkeit in ihrem ganzen Umfang (1914)

Lammasch, H.: Die Rechtskraft internationaler Schiedssprüche (1913)

Lillich, R. B. (ed.): Fact-Finding before International Tribunals (1992)

Loder, B. C. J.: La différence entre l'arbitrage international et la justice internationale (1923)

Mahrouk, M.: Les exceptions de procédure devant les juridictions internationales (1966)

Malca, C.: El arbitraje internacional (1948)

von Mangoldt, H.: Die Schiedsgerichtsbarkeit als Mittel internationaler Streitschlichtung. Zur Beilegung von Rechtsstreitigkeiten auf der Grundlage der Achtung vor dem Rechte (Beiträge zum ausländischen öffentlichen Recht und Völkerrecht, Vol. 63) (1974)

Mani, V.: International Adjudication. Procedural Aspects (1980)

Mavungu, Mvumbi-di-Ngoma: Le règlement judiciaire des différends en Afrique (1992)

McNair, A.: The Development of International Justice (1954)

Merrills, J. G.: International Dispute Settlement (1998)

Morelli, G.: Nuovi studi sul processo internazionale (1972)

Nantwi, E. K.: The Enforcement of International Judicial Decisions and Arbitral Awards in Public International Law (1966)

Neuhold, H.: Internationale Konflikte — verbotene und erlaubte Mittel ihrer Austragung (1977)

Nippold, O.: Die Fortbildung des Verfahrens in völkerrechtlichen Streitigkeiten (1907)

Oppenheim, L./H. Lauterpacht: Oppenheim's International Law, Vol. 1: Peace (9th ed. 1992);

Pacific settlement of disputes: diplomatic, judicial, political (1991), Thesaurus acroasium of the Institute of public international law and international relations of Thessaloniki

Pazartzis, P.: Les engagements internationaux en matière de règlement pacifique des différends entre états (1992)

Politis, N.: La Justice internationale (1924)

Procédure arbitrale, Ann.IDI Vol. 33 (1927 II), pp. 565–668

Il processo internazionale. Studi in onore di Gaetano Morelli, Comunicazioni e Studi Vol. 14 (1975)

Ralston, J. H.: International Arbitration from Athens to Locarno (1929)

Ralston, J. H.: The Law and Procedure of International Tribunals (1926), Suppl. to 1926 (rev. ed. 1936)

Reisman, W. M.: Nullity and Revision (1971)

Reisman, W. M.: The supervisory jurisdiction of the International Court of Justice: international arbitration and international adjudication, RdC Vol. 258 (1996), 13–394

Reisman, W. M. (ed.): Jurisdiction in International Law (1999)

Rideau, J.: Juridictions internationales et contrôle du respect des traités constitutifs des organisations internationales (1969)

Rosenne, S.: The Law and Practice of the International Court, 1920–1996 (1997)

Il ruolo del giudice internazionale nell'evoluzione del diritto internazionale e comunitario: atti del Convegno di studi in memoria di Gaetano Morelli organizzato dall'Università di Reggio Calabria (1995)

Sandifer, D. V.: Evidence Before International Tribunals (1975)

Schindler, D.: Die Schiedsgerichtsbarkeit seit 1914 (1938)

Seidl-Hohenveldern, I.: Die Grenzen rechtlicher Streiterledigung im Völkerrecht und in internationalen Organisationen, Berichte der Deutschen Gesellschaft für Völkerrecht, Vol. 9 (1969), pp. 1–75

Sereni, A. P.: Principi generali di diritto e processo internazionale (1955)

Simpson, J. L./H. Fox: International Arbitration (1959)

Sohn, L. B.: The Function of International Arbitration Today, RdC Vol. 108 (1963 I), pp. 1–113

Sohn, L. B.: Report on International Arbitration. International Law Association, Report of the Fifty-Second Conference (1966), pp. 323–356

Sohn, L. B.: Settlement of Disputes relating to the Interpretation and Application of Treaties, RdC Vol. 150 (1976 II), pp.195–254

Stone, J.: Legal Controls of International Conflict (2nd. ed. 1959)

Stoykovitch, S.: De l'autorité de la sentence arbitrale en droit international public (1924)

Stuyt, A. M.: The General Principles of Law as Applied by International Tribunals to Disputes on Attribution and Exercise of State Jurisdiction (1946)

Teymouri, E.: L'évolution de l'Arbitrage international au XXème siècle (1958)

Treves, T.: Le controversie internazionali: nuove tendenze, nuovi tribunali (1999)

del Vecchio, A.: Le parti nel processo internazionale (1975)

Verzijl, J. H. W.: International Law in Historical Perspective, Part 8: Inter-State Disputes and their Settlement (1976)

Weckel, P. (ed.): Le juge international et l'aménagement de l'espace: la spécificité du contentieux territorial (1998)

Wetter, J.: The International Arbitral Process: Public and Private (1979)

Witenberg, J. C.: L'organisation judiciaire. La procédure et la sentence internationales. Traité pratique (1937)

Wühler, N.: Die internationale Schiedsgerichtsbarkeit in der völkerrechtlichen Praxis der Bundesrepublik Deutschland (1985)

Volume I

First Part:
General Agreements

I. Universal Agreements

1. Hague Convention for the Pacific Settlement of International Disputes

When the Czarist government invited other States to hold a conference in 1898 to serve the maintenance of peace and to reduce excessive armaments as well as to promote peaceful means for avoiding armed conflicts, it initiated one of the crucial developments towards the pacific settlement of international disputes on a universal basis. The acceptance of established procedures for the settlement of disputes was widely regarded as the only alternative to the resort to arms. Thus, the codification and further development of previous procedures of dispute settlement, particularly arbitration, became principal subjects of the first Hague Peace Conference which adopted the Convention for the Pacific Settlement of International Disputes. This Convention of July 29, 1899 contained detailed provisions for various methods of pacific settlement of disputes, namely arbitration, good offices and mediation.

Concerning arbitration, the Convention provided, in Title IV, for the creation of a permanent mechanism to enable arbitral tribunals to be set up as necessary consisting of a panel of jurists known as the Permanent Court of Arbitration. The panel members were designated by the States party to the Convention, each State being entitled to designate up to four jurists. The Permanent Court of Arbitration was established in 1900 and began operating in 1902. The Convention further created a permanent Bureau located at The Hague with functions corresponding to those of a court registry or a Secretariat and laid down a set of rules of procedure to govern the conduct of an arbitration.

In 1907, at the second Hague Peace Conference, the second Convention for the Pacific Settlement of International Disputes was adopted. This Convention left essentially intact the institution of the Permanent Court as well as the rules governing the arbitral and conciliation procedure. It set forth a procedure for international inquiry commissions and, in Art. 53, provided for cases in which the parties would not agree upon an arbitration treaty (compromis). According to Art. 45 the parties are only entitled to choose one jurist of their own nationality in designating the judges for an arbitral tribunal. Agreement to create a permanent tribunal of judges serving exclusively this purpose, though supported by several members of the Conference, could not be reached at that time. Nevertheless, the Permanent Court of Arbitration has made a positive contribution to the development of international law. There are presently 85 parties to the Convention entitled to designate jurists on the Court's panel. Until 1928, the Permanent Court of Arbitration was resorted to in 19 cases; since then six special arbitral tribunals have been drawn from the panel of the Permanent Court.

As the use made of the Permanent Court of Arbitration was not considered to be satisfactory, the Administrative Council of the Court charged the Bureau in 1959 to examine the question in which way the Permanent Court of Arbitration might play a more active role in the pacific settlement of disputes. In a note of March 3, 1960 (AJIL 54 (1960) 933–941) the Secretary General stated *inter alia* that the Permanent Court of Arbitration was also open for disputes in cases in which only one party was a State. Rules for such a procedure were elaborated in 1962 (text in J. G. Wetter, The International Arbitral Process: Public and Private, 1979, Vol. V, 53–64). In 1991 a Working Group was created in order to analyse the reason for the still relative indifference to the Permanent Court of Arbitration by States. As a follow-up of its analysis the International Bureau adopted various means to make the potential and flexibility of dispute settlement procedure by the Permanent Court of Arbitration better known. Furthermore, a new set of procedural rules were adopted, namely the 1992 "Optional Rules for Arbitrating Disputes Between Two States" (see infra b)), and in 1993 the "Arbitration Rules for Arbitrating Disputes between Two Parties of which only one is a State (effective on July 6, 1993) and the "Optional Rules for Arbitration involving International Organizations and States", effective July 1, 1996 as well as the "Optional Rules for Arbitration Between International Organizations and Private Parties, effective July 1, 1996 (all published by the Permanent Court of Arbitration). These rules follow the same pattern and differ only in details due to the particularity of the kind of arbitration concerned. As an example, only the "Rules for Arbitrating Disputes between two States" are reproduced.

Texts

Conventions pour le règlement pacifique des conflits internationaux 1899: Martens NRG2 Vol. 26, pp. 920–946; 1907: Martens NRG3 Vol. 3, pp. 360–407 (French)

RGBl. 1910, pp. 5–54 (French and German)

J. B. Scott (ed.), The Hague Conventions and Declarations of 1899 and 1907 (1915) (English)

Carnegie Endowment for International Peace, The Proceedings of the Hague Peace Conferences, Translation of the official texts, 5 vols. (1920)

Max Habicht, Post-War Treaties for the Pacific Settlement of International Disputes, 1931, p. 902 ss

Bibliographical notes

Ch. Meurer, Das Friedensrecht der Haager Konferenz (Die Haager Friedenskonferenz, Vol. 1, passim; Vol. 2, pp. 211–291) (1905)

H. Wehberg, Kommentar zu dem Haager Abkommen betreffend die friedliche Erledigung von internationalen Streitigkeiten vom 18. Oktober 1907 (1911)

M. O. Hudson, The Permanent Court of Arbitration, AJIL Vol. 27 (1933), pp. 440–460

J. P. A. François, La Cour Permanente d'Arbitrage, RdC Vol. 87 (1955 I), pp. 460–551

J. P. A. François, Le développement future de la Cour Permanente d'Arbitrage, NTIR Vol. 9 (1962), pp. 264 – 272

H.-J. Schlochauer, Permanent Court of Arbitration, in: R. Bernhardt (ed.), Encyclopedia of Public International Law, Vol. III (1997), pp. 981–988 with further bibliographical indications

W.E. Butler, The Hague Permanent Court of Arbitration, in: M.W. Janis (ed.), International Courts for the Twenty-First Century (1992), pp. 43–53

J.L. Bleich, A New Direction for the PCA: The Work of the Expert Group, Leiden Journal of International Law, Vol. 6 (1993), pp. 215–240

Collection of cases

W. Schücking, Das Werk vom Haag, Series 2, Vol. 1: Die Judikatur des Ständigen Schiedshofs von 1899–1913 (Parts 1–3) (1914–1917)

Fontes Iuris Gentium A I 2, Digest of the Decisions of the Permanent Court of Arbitration 1902– 1928 (1931)

J.B. Scott (ed.), The Hague Court reports, Vols. 1–2 (1916–1932)

Bureau de la Cour Permanente d'Arbitrage: Analyses des sentences rendues par les Tribunaux d'arbitrage constitués conformément aux stipulations des Conventions de La Haye de 1899 et 1907 (1934)

O. Brintzinger, Die bisher ergangenen Schiedssprüche des Ständigen Schiedshofes, JIR Vol. 10 (1961/62), pp. 273–284

a) Convention for the Pacific Settlement of International Disputes Signed at The Hague on October 18, 1907 (Second Hague Convention)

PART I. — THE MAINTENANCE OF GENERAL PEACE

Art. 1   With a view to obviating as far as possible recourse to force in the relations between States, the contracting Powers agree to use their best efforts to insure the pacific settlement of international differences.

PART II. — GOOD OFFICES AND MEDIATION

Art. 2   In case of serious disagreement or dispute, before an appeal to arms, the contracting Powers agree to have recourse, as far as circumstances allow, to the good offices or mediation of one or more friendly Powers.

Art. 3   Independently of this recourse, the contracting Powers deem it expedient and desirable that one or more Powers, strangers to the dispute, should, on their own initiative and as far as circumstances may allow, offer their good offices or mediation to the States at variance.

Powers strangers to the dispute have the right to offer good offices or mediation even during the course of hostilities.

The exercise of this right can never be regarded by either of the parties in dispute as an unfriendly act.

Art. 4   The part of the mediator consists in reconciling the opposing claims and appeasing the feelings of resentment which may have arisen between the States at variance.

Art. 5   The functions of the mediator are at an end when once it is declared, either by one of the parties to the dispute or by the mediator himself, that the means of reconciliation proposed by him are not accepted.

Art. 6   Good offices and mediation undertaken either at the request of the parties in dispute or on the initiative of Powers strangers to the dispute have exclusively the character of advice, and never have binding force.

Art. 7   The acceptance of mediation can not, unless there be an agreement to the contrary, have the effect of interrupting, delaying, or hindering mobilization or other measures of preparation for war.

If it takes place after the commencement of hostilities, the military operations in progress are not interrupted in the absence of an agreement to the contrary.

Art. 8   The contracting Powers are agreed in recommending the application, when circumstances allow, of special mediation in the following form: In case of a serious difference endangering peace, the States at variance choose respectively a Power, to which they intrust the mission of entering into direct communication with the Power chosen on the other side, with the object of preventing the rupture of pacific relations.

For the period of this mandate, the term of which, unless otherwise stipulated, can not exceed thirty days, the States in dispute cease from all direct communication on the subject of the dispute, which is regarded as referred exclusively to the mediating Powers, which must use their best efforts to settle it.

In case of a definite rupture of pacific relations, these Powers are charged with the joint task of taking advantage of any opportunity to restore peace.

PART III. — INTERNATIONAL COMMISSIONS OF INQUIRY

Art. 9   In disputes of an international nature involving neither honor nor vital interests, and arising from a difference of opinion on points of fact, the contracting Powers deem it expedient and desirable that the parties who have not been able to come to an agreement by means of diplomacy, should, as far as circumstances allow, institute an international commission of inquiry, to facilitate a solution of these disputes by elucidating the facts by means of an impartial and conscientious investigation.

Art. 10   International commissions of inquiry are constituted by special agreement between the parties in dispute.

The inquiry convention defines the facts to be examined; it determines the mode and time in which the commission is to be formed and the extent of the powers of the commissioners.

It also determines, if there is need, where the commission is to sit, and whether it may remove to another place, the language the commission shall use and the languages the use of which shall be authorized before it, as well as the date on which each party must deposit its statement of facts, and, generally speaking, all the conditions upon which the parties have agreed.

If the parties consider it necessary to appoint assessors, the convention of inquiry shall determine the mode of their selection and the extent of their powers.

Art. 11   If the inquiry convention has not determined where the commission is to sit, it will sit at The Hague.

The place of meeting, once fixed, can not be altered by the commission except with the assent of the parties.

If the inquiry convention has not determined what languages are to be employed, the question shall be decided by the commission.

Art. 12   Unless an undertaking is made to the contrary, commissions of inquiry shall be formed in the manner determined by Articles 45 and 57 of the present Convention.

Art. 13   Should one of the commissioners or one of the assessors, should there be any, either die, or resign, or be unable for any reason whatever to discharge his functions, the same procedure is followed for filling the vacancy as was followed for appointing him.

Art. 14   The parties are entitled to appoint special agents to attend the commission of inquiry, whose duty it is to represent them and to act as intermediaries between them and the commission.

They are further authorized to engage counsel or advocates, appointed by themselves, to state their case and uphold their interests before the commission.

Art. 15   The International Bureau of the Permanent Court of Arbitration acts as registry for the commissions which sit at The Hague, and shall place its offices and staff at the disposal of the contracting Powers for the use of the commission of inquiry.

Art. 16   If the commission meets elsewhere than at The Hague, it appoints a secretary general, whose office serves as registry.

It is the function of the registry, under the control of the president, to make the necessary arrangements for the sittings of the commission, the preparation of the minutes, and, while the inquiry lasts, for the charge of the archives, which shall subsequently be transferred to the International Bureau at The Hague.

Art. 17   In order to facilitate the constitution and working of commissions of inquiry, the contracting Powers recommend the following rules, which shall be applicable to the inquiry procedure in so far as the parties do not adopt other rules.

Art. 18   The commission shall settle the details of the procedure not covered by the special inquiry convention or the present Convention, and shall arrange all the formalities required for dealing with the evidence.

Art. 19   On the inquiry both sides must be heard.

At the dates fixed, each party communicates to the commission and to the other party the statements of facts, if any, and, in all cases, the instruments, papers, and documents which it considers useful for ascertaining the truth, as well as the list of witnesses and experts whose evidence it wishes to be heard.

Art. 20   The commission is entitled, with the assent of the Powers, to move temporarily to any place where it considers it may be useful to have recourse to this means of inquiry or to send one or more of its members. Permission must be obtained from the State on whose territory it is proposed to hold the inquiry.

Art. 21   Every investigation, and every examination of a locality, must be made in the presence of the agents and counsel of the parties or after they have been duly summoned.

Art. 22   The commission is entitled to ask from either party for such explanations and information as it considers necessary.

Art. 23   The parties undertake to supply the commission of inquiry, as fully as they may think possible, with all means and facilities necessary to enable it to become completely acquainted with, and to accurately understand, the facts in question.

They undertake to make use of the means at their disposal, under their municipal law, to insure the appearance of the witnesses or experts who are in their territory and have been summoned before the commission.

If the witnesses or experts are unable to appear before the commission, the parties will arrange for their evidence to be taken before the qualified officials of their own country.

Art. 24   For all notices to be served by the commission in the territory of a third contracting Power, the commission shall apply direct to the Government of the said Power. The same rule applies in the case of steps being taken on the spot to procure evidence.

The requests for this purpose are to be executed so far as the means at the disposal of the Power applied to under its municipal law allow. They can not be rejected unless the Power in question considers they are calculated to impair its sovereign rights or its safety.

The commission will equally be always entitled to act through the Power on whose territory it sits.

Art. 25   The witnesses and experts are summoned on the request of the parties or by the commission of its own motion, and, in every case, through the Government of the State in whose territory they are.

The witnesses are heard in succession and separately, in the presence of the agents and counsel, and in the order fixed by the commission.

Art. 26   The examination of witnesses is conducted by the president.

The members of the commission may however put to each witness questions which they consider likely to throw light on and complete his evidence, or get information on any point concerning the witness within the limits of what is necessary in order to get at the truth.

The agents and counsel of the parties may not interrupt the witness when he is making his statement, nor put any direct question to him, but they may ask the president to put such additional questions to the witness as they think expedient.

Art. 27   The witness must give his evidence without being allowed to read any written draft. He may, however, be permitted by the president to consult notes or documents if the nature of the facts referred to necessitates their employment.

Art. 28   A minute of the evidence of the witness is drawn up forthwith and read to the witness. The latter may make such alterations and additions as he thinks necessary, which will be recorded at the end of his statement.

When the whole of his statement has been read to the witness, he is asked to sign it.

Art. 29   The agents are authorized, in the course of or at the close of the inquiry, to present in writing to the commission and to the other party such statements, requisitions, or summaries of the facts as they consider useful for ascertaining the truth.

Art. 30   The commission considers its decisions in private and the proceedings are secret.

All questions are decided by a majority of the members of the commission.

If a member declines to vote, the fact must be recorded in the minutes.

Art. 31   The sittings of the commission are not public, nor the minutes and documents connected with the inquiry published except in virtue of a decision of the commission taken with the consent of the parties.

Art. 32   After the parties have presented all the explanations and evidence, and the witnesses have all been heard, the president declares the inquiry terminated, and the commission adjourns to deliberate and to draw up its report.

Art. 33   The report is signed by all the members of the commission.

If one of the members refuses to sign, the fact is mentioned; but the validity of the report is not affected.

Art. 34   The report of the commission is read at a public sitting, the agents and counsel of the parties being present or duly summoned.

A copy of the report is given to each party.

Art. 35   The report of the commission is limited to a statement of facts, and has in no way the character of an award. It leaves to the parties entire freedom as to the effect to be given to the statement.

Art. 36   Each party pays its own expenses and an equal share of the expenses incurred by the commission.

PART IV. — INTERNATIONAL ARBITRATION

CHAPTER I. — THE SYSTEM OF ARBITRATION

Art. 37   International arbitration has for its object the settlement of disputes between States by judges of their own choice and on the basis of respect for
law.

Recourse to arbitration implies an engagement to submit in good faith to
the award.

Art. 38   In questions of a legal nature, and especially in the interpretation or application of international conventions, arbitration is recognised by the contracting Powers as the most effective, and, at the same time, the most equitable means of settling disputes which diplomacy has failed to settle.

Consequently, it would be desirable that, in disputes about the above-
mentioned questions, the contracting Powers should, if the case arose,
have recourse to arbitration, in so far as circumstances permit.

Art. 39   The arbitration convention is concluded for questions already existing or
for questions which may arise eventually.

It may embrace any dispute or only disputes of a certain category.

Art. 40   Independently of general or private treaties expressly stipulating recourse
to arbitration as obligatory on the contracting Powers, the said Powers
reserve to themselves the right of concluding new agreements, general or
particular, with a view to extending compulsory arbitration to all cases
which they may consider it possible to submit to it.

CHAPTER II. — THE PERMANENT COURT OF ARBITRATION

Art. 41   With the object of facilitating an immediate recourse to arbitration for
international differences, which it has not been possible to settle by diplomacy, the contracting Powers undertake to maintain the Permanent
Court of Arbitration, as established by the First Peace Conference, accessible at all times, and operating, unless otherwise stipulated by the parties,
in accordance with the rules of procedure inserted in the present Convention.

Art. 42   The Permanent Court is competent for all arbitration cases, unless the
parties agree to institute a special tribunal.

Art. 43   The Permanent Court sits at The Hague.

An International Bureau serves as registry for the Court. It is the channel
for communications relative to the meetings of the Court; it has charge of
the archives and conducts all the administrative business.

The contracting Powers undertake to communicate to the Bureau, as soon
as possible, a certified copy of any conditions of arbitration arrived at

between them and of any award concerning them delivered by a special tribunal.

They likewise undertake to communicate to the Bureau the laws, regulations, and documents eventually showing the execution of the awards given by the Court.

Art. 44   Each contracting Power selects four persons at the most, of known competency in questions of international law, of the highest moral reputation, and disposed to accept the duties of arbitrator.

The persons thus selected are inscribed, as members of the Court, in a list which shall be notified to all the contracting Powers by the Bureau.

Any alteration in the list of arbitrators is brought by the Bureau to the knowledge of the contracting Powers.

Two or more Powers may agree on the selection in common of one or more members.

The same person can be selected by different Powers.

The members of the Court are appointed for a term of six years. These appointments are renewable.

Should a member of the Court die or resign, the same procedure is followed for filling the vacancy as was followed for appointing him. In this case the appointment is made for a fresh period of six years.

Art. 45   When the contracting Powers wish to have recourse to the Permanent Court for the settlement of a difference which has arisen between them, the arbitrators called upon to form the tribunal with jurisdiction to decide this difference must be chosen from the general list of members of the Court.

Failing the direct agreement of the parties on the composition of the arbitration tribunal, the following course shall be pursued:

Each party appoints two arbitrators, of whom one only can be its national or chosen from among the persons selected by it as members of the Permanent Court. These arbitrators together choose an umpire.

If the votes are equally divided, the choice of the umpire is intrusted to a third Power, selected by the parties by common accord.

If an agreement is not arrived at on this subject each party selects a different Power, and the choice of the umpire is made in concert by the Powers thus selected.

If, within two months' time, these two Powers can not come to an agreement, each of them presents two candidates taken from the list of members of the Permanent Court, exclusive of the members selected by the parties and not being nationals of either of them. Drawing lots determines which of the candidates thus presented shall be umpire.

Art. 46   The tribunal being thus composed, the parties notify to the Bureau their determination to have recourse to the Court, the text of their compromis, and the names of the arbitrators.

The Bureau communicates without delay to each arbitrator the compromis, and the names of the other members of the tribunal.

The tribunal assembles at the date fixed by the parties. The Bureau makes the necessary arrangements for the meeting.

The members of the tribunal, in the exercise of their duties and out of their own country, enjoy diplomatic privileges and immunities.

Art. 47   The Bureau is authorized to place its offices and staff at the disposal of the contracting Powers for the use of any special board of arbitration.

The jurisdiction of the Permanent Court may, within the conditions laid down in the regulations, be extended to disputes between non-contracting Powers or between contracting Powers and non-contracting Powers, if the parties are agreed on recourse to this tribunal.

Art. 48   The contracting Powers consider it their duty, if a serious dispute threatens to break out between two or more of them, to remind these latter that the Permanent Court is open to them.

Consequently, they declare that the fact of reminding the parties is at variance of the provisions of the present Convention, and the advice given to them, in the highest interests of peace, to have recourse to the Permanent Court, can only be regarded as friendly actions.

In case of dispute between two Powers, one of them can always address to the International Bureau a note containing a declaration that it would be ready to submit the dispute to arbitration.

The Bureau must at once inform the other Power of the declaration.

Art. 49   The Permanent Administrative Council, composed of the diplomatic representatives of the contracting Powers accredited to The Hague and of the Netherland Minister for Foreign Affairs, who will act as president, is charged with the direction and control of the International Bureau.

The Council settles its rules of procedure and all other necessary regulations.

It decides all questions of administration which may arise with regard to the operations of the Court.

It has entire control over the appointment, suspension, or dismissal of the officials and employees of the Bureau.

It fixes the payments and salaries, and controls the general expenditure.

At meetings duly summoned the presence of nine members is sufficient to render valid the decisions of the Council. The decisions are taken by a majority of votes.

The Council communicates to the contracting Powers without delay the regulations adopted by it. It furnishes them with an annual report on the labors of the Court, the working of the administration, and the expenditure. The report likewise contains a résumé of what is important in the documents communicated to the Bureau by the Powers in virtue of Article 43, paragraphs 3 and 4.

Art. 50   The expenses of the Bureau shall be borne by the contracting Powers in the proportion fixed for the International Bureau of the Universal Postal Union.

The expenses to be charged to the adhering Powers shall be reckoned from the date on which their adhesion comes into force.

CHAPTER III. — ARBITRATION PROCEDURE

Art. 51   With a view to encouraging the development of arbitration, the contracting Powers have agreed on the following rules, which are applicable to arbitration procedure, unless other rules have been agreed on by the parties.

Art. 52   The Powers which have recourse to arbitration sign a compromis, in which the subject of the dispute is clearly defined, the time allowed for appointing arbitrators, the form, order, and time in which the communication referred to in Article 63 must be made, and the amount of the sum which each party must deposit in advance to defray the expenses.

The compromis likewise defines, if there is occasion, the manner of appointing arbitrators, any special powers which may eventually belong to the tribunal, where it shall meet, the language it shall use, and the languages the employment of which shall be authorised before it, and, generally speaking, all the conditions on which the parties are agreed.

Art. 53   The Permanent Court is competent to settle the compromis, if the parties are agreed to have recourse to it for the purpose.

It is similarly competent, even if the request is only made by one of the parties, when all attempts to reach an understanding through the diplomatic channel have failed, in the case of —

(1) A dispute covered by a general treaty of arbitration concluded or renewed after the present Convention has come into force, and providing for a compromis in all disputes and not either explicitly or implicitly excluding the settlement of the compromis from the competence of the Court. Recourse can not, however, be had to the Court if the other party declares that in its opinion the dispute does not belong to the category of disputes which can be submitted to compulsory arbitration, unless the treaty of arbitration confers upon the arbitration tribunal the power of deciding this preliminary question.

(2) A dispute arising from contract debts claimed from one Power by another Power as due to its nationals, and for the settlement of which the offer of arbitration has been accepted. This arrangement is not applicable if acceptance is subject to the condition that the compromis should be settled in some other way.

Art. 54   In the cases contemplated in the preceding article, the compromis shall be settled by a commission consisting of five members selected in the manner arranged for in Article 45, paragraphs 3 to 6.

The fifth member is president of the commission ex officio.

Art. 55   The duties of arbitrator may be conferred on one arbitrator alone or on several arbitrators selected by the parties as they please, or chosen by them from the members of the Permanent Court of Arbitration established by the present Convention.

Failing the constitution of the tribunal by direct agreement between the parties, the course referred to in Article 45, paragraphs 3 to 6, is followed.

Art. 56   When a sovereign or the chief of a State is chosen as arbitrator, the arbitration procedure is settled by him.

Art. 57   The umpire is president of the tribunal ex officio.

When the tribunal does not include an umpire, it appoints its own president.

Art. 58   When the compromis is settled by a commission, as contemplated in Article 54, and in the absence of an agreement to the contrary, the commission itself shall form the arbitration tribunal.

Art. 59   Should one of the arbitrators either die, retire, or be unable for any reason whatever to discharge his functions, the same procedure is followed for filling the vacancy as was followed for appointing him.

Art. 60   The tribunal sits at The Hague, unless some other place is selected by the parties.

The tribunal can only sit in the territory of a third Power with the latter's consent.

The place of meeting once fixed can not be altered by the tribunal, except with the consent of the parties.

Art. 61   If the question as to what languages are to be used has not been settled by the compromis, it shall be decided by the tribunal.

Art. 62   The parties are entitled to appoint special agents to attend the tribunal to act as intermediaries between themselves and the tribunal.

They are further authorised to retain for the defence of their rights and interests before the tribunal counsel or advocates appointed by themselves for this purpose.

The members of the Permanent Court may not act as agents, counsel, or advocates except on behalf of the Power which appointed them members of the Court.

Art. 63   As a general rule, arbitration procedure comprises two distinct phases: pleadings and oral discussions.

The pleadings consist in the communication by the respective agents to the members of the tribunal and the opposite party of cases, counter-cases, and, if necessary, of replies; the parties annex thereto all papers and documents called for in the case. This communication shall be made either directly or through the intermediary of the International Bureau, in the order and within the time fixed by the compromis.

The time fixed by the compromis may be extended by mutual agreement by the parties, or by the tribunal when the latter considers it necessary for the purpose of reaching a just decision.

The discussions consist in the oral development before the tribunal of the arguments of the parties.

Art. 64   A certified copy of every document produced by one party must be communicated to the other party.

Art. 65   Unless special circumstances arise, the tribunal does not meet until the pleadings are closed.

Art. 66   The discussions are under the control of the president.

They are only public if it be so decided by the tribunal, with the assent of the parties.

They are recorded in minutes drawn up by the secretaries appointed by the president. These minutes are signed by the president and by one of the secretaries and alone have an authentic character.

Art. 67   After the close of the pleadings, the tribunal is entitled to refuse discussion of all new papers or documents which one of the parties may wish to submit to it without the consent of the other party.

Art. 68   The tribunal is free to take into consideration new papers or documents to which its attention may be drawn by the agents or counsel of the parties.

In this case, the tribunal has the right to require the production of these papers or documents, but is obliged to make them known to the opposite party.

Art. 69   The tribunal can, besides, require from the agents of the parties the production of all papers, and can demand all necessary explanations. In case of refusal the tribunal takes note of it.

Art. 70   The agents and the counsel of the parties are authorized to present orally to the tribunal all the arguments they may consider expedient in defense of their case.

Art. 71   They are entitled to raise objections and points. The decisions of the tribunal on these points are final and can not form the subject of any subsequent discussion.

Art. 72 The members of the tribunal are entitled to put questions to the agents and counsel of the parties, and to ask them for explanations on doubtful points.

His Neither the questions put, nor the remarks made by members of the tribunal in the course of the discussions, can be regarded as an expression of opinion by the tribunal in general or by its members in particular.

Art. 73 The tribunal is authorized to declare its competence in interpreting the compromis, as well as the other papers and documents which may be invoked, and in applying the principles of law.

Art. 74 The tribunal is entitled to issue rules of procedure for the conduct of the case, to decide the forms, order, and time in which each party must conclude its arguments, and to arrange all the formalities required for dealing with the evidence.

Art. 75 The parties undertake to supply the tribunal, as fully as they consider possible, with all the information required for deciding the case.

Art. 76 For all notices which the tribunal has to serve in the territory of a third contracting Power, the tribunal shall apply direct to the Government of that Power. The same rule applies in the case of steps being taken to procure evidence on the spot.

The requests for this purpose are to be executed as far as the means at the disposal of the Power applied to under its municipal law allow. They can not be rejected unless the Power in question considers them calculated to impair its own sovereign rights or its safety.

The Court will equally be always entitled to act through the Power on whose territory it sits.

Art. 77 When the agents and counsel of the parties have submitted all the explanations and evidence in support of their case the president shall declare the discussion closed.

Art. 78 The tribunal considers its decisions in private and the proceedings remain secret.

All questions are decided by a majority of the members of the tribunal.

Art. 79 The award must give the reasons on which it is based. It contains the names of the arbitrators; it is signed by the president and registrar or by the secretary acting as registrar.

Art. 80 The award is read out in public sitting, the agents and counsel of the parties being present or duly summoned to attend.

Art. 81 The award, duly pronounced and notified to the agents of the parties, settles the dispute definitively and without appeal.

Art. 82 Any dispute arising between the parties as to the interpretation and execution of the award shall, in the absence of an agreement to the contrary, be submitted to the tribunal which pronounced it.

Art. 83   The parties can reserve in the compromis the right to demand the revision of the award.

In this case and unless there be an agreement to the contrary, the demand must be addressed to the tribunal which pronounced the award. It can only be made on the ground of the discovery of some new fact calculated to exercise a decisive influence upon the award and which was unknown to the tribunal and to the party which demanded the revision at the time the discussion was closed.

Proceedings for revision can only be instituted by a decision of the tribunal expressly recording the existence of the new fact, recognizing in it the character described in the preceding paragraph, and declaring the demand admissible on this ground.

The compromis fixes the period within which the demand for revision must be made.

Art. 84   The award is not binding except on the parties in dispute.

When it concerns the interpretation of a Convention to which Powers other than those in dispute are parties, they shall inform all the signatory Powers in good time. Each of these Powers is entitled to intervene in the case. If one or more avail themselves of this right, the interpretation contained in the award is equally binding on them.

Art. 85   Each party pays its own expenses and an equal share of the expenses of the tribunal.

CHAPTER IV. — ARBITRATION BY SUMMARY PROCEDURE

Art. 86   With a view to facilitating the working of the system of arbitration in disputes admitting of a summary procedure, the contracting Powers adopt the following rules, which shall be observed in the absence of other arrangements and subject to the reservation that the provisions of Chapter III apply so far as may be.

Art. 87   Each of the parties in dispute appoints an arbitrator. The two arbitrators thus selected choose an umpire. If they do not agree on this point, each of them proposes two candidates taken from the general list of the members of the Permanent Court exclusive of the members appointed by either of the parties and not being nationals of either of them; which of the candidates thus proposed shall be the umpire is determined by lot.

The umpire presides over the tribunal, which gives its decisions by a majority of votes.

Art. 88   In the absence of any previous agreement the tribunal, as soon as it is formed, settles the time within which the two parties must submit their respective cases to it.

Art. 89   Each party is represented before the tribunal by an agent, who serves as intermediary between the tribunal and the Government who appointed him.

Art. 90   The proceedings are conducted exclusively in writing. Each party, however, is entitled to ask that witnesses and experts should be called. The tribunal has for its part, the right to demand oral explanations from the agents of the two parties, as well as from the experts and witnesses whose appearance in Court it may consider useful.

PART V. — FINAL PROVISIONS

Art. 91   The present Convention, duly ratified, shall replace, as between the contracting Powers, the Convention for the pacific settlement of international disputes of the 28th July, 1899.

Art. 92   The present Convention shall be ratified as soon as possible.

The ratifications shall be deposited at The Hague.

The first deposit of ratifications shall be recorded in a procès-verbal signed by the representatives of the Powers which take part therein and by the Netherland Minister for Foreign Affairs.

The subsequent deposits of ratifications shall be made by means of a written notification, addressed to the Netherland Government and accompanied by the instrument of ratification.

A duly certified copy of the procès-verbal relative to the first deposit of ratifications, of the notifications mentioned in the preceding paragraph, and of the instruments of ratification, shall be immediately sent by the Netherland Government, through the diplomatic channel, to the Powers invited to the Second Peace Conference, as well as to those Powers which have adhered to the Convention. In the cases contemplated in the preceding paragraph, the said Government shall at the same time inform the Powers of the date on which it received the notification.

Art. 93   Non-signatory Powers which have been invited to the Second Peace Conference may adhere to the present Convention.

The Power which desires to adhere notifies its intention in writing to the Netherland Government, forwarding to it the act of adhesion, which shall be deposited in the archives of the said Government.

This Government shall immediately forward to all the other Powers invited to the Second Peace Conference a duly certified copy of the notification as well as of the act of adhesion, mentioning the date on which it received the notification.

Art. 94   The conditions on which the Powers which have not been invited to the Second Peace Conference may adhere to the present Convention shall form the subject of a subsequent agreement between the contracting Powers.

Art. 95   The present Convention shall take effect, in the case of the Powers which were not a party to the first deposit of ratifications, sixty days after the date of the procès-verbal of this deposit, and, in the case of the Powers which ratify subsequently or which adhere, sixty days after the notification of their ratification or of their adhesion has been received by the Netherland Government.

Art. 96   In the event of one of the contracting Powers wishing to denounce the present Convention, the denunciation shall be notified in writing to the Netherland Government which shall immediate communicate a duly certified copy of the notification to all the other Powers informing them of the date on which it was received.

The denunciation shall only have effect in regard to the notifying Power, and one year after the notification has reached the Netherland Government.

Art. 97   A register kept by the Netherland Minister for Foreign Affairs shall give the date of the deposit of ratifications effected in virtue of Article 92, paragraphs 3 and 4, as well as the date on which the notifications of adhesion (Article 93, paragraph 2) or of denunciation (Article 96, paragraph 1) have been received.

Each contracting Power is entitled to have access to this register and to be supplied with duly certified extracts from it.

b) Permanent Court of Arbitration Optional Rules for Arbitrating Disputes Between Two States

SECTION I. INTRODUCTORY RULES

SCOPE OF APPLICATION

Art. 1   1. Where the parties to a treaty or other agreement have agreed in writing that disputes shall be referred to arbitration under the Permanent Court of Arbitration Optional Rules for Arbitrating Disputes Between Two States, then such disputes shall be settled in accordance with these Rules subject to such modification as the parties may agree in writing.

2. The International Bureau of the Permanent Court of Arbitration ('the International Bureau') shall take charge of the archives of the arbitration proceeding. In addition, upon written request of all the parties or of the arbitral tribunal, the International Bureau shall act as a channel of communication between the parties and the arbitral tribunal, provide secretariat services and/or serve as registry.

3. If on the date the arbitration commences either The Hague Convention for the Pacific Settlement of International Disputes of 1899 or The Hague Convention for the Pacific Settlement of International Disputes of 1907 is

in force between the parties, the applicable Convention shall remain in force, and the parties, in the exercise of their rights under the Convention, agree that the procedures set forth in these Rules shall govern the arbitration as provided for in the parties' agreement.

NOTICE, CALCULATION OF PERIODS OF TIME

Art. 2   1. For the purposes of these Rules, any notice, including a notification, communication or proposal, is deemed to have been received when it has been delivered to the addressee through diplomatic channels. Notice shall be deemed to have been received on the day it is so delivered.

2. For the purposes of calculating a period of time under these Rules, such period shall begin to run on the day following the day when a notice, notification, communication or proposal is received. If the last day of such period is an official holiday or a non-work day in the State of the addressee, the period is extended until the first work day which follows. Official holidays or non-work days occurring during the running of the period of time are included in calculating the period.

NOTICE OF ARBITRATION

Art. 3   1. The party initiating recourse to arbitration (hereinafter called the 'claimant') shall give to the other party (hereinafter called the 'respondent') a notice of arbitration.

2. Arbitral proceedings shall be deemed to commence on the date on which the notice of arbitration is received by the respondent.

3. The notice of arbitration shall include the following:

(a) A demand that the dispute be referred to arbitration;

(b) The names and addresses of the parties;

(c) A reference to the arbitration clause or the separate arbitration agreement that is invoked;

(d) A reference to the treaty or other agreement out of or in relation to which the dispute arises;

(e) The general nature of the claim and an indication of the amount involved, if any;

(f) The relief or remedy sought;

(g) A proposal as to the number of arbitrators (i.e., one, three or five), if the parties have not previously agreed thereon.

4. The notice of arbitration may also include the statement of claim referred to in article 18.

REPRESENTATION AND ASSISTANCE

Art. 4   Each party shall appoint an agent. The parties may also be assisted by persons of their choice. The name and address of the agent must be communicated in writing to the other party, to the International Bureau and to the arbitral tribunal after it has been appointed.

SECTION II. COMPOSITION OF THE ARBITRAL TRIBUNAL

NUMBER OF ARBITRATORS

Art. 5   If the parties have not previously agreed on the number of arbitrators (i.e., one, three, or five), and if within thirty days after the receipt by the respondent of the notice of arbitration the parties have not agreed on the number of arbitrators, three arbitrators shall be appointed.

APPOINTMENT OF ARBITRATORS (ARTICLES 6 TO 8)

Art. 6   1. If a sole arbitrator is to be appointed, either party may propose to the other:

(a) The names of one or more persons, one of whom would serve as the sole arbitrator; and

(b) If no appointing authority has been agreed upon by the parties, the name or names of one or more institutions or persons, one of whom would serve as appointing authority.

2. If within sixty days after receipt by a party of a proposal made in accordance with paragraph 1 the parties have not reached agreement on the choice of a sole arbitrator, the sole arbitrator shall be appointed by the appointing authority agreed upon by the parties. If no appointing authority has been agreed upon by the parties, or if the appointing authority agreed upon refuses to act or fails to appoint the arbitrator within sixty days of the receipt of a party's request therefor, either party may request the Secretary-General of the Permanent Court of Arbitration at The Hague ('the Secretary-General') to designate an appointing authority.

3. The appointing authority shall, at the request of one of the parties, appoint the sole arbitrator as promptly as possible. In making the appointment the appointing authority shall use the following list-procedure, unless both parties agree that the list-procedure should not be used or unless the appointing authority determines in its discretion that the use of the list-procedure is not appropriate for the case:

(a) At the request of one of the parties the appointing authority shall communicate to both parties an identical list containing at least three names;

(b) Within thirty days after the receipt of this list, each party may return the list to the appointing authority after having deleted the name or names to which it objects and numbered the remaining names on the list in the order of its preference;

(c) After the expiration of the above period of time the appointing authority shall appoint the sole arbitrator from among the names approved on the lists returned to it and in accordance with the order of preference indicated by the parties;

(d) If for any reason the appointment cannot be made according to this procedure, the appointing authority may exercise its discretion in appointing the sole arbitrator.

4. In making the appointment, the appointing authority shall have regard to such considerations as are likely to secure the appointment of an independent and impartial arbitrator and shall take into account as well the advisability of appointing an arbitrator of a nationality other than the nationalities of the parties.

Art. 7   1. If three arbitrators are to be appointed, each party shall appoint one arbitrator. The two arbitrators thus appointed shall choose the third arbitrator who will act as the presiding arbitrator of the tribunal. If five arbitrators are to be appointed, the two party-appointed arbitrators shall choose the remaining three arbitrators and designate one of those three as the presiding arbitrator of the tribunal.

2. If within thirty days after the receipt of a party's notification of the appointment of an arbitrator the other party has not notified the first party of the arbitrator it has appointed:

(a) The first party may request the appointing authority previously designated by the parties to appoint the second arbitrator, or

(b) If no such authority has been previously designated by the parties, or if the appointing authority previously designated refuses to act or fails to appoint the arbitrator within sixty days after receipt of a party's request therefor, the first party may request the Secretary-General of the Permanent Court of Arbitration at The Hague to designate the appointing authority. The first party may then request the appointing authority so designated to appoint the second arbitrator. In either case, the appointing authority may exercise its discretion in appointing the arbitrator.

3. If within sixty days after the appointment of the second arbitrator the two arbitrators have not agreed on the choice of the remaining arbitrators and/or presiding arbitrator, the remaining arbitrators and/or presiding arbitrator shall be appointed by an appointing authority in the same way as a sole arbitrator would be appointed under article 6.

Art. 8   1. When an appointing authority is requested to appoint an arbitrator pursuant to article 6 or article 7, the party which makes the request shall send to the appointing authority a copy of the notice of arbitration, a copy of the treaty or other agreement out of or in relation to which the dispute has arisen and a copy of the arbitration agreement if it is not contained in the treaty or other agreement. The appointing authority may request from either party such information as it deems necessary to fulfil its function.

2. Where the names of one or more persons are proposed for appointment as arbitrators, their full names, addresses and nationalities shall be indicated, together with a description of their qualifications.

3. In appointing arbitrators pursuant to these Rules, the parties and the appointing authority are free to designate persons who are not members of the Permanent Court of Arbitration at The Hague.

CHALLENGE OF ARBITRATORS (ARTICLES 9 TO 12)

Art. 9   A prospective arbitrator shall disclose to those who approach him/her in connection with his/her possible appointment any circumstances likely to give rise to justifiable doubts as to his/her impartiality or independence. An arbitrator, once appointed or chosen, shall disclose such circumstances to the parties unless they have already been informed by him/her of these circumstances.

Art. 10   1. Any arbitrator may be challenged if circumstances exist that give rise to justifiable doubts as to the arbitrator's impartiality or independence.

2. A party may challenge the arbitrator appointed by him/her only for reasons of which he/she becomes aware after the appointment has been made.

Art. 11   1. A party who intends to challenge an arbitrator shall send notice of its challenge within thirty days after the appointment of the challenged arbitrator has been notified to the challenging party or within thirty days after the circumstances mentioned in articles 9 and 10 became known to that party.

2. The challenge shall be notified to the other party, to the arbitrator who is challenged and to the other members of the arbitral tribunal. The notification shall be in writing and shall state the reasons for the challenge.

3. When an arbitrator has been challenged by one party, the other party may agree to the challenge. The arbitrator may also, after the challenge, withdraw from his/her office. In neither case does this imply acceptance of the validity of the grounds for the challenge. In both cases the procedure provided in article 6 or 7 shall be used in full for the appointment of the substitute arbitrator, even if during the process of appointing the challenged arbitrator a party had failed to exercise his/her right to appoint or to participate in the appointment.

Art. 12   1. If the other party does not agree to the challenge and the challenged arbitrator does not withdraw, the decision on the challenge will be made:

(a) When the initial appointment was made by an appointing authority, by that authority;

(b) When the initial appointment was not made by an appointing authority, but an appointing authority has been previously designated, by that authority;

(c) In all other cases, by the appointing authority to be designated in accordance with the procedure for designating an appointing authority as provided for in article 6.

2. If the appointing authority sustains the challenge, a substitute arbitrator shall be appointed or chosen pursuant to the procedure applicable to the appointment or choice of an arbitrator as provided in articles 6 to 9 except that, when this procedure would call for the designation of an appointing authority, the appointment of the arbitrator shall be made by the appointing authority which decided on the challenge.

REPLACEMENT OF AN ARBITRATOR

Art. 13   1. In the event of the death or resignation of an arbitrator during the course of the arbitral proceedings, a substitute arbitrator shall be appointed or chosen pursuant to the procedure provided for in articles 6 to 9 that was applicable to the appointment or choice of the arbitrator being replaced. Any resignation by an arbitrator shall be addressed to the arbitral tribunal and shall not be effective unless the arbitral tribunal determines that there are sufficient reasons to accept the resignation, and if the arbitral tribunal so determines the resignation shall become effective on the date designated by the arbitral tribunal. In the event that an arbitrator whose resignation is not accepted by the tribunal nevertheless fails to participate in the arbitration, the provisions of paragraph 3 of this article shall apply.

2. In the event that an arbitrator fails to act or in the event of the *de jure* or *de facto* impossibility of his/her performing his/her functions, the procedure in respect of the challenge and replacement of an arbitrator as provided in the preceding articles shall apply, subject to the provisions of paragraph 3 of this article 13.

3. If an arbitrator on a three- or five-person tribunal fails to participate in the arbitration, the other arbitrators shall, unless the parties agree otherwise, have the power in their sole discretion to continue the arbitration and to make any decision, ruling or award, notwithstanding the failure of one arbitrator to participate. In determining whether to continue the arbitration or to render any decision, ruling, or award without the participation of an arbitrator, the other arbitrators shall take into account the stage of the arbitration, the reason, if any, expressed by the arbitrator for such non-participation, and such other matters as they consider appropriate in the circumstances of the case. In the event that the other arbitrators determine not to continue the arbitration without the non-participating arbitrator, the arbitral tribunal shall declare the office vacant, and a sub-

stitute arbitrator shall be appointed pursuant to the provisions of articles 6 to 9, unless the parties agree on a different method of appointment.

REPETITION OF HEARINGS IN THE EVENT OF THE REPLACEMENT OF AN ARBITRATOR

Art. 14   If under articles 11 to 13 the sole arbitrator or presiding arbitrator is replaced, any hearings held previously shall be repeated; if any other arbitrator is replaced, such prior hearings may be repeated at the discretion of the arbitral tribunal.

SECTION III. ARBITRAL PROCEEDINGS

GENERAL PROVISIONS

Art. 15   1. Subject to these Rules, the arbitral tribunal may conduct the arbitration in such manner as it considers appropriate, provided that the parties are treated with equality and that at any stage of the proceedings each party is given a full opportunity of presenting its case.

2. If either party so requests at any appropriate stage of the proceedings, the arbitral tribunal shall hold hearings for the presentation of evidence by witnesses, including expert witnesses, or for oral argument. In the absence of such a request, the arbitral tribunal shall decide whether to hold such hearings or whether the proceedings shall be conducted on the basis of documents and other materials.

3. All documents or information supplied to the arbitral tribunal by one party shall at the same time be communicated by that party to the other party and a copy shall be filed with the International Bureau.

PLACE OF ARBITRATION

Art. 16   1. Unless the parties have agreed otherwise, the place where the arbitration is to be held shall be The Hague, The Netherlands. If the parties agree that the arbitration shall be held at a place other than The Hague, the International Bureau of the Permanent Court of Arbitration shall inform the parties and the arbitral tribunal whether it is willing to provide the secretariat and registrar services referred to in article 1, paragraph 1, and the services referred to in article 25, paragraph 3.

2. The arbitral tribunal may determine the locale of the arbitration within the country agreed upon by the parties. It may hear witnesses and hold meetings for consultation among its members at any place it deems appropriate, having regard to the circumstances of the arbitration.

3. After inviting the views of the parties, the arbitral tribunal may meet at any place it deems appropriate for the inspection of property or docu-

ments. The parties shall be given sufficient notice to enable them to be present at such inspection.

4. The award shall be made at the place of arbitration.

LANGUAGE

Art. 17 1. Subject to an agreement by the parties, the arbitral tribunal shall, promptly after its appointment, determine the language or languages to be used in the proceedings. This determination shall apply to the statement of claim, the statement of defence, and any further written statements and, if oral hearings take place, to the language or languages to be used in such hearings.

2. The arbitral tribunal may order that any documents annexed to the statement of claim or statement of defence, and any supplementary documents or exhibits submitted in the course of the proceedings, delivered in their original language, shall be accompanied by a translation into the language or languages agreed upon by the parties or determined by the arbitral tribunal.

STATEMENT OF CLAIM

Art. 18 1. Unless the statement of claim was contained in the notice of arbitration, within a period of time to be determined by the arbitral tribunal, the claimant shall communicate its statement of claim in writing to the respondent and to each of the arbitrators. A copy of the treaty or other agreement and of the arbitration agreement if not contained in the treaty or agreement, shall be annexed thereto.

2. The statement of claim shall include a precise statement of the following particulars:

(a) The names and addresses of the parties;

(b) A statement of the facts supporting the claim;

(c) The points at issue;

(d) The relief or remedy sought.

The claimant may annex to its statement of claim all documents it deems relevant or may add a reference to the documents or other evidence it will submit.

STATEMENT OF DEFENCE

Art. 19 1. Within a period of time to be determined by the arbitral tribunal, the respondent shall communicate its statement of defence in writing to the claimant and to each of the arbitrators.

2. The statement of defence shall reply to the particulars (b), (c) and (d) of the statement of claim (article 18, para.2). The respondent may annex to

its statement the documents on which it relies for its defence or may add a reference to the documents or other evidence it will submit.

3. In its statement of defence, or at a later stage in the arbitral proceedings if the arbitral tribunal decides that the delay was justified under the circumstances, the respondent may make a counter-claim arising out of the same treaty or other agreement or rely on a claim arising out of the same treaty or other agreement for the purpose of a set-off.

4. The provisions of article 18, paragraph 2, shall apply to a counter-claim and a claim relied on for the purpose of a set-off.

AMENDMENTS TO THE CLAIM OR DEFENCE

Art. 20   During the course of the arbitral proceedings either party may amend or supplement its claim or defence unless the arbitral tribunal considers it inappropriate to allow such amendment having regard to the delay in making it or prejudice to the other party or any other circumstances. However, a claim may not be amended in such a manner that the amended claim falls outside the scope of the arbitration clause or separate arbitration agreement.

PLEAS AS TO THE JURISDICTION OF THE ARBITRAL TRIBUNAL

Art. 21   1. The arbitral tribunal shall have the power to rule on objections that it has no jurisdiction, including any objections with respect to the existence or validity of the arbitration clause or of the separate arbitration agreement.

2. The arbitral tribunal shall have the power to determine the existence or the validity of the treaty or other agreement of which an arbitration clause forms a part. For the purposes of article 21, an arbitration clause which forms part of the treaty or agreement and which provides for arbitration under these Rules shall be treated as an agreement independent of the other terms of the treaty or agreement. A decision by the arbitral tribunal that the treaty or agreement is null and void shall not entail *ipso jure* the invalidity of the arbitration clause.

3. A plea that the arbitral tribunal does not have jurisdiction shall be raised not later than in the statement of defence or, with respect to a counter-claim, in the reply to the counter-claim.

4. In general, the arbitral tribunal should rule on a plea concerning its jurisdiction as a preliminary question. However, the arbitral tribunal may proceed with the arbitration and rule on such a plea in its final award.

FURTHER WRITTEN STATEMENTS

Art. 22   The arbitral tribunal shall, after inviting the views of the parties, decide which further written statements, in addition to the statement of claim and the statement of defence, shall be required from the parties or may be presented by them and shall fix the period of time for communicating such statements.

PERIODS OF TIME

Art. 23   The periods of time fixed by the arbitral tribunal for the communication of written statements (including the statement of claim and statement of defence) should not exceed ninety days. However, the arbitral tribunal may set longer time limits, if it concludes that an extension is justified.

EVIDENCE AND HEARINGS (ARTICLES 24 AND 25)

Art. 24   1. Each party shall have the burden of proving the facts relied on to support its claim or defence.

2. The arbitral tribunal may, if it considers it appropriate, require a party to deliver to the tribunal and to the other party, within such a period of time as the arbitral tribunal shall decide, a summary of the documents and other evidence which that party intends to present in support of the facts in issue set out in its statement of claim or statement of defence.

3. At any time during the arbitral proceedings the arbitral tribunal may call upon the parties to produce documents, exhibits or other evidence within such a period of time as the tribunal shall determine. The Tribunal shall take note of any refusal to do so as well as any reasons given for such refusal.

Art. 25   1. In the event of an oral hearing, the arbitral tribunal shall give the parties adequate advance notice of the date, time and place thereof.

2. If witnesses are to be heard, at least thirty days before the hearing each party shall communicate to the arbitral tribunal and to the other party the names and addresses of the witnesses it intends to present, the subject upon and the languages in which such witnesses will give their testimony.

3. The International Bureau shall make arrangements for the translation of oral statements made at a hearing and for a record of the hearing if either is deemed necessary by the tribunal under the circumstances of the case, or if the parties have agreed thereto and have communicated such agreement to the tribunal and the International Bureau at least thirty days before the hearing or such longer period before the hearing as the arbitral tribunal may determine.

4. Hearings shall be held *in camera* unless the parties agree otherwise. The arbitral tribunal may require the retirement of any witness or witnesses during the testimony of other witnesses. The arbitral tribunal is free to determine the manner in which witnesses are examined.

5. Evidence of witnesses may also be presented in the form of written statements signed by them.

6. The arbitral tribunal shall determine the admissibility, relevance, materiality and weight of the evidence offered.

INTERIM MEASURES OF PROTECTION

Art. 26   1. Unless the parties otherwise agree, the arbitral tribunal may, at the request of either party, take any interim measures it deems necessary to preserve the respective rights of either party.

2. Such interim measures may be established in the form of an interim award. The arbitral tribunal shall be entitled to require security for the costs of such measures.

3. A request for interim measures addressed by any party to a judicial authority shall not be deemed incompatible with the agreement to arbitrate, or as a waiver of that agreement.

EXPERTS

Art. 27   1. The arbitral tribunal may appoint one or more experts to report to it, in writing, on specific issues to be determined by the tribunal. A copy of the expert's terms of reference, established by the arbitral tribunal, shall be communicated to the parties.

2. The parties shall give the expert any relevant information or produce for his/her inspection any relevant documents or goods that he/she may request of them. Any dispute between a party and such expert as to the relevance and appropriateness of the required information or production shall be referred to the arbitral tribunal for decision.

3. Upon receipt of the expert's report, the arbitral tribunal shall communicate a copy of the report to the parties who shall be given the opportunity to express, in writing, their opinion on the report. A party shall be entitled to examine any document on which the expert has relied in his/her report.

4. At the request of either party the expert, after delivery of the report, may be heard at a hearing where the parties shall have the opportunity to be present and to interrogate the expert. At this hearing either party may present expert witnesses in order to testify on the points at issue. The provisions of article 25 shall be applicable to such proceedings.

FAILURE TO APPEAR OR TO MAKE SUBMISSIONS

Art. 28   1. If, within the period of time fixed by the arbitral tribunal, the claimant has failed to communicate its claim without showing sufficient cause for such failure, the arbitral tribunal shall issue an order for the termination of the arbitral proceedings. If, within the period of time fixed by the arbitral tribunal, the respondent has failed to communicate its statement of defence without showing sufficient cause for such failure, the arbitral tribunal shall order that the proceedings continue.

2. If one of the parties, duly notified under these Rules, fails to appear at a hearing, without showing sufficient cause for such failure, the arbitral tribunal may proceed with the arbitration.

3. If one of the parties, duly invited to produce documentary evidence, fails to do so within the established period of time, without showing sufficient cause for such failure, the arbitral tribunal may make the award on the evidence before it.

CLOSURE OF HEARINGS

Art. 29   1. The arbitral tribunal may inquire of the parties if they have any further proof to offer or witnesses to be heard or submissions to make and, if there are none, it may declare the hearings closed.

2. The arbitral tribunal may, if it considers it necessary owing to exceptional circumstances, decide, on its own motion or upon application of a party, to reopen the hearings at any time before the award is made.

WAIVER OF RULES

Art. 30   A party who knows that any provision of, or requirement under, these Rules has not been complied with and yet proceeds with the arbitration without promptly stating its objection to such non-compliance, shall be deemed to have waived its right to object.

SECTION IV. THE AWARD

DECISIONS

Art. 31   1. When there are three or five arbitrators, any award or other decision of the arbitral tribunal shall be made by a majority of the arbitrators.

2. In the case of questions of procedure, when there is no majority or when the arbitral tribunal so authorises, the presiding arbitrator may decide on his/her own, subject to revision, if any, by the arbitral tribunal.

FORM AND EFFECT OF THE AWARD

Art. 32   1. In addition to making a final award, the arbitral tribunal shall be entitled to make interim, interlocutory, or partial awards.

2. The award shall be made in writing and shall be final and binding on the parties. The parties undertake to carry out the award without delay.

3. The arbitral tribunal shall state the reasons upon which the award is based, unless the parties have agreed that no reasons are to be given.

4. An award shall be signed by the arbitrators and it shall contain the date on which and the place where the award was made. Where there are three or five arbitrators and any one of them fails to sign, the award shall state the reason for the absence of the signature(s).

5. The award may be made public only with the consent of both parties.

6. Copies of the award signed by the arbitrators shall be communicated to the parties by the International Bureau.

APPLICABLE LAW

Art. 33   1. The arbitral tribunal shall apply the law chosen by the parties, or in the absence of an agreement, shall decide such disputes in accordance with international law by applying:

(a)   international conventions, whether general or particular, establishing rules expressly recognized by the contesting States;

(b)   international custom, as evidence of a general practice accepted as law;

(c)   the general principles of law recognised by civilized nations;

(d)   judicial and arbitral decisions and the teachings of the most highly qualified publicists of the various nations, as subsidiary means for the determination of rules of law.

2. This provision shall not prejudice the power of the arbitral tribunal to decide a case ex aequo et bono, if the parties agree thereto.

SETTLEMENT OR OTHER GROUNDS FOR TERMINATION

Art. 34   1. If, before the award is made, the parties agree on a settlement of the dispute, the arbitral tribunal shall either issue an order for the termination of the arbitral proceedings or, if requested by both parties and accepted by the tribunal, record the settlement in the form of an arbitral award on agreed terms. The arbitral tribunal is not obliged to give reasons for such an award.

2. If, before the award is made, the continuation of the arbitral proceedings becomes unnecessary or impossible for any reason not mentioned in paragraph 1, the arbitral tribunal shall inform the parties of its intention to issue an order for the termination of the proceedings. The arbitral tribunal shall have the power to issue such an order unless a party raises justifiable grounds for objection.

3. Copies of the order for termination of the arbitral proceedings or of the arbitral award on agreed terms, signed by the arbitrators, shall be communicated to the parties by the International Bureau. Where an arbitral award on agreed terms is made, the provisions of article 32, paragraphs 2 and 4 to 6, shall apply.

INTERPRETATION OF THE AWARD

Art. 35   1. Within sixty days after the receipt of the award, either party, with notice to the other party, may request that the arbitral tribunal give an interpretation of the award.

2. The interpretation shall be given in writing within forty-five days after
the receipt of the request. The interpretation shall form part of the award
and the provisions of article 32, paragraphs 2 to 6, shall apply.

CORRECTION OF THE AWARD

Art. 36   1. Within sixty days after the receipt of the award, either party, with notice to the other party, may request the arbitral tribunal to correct in the
award any errors in computation, any clerical or typographical errors, or
any errors of similar nature. The arbitral tribunal may within thirty days
after the communication of the award make such corrections on its own
initiative.

2. Such corrections shall be in writing, and the provisions of article 32,
paragraphs 2 to 6, shall apply.

ADDITIONAL AWARD

Art. 37   1. Within sixty days after the receipt of the award, either party, with notice to the other party, may request the arbitral tribunal to make an additional award as to claims presented in the arbitral proceedings but omitted
from the award.

2. If the arbitral tribunal considers the request for an additional award to
be justified and considers that the omission can be rectified without any
further hearings or evidence, it shall complete its award within sixty days
after the receipt of the request.

3. When an additional award is made, the provisions of article 32, paragraphs 2 to 6, shall apply.

COSTS (ARTICLES 38 TO 40)

Art. 38   The arbitral tribunal shall fix the costs of arbitration in its award. The
term 'costs' includes only:

(a)   The fees of the arbitral tribunal;

(b)   The travel and other expenses incurred by the arbitrators;

(c)   The costs of expert advice and of other assistance required by the arbitral tribunal;

(d)   The travel and other expenses of witnesses to the extent such expenses are approved by the arbitral tribunal;

(e) Any fees and expenses of the appointing authority as well as the expenses of the Secretary-General of the Permanent Court of Arbitration at The Hague and the International Bureau.

Art. 39 1. The fees of the arbitral tribunal shall be reasonable in amount, taking into account the complexity of the subject-matter, the time spent by the arbitrators, the amount in dispute, if any, and any other relevant circumstances of the case.

2. When a party so requests, the arbitral tribunal shall fix its fees only after consultation with the Secretary-General of the Permanent Court of Arbitration who may make any comment he/she deems appropriate to the arbitral tribunal concerning the fees.

Art. 40 1. Each party shall bear its own costs of arbitration. However, the arbitral tribunal may apportion each of such costs between the parties if it determines that apportionment is reasonable, taking into account the circumstances of the case.

2. When the arbitral tribunal issues an order for the termination of the arbitral proceedings or makes an award on agreed terms, it shall fix the costs of arbitration referred to in article 38 and article 39, paragraph 1, in the text of that order or award.

3. No additional fees may be charged by an arbitral tribunal for interpretation or correction or completion of its award under articles 35 to 37.

DEPOSIT OF COSTS

Art. 41 1. The International Bureau following the commencement of the arbitration, may request each party to deposit an equal amount as an advance for the costs referred to in article 38, paragraphs (a), (b), (c) and (e). All amounts deposited by the parties pursuant to this paragraph and paragraph 2 of this article shall be directed to the International Bureau, and disbursed by it for such costs, including, *inter alia*, fees to the arbitrators, the Secretary-General and the International Bureau.

2. During the course of the arbitral proceedings the arbitral tribunal may request supplementary deposits from the parties.

3. If the requested deposits are not paid in full within sixty days after the receipt of the request, the arbitral tribunal shall so inform the parties in order that one or another of them may make the required payment. If such payment is not made, the arbitral tribunal may order the suspension or termination of the arbitral proceedings.

4. After the award has been made, the International Bureau shall render an accounting to the parties of the deposits received and return any unexpended balance to the parties.

c) Model Arbitration Clauses for Use in Connection with Permanent Court of Arbitration Optional Rules for Arbitrating Disputes Between Two States

FUTURE DISPUTES

Parties to a bilateral treaty or other agreement who wish to have any dispute referred to arbitration under these Rules may insert in the treaty or agreement an arbitration clause in the following form:[1]

1. If any dispute arises between the parties as to the interpretation, application or performance of this [treaty] [agreement], including its existence, validity or termination, either party may submit the dispute to final and binding arbitration in accordance with the Permanent Court of Arbitration Optional Rules for Arbitrating Disputes Between Two States, as in effect on the date of this [treaty] [agreement].

Parties may wish to consider adding:

2. The number of arbitrators shall be .... [insert 'one', 'three', or 'five']*[2]*

3. The language(s) to be used in the arbitral proceedings shall be ... [insert choice of one or more languages]*[3]*

4. The appointing authority shall be .... [insert choice]*[4]*

EXISTING DISPUTES

If the parties have not already entered into an arbitration agreement, or if they mutually agree to change a previous agreement in order to provide for arbitration under these Rules, they may enter into an agreement in the following form:

The parties agree to submit the following dispute to final and binding arbitration in accordance with the Permanent Court of Arbitration Optional Rules for Arbitrating Disputes Between Two States, as in effect on the date of this agreement: .... [insert brief description of dispute.]

Parties may wish to consider adding paragraphs 2–4 of the arbitration clause for future disputes as set forth above.

NOTES

1) Parties may agree to vary this model clause. If they consider doing so, they may consult with the Secretary-General of the Permanent Court of Arbitration to ensure that the clause to which they agree will be appropriate in the context of the Rules, and that the functions of the Secretary-General and the International Bureau can be carried out effectively.

2) If the parties do not agree on the number of arbitrators, the number shall be three, in accordance with article 5 of the Rules.

3) If the parties do not agree on the language, or languages, to be used in the arbitral proceedings, this shall be determined by the arbitral tribunal in accordance with article 17 of the Rules.

4) Parties are free to agree upon any appointing authority, e.g., the President of the International Court of Justice, or the head of a specialized body expert in the relevant subject-matter, or an ad hoc panel chosen by the parties, or any other officer, institution or individual. The Secretary-General of the Permanent Court of Arbitration will consider accepting designation as appointing authority in appropriate cases. Before inserting the name of an appointing authority in an arbitration clause, it is advisable for the parties to inquire whether the proposed authority is willing to act. If the parties do not agree on the appointing authority, the Secretary-General of the Permanent Court of Arbitration at The Hague will designate the appointing authority in accordance with article 6 or 7 of the Rules, as the case may be.

d) Guidelines for Adapting these Rules for Use in Arbitrating Multiparty Disputes

The Permanent Court of Arbitration Optional Rules for Arbitration involving International Organizations and States can be adapted for use in resolving disputes arising under a multilateral treaty, convention or arrangement. All of the provisions in these Rules are appropriate, except that modifications are needed in the mechanisms for naming arbitrators and sharing costs.

Particular care should be taken in drafting the provisions for appointing arbitrators where there may be so many parties in the arbitration that the tribunal would be of impractical size or structure if each party appointed an arbitrator. One solution sometimes considered in multiparty arbitrations is for the parties to agree that the appointing authority will designate all of the arbitrators if the parties do not do so within a specified period.

Modifications may also be needed in the provisions for sharing the costs of the arbitration.

It is recommended that parties that contemplate including an arbitration provision in a multilateral instrument consult in advance with the Secretary-General concerning the drafting of that provision in order to ensure that the proposed modifications are appropriate in the context of the Rules and that the functions of the Secretary-General and the International Bureau can be carried out effectively.

2. International Court of Justice

The International Court of Justice is the principal judicial organ of the United Nations as defined in Chapter XIV of the Charter of the United Nations. Its Statute forms an integral part of the Charter and elaborates the principles laid down there. The Rules of Procedure adopted by the Court in their original form on May 6, 1946 further refine the provisions of the Statute.

The International Court of Justice is the successor to the Permanent Court of International Justice which had been created in 1922. Although World War II interrupted the activity of the Permanent Court, the idea of establishing a new international court or re-establishing the Permanent Court was always upheld. Finally, the creation of a new court seemed more consistent with the founding of the United Nations Organization and led to the dissolution of the Permanent Court of International Justice in 1946. Despite the establishment of a new Court, the Statute and Rules of the International Court of Justice are nearly identical to those of the Permanent Court of international Justice. The continuity between the two Courts is further realized by the survival of certain obligations which States had contracted in relation to the Permanent Court of International Justice (Art. 36 (5) and Art. 37 of the Statute).

Unlike international arbitral tribunals which exist on an institutional basis for particular subjects or for certain periods of time or may be created *ad hoc* the International Court of Justice is a permanently constituted body. The organisation and procedure of the Court are governed by the previously fixed Statute and Rules of Procedure which are binding on parties having recourse to it.

In contentious cases the International Court of Justice is accessible only to States. The rights and interests of individuals are treated before the Court only in cases involving diplomatic protection in which grievances may be brought before the Court by the State of which the individual is a national.

The International Court of Justice is also empowered to give advisory opinions upon any question referred to it by the General Assembly and the Security Council (Art. 96 of the Charter) as well as to 20 United Nations institutions and specialised agencies (Yearbook of the ICJ 1994–1995, p. 74/75) upon authorisation of the General Assembly. In particular cases the International Court of Justice functions like a Court of Appeals with respect to decisions of other international tribunals such as the United Nations Administrative Tribunal and the International Labour Organisation Administrative Tribunal.

The International Court of Justice is open as a practical matter to all States. The wording of the Statute restricts access to the Court in contentious cases to signatories of the Statute. Under Art. 93 of the Charter these are *ipso facto* all member States of the United Nations. Other States may become parties to the Statute under the conditions determined by the General Assembly upon recommendation by the Security Council (Art. 93 (2) of the Charter). Under this provision Switzerland (July 28, 1948) and Nauru (January 19, 1988) have become parties to the Statute.

Any other State which is neither a member of the United Nations nor a party to the Statute of the International Court of Justice may be admitted to the proceedings by depositing with the Registrar of the Court a declaration that satisfies the jurisdictional requirements laid down in the Security Council resolution of October 15, 1946. Such a declaration may be in respect to a particular dispute which has already arisen or in respect to pending or future disputes of a particular class or classes.

This *ratione personae* jurisdiction of the Court however, is not sufficient in practical terms since the consent of the disputing States is essential for the judicial resolution of international disputes. Accordingly, a State can be made a party to proceedings before the Court only by consent. It is such consent that determines the jurisdiction of the Court in any particular dispute: jurisdiction *ratione materiae*. This consent may be given by specific agreements concerning the Court's jurisdiction and may apply to all or particular classes of existing or future disputes. Methods of manifesting consent are defined in Art. 36 of the Statute. Paragraph 1 envisages the possibility that the parties bilaterally agree to submit an already existing dispute to the Court (special agreement or *compromis*) or that the jurisdiction of the Court is provided for in pre-existing treaties or conventions. The other possibility, according to paragraph 2 of Art. 36 (optional clause), is the acceptance of the so-called compulsory jurisdiction of the Court concerning all or particular classes of existing or future disputes. Here unilateral application to the Court for relief is possible in respect to all States who have accepted the optional clause. Finally, if proceedings are instituted against a State which has not accepted the jurisdiction of the Court, such a State may recognize ad hoc the Court's jurisdiction for the particular case (*forum prorogatum*).

A list of States to which the Court provides a forum and a list of instruments governing its jurisdiction, as well as those declarations of acceptance of the Court's compulsory jurisdiction that are in force, and a list of treaties and conventions providing for the jurisdiction of the Court are published each year in the International Court of Justice Yearbook.

Texts

Actes et documents relatifs à l'organisation de la Cour — Acts and Documents concerning the Organization of the Court, Nos. 1–4. Charter of the United Nations, Statute and Rules of Court and Other Documents (1947–1978) (French and English)
BGBl. 1973 II, pp. 505–531 (German)

Bibliographical notes

a) Publications of the Court

Yearbooks-Annuaires (1946/47 to date)

Bibliographies (1964/65 to date)

The International Court of Justice (1978) (available also in French, German, Spanish, translations into other languages are in preparation)

b) Other publications

B. Schenck von Stauffenberg, Statut et Règlement de la Cour permanente de Justice internationale — Eléments d'interprétation (1934)

M. O. Hudson, The Permanent Court of International Justice 1920–1942 (Reprint 1972)

Judicial Settlement of International Disputes, An International Symposium (1972), especially report of H. Steinberger, The International Court of Justice, pp. 193–283

G. Guyomar, Commentaire du règlement de la Cour internationale de justice. Adopté le 14 Avril 1978. Interprétation et pratique (1983)

S. Rosenne, Procedure in the International Court. A Commentary on the 1978 Rules of the International Court of Justice (1983)

H. Mosler, Chapter XIV. The International Court of Justice, in: B. Simma (ed.), The Charter of the United Nations (1994)

H.-J. Schlochauer, International Court of Justice, up-dated by K. Oellers-Frahm, in: R. Bernhardt (ed.), Encyclopedia of Public International Law, Vol. II (1995), pp. 1084–1107, with detailed bibliographical indications

A. Eyffinger, The International Court of Justice 1946–1996 (1996)

S. Rosenne, The Law and Practice of the International Court, 1920–1996, 5 vols. (1997)

A.S. Muller, D. Raic, J.M. Thuransky, The International Court of Justice — Its Future Role after fifty years (1997)

Collections of cases

Reports of Judgments, Advisory Opinions and Orders — Recueil des arrêts, avis consultatifs et ordonnances (1947/48 to date) (Publication of the Court)

Pleadings, Oral Arguments, Documents — Mémoires, plaidoiries et documents (1948 to date) (Publication of the Court)

E. Hambro and A. Rovine, The Case Law of the International Court, A Repertoire of the Judgments, Advisory Opinions and Orders of the International Court of Justice, 12 vols. (1952–1974)

Fontes Iuris Gentium, Digest of the Decisions of the International Court of Justice, Series A, Section I, vols.1, 3, 4, 5, 6, 7

World Court Digest (formerly Fontes Iuris Gentium), vol. 1, vol. 2

P. M. Eisemann et al., Petit manuel de la jurisprudence de la Cour Internationale de Justice (1980)

G. Ziccardi-Capaldo, Répertoire de la jurisprudence de la Cour internationale de Justice (1947–1992) — Repertory of Decisions of the International Court of Justice (1947–1992) 1995

of Arbitration by Article 44 of the Convention of The Hague of 1907 for the pacific settlement of international disputes.

3. The conditions under which a State which is a party to the present Statute but is not a Member of the United Nations may participate in electing the Members of the Court shall, in the absence of a special agreement, be laid down by the General Assembly upon recommendation of the Security Council.

Art. 5   1. At least three months before the date of the election, the Secretary-General of the United Nations shall address a written request to the members of the Permanent Court of Arbitration belonging to the States which are parties to the present Statute, and to the members of the national groups appointed under Article 4, paragraph 2, inviting them to undertake, within a given time, by national groups, the nomination of persons in a position to accept the duties of a Member of the Court.

2. No group may nominate more than four persons, not more than two of whom shall be of their own nationality. In no case may the number of candidates nominated by a group be more than double the number of seats to be filled.

Art. 6   Before making these nominations, each national group is recommended to consult its highest court of justice, its legal faculties and schools of law, and its national academies and national sections of international academies devoted to the study of law.

Art. 7   1. The Secretary-General shall prepare a list in alphabetical order of all the persons thus nominated. Save as provided in Article 12, paragraph 2, these shall be the only persons eligible.

2. The Secretary-General shall submit this list to the General Assembly and to the Security Council.

Art. 8   The General Assembly and the Security Council shall proceed independently of one another to elect the Members of the Court.

Art. 9   At every election, the electors shall bear in mind not only that the persons to be elected should individually possess the qualifications required, but also that in the body as a whole the representation of the main forms of civilisation and of the principal legal systems of the world should be assured.

Art. 10   1. Those candidates who obtain an absolute majority of votes in the General Assembly and in the Security Council shall be considered as elected.

2. Any vote of the Security Council, whether for the election of judges or for the appointment of members of the conference envisaged in Article 12, shall be taken without any distinction between permanent and non-permanent members of the Security Council.

3. In the event of more than one national of the same State obtaining an absolute majority of the votes both of the General Assembly and of the Security Council, the eldest of these only shall be considered as elected.

Art. 11   If, after the first meeting held for the purpose of the election, one or more seats remain to be filled, a second and, if necessary, a third meeting shall take place.

Art. 12   1. If, after the third meeting, one or more seats still remain unfilled, a joint conference consisting of six members, three appointed by the General Assembly and three by the Security Council, may be formed at any time at the request of either the General Assembly or the Security Council, for the purpose of choosing by the vote of an absolute majority one name for each seat still vacant, to submit to the General Assembly and the Security Council for their respective acceptance.

2. If the joint conference is unanimously agreed upon any person who fulfils the required conditions, he may be included in its list, even though he was not included in the list of nominations referred to in Article 7.

3. If the joint conference is satisfied that it will not be successful in procuring an election, those Members of the Court who have already been elected shall, within a period to be fixed by the Security Council, proceed to fill the vacant seats by selection from among those candidates who have obtained votes either in the General Assembly or in the Security Council.

4. In the event of an equality of votes among the judges, the eldest judge shall have a casting vote.

Art. 13   1. The Members of the Court shall be elected for nine years and may be re-elected; provided, however, that of the judges elected at the first election, the terms of five judges shall expire at the end of three years and the terms of five more judges shall expire at the end of six years.

2. The judges whose terms are to expire at the end of the abovementioned initial periods of three and six years shall be chosen by lot to be drawn by the Secretary-General immediately after the first election has been completed.

3. The Members of the Court shall continue to discharge their duties until their places have been filled. Though replaced, they shall finish any cases which they may have begun.

4. In the case of the resignation of a Member of the Court, the resignation shall be addressed to the President of the Court for transmission to the Secretary-General. This last notification makes the place vacant.

Art. 14   Vacancies shall be filled by the same method as that laid down for the first election, subject to the following provision: the Secretary-General shall, within one month of the occurrence of the vacancy, proceed to issue the invitations provided for in Article 5, and the date of the election shall be fixed by the Security Council.

Art. 15   A Member of the Court elected to replace a member whose term of office has not expired shall hold office for the remainder of his predecessor's term.

Art. 16   1. No Member of the Court may exercise any political or administrative function, or engage in any other occupation of a professional nature.

2. Any doubt on this point shall be settled by the decision of the Court.

Art. 17   1. No Member of the Court may act as agent, counsel, or advocate in any case.

2. No Member may participate in the decision of any case in which he has previously taken part as agent, counsel, or advocate for one of the parties, or as a member of a national or international court, or of a commission of enquiry, or in any other capacity.

3. Any doubt on this point shall be settled by the decision of the Court.

Art. 18   1. No Member of the Court can be dismissed unless, in the unanimous opinion of the other Members, he has ceased to fulfil the required conditions.

2. Formal notification thereof shall be made to the Secretary-General by the Registrar.

3. This notification makes the place vacant.

Art. 19   The Members of the Court, when engaged on the business of the Court, shall enjoy diplomatic privileges and immunities.

Art. 20   Every Member of the Court shall, before taking up his duties, make a solemn declaration in open court that he will exercise his powers impartially and conscientiously.

Art. 21   1. The Court shall elect its President and Vice-President for three years; they may be re-elected.

2. The Court shall appoint its Registrar and may provide for the appointment of such other officers as may be necessary.

Art. 22   1. The seat of the Court shall be established at The Hague. This, however, shall not prevent the Court from sitting and exercising its functions elsewhere whenever the Court considers it desirable.

2. The President and the Registrar shall reside at the seat of the Court.

Art. 23   1. The Court shall remain permanently in session, except during the judicial vacations, the dates and duration of which shall be fixed by the Court.

2. Members of the Court are entitled to periodic leave, the dates and duration of which shall be fixed by the Court, having in mind the distance between The Hague and the home of each judge.

3. Members of the Court shall be bound, unless they are on leave or prevented from attending by illness or other serious reasons duly explained to the President, to hold themselves permanently at the disposal of the Court.

Art. 24 1. If, for some special reason, a Member of the Court considers that he should not take part in the decision of a particular case, he shall so inform the President.

2. If the President considers that for some special reason one of the Members of the Court should not sit in a particular case, he shall give him notice accordingly.

3. If in any such case the Member of the Court and the President disagree, the matter shall be settled by the decision of the Court.

Art. 25 1. The full Court shall sit except when it is expressly provided otherwise in the present Statute.

2. Subject to the condition that the number of judges available to constitute the Court is not thereby reduced below eleven, the Rules of the Court may provide for allowing one or more judges, according to circumstances and in rotation, to be dispensed from sitting.

3. A quorum of nine judges shall suffice to constitute the Court.

Art. 26 1. The Court may from time to time form one or more chambers, composed of three or more judges as the Court may determine, for dealing with particular categories of cases; for example, labour cases and cases relating to transit and communications.

2. The Court may at any time form a chamber for dealing with a particular case. The number of judges to constitute such a chamber shall be determined by the Court with the approval of the parties.

3. Cases shall be heard and determined by the chambers provided for in this article if the parties so request.

Art. 27 A judgment given by any of the chambers provided for in Articles 26 and 29 shall be considered as rendered by the Court.

Art. 28 The chambers provided for in Articles 26 and 29 may, with the consent of the parties, sit and exercise their functions elsewhere than at The Hague.

Art. 29 With a view to the speedy dispatch of business, the Court shall form annually a chamber composed of five judges which, at the request of the parties, may hear and determine cases by summary procedure. In addition, two judges shall be selected for the purpose of replacing judges who find it impossible to sit.

Art. 30 1. The Court shall frame rules for carrying out its functions. In particular, it shall lay down rules of procedure.

2. The Rules of the Court may provide for assessors to sit with the Court or with any of its chambers, without the right to vote.

Art. 31 1. Judges of the nationality of each of the parties shall retain their right to sit in the case before the Court.

2. If the Court includes upon the Bench a judge of the nationality of one of the parties, any other party may choose a person to sit as judge. Such

person shall be chosen preferably from among those persons who have been nominated as candidates as provided in Articles 4 and 5.

3. If the Court includes upon the Bench no judge of the nationality of the parties, each of these parties may proceed to choose a judge as provided in paragraph 2 of this Article.

4. The provisions of this Article shall apply to the case of Articles 26 and 29. In such cases, the President shall request one or, if necessary, two of the Members of the Court forming the chamber to give place to the Members of the Court of the nationality of the parties concerned, and, failing such, or if they are unable to be present, to the judges specially chosen by the parties.

5. Should there be several parties in the same interest, they shall, for the purpose of the preceding provisions, be reckoned as one party only. Any doubt upon this point shall be settled by the decision of the Court.

6. Judges chosen as laid down in paragraphs 2, 3, and 4 of this Article shall fulfil the conditions required by Articles 2, 17 (paragraph 2), 20, and 24 of the present Statute. They shall take part in the decision on terms of complete equality with their colleagues.

Art. 32   1. Each member of the Court shall receive an annual salary.

2. The President shall receive a special annual allowance.

3. The Vice-President shall receive a special allowance for every day on which he acts as President.

4. The judges chosen under Article 31, other than Members of the Court, shall receive compensation for each day on which they exercise their functions.

5. These salaries, allowances, and compensation shall be fixed by the General Assembly. They may not be decreased during the term of office.

6. The salary of the Registrar shall be fixed by the General Assembly on the proposal of the Court.

7. Regulations made by the General Assembly shall fix the conditions under which retirement pensions may be given to Members of the Court and to the Registrar, and the conditions under which Members of the Court and the Registrar shall have their travelling expenses refunded.

8. The above salaries, allowances, and compensation shall be free of all taxation.

Art. 33   The expenses of the Court shall be borne by the United Nations in such a manner as shall be decided by the General Assembly.

CHAPTER II. COMPETENCE OF THE COURT

Art. 34   1. Only States may be parties in cases before the Court.

2. The Court, subject to and in conformity with its Rules, may request of public international organisations information relevant to cases before it,

and shall receive such information presented by such organisations on their own initiative.

3. Whenever the construction of the constituent instrument of a public international organisation or of an international convention adopted thereunder is in question in a case before the Court, the Registrar shall so notify the public international organization concerned and shall communicate to it copies of all the written proceedings.

Art. 35   1. The Court shall be open to the States parties to the present Statute.

2. The conditions under which the Court shall be open to other States shall, subject to the special provisions contained in treaties in force, be laid down by the Security Council, but in no case shall such conditions place the parties in a position of inequality before the Court.

3. When a State which is not a Member of the United Nations is a party to a case, the Court shall fix the amount which that party is to contribute towards the expenses of the Court. This provision shall not apply if such State is bearing a share of the expenses of the Court.

Art. 36   1. The jurisdiction of the Court comprises all cases which the parties refer to it and all matters specially provided for in the Charter of the United Nations or in treaties and conventions in force.

2. The States parties to the present Statute may at any time declare that they recognize as compulsory ipso facto and without special agreement, in relation to any other State accepting the same obligation, the jurisdiction of the Court in all legal disputes concerning:

(a) the interpretation of a treaty;

(b) any question of international law;

(c) the existence of any fact which, if established, would constitute a breach of an international obligation;

(d) the nature or extent of the reparation to be made for the breach of an international obligation.

3. The declarations referred to above may be made unconditionally or on condition of reciprocity on the part of several or certain States, or for a certain time.

4. Such declarations shall be deposited with the Secretary-General of the United Nations, who shall transmit copies thereof to the parties to the Statute and to the Registrar of the Court.

5. Declarations made under Article 36 of the Statute of the Permanent Court of International Justice and which are still in force shall be deemed, as between the parties to the present Statute, to be acceptances of the compulsory jurisdiction of the International Court of Justice for the period which they still have to run and in accordance with their terms.

6. In the event of a dispute as to whether the Court has jurisdiction, the matter shall be settled by the decision of the Court.

Art. 37   Whenever a treaty or convention in force provides for reference of a matter to a tribunal to have been instituted by the League of Nations, or to the Permanent Court of International Justice, the matter shall, as between the parties to the present Statute, be referred to the International Court of Justice.

Art. 38   1. The Court, whose function is to decide in accordance with international law such disputes as are submitted to it, shall apply:

(a) international conventions, whether general or particular, establishing rules expressly recognised by the contesting States;

(b) international custom, as evidence of a general practice accepted as law;

(c) the general principles of law recognised by civilised nations;

(d) subject to the provisions of Article 59, judicial decisions and the teachings of the most highly qualified publicists of the various nations, as subsidiary means for the determination of rules of law.

2. This provision shall not prejudice the power of the Court to decide a case *ex aequo et bono*, if the parties agree thereto.

CHAPTER III. PROCEDURE

Art. 39   1. The official languages of the Court shall be French and English. If the parties agree that the case shall be conducted in French, the judgment shall be delivered in French. If the parties agree that the case shall be conducted in English, the judgment shall be delivered in English.

2. In the absence of an agreement as to which language shall be employed, each party may, in the pleadings, use the language which it prefers; the decision of the Court shall be given in French and English. In this case the Court shall at the same time determine which of the two texts shall be considered as authoritative.

3. The Court shall, at the request of any party, authorise a language other than French or English to be used by that party.

Art. 40   1. Cases are brought before the Court, as the case may be, either by the notification of the special agreement or by a written application addressed to the Registrar. In either case the subject of the dispute and the parties shall be indicated.

2. The Registrar shall forthwith communicate the application to all concerned.

3. He shall also notify the Members of the United Nations through the Secretary-General, and also any other States entitled to appear before the Court.

Art. 41   1. The Court shall have the power to indicate, if it considers that circumstances so require, any provisional measures which ought to be taken to preserve the respective rights of either party.

2. Pending the final decision, notice of the measures suggested shall forthwith be given to the parties and to the Security Council.

Art. 42   1. The parties shall be represented by agents.

2. They may have the assistance of counsel or advocates before the Court.

3. The agents, counsel, and advocates of parties before the Court shall enjoy the privileges and immunities necessary to the independent exercise of their duties.

Art. 43   1. The procedure shall consist of two parts: written and oral.

2. The written proceedings shall consist of the communication to the Court and to the parties of memorials, counter-memorials and, if necessary, replies; also all papers and documents in support.

3. These communications shall be made through the Registrar, in the order and within the time fixed by the Court.

4. A certified copy of every document produced by one party shall be communicated to the other party.

5. The oral proceedings shall consist of the hearing by the Court of witnesses, experts, agents, counsel, and advocates.

Art. 44   1. For the service of all notices upon persons other than the agents, counsel, and advocates, the Court shall apply direct to the government of the State upon whose territory the notice has to be served.

2. The same provision shall apply whenever steps are to be taken to procure evidence on the spot.

Art. 45   The hearing shall be under the control of the President, or, if he is unable to preside, of the Vice-President; if neither is able to preside, the senior judge present shall preside.

Art. 46   The hearing in Court shall be public, unless the Court shall decide otherwise, or unless the parties demand that the public be not admitted.

Art. 47   1. Minutes shall be made at each hearing and signed by the Registrar and the President.

2. These minutes alone shall be authentic.

Art. 48   The Court shall make orders for the conduct of the case, shall decide the form and time in which each party must conclude its arguments, and make all arrangements connected with the taking of evidence.

Art. 49   The Court may, even before the hearing begins, call upon the agents to produce any document or to supply any explanations. Formal note shall be taken of any refusal.

Art. 50   The Court may, at any time, entrust any individual, body, bureau, commission, or other organisation that it may select, with the task of carrying out an enquiry or giving an expert opinion.

Art. 51   During the hearing any relevant questions are to be put to the witnesses and experts under the conditions laid down by the Court in the rules of procedure referred to in Article 30.

Art. 52   After the Court has received the proofs and evidence within the time specified for the purpose, it may refuse to accept any further oral or written evidence that one party may desire to present unless the other side consents.

Art. 53   1. Whenever one of the parties does not appear before the Court, or fails to defend its case, the other party may call upon the Court to decide in favour of its claim.

2. The Court must, before doing so, satisfy itself, not only that it has jurisdiction in accordance with Articles 36 and 37, but also that the claim is well founded in fact and law.

Art. 54   1. When, subject to the control of the Court, the agents, counsel, and advocates have completed their presentation of the case, the President shall declare the hearing closed.

2. The Court shall withdraw to consider the judgment.

3. The deliberations of the Court shall take place in private and remain secret.

Art. 55   1. All questions shall be decided by a majority of the judges present.

2. In the event of an equality of votes, the President or the judge who acts in his place shall have a casting vote.

Art. 56   1. The judgment shall state the reasons on which it is based.

2. It shall contain the names of the judges who have taken part in the decision.

Art. 57   If the judgment does not represent in whole or in part the unanimous opinion of the judges, any judge shall be entitled to deliver a separate opinion.

Art. 58   The judgment shall be signed by the President and by the Registrar. It shall be read in open court, due notice having been given to the agents.

Art. 59   The decision of the Court has no binding force except between the parties and in respect of that particular case.

Art. 60   The judgment is final and without appeal. In the event of dispute as to the meaning or scope of the judgment, the Court shall construe it upon the request of any party.

Art. 61   1. An application for revision of a judgment may be made only when it is based upon the discovery of some fact of such a nature as to be a decisive factor, which fact was, when the judgment was given, unknown to the Court and also to the party claiming revision, always provided that such ignorance was not due to negligence.

2. The proceedings for revision shall be opened by a judgment of the Court expressly recording the existence of the new fact, recognising that it has such a character as to lay the case open to revision, and declaring the application admissible on this ground.

3. The Court may require previous compliance with the terms of the judgment before it admits proceedings in revision.

4. The application for revision must be made at latest within six months of the discovery of the new fact.

5. No application for revision may be made after the lapse of ten years from the date of the judgment.

Art. 62   1. Should a State consider that it has an interest of a legal nature which may be affected by the decision in the case, it may submit a request to the Court to be permitted to intervene.

2. It shall be for the Court to decide upon this request.

Art. 63   1. Whenever the construction of a convention to which States other than those concerned in the case are parties is in question, the Registrar shall notify all such States forthwith.

2. Every State so notified has the right to intervene in the proceedings; but if it uses this right, the construction given by the judgment will be equally binding upon it.

Art. 64   Unless otherwise decided by the Court, each party shall bear its own costs.

CHAPTER IV. ADVISORY OPINIONS

Art. 65   1. The Court may give an advisory opinion on any legal question at the request of whatever body may be authorised by or in accordance with the Charter of the United Nations to make such a request.

2. Questions upon which the advisory opinion of the Court is asked shall be laid before the Court by means of a written request containing an exact statement of the question upon which an opinion is required, and accompanied by all documents likely to throw light upon the question.

Art. 66   1. The Registrar shall forthwith give notice of the request for an advisory opinion to all States entitled to appear before the Court.

2. The Registrar shall also, by means of a special and direct communication, notify any State entitled to appear before the Court or international organisation considered by the Court, or, should it not be sitting, by the President, as likely to be able to furnish information on the question, that the Court will be prepared to receive, within a time-limit to be fixed by the President, written statements, or to hear, at a public sitting to be held for the purpose, oral statements relating to the question.

3. Should any such State entitled to appear before the Court have failed to receive the special communication referred to in paragraph 2 of this Article, such State may express a desire to submit a written statement or to be heard; and the Court will decide.

4. States and organisations having presented written or oral statements or both shall be permitted to comment on the statements made by other States or organisations in the form, to the extent, and within the time-limits which the Court, or, should it not be sitting, the President, shall decide in each particular case. Accordingly, the Registrar shall in due time communicate any such written statements to States and organisations having submitted similar statements.

Art. 67   The Court shall deliver its advisory opinions in open court, notice having been given to the Secretary-General and to the representatives of Members of the United Nations, of other States and of international organisations immediately concerned.

Art. 68   In the exercise of its advisory functions the Court shall further be guided by the provisions of the present Statute which apply in contentious cases to the extent to which it recognises them to be applicable.

CHAPTER V. AMENDMENT

Art. 69   Amendments to the present Statute shall be effected by the same procedure as is provided by the Charter of the United Nations for amendments to that Charter, subject however to any provisions which the General Assembly upon recommendation of the Security-Council may adopt concerning the participation of States which are parties to the present Statute but are not Members of the United Nations.

Art. 70   The Court shall have power to propose such amendments to the present Statute as it may deem necessary, through written communications to the Secretary-General, for consideration in conformity with the provisions of Article 69.

c) Rules of the International Court of Justice of April 14, 1978

PREAMBLE

The Court,
Having regard to Chapter XIV of the Charter of the United Nations;
Having regard to the Statute of the Court annexed thereto;
Acting in pursuance of Article 30 of the Statute;

Adopts the following revised Rules of Court, approved on 14 April 1978, which shall come into force on 1 July 1978, and shall as from that date replace the Rules adopted by the Court on 6 May 1946 and amended on 10 May 1972, save in respect of any case submitted to the Court before 1 July 1978, or any phase of such a case, which shall continue to be governed by the Rules in force before that date.

PART I. THE COURT

SECTION A. JUDGES AND ASSESSORS

Subsection I. The Members of the Court

Art. 1   1. The Members of the Court are the judges elected in accordance with Articles 2 to 15 of the Statute.

2. For the purposes of a particular case, the Court may also include upon the Bench one or more persons chosen under Article 31 of the Statute to sit as judges *ad hoc*.

3. In the following Rules, the term "Member of the Court" denotes any elected judge; the term "judge" denotes any Member of the Court, and any judge *ad hoc*.

Art. 2   1. The term of office of Members of the Court elected at a triennial election shall begin to run from the sixth of February[1] in the year in which the vacancies to which they are elected occur.

2. The term of office of a Member of the Court elected to replace a Member whose term of office has not expired shall begin to run from the date of the election.

Art. 3   1. The Members of the Court, in the exercise of their functions, are of equal status, irrespective of age, priority of election or length of service.

2. The Members of the Court shall, except as provided in paragraphs 4 and 5 of this Article, take precedence according to the date on which their terms of office respectively began, as provided for by Article 2 of these Rules.

3. Members of the Court whose terms of office began on the same date shall take precedence in relation to one another according to seniority of age.

4. A Member of the Court who is re-elected to a new term of office which is continuous with his previous term shall retain his precedence.

5. The President and the Vice-President of the Court, while holding these offices, shall take precedence before all other Members of the Court.

---

[1]   This is the date on which the terms of office of the Members of the Court elected at the first election began in 1946.

6. The Member of the Court who, in accordance with the foregoing paragraphs, takes precedence next after the President and the Vice-President is in these Rules designated the "senior judge". If that Member is unable to act, the Member of the Court who is next after him in precedence and able to act is considered as senior judge.

Art. 4   1 The declaration to be made by every Member of the Court in accordance with Article 20 of the Statute shall be as follows:

"I solemnly declare that I will perform my duties and exercise my powers as judge honourably, faithfully, impartially and conscientiously."

2. This declaration shall be made at the first public sitting at which the Member of the Court is present. Such sitting shall be held as soon as practicable after his term of office begins and, if necessary, a special sitting shall be held for the purpose.

3. A Member of the Court who is re-elected shall make a new declaration only if his new term is not continuous with his previous one.

Art. 5   1. A Member of the Court deciding to resign shall communicate his decision to the President, and the resignation shall take effect as provided in Article 13, paragraph 4, of the Statute.

2. If the Member of the Court deciding to resign from the Court is the President, he shall communicate his decision to the Court, and the resignation shall take effect as provided in Article 13, paragraph 4, of the Statute.

Art. 6   In any case in which the application of Article 18 of the Statute is under consideration, the Member of the Court concerned shall be so informed by the President or, if the circumstances so require, by the Vice-President, in a written statement which shall include the grounds therefor and any relevant evidence. He shall subsequently, at a private meeting of the Court specially convened for the purpose, be afforded an opportunity of making a statement, of furnishing any information or explanations he wishes to give, and of supplying answers, orally or in writing, to any questions put to him. At a further private meeting, at which the Member of the Court concerned shall not be present, the matter shall be discussed; each Member of the Court shall state his opinion, and if requested a vote shall be taken.

Subsection 2. Judges ad hoc

Art. 7   1. Judges *ad hoc*, chosen under Article 31 of the Statute for the purposes of particular cases, shall be admitted to sit on the Bench of the Court in the circumstances and according to the procedure indicated in Article 17, paragraph 2, Articles 35, 36, 37, Article 91, paragraph 2, and Article 102, paragraph 3, of these Rules.

2. They shall participate in the case in which they sit on terms of complete equality with the other judges on the Bench.

3. Judges *ad hoc* shall take precedence after the Members of the Court and in order of seniority of age.

Art. 8 1. The solemn declaration to be made by every judge *ad hoc* in accordance with Articles 20 and 31, paragraph 6, of the Statute shall be as set out in Article 4, paragraph 1, of these Rules.

2. This declaration shall be made at a public sitting in the case in which the judge *ad hoc* is participating. If the case is being dealt with by a chamber of the Court, the declaration shall be made in the same manner in that chamber.

3. Judges *ad hoc* shall make the declaration in relation to any case in which they are participating, even if they have already done so in a previous case, but shall not make a new declaration for a later phase of the same case.

Subsection 3. Assessors

Art. 9 1. The Court may, either *proprio motu* or upon a request made not later than the closure of the written proceedings, decide, for the purpose of a contentious case or request for advisory opinion, to appoint assessors to sit with it without the right to vote.

2. When the Court so decides, the President shall take steps to obtain all the information relevant to the choice of the assessors.

3. The assessors shall be appointed by secret ballot and by a majority of the votes of the judges composing the Court for the case.

4. These same powers shall belong to the Chambers provided for by Articles 26 and 29 of the Statute and to the presidents thereof, and may be exercised in the same manner.

5. Before entering upon their duties, assessors shall make the following declaration at a public sitting:

> "I solemnly declare that I will perform my duties as an assessor honourably, impartially and conscientiously, and that I will faithfully observe all the provisions of the Statute and of the Rules of the Court."

SECTION B. THE PRESIDENCY

Art. 10 1. The term of office of the President and that of the Vice-President shall begin to run from the date on which the terms of office of the Members of the Court elected at a triennial election begin in accordance with Article 2 of these Rules.

2. The elections to the presidency and vice-presidency shall be held on that date or shortly thereafter. The former President, if still a Member of

the Court, shall continue to exercise his functions until the election to the presidency has taken place.

Art. 11   1. If, on the date of the election to the presidency, the former President is still a Member of the Court, he shall conduct the election. If he has ceased to be a Member of the Court, or is unable to act, the election shall be conducted by the Member of the Court exercising the functions of the presidency by virtue of Article 13, paragraph 1, of these Rules.

2. The election shall take place by secret ballot, after the presiding Member of the Court has declared the number of affirmative votes necessary for election; there shall be no nominations. The Member of the Court obtaining the votes of a majority of the Members composing it at the time of the election shall be declared elected, and shall enter forthwith upon his functions.

3. The new President shall conduct the election of the Vice-President either at the same or at the following meeting. The provisions of paragraph 2 of this Article shall apply equally to this election.

Art. 12   The President shall preside at all meetings of the Court; he shall direct the work and supervise the administration of the Court.

Art. 13   1. In the event of a vacancy in the presidency or of the inability of the President to exercise the functions of the presidency, these shall be exercised by the Vice-President, or failing him, by the senior judge.

2. When the President is precluded by a provision of the Statute or of these Rules either from sitting or from presiding in a particular case, he shall continue to exercise the functions of the presidency for all purposes save in respect of that case.

3. The President shall take the measures necessary in order to ensure the continuous exercise of the functions of the presidency at the seat of the Court. In the event of his absence, he may, so far as is compatible with the Statute and these Rules, arrange for these functions to be exercised by the Vice-President, or failing him, by the senior judge.

4. If the President decides to resign the presidency, he shall communicate his decision in writing to the Court through the Vice-President, or failing him, the senior judge. If the Vice-President decides to resign his office, he shall communicate his decision to the President.

Art. 14   If a vacancy in the presidency or the vice-presidency occurs before the date when the current term is due to expire under Article 21, paragraph 1, of the Statute and Article 10, paragraph 1, of these Rules, the Court shall decide whether or not the vacancy shall be filled during the remainder of the term.

SECTION C. THE CHAMBERS

Art. 15   1. The Chamber of Summary Procedure to be formed annually under Article 29 of the Statute shall be composed of five Members of the Court, comprising the President and Vice-President of the Court, acting ex officio, and three other members elected in accordance with Article 18, paragraph 1, of these Rules. In addition, two Members of the Court shall be elected annually to act as substitutes.

2. The election referred to in paragraph 1 of this Article shall be held as soon as possible after the sixth of February in each year. The members of the Chamber shall enter upon their functions on election and continue to serve until the next election; they may be re-elected.

3. If a member of the Chamber is unable, for whatever reason, to sit in a given case, he shall be replaced for the purposes of that case by the senior in precedence of the two substitutes.

4. If a member of the Chamber resigns or otherwise ceases to be a member, his place shall be taken by the senior in precedence of the two substitutes, who shall thereupon become a full member of the Chamber and be replaced by the election of another substitute. Should vacancies exceed the number of available substitutes, elections shall be held as soon as possible in respect of the vacancies still existing after the substitutes have assumed full membership and in respect of the vacancies in the substitutes.

Art. 16   1. When the Court decides to form one or more of the Chambers provided for in Article 26, paragraph 1, of the Statute, it shall determine the particular category of cases for which each Chamber is formed, the number of its members, the period for which they will serve, and the date at which they will enter upon their duties.

2. The members of the Chamber shall be elected in accordance with Article 18, paragraph 1, of these Rules from among the Members of the Court, having regard to any special knowledge, expertise or previous experience which any of the Members of the Court may have in relation to the category of case the Chamber is being formed to deal with.

3. The Court may decide upon the dissolution of a Chamber, but without prejudice to the duty of the Chamber concerned to finish any cases pending before it.

Art. 17   1. A request for the formation of a Chamber to deal with a particular case, as provided for in Article 26, paragraph 2, of the Statute, may be filed at any time until the closure of the written proceedings. Upon receipt of a request made by one party, the President shall ascertain whether the other party assents.

2. When the parties have agreed, the President shall ascertain their views regarding the composition of the Chamber, and shall report to the Court accordingly. He shall also take such steps as may be necessary to give effect to the provisions of Article 31, paragraph 4, of the Statute.

3. When the Court has determined, with the approval of the parties, the number of its Members who are to constitute the Chamber, it shall proceed to their election, in accordance with the provisions of Article 18, paragraph 1, of these Rules. The same procedure shall be followed as regards the filling of any vacancy that may occur on the Chamber.

4. Members of a Chamber formed under this Article who have been replaced, in accordance with Article 13 of the Statute following the expiration of their terms of office, shall continue to sit in all phases of the case, whatever the stage it has then reached.

Art. 18 1. Elections to all Chambers shall take place by secret ballot. The Members of the Court obtaining the largest number of votes constituting a majority of the Members of the Court composing it at the time of the election shall be declared elected. If necessary to fill vacancies, more than one ballot shall take place, such ballot being limited to the number of vacancies that remain to be filled.

2. If a Chamber when formed includes the President or Vice-President of the Court, or both of them, the President or Vice-President, as the case may be, shall preside over that Chamber. In any other event, the Chamber shall elect its own president by secret ballot and by a majority of votes of its members. The Member of the Court who, under this paragraph, presides over the Chamber at the time of its formation shall continue to preside so long as he remains a member of that Chamber.

3. The president of a Chamber shall exercise, in relation to cases being dealt with by that Chamber, all the functions of the President of the Court in relation to cases before the Court.

4. If the president of a Chamber is prevented from sitting or from acting as president, the functions of the presidency shall be assumed by the member of the Chamber who is the senior in precedence and able to act.

SECTION D. INTERNAL FUNCTIONING OF THE COURT

Art. 19 The internal judicial practice of the Court shall, subject to the provisions of the Statute and these Rules, be governed by any resolutions on the subject adopted by the Court[1].

Art. 20 1. The quorum specified by Article 25, paragraph 3, of the Statute applies to all meetings of the Court.

2. The obligation of Members of the Court under Article 23, paragraph 3, of the Statute, to hold themselves permanently at the disposal of the Court, entails attendance at all such meetings, unless they are prevented from attending by illness or for other serious reasons duly explained to the President, who shall inform the Court.

---

[1] The resolution now in force was adopted on 12 April 1976 (see pp. 84 below).

3. Judges *ad hoc* are likewise bound to hold themselves at the disposal of the Court and to attend all meetings held in the case in which they are participating. They shall not be taken into account for the calculation of the quorum.

4. The Court shall fix the dates and duration of the judicial vacations and the periods and conditions of leave to be accorded to individual Members of the Court under Article 23, paragraph 2, of the Statute, having regard in both cases to the state of its General List and to the requirements of its current work.

5. Subject to the same considerations, the Court shall observe the public holidays customary at the place where the Court is sitting.

6. In case of urgency the President may convene the Court at any time.

Art. 21 1. The deliberations of the Court shall take place in private and remain secret. The Court may however at any time decide in respect of its deliberations on other than judicial matters to publish or allow publication of any part of them.

2. Only judges, and the assessors, if any, take part in the Court's judicial deliberations. The Registrar, or his deputy, and other members of the staff of the Registry as may be required shall be present. No other person shall be present except by permission of the Court.

3. The minutes of the Court's judicial deliberations shall record only the title or nature of the subjects or matters discussed, and the results of any vote taken. They shall not record any details of the discussions nor the views expressed, provided however that any judge is entitled to require that a statement made by him be inserted in the minutes.

PART II. THE REGISTRY

Art. 22 1. The Court shall elect its Registrar by secret ballot from amongst candidates proposed by Members of the Court. The Registrar shall be elected for a term of seven years. He may be re-elected.

2. The President shall give notice of a vacancy or impending vacancy to Members of the Court, either forthwith upon the vacancy arising, or, where the vacancy will arise on the expiration of the term of office of the Registrar, not less than three months prior thereto. The President shall fix a date for the closure of the list of candidates so as to enable nominations and information concerning the candidates to be received in sufficient time.

3. Nominations shall indicate the relevant information concerning the candidate, and in particular information as to his age, nationality, and present occupation, university qualifications, knowledge of languages, and any previous experience in law, diplomacy or the work of international organisations.

4. The candidate obtaining the votes of the majority of the Members of the Court composing it at the time of the election shall be declared elected.

Art. 23   The Court shall elect a Deputy-Registrar: the provisions of Article 22 of these Rules shall apply to his election and term of office.

Art. 24   1. Before taking up his duties, the Registrar shall make the following declaration at a meeting of the Court:

> "I solemnly declare that I will perform the duties incumbent upon me as Registrar of the International Court of Justice in all loyalty, discretion and good conscience, and that I will faithfully observe all the provisions of the Statute and of the Rules of the Court."

2. The Deputy-Registrar shall make a similar declaration at a meeting of the Court before taking up his duties.

Art. 25   1. The staff-members of the Registry shall be appointed by the Court on proposals submitted by the Registrar. Appointments to such posts as the Court shall determine may however be made by the Registrar with the approval of the President.

2. Before taking up his duties, every staff-member shall make the following declaration before the President, the Registrar being present:

> "I solemnly declare that I will perform the duties incumbent upon me as an official of the International Court of Justice in all loyalty, discretion and good conscience, and that I will faithfully observe all the provisions of the Statute and of the Rules of the Court."

Art. 26   1. The Registrar, in the discharge of his functions, shall:

(a) be the regular channel of communications to and from the Court and in particular shall effect all communications, notifications and transmission of documents required by the Statute or by these Rules and ensure that the date of despatch and receipt thereof may be readily verified;

(b) keep, under the supervision of the President, and in such form as may be laid down by the Court, a General List of all cases, entered and numbered in the order in which the documents instituting proceedings or requesting an advisory opinion are received in the Registry;

(c) have the custody of the declarations accepting the jurisdiction of the Court made by States not parties to the Statute in accordance with any resolution adopted by the Security Council under Article 35, paragraph 2, of the Statute[1], and transmit certified copies thereof to all States parties to the Statute, to such other States as shall have deposited declarations, and to the Secretary-General of the United Nations;

---

[1]   See pp. 88 below.

(d) transmit to the parties copies of all pleadings and documents annexed upon receipt thereof in the Registry;

(e) communicate to the government of the country in which the Court or a Chamber is sitting, and any other governments which may be concerned, the necessary information as to the persons from time to time entitled, under the Statute and relevant agreements, to privileges, immunities, or facilities;

(f) be present, in person or by his deputy, at meetings of the Court, and of the Chambers, and be responsible for the preparation of minutes of such meetings;

(g) make arrangements for such provision or verification of translations and interpretations into the Court's official languages as the Court may require;

(h) sign all judgments, advisory opinions and orders of the Court, and the minutes referred to in subparagraph (f);

(i) be responsible for the printing and publication of the Court's judgments, advisory opinions and orders, the pleadings and statements, and minutes of public sittings in cases, and of such other documents as the Court may direct to be published;

(j) be responsible for all administrative work and in particular for the accounts and financial administration in accordance with the financial procedures of the United Nations;

(k) deal with enquiries concerning the Court and its work;

(l) assist in maintaining relations between the Court and other organs of the United Nations, the specialised agencies, and international bodies and conferences concerned with the codification and progressive development of international law;

(m) ensure that information concerning the Court and its activities is made accessible to governments, the highest national courts of justice, professional and learned societies, legal faculties and schools of law, and public information media;

(n) have custody of the seals and stamps of the Court, of the archives of the Court, and of such other archives as may be entrusted to the Court[1].

2. The Court may at any time entrust additional functions to the Registrar.

---

[1] The Registrar also keeps the Archives of the Permanent Court of International Justice, entrusted to the present Court by decision of the Permanent Court of October 1945 (I.C.J. Yearbook 1946-1947, p. 26), and the Archives of the Trial of the Major War Criminals before the International Military Tribunal at Nuremberg (1945-1946), entrusted to the Court by decision of that Tribunal of 1 October 1946; the Court authorized the Registrar to accept the latter Archives by decision of 19 November 1949.

3. In the discharge of his functions the Registrar shall be responsible to the Court.

Art. 27   1. The Deputy-Registrar shall assist the Registrar, act as Registrar in the latter's absence and, in the event of the office becoming vacant, exercise the functions of Registrar until the office has been filled.

2. If both the Registrar and the Deputy-Registrar are unable to carry out the duties of Registrar, the President shall appoint an official of the Registry to discharge those duties for such time as may be necessary. If both offices are vacant at the same time, the President, after consulting the Members of the Court, shall appoint an official of the Registry to discharge the duties of Registrar pending an election to that office.

Art. 28   1. The Registry shall comprise the Registrar, the Deputy-Registrar, and such other staff as the Registrar shall require for the efficient discharge of his functions.

2. The Court shall prescribe the organisation of the Registry, and shall for this purpose request the Registrar to make proposals.

3. Instructions for the Registry shall be drawn up by the Registrar and approved by the Court.

4. The staff of the Registry shall be subject to Staff Regulations drawn up by the Registrar, so far as possible in conformity with the United Nations Staff Regulations and Staff Rules, and approved by the Court.

Art. 29   1. The Registrar may be removed from office only if, in the opinion of two-thirds of the Members of the Court, he has either become permanently incapacitated from exercising his functions, or has committed a serious breach of his duties.

2. Before a decision is taken under this Article, the Registrar shall be informed by the President of the action contemplated, in a written statement which shall include the grounds therefor and any relevant evidence. He shall subsequently, at a private meeting of the Court, be afforded an opportunity of making a statement, of furnishing any information or explanations he wishes to give, and of supplying answers, orally or in writing, to any questions put to him.

3. The Deputy-Registrar may be removed from office only on the same grounds and by the same procedure.

PART III. PROCEEDINGS IN CONTENTIOUS CASES

SECTION A. COMMUNICATIONS TO THE COURT AND CONSULTATIONS

Art. 30   All communications to the Court under these Rules shall be addressed to the Registrar unless otherwise stated. Any request made by a party shall likewise be addressed to the Registrar unless made in open court in the course of the oral proceedings.

Art. 31   In every case submitted to the Court, the President shall ascertain the views of the parties with regard to questions of procedure. For this purpose he shall summon the agents of the parties to meet him as soon as possible after their appointment, and whenever necessary thereafter.

SECTION B. THE COMPOSITION OF THE COURT FOR PARTICULAR CASES

Art. 32   1. If the President of the Court is a national of one of the parties in a case he shall not exercise the functions of the presidency in respect of that case. The same rule applies to the Vice-President, or to the senior judge, when called on to act as President.

2. The Member of the Court who is presiding in a case on the date on which the Court convenes for the oral proceedings shall continue to preside in that case until completion of the current phase of the case, notwithstanding the election in the meantime of a new President or Vice-President. If he should become unable to act, the presidency for the case shall be determined in accordance with Article 13 of these Rules, and on the basis of the composition of the Court on the date on which it convened for the oral proceedings.

Art. 33   Except as provided in Article 17 of these Rules, Members of the Court who have been replaced, in accordance with Article 13, paragraph 3, of the Statute following the expiration of their terms of office, shall discharge the duty imposed upon them by that paragraph by continuing to sit until the completion of any phase of a case in respect of which the Court convenes for the oral proceedings prior to the date of such replacement.

Art. 34   1. In case of any doubt arising as to the application of Article 17, paragraph 2, of the Statute or in case of a disagreement as to the application of Article 24 of the Statute, the President shall inform the Members of the Court, with whom the decision lies.

2. If a party desires to bring to the attention of the Court facts which it considers to be of possible relevance to the application of the provisions of the Statute mentioned in the previous paragraph, but which it believes may not be known to the Court, that party shall communicate confidentially such facts to the President in writing.

Art. 35   1. If a party proposes to exercise the power conferred by Article 31 of the Statute to choose a judge *ad hoc* in a case, it shall notify the Court of its intention as soon as possible. If the name and nationality of the judge selected are not indicated at the same time, the party shall, not later than two months before the time-limit fixed for the filing of the Counter-Memorial, inform the Court of the name and nationality of the person chosen and supply brief biographical details. The judge *ad hoc* may be of a nationality other than that of the party which chooses him.

2. If a party proposes to abstain from choosing a judge *ad hoc*, on condition of a like abstention by the other party, it shall so notify the Court which shall inform the other party. If the other party thereafter gives notice of its intention to choose, or chooses, a judge *ad hoc*, the time-limit for the party which has previously abstained from choosing a judge may be extended by the President.

3. A copy of any notification relating to the choice of a judge *ad hoc* shall be communicated by the Registrar to the other party, which shall be requested to furnish, within a time-limit to be fixed by the President, such observations as it may wish to make. If within the said time-limit no objection is raised by the other party, and if none appears to the Court itself, the parties shall be so informed.

4. In the event of any objection or doubt, the matter shall be decided by the Court, if necessary after hearing the parties.

5. A judge *ad hoc* who has accepted appointment but who becomes unable to sit may be replaced.

6. If and when the reasons for the participation of a judge *ad hoc* are found no longer to exist, he shall cease to sit on the Bench.

Art. 36   1. If the Court finds that two or more parties are in the same interest, and therefore are to be reckoned as one party only, and that there is no Member of the Court of the nationality of any one of those parties upon the Bench, the Court shall fix a time-limit within which they may jointly choose a judge *ad hoc*.

2. Should any party amongst those found by the Court to be in the same interest allege the existence of a separate interest of its own, or put forward any other objection, the matter shall be decided by the Court, if necessary after hearing the parties.

Art. 37   1. If a Member of the Court having the nationality of one of the parties is or becomes unable to sit in any phase of a case, that party shall thereupon become entitled to choose a judge *ad hoc* within a time-limit to be fixed by the Court, or by the President if the Court is not sitting.

2. Parties in the same interest shall be deemed not to have a judge of one of their nationalities upon the Bench if the Member of the Court having one of their nationalities is or becomes unable to sit in any phase of the case.

3. If the Member of the Court having the nationality of a party becomes able to sit not later than the closure of the written proceedings in that phase of the case, that Member of the Court shall resume his seat on the Bench in the case.

SECTION C. PROCEEDINGS BEFORE THE COURT

Subsection 1. Institution of Proceedings

Art. 38   1. When proceedings before the Court are instituted by means of an application addressed as specified in Article 40, paragraph 1, of the Statute, the application shall indicate the party making it, the State against which the claim is brought, and the subject of the dispute.

2. The application shall specify as far as possible the legal grounds upon which the jurisdiction of the Court is said to be based; it shall also specify the precise nature of the claim, together with a succinct statement of the facts and grounds on which the claim is based.

3. The original of the application shall be signed either by the agent of the party submitting it, or by the diplomatic representative of that party in the country in which the Court has its seat, or by some other duly authorized person. If the application bears the signature of someone other than such diplomatic representative, the signature must be authenticated by the latter or by the competent authority of the applicant's foreign ministry.

4. The Registrar shall forthwith transmit to the respondent a certified copy of the application.

5. When the applicant State proposes to found the jurisdiction of the Court upon a consent thereto yet to be given or manifested by the State against which such application is made, the application shall be transmitted to that State. It shall not however be entered in the General list, nor any action be taken in the proceedings, unless and until the State against which such application is made consents to the Court's jurisdiction for the purposes of the case.

Art. 39   1. When proceedings are brought before the Court by the notification of a special agreement, in conformity with Article 40, paragraph 1, of the Statute, the notification may be effected by the parties jointly or by any one or more of them. If the notification is not a joint one, a certified copy of it shall forthwith be communicated by the registrar to the other party.

2. In each case the notification shall be accompanied by an original or certified copy of the special agreement. The notification shall also, in so far as this is not already apparent from the agreement, indicate the precise subject of the dispute and identify the parties to it.

Art. 40   1. Except in the circumstances contemplated by Article 38, paragraph 5, of these Rules, all steps on behalf of the parties after proceedings have been instituted shall be taken by agents. Agents shall have an address for service at the seat of the Court to which all communications concerning the case are to be sent. Communications addressed to the agents of the parties shall be considered as having been addressed to the parties themselves.

2. When proceedings are instituted by means of an application, the name of the agent for the applicant shall be stated. The respondent, upon receipt of the certified copy of the application, or as soon as possible thereafter, shall inform the Court of the name of its agent.

3. When proceedings are brought by notification of a special agreement, the party making the notification shall state the name of its agent. Any other party to the special agreement, upon receiving from the Registrar a certified copy of such notification, or as soon as possible thereafter, shall inform the Court of the name of its agent if it has not already done so.

Art. 41   The institution of proceedings by a State which is not a party to the Statute but which, under Article 35, paragraph 2, thereof, has accepted the jurisdiction of the Court by a declaration made in accordance with any resolution adopted by the Security Council under that Article[1], shall be accompanied by a deposit of the declaration in question, unless the latter has previously been deposited with the Registrar. If any question of the validity or effect of such declaration arises, the Court shall decide.

Art. 42   The Registrar shall transmit copies of any application or notification of a special agreement instituting proceedings before the Court to: (a) the Secretary-General of the United Nations; (b) the Members of the United Nations; (c) other States entitled to appear before the Court.

Art. 43   Whenever the construction of a convention to which States other than those concerned in the case are parties may be in question within the meaning of Article 63, paragraph 1, of the Statute, the Court shall consider what directions shall be given to the Registrar in the matter.

Subsection 2. The Written Proceedings

Art. 44   1. In the light of the information obtained by the President under Article 31 of these Rules, the Court shall make the necessary orders to determine, *inter alia*, the number and the order of filing of the pleadings and the time-limits within which they must be filed.

2. In making an order under paragraph 1 of this Article, any agreement between the parties which does not cause unjustified delay shall be taken into account.

3. The Court may, at request of the party concerned, extend any time-limit, or decide that any step taken after the expiration of the time-limit fixed therefor shall be considered as valid, if it is satisfied that there is adequate justification for the request. In either case the other party shall be given an opportunity to state its views.

4. If the Court is not sitting, its powers under this Article shall be exercised by the President, but without prejudice to any subsequent decision of the Court. If the consultation referred to in Article 31 reveals persis-

---

[1]   The resolution now in force was adopted on 15 October 1946 (see p. 88, below).

tent disagreement between the parties as to the application of Article 45, paragraph 2, or Article 46, paragraph 2, of these Rules, the Court shall be convened to decide the matter.

Art. 45   1. The pleadings in a case begun by means of an application shall consist, in the following order, of: a Memorial by the applicant; a Counter-Memorial by the respondent.

2. The Court may authorize or direct that there shall be a Reply by the applicant and a Rejoinder by the respondent if the parties are so agreed, or if the Court decides, *proprio motu* or at the request of one of the parties, that these pleadings are necessary.

Art. 46   1. In a case begun by the notification of a special agreement, the number and order of the pleadings shall be governed by the provisions of the agreement, unless the Court, after ascertaining the views of the parties, decides otherwise.

2. If the special agreement contains no such provision, and if the parties have not subsequently agreed on the number and order of pleadings, they shall each file a Memorial and Counter-Memorial, within the same time-limits. The Court shall not authorise the presentation of Replies unless it finds them to be necessary.

Art. 47   The Court may at any time direct that the proceedings in two or more cases be joined. It may also direct that the written or oral proceedings, including the calling of witnesses, be in common; or the Court may, without effecting any formal joinder, direct common action in any of these respects.

Art. 48   Time-limits for the completion of steps in the proceedings may be fixed by assigning a specified period but shall always indicate definite dates. Such time-limits shall be as short as the character of the case permits.

Art. 49   1. A Memorial shall contain a statement of the relevant facts, a statement of law, and the submissions.

2. A Counter-Memorial shall contain: an admission or denial of the facts stated in the Memorial; any additional facts, if necessary; observations concerning the statement of law in the Memorial; a statement of law in answer thereto; and the submissions.

3. The Reply and Rejoinder, whenever authorised by the Court, shall not merely repeat the parties' contentions, but shall be directed to bringing out the issues that still divide them.

4. Every pleading shall set out the party's submissions at the relevant stage of the case, distinctly from the arguments presented, or shall confirm the submissions previously made.

Art. 50   1. There shall be annexed to the original of every pleading certified copies of any relevant documents adduced in support of the contentions contained in the pleading.

2. If only parts of a document are relevant, only such extracts as are necessary for the purpose of the pleading in question need be annexed. A copy of the whole document shall be deposited in the Registry, unless it has been published and is readily available.

3. A list of all documents annexed to a pleading shall be furnished at the time the pleading is filed.

Art. 51   1. If the parties are agreed that the written proceedings shall be conducted wholly in one of the two official languages of the Court, the pleadings shall be submitted only in that language. If the parties are not so agreed, any pleading or any part of a pleading shall be submitted in one or other of the official languages.

2. If in pursuance of Article 39, paragraph 3, of the Statute a language other than French or English is used, a translation into French or English certified as accurate by the party submitting it, shall be attached to the original of each pleading.

3. When a document annexed to a pleading is not in one of the official languages of the Court, it shall be accompanied by a translation into one of these languages certified by the party submitting it as accurate. The translation may be confined to part of an annex, or to extracts therefrom, but in this case it must be accompanied by an explanatory note indicating what passages are translated. The Court may however require a more extensive or a complete translation to be furnished.

Art. 52[1]   1. The original of every pleading shall be signed by the agent and filed in the Registry. It shall be accompanied by a certified copy of the pleading, documents annexed, and any translations, for communication to the other party in accordance with Article 43, paragraph 4, of the Statute, and by the number of additional copies required by the Registry, but without prejudice to an increase in that number should the need arise later.

2. All pleadings shall be dated. When a pleading has to be filed by a certain date, it is the date of the receipt of the pleading in the Registry which will be regarded by the Court as the material date.

3. If the Registrar arranges for the printing of a pleading at the request of a party, the text must be supplied in sufficient time to enable the printed pleading to be filed in the Registry before the expiration of any time-limit which may apply to it. The printing is done under the responsibility of the party in question.

4. The correction of a slip or error in any document which has been filed may be made at any time with the consent of the other party or by leave of the President. Any correction so effected shall be notified to the other party in the same manner as the pleading to which it relates.

---

[1]   The agents of the parties are requested to ascertain from the Registry the usual format of the pleadings, and the conditions on which the Court may bear part of the cost of printing.

Art. 53   1. The Court, or the President if the Court is not sitting, may at any time decide, after ascertaining the views of the parties, that copies of the pleadings and documents annexed shall be made available to a State entitled to appear before it which has asked to be furnished with such copies.

2. The Court may, after ascertaining the views of the parties, decide that copies of the pleadings and documents annexed shall be made accessible to the public on or after the opening of the oral proceedings.

Subsection 3. The Oral Proceedings

Art. 54   1. Upon the closure of the written proceedings, the case is ready for hearing. The date for the opening of the oral proceedings shall be fixed by the Court, which may also decide, if occasion should arise, that the opening or the continuance of the oral proceedings be postponed.

2. When fixing the date for, or postponing, the opening of the oral proceedings the Court shall have regard to the priority required by Article 74 of these Rules and to any other special circumstances, including the urgency of a particular case.

3. When the Court is not sitting, its powers under this Article shall be exercised by the President.

Art. 55   The Court may, if it considers it desirable, decide pursuant to Article 22, paragraph 1, of the Statute that all or part of the further proceedings in a case shall be held at a place other than the seat of the Court. Before so deciding, it shall ascertain the views of the parties.

Art. 56   1. After the closure of the written proceedings, no further documents may be submitted to the Court by either party except with the consent of the other party or as provided in paragraph 2 of this Article. The party desiring to produce a new document shall file the original or a certified copy thereof, together with the number of copies required by the Registry, which shall be responsible for communicating it to the other party and shall inform the Court. The other party shall be held to have given its consent if it does not lodge an objection to the production of the document.

2. In the absence of consent, the Court, after hearing the parties, may, if it considers the document necessary, authorise its production.

3. If a new document is produced under paragraph 1 or paragraph 2 of this Article, the other party shall have an opportunity of commenting upon it and of submitting documents in support of its comments.

4. No reference may be made during the oral proceedings to the contents of any document which has not been produced in accordance with Article 43 of the Statute or this Article, unless the document is part of a publication readily available.

5. The application of the provisions of this Article shall not in itself constitute a ground for delaying the opening or the course of the oral proceedings.

Art. 57   Without prejudice to the provisions of the Rules concerning the production of documents, each party shall communicate to the Registrar, in sufficient time before the opening of the oral proceedings, information regarding any evidence which it intends to produce or which it intends to request the Court to obtain. This communication shall contain a list of the surnames, first names, nationalities, descriptions and places of residence of the witnesses and experts whom the party intends to call, with indications in general terms of the point or points to which their evidence will be directed A copy of the communication shall also be furnished for transmission to the other party.

Art. 58   1. The Court shall determine whether the parties should present their arguments before or after the production of the evidence; the parties shall, however, retain the right to comment on the evidence given.

           2. The order in which the parties will be heard, the method of handling the evidence and of examining any witnesses and experts, and the number of counsel and advocates to be heard on behalf of each party, shall be settled by the Court after the views of the parties have been ascertained in accordance with Article 31 of these Rules.

Art. 59   The hearing in Court shall be public, unless the Court shall decide otherwise, or unless the parties demand that the public be not admitted. Such a decision or demand may concern either the whole or part of the hearing, and may be made at any time.

Art. 60   1. The oral statements made on behalf of each party shall be as succinct as possible within the limits of what is requisite for the adequate presentation of that party's contentions at the hearing. Accordingly, they shall be directed to the issues that still divide the parties, and shall not go over the whole ground covered by the pleadings, or merely repeat the facts and arguments these contain.

           2. At the conclusion of the last statement made by a party at the hearing, its agent, without recapitulation of the arguments, shall read that party's final submissions. A copy of the written text of these, signed by the agent, shall be communicated to the Court and transmitted to the other party.

Art. 61   1. The Court may at any time prior to or during the hearing indicate any points or issues to which it would like the parties specially to address themselves, or on which it considers that there has been sufficient argument.

           2. The Court may, during the hearing, put questions to the agents, counsel and advocates, and may ask them for explanations.

3. Each judge has a similar right to put questions, but before exercising it he should make his intention known to the President, who is made responsible by Article 45 of the Statute for the control of the hearing.

4. The agents, counsel and advocates may answer either immediately or within a time-limit fixed by the President.

Art. 62   1. The Court may at any time call upon the parties to produce such evidence or to give such explanations as the Court may consider to be necessary for the elucidation of any aspect of the matters in issue, or may itself seek other information for this purpose.

2. The Court may, if necessary, arrange for the attendance of a witness or expert to give evidence in the proceedings.

Art. 63   1. The parties may call any witnesses or experts appearing on the list communicated to the Court pursuant to Article 57 of these Rules. If at any time during the hearing a party wishes to call a witness or expert whose name was not included in that list, it shall so inform the Court and the other party, and shall supply the information required by Article 57. The witness or expert may be called either if the other party makes no objection or if the Court is satisfied that his evidence seems likely to prove relevant.

2. The Court, or the President if the Court is not sitting, shall, at the request of one of the parties or *proprio motu*, take the necessary steps for the examination of witnesses otherwise than before the Court itself.

Art. 64   Unless on account of special circumstances the Court decides on a different form of words,

(a) every witness shall make the following declaration before giving any evidence:
"I solemnly declare upon may honour and conscience that I will speak the truth, the whole truth and nothing but the truth";

(b) every expert shall make the following declaration before making any statement:
"I solemnly declare upon my honour and conscience that I will speak the truth, the whole truth and nothing but the truth, and that my statement will be in accordance with my sincere belief."

Art. 65   Witnesses and experts shall be examined by the agents, counsel or advocates of the parties under the control of the President. Questions may be put to them by the President and by the judges. Before testifying, witnesses shall remain out of court.

Art. 66   The Court may at any time decide, either *proprio motu* or at the request of a party, to exercise its functions with regard to the obtaining of evidence at a place or locality to which the case relates, subject to such conditions as the Court may decide upon after ascertaining the views of the parties. The necessary arrangements shall be made in accordance with Article 44 of the Statute.

Art. 67   1. If the Court considers it necessary to arrange for an enquiry or an expert opinion, it shall, after hearing the parties, issue an order to this effect,
defining the subject of the enquiry or expert opinion, stating the number
and mode of appointment of the persons to hold the enquiry or of the experts, and laying down the procedure to be followed. Where appropriate,
the Court shall require persons appointed to carry out an enquiry, or to
give an expert opinion, to make a solemn declaration.

2. Every report or record of an enquiry and every expert opinion shall be
communicated to the parties, which shall be given the opportunity of
commenting upon it.

Art. 68   Witnesses and experts who appear at the instance of the Court under Article 62, paragraph 2, and persons appointed under Article 67, paragraph
1, of these Rules, to carry out an enquiry or to give an expert opinion,
shall, where appropriate, be paid out of the funds of the Court.

Art. 69   1. The Court may, at any time prior to the closure of the oral proceedings, either *proprio motu* or at the request of one of the parties communicated as provided in Article 57 of these Rules, request a public international organisation, pursuant to Article 34 of the Statute, to furnish information relevant to a case before it. The Court, after consulting the
chief administrative officer of the organisation concerned, shall decide
whether such information shall be presented to it orally or in writing, and
the time-limits for its presentation.

2. When a public international organisation sees fit to furnish, on its own
initiative, information relevant to a case before the Court, it shall do so in
the form of a Memorial to be filed in the Registry before the closure of
the written proceedings. The Court shall retain the right to require such
information to be supplemented, either orally or in writing, in the form of
answers to any questions which it may see fit to formulate, and also to
authorise the parties to comment, either orally or in writing, on the information thus furnished.

3. In the circumstances contemplated by Article 34, paragraph 3, of the
Statute, the Registrar on the instructions of the Court, or of the President
if the Court is not sitting, shall proceed as prescribed in that paragraph.
The Court, or the President if the Court is not sitting, may, as from the
date on which the Registrar has communicated copies of the written proceedings and after consulting the chief administrative officer of the public
international organisation concerned, fix a time-limit within which the
organisation may submit to the Court its observations in writing. These
observations shall be communicated to the parties and may be discussed
by them and by the representative of the said organisation during the oral
proceedings.

4. In the foregoing paragraphs, the term "public international organisation" denotes an international organisation of States.

Art. 70   1. In the absence of any decision to the contrary by the Court, all speeches and statements made and evidence given at the hearing in one of the official languages of the Court shall be interpreted into the other official language. If they are made or given in any other language, they shall be interpreted into the two official languages of the Court.

2. Whenever, in accordance with Article 39, paragraph 3, of the Statute, a language other than French or English is used, the necessary arrangements for interpretation into one of the two official languages shall be made by the party concerned; however, the Registrar shall make arrangements for the verification of the interpretation provided by a party of evidence given on the party's behalf. In the case of witnesses or experts who appear at the instance of the Court, arrangements for interpretation shall be made by the Registry.

3. A party on behalf of which speeches or statements are to be made, or evidence given, in a language which is not one of the official languages of the Court, shall so notify the Registrar in sufficient time for him to make the necessary arrangements.

4. Before first interpreting in the case, interpreters provided by a party shall make the following declaration in open court:

"I solemnly declare upon my honour and conscience that my interpretation will be faithful and complete."

Art. 71   1. A verbatim record shall be made by the Registrar of every hearing, in the official language of the Court which has been used. When the language used is not one of the two official languages of the Court, the verbatim record shall be prepared in one of the Court's official languages.

2. When speeches or statements are made in a language which is not one of the official languages of the Court, the party on behalf of which they are made shall supply to the Registry in advance a text thereof in one of the official languages, and this text shall constitute the relevant part of the verbatim record.

3. The transcript of the verbatim record shall be preceded by the names of the judges present, and those of the agents, counsel and advocates of the parties.

4. Copies of the transcript shall be circulated to the judges sitting in the case, and to the parties. The latter may, under the supervision of the Court, correct the transcripts of speeches and statements made on their behalf, but in no case may such corrections affect the sense and bearing thereof. The judges may likewise make corrections in the transcript of anything they may have said.

5. Witnesses and experts shall be shown that part of the transcript which relates to the evidence given, or the statements made by them, and may correct it in like manner as the parties.

6. One certified true copy of the eventual corrected transcript, signed by the President and the Registrar, shall constitute the authentic minutes of

the sitting for the purposes of Article 47 of the Statute. The minutes of public hearings shall be printed and published by the Court.

Art. 72   Any written reply by a party to a question put under Article 61, or any evidence or explanation supplied by a party under Article 62 of these Rules, received by the Court after the closure of the oral proceedings, shall be communicated to the other party, which shall be given the opportunity of commenting upon it. If necessary the oral proceedings may be reopened for that purpose.

SECTION D. INCIDENTAL PROCEEDINGS

Subsection 1. Interim Protection

Art. 73   1. A written request for the indication of provisional measures may be made by a party at any time during the course of the proceedings in the case in connection with which the request is made.

2. The request shall specify the reasons therefor, the possible consequences if it is not granted, and the measures requested. A certified copy shall forthwith be transmitted by the Registrar to the other party.

Art. 74   1. A request for the indication of provisional measures shall have priority over all other cases.

2. The Court, if it is not sitting when the request is made, shall be convened forthwith for the purpose of proceeding to a decision on the request as a matter of urgency.

3. The Court, or the President if the Court is not sitting, shall fix a date for a hearing which will afford the parties an opportunity of being represented at it. The Court shall receive and take into account any observations that may be presented to it before the closure of the oral proceedings.

4. Pending the meeting of the Court, the President may call upon the parties to act in such a way as will enable any order the Court may make on the request for provisional measures to have its appropriate effects.

Art. 75   1. The Court may at any time decide to examine *proprio motu* whether the circumstances of the case require the indication of provisional measures which ought to be taken or complied with by any or all of the parties.

2. When a request for provisional measures has been made, the Court may indicate measures that are in whole or in part other than those requested, or that ought to be taken or complied with by the party which has itself made the request.

3. The rejection of a request for the indication of provisional measures shall not prevent the party which made it from making a fresh request in the same case based on new facts.

Art. 76 1. At the request of a party the Court may, at any time before the final judgment in the case, revoke or modify any decision concerning provisional measures if, in its opinion, some change in the situation justifies such revocation or modification.

2. Any application by a party proposing such a revocation or modification shall specify the change in the situation considered to be relevant.

3. Before taking any decision under paragraph 1 of this Article the Court shall afford the parties an opportunity of presenting their observations on the subject.

Art. 77 Any measures indicated by the Court under Articles 73 and 74 of these Rules, and any decision taken by the Court under Article 76, paragraph 1, of these Rules, shall forthwith be communicated to the Secretary-General of the United Nations for transmission to the Security Council in pursuance of Article 41, paragraph 2, of the Statute.

Art. 78 The Court may request information from the parties on any matter connected with the implementation of any provisional measures it has indicated.

Subsection 2. Preliminary Objections

Art. 79 1. Any objection by the respondent to the jurisdiction of the Court or to the admissibility of the application, or other objection the decision upon which is requested before any further proceedings on the merits, shall be made in writing within the time-limit fixed for the delivery of the Counter-Memorial. Any such objection made by a party other than the respondent shall be filed within the time-limit fixed for the delivery of that party's first pleading.

2. The preliminary objection shall set out the facts and the law on which the objection is based, the submissions and a list of the documents in support; it shall mention any evidence which the party may desire to produce. Copies of the supporting documents shall be attached.

3. Upon receipt by the Registry of a preliminary objection, the proceedings on the merits shall be suspended and the Court, or the President if the Court is not sitting, shall fix the time-limit within which the other party may present a written statement of its observations and submissions; documents in support shall be attached and evidence which it is proposed to produce shall be mentioned.

4. Unless otherwise decided by the Court, the further proceedings shall be oral.

5. The statements of fact and law in the pleadings referred to in paragraphs 2 and 3 of this Article, and the statements and evidence presented at the hearings contemplated by paragraph 4, shall be confined to those matters that are relevant to the objection.

6. In order to enable the Court to determine its jurisdiction at the preliminary stage of the proceedings, the Court, whenever necessary, may request the parties to argue all questions of law and fact, and to adduce all evidence, which bear on the issue.

7. After hearing the parties, the Court shall give its decision in the form of a judgment, by which it shall either uphold the objection, reject it, or declare that the objection does not possess, in the circumstances of the case, an exclusively preliminary character. If the Court rejects the objection or declares that it does not possess an exclusively preliminary character, it shall fix time-limits for the further proceedings.

8. Any agreement between the parties that an objection submitted under paragraph 1 of this Article be heard and determined within the framework of the merits shall be given effect by the Court.

Subsection 3. Counter-Claims

Art. 80   1. A counter-claim may be presented provided that it is directly connected with the subject-matter of the claim of the other party and that it comes within the jurisdiction of the Court.

2. A counter-claim shall be made in the Counter-Memorial of the party presenting it, and shall appear as part of the submissions of that party.

3. In the event of doubt as to the connection between the question presented by way of counter-claim and the subject-matter of the claim of the other party the Court shall, after hearing the parties, decide whether or not the question thus presented shall be joined to the original proceedings.

Subsection 4. Intervention

Art. 81   1. An application for permission to intervene under the terms of Article 62 of the Statute, signed in the manner provided for in Article 38, paragraph 3, of these Rules, shall be filed as soon as possible, and not later than the closure of the written proceedings. In exceptional circumstances, an application submitted at a later stage may however be admitted.

2. The application shall state the name of an agent. It shall specify the case to which it relates, and shall set out:

(a) the interest of a legal nature which the State applying to intervene considers may be affected by the decision in that case;

(b) the precise object of the intervention;

(c) any basis of jurisdiction which is claimed to exist as between the State applying to intervene and the parties to the case.

3. The application shall contain a list of the documents in support, which documents shall be attached.

Art. 82 1. A State which desires to avail itself of the right of intervention conferred upon it by Article 63 of the Statute shall file a declaration to that effect, signed in the manner provided for in Article 38, paragraph 3, of these Rules. Such a declaration shall be filed as soon as possible, and not later than the date fixed for the opening of the oral proceedings. In exceptional circumstances a declaration submitted at a later stage may however be admitted.

2. The declaration shall state the name of an agent. It shall specify the case and the convention to which it relates and shall contain:

(a) particulars of the basis on which the declarant State considers itself a party to the convention;

(b) identification of the particular provisions of the convention the construction of which it considers to be in question;

(c) statement of the construction of those provisions for which it contends;

(d) a list of the documents in support, which documents shall be attached.

3. Such a declaration may be filed by a State that considers itself a party to the convention the construction of which is in question but has not received the notification referred to in Article 63 of the Statute.

Art. 83 1. Certified copies of the application for permission to intervene under Article 62 of the Statute, or of the declaration of intervention under Article 63 of the Statute, shall be communicated forthwith to the parties to the case, which shall be invited to furnish their written observations within a time-limit to be fixed by the Court or by the President if the Court is not sitting.

2. The Registrar shall also transmit copies to: (a) the Secretary-General of the United Nations; (b) the Members of the United Nations; (c) other States entitled to appear before the Court; (d) any other States which have been notified under Article 63 of the Statute.

Art. 84 1. The Court shall decide whether an application for permission to intervene under Article 62 of the Statute should be granted, and whether an intervention under Article 63 of the Statute is admissible, as a matter of priority unless in view of the circumstances of the case the Court shall otherwise determine.

2. If, within the time-limit fixed under Article 83 of these Rules, an objection is filed to an application for permission to intervene, or to the admissibility of a declaration of intervention, the Court shall hear the State seeking to intervene and the parties before deciding.

Art. 85 1. If an application for permission to intervene under Article 62 of the Statute is granted, the intervening State shall be supplied with copies of the pleadings and documents annexed and shall be entitled to submit a written statement within a time-limit to be fixed by the Court. A further time-limit shall be fixed within which the parties may, if they so desire, furnish their written observations on that statement prior to the oral proceedings. If the Court is not sitting, these time-limits shall be fixed by the President.

2. The time-limits fixed according to the preceding paragraph shall, so far as possible, coincide with those already fixed for the pleadings in the case.

3. The intervening State shall be entitled, in the course of the oral proceedings, to submit its observations with respect to the subject-matter of the intervention.

Art. 86   1. If an intervention under Article 63 of the Statute is admitted, the intervening State shall be furnished with copies of the pleadings and documents annexed, and shall be entitled, within a time-limit to be fixed by the Court, or by the President if the Court is not sitting, to submit its written observations on the subject-matter of the intervention.

2. These observations shall be communicated to the parties and to any other State admitted to intervene. The intervening State shall be entitled, in the course of the oral proceedings, to submit its observations with respect to the subject-matter of the intervention.

Subsection 5. Special Reference to the Court

Art. 87   1. When in accordance with a treaty or convention in force a contentious case is brought before the Court concerning a matter which has been the subject of proceedings before some other international body, the provisions of the Statute and of the Rules governing contentious cases shall apply.

2. The application instituting proceedings shall identify the decision or other act of the international body concerned and a copy thereof shall be annexed; it shall contain a precise statement of the questions raised in regard to that decision or act, which constitute the subject of the dispute referred to the Court.

Subsection 6. Discontinuance

Art. 88   1. If at any time before the final judgment on the merits has been delivered the parties, either jointly or separately, notify the Court in writing that they have agreed to discontinue the proceedings, the Court shall make an order recording the discontinuance and directing that the case be removed from the list.

2. If the parties have agreed to discontinue the proceedings in consequence of having reached a settlement of the dispute and if they so desire, the Court may record this fact in the order for the removal of the case from the list, or indicate in, or annex to, the order, the terms of the settlement.

3. If the Court is not sitting, any order under this Article may be made by the President.

Art. 89   1. If in the course of proceedings instituted by means of an application, the applicant informs the Court in writing that it is not going on with the proceedings, and if, at the date on which this communication is received by the Registry, the respondent has not yet taken any step in the proceedings, the Court shall make an order officially recording the discontinuance of the proceedings and directing the removal of the case from the list. A copy of this order shall be sent by the Registrar to the respondent.

2. If, at the time when the notice of discontinuance is received, the respondent has already taken some step in the proceedings, the Court shall fix a time-limit within which the respondent may state whether it opposes the discontinuance of the proceedings If no objection is made to the discontinuance before the expiration of the time-limit, acquiescence will be presumed and the Court shall make an order officially recording the discontinuance of the proceedings and directing the removal of the case from the list. If objection is made, the proceedings shall continue.

3. If the Court is not sitting, its powers under this Article may be exercised by the President.

SECTION E. PROCEEDINGS BEFORE THE CHAMBERS

Art. 90   Proceedings before the Chambers mentioned in Articles 26 and 29 of the Statute shall, subject to the provisions of the Statute and of these Rules relating specifically to the Chambers, be governed by the provisions of Parts I to III of these Rules applicable in contentious cases before the Court.

Art. 91   1. When it is desired that a case should be dealt with by one of the Chambers which has been formed in pursuance of Article 26, paragraph 1, or Article 29 of the Statute, a request to this effect shall either be made in the document instituting the proceedings or accompany it. Effect will be given to the request if the parties are in agreement.

2. Upon receipt by the Registry of this request, the President of the Court shall communicate it to the members of the Chamber concerned. He shall take such steps as may be necessary to give effect to the provisions of Article 31, paragraph 4, of the Statute.

3. The President of the Court shall convene the Chamber at the earliest date compatible with the requirements of the procedure.

Art. 92   1. Written proceedings in a case before a Chamber shall consist of a single pleading by each side. In proceedings begun by means of an application, the pleadings shall be delivered within successive time-limits. In proceedings begun by the notification of a special agreement, the pleadings shall be delivered within the same time-limits, unless the parties have agreed on successive delivery of their pleadings. The time-limits referred to in this paragraph shall be fixed by the Court, or by the President if the Court is not sitting, in consultation with the Chamber concerned if it is already constituted.

2. The Chamber may authorise or direct that further pleadings be filed if the parties are so agreed, or if the Chamber decides, *proprio motu* or at the request of one of the parties, that such pleadings are necessary.

3. Oral proceedings shall take place unless the parties agree to dispense with them, and the Chamber consents. Even when no oral proceedings take place, the Chamber may call upon the parties to supply information or furnish explanations orally.

Art. 93   Judgments given by a Chamber shall be read at a public sitting of that Chamber.

SECTION F. JUDGMENTS, INTERPRETATION AND REVISION

Subsection 1 . Judgments

Art. 94   1. When the Court has completed its deliberations and adopted its judgment, the parties shall be notified of the date on which it will be read.

2. The judgment shall be read at a public sitting of the Court and shall become binding on the parties on the day of the reading.

Art. 95   1. The judgment, which shall state whether it is given by the Court or by a Chamber, shall contain:

the date on which it is read;

the names of the judges participating in it;

the names of the parties;

the names of the agents, counsel and advocates of the parties;

a summary of the proceedings;

the submissions of the parties;

a statement of the facts;

the reasons in point of law;

the operative provisions of the judgment;

the decision, if any, in regard to costs;

the number and names of the judges constituting the majority;

a statement as to the text of the judgment which is authoritative.

2. Any judge may, if he so desires, attach his individual opinion to the judgment, whether he dissents from the majority or not; a judge who wishes to record his concurrence or dissent without stating his reasons may do so in the form of a declaration. The same shall also apply to orders made by the Court.

3. One copy of the judgment duly signed and sealed, shall be placed in the archives of the Court and another shall be transmitted to each of the par-

ties. Copies shall be sent by the Registrar to: (a) the Secretary-General of the United Nations; (b) the Members of the United Nations; (c) other States entitled to appear before the Court.

Art. 96   When by reason of an agreement reached between the parties, the written and oral proceedings have been conducted in one of the Court's two official languages, and pursuant to Article 39, paragraph 1, of the Statute the judgment is to be delivered in that language, the text of the judgment in that language shall be the authoritative text.

Art. 97   If the Court, under Article 64 of the Statute, decides that all or part of a party's costs shall be paid by the other party, it may make an order for the purpose of giving effect to that decision.

Subsection 2. Requests for the Interpretation or Revision of a Judgment

Art. 98   1. In the event of dispute as to the meaning or scope of a judgment any party may make a request for its interpretation, whether the original proceedings were begun by an application or by the notification of a special agreement.

2. A request for the interpretation of a judgment may be made either by an application or by the notification of a special agreement to that effect between the parties; the precise point or points in dispute as to the meaning or scope of the judgment shall be indicated.

3. If the request for interpretation is made by an application, the requesting party's contentions shall be set out therein, and the other party shall be entitled to file written observations thereon within a time-limit fixed by the Court, or by the President if the Court is not sitting.

4. Whether the request is made by an application or by notification of a special agreement, the Court may, if necessary, afford the parties the opportunity of furnishing further written or oral explanations.

Art. 99   1. A request for the revision of a judgment shall be made by an application containing the particulars necessary to show that the conditions specified in Article 61 of the Statute are fulfilled. Any documents in support of the application shall be annexed to it.

2. The other party shall be entitled to file written observations on the admissibility of the application within a time-limit fixed by the Court, or by the President if the Court is not sitting. These observations shall be communicated to the party making the application.

3. The Court, before giving its judgment on the admissibility of the application may afford the parties a further opportunity of presenting their views thereon.

4. If the Court finds that the application is admissible it shall fix time-limits for such further proceedings on the merits of the application as, after ascertaining the views of the parties, it considers necessary.

5. If the Court decides to make the admission of the proceedings in revision conditional on previous compliance with the judgment, it shall make an order accordingly.

Art. 100   1. If the judgment to be revised or to be interpreted was given by the Court, the request for its revision or interpretation shall be dealt with by the Court. If the judgment was given by a Chamber, the request for its revision or interpretation shall be dealt with by that Chamber.

2. The decision of the Court, or of the Chamber, on a request for interpretation or revision of a judgment shall itself be given in the form of a judgment.

SECTION G. MODIFICATIONS PROPOSED BY THE PARTIES

Art. 101   The parties to a case may jointly propose particular modifications or additions to the rules contained in the present Part (with the exception of Articles 93 to 97 inclusive), which may be applied by the Court or by a Chamber if the Court or the Chamber considers them appropriate in the circumstances of the case.

PART IV. ADVISORY PROCEEDINGS

Art. 102   1. In the exercise of its advisory functions under Article 65 of the Statute, the Court shall apply, in addition to the provisions of Article 96 of the Charter and Chapter IV of the Statute, the provisions of the present Part of the Rules.

2. The Court shall also be guided by the provisions of the Statute and of these Rules which apply in contentious cases to the extent to which it recognises them to be applicable. For this purpose, it shall above all consider whether the request for the advisory opinion relates to a legal question actually pending between two or more States.

3. When an advisory opinion is requested upon a legal question actually pending between two or more States, Article 31 of the Statute shall apply, as also the provisions of these Rules concerning the application of that Article.

Art. 103   When the body authorised by or in accordance with the Charter of the United Nations to request an advisory opinion informs the Court that its request necessitates an urgent answer, or the Court finds that an early answer would be desirable, the Court shall take all necessary steps to accelerate the procedure, and it shall convene as early as possible for the purpose of proceeding to a hearing and deliberation on the request.

Art. 104   All requests for advisory opinions shall be transmitted to the Court by the Secretary-General of the United Nations or, as the case may be, the chief administrative officer of the body authorised to make the request. The documents referred to in Article 65, paragraph 2, of the Statute shall be transmitted to the Court at the same time as the request or as soon as possible thereafter, in the number of copies required by the Registry.

Art. 105   1. Written statements submitted to the Court shall be communicated by the Registrar to any States and organisations which have submitted such statements.

2. The Court, or the President if the Court is not sitting, shall:

(a) determine the form in which, and the extent to which, comments permitted under Article 66, paragraph 4, of the Statute shall be received, and fix the time-limit for the submission of any such comments in writing;

(b) decide whether oral proceedings shall take place at which statements and comments may be submitted to the Court under the provisions of Article 66 of the Statute, and fix the date for the opening of such oral proceedings.

Art. 106   The Court, or the President if the Court is not sitting, may decide that the written statements and annexed documents shall be made accessible to the public on or after the opening of the oral proceedings. If the request for advisory opinion relates to a legal question actually pending between two or more States, the views of those States shall first be ascertained.

Art. 107   1. When the Court has completed its deliberations and adopted its advisory opinion, the opinion shall be read at a public sitting of the Court.

2. The advisory opinion shall contain:

the date on which it is delivered;

the names of the judges participating;

a summary of the proceedings;

a statement of the facts;

the reasons in point of law;

the reply to the question put to the Court;

the number and names of the judges constituting the majority;

a statement as to the text of the opinion which is authoritative.

3. Any judge may, if he so desires, attach his individual opinion to the advisory opinion of the Court, whether he dissents from the majority or not; a judge who wishes to record his concurrence or dissent without stating his reasons may do so in the form of a declaration.

Art. 108   The Registrar shall inform the Secretary-General of the United Nations, and, where appropriate, the chief administrative officer of the body which requested the advisory opinion, as to the date and the hour fixed for the public sitting to be held for the reading of the opinion. He shall also inform the representatives of the Members of the United Nations and other States, specialised agencies and public international organizations immediately concerned.

Art. 109   One copy of the advisory opinion, duly signed and sealed, shall be placed
            in the archives of the Court, another shall be sent to the Secretary-
            General of the United Nations and, where appropriate, a third to the
            chief administrative officer of the body which requested the opinion of
            the Court. Copies shall be sent by the Registrar to the Members of the
            United Nations and to any other States, specialised agencies and public
            international organisations immediately concerned.

d) Resolution Concerning the Internal Judicial Practice of the Court of April 12, 1976

(Rules of Court, Article 19)

The Court decides to revise its Resolution concerning the Internal Judicial Practice of the Court of 5 July 1968[1] and to adopt the articles concerning its internal judicial practice which are set out in the present
Resolution. The Court remains entirely free to depart from the present
Resolution, or any part of it, in a given case, if it considers that the circumstances justify that course.

Art. 1   (i) After the termination of the written proceedings and before the begin-
          ning of the oral proceedings, a deliberation is held at which the judges ex-
          change views concerning the case, and bring to the notice of the Court
          any point in regard to which they consider it may be necessary to call for
          explanations during the course of the oral proceedings.

          (ii) In cases where two exchanges of oral arguments take place, after the
          first such exchange has been concluded, a further deliberation is held
          having the same objects.

          (iii) The Court also meets in private from time to time during the oral
          proceedings to enable judges to exchange views concerning the case and
          to inform each other of possible questions which they may intend to put
          in the exercise of their right under Article 61, paragraph 3, of the Rules.

Art. 2   After the termination of the oral proceedings, an appropriate period is
          allowed to the judges in order that they may study the arguments pre-
          sented to the Court.

Art. 3   (i) At the expiration of this period a deliberation is held at which the
          President outlines the issues which in his opinion will require discussion
          and decision by the Court. Any judge may then comment on the state-
          ment or call attention to any other issue or question which he considers

---

[1]   Prior to 1968, the internal judicial practice of the Court was governed by the Reso-
       lution of the Permanent Court of International Justice of 20 February 1931 (as
       amended on 17 March 1936), by virtue of a decision of the International Court of
       Justice of 1946 to adopt provisionally the practice of the Permanent Court.

relevant, and may at any time during or at the close of the deliberation cause to be distributed a text formulating a new question or reformulating a question already brought to notice.

(ii) During this deliberation any judge may comment on the pertinence of any issues or questions arising in the case. The President also invites judges to indicate their preliminary impressions regarding any issue or question.

(iii) Judges will be called on by the President in the order in which they signify their desire to speak.

Art. 4   (i) At a suitable interval of time after this deliberation, each judge prepares a written note which is distributed to the other judges.

(ii) The written note expresses the judge's views on the case, indicating, *inter alia*:

(a) whether any questions which have been called to notice should be eliminated from further consideration or should not, or need not, be decided by the Court;

(b) the precise questions which should be answered by the Court;

(c) his tentative opinion as to the answers to be given to the questions in (b) and his reasons therefor;

(d) his tentative conclusion as to the correct disposal of the case.

Art. 5   (i) After the judges have had an opportunity to examine the written notes, a further deliberation is held, in the course of which all the judges, called upon by the President as a rule in inverse order of seniority, must declare their views. Any judge may address comments to or ask for further explanations from a judge concerning the latter's statement declaring his views.

(ii) During this deliberation any judge may circulate an additional question or a reformulation of a question already brought to notice.

(iii) On the request of any judge the President shall ask the Court to decide whether a vote shall be taken on any question.

Art. 6   (i) On the basis of the views expressed in the deliberations and in the written notes, the Court proceeds to choose a drafting committee by secret ballot and by an absolute majority of votes of the judges present. Two members are elected who should be chosen from among those judges whose oral statements and written notes have most closely and effectively reflected the opinion of the majority of the Court as it appears then to exist.

(ii) The President shall ex officio be a member of the drafting committee unless he does not share the majority opinion of the Court as it appears then to exist, in which case his place shall be taken by the Vice-President. If the Vice-President is ineligible for the same reason, the Court shall proceed, by the process already employed, to the election of a third member, in which case the senior of the elected judges shall preside in the drafting committee.

(iii) If the President is not a member of the drafting committee, the committee shall discuss its draft with him before submitting it to the Court. If the President proposes amendments which the committee does not find it possible to adopt, it shall submit the President's proposals to the Court together with its own draft.

Art. 7   (i) A preliminary draft of the decision is circulated to the judges, who may submit amendments in writing. The drafting committee, having considered these amendments, submits a revised draft for discussion by the Court in first reading.

(ii) Judges who wish to deliver separate or dissenting opinions make the text thereof available to the Court after the first reading is concluded and within a time-limit fixed by the Court.

(iii) The drafting committee circulates an amended draft of the decision for the second reading, at which the President enquires whether any judge wishes to propose further amendments.

(iv) Judges who are delivering separate or dissenting opinions may make changes in or additions to their opinions only to the extent that changes have been made in the draft decision. During the second reading they inform the Court of any changes in or additions to their opinions which they propose to make for that reason. A time-limit is fixed by the Court for the filing of the revised texts of separate or dissenting opinions, copies of which are distributed to the Court.

Art 8   (i) At or after a suitable interval following upon the termination of the second reading, the President calls upon the judges to give their final vote on the decision or conclusion concerned in inverse order of seniority, and in the manner provided for by paragraph (v) of this Article.

(ii) Where the decision deals with issues that are separable, the Court shall in principle, and unless the exigencies of the particular case require a different course, proceed on the following basis, namely that:

(a)   any judge may request a separate vote on any such issue;

(b)   wherever the question before the Court is whether the Court is competent or the claim admissible, any separate vote on particular issues of competence or admissibility shall (unless such vote has shown some preliminary objection to be well-founded under the Statute and the Rules of Court) be followed by a vote on the question of whether the Court may proceed to entertain the merits of the case or, if that stage has already been reached, on the global question of whether, finally, the Court is competent or the claim admissible.

(iii) In any case coming under paragraph (ii) of this Article, or in any other case in which a judge so requests, the final vote shall take place only after a discussion on the need for separate voting, and whenever possible after a suitable interval following upon such discussion.

(iv) Any question whether separate votes as envisaged in paragraph (ii) of this Article should be recorded in the decision shall be decided by the Court.

(v) Every judge, when called upon by the President to record his final vote in any phase of the proceedings, or to vote upon any question relative to the putting to the vote of the decision or conclusion concerned, shall do so only by means of an affirmative or negative.

Art. 9   (i) Although because of illness or other reason deemed adequate by the President, a judge may have failed to attend part of the public hearing or of the Court's internal proceedings under Articles 1 to 7 inclusive of this Resolution, he may nevertheless participate in the final vote provided that:

(a) during most of the proceedings, he shall have been, or remained, at the seat of the Court or other locality in which the Court is sitting and exercising its functions for the purposes of the case under paragraph 1 of Article 22 of the Statute;

(b) as regards the public hearing, he shall have been able to read the official transcript of the proceedings;

(c) as regards the internal proceedings under Articles 1 to 7 inclusive, he shall have been able at least to submit his own written note, read those of the other judges, and study the drafts of the drafting committee; and

(d) as regards the proceedings as a whole, he shall have taken a sufficient part in the public hearing and in the internal proceedings under Articles 1 to 7 inclusive to enable him to arrive at a judicial determination of all issues of fact and law material to the decision of the case.

(ii) A judge who is qualified to participate in the final vote must record his vote in person. In the event of a judge who is otherwise in a fit condition to record his vote being unable because of physical incapacity or other compelling reason to attend the meeting at which the vote is to be taken, the vote shall, if the circumstances permit, be postponed until he can attend. If, in the opinion of the Court, the circumstances do not permit of such a postponement, or render it inadvisable, the Court may, for the purpose of enabling the judge to record his vote, decide to convene elsewhere than at its normal meeting place. If neither of these alternatives is practicable, the judge may be permitted to record his vote in any other manner which the Court decides to be compatible with the Statute.

(iii) In the event of any doubt arising as to whether a judge may vote in the circumstances contemplated by paragraphs (i) and (ii) hereof — and if this doubt cannot be resolved in the course of discussion — the matter shall, upon the proposal of the President, or at the request of any other Member of the Court, be decided by the Court.

(iv) When a judge casts his final vote in the circumstances contemplated by paragraphs (i) and (ii) of the present Article, paragraph (v) of Article 8 shall apply.

Art. 10   The foregoing provisions shall apply whether the proceedings before the Court are contentious or advisory.

e) Access to the Court of States Not Parties to the Statute, Security Council Resolution 9 (1946) of October 15, 1946

The Security Council of the United Nations, in virtue of the powers conferred upon it by Article 35, paragraph 2, of the Statute of the International Court of Justice, and subject to the provisions of that Article, resolves that:

(1) The International Court of Justice shall be open to a State which is not a party to the Statute of the International Court of Justice, upon the following condition, namely: that such State shall previously have deposited with the Registrar of the Court a declaration by which it accepts the jurisdiction of the Court, in accordance with the Charter of the United Nations and with the terms and subject to the conditions of the Statute and Rules of the Court, and undertakes to comply in good faith with the decision or decisions of the Court and to accept all the obligations of a Member of the United Nations under Article 94 of the Charter.

(2) Such declaration may be either particular or general.

A particular declaration is one accepting the jurisdiction of the Court in respect only of a particular dispute or disputes which have already arisen.

A general declaration is one accepting the jurisdiction generally in respect of all disputes or of a particular class or classes of disputes which have already arisen, or which may arise in the future.

A State in making such a general declaration may, in accordance with Article 36, paragraph 2, of the Statute, recognise as compulsory, *ipso facto*, and without special agreement, the jurisdiction of the Court, provided, however, that such acceptance may not, without explicit agreement, be relied upon vis-a-vis States parties to the Statute, which have made the declaration in conformity with Article 36, paragraph 2, of the Statute of the International Court of Justice.

(3) The original declarations made under the terms of this Resolution shall be kept in the custody of the Registrar of the Court, in accordance with the practice of the Court. Certified true copies thereof shall be transmitted, in accordance with the practice of the Court, to all States parties to the Statute of the International Court of Justice, and to such other States as shall have deposited a declaration under the terms of this Resolution, and to the Secretary-General of the United Nations.

(4) The Security Council of the United Nations reserves the right to rescind or amend this Resolution by a resolution which shall be communicated to the Court, and on the receipt of such communication and to the extent determined by the new resolution existing declarations shall cease to be effective except in regard to disputes which are already before the Court.

(5) All questions as to the validity or the effect of a declaration made under the terms of this Resolution shall be decided by the Court.

f) Secretary-General's Trust Fund to Assist States in the Settlement of Disputes through the International Court of Justice of November 1, 1989

TERMS OF REFERENCE, GUIDELINES AND RULES OF THE SECRETARY-GENERAL'S TRUST FUND TO ASSIST STATES IN THE SETTLEMENT OF DISPUTES THROUGH THE INTERNATIONAL COURT OF JUSTICE

REASONS FOR ESTABLISHING THE TRUST FUND

1. The United Nations has a special role in the maintenance of peace and security. The Charter recognises settlement of disputes by peaceful means, and in conformity with the principles of justice and international law. as a basic purpose of the United Nations and as an essential tool for the maintenance of international peace and security. The importance of peaceful settlement of disputes has been reiterated in numerous UN legal instruments, including the Declaration on Principles of International Law Concerning the Friendly Relations and Cooperation among States of 24 October 1970 and the Manila Declaration on the Peaceful Settlement of Disputes of 15 November 1982. In the Manila Declaration the General Assembly stressed once again that States should be encouraged to settle disputes by making full use of the provisions of the Charter of the United Nations, in particular those concerning the peaceful settlement of disputes. At the same time the Manila Declaration also states that recourse to judicial settlement of legal disputes, particularly referral to the International Court of Justice, should not be considered an unfriendly act between States.

2. The Court is the principal judicial organ of the United Nations. Its judgments represent the most authoritative pronouncement on international law. As follows from Article 36(3) of the Charter, the Court is also the principal organ for resolving legal disputes between States. The Secretary-General, as the Chief Administrative Officer of the Organization, has, therefore, a special responsibility to promote judicial settlement through the Court.

3. Legal disputes may arise in various parts of the world over a wide variety of issues. There are occasions where the Parties concerned are prepared to seek settlement of their disputes through the International Court of Justice, but cannot proceed because of the lack of legal expertise or funds. There may also be cases where the parties are unable to implement an ICJ decision because of the same reasons. In all such cases the availability of funds would advance the peaceful settlement of disputes.

4. The cost which may be incurred by ICJ proceedings is a factor which may in some instances discourage States from resorting to the Court. In arbitration, the parties bear the costs of the arbitrators and the maintenance of the tribunal (e.g. the registry etc.). The administrative costs of the International Court of Justice are borne by the United Nations. But, as in arbitration, the parties must bear the costs of agents, counsels, experts, witnesses, and the preparation of memorials and counter-memorials, etc. The total can be considerable. Thus, costs can be a factor in deciding whether a dispute should be referred to the International Court of Justice. The availability of funds would therefore be helpful for States which lack the necessary funds.

5. The United Nations has extensive experience in providing assistance to countries for their industrial and economic development. This experience could be utilised to assist States in obtaining the necessary legal expertise to facilitate settlement of disputes.

OBJECT AND PURPOSE OF THE TRUST FUND

6. This Trust Fund (hereinafter referred to as "the Fund") is established by the Secretary-General under the Financial Regulations and Rules of the United Nations. The purpose of the Fund is to provide, in accordance with the terms and conditions specified herein, financial assistance to States for expenses incurred in connexion with: (i) a dispute submitted to the International Court of Justice by way of a special agreement, or (ii) the execution of a Judgment of the Court resulting from such special agreement.

CONTRIBUTIONS TO THE FUND

7. The Secretary-General invites States, intergovernmental organizations, national institutions, non-governmental organisations, as well as natural and juridical persons to make voluntary financial contributions to the Fund.

APPLICATION FOR FINANCIAL ASSISTANCE

8. An application for financial assistance from the Fund may be submitted by any Member State of the United Nations, any State party to the Stat-

ute of the International Court of Justice or a Non-Member State having complied with Security Council resolution 9 (1946), which has concluded a special agreement for the purpose of submitting a specific dispute to the International Court of Justice for judgment. The application shall be accompanied by:

(i)   a copy of the special agreement referred to;

(ii) an itemised statement of the estimated costs for which financial assistance is requested from the Fund;

(iii) an undertaking that the requesting State shall supply a final statement of account providing details of the expenditures made from the approved amounts, to be certified by an auditor acceptable to the United Nations.

ESTABLISHMENT OF PANEL OF EXPERTS

9. For each request for financial assistance, the Secretary-General will establish a Panel of Experts composed of three persons of the highest judicial and moral standing. The task of the Panel is to examine the application on the basis of paragraph 8 above, to recommend to the Secretary-General the amount of financial assistance to be given and the types of expenses for which the assistance may be used: e.g. preparation of memorials, counter-memorials and replies; fees for agents, counsel, advocates, experts or witnesses; legal research fees; costs related to oral proceedings: e.g. interpretation into and/or from languages other than English and French; expenses of producing technical materials (e.g. reproduction of cartographic evidence), costs relating to the execution of an ICJ Judgment (e.g. demarcation of boundaries).

10. The work of the Panel of Experts shall be conducted in strict confidentiality.

11. In considering an application, the Panel of Experts shall be guided solely by the financial needs of the requesting State and availability of funds.

12. Travel expenses and subsistence allowance are payable to members of the Panel from the Fund.

GRANTING OF ASSISTANCE

13. The Secretary-General will provide financial assistance from the Fund on the basis of the evaluation and recommendations of the Panel of Experts. Payments will be made against receipts evidencing actual expenditures for approved costs.

APPLICATION OF UN FINANCIAL REGULATIONS AND RULES

14. The Financial Regulations and Rules of the United Nations shall apply to the administration of the Trust Fund. The Fund shall be subject to the auditing procedures provided therein.

REPORTING

15. An annual report on the activities of the Fund will be made to the General Assembly.

IMPLEMENTING OFFICE

16. The Office of Legal Affairs is the Implementing Office for the Trust Fund and provides the services required for the operation of the Fund.

REVISION

17. The Secretary-General may revise the above, if circumstances so require.

3. Geneva General Act for the Pacific Settlement of International Disputes of September 26, 1928 and April 28, 1949

As in the case of the Hague Convention, the General Act for the Pacific Settlement of Disputes was conceived as a universal instrument for the peaceful settlement of international disputes. The basic premise of the General Act is the feasibility of settling all disputes whether legal or non-legal ones by conciliation, arbitration or adjudication.

Under the terms of the General Act all legal disputes are subject to compulsory adjudication by the International Court of Justice although an optional conciliation procedure may precede adjudication; all non-legal disputes are subject to compulsory conciliation with subsequent compulsory arbitration if the conciliation procedure had failed. As to legal disputes arbitration and conciliation are envisaged only as a subsidiary means of dispute settlement.

While the General Act provides for the creation of permanent conciliation commissions between pairs of signatory States this does not preclude the possibility of forming ad hoc commissions for the settlement of a particular dispute. According to the General Act not only the parties to a dispute but all signatory States are obliged to abstain from all measures likely to impair the efforts of the commissions or the execution of the arrangements proposed by them.

In regard to arbitration the General Act refers largely to the Hague Convention of 1907 unless the parties have otherwise provided. Although the arbitral tribunals do not, in general, decide upon legal disputes, they have to apply international law. If international law does not provide an applicable rule the decision is taken *ex aequo et bono*. The General Act is the first instrument which aims at institutionalizing obligatory arbitration in the case of failure of previous conciliation as a means of settling non-legal disputes.

Further advantages of the Act are the limitation of possible reservations to certain specially enumerated categories as well as the faculty granted to the arbitral tribunals and the International Court of Justice to order interim measures of protection.

States may accede to the General Act as a whole or to only a portion of it. In practice, no more than 24 States acceded to the Act most of them making reservations.

In 1939 Great Britain, France, India, New Zealand and Australia emptied the General Act of its most substantive effect by making reservations declaring it inapplicable if war was either imminent or had broken out or to conflicts arising out of events occurring during the war. Although the General Act never applied as intended it survived the war and the League of Nations. In 1949 the United Nations General Assembly attempted to revive the Act by adapting it to the new international circumstances. This effort was rather unsuccessful: as of 1999 only eight States had declared their accession to the Act and it is doubtful whether the original 1928 General Act is still in force between the States which acceded to it. This question was raised before the International Court of Justice in the Pakistani Prisoners of War Case, the Nuclear Tests Cases and the Aegean Sea Continental Shelf Case, but remained undecided.

Texts

General Act for the Pacific Settlement of International Disputes: LNTS Vol. 93, pp. 344–363 (French and English)

M. O. Hudson (ed.), International Legislation, Vol. 4 (1931), pp. 2529–2544

F. Berber, Völkerrecht, Dokumentensammlung, Vol. 2 (1967), pp. 1734 et seq.

Revised General Act for the Pacific Settlement of Disputes: UNTS Vol.71, pp. 101–127 (French and English)

United Nations Textbook (3rd ed. 1958), pp. 108–119

Bibliographical notes

E. Borel, L'Acte Général de Genève, RdC Vol. 27 (1929 II), pp. 499–592

S. Dotremont, L'arbitrage international et le Conseil de la Société des Nations (1929)

H. Sandelmann, Die Generalakte der Neunten Völkerbundsversammlung, Friedens-Warte, Vol. 29 (1920), pp. 196 – 200

H. Wehberg, Die Generalakte zur friedlichen Erledigung internationaler Streitigkeiten, Friedens-Warte, Vol. 29 (1929), pp. 300–308

J. L. Brierly, The General Act of Geneva 1928, BYIL 11 (1930), pp. 119–133

M. Gonsiorowski, Political Arbitration under the General Act for the Pacific Settlement of International Disputes, AJIL Vol. 27 (1933), pp. 469–490

M. Faroggi, L'Acte Général d'Arbitrage (1935)

K. H. Kunzmann, Die Generalakte von New York und Genf als Streitschlichtungsvertrag der Vereinten Nationen, Friedens-Warte, Vol. 56 (1961), pp. 1–33

J. G. Merrills, The International Court of Justice and the General Act of 1928, Cambridge LJ Vol. 39 (1980), pp. 137–171

F. A. Freiherr von der Heydte, General Act for the Pacific Settlement of International Disputes 1928 and 1949, in: R. Bernhardt (ed.), Encyclopedia of Public International Law, Vol. II (1995), pp. 499–502

General Act for the Pacific Settlement of International Disputes of September 26, 1928 and April 28, 1949[1]

CHAPTER I. CONCILIATION

Art. 1   Disputes of every kind between two or more Parties to the present General Act which it has not been possible to settle by diplomacy shall, subject to such reservations as may be made under Article 39, be submitted, under the conditions laid down in the present Chapter, to the procedure of conciliation.

Art. 2   The disputes referred to in the preceding article shall be submitted to a permanent or special Conciliation Commission constituted by the parties to the dispute.

Art. 3   On a request to that effect being made by one of the Contracting Parties to another Party, a permanent Conciliation Commission shall be constituted within a period of six months.

Art. 4   Unless the parties concerned agree otherwise, the Conciliation Commission shall be constituted as follows:

(1) The Commission shall be composed of five members. The parties shall each nominate one commissioner, who may be chosen from among their respective nationals. The three other commissioners shall be appointed by agreement from among the nationals of third Powers. These three commissioners must be of different nationalities and must not be habitually resident in the territory nor be in the service of the parties. The parties shall appoint the President of the Commission from among them.

(2) The commissioners shall be appointed for three years. They shall be re-eligible. The commissioners appointed jointly may be replaced during the course of their mandate by agreement between the parties. Either party may, however, at any time replace a commissioner whom it has appointed. Even if replaced, the commissioners shall continue to exercise their functions until the termination of the work in hand.

(3) Vacancies which may occur as a result of death, resignation or any other cause shall be filled within the shortest possible time in the manner fixed for the nominations.

Art. 5   If, when a dispute arises, no permanent Conciliation Commission appointed by the parties is in existence, a special commission shall be constituted for the examination of the dispute within a period of three months from the date at which a request to that effect is made by one of the parties to the other party. The necessary appointments shall be made

---

[1]   Footnotes indicate the differences in the text of the 1949 General Act.

in the manner laid down in the preceding article, unless the parties decide otherwise.

Art. 6   1. If the appointment of the commissioners to be designated jointly is not made within the periods provided for in Articles 3 and 5, the making of the necessary appointments shall be entrusted to a third Power, chosen by agreement between the parties, or on request of the parties, to the[1] Acting President of the Council of the League of Nations.

2. If no agreement is reached on either of these procedures, each party shall designate a different Power, and the appointment shall be made in concert by the Powers thus chosen.

3. If, within a period of three months, the two Powers have been unable to reach an agreement, each of them shall submit a number of candidates equal to the number of members to be appointed. It shall then be decided by lot which of the candidates thus designated shall be appointed.

Art. 7   1. Disputes shall be brought before the Conciliation Commission by means of an application addressed to the President by the two parties acting in agreement, or in default thereof by one or other of the parties.

2. The application, after giving a summary account of the subject of the dispute, shall contain the invitation to the Commission to take all necessary measures with a view to arriving at an amicable solution.

3. If the application emanates from only one of the parties, the other party shall, without delay, be notified by it.

Art. 8   1. Within fifteen days from the date on which a dispute has been brought by one of the parties before a permanent Conciliation Commission, either party may replace its own commissioner, for the examination of the particular dispute, by a person possessing special competence in the matter.

2. The party making use of this right shall immediately notify the other party; the latter shall, in such case, be entitled to take similar action within fifteen days from the date on which it received the notification.

Art. 9   1. In the absence of agreement to the contrary between the parties, the Conciliation Commission shall meet at the seat of the[2] League of Nations, or at some other place selected by its President.

2. The Commission may in all circumstances request the Secretary-General of the League of Nations to afford it his assistance.

Art. 10 The work of the Conciliation Commission shall not be conducted in public unless a decision to that effect is taken by the Commission with the consent of the parties.

---

[1]   President of the General Assembly, or, if the latter is not in session, to the last President.

[2]   United Nations.

Art. 11   1. In the absence of agreement to the contrary between the parties, the Conciliation Commission shall lay down its own procedure, which in any case must provide for both parties being heard. In regard to enquiries, the Commission, unless it decides unanimously to the contrary, shall act in accordance with the provisions of Part III of the Hague Convention of October 18, 1907, for the Pacific Settlement of International Disputes.

2. The parties shall be represented before the Conciliation Commission by agents, whose duty shall be to act as intermediaries between them and the Commission; they may, moreover, be assisted by counsel and experts appointed by them for that purpose and may request that all persons whose evidence appears to them desirable shall be heard.

3. The Commission, for its part, shall be entitled to request oral explanations from the agents, counsel and experts of both parties, as well as from all persons it may think desirable to summon with the consent of their Governments.

Art. 12   In the absence of agreement to the contrary between the parties, the decisions of the Conciliation Commission shall be taken by a majority vote, and the Commission may only take decisions on the substance of the dispute if all its members are present.

Art. 13   The parties undertake to facilitate the work of the Conciliation Commission, and particularly to supply it to the greatest possible extent with all relevant documents and information, as well as to use the means at their disposal to allow it to proceed in their territory, and in accordance with their law, to the summoning and hearing of witnesses or experts and to visit the localities in question.

Art. 14   1. During the proceedings of the Commission, each of the commissioners shall receive emoluments the amount of which shall be fixed by agreement between the parties, each of which shall contribute an equal share.

2. The general expenses arising out of the working of the Commission shall be divided in the same manner.

Art. 15   1. The task of the Conciliation Commission shall be to elucidate the questions in dispute, to collect with that object all necessary information by means of enquiry or otherwise, and to endeavour to bring the parties to an agreement. It may, after the case has been examined, inform the parties of the terms of settlement which seem suitable to it, and lay down the period within which they are to make their decision.

2. At the close of the proceedings the Commission shall draw up a procès-verbal stating, as the case may be, either that the parties have come to an agreement and, if need arises, the terms of the agreement, or that it has been impossible to effect a settlement. No mention shall be made in the procès-verbal of whether the Commission's decisions were taken unanimously or by a majority vote.

3. The proceedings of the Commission must, unless the parties otherwise agree, be terminated within six months from the date on which the Commission shall have been given cognisance of the dispute.

Art. 16   The Commission's procès-verbal shall be communicated without delay to the parties. The parties shall decide whether it shall be published.

CHAPTER II. JUDICIAL SETTLEMENT

Art. 17   All disputes with regard to which the parties are in conflict as to their respective rights shall, subject to any reservations which may be made under Article 39, be submitted for decision to the[1] Permanent Court of International Justice, unless the parties agree, in the manner hereinafter provided, to have resort to an arbitral tribunal.

It is understood that the disputes referred to above include in particular those mentioned in Article 36 of the Statute of the[1] Permanent Court of International Justice.

Art. 18   If the parties agree to submit the disputes mentioned in the preceding article to an arbitral tribunal, they shall draw up a special agreement in which they shall specify the subject of the dispute, the arbitrators selected, and the procedure to be followed. In the absence of sufficient particulars in the special agreement, the provisions of the Hague Convention of October 18th, 1907, for the Pacific Settlement of International Disputes shall apply so far as is necessary. If nothing is laid down in the special agreement as to the rules regarding the substance of the dispute to be followed by the arbitrators, the tribunal shall apply the substantive rules enumerated in Article 38 of the Statute of the[1] Permanent Court of International Justice.

Art. 19   If the parties fail to agree concerning the special agreement referred to in the preceding article, or fail to appoint arbitrators, either party shall be at liberty, after giving three months' notice, to bring the dispute by an application direct before the[1] Permanent Court of International Justice.

Art. 20   1. Notwithstanding the provisions of Article 1, disputes of the kind referred to in Article 17 arising between parties who have acceded to the obligations contained in the present chapter shall only be subject to the procedure of conciliation if the parties so agree.

2. The obligation to resort to the procedure of conciliation remains applicable to disputes which are excluded from judicial settlement only by the operation of reservations under the provision of Article 39.

3. In the event of recourse to and failure of conciliation, neither party may bring the dispute before the[1] Permanent Court of International Justice or call for the constitution of the arbitral tribunal referred to in Article 18

---

[1]   International Court of Justice.

before the expiration of one month from the termination of the proceedings of the Conciliation Commission.

CHAPTER III. ARBITRATION

Art. 21   Any dispute not of the kind referred to in Article 17 which does not, within the month following the termination of the work of the Conciliation Commission provided for in Chapter I, form the object of an agreement between the parties, shall, subject to such reservations as may be made under Article 39, be brought before an arbitral tribunal which, unless the parties otherwise agree, shall be constituted in the manner set out below.

Art. 22   The Arbitral Tribunal shall consist of five members. The parties shall each nominate one member, who may be chosen from among their respective nationals. The two other arbitrators and the Chairman shall be chosen by common agreement from among the nationals of third Powers. They must be of different nationalities and must not be habitually resident in the territory nor be in the service of the parties.

Art. 23   1. If the appointment of the members of the Arbitral Tribunal is not made within a period of three months from the date on which one of the parties requested the other party to constitute an arbitral tribunal, a third Power, chosen by agreement between the parties, shall be requested to make the necessary appointments.

2. If no agreement is reached on this point, each party shall designate a different Power, and the appointments shall be made in concert by the Powers thus chosen.

3. If, within a period of three months, the two Powers so chosen have been unable to reach an agreement, the necessary appointments shall be made by the President of the[1] Permanent Court of International Justice. If the latter is prevented from acting or is a subject of one of the parties, the nominations shall be made by the Vice-President. If the latter is prevented from acting or is a subject of one of the parties, the appointments shall be made by the oldest member of the Court who is not a subject of either party.

Art. 24   Vacancies which may occur as a result of death, resignation or any other cause shall be filled within the shortest possible time in the manner fixed for the nominations.

Art. 25   The parties shall draw up a special agreement determining the subject of the disputes and the details of procedure.

Art. 26   In the absence of sufficient particulars in the special agreement regarding the matters referred to in the preceding article, the provisions of the

---

[1]   International Court of Justice.

Hague Convention of October 18th, 1907, for the Pacific Settlement of International Disputes shall apply so far as is necessary.

Art. 27   Failing the conclusion of a special agreement within a period of three months from the date on which the Tribunal was constituted, the dispute may be brought before the Tribunal by an application by one or other party.

Art. 28   If nothing is laid down in the special agreement or no special agreement has been made, the Tribunal shall apply the rules in regard to the substance of the dispute enumerated in Article 38 of the Statute of the[1] Permanent Court of International Justice. In so far as there exists no such rule applicable to the dispute, the Tribunal shall decide *ex aequo et bono*.

CHAPTER IV. GENERAL PROVISIONS

Art. 29   1. Disputes for the settlement of which a special procedure is laid down in other conventions in force between the parties to the dispute shall be settled in conformity with the provisions of those conventions.

2. The present General Act shall not affect any agreements in force by which conciliation procedure is established between the Parties or they are bound by obligations to resort to arbitration or judicial settlement which ensure the settlement of the dispute. If, however, these agreements provide only for a procedure of conciliation, after such procedure has been followed without result, the provisions of the present General Act concerning judicial settlement or arbitration shall be applied in so far as the parties have acceded thereto.

Art. 30   If a party brings before a Conciliation Commission a dispute which the other party, relying on conventions in force between the parties, has submitted to the[1] Permanent Court of International Justice or an Arbitral Tribunal, the Commission shall defer consideration of the dispute until the Court or the Arbitral Tribunal has pronounced upon the conflict of competence. The same rule shall apply if the Court or the Tribunal is seized of the case by one of the parties during the conciliation proceedings.

Art. 31   1. In the case of a dispute the occasion of which, according to the municipal law of one of the parties, falls within the competence of its judicial or administrative authorities, the party in question may object to the matter in dispute being submitted for settlement by the different methods laid down in the present General Act until a decision with final effect has been pronounced, within a reasonable time, by the competent authority.

2. In such a case, the party which desires to resort to the procedures laid down in the present General Act must notify the other party of its inten-

---

[1]   International Court of Justice.

tion within a period of one year from the date of the aforementioned decision.

Art. 32   If, in a judicial sentence or arbitral award, it is declared that a judgment, or a measure enjoined by a court of law or other authority of one of the parties to the dispute, is wholly or in part contrary to international law, and if the constitutional law of that party does not permit or only partially permits the consequences of the judgment or measure in question to be annulled, the parties agree that the judicial sentence or arbitral award shall grant the injured party equitable satisfaction.

Art. 33   1. In all cases where a dispute forms the object of arbitration or judicial proceedings, and particularly if the question on which the parties differ arises out of acts already committed or on the point of being committed, the[1] Permanent Court of International Justice, acting in accordance with Article 41 of its Statute, or the Arbitral Tribunal, shall lay down within the shortest possible time the provisional measures to be adopted. The parties to the dispute shall be bound to accept such measures.

2. If the dispute is brought before a Conciliation Commission, the latter may recommend to the parties the adoption of such provisional measures as it considers suitable.

3. The parties undertake to abstain from all measures likely to react prejudicially upon the execution of the judicial or arbitral decision or upon the arrangements proposed by the Conciliation Commission and, in general, to abstain from any sort of action whatsoever which may aggravate or extend the dispute.

Art. 34   Should a dispute arise between more than two Parties to the present General Act, the following rules shall be observed for the application of the forms of procedure described in the foregoing provisions:

(a)   In the case of conciliation procedure, a special commission shall invariably be constituted. The composition of such commission shall differ according as the parties all have separate interests or as two or more of their number act together.

In the former case, the parties shall each appoint one commissioner and shall jointly appoint commissioners nationals of third Powers not parties to the dispute, whose number shall always exceed by one the number of commissioners appointed separately by the parties.

In the second case, the parties who act together shall appoint their commissioner jointly by agreement between themselves and shall combine with the other party or parties in appointing third commissioners.

In either event, the parties, unless they agree otherwise, shall apply Article 5 and the following articles of the present Act, so far as they are compatible with the provisions of the present article.

---

[1]   International Court of Justice.

(b) In the case of judicial procedure, the Statute of the[1] Permanent Court of International Justice shall apply.

(c) In the case of arbitral procedure, if agreement is not secured as to the composition of the tribunal, in the case of the disputes mentioned in Article 17, each party shall have the right, by means of an application, to submit the dispute to the[1] Permanent Court of International Justice; in the case of the disputes mentioned in Article 21, the above Article 22 and following articles shall apply, but each party having separate interests shall appoint one arbitrator and the number of arbitrators separately appointed by the parties to the dispute shall always be one less than that of the other arbitrators.

Art. 35   1. The present General Act shall be applicable as between the Parties thereto, even though a third Power, whether a party to the Act or not, has an interest in the dispute.

2. In conciliation procedure, the parties may agree to invite such third Power to intervene.

Art. 36   1. In judicial or arbitral procedure, if a third Power should consider that it has an interest of a legal nature which may be affected by the decision in the case, it may submit to the[1] Permanent Court of International Justice or to the arbitral tribunal a request to intervene as a third Party.

2. It will be for the Court or the tribunal to decide upon this request.

Art. 37   1. Whenever the construction of a convention to which States other than those concerned in the case are parties is in question, the Registrar of the[1] Permanent Court of International Justice or the arbitral tribunal shall notify all such States forthwith.

2. Every State so notified has the right to intervene in the proceedings; but, if it uses this right, the construction given by the decision will be binding upon it.

Art. 38   Accessions to the present General Act may extend:

A.   Either to all the provisions of the Act (Chapters I, II, III and IV);

B.   Or to those provisions only which relate to conciliation and judicial settlement (Chapters I and II), together with the general provisions dealing with these procedures (Chapter IV);

C.   Or to those provisions only which relate to conciliation (Chapter I, together with the general provisions concerning that procedure (Chapter IV).

The Contracting Parties may benefit by the accessions of other Parties only in so far as they have themselves assumed the same obligations.

Art. 39   1. In addition to the power given in the preceding article, a Party, in acceding to the present General Act, may make his acceptance conditional

---

[1]   International Court of Justice.

upon the reservations exhaustively enumerated in the following paragraph. These reservations must be indicated at the time of accession.

2. These reservations may be such as to exclude from the procedure described in the present Act:

(a) Disputes arising out of facts prior to the accession either of the Party making the reservation or of any other Party with whom the said Party may have a dispute;

(b) Disputes concerning questions which by international law are solely within the domestic jurisdiction of States;

(c) Disputes concerning particular cases or clearly specified subject-matters, such as territorial status, or disputes falling within clearly defined categories.

3. If one of the parties to a dispute has made a reservation, the other parties may enforce the same reservation in regard to that party.

4. In the case of Parties, who have acceded to the provisions of the present General Act relating to judicial settlement or to arbitration, such reservations as they may have made shall, unless otherwise expressly stated, be deemed not to apply to the procedure of conciliation.

Art. 40   A Party whose accession has been only partial, or was made subject to reservations, may at any moment, by means of a simple declaration, either extend the scope of his accession or abandon all or part of his reservations.

Art. 41   Disputes relating to the interpretation or application of the present General Act, including those concerning the classification of disputes and the scope of reservations, shall be submitted to the[1] Permanent Court of International Justice.

Art. 42   The present General Act[2], of which the French and English texts shall both be authentic, shall bear the date of the 26th of September, 1928.

Art. 43   1. The present General Act shall be open to accession by all the Heads of States or other competent authorities of the Members of the League of Nations and the non-Member States to which the Council of the League of Nations has communicated a copy for this purpose.

2. The instruments of accession and the additional declarations provided for by Article 40 shall be transmitted to the Secretary-General of the[3] League of Nations, who shall notify their receipt to all the Members of the[2] League and to the non-Member States referred to in the preceding paragraph.

---

[1]   International Court of Justice.
[2]   shall bear the date of 28 April 1949.
[3]   United Nations.

3. The Secretary-General of the[2] League of Nations shall draw up three lists, denominated respectively by the letters A, B and C, corresponding to the three forms of accession to the present Act provided for in Article 38, in which shall be shown the accessions and additional declarations of the Contracting Parties. These lists, which shall be continually kept up to date, shall be published in the annual report presented to the Assembly of the[2] League of Nations by the Secretary-General.

Art. 44 1. The present General Act shall come into force on the ninetieth day following the receipt by the Secretary-General of the[2] League of Nations of the accession of not less than two Contracting Parties.

2. Accessions received after the entry into force of the Act, in accordance with the previous paragraph, shall become effective as from the ninetieth day following the date of receipt by the Secretary-General of the[2] League of Nations. The same rule shall apply to the additional declaration provided for by Article 40.

Art. 45 1. The present General Act shall be concluded for a period of five years, dating from its entry into force.

2. It shall remain in force for further successive periods of five years in the case of Contracting Parties which do not denounce it at least six months before the expiration of the current period.

3. Denunciation shall be effected by a written notification addressed to the Secretary-General of the[2] League of Nations, who shall inform all the Members of the[2] League and the non-Member States referred to in Article 43.

4. A denunciation may be partial only, or may consist in notification of reservations not previously made.

5. Notwithstanding denunciation by one of the Contracting Parties concerned in a dispute, all proceedings pending at the expiration of the current period of the General Act shall be duly completed.

Art. 46 A copy of the present General Act, signed by the President of the[1] Assembly and by the Secretary-General of the[2] League of Nations, shall be deposited in the archives of the Secretariat; a certified true copy shall be delivered by the Secretary-General to all the Members of the[3] League of Nations and to the non-Member States[3] indicated by the Council of the League of Nations.

Art. 47 The present General Act shall be registered by the Secretary-General of the[2] League of Nations on the date of its entry into force.

---

[1] General Assembly.

[2] United Nations.

[3] which shall have become parties to the Statute of the International Court of Justice and to those designated by the General Assembly of the United Nations.

4. ILC Model Rules on Arbitral Procedure of June 27, 1958

The United Nations International Law Commission has viewed arbitral procedures as a subject ready for codification since it began its activities in 1949. The first effort in this direction, drafted by *G. Scelle*, was adopted by the General Assembly in 1958 after slight modification. The General Assembly intentionally adopted the Model Rules in the form of a Resolution (1262 (XIII)) rather than a convention.

The Model Rules were meant to set forth the essential procedure governing arbitration between States. However, the Model Rules were not supposed to embody detailed rules of procedure such as those found in the Rules of Procedure of the International Court of Justice, because such rules are liable to vary according to the circumstances of each arbitration. The Draft therefore concentrated on safeguarding the effectiveness of arbitration agreements accepted by the parties for the settlement of an actual dispute. As a result of this approach, the Draft contains provisions for ensuring that the obligation to arbitrate shall not be frustrated at any point by a subsequent failure of one of the parties to fulfil that obligation. Such provisions include the following devices: decision by the International Court of Justice concerning the existence of a dispute or concerning the obligation to go to arbitration, third party appointment of arbitrators not designated by a party despite its obligation, establishment of the compromis failing agreement of the parties, procedural safeguards to secure the functioning of the tribunal until the award has been rendered, decision by default, ordering of interim measures of protection, and exclusion of a non liquet.

This form of "judicial" arbitration was met with reluctance by States which felt that the Draft distorted traditional arbitration practice by making it a quasi-compulsory judicial procedure. While most States would probably be prepared to accept this concept of arbitration for the purposes of submitting particular dispute to arbitration, they are not prepared to accept in advance such a multilateral treaty of arbitration to be applied automatically to the settlement of all future disputes between them. Thus, the Draft of the International Law Commission at this point only represents model rules for an extremely rigid arbitral procedure not yet applied in a single case.

Texts

General Assembly Resolution, Doc. A/CN.4/113, March 6, 1958 (French and English)

Rapport de la Commission du Droit International, Assemblée Générale, Documents officiels: Treizième Session, Supplément No. 9 (A/3859)

General Assembly Resolution 1262 (XIII), November 14, 1958, AJIL Vol. 53 (1959), pp. 239 et seq. (English)

F. Berber, Völkerrecht, Dokumentensammlung, Vol. 2 (1967), pp. 1760–1771 (English)

Bibliographical notes

U. S. Carlston, Draft Convention on Arbitral Procedure of the International Law Commission, AJIL Vol. 48 (1954), pp. 296–299

M. Bos, The International Law Commission's Draft Convention on Arbitral Procedure in the General Assembly of the United Nations, NTIR Vol. 3 (1959), pp. 234–261

Model Rules on Arbitral Procedure
(Draft of the International Law Commission)
(27. 6. 1958)

PREAMBLE

The undertaking to arbitrate is based on the following fundamental rules:

1. Any undertaking to have recourse to arbitration in order to settle a dispute between states constitutes a legal obligation which must be carried out in good faith.

2. Such an undertaking results from agreement between the parties and may relate to existing disputes or to disputes arising subsequently.

3. The undertaking must be embodied in a written instrument, whatever the form of the instrument may be.

4. The procedures suggested to states parties to a dispute by these model rules shall not be compulsory unless the states concerned have agreed, either in the *compromis* or in some other undertaking, to have recourse thereto.

5. The parties shall be equal in all proceedings before the arbitral tribunal.

THE EXISTENCE OF A DISPUTE AND THE SCOPE OF THE UNDERTAKING TO ARBITRATE

Art. 1   1. If, before the constitution of the arbitral tribunal, the parties to an undertaking to arbitrate disagree as to the existence of a dispute, or as to whether the existing dispute is wholly or partly within the scope of the obligation to go to arbitration, such preliminary question shall, at the request of any of the parties and failing agreement between them upon the adoption of another procedure, be brought before the International Court of Justice for decision by means of its summary procedure.

2. The Court shall have the power to indicate, if it considers that circumstances so require, any provisional measures which ought to be taken to preserve the respective rights of either party.

3. If the arbitral tribunal has already been constituted, any dispute concerning arbitrability shall be referred to it.

THE COMPROMIS

Art. 2   1. Unless there are earlier agreements which suffice for the purpose, for example in the undertaking to arbitrate itself, the parties having recourse to arbitration shall conclude a *compromis* which shall specify, as a minimum:

(a)   The undertaking to arbitrate according to which the dispute is to be submitted to the arbitrators,

(b)   The subject-matter of the dispute and, if possible, the points on which the parties are or are not agreed;

(c)   The method of constituting the tribunal and the number of arbitrators.

2. In addition, the *compromis* shall include any other provisions deemed desirable by the parties, in particular:

(i)   The rules of law and the principles to be applied by the tribunal, and the right, if any, conferred on it to decide *ex aequo et bono* as though it had legislative functions in the matter;

(ii)   The power, if any, of the tribunal to make recommendations to the parties;

(iii)   Such power as may be conferred on the tribunal to make its own rules of procedure;

(iv)   The procedure to be followed by the tribunal; provided that, once constituted, the tribunal shall be free to override any provisions of the *compromis* which may prevent it from rendering its award;

(v)   The number of members required for the constitution of a *quorum* for the conduct of the hearings;

(vi)   The majority required for the award;

(vii)   The time limit within which the award shall be rendered;

(viii) The right of the members of the tribunal to attach dissenting or individual opinions to the award, or any prohibition of such opinions;

(ix)   The languages to be employed in the course of the proceedings;

(x)   The manner in which the costs and disbursements shall be apportioned;

(xi)   The services which the International Court of Justice may be asked to render.

This enumeration is not intended to be exhaustive.

CONSTITUTION OF THE TRIBUNAL

Art. 3   1. Immediately after the request made by one of the states parties to the dispute for the submission of the dispute to arbitration, or after the decision on the arbitrability of the dispute, the parties to an undertaking to arbitrate shall take the necessary steps, either by means of the *compromis* or by special agreement, in order to arrive at the constitution of the arbitral tribunal.

2. If the tribunal is not constituted within three months from the date of the request made for the submission of the dispute to arbitration, or from the date of the decision on arbitrability, the President of the International Court of Justice shall, at the request of either party, appoint the arbitra-

tors not yet designated. If the President is prevented from acting or is a national of one of the parties, the appointments shall be made by the Vice-President. If the Vice-President is prevented from acting or is a national of one of the parties, the appointments shall be made by the oldest member of the Court who is not a national of either party.

3. The appointments referred to in paragraph 2 shall, after consultation with the parties, be made in accordance with the provisions of the *compromis* or of any other instrument consequent upon the undertaking to arbitrate. In the absence of such provisions, the composition of the tribunal shall, after consultation with the parties, be determined by the President of the International Court of Justice or by the judge acting in his place. It shall be understood that in this event the number of the arbitrators must be uneven and should preferably be five.

4. Where provision is made for the choice of a president of the tribunal by the other arbitrators, the tribunal shall be deemed to be constituted when the president is selected. If the president has not been chosen within two months of the appointment of the arbitrators, he shall be designated in accordance with the procedure in paragraph 2.

5. Subject to the special circumstances of the case, the arbitrators shall be chosen from among persons of recognized competence in international law.

Art. 4 1. Once the tribunal has been constituted, its composition shall remain unchanged until the award has been rendered.

2. A party may, however, replace an arbitrator appointed by it, provided that the tribunal has not yet begun its proceedings. Once the proceedings have begun, an arbitrator appointed by a party may not be replaced except by mutual agreement between the parties.

3. Arbitrators appointed by mutual agreement between the parties, or by agreement between arbitrators already appointed, may not be changed after the proceedings have begun, save in exceptional circumstances. Arbitrators appointed in the manner provided for in Article 3, paragraph 2, may not be changed even by agreement between the parties.

4. The proceedings are deemed to have begun when the president of the tribunal or the sole arbitrator has made the first procedural order.

Art. 5 If, whether before or after the proceedings have begun, a vacancy should occur on account of the death, incapacity or resignation of an arbitrator, it shall be filled in accordance with the procedure prescribed for the original appointment.

Art. 6 1. A party may propose the disqualification of one of the arbitrators on account of a fact arising subsequently to the constitution of the tribunal. It may only propose the disqualification of one of the arbitrators on account of a fact arising prior to the constitution of the tribunal if it can show that the appointment was made without knowledge of that fact or as a result of fraud. In either case, the decision shall be taken by the other members of the tribunal.

2. In the case of a sole arbitrator or of the president of the tribunal, the question of disqualification shall, in the absence of agreement between the parties, be decided by the International Court of Justice on the application of one of them.

3. Any resulting vacancy or vacancies shall be filled in accordance with the procedure prescribed for the original appointments.

Art. 7   Where a vacancy has been filled after the proceedings have begun, the proceedings shall continue from the point they had reached at the time the vacancy occurred. The newly appointed arbitrator may, however, require that the oral proceedings shall be recommenced from the beginning, if these have already been started.

POWERS OF THE TRIBUNAL AND THE PROCESS OF ARBITRATION

Art. 8   1. When the undertaking to arbitrate or any supplementary agreement contains provisions which seem sufficient for the purpose of a *compromis*, and the tribunal has been constituted, either party may submit the dispute to the tribunal by application. If the other party refuses to answer the application on the ground that the provisions above referred to are insufficient, the tribunal shall decide whether there is already sufficient agreement between the parties on the essential elements of a *compromis* set forth in Article 2. In the case of an affirmative decision, the tribunal shall prescribe the necessary measures for the institution or continuation of the proceedings. In the contrary case, the tribunal shall order the parties to complete or conclude the *compromis* within such time limits as it deems reasonable.

2. If the parties fail to agree or to complete the *compromis* within the time limit fixed in accordance with the preceding paragraph, the tribunal, within three months after the parties report failure to agree — or after the decision, if any, on the arbitrability of the dispute — shall proceed to hear and decide the case on the application of either party.

Art. 9   The arbitral tribunal, which is the judge of its own competence, has the power to interpret the *compromis* and the other instruments on which that competence is based.

Art. 10   1. In the absence of any agreement between the parties concerning the law to be applied, the tribunal shall apply:

(a) International conventions, whether general or particular, establishing rules expressly recognised by the contesting states;

(b) International custom, as evidence of a general practice accepted as law;

(c) The general principles of law recognised by civilised nations;

(d) Judicial decisions and the teachings of the most highly qualified publicists of the various nations, as subsidiary means for the determination of rules of law.

2. If the agreement between the parties so provides, the tribunal may also decide *ex aequo et bono*.

Art. 11   The tribunal may not bring in a finding of *non liquet* on the ground of the silence or obscurity of the law to be applied.

Art. 12   1. In the absence of any agreement between the parties concerning the procedure of the tribunal. or if the rules laid down by them are insufficient, the tribunal shall be competent to formulate or complete the rules of procedure.

2. All decisions shall be taken by a majority vote of the members of the tribunal.

Art. 13   If the languages to be employed are not specified in the *compromis*, this question shall be decided by the tribunal.

Art. 14   1. The parties shall appoint agents before the tribunal to act as intermediaries between them and the tribunal.

2. They may retain counsel and advocates for the prosecution of their rights and interests before the tribunal.

3. The parties shall be entitled through their agents, counsel or advocates to submit in writing and orally to the tribunal any arguments they may deem expedient for the prosecution of their case. They shall have the right to raise objections and incidental points. The decisions of the tribunal on such matters shall be final.

4. The members of the tribunal shall have the right to put questions to agents, counsel or advocates, and to ask them for explanations. Neither the questions put nor the remarks made during the hearing are to be regarded as an expression of opinion by the tribunal or by its members.

Art. 15   1. The arbitral procedure shall in general comprise two distinct phases: pleadings and hearing.

2. The pleadings shall consist in the communication by the respective agents to the members of the tribunal and to the opposite party of memorials, counter-memorials and, if necessary, of replies and rejoinders. Each party must attach all papers and documents cited by it in the case.

3. The time limits fixed by the *compromis* may be extended by mutual agreement between the parties, or by the tribunal when it deems such extension necessary to enable it to reach a just decision.

4. The hearing shall consist in the oral development of the parties' arguments before the tribunal.

5. A certified true copy of every document produced by either party shall be communicated to the other party.

Art. 16   1. The hearing shall be conducted by the president. It shall be public only if the tribunal so decides with the consent of the parties.

2. Records of the hearing shall be kept and signed by the president, registrar or secretary; only those so signed shall be authentic.

Art. 17   1. After the tribunal has closed the written pleadings, it shall have the right to reject any papers and documents not yet produced which either party may wish to submit to it without the consent of the other party. The tribunal shall, however, remain free to take into consideration any such papers and documents which the agents, advocates or counsel of one or other of the parties may bring to its notice, provided that they have been made known to the other party. The latter shall have the right to require a further extension of the written pleadings so as to be able to give a reply in writing.

2. The tribunal may also require the parties to produce all necessary documents and to provide all necessary explanations. It shall take note of any refusal to do so.

Art. 18   1. The tribunal shall decide as to the admissibility of the evidence that may be adduced, and shall be the judge of its probative value. It shall have the power, at any stage of the proceedings, to call upon experts and to require the appearance of witnesses. It may also, if necessary, decide to visit the scene connected with the case before it.

2. The parties shall co-operate with the tribunal in dealing with the evidence and in the other measures contemplated by paragraph 1. The tribunal shall take note of the failure of any party to comply with the obligations of this paragraph.

Art. 19   In the absence of any agreement to the contrary implied by the undertaking to arbitrate or contained in the *compromis*, the tribunal shall decide on any ancillary claims which it considers to be inseparable from the subject-matter of the dispute and necessary for its final settlement.

Art. 20   The tribunal, or in case of urgency its president subject to confirmation by the tribunal, shall have the power to indicate, if it considers that circumstances so require, any provisional measures which ought to be taken to preserve the respective rights of either party.

Art. 21   1. When, subject to the control of the tribunal, the agents, advocates and counsel have completed their presentation of the case, the proceedings shall be formally declared closed.

2. The tribunal shall, however, have the power, so long as the award has not been rendered, to re-open the proceedings after their closure, on the ground that new evidence is forthcoming of such a nature as to constitute a decisive factor, or if it considers, after careful consideration, that there is a need for clarification on certain points.

Art. 22   1. Except where the claimant admits the soundness of the defendant's case, discontinuance of the proceedings by the claimant party shall not be accepted by the tribunal without the consent of the defendant.

2. If the case is discontinued by agreement between the parties, the tribunal shall take note of the fact.

Art. 23   If the parties reach a settlement, it shall be taken note of by the tribunal. At the request of either party, the tribunal may, if it thinks fit, embody the settlement in an award.

Art. 24   The award shall normally be rendered within the period fixed by the *compromis*, but the tribunal may decide to extend this period if it would otherwise be unable to render the award.

Art. 25   1. Whenever one of the parties has not appeared before the tribunal, or has failed to present its case, the other party may call upon the tribunal to decide in favour of its case.

2. The arbitral tribunal may grant the defaulting party a period of grace before rendering the award.

3. On the expiry of this period of grace, the tribunal shall render an award after it has satisfied itself that it has jurisdiction. It may only decide in favour of the submissions of the party appearing, if satisfied that they are well founded in fact and in law.

DELIBERATIONS OF THE TRIBUNAL

Art. 26   The deliberations of the tribunal shall remain secret.

Art. 27   1. All the arbitrators shall participate in the decisions.

2. Except in cases where the *compromis* provides for a quorum, or in cases where the absence of an arbitrator occurs without the permission of the president of the tribunal, the arbitrator who is absent shall be replaced by an arbitrator nominated by the President of the International Court of Justice. In the case of such replacement the provisions of Article 7 shall apply.

THE AWARD

Art. 28   1. The award shall be rendered by a majority vote of the members of the tribunal. It shall be drawn up in writing and shall bear the date on which it was rendered. It shall contain the names of the arbitrators and shall be signed by the president and by the members of the tribunal who have voted for it. The arbitrators may not abstain from voting.

2. Unless otherwise provided in the *compromis*, any member of the tribunal may attach his separate or dissenting opinion to the award.

3. The award shall be deemed to have been rendered when it has been read in open court, the agents of the parties being present or having been duly summoned to appear.

4. The award shall immediately be communicated to the parties.

Art. 29   The award shall, in respect of every point on which it rules, state the reasons on which it is based.

Art. 30   Once rendered, the award shall be binding upon the parties. It shall be carried out in good faith immediately, unless the tribunal has allowed a time limit for the carrying out of the award or of any part of it.

Art. 31   During a period of one month after the award has been rendered and communicated to the parties, the tribunal may, either of its own accord or at the request of either party, rectify any clerical, typographical or arithmetical error in the award, or any obvious error of a similar nature.

Art. 32   The arbitral award shall constitute a definitive settlement of the dispute.

INTERPRETATION OF THE AWARD

Art. 33   1. Any dispute between the parties as to the meaning and scope of the award shall, at the request of either party and within three months of the rendering of the award, be referred to the tribunal which rendered the award.

2. If, for any reason, it is found impossible to submit the dispute to the tribunal which rendered the award, and if within the above-mentioned time limit the parties have not agreed upon another solution, the dispute may be referred to the International Court of Justice at the request of either party.

3. In the event of a request for interpretation, it shall be for the tribunal or for the International Court of Justice, as the case may be, to decide whether and to what extent execution of the award shall be stayed pending a decision on the request.

Art. 34   Failing a request for interpretation, or after a decision on such a request has been made, any pleadings and documents in the case shall be deposited by the president of the tribunal with the International Bureau of the Permanent Court of Arbitration or with another depositary selected by agreement between the parties.

VALIDITY AND ANNULMENT OF THE AWARD

Art. 35   The validity of an award may be challenged by either party on one or more of the following grounds:

(a)   That the tribunal has exceeded its powers;

(b)   That there was corruption on the part of a member of the tribunal;

      (c)   That there has been a failure to state the reasons for the award or a serious departure from a fundamental rule of procedure;

      (d)   That the undertaking to arbitrate or the *compromis* is a nullity.

Art. 36   1. If, within three months of the date on which the validity of the award is contested, the parties have not agreed on another tribunal, the International Court of Justice shall be competent to declare the total or partial nullity of the award on the application of either party.

           2. In the cases covered by Article 35, sub-paragraphs (a) and (c),validity must be contested within six months of the rendering of the award, and in the cases covered by sub-paragraphs (b) and (d) within six months of the discovery of the corruption or of the facts giving rise to the claim of nullity, and in any case within ten years of the rendering of the award.

           3. The Court may, at the request of the interested party, and if circumstances so require, grant a stay of execution pending the final decision on the application for annulment.

Art. 37   If the award is declared invalid by the International Court of Justice, the dispute shall be submitted to a new tribunal constituted by agreement between the parties, or, failing such agreement, in the manner provided by Article 3.

REVISION OF THE AWARD

Art. 38   1. An application for the revision of the award may be made by either party on the ground of the discovery of some fact of such a nature as to constitute a decisive factor, provided that when the award was rendered that fact was unknown to the tribunal and to the party requesting revision, and that such ignorance was not due to the negligence of the party requesting revision.

           2. The application for revision must be made within six months of the discovery of the new fact, and in any case within ten years of the rendering of the award.

           3. In the proceedings for revision, the tribunal shall, in the first instance, make a finding as to the existence of the alleged new fact and rule on the admissibility of the application.

           4. If the tribunal finds the application admissible, it shall then decide on the merits of the dispute.

           5. The application for revision shall, whenever possible, be made to the tribunal which rendered the award.

           6. If, for any reason, it is not possible to make the application to the tribunal which rendered the award, it may, unless the parties otherwise agree, be made by either of them to the International Court of Justice.

7. The tribunal or the Court may, at the request of the interested party, and if circumstances so require, grant a stay of execution pending the final decision on the application for revision.

5. United Nations: Draft Rules for the Conciliation of Disputes between States of November 28, 1990

In its report of November 20, 1990, the Sixth Committee of the United Nations recommended that the General Assembly adopt a decision on the "United Nations rules for the conciliation of disputes between States" in order to enhance the role of conciliation in international dispute settlement. The General Assembly adopted the decision on November 28, 1990 requesting the Secretary-General to circulate the draft rules for comment and to report accordingly. However, until now, it remains to be seen what will be the concrete outcome of this draft which incorporates the results of the most recent studies and experience in the field of international conciliation. The rules thus contain the traditional scheme of conciliation through one conciliator or a conciliation commission as well as the guiding principles for the procedure which, however, are open to amendment by States in a particular case. The rules should be applied for the conciliation of disputes between States which it has not been possible to settle by direct negotiations and are meant to facilitate the agreement on conciliation by providing a model set of rules of procedure.

Texts

ILM XXX (1990), 229
UN Doc. A/45/742 of November 20, 1990

Bibliographical notes

R.L. Bindschedler, Conciliation and Mediation, in: R. Bernhardt (ed.), EPIL, Vol. I (1992), 721–725

a) United Nations Rules for the Conciliation of Disputes between States

CHAPTER I. APPLICATION OF THE RULES

Art. 1   1. These rules apply to the conciliation of disputes between States which it has not been possible to settle by means of negotiation or amicable methods of settlement other than conciliation, whether the disputes are of a legal nature or not. These rules do not apply, however, to disputes of a purely legal nature in which no questions of responsibility or reparation arise and in which there is no disagreement as regards the facts.

2. The States applying these rules may at any time agree to exclude or amend any of their provisions. The State initiating the conciliation may propose an amended version of the rules. The State to which these rules are proposed may do the same.

CHAPTER II. INITIATION OF THE CONCILIATION PROCEEDINGS

Art. 2   1. The State which initiates conciliation proceedings in accordance with these rules shall send the other State a written invitation to conduct a process of conciliation in accordance with these rules, and identifying and describing the subject of the dispute. In the invitation, the State initiating the conciliation proceedings shall indicate the amendments it proposes to the rules, if any, and its choice as regards the number of conciliators. The invitation shall also indicate the language or languages which are to be used in the conciliation proceedings and also the linguistic or other services which the conciliator or conciliators may need.

2. For the preparation of the invitation, the State initiating the proceedings may request the assistance and advice of the Secretary-General of the United Nations.

3. The conciliation proceedings shall begin as soon as possible after the State to which the invitation has been sent has accepted it or, if it is not accepted, the States have agreed to apply an amended version of these rules.

4. If the States cannot reach agreement on the definition of the dispute, they may jointly request the assistance of the Secretary-General of the United Nations to resolve the difficulty.

CHAPTER III. CASES IN WHICH MORE THAN ONE STATE HAS THE SAME INTEREST WITH REGARD TO THE DISPUTE

Art. 3   When more than two States are involved in the same dispute, the States which have the same viewpoints and the same interest shall be considered and shall act jointly as a single party.

CHAPTER IV. NUMBER OF CONCILIATORS

Art. 4   There may be a sole conciliator, three conciliators or five conciliators. In the two latter cases the conciliators shall form a commission.

CHAPTER V. APPOINTMENT OF CONCILIATORS

Art. 5   For the appointment of conciliators the parties shall take into account the system of investigation and conciliation envisaged in General Assembly resolution 268 D (III) of 28 April 1949 and any other similar system established by a regional body in which both parties participate. If the dispute involves issues of fact only, they shall take into account the system envisaged in General Assembly resolution 2329 (XXII).

Art. 6   If the parties have agreed that a sole conciliator shall be appointed, that conciliator shall be appointed by agreement between them. If such an agreement is not reached within two months, the conciliator shall be appointed by the government of a third State, chosen by agreement between the parties or, if no such agreement is reached within two months, by the President of the International Court of Justice. If the President is a national of one of the parties, the appointment shall be made by the Vice-President or the next judge of the Court in order of seniority who is not a national of the parties. The conciliator shall not have the nationality of any of the parties, shall not reside or have resided habitually in their territory and shall not be or have been in the service of any of them.

Art. 7   If the parties have agreed that three conciliators shall be appointed, each one of them shall appoint a conciliator who may be of its own nationality. The parties shall appoint by mutual agreement the third conciliator, who may not be of the nationality of any of the parties or of the other conciliators. The third conciliator shall act as chairman of the commission. If he is not appointed within two months of the appointment of the conciliators appointed individually by the parties, the third conciliator shall be appointed by the government of a third State chosen by agreement between the parties or, if such agreement is not obtained within two months, by the President of the International Court of Justice. If the President is a national of one of the Parties, the appointment shall be made by the Vice-President or the next judge of the Court in order of seniority who is not a national of the parties. The third conciliator shall not reside or have resided habitually in the territory of the parties nor be or have been in their service.

Art. 8   1. If the parties have agreed that five conciliators should be appointed, each one of them shall appoint a conciliator who may be chosen from among its nationals. The other three conciliators, one of whom shall be chosen with a view to his acting as chairman, shall be appointed by agreement between the parties from among nationals of third States and shall be of different nationalities. None of them shall reside or have resided habitually in the territory of the parties or be or have been in their service. None of them shall have the same nationality as that of the other two conciliators.

2. If the appointment of the conciliators whom the parties are to appoint jointly has not been effected within three months, they shall be appointed by the government of a third State chosen by agreement between the parties or, if such an agreement is not reached within three months, by the President of the International Court of Justice. If the President is a national of one of the parties, the appointment shall be made by the Vice-President or the next judge in order of seniority who is not a national of the parties. The Government or member of the International Court of Justice making the appointment shall also decide which of the three conciliators shall act as chairman.

3. If at the end of the three-month period referred to in the preceding paragraph, the parties have been able to appoint only one or two conciliators, the two conciliators or the conciliator still required shall be appointed in the manner described in the preceding paragraph. If the parties have not agreed that the conciliator or one of the two conciliators whom they have appointed shall act as chairman, the Government or member of the International Court of Justice appointing the two conciliators or the conciliator still required shall also decide which of the three conciliators shall act as chairman.

4. If, at the end of the three-month period referred to in paragraph 2 of this article the parties have appointed three conciliators but have not been able to agree which of them shall act as chairman, the chairman shall be chosen in the manner described in that paragraph.

Art. 9   In the event that a sole conciliator dies, resigns or for any other reason is prevented from continuing to discharge his duties, a successor shall be appointed as soon as possible in the same way as the original conciliator was appointed. The vacancies which may occur in a conciliation commission as a result of death, resignation or any other cause shall be filled as soon as possible by the method established for appointing the members to be replaced.

CHAPTER VI. RULES APPLICABLE TO CONCILIATION BY A SOLE CONCILIATOR

Art. 10   The conciliator, acting in an independent and impartial manner, shall seek to ensure that the parties reach an amicable settlement of the dispute. To that end, he shall be guided by principles of objectivity, fairness and justice, giving consideration to, among other factors, the rights and obligations of the parties and the facts and circumstances of the case. If no settlement is reached during consideration of the dispute, he shall draw up and communicate to the parties, in writing, such terms of settlement as he deems appropriate.

Art. 11   1. After his appointment, the conciliator shall request each of the parties to submit to him a statement, in writing, describing the elements of the dispute and the points at issue, accompanied by any information or evidence which the party considers necessary or useful. Each party shall send the other a copy of this statement and the annexes thereto.

2. The conciliator may request any of the parties to submit to him an additional statement, in writing, concerning its original statement and concerning the facts and grounds in support thereof, accompanied by any information or evidence which the party considers necessary or useful. The submitting party shall send a copy of the additional statement and the annexes thereto to the other party.

3. At any stage of the conciliation proceedings, the conciliator may request any of the parties to submit any other documents or information which he considers necessary or useful; such documents or information shall be communicated to the other party.

Art. 12   1. The conciliator shall conduct the proceedings in such a manner as he considers appropriate, taking into account the circumstances of the case, the wishes the parties may express, and the need for a speedy settlement of the dispute.

2. The conciliator may hear the parties jointly or separately and in any place.

3. At any stage of the proceedings, the conciliator may make proposals for a settlement of the dispute.

4. In putting forward proposals and terms of settlement, the conciliator shall refrain from presenting any final conclusions with regard to the facts at issue or from ruling formally on issues of law, unless the parties have jointly requested him to do so.

5. No minutes shall be drawn up of the meetings between the parties, or one of them, and the conciliator, nor of the evidence submitted.

6. A certified copy of any document submitted by a party as evidence shall be provided to the other party.

7. If a party submits an original document as evidence, it shall be entitled to have that document returned to it: a certified copy of the document shall remain in the possession of the conciliator.

Art. 13   1. The work of the conciliator, including his meetings with one or both the parties, which shall be private, shall be secret. The conciliator and the parties shall refrain from divulging any documents or oral statements, or any communication concerning the progress of the proceedings, without the prior approval of both parties.

2. If any indiscretion occurs during the proceedings, the conciliator may determine its possible effect on the continuation of such proceedings.

3. Except in the case of evidence submitted during the conciliation proceedings which the parties may submit in any judicial or arbitral proceedings held after the conclusion of the conciliation proceedings, the obligation to respect the secrecy of the conciliation proceedings shall remain in effect for the parties and for the conciliator after the proceedings are concluded and shall extend to the terms of settlement and any proposal made by the conciliator, whether accepted by the parties or not. After the conclusion of the proceedings the parties may, by agreement, make all or some of the documents available to the public or authorize the publication of all or some of them.

4. Upon conclusion of the proceedings, the conciliator shall destroy every original or copy in his possession of any written material submitted in accordance with article 38.

5. Upon conclusion of the proceedings, the conciliator shall deposit a set of the documents with each of the parties.

Art. 14   1. If the terms of settlement are not accepted by both parties and the latter do not wish further efforts to be made to reach agreement on different terms, the proceedings shall be terminated.

2. If the terms of settlement are not accepted by both parties but the latter wish efforts to reach agreement on different terms to continue, new proceedings shall be initiated, to which all the provisions of the present chapter shall apply, except that, if the conciliator has no objection, the parties may, with respect to the new proceedings, reduce by mutual agreement the time-limit mentioned in article 15.

Art. 15   Without prejudice to the right of the parties, acting by mutual agreement, and of the conciliator, to extend this time-limit and the possible application of article 13, paragraph 2, or of article 45, the conciliator shall conclude his work within two months from the date on which the procedures mentioned in article 11, paragraph 1, were completed.

Art. 16   The conciliator may, at any time, request the Secretary-General of the United Nations for advice and assistance with regard to the administrative and procedural aspects of his work.

CHAPTER VII. RULES APPLICABLE TO CONCILIATION BY COMMISSION

FUNDAMENTAL PRINCIPLES

Art. 17   The commission shall attempt to clarify the issues in dispute and to help the parties reach an agreement. It shall seek to obtain all information necessary or useful for the attainment of those objectives. If no settlement is reached during consideration of the dispute, the commission shall draw up and communicate to the parties, through a report of its chairman, such terms of settlement as it deems appropriate.

Art. 18   The commission shall be guided by principles of objectivity, fairness and justice, giving consideration to, among other things, the rights and obligations of the parties and the facts and circumstances of the case.

PROCEDURES OF THE COMMISSION

Art. 19   While adhering to the procedural provision contained in chapters VII and XVIII of these rules, the commission shall adopt its own procedures.

Art. 20   1. Before the commission begins its work, the parties shall designate their representatives and shall communicate the names of such representatives to the chairman of the commission. The chairman shall determine, in agreement with the parties, the place and date of the commission's first meeting, to which the members of the commission and the representatives shall be convoked.

2. Before the first meeting of the commission, its members may meet informally to deal with administrative and procedural matters.

Art. 21   The representatives of the parties may be assisted by counsel and experts appointed by the parties.

Art. 22   1. At its first meeting, the commission shall appoint a secretary, who may be a United Nations official. It shall then hear initial statements from the parties. If it decides that the information provided by the parties so permits, the commission shall agree on the method to be used to consider the dispute and, in particular, whether the parties should be invited to submit written statements and in what order and within what time-limits such statements must be submitted, as well as the dates when, if this is required, representatives and counsel will be heard. The decisions taken by the commission in this regard may be amended at any later stage of the proceedings.

2. The secretary of the commission shall not have the nationality of any of the parties, shall not reside or have resided habitually in their territory and shall not be or have been in the service of any of them.

3. Except as provided in article 28, paragraph 1, the commission shall not hear statements by the representative or counsel of a party without having

given the other party the opportunity to be represented at the hearing in question.

Art. 23   1. The parties shall facilitate the commission's work and, in particular, shall do everything possible to provide it with whatever documents and information may be relevant.

2. The commission shall accept any request by the parties that persons whose testimony they consider necessary or useful be heard, that experts be consulted or that local investigations be conducted. It may, however, in any case in which it considers it neither necessary nor useful to accept such a request, ask the party making the request to reconsider it.

3. The parties shall use the means available to them to enable the commission to enter their territory and, in accordance with their laws, to convoke and hear witnesses or experts and visit any part of their territory to conduct local investigations. Articles 19 to 29 of the Hague Convention for the Pacific Settlement of International Disputes of 18 October 1907 shall apply in such cases.

Art. 24   If the commission establishes that the parties disagree on issues of fact, or considers it necessary or useful to clarify facts which the parties do not seem to have taken into account, it may, *motu proprio*, consult experts, conduct local investigations or question witnesses. In such cases, article 23, paragraph 3, shall apply. Before using the powers conferred by the present article with regard to facts which the parties do not seem to have taken into account, the commission shall consult the parties.

Art. 25   The commission may propose to the parties that they jointly appoint expert advisers to assist them in the consideration of technical aspects of the dispute. If the proposal is accepted, its implementation shall be conditional upon the expert advisers being appointed by the parties by mutual agreement and accepted by the commission and upon the parties fixing the emoluments of the expert advisers.

Art. 26   If the commission is unable to reach unanimous agreement, it may take its decisions by a majority of votes of its members without being required to indicate the number of votes. Except in matters of procedure, the presence of all members shall be required in order for a decision to be valid.

Art. 27   1. The commission shall meet at United Nations Headquarters.

2. The commission may, at any time, request the Secretary-General of the United Nations for advice or assistance with regard to the administrative and procedural aspects of its work.

CONCLUSION OF THE COMMISSION'S WORK

Art. 28   1. On concluding its consideration of the dispute, the commission shall define the terms of settlement which are likely to be acceptable to the parties, unless the dispute involves issues of fact only. In this connection, the commission may hold an exchange of views with the representatives of the parties, who may be heard jointly or separately.

2. Once the proposed terms of settlement have been drawn up, they shall be communicated by the chairman of the commission in a report to the representatives of the parties, with a request that the representatives inform the commission, within a given period, whether the parties accept them. The chairman may include in his report the reasons which, in the commission's view, might prompt the parties to accept the proposed terms of settlement. The chairman shall refrain in his report from presenting any final conclusions with regard to facts or from ruling formally on issues of law, unless the parties have jointly asked the commission to do so.

3. If the dispute involves issues of fact only, the chairman shall hand over to the representatives of the parties, once it is complete, a report setting forth the commission's findings in that regard. The proceedings shall be concluded when his report is handed over.

Art. 29   If the parties accept the terms of settlement proposed by the commission, a document shall be drawn up setting forth those terms. The document shall be signed by the chairman and the secretary. A copy signed by the secretary shall be provided to each party, and this shall conclude the proceedings.

Art. 30   1. If the terms of settlement are not accepted by both parties and the latter do not wish further efforts to be made to reach agreement on different terms, a document shall be drawn up as stipulated in article 29, but omitting the proposed terms and indicating that the parties were unable to accept them and do not wish further efforts to be made to reach agreement on different forms. The proceedings shall be concluded when each party has received a copy of the document signed by the secretary.

2. If the forms of settlement are not accepted by both parties but the latter wish efforts to reach agreement on different terms to continue, new proceedings shall be initiated, to which all the provisions of chapters VII and VIII of these rules used in the first proceedings shall apply, except that it shall not be necessary to appoint a new secretary and, if the commission has no objection, the parties may, with respect to the new proceedings, reduce by mutual agreement the time-limit mentioned in article 31.

Art. 31   Without prejudice to the right of the parties, acting by mutual agreement, and of the commission, to extend the relevant time-limit and the possible application of article 32, paragraph 2, or article 45, the commission shall conclude its work within three months from the date on which, in accordance with article 22, paragraph 1, the initial statements of the parties were made, if it consists of three members, and within five months of that date if it consists of five members.

SECRECY OF THE COMMISSION'S WORK AND OF THE DOCUMENTS
INVOLVED

Art. 32   1. The commission's meetings shall be closed. Members of the commission and its expert advisers, together with representatives, counsel and experts, and the secretary and secretariat staff, shall refrain from divulging any documents or statements, or any communication concerning the progress of the proceedings, without the prior approval of both representatives.

2. If any indiscretion occurs during the proceedings, the commission may determine its possible effect on the continuation of such proceedings.

Art. 33   Except as provided in articles 29 and 30, no decision, statement or communication concerning the substance of the dispute shall be reflected in the minutes of the commission's meetings at which one or both parties were represented.

Art. 34   1. Certified copies of the minutes of the commission's meetings and of the annexes thereto shall be provided to the representatives through the secretary of the commission, except in the case of the minutes of meetings of the commission to which neither of the parties were invited; the parties shall not receive copies of the minutes of those meetings.

2. Originals of the minutes of the commission's meetings to which neither of the parties were invited and copies of those minutes in the possession of the secretariat at the conclusion of the proceedings shall be destroyed at that time by the secretary.

3. Upon conclusion of the proceedings the secretary shall destroy all originals or copies of any written materials submitted in accordance with article 38 that are in his possession.

4. A certified copy of any document submitted by a party as evidence shall be provided to the other party.

5. If a party submits an original document as evidence, it shall be entitled to have that document returned to it: a certified copy of the document shall remain in the possession of the secretariat.

6. The parties shall receive certified copies of the records of evidence drawn from experts' reports, investigations and the questioning of witnesses.

Art. 35   Except with regard to evidence drawn from experts' reports, investigations and the questioning of witnesses and documentary evidence which the parties may submit in any judicial or arbitral proceedings held after the conclusion of the conciliation proceedings, the obligation to respect the secrecy of the proceedings and of the deliberations shall remain in effect for the parties and for members of the commission, expert advisers and secretariat staff after the proceedings are concluded and shall extend to the terms of settlement, whether accepted or not, and to any proposals made, whether accepted or not. Except for the documents referred to in article 32, paragraph 1, no document shall be communicated to the public before the conclusion of the proceedings. Upon conclusion of the proceedings, the parties may, by mutual agreement, make available to the public all or some of the documents or authorise the publication of all or some of them.

Art. 36   Upon conclusion of the proceedings, the chairman of the commission shall deliver the documents in the possession of the secretariat of the commission to the Secretary-General of the United Nations, who shall preserve their secrecy within the limits indicated above.

CHAPTER VIII. RULES APPLICABLE TO ALL CONCILIATION PROCEEDINGS CONDUCTED IN ACCORDANCE WITH THESE RULES

Art. 37   No admission or proposal made or view expressed during the conciliation proceedings by one of the parties, the commission, a member of the commission or the sole conciliator, as the case may be, shall be considered to prejudge or in any way affect the rights or claims of any of the parties should the proceedings fail. Likewise, a party's acceptance of a proposal or terms of settlement in no way implies acceptance by that party of the arguments of law or of fact on which the proposal or terms of settlement may be based.

Art. 38   1. Any of the parties to conciliation proceedings governed by these rules may provide the sole conciliator or the commission, as the case may be, with comments on situations or facts relating to the dispute and on arguments acquitted by the other party, on the understanding that the origin of the comments shall not be revealed to the latter.

2. Materials in writing submitted in accordance with this article shall not have any evidentiary effect if it affirms or refutes facts.

Art. 39   The parties undertake that no conciliator or expert adviser who takes part in proceedings conducted in conformity with these rules shall act as a judge *ad hoc*, arbitrator, representative, counsel or expert of a party in any arbitral or judicial proceedings in respect of the dispute that was the subject of the conciliation proceedings. The parties also undertake not to present a conciliator or expert adviser as a witness or expert in any such proceedings.

Art. 40   Each party may at any time, at its own initiative or at the initiative of the sole conciliator or the commission, as the case may be, make proposals for the settlement of the dispute. Any proposal made in accordance with this article shall be communicated immediately to the sole conciliator or to the commission, as the case may be.

Art. 41   At any stage of the conciliation proceedings, the sole conciliator or the commission, as the case may be, may recommend any provisional measure which should be taken to preserve the corresponding rights of a party.

Art. 42   At any stage of the proceedings, the sole conciliator or the commission, as the case may be, may draw the attention of the parties to any measures which might facilitate an amicable settlement.

Art. 43   Neither of the parties shall initiate, during the conciliation proceedings, any arbitral or judicial proceedings in respect of the dispute which is the subject of the conciliation proceedings. Each party may, however, initiate arbitral or judicial proceedings where such proceedings are necessary for preserving its rights.

Art. 44   The parties shall refrain from any measures which might have an adverse effect on the terms of settlement proposed by the sole conciliator or the commission, as the case may be, until those forms have been explicitly rejected by both or one of the parties. The parties shall also, in general, refrain from any measure which might aggravate or exacerbate the dispute.

Art. 45   If the sole conciliator or the commission, as the case may be, finds one or both of the parties to be systematically and persistently refraining from extending the co-operation necessary for the satisfactory progress of the conciliation proceedings, impeding those proceedings or violating provisions of these rules, the conciliator or the commission may terminate the proceedings without proposing terms of settlement or, in the case of a dispute involving issues of fact only, without formulating findings in that regard. If the sole conciliator or the commission, as the case may be, makes use of this power, the conciliator or the commission shall communicate to the parties in writing, in a thorough and precise manner, the reasons why this step has been taken.

Art. 46   The sole conciliator or, if the conciliation proceedings are conducted by commission, each member of the commission shall receive emoluments in an amount and on terms agreed by the parties who may, if they so wish, request the opinion of the Secretary-General of the United Nations on this matter. The emoluments and the terms of their payment must be fixed before the conciliators are appointed and be communicated to them before they take up office. The same rules apply to the emoluments of the secretary of the commission and any staff he recruits.

Art. 47   The costs of the conciliation proceedings, including those occasioned by any investigations agreed upon by a commission *motu proprio* and the emoluments of expert advisers appointed in accordance with article 25, shall be borne by the parties in equal shares.

Art. 48   The terms of settlement proposed by a sole conciliator or by a commission, as the case may be, shall in no way be binding on the parties with regard to their substance. They shall be simply recommendations submitted to the parties for consideration in order to facilitate an amicable settlement of the dispute. The parties nevertheless undertake to study them carefully and objectively. If one of the parties rejects terms of settlement which the other party accepts, it shall inform the latter, in writing, of the reasons why it could not accept them.

b) Explanatory Commentary on the Application of the United Nations Rules for the Conciliation of Disputes between States

1. The rules in annex I are a model set of norms which States between whom a dispute has arisen can adopt either through a bilateral agreement simply referring to the rules, if they wish to apply them without amendment, or otherwise through a bilateral agreement adopting an amended version of the rules. The rules are sufficiently broad to serve as a basis for conciliation proceedings without it being necessary to incorporate additional norms in them.

2. It is possible that States wishing to set up an *ad hoc* conciliation mechanism to assist them in settling a dispute between them may be parties to a bilateral or multilateral convention which requires them to resort to conciliation to settle disputes arising between them.

3. If the convention is bilateral, there is of course nothing to prevent the States from using the rules instead of the convention, without amending the rules, if the convention provides for *ad hoc* conciliation, in other words, if there is no pre-established conciliation body. If such a body does exist, they could, if they prefer to apply the rules rather than the convention establishing such a body, apply the rules with the necessary amendments so that the pre-established commission can handle the dispute.

4. If the pre-existing convention is multilateral, the States may act as indicated in the preceding paragraph, but taking into account, if the rules, with the agreed amendments, are not fully compatible with the conciliation provisions in the convention, that article 41 of the Vienna Convention on the Law of Treaties requires them to inform States parties to the convention in question of the amendments that they have made in the light of their decision to apply the rules. This requirement may be fulfilled through the depositary of the convention.

5. If the dispute prompting recourse to the rules comes within the terms of a clause of a bilateral or multilateral convention requiring the parties to resort to arbitration or to the International Court of Justice, or if the latter has competence to hear the dispute by virtue of declarations made under Article 36, paragraph 2, of its Statute, States may normally agree that the dispute will none the less first be referred to conciliation on the basis of the rules, and that recourse to arbitration or to the Court will be required only if such conciliation proceedings fail.

6. The provisions of article 43 of the rules are relevant to the comments in the preceding paragraph.

7. It should be noted that the conciliation commissions, which enjoy far-reaching powers of investigation under articles 23 and 24, may serve as investigatory commissions in any case where the dispute involves issues of fact only. In such a case, the sole purpose of the proceedings will be to investigate the facts (see art. 28, para. 3).

8. The procedure involving conciliation by a sole conciliator is far more flexible and informal than the procedure involving the commissions. The rules do not envisage the application of the former type of conciliation to disputes on issues of fact only. Moreover, inasmuch as neither paragraph 3 of article 23 nor article 24 applies to the sole conciliator, that procedure is often not as well suited to the settlement of disputes on issues of fact as the procedure involving commissions. It should also be noted that because of its flexible and informal nature, the procedure involving a sole conciliator is somewhat similar to mediation.

9. Unlike what happens in the case of five-member commissions, members appointed individually by the parties are in the majority on three-member commissions. If the dispute has caused serious uneasiness between the parties, that factor could put the chairman of the commission in an awkward position. Accordingly, establishing a three-member commission would appear to be advisable only when, despite the dispute, relations between the parties are still relatively amicable.

10. If — as happens, for example, when injury is sustained by a national of one party in the territory of the other — the dispute comes within the purview of the courts of one of the parties, it would be better not to initiate conciliation proceedings until that party's highest judicial authority has issued a final ruling on the matter.

II. Compromissory Clauses in Universal Agreements[1]

1. Vienna Convention on Diplomatic Relations of April 18, 1961: Optional Protocol Concerning the Compulsory Settlement of Disputes

The Vienna Convention on Diplomatic Relations provides for a dispute settlement procedure to which States Parties to the Convention may accede. Thus, the dispute settlement procedure is not applicable to States which have only ratified the Convention and not the Optional Protocol. For those States Parties to the Convention and the Optional Protocol any dispute arising out of the interpretation or application of the Convention lies within the compulsory jurisdiction of the International Court of Justice. If the parties so agree within a period of two months they may, however, bring the dispute before an arbitral tribunal instead of the International Court of Justice or may adopt a conciliation procedure before resorting to the International Court of Justice.

An Optional Protocol of identical wording was adopted together with the Vienna Convention on Consular Relations of April 24, 1963 (AJIL 57 (1963), 995). It was the basis of jurisdiction in the 1998 case brought by Paraguay against the United States of America on the question of consular assistance to persons of their nationality on case of arrest in the receiving State. In this case the International Court of Justice stated that the Parties to the Convention having ratified the Optional Protocol may apply directly to the Court without first resorting to arbitration or conciliation.

Text

UNTS Vol. 500 (1964), 95–221

Bibliographical notes

C. A. Colliard, La Convention de Vienne sur les Relations Diplomatiques, AFDI 7 (1961), 3–21

R. L. Bindschedler, Die Wiener Konvention über die diplomatischen Beziehungen, SchweizJIR 18 (1963), 29–44

Sir E. Satow, Guide to Diplomatic Practice (5th ed. by Lord Gore-Booth) 1979

---

[1] The following texts provide some examples of compromissory clauses in universal agreements; they are not meant to be exhaustive.

Y. Z. Blum, Diplomatic Agents and Missions, in: R. Bernhardt (ed.), Encyclopedia of Public International Law, Vol. I (1992), 1034 et seq. with further bibliographical indications

E. Denza, Diplomatic Law: commentary on the Vienna Convention on Diplomatic Relations (1998)

Optional Protocol Concerning the Compulsory Settlement of Disputes

Art. I   Disputes arising out of the interpretation or application of the Convention shall lie within the compulsory jurisdiction of the International Court of Justice and may accordingly be brought before the Court by an application made by any party to the dispute being a Party to the present Protocol.

Art. II   The parties may agree, within a period of two months after one party has notified its opinion to the other that a dispute exists, to resort not to the International Court of Justice but to an arbitral tribunal. After the expiry of the said period, either party may bring the dispute before the Court by an application.

Art. III 1. Within the same period of two months, the parties may agree to adopt a conciliation procedure before resorting to the International Court of Justice.

2. The conciliation commission shall make its recommendations within five months after its appointment. If its recommendations are not accepted by the parties to the dispute within two months after they have been delivered, either party may bring the dispute before the Court by an application.

Art. IV   States Parties to the Convention, to the Optional Protocol concerning Acquisition of Nationality, and to the present Protocol may at any time declare that they will extend the provisions of the present Protocol to disputes arising out of the interpretation or application of the Optional Protocol concerning Acquisition of Nationality. Such declarations shall be notified to the Secretary-General of the United Nations.

Art. V   The present Protocol shall be open for signature by all States which may become Parties to the Convention, as follows: until 31 October 1961 at the Federal Ministry for Foreign Affairs of Austria and subsequently, until 31 March 1962, at the United Nations Headquarters in New York.

Art. VI   The present Protocol is subject to ratification. The instruments of ratification shall be deposited with the Secretary-General of the United Nations.

Art. VII The present Protocol shall remain open for accession by all States which may become Parties to the Convention. The instruments of accession shall be deposited with the Secretary-General of the United Nations.

Art. VIII 1. The present Protocol shall enter into force on the same day as the Convention or on the thirtieth day following the date of deposit of the second instrument of ratification or accession to the Protocol with the Secretary-General of the United Nations, whichever day is the later.

2. For each State ratifying or acceding to the present Protocol after its entry into force in accordance with paragraph 1 of this Article, the Protocol shall enter into force on the thirtieth day after deposit by such State of its instrument of ratification or accession.

Art. IX   The Secretary-General of the United Nations shall inform all States which may become Parties to the Convention:

(a)   of signatures to the present Protocol and of the deposit of instruments of ratification or accession, in accordance with Articles V, VI and VII;

(b)   of declarations made in accordance with Article IV of the present Protocol;

(c)   of the date on which the present Protocol will enter into force, in accordance with Article VIII.

Art. X   The original of the present Protocol, of which the Chinese, English, French, Russian and Spanish texts are equally authentic, shall be deposited with the Secretary-General of the United Nations, who shall send certified copies thereof to all States referred to in Article V.

In WITNESS WHEREOF the undersigned Plenipotentiaries, being duly authorised thereto by their respective Governments, have signed the present Protocol.

DONE at Vienna, this eighteenth day of April one thousand nine hundred and sixty-one.

2. Vienna Convention on the Law of Treaties

The Vienna Convention on the Law of Treaties of May 23, 1969 contains provisions for the settlement of disputes concerning that part of the Convention which deals with the invalidity and termination of treaties (Part V). Any party invoking grounds for impeaching the validity of a treaty or for terminating it must notify the other parties of its claim. If an objection is raised, a solution shall be sought under the provisions of Art. 33 of the United Nations Charter.

Should the matter remain unresolved twelve months after the objection was raised, two means of compulsory settlement are available, depending on the disputed provisions. In disputes concerning the application or interpretation of the *"jus cogens"* (Articles 53 and 64), the International Court of Justice may be seised by unilateral application; however, the parties may also agree to submit the dispute to *ad hoc* arbitration. In all other disputes concerning the application or interpretation of the provisions of Part V of the Convention, the conciliation procedure specified in the Annex to the Convention comes into play. Five conciliators are selected from a list to which qualified persons may be nominated by the contracting parties or by any member State of the United Nations for a five year-term. The Secretary-General of the United Nations shall appoint necessary conciliators if the parties fail to do so. The report issued by the Conciliation Commission is not binding on the parties to the dispute, but is rather meant to facilitate an amicable settlement.

Texts

ILM Vol. 8 (1969), p. 679 (English; Chinese, French, Russian, Spanish also official)
BGBl. (Austria) 1980, p. 775 (English, French, German)
Cmnd. 7964, TS 58 (1980) (English)

Bibliographical notes

S. Verosta, Die Vertragsrechts-Konferenz der Vereinten Nationen 1968/69 und die Wiener Konvention über das Recht der Verträge, ZaöRV Vol. 29 (1969), pp. 654–710
S. Rosenne, The Law of Treaties. A guide to the legislative history of the Vienna Convention (1970)
E. Castren, La Convention de Vienne sur le droit des traites, in: Internationale Festschrift Alfred Verdross (1971), pp. 71–83
C.-A. Fleischhauer, Die Wiener Vertragsrechtskonferenz, JIRVol. 15 (1971), pp. 202–241

H. Neuhold, Die Wiener Vertragsrechtskonvention 1969, ArchVR Vol. 15 (1971), pp. 1–55

S. Rosenne, The Settlement of Treaty Disputes under the Vienna Convention of 1969, ZaöRV Vol. 31 (1971), pp. 1–62

P. K. Menon, The Law of Treaties with Special Reference to the Vienna Convention of 1969, Revue de Droit International de Sciences Diplomatiques et Politiques (The International Law Review) Vol. 56 (1978), pp. 133–155, 213–270

J. Sinclair, The Vienna Convention on the Law of Treaties, 1984

K. Rosenne, The Vienna Convention on the Law of Treaties in: R. Bernhardt (ed.) Encyclopedia of Public International Law, Instalment 7 (1984), 525–533

M. E. Villiger, Customary international law and treaties: a study of their interactions and interrelations with special consideration of the 1969 Vienna convention on the law of treaties (1985)

a) Convention of May 23, 1969

Art. 66 *Procedures for judicial settlement, arbitration and conciliation.* If, under paragraph 3 of article 65, no solution has been reached within a period of twelve months following the date on which the objection was raised, the following procedures shall be followed:

(a) any one of the parties to a dispute concerning the application or the interpretation of article 53 or 64 may, by a written application, submit it to the International Court of Justice for a decision unless the parties by common consent agree to submit the dispute to arbitration;

(b) any one of the parties to a dispute concerning the application or the interpretation of any of the other articles in Part V of the present Convention may set in motion the procedure specified in the Annex to the Convention by submitting a request to that effect to the Secretary-General of the United Nations.

b) Annex to the Convention, Conciliation Commission

1. A list of conciliators consisting of qualified jurists shall be drawn up and maintained by the Secretary-General of the United Nations. To this end, every State which is a Member of the United Nations or a party to the present Convention shall be invited to nominate two conciliators, and the names of the persons so nominated shall constitute the list. The term of a conciliator, including that of any conciliator nominated to fill a casual vacancy, shall be five years and may be renewed. A conciliator whose term expires shall continue to fulfil any function for which he shall have been chosen under the following paragraph.

2. When a request has been made to the Secretary-General under article 66, the Secretary-General shall bring the dispute before a conciliation commission constituted as follows:

The State or States constituting one of the parties to the dispute shall appoint:

(a) one conciliator of the nationality of that State or of one of those States, who may or may not be chosen from the list referred to in paragraph 1; and

(b) one conciliator not of the nationality of that State or of any of those States, who shall be chosen from the list.

The State or States constituting the other party to the dispute shall appoint two conciliators in the same way. The four conciliators chosen by the parties shall be appointed within sixty days following the date on which the Secretary-General receives the request.

The four conciliators shall, within sixty days following the date of the last of their own appointments, appoint a fifth conciliator chosen from the list, who shall be chairman.

If the appointment of the chairman or of any of the other conciliators has not been made within the period prescribed above for such appointment, it shall be made by the Secretary-General within sixty days following the expiry of that period. The appointment of the chairman may be made by the Secretary-General either from the list or from the membership of the International Law Commission. Any of the periods within which appointments must be made may be extended by agreement between the parties to the dispute.

Any vacancy shall be filled in the manner prescribed for the initial appointment.

3. The Conciliation Commission, shall decide its own procedure. The Commission, with the consent of the parties to the dispute, may invite any party to the treaty to submit to it its views orally or in writing. Decisions and recommendations of the Commission shall be made by a majority vote of the five members.

4. The Commission may draw the attention of the parties to the dispute to any measures which might facilitate an amicable settlement.

5. The Commission shall hear the parties, examine the claims and objections, and make proposals to the parties with a view to reaching an amicable settlement of the dispute.

6. The Commission shall report within twelve months of its constitution. Its report shall be deposited with the Secretary-General and transmitted to the parties to the dispute. The report of the Commission, including any conclusions stated therein regarding the facts or questions of law, shall not be binding upon the parties and it shall have no other character than that of recommendations submitted for the consideration of the parties in order to facilitate an amicable settlement of the dispute.

7. The Secretary-General shall provide the Commission with such assistance and facilities as it may require. The expenses of the Commission shall be borne by the United Nations.

3. Vienna Convention on Succession of States in Respect of State Property, Archives and Debts of April 8, 1983 (Identical with the Vienna Convention on Succession of States in Respect of Treaties of August 23, 1978)

The Vienna Convention on Succession of States in respect of Treaties and the Vienna Convention on Succession of States in respect of State Property, Archives and Debts contain identical provisions for the settlement of disputes arising out of the interpretation or application of the respective convention. According to the provisions the parties may resort to different means of dispute settlement comprising negotiation, conciliation, arbitration and judicial settlement by the International Court of Justice. Resort to arbitration or the International Court of Justice presupposes, however, a special declaration to this effect, while without such special declaration states shall, in case of a dispute, first try to seek a resolution by negotiation. If the dispute is not settled by negotiation within six months, any party may submit the dispute to a conciliation procedure the rules of which are laid down in the Annex to the Convention.

Texts

Vienna Convention on Succession of States in respect of Treaties, ILM XVII (1978), 1488–1517

Vienna Convention on Succession of States in respect to Property, Archives and Debts, ILM XXII (1983), 306–329

Bibliographical notes

Commentary of the ILC in ILC Yearbook 1974, Vol.2, part 1, 174–269

Commentary of the ILC in Yearbook 1981, Vol. 2, part 2, 20–113

R. Lavalle, Dispute Settlement under the Vienna Convention on Succession of States in Respect of Treaties, AJIL 37 (1979), 407–425

J. Oesterhelt, Vienna Convention on Succession of States in Respect of Property, Archives and Debts, in: R. Bernhardt (ed.), EPIL, Instalment 10 (1987), 521–523

H. D. Treviranus, Vienna Convention on Succession of States in Respect of Treaties, in: R. Bernhardt (ed.), EPIL, Instalment 10 (1987), 523–526

P. K. Menon, The succession of States in respect to treaties, state property, archives and debts (1991)

Sur la succession d'états en matière de traités/Comité 21 de l'Association du Droit International, in: Rivista di studi politici internazionali 63 (1996), 504–544

a) Part V: Settlement of Disputes

Art. 42   Consultation and negotiation

If a dispute regarding the interpretation or application of the present Convention arises between two or more Parties to the Convention, they shall, upon the request of any of them, seek to resolve it by a process of consultation and negotiation.

Art. 43   Conciliation

If the dispute is not resolved within six months of the date on which the request referred to in article 42 has been made, any party to the dispute may submit it to the conciliation procedure specified in the Annex to the present Convention by submitting a request to that effect to the Secretary-General of the United Nations and informing the other party or parties to the dispute of the request.

Art. 44   Judicial settlement and arbitration

Any State at the time of signature or ratification of the present Convention or accession thereto or at any time thereafter, may, by notification to the depositary, declare that, where a dispute has not been resolved by the application of the procedures referred to in articles 42 and 43, that dispute may be submitted for a decision to the International Court of Justice by a written application of any party to the dispute, or in the alternative to arbitration, provided that the other party to the dispute has made a like declaration.

Art. 45   Settlement by common consent

Notwithstanding articles 42, 43 and 44, if a dispute regarding the interpretation or application of the present Convention arises between two or more Parties to the Convention, they may by common consent agree to submit it to the International Court of Justice, or to arbitration, or to any other appropriate procedure for the settlement of disputes.

Art. 46   Other provisions in force for the settlement of disputes

Nothing in articles 42 to 45 shall affect the rights or obligations of the Parties to the present Convention under any provisions in force binding them with regard to the settlement of disputes.

b) Annex to the Convention

1. A list of conciliators consisting of qualified jurists shall be drawn up and maintained by the Secretary-General of the United Nations. To this end, every State which is a Member of the United Nations or a Party to the present Convention shall be invited to nominate two conciliators, and the names of the persons so nominated shall constitute the list. The term

of a conciliator, including that of any conciliator nominated to fill a casual vacancy, shall be five years and may be renewed. A conciliator whose term expires shall continue to fulfil any function for which he shall have been chosen under the following paragraph.

2. When a request has been made to the Secretary-General under article 43, the Secretary-General shall bring the dispute before a conciliation commission constituted as follows:

The State or States constituting one of the parties to the dispute shall appoint:

(a) one conciliator of the nationality of that State or of one of those States, who may or may not be chosen from the list referred to in paragraph 1; and

(b) one conciliator not of the nationality of that State or of any of those States, who shall be chosen from the list.

The State or States constituting the other party to the dispute shall appoint two conciliators in the same way. The four conciliators chosen by the parties shall be appointed within sixty days following the date on which the Secretary-General receives the request.

The four conciliators shall, within sixty days following the date of the appointment of the last of them, appoint a fifth conciliator chosen from the list, who shall be chairman.

If the appointment of the chairman or of any of the other conciliators has not been made within the period prescribed above for such appointment, it shall be made by the Secretary-General within sixty days following the expiry of that period. The appointment of the chairman may be made by the Secretary-General either from the list or from the membership of the International Law Commission. Any of the periods within which appointments must be made may be extended by agreement between the parties to the dispute.

Any vacancy shall be filled in the manner prescribed for the initial appointment.

3. The Conciliation Commission shall decide its own procedure. The Commission, with the consent of the parties to the dispute, may invite any Party to the present Convention to submit to it its views orally or in writing. Decisions and recommendations of the Commission shall be made by a majority vote of the five members.

4. The Commission may draw the attention of the parties to the dispute to any measures which might facilitate an amicable settlement.

5. The Commission shall hear the parties, examine the claims and objections, and make proposals to the parties with a view to reaching an amicable settlement of the dispute.

6. The Commission shall report within twelve months of its constitution. Its report shall be deposited with the Secretary-General and transmitted to the parties to the dispute. The report of the Commission, including any

conclusions stated therein regarding the facts or questions of law, shall not be binding upon the parties and it shall have no other character than that of recommendations submitted for the consideration of the parties in order to facilitate an amicable settlement of the dispute.

7. The Secretary-General shall provide the Commission with such assistance and facilities as it may require. The expenses of the Commission shall be borne by the United Nations.

4. Vienna Convention on the Law of Treaties between States and International Organizations or between International Organizations

In 1986, a special convention on the law of treaties concerning treaties concluded between States and international organizations or between international organizations was signed. Similarly to the Vienna Convention on the Law of Treaties, this convention provides for the settlement of disputes concerning Part V of the Convention which is concerned with the invalidity or termination of treaties. Parties to such a dispute shall first try to reach a solution under Art. 33 of the United Nations Charter. If no solution is reached, any of the parties to the dispute may set in motion the conciliation procedure specified in the Annex to the Convention.

In disputes concerning the application or interpretation of "jus cogens" (Articles 53 and 64), the International Court of Justice may be seized by unilateral application, unless the parties agree to submit the dispute to ad hoc arbitration. Resort to the contentious procedure of the International Court of Justice is, however, only possible if the parties to the dispute are States; if not all parties to the dispute are States, the International Court of Justice may only be requested in accordance with Article 96 of the Charter and Article 65 of the Statute to give an advisory opinion which shall be accepted as decisive by all the parties to the dispute concerned. If resort to the International Court of Justice is not open, any of the parties to the dispute may submit the dispute to arbitration in accordance with the provisions laid down in the Annex to the Convention.

Texts

ILM Vol. XXV (1986), 543–592
UN Doc. A/CONF.129/15

Bibliographical notes

E. Klein/M. Pechstein, Das Vertragsrecht internationaler Organisationen (1985)

F. Gaja, A "New" Vienna Convention on Treaties Between States and International Organizations: A Critical Commentary, BYIL 58 (1987), 253 et seq.

G. K. Menon, The Law of Treaties between States and International Organizations (1992)

K. Zemanek, International Organizations, Treaty-Making Power, in: R. Bernhardt (ed.), EPIL, Vol. II (1995), 1343–1346 with further bibliographical indications

a) Art. 66 of the Convention

Art. 66   Procedures for judicial settlement, arbitration and conciliation

1. If, under paragraph 3 of article 65, no solution has been reached within a period of twelve months following the date on which the objection was raised, the procedures specified in the following paragraphs shall be followed.

2. With respect to a dispute concerning the application or the interpretation of article 53 or 64:

(a) if a State is a party to the dispute with one or more States, it may, by a written application, submit the dispute to the International Court of Justice for a decision;

(b) if a State is a party to the dispute to which one or more international organizations are parties, the State may, through a Member State of the United Nations if necessary, request the General Assembly or the Security Council or, where appropriate, the competent organ of an international organisation which is a party to the dispute and is authorised in accordance with Article 96 of the Charter of the United Nations, to request an advisory opinion of the International Court of Justice in accordance with article 65 of the Statute of the Court;

(c) if the United Nations or an international organisation that is authorised in accordance with Article 96 of the Charter of the United Nations is a party to the dispute, it may request an advisory opinion of the International Court of Justice in accordance with article 65 of the Statute of the Court;

(d) if an international organisation other than those referred to in subparagraph (c) is a party to the dispute, it may, through a Member State of the United Nations, follow the procedure specified in subparagraph (b);

(e) the advisory opinion given pursuant to sub-paragraph (b), (c) or (d) shall be accepted as decisive by all the parties to the dispute concerned;

(f) if the request under sub-paragraph (b), (c) or (d) for an advisory opinion of the Court is not granted, any one of the parties to the dispute may, by written notification to the other party or parties, submit it to arbitration in accordance with the provisions of the Annex to the present Convention.

3. The provisions of paragraph 2 apply unless all the parties to a dispute referred to in that paragraph by common consent agree to submit the dispute to an arbitration procedure, including the one specified in the Annex to the present Convention.

4. With respect to a dispute concerning the application or the interpretation of any of the articles in Part V, other than articles 53 and 64, of the present Convention, any one of the parties to the dispute may set in mo-

tion the Conciliation procedure specified in the Annex to the Convention by submitting a request to that effect to the Secretary-General of the United Nations.

b) Annex to the Convention

ARBITRATION AND CONCILIATION PROCEDURES ESTABLISHED IN APPLICATION OF ARTICLE 66

I. ESTABLISHMENT OF THE ARBITRAL TRIBUNAL OR CONCILIATION COMMISSION

1. A list consisting of qualified jurists, from which the parties to a dispute may choose the persons who are to constitute an arbitral tribunal or, as the case may be, a conciliation commission, shall be drawn up and maintained by the Secretary-General of the United Nations. To this end, every State which is a Member of the United Nations and every party to the present Convention shall be invited to nominate two persons, and the names of the persons so nominated shall constitute the list, a copy of which shall be transmitted to the President of the International Court of Justice. The term of office of a person on the list, including that of any person nominated to fill a casual vacancy, shall be five years and may be renewed. A person whose term expires shall continue to fulfil any function for which he shall have been chosen under the following paragraphs.

2. When notification has been made under article 66, paragraph 2, sub-paragraph (f), or agreement on the procedure in the present Annex has been reached under paragraph 3, the dispute shall be brought before an arbitral tribunal. When a request has been made to the Secretary-General under article 66, paragraph 4, the Secretary-General shall bring the dispute before a conciliation commission. Both the arbitral tribunal and the conciliation commission shall be constituted as follows:

The States, international organisations or, as the case may be, the States and organisations which constitute one of the parties to the dispute shall appoint by common consent:

(a) one arbitrator or, as the case may be, one conciliator, who may or may not be chosen from the list referred to in paragraph 1; and

(b) one arbitrator or, as the case may be, one conciliator, who shall be chosen from among those included in the list and shall not be of the nationality of any of the States or nominated by any of the organisations which constitute that party to the dispute, provided that a dispute between two international organisations is not considered by nationals of one and the same State.

The States, international organisations or, as the case may be, the States and organisations which constitute the other party to the dispute shall appoint two arbitrators or, as the case may be, two conciliators, in the same way. The four persons chosen by the parties shall be appointed within sixty days following the date on which the other party to the dispute receives notification under article 66, paragraph 2, sub-paragraph (f), or on which the agreement on the procedure in the present Annex under paragraph 3 is reached, or on which the Secretary-General receives the request for conciliation.

The four persons so chosen shall, within sixty days following the date of the last of their own appointments, appoint from the list a fifth arbitrator or, as the Case may be, conciliator, who shall be chairman.

If the appointment of the chairman, or any of the arbitrators or, as the case may be, conciliators, has not been made within the period prescribed above for such appointment, it shall be made by the Secretary-General of the United Nations within sixty days following the expiry of that period. The appointment of the chairman may be made by the Secretary-General either from the list or from the membership of the International Law Commission. Any of the periods within which appointments must be made may be extended by agreement between the parties to the dispute. If the United Nations is a party or is included in one of the parties to the dispute, the Secretary-General shall transmit the above-mentioned request to the President of the International Court of Justice, who shall perform the functions conferred upon the Secretary-General under this sub-paragraph.

Any vacancy shall be filled in the manner prescribed for the initial appointment.

The appointment of arbitrators or conciliators by an international organisation provided for in paragraphs 1 and 2 shall be governed by the rules of that organisation.

II. FUNCTIONING OF THE ARBITRAL TRIBUNAL

3. Unless the parties to the dispute otherwise agree, the Arbitral Tribunal shall decide its own procedure, assuring to each party to the dispute a full opportunity to be heard and to present its case.

4. The Arbitral Tribunal, with the consent of the parties to the dispute, may invite any interested State or international organisation to submit to it its views orally or in writing.

5. Decisions of the Arbitral Tribunal shall be adopted by a majority vote of the members. In the event of an equality of votes, the vote of the Chairman shall be decisive.

6. When one of the parties to the dispute does not appear before the Tribunal or fails to defend its case, the other party may request the Tribunal to continue the proceedings and to make its award. Before making its

award, the Tribunal must satisfy itself not only that it has jurisdiction over the dispute but also that the claim is well founded in fact and law.

7. The award of the Arbitral Tribunal shall be confined to the subject-matter of the dispute and state the reasons on which it is based. Any member of the Tribunal may attach a separate or dissenting opinion to the award.

8. The award shall be final and without appeal. It shall be complied with by all parties to the dispute.

9. The Secretary-General shall provide the Tribunal with such assistance and facilities as it may require. The expenses of the Tribunal shall be borne by the United Nations.

III. FUNCTIONING OF THE CONCILIATION COMMISSION

10. The Conciliation Commission shall decide its own procedure. The Commission, with the consent of the parties to the dispute, may invite any party to the treaty to submit to it its views orally or in writing. Decisions and recommendations of the Commission shall be made by a majority vote of the five members.

11. The Commission may draw the attention of the parties to the dispute to any measures which might facilitate an amicable settlement.

12. The Commission shall hear the parties, examine the claims and objections, and make proposals to the parties with a view to reaching an amicable settlement of the dispute.

13. The Commission shall report within twelve months of its constitution. Its report shall be deposited with the Secretary-General and transmitted to the parties to the dispute. The report of the Commission, including any conclusions stated therein regarding the facts or questions of law, shall not be binding upon the parties and it shall have no other character than that of recommendations submitted for the consideration of the pasties in order to facilitate an amicable settlement of the dispute.

14. The Secretary-General shall provide the Commission with such assistance and facilities as it may require. The expenses of the Commission shall be borne by the United Nations.

III. Regional Agreements

1. Europe

a) European Convention for the Peaceful Settlement of Disputes of April 29, 1957

The European Convention for the Peaceful Settlement of Disputes was drafted within the framework of the Council of Europe and is limited in its applicability to the member States of the Council of Europe.

The Convention is modelled essentially on the Geneva General Act of 1928 and is similar to the Pact of Bogotá as a regional agreement for the pacific settlement of disputes.

The Convention provides for the settlement of legal as well as non-legal disputes. As to international legal disputes, defined in Art. 36 para. 2 of the Statute of the International Court of Justice, the Convention provides for the compulsory jurisdiction of the International Court of Justice. For these disputes an optional conciliation procedure may precede adjudication by the International Court of Justice; the conciliation procedure is, on the other hand, compulsory concerning non-legal disputes and may be followed, if necessary, by compulsory arbitration. The rules of procedure applicable in conciliation and arbitration procedures are those defined in the Hague Convention of October 18, 1907 on the Pacific Settlement of International Disputes. Disagreement as to the legal or non-legal character of a dispute is resolved by the International Court of Justice.

In ratifying the European Convention, States must accept on the basis of reciprocity at least the compulsory jurisdiction of the International Court of Justice for legal disputes; they may, however, declare that they will not be bound by the provisions relating to arbitration or to conciliation and arbitration (Art. 34). The result of this possibility of partial acceptance of the Convention as well as the possibility of making reservations concerning the jurisdiction of the International Court of Justice is that arbitration remains compulsory only for half of the 13 States that have ratified the Convention, namely Austria, Germany, Switzerland, Luxembourg, Denmark and Norway and Liechtenstein.

The Convention, in force since April 30, 1958, has been ratified by thirteen member States of the Council of Europe (Belgium, Denmark, Federal Republic of Germany, Italy, Liechtenstein, Luxembourg, Malta, the Netherlands, Norway, Austria, Sweden, Switzerland, Great Britain. Turkey only signed the Convention (dates taken of the Council of Europe Treaty Series Update of March 1997).

Texts

UNTS Vol. 320, pp. 243–267 (English and French)
European Treaty Series, No. 23
BGBl. 1961 II, pp. 82 et seq. (German)

Bibliographical notes

J. P. A. François, La Convention européenne pour le règlement pacifique des différends, 29 avril 1957, Annuaire européenne — European Yearbook, Vol. 6 (1958),
pp. 54 et seq.

K. H. Kunzmann, Die Europäische Konvention über die friedliche Beilegung von
Streitigkeiten, EA Vol. 14 (1959), pp. 125 et seq.

H. Rolin, L'arbitrage international: Une panacée illusoire, NTIR Vol. 6 (1959),
Special Issue, Liber Amicorum J.P.A. François, pp. 254 et seq.

J. Salmon, La convention européenne pour le règlement pacifique des différends,
RGDIP Vol. 63 (1959), pp. 21 et seq.

H. Wehberg, La convention européenne pour le règlement pacifique des différends,
NTIR Vol. 6 (1959), Special Issue, Liber Amicorum J.P.A. François, pp. 391 et
seq.

A. C. Kiss, Le Conseil de L'Europe et le règlement pacifique des différends, AFDI
Vol. 11 (1965), pp. 668–686

M. O. Wiederkehr, Les clauses de règlement des différends dans les conventions et
accords du Conseil de l'Europe, AFDI Vol. 24 (1978), pp. 942–960

Parliamentary Assembly, Council of Europe, Legal Affairs Committee, Report on
Peaceful Settlement of Disputes (Rapporteur: Mr. Grieve), September 24, 1979,
Council of Europe Document No. 4406

K. Ginther, European Convention for the Peaceful Settlement of Disputes, in: R.
Bernhardt (ed.), EPIL, Vol. II (1995), 186–188

a) European Convention for the Peaceful Settlement of Disputes of April 29, 1957

The Governments signatory hereto, being Members of the Council of Europe,

Considering that the aim of the Council of Europe is to achieve a greater unity between its Members;

Convinced that the pursuit of peace based upon justice is vital for the preservation of human society and civilisation;

Resolved to settle by peaceful means any disputes which may arise between them,

Have agreed as follows:

CHAPTER I. JUDICIAL SETTLEMENT

Art. 1   The High Contracting Parties shall submit to the judgement of the International Court of Justice all international legal disputes which may arise between them including, in particular, those concerning:

(a) the interpretation of a treaty;

(b) any question of international law;

(c) the existence of any fact which, if established, would constitute a breach of an international obligation;

(d) the nature or extent of the reparation to be made for the breach of an international obligation.

Art. 2   1. The provisions of Article 1 shall not affect undertakings by which the High Contracting Parties have accepted or may accept the jurisdiction of the International Court of Justice for the settlement of disputes other than those mentioned in Article 1.

2. The parties to a dispute may agree to resort to the procedure of conciliation before that of judicial settlement.

Art. 3   The High Contracting Parties which are not parties to the Statute of the International Court of Justice shall carry out the measures necessary to enable them to have access thereto.

CHAPTER II. CONCILIATION

Art. 4   1. The High Contracting Parties shall submit to conciliation all disputes which may arise between them, other than disputes falling within the scope of Article 1.

2. Nevertheless, the parties to a dispute falling within the scope of this Article may agree to submit it to an arbitral tribunal without prior recourse to the procedure of conciliation.

Art. 5   When a dispute arises which falls within the scope of Article 4, it shall be referred to a Permanent Conciliation Commission competent in the matter, previously set up by the parties concerned. If the parties agree not to have recourse to that Commission or if there is no such Commission, the dispute shall be referred to a special Conciliation Commission, which shall be set up by the parties within a period of three months from the date on which a request to that effect is made by one of the parties to the other party.

Art. 6   In the absence of agreement to the contrary between the parties concerned, the Special Conciliation Commission shall be constituted as follows:

The Commission shall be composed of five members. The parties shall each nominate one Commissioner, who may be chosen from among their respective nationals. The three other Commissioners, including the President, shall be chosen by agreement from among the nationals of third States. These three Commissioners shall be of different nationalities and shall not be habitually resident in the territory nor be in the service of the parties.

Art. 7   If the nomination of the Commissioners to be designated jointly is not made within the period provided for in Article 5, the task of making the necessary nominations shall be entrusted to the Government of a third State, chosen by agreement between the parties, or, failing such agreement being reached within three months, to the President of the International Court of Justice. Should the latter be a national of one of the parties to the dispute, this task shall be entrusted to the Vice-President of the Court or to the next senior judge of the Court who is not a national of the parties.

Art. 8   Vacancies which may occur as a result of death, resignation or any other cause shall be filled within the shortest possible time in the manner fixed for the nominations.

Art. 9   1. Disputes shall be brought before the Special Conciliation Commission by means of an application addressed to the President by the two Parties acting in agreement or, in default thereof, by one or other of the parties.

2. The application, after giving a summary account of the subject of the dispute, shall contain the invitation to the Commission to take all necessary measures with a view to arriving at an amicable solution.

3. If the application emanates from only one of the parties, the other party shall, without delay, be notified of it by that party.

Art. 10   1. In the absence of agreement to the contrary between the parties, the Special Conciliation Commission shall meet at the seat of the Council of Europe or at some other place selected by its President.

2. The Commission may at all times request the Secretary-General of the Council of Europe to afford it his assistance.

Art. 11   The work of the Special Conciliation Commission shall not be conducted in public unless the Commission with the consent of the parties so decides.

Art. 12   1. In the absence of agreement to the contrary between the parties, the Special Conciliation Commission shall lay down its own procedure, which in any case must provide for both parties being heard. In regard to enquiries, subject to the provisions of this Convention, the Commission, unless it decides unanimously to the contrary, shall act in accordance with the provisions of Part III of the Hague Convention for the Pacific Settlement of International Disputes of 18th October 1907.

2. The parties shall be represented before the Conciliation Commission by agents whose duty shall be to act as intermediaries between them and the Commission; they may be assisted by counsel and experts appointed by them for that purpose and may request that all persons whose evidence appears to them desirable shall be heard.

3. The Commission shall be entitled to request oral explanations from the agents, counsel and experts of both parties, as well as from all persons it may think desirable to summon with the consent of their Governments.

Art. 13   In the absence of agreement to the contrary between the parties, the decisions of the Special Conciliation Commission shall be taken by a majority vote and, except in relation to questions of procedure, decisions of the Commission shall be valid only if all its members are present.

Art. 14   The parties shall facilitate the work of the Special Conciliation Commission and, in particular, shall supply it to the greatest possible extent with all relevant documents and information. They shall use the means at their disposal to allow it to proceed in their territory, and in accordance with their law, to the summoning and hearing of witnesses or experts and to visit the localities in question.

Art. 15   1. The task of the Special Conciliation Commission shall be to elucidate the questions in dispute, to collect with that object all necessary information by means of enquiry or otherwise, and to endeavour to bring the parties to an agreement. It may, after the case has been examined, inform the parties of the terms of settlement which seem suitable to it and lay down the period within which they are to make their decision.

2. At the close of its proceedings, the Commission shall draw up a procès-verbal stating, as the case may be, either that the parties have come to an agreement and, if need arises, the terms of the agreement, or that it has been impossible to effect a settlement. No mention shall be made in the procès-verbal of whether the Commission's decisions were taken unanimously or by a majority vote.

3. The proceedings of the Commission shall, unless the parties otherwise agree, be terminated within six months from the date on which the Commission shall have been given cognizance of the dispute.

Art. 16   The Commission's procès-verbal shall be communicated without delay to the parties. It shall only be published with their consent.

Art. 17   1. During the proceedings of the Commission, each of the Commissioners shall receive emoluments, the amount of which shall be fixed by agreement between the parties, each of which shall contribute an equal share.

2. The general expenses arising out of the working of the Commission shall be divided in the same manner.

Art. 18   In the case of a mixed dispute involving both questions for which conciliation is appropriate and other questions for which judicial settlement is appropriate, any party to the dispute shall have the right to insist that the judicial settlement of the legal questions shall precede conciliation.

CHAPTER III. ARBITRATION

Art. 19   The High Contracting Parties shall submit to arbitration all disputes which may arise between them other than those mentioned in Article 1 and which have not been settled by conciliation, either because the parties have agreed not to have prior recourse to it or because conciliation has failed.

Art. 20   1. The party requesting arbitration shall inform the other party of the claim which it intends to submit to arbitration, of the grounds on which such claim is based and of the name of the arbitrator whom it has nominated.

2. In the absence of agreement to the contrary between the parties concerned, the Arbitral Tribunal shall be constituted as follows:

The Arbitral Tribunal shall consist of five members. The parties shall each nominate one member, who may be chosen from among their respective nationals. The other three arbitrators, including the President, shall be chosen by agreement from among the nationals of third States. They shall be of different nationalities and shall not be habitually resident in the territory nor be in the service of the parties.

Art. 21   If the nomination of the members of the Arbitral Tribunal is not made within a period of three months from the date on which one of the parties requested the other party to constitute an Arbitral Tribunal, the task of making the necessary nominations shall be entrusted to the Government of a third State, chosen by agreement between the parties, or, failing agreement within three months, to the President of the International Court of Justice. Should the latter be a national of one of the parties to the dispute, this task shall be entrusted to the Vice-President of the Court, or to the next senior judge of the Court who is not a national of the parties.

Art. 22   Vacancies which may occur as a result of death, resignation or any other cause shall be filled within the shortest possible time in the manner fixed for the nomination.

Art. 23   The parties shall draw up a special agreement determining the subject of the dispute and the details of procedure.

Art. 24   In the absence of sufficient particulars in the special agreement regarding the matters referred to in Article 23, the provisions of Part IV of the Hague Convention of 18th October 1907 for the Pacific Settlement of International Disputes shall apply so far as possible.

Art. 25   Failing the conclusion of a special agreement within a period of three months from the date on which the Arbitral Tribunal was constituted, the dispute may be brought before the Tribunal upon application by one or other party.

Art. 26   If nothing is laid down in the special agreement or no special agreement has been made, the Tribunal shall decide *ex aequo et bono*, having regard to the general principles of international law, while respecting the contractual obligations and the final decisions of international tribunals which are binding on the parties.

CHAPTER IV. GENERAL PROVISIONS

Art. 27   The provisions of this Convention shall not apply to:
   (a)   disputes relating to facts or situations prior to the entry into force of this Convention as between the parties to the dispute;
   (b)   disputes concerning questions which by international law are solely within the domestic jurisdiction of States.

Art 28   1. The provisions of this Convention shall not apply to disputes which the parties have agreed or may agree to submit to another procedure of peaceful settlement. Nevertheless, in respect of disputes falling within the scope of Article 1, the High Contracting Parties shall refrain from invoking as between themselves agreements which do not provide for a procedure entailing binding decisions.

2. This Convention shall in no way affect the application of the provisions of the Convention for the Protection of Human Rights and Fundamental Freedoms signed on 4th November 1950, or of the Protocol thereto signed on 20th March 1952.

Art. 29   1. In the case of a dispute the subject of which, according to the municipal law of one of the parties, falls within the competence of its judicial or administrative authorities, the party in question may object to the dispute being submitted for settlement by any of the procedures laid down in this Convention until a decision with final effect has been pronounced, within a reasonable time, by the competent authority.

2. If a decision with final effect has been pronounced in the State concerned, it will no longer be possible to resort to any of the procedures laid down in this Convention after the expiration of a period of five years from the date of the aforementioned decision.

Art. 30   If the execution of a judicial sentence or arbitral award would conflict with a judgement or measure enjoined by a court of law or other authority of one of the parties to the dispute, and if the municipal law of that party does not permit or only partially permits the consequences of the judgement or measure in question to be annulled, the Court or the Arbitral Tribunal shall, if necessary, grant the injured party equitable satisfaction.

Art. 31   1. In all cases where a dispute forms the subject of arbitration or judicial proceedings, and particularly if the question on which the parties differ arises out of acts already committed or on the point of being committed, the International Court of Justice, acting in accordance with Article 41 of its Statute, or the Arbitral Tribunal, shall lay down within the shortest possible time the provisional measures to be adopted. The parties to the dispute shall be bound to accept such measures.

2. If the dispute is brought before a Conciliation Commission the latter may recommend to the parties the adoption of such provisional measures as it considers suitable.

3. The Parties shall abstain from all measures likely to react prejudicially upon the execution of the judicial or arbitral decision or upon the arrangements proposed by the Conciliation Commission and, in general, shall abstain from any sort of action whatsoever which may aggravate or extend the dispute.

Art. 32   1. This Convention shall remain applicable as between the Parties thereto, even though a third State, whether a Party to the Convention or not, has an interest in the dispute.

2. In the procedure of conciliation the parties may agree to invite such a third State to intervene.

Art. 33   1. In judicial or arbitral procedure, if a third State should consider that its legitimate interests are involved, it may submit to the International Court of Justice or to the Arbitral Tribunal a request to intervene as a third party.

2. It will be for the Court or the Tribunal to decide upon this request.

Art. 34   1. On depositing its instrument of ratification, any one of the High Contracting Parties may declare that it will not be bound by:

(a)   Chapter III relating to arbitration; or

(b)   Chapters II and III relating to conciliation and arbitration.

2. A High Contracting Party may only benefit from those provisions of this Convention by which it is itself bound.

Art. 35   1. The High Contracting Parties may only make reservations which exclude from the application of this Convention disputes concerning particular cases or clearly specified subject matters, such as territorial status, or disputes falling within clearly defined categories. If one of the High Contracting Parties has made a reservation, the other Parties may enforce the same reservation in regard to that Party.

2. Any reservation made shall, unless otherwise expressly stated, be deemed not to apply to the procedure of conciliation.

3. Except as provided in paragraph 4 of this Article, any reservations must be made at the time of depositing instruments of ratification of the Convention.

4. If a High Contracting Party accepts the compulsory jurisdiction of the International Court of Justice under paragraph 2 of Article 36 of the Statute of the said Court, subject to reservations, or amends any such reservations, that High Contracting Party may by a simple declaration, and subject to the provisions of paragraphs 1 and 2 of this Article, make the same reservations to this Convention. Such reservations shall not release the High Contracting Party concerned from its obligations under this Convention in respect of disputes relating to facts or situations prior to the date of the declaration by which they are made. Such disputes shall, however, be submitted to the appropriate procedure under the terms of this Convention within a period of one year from the said date.

Art. 36   A Party which is bound by only part of this Convention, or which has made reservations, may at any time, by a simple declaration, either extend the scope of its obligations or abandon all or part of its reservations.

Art. 37   The declarations provided for in paragraph 4 of Article 35 and in Article 36 shall be addressed to the Secretary-General of the Council of Europe, who shall transmit copies to each of the other High Contracting Parties.

Art. 38   1. Disputes relating to the interpretation or application of this Convention, including those concerning the classification of disputes and the scope of reservations, shall be submitted to the International Court of Justice. However, an objection concerning the obligation of a High Contracting Party to submit a particular dispute to arbitration can only be submitted to the Court within a period of three months after the notification by one party to the other of its intention to resort to arbitration. Any such objection made after that period shall be decided upon by the arbitral tribunal. The decision of the Court shall be binding on the body dealing with the dispute.

2. Recourse to the International Court of Justice in accordance with the above provisions shall have the effect of suspending the conciliation or arbitration proceeding concerned until the decision of the Court is known.

Art. 39   1. Each of the High Contracting Parties shall comply with the decision of the International Court of Justice or the award of the Arbitral Tribunal in any dispute to which it is a party.

2. If one of the parties to a dispute fails to carry out its obligations under a decision of the International Court of Justice or an award of the Arbitral Tribunal, the other party to the dispute may appeal to the Committee of Ministers of the Council of Europe. Should it deem necessary, the latter, acting by a two-third majority of the representatives entitled to sit on the Committee, may make recommendations with a view to ensuring compliance with the said decision or award.

Art. 40   1. This Convention may be denounced by a High Contracting Party only after the conclusion of a period of five years from the date of its entry into force for the Party in question. Such denunciation shall be subject to six months' notice, which shall be communicated to the Secretary-General of the Council of Europe, who shall inform the other Contracting Parties.

2. Denunciation shall not release the High Contracting Party concerned from its obligations under this Convention in respect of disputes relating to facts or situations prior to the date of the notice referred to in the preceding paragraph. Such dispute shall, however, be submitted to the appropriate procedure under the terms of this Convention within a period of one year from the said date.

3. Subject to the same conditions, any High Contracting Party which ceases to be a Member of the Council of Europe shall cease to be a party to this Convention within a period of one year from the said date.

Art. 41   1. This Convention shall be open for signature by the Members of the Council of Europe. It shall be ratified. Instruments of ratification shall be deposited with the Secretary-General of the Council of Europe.

2. This Convention shall enter into force on the date of the deposit of the second instrument of ratification.

3. As regards any signatory ratifying subsequently, the Convention shall enter into force on the date of the deposit of its instrument of ratification.

4. The Secretary-General of the Council of Europe shall notify all the Members of the Council of Europe of the entry into force of the Convention, the names of the High Contracting Parties who have ratified it and the deposit of all instruments of ratification which may be effected subsequently.

In witness whereof the undersigned, being duly authorised thereto, have signed the present Convention.

Done at Strasbourg, this 29th day of April 1957, in English and French, both texts being equally authoritative, in a single copy which shall remain deposited in the Archives of the Council of Europe. The Secretary-General shall transmit certified copies to each of the Signatories.

b) Conference/Organisation on Security and Cooperation in Europe (CSCE/OSCE)

In the framework of the creation of the Conference on Security and Cooperation in Europe one of the principle aims has always been the creation of a procedure for the peaceful settlement of disputes. However, the Final Act of Helsinki of August 1, 1975 contained only a general commitment to peaceful settlement of disputes, Principle V, without any mandatory component. The comprehensive draft on dispute settlement introduced by the Swiss delegation already in 1973 (cf. Dispute Settlement in Public International Law, first edition, 1984, 101–116) could not find sufficient support notwithstanding lengthy debates in a special working group. However, it was in particular the Swiss delegation which kept the question on the agenda and came forward with a new draft convention on binding dispute settlement in the subsequent meetings of experts on peaceful settlement in Montreux 1978 (cf. Dispute Settlement in Public International Law, first edition, 1984, 116–118) and Athens 1984, again without yielding substantial result.

The first substantial progress was reached after the break-down of the bloc system which enabled the 1991 expert meeting on peaceful settlement of disputes (La Valletta, January 15 to February 8, 1991) to agree on a mechanism on dispute settlement (infra aa). This mechanism provided for mandatory third party involvement without, however, finding agreement on binding decision by the involved neutral third, but only instituting a kind of compulsory conciliation procedure. According to this mechanism a commission, the composition of which cannot be prevented by one of the parties, has in a first step only the task to search together with the parties to the dispute a solution acceptable for all. If no solution is reached the commission may, in a second step, make proposals to the parties how to settle the dispute. These proposals, however, become binding only after having been accepted by the parties. This mechanism, which does not at all constitute a satisfactory procedure for the settlement of disputes, even provides for further restriction in that the mechanism will not be established or continue its work if one of the parties to the dispute considers that its territorial integrity, or national defence, title to sovereignty over land territory, or competing claims with regard to the jurisdiction over other areas is concerned. Thus the only advantage of this mechanism is the fact that no state may escape definitively to any attempt of a peaceful settlement of a dispute.

Since it was evident that this procedure of dispute settlement was not satisfactory, a group of experts was charged with the elaboration of a statute for a CSCE procedure on conciliation and arbitration which was adopted in December 1992 at the Stockholm Meeting together with an amendment of the Valletta Mechanism, Provisions for a CSCE Conciliation Commission and Provisions for Directed Conciliation.

The Convention on Conciliation and Arbitration within the CSCE creates two organs which, as is the case of the Permanent Court of Arbitration, consist of two lists: one containing the names of conciliators nominated by the States Parties, the other one containing the names of the arbitrators nominated by the States Parties. Both, the conciliation commissions and the arbitral tribunals follow in their composition the usual model of such organs. They are instituted by parties to the Convention by unilateral application; they may, however, also be instituted by agreement, if at least one party to the dispute is a party to the Convention. Similar to the International Court of Justice, the Convention contains an optional clause, Art. 26, paragraph 2, corresponding to Art. 36, paragraph 2 of the Statute of the International Court of Justice, according to which arbitration becomes compulsory with regard to all Parties which have made the same declaration. In the case, however, of bringing a dispute on the basis of the optional clause, the parties are obliged first to go to conciliation; otherwise a conciliation procedure is not required before resorting to arbitration.

The Convention is a treaty under international law and not a CSCE document. In contrast to the European Convention for the Peaceful Settlement of Disputes of 1957, the Convention can only be ratified in whole; that means that the States are not free to submit only to conciliation or to arbitration. In order to make conciliation available also to participant States of the CSCE which have not become Parties to the Convention, a special conciliation on an ad hoc basis was instituted together with the adoption of the Convention which is open to all participants of the CSCE. The members of the conciliation commissions established under these provisions are nominated from the list instituted under the Valletta mechanism. Since it was not possible to include the competence to give advisory opinions into the Convention a special instrument was adopted together with the convention which provides for directed conciliation. According to these provisions, a conciliation procedure may be initiated by the Council of Ministers or the Committee of Senior Officials in case that the parties to the dispute are not willing to submit their dispute to conciliation or arbitration. Also in this case, the solution found by the Commission becomes binding only after acceptance of the Parties so that mandatory dispute settlement is not possible without the consent of the parties to the dispute. Until now, none of the different procedure for the settlement of disputes existing within the framework of the CSCE has been used, a fact that may be attributed to the subsidiarity of those procedures with regard to other commitments of the parties to dispute settlement procedures.

Texts

Valletta Mechanism
    ILM XXX (1991), 382–396
    U. Fastenrath, Dokumente der KSZE, Bd. 1, E.1, 1–12
    CSCE Document of the Meeting of the Council of Foreign Ministers at Berlin, 20 June, 1991
    T. Schweisfurth/K. Oellers-Frahm, KSZE-Dokumente (1993), 470–479
Amendment of Section V of the Valletta Mechanism
    ILM XXXII (1993), 556
    Schweisfurth/Oellers-Frahm, op. cit., 707
Convention on Conciliation and Arbitration Within the CSCE
    ILM XXXII (1993), 557–567
    Schweisfurth/Oellers-Frahm, op. cit., 708–722
    Fastenrath, op. cit., Bd. 1, E.4, 1-19

Rules of Procedure
    L. Caflisch (ed.), The Peaceful Settlement of Disputes between States: Universal
    and European Perspectives (1998), Annex IV (B), p. 135 et seq.
Provisions for a CSCE Conciliation Commission
    ILM XXXII (1993), 568–570
    Fastenrath, op. cit., Bd. 1, E.5, 1-6
    Schweisfurth/Oellers-Frahm, op. cit., 722–725
Provisions for Directed Conciliation
    ILM XXXII (1993), 570–571
    Fastenrath, op. cit., Bd. 1, E.6, 1-2
    Schweisfurth/Oellers-Frahm, op. cit., 725–726

Bibliographical notes

V.-Y. Ghébali, La CSCE et la transformation des relations internationales en
    Europe, in: Le règlement pacifique des différends en Europe, Perspectives
    d'avenir, Académie de droit international de La Haye (1991), 529–566
P. H. Kooijmans, The Mountain produced a Mouse — The CSCE Meeting of
    Experts on Peaceful Settlement of Disputes, Valletta 1991, Leiden Journal of
    International Law 1992, 90 et seq.
C. Leben, La création d'un organisme CSCE pour le règlement des différends,
    RGDIP 1991, 857 et seq.
K. Oellers-Frahm, The Mandatory Component in the CSCE Dispute Settlement
    System, in: M. W. Janis, International Courts for the Twenty-First Century
    (1992), 195–211
L. Caflisch, Règlement pacifique des différends en Europe: la procédure de La
    Valette et les perspectives d'avenir, in: C. Dominicé/R. Patry/C. Reymond
    (éds.), Etudes de droit international en l'honneur de Pierre Lalive (1993), 437 et
    seq.
L. Condorelli, En attendant la "Cour de conciliation et d'arbitrage de la CSCE":
    quelques remarques sur le droit applicable, ibid., 457 et seq.
A. Pellet, Note sur la Cour de Conciliation et d'Arbitrage de la CSCE, in: E.
    Décaux/L.A. Sicilianos (ed.), La CSCE: Dimension humaine et règlement des
    différends (1993), 189–217
L. A. Sicilianos, Le mécanisme de règlement pacifique des différends au sein de la
    CSCE approuvé à Stockholm, AFDI 39 (1993), 889–918
G. Hafner, Das Streitbeilegungsübereinkommen der KSZE: Cui bono?, in: K. Gin-
    ther/G. Hafner/W. Lang/H. Neuhold/L. Suchapira-Behrmann (ed.), Festschrift
    für Karl Zemanek zum 65. Geburtstag (1994), 115 et seq.
G. Tanja, Peaceful Settlement of Disputes within the framework of the CSCE: A
    Legal Novelty in a Political-Diplomatic Environment, in: A. Bloed (ed.), The
    Challenges of Change (1994), 67–94
C. Leben, La mise en place de la cour de conciliation et d'arbitrage au sein de la
    C.S.C.E., RGDIP 1996, 135 et seq.
M. Wenig, Möglichkeiten und Grenzen der Streitbeilegung ethnischer Konflikte
    durch die OSZE — dargestellt am Konflikt im ehemaligen Jugoslawien (1996)

L. Caflisch, La subsidiarité des mécanismes de la Convention de 1992, in: L. Caflisch (ed.), The Peaceful Settlement of Disputes between States: Universal and European Perspectives (1998), 55–65

E. Décaux, La place de la Convention de 1992 au sein de l'OSCE, ibid., 45–53

K. Oellers-Frahm, The Arbitration Procedure Established by the Convention on Conciliation and Arbitration within the OSCE, ibid., 79–92

H. Steinberger, The Conciliation Procedure Established by the Convention on Conciliation and Arbitration within the OSCE, ibid., 67–77

C. Lüthy, Verfahren zur friedlichen Beilegung internationaler Streitigkeiten im Rahmen der OSZE (1998)

aa) Report of the CSCE Meeting of Experts on Peaceful Settlement of Disputes Adopted at La Valletta, February 8, 1991

The representatives of Austria, Belgium, Bulgaria, Canada, Cyprus, the Czech and Slovak Federal Republic, Denmark, Finland, France, Germany, Greece the Holy See, Hungary, Iceland, Ireland, Italy, Liechtenstein, Luxembourg, European Community, Malta, Monaco, the Netherlands, Norway, Poland, Portugal, Romania, San Marino, Spain, Sweden, Switzerland, Turkey, the Union of Soviet Socialist Republics, the United Kingdom, the United States of America and Yugoslavia met in Valletta from 15 January to 8 February 1991 in accordance with the relevant provisions of the Concluding Document of the Vienna CSCE Meeting 1986 and the Charter of Paris for a New Europe, to consider the question of Peaceful Settlement of Disputes.

The representative of Albania attended the Meeting as observer.

The formal Opening was attended by H.E. Dr. Censu Tabone, President of Malta, who gave an address of welcome. The Meeting was opened by the Hon. Professor Guido de Marco, Deputy Prime Minister and Minister of Foreign Affairs and Justice of Malta, who delivered the opening address on behalf of the host country. He also closed the Meeting.

Opening statements were made by Heads of Delegation of the participating States.

The Hon. Gianni de Michelis, Minister of Foreign Affairs of Italy, addressed the meeting.

A number of proposals were submitted for consideration by the Meeting.

The representatives of the participating States held a general exchange of views on the peaceful settlement of disputes. It was observed that developments in Europe and the world since the Vienna Follow-up Meeting had enhanced the importance of the Meeting, and that this was also reflected in the Charter of Paris for a New Europe, signed by the Heads of State or Government of the participating States an 21 November 1990.

During their deliberations, the representatives of the participating stamps took note of the fact that the States were already bound by a number of agreements containing various methods for a peaceful settlement of disputes; and that, in practice, they made use of an even greater variety of such methods. It was noted in particular that many participating States have devised innovative approaches to dispute settlement designed to suit the characteristics of particular disputes, as well as developed arrangements aimed at preventing or managing disputes, such as notification and consultation arrangements, and the establishment of *ad hoc* and permanent joint commissions. It was also noted that many participating States were parties to the 1899 and/or 1907 Hague Conventions for the Pacific Settlement of International Disputes, and that many of them have accepted the jurisdiction of the International Court of Justice, in accordance with the Statute of the Court.

Following their deliberations, the representatives of the participating
States adopted this Report.

PRINCIPLES FOR DISPUTE SETTLEMENT AND PROVISIONS FOR A CSCE PROCEDURE FOR PEACEFUL SETTLEMENT OF DISPUTES

INTRODUCTION

The commitment of the participating States in the Conference on Security
and Co-operation in Europe (CSCE), laid down in Principle V of the Helsinki Final Act, to settle disputes among them by peaceful means represents one of the cornerstones of the CSCE process. This commitment is
reaffirmed in the Vienna Concluding Document and the Charter of Paris
for a New Europe.

In accordance with the Helsinki Final Act, all ten principles of the Declaration on Principles Guiding Relations between Participating States are of
primary significance and, accordingly, apply equally and unreservedly,
each of them being interpreted taking into account the others.

In the Charter of Paris for a New Europe the participating States solemnly
pledged their full commitment to these ten principles, in order to uphold
and promote democracy, peace and unity in Europe. They expressed their
conviction that in order to strengthen peace and security among the participating States, the advancement of, and respect for and effective exercise
of human rights, are indispensable. They also reaffirmed the equal rights
of peoples and their right to self-determination in conformity with the
Charter of the United Nations and with the relevant norms of international law, including those relating to territorial integrity of States.

Full implementation of all CSCE principles and commitments constitutes
in itself an essential element in preventing disputes among the participating States.

In accordance with international law and in particular the Charter of the
United Nations, and also in accordance with the relevant principles of the
Helsinki Final Act, threat or use of force must not be resorted to in order
to settle disputes between States. Such disputes must be settled through
peaceful means in accordance with international law. All States must comply in good faith with their obligations under the generally recognised
principles and rules of international law with respect to the maintenance
of international peace and security.

The existence of appropriate dispute settlement procedures is indispensable for the implementation of the principle that all disputes should be settled exclusively by peaceful means. Such procedures are an essential contribution to the strengthening of the rule of law at the international level
and of international peace and security, and justice.

International disputes are to be settled on the basis of the sovereign equality of States and in accordance with the principle of the free choice of

means in conformity with international obligations and commitments and with the principles of justice and international law.

Agreement, whether *ad hoc* or given in advance, between the parties to a dispute upon procedures for its settlement, appropriate for the parties concerned and the characteristics of the dispute, is essential for an effective and lasting system for the peaceful settlement of disputes.

Compliance with binding decisions reached through procedures for the peaceful settlement of disputes is an essential element in any overall structure for the peaceful settlement of disputes.

PRINCIPLES FOR DISPUTE SETTLEMENT

General

1. The participating States reaffirm their commitment to abide by international law and their determination to respect and fully implement all CSCE principles and provisions.

2. In conformity with international law, including the Charter of the United Nations, and in accordance with the relevant CSCE principles and provisions the participating States will refrain from resorting to the threat or use of force to settle their disputes, and will seek a peaceful settlement thereof.

3. The participating States recognize that recourse to, or acceptance of, a settlement procedure freely agreed to by States with regard to existing or future disputes to which they are parties is not incompatible with the sovereign equality of States. A request to have recourse to a settlement procedure does not constitute an unfriendly act.

Dispute prevention

4. The participating States will seek to prevent disputes and to develop, utilize, and improve mechanisms designed to prevent disputes from occurring, including, as appropriate, arrangements and procedures for prior notification and consultation regarding actions by one State likely to affect significantly the interests of another State.

Dispute management

5. Should disputes nevertheless occur, the participating States will take particular care not to let any dispute among then develop in such a way that it will endanger international peace and security, and justice. They will take appropriate steps to manage their disputes pending their settlement. To that end, the participating States will:

(a)   address disputes at an early stage;

(b) refrain throughout the course of a dispute from any action which may aggravate the situation and make more difficult or impede the peaceful settlement of the dispute;

(c) seek by all appropriate means to make arrangements enabling the maintenance of good relations between them, including, where appropriate, the adoption of interim measures which are without prejudice to their legal positions in the dispute.

Dispute solution

6. As laid down in the Helsinki Final Act and subsequent relevant documents, the participating States will endeavour in good faith and in a spirit of co-operation to reach a rapid and equitable solution of their disputes on the basis of international law, and will for this purpose use such means as negotiation, enquiry, good offices, mediation, conciliation, arbitration, judicial settlement or other peaceful means of their own choice, including any settlement procedure agreed to in advance of disputes to which they are parties. To that end, the participating States concerned will in particular:

(a) consult with each other at as early a stage as possible;

(b) in case they cannot settle the dispute among themselves, endeavour to agree upon a settlement procedure suited to the nature and characteristics of the particular dispute;

(c) where a dispute is subject to a dispute settlement procedure agreed upon between the parties, settle the dispute through such procedure, unless they agree otherwise;

(d) accept, in the context of the CSCE Procedure for Peaceful Settlement of Disputes and its scope of applicability, the mandatory involvement of a third party when a dispute cannot be settled by other peaceful means.

Information from participating States

7. The participating States will, upon request from a participating State involved in a dispute, make best efforts to provide information regarding appropriate methods for the settlement of such dispute.

Continued efforts

8. In the event of failure to reach a solution within a reasonable time through the method agreed upon, the participating States parties to the dispute will continue to seek a way to settle the dispute peacefully.

Strengthening of commitment

9. The participating States will strengthen their commitment relating to the peaceful settlement of disputes. To that end, they will in particular:

(a) endeavour to include, in their future treaties, clauses providing for the settlement of disputes arising from the interpretation or application of those treaties, and to consider whether or not there is an appropriate role for a third party, be it mandatory or non-mandatory;

(b) refrain to the extent possible from making reservations to dispute settlement procedures;

(c) consider withdrawing reservations they may have made regarding dispute settlement procedures embodied in multilateral treaties;

(d) consider accepting the compulsory jurisdiction of the International Court of Justice, either by treaty or by unilateral declaration under Article 36, paragraph 2, of the Statute of the Court, and minimizing, where possible, any reservations attached to such a declaration;

(e) if they have made such a declaration accompanied by one or more reservations or if they do so in the future withdrawing such reservations;

(f) consider submitting by special agreement to the International Court of Justice or to arbitration, using the Permanent Court of Arbitration, as appropriate, those disputes which lend themselves to such procedures;

(g) to the extent feasible, become party to other appropriate treaties, and other international agreements on dispute settlement;

(h) make wider use of international dispute settlement institutions;

(i) consider accepting the jurisdiction of international bodies for the peaceful settlement of disputes or control mechanisms, established by multilateral treaties pertaining, *inter alia*, to the protection of human rights, or, as the case may be, withdrawing existing reservations in respect of such mechanisms;

(j) examine means of establishing and strengthening mechanisms for securing compliance with binding decisions taken in the framework of the peaceful settlement of disputes;

(k) work actively within the international community for the advancement of methods for the peaceful settlement of disputes.

Information to natural or legal persons

10. In relation to disputes between them that are of special relevance to particular natural or legal persons, the participating States will, as they deem appropriate, provide information to those persons and hear their views.

PROVISIONS FOR A CSCE PROCEDURE FOR PEACEFUL SETTLEMENT OF
DISPUTES

Section I

If a dispute arises between participating States, they will, without undue
delay and in good faith, seek to settle the dispute through a process of direct consultation and negotiation, or seek to agree upon an appropriate
alternative procedure of settling the dispute.

Section II

Without prejudice to the right of any participating State to raise an issue
within the CSCE process, a dispute of importance to peace, security, or
stability among the participating States may be brought before the Committee of Senior Officials by any party to the dispute.

Section III

The procedure described below will not apply if the dispute has previously been dealt with, or is being addressed, under some other procedure
for the settlement of disputes, as referred to in Section VIII, or is covered
by any other process which parties to the dispute have accepted.

Section IV

If the parties are unable, within a reasonable period of time, in the light of
all circumstances of the dispute, to settle the dispute in direct consultation
or negotiation, or to agree upon an appropriate procedure for settling the
dispute, any party to the dispute may request the establishment of a
CSCE Dispute Settlement Mechanism by notifying the other party or
parties to the dispute.

Section V

1. A CSCE Dispute Settlement Mechanism consists of one or more members, selected by common agreement of the parties to a dispute from a
register of qualified candidates maintained by the nominating institution.
The register comprises the names of up to four persons nominated by each
participating state desiring to do so. No member of a Mechanism may be a
national of, or permanently resident in the territory of any State involved
in the dispute. By agreement between the parties, a Mechanism may include members whose names are not included in the register.

2. If the parties to a dispute have not reached agreement on the composition of a Mechanism within three months from the initial request of a
party for the establishment of a Mechanism, the Senior Official of the
nominating institution will, in consultation with the parties to the dispute,

select from the register a number of names less than six. If the Senior Official of the nominating institution is a national of any of the States involved in the dispute, his functions will be performed by the next most senior official who is not such a national.

3. Each party([1]) to the dispute has the right to reject up to three of the nominees. The parties will inform the nominating institution of the rejections, if any, within one month of having been informed of the nominations. This information will be confidential. After one month from the date of informing the parties of the nominations, the nominating institution will notify the parties of the composition of the Mechanism.

4. If the result of the above process is that all the nominees have been rejected, the nominating institution will select from the register an additional five names which have not been included in the initial nominations.

5. Each party to the dispute has now the right to reject one nominee. The parties will inform the nominating institution of the rejections, if any, within fourteen days of having been informed of the nominations. This information will be confidential. After the expiry of fourteen days from the date of informing the parties of the nominations, the nominating institution will notify the parties of the composition of the Mechanism.

Section VI

When the Mechanism has been established, it will seek appropriate contact with the parties to the dispute, separately or jointly. The Mechanism will adapt its methods of work, proceeding in such informal and flexible manner as it may deem practical.

2. Unless the parties agree otherwise, the proceedings of the Mechanism and any comment or advice offered by it will be confidential, although the fact that the Mechanism has been established may be acknowledged publicly.

3. The Mechanism may, if the parties so agree, use the premises and facilities of the International Bureau of the Permanent Court of Arbitration.

Section VII

The Mechanism will seek such information and comments from the parties as will enable it to assist the parties in identifying suitable procedures for the settlement of the dispute. The Mechanism may offer general or specific comment or advice.

---

[1] The problems arising when the parties are more than two will require further consideration.

Section VIII

The comment or advice of the Mechanism may relate to the inception or resumption of a process of negotiation among the parties, or to the adoption of any other dispute settlement procedure, such as fact-finding, conciliation, mediation, good offices, arbitration or adjudication or any adaptation of any such procedure or combination thereof, or any other procedure which it may indicate in relation to the circumstances of the dispute, or to any aspect of any such procedure.

Section IX

The parties will consider in good faith and in a spirit of co-operation any comment or advice of the Mechanism. If, on the basis of the proceedings of the Mechanism and of any comment or advice offered, the parties are nevertheless unable, within a reasonable time, to settle the dispute or to agree upon a procedure for its settlement, any party to the dispute may so notify the Mechanism and the other party to the dispute. Any party may thereupon, consistently with the provisions of Section VI, paragraph 2, bring that circumstance to the attention of the Committee of Senior Officials.

Section X

The failure of a party to act upon any comment or advice of the Mechanism with regard to a procedure for the settlement of a dispute does not relieve any of the parties of the duty to pursue its efforts to settle the dispute by peaceful means.

Section XI

In the event referred to in the second sentence of Section IX, any party to the dispute may, within a period of three months from any notification, request the Mechanism to provide general or specific comment or advice on the substance of the dispute, in order to assist the parties in finding a settlement in accordance with international law and their CSCE commitments. The parties will consider in good faith and in a spirit of co-operation any such comment or advice of the Mechanism.

Section XII

1. Notwithstanding a request by a party under either Section IV or Section XI, the Mechanism will not be established or continued, as the case may be, if another party to the dispute considers that because the dispute raises issues concerning its territorial integrity, or national defence, title to sovereignty over land territory, or competing claims with regard to the ju-

risdiction over other areas, the Mechanism should not be established or continued.

2. In that event, any other party to the dispute may bring that circumstance to the attention of the Committee of Senior Officials.

Section XIII

The parties to a dispute may at any time by mutual agreement modify or adapt the present procedure as they may consider appropriate to facilitate the settlement of their dispute, *inter alia*, by agreeing:

(a) to authorise the Mechanism either to conduct a process of fact-finding, or to entrust one or more persons, one or more participating States, or any competent CSCE institution, or any other body, with a fact-finding mission;

(b) to request the Mechanism to undertake or organize any expert function in regard to the subject-matter of the dispute;

(c) to request the Mechanism to report in any other form than provided in the foregoing;

(d) to accept any comment or advice of the Mechanism as binding, in part or in full, with regard to the settlement of the dispute.

Section XIV

Any expenses incurred in utilising the CSCE Dispute Settlement Mechanism, other than those incurred by the parties to the dispute for the conduct of the proceedings, will be shared equally between the parties to the dispute unless they agree otherwise.

Section XV

Nothing stated in the foregoing will in any way affect the unity of the CSCE principles, or the right of participating States to raise within the CSCE process any issue relating to the implementation of any CSCE commitment concerning the principle of the peaceful settlement of disputes, or relating to any other CSCE commitment or provision.

Section XVI

All parties to a dispute will implement meaningfully and in good faith the CSCE Dispute Settlement Procedure.

The representatives of the participating States noted that the Council of Ministers for Foreign Affairs will take into account the Report of the Valletta Meeting at its first meeting in Berlin. In this context, the representatives of the participating States recommend that the Council establish the necessary arrangements in accordance with the Charter of Paris for a

New Europe. They furthermore noted that the next CSCE Follow-up Meeting in Helsinki will assess the progress achieved at the Valletta Meeting. In this context, the representatives of the participating States consider that the commitments contained in the present Report as well as their implementation should be kept under review, bearing in mind the importance of enhancing the effectiveness of the procedure.

The representatives of the participating States expressed their deep gratitude to the people and the Government of Malta for the excellent organisation of the Meeting and for the warm hospitality extended to them during their stay in Malta.

Valletta, 8 February 1991

bb) Modification to Section V of the Valletta Provisions for a CSCE Procedure for Peaceful Settlement of Disputes

Section V of the Valletta Provisions for a CSCE Procedure for Peaceful Settlement of Disputes should read as follows:

Section V

1. A CSCE Dispute Settlement Mechanism consists of one or more members, selected by common agreement of the parties to a dispute from a register of qualified candidates maintained by the nominating institution. The register comprises the names of up to four persons nominated by each participating State desiring to do so. No member of a Mechanism may be a national of, or permanently resident in the territory of any State involved in the dispute. By agreement between the parties, a Mechanism may include members whose names are not included in the register.

2. If the parties to a dispute have not reached agreement on the composition of a Mechanism within two months from the initial request of a party for the establishment of a Mechanism, the Senior Official of the nominating institution will, in consultation with the parties to the dispute, select seven names from the register. If the Senior Official of the nominating institution is a national of any of the States involved in the dispute, his functions will be performed by the next most senior official who is not such a national.

3. Each party ([1]) to the dispute has the right to reject up to three of the nominees. The parties will inform the nominating institution of the rejections, if any, within one month of having been informed of the nominations. This information will be confidential. After one month from the

---

[1]   The problems arising when the parties are more than two will require further consideration.

date of informing the parties of the nominations, the nominating institution will notify the parties of the composition of the Mechanism.

Note: The modification means that the time period under paragraph 2 is shortened by one month, that seven names should be selected instead of "less than six" and that paragraphs 4 and 5 will no longer apply.

cc) Convention on Conciliation and Arbitration within the CSCE of December 15, 1992

The States parties to this Convention, being States participating in the Conference on Security and Co-operation in Europe,

Conscious of their obligation, as provided for in Article 2, paragraph 3, and Article 33 of the Charter of the United Nations, to settle their disputes peacefully;

Emphasizing that they do not in any way intend to impair other existing institutions or mechanisms, including the International Court of Justice, the European Court of Human Rights, the Court of Justice of the European Communities and the Permanent Court of Arbitration;

Reaffirming their solemn commitment to settle their disputes through peaceful means and their decision to develop mechanisms to settle disputes between participating states;

Recalling that full implementation of all CSCE principles and commitments constitutes in itself an essential element in preventing disputes between the CSCE participating States;

Concerned to further and strengthen the commitments stated, in particular, in the Report of the Meeting of Experts on Peaceful Settlement of Disputes adopted at Valletta and endorsed by the CSCE Council of Ministers of Foreign Affairs at its meeting in Berlin on 19 and 20 June 1991,

Have agreed as follows:

CHAPTER I — GENERAL PROVISIONS

Art. 1   Establishment of the Court

A Court of Conciliation and Arbitration shall be established to settle, by means of conciliation and, where appropriate, arbitration, disputes which are submitted to it in accordance with the provisions of this Convention.

Art. 2   Conciliation Commissions and Arbitral Tribunals

1. Conciliation shall be undertaken by a Conciliation Commission constituted for each dispute. The Commission shall be made up of conciliators drawn from a list established in accordance with the provisions of Article 3.

2. Arbitration shall be undertaken by an Arbitral Tribunal constituted for each dispute. The Tribunal shall be made up of arbitrators drawn from a list established in accordance with the provisions of Article 4.

3. Together, the conciliators and arbitrators shall constitute the Court of Conciliation and Arbitration within the CSCE, hereinafter referred to as "the Court".

Art. 3   Appointment of Conciliators

1. Each State party to this Convention shall appoint, within two months following its entry into force, two conciliators of whom at least one is a national of that state. The other may be a national of another CSCE participating State. A State which becomes party to this Convention after its entry into force shall appoint its conciliators within two months following the entry into force of this Convention for the State concerned.

2. The conciliators must be persons holding or having held senior national or international positions and possessing recognised qualifications in international law, international relations, or the settlement of disputes.

3. Conciliators shall be appointed for a renewable period of six years. Their functions may not be terminated by the appointing State during their term of office. In the event of death, resignation or inability to attend recognized by the Bureau, the State concerned shall appoint a new conciliator; the term of office of the new conciliator shall be the remainder of the term of office of the predecessor.

4. Upon termination of their period of office, conciliators shall continue to hear any cases that they are already dealing with.

5. The names of the conciliators shall be notified to the Registrar, who shall enter them into a list, which shall be communicated to the CSCE Secretariat for transmission to the CSCE participating States.

Art. 4   Appointment of Arbitrators

1. Each State party to this Convention shall appoint, within two months following its entry into force, one arbitrator and one alternate, who may be its nationals or nationals of any other CSCE participating State. A State which becomes Party to this Convention after its entry into force shall appoint its arbitrator and the alternate within two months of the entry into force of this Convention for that State.

2. Arbitrators and their alternates must possess the qualifications required in their respective countries for appointment to the highest judicial offices or must be jurisconsults of recognised competence in international law.

3. Arbitrators and their alternates are appointed for a period of six years, which may be renewed once. Their functions may not be terminated by the appointing State party during their term of office. In the event of death, resignation or inability to attend, recognised by the Bureau, the arbitrator shall be replaced by his or her alternate.

4. If an arbitrator and his or her alternate die, resign or are both unable to attend, the fact being recognised by the Bureau, new appointments will be

made in accordance with paragraph 1. The new arbitrator and his or her alternate shall complete the term of office of their predecessors.

5. The Rules of the Court may provide for a partial renewal of the arbitrators and their alternates.

6. Upon expiry of their term of office, arbitrators shall continue to hear any cases that they are already dealing with.

7. The names of the arbitrators shall be notified to the Registrar, who shall enter them into a list, which shall be communicated to the CSCE Secretariat for transmission to the CSCE participating States.

Art. 5   Independence of the Members of the Court and of the Registrar

The conciliators, the arbitrators and the Registrar shall perform their functions in full independence. Before taking up their duties, they shall make a declaration that they will exercise their powers impartially and conscientiously.

Art. 6   Privileges and Immunities

The conciliators, the arbitrators, the Registrar and the agents and counsel of the parties to a dispute shall enjoy, while performing their functions in the territory of the States parties to this Convention, the privileges and immunities accorded to persons connected with the International Court of Justice.

Art. 7   Bureau of the Court

1. The Bureau of the Court shall consist of a President, a Vice-President and three other members.

2. The President of the Court shall be elected by the members of the Court from among their number. The President presides over the Bureau.

3. The conciliators and the arbitrators shall each elect from among their number two members of the Bureau and their alternates.

4. The Bureau shall elect its Vice-President from among its members. The Vice-President shall be a conciliator if the President is an arbitrator, and an arbitrator if the President is a conciliator.

5. The Rules of the Court shall establish the procedures for the election of the President as well as of the other members of the Bureau and their alternates.

Art. 8   Decision Making Procedure

1. The decisions of the Court shall be taken by a majority of the members participating in the vote. Those abstaining shall not be considered participating in the vote.

2. The decisions of the Bureau shall be taken by a majority of its members.

3. The decisions of the Conciliation Commissions and the Arbitral Tribunals shall be taken by a majority of their members, who may not abstain from voting.

4. In the event of a tied vote, the vote of the presiding officer shall prevail.

Art. 9   Registrar

The Court shall appoint its Registrar and may provide for the appointment of such other officers as may be necessary. The staff regulations of the Registry shall be drawn up by the Bureau and adopted by the States parties to this Convention.

Art. 10   Seat

1. The seat of the Court shall be established in Geneva.

2. At the request of the parties to the dispute and in agreement with the Bureau, a Conciliation Commission or an Arbitral Tribunal may meet at another location.

Art. 11   Rules of the Court

1. The Court shall adopt its own Rules, which shall be subject to approval by States parties to this Convention.

2. The Rules of the Court shall establish, in particular, the rules of procedure to be followed by the Conciliation Commissions and Arbitral Tribunals constituted pursuant to this Convention. They shall state which of these rules may not be waived by agreement between the parties to the dispute.

Art. 12   Working Languages

The Rules of the Court shall establish rules on the use of languages.

Art. 13   Financial Protocol

Subject to the provisions of Article 17, all the costs of the Court shall be met by the States parties to this Convention. The provisions for the calculation of the costs; for the drawing up and approval of the annual budget of the Court; for the distribution of the costs among the States parties to this Convention; for the audit of the accounts of the Court; and for related matters, shall be contained in a Financial Protocol to be adopted by the Committee of Senior Officials. A State becomes bound by the Protocol on becoming a party to this Convention.

Art. 14   Periodic Report

The Bureau shall annually present to the CSCE Council through the Committee of Senior Officials a report on the activities under this Convention.

Art. 15   Notice of Requests for Conciliation or Arbitration

The Registrar of the Court shall give notice to the CSCE Secretariat of all requests for conciliation or arbitration, for immediate transmission to the CSCE participating States.

Art. 16   Conduct of Parties — Interim Measures

1. During the proceedings, the parties to the dispute shall refrain from any action which may aggravate the situation or further impede or prevent the settlement of the dispute.

2. The Conciliation Commission may draw the attention of the parties to the dispute submitted to it to the measures the parties could take in order to prevent the dispute from being aggravated or its settlement made more difficult.

3. The Arbitral Tribunal constituted for a dispute may indicate the interim measures that ought to be taken by the parties to the dispute in accordance with the provisions of Article 26, paragraph 4.

Art. 17   Procedural Costs

The parties to a dispute and any intervening party shall each bear their own costs.

CHAPTER II — COMPETENCE

Art. 18   Competence of the Commission and of the Tribunal

1. Any State party to this Convention may submit to a Conciliation Commission any dispute with another State party which has not been settled within a reasonable period of time through negotiation.

2. Disputes may be submitted to an Arbitral Tribunal under the conditions stipulated in Article 26.

Art. 19   Safeguarding the Existing Means of Settlement

1. A Conciliation Commission or an Arbitral Tribunal constituted for a dispute shall take no further action in the case:

(a) If, prior to being submitted to the Commission or the Tribunal, the dispute has been submitted to a court or tribunal whose jurisdiction in respect of the dispute the parties thereto are under a legal obligation to accept, or if such a body has already given a decision on the merits of the dispute;

(b) If the parties to the dispute have accepted in advance the exclusive jurisdiction of a jurisdictional body other than a Tribunal in accordance with this Convention which has jurisdiction to decide, with binding force, on the dispute submitted to it, or if the parties thereto have agreed to seek to settle the dispute exclusively by other means.

2. A Conciliation Commission constituted for a dispute shall take no further action if, even after the dispute has been submitted to it, one or all of the parties refer the dispute to a court or tribunal whose jurisdiction in respect of the dispute the parties thereto are under a legal obligation to accept.

3. A Conciliation Commission shall postpone examining a dispute if this dispute has been submitted to another body which has competence to formulate proposals with respect to this dispute. If those prior efforts do not lead to a settlement of the dispute, the Commission shall resume its work at the request of the parties or one of the parties to the dispute, subject to the provisions of Article 26, paragraph 1.

4. A State may, at the time of signing, ratifying or acceding to this Convention, make a reservation in order to ensure the compatibility of the mechanism of dispute settlement that this Convention establishes with other means of dispute settlement resulting from international undertakings applicable to that State.

5. If, at any time, the parties arrive at a settlement of their dispute, the Commission or Tribunal shall remove the dispute from its list, on receiving written confirmation from all the parties thereto that they have reached a settlement of the dispute.

6. In the event of disagreement between the parties to the dispute with regard to the competence of the Commission or the Tribunal, the decision in the matter shall rest with the Commission or the Tribunal.

CHAPTER III — CONCILIATION

Art. 20 Request for the Constitution of a Conciliation Commission

1. Any State party to this Convention may lodge an application with the Registrar requesting the constitution of a Conciliation Commission for a dispute between it and one or more other States parties. Two or more States parties may also jointly lodge an application with the Registrar.

2. The constitution of a Conciliation Commission may also be requested by agreement between two or more States parties or between one or more States parties and one or more other CSCE participating States. The agreement shall be notified to the Registrar.

Art. 21 Constitution of the Conciliation Commission

1. Each party to the dispute shall appoint, from the list of conciliators established in accordance with Article 3, one conciliator to sit on the Commission.

2. When more than two States are parties to the same dispute, the States asserting the same interest may agree to appoint one single conciliator. If they do not so agree, each of the two sides to the dispute shall appoint the same number of conciliators up to a maximum decided by the Bureau.

3. Any State which is a party to a dispute submitted to a Conciliation Commission and which is not a party to this Convention, may appoint a person to sit on the Commission, either from the list of conciliators established in accordance with Article 3, or from among other persons who are nationals of a CSCE participating State. In this event, for the purpose of examining the dispute, such persons shall have the same rights and the same obligations as the other members of the Commission. They shall perform their functions in full independence and shall make the declaration required by Article 5 before taking their seats on the Commission.

4. As soon as the application or the agreement whereby the parties to a dispute have requested the constitution of a Conciliation Commission is received, the President of the Court shall consult the parties to the dispute as to the composition of the rest of the Commission.

5. The Bureau shall appoint three further conciliators to sit on the Commission. This number can be increased or decreased by the Bureau, provided it is uneven. Members of the Bureau and their alternates, who are on the list of conciliators, shall be eligible for appointment to the Commission.

6. The Commission shall elect its Chairman from among the members appointed by the Bureau.

7. The Rules of the Court shall stipulate the procedures applicable if an objection is raised to one of the members appointed to sit on the Commission or if that member is unable to or refuses to sit at the commencement or in the course of the proceedings.

8. Any question as to the application of this article shall be decided by the Bureau as a preliminary matter.

Art. 22   Procedure for the Constitution of a Conciliation Commission

1. If the constitution of a Conciliation Commission is requested by means of an application, the application shall state the subject of the dispute, the name of the party or parties against which the application is directed, and the name of the conciliator or conciliators appointed by the requesting party or parties to the dispute. The application shall also briefly indicate the means of settlement previously resorted to.

2. As soon as an application has been received, the Registrar shall notify the other party or parties to the dispute mentioned in the application. Within a period of fifteen days from the notification, the other party or parties to the dispute shall appoint the conciliator or conciliators of their choice to sit on the Commission. If, within this period, one or more parties to the dispute have not appointed the member or members of the Commission whom they are entitled to appoint, the Bureau shall appoint the appropriate number of conciliators. Such appointment shall be made from among the conciliators appointed in accordance with Article 3 by the party or each of the parties involved or, if those parties have not yet appointed conciliators, from among the other conciliators not appointed by the other party or parties to the dispute.

3. If the constitution of a Conciliation Commission is requested by means of an agreement, the agreement shall state the subject of the dispute. If there is no agreement, in whole or in part, concerning the subject of the dispute, each party thereto may formulate its own position in respect of such subject.

4. At the same time as the parties request the constitution of a Conciliation Commission by agreement, each party shall notify the Registrar of the name of the conciliator or conciliators whom it has appointed to sit on the Commission.

Art. 23   Conciliation Procedure

1. The conciliation proceedings shall be confidential and all parties to the dispute shall have the right to be heard. Subject to the provisions of Articles 10 and 11 and the Rules of the Court, the Conciliation Commission

shall, after consultation with the parties to the dispute, determine the procedure.

2. If the parties to the dispute agree thereon, the Conciliation Commission may invite any State party to this Convention which has an interest in the settlement of the dispute to participate in the proceedings.

Art. 24   Objective of Conciliation

The Conciliation Commission shall assist the parties to the dispute in finding a settlement in accordance with international law and their CSCE commitments.

Art. 25   Result of the Conciliation

1. If, during the proceedings, the parties to the dispute, with the help of the Conciliation Commission, reach a mutually acceptable settlement, they shall record the terms of this settlement in a summary of conclusions signed by their representatives and by the members of the Commission. The signing of the document shall conclude the proceedings. The CSCE Council shall be informed through the Committee of Senior Officials of the success of the conciliation.

2. When the Conciliation Commission considers that all the aspects of the dispute and all the possibilities of finding a solution have been explored, it shall draw up a final report. The report shall contain the proposals of the Commission for the peaceful settlement of the dispute.

3. The report of the Conciliation Commission shall be notified to the parties to the dispute, which shall have a period of thirty days in which to examine it and inform the Chairman of the Commission whether they are willing to accept the proposed settlement.

4. If a party to the dispute does not accept the proposed settlement, the other party or parties are no longer bound by their own acceptance thereof.

5. If, within the period prescribed in paragraph 3, the parties to the dispute have not accepted the proposed settlement, the report shall be forwarded to the CSCE Council through the Committee of Senior Officials.

6. A report shall also be drawn up which provides immediate notification to the CSCE Council through the Committee of Senior Officials of circumstances where a party fails to appear for conciliation or leaves a procedure after it has begun.

CHAPTER IV — ARBITRATION

Art. 26   Request for the Constitution of an Arbitral Tribunal

1. A request for arbitration may be made at any time by agreement between two or more States parties to this Convention or between one or more States parties to this Convention and one or more other CSCE participating States.

2. The States parties to this Convention may at any time by a notice addressed to the Depositary declare that they recognise as compulsory, *ipso facto* and without special agreement, the jurisdiction of an Arbitral Tribunal, subject to reciprocity. Such a declaration may be made for an unlimited period or for a specified time. It may cover all disputes or exclude disputes concerning a State's territorial integrity, national defence, title to sovereignty over land territory, or competing claims with regard to jurisdiction over other areas.

3. A request for arbitration against a State party to this Convention which has made the declaration specified in paragraph 2 may be made by means of an application to the Registrar only after a period of thirty days after the report of the Conciliation Commission which has dealt with the dispute has been transmitted to the CSCE Council in accordance with the provisions of Article 25, paragraph 5.

4. When a dispute is submitted to an Arbitral Tribunal in accordance with this article, the Tribunal may, on its own authority or at the request of one or all of the parties to the dispute, indicate interim measures that ought to be taken by the parties to the dispute to avoid an aggravation of the dispute, greater difficulty in reaching a solution, or the possibility of a future award of the Tribunal becoming unenforceable owing to the conduct of one or more of the parties to the dispute.

Art. 27   Cases Brought before an Arbitral Tribunal

1. If a request for arbitration is made by means of an agreement, it shall indicate the subject of the dispute. If there is no agreement, in whole or in part, concerning the subject of the dispute, each party thereto may formulate its own position in respect of such subject.

2. If a request for arbitration is made by means of an application, it shall indicate the subject of the dispute, the States party or parties to this Convention against which it is directed, and the main elements of fact and law on which it is grounded. As soon as the application is received, the Registrar shall notify the other States party or parties mentioned in the application.

Art. 28   Constitution of the Arbitral Tribunal

1. When a request for arbitration is submitted, an Arbitral Tribunal shall be constituted.

2. The arbitrators appointed by the parties to the dispute in accordance with Article 4 are *ex officio* members of the Tribunal. When more than two States are parties to the same dispute, the States asserting the same interest may agree to appoint one single arbitrator.

3. The Bureau shall appoint, from among the arbitrators, a number of members to sit on the Tribunal so that the members appointed by the Bureau total at least one more than the *ex officio* members. Members of the Bureau and their alternates, who are on the list of arbitrators, shall be eligible for appointment to the Tribunal.

4. If an *ex officio* member is unable to attend or has previously taken part in any capacity in the hearings of the case arising from the dispute submitted to the Tribunal, that member shall be replaced by his or her alternate. If the alternate is in the same situation, the State involved shall appoint a member to examine the dispute pursuant to the terms and conditions specified in paragraph 5. In the event of a question arising as to the capacity of a member or of his or her alternate to sit on the Tribunal, the matter shall be decided by the Bureau.

5. Any State, which is a party to a dispute submitted to an Arbitral Tribunal and which is not party to this Convention, may appoint a person of its choice to sit on the Tribunal, either from the list of arbitrators established in accordance with Article 4 or from among other persons who are nationals of a CSCE participating State. Any person thus appointed must meet the conditions specified in Article 4, paragraph 2, and for the purpose of examining the dispute, shall have the same rights and obligations as the other members of the Tribunal. The person shall perform his or her functions in full independence and shall make the declaration required by Article 5 before sitting on the Tribunal.

6. The Tribunal shall appoint its Chairman from among the members appointed by the Bureau.

7. In the event that one of the members of the Tribunal appointed by the Bureau is unable to attend the proceedings, that member shall not be replaced unless the number of members appointed by the Bureau falls below the number of *ex officio* members, or members appointed by the parties to the dispute in accordance with paragraph 5. In this event, one or more new members shall be appointed by the Bureau pursuant to paragraphs 3 and 4 of this article. A new Chairman will not be elected if one or more new members are appointed, unless the member unable to attend is the Chairman of the Tribunal.

Art. 29   Arbitration Procedure

1. All the parties to the dispute shall have the right to be heard during the arbitration proceedings, which shall conform to the principles of a fair trial. The proceedings shall consist of a written part and an oral part.

2. The Arbitral Tribunal shall have, in relation to the parties to the dispute, the necessary fact-finding and investigative powers to carry out its tasks.

3. Any CSCE participating State which considers that it has a particular interest of a legal nature likely to be affected by the ruling of the Tribunal may, within fifteen days of the transmission of the notification by the CSCE Secretariat as specified in Article 15, address to the Registrar a request to intervene. This request shall be immediately transmitted to the parties to the dispute and to the Tribunal constituted for the dispute.

4. If the intervening State establishes that it has such an interest, it shall be authorised to participate in the proceedings in so far as may be required

for the protection of this interest. The relevant part of the ruling of the Tribunal is binding upon the intervening State.

5. The parties to the dispute have a period of thirty days in which to address their observations regarding the request for intervention to the Tribunal. The Tribunal shall render its decision on the admissibility of the request.

6. The hearings in the Tribunal shall be held *in camera*, unless the Tribunal decides otherwise at the request of the parties to the dispute.

7. In the event that one or more parties to the dispute fail to appear, the other party or parties thereto may request the Tribunal to decide in favour of its or their claims. Before doing so, the Tribunal must satisfy itself that it is competent and that the claims of the party or parties taking part in the proceedings are well founded.

Art. 30   Function of the Arbitral Tribunal

The function of the Arbitral Tribunal shall be to decide, in accordance with international law, such disputes as are submitted to it. This provision shall not prejudice the power of the tribunal to decide a case *ex aequo et bono*, if the parties to the dispute so agree.

Art. 31   Arbitral Award

1. The award of the Arbitral Tribunal shall state the reasons on which it is based. If it does not represent in whole or in part the unanimous opinion of the members of the Arbitral Tribunal, any member shall be entitled to deliver a separate or dissenting opinion.

2. Subject to Article 29, paragraph 4, the award of the Tribunal shall have binding force only between the parties to the dispute and in respect of the case to which it relates.

3. The award shall be final and not subject to appeal. However, the parties to the dispute or one of them may request that the Tribunal interpret its award as to the meaning or scope. Unless the parties to the dispute agree otherwise, such request shall be made at the latest within six months after the communication of the award. After receiving the observations of the parties to the dispute, the Tribunal shall render its interpretation as soon as possible.

4. An application for revision of the award may be made only when it is based upon the discovery of some fact which is of such a nature as to be a decisive factor and which, when the award was rendered, was unknown to the Tribunal and to the party or parties to the dispute claiming revision. The application for revision must be made at the latest within six months of the discovery of the new fact. No application for revision may be made after the lapse of ten years from the date of the award.

5. As far as possible, the examination of a request for interpretation or an application for revision should be carried out by the Tribunal which made the award in question. If the Bureau should find this to be impossible, another Tribunal shall be constituted in accordance with the provisions of Article 28.

Art. 32   Publication of the Arbitral Award

The award shall be published by the Registrar. A certified copy shall be communicated to the parties to the dispute and to the CSCE Council through the Committee of Senior Officials

CHAPTER V — FINAL PROVISIONS

Art. 33   Signature and Entry into Force

1. This Convention shall be open for signature with the Government of Sweden by the CSCE participating States until 31 March 1993. It shall be subject to ratification.

2. The CSCE participating States which have not signed this Convention may subsequently accede thereto.

3. This Convention shall enter into force two months after the date of deposit of the twelfth instrument of ratification or accession.

4. For every State which ratifies or accedes to this Convention after the deposit of the twelfth instrument of ratification or accession, the Convention shall enter into force two months after its instrument of ratification or accession has been deposited.

5. The Government of Sweden shall serve as depositary of this Convention.

Art. 34   Reservations

This Convention may not be the subject of any reservation that it does not expressly authorise.

Art. 35   Amendments

1. Amendments to this Convention must be adopted in accordance with the following paragraphs.

2. Amendments to this Convention may be proposed by any State party thereto, and shall be communicated by the Depositary to the CSCE Secretariat for transmission to the CSCE participating States.

3. If the CSCE Council adopts the proposed text of the amendment, the text shall be forwarded by the Depositary to States parties to this Convention for acceptance in accordance with their respective constitutional requirements.

4. Any such amendment shall come into force on the thirtieth day after all States parties to this Convention have informed the Depositary of their acceptance thereof.

Art. 36   Denunciation

1. Any State party to this Convention may, at any time, denounce this Convention by means of a notification addressed to the Depositary.

2. Such denunciation shall become effective one year after the date of receipt of the notification by the Depositary.

3. This Convention shall, however, continue to apply for the denouncing party with respect to proceedings which are under way at the time the denunciation enters into force. Such proceedings shall be pursued to their conclusion.

Art. 37   Notifications and Communications

The notifications and communications to be made by the Depositary shall be transmitted to the Registrar and to the CSCE Secretariat for further transmission to the CSCE participating States.

Art. 38   Non-Parties

In conformity with international law, it is confirmed that nothing in this Convention shall be interpreted to establish any obligations or commitments for CSCE participating States that are not parties to this Convention if not expressly provided for and expressly accepted by such States in writing.

Art. 39   Transitional Provisions

1. The Court shall proceed, within four months of the entry into force of this Convention, to elect the Bureau, to adopt its rules and to appoint the Registrar in accordance with the provisions of Articles 7, 9 and 11. The host Government of the Court shall, in co-operation with the Depositary, make the arrangements required.

dd) Financial Protocol

FINANCIAL PROTOCOL ESTABLISHED IN ACCORDANCE WITH ARTICLE 13 OF THE CONVENTION ON CONCILIATION AND ARBITRATION WITHIN THE CSCE

Art. 1   Costs of the Court

1. All the costs of the Court established by the Convention on Conciliation and Arbitration within the CSCE (hereinafter referred to as "the Convention") shall be met by the States parties to the Convention. Costs of conciliators and arbitrators shall be costs of the Court.

2. The obligations of the host State with respect to expenditures in connection with the premises and furniture for use by the Court, their maintenance, insurance and security, as well as utilities, shall be set out in an exchange of letters between the Court acting with the consent of and on behalf of the States parties to the Convention, and the host State.

Art. 2   Contributions to the Budget of the Court

1. Contributions to the budget of the Court shall be divided among the States parties to the Convention according to the scale of distribution applicable within the CSCE, adjusted to take into account the difference in

number between the CSCE participating States and the States parties to the Convention.

2. If a State ratifies or accedes to the Convention after its entry into force, its contribution shall be equal, for the current financial year, to one-twelfth of its portion of the adjusted scale, as established according to paragraph 1 of this Article, for each full month of that financial year which remains after the date on which the Convention enters into force in respect of it.

3. If a State which is not a party to the Convention submits a dispute to the Court pursuant to the provisions of Article 20, paragraph 2, or Article 26, paragraph 1 of the Convention, it shall contribute to the financing of the budget of the Court, for the duration of the proceedings, as if it were a party to the Convention.

For the application of this paragraph, the conciliation shall be presumed to commence on the day the Registrar receives notice of the agreement of the parties to set up a Commission and to end on the day the Commission notifies its report to the parties. If a party withdraws from the proceedings, these proceedings shall be considered as ended on the day of notice of the report specified in Article 25, paragraph 6 of the Convention. The arbitration proceedings shall be presumed to start on the day the Registrar receives notice of the agreement of the parties to establish a Tribunal and to end on the day the Tribunal renders its award.

Art. 3   Financial Year and Budget

1. The financial year shall be from 1 January to 31 December.

2. The Registrar, acting with the concurrence of the Bureau of the Court, shall establish each year a budget proposal for the Court. The budget proposal for the ensuing financial year shall be submitted to the States parties to the Convention before 15 September.

3. The budget shall be approved by the representatives of the States parties to the Convention. Consideration and approval of the budget shall take place in Vienna unless the States parties to the Convention otherwise agree. On approval of the budget for the financial year the Registrar shall request the States parties to the Convention to remit their contributions.

If the budget is not approved by 31 December the Court will operate on the basis of the preceding budget and, without prejudice to later adjustments, the Registrar shall request the States parties to the Convention to remit their contributions in accordance with this budget.

The Registrar shall request States parties to the Convention to make fifty per cent of their contributions available on 1 January and the remaining fifty per cent on 1 April.

4. Barring a decision to the contrary by the representatives of the States parties to the Convention, the budget shall be established in Swiss francs and the contributions of the States shall be paid in this currency.

5. A State which ratifies or accedes to the Convention after its entry into force shall pay its first contribution to the budget within two months after the request by the Registrar.

6. States which, without being parties to the Convention, have submitted a dispute to the Court, shall pay their contribution within two months after the request by the Registrar.

7. The year the Convention enters into force, the States parties to the Convention shall pay their contribution to the budget within two months following the date of deposit of the twelfth instrument of ratification of the Convention. This budget is preliminarily fixed at 250,000 Swiss francs.

Art. 4   Obligations, Payments and Revised Budget

1. The approved budget shall constitute authorization to the Registrar, acting under the responsibility of the Bureau of the Court, to incur obligations and make payments up to the amounts and for the purposes approved.

2. The Registrar, acting under the responsibility of the Bureau of the Court, is authorized to make transfers between items and sub-items of up to 15 per cent of items/sub-items. All such transfers must be reported by the Registrar in connection with the financial statement mentioned in Article 9 of this Protocol.

3. Obligations remaining undischarged at the end of the financial year shall be carried over to the next financial year.

4. If so obliged by circumstances and following careful examination of available resources with a view to identifying savings, the Registrar is authorized to submit a revised budget, which may entail requests for supplementary appropriations, for the approval of the representatives of the States parties to the Convention.

5. Any surplus for a given financial year shall be deducted from the assessed contributions for the financial year following the one in which the accounts have been approved by the representatives of the States parties to the Convention. Any deficit shall be charged to the ensuing financial year unless the representatives of the States parties to the Convention decide on supplementary contributions.

Art. 5   Working Capital Fund

A working capital fund may be established in case the States parties to the Convention deem it necessary. It will be funded by the States parties to the Convention.

Art. 6   Allowances and Nominal Retainers

1. Members of the Bureau of the Court, of the Conciliation Commissions and of the Arbitral Tribunals shall receive, for each day on which they exercise their functions, a daily allowance.

2. Members of the Bureau of the Court shall additionally receive a nominal annual retainer.

3. The daily allowance and the nominal annual retainer shall be determined by the representatives of the States parties to the Convention.

Art. 7   Salaries, Social Security and Pensions

1. The Registrar and any other registry staff appointed in accordance with Article 9 of the Convention shall receive a salary to be determined by the representatives of the States parties to the Convention.

2. The registry staff shall be limited to the strict minimum needed to ensure the operation of the Court.

3. The representatives of the States parties to the Convention shall ensure that the Registrar and the registry staff are afforded an adequate social security scheme and retirement pension.

Art. 8   Travel Expenses

1. Travel expenses which are absolutely necessary for exercising their functions shall be paid to the members of the Bureau of the Court, of the Conciliation Commissions and of the Arbitral Tribunals and to the Registrar and the registry staff.

2. Travel expenses shall comprise actual transportation costs, including expenses normally incidental to transportation, and a daily subsistence allowance to cover all charges of meals, lodging, fees and gratuities and other personal expenses. The daily subsistence allowance shall be determined by the representatives of the States parties to the Convention.

Art. 9   Records and Accounts

1. The Registrar, acting under the authority of the Bureau of the Court, shall ensure that appropriate records and accounts are kept of the transactions and that all payments are properly authorized.

2. The Registrar, acting under the authority of the Bureau of the Court, shall submit to the States parties to the Convention, not later than 1 March, an annual financial statement showing, for the preceding financial year:

(a)   the income and expenditures relating to all accounts;

(b)   the situation with regard to budget provisions;

(c)   the financial assets and liabilities at the end of the financial year.

Art. 10   Audit

1. The accounts of the Court shall be audited by two auditors, of different nationalities, appointed for renewable periods of three years by the representatives of the States parties to the Convention.

Persons appearing or having appeared on the lists of conciliators or arbitrators or having received payment by the Court pursuant to Article 7 of this Protocol may not be auditors.

2. Auditors shall annually conduct audits. They shall, in particular, check the accuracy of the books, the statement of assets and liabilities, and the accounts. The accounts shall be available for the annual auditing and inspection not later than 1 March.

3. Auditors shall perform such audits as they deem necessary to certify:

(a) that the annual financial statement submitted to them is correct and in accordance with the books and records of the Court,

(b) that the financial transactions recorded in this statement have been effected in accordance with the relevant rules, the budgetary provisions and other directives which may be applicable, and

(c) that the funds on deposit and on hand have been verified by certificates received directly from the depositories or by actual count.

4. The Registrar shall give auditors such assistance and facilities as may be needed for the proper discharge of their duties. Auditors shall, in particular, have free access to the books of account, records and documents which, in their opinion, are necessary for the audit.

5. Auditors shall annually draw up a report certifying the accounts and setting forth the comments warranted by the audit. They may, in this context, also make such observations as they deem necessary regarding the efficiency of financial procedures, the accounting system and the internal financial control.

6. The report shall be submitted to the representatives of the States parties to the Convention not later than four months after the end of the financial year to which the accounts refer. The report shall be transmitted to the Registrar beforehand, so that he will have at least 15 days in which to furnish such explanations and justifications as he may consider necessary.

7. In addition to the annual auditing, auditors will at any time have free access to check the books, the statement of assets and liabilities, and accounts.

8. On the basis of the audit report, the representatives of the States parties to the Convention shall signify their acceptance of the annual financial statement or take such other action as may be considered appropriate.

Art. 11   Special Disbursement Account

1. A special disbursement account may be established by the States parties to the Convention aimed at lowering the procedural costs for the States parties to disputes submitted to the Court which have difficulties paying these costs. It will be funded by voluntary contributions from States parties to the Convention.

2. A State party to a dispute submitted to the Court that wishes to receive funds from the special disbursement account shall file a request to the Registrar, with a detailed statement estimating procedural costs.

The Bureau of the Court shall examine the request and forward its recommendation to the representatives of the States parties to the Convention which shall decide whether to grant this request and to what extent.

After the case has been heard, the State having received funds from the special disbursement account shall address to the Registrar, for study by the Bureau, a detailed statement of procedural costs actually expended and shall proceed, if need be, with reimbursing the sums in excess of the actual costs.

Art. 12   Decision Making

All decisions by the States parties to the Convention or their representatives under this Protocol shall be taken by consensus.

Art. 13   Amendments

Amendments to this Protocol shall be adopted in accordance with the provisions of Article 35 of the Convention. The Bureau of the Court may address its opinion on the proposed amendments to the CSCE Secretariat for transmission to the CSCE participating States.

This Protocol, established in the English, French, German, Italian, Russian and Spanish languages, all six language versions being equally authentic, having been adopted by the Committee of Senior Officials at Prague, on 28 April 1993 in accordance with Article 13 of the Convention on Conciliation and Arbitration within the CSCE is deposited with the Government of Sweden.

ee) Rules of the Court of Conciliation and Arbitration within the OSCE of February 1, 1997

CHAPTER I: GENERAL AND INSTITUTIONAL PROVISIONS

1. GENERAL PROVISION

Art. 1   Rules of the Court

1. The present Rules, adopted by the Court of Conciliation and Arbitration (hereinafter: the Court) and approved by the States Parties to the Stockholm Convention of 15 December 1992 on Conciliation and Arbitration within the OSCE (hereinafter: the Convention), shall govern, in accordance with Article 11, paragraph 1, of the Convention, the activities of the Court and of the organs established within the Court.

2. In the event of a conflict between provisions of the Convention and of the Rules, the former shall prevail.

2. THE COURT

Art. 2   Solemn Declaration

Upon taking up their duties, conciliators, arbitrators and their alternates shall make the following solemn declaration: "I solemnly declare that I shall fulfil impartially and conscientiously, to the best of my ability, my duties as member of the Court of Conciliation and Arbitration established by the Convention on Conciliation and Arbitration within the OSCE."

Art. 3   Working Languages

1. The languages of the Court and of the organs established within the Court shall be the official languages of the OSCE (English, French, German, Italian, Russian and Spanish).

2. From among those languages, in each case, the conciliation commission or the arbitral tribunal concerned, after hearing the parties, shall determine, in its rules of procedure, the language or languages to be used.

3. Any party to a dispute may however request to express itself in another language. In that event, it shall bear the additional expenses arising from the use of that language.

Art. 4   Notice of Requests and List of Cases

1. In accordance with Article 15 of the Convention, all requests for conciliation or arbitration addressed to the Court shall be communicated by the Registrar to the Secretariat of the OSCE, which shall transmit them forthwith to the States participating in the OSCE.

2. The Court shall establish a list of the cases brought before it. The list shall be kept by the Registrar.

Art. 5   Decision-Making

1. The decision-making procedure of the Court, the Bureau and the organs established within the Court shall be governed by Article 8 of the Convention.

2. The Court, the Bureau and the organs established within the Court may decide to take decisions by correspondence or facsimile.

Art. 6   Procedural Costs

1. In accordance with Article 17 of the Convention, the parties to a dispute and any intervening party shall each bear their own costs.

2. This rule shall apply to the circumstances contemplated in Article 23, paragraph 2, of the Convention.

Art. 7   Publications of the Court

1. In accordance with Article 32 of the Convention, the Court shall publish the awards rendered by arbitral tribunals established within it.

2. The Court may also publish the Annual Report on its activities submitted by the Bureau to the OSCE Council pursuant to Article 14 of the Convention.

3. The Court shall not publish the final reports of conciliation commissions established within it, unless the parties so agree.

3. THE BUREAU OF THE COURT

Art. 8   Composition

1. The Bureau of the Court shall consist of the President of the Court, the Vice-President of the Bureau and three other members of the Court.

2. The alternates of the four members of the Bureau other than the President shall participate in the work of the Bureau without vote.

Art. 9   Election of the President of the Court, the Other Members of the Bureau and the Vice-President of the Bureau

1. Nominations for President of the Court and for membership of the Bureau may be submitted by any member of the Court. They shall be announced to the Depositary State twenty days at least before the date set for the election.

2. In accordance with Article 7, paragraph 2, of the Convention, the President of the Court shall be elected for a six-year term by all the members of the Court. The candidate obtaining the highest number of votes shall be elected. In the event of a tie, a second ballot shall be held. In the event of a further tie, the election shall be decided by lot. The election of the President shall take place under the chairmanship of a representative of the Depositary State.

3. In accordance with Article 7, paragraph 3, of the Convention, the conciliators and the arbitrators shall then each elect, from among their number, two members of the Bureau for six-year terms. The two candidates obtaining the highest number of votes shall be elected. In the event of a tie, a second ballot shall be held. In the event of a further tie, the election shall be decided by lot. Elections under this paragraph shall take place under the chairmanship of the President of the Court.

4. Two alternates each shall be elected by the conciliators and by the arbitrators from among their number, following the procedure laid down in the preceding paragraph. The Bureau shall subsequently indicate which alternate would be called upon to take the place of which member of the Bureau.

5. The Vice-President shall be elected by the Bureau from among its members, in accordance with Article 7, paragraph 4, of the Convention.

6. The President, the other members of the Bureau and the alternates may be re-elected.

7. In the event of the death, resignation or prolonged inability of the President to fulfil his or her duties, a new President shall be elected, following the procedure laid down in paragraphs 1 and 2 of this Article, to serve out the term of the former President.

8. In the event of the death, resignation or prolonged inability of a member of the Bureau other than the President to fulfil his or her duties, the alternate appointed under paragraph 4 of this Article shall serve out the term of the member concerned. In the event of the death, resignation or prolonged inability of an alternate to fulfil his or her duties, a new alternate shall be elected, following the procedure laid down in paragraph 4 of this Article, to serve out the former alternate's term.

Art. 10   Functions of the Bureau

1. The Bureau is the permanent executive body of the Court. It shall meet regularly to ensure the satisfactory operation of the Court and carry out the duties entrusted to it under the Convention, the Financial Protocol and the present Rules.

2. The Bureau shall appoint the conciliators and arbitrators as provided by Articles 21 and 28 of the Convention.

3. An exchange of letters shall take place between the Bureau and the host State concerning the obligations assumed by that State in accordance with Article 1 of the Financial Protocol. A further exchange of letters between the Bureau and that State shall specify the legal status, on the territory of the host State, of the members, the Registrar and the officials of the Court, as well as of the agents, counsel and experts of the States parties to a dispute brought before the Court. Such exchanges of letters shall be approved by the States Parties.

4. THE REGISTRAR

Art. 11   Appointment of the Registrar and of Registry Officials

1. The Registrar shall be appointed by the Court for a maximum term of six years on the proposal of the Bureau of the Court.

2. The Court may appoint such other officials as it requires and its financial resources permit. It may delegate that function to the Bureau.

Art. 12   Functions of the Registrar

1. The Registrar shall supervise the Court's officials under the authority and control of the Bureau of the Court.

2. The Registrar and, under his or her authority, the officials of the Court shall perform all the duties laid upon them by the Convention, the Financial Protocol and the present Rules.

3. The Registrar shall serve as secretary of the Court, of its Bureau, and of the conciliation commissions and arbitral tribunals established within the Court. The Registrar shall draw up the minutes of the meetings of such organs.

4. The Registrar shall be responsible for the Archives of the Court.

5. The Registrar shall fulfil such other duties as may be entrusted to him or her by the Court, its Bureau or the conciliation commissions and arbitral tribunals established within the Court.

6. The Registrar may, as necessary, delegate duties to other officials of the Court.

Art. 13   Solemn Declaration

Upon taking up their duties, the Registrar and the other officials of the Court shall make the following solemn declaration: "I solemnly declare that I shall fulfil impartially and conscienciously, to the best of my ability, my duties at the Court of Conciliation and Arbitration established by the Convention on Conciliation and Arbitration within the OSCE."

CHAPTER II: CONCILIATION

Art. 14   Purpose

1. The purpose of conciliation is to assist the parties to a dispute in finding a settlement in accordance with international law and their OSCE commitments. The conciliation commission may submit to the parties proposals with a view to bringing about a settlement of the dispute.

2. The parties may request the conciliation commission to clarify questions of fact. Its findings shall not be binding upon the parties, unless they otherwise agree.

3. Conciliation proceedings may be initiated only after a fact-finding procedure set in motion under paragraph 2 of this Article has been concluded.

Art. 15   Request for Conciliation

1. Any dispute between States Parties to the Convention may be submitted to conciliation by unilateral or joint application, as laid down in Articles 18, paragraph 1, and 20, paragraph 1, of the Convention. The application shall specify the facts, the subject of the dispute, the parties thereto, the name or names of the conciliator or conciliators appointed by the applicant or applicants, and the means of settlement previously used.

2. Disputes between two or more States Parties to the Convention, or between one or more States Parties to the Convention and one or more other OSCE participating States, may be submitted to conciliation by an agreement notified to the Registrar, in accordance with Article 20, paragraph 2, of the Convention. That agreement shall specify the subject of the dispute; in the event of total or partial disagreement concerning the subject of the dispute, each party shall state its own position. When notifying the agreement, the parties shall inform the Registrar of the name or names of the conciliator or conciliators appointed by them.

Art. 16   Composition and Constitution of Conciliation Commissions

1. The conciliation commission shall be composed and constituted in accordance with Articles 21 and 22 of the Convention.

2. If more than two States are parties to a dispute, and the parties in the same interest are unable to agree on the appointment of a single conciliator, as contemplated by Article 21, paragraph 2, of the Convention, each of the two sides shall appoint the same number of conciliators, up to a maximum decided by the Bureau of the Court.

3. If more than two States are parties to a dispute, and there are no parties in the same interest, each State may appoint one conciliator.

4. In accordance with Article 21, paragraph 5, of the Convention, the Bureau shall appoint three conciliators. It may increase or decrease this number after consulting the parties. If more than two States are parties to the dispute, the number of members appointed to the conciliation commission by the Bureau shall total one more than the members appointed by the parties.

5. When all its members have been appointed, the conciliation commission shall hold its constitutive meeting. At that meeting, it shall elect its chairman in accordance with Article 21, paragraph 6, of the Convention.

Art. 17   Objection and Refusal or Inability to Sit

1. If a party to the dispute objects to a conciliator, the Bureau of the Court shall rule on the objection. Any objection shall be made within thirty days of the notification of the conciliator's appointment. If the objection is upheld, the conciliator concerned shall be replaced according to the provisions laid down for his or her own appointment.

2. If a conciliator, having previously taken part in the case or for any other reason, refuses to sit, he or she shall be replaced according to the provisions laid down for his or her own appointment.

3. In the event of death or of a prolonged inability or refusal to sit during the proceedings, the conciliator concerned shall be replaced according to the provisions laid down for his or her own appointment if this is considered necessary by the Bureau.

Art. 18   Safeguarding Existing Means of Settlement

1. In the situations referred to by Article 19, paragraphs 1 and 2, of the Convention, the conciliation commission shall take no further action and have the case removed from the List.

2. In the situation referred to by Article 19, paragraph 3, of the Convention, the commission shall suspend the conciliation proceedings. The proceedings shall be resumed, at the request of the parties or one of them, if the procedure resulting in the suspension failed to produce a settlement of the dispute.

3. In the situation referred to by Article 19, paragraph 4, of the Convention, the commission shall take no further action and have the case removed from the List upon the request of one of the parties if it is satisfied that the dispute is covered by the reservation.

Art. 19   Rules of Procedure

In accordance with Article 23, paragraph 1, of the Convention, the conciliation commission shall determine its own rules of procedure after consulting the parties to the dispute. The rules of procedure laid down by the commission, which are subject to approval by the Bureau of the Court, may not derogate from the following rules:

(a) Each party shall appoint a representative to the commission no later than at the time of its constitution.

(b) The parties shall participate in all the proceedings and co-operate with the commission, in particular by providing the documents and information it may require.

Art. 20   Interlocutory Matters

1. The conciliation commission may, *proprio motu* or at the request of the parties to the dispute or one of them, call the parties' attention to the measures they could take in order to prevent the dispute from being aggravated or its settlement made more difficult.

2. In accordance with Article 23, paragraph 2, of the Convention, the commission may, with the parties' consent, invite to participate in the

proceedings any other State Party to the Convention which has an interest in the settlement of the dispute.

Art. 21   Result of Conciliation

1. The conciliation proceedings shall be concluded by the signature, by the representatives of the parties, of the summary of conclusions referred to in Article 25, paragraph 1, of the Convention. The summary of conclusions shall be tantamount to an agreement settling the dispute.

2. Failing such an agreement, the conciliation commission shall draw up a final report when it considers that all possibilities of reaching an amicable settlement have been exhausted. The report, which shall be communicated to the parties, shall include a statement of the facts and claims of the parties, a record of the proceedings and proposals made by the commission for the peaceful settlement of the dispute.

3. The parties may agree in advance to accept the proposals of the commission. Failing such an agreement, they shall, within thirty days of the notification of the report under Article 25, paragraph 3, of the Convention, inform the chairman of the commission whether they accept the proposals for a settlement contained in the final report.

4. The acceptance of such proposals by the parties shall be tantamount to an agreement settling the dispute. If one of the parties rejects the proposals, the other party or parties shall no longer be bound by their own acceptance, in accordance with Article 25, paragraph 4, of the Convention.

5. In the event of a party failing to appear, the commission shall draw up a report for the OSCE Council in accordance with Article 25, paragraph 6, of the Convention.

CHAPTER III: ARBITRATION

Art. 22   Purpose

The role of an arbitral tribunal is to settle, in accordance with international law, such disputes as are submitted to it. If the parties to the dispute agree, the tribunal may decide *ex aequo et bono*.

Art. 23   Institution of Proceedings

1. Any dispute between two or more States Parties to the Convention, or between one or more States Parties to the Convention and one or more States participating in the OSCE, may be submitted to arbitration, as provided by Article 26 of the Convention.

2. When a request for arbitration is made by means of an agreement, in accordance with Article 26, paragraph 1, of the Convention, such agreement, notified to the Registrar by the parties to the dispute or by one of them, shall indicate the subject of the dispute. In the event of total or partial disagreement concerning the subject of the dispute, each party may state its own position in that respect.

3. When a request for arbitration is made by means of an application addressed to the Registrar, in accordance with Article 26, paragraphs 2 and 3, of the Convention, the application shall indicate the facts giving rise to the dispute, the subject of the dispute, the parties, the means of settlement previously used and the main legal arguments invoked.

Art. 24   Composition and Constitution of Arbitral Tribunals

1. The arbitral tribunal shall be composed and constituted in accordance with Article 28 of the Convention.

2. If more than two States are parties to a dispute and the parties in the same interest are unable to agree on the appointment of a single arbitrator, as contemplated by Article 28, paragraph 2, of the Convention, the arbitrators designated by each party under Article 28, paragraphs 2, 4 or 5, of the Convention shall be *ex officio* members of the tribunal.

3. In accordance with Article 28, paragraph 3, of the Convention, the Bureau of the Court shall appoint a number of members to sit on the tribunal totalling at least one more than the *ex officio* members under paragraph 2 of this Article. The Bureau may consult the parties in this matter.

4. When all its members have been appointed, the tribunal shall hold its constitutive meeting. At that meeting, it shall elect its chairman in accordance with Article 28, paragraph 6, of the Convention.

Art. 25   Objection and Refusal or Inability to Sit

1. If a party to the dispute objects to an arbitrator, the Bureau of the Court shall rule on the objection. Any objection shall be made within thirty days of the notification of the arbitrator's appointment. If the objection is upheld, the arbitrator concerned shall be replaced according to the provisions laid down for his or her own appointment, except for *ex officio* members of the tribunal who shall be replaced by their alternates. If the alternate is in the same situation, the State concerned shall appoint a member according to the procedure laid down in Article 28, paragraph 5, of the Convention.

2. If an arbitrator, having previously taken part in the case or for any other reason, refuses to sit, he or she shall be replaced according to the procedure laid down for his or her own appointment, except for *ex officio* members of the tribunal who shall be replaced by their alternates. If the alternate is in the same situation, the State concerned shall appoint a member according to the procedure laid down in Article 28, paragraph 5, of the Convention.

3. In the event of death, or of a prolonged inability or refusal to sit during the proceedings, an *ex officio* member of the tribunal shall be replaced by his or her alternate. If the alternate is in the same situation, the State concerned shall appoint a member according to the procedure laid down in Article 28, paragraph 5, of the Convention. A member appointed by the Bureau shall only be replaced, in accordance with Article 28, paragraph 7, of the Convention, if the number of members appointed by the Bureau falls below the number of *ex officio* members or members appointed by

the parties to the dispute under paragraph 5 of the same Article. If the member concerned was the chairman of the tribunal, a new chairman shall then be elected.

Art. 26   Safeguarding Existing Means of Settlement

1. In the situations referred to by Article 19, paragraph 1, of the Convention, the arbitral tribunal shall take no further action and have the case removed from the List.

2. In the situation referred to by Article 19, paragraph 4, of the Convention, the tribunal shall take no further action and have the case removed from the List upon the request of one of the parties or if it is satisfied that the dispute is covered by the reservation. To be admissible, the request must be formulated within the time-limit set under Article 29, paragraph 1, of the present Rules.

Art. 27   Rules of Procedure

1. The arbitral tribunal shall lay down its own rules of procedure after consulting the parties to the dispute. The rules of procedure laid down by the tribunal, which are subject to approval by the Bureau of the Court, may not derogate from the rules that follow.

2. All the parties to the dispute shall have the right to be heard in the course of the proceedings, which shall conform to the principles of a fair trial.

3. Each party shall appoint an agent to represent it before the tribunal no later than at the time of its constitution.

4. The parties shall participate in all the proceedings and co-operate with the tribunal, in particular by providing the documents and information it may require.

5. A certified copy of every document produced by one party shall immediately be communicated to the other party or parties.

6. The proceedings shall consist of a written phase and hearings. The hearings shall be held *in camera*, unless the tribunal decides otherwise at the request of the parties.

7. The tribunal shall have all the necessary fact-finding and investigative powers to carry out its task. It may, in particular:

(a)   make any orders necessary for the good conduct of the proceedings;

(b)   determine the number and order of, and the time-limits for, the written phase;

(c)   order the production of evidence and make all other arrangements for the taking of evidence;

(d)   refuse to admit, after the closure of the written phase, any new documents a party may wish to submit without the consent of the other party or parties;

(e)   visit the site;

(f)   appoint experts;

(g) examine witnesses and request clarifications from the agents, counsel or experts of the parties.

8. As soon as the hearings have been completed, the tribunal shall declare the proceedings closed and begin its deliberations. It may however, during its deliberations, request the parties to provide any additional information or clarification it considers necessary.

Art. 28   Interim Measures

1. Before indicating any interim measures under Article 26, paragraph 4, of the Convention, the arbitral tribunal shall hear the parties to the dispute.

2. The tribunal may at any time request the parties to provide information on the implementation of the measures indicated by it.

3. The tribunal may at any time examine, *proprio motu* or at the request of the parties or one of them, whether the situation requires the maintenance, modification or cancellation of the measures indicated. Before taking any decision, it shall hear the parties.

4. The measures indicated by the tribunal shall cease to apply upon the rendering of the arbitral award.

Art. 29   Objections Concerning Jurisdiction and Admissibility

1. Any objection concerning jurisdiction or admissibility shall be made in writing to the Registrar within thirty days of the transmission of the notice of the request for arbitration referred to in Article 15 of the Convention. The preliminary objection shall set out the facts and the law on which the objection is based, the submissions of the objecting party and any evidence it may wish to produce. The other party shall have a period of thirty days to communicate its written observations on the objection.

2. The tribunal shall decide, in an order, whether it upholds or rejects the objection, or declare that the objection is not, in the circumstances of the case, exclusively preliminary in character. If it upholds the objection, the tribunal shall have the case removed from the List. If it rejects the objection or considers that it is not exclusively preliminary in character, the tribunal shall fix time-limits for the further proceedings.

Art. 30   Counter-claims

1. The tribunal may examine counter-claims directly connected with the subject-matter of the main claim if they are within its jurisdiction.

2. Counter-claims shall be submitted within the time-limit set for the filing of the Counter-Memorial.

3. After hearing the parties, the tribunal shall decide on the admissibility of the counter-claim in the form of an order.

Art. 31   Intervention

1. In accordance with Article 29, paragraph 3, of the Convention, any OSCE participating State which considers that it has a particular interest of a legal nature likely to be affected by the award of the tribunal may,

within fifteen days of the transmission of the notice of the request for arbitration, as referred to in Article 15 of the Convention, address to the Registrar of the Court a request to intervene indicating the legal interest concerned and the precise object of its intervention. Such request, which shall be immediately transmitted to the tribunal and the parties to the dispute, shall also include, as appropriate, a list of the documents submitted in support of the request and which shall be attached to the request.

2. The parties shall have thirty days to comment in writing on the request for intervention.

3. The tribunal shall decide on the request for intervention in the form of an order. If the request is granted, the intervening State shall participate in the proceedings to the extent required to protect its interest. The relevant part of the award shall be binding upon the intervening State in accordance with Article 29, paragraph 4, of the Convention.

Art. 32   Failure to Appear

In the event that one or more parties to the dispute fail to appear, the tribunal shall apply Article 29, paragraph 7, of the Convention.

Art. 33   Discontinuance of Proceedings

1. If, at any time prior to the rendering of the arbitral award, all the parties to the dispute, jointly or separately, notify the arbitral tribunal in writing that they have agreed to discontinue the proceedings, the tribunal shall make an order noting the discontinuance and have the case removed from the List.

2. If, in the course of proceedings initiated by an application, the applicant informs the tribunal that it wishes to discontinue the proceedings, the tribunal shall set a time-limit for the respondent to state its position. If the respondent does not object to the discontinuance, the tribunal shall make an order noting the discontinuance and have the case removed from the List.

Art. 34   The Arbitral Award

1. When the tribunal has concluded its deliberations, which shall be secret, and adopted the arbitral award, it shall render the award by communicating to the agent of each party to the dispute an authentic copy bearing the seal of the Court and the signatures of the chairman of the tribunal and the Registrar of the Court. A further authentic copy shall be placed in the Archives of the Court.

2. The award, which shall mention the names of all the arbitrators, shall state the reasons on which it is based. Any member of the tribunal may, if he or she so desires, attach a dissenting or separate opinion. The same shall apply to the orders of the tribunal.

3. The award shall have binding force only between the parties to the dispute and in respect of the case to which it relates, subject to Article 29, paragraph 4, of the Convention and Article 30, paragraph 3, of the present Rules. The same shall apply to the orders of the tribunal.

4. The award shall be final and not subject to appeal. The same shall apply to orders made by the tribunal under Articles 2, 30, paragraph 3, 31, paragraph 3, and 37, paragraph 3, as well as to the awards rendered under Articles 35 and 36 of the present Rules.

Art. 35   Interpretation of the Arbitral Award

1. Any request for interpretation of the arbitral award the meaning or scope of which is in dispute shall be in the form of a written application made under the conditions laid down by Article 31, paragraph 3, of the Convention. The application shall indicate the precise point or points in dispute.

2. Requests for interpretation shall be examined by the arbitral tribunal which rendered the award. If the Bureau of the Court should find this to be impossible, a new arbitral tribunal shall be constituted in accordance with Article 28 of the Convention and Article 24 of the present Rules.

3. Before interpreting the award by means of an additional award, the tribunal shall set a time-limit for the parties to communicate their written observations.

4. It is up to the tribunal to decide whether and to what extent the implementation of the award is to be suspended pending the communication of the additional award.

Art. 36   Revision

1. Any request for revision of the arbitral award shall be in the form of a written application made under the conditions laid down by Article 31, paragraph 4, of the Convention. The application shall indicate the precise grounds for revision according to the party claiming revision.

2. A request for revision shall be examined by the arbitral tribunal which rendered the award. If the Bureau of the Court should find this to be impossible, a new arbitral tribunal shall be constituted in accordance with Article 28 of the Convention and Article 24 of the present Rules.

3. The other party or parties may, within a time-limit set by the tribunal, make written observations on the admissibility of the request for revision.

4. If the tribunal, by an order, declares the application admissible, it shall set time-limits for the subsequent proceedings on the merits.

5. At the request of the party claiming revision, and if the circumstances so justify, the tribunal may suspend the implementation of the award pending its revision.

6. The tribunal shall decide on the merits in the form of a new arbitral award.

CHAPTER IV: FINAL PROVISIONS

Art. 37   Amendments

1. The Court, any member of the Court and any State Party to the Convention may propose amendments to the present Rules.

2. Proposals for amendment shall be communicated to the Court for comment and approved by consensus of the States Parties to the Convention.

3. Amendments shall come into force upon their approval by the States Parties to the Convention but shall not apply to cases pending at the time of their entry into force.

Art. 38   Entry into Force of the Present Rules

The present Rules shall enter into force on 1 February 1997, date of their approval by consensus of the States Parties to the Convention.

ff) Provisions for a CSCE Conciliation Commission

The participating States in the Conference on Security and Co-operation in Europe (CSCE) hereby establish a procedure to complement the Valletta Procedure for the Peaceful Settlement of Disputes endorsed by the Berlin Meeting, by the establishment of a Conciliation Commission ("the Commission") in accordance with the following provisions.

SECTION I

A dispute between two CSCE participating States may be brought before the Commission if the parties to it so agree.

SECTION II

A participating State may at any time declare that it will accept, on condition of reciprocity, conciliation by the Commission for disputes between it and other participating states. The declaration may not include conditions which would affect the procedures described in Sections III to XVII below. The declaration will be deposited with the Secretary of the Commission ("the Secretary") who will transmit copies to all the participating States.

SECTION III

1. Where the parties to a dispute have agreed to bring it before the Commission, the procedure will be invoked by a joint written request by the parties to the Secretary.

2. Where both parties to a dispute have made declarations under Section II which apply to that dispute, the procedure may be invoked by a written request by either party to the other and to the Secretary.

SECTION IV

1. As soon as the Secretary has received a request made in accordance with Section III, the Commission will be constituted in accordance with Section V.

2. Any question as to the application of Section II with respect to the dispute, and in particular as to reciprocity of the declarations made thereunder, will be decided by the Commission as a preliminary question. For this purpose the parties will proceed directly to the appointment of the conciliators.

SECTION V

1. The parties to the dispute will, within 20 days of the receipt by the Secretary of a written request under Section III, appoint one conciliator from the Register maintained for the purposes of the Valletta Procedure for the Peaceful Settlement of Disputes ("the Valletta Register"). A party which invokes the procedure in accordance with Section III, paragraph 2, should name its conciliator in its written request.

2. The conciliators will, within 20 days of the date of the second of their own appointments, appoint a third conciliator chosen from the Valletta Register, who will act as Chairman of the Commission. He will not be a national of either of the parties or have been nominated by either of them to the Register.

3. If the appointment of the Chairman, or of any of the other conciliators, has not been made within the prescribed period, it will be made within 20 days of the expiry of the relevant period by the Secretary-General of the Permanent Court of Arbitration, after consultations with the parties.

4. Any vacancies will be filled in the manner prescribed for the initial appointment.

SECTION VI

1. The Commission will consult the parties on the procedure to be followed in the exercise of its responsibilities as described herein. The Commission will give effect to any agreement between the parties on procedure. In the absence of agreement on any point, the Commission may decide the matter.

2. Decisions and recommendations of the Commission will be made by a majority vote of the members.

SECTION VII

The Commission may, with the consent of the parties, invite any participating State to submit its views orally or in writing.

SECTION VIII

The parties will refrain throughout the course of the procedure from any action which may aggravate the situation and make more difficult or impede the peaceful settlement of the dispute. In this connection, the Commission may draw the attention of the parties to any measures which it considers might facilitate an amicable settlement.

SECTION IX

The Commission will seek to clarify the points in dispute between the parties and endeavour to bring about a resolution of the dispute on mutually agreeable terms.

SECTION X

If the Commission considers that to do so will facilitate an amicable settlement of the dispute, it may suggest possible terms of settlement and set a time limit within which the parties should inform the Commission whether they accept such recommendations.

SECTION XI

Each party will, within the time limit set under Section X, inform the Secretary and the other party whether or not it accepts the proposed terms of settlement. If both parties have not notified such acceptance within such time limit the Secretary will forward a report from the Commission to the Committee of Senior Officials of the CSCE. The report will not include the matters referred to in Section XII.

SECTION XII

Any measures recommended under Section VIII, and any information and comments provided to the Commission by the parties in confidence, will remain confidential unless the parties agree otherwise.

SECTION XIII

Each party to the dispute will bear its own costs and the costs of the conciliator appointed by it. The rest of the costs of the Commission will be shared equally by the parties.

SECTION XIV

A participating State may at any time, whether before or after a dispute has been referred to the Commission, declare, either generally or in relation to a particular dispute, that it will accept as binding, on condition of reciprocity, any terms of settlement proposed by the Commission. Such declaration will be deposited with the Secretary who will transmit copies to all the participating States.

SECTION XV

A declaration made under Section II or Section XIV may be withdrawn or modified by written notification to the Secretary who will transmit copies to all the participating States. A declaration made under Section II or Section XIV may not be withdrawn or modified in relation to a dispute to which it applies once a written request for conciliation of the dispute has been made under Section III, and the other party to the dispute has already made such a declaration.

SECTION XVI

The parties may agree to modify the procedure set out in the preceding sections with respect to their particular dispute.

SECTION XVII

The Director of the Conflict Prevention Centre will act as Secretary of the Commission. In carrying out his functions the Director may consult the Committee of Senior Officials as and when he deems necessary. If the Director is a national of one of the parties to a dispute, his functions in respect of that dispute will be performed by the next most senior official of the Conflict Prevention Centre who is not such a national.

gg) Provisions for Directed Conciliation

1. The Council of Ministers or the Committee of Senior Officials (CSO) may direct any two participating States to seek conciliation to assist them in resolving a dispute that they have not been able to settle within a reasonable period of time.

2. In using this authority, the Council or the CSO may direct that the parties to the dispute use the provisions for conciliation described in Annex 3, on the same basis as if the parties had made a joint written request to bring the dispute before the Conciliation Commission established by that Annex. However, in such situations:

(a) the Council or the CSO may decide, in view of the nature of the particular dispute or other relevant factors, either to increase or to decrease any of the twenty-day periods for appointment by the parties of the two members of the Conciliation Commission or for selection of the Chairman; and

(b) the work of the Commission will not be conducted in public, unless the parties agree otherwise.

3. Moreover, in cases involving disputes between two parties to the Convention on Conciliation and Arbitration within the CSCE, the Council or the CSO may direct that the parties use the provisions for conciliation established under that Convention, once that Convention enters into force.

4. The parties to the dispute may exercise any rights they otherwise have to participate in all discussions within the Council or CSO regarding the dispute, but they will not take part in the decision by the Council or the CSO directing the parties to conciliation, or in decisions described in paragraph 2(a).

5. The Council or the CSO will not direct parties to dispute to seek conciliation under this Annex:

(a) if the dispute is being addressed under some other procedure for the peaceful settlement of disputes;

(b) if the dispute is covered by any process outside the CSCE which the parties to the dispute have accepted, including under an agreement in which the parties have undertaken to address certain disputes only through negotiations; or

(c) if either party to the dispute considers that, because the dispute raises issues concerning its territorial integrity, or national defence, title to sovereignty over land territory, or competing claims with regard to the jurisdiction over other areas, the provisions of this Annex should not be applied.

6. The parties to the dispute will bear their own expenses. Except for disputes covered in paragraph 3, any other expenses incurred under the procedure will be shared by all participating States in accordance with the CSCE scale of distribution, subject to any procedures that the CSO may adopt to ensure that expenses are limited to those reasonable. With respect to disputes covered by paragraph 3, responsibility for such other expenses will be borne in accordance with the provisions of the Convention on Conciliation and Arbitration within the CSCE.

7. In addition to any reports otherwise provided for under the conciliation provisions described in paragraphs 2 and 3, the Council or the CSO may request the Commission to report on the results of the conciliation. The report will not reflect matters that are considered confidential under the applicable provisions, unless the parties agree otherwise.

2. America and the Caribbean

a) Central American Court of Justice

The Central American Court of Justice was the first functioning international court in this part of the world. Its creation was due to the fact that the five Central American Republics Costa Rica, Guatemala, Honduras, Nicaragua and El Salvador had formed a single administrative unit while under Spanish rule and had endeavoured, during the 19th century, to form a confederation, in spite of repeated setbacks. After further tension in 1906/07 had been eased with the aid of the United States and Mexico a peace conference was held in Washington, D.C. in November and December 1907 which ended with the adoption of nine international instruments including the Convention on the Central American Court of Justice. The function of the Court was expressed in the fundamental political instrument, the General Treaty of Peace and Amity, Art. I, which provided that the parties were bound to "decide every difference or difficulty that may arise between them, of whatever nature it may be, by means of the Central American Court of Justice ...". The Court was first constituted in May 1908 and sat in Cartago and later in San Jose, Costa Rica.

In practice, the functions of the Court were much too wide. Apart from its function in settling disputes between States, which could unilaterally apply to the Court for relief, it was empowered to decide on complaints by individuals of any of the Central American Republics against the Government of another Member State, an innovation as to the function of an international court. Moreover, the Member States had the right to seek relief from the Court in any other dispute between themselves and third States, or even individuals. Except for Costa Rica, the Member States had invested the Court with the power to act as a constitutional body for settling disputes among the executive, legislative and judicial institutions of Member States.

Although the five judges constituting the Court were to be appointed by the legislative organs of each Member State, they were obligated to serve the common interest and to "personify the national conscience of Central America" (Art. XIII).

The functions of the Court came to an end after ten years following unsuccessful efforts to place it on a new contractual footing.

In total, the Court dealt with ten cases, five concerning individual complaints and five truly international disputes. All five cases concerning individuals were rejected on the merits. They nearly all relied on Art. VI of the General Treaty of Peace and Amity concerning national treatment of aliens who were nationals of one of the other Republics party to the Treaty. The other five cases were heard either on application of the parties or on the Court's own initiative; here the Court acted more as a mediator than a judge.

The failure of the Central American Court of Justice is generally thought to stem from the rules concerning the appointment and remuneration of judges by their respective States, since the judges, in all important cases, voted in accordance with the interests of the countries they represented.

Texts

Martens NRG 3 Vol. 3, pp. 94 et seq. (Spanish and English)
Papers Relating to the Foreign Relations of the United States (1907), pp. 665–727
Anales de la Corte de Justicia Centroamericana (1911–1918)

Bibliographical notes

N. Politis, Une expérience de tribunal international permanent en Amérique centrale, Revue d'histoire diplomatique, Vol. 36 (1922), pp. 123–127
M. O. Hudson, The Central American Court of Justice, AJIL Vol. 26 (1932), pp. 759–786
C. Arevalo y Carreño, Hacia una Corte Interamericana de Justicia (1944)
E. Kraske, Der Mittelamerikanische Gerichtshof 1908–1918, ArchVR Vol. 2 (1950), pp. 204–212
Ch. Tomuschat, International Courts and Tribunals with Regionally Restricted and/or Specialized Jurisdiction, in: Judicial Settlement of International Disputes (Beiträge zum ausländischen öffentlichen Recht und Völkerrecht, Vol. 62) (1974), pp. 315–322
C. J. Gutierrez, La Corte de Justicia Centro-americana (1978)
L. A. Haward, The Local and General Context of the Central American Court of Justice (1984)
H. M. Hill, Central American Court of Justice, in: R. Bernhardt (ed.), Encyclopedia of Public International Law, Vol. I (1992), 551–554

aa) General Treaty of Peace and Amity of December 20, 1907

Art. I   The Republics of Central America consider as one of their first duties, in
           their mutual relations, the maintenance of peace; and they bind themselves
           to always observe the most complete harmony, and decide every differ-
           ence or difficulty that may arise amongst them, of whatsoever nature it
           may be, by means of the Central American Court of Justice, created by
           the Convention which they have concluded for that purpose on this date.

bb) Convention for the Establishment of a Central American Court of Justice of December 20, 1907

Art. I   The High Contracting Parties agree by the present Convention to consti-
           tute and maintain a permanent tribunal which shall be called the "Central
           American Court of Justice", to which they bind themselves to submit all
           controversies or questions which may arise among them, of whatsoever
           nature and no matter what their origin may be, in case the respective De-
           partments of Foreign Affairs should not have been able to reach an under-
           standing.

Art. II   This Court shall also take cognizance of the questions which individuals
           of one Central American country may raise against any of the other con-
           tracting Governments, because of the violation of treaties or conventions,
           and other cases of an international character; no matter whether their own
           Government supports said claim or not; and provided that the remedies
           which the laws of the respective country provide against such violation
           shall have been exhausted or that denial of justice shall have been shown.

Art. III   It shall also have jurisdiction over cases arising between any of the con-
           tracting Governments and individuals, when by common accord they are
           submitted to it.

Art. IV   The Court can likewise take cognizance of the international questions
           which by special agreement any one of the Central American Govern-
           ments and a foreign Government may have determined to submit to it.

Art. V   The Central American Court of Justice shall sit at the City of Cartago in
           the Republic of Costa Rica, but it may temporarily transfer its residence
           to another point in Central America whenever it deems it expedient for
           reasons of health, or in order to insure the exercise of its functions, or of
           the personal safety of its members.

Art. VI   The Central American Court of Justice shall consist of five Justices, one
           being appointed by each Republic and selected from among the jurists
           who possess the qualifications which the laws of each country prescribe
           for the exercise of high judicial office, and who enjoy the highest consid-

eration, both because of their moral character and their professional ability.

Vacancies shall be filled by substitute Justices, named at the same time and in the same manner as the regular Justices and who shall unite the same qualifications as the latter.

The attendance of the five justices who constitute the Tribunal is indispensable in order to make a legal quorum in the decisions of the Court.

Art. VII   The Legislative Power of each one of the five contracting Republics shall appoint their respective Justices, one regular and two substitutes.

The salary of each Justice shall be eight thousand dollars, gold, per annum, which shall be paid them by the Treasury of the Court. The salary of the Justice of the country where the Court resides shall be fixed by the Government thereof. Furthermore each State shall contribute two thousand dollars, gold, annually toward the ordinary and extraordinary expenses of the Tribunal. The Governments of the contracting Republics bind themselves to include their respective contributions in their estimates of expenses and to remit quarterly in advance to the Treasury of the Court the share they may have to bear on account of such services.

Art. VIII   The regular and substitute Justices shall be appointed for a term of five years, which shall be counted from the day on which they assume the duties of their office, and they may be reelected.

In case of death, resignation or permanent incapacity of any of them, the vacancy shall be filled by the respective Legislature, and the Justice elected shall complete the term of his predecessor.

Art. IX   The regular and substitute Justices shall take oath or make affirmation prescribed by law before the authority that may have appointed them, and from that moment they shall enjoy the immunities and prerogatives which the present Convention confers upon them. The regular Justices shall likewise enjoy thenceforth the salary fixed in Article VII.

Art. X   Whilst they remain in the country of their appointment the regular and substitute Justices shall enjoy the personal immunity which the respective laws grant to the magistrates of the Supreme Court of Justice, and in the other contracting Republics they shall have the privileges and immunities of Diplomatic Agents.

Art. XI   The office of Justice whilst held is incompatible with the exercise of his profession, and with the holding of public office. The same incompatibility applies to the substitute Justices so long as they may actually perform their duties.

Art. XII   At its first annual session the Court shall elect from among its own members a President and Vice-President; it shall organise the personnel of its office by designating a Clerk, a Treasurer, and such other subordinate employees as it may deem necessary, and it shall draw up the estimate of its expenses.

Art. XIII The Central American Court of Justice represents the national conscience of Central America, wherefore the Justices who compose the Tribunal shall not consider themselves barred from the discharge of their duties because of the interest which the Republics, to which they owe their appointment, may have in any case or question. With regard to allegations of personal interest, the rules of procedure which the Court may fix, shall make proper provision.

Art. XIV When differences or questions subject to the jurisdiction of the Tribunal arise, the interested party shall present a complaint which shall comprise all the points of fact and law relative to the matter, and all pertinent evidence. The Tribunal shall communicate without loss of time a copy of the complaint to the Governments or individuals interested, and shall invite them to furnish their allegations and evidence within the term that it may designate to them, which, in no case, shall exceed sixty days counted from the date of notice of the complaint.

Art. XV If the term designated shall have expired without answer having been made to the complaint, the Court shall require the complainant or complainants to do so within a further term not to exceed twenty days, after the expiration of which and in view of the evidence presented and of such evidence as it may *ex officio* have seen fit to obtain, the Tribunal shall render its decision in the case, which decision shall be final.

Art. XVI If the Government, Governments, or individuals sued shall have appeared in time before the Court, presenting their allegations and evidence, the Court shall decide the matter within thirty days following, without further process or proceedings; but if a new term for the presentation of evidence be solicited, the Court shall decide whether or not there is occasion to grant it; and in the affirmative it shall fix therefor a reasonable time. Upon the expiration of such term, the Court shall pronounce its final judgment within thirty days.

Art. XVII Each one of the Governments or individuals directly concerned in the questions to be considered by the Court has the right to be represented before it by a trustworthy person or persons, who shall present evidence, formulate arguments, and shall, within the terms fixed by this Convention and by the rules of the Court of Justice do everything that in their judgment shall be beneficial to the defense of the rights they represent.

Art. XVIII From the moment in which any suit is instituted against any one or more governments up to that in which a final decision has been pronounced, the court may at the solicitation of any one of the parties fix the situation in which the contending parties must remain, to the end that the difficulty shall not be aggravated and that things shall be conserved in *statu quo* pending a final decision.

Art. XIX For all the effects of this Convention, the Central American Court of Justice may address itself to the Governments or tribunals of justice of the contracting States, through the medium of the Ministry of Foreign Relations or the office of the Clerk of the Supreme Court of Justice of the respective country, according to the nature of the requisite proceeding, in order to have the measures that it may dictate within the scope of its jurisdiction carried out.

Art. XX   It may also appoint special commissioners to carry out the formalities above referred to, when it deems it expedient for their better fulfillment. In such case, it shall ask of the Government where the proceeding is to be had, its cooperation and assistance, in order that the Commissioner may fulfill his mission. The contracting Governments formally bind themselves to obey and to enforce the orders of the Court, furnishing all the assistance that may be necessary for their best and most expeditious fulfillment.

Art. XXI   In deciding points of fact that may be raised before it, the Central American Court of Justice shall be governed by its free judgment, and with respect to points of law, by the principles of International Law. The final judgment shall cover each one of the points in litigation.

Art. XXII   The Court is competent to determine its jurisdiction, interpreting the Treaties and Conventions germane to the matter in dispute, and applying the principles of international law.

Art. XXIII   Every final or interlocutory decision shall be rendered with the concurrence of at least three of the Justices of the Court. In case of disagreement, one of the substitute Justices shall be chosen by lot, and if still a majority of three be not thus obtained other Justices shall be successively chosen by lot until three uniform votes shall have been obtained.

Art. XXIV   The decisions must be in writing and shall contain a statement of the reasons upon which they are based. They must be signed by all the Justices of the Court and countersigned by the Clerk. Once they have been notified they can not be altered on any account; but, at the request of any of the parties, the Tribunal may declare the interpretation which must be given to its judgments.

Art. XXV   The judgments of the Court shall be communicated to the five Governments of the contracting Republics. The interested parties solemnly bind themselves to submit to said judgments, and all agree to lend all moral support that may be necessary in order that they may be properly fulfilled, thereby constituting a real and positive guarantee of respect for this Convention and for the Central American Court of Justice.

Art. XXVI   The Court is empowered to make its rules, to formulate the rules of procedure which may be necessary, and to determine the forms and terms not prescribed in the present Convention. All the decisions which may be rendered in this respect shall be communicated immediately to the High Contracting Parties.

Art. XXVII   The High Contracting Parties solemnly declare that on no ground nor in any case will they consider the present Convention as void; and that, therefore, they will consider it as being always in force during the term of ten years counted from the last ratification. In the event of the change or alteration of the political status of one or more of the Contracting Republics, the functions of the Central American Court of Justice created by this Convention shall be suspended *ipso facto*; and a conference to adjust the constitution of said Court to the new order of things shall be forthwith convoked by the respective Governments; in case they do not unanimously agree the present Convention shall be considered as rescinded.

Art. XXVIII	The exchange of ratifications of the present Convention shall be made in accordance with Article XXI of the General Treaty of Peace and Amity concluded on this date.
Provisional Art.	As recommended by the five Delegations an Article is annexed which contains an amplification of the jurisdiction of the Central American Court of Justice, in order that the Legislatures may, if they see fit, include it in this Convention upon ratifying it.
Annexed Art.	The Central American Court of Justice shall also have jurisdiction over the conflicts which may arise between the Legislative, Executive and Judicial Powers, and when as a matter of fact the judicial decisions and resolutions of the National Congress are not respected.

Signed at the city of Washington on the twentieth day of December, one thousand nine hundred and seven.

cc) Rules of Procedure of December 2, 1911

CAPÍTULO PRIMERO. DEL CARÁCTER Y ORGANIZACIÓN DE LA CORTE

Art. 1	La Corte de Justicia Centroamericana tiene por objeto garantizar con su autoridad, basada en el honor de los Estados, y dentro de los límites de la intervención que le ha sido concedida, los derechos de cada uno de ellos en sus recíprocas relaciones así como mantener en éstas la paz y la armonía, y es, por su naturaleza, por sus atribuciones y por el carácter de su jurisdicción, un Tribunal Permanente de Justicia Internacional, con potestad para juzgar y resolver, á petición de parte, todos los asuntos comprendidos en su ley constitutiva, y para sostener y administrar, conforme á la misma, la oficina de su despacho y los intereses de ésta.
Art. 2	La personalidad jurídica de la Corte existe en la integridad de su composición, ó sea, en virtud de la concurrencia de un Magistrado por cada una de las Repúblicas de que es exponente, y ella deberá por lo tanto, en caso de faltar alguno de sus miembros, procurar sin demora que el Estado ó Estados respectivos restablezcan su representación.
Art. 3	Cuando por fallecimiento, renuncia ó incapacidad haya de procederse al reemplazo de un Magistrado, ocupará su puesto uno de los suplentes de la

República á quien corresponda el nombramiento de sucesor, mientras éste no entre á ejercer sus funciones, é igual disposición regirá, si á causa de abandono de destino, quedaré vacante alguna Magistratura.

Si la vacante ocurriere durante licencia concedida al Magistrado que cesa, continuará en su lugar durante el tiempo antes indicado, el suplente que por aquel motivo estuviere en ejercicio.

Tratándose de faltas temporales ó de separación de un Magistrado del conocimiento de determinado negocio, se llamará también a uno de sus suplentes á ejercer el cargo, durante la ausencia del proprietario ó en el juicio á que la excusa o recusación se refieran.

Art. 4   Siempre que la Corte se desintegre por cualquier motivo, los Magistrados presentes quedarán constituídos en Comisión Permanente pare el efecto de dirigir á quien corresponda las instancias tendientes á completar el quorum de ley, para el de servir la correspondencia oficial y para atender la administración de la Oficina, en todo aquello que fuere urgente é indispensable.

Art. 5   La Corte podrá otorgar licencia á los Magistrados, sin goce de sueldo y por tiempo determinado, siempre que la petición se apoye en justa causa, á juicio de la misma, no debiendo el término del permiso exceder de seis meses, ni bajar de tres.

El mínimum indicado será de un mes, si se tratare del Magistrado de la República donde el Tribunal resida.

Art. 6   Salvo el caso de licencia, fundada en razones que la Corte califique de perentorias, el Magistrado que la hubiere obtenido no podrá separarse de su puesto, mientras el Suplente llamado á sustituirlo no se haya presentado en el Tribunal con tal objeto.

Durante la desintegración del Tribunal que pueda ocurrir conforme á este artículo, el Magistrado ausente en virtud de licencia, gotará del sueldo de su cargo.

Art. 7   Pendiente la tramitación de un juicio no podrá concederse licencia á ningún Magistrado, sino por grave enfermedad suya, de sus ascendientes, descendientes ó esposa, ó por otra causa de igual importancia, según el criterio del Tribunal.

Art. 8   La licencia es irrenunciable, si ya estuviere en ejercicio de sus funciones el sustituto respectivo, ó si hubiere salido de su país con el fin de llenar la plaza; á menos que, en una ú otra hipótesis, el suplente asintiere y se abonaren á la Tesorería de la Corte los gastos que el viaje le ocasione.

Art. 9   Los gastos de viaje del suplente serán de cuenta del Tribunal, sólo cuando el llamamiento obedezca á licencia concedida al propietario ó provenga de algún auto pronunciado en el curso de un litigio.

Art. 10   Sin perjuicio de lo dispuesto en materia de licencias para los Magistrados en funciones, los Magistrados Propietarios ó Suplentes que tuvieren que salir de Centro América, lo avisarán anticipadamente á la Corte, indicando su dirección y el tiempo probable de su ausencia.

Art. 11 Si un Magistrado abandonare de hecho su puesto, ó si habiendo obtenido licencia, permaneciere ausente por más de un mes después de vencida ella, sin obtener prórroga del plazo, cuando cupiere dentro del máximum fijado en el artículo 5, el Tribunal dará cuenta de esa circunstancia al Estado respectivo, para que estime sus efectos jurídicos conforme á las reglas de su Derecho Público interno.

Art. 12 El nombramiento de un Magistrado Propietario ó Suplente debe estimarse como acto de la exclusiva responsabilidad del Estado que lo efectuare é implica calificación con fuerza de ley de la habilidad y demás condiciones del funcionario designado, para el ejercicio de la Magistratura conferida.

Art. 13 Conforme al artículo XXVII de la Convención, la Corte suspenderá sus funciones, si por una causa cualquiera llegare á alterarse la composición política de Centro América, de manera que exija aumento ó disminución de las Magistraturas representativas de los Estados en el seno del Tribunal, y éstos declararen haberse realizado tal evento.

Art. 14 La Corte no se disolverá, ni suspenderá sus funciones por inobservancia de sus fallos ó mandatos, ó por desconocimiento de sus atribuciones ó prerrogativas. Llegado ese caso, dirigirá al Gobierno respectivo las observaciones convenientes, y si estas fueren desatendidas, dará cuenta de lo ocurrido á los otros Gobiernos.

Art. 15 La desintegración del Tribunal, prevista en el artículo 4, interrumpe la tramitación de todos los juicios pendientes, con suspensión de los términos ó plazos judiciales.

CAPÍTULO SEGUNDO. DE LA JURISDICCIÓN Y ATRIBUCIONES DE LA CORTE

Art. 16 La Corte de Justicia Centroamericana no tiene en los negocios de su jurisdicción ordinaria más autoridad, ni atribuciones que las que expresamente le confiere su Ley Constitutiva; y desde el momento en que se inicie una demanda, posee la facultad de fijar su competencia, así sobre el asunto principal controvertido, como sobre las cuestiones incidentales, que en la tramitación ocurran, interpretando los Tratados y Convenciones y aplicando los princípios de Derecho Internacional referentes al punto ó puntos en cuestión.

Art. 17 La jurisdicción ordinaria de la Corte comprende:

1° Todas las cuestiones ó controversias, que entre los Estados Centroamericanos ocurran, cualesquiera que seen su origen y naturaleza, si las Cancillerías interesadas no hubieren podido llegar á un avenimiento; ya se demuestre esto por actas ú otra clase de documentos eficientes, ya por el hecho de hallarse las Partes en estado de guerra;

2° Los litigios que un centroamericano establezca contra alguno de los Estados contratantes, que no sea el suyo, cuando se refieran á violación de Tratados ó Convenciones ó á otros asuntos de carácter internacional, á condición de que haya agotado los recursos que las leyes del respectivo país le otorguen, contra los actos motivadores de la acción judicial, ó que se demuestre denegación de justicia.

3° La potestad de fijar en armonía con el artículo XVIII de la Convención, la situación en que las Partes contendientes deban permanecer durante el juicio entre ellas iniciado, y en consecuencia, la de dictar todas las providencias precautorias, que al efecto estime indispensables, así como la de modificarlas, suspenderlas ó revocarlas, según las circunstancias;

4° Los casos de Derecho Público interno, comprendidos en el Artículo Anexo de la citada Convención, respecto de los Estados que incluyeron esa cláusula en la ratificación legislativa del Pacto.

Art. 18 La jurisdicción ordinaria se ejercerá con arreglo á las formas y plazos fijados en la Convención de Washington, y á las reglas complementarias que la Corte estatuya en su Ordenanza Procesal.

Art. 19 Constituyen la jurisdicción extraordinaria ó compromisoria:

1° Las cuestiones no comprendidas en el inciso 2° del artículo 17, que sobrevengan entre uno de los Gobiernos Centroamericanos y personas particulares, cuando de común acuerdo le fueren sometidas;

2° Las controversias de orden internacional, entre alguno de los Gobiernos de Centro América y el de una Nación extranjera, que, por Convención celebrada al efecto decidan las Partes ventilar y dirimir ante la Corte.

Art. 20 En los asuntos mencionados en el inciso 1° del artículo anterior, la extensión de las facultades de la Corte, así como el procedimiento judicial aplicable, serán los que exprese el acuerdo ó compromiso de las partes; y á falta de determinación al respecto, se presumirá conferida al Tribunal, para la litis, la misma suma de facultades anexas á su jurisdicción ordinaria, con observancia de los procedimientos á ésta inherentes.

Art. 21 En las controversias á que alude el inciso 2° del artículo 19, es potestativa para la Corte su intervención judicial; y en ellas no tendrá más facultades, ni usará de otros procedimientos, que los estatuidos en el pacto compromisorio.

Art. 22 La jurisdicción de la Corte en cada uno de los negocios que ante ella se ventilen, cesa en virtud de la notificación de la sentencia definitiva, sin perjuicio de la facultad de interpretar el fallo pronunciado, conforme al artículo XXIV de la Convención.

CAPÍTULO TERCERO. DE LOS IMPEDIMENTOS, RECUSACIONES Y EXCUSAS

Art. 23   Los Magistrados en ejercicio están obligados á integrar el quorum de ley para el pronunciamiento de las resoluciones del Tribunal, sin que, en caso alguno, puedan abstenerse de ello por disentimiento de pareceres ú otro motivo, ni negarse á dar su voto, sobre el asunto en cuestión.

Art. 24   Constituyen causa de impedimento de los Magistrados, para conocer en los juicios sometidos á la jurisdicción del Tribunal:

1° Tener ellos interés directo y personal en la controversia, ó tenerlo sus cónyuges ó sus ascendientes, descendientes y hermanos consanguíneos ó por afinidad;

2° Haber concurrido en el ejercicio de funciones judiciales á la decisión de un tribunal nacional, sobre el asunto en cuestión, ó á la de un Tribunal de Arbitramento, ó á la de una Comisión Internacional de Investigación.

Art. 25   Son causas de recusación de un Magistrado para conocer en un juicio:

1° Las que constituyen impedimento;

2° Haber sido abogado ó personero de alguna de las partes en el juicio pendiente, ó haberlo sido, ante un tribunal nacional ó un Tribunal de Arbitramento ó Comisión de Investigación Internacional, al controvertirse el asunto que hubiere dado margen á dicho juicio;

3° Haber cooperado directamente, con carácter público, ya sea político, administrativo ó militar, ó con carácter particular, en los actos ú omisiones motivadores del juicio; ó haberlo hecho alguno de los deudos comprendidos en el número 1° del artículo anterior;

4° Haber emitido por escrito opinión concreta, fuera del ejercicio de sus funciones, acerca de la acción controvertida.

Art. 26   Los Magistrados están obligados á excusarse de intervenir en un juicio, siempre que tuvieren alguna de las causales de impedimento establecidas por el artículo 24; pero no contraen responsabilidad alguna por dejar de hacerlo ó retardarlo, cuando la causal consistiere en interés directo y personal de los parientes designados en el número 1° de dicho artículo, y el Magistrado jurare haberlo ignorado.

Art. 27   Es facultativo para los Magistrados excusarse de conocer en un juicio, cuando ocurriere respecto de ellos alguno de los motivos de recusación, expuestos en los números 2°, 3° y 4° del artículo 25; pero las partes tienen derecho á recusarlos y, una vez rendida la prueba del caso, á obtener su separación.

Art. 28   Tanto para la excusa, como para la recusación, deberá invocarse una de las causales previstas en los artículos 24 y 25 de este Reglamento, expresándola clara y concretamente, y el incidente respectivo se tramitará conforme á las reglas establecidas en la Ordenanza de Procedimientos.

Art. 29   Fuera de las providencias relativas á la inhibición ó separación, son anulables, á petición de cualquiera de las partes contendientes, las resoluciones dictadas por la Corte en el curso de una controversia, con la concurrencia de un Magistrado que se halle impedido, siempre que el incidente de nulidad se promueva antes del auto en que el Tribunal, teniendo por concluídos los trámites del juicio, declare que debe procederse al pronunciamiento del fallo definitivo.

CAPÍTULO CUARTO. DE LA INVESTIDURA, FUNCIONES Y PRERROGATIVAS DE LOS MAGISTRADOS

Art. 30   Los Magistrados Propietarios ó Suplentes adquieren su investidura en virtud del nombramiento decretado por el Poder Legislativo de la Nación a que pertenecen, y de la prestación del juramento de posesión del cargo, conforme al artículo IX de la Convención.

Art. 31   El ingreso de los Magistrados Propietarios en la Corte para el ejercicio de sus funciones, así como la incorporación de los Suplentes que deban sustituirlos en los casos de ley, se realiza por la presentación de ellos en el Tribunal, con los documentos fehacientes, en que consten el nombramiento y toma de posesión indicados en el artículo anterior.

Art. 32   Los Magistrados en funciones son iguales, y su precedencia, después del Presidente y el Vice-Presidente, se determinará por una de estas causas, en el orden en que se exponen:

1° La fecha de su nombramiento;

2° La de toma de posesión;

3° La de su ingreso en la Corte;

4° La del título profesional.

Los propietarios precederán á los suplentes.

Art. 33   Los Magistrados Propietarios y Suplentes gozan, en los Estados Centroamericanos que no sean el de su nacionalidad, de los privilegios é inmunidades de los Agentes Diplomáticos, y podrán usar, como éstos, el escudo y la bandera del país de que proceden.

Art. 34   Sin perjuicio de lo dispuesto en el artículo IX de la Convención y en la fracción final del artículo 6° del presente Reglamento, los Magistrados sólo gozarán de sueldo durante el ejercicio de sus funciones. A los Magistrados Suplentes llamados á integrar el Tribunal conforme á la ley, se les abonará un viático, que la Corte fijará, cuando ella deba satisfacerlo, según lo dispuesto en el artículo 9° de dicho Reglamento.

Capítulo Quinto. Incompatibilidades y Prohibiciones Relativas á la Magistratura

Art. 35   El cargo de Magistrado en funciones, sea Propietario ó Suplente, es incompatible:

1° Con el ejercicio de la profesión de abogado;

2° Con el desempeño de cargos públicos.

Art. 36   Para los efectos del anterior artículo se entenderá por cargo público, el que implique posesión de autoridad, jurisdicción ó representación política interna ó internacional.

Art. 37   Los Magistrados Propietarios y Suplentes, aunque no se hallen en el ejercicio de su ministerio, están imposibilitados de intervenir como abogados ó consejeros de alguna de las partes, en los asuntos que ante la Corte se ventilen.

Art. 38   Es prohibido á los Magistrados en funciones:

1° Ser miembros de Tribunales Especiales de Arbitramento, ó de Comisiones Internacionales de Investigación, que se organicen por acuerdo de dos ó más Gobiernos Centroamericanos;

2° Ser órganos de comunicación de ningún Gobierno ante la Corte;

3° Provocar ó sostener polémicas por la prensa, sobre asuntos de política actual de Centro América, ó tomar parte en manifestaciones de aplauso ó de censura para algún Gobierno Centroamericano.

Capítulo Sexto. Del Modo de Funcionar la Corte

Art. 39   Todo acto del Tribunal se ejecutará en sesión ordinaria ó extraordinaria, con asistencia de los cinco Magistrados que lo componen.

Art. 40   Para que haya acuerdo ó resolución de la Corte, es indispensable, por lo menos, una mayoría de tres votos conformes; y á fin de obtenerla se aplicará, en caso necesario, la regla establecida en el artículo XXIII de la Convención.

Art. 41   La elección de Presidente, Vice-Presidente, Secretario y empleados subalternos de la oficina, se hará por votación; pero si después de dos escrutinios no resultare mayoría de votos, la suerte decidirá entre los candidatos propuestos. La Corte procurará, al hacer la elección de Presidente, que en ese puesto alternen, durante el quinquenio, todos los Magistrados que la componen.

Art. 42   La Corte celebrará sesiones ordinarias los lunes, miércoles y viernes de cada semana, comenzando á la una de la tarde; y extraordinarias, cuando el Presidente lo estimare oportuno. El despacho ordinario de los asuntos se hará diariamente, entre las doce y media y las cinco y media de la tarde, exceptuándose los días de fiesta y demás feriados por la ley del domicilio ó residencia de la Corte. Esta reserva no regirá en caso de urgencia.

El Secretario asistirá á todas las sesiones.

Art. 43   De cada sesión de la Corte se asentará acta con todos los detalles posibles y necesarios; y en ella se harán constar las disposiciones que se dicten y la tramitación dada á los asuntos judiciales en curso.

Art. 44   En cada sesión se leerá el acta de la anterior, y una vez aprobada con ó sin reformas, se consignará en el libro destinado al efecto y se firmará por todos los Magistrados y por el Secretario.

La discusión del acta se limitará á la exactitud de la relación en ella contenida.

Las actas deben escribirse sucesivamente, sin dejar entre ellas espacios innecesarios.

Art. 45   Es derecho de los Magistrados hacer constar los motivos de sus mociones y votos.

Las exposiciones que al efecto formularen se asentarán con clara referencia al acta respectiva, en un libro especial denominado Libro de Votos.

No podrán los Magistrados formular protestas contra los acuerdos del Tribunal, ó contra las opiniones de sus colegas.

Art. 46   Los acuerdos votados en una sesión podrán ser reconsiderados en la siguiente, si así lo decidiere la Corte á solicitud de alguno de los Magistrados.

La revisión deberá ser pedida inmediatamente después de aprobada el acta respectiva, y no podrán ser objeto de ella, los acuerdos que se hubieren emitido con el propósito de que sean inmediatamente ejecutados, ni los que contengan sentencia definitiva ó interlocutoria.

En los asuntos concernientes á la administración y disciplina interna de la oficina, la Corte conserva la facultad de reformar ó revocar, en cualquier tiempo, las disposiciones que emita.

Art. 47   En la primera sesión anual, que se celebrará el 25 de mayo, salvo caso de imposibilidad, fijará la Corte el Presupuesto de gastos del año y hará el nombramiento de Presidente, Vice-Presidente, Secretario, Tesorero y empleados subalternos de la oficina, para el nuevo período. La elección de Presidente, Vice-Presidente y Secretario se comunicará á los Gobiernos de Centro América y á las Cortes Supremas de Justicia de las cinco Repúblicas, á quienes se dará á conocer, además, la firma de dichos funcionarios.

Art. 48   Cuando no sea posible hacer, al terminar el año, la elección de Presidente y de Vice-Presidente, así como el nombramiento de Secretario y demás empleados del Tribunal, se entenderán prorrogadas las funciones de los dos primeros, hasta la fecha de su reposición, y continuarán los últimos en el desempeño interino de sus cargos.

Art. 49   Las sesiones de la Corte serán secretas, salvo que se acuerde lo contrario respecto de alguna ó de algunas de ellas.

Art. 50   La Corte no podrá variar de modo definitivo el domicilio que le señala la Convención respectiva, ni podrá cambiarlo accidentalmente, sin acuerdo previo, fundado en alguno de los motivos prescritos en el artículo V de dicha Convención.

Art. 51   El idioma del Tribunal es el castellano.

Las partes contendientes deberán dirigir en él sus peticiones, y cuando tuvieren necesidad de valerse de documentos escritos en otra lengua, agregarán una traducción fehaciente.

La Corte hará traducir por medio de intérpretes y con las formalidades perceptuadas en la Ordenanza de Procedimientos, los documentos en idioma extranjero que de oficio hiciere introducir á los autos, así como las declaraciones de los testigos que no hablaren castellano, y podrá comprobar en la misma forma la exactitud de las traducciones que las partes presentaren.

Art. 52   Todos los empleados de la Corte prometerán ante ella el buen desempeño de su cargo.

CAPÍTULO SÉTIMO. DEL PRESIDENTE Y VICE-PRESIDENTE

Art. 53   El Presidente y el Vice-Presidente de la Corte serán electos anualmente, según lo prevenido por el artículo XII de la Convención; y si en el curso del año ambos funcionarios llegaren á faltar por causa que determine vacante, ó por licencia, presidirá el Tribunal durante la vacante ó licencia, el Magistrado presente que tuviere la primacía por razón de precedencia.

Art. 54   Son atribuciones del Presidente de la Corte, y en su defecto, del Vice-Presidente:

1° Dirigir las sesiones y fijar el orden en que deban tratarse los asuntos;

2° Convocar á los Magistrados á sesiones extraordinarias, siempre que así lo requiera el pronto despacho de los asuntos pendientes;

3° Firmar la correspondencia postal ó telegráfica que ocurra con los Presidentes de los Supremos Poderes de los Estados Centroamericanos ó de Naciones extranjeras ó con los Presidentes de Tribunales y demás corporaciones de carácter internacional;

4° Vigilar los trabajos de la oficina para que sean en todo concepto satisfactorios;

5° Firmar junto con el Secretario las órdenes de pago que la Tesorería deba cubrir por sueldos, servicios y menesteres de la oficina, de conformidad con el presupuesto y demás acuerdos de la Corte, relativos á la administración económica de la oficina;

6° Conceder licencia hasta por ocho días á los empleados del Tribunal, sin goce de sueldo;

7° Nombrar las comisiones que deban dar dictamen, en los negocios que lo requieran, á juicio de la Corte.

CAPÍTULO OCTAVO. DEL SECRETARIO

Art. 55   El Secretario es el órgano de comunicación de la Corte y el jefe inmediato de la oficina de la misma, cuyos servicios reglamentará con aprobación del Presidente.

Art. 56   A falta del Secretario hará sus veces el Oficial Mayor de la Corte.

Art. 57   El Secretario asistirá diariamente á la oficina durante las horas de despacho.

Art. 58   Sus atribuciones son:

1° Asistir á las sesiones del Tribunal y darle cuenta de los negocios que ocurran;

2° Redactar las actas de las sesiones y asentarlas en el libro respectivo;

3° Dirigir, conforme á instrucciones, la correspondencia del Tribunal, de la cual dejará copia íntegra;

4° Ordenar la Biblioteca y el Archivo de la Corte, inventariar sus propiedades y cuidar de que todo se conserve en buen estado;

5° Ejercer en los asuntos judiciales las funciones correspondientes á la Secretaría de un Tribunal de Justicia, según la práctica común;

6° Disponer, con aprobación del Presidente, todo lo relativo al régimen interno de la oficina del Tribunal;

7° Desempeñar transitoriamente la Tesorería del Tribunal, mientras éste no acuerde separar esa función;

8° Dirigir las publicaciones de la Corte, en tanto no se dispusiere otra cosa.

CAPÍTULO NOVENO. DEL TESORERO

Art. 59   Son atribuciones del Tesorero:

1° Cuidar de que ingresen puntualmente en la Tesorería los sueldos y contribuciones que los Gobiernos deben suministrar para el sostenimiento del Tribunal, conforme al artículo VII de la Convención de Wáshington; y cuando encontrare dificultades para ello, dar cuenta á la Corte, á fin de que acuerde lo conducente;

2° Legalizar en forma los giros y recibos correspondientes a los sueldos de los Magistrados en funciones, las listas de servicio mensuales de la Oficina y los documentos relativos á gastos extraordinarios; todo conforme al presupuesto de la Corte;

3° Llevar la contabilidad de la Tesorería por el sistema de partida doble, con los libros principales y auxiliares que sean necesarios, y presentar mensualmente un estado de sus cuentas á la Corte.

Art. 60   La Corte guardará sus fondos en un banco de su domicilio, y mientras no disponga otra cosa, continuará siendo depositario de ellos el Banco de Costa Rica.

CAPÍTULO DÉCIMO. DE LA REFORMA DE ESTE REGLAMENTO

Art. 61   Este Reglamento no podrá reformarse, en todo ó en parte, sino en virtud de proposición que un Magistrado presentare por escrito, expresando las razones ó motivos de ella, que obtenga aprobación unánime ó de una mayoría de cuatro votos, en dos sesiones sucesivas, celebradas con un intervalo no menor de quince días.

b) Organization of American States

Although discussed since the fifth International Conference of American States at Santiago in 1923 the creation of an inter-American Court of Justice proved unsuccessful. However, agreement was reached at the ninth Conference at Bogotá in 1948, in the form of the American Treaty on Pacific Settlement (Pact of Bogotá). Concerning an inter-American judicial procedure the Pact was to replace the previous inter-American treaties, conventions and protocols governing the peaceful settlement of disputes among the ratifying States. The Pact served, as stated in Chapter IV (now Chapter V, Art. 26) of the Bogotá Charter ratified on the same day, to establish a procedure for the definitive settlement of all inter-State disputes within reasonable time-limits by mediation, conciliation, arbitration and adjudication. Excepted from this system were disputes falling exclusively within domestic jurisdiction or those already settled or governed by agreements in force prior to the Pact. One special feature of this Pact is that, after the failure of conciliation and in the absence of a *compromis* to arbitrate, unilateral application to the International Court of Justice is permitted (Art. 32). Should the International Court of Justice declare itself without jurisdiction in a specific case, compulsory arbitration is provided for (Art. 35). In such a case, as well as when a special arbitration agreement has been concluded, the Pact provides for remedies if one party withdraws unilaterally from the proceedings (Arts. 43, 45, 47, 48, 50).

Owing to the compulsory nature of its system of pacific settlement, States have attached broad reservations in ratifying the Pact. Since some of the more important States, however, did not adhere to it, the Charter of the OAS was amended in 1967 in order to provide itself for some kind of dispute settlement. The amendment which entered into force on February 27, 1970 added a new chapter to the Charter which contained provisions for the peaceful settlement of disputes by means of a Permanent Council and an Inter-American Committee on Peaceful Settlement as a subsidiary organ to the Council. The Committee comes into play when the parties fail to agree upon one of the procedures provided for in Art. 24 (formerly Art. 21) of the Charter. A further amendment of the Charter by the Protocol of Cartagena de Indias of 1985 enhanced this dispute settlement procedure by providing that any party can now unilaterally call upon the Permanent Council to obtain its good offices for the settlement of the dispute. The Permanent Council may also establish ad hoc committees, however, only with the consent of the parties. The solution found for the settlement of the dispute has in any way to be accepted by the parties, which means that this form of dispute settlement does not lead to a mandatory decision. This system of dispute settlement has thus to be characterized as a political mediation or conciliation procedure rather than as a legal procedure of dispute settlement.

Only one case has been settled by resorting to the Pact: the border dispute between Honduras and Nicaragua in 1957, which was based on a disagreement concerning the Arbitral Award of the King of Spain of December 23, 1906. By agreement between the two States the case was brought before the International Court of Justice. In the case concerning Border and Transborder Armed Actions between Nicaragua and Honduras Nicaragua based the jurisdiction of the International

Court of Justice, besides on Art. 36, paragraph 2 of the Statute of the Court, also on Article XXXI of the Pact of Bogotà. Honduras objected, however, that the Pact did not provide a basis for jurisdiction. In a judgement of December 20, 1988, the International Court of Justice found that Article XXXI of the Pact conferred jurisdiction upon it to entertain the dispute submitted to it. In 1992, Nicaragua informed the Court that the Parties had reached an out-of-court agreement and did not wish to go on with the proceedings. On May 27, 1992, the Court made an order directing the removal of the case from the Court's list.

Texts

Text of the Charter
   UNTS Vol. 119, pp. 3 et seq. (Spanish, Portuguese, English and French)
   F. Berber, Völkerrecht, Dokumentensammlung, Vol. 1 (1967), pp. 678–699
Text of the Protocol of Amendment of Buenos Aires
   UNTS Vol. 721, pp. 267 et seq. (Spanish, Portuguese, English and French)
Integrated Text of the Charter including the texts of the Protocols of Amendment of
   Buenos Aires, Cartagena, Washington and Managua
   ILM 33 (1994), 981 et seq.
   OAS Treaty Series No 1-E
   OEA /Ser.A/2, Rev. 3 (English)
Text of the Pact
   UNTS Vol. 30, pp. 55 et seq. (Spanish, Portuguese, English and French)
   F. Berber, Völkerrecht, Dokumentensammlung, Vol. 2 (1967), pp. 1701–1714
   Inter-American Juridical Yearbook 1948, pp. 347 et seq.

Bibliographical notes

H. Accioly, El Pacto de Bogotá, Inter-American Juridical Yearbook 1948, pp. 3 et seq.

J. L. Kunz, The Pact of Bogotá, The Arbitration Journal, Vol. 3 (1948), pp. 147 et seq.

E. Turlington, The Pact of Bogotá, AJIL Vol. 42 (1948), pp. 608 et seq.

J. L. Kunz, Die Bogotá-Charter, Reorganisation Panamerikas, ArchVR Vol. 1 (1948/49), pp. 399 et seq.

J. L. Kunz, Interamerikanische Streitschlichtung unter dem Pakt von Bogotá, ÖZöR Vol. 2 (1950), pp. 486 et seq.

Ch. G. Fenwick, Revision of the Pact of Bogotá, AJIL Vol. 48 (1954), pp. 123 et seq.

M. M. Ball, The OAS in Transition (1969)

H. Lehmann, Das interamerikanische System zur friedlichen Beilegung von Streitigkeiten (1969)

R. M. Cattáneo, La solución pacifica de controversias en la nueva carta de la O.E.A., Revista de Derecho Internacional y Ciencias Diplomáticas, Vol. 19 (1970), pp. 138–146

G. Kutzner, Die Organisation der Amerikanischen Staaten (1970)

R. Gerold, Die Sicherung des Friedens durch die Organisation der Amerikanischen Staaten (OAS) (1971)

J.-P. Hubert, L'Organisation des Etats Américains. Le rôle des organisations régionales dans les conflits entre leurs membres, RFSP Vol. 21 (1971), pp. 339–361

T. Infante Caffé, La solución pacifica de las controversias. Antecedentes, balance y perspectivas del sistema interamericano (Santiago 1977), pp. 149–182

C. Honegger, Friedliche Streitbeilegung durch regionale Organisationen — Theorie und Praxis der Friedenssicherungssysteme der OAS, der Liga der Arabischen Staaten und der OAU im Vergleich (1983)

D. Uribe Vargas, La transformation du système interaméricain: tribunaux de juridiction ouverte (1984)

R. Dolzer, Enforcement of International Obligations Through Regional Arrangements; Structures and Experiences of the OAS, ZaöRV 47 (1987), 113–133

O. C. Stoetzer, The Organization of American States, (2nd ed., 1993)

V. Vaky/H. Munoz (ed.), The Future of the Organization of American States (1995)

aa) Integrated Text of the Charter as Amended by the Protocols of Buenos Aires and Cartagena de Indias, the Protocol of Amendment of Washington; and the Protocol of Amendment of Managua; June 10, 1993

CHAPTER V. PACIFIC SETTLEMENT OF DISPUTES

Art. 23   International disputes between Member States shall be submitted to the peaceful procedures set forth in this Charter.

This provision shall not be interpreted as an impairment of the rights and obligations of the Member States under Articles 34 and 35 of the Charter of the United Nations.

Art. 24   The following are peaceful procedures: direct negotiation, good offices, mediation, investigation and conciliation, judicial settlement, arbitration, and those which the parties to the dispute may especially agree upon at any time.

Art. 25   In the event that a dispute arises between two or more American States which, in the opinion of one of them, cannot be settled through the usual diplomatic channels, the parties shall agree on some other peaceful procedure that will enable them to reach a solution.

Art. 26   A special treaty will establish adequate means for the settlement of disputes and will determine pertinent procedures for each peaceful means such that no dispute between American States may remain without definitive settlement within a reasonable period of time.

CHAPTER XII. THE PERMANENT COUNCIL OF THE ORGANIZATION

Art. 79   The Permanent Council of the Organization is composed of one representative of each Member State, especially appointed by the respective Government, with the rank of ambassador. Each Government may accredit an acting representative, as well as such alternates and advisers as it considers necessary.

Art. 80   The office of Chairman of the Permanent Council shall be held by each of the representatives, in turn, following the alphabetic order in Spanish of the names of their respective countries. The office of Vice Chairman shall be filled in the same way, following reverse alphabetic order.

The Chairman and the Vice Chairman shall hold office for a term of not more than six months, which shall be determined by the statutes.

Art. 81   Within the limits of the Charter and of inter-American treaties and agreements, the Permanent Council takes cognizance of any matter referred to it by the General Assembly or the Meeting of Consultation of Ministers of Foreign Affairs.

Art. 82   The Permanent Council shall serve provisionally as the Organ of Consultation in conformity with the provisions of the special treaty on the subject.

Art. 83   The Permanent Council shall keep vigilance over the maintenance of friendly relations among the Member States, and for that purpose shall effectively assist them in the peaceful settlement of their disputes, in accordance with the following provisions.

Art. 84   In accordance with the provisions of this Charter, any party to a dispute in which none of the peaceful procedures provided for in the Charter is under way may resort to the Permanent Council to obtain its good offices. The Council, following the provisions of the preceding article, shall assist the parties and recommend the procedures it considers suitable for peaceful settlement of the dispute.

Art. 85   In the exercise of its functions and with the consent of the parties to the dispute, the Permanent Council may establish ad hoc committees.

The ad hoc committees shall have the membership and the mandate that the Permanent Council agrees upon in each individual case, with the consent of the parties to the dispute.

Art. 86   The Permanent Council may also, by such means as it deems advisable, investigate the facts in the dispute, and may do so in the territory of any of the parties, with the consent of the Government concerned.

Art. 87   If the procedure for peaceful settlement of disputes recommended by the Permanent Council or suggested by the pertinent ad hoc committee under the terms of its mandate is not accepted by one of the parties, or one of the parties declares that the procedure has not settled the dispute, the Permanent Council shall so inform the General Assembly, without prejudice to its taking steps to secure agreement between the parties or to restore relations between them.

Art. 88   The Permanent Council, in the exercise of these functions, shall take its decisions by an affirmative vote of two thirds of its members, excluding the parties to the dispute, except for such decisions as the rules of procedure provide shall be adopted by a simple majority.

Art. 89   In performing their functions with respect to the peaceful settlement of disputes, the Permanent Council and the respective ad hoc committee shall observe the provisions of the Charter and the principles and standards of international law, as well as take into account the existence of treaties in force between the parties.

Art. 90   The Permanent Council shall also:

a)   Carry out those decisions of the General Assembly or of the Meeting of Consultation of Ministers of Foreign Affairs the implementation of which has not been assigned to any other body;

b)   Watch over the observance of the standards governing the operation of the General Secretariat and, when the General Assembly is not in session, adopt provisions of a regulatory nature that enable the General Secretariat to carry out its administrative functions;

c) Act as the Preparatory Committee of the General Assembly, in accordance with the terms of Article 59 of the Charter, unless the General Assembly should decide otherwise;

d) Prepare, at the request of the Member States and with the cooperation of the appropriate organs of the Organization, draft agreements to promote and facilitate cooperation between the Organization of American States and the United Nations or between the Organization and other American agencies of recognised international standing. These draft agreements shall be submitted to the General Assembly for approval;

e) Submit recommendations to the General Assembly with regard to the functioning of the Organization and the coordination of its subsidiary organs, agencies, and committees;

f) Consider the reports of the other Councils, of the Inter-American Juridical Committee, of the Inter-American Commission on Human Rights, of the General Secretariat, of specialised agencies and conferences, and of other bodies and agencies, and present to the General Assembly any observations and recommendations it deems necessary; and

g) Perform the other functions assigned to it in the Charter.

Art. 91 The Permanent Council and the General Secretariat shall have the same seat.

CHAPTER XVI. THE INTER-AMERICAN COMMISSION ON HUMAN RIGHTS

Art. 111 There shall be an Inter-American Commission on Human Rights, whose principal function shall be to promote the observance and protection of human rights and to serve as a consultative organ of the Organization in these matters.

An inter-American convention on human rights shall determine the structure, competence, and procedure of this Commission, as well as those of other organs responsible for these matters.

bb) American Treaty on Pacific Settlement (Pact of Bogotá) of April 13, 1948

In the name of their peoples, the Governments represented at the Ninth International Conference of American States have resolved, in fulfilment of Article XXIII of the Charter of the Organization of American States, to conclude the following Treaty:

CHAPTER ONE. GENERAL OBLIGATION TO SETTLE DISPUTES BY PACIFIC MEANS

Art. I   The High Contracting Parties, solemnly reaffirming their commitments made in earlier international conventions and declarations, as well as in the Charter of the United Nations agree to refrain from the threat or the use of force, or from any other means of coercion for the settlement of their controversies, and to have recourse at all times to pacific procedures.

Art. II   The High Contracting Parties recognise the obligation to settle international controversies by regional pacific procedures before referring them to the Security Council of the United Nations.

Consequently, in the event that a controversy arises between two or more signatory states which, in the opinion of the parties, cannot be settled by direct negotiations through the usual diplomatic channels, the parties bind themselves to use the procedures established in the present Treaty, in the manner and under the conditions provided for in the following articles, or, alternatively, such special procedures as, in their opinion, will permit them to arrive at a solution.

Art. III The order of the pacific procedures established in the present Treaty does not signify that the parties may not have recourse to the procedure which they consider most appropriate in each case, or that they should use all these procedures, or that any of them have preference over others except as expressly provided.

Art. IV   Once any pacific procedure has been initiated, whether by agreement between the parties or in fulfillment of the present Treaty or a previous pact, no other procedure may be commenced until that procedure is concluded.

Art. V   The aforesaid procedures may not be applied to matters which, by their nature, are within the domestic jurisdiction of the state. If the parties are not in agreement as to whether the controversy concerns a matter of domestic jurisdiction, this preliminary question shall be submitted to decision by the International Court of Justice, at the request of any of the parties.

Art. VI   The aforesaid procedures, furthermore, may not be applied to matters already settled by arrangements between the parties, or by arbitral award or by decision of an international court, or which are governed by agreements or treaties in force on the date of the conclusion of the present Treaty.

Art. VII The High Contracting Parties bind themselves not to make diplomatic representations in order to protect their nationals, or to refer a controversy to a court of international jurisdiction for that purpose, when the said nationals have had available the means to place their case before competent domestic courts of the respective state.

Art. VIII Neither recourse to pacific means for the solution of controversies, nor the recommendation of their use, shall, in the case of an armed attack, be ground for delaying the exercise of the right of individual or collective self-defence, as provided for in the Charter of the United Nations.

CHAPTER TWO. PROCEDURES OF GOOD OFFICES AND MEDIATION

Art. IX The procedure of good offices consists in the attempt by one or more American Governments not parties to the controversy, or by one or more eminent citizens of any American State which is not a party to the controversy, to bring the parties together, so as to make it possible for them to reach an adequate solution between themselves.

Art. X Once the parties have been brought together and have resumed direct negotiations, no further action is to be taken by the states or citizens that have offered their good offices or have accepted an invitation to offer them; they may, however, by agreement between the parties, be present at the negotiations.

Art. XI The procedure of mediation consists in the submission of the controversy to one or more American Governments not parties to the controversy, or to one or more eminent citizens of any American State not a party to the controversy. In either case the mediator or mediators shall be chosen by mutual agreement between the parties.

Art. XII The functions of the mediator or mediators shall be to assist the parties in the settlement of controversies in the simplest and most direct manner, avoiding formalities and seeking and acceptable solution. No report shall be made by the mediator and, so far as he is concerned, the proceedings shall be wholly confidential.

Art. XIII In the event that the High Contracting Parties have agreed to the procedure of mediation but are unable to reach an agreement within two months on the selection of the mediator or mediators, or no solution to the controversy has been reached within five months after mediation has begun, the parties shall have recourse without delay to any one of the other procedures of peaceful settlement established in the present Treaty.

Art. XIV The High Contracting Parties may offer their mediation, either individually or jointly, but they agree not to do so while the controversy is in process of settlement by any of the other procedures established in the present Treaty.

CHAPTER THREE. PROCEDURE OF INVESTIGATION AND CONCILIATION

Art. XV The procedure of investigation and conciliation consists in the submission of the controversy to a Commission of Investigation and Conciliation, which shall be established in accordance with the provisions established in subsequent articles of the present Treaty, and which shall function within the limitations prescribed therein.

Art. XVI   The party initiating the procedure of investigation and conciliation shall request the Council of the Organisation of American States to convoke the Commission of Investigation and Conciliation. The Council for its part shall take immediate steps to convoke it.

Once the request to convoke the Commission has been received, the controversy between the parties shall immediately be suspended, and the parties shall refrain from any act that might make conciliation more difficult. To that end, at the request of one of the parties, the Council of the Organization of American States may, pending the convocation of the Commission, make appropriate recommendations to the parties.

Art. XVII   Each of the High Contracting Parties may appoint, by means of a bilateral Agreement consisting of a simple exchange of notes with each of the other signatories, two members of the Commission of Investigation and Conciliation, only one of whom may be of its own nationality. The fifth member, who shall perform the functions of chairman, shall be selected immediately by common agreement of the members thus appointed.

Any one of the contracting parties may remove members whom it has appointed, whether nationals or aliens; at the same time it shall appoint the successor. If this is not done, the removal shall be considered as not having been made. The appointments and substitutions shall be registered with the Pan American Union, which shall endeavor to ensure that the commissions maintain their full complement of five members.

Art. XVIII   Without prejudice to the provisions of the foregoing article, the Pan American Union shall draw up a permanent panel of American conciliators, to be made up as follows:

a)   Each of the High Contracting Parties shall appoint, for three year periods, two of their nationals who enjoy the highest reputation for fairness, competence and integrity;

b)   The Pan American Union shall request of the candidates notice of their formal acceptance, and it shall place on the panel of conciliators the names of the persons who so notify it;

c)   The governments may, at any time, fill vacancies occurring among their appointees; and they may reappoint their members.

Art. XIX   In the event that a controversy should arise between two or more American States that have not appointed the Commission referred to in Article XVII, the following procedure shall be observed:

a)   Each party shall designate two members from the permanent panel of American conciliators, who are not of the same nationality as the appointing party.

b)   These four members shall in turn choose a fifth member, from the permanent panel, not of the nationality of either party.

c) If, within a period of thirty days following the notification of their selection, the four members are unable to agree upon a fifth member, they shall each separately list the conciliators composing the permanent panel, in order of their preference, and upon comparison of the lists so prepared, the one who first receives a majority of votes shall be declared elected. The person so elected shall perform the duties of chairman of the Commission.

Art. XX   In convening the Commission of Investigation and Conciliation, the Council of the Organization of American States shall determine the place where the Commission shall meet. Thereafter, the Commission may determine the place or places in which it is to function, taking into account the best facilities for the performance of its work.

Art. XXI   When more than two states are involved in the same controversy, the states that hold similar points of view shall be considered as a single party. If they have different interests they shall be entitled to increase the number of conciliators in order that all parties may have equal representation. The chairman shall be elected in the manner set forth in Article XIX.

Art. XXII   It shall be the duty of the Commission of Investigation and Conciliation to clarify the points in dispute between the parties and to endeavor to bring about an agreement between them upon mutually acceptable terms. The Commission shall institute such investigations of the Acts involved in the controversy as it may deem necessary for the purpose of proposing acceptable bases of settlement.

Art. XXIII   It shall be the duty of the parties to facilitate the work of the Commission and to supply it, to the fullest extent possible, with all useful documents and information, and also to use the means at their disposal to enable the Commission to summon and hear witnesses or experts and perform other tasks in the territories of the parties, in conformity with their laws.

Art. XXIV   During the proceedings before the Commission, the parties shall be represented by plenipotentiary delegates or by agents, who shall serve as intermediaries between them and the Commission. The parties and the Commission may use the services of technical advisers and experts.

Art. XXV   The Commission shall conclude its work within a period of six months from the date of its installation; but the parties may, by mutual agreement, extend the period.

Art. XXVI   If, in the opinion of the parties, the controversy relates exclusively to questions of fact, the Commission shall limit itself to investigating such questions, and shall conclude its activities with an appropriate report.

Art. XXVII   If an agreement is reached by conciliation, the final report of the Commission shall be limited to the text of the agreement and shall be published after its transmittal to the parties, unless the parties decide otherwise. If no agreement is reached, the final report shall contain a summary of the work of the Commission; it shall be delivered to the parties, and shall be published after the expiration of six months unless the parties decide otherwise. In both cases, the final report shall be adopted by a majority vote.

Art. XXVIII   The reports and conclusions of the Commission of Investigation and Conciliation shall not be binding upon the parties, either with respect to the statement of facts or in regard to questions of law, and they shall have no other character than that of recommendations submitted for the consideration of the parties in order to facilitate a friendly settlement of the controversy.

Art. XXIX   The Commission of Investigation and Conciliation shall transmit to each of the parties, as well as to the Pan American Union, certified copies of the minutes of its proceedings. These minutes shall not be published unless the parties so decide.

Art. XXX   Each member of the Commission shall receive financial remuneration, the amount of which shall be fixed by agreement between the parties. If the parties do not agree thereon, the Council of the Organization shall determine the remuneration. Each government shall pay its own expenses and an equal share of the common expenses of the Commission, including the aforementioned remunerations.

CHAPTER FOUR. JUDICIAL PROCEDURE

Art. XXXI   In conformity with Article 36, paragraph 2, of the Statute of the International Court of Justice, the High Contracting Parties declare that they recognise, in relation to any other American State, the jurisdiction of the Court as compulsory *ipso facto*, without the necessity of any special agreement so long as the present Treaty is in force, in all disputes of a juridical nature that arise among them concerning:

a)   The interpretation of a treaty;

b)   Any question of international law;

c)   The existence of any fact which, if established, would constitute the breach of an international obligation;

d)   The nature or extent of the reparation to be made for the breach of an international obligation.

Art. XXXII   When the conciliation procedure previously established in the present Treaty or by agreement of the parties does not lead to a solution, and the said parties have not agreed upon an arbitral procedure, either of them shall be entitled to have recourse to the International Court of Justice in the manner prescribed in Article 40 of the Statute thereof. The Court shall have compulsory jurisdiction in accordance with Article 36, paragraph 1, of the said Statute.

Art. XXXIII   If the parties fail to agree as to whether the Court has jurisdiction over the controversy, the Court itself shall first decide that question.

Art. XXXIV   If the Court, for the reasons set forth in Articles V, VI and VII of this Treaty, declares itself to be without jurisdiction to hear the controversy, such controversy shall be declared ended.

Art. XXXV   If the Court for any other reason declares itself to be without jurisdiction to hear and adjudge the controversy, the High Contracting Parties obligate themselves to submit it to arbitration, in accordance with the provisions of Chapter Five of this Treaty.

Art. XXXVI   In the case of controversies submitted to the judicial procedure to which this Treaty refers, the decision shall devolve upon the full Court, or, if the parties so request, upon a special chamber in conformity with Article 26 of the Statute of the Court. The parties may agree, moreover, to have the controversy decided *ex aequo et bono.*

Art. XXXVII   The procedure to be followed by the Court shall be that established in the Statute thereof.

CHAPTER FIVE. PROCEDURE OF ARBITRATION

Art. XXXVIII   Notwithstanding the provisions of Chapter Four of this Treaty, the High Contracting Parties may, if they so agree, submit to arbitration differences of any kind, whether juridical or not, that have arisen or may arise in the future between them.

Art. XXXIX   The Arbitral Tribunal to which a controversy is to be submitted shall, in the cases contemplated in Articles XXXV and XXXVIII of the present Treaty, be constituted in the following manner, unless there exists an agreement to the contrary.

Art. XL   (1) Within a period of two months after notification of the decision of the Court in the case provided for in Article XXXV, each party shall name one arbiter of recognised competence in questions of international law and of the highest integrity, and shall transmit the designation to the Council of the Organization. At the same time, each party shall present to the Council a list of ten jurists chosen from among those on the general panel of members of the Permanent Court of Arbitration of The Hague who do not belong to its national group and who are willing to be members of the Arbitral Tribunal.

(2) The Council of the Organization shall, within the month following the presentation of the lists, proceed to establish the Arbitral Tribunal in the following manner:

a)   If the lists presented by the parties contain three names in common, such persons, together with the two directly named by the parties, shall constitute the Arbitral Tribunal;

b)   In case these lists contain more than three names in common, the three arbiters needed to complete the Tribunal shall be selected by lot;

c)   In the circumstances envisaged in the two preceding clauses, the five arbiters designated shall choose one of their number as presiding officer;

d)   If the lists contain only two names in common, such candidates and the two arbiters directly selected by the parties shall by common agreement choose the fifth arbiter, who shall preside over the Tribunal. The choice shall devolve upon a jurist on the aforesaid general panel of the Permanent Court of Arbitration of The Hague who has not been included in the lists drawn up by the parties;

e)   If the lists contain only one name in common, that person shall be a member of the Tribunal, and another name shall be chosen by lot from among the eighteen jurists remaining on the above-mentioned lists. The presiding officer shall be elected in accordance with the procedure established in the preceding clause;

f)   If the list contain no names in common, one arbiter shall be chosen by lot from each of the lists; and the fifth arbiter, who shall act as presiding officer, shall be chosen in the manner previously indicated;

g)   If the four arbiters cannot agree upon a fifth arbiter within one month after the Council of the Organization has notified them of their appointment, each of them shall separately arrange the list of jurists in the order of their preference and, after comparison of the lists so formed, the person who first obtains a majority vote shall be declared elected.

Art. XLI   The parties may by mutual agreement establish the Tribunal in the manner they deem most appropriate; they may even select a single arbiter, designating in such case a chief of state, an eminent jurist, or any court of justice in which the parties have mutual confidence.

Art. XLII   When more than two states are involved in the same controversy, the states defending the same interests shall be considered as a single party. If they have opposing interests they shall have the right to increase the number of arbiters so that all parties may have equal representation. The presiding officer shall be selected by the method established in Article XL.

Art. XLIII   The parties shall in each case draw up a special agreement clearly defining the specific matter that is the subject of the controversy, the seat of the Tribunal, the rules of procedure to be observed, the period within which the award is to be handed down, and such other conditions as they may agree upon among themselves.

If the special agreement cannot be drawn up within three months after the date of the installation of the Tribunal, it shall be drawn up by the International Court of Justice through summary procedure, and shall be binding upon the parties.

Art. XLIV   The parties may be represented before the Arbitral Tribunal by such persons as they may designate.

Art.
XLV

If one of the parties fails to designate its arbiter and present its list of candidates within the period provided for in Article XL, the other party shall have the right to request the Council of the Organization to establish the Arbitral Tribunal. The Council shall immediately urge the delinquent party to fulfill its obligations within an additional period of fifteen days, after which time the Council itself shall establish the Tribunal in the following manner:

a) It shall select a name by lot from the list presented by the petitioning party.

b) It shall choose, by absolute majority vote, two jurists from the general panel of the Permanent Court of Arbitration of The Hague who do not belong to the national group of any of the parties.

c) The three persons so designated, together with the one directly chosen by the petitioning party, shall select the fifth arbiter, who shall act as presiding officer, in the manner provided for in Article XL.

d) Once the Tribunal is installed, the procedure established in Article XLIII shall be followed.

Art.
XLVI

The award shall be accompanied by a supporting opinion, shall be adopted by a majority vote, and shall be published after notification thereof has been given to the parties. The dissenting arbiter or arbiters shall have the right to state the grounds for their dissent.

The award, once it is duly handed down and made known to the parties, shall settle the controversy definitively, shall not be subject to appeal, and shall be carried out immediately.

Art.
XLVII

Any differences that arise in regard to the interpretation or execution of the award shall be submitted to the decision of the Arbitral Tribunal that rendered the award.

Art.
XLVIII

Within a year after notification thereof, the award shall be subject to review by the same Tribunal at the request of one of the parties, provided a previously existing fact is discovered unknown to the Tribunal and to the party requesting the review, and provided the Tribunal is of the opinion that such fact might have a decisive influence on the award.

Art.
XLIX

Every member of the Tribunal shall receive financial remuneration, the amount of which shall be fixed by agreement between the parties. If the parties do not agree on the amount, the Council of the Organization shall determine the remuneration. Each Government shall pay its own expenses and an equal share of the common expenses of the Tribunal, including the aforementioned remunerations.

CHAPTER SIX. FULFILLMENT OF DECISIONS

Art. L

If one of the High Contracting Parties should fail to carry out the obligations imposed upon it by a decision of the International Court of Justice or by an arbitral award, the other party or parties concerned shall, before resorting to the Security Council of the United Nations, propose a Meeting of Consultation of Ministers of Foreign Affairs to agree upon appropriate measures to ensure the fulfilment of the judicial decision or arbitral award.

CHAPTER SEVEN. ADVISORY OPINIONS

Art. LI   The parties concerned in the solution of a controversy may, by agreement, petition the General Assembly or the Security Council of the United Nations to request an advisory opinion of the International Court of Justice on any juridical question.

The petition shall be made through the Council of the Organization of American States.

CHAPTER EIGHT. FINAL PROVISIONS

Art. LII   The present Treaty shall be ratified by the High Contracting Parties in accordance with their constitutional procedures. The original instrument shall be deposited in the Pan American Union, which shall transmit an authentic certified copy to each Government for the purpose of ratification. The instruments of ratification shall be deposited in the archives of the Pan American Union, which shall notify the signatory governments of the deposit. Such notification shall be considered as an exchange of ratifications.

Art. LIII   This Treaty shall come into effect between the High Contracting Parties in the order in which they deposit their respective ratifications.

Art. LIV   Any American State which is not a signatory to the present Treaty, or which has made reservations thereto, may adhere to it, or may withdraw its reservations in whole or in part, by transmitting an official instrument to the Pan American Union, which shall notify the other High Contracting Parties in the manner herein established.

Art. LV   Should any of the High Contracting Parties make reservations concerning the present Treaty, such reservations shall, with respect to the state that makes them, apply to all signatory states on the basis of reciprocity.

Art. LVI   The present Treaty shall remain in force indefinitely, but may be denounced upon one year's notice, at the end of which period it shall cease to be in force with respect to the state denouncing it, but shall continue in force for the remaining signatories. The denunciation shall be addressed to the Pan American Union, which shall transmit it to the other Contracting Parties.

The denunciation shall have no effect with respect to pending procedures initiated prior to the transmission of the particular notification.

Art. LVII   The present Treaty shall be registered with the Secretariat of the United Nations through the Pan American Union.

Art.
LVIII
As this Treaty comes into effect through the successive ratifications of the High Contracting Parties, the following treaties, conventions and protocols shall cease to be in force with respect to such parties:

Treaty to Avoid or Prevent Conflicts between the American States, of May 3, 1923;

General Convention of Inter-American Conciliation, of January 5, 1929;

General Treaty of Inter-American Arbitration and Additional Protocol of Progressive Arbitration, of January 5, 1929;

Additional Protocol to the General Convention of Inter-American Conciliation, of December 26, 1933;

Anti-War Treaty of Non-Aggression and Conciliation, of October 10, 1933;

Convention to Coordinate, Extend and Assure the Fulfillment of the Existing Treaties between the American States, of December 23, 1936;

Inter-American Treaty on Good Offices and Mediation, of December 23, 1936;

Treaty on the Prevention of Controversies, of December 23, 1936.

Art. LIX The provisions of the foregoing Article shall not apply to procedures already initiated or agreed upon in accordance with any of the above-mentioned international instruments.

Art. LX The present Treaty shall be called the "Pact of Bogotá."

In Witness whereof, the undersigned Plenipotentiaries, having deposited their full powers, found to be in good and due form, sign the present Treaty, in the name of their respective Governments, on the dates appearing below their signatures.

Done at the City of Bogotá, in four texts, in the English, French, Portuguese and Spanish languages respectively, on the thirtieth day of April, nineteen hundred forty-eight.

c) Central American Integration System (SICA)

The five States, Costa Rica, El Salvador, Guatemala, Honduras and Nicaragua, which concluded the 1907 Convention creating the Central American Court of Justice found themselves unable to prolong the life of the Convention or to create a new Court. However, in 1962, when they established the Charter of the Organization of Central American States (ODECA) which was designed to strengthen economic and social progress, they provided for a Central American Court of Justice. Despite this step, the Charter paid only little attention to the Court.

According to Arts. 14–16 the Court was composed of the President of the Judicial Branch of each of the member States; its jurisdiction or functions were limited to resolving conflicts of a legal nature which member States agreed to submit to it and to the preparation and rendering of opinions on proposals for the unification of Central American legislation when so requested by two other organs, the Conference of Foreign Ministers and the Executive Council. The Court thus represented a wide departure from the 1907 Central American Court of Justice, first, because it was not a permanent court, and second, because its jurisdiction was much different. The Court received only little attention. It met only once to approve its regulations, but does not seem to have elaborated its statute or rules, although information on this point is not clear.

The ODECA basically failed to achieve its goals, namely the creation of a political and economic community within Central America. Therefore the five original member States of ODECA and Panama signed on December 13, 1991 the Protocol of Tegucigalpa, which entered into force on July 23, 1992. This Protocol reformed the Charter of the ODECA by transformation of the latter into the Central American Integration System (Sistema de la Integración Centroamericano, SICA). The SICA constitutes a new institutional framework for the regional integration of Central America. The organs of SICA are the Meeting of the Presidents, the Council of Ministers, an Executive Committee and a permanent Secretariat. In addition there are other institutions which take part in the System, namely the Meeting of the Vice-Presidents, the Central American Parliament, a Consultative Committee and the Central American Court of Justice with jurisdiction over the interpretation of the Protocol and the acts of SICA's organs. A Statute regulates the Court's composition and procedure.

Texts

Charter of the ODECA

Inter-American Institute of International Legal Studies, Instruments of Economic Integration in Latin America and the Caribbean, Vol. 2 (1975) 561–566

Inter-American Institute of International Legal Studies, Derecho Comunitario Centroamericano (1968)

UNTS Vol. 552, pp. 15 et seq. (Spanish, English, French)

AJIL Vol. 58 (1964), pp. 134 et seq.

Protocol of Tegucigalpa, Rules of the Central American Court of Justice and
    Internal Rules of Procedure
    El tribunal centroamericano: La Corte centroamericana de justicia, Universidad
    Nacional Autónoma de Honduras, Colección cuadernos juridicos no. 21 (1995),
    159–175; 197–207; 219–234
Statute of the Court of the SICA
    ILM 34 (1995), 921 et seq.

Bibliographical notes

Derecho Comunitario Centroamericano (1968), Instituto Interamericano de
    Estudios Juridicos Internacionales
V. Gessner, Der Richter im Staatenkonflikt (1969)
F. Villagrán-Kramer, Integración Economica Centroamericana (1970), p. 119
M. Fuentes Irurozqui, Centro América y la Organización de Estados Centro
    Americanos (ODECA), Revista de Política Internacional 1976 No. 146, pp. 53–
    69
El tribunal centroamericano: La Corte centroamericana de justicia, Universidad
    Nacional Autónoma de Honduras, Colección cuadernos juridicos no. 21 (1995)
K.R. Simmonds/H.-K. Ress, Organization of Central American States, in: R. Bern-
    hardt (ed.) EPIL, Vol. III (1997), 823–824

aa) Protocol of Tegucigalpa Reforming the Charter of the Organization of Central American States (ODECA) Constituting the Central American Integration System (SICA) of December 13, 1991

Art. 12　　Para la realización de los fines del SISTEMA DE LA INTEGRACIÓN CENTROAMERICANA se establecen los siguientes Organos:

La Reunión de Presidentes;

El Consejo de Ministros,

El Comité Ejecutivo, y

La Secretaría General.

Forman parte de este Sistema:

La Reunión de Vicepresidentes y Designados a la Presidencia de la República, que será un Organo de Asesoría y Consulta. Dicha Reunión se realizará ordinariamente cada semestre y extraordinariamente, cuando los Vicepresidentes así lo deseen. Sus resoluciones serán adoptadas por consenso.

Sin perjuicio de lo establecido en el artículo 4 de las Disposiciones Transitorias, el Parlamento Centroamericano (PARLACEN) como Organo de Planteamiento, Análisis y Recomendación, cuyas funciones y atribuciones son las que establecen su Tratado Constitutivo y Protocolos vigentes.

La Corte Centroamericana de Justicia, que garantizará el respeto del derecho, en la interpretación y ejecución del presente Protocolo y sus instrumentos complementarios o actos derivados del mismo. La integración, funcionamiento y atribuciones de La Corte Centroamericana de Justicia deberán regularse en el Estatuto de la misma, el cual deberá ser negociado y suscrito por los Estados Miembros dentro de los noventa días posteriores a la entrada en vigor del presente Protocolo.

El Comité Consultivo estará integrado por los sectores empresarial, laboral, académico y otras principales fuerzas vivas del Istmo Centroamericano representativas de los sectores económicos, sociales y culturales, comprometidos con el esfuerzo de integración ístmica.

Este Comité tendrá como función asesorar a la Secretaría General sobre la política de la organización en el desarrollo de los programas que lleva a cabo.

bb) Statute of the Central American Court of Justice

CHAPTER I. ATTRIBUTES AND ORGANIZATION

Art. 1　　The Central American Court of Justice, established through Article 12 of the "Protocol of Tegucigalpa to the Charter of the Organization of Central American States (ODECA)", is established and shall function according to the provisions of the present Statute and the ordinances, rules and resolutions issued by the Court itself.

The Central American Court of Justice is the principal and permanent judicial organ of the "Central American Integration System". It shall have mandatory regional jurisdiction and competence over all the Member States.

In the text of this Convention, the Central American Court of Justice shall also be referred to as "the Court".

Art. 2   The Court shall guarantee respect for the law, both in the interpretation and execution of the "Protocol of Tegucigalpa of Reforms to the Charter of the Organization of Central American States (ODECA)", and of its related instruments and acts.

Art. 3   The Court shall have its own competence and jurisdiction. It shall have the authority to render judgments at the request of a party and to resolve issues with the effect of res judicata. The Court's doctrine shall have a unifying effect on all the states, organs and organisations that form or participate in the "Central American Integration System", and on issues of private law.

Art. 4   The Court shall issue procedural ordinances and general rules, whether substantive or otherwise, through which the Court shall determine the process and manner by which it will exercise its functions. However, these ordinances and rules may not contain norms that are in conflict with the present Statute.

Art. 5   The goal of the procedures anticipated by this Statute and of the procedures that will be established in the rules and ordinances shall be to safeguard the aims and principles of the "Central American Integration System", the availability of rights, the equality of parties and the guarantee of due process.

Art. 6   The Court embodies the national conscience of Central America and is considered the depositary and the guardian of the values that form the Central American nationality. By virtue of this role, the Magistrates of the Court shall not permit the interest of the states that nominated them to interfere with the exercise of their functions.

Art. 7   The Court shall exercise its functions in plenary sessions. Nonetheless it shall have authority to separate or distribute its competence and jurisdiction to Tribunals or Chambers in order to hear controversies that may be submitted for decision. These Tribunals or Chambers shall issue their judgments or resolutions as courts of sole resort.

The Court shall be headquartered in the city of Managua, Republic of Nicaragua, where it shall function indefinitely. Nevertheless, it may hold sessions in the territory of any of the Member States.

Art. 8   The Court shall be composed of one or more Magistrates from each state. Each Magistrate shall have an alternate who must possess the same qualifications as the Magistrate.

Art. 9   The Magistrates must be individuals who are held in high moral esteem and must possess the qualifications required for holding the highest judicial positions in their country. The age requirement for jurists of notorious competence may be waived by the court of their respective country.

Art. 10   The Magistrates and their alternates shall be elected by the supreme courts of justice of the Member States.

Art. 11   The Magistrates of the Court shall perform their duties for a period of ten years and may be reelected. Those Magistrates elected for a stated period shall continue to exercise their duties until replaced by their successor.

Art. 12   The Magistrates of the Court and their alternates may only be removed for the causes and pursuant to the procedures established in the rules, provided that the decision to remove is approved by a two-thirds affirmative vote of the remaining Magistrates.

Art. 13   In the event that a Magistrate is temporarily absent from the Court, the President will call the respective alternate who will perform the duties of Magistrate during his or her absence. If the absence is permanent, the President shall bring the matter to the attention of the respective organ or judicial authority so that it may proceed to nominate a new Magistrate for a full term. The foregoing shall not interfere with the alternate's exercise of his or her functions, until the new Magistrate assumes his or her post.

Art. 14   In the exercise of their functions the Magistrates shall enjoy complete independence — including independence from the states of which they are nationals — and they shall exercise their functions impartially.

Art. 15   The Magistrates may not perform other professional activities, whether remunerated or not, except for those of an academic nature. They shall also abstain from engaging in any activities that are incompatible with the character and dignity of their post.

Art. 16   The Court shall have a president and a vice-president, who will perform their functions for one year. The Presidency will be held successively by one of the Magistrates in alphabetical order according to the names of their respective states. The Vice-President shall be elected by the Court according to the Court's rules and must be of a different nationality than that of the President.

Art. 17   In the event that the President is temporarily absent, the Presidency shall be held by the Vice-President. If the absence is permanent, the Vice-President shall continue to exercise the presidential functions for the remainder of the President's term.

Art. 18   The President shall be the representative of the Court. Such representation shall be exercised by the Vice-President in the event referred to in the previous article. In the absence of both the President and the Vice-President, such representation may be delegated to another Magistrate.

Art. 19 The Court shall name its Secretary General and may arrange for the nomination of the other officials when necessary. These officials shall exercise discretion over the cases that are discussed before the Court.

Art. 20 The rules of the court shall establish the qualifications that the Secretary General and other officials must possess.

Art. 21 The Magistrates of the Court and the Secretary General shall reside in the country where the Court is headquartered. The Magistrates of the Court must participate in the exercise of the Court's functions throughout the duration of their respective terms. In the event that a Magistrate is prevented from participating, he or she must inform the President or whomever is performing the functions of the President.

CHAPTER II. COMPETENCE AND AUTHORITY

Art. 22 The Court's competence includes the following:

a) To hear, at the request of any of the Member States, the controversies that arise among them. Excepted are frontier, territorial or maritime controversies, which may not be heard without the consent of all parties concerned.

Prior to commencement of trial, the respective chanceries must seek to obtain an agreement on the issues, but may also attempt to obtain an agreement during a later stage in the proceedings.

b) To hear actions that relate to the nullification or nonfulfillment of the agreements of the organisms of the Central American Integration System.

c) To hear, at the request of any interested party, any matter related to the legal, regulatory or administrative provisions or any other type of rules prescribed by a state, when such provisions or rules affect the conventions, treaties or any other norm of the Law of Central American Integration, or the agreements or resolutions of its organs or organisms;

ch) To hear and issue verdicts, if it so decides, relating to matters which the parties have requested the Court to hear as a competent tribunal. The Court may also hear, decide, and resolve disputes *ex aequo et bono*, if the interested parties so agree;

d) To act as Tribunal of Permanent Consultation to the supreme courts of justice of the Member States;

e) To act as a consultant to the organs and organisms of the Central American Integration System in the interpretation and application of the "Protocol of Tegucigalpa of Reforms to the Charter of the Organization of Central American States (ODECA)" and of the complementary instruments and acts derived from the same;

f) To hear and resolve, at the request of aggrieved parties, conflicts that may arise among the fundamental powers or organs of the Member States, and disputes which may arise when judicial verdicts are not respected;

g) To hear matters that are submitted directly by individuals who are affected by the agreements of the organs or organisms of the Central American Integration System;

h) To hear controversies or questions that may arise between a Central American state and another non-Central American state when such controversies are submitted to the Court by mutual agreement;

i) To undertake comparative studies of Central American legislation in order to achieve the harmonization of laws and to complete drafts of uniform laws so as to achieve the legal integration of Central America.

This task shall be performed either directly or by means of a specialized institute or organism such as the Central American Judicial Council or the Central American Institute of the Law of Integration;

j) To hear on appeal, as court of last resort, the administrative resolutions prescribed by the organs or organisms of the Central American Integration System which directly affect a member of the staff of the same and whose reinstatement has been denied.

k) To resolve all prejudicial consultations as requested by any judge or judicial tribunal which is hearing a pending case or which wants to obtain a uniform application or interpretation of the norms that conform to the legal principles of the "Central American Integration System" created by the "Protocol of Tegucigalpa", its complementary instruments or acts derived from the same.

Art. 23 The Member States shall be permitted to formulate and propose questions to the Court which relate to the interpretation of any treaty or international convention in force, or to conflicts between treaties, or between treaties and the national laws of each Member State.

Art. 24 Questions decided by the Court pursuant to this Statute, rules or regulations which involve the Central American Integration System, shall be binding on all the states that comprise the system.

Art. 25 The Court's competence does not extend to the area of human rights which falls under the exclusive jurisdiction of the Inter-American Court of Human Rights.

Art. 26 The Member States are obligated to grant to the Court all necessary facilities for the adequate performance of its functions.

Art. 27 The Court and its Magistrates shall enjoy in all the Member States the immunities recognized by international custom and by the Vienna Convention on Diplomatic Relations with respect to the inviolability of its archives and official correspondence and with respect to all that relates to its jurisdiction, both civil and penal.

Art. 28   The Court shall possess a legal personality and shall enjoy, in all the Member States, the privileges and immunities that it is due as an organ of the Central American Integration System. These privileges and immunities shall ensure the independent exercise of the Court's functions and the realisation of the objectives for which it was created. The Magistrates, the Secretary General of the Court and the officials designated by the Court as international employees shall enjoy the immunities and privileges due to their posts. To that end, the Magistrates shall possess a rank equivalent to that of Ambassadors and the other officials shall possess a rank as established by mutual agreement of the Court and the Government of the country where the Court is headquartered.

Art. 29   The Magistrates shall be immune from all responsibility associated with the execution of acts and the issuance of opinions in the fulfillment of their official functions and shall continue to enjoy such immunity after having ceased performing these functions.

Art. 30   Consistent with the norms heretofore established, the Court possesses the authority to determine its competence in each case by interpreting the treaties and conventions pertinent to the matter at hand and by applying the principles of both the Law of Integration and International Law.

Art. 31   The Court shall be authorised to prescribe pretrial or protective measures which it considers advisable to safeguard the rights of the parties from the moment that a claim is made against one or more states, organs or organisms of the Central American Integration System until a definitive verdict is issued. This authority shall permit the Court to stabilize the situation in which the contending parties are to remain, so as not to aggravate the harm and so as to maintain matters in the same state pending resolution.

Art. 32   The rules of evidence will be established in the Court's rules. The court shall be able to request or accept evidence which it considers useful to define, establish or uphold the rights that the parties hold or claim.

Art. 33   In the area of the admission and use of evidence, the orders issued by the Court shall not require ratification or approval prior to their execution, and must be executed by the Court's officials, judicial or administrative authorities, or by whomever receives an order from the Court.

Art. 34   The documents from any country, regardless of their form, which are presented as evidence in trials, need only be authenticated in the place of origin by competent officials of that country or by a notary in the exercise of his or her functions. The rules of evidence to be observed in any one of the territories of the Member States shall comply with the rules prescribed by the Court.

THE VERDICT AND ITS EXECUTION

Art. 35   The Court shall evaluate the evidence as a whole, using its judgment as the evaluating criteria.

Art. 36   All of the Court's decisions and those of its Tribunals and Chambers shall be reached by a vote of at least an absolute majority of the members of the relevant decision-making body. The dissenting or concurring Magistrate or Magistrates shall have the right to have their opinion set apart in writing. The resolution shall set forth the grounds on which it is based, shall mention the names of the Magistrates who have taken part in it and shall contain their signatures in the absence of justification for not including their signatures.

Art. 37   The judgment shall resolve every point in dispute. However, the judgment shall only be binding upon the parties to the dispute.

Art. 38   The judgement shall be definitive and shall not be appealable; nevertheless the Court may, either on its own initiative or at the request of a party, clarify or expand the reasoning of the decision within thirty days following the decision.

Art. 39   The interlocutory decisions and definitive sentences prescribed by the Court shall not be appealable. All such decisions are binding upon the Member States and upon the organs or organisms of the Central American Integration System and upon natural and legal persons, and shall be executed as would a resolution, award or sentence of a national court. Moreover, the certification issued by the Secretary General of the Court shall suffice for such execution. In the event that the Court's judgments or resolutions are not enforced by a Member State, the Court shall inform the other Member States, so that they may ensure the execution through appropriate means.

Art. 40   In cases submitted to the jurisdictional ambit of the Court, the Court may not avoid passing judgment by alleging silence or uncertainty in the Convention or Treaties alleged to be applicable.

CHAPTER VI. GENERAL PROVISIONS, TRANSITORY PROVISIONS AND DATES OF EFFECTIVENESS

Art. 41   The Member States shall bear the expenses for the Court's general budget equally.

Art. 42   In the budget of each Member State a specific item must provide for the Court's budget. Each Member State shall pay its contribution within the three months before the beginning of the calendar year.

Art. 43   In order to issue and reform rules and regulations that govern proceedings, the affirmative votes of the majority of the Magistrates shall be required. These modifications shall have no retroactive effect.

Art. 44   Each Magistrate of the Court shall earn a salary and shall have a right to be compensated for incidental expenses, travel expenses and expenses associated with food and lodging. Magistrates who have completed their terms shall be entitled to a retirement pension in an amount and subject to conditions established by the Court.

Art. 45   While the Court is not yet composed or established, the application, interpretation and execution of the provisions contained in the present Statute will be the responsibility of the Central American Judicial Council, made up of the Presidents of the supreme courts of justice of the Member States. The Central American Judicial Council shall also be responsible for undertaking all appropriate measures and whatever steps that are necessary to ensure the prompt installation and operation of the Court.

Art. 46   The Central American Judicial Council shall, in addition to those duties already stated, fix the date of solemn establishment and commencement of the functions of the Central American Court of Justice; draft its rules and regulations, which are to govern proceedings and budgets; and fix the initial number of Magistrates who will compose the Court.

Art. 47   Before the Court begins its functions, the Member States must endow the Court with sufficient financial resources so that it may adequately carry out its critical and lofty functions.

Art. 48   This Statute does not permit any reservations. Its duration shall be indefinite and it shall enter into force eight days after the date on which the Member States, who have ratified the Protocol of Tegucigalpa to the Charter of the Organization of Central American States (ODECA), which constitutes the "Central American Integration System", have deposited the appropriate documents pursuant to what is established in Article 36 of the aforementioned Protocol. Those Member States which, on the day of entry into force of the Statute, have yet to ratify the aforementioned Protocol, may participate in the composition of the Court prior to the ratification and deposit of instruments in accordance with the procedures stated in those instruments.

cc) Reglamento de la Corte Centroamericana de Justicia

CAPÍTULO I. INTEGRACIÓN DE LA CORTE Y SUS FUNCIONES ADMINISTRATIVAS

Art. 1   La Corte Centroamericana de Justicia tiene su Sede en la ciudad de Managua, República de Nicaragua; está integrada por Magistrados Titulares y Suplentes y podrá dividirse en Salas o Cámaras, de acuerdo con lo que establece su Estatuto. Tendrá un Presidente y un Vicepresidente, los cuales ejercerán sus cargos por un año.

Art. 2   El período de los Magistrados Titulares y Suplentes es de diez años y se contará a partir de la fecha de su toma de posesión.

Art. 3   A más tardar treinta días después de su designación, el Magistrado prestará ante el Consejo Judicial Centroamericano, el juramento de que ejercerá sus funciones a conciencia y con justicia, absoluta imparcialidad e independencia, que guardará el secreto de las deliberaciones de La Corte y que cumplirá con los deberes inherentes a su cargo.

Posteriormente el Presidente de La Corte o quien haga sus veces, pondrá en posesión del cargo al Magistrado, quien entrará en ese momento en el ejercicio de sus funciones. De esa sesión se levantará un acta que deberá ser firmada por el Presidente, el Secretario y el Magistrado.

Art. 4   Los Magistrados Titulares y Suplentes gozan en todos los Estados Miembros de las mismas inmunidades prerrogativas y privilegios.

Para los efectos del artículo 12 del Estatuto, los Magistrados Titulares y Suplentes sólo podrán ser removidos de su cargo, mediante decisión adoptada por el voto afirmativo de los dos tercios de los otros Magistrados, y únicamente cuando hayan incurrido en falta grave.

Se consideran faltas graves:

a)   La notoria mala conducta;

b)   Actuar en forma indebida con el carácter y dignidad de su cargo;

c)   Contrariar lo preceptuado en el artículo 15 del Estatuto ejerciendo la profesión de Abogado o desempeñando cargos que le impidan cumplir adecuadamente sus funciones; y

d)   Por violación del juramento a que se refiere el artículo anterior.

No obstante, a los Magistrados Suplentes que no estén desempeñando el cargo de titular y a los Titulares con permiso para desempeñar otro trabajo en sus respectivos países u organismos internacionales, no les será aplicable el literal c) del presente artículo.

Art. 5   Los Suplentes, serán llamados por el Presidente y reemplazarán al Magistrado Titular en los siguientes casos:

a)   Si el Magistrado Titular, sin justificación alguna, no se presentare a la juramentación o a la toma de posesión;

b)   Por fallecimiento, ausencia indefinida, renuncia, remoción o vacancia del cargo, de conformidad a lo establecido en el artículo 13 del Estatuto de La Corte;

c)   Por permisos mayores de un mes; y

d)   En los casos de impedimento o recusación declarados con lugar y solamente respecto de la audiencia y sentencia del proceso correspondiente.

El Magistrado Suplente que fuere llamado, se le dará posesión de su cargo y entrará de inmediato al ejercicio de sus funciones.

Art. 6   Los Magistrados Titulares de La Corte, están obligados a residir y permanecer en la Sede del Tribunal, excepto cuando tengan que ausentarse por razón del servicio, vacaciones, licencias, permisos o durante días feriados.

Los Magistrados Titulares y los Suplentes, en su caso, están obligados a asistir a su despacho todos los días hábiles y a permanecer en él, desempeñando sus funciones durante cinco horas diarias como mínimo.

Los Magistrados tienen la obligación de asistir a sesión del Pleno de La Corte y a permanecer durante su desarrollo, salvo causa o motivo justificable.

Art. 7 Los Magistrados en funciones son iguales, y su precedencia, después del Presidente y del Vicepresidente, se determinará por una de estas causas, en el orden en que se exponen:

1. La fecha de su nombramiento;

2. La de toma de posesión;

3. La de su ingreso en La Corte; y

4. La del Título Profesional.

Los Titulares precederán a los Suplentes.

Art. 8 En caso de ausencia temporal del Presidente, la Presidencia será ejercida por el Vicepresidente. Si ésta fuere definitiva, el Vicepresidente ejercerá por el resto del período de su predecesor.

Si la ausencia del Presidente y del Vicepresidente fueren simultáneas y definitivas, se elegirán sus respectivos sustitutos de la misma nacionalidad de los ausentes, para que concluyan el período de sus predecesores.

Art. 9 Corresponde a La Corte ejercer, además de la función jurisdiccional que le señala su Estatuto, las funciones administrativas, disciplinarias y económicas sobre todas sus dependencies.

Art. 10 La Corte, a solicitud de cualesquiera de los Estados Miembros, podrá levantar la inmunidad a que se refieren los artículos 27, 28 y 29 del Estatuto, en el caso de incurrir en faltas graves, por el voto afirmativo de los dos tercios de los otros Magistrados. En este caso, y en sesión plenaria, una vez examinados los antecedentes, La Corte, previa audiencia del Magistrado infractor, dictará resolución motivada.

Si la inmunidad fuere levantada, y el Magistrado es sometido a juicio, éste habrá de desarrollarse ante la jurisdicción competente para juzgar a los más altos Magistrados del Estado Miembro donde se tramite la causa; y en tal caso, si la sentencia fuere condenatoria, ésta determinará la vacancia del cargo.

Art. 11 Cuando en el ejercicio de sus funciones un Magistrado incurriere en alguna de las faltas graves contempladas en el artículo 4, cualquiera de los Estados Miembros podrá formular la solicitud, por medio de su Corte Suprema de Justicia.

Art. 12 En el ejercicio de la función disciplinaria, La Corte podrá corregir por si misma las faltas o abusos que cometieren los Magistrados, funcionarios o empleados, en el desempeño de sus cargos.

Art. 13   En el ejercicio de las funciones expresadas en el artículo anterior La Corte podrá:

        a)   Amonestar o censurar la conducta inadecuada de Magistrados, funcionarios o empleados;

        b)   Imponer multas correctivas a funcionarios y empleados, no inferiores a cinco días de sueldo, ni superiores a treinta días;

        c)   Decretar la suspensión del cargo a funcionarios y empleados, en su caso, hasta por tres meses, sin derecho a remuneración, previa información sumaria;

        d)   Destituir a los funcionarios o empleados de su nombramiento, por mala conducta o por faltas graves en el ejercicio de sus funciones, mediante información sumaria y audiencia del funcionario o empleado a quien se deba destituir.

Si la falta o abuso fuere de un Magistrado de La Corte, ésta decidirá con el voto de dos tercios de sus integrantes, excluyendo la participación y el voto del inculpado, si ha o no lugar a la formación del expediente y, en su caso, impondrá la sanción disciplinaria correspondiente.

CAPÍTULO II. DE LA CORTE PLENA, SU INTEGRACIÓN Y PROCEDIMIENTO DE LAS SESIONES

Art. 14   Para que La Corte pueda celebrar válidamente sesiones, se requiere que estén presentes la mitad más uno de los Magistrados en funciones.

Art. 15   La Corte celebrará sesiones los días que fueren necesarios para la marcha expedita de los asuntos, debiéndose realizar una sesión semanal, por lo menos.

Art. 16   El Magistrado Presidente de La Corte dirigirá las sesiones en el siguiente orden: Declarará abierta la sesión y el Secretario dará lectura al Acta de la sesión anterior, la que inmediatamente después se pondrá a discusión antes de ser aprobada, a efecto de que se hagan las correcciones o rectificaciones si procedieren.

Aprobada el Acta el Secretario dará cuenta de la correspondencia recibida y despachada, de las solicitudes presentadas y de los asuntos pendientes. En lo que respecta a la discusión de las sentencias, se estará a lo que dispongan el Estatuto, las Ordenanzas y los Reglamentos.

CAPÍTULO III. DEL PRESIDENTE Y DEL VICEPRESIDENTE DE LA CORTE

Art. 17   La Presidencia será ejercida sucesivamente por uno de los Magistrados Titulares en el orden alfabético de los nombres de sus respectivos Estados.

En caso de incorporación y toma de posesión de Magistrados de Estados Miembros que se integren a La Corte, les corresponderá el ejercicio de la Presidencia respetando el orden alfabético, después que se haya agotado el orden de los integrantes iniciales que determinaron su vigencia.

Art. 18 Al Presidente le corresponden las siguientes atribuciones:

a) Presidir La Corte Centroamericana de Justicia y representarla en los actos oficiales y públicos;

b) Ordenar la tramitación de los asuntos que deba resolver La Corte;

c) Anticipar o prorrogar las horas de despacho cuando así lo requieran asuntos graves o urgentes y convocar a sesiones extraordinarias, cuando las circunstancias así lo exijan;

d) Impartir las órdenes convenientes para integrar el Tribunal, cuando por impedimento, licencia o cualquier otro motivo, faltare alguno de los Magistrados Titulares;

e) Velar por el mantenimiento del orden dentro del Tribunal, adoptando las medidas que juzgue necesarias para ello;

f) Dirigir los debates concediendo el uso de la palabra a los Magistrados, en el orden que la hubieren solicitado;

g) Fijar los puntos o cuestiones que hayan de discutirse y las proposiciones sobre las cuales haya de recaer la votación;

h) Poner a votación las materias que hayan sido discutidas;

i) Dirigir la publicación de la Gaceta con la cooperación de los demás Magistrados;

j) Nombrar Comisiones permanentes integradas por tres Magistrados que respectivamente atiendan el desarrollo físico de las instalaciones, los asuntos jurídicos y la eficiencia administrativa; y las especiales que fueren necesarias;

k) Elaborar dentro de los dos meses siguientes a la expiración del año económico, el informe de las labores realizadas en dicho año, incluyendo datos estadísticos;

l) Ejercer la más estricta vigilancia sobre la ejecución del Presupuesto;

ll) Ejercer, a través de las dependencias correspondientes, la vigilancia judicial y la función disciplinaria que le confieren el Estatuto, Ordenanzas y Reglamentos;

m) Determinar el orden en que deban verse los asuntos sujetos al conocimiento del Tribunal; y

n) Ejercer cualquier otra atribución que le corresponda conforme al Estatuto, Ordenanzas y Reglamentos.

Art. 19 El Vicepresidente se elegirá por La Corte, debiendo ser siempre un titular de distinta nacionalidad a la del Presidente.

Art. 20 El Vicepresidente ejercerá las facultades que se le señalan en el presente Reglamento y las que le delegue el Presidente.

CAPÍTULO IV. DE LA SECRETARÍA GENERAL DE LA CORTE

Art. 21 La Secretaría General es el órgano de comunicación de La Corte.

Art. 22   La Corte nombrará su Secretario General, quien deberá rendir promesa de reserva de los casos que allí se ventilen. Este será el Jefe inmediato de las Oficinas de la misma, cuyos servicios regulará con aprobación del Presidente.

Art. 23   Para ser Secretario de La Corte se requiere:

1. Ser mayor de veinticinco años;

2. Ser Centroamericano de origen en el ejercicio de sus derechos;

3. Ser de notoria buena conducta;

4. Ser Abogado en ejercicio; y,

5. Tener experiencia profesional no menor de cinco años.

Art. 24   El Secretario General, al tomar posesión de su cargo, prestará ante La Corte el juramento a que se refiere el artículo 3.

Art. 25   La falta temporal del Secretario General, por cualquier motivo legal, será suplida por un Secretario Interino designado por el Presidente.

En los casos de ausencia definitiva, vacancia o abandono del cargo, La Corte nombrará nuevo Secretario General.

Art. 26   Si el Secretario General incurriere en las faltas graves previstas en el artículo 4, La Corte examinará el caso, escuchará al afectado y adoptará, en sesión plenaria, resolución por mayoría.

Art. 27   El Secretario General tendrá las siguientes obligaciones:

a)   Residir en el país de la Sede;

b)   Dirigir, bajo la autoridad del Presidente y Vicepresidente en su caso, la Secretaría de La Corte;

c)   Dar fe, expedir certificaciones y copias, con autorización de La Corte;

d)   Llevar un libro en que los Magistrados registren las firmas, medias firmas y rúbricas que usen;

e)   Autorizar con su firma los acuerdos y las resoluciones de La Corte y las que dicte el Presidente;

f)   Despachar oportunamente la correspondencia oficial de La Corte;

g)   Llevar un registro que contendrá lo esencial y en extracto, día a día, de las resoluciones que se dicten en el Tribunal;

h)   Custodiar los sellos y libros de La Corte y de la Secretaría;

i)   Cumplir y hacer cumplir inmediatamente las órdenes verbales o escritas emanadas de La Corte o del Presidente;

j)   Atender, conforme a instrucciones del Presidente, el despacho judicial de La Corte, la recepción, trámite y custodia de todos los documentos, autos y notificaciones requeridos en el presente Reglamento, así como la organización y mantenimiento del registro general de los asuntos sometidos al Tribunal;

k)   Cumplir con las demás obligaciones y ejercer las atribuciones que le señale el presente Reglamento y las Ordenanzas.

Art. 28   En las oficinas de la Secretaría se observará el orden y respeto debidos. En consecuencia, se prohiben las conversaciones y tertulias que perturben la marcha normal de los asuntos.

Art. 29   El Secretario deberá llevar en forma ordenada los datos estadísticos de las resoluciones y acuerdos emitidos por La Corte Plena y de los trabajos realizados por las Salas o Cámaras en su caso, debiendo al fin de cada mes hacer el cuadro del movimiento habido durante el mismo, enviando copia de todo ello a los Magistrados.

Capítulo V. De la Organización, el Personal y la Administración

Art. 30   Para la mejor administración, La Corte contará, además de la Secretaría General, con una Dirección Administrativa y Financiera, Auditoría Externa, Departamento de Publicaciones y los demás que en el futuro se organicen.

Art. 31   La Corte, en sesión plenaria, definirá la estructura organica de la Secretaría General y de la Administración.

Art. 32   En la contratación del personal indispensable para el cumplimiento de sus funciones, La Corte tendrá en cuenta únicamente la idoneidad, competencia y honorabilidad de los candidatos y procurará, en cuanto ello no fuere incompatible con los criterios anteriores, que en la provisión de los cargos haya una distribución geográfica regional tan amplia y proporcional como sea posible.

Art. 33   La Corte establecerá los procedimientos de selección, modalidades de contratación, categorías y períodos, así como el régimen de derechos y obligaciones de sus funcionarios y empleados.

Art. 34   Antes de asumir el cargo, los funcionarios prestarán ante el Presidente, y en presencia del Secretario General, el juramento de que guardarán la debida reserva y cumplirán con absoluta lealtad, imparcialidad, discreción y conciencia, las funciones que se les han conferido.

Art. 35   La Corte preparará el Proyecto del Presupuesto Anual y el Presidente lo enviará a cada uno de los Gobiernos de los Estados Miembros para los cuales esté vigente el Estatuto de La Corte, a fin de que procedan de conformidad a lo establecido en los artículos 41 y 42 del referido instrumento.

Capítulo VI. Disposiciones Varias

Art. 36   En lo no previsto en este Reglamento se estará a lo que dispongan los acuerdos que La Corte emita.

Art. 37   Este Reglamento podrá ser derogado o reformado con el voto favorable de la mayoría de los Magistrados y entra en vigencia a partir del doce de octubre de mil novecientos noventa y cuatro.

d) Organization of Eastern Caribbean States*

In 1968 after the creation of the East Caribbean Common Market and, in 1973, the Caribbean Community, the Treaty establishing the Organization of Eastern Caribbean States was concluded in 1981 constituting a sort of common link uniting the former two organisations.

The scope of the Organization of Eastern Caribbean States is the promotion of cooperation among the Member States at the regional and international levels having due regard to the Treaty establishing the Caribbean Community and the Charter of the United Nations as well as the promotion of unity and solidarity, economic integration according to the Agreement establishing the Caribbean Common Market and the harmonisation of foreign policy among the Member States.

Art. 14 of the Agreement concerns the peaceful settlement of disputes which has to be reached, if direct negotiations are unsuccessful, by a conciliation procedure with binding effect. Annex A of the Agreement contains the ruling concerning the Conciliation Commission. According to these provisions, the conciliators are to be appointed out of a panel maintained by the Director-General of the Organization. Each party has to appoint one conciliator of its own nationality and one non-national; the four conciliators, then, have to choose the fifth member, the chairman.

Despite the fact that the parties to the dispute appoint the conciliation commission, the request is brought before the commission not by the parties but by the Director-General to whom either of the parties has to submit the claim.

The decision of the commission is not a judgment in the narrow legal sense but a report which is, however, final and binding upon the parties thus conferring, to the conciliation commission a character analogous to that of an arbitral tribunal.

Member States: Antigua, Dominica, Grenada, Montserrat, St. Kitts-Nevis, Saint Lucia, Saint Vincent and the Grenadines.

Texts

Text of the Agreement and Annex A: ILM Vol. 20 (1981), pp. 1166–1189 (English)

---

*   See also Supplement 1.

Organization of Eastern Caribbean States of June 18, 1981

aa) Treaty of June 18, 1981

Art. 14   Procedure for the Settlement of Disputes

1. Any dispute that may arise between two or more of the Member States regarding the interpretation and application of this Treaty shall, upon the request of any of them, be amicably resolved by direct agreement.

2. If the dispute is not resolved within three months of the date on which the request referred to in the preceding paragraph has been made, any party to the dispute may submit it to the conciliation procedure provided for in Annex A to this Treaty by submitting a request to that effect to the Director-General of the Organisation and informing the other party or parties to the dispute of the request.

3. Member States undertake to accept the conciliation procedure referred to in the preceding paragraph as compulsory. Any decisions or recommendations of the Conciliation Commission in resolution of the dispute shall be final and binding on the Member States.

bb) Conciliation Commission

ANNEX A. CONCILIATION COMMISSION

1. A list of conciliators consisting of qualified jurists shall be drawn up and maintained by the Director-General of the Organisation. To this end, every Member State shall be invited to nominate two conciliators, and the names of the persons so nominated shall constitute the list. The term of a conciliator, including that of any conciliator nominated to fill a casual vacancy, shall be five years and may be renewed. A conciliator whose term expires shall continue to fulfil any function for which he shall have been chosen under the following paragraph.

2. (a) When a request has been made to the Director-General under Article 14, the Director-General shall bring the dispute before a Conciliation Commission constituted as follows:

The Member State or Member States constituting one of the parties to the dispute shall appoint:

(i) one conciliator who is a citizen of that State or of one of those States and who may or may not be chosen from the list referred to in paragraph 1; and

(ii) one conciliator who is not a citizen of that State or of any of those States and who shall be chosen from the list.

(b) The Member State or Member States constituting the other party to the dispute shall appoint two conciliators in the same way. The four conciliators chosen by the parties shall be appointed within thirty days following the date on which the Director-General received the request.

c) The four conciliators shall, within thirty days following the date of the last of their own appointments, appoint a fifth conciliator chosen from the list, who shall be chairman.

(d) If the appointment of the Chairman or of any of the other conciliators has not been made within the period prescribed above for such appointment, it shall be made by the Director-General within thirty days following the expiry of that period. The appointment of the Chairman may be made by the Director-General either from the list or from the membership of the International Law Commission. Any of the periods within which appointments must be made may be extended by agreement between the parties to the dispute.

(e) Any vacancy shall be filled in the manner prescribed for the initial appointment.

3. The Conciliation Commission shall decide its own procedure. The Commission with the consent of the parties to the dispute, may invite any Member State of the Organisation to submit to it its views orally or in writing. Decisions and recommendations of the Commission shall be made by a majority vote of the five members.

4. The Commission may draw the attention of the parties to the dispute to any measures which might facilitate an amicable settlement.

5. The Commission shall hear the parties, examine the claims and objections, and make proposals to the parties with a view to reaching an amicable settlement of the dispute.

6. The Commission shall report within six months of its constitution. Its report shall be deposited with the Director-General and transmitted to the parties to the dispute. The report of the Commission, including any conclusions stated therein regarding the facts or questions of law, shall be binding upon the parties.

7. The Director-General shall provide the Commission with such assistance and facilities as it may require. The expenses of the Commission shall be borne by the Organisation.

3. Africa and Arab Region

a) Organization of African Unity (OAU)

At the Addis Ababa Conference in May 1963, all independent African States, with the exception of Morocco and Togo, finally succeeded in establishing a pan-continental organisation, the Organization of African Unity (OAU). The OAU Charter was eventually adopted by all independent African States including Morocco and Togo and came into force on September 13, 1963. The OAU Charter obliges its members to coordinate and harmonize their national policies, to defend their sovereignty and territorial integrity against colonialism, to pursue a policy of non-alignment, and to eradicate all forms of colonialism in Africa, for which purpose the OAU created a special Committee for de-colonization. One of the main organs of the OAU is the Commission of Mediation, Conciliation and Arbitration, which was meant to facilitate the pacific settlement of all disputes arising among the member States. Details with respect to the functioning of this Commission are contained in the Protocol of the Commission of Mediation, Conciliation and Arbitration of July 21, 1964. The Protocol is an integral part of the OAU Charter and therefore binding upon all member States without special ratification. Despite rejection of the Hague Court of Arbitration by the majority of African States, these States have nevertheless been successful in reaching a regional solution modelled after the Hague Court, but strengthened by making the President and two Vice-Presidents permanent institutional organs. The holders of these offices were required to be full-time members of the Commission. Apart from this difference, the Commission resembles the Hague Permanent Court of Arbitration in consisting of a panel of persons elected by the Conference of the Heads of State and Government for a 5-year term with the possibility of re-election. Member States as well as the organs of the OAU may have recourse to the Commission. The system adopted by the OAU relies on the basic principles of a voluntary settlement of disputes through special independent organs created on an ad hoc basis. The arbitration procedure is possible only after the conclusion of a *compromis* between the parties to the dispute. Mediation and conciliation may be initiated unilaterally. However, if one party refuses to submit to the jurisdiction of the Commission, the Bureau may entrust the matter to the Council of Ministers of the OAU for review.

The Commission did not begin to function until 1968 and Member States have not shown much interest in dispute settlement by conciliation or arbitration; since its creation, no dispute has been referred to the Commission. States preferred instead to have resort to political mediation by Heads of States on an ad hoc basis. Accordingly, in 1977 it was decided to reorganise the Commission in order to promote greater use of the Commission and more flexibility in its activity. The consensus was that there should be no election to replace members of the Commission whose term of office ended in June of that year. Instead, an ad hoc Committee was created on provisional basis which, however, was just as little successful as the Commission. What happened exactly to the Commission is not absolutely clear, according to one authority (Sanders) the Commission must, however, be supposed to be defunct. In 1993, the Assembly of Heads of State and Government adopted a Mechanism for Conflict Prevention, Management and Resolution. This mechanism is composed of a Central Organ, consisting of the member States of the OAU summit bureau, with the Secretary-General and the Secretariat as its operational arm. Its primary objectives are the anticipation and prevention of conflicts. Civil or military observer groups may be deployed and the assistance of the UN will be sought in any case of degeneration of a conflict. The Central Organ of the mechanism has already reviewed various conflict situations in Africa, including internal conflicts (cf. UN Docs. S/1994/351; S/1994, 945). It has, however, to be stressed that this mechanism is only meant to operate for conflict prevention and peace-building or peace-keeping, and not for legal dispute settlement, which is still not provided for in a formal manner in the now existing system within the Organization of African States.

Texts

UNTS Vol. 479, pp. 39 et seq. (Amharic, Arabic, English and French)

ILM Vol. 2 (1963), pp. 766 et seq. (English)

EA Vol. 18 (1963), D 314 (German)

F. Berber, Völkerrecht, Dokumentensammlung, Vol. 1 (1967), pp. 717 et seq. (German)

Text of the Protocol of the Commission of Mediation, Conciliation and Arbitration: ILM Vol. 3 (1964), pp. 1116 et seq.

Text of the Document concerning the Settlement of Inter-African Disputes: Documents d'actualité internationale 1977 No. 49, pp. 950–951

Text of the Declaration of the Assembly of Heads of State and Government on the Establishment within the OAU of a Mechanism for Conflict Prevention, Management and Resolution: Doc. AHG/Decl. 3 (XXIX) Rev.1; UN Doc. A/48/322; ZaöRV 54 (1994), 1043–1047

E. G. Bello/J. Hilf, Organization of African Unity, in: R. Bernhardt (ed.), EPIL, Vol. III (1997), 802–810

Bibliographical notes

Z. Červenka, The Organisation of African Unity and its Charter (2nd ed. 1968)

B. Boutros-Ghali, L'Organisation de l'Unité Africaine (1969)

J.-M. Bipoun-Woum, Le droit international africain (1970)

M. Manigat, L'Organisation de l'Unité Africaine, RFSP Vol. 21 (1971), pp. 382 et seq.

M. Bedjaoui, Le règlement pacifique des différends africains, AFDI 1972, pp. 85–99

Z. Červenka, The Settlement of Disputes among Members of the Organisation of African Unity, VRÜ Vol. 7 (1974), pp. 117–138

K. Morjane, L'Organisation de l'Unité Africaine et le règlement pacifique des différends interafricains, Rev. égypt. Vol. 31 (1975), pp. 17–73 (with detailed bibliographical indications)

J. Polhemus, The Birth and Irrelevance of the Commission of Mediation, Conciliation and Arbitration of the OAU, in: Nigerian Journal of International Affairs 3 (1977), 1 et seq.

P. Vellas, La revision des procédures de règlement des conflits dans le cadre de l'Organisation de l'Unité Africaine, Rev. belge Vol. 14 (1978/79), pp. 157–166

AJGM Sanders, International Jurisprudence in African Context (1979)

C.O.C. Amate, Inside the OAU: Pan-Africanism in Practice (1986)

B. Oyebade, The Organisation of African Unity and Peaceful Settlement of Disputes: An Assessment, in: Nigerian Forum 9 (1989), 230 et seq.

M.C.D. Wembou, A propos du nouveau mécanisme de l'OAU sur les conflits, African Journal of International and Comparative Law 5 (1993), 725 et seq.

J. Hilf, Der neue Konfliktregelungsmechanismus der OAU: Deklaration der Versammlung der Staats- und Regierungschefs der OAU über die Einrichtung eines Mechanismus für Konfliktverhütung, -bewältigung und -lösung vom 30. Juni 1993, ZaöRV 54 (1994), 1023–1047

aa) Charter of the OAU of May 25, 1963

COMMISSION OF MEDIATION, CONCILIATION AND ARBITRATION

Art. XIX   Member States pledge to settle all disputes among themselves by peaceful means and, to this end decide to establish a Commission of Mediation, Conciliation and Arbitration, the composition of which and conditions of service shall be defined by a separate Protocol to be approved by the Assembly of Heads of State and Government. Said Protocol shall be regarded as forming an integral part of the present Charter.

bb) Protocol of the Commission of Mediation, Conciliation and Arbitration of July 21, 1964

PART I. ESTABLISHMENT AND ORGANIZATION

Art. I   The Commission of Mediation, Conciliation and Arbitration established by Article XIX of the Charter of the Organization of African Unity shall be governed by the provisions of the present Protocol.

Art. II   1. The Commission shall consist of twenty-one members elected by the Assembly of Heads of State and Government.

2. No two Members shall be nationals of the same State.

3. The Members of the Commission shall be persons with recognised professional qualifications.

4. Each Member State of the Organization of African Unity shall be entitled to nominate two candidates.

5. The Administrative Secretary-General shall prepare a list of the candidates nominated by Member States and shall submit it to the Assembly of Heads of State and Government.

Art. III   1. Members of the Commission shall be elected for a term of five years and shall be eligible for re-election.

2. Members of the Commission whose terms of office have expired shall remain in office until the election of a new Commission.

3. Notwithstanding the expiry of their terms of office, Members shall complete any proceedings in which they are already engaged.

Art. IV   Members of the Commission shall not be removed from office except by decision of the Assembly of Heads of State and Government, by a two-thirds majority of the total membership, on the grounds of inability to perform the functions of their office or of proved misconduct.

Art. V   1. Whenever a vacancy occurs in the Commission, it shall be filled in conformity with the provisions of Article II.

2. A Member of the Commission elected to fill a vacancy shall hold office for the unexpired term of the Member he has replaced.

Art. VI   1. A President and two Vice-Presidents shall be elected by the Assembly of Heads of State and Government from among the Members of the Commission who shall each hold office for five years. The President and the two Vice-Presidents shall not be eligible for reelection as such officers.

2. The President and the two Vice-Presidents shall be full-time members of the Commission, while the remaining eighteen shall be part-time Members.

Art. VII   The President and the two Vice-Presidents shall constitute the Bureau of the Commission and shall have the responsibility of consulting with the parties as regards the appropriate mode of settling the dispute in accordance with this Protocol.

Art. VIII The salaries and allowances of the Members of the Bureau and the remuneration of the other Members of the Commission shall be determined in accordance with the provisions of the Charter of the Organization of African Unity.

Art. IX   1. The Commission shall appoint a Registrar and may provide for such other officers as may be deemed necessary.

2. The terms and conditions of service of the Registrar and other administrative officers of the Commission shall be governed by the Commission's Staff Regulations.

Art. X   The Administrative expenses of the Commission shall be borne by the Organization of African Unity. All other expenses incurred in connection with the proceedings before the Commission shall be met in accordance with the Rules of Procedure of the Commission.

Art. XI   The Seat of the Commission shall be at Addis Ababa, Ethiopia.

PART II. GENERAL PROVISIONS

Art. XII   The Commission shall have jurisdiction over disputes between States only.

Art. XIII 1. A dispute may be referred to the Commission jointly by the parties concerned, by a party to the dispute, by the Council of Ministers or by the Assembly of Heads of State and Government.

2. Where a dispute has been referred to the Commission as provided in paragraph 1, and one or more of the parties have refused to submit to the jurisdiction of the Commission, the Bureau shall refer the matter to the Council of Ministers for consideration.

Art. XIV   The consent of any party to a dispute to submit to the jurisdiction of the Commission may be evidenced by:

(a) a prior written undertaking by such party that there shall be recourse to Mediation, Conciliation or Arbitration;

(b) reference of a dispute by such party to the Commission; or

(c) submission by such party to the jurisdiction in respect of a dispute referred to the Commission by another State, by the Council of Ministers, or by the Assembly of Heads of State and Government.

Art. XV Member States shall refrain from any act or omission that is likely to aggravate a situation which has been referred to the Commission.

Art. XVI Subject to the provisions of this Protocol and any special agreement between the parties, the Commission shall be entitled to adopt such working methods as it deems to be necessary and expedient and shall establish appropriate rules of procedure.

Art. XVII The Members of the Commission, when engaged in the business of the Commission, shall enjoy diplomatic privileges and immunities as provided for in the Convention on Privileges and Immunities of the Organization of African Unity.

Art. XVIII Where, in the course of Mediation, Conciliation or Arbitration, it is deemed necessary to conduct an investigation or inquiry for the purpose of elucidating facts or circumstances relating to a matter in dispute, the parties concerned and all other Member States shall extend to those engaged in any such proceedings the fullest cooperation in the conduct of such investigation or inquiry.

Art. XIX In case of a dispute between Member States, the parties may agree to resort to any one of these modes of settlement: Mediation, Conciliation and Arbitration.

PART III. MEDIATION

Art. XX When a dispute between Member States is referred to the Commission for Mediation, the President shall, with the consent of the parties, appoint one or more members of the Commission to mediate the dispute.

Art. XXI 1. The role of the mediator shall be confined to reconciling the views and claims of the parties.

2. The mediator shall make written proposals to the parties as expeditiously as possible.

3. If the means of reconciliation proposed by the mediator are accepted, they shall become the basis of a protocol of arrangement between the parties.

PART IV. CONCILIATION

Art.
XXII

1. A request for the settlement of a dispute by conciliation may be submitted to the Commission by means of a petition addressed to the President by one or more of the parties to the dispute.

2. If the request is made by only one of the parties, that party shall indicate that prior written notice has been given to the other party.

3. The petition shall include a summary explanation of the grounds of the dispute.

Art.
XXIII

1. Upon receipt of the petition, the President shall, in agreement with the parties, establish a Board of Conciliators, of whom three shall be appointed by the President from among the Members of the Commission, and one each by the parties.

2. The Chairman of the Board shall be a person designated by the President from among the three Members of the Commission.

3. In nominating persons to serve as Members of the Board, the parties to the dispute shall designate persons in such a way that no two Members of it shall be nationals of the same State.

Art.
XXIV

1. It shall be the duty of the Board of Conciliators to clarify the issues in dispute and to endeavour to bring about an agreement between the parties upon mutually acceptable terms.

2. The Board shall consider all questions submitted to it and may undertake any inquiry or hear any person capable of giving relevant information concerning the dispute.

3. In the absence of disagreement between the parties, the Board shall determine its own procedure.

Art.
XXV

The parties shall be represented by agents, whose duty shall be to act as intermediaries between them and the Board. They may moreover be assisted by counsel and experts and may request that all persons whose evidence appears to the Board to be relevant shall be heard.

Art.
XXVI

1. At the close of the proceedings, the Board shall draw up a report stating either:

(a) that the parties have come to an agreement and, if the need arises, the terms of the agreement and any recommendations for settlement made by the Board; or

(b) that it has been impossible to effect a settlement.

2. The Report of the Board of Conciliators shall be communicated to the parties and to the President of the Commission without delay and may be published only with the consent of the parties.

PART V. ARBITRATION

Art.
XXVII

1. Where it is agreed that arbitration should be resorted to, the Arbitral Tribunal shall be established in the following manner:

(a) each party shall designate one arbitrator from among the Members of the Commission having legal qualifications;

(b) the two arbitrators thus designated shall, by common agreement, designate from among the Members of the Commission a third person who shall act as Chairman of the Tribunal;

(c) where the two arbitrators fail to agree, within one month of their appointment, in the choice of the person to be Chairman of the Tribunal, the Bureau shall designate the Chairman.

2. The President may, with the agreement of the parties, appoint to the Arbitral Tribunal two additional Members who need not be Members of the Commission but who shall have the same powers as the other Members of the Tribunal.

3. The arbitrators shall not be nationals of the parties, or have their domicile in the territories of the parties, or be employed in their service, or have served as mediators or conciliators in the same dispute. They shall all be of different nationalities.

Art.
XXVIII

Recourse to arbitration shall be regarded as submission in good faith to the award of the Arbitral Tribunal.

Art.
XXIX

1. The parties shall, in each case, conclude a *compromis* which shall specify:

(a) the undertaking of the parties to go to arbitration, and to accept as legally binding, the decision of the Tribunal;

(b) the subject matter of the controversy; and

(c) the seat of the Tribunal.

2. The *compromis* may specify the law to be applied by the Tribunal and the power, if the parties so agree, to adjudicate *ex aequo et bono*, the time-limit within which the award of the arbitrators shall be given, and the appointment of agents and counsel to take part in the proceedings before the Tribunal.

Art.
XXX

In the absence of any provision in the *compromis* regarding the applicable law, the Arbitral Tribunal shall decide the dispute according to treaties concluded between the parties, International Law, the Charter of the Organization of African Unity, the Charter of the United Nations and, if the parties agree, *ex aequo et bono*.

Art.
XXXI

1. Hearings shall be held *in camera* unless the arbitrators decide otherwise.

2. The record of the proceedings signed by the arbitrators and the Registrar shall alone be authoritative.

3. The arbitral award shall be in writing and shall, in respect of every point decided, state the reasons on which it is based.

cc) Document Concerning the Settlement of Inter-African Disputes of July 1977[1]

Relative au règlement des litiges intra-africains

La Conférence des chefs d'Etat et de gouvernement, réunie en sa 14e session ordinaire, à Libreville, Gabon, du 2 au 5 juillet 1977,

Après avoir entendu le rapport du secrétaire général administratif sur la Commission de médiation, de conciliation et d'arbitrage de l'O.U.A., Document AHG/86 (XIV);

Ayant examiné le rapport présenté par le Nigéria sur la question des litiges intra-africains;

Rappelant les idéaux élevés et les objectifs de promotion de la paix et de l'harmonie sur le continent africain qui ont présidé à la création de l'O.U.A.;

Consciente des conflits nombreux et sans cesse croissants qui ont eu tendance à freiner la coopération intra-africaine, notamment sur le plan politique et particulièrement au cours de l'année dernière;

Consciente que la persistence de cette tendance indésirable serait gravement préjudiciable à la réalisation des objectifs de la Charte de l'Organisation de l'unité africaine;

Notant avec préoccupation que ces différends fréquents entre Etats africains retardent nécessairement le développement socio-économique accéléré, souhaité pour l'Afrique, ainsi que le bien-être de nos peuples;

Réaffirmant, sans réserve, son engagement continu pour le principe d'un règlement pacifique des différends comme stipulé dans la Charte de l'O.U.A.;

Notant avec regret que les mécanismes mis en place dans la Commission de médiation, de conciliation et d'arbitrage de l'O.U.A. ne peuvent pas, de par leur nature même, opérer de façon spontanée pour répondre à l'action urgente souvent nécessaire au moment des disputes;

Profondément convaincue que si la fréquence actuelle des conflits intra-africains n'est pas freinée, elle peut avoir pour grave conséquence de détourner l'attention de la guerre de libération en Afrique australe;

1. Demande en conséquence au secrétaire général administratif de l'O.U.A. de réexaminer d'urgence les procédures contenues dans le protocole relatives à la Commission de médiation, de conciliation et d'arbitrage de l'O.U.A. pour faire recommandations en vue de leur modification pour permettre ainsi à la Commission de réagir plus rapidement lors

---

d'apparition de situations de crise partout en Afrique, et de présenter en retour un rapport à la 30e session ordinaire du Conseil des ministres sur toutes améliorations souhaitables à apporter au Protocole;

2. Décide de surseoir au renouvellement par élection des membres de la Commission de médiation, de conciliation et d'arbitrage de l'O.U.A. dont le mandat est arrivé à expiration en juin 1977;

3. Décide en outre, à titre provisoire, de mettre sur pied un Comité ad hoc chargé du règlement des différends entre Etats membres et composé des pays suivants: Gabon, Togo, Tunisie, Madagascar, Zambie, Nigéria, Zaire, Gambie, Empire centrafricain.

Dans sa sagesse, le président en exercice de l'O.U.A. peut désigner trois autre Etats membres dont il estime utile la participation aux travaux du Comité ad hoc.

4. Engage, par ailleurs, le secrétaire général administratif, comme mesure intérimaire à prendre toutes les dispositions nécessaires pour mener une enquête en tant que procédure régulière sur tous cas de dispute qui pourraient à son avis rompre la paix et la sécurité en Afrique et à présenter sans tarder un rapport sur ses découvertes au président en exercice de la Conférence au sommet des chefs d'Etat et de gouvernement; celui-ci, dans la mesure de ses possibilités, prendra toutes les mesures nécessaires pour mettre fin à la détérioration des relations dans la région concernée.

dd) Declaration of the Assembly of Heads of State and Government on the Establishment within the OAU of a Mechanism for Conflict Prevention, Management and Resolution

We, the Heads of State and Government of the Organization of African Unity, meeting in our Twenty-nineth Ordinary Session in Cairo, Egypt, from 28 to 30 June 1993, having considered the situations of conflict on our Continent and recalling the Declaration we adopted on 11th July 1990, on the Political and Socio-Economic Situation in Africa and the Fundamental Changes Taking Place in the World, declare as follows:

1. In May 1963, when the Founding Fathers met in Addis Ababa, Ethiopia, to found the Organization of African Unity, they were guided by their collective conviction that freedom, equality, justice and dignity are legitimate aspirations of the African peoples, and by their desire to harness the natural and human resources for the advancement of the Continent in all spheres of human endeavour. The Founding Fathers were inspired by an equally common determination to promote understanding between the African peoples and co-operation among the African States, and to rekindle the aspirations of the African people for brotherhood and solidarity in a larger unity transcending linguistic, ideological, ethnic and national differences.

2. The Founding Fathers were fully convinced that to achieve these lofty objectives, conditions for peace and security must be established and maintained.

3. It was with this overriding conviction, and guided also by the Charter of the United Nations and the Universal Declaration of Human Rights, that our countries began on the arduous task of meeting the triple challenge of decolonisation, economic development and maintenance of peace and security.

4. Today, thirty years later, we can look back with pride at the achievements which the Organization of African Unity has been able to make against heavy odds and the many obstacles it has had to surmount.

5. The ranks of independent countries have been strengthened; and the membership of the OAU has increased from thirty-two at its founding to fifty-two today. The frontiers of freedom in Africa have been pushed to the doors of Apartheid South Africa. And even there, significant progress has been made; and we have reasonable cause for optimism that we shall soon see the total eradication of the remaining vestiges of colonialism, racism, racial discrimination and apartheid.

6. We, however, continue to be faced by the daunting dual challenge of economic development and democratic transformation. Our countries have made tremendous efforts both individually and collectively to arrest and reverse the decline in our economies. Notwithstanding the many serious difficulties they have encountered, and the magnitude of what remains to be done, appreciable progress has been made in the social and economic fields.

7. The socio-economic situation on our Continent remains nonetheless in a precarious state. Factors including poverty, deterioration of the terms of trade, plummeting prices of the commodities we produce, the excruciating external indebtedness and the resultant reverse flow of resources have combined to undermine the ability of our countries to provide for the basic needs of our people. In some cases, this situation has been further compounded by external political factors.

8. We do recognize, however, that there have also been certain internal human factors and policies which have negatively contributed to the present state of affairs on the Continent.

9. No single internal factor has contributed more to the present socio-economic problems on the Continent than the scourge of conflicts within and between our countries. They have brought about death and human suffering, engendered hate and divided nations and families. Conflicts have forced millions of our people into a drifting life as refugees and internally displaced persons, deprived of their means of livelihood, human dignity and hope. Conflicts have gobbled-up scarce resources, and undermined the ability of our countries to address the many compelling needs of our people.

10. While reaffirming our commitment to the Declaration on the Political and Socio-Economic Situation in Africa and the Fundamental Changes

Taking Place in the World which we adopted during the 26th Session of our Assembly, in Addis Ababa, in July 1990, we renew our determination to work in concert in the search for speedy and peaceful resolution to all the conflicts in Africa.

11. In June last year at the Twenty-eighth meeting of our Assembly in Dakar-Senegal, we decided in principle to establish within the OAU, and in keeping with the principles and objectives of the Charter of the Organization, a Mechanism for Conflict Prevention, Management and Resolution. We took that decision against the background of the history of many prolonged and destructive conflicts on our continent and of our limited success at finding lasting solutions to them, notwithstanding the many efforts we and our predecessors had expended. In so doing, we were also guided by our determination to ensure that Africa through the Organization of African Unity plays a central role in bringing about peace and stability on the Continent.

12. We saw in the establishment of such a Mechanism the opportunity to bring to the processes of dealing with conflicts on our continent a new institutional dynamism, enabling speedy action to prevent or manage and ultimately resolve conflicts when and where they occur.

13. Now, having considered the report on the Mechanism prepared by the Secretary General pursuant to our decision on the principle of its creation, we hereby establish, within the OAU, a Mechanism for preventing, managing and resolving conflicts in Africa.

14. The Mechanism will be guided by the objectives and principles of the OAU Charter; in particular, the sovereign equality of Member States, non-interference in the internal affairs of States, the respect of the sovereignty and territorial integrity of Member States, their inalienable right to independent existence, the peaceful settlement of disputes as well as the inviolability of borders inherited from colonialism. It will also function on the basis of the Consent and the co-operation of the parties to a conflict.

15. The Mechanisms will have as a primary objective, the anticipation and prevention of conflicts. In circumstances where conflicts have occurred, it will be its responsibility to undertake peace-making and peace-building functions in order to facilitate the resolution of these conflicts. In this respect, civilian and military missions of observation and monitoring of limited scope and duration may be mounted and deployed. In setting these objectives, we are fully convinced that prompt and decisive action in these spheres will, in the first instance, prevent the emergence of conflicts, and where they do inevitably occur, stop them from degenerating into intense or generalized conflicts. Emphasis on anticipatory and preventive measures, and concerted action in peace-making and peace-building will obviate the need to resort to the complex and resource-demanding peace-keeping operations, which our countries will find difficult to finance.

16. However, in the event that conflicts degenerate to the extent of requiring collective international intervention and policing, the assistance or where appropriate the services of the United Nations will be sought under

the general terms of its Charter. In this instance, our respective countries will examine ways and modalities through which they can make practical contribution to such a United Nations undertaking and participate effectively in the peace-keeping operations in Africa.

17. The Mechanism will be built around a Central Organ with the Secretary General and the Secretariat as its operational arm.

18. The Central Organ of the Mechanism shall be composed of the States members of the Bureau of the Assembly of Heads of State and Government elected annually, bearing in mind the principles of equitable regional representation and rotation. In order to ensure continuity, the States of the outgoing Chairman and (where known) the incoming Chairman shall also be members of the Central Organ. In between Ordinary Sessions of the Assembly, it will assume overall direction and coordinate the activities of the Mechanisms.

19. The Central Organ shall function at the level of Heads of State as well as that of Ministers and Ambassadors accredited to the OAU or duly authorized representatives. It may, where necessary, seek the participation of other OAU Member States in its deliberations particularly, the neighbouring countries. It may also seek, from within the Continent, such military, legal and other forms of expertise as it may require in the performance of its functions.

20. The proceedings of the Central Organ shall be governed by the pertinent Rules of Procedure of the Assembly of Heads of State and Government. The Central Organ shall be convened by the Chairman or at the request of the Secretary General or any Member State. It will meet at least once a year at the level of Heads of State and Government; twice a year at the Ministerial level; and once a month at Ambassadorial and duly authorised representatives level. The quorum of the Central Organ shall be two thirds of its members. In deciding on its recommendations and without prejudice to the decision-making methods provided for in the Rules of Procedure of the Assembly of Heads of State and Government, it shall generally be guided by the principle of consensus. The Central Organ shall report on its activities to the Assembly of Heads of State and Government.

21. The venue of its meetings shall ordinarily be at the Headquarters of the Organization. Meetings may also be held elsewhere if so decided through consultations among its members. The provisional agenda of the Central Organ shall be prepared by the Secretary General in consultation with the Chairman.

22. The Secretary General shall, under the authority of the Central Organ and in consultation with the parties involved in the conflict, deploy efforts and take all appropriate initiatives to prevent, manage and resolve conflicts. To this end, the Secretary General shall rely upon the human and material resources available at the General Secretariat. Accordingly, we direct the Council of Ministers, in consultation with the Secretary General, to examine ways and means in which the capacity within the General Sec-

retariat can be built and brought to a level commensurate with the magnitude of the tasks at hand and the responsibilities expected of the Organization. In his efforts, the Secretary General may also resort to eminent African personalities in consultation with the Authorities of their countries of origin. Where necessary, he may make use of other relevant expertise, send special envoys or special representatives as well as despatch fact-finding missions to conflict areas.

23. A special Fund governed by the relevant OAU Financial Rules and Regulations shall be established for the purpose of providing financial resources to support exclusively the OAU operational activities relating to conflict management and resolution. It will be made up of financial appropriations from the regular budget of the OAU, voluntary contributions from Member States as well as from other sources within Africa. The Secretary General may, with the consent of the Central Organ, and in conformity with the principles and objectives of the OAU Charter, also accept voluntary contributions from sources outside Africa. Disbursement from the Special Fund shall be subject to the approval of the Central Organ.

24. Within the context of the Mechanism for Conflict Prevention, Management and Resolution, the OAU shall closely coordinate its activities with the African regional and sub-regional organizations and shall cooperate as appropriate with the neighbouring countries with respect to conflicts which may arise in the different sub-regions of the Continent.

25. The OAU shall also co-operate and work closely with the United Nations not only with regard to issues relating to peace-making but, and especially, also those relating to peace-keeping. Where necessary, recourse will be had to the United Nations to provide the necessary financial, logistical and military support for the OAU's activities in Conflict Prevention, Management and Resolution in Africa in keeping with the provisions of Chapter VIII of the UN Charter on the role of regional organisations in the maintenance of international peace and security. In the like manner, the Secretary General of the OAU shall maintain close co-operation with other international organisations.

(Reservations by Sudan and Eritrea)

b) League of the Arab States

The League of Arab States was founded in 1945 in order to strengthen relations between the Arab States. Art. 5 of the Pact of March 22, 1945 invests the Council of the League with authority to act as arbitrator in disputes which both parties have voluntarily brought before it, provided that the dispute does not involve the independence, sovereignty, or the territorial integrity of the disputing parties. Those disputes which may lead to war are to be submitted to compulsory mediation by the Council. Further rules concerning the settlement of disputes are not provided neither in the Pact nor in additional instruments.

The special Arab Arbitration Tribunal provided for in Art. 19 has never been set up nor has the projected Arab Court of Justice ever been created. Thus, the dispute settlement system of the Pact is to be regarded as a step back rather than a step forward concerning the development of the concept of arbitration.

Texts

UNTS Vol. 70, pp. 237 et seq. (Arabic, English and French)
F. Berber, Völkerrecht, Dokumentensammlung, Vol. 1 (1967), pp. 816–822

Bibliographical notes

E. Fonda, The Projected Arab Court of Justice (1957)
R. W. McDonald, The League of Arab States (1965)
O. Cassé, La Ligue des Etats Arabes. Le rôle des organisations régionales dans les conflits entre leurs membres, RFSP Vol. 21 (1971), pp. 362–381
C. Wissa-Wassef, La Ligue des Etats Arabes face aux conflits inter-arabes, Politique étrangère, Vol. 38 (1973), pp. 51–83
S. J. Al Kadhem, The Role of the League of Arab States in Settling Inter-Arab Disputes, Rev. égypt. Vol. 32 (1976), pp. 1–31
S. Chaabane, La réforme du Pacte de la Ligue des Etats arabes, RGDIP 86 (1982), pp 509 – 542
C. Honegger, Friedliche Streitbeilegung durch regionale Organisationen — Theorie und Praxis der Friedenssicherungssysteme der OAS, der Liga der Arabischen Staaten und der OAU im Vergleich (1983)
M. Shihab, Arab States, League of, in: R. Bernhardt (ed.), EPIL, Vol. I (1992), 202–207

    c)   The Commission's recommendations or opinions shall spell out the reasons on which they were based and shall be signed by the chairman and recorder.

    d)   If an opinion is passed wholly or partially by unanimous vote of the members, the dissenting members shall be entitled to document their dissenting opinion.

Art. 10   Immunities and Privileges

The Commission and its members shall enjoy such immunities and privileges in the territories of the member states as are required to realize its objectives and in accordance with Article Seventeen of the Cooperation Council Charter.

Art. 11   Commission's Budget

The Commission's budget shall be considered part of the Secretariat General's budget. Remunerations of the Commission's members shall be established by the Supreme Council.

Art. 12   Amendments

    a)   Any member state may request for amendments of these Rules of Procedures.

    b)   Requests for amendments shall be submitted to the Secretary-General who shall relay them to the member states by at least four months before submission to the Ministerial Council.

    c)   An amendment shall be effective if approved unanimously by the Supreme Council.

Art. 13   Effective Date

These Rules of Procedures shall go into effect as of the date of approval by the Supreme Council.

These Rules of Procedures were signed at Abu Dhabi City, United Arab Emirates on 21 Rajab 1401 AH corresponding to 25 May 1981 AD.

d) Organization of the Islamic Conference

The Organization of the Islamic Conference was established following a meeting of Muslim Heads of States held at Rabat in September 1969 and the Islamic Foreign Ministers' Conference in Jedda in March 1970. The Organization shall promote Islamic solidarity among the member States. It aims particularly at enhancing economic, cultural and political cooperation as well as to provide humanitarian assistance to Muslim communities affected by wars and natural disasters. The membership of the Organization comprises about 50 States.

During the Third Summit Conference in Mecca and Ta'if in 1981 it was decided to establish an Islamic Court of Justice (Decision No. 11/3) as a judicial organ of the Conference. The Court is competent for the settlement of disputes arising out of the interpretation or implementation of the Organization's Charter as well as disputes arising between the member States of the Organization. Furthermore, the Court may give advisory opinions on legal matters which are requested by the Conference of Kings and Heads of State and Government, the Foreign Ministers' Conference or organs of the Organization on approval of the Foreign Ministers' Conference. The Court is composed of seven judges. The applicable law is the Shari'a; however, also international law as mentioned in Art. 38 of the Statute of the International Court of Justice may be consulted. The judgements are final and binding on the parties. If a party fails to implement a judgement, the case is referred to the Foreign Ministers' Conference.

Texts

Decision No. 11/13 on the Islamic Court of Justice Doc. A/36/138, Annex I, p. 59

Bibliographical notes

H. Moinuddin, Die Organisation der Islamischen Konferenz (OIC) als Forum politischer und wirtschaftlicher Kooperation (1984)

H. Moinuddin, The Charter of the Islamic Conference (1987)

M. Shihab, Organization of the Islamic Conference, in: R. Bernhardt (ed.) EPIL, Vol. III (1997), 824–828

casioned by the lawful impediments aforesaid, and is not to extend to losses occasioned by such insolvency of the debtors, or other causes as would equally have operated to produce such loss, if the said impediments had not existed; nor to such losses or damages as have been occasioned by the manifest delay or negligence, or wilful omission of the claimant.

For the purpose of ascertaining the amount of any such losses and damages, five commissioners shall be appointed, and authorised to meet and act in manner following, viz. Two of them shall be appointed by his Majesty, two of them by the President of the United States by and with the advice and consent of the Senate thereof, and the fifth by the unanimous voice of the other four; and if they should not agree in such choice, then the commissioners named by the two parties shall respectively propose one person, and of the two names so proposed, one shall be drawn by lot, in the presence of the four original commissioners. When the five commissioners thus appointed shall first meet, they shall, before they proceed to acts respectively take the following oath, or affirmation, in the presence of each other; which oath, or affirmation, being so taken and duly attested, shall be entered on the record of their proceedings, viz. I, A. B. one of the commissioners appointed in pursuance of the sixth article of the treaty of amity, commerce, and navigation, between his Britannic Majesty and the United States of America do solemnly swear (or affirm) that I will honestly, diligently, impartially, and carefully examine, and to the best of my judgment, according to justice and equity, decide all such complaints, as under the said article shall be preferred to the said commissioners: and that I will forbear to act as a commissioner, in any case in which I may be personally interested.

Three of the said commissioners shall constitute a board, and shall have power to do any act appertaining to the said commission, provided that one of the commissioners named on each side, and the fifth commissioner shall be present, and all decisions shall be made by the majority of the voices of the commissioners then present. Eighteen months from the day on which the said commissioners shall form a board, and be ready to proceed to business, are assigned for receiving complaints and applications; but they are nevertheless authorised, in any particular cases in which it shall appear to them to be reasonable and just, to extend the said term of eighteen months, for any term not exceeding six months, after the expiration thereof. The said commissioners shall first meet at Philadelphia, but they shall have power to adjourn from place to place as they shall see cause.

The said commissioners in examining the complaints and applications so preferred to them, are empowered and required, in pursuance of the true intent and meaning of this article, to take into their consideration all claims, whether of principal or interest, or balances of principal and interest, and to determine the same respectively, according to the merits of the several cases, due regard being had to all the circumstances thereof, and as equity and justice shall appear to them to require. And the said commissioners shall have power to examine all such persons as shall come before them, on oath or affirmation, touching the premises; and also to receive in evidence, according as they may think most consistent with equity and justice, all written depositions, or books, or papers, or copies, or extracts thereof; every such deposition, book, or paper, or copy, or extract, being duly authenticated, either according to the legal forms now respectively existing in the two countries, or in such other manner as the said commissioners shall see cause to require or allow.

The award of the said commissioners, or of any three of them as aforesaid, shall in all cases be final and conclusive, both as to the justice of the claim, and to the amount of the sum to be paid to the creditor or claimant: And the United States undertake to cause the sum so awarded to be paid in specie to such creditor or claimant without deduction; and at such time or times, and at such place or places, as shall be awarded by the said commissioners; and on condition of such releases or assignments to be given by the creditor or claimant, as by the said commissioners may be directed: Provided always, that no such payment shall be fixed by the said commissioners to take place sooner than twelve months from the day of the exchange of the ratifications of this treaty.

Art. VII Whereas complaints have been made by divers merchants and others, citizens of the United States, that during the course of the war in which his Majesty is now engaged, they have sustained considerable losses and damage, by reason of irregular or illegal captures or condemnations of their vessels and other property, under colour of authority or commissions from his Majesty, and that from various circumstances belonging to the said cases, adequate compensation for the losses and damages so sustained cannot now be actually obtained, had and received by the ordinary course of judicial proceedings; it is agreed, that in all such cases, where adequate compensation cannot, for whatever reason, be now actually obtained, had and received by the said merchants and others, in the ordinary course of justice, full and complete compensation for the same will be made by the British government to the said complainants. But it is distinctly understood, that this provision is not to extend to such losses or damages as have been occasioned by the manifest delay or negligence, or wilful omission of the claimant.

That for the purpose of ascertaining the amount of any such losses and damages, five commissioners shall be appointed and authorised to act in London, exactly in the manner directed with respect to those mentioned in the preceding article, and after having taken the same oath or affirmation (mutatis mutandis) the same term of eighteen months is also assigned for the reception of claims, and they are in like manner authorised to extend the same in particular cases. They shall receive testimony, books, papers and evidence in the same latitude, and exercise the like discretion and powers respecting that subject; and shall decide the claims in question according to the merits of the several cases, and to justice, equity, and the laws of nations. The award of the said commissioners, or any such three of them as aforesaid, shall in all cases be final and conclusive, both as to the justice of the claim, and the amount of the sum to be paid to the claimant; and his Britannic Majesty undertakes to cause the same to be paid to such claimant in specie, without any deduction, at such place or places, and at such time or times, as shall be awarded by the said commissioners, and on condition of such releases or assignments to be given by the claimant, as by the said commissioners may be directed.

And whereas certain merchants and others his Majesty's subjects, complain, that in the course of the war they have sustained loss and damage, by reason of the capture of their vessels and merchandise, taken within the limits and jurisdiction of the states, and brought into the ports of the same, or taken by vessels originally armed in ports of the said states.

It is agreed that in all such cases where restitution shall not have been made agreeably to the tenor of the letter from Mr. Jefferson to Mr. Hammond, dated at Philadelphia, Sept. 5, 1793, a copy of which is annexed to this treaty; the complaints of the parties shall be and hereby are referred to the commissioners to be appointed by virtue of this article, who are hereby authorised and required to proceed in the like manner relative to these as to the other cases committed to them; and the United States undertake to pay to the complainants or claimants in specie, without deduction, the amount of such sums as shall be awarded to them respectively by the said commissioners, and at the times and places which in such awards shall be specified; and on condition of such releases or assignments to be given by the claimants as in the said awards may be directed: And it is further agreed, that not only the now-existing cases of both descriptions, but also all such as shall exist at the time of exchanging the ratifications of this treaty, shall be considered as being within the provisions, intent, and meaning of this article.

2. Bryan Arbitration Treaties of 1913/14

The Bryan Treaties between the United States of America and several other States were the result of American Secretary of State Bryan's initiative. The idea originated during discussion of a General Model Arbitration Treaty in 1905. It first acquired form in a Draft Bilateral Convention presented by Bryan at the 14th Interparlamentarian Conference.

These treaties aimed at settling non-arbitrable disputes by establishing permanent commissions to examine them. The Bryan Treaties supplemented arbitration treaties containing honour and interest clauses, which only allowed for the settlement of arbitrable disputes. However, the examining commissions were created without the authority to render binding decisions, but could only issue non-binding "reports". By failing to appoint or by withdrawing its delegates to the commission a party could avoid the proceedings entirely.

The permanent commissions were instituted as permanently joint organs of the States parties to the treaties and consisted of five members. Two of the members were chosen by each party and the fifth by common agreement. The treaties provided for unilateral requests for examination of a dispute and in some cases even allowed for *ex officio* activity by a commission. The procedure of the commissions was that provided for in Arts. 9–36 of the Hague Convention for the Pacific Settlement of International Disputes of 1907. Although a commission could not render a binding decision, it is generally accepted that it had the power to set forth concrete proposals regarding the settlement of a dispute.

Despite the fact that the Bryan Treaties never found application, they are of considerable importance because the extension of the obligatorium they reached, although this was achieved at the expense of the binding character of the commissions' decisions. These treaties mark the beginning of the development of conciliation.

The Model Treaty was concluded between the United States of America and San Salvador on August 7, 1913. It was followed by a series of twenty bilateral treaties of which only sixteen were ratified. Of special political importance were the treaties between the United States of America and France (September 15,1914), the United States and Great Britain (September 15, 1914), and the United States and Russia (October 1, 1914). In 1928/29 further treaties were concluded, so that by 1930, nineteen such bilateral treaties were in force and are, in part, presently in force.

Texts

Martens NRG3 Vol. 9, pp. 106–112 (English and language of the other Contracting Party)

K. Strupp, Die Schiedsgerichts-, Gerichts und Vergleichsverträge des Deutschen Reiches (1929), pp. 68 et seq.

G. H. Hackworth, Digest of International Law, Vol. 6 (1943), p. 5
Report of the UN Secretary-General, Doc. A/5694, in: GAOR 20th Session, Annexes, agenda items 90 and 94
AJIL Vol. 10 (1916), pp. 882 et seq.

Bibliographical notes

The Bryan Treaties, AJIL Vol. 7 (1913), pp. 823–839
B. de Jong van Beck en Dong, Der Bryansche Friedensplan, ZV Vol. 7 (1913), pp. 533–553
G. A. Finch, The Bryan Peace Treaties, AJIL Vol. 10 (1916), pp. 882–890
C. L. Lange, Die amerikanischen Friedensverträge (1916) (with treaty texts)
J. B. Scott, Treaties for the Advancement of Peace between the United States and other Powers Negotiated by the Honorable William J. Bryan (1920)
H. Scherer, Das Vergleichsverfahren — Der Bryansche Friedensplan und seine Fortentwicklung bis zur Neuzeit (1928)
H.-J. Schlochauer, Bryan Treaties (1913/1914), in: R. Bernhardt (ed.), Encyclopedia of Public International Law, Vol. I (1992), pp. 509–511

a) United States of America-France, Treaty of September 15, 1914

Art. 1   Any disputes arising between the Government of the United States of
           America and the Government of the French Republic, of whatever nature
           they may be, shall, when ordinary diplomatic proceedings have failed and
           the High Contracting Parties do not have recourse to arbitration, be sub-
           mitted for investigation and report to a Permanent International Commis-
           sion constituted in the manner prescribed in the following article.

           The High Contracting Parties agree not to resort, with respect to each
           other, to any act of force during the investigation to be made by the
           Commission and before its report is handed in.

Art. 2   The International Commission shall be composed of five members ap-
           pointed as follows: Each Government shall designate two members, only
           one of whom shall be of its own nationality; the fifth member shall be
           designated by common consent and shall not belong to any of the nation-
           alities already represented on the Commission; he shall perform the duties
           of President.

           In case the two Governments should be unable to agree on the choice of
           the fifth commissioner, the other four shall be called upon to designate
           him, and failing an understanding between them, the provisions of article
           45 of The Hague Convention of 1907 shall be applied.

           The Commission shall be organized within six months from the exchange
           of ratifications of the present convention.

           The members shall be appointed for one year and their appointment may
           be renewed. They shall remain in office until superseded or reappointed,
           or until the work on which they are engaged at the time their office ex-
           pires is completed.

           Any vacancies which may arise (from death, resignation, or cases of
           physical or moral incapacity) shall be filled within the shortest possible
           period in the manner followed for the original appointment.

           The High Contracting Parties shall, before designating the Commission-
           ers, reach an understanding in regard to their compensation. They shall
           bear by halves the expenses incident to the meeting of the Commission.

Art. 3   In case a dispute should arise between the High Contracting Parties which
           is not settled by the ordinary methods, each Party shall have a right to ask
           that the investigation thereof be intrusted to the International Commis-
           sion charged with making a report. Notice shall be given to the President
           of the International Commission, who shall at once communicate with his
           colleagues.

           In the same case the President may, after consulting his colleagues and
           upon receiving the consent of a majority of the members of the Commis-
           sion, offer the services of the latter to each of the Contracting Parties. Ac-
           ceptance of that offer declared by one of the two Governments shall be
           sufficient to give jurisdiction of the case to the Commission in accordance
           with the foregoing paragraph.

The place of meeting shall be determined by the Commission itself.

Art. 4   The two High Contracting Parties shall have a right, each on its own part, to state to the President of the Commission what is the subject-matter of the controversy. No difference in these statements, which shall be furnished by way of suggestion, shall arrest the action of the Commission.

In case the cause of the dispute should consist of certain acts already committed or about to be committed, the Commission shall as soon as possible indicate what measures to preserve the rights of each party ought in its opinion to be taken provisionally and pending the delivery of its report.

Art. 5   As regards the procedure which it is to follow, the Commission shall as far as possible be guided by the provisions contained in articles 9 to 36 of Convention 1 of The Hague of 1907.

The High Contracting Parties agree to afford the Commission all means and all necessary facilities for its investigation and report.

The work of the Commission shall be completed within one year from the date on which it has taken jurisdiction of the case, unless the High Contracting Parties should agree to set a different period.

The conclusion of the Commission and the terms of its report shall be adopted by a majority. The report, signed only by the President acting by virtue of his office, shall be transmitted by him to each of the Contracting Parties.

The High Contracting Parties reserve full liberty as to the action to be taken on the report of the Commission.

Art. 6   The present treaty shall be ratified by the President of the United States of America, with the advice and consent of the Senate of the United States, and by the President of the French Republic, in accordance with the constitutional laws of France.

It shall go into force immediately after the exchange of ratifications and shall last five years.

Unless denounced six months at least before the expiration of the said period of five years, it shall remain in force until the expiration of a period of twelve months after either party shall have notified the other of its intention to terminate it.

In witness whereof the respective plenipotentiaries have signed the present treaty and have affixed thereunto their seals.

Done at Washington this 15th day of September, in the year nineteen hundred and fourteen.

b) United States of America-Great Britain, Treaty of September 15, 1914

Art. I   The High Contracting Parties agree that all disputes between them, of every nature whatsoever, other than disputes the settlement of which is provided for and in fact achieved under existing agreements between the High Contracting Parties, shall, when diplomatic methods of adjustment have failed, be referred for investigation and report to a permanent International Commission, to be constituted in the manner prescribed in the next succeeding article; and they agree not to declare war or begin hostilities during such investigation and before the report is submitted.

Art. II   The International Commission shall be composed of five members, to be appointed as follows: One member shall be chosen from each country, by the Government thereof; one member shall be chosen by each Government from some third country; the fifth member shall be chosen by common agreement between the two Governments, it being understood that he shall not be a citizen of either country. The expenses of the Commission shall be paid by the two Governments in equal proportions.

The International Commission shall be appointed within six months after the exchange of the ratifications of this treaty; and vacancies shall be filled according to the manner of the original appointment.

Art. III In case the High Contracting Parties shall have failed to adjust a dispute by diplomatic methods, they shall at once refer it to the International Commission for investigation and report. The International Commission may, however, spontaneously by unanimous agreement offer its services to that effect, and in such case it shall notify both Governments and request their cooperation in the investigation.

In the event of its appearing to His Majesty's Government that the British interests affected by the dispute to be investigated are not mainly those of the United Kingdom but are mainly those of some one or more of the self governing dominions, namely, the Dominion of Canada, the Commonwealth of Australia, the Dominion of New Zealand, the Union of South Africa, and Newfoundland, His Majesty's Government shall be at liberty to substitute as the member chosen by them to serve on the International Commission for such investigation and report another person selected from a list of persons to be named one for each of the self governing dominions but only one shall act, namely, that one who represents the dominion immediately interested.

The High Contracting Parties agree to furnish the Permanent International Commission with all the means and facilities required for its investigation and report.

The report of the International Commission shall be completed within one year after the date on which it shall declare its investigation to have begun, unless the High Contracting Parties shall limit or extend the time by mutual agreement. The report shall be prepared in triplicate; one copy shall be presented to each Government, and the third retained by the Commission for its files.

The High Contracting Parties reserve the right to act independently on the subject matter of the dispute after the report of the Commission shall have been submitted.

Art. IV   The treaty shall not affect in any way the provisions of the Treaty of the 11th January, 1909, relating to questions arising between the United States and the Dominion of Canada.

Art. V   The present treaty shall be ratified by the President of the United States of America, by and with the advice and consent of the Senate thereof, and by His Britannic Majesty; and the ratifications shall be exchanged at Washington as soon as possible. It shall take effect immediately after the exchange of ratifications, and shall continue in force for a period of five years; and it shall thereafter remain in force until twelve months after one of the High Contracting Parties have given notice to the other of an intention to terminate it.

In witness whereof the respective plenipotentiaries have signed the present treaty and have affixed thereunto their seals.

Done in duplicate at Washington on the 15th day of September, in the year of our Lord nineteen hundred and fourteen.

3. German-Swiss Treaty on Arbitration and Conciliation

While prior arbitration treaties were minimally effective because they frequently included honour and interest clauses and because the parties themselves were to decide whether the clauses applied in a specific case, the German-Swiss Arbitration Treaty of December 3, 1921 marked a turning point in compulsory arbitration. This Treaty was the first to provide for the justiciability of the honour and interest clauses (Art. 4). Finally such Clauses were eliminated totally by the Protocol of Amendment of August 29, 1928. In addition, the 1921 Treaty provided for the possibility of using a third party to establish the special agreement or to appoint arbitrators when the parties failed to fulfil their obligations. In these cases a permanent conciliation commission set up under the Treaty replaces the party impeding the procedure (Art. 8). This provision has been amended by the Protocol of 1928 in the sense that failing agreement upon the *compromis* or appointment of the arbitrators within two months unilateral application to the Permanent International Court of Justice has been permitted. Similar treaties have been concluded by Switzerland with Austria (1924), Belgium (1927), Brazil (1924), Columbia (1927), Denmark (1924), Spain (1926), United States of America (1931), Finland (1927), France (1925), Greece (1925), Hungary (1924), Italy (1924), Japan (1924), Luxembourg (1929), Norway (1925), The Netherlands (1925), Portugal (1928), Romania (1926), Sweden (1924), Tchecoslovakia (1929) and Turkey (1928).

Texts

RGBl. 1922, p. 217 (German)
LNTS Vol. 12, pp. 280 et seq. (English and French)
Text of the 1928 Protocol: M. Habicht, Post-War Treaties (1931), pp. 34 f.
Systematische Sammlung des Bundesrechts der Schweiz, Band 0.1, 2, 1970

Bibliographical notes

R. Probst, Die Schweiz und die internationale Schiedsgerichtsbarkeit, Schweiz. JIR Vol. 17 (1960), pp. 99–146

F. Münch, Die schweizerische Initiative zu zweiseitigen Abmachungen über die friedliche Beilegung von Streitigkeiten, ZaöRV Vol. 26 (1966), pp. 705–746

a) Germany-Switzerland: Treaty of Conciliation, Arbitration, and Compulsory Adjudication

Art. 1   The Contracting Parties undertake to refer to the procedure of arbitration or conciliation disputes of any nature whatsoever which may arise between them and which it has not been possible to settle, within a reasonable period, by diplomatic means.

Disputes for the solution of which a special procedure has been laid down in other Conventions in force between the Contracting Parties, shall be settled in accordance with the provisions of such Conventions.

Art. 2   At the request of one of the Parties, disputes regarding the following subjects shall, unless otherwise provided for in Articles 3 and 4, be submitted to arbitration:

Firstly, the contents, interpretation and application of any treaty concluded between the two Parties;

Secondly, any point of international law;

Thirdly, the existence of any fact which, if established, would constitute a violation of an international engagement;

Fourthly, the extent and nature of the reparation due for such violation.

In case of disagreement as to whether the dispute falls under one of the above categories, this preliminary question shall be referred to arbitration.

Art. 3   In regard to questions which, under the national laws of the Party against which an action has been brought, are within the competence of judicial authorities, including administrative tribunals, the defendant Party may require, on the one hand, that the dispute shall not be submitted to arbitral award until a final decision has been pronounced by these judicial authorities and, on the other hand, that the matter shall be brought before the Tribunal not later than six months after the date of such decision. The above provisions shall not apply if justice has been refused and if the matter has been brought before the courts of appeal provided for by law.

In the case of disputes regarding the application of the preceding provision, the Arbitral Tribunal shall decide.

Art. 4   If, in a dispute coming under one of the categories mentioned in Article 2, one of the Parties pleads that the question at issue is one which affects its independence, the integrity of its territory or other vital interests of the highest importance, and if the opposing Party admits that the plea is well founded, the dispute shall not be subject to arbitration, but to the procedure of conciliation. If, however, the plea is not recognised as well founded by the opposing Party, this point shall be settled by means of arbitration.

The above provisions shall apply if, in a dispute coming under one of the categories mentioned in Article 2, one Party, although not pleading its independence, the integrity of its territory, or other vital interests of the highest importance, pleads that the dispute is mainly political and, for this reason, does not allow of a decision based exclusively on legal principles. At the same time, as an exception to the provision laid down in Article 9, the Tribunal can only recognise the validity of this plea if all its members unanimously agree thereto, or if there is only one dissentient.

If the Tribunal recognises the validity of such pleas it shall refer the dispute for settlement to the procedure of conciliation. If the contrary is the case, it shall give an award on the dispute itself.

A Party which does not recognise the validity of one of the pleas of exception put forward by the opposing Party, may, nevertheless, without first having recourse to arbitration, agree to the application of the procedure of conciliation. It may, however, stipulate that if the proposal for settlement by conciliation is not accepted by both parties, the Tribunal shall be required to give a decision regarding the plea of exception, and, if necessary, regarding the dispute itself.

Art. 5   The Tribunal shall apply:

Firstly: the conventions in force between the Parties, whether general or special, and the principles of law arising therefrom;

Secondly: international custom as evidence of a general practice accepted as law;

Thirdly: the general principles of law recognised by civilised nations.

If, in a particular case, the legal bases mentioned above are inadequate, the Tribunal shall give an award in accordance with the principles of law which, in its opinion, should govern international law.

For this purpose it shall be guided by decisions sanctioned by legal authorities and by jurisprudence.

If the Parties agree, the Tribunal may, instead of basing its decision on legal principles, give an award in accordance with considerations of equity.

Art. 6   Subject to special agreement to the contrary in each particular case, the Tribunal shall be constituted as follows:

The judges shall be chosen from the list of Members of the Permanent Court of Arbitration established by The Hague Convention, dated October 18, 1907, for the pacific settlement of international disputes.

Each Party shall appoint its own arbiter. The Parties shall jointly nominate three other arbiters, one of whom shall be the umpire. If, after having been appointed, one of the judges jointly elected acquires the nationality of one of the Parties, appoints his domicile in its territory or enters its service, either of the Parties may claim that he be replaced. Any disputes which may arise as to whether either of these conditions exists shall be settled by the other four judges; the eldest of the judges jointly elected shall take the chair in these cases, and if the votes are equally divided, he shall give a casting vote.

For each individual dispute there shall be a fresh election of judges. The Contracting Parties, however, reserve the right to act in concert regarding these elections, so that for a certain class of dispute arising within a fixed period, the same judges shall be seated on the Tribunal.

In case of the death of members of the Tribunal, or of their retirement, for any reason whatever, they shall be replaced according to the manner determined for their appointment.

Art. 7   In each individual case the Contracting Parties shall, in pursuance of the present Treaty, draw up an agreement of reference ("compromis"), to determine the subject of the dispute, any special terms of reference which may be accorded to the Tribunal, its composition, the place where it shall meet, the total amount that each Party concerned shall be obliged to deposit in advance to cover expenses, the rules to be observed with regard to the form and time limits of the proceedings, and any other detail that may be considered necessary.

Any disputes arising out of the terms of the agreement of reference, shall, subject to the terms of Article 8, be referred to arbitration.

Art. 8   If the agreement of reference has not been determined within a period of six months after one Party concerned has notified the other of its intention to refer the dispute to arbitration, either Party may request the Permanent Board of Conciliation provided for under Article 14, to establish the agreement of reference. The Permanent Board of Conciliation shall, within two months after having been convened, settle the terms of the agreement of reference abiding by the conclusions of each Party when determining the subject of the dispute.

The same procedure shall apply when one Party has not nominated the arbitrators for whose appointment it is responsible, or when the Parties concerned cannot agree upon the choice of judges to be jointly appointed, or upon the umpire.

Pending the constitution of the Tribunal, the Permanent Board of Conciliation shall also be competent to give an award upon any other dispute arising out of the agreement of reference.

Art. 9   The decisions of the Tribunal shall be based upon a majority vote.

Art. 10   The arbitration award shall specify the manner in which it is to be carried out, especially as regards the time-limits to be observed.

If in an arbitration award it is proved that a decision or measure of a court of law or other authority of one of the Parties is wholly or in part contrary to international law, and if the constitutional law of that Party does not permit, or only partially permits, the consequences of the decision or measure in question, to be annulled by administrative measures, the arbitration award shall award the injured Party equitable satisfaction of another kind.

Art. 11   Subject to compromissorial clauses to the contrary, either Party may claim a revision of the award by the Tribunal which gave the award. This demand shall only be warranted by the discovery of a fact, which exercises a decisive influence on the award, and which, at the time of the close of the discussion in Court was unknown to the Tribunal itself and to the Party demanding the revision, unless that Party ought to have been aware of it.

If, for any reason, any Members of the Tribunal do not take part in the revision proceedings, substitutes for them shall be appointed in the manner determined for their own appointment.

The limit of time within which the demand provided for in the first paragraph may be presented, shall be fixed in the arbitral award, unless it has already been fixed in the agreement of reference.

Art. 12 Any dispute arising between the Parties concerned as to the interpretation and execution of the award shall, in the absence of an agreement to the contrary, be submitted to the Tribunal which pronounced it. In the latter case the provision contained in Article 11, paragraph 2, shall also apply.

Art. 13 Any dispute which, under the terms of the present Treaty, cannot be referred to arbitration, shall, at the request of one of the Parties concerned, be submitted to the procedure of conciliation.

If the opposing Party claims that a dispute, for which conciliation procedure has been initiated, should be settled by the Tribunal, the latter shall first pronounce judgment upon this preliminary question.

The Governments of the Contracting Parties shall be entitled to agree that a dispute which, under the terms of the present Treaty, can be settled by arbitration, shall be referred to the conciliation procedure, either without appeal or subject to appeal to the Tribunal.

Art. 14 A Permanent Board of Conciliation shall be constituted for the procedure of conciliation.

The Permanent Board of Conciliation shall consist of five members. The Contracting Parties shall appoint one member each of their own choice, and nominate the other three members by mutual agreement. These three members shall not be nationals of the Contracting Parties, nor shall they be domiciled on their territory, nor employed in their service. The Contracting Parties shall by mutual agreement elect the President from among these three Members.

Either of the Contracting Parties shall at any time, if no procedure is pending or if no procedure has been proposed by one of the Parties, have the right to recall the member appointed by it, and to appoint a successor. In the same circumstances either Contracting Party shall be entitled to withdraw its consent to the appointment of any one of the three Members jointly elected. In that case a new member shall be appointed, without delay, by joint nomination.

While the procedure is actually in progress, the Members shall receive remuneration, the amount of which shall be fixed by the Parties concerned. The expenses of the Permanent Board of Conciliation shall be divided equally between the Contracting Parties.

The Permanent Board of Conciliation shall be constituted in the course of the six months following the exchange of ratifications of the present

Treaty. Retiring members shall be replaced as soon as possible in the manner laid down for the first election.

The Permanent Board of Conciliation shall determine its own meeting-place, and shall be at liberty to transfer it.

The Permanent Board of Conciliation shall, if need be, establish a registry. If it appoints nationals of the Contracting Parties to positions in this office, it shall treat both Parties alike.

If the nomination of the members to be appointed in common has not taken place within the six months following the exchange of ratifications, or, in the case of a vacancy on the Permanent Board of Conciliation, within the three months dating from the retirement or death of a member, the provisions of Article 45, paragraphs 4 to 6, of the Hague Convention, dated October 18, 1907, for the Pacific Settlement of International Disputes, shall be applicable by analogy as regards the appointment of members.

Art. 15   The Permanent Board of Conciliation shall draw up a report which shall determine the facts of the case and shall contain proposals for settling the dispute.

The report shall be submitted within six months from the day on which the dispute was laid before the Permanent Board of Conciliation, unless the Parties shall agree to cancel or extend this time-limit. The report shall be drawn up in three copies, one of which shall be handed to each of the Parties and the third preserved in the archives of the Permanent Board of Conciliation.

The report shall not, either as regards statement of facts or as regards legal considerations, be in the nature of a final judgment binding upon the parties. Each Party shall, however, state, within a time-limit to be fixed by the report, whether it and within what limits it recognises the accuracy of the facts noted in the report and accepts the proposals which it contains. The duration of this time-limit shall not exceed three months.

Art. 16   The Permanent Board of Conciliation shall begin work as soon as the question shall have been submitted to it by one of the Parties. That Party shall communicate its request to the President of the Permanent Board of Conciliation and at the same time to the opposing Party.

The Contracting Parties shall undertake to facilitate in all cases and in all respects, the work of the Permanent Board of Conciliation, and in particular, to grant it all legal assistance through the agency of competent authorities. The Permanent Board of Conciliation shall be entitled, within the limits of the competence of the local Courts, to summon and examine witnesses and experts and search premises in the territory of the Contracting Parties. It may draw up the procedure for the taking of evidence at a plenary meeting, or entrust this task to one or several [of the][1] members chosen by common agreement.

---

[1]   These words may have been omitted by oversight. Cf. the German text.

Art. 17   Every decision shall be taken by a majority of the members of the Permanent Board of Conciliation. Its deliberations shall be valid if all the Members have been duly convoked and if all the members elected by common agreement are present at the meeting.

Art. 18   The award pronounced as the result of the procedure of arbitration shall be carried out in good faith by the Parties concerned.

The Contracting Parties shall undertake during the course of the arbitration or conciliation proceedings to refrain as far as possible from any action liable to have a prejudicial effect on the execution of the award or on the acceptance of the proposals of the Permanent Board of Conciliation. They shall refrain from any act of a legal nature in connection with the conciliation proceedings until the expiration of the time limit fixed by the Permanent Board of Conciliation for the acceptance of its proposals.

At the request of one of the Parties, the Tribunal may order provisional measures to be taken in so far as the Parties are in a position to secure their execution, through administrative channels; the Permanent Board of Conciliation may also formulate proposals to the same effect.

Art. 19   Subject to the contrary provisions laid down in the present Treaty or the agreement of reference, the procedure of arbitration and conciliation is regulated by the Hague Convention for the pacific settlement of international disputes, of October 18, 1907.

In as far as the present Treaty refers to the stipulations of the Hague Convention, the latter shall continue to be applicable to relations between the Contracting Parties, even if one or both of them denounce the Convention.

The Tribunal or the Permanent Board of Conciliation shall be competent to decide as to the necessary provisions with regard to periods of grace or other details connected with the method of arbitration or conciliation, in so far as neither the present Treaty nor the agreement of reference, nor other Conventions in force between the Parties contain stipulations on these points.

Art. 20   The present Treaty shall be ratified[1] as soon as possible. The instruments of ratification shall be exchanged at Berne.

The Treaty shall come into force one month after the exchange of ratifications.

It is valid for a period of ten years. If, however, it is not denounced six months before the expiration of this period, it shall remain in force for a further period of two years, and so on, as long as it has not been denounced within the prescribed period.

If a dispute which has been referred to arbitration or conciliation has not been settled when the present Treaty expires, the case shall be proceeded

---

[1]   Here we have corrected the League of Nations translation by substituting "be ratified" for "come into force".

with according to the stipulations of the Treaty or of any other Convention which the Contracting Parties may agree to substitute therefor.

Final Protocol

(1) The Contracting Parties are agreed that in doubtful cases the stipulations of the present Treaty shall be interpreted in favour of the application of the principle of settlement of disputes by arbitration. In particular, the Contracting Parties declare that ordinary frontier disputes shall not be considered as disputes affecting their territorial integrity in the sense provided in Article 4 of the Treaty.

(2) The Contracting Parties declare that the Treaty shall apply equally to disputes arising out of events which occurred prior to its conclusion. In consideration of their general political bearing. an exception shall, however, be made with regard to disputes arising directly out of the world-war.

(3) The Treaty shall not cease to be applicable if a third State is concerned in a dispute. The Contracting Parties shall endeavour, if necessary, to induce the third State to agree to refer the dispute to arbitration or conciliation. In this case the two Governments may, if they so desire, jointly provide that the Tribunal or the Permanent Board of Conciliation shall be composed of members specially chosen for the case. If no agreement is reached with the third State within a reasonable period, the Contracting Parties shall proceed with the case in accordance with the provisions of the Treaty.

(4) The Contracting Parties declare that disputes between Germany and a Third State, in which Switzerland might be interested as a Member of the League of Nations, cannot be considered as disputes between the Contracting Parties in the sense intended by the present Treaty.

b) Amendment of the Treaty

Protocol Signed at Berne August 29, 1928;
Ratifications Exchanged June 13, 1929

(Translation)

With the object of amending the Arbitration and Conciliation Treaty concluded on December 3rd, 1921, between Switzerland and Germany with reference to the declarations made by Switzerland and Germany in connexion with Article 36, paragraph 2, of the Statute of the Permanent Court of International Justice at the Hague, the undersigned Plenipotentiaries of the Swiss Confederation and the German Reich have agreed as follows:

Art. 1   Article 4 of the Treaty of December 3rd shall be annulled; and conse-quentially the words "unless otherwise provided for in Articles 3 and 4" shall be replaced by the words "unless otherwise provided for in Article 3."

Art. 2   Article 8 of the Treaty of December 3rd, 1921, shall be replaced by the following clause: "If the arbitration agreement is not reached between the Parties within two months after one of the Parties has informed the other of its desire for the settlement of a dispute by arbitration, or if the court of arbitration has not been constituted within that period, either Party may submit the dispute direct to the Permanent Court of International Justice at the Hague."

In witness whereof the undersigned Plenipotentiaries have drawn up this Protocol, which shall be ratified and come into force on the day of the exchange of ratifications.

4. Swiss Model of a Treaty for Conciliation, Judicial Settlement and Arbitration of 1960

The Swiss Model of a Treaty for Conciliation, Judicial Settlement and Arbitration has the same scope as the European Convention for the Peaceful Settlement of Disputes of 1957. However, the system applied in the Swiss Model Treaty differs largely from that of the European Convention. In a first phase, the Model Treaty eliminates the difference between legal and non-legal, political, disputes by stipulating that "all disputes, of any nature whatsoever" are to be submitted to conciliation. Only if conciliation has failed is the dispute submitted to a procedure culminating in a binding decision. Once conciliation fails, the different categories of disputes become relevant in that legal disputes as defined in the Statute of the International Court of Justice (Art. 36, para. 2) are to be submitted to the International Court of Justice and non-legal disputes are to be submitted to an arbitral tribunal. The latter decided *ex aequo et bono*, but must respect the general principles of law as well as the legal interests of the parties to the dispute. When a legal dispute is submitted, by special agreement of the parties, to the arbitral tribunal instead of to the International Court of Justice, the arbitral tribunal must apply international law in reaching its decision.

While the conciliation commission is conceived of as a permanent body, the arbitral tribunal is to be instituted ad hoc. Both consist of five members. Each party to the dispute nominates one member leaving three neutral members. Local remedies must be exhausted before the procedures provided for in the Treaty are available. As is usual, the proceedings of the conciliation commission shall not be made public. An important feature of the Treaty is the fact that the various procedures may be invoked on the application of one party only. If one of the parties does not cooperate in creating the conciliation commission, the President of the International Court of Justice may be entrusted to make the necessary appointments; the same mechanism is provided for the appointment of the arbitrators. Even the special agreement may be drawn up by the Court upon unilateral action of one of the parties failing cooperation of the other one within three months. If the special agreement does not contain sufficient provisions for the functioning of an arbitral tribunal, the rules of procedure of the International Court of Justice apply.

By this Model Treaty, Switzerland continues her traditional practice concerning peaceful settlement of disputes as documented by the treaties concluded with Germany on December 3, 1921, with Columbia on August 20, 1927 and with France on April 6, 1925 (in force only 1934). The main feature of Swiss practice is the settlement of all disputes, whether legal or non-legal, by a binding decision.

The difficulty with this concept became evident, when Great Britain refused to commit herself to such binding arbitration procedures on non-legal issues.

Presently, the Treaty is in force between Switzerland and Cameroons (1963), Costa Rica (1965), Ivory Coast (1962), Great Britain and Northern Ireland (1965), Israel (1965), Liberia(1963), Madagaskar (1965), Niger (1963) (position 1977 taken from "Systematische Sammlung des Bundesrechts", Vol. 0.1/2)

These treaties follow in principle the model, contain, however, differences of detail. In order to give an example, the treaty concluded according to this model with Great-Britain and Northern Ireland shall be reproduced below because it is one of the most detailed examples and is available in an English version. For the original French text see Dispute Settlement in Public International Law, Texts and Materials, compiled by K. Oellers-Frahm and Norbert Wühler, 1984, p. 83 et seq.

Treaty for Conciliation, Judicial Settlement and Arbitration between the United Kingdom of Great Britain and Northern Ireland and the Swiss Confederation of July 7, 1965

The Government of the United Kingdom of Great Britain and Northern Ireland and the Swiss Federal Council:

Being desirous of strengthening the ties of friendship which unite the United Kingdom of Great Britain and Northern Ireland and the Swiss Confederation and of furthering, in the general interest of peace, the development of the procedures leading to the peaceful settlement of international disputes:

Have agreed as follows:

CHAPTER I. THE PRINCIPLE OF PEACEFUL SETTLEMENT OF DISPUTES

Art. 1   (1) The Contracting Parties undertake to submit to a procedure of conciliation all disputes, of any nature whatsoever, which may arise between them and which may not have been settled within a reasonable time by diplomacy.

(2) If the procedure of conciliation has failed, a dispute may be submitted in accordance with the relevant provisions of this Treaty either to judicial settlement or to arbitration.

(3) The Contracting Parties may however at any time agree that a particular dispute shall be referred directly to judicial settlement or, if the dispute is of a legal nature. to arbitration, without prior recourse to the procedure of conciliation.

CHAPTER II. CONCILIATION

Art. 2   (1) The Contracting Parties shall establish a Permanent Conciliation Commission (hereinafter referred to as "the Commission") composed of five members.

(2) The Contracting Parties shall each appoint a Commissioner, who may be chosen from among their respective nationals. The Contracting Parties shall jointly appoint the three other Commissioners from among the nationals of third States. These three Commissioners must be of different nationalities. They shall not be habitually resident in the territory of the Contracting Parties, nor be employed in their service.

(3) The President of the Commission shall be appointed by agreement between the Contracting Parties from among the jointly appointed Commissioners.

Art. 3   (1) The Commissioners shall be appointed for three years. Their appointment shall continue until their replacement and, in any event, until the termination of the work in hand at the expiry of their term of office. If it is intended to replace a Commissioner at the end of any period of three years, he shall be given at least six months' prior notice of such intention. A Commissioner who has not been given such notice shall be deemed to have been appointed for another period of three years, and so on.

(2) Vacancies which may occur as a result of death, resignation, or any other cause. shall be filled within the shortest possible time in the manner fixed for the original appointments.

(3) If any member of the Commission is unable to participate in the work of the Commission as a result of illness or any other circumstance, the Contracting Party or Parties, which appointed him, shall designate a substitute, who shall temporarily take his place.

Art. 4   Each of the Contracting Parties may replace the Commissioner chosen by it by someone possessing special competence in the matter in dispute. If either Contracting Party intends to do so, it shall inform the other Contracting Party of its intention at the time of the application for conciliation or not later than fifteen days after receipt of the notification of such application, as the case may be. Either Contracting Party may then, within six weeks, replace its own Commissioner, if it so desires.

Art. 5   (1) The Commission shall be set up within six months after the exchange of instruments of ratification of this Treaty.

(2) If any of the Commissioners to be jointly appointed are not appointed within the time-limit provided for in paragraph (1) of this Article or, in the case of replacement under paragraph (2) of Article 3, within three months from the date on which the seat became vacant, the task of making the necessary appointments may be entrusted to the President of the International Court of Justice at the request of either Contracting Party. Should the President be prevented from acting or be a national of either of the Contracting Parties, the task shall be entrusted to the Vice-President of the Court. If the latter is prevented from acting, or is a national of either of the Contracting Parties, the next senior Judge of the Court, who is not a national of either of the Contracting Parties, shall proceed to make these appointments.

(3) Should the Commissioners to be appointed by each of the Contracting Parties not be appointed within the time-limit provided for in paragraph (1) of this Article or, in the case of replacement under paragraph (2) of Article 3, within three months from the date on which the seat became vacant, the Commissioners shall be appointed in accordance with the procedure laid down in paragraph (2) of this Article.

(4) If the President of the Commission is not appointed by the Contracting Parties within two months following the constitution of the Commission or (when a vacancy has arisen) the reconstitution of the Commission, he shall be appointed in accordance with the procedure laid down in paragraph (2) of this Article.

Art. 6   (1) Disputes shall be brought before the Commission by means of an application addressed to the President by one of the Contracting Parties.

That Contracting Party shall at the same time inform the other of the application.

(2) The application, after having given a summary account of the subject of the dispute, shall contain the invitation to the Commission to take all necessary measures with a view to arriving at an amicable settlement.

Art. 7   The Commission shall after hearing the agents of the Contracting Parties, lay down the rules of procedure to be followed in each particular case. The rules of procedure shall be consistent with the provisions of this Treaty and shall ensure that at all stages of the proceedings the Contracting Parties have equal opportunity to present their cases. Moreover the rules of procedure set out in Annex I to this Treaty shall be followed unless the Commission, with the consent of the Contracting Parties, otherwise decides.

Art. 8   In the absence of agreement to the contrary between the Contracting Parties, the Commission shall meet at the place chosen by its President.

Art. 9   (1) The Contracting Parties shall be represented before the Commission by agents whose duty shall be to act as intermediaries between them and the Commission. The agents may, moreover, be assisted by counsel, experts and staff appointed by them for that purpose and may request that all persons whose evidence appears to them useful should be heard.

(2) The Commission shall be entitled to request oral explanations from the agents, counsel and experts of both Contracting Parties, as well as from all persons it may think desirable to summon before it with the consent of their Governments.

Art. 10   (1) In the absence of agreement to the contrary between the Contracting Parties, the decisions of the Commission shall be taken by a majority vote of its members and, except in relation to questions of procedure, decisions of the Commission shall be valid only if all members are present.

(2) A question of procedure may, if the Commission is not sitting and provided that the question is of an urgent nature, be decided by the President.

Art. 11   The Contracting Parties shall facilitate the work of the Commission and, in particular, shall supply it to the greatest possible extent with all relevant documents and information. They shall use the means at their disposal to allow it to proceed, in their territory and in accordance with their law, to summon and hear witnesses or experts and to visit the localities in question.

Art. 12   The proceedings of the Commission shall not be made public, except when a decision to that effect has been taken by the Commission with the consent of the Contracting Parties.

Art. 13   (1) The task of the Commission shall be to elucidate questions in dispute and, to that end, to collect information by means of enquiries or otherwise, and to endeavour to bring the Contracting Parties to an agreement.

(2) The Commission shall, unless the Contracting Parties agree to an extension of this period, present its report within six months from the date on which the dispute shall have been referred to the Commission. If the circumstances allow, the report shall contain a draft settlement of the dispute.

(3) Each Contracting Party shall receive a copy of the aforesaid report. The report has in no way the character of an arbitral award. It leaves to the Contracting Parties entire freedom as to the effect to be given to the findings or recommendations.

(4) If the Commission formulates recommendations. it shall, whenever possible, fix the period within which each Contracting Party shall inform the other whether it is prepared to give effect to them.

(5) No admission or proposal formulated during the course of the procedure of conciliation, either by one of the Contracting Parties or by the Commission, shall prejudice or affect in any manner the rights or the contentions of either Contracting Party in the event of the failure of the procedure of conciliation. Similarly, the acceptance by a Contracting Party of a finding, recommendation or draft settlement, formulated by the Commission, shall in no way imply any admission of the considerations of law or of fact upon which such finding, recommendation or draft settlement may have been based.

CHAPTER III. JUDICIAL SETTLEMENT

Art. 14   (1) If the procedure of conciliation has failed, or if the Contracting Parties have agreed not to have prior recourse to it, the Contracting Parties may refer the dispute to the International Court of Justice by means of a special agreement or by unilateral application in accordance with the provisions of its Statute, provided that the dispute is of a legal nature concerning:

a)   the interpretation of a treaty:

b)   any question of international law:

c)   the existence of any fact which, if established, would constitute a breach of an international obligation:

d)   the nature or extent of the reparation to be made for the breach of an international obligation.

(2) In the event of a dispute as to whether the Court has jurisdiction, the matter shall be settled by the decision of the Court.

(3) By special agreement between the Contracting Parties, disputes other than those mentioned in paragraph (1) of this Article may also be submitted to the Court. This provision shall not prejudice the power of the Court to decide a case *ex aequo et bono* if the Contracting Parties so agree.

CHAPTER IV. ARBITRATION

Art. 15   If the procedure of conciliation has failed, or if the Contracting Parties have agreed not to have prior recourse to it, the Contracting Parties may by special agreement refer a dispute of a legal nature to the procedure of arbitration provided for in this Chapter. The Arbitral Tribunal, of which it shall be the task to decide the questions in dispute, shall, in the absence of agreement to the contrary between the Contracting Parties, be constituted in each specific case as provided in Articles 16 to 19.

Art. 16   (1) The Arbitral Tribunal shall consist of five members. The Contracting Parties shall each appoint one member, who may be chosen from among their respective nationals. The Contracting Parties shall jointly appoint three other Arbitrators from among the nationals of third States. These three Arbitrators must be of different nationalities. They shall not be habitually resident in the territory of the Contracting Parties, nor be employed in their service.

(2) The President of the Arbitral Tribunal shall be appointed by agreement between the Contracting Parties from among the jointly appointed Arbitrators.

Art. 17   (1) If any of the Arbitrators to be jointly appointed are not appointed within a period of three months following the date of the special agreement concluded in accordance with Article 15, or in the case of replacement under paragraph (1) or Article 19 within three months from the date upon which the seat became vacant, the task of making the necessary appointments may he entrusted to the President of the International Court of Justice at the request of either Contracting Party. Should the President be prevented from acting or be a national of either of the Contracting Parties, the task shall be entrusted to the Vice-President of the Court. If the latter is prevented from acting, or is a national of either of the Contracting Parties, the next senior Judge of the Court, who is not a national of either of the Contracting Parties, shall proceed to make the appointments.

(2) If the Arbitrators to he appointed by each Contracting Party are not appointed within a period of three months following the date of the special agreement concluded in accordance with Article 15, or in the case of replacement under paragraph (1) of Article 14 within three months from the date upon which the seat became vacant, they shall be appointed in accordance with the procedure laid down in paragraph (1) of this Article.

(3) Should the President of the Arbitral Tribunal not be appointed by the Contracting Parties within two months following the constitution of the Arbitral Tribunal, or (when a vacancy has arisen), the reconstitution of the Arbitral Tribunal, he shall be appointed in accordance with the procedure provided for in paragraph (1) of this Article.

Art. 18 (1) Subject to the provisions of this Article and of Article 19 once the Arbitral Tribunal has been constituted the composition shall not be altered until it has given its award.

(2) However, as long as the procedure before the Arbitral Tribunal has not begun, each Contracting Party shall be entitled to replace the Arbitrator appointed by it by another person. After the commencement of the procedure, such replacement of an Arbitrator is subject to agreement between the Contracting Parties.

(3) The procedure shall be deemed to have begun as soon as the President of the Arbitral Tribunal has made the first procedural order.

Art. 19 (1) Vacancies which may occur as a result of death or resignation, shall be filled within the shortest possible time in the manner fixed for the original appointments.

(2) Each Contracting Party is entitled to appoint a deputy to replace, temporarily, the Arbitrator appointed by it if the latter is unavoidably prevented by illness or for any other reason from taking part in the proceedings. The Contracting Party, which intends to avail itself of this right, shall inform the other without delay.

Art. 20 The special agreement concluded in accordance with Article 15 shall specify the subject-matter of the dispute, the competence of the Arbitral Tribunal, the Procedure to be adopted, as well as any other conditions agreed upon between the Contracting Parties.

Art. 21 The Arbitral Tribunal shall be empowered to interpret the special agreement.

Art. 22 The rules of procedure set out in the special agreement shall be consistent with the provisions of this Treaty. Where the special agreement does not contain specific rules of procedure, the rules set out in Annex II to this Treaty shall apply.

Art. 23 (1) The Contracting Parties shall be represented before the Arbitral Tribunal by agents whose duty shall be to act as intermediaries between them and the Arbitral Tribunal. The agents may moreover be assisted by counsel, experts and staff appointed by them for that purpose and may request that all persons whose evidence appears to them useful should be heard.

(2) The Arbitral Tribunal shall be entitled to request oral explanations from the agents, counsel and experts of both Contracting Parties, as well as from all persons it may think desirable to summon before it with the consent of their Governments.

Art. 24 (1) All decisions of the Arbitral Tribunal shall be taken by a vote of a majority of its members.

(2) Any question of procedure, for which provision has not been made in this Treaty or in the special agreement between the Contracting Parties or in the rules of procedure set out in Annex II to this Treaty, shall be de-

cided by the Arbitral Tribunal, or if the Arbitral Tribunal is not sitting and the question is of an urgent nature, by the President.

Art. 25   All the proceedings and deliberations of the Arbitral Tribunal shall be conducted in private. There shall be no publication of the written proceedings, records, minutes, the award or any other document, except as may be agreed between the Contracting Parties.

Art. 26   The Arbitral Tribunal shall apply:

   (a)   international conventions, whether general or particular, establishing rules expressly recognised by the contesting States;

   (b)   international custom, as evidence of a general practice accepted as law;

   (c)   the general principles of law recognised by civilized nations;

   (d)   judicial decisions and the teachings of the most highly qualified publicists of the various nations, as subsidiary means for the determination of rules of law.

Art. 27   The award shall state the reasons on which it is based. A copy of the award shall be furnished to each Contracting Party.

CHAPTER V. GENERAL PROVISIONS

Art. 28   (1) The provisions of this Treaty shall not apply to:

   (a)   disputes relating to facts or situations prior to the entry into force of this Treaty;

   (b)   disputes concerning questions which by international law are solely within the domestic jurisdiction of either Contracting Party

   (c)   disputes in regard to which the Contracting Parties have agreed or shall agree to have recourse to some other method of peaceful settlement.

   (2) If after the initiation of the procedure of conciliation, judicial settlement, or arbitration, any disagreement arises between the Contracting Parties as to whether any question falls within the scope of this Article, the matter shall be settled by the Permanent Conciliation Commission, the International Court of Justice or the Arbitral Tribunal, as the case may be.

Art. 29   (1) In the case of a dispute the subject-matter of which, according to the municipal law of either Contracting Party, falls within the competence of its judicial or administrative authorities, the dispute shall not be submitted to conciliation, judicial settlement or arbitration in accordance with this Treaty, until a decision with final effect has been pronounced, within a reasonable time, by the competent national judicial or administrative authority.

(2) If such a decision has been given in the State concerned, no recourse to the procedures provided for in this Treaty shall be possible after the expiration of a period of five years following the said decision.

Art. 30 (1) In all cases where a dispute is referred to judicial settlement or to arbitration, and particularly if the question on which the Contracting Parties differ arises out of acts already committed or on the point of being committed, the International Court of Justice, acting in accordance with Article 41 of its Statute, or the Arbitral Tribunal, shall have power to indicate within the shortest possible time the provisional measures necessary to preserve the respective rights of the Contracting Parties. The Contracting Parties shall be bound to take such measures as are indicated by the Court or the Arbitral Tribunal.

(2) If the dispute is brought before the Permanent Conciliation Commission, it may recommend to the Contracting Parties the adoption of such provisional measures as it considers suitable.

Art. 31 The Contracting Parties shall abstain from all measures likely to react prejudicially upon the execution the judicial decision or arbitral award or upon the findings or recommendations of the Permanent Conciliation Commission and, in general, shall abstain from any sort of action whatsoever which may aggravate or extend the dispute.

Art. 32 The Contracting Parties shall comply with the decision of the International Court of Justice or the award of the Arbitral Tribunal. The decision or award shall be acted upon in good faith. It shall be acted upon immediately unless the Court or the Arbitral Tribunal has fixed a time-limit for the execution of the whole or part of the decision or award.

Art. 33 If the execution of a judicial decision or arbitral award would conflict with a judgment or measure enjoined by a court of law or other authority of either of the Contracting Parties and if the municipal law of that Contracting Party does not permit or only partially permits the consequences of the judgment or measure in question to be annulled, the International Court of Justice or the Arbitral Tribunal shall determine the nature or extent of the reparation to be awarded to the injured party.

Art. 34 Difficulties arising out of the interpretation of a judicial decision or arbitral award shall, upon unilateral application of either Contracting Party and within a period of three months following the date of the judgment or award, be submitted to the International Court of Justice or to the Arbitral Tribunal, as the case may be.

Art. 35 An application for revision of a judicial decision or arbitral award may be made only when it is based upon the discovery of some fact of such a nature as to be a decisive factor, which fact was, when the judicial decision or arbitral award was given, unknown to the International Court of Justice or the Arbitral Tribunal and also the Contracting Party claiming revision, always provided that such ignorance was not due to negligence. The proceedings for revision shall be opened by a decision of the International

Court of Justice or the Arbitral Tribunal expressly recording the existence of the new fact, recognising that it has such a character as to lay the case open to revision and declaring the application admissible on this ground. The application for revision must be made at latest within six months of the discovery of the new fact. No application for revision may be made after the lapse of ten years from the date of the award.

Art. 36   (1) This Treaty shall remain applicable as between the Contracting Parties, even though a third State has an interest in the dispute.

(2) In the procedure of conciliation the Contracting Parties may agree to invite a third State to intervene.

(3) In judicial or arbitral procedure, if a third State should consider that its legal interests are involved, it may submit to the International Court of Justice or to the Arbitral Tribunal a request to be permitted to intervene as a third party. It shall be for the Court or the Arbitral Tribunal to decide upon this request.

Art. 37   (1) For the actual duration of the procedure of conciliation or arbitration the jointly appointed members of the Permanent Conciliation Commission and of the Arbitral Tribunal shall receive emoluments the amount of which shall be fixed by agreement between the Contracting Parties, each of which shall contribute an equal share.

(2) Each Contracting Party shall bear its own expenses and an equal share of the costs arising out of the work of the Permanent Conciliation Commission and of the Arbitral Tribunal.

Art. 38   (1) Subject to paragraph (a) of Article 28 of this Treaty, disputes relating to the interpretation or execution of this Treaty may be submitted to the international Court of Justice by means of a unilateral application.

(2) Recourse to the International Court of Justice in accordance with paragraph (1) of this Article shall have the effect of suspending the conciliation or arbitration proceedings until the Court gives its decision.

(3) The provisions of Article 32 of this Treaty apply to such decisions of the Court.

Art. 39   (1) This Treaty shall not apply to disputes relating to anything done or omitted to be done in or in relation to any territory (other than the United Kingdom) for the international relations of which the Government of the United Kingdom of Great Britain and Northern Ireland are responsible unless this Treaty has been extended to such territory. Any such extension shall take effect from such date and subject to such modifications and conditions (including conditions as to termination) as may be specified and agreed between the Contracting Parties in Notes to be exchanged for this purpose.

(2) The termination of this Treaty in accordance with paragraph (2) of Article 40 shall, unless otherwise expressly agreed between the Contracting Parties, terminate the extension of this Treaty to any territory to which it has been extended under this Article.

Art. 40   (1) This Treaty shall be ratified. The instruments of ratification shall be exchanged at Berne as soon as possible.

(2) This Treaty shall enter into force as soon as the instruments of ratification have been exchanged.[1] It shall remain in force for five years from the date of its entry into force, and it shall thereafter remain in force for successive periods of five years. unless denounced by either Contracting Party by notice given in writing to the other at least six months before the expiration of any five-year period.

(3) If a procedure of conciliation, or judicial settlement or arbitration has been commenced at the time of the expiration of this Treaty, it shall be completed in accordance with the provisions of this Treaty or any other convention which the Contracting Parties may have agreed to substitute therefor.

Annex I

PERMANENT CONCILIATION COMMISSION

RULES OF PROCEDURE

1. The place of sitting once fixed in accordance with Article 8 of the Treaty, shall not be changed except by a decision of the Commission taken with the consent of the Contracting Parties.

2. The official languages of the Commission shall be English and French. Written pleadings and statements may be submitted either in English or in French. Oral proceedings shall be translated from one official language into the other, unless the Commission, with the consent of the agents, decides that translation may be dispensed with for the whole or any part of the proceedings.

3. The Commission may, if it deems it necessary, appoint a Registrar who, under the control of the President, will make the necessary arrangements for the sittings of the Commission, the taking of records and the preparation of minutes and discharge such other functions for the assistance of the Commission, as the Commission may require.

4. The Commission shall fix the dates on which each Contracting Party shall communicate to the Commission and to the other Contracting Party its statement of facts and the instruments, papers and documents which it considers useful for ascertaining the truth, as well as the list of witnesses and experts whose evidence it wishes to be heard.

5. The Commission may move temporarily to any place where it considers it may be useful to take evidence. Permission must be obtained from any third State on the territory of which evidence is to be taken.

---

[1]   The Treaty entered into force on 9 February 1967.

6. Every investigation and every examination of a locality must be made in the presence of the agents, counsel and experts of the Contracting Parties or after they have been duly summoned.

7. After the Contracting Parties have presented all their explanations and evidence and the witnesses have all been heard, the President shall declare the enquiry terminated and the Commission shall adjourn to deliberate and draw up its report.

8. The report shall be signed by all the members of the Commission. If one of the members refuses to sign, the fact shall be mentioned but the validity of the report shall not be affected.

Annex II

ARBITRAL TRIBUNAL

RULES OF PROCEDURE

1. If the place of sitting has not been agreed between the Contracting Parties, the Arbitral Tribunal shall meet at the place chosen by its President. The place of sitting, once fixed, shall not be changed except by a decision of the Arbitral Tribunal taken with the consent of the Contracting Parties.

2. The official languages of the Arbitral Tribunal shall be English and French. Written pleadings and statements may be submitted either in English or in French. Oral proceedings shall be translated from one official language into the other, unless the Arbitral Tribunal, with the consent of the agents, decides that translation may be dispensed with for the whole or any part of the proceedings.

3. The Arbitral Tribunal may, if it deems it necessary, appoint a Registrar who, under the control of the President, will make the necessary arrangements for the sittings of the Arbitral Tribunal, the taking of records and the preparation of minutes and discharge such other functions for the assistance of the Arbitral Tribunal, as the Arbitral Tribunal may require.

4. The procedure shall consist of two parts: written and oral. The written procedure shall consist of the communication to the Arbitral Tribunal and to the Contracting Parties of Memorials, Counter-Memorials and, if necessary, Replies and also all papers and documents in support. The oral proceedings shall consist of the hearing by the Arbitral Tribunal of witnesses, experts, agents and counsel.

5. In every case submitted to the Arbitral Tribunal, the President will ascertain the views of the Contracting Parties with regard to questions of procedure. For this purpose he may summon the agents to meet him as soon as they have been appointed. In the light of information obtained from the agents and with due regard to any agreement between the Contracting Parties, the President will make the necessary orders to determine inter alia the number and the order of filing of the pleadings and the time

limits within which they must be filed. The President may extend any time limit which has been fixed.

6. There must be annexed to every Memorial, Counter-Memorial, or other Pleadings, copies of all the relevant documents, a list of which shall be given after the submissions. If on account of the length of a document extracts only are attached, the document itself or a complete copy of it must, unless the document has been published and is available to the public, be furnished to the Registrar for the use of the Arbitral Tribunal and of the other Contracting Party. Every document which is in a language other than French or English must be accompanied by a translation either into French or English. In the case of lengthy documents translations of extracts may be submitted, subject however to any subsequent decision by the President or by the Arbitral Tribunal.

7. Each Contracting Party shall communicate to the President of the Arbitral Tribunal, in sufficient time before the commencement of the oral proceedings, information regarding the evidence which it intends to produce or which it intends to request the Arbitral Tribunal to obtain. This communication shall contain a list of the surnames, first names, descriptions and places of residence of the witnesses and experts whom the Contracting Party intends to call, with indications in general terms of the point or points to which their evidence will be directed.

8. The Arbitral Tribunal may move temporarily to any place where it considers it may be useful to take evidence. Permission must be obtained from any third State on the territory of which evidence is to be taken.

9. Every investigation and every examination of a locality must be made in the presence of the agents, counsel and experts of the Contracting Parties or after they have been duly summoned.

10. After the Contracting Parties have presented all their explanations and evidence and the witnesses have all been heard, the President shall declare the proceedings closed and the Arbitral Tribunal shall adjourn to deliberate and draw up its award.

Second Part:
Human Rights

I. UN Instruments on Human Rights

One of the primary goals of the United Nations is the realization of human rights as defined by the General Assembly in the Universal Declaration of Human Rights and Fundamental Freedoms of December 10, 1948. For making effective the respect of human rights, a Commission on Human Rights was created under the auspices of ECOSOC according to Art. 68 of the United Nations Charter. The functions of this Commission, however, are limited to the discussion of violations of human rights and are, thus, not very effective. On December 19, 1966 the United Nations successfully extended the general concepts of the Declaration into two covenants, the International Covenant on Civil and Political Rights and the International Covenant on Economic, Social and Cultural Rights, of which only one, the Covenant on Civil and Political Rights, established a special machinery for the more effective realization of those rights. Part IV of the Covenant provides for a Human Rights Committee and lays down detailed rules as to its composition and competence. However, this Committee, whose members have much the same status as judges, lack real decision-making power. Proceedings may be initiated by States according to Part IV of the Covenant, as well as by individuals under the Optional Protocol.

States may bring communications before the Committee to the effect that another State party has violated its obligations (Art. 41, para. 1). The competence of the Committee is, however, dependent upon the declaration of the States concerned, recognizing such competence. In these cases, the Committee is principally intended to make available to the parties its good offices (Art. 41, para. 1e). If no settlement can be reached in this way, the Committee is only empowered to draw up a report briefly stating the facts. In the second phase of the proceedings, an *ad hoc* conciliation commission may be set up with the consent of the States concerned. If this means of settling the dispute is also unsuccessful, the commission may communicate to the parties "its views on the possibility of an amicable solution of the matter" (Art. 42, para. 7c).

In the case of communications by individuals asserting a violation of rights protected under the Covenant, examination as to the merits is solely possible on the supplementary condition that the State in question has agreed to the Optional Protocol. In proceedings of this kind, the Committee does not make a binding decision, but is limited to communicating its "views" to the State and individual concerned. It is doubtful whether such "jurisdiction" may be said to include "judicial" powers of settlement.

The same procedure of implementation is applicable for the States parties to the Second Optional Protocol to the International Covenant on Civil and Political Rights Aiming at the Abolition of the Death Penalty of December 15, 1989 (text in

ILM 29 (1990) 1447), unless the State party concerned has made a statement to the contrary when acceding to the second optional protocol.

As mentioned above, the International Covenant on Economic, Social and Cultural Rights did not provide for an effective review mechanism. However, a revision on this topic has taken place by changing the composition of the Committee on Economic, Social and Cultural Rights which comprises no longer fifteen members elected by ECOSOC as originally provided, but, since 1987, eighteen independent experts. The primary task of the Committee lies in examining States' reports. The problem of overdue reports led the Committee to creating a procedure allowing for the consideration of the situation of particular States where those States had not produced reports for a long time and to request additional information from States parties where this seems necessary. The Committee cannot, however, hear individual petitions, nor has it an interstate complaints competence. In 1992, the Committee has proposed that an optional protocol providing for some kind of petition procedure be drafted and adopted.

Similar to the human rights protection in the framework of the Covenant on Civil and Political rights the UN Committee on the Elimination of Racial Discrimination established under Art. 8 of the International Convention on the Elimination of All Forms of Racial Discrimination provides for a special mechanism of protection. Besides the function to consider reports submitted by States parties to the Convention, to make suggestions and general recommendations, to assist in settling disputes among States parties, this Committee is competent to deal with "communications" from States (Art. 11, para. 1) as well as individuals (Art. 14, para. 1), provided the State concerned has made a declaration accepting this procedure. In the case of the institution of proceedings by a State, an *ad hoc* conciliation commission is appointed to deal with the matter if, during the first phase before the Committee, a solution acceptable to both parties has not been reached. The competence of the commission is limited to the formulation of "recommendations". No formal conclusion exists for proceedings instituted by an individual. The Convention requires only that the Committee shall "forward its suggestions and recommendations, if any, to the State party concerned and to the petitioner". These recommendations are published in the annual report of the Committee. This Covenant, however, in distinction to that on civil and political rights, provides for the possibility of unilaterally referring to the International Court of Justice a dispute concerning the interpretation or application of the Convention which has not been settled by negotiation or by the procedures provided for in the Covenant (Art. 22).

Also other UN instruments concerning particular question of human rights, such as the Convention on the Elimination of all Forms of Discrimination against Women of 1979, the Convention against Torture and other Cruel, Inhuman or Degrading Treatment or Punishment of 1984 as well as the Convention on the Right of the Child of 1989, provide for implementation mechanisms. Thus, the Convention against all Forms of Discrimination against Women provides in Art. 17 et seq. for the establishment of a Committee monitoring the implementation of the Convention. This Committee examines reports from States parties and makes general recommendations in much the same way as the CERD. On October 15, 1999 an Optional Protocol was adopted in order to empower the Committee to receive also communications from individuals or groups and to make inquiries and thus to render more effective the implementation procedures concerning the Convention. As to the Committee established according to Art. 17 et seq. of the Convention against Torture, it is enabled, as is the Committee under the Covenant on Civil and Political Rights, not only to examine states' reports, but also to receive communications from individuals and States, however it has not the competence to take binding decisions. As concerns the Convention on the Rights of the Child, the Committee provided for in Art. 42 et seq. has the competence to hear states' reports. It can only formulate concluding observations or request further information; it cannot take binding decisions.

Texts

International Convention on the Elimination of All Forms of Racial Discrimination:
    UNTS Vol. 660, pp. 195–318 (Chinese, English, French, Russian and Spanish)
    BGBl. 1969 II, pp. 962 et seq. (German)
Rules of Procedure of the Committee:
    CERD/C/35/Rev. 3 (1986)
International Covenant on Civil and Political Rights:
    A/Res./2200 (XXI) of December 19, 1966
    UNTS, Vol. 999 (1983), 172–346
    ILM Vol. 6 (1967), pp. 368 et seq. (English)
    BGBI. 1973 II pp. 1534 et seq. (German)
Optional Protocol:
    A/Res./2200 (XXI) of December 19, 1966 (English)
    Vereinte Nationen 1974, pp. 20 f. (German)
    ILM Vol. 6 (1967), pp. 383 et seq. (English)
Rules of Procedure of the Committee:
    GAOR, Report of the Human Rights Committee, 32nd Session
    Menschenrechte. Ihr internationaler Schutz (Beck-Texte) (1992) (German)
International Covenant on Economic, Social and Cultural Rights
    UN GA Res. 2200 A, December 16, 1966
    UNTS Vol. 993 (1983) 3–106
    Draft Optional Protocol Doc. E/CN. 4/1997/105
Convention on the Elimination of All Forms of Discrimination Against Women
    UNTS 13, 1249
    ILM 19 (1980, 33)
    BGBl. 1992 II, S. 122
Rules of Procedure of the Committee:
    GAOR 38th Session, Suppl. No. 45 (A/38/45)
    Report of the Committee on the Elimination for Discrimination Against Women (1983), p. 19
Convention Against Torture and Other Cruel, Inhuman or Degrading Treatment or Punishment
    ILM 23 (1984) 1027
    BGBl 1990 II, 247

Convention on the Rights of the Child
   ILM 28 (1989)
   BGBl 1992 II 122

Bibliographical notes

E. Schwelb, The International Convention on the Elimination of All Forms of Racial Discrimination, ICLQ Vol. 15 (1966), pp. 996–1059

U. P. Saskena, International Covenants on Human Rights, Indian Yearbook of International Affairs, Vol. 15/16 (1966/67), pp. 596 et seq.

J. Mourgeon, Les pactes internationaux relatifs aux droits de l'homme, AFDI 13 (1967), pp. 326 et seq.

J. P. Humphrey, International Committee on Human Rights — Report of the 53rd Conference, Buenos Aires (1968), pp. 437 et seq.

K. J. Partsch, Rassendiskriminierung. Die UN-Konventionen und ihre Wirkungsweise (1971), pp. 18 et seq.

E. Schwelb, Zur Frage der Anrufung der UN-Menschenrechtskommission durch Individuen und nichtstaatliche Organisationen, Vereinte Nationen, Vol. 19 (1971), pp. 27–55

R. Cassin, La Commission des droits de l'homme de l'ONU, 1947–1971, Miscellanea Ganshof van der Meersch (1972), pp. 397–433

F. Meissner, Die Menschenrechtsbeschwerde vor den Vereinten Nationen (1976)

M. E. Tardu, The Protocol to the United Nations Covenant on Civil and Political Rights and the Inter-American System: A Study of Co-Existing Petition Procedures, AJIL Vol. 70 (1976), pp. 778 et seq.

M. Bossuyt, Le Règlement Intérieur du Comité des Droits de l'Homme, Rev. belge Vol. 14 (1978/79), pp. 79 et seq.

K. Hüfner (ed.), Zur Kodifizierung der Menschenrechte durch das UNO-System (1978)

K. Vasak (ed.), Les dimensions internationales des droits de l'homme (1978), pp. 253–506: Human Rights in Special Organizations of the UN

G. Zieger et al., Die Ausübung staatlicher Gewalt in Ost und West nach Inkrafttreten der UN-Konvention über zivile und politische Rechte (1978)

M. Lippman, Human Rights Revisited: The Protection of Human Rights under the International Covenant on Civil and Political Rights, NILR Vol. 26 (1979), pp. 221–277

B. S. Ramcharan, Implementing the International Covenants on Human Rights, in: Thirty Years after the Universal Declaration (1979), 159 et seq.

N. Lerner, The UN Convention on the Elimination of All Forms of Racial Discrimination (1980)

J.-B. Marie, La pratique de la Commission des droits de l'homme de l'O.N.U. en matière de violation des droits de l'homme, Rev. belge Vol. 15 (1980) pp. 355–380

J. Delbrück, Die Konvention der Vereinten Nationen zur Beseitigung jeder Form der Diskriminierung der Frau von 1979 im Kontext der Bemühungen um einen völkerrechtlichen Schutz der Menschenrechte, in: Festschrift für Hans-Jürgen Schlochauer (1981), pp. 247–270

E. Mose/T. Opsahl, The Optional Protocol to the International Covenant on Civil and Political Rights, Santa Clara Law Review Vol. 21 (1981), pp. 271–331

M. Nowak, The Effectiveness of the International Covenant on Civil and Political Rights — Stocktaking After the First Eleven Sessions of the UN-Human Rights Committee, HRLJ Vol. 1 (1980), pp. 136 – 170

Ch. Tomuschat, Equality and Non-Discrimination under the International Covenant on Civil and Political Rights, in: Festschrift für Hans-Jürgen Schlochauer (1981), pp. 691–716

H. Tolley jr., Decision Making at the United Nations Commission on Human Rights (1979–1982), Human Rights Quarterly Vol. 5 (1983), 27–57

P. Alston, Out of the Abyss: The Challenge Confronting the New UN Committee on Economic, Social and Cultural Rights, Human Rights Quarterly 9 (1987), 332 et seq.

A. Byrnes, The "Other" Human Rights Body: The Work of the Committee on the Elimination of Discrimination Against Women, Yale Journal of International Law 14 (1989), 1 et seq.

A. Byrnes, The Committee against Torture, in: The United Nations and Human Rights, 509 et seq.

R. Jacobson, The Committee on the Elimination of Discrimination against Women, in: The United Nations and Human Rights, 444 et seq.

A. Dormenval, UN Committee Against Torture: Practice and Perspectives NQHR 8 (1990), 26 et seq.

A. Cassese (ed.), The international fight against torture (1991)

M. Santos Paisa, The Convention on the Rights of the Child and the Work of the Committee, Israel Law Review 26 (1992), 16 et seq.

M. Nowak, UN Covenant on Civil and Political Rights: CCPR Commentary (1993)

L.B. Sohn, Guide to the interpretation of the International Covenant on economic, social and cultural rights (1993)

R. Cook (ed.), Human Rights of Women: National and International Perspectives (1994)

D. McGoldrick, The Human Rights Committee. Its Role in the Development of the International Covenant on Civil and Political Rights (2nd ed. 1994)

G. Van Bueren, The International Law on the Rights of the Child (1995)

C. Tomuschat, International Covenant on Civil and Political Rights, Human Rights Committee, in: Bernhardt (ed.) EPIL, vol. II (1995), 1115–1119 with further bibliographical indications

M.C.R. Craves, The International Covenant on economic, social and cultural rights: a perspective of its development (1995)

G. Cohen-Jonathan, Human Rights Covenants, in: Bernhardt (ed.) EPIL, Vol. II (1995), 915 et seq. with further bibliographical indications

M.-C. Castrermans-Holleman, The protection of economic, social and cultural rights within the UN-framework, Netherlands international law review 42 (1995), 353–373

M. Nowak, The activities of the UN Human Rights Committee: developments from 1 August 1992 to 31 July 1995, Human rights law journal 16 (1995), 377–397

J. Boerefijn, Towards a strong system of supervision: The Human Rights Committee's role in reforming the reporting procedure under Article 40 of the Covenant on Civil and Political Rights, Human Rights Quarterly 17 (1995), 766–793

G. v. Bueren, The International Law on the Rights of the Child (1995)

I.J. LeBlanc, The Convention on the Rights of the Child: United Nations Lawmaking on Human Rights (1995)

R. Chapman, A "violation approach" for monitoring the International Covenant on Economic, Social and Cultural Rights, Human rights quarterly 18 (1996), 23–66

J. Dhommeaux, Jurisprudence du Comité des droits de l'homme des Nations Unies, Novembre 1993–Juillet 1996, AFDI 42 (1996), 679–714

R. Wolfrum, The implementation of international standards on prevention and elimination of racial discrimination: achievements and challenges, in: The Struggle against discrimination (Paris 1996), 45–78

R. deGouttes, La Convention internationale et le Comité des Nations Unies sur l'élimination de la discrimination raciale, Revue trimestrielle des droits de l'homme 7 (1996), 515–539

K. Koufa, Elimination of racial discrimination and the role of the United Nations Sub-Commission on Prevention of Discrimination and Protection of Minorities, International Geneva Yearbook 10 (1996), 44–63

Activity of the Committees

For the activity of the different Committees reference is made to the Annual Reports of the Committees to the Secretary-General of the United Nations

1. UN Commission on Human Rights

a) Resolution E/20 of February 15, 1946

Resolution of the Economic and Social Council of 16 February 1946 (document E/20 of 15 February 1946), on the establishment of a Commission on Human Rights and a Sub-Commission on the Status of Women, supplemented by the action taken by the Council on 18 February 1946, completing paragraphs 6 and 7 of section A and paragraphs 4 and 5 of section B concerning the initial composition of these bodies.

Section A

1. *The Economic and Social Council*, being charged under the Charter with the responsibility of promoting universal respect for, and observance of, human rights and fundamental freedoms for all without distinction as to race, sex, language or religion, and requiring advice and assistance to enable it to discharge this responsibility,

Establishes a Commission on Human Rights.

2. The work of the Commission shall be directed towards submitting proposals, recommendations and reports to the Council regarding:

(a) An international bill of rights;

(b) International declarations or conventions on civil liberties, the status of women, freedom of information and similar matters;

(c) The protection of minorities;

(d) The prevention of discrimination on grounds of race, sex, language or religion.

3. The Commission shall make studies and recommendations and provide information and other services at the request of the Economic and Social Council.

4. The Commission may propose to the Council any changes in its terms of reference.

5. The Commission may make recommendations to the Council concerning any sub-commission which it considers should be established.

6. Initially, the Commission shall consist of a nucleus of nine members appointed in their individual capacity for a term of office expiring on 31 March 1947. They are eligible for re-appointment. In addition to exercis-

ing the functions enumerated in paragraphs 2, 3 and 4, the Commission thus constituted shall make recommendations on the definitive composition of the Commission to the second session of the Council.

7. The Council hereby appoints the following persons as initial members of the Commission:

SECTION B

1. *The Economic and Social Council*, considering that the Commission on Human Rights will require special advice on problems relating to the status of women,

Establishes a Sub-Commission on the Status of Women.

2. The Sub-Commission shall submit proposals, recommendations and reports to the Commission on Human Rights regarding the status of women.

3. The Sub-Commission may submit proposals to the Council, through the Commission on Human Rights, regarding its terms of reference.

4. Initially, the Sub-Commission shall consist of a nucleus of nine members appointed in their individual capacity for a term of office expiring on 31 March 1947. They are eligible for re-appointment. In addition to exercising the functions enumerated in paragraphs 2 and 3, the Sub-Commission thus constituted shall make recommendations on the definitive composition of the Sub-Commission to the second session of the Council through the Commission on Human Rights.

5. The Council hereby appoints the following persons as initial members of this Sub-Commission: ... and, in addition, the names of one national each from Poland and the Union of Soviet Socialist Republics to be transmitted to the Secretary-General, not later than 31 March 1946, by the member of the Council for the Union of Soviet Socialist Republics, and three members appointed by the Commission on Human Rights to serve as *ex officio* members of this Sub-Commission.

b) Resolution E/56/Rev. 1 and E/84 of June 21, 1946

Resolution adopted on 21 June 1946 (documents E/56/Rev. I and E/84, paragraph 4, both as amended by the Council)

The Economic and Social Council, having considered the report of the nuclear Commission on Human Rights of 21 May 1946 (document E/38/Rev. 1)

Decides as follows:

1. FUNCTIONS

The functions of the Commission on Human Rights shall be those set forth in the terms of reference of the Commission, approved by the Economic and Social Council in its resolution of 16 February 1946, with the addition to paragraph 2 of that resolution of a new sub-paragraph (e) as follows:

(e) Any other matter concerning human rights not covered by items (a), (b), (c) and (d).

2. COMPOSITION

(a) The Commission on Human Rights shall consist of one representative from each of eighteen members of the United Nations selected by the Council.

(b) With a view to securing a balanced representation in the various fields covered by the Commission, the Secretary-General shall consult with the Governments so selected before the representatives are finally nominated by these Governments and confirmed by the Council.

(c) Except for the initial period, the term of office shall be for three years. For the initial period, one-third of the members shall serve for two years, one-third for three years, and one-third for four years, the term of each member to be determined by lot.

(d) Retiring members shall be eligible for re-election.

(e) In the event that a member of the Commission is unable to serve for the full three-year term, the vacancy thus arising shall be filled by a representative designated by the Member Government, subject to the provisions of paragraph (b) above.

3. WORKING GROUPS OF EXPERTS

The Commission is authorized to call in *ad hoc* working groups of non-governmental experts in specialized fields or individual experts, without further reference to the Council, but with the approval of the President of the Council and the Secretary-General.

4. DOCUMENTATION

The Secretary-General is requested to make arrangements for:

(a) The compilation and publication of a year-book on law and usage relating to human rights, the first edition of which should include all declarations and bills on human rights now in force in the various countries;

(b) The collection and publication of information on the activities concerning human rights of all organs of the United Nations;

(c) The collection and publication of information concerning human rights arising from trials of war criminals, quisling and traitors, and in particular from the Nuremberg and Tokyo trials;

(d) The preparation and publication of a survey of the development of human rights;

(e) The collection and publication of plans and declarations on human rights by specialized agencies and non-governmental national and international organizations.

5. INFORMATION GROUPS

Members of the United Nations are invited to consider the desirability of establishing information groups or local human rights committees within their respective countries to collaborate with them in furthering the work of the Commission on Human Rights.

6. HUMAN RIGHTS IN INTERNATIONAL TREATIES

Pending the adoption of an international bill of rights, the general principle shall be accepted that international treaties involving basic human rights, including to the fullest extent practicable treaties of peace, shall conform to the fundamental standards relative to such rights set forth in the Charter.

7. PROVISIONS FOR IMPLEMENTATION

Considering that the purpose of the United Nations with regard to the promotion and observance of human rights, as defined in the Charter of the United Nations, can only be fulfilled if provisions are made for the implementation of human rights and of an international bill of rights, the Council requests the Commission on Human Rights to submit at an early date suggestions regarding the ways and means for the effective implementation of human rights and fundamental freedoms, with a view to assisting the Economic and Social Council in working out arrangements for such implementation with other appropriate organs of the United Nations.

8. SUB-COMMISSION ON FREEDOM OF INFORMATION AND OF THE PRESS

(a) The Commission on Human Rights is empowered to establish a sub-commission on freedom of information and of the press.

(b) The function of the sub-commission shall be, in the first instance, to examine what rights, obligations and practices should be included in the concept of freedom of information, and to report to the Commission on Human Rights on any issues that may arise from such examination.

9. Sub-Commission on the Protection of Minorities

a) The Commission on Human Rights is empowered to establish a sub-commission on the protection of minorities.

(b) Unless the Commission otherwise decides, the function of the sub-commission shall be, in the first instance, to examine what provisions should be adopted in the definition of the principles which are to be applied in the field of protection of minorities, and to deal with the urgent problems in this field by making recommendations to the Commission.

10. Sub-Commission on the Prevention of Discrimination

a) The Commission on Human Rights is empowered to establish a sub-commission on the prevention of discrimination on the grounds of race, sex, language or religion.

(b) Unless the Commission otherwise decides, the functions of the sub-commission shall be, in the first instance, to examine what provisions should be adopted in the definition of the principles which are to be applied in the field of the prevention of discrimination, and to deal with the urgent problems in this field by making recommendations to the Commission.

c) Resolution 728 F of July 30, 1959

The Economic and Social Council,

Having considered chapter V of the report of the Commission on Human Rights on its first session[1], concerning communications, and chapter IX of the report of the Commission on its fifteenth session[2],

1. *Approves* the statement that the Commission on Human Rights recognizes that it has no power to take any action in regard to any complaints concerning human rights;

2. *Requests* the Secretary-General:

(a) To compile and distribute to members of the Commission on Human Rights before each session a non-confidential list containing a brief indication of the substance of each communication, however addressed, which deals with the principles involved in the promotion of universal re-

---

[1]   ESCOR, Fourth Session, Supplement No. 3 (E/259).
[2]   ESCOR, Twenty-eighth Session, Supplement No. 8 (E/3229).

spect for, and observance of human rights and to divulge the identity of the authors of such communications unless they indicate that they wish their names to remain confidential;

(b) To compile before each session of the Commission a confidential list containing a brief indication of the substance of other communications concerning human rights, however addressed, and to furnish this list to members of the Commission, in private meeting, without divulging the identity of the authors of communications except in cases where the authors state that they have already divulged or intend to divulge their names or that they have no objection to their names being divulged;

(c) To enable the members of the Commission, upon request, to consult the originals of communications dealing with the principles involved in the promotion of universal respect for, and observance of, human rights;

(d) To inform the writers of all communications concerning human rights, however addressed, that their communications will be handled in accordance with this resolution, indicating that the Commission has no power to take any action in regard to any complaint concerning human rights;

(e) To furnish each Member State concerned with a copy of any communication concerning human rights which refers explicitly to that State or to territories under its jurisdiction, without divulging the identity of the author, except as provided for in sub-paragraph (b) above;

(f) To ask Governments sending replies to communications brought to their attention in accordance with sub-paragraph (e) whether they wish their replies to be presented to the Commission in summary form or in full;

3. *Resolves* to give members of the Sub-Commission on Prevention of Discrimination and Protection of Minorities, with respect to communications dealing with discrimination and minorities, the same facilities as are enjoyed by members of the Commission on Human Rights under the present resolution;

4. *Suggests* to the Commission on Human Rights that it should at each session appoint an *ad hoc* committee to meet shortly before its next session for the purpose of reviewing the list of communications prepared by the Secretary-General under paragraph 2 (a) above and of recommending which of these communications, in original, should, in accordance with paragraph 2 (c) above, be made available to members of the commission on request.

d) Resolution 1235 (XLII) of July 6, 1967

Question of the violation of human rights and fundamental freedoms, including policies of racial discrimination and segregation and of apartheid, in all countries, with particular reference to colonial and other dependent countries and territories

The Economic and Social Council,

Noting resolutions 8 (XXIII) and 9 (XX111) of the Commission on Human Rights,

1. *Welcomes* the decision of the Commission on Human Rights to give annual consideration to the item entitled "Question of the violation of human rights and fundamental freedoms, including policies of racial discrimination and segregation and of apartheid, in all countries, with particular reference to colonial and other dependent countries and territories," without prejudice to the functions and powers of organs already in existence or which may be established within the framework of measures of implementation included in international covenants and conventions on the protection of human rights and fundamental freedoms; and concurs with the requests for assistance addressed to the Sub-Commission on Prevention of Discrimination and Protection of Minorities and to the Secretary-General;

2. *Authorizes* the Commission on Human Rights and the Sub-Commission on Prevention of Discrimination and Protection of Minorities, in conformity with the provisions of paragraph 1 of the Commission's resolution 8 (XXIII) to examine information relevant to gross violations of human rights and fundamental freedoms, as exemplified by the policy of apartheid as practised in the Republic of South Africa and in the Territory of South West Africa under the direct responsibility of the United Nations and now illegally occupied by the Government of the Republic of South Africa, and to racial discrimination as practised notably in Southern Rhodesia, contained in the communications listed by the Secretary-General pursuant to Economic and Social Council resolution 728 F (XXV111) of 30 July 1959;

3. *Decides* that the Commission on Human Rights may, in appropriate cases, and after careful consideration of the information thus made available to it, in conformity with the provisions of paragraph 1 above, make a thorough study of situations which reveal a consistent pattern of violations of human rights, as exemplified by the policy of apartheid as practised in the Republic of South Africa and in the Territory of South West Africa under the direct responsibility of the United Nations and now illegally occupied by the Government of the Republic of South Africa, and racial discrimination as practised notably in Southern Rhodesia, and report, with recommendations thereon, to the Economic and Social Council;

4. *Decides* to review the provisions of paragraphs 2 and 3 of the present resolution after the entry into force of the International Covenants on Human Rights;

5. *Takes note* of the fact that the Commission on Human Rights, in its resolution 6 (XXIII), has instructed an *ad hoc* study group to study in all

its aspects the question of the ways and means by which the Commission
might be enabled or assisted to discharge functions in relation to violations of human rights and fundamental freedoms, whilst maintaining and
fulfilling its other functions;

6. *Requests* the Commission on Human Rights to report to it on the result
of this study after having given consideration to the conclusions of the *ad
hoc* study group referred to in paragraph 5 above.

e) Resolution 1503 (XLVIII) of May 27, 1970

Procedure for dealing with communications relating to violations of human rights and fundamental freedoms

The Economic and Social Council,

Noting resolutions 7 (XXVI)[1] and 17 (XXV)[2] of the Commission on Human Rights and resolution 2 (XXI)[3] of the Sub-Commission on Prevention of Discrimination and Protection of Minorities,

1. *Authorizes* the Sub-Commission on Prevention of Discrimination and
Protection of Minorities to appoint a working group consisting of not
more than five of its members, with due regard to geographical distribution, to meet once a year in private meetings for a period not exceeding
ten days immediately before the sessions of the Sub-Commission to consider all communications, including replies of Governments thereon, received by the Secretary-General under Council resolution 728 F
(XXVIII) of 30 July 1959 with a view to bringing to the attention of the
Sub-Commission those communications, together with replies of Governments, if any, which appear to reveal a consistent pattern of gross and
reliably attested violations of human rights and fundamental freedoms
within the terms of reference of the Sub-Commission;

2. *Decides* that the Sub-Commission on Prevention of Discrimination and
Protection of Minorities should, as the first stage in the implementation
of the present resolution, devise at its twenty-third session appropriate
procedures for dealing with the question of admissibility of communications received by the Secretary-General under Council resolution 728 F
(XXVIII) and in accordance with Council resolution 1235 (XLII) of 6
June 1967;

3. *Requests* the Secretary-General to prepare a document on the question
of admissibility of communications for the Sub-Commission's consideration at its twenty-third session;

---

[1] See Official Records of the Economic and Social Council, Forty-eighth Session,
Supplement No. 5 (E/4816), chap. XXIII.

[2] Ibid., Forty-sixth Session, document E/4621, chap XVIII.

[3] E/CN.4/976, chap. VI.

4. *Further requests* the Secretary-General:

(a) To furnish to the members of the Sub-Commission every month a list of communications prepared by him in accordance with Council resolution 728 F (XXVIII) and a brief description of them, together with the text of any replies received from Governments;

(b) To make available to the members of the working group at their meetings the originals of such communications listed as they may request, having due regard to the provisions of paragraph 2 (b) of Council resolution 728 F (XXVIII) concerning the divulging of the identity of the authors of communications;

(c) To circulate to the members of the Sub-Commission, in the working languages, the originals of such communications as are referred to the Sub-Commission by the working group;

5. *Requests* the Sub-Commission on Prevention of Discrimination and Protection of Minorities to consider in private meetings, in accordance with paragraph 1 above, the communications brought before it in accordance with the decision of a majority of the members of the working group and any replies of Governments relating thereto and other relevant information, with a view to determining whether to refer to the Commission on Human Rights particular situations which appear to reveal a consistent pattern of gross and reliably attested violations of human rights requiring consideration by the Commission;

6. *Requests* the Commission on Human Rights after it has examined any situation referred to it by the Sub-Commission to determine:

(a) Whether it requires a thorough study by the Commission and a report and recommendations thereon to the Council in accordance with paragraph 3 of Council resolution 1235 (XLII);

(b) Whether it may be a subject of an investigation by an *ad hoc* committee to be appointed by the Commission which shall be undertaken only with the express consent of the State concerned and shall be conducted in constant co-operation with that State and under conditions determined by agreement with it. In any event, the investigation may be undertaken only if:

(i) All available means at the national level have been resorted to and exhausted;

(ii) The situation does not relate to a matter which is being dealt with under other procedures prescribed in the constituent instruments of, or conventions adopted by, the United Nations and the specialized agencies, or in regional conventions, or which the State concerned wishes to submit to other procedures in accordance with general or special international agreements to which it is a party.

7. *Decides* that if the Commission on Human Rights appoints an *ad hoc* committee to carry on an investigation with the consent of the State concerned:

(a) The composition of the committee shall be determined by the Commission. The members of the committee shall be independent persons whose competence and impartiality is beyond question. Their appointment shall be subject to the consent of the Government concerned;

(b) The committee shall establish its own rules of procedure. It shall be subject to the quorum rule. It shall have authority to receive communications and hear witnesses, as necessary. The investigation shall be conducted in co-operation with the Government concerned;

(c) The committee's procedure shall be confidential, its proceedings shall be conducted in private meetings and its communications shall not be publicized in any way;

(d) The committee shall strive for friendly solutions before, during and even after the investigation;

(e) The committee shall report to the Commission on Human Rights with such observations and suggestions as it may deem appropriate;

8. *Decides* that all actions envisaged in the implementation of the present resolution by the Sub-Commission on Prevention of Discrimination and Protection of Minorities or the Commission on Human Rights shall remain confidential until such time as the Commission may decide to make recommendations to the Economic and Social Council;

9. *Decides* to authorize the Secretary-General to provide all facilities which may be required to carry out the present resolution, making use of the existing staff of the Division of Human Rights of the United Nations Secretariat;

10. *Decides* that the procedure set out in the present resolution for dealing with communications relating to violations of human rights and fundamental freedoms should be reviewed if any new organ entitled to deal with such communications should be established within the United Nations or by international agreement.

f) Resolution 1 (XXIV) of August 13, 1971

Question of the Violation of Human Rights and Fundamental Freedoms, Including Policies of Racial Discrimination and Segregation and of Apartheid, in all Countries, with Particular Reference to Colonial and Other Dependent Countries and Territories

The Sub-Commission on Prevention of Discrimination and Protection of Minorities,

Considering that the Economic and Social Council, by its resolution 1503 (XLVIII), decided that the Sub-Commission should devise appropriate procedures for dealing with the question of admissibility of communications received by the Secretary-General under Council resolution 728 F

(XXVIII) of 30 July 1959 and in accordance with Council resolution 1235 (XLII) of 6 June 1967,

Adopts the following provisional procedures for dealing with the question of admissibility of communications referred to above:

(1) STANDARDS AND CRITERIA

(a) The object of the communication must not be inconsistent with the relevant principles of the Charter, of the Universal Declaration of Human Rights and of the other applicable instruments in the field of human rights.

(b) Communications shall be admissible only if, after consideration thereof, together with the replies if any of the Governments concerned, there are reasonable grounds to believe that they may reveal a consistent pattern of gross and reliably attested violations of human rights and fundamental freedoms, including policies of racial discrimination and segregation and of *apartheid*, in any country, including colonial and other dependent countries and peoples.

(2) SOURCE OF COMMUNICATIONS

(a) Admissible communications may originate from a person or group of persons who, it can be reasonably presumed, are victims of the violations referred to in sub-paragraph (1) (b) above, any person or group of persons who have direct and reliable knowledge of those violations, or non-governmental organizations acting in good faith in accordance with recognized principles of human rights, not resorting to politically motivated stands contrary to the provisions of the Charter of the United Nations and having direct and reliable knowledge of such violations.

(b) Anonymous communications shall be inadmissible; subject to the requirements of subparagraph 2 (b) of resolution 728 F (XXVIII) of the economic and Social Council, the author of a communication, whether an individual, a group of individuals or an organization, must be clearly identified.

(c) Communications shall not be inadmissible solely because the knowledge of the individual authors is second-hand, provided that they are accompanied by clear evidence.

(3) CONTENTS OF COMMUNICATIONS AND NATURE OF ALLEGATIONS

(a) The communication must contain a description of the facts and must indicate the purpose of the petition and the rights that have been violated.

(b) Communications shall be inadmissible if their language is essentially abusive and in particular if they contain insulting references to the State against which the complaint is directed. Such communications may be considered if they meet the other criteria for admissibility after deletion of the abusive language.

(c) A communication shall be inadmissible if it has manifestly political motivations and its subject is contrary to the provisions of the Charter of the United Nations.

(d) A communication shall be inadmissible if it appears that it is based exclusively on reports disseminated by mass media.

(4) EXISTENCE OF OTHER REMEDIES

(a) Communications shall be inadmissible if their admission would prejudice the functions of the specialized agencies of the United Nations system.

(b) Communications shall be inadmissible if domestic remedies have not been exhausted, unless it appears that such remedies would be ineffective or unreasonably prolonged. Any failure to exhaust remedies should be satisfactorily established.

(c) Communications relating to cases which have been settled by the State concerned in accordance with the principles set forth in the Universal Declaration of Human Rights and other applicable documents in the field of human rights will not be considered.

(5) TIMELINESS

A communication shall be inadmissible if it is not submitted to the United Nations within a reasonable time after the exhaustion of the domestic remedies as provided above.

g) Resolution 2 (XXIV) of August 16, 1971

Question of the Violation of Human Rights and Fundamental Freedoms, Including Policies of Racial Discrimination and Segregation and of Apartheid, in all Countries with Particular Reference to Colonial and Other Dependent Countries and Territories

The Sub-Commission on Prevention of Discrimination and Protection of Minorities,

Considering that the Economic and Social Council in paragraph 1 of resolution 1503 (XLVIII), adopted on 27 May 1970, authorized the Sub-Commission to appoint a working group consisting of not more than five of its members, with due regard to geographical distribution, to meet once a year in private meetings for a period not exceeding 10 days immediately before the sessions of the Sub-Commission to consider all communications, including replies of Governments thereon, received by the Secretary-General under Council resolution 728 F (XXVIII) of 30 July 1959 with a view to bringing to the attention of the Sub-Commission those communications, together with replies of Governments, if any, which appear to reveal a consistent pattern of gross and reliably attested violations of human rights and fundamental freedoms within the terms of reference of the Sub-Commission,

1. *Decides* that the working group referred to in paragraph 1 of Economic and Social Council resolution 1503 (XLVIII) shall be constituted in the manner set out below:

(a) Before the end of each session of the Sub-Commission, the names of five members of the Sub-Commission shall be selected by the Chairman, after Consultations with the members of each geographical area to constitute the working group for the next session, one from each of the following geographical areas, namely (i) African, (ii) Asian, (iii) Eastern European, (iv) Western European and other States, (v) Latin American.

(b) If necessary, the Chairman or the outgoing Chairman may at any time, in order to fill a vacancy, designate a member from among the names of all Sub-Commission members of the same geographical area.

2. *Further decides* that the Working Group shall hold closed meetings and that the results of the Working Group's work shall be communicated to the Sub-Commission confidentially.

2. International Convention on the Elimination of All Forms of Racial Discrimination

a) Convention of March 7, 1966, Part II

PART II

Art. 8   1. There shall be established a Committee on the Elimination of Racial Discrimination (hereinafter referred to as the Committee) consisting of eighteen experts of high moral standing and acknowledged impartiality elected by States Parties from among their nationals, who shall serve in their personal capacity, consideration being given to equitable geographical distribution and to the representation of the different forms of civilization as well as of the principal legal systems.

2. The members of the Committee shall be elected by secret ballot from a list of persons nominated by the States Parties. Each State Party may nominate one person from among its own nationals.

3. The initial election shall be held six months after the date of the entry into force of this Convention. At least three months before the date of each election the Secretary-General of the United Nations shall address a letter to the States Parties inviting them to submit their nominations within two months. The Secretary-General shall prepare a list in alphabetical order of all persons thus nominated, indicating the States Parties which have nominated them, and shall submit it to the States Parties.

4. Elections of the members of the Committee shall be held at a meeting of States Parties convened by the Secretary-General at United Nations Headquarters. At that meeting, for which two-thirds of the States Parties shall constitute a quorum, the persons elected to the Committee shall be those nominees who obtain the largest number of votes and an absolute majority of the votes of the representatives of States Parties present and voting.

5. (a) The members of the Committee shall be elected for a term of four years. However, the terms of nine of the members elected at the first election shall expire at the end of two years; immediately after the first election the names of these nine members shall be chosen by lot by the Chairman of the Committee.

(b) For the filling of casual vacancies, the State Party whose expert has ceased to function as a member of the Committee shall appoint another expert from among its nationals, subject to the approval of the Committee.

6. States Parties shall be responsible for the expenses of the members of the Committee while they are in performance of Committee duties.

Art. 9   1. States Parties undertake to submit to the Secretary-General of the United Nations, for consideration by the Committee, a report on the legislative, judicial, administrative or other measures which they have adopted and which give effect to the provisions of this Convention:

(a) within one year after the entry into force of the Convention for the State concerned: and

(b) thereafter every two years and whenever the Committee so requests. The Committee may request further information from the States Parties.

2. The Committee shall report annually, through the Secretary-General, to the General Assembly of the United Nations on its activities and may make suggestions and general recommendations based on the examination of the reports and information received from the States Parties. Such suggestions and general recommendations shall be reported to the General Assembly together with comments, if any, from States Parties.

Art. 10   1. The Committee shall adopt its own rules of procedure.

2. The Committee shall elect its officers for a term of two years.

3. The secretariat of the Committee shall be provided by the Secretary-General of the United Nations.

4. The meetings of the Committee shall normally be held at United Nations Headquarters.

Art. 11   1. If a State Party considers that another State Party is not giving effect to the provisions of this Convention, it may bring the matter to the attention of the Committee. The Committee shall then transmit the communication to the State Party concerned. Within three months, the receiving State shall submit to the Committee written explanations or statements clarifying the matter and the remedy, if any, that may have been taken by that State.

2. If the matter is not adjusted to the satisfaction of both parties, either by bilateral negotiations or by any other procedure open to them, within six months after the receipt by the receiving State of the initial communication, either State shall have the right to refer the matter again to the Committee by notifying the Committee and also the other State.

3. The Committee shall deal with a matter referred to it in accordance with paragraph 2 of this article after it has ascertained that all available domestic remedies have been invoked and exhausted in the case, in conformity with the generally recognized principles of international law. This shall not be the rule where the application of the remedies is unreasonably prolonged.

4. In any matter referred to it, the Committee may call upon the States Parties concerned to supply any other relevant information.

5. When any matter arising out of this article is being considered by the Committee, the States Parties concerned shall be entitled to send a representative to take part in the proceedings of the Committee, without voting rights, while the matter is under consideration.

Art. 12   1. (a) After the Committee has obtained and collated all the information it deems necessary, the Chairman shall appoint an *ad hoc* Conciliation Commission (hereinafter referred to as the Commission) comprising five persons who may or may not be members of the Committee. The members of the Commission shall be appointed with the unanimous consent of the parties to the dispute, and its good offices shall be made available to the States concerned with a view to an amicable solution of the matter on the basis of respect for this Convention.

(b) If the States parties to the dispute fail to reach agreement within three months on all or part of the composition of the Commission, the members of the Commission not agreed upon by the States parties to the dispute shall be elected by secret ballot by a two-thirds majority vote of the Committee from among its own members.

2. The members of the Commission shall serve in their personal capacity. They shall not be nationals of the States parties to the dispute or of a State not Party to this Convention.

3. The Commission shall elect its own Chairman and adopt its own rules of procedure.

4. The meetings of the Commission shall normally be held at United Nations Headquarters or at any other convenient place as determined by the Commission.

5. The secretariat provided in accordance with article 10, paragraph 3, of this Convention shall also service the Commission whenever a dispute among States Parties brings the Commission into being.

6. The States parties to the dispute shall share equally all the expenses of the members of the Commission in accordance with estimates to be provided by the Secretary-General of the United Nations.

7. The Secretary-General shall be empowered to pay the expenses of the members of the Commission, if necessary, before reimbursement by the States parties to the dispute in accordance with paragraph 6 of this article.

8. The information obtained and collated by the Committee shall be made available to the Commission, and the Commission may call upon the States concerned to supply any other relevant information.

Art 13   1. When the Commission has fully considered the matter, it shall prepare and submit to the Chairman of the Committee a report embodying its findings on all questions of fact relevant to the issue between the parties and containing such recommendations as it may think proper for the amicable solution of the dispute.

2. The Chairman of the Committee shall communicate the report of the Commission to each of the States parties to the dispute. These States shall, within three months, inform the Chairman of the Committee whether or not they accept the recommendations contained in the report of the Commission.

3. After the period provided for in paragraph 2 of this article, the Chairman of the Committee shall communicate the report of the Commission and the declarations of the States Parties concerned to the other States Parties to this Convention.

Art. 14   1. A State Party may at any time declare that it recognizes the competence of the Committee to receive and consider communications from individuals or groups of individuals within its jurisdiction claiming to be victims of a violation by that State Party of any of the rights set forth in this Convention. No communication shall be received by the Committee if it concerns a State Party which has not made such a declaration.

2. Any State Party which makes a declaration as provided for in paragraph 1 of this article may establish or indicate a body within its national legal order which shall be competent to receive and consider petitions from individuals and groups of individuals within its jurisdiction who claim to be victims of a violation of any of the rights set forth in this Convention and who have exhausted other available local remedies.

3. A declaration made in accordance with paragraph 1 of this article and the name of any body established or indicated in accordance with paragraph 2 of this article shall be deposited by the State Party concerned with the Secretary-General of the United Nations, who shall transmit copies thereof to the other States Parties. A declaration may be withdrawn at any time by notification to the Secretary-General, but such a withdrawal shall not affect communications pending before the Committee.

4. A register of petitions shall be kept by the body established or indicated in accordance with paragraph 2 of this article, and certified copies of the register shall be filed annually through appropriate channels with the Secretary-General on the understanding that the contents shall not be publicly disclosed.

5. In the event of failure to obtain satisfaction from the body established or indicated in accordance with paragraph 2 of this article, the petitioner shall have the right to communicate the matter to the Committee within six months.

6. (a) The Committee shall confidentially bring any communication referred to it to the attention of the State Party alleged to be violating any provision of this Convention, but the identity of the individual or groups of individuals concerned shall not be revealed without his or their express consent. The Committee shall not receive anonymous communications.

(b) Within three months, the receiving State shall submit to the Committee written explanations or statements clarifying the matter and the remedy, if any, that may have been taken by that State.

7. (a) The Committee shall consider communications in the light of all information made available to it by the State Party concerned and by the petitioner. The Committee shall not consider any communication from a petitioner unless it has ascertained that the petitioner has exhausted all available domestic remedies. However, this shall not be the rule where the application of the remedies is unreasonably prolonged.

(b) The Committee shall forward its suggestions and recommendations, if any, to the State Party concerned and to the petitioner.

8. The Committee shall include in its annual report a summary of such communications and, where appropriate, a summary of the explanations and statements of the States Parties concerned and of its own suggestions and recommendations.

9. The Committee shall be competent to exercise the functions provided for in this article only when at least ten States Parties to this Convention are bound by declarations in accordance with paragraph 1 of this article.

Art. 15   1. Pending the achievement of the objectives of the Declaration on the Granting of Independence to Colonial Countries and Peoples, contained in General Assembly resolution 1514 (XV) of 14 December 1960, the provisions of this Convention shall in no way limit the right of petition granted to these peoples by other international instruments or by the United Nations and its specialized agencies.

2. (a) The Committee established under article 8, paragraph 1, of this Convention shall receive copies of the petitions from, and submit expressions of opinion and recommendations on these petitions to, the bodies of the United Nations which deal with matters directly related to the principles and objectives of this Convention in their consideration of petitions from the inhabitants of Trust and Non-Governing Territories and all other territories to which General Assembly resolution 1514 (XV) applies, relating to matters covered by this Convention which are before these bodies.

(b) The Committee shall receive from the competent bodies of the United Nations copies of the reports concerning the legislative, judicial, administrative or other measures directly related to the principles and objectives of this Convention applied by the administering Powers within the Territories mentioned in sub-paragraph (a) of this paragraph, and shall express opinions and make recommendations to these bodies.

3. The Committee shall include in its report to the General Assembly a summary of the petitions and reports it has received from United Nations bodies, and the expressions of opinion and recommendations of the Committee relating to the said petitions and reports.

4. The Committee shall request from the Secretary-General of the United Nations all information relevant to the objectives of this Convention and available to him regarding the Territories mentioned in paragraph 2 (a) of this article.

Art. 16   The provisions of this Convention concerning the settlement of disputes or complaints shall be applied without prejudice to other procedures for settling disputes or complaints in the field of discrimination laid down in the constituent instruments of, or in conventions adopted by, the United Nations and its specialized agencies, and shall not prevent the States Parties from having recourse to other procedures for settling a dispute in accordance with general or special international agreements in force between them.

b) Rules Relating to the Functions of the Committee of July 31, 1984

XV. Reports and Information from States Parties Under Article 9 of the Convention

Form and contents of reports

Rule 63   The Committee may, through the Secretary-General, inform the States parties of its wishes regarding the form and contents of the periodic reports required to be submitted under article 9 of the Convention.

Attendance by States parties at examination of reports

Rule 64   The Committee shall, through the Secretary-General, notify the States parties (as early as possible) of the opening date, duration and place of the session at which their respective reports will be examined. Representatives of the States parties may be present at the meetings of the Committee when their reports are examined. The Committee may also inform a State party from which it decides to seek further information that it may authorize its representative to be present at a specified meeting. Such a representative should be able to answer questions which may be put to him by the Committee and make statements on reports already submitted by his State, and may also submit additional information from his State.

Request for additional information

Rule 65   If the Committee decides to request an additional report or further information from a State party under the provisions of article 9, paragraph 1, of the Convention, it may indicate the manner as well as the time within which such additional report or further information shall be supplied and shall transmit its decision to the Secretary-General for communication, within two weeks, to the State party concerned.

Non-receipt of reports

Rule 66   1. At each session, the Secretary-General shall notify the Committee of all cases of non-receipt of reports or additional information, as the case may be, provided for under article 9 of the Convention. The Committee, in such cases, may transmit to the State party concerned, through the Secretary-General, a reminder concerning the submission of the report or additional information.

2. If even after the reminder, referred to in paragraph 1 of this rule, the State party does not submit the report or additional information required under article 9 of the Convention, the Committee shall include a reference to this effect in its annual report to the General Assembly.

Suggestions and general recommendations

Rule 67   1. When considering a report submitted by a State party under article 9, the Committee shall first determine whether the report provides the information referred to in the relevant communications of the Committee.

2. If a report of the State party to the Convention, in the opinion of the Committee, does not contain sufficient information, the Committee may request that State to furnish additional information.

3. If, on the basis of its examination of the reports and information supplied by the State party, the Committee determines that some of the obligations of that State under the Convention have not been discharged, it may make suggestions and general recommendations in accordance with article 9, paragraph 2, of the Convention.

Transmission of suggestions and general recommendations

Rule 68   1. Suggestions and general recommendations made by the Committee based on the examination of the reports and information received from States parties under article 9, paragraph 2, of the Convention shall be communicated by the Committee through the Secretary-General to the States parties for their comments.

2. The Committee may, where necessary, indicate a time-limit within which comments from States parties are to be received.

3. Suggestions and general recommendations of the Committee, referred to in paragraph 1, shall be reported to the General Assembly, together with comments, if any, from States parties.

XVI. COMMUNICATIONS FROM STATES PARTIES UNDER ARTICLE 11 OF THE CONVENTION

Method of dealing with communications from States parties

Rule 69   1. When a matter is brought to the attention of the Committee by a State party in accordance with article 11, paragraph 1, of the Convention, the Committee shall examine it at a private meeting and shall then transmit it to the State party concerned through the Secretary-General. The Committee in examining the communications shall not consider its substance. Any action at this stage by the Committee in respect of the communication shall in no way be construed as an expression of its views on the substance of the communication.

2. If the Committee is not in session, the Chairman shall bring the matter to the attention of its members by transmitting copies of the communication and requesting their consent to transmit such communication on behalf of the Committee, to the State party concerned in compliance with article 11, paragraph 1. The Chairman shall also specify a time-limit of three weeks for their replies.

3. Upon receipt of the consent of the majority of the members, or, if within the specified time-limit no replies are received, the Chairman shall transmit the communication to the State party concerned, through the Secretary-General, without delay.

4. In the event of any replies being received which represent the views of the majority of the Committee, the Chairman, while acting in accordance with such replies, shall bear in mind the requirement of urgency in transmitting the communication to the State party concerned on behalf of the Committee.

5. The Committee, or the Chairman on behalf of the Committee, shall remind the receiving State that the time-limit for submission of its written explanations or statement under the Convention is three months.

6. When the Committee receives the explanations or statements of the receiving State, the procedure laid down above shall be followed with respect to the transmission of those explanations or statements to the State party submitting the initial communication.

Request for information

Rule 70   The Committee may call upon the States parties concerned to supply information relevant to the application of article 11 of the Convention. The Committee may indicate the manner as well as the time within which such information shall be supplied.

Notification to the States parties concerned

Rule 71   If any matter is submitted for consideration by the Committee under
          paragraph 2 of article 11 of the Convention, the Chairman, through the
          Secretary-General, shall inform the States parties concerned of the forth-
          coming consideration of this matter not later than 30 days in advance of
          the first meeting of the Committee, in the case of a regular session, and at
          least 18 days in advance of the first meeting of the Committee, in the case
          of a special session.

XVII. ESTABLISHMENT AND FUNCTIONS OF THE AD HOC CONCILIATION COMMISSION UNDER ARTICLES 12 AND 13 OF THE CONVENTION

Consultations on the composition of the Commission

Rule 72   After the Committee has obtained and collated all the information it
          thinks necessary as regards a dispute that has arisen under article 11,
          paragraph 2, of the Convention, the Chairman shall notify the States par-
          ties to the dispute and undertake consultations with them concerning the
          composition of the Ad Hoc Conciliation Commission (hereinafter re-
          ferred to as "the Commission"), in accordance with article 12 of the Con-
          vention.

Appointment of members of the Commission

Rule 73   Upon receiving the unanimous consent of the States parties to the dispute
          regarding the composition of the Commission, the Chairman shall pro-
          ceed to the appointment of the members of the Commission and shall
          inform the States parties to the dispute of the composition of the Com-
          mission.

Rule 74   If within three months of the Chairman's notification as provided in rule
          72 above, the States parties to the dispute fail to reach agreement on all or
          part of the composition of the Commission, the Chairman shall then
          bring the situation to the attention of the Committee which shall proceed
          according to article 12, paragraph 1 (b), of the Convention at its next ses-
          sion.

          2. Upon the completion of the election, the Chairman shall inform the
          States parties to the dispute of the composition of the Commission.

Solemn declaration by members of the Commission

Rule 75   Upon assuming his duties, each member of the Commission shall make
          the following solemn declaration at the first meeting of the Commission:

"I solemnly declare that I will perform my duties and exercise my powers as a member of the Ad Hoc Conciliation Commission honourably, faithfully, impartially and conscientiously".

Filling of vacancies in the Commission

Rule 76 Whenever a vacancy arises in the Commission, the Chairman of the Committee shall fill the vacancy as soon as possible in accordance with procedures laid down in rules 72 to 74. He shall proceed with filling such vacancy upon receipt of a report from the Commission or upon a notification by the Secretary-General.

Transmission of information to members of the Commission

Rule 77 The information obtained and collated by the Committee shall be made available by its Chairman, through the Secretary-General, to the members of the Commission at the time of notifying the members of the Commission of the date of the first meeting of the Commission.

Report of the Commission

Rule 78 1. The Chairman of the Committee shall communicate the report of the Commission referred to in article 13 of the Convention as soon as possible after its receipt to each of the States parties to the dispute and to the members of the Committee.

2. The States parties to the dispute, shall, within three months after the receipt of the Commission's report, inform the Chairman of the Committee whether or not they accept the recommendations contained in the report of the Commission. The Chairman shall transmit the information received from the States parties to the dispute to the members of the Committee.

3. After the expiry of the time-limit provided for in the preceding paragraph, the Chairman of the Committee shall communicate the report of the Commission and any declaration of States parties concerned to the other States parties to the Convention.

Keeping members of the Committee informed

Rule 79 The Chairman of the Committee shall keep the members of the Committee informed of his actions under rules 73 to 78.

XVIII. Procedure for Considering Communications from Individuals or Groups of Individuals Under Article 14 of the Convention

A. General provisions

Competence of the Committee

Rule 80   1. The Committee shall be competent to receive and consider communications and exercise the functions provided for in article 14 of the Convention only when at least 10 States parties are bound by declarations recognizing the competence of the Committee in conformity with paragraph 1 thereof.

2. The Secretary-General shall transmit to the other States parties copies of the declarations deposited with him by States parties recognizing the competence of the Committee.

3. Consideration of communications pending before the Committee shall not be affected by the withdrawal of a declaration made under article 14 of the Convention.

4. The Secretary-General shall inform the other States parties of the name, composition and functions of any national legal body which has been established or indicated by a State party, in conformity with paragraph 3 of article 14.

National bodies

Rule 81   The Secretary-General shall keep the Committee informed of the name, composition and functions of any national legal body established or indicated under paragraph 2 of article 14 as competent to receive and consider petitions from individuals or groups of individuals claiming to be victims of a violation of any of the rights set forth in the Convention.

Certified copies of registers of petitions

Rule 82   1. The Secretary-General shall keep the Committee informed of the contents of all certified copies of the register of petitions filed with him in accordance with paragraph 4 of article 14.

2. The Secretary-General may request clarifications from the States parties concerning the certified copies of the registers of petitions emanating from the national legal bodies responsible for such registers.

3. The contents of the certified copies of the registers of petitions transmitted to the Secretary-General shall not be publicly disclosed.

Record of communications received by the Secretary-General

Rule 83   1. The Secretary-General shall keep a record of all communications which are or appear to be submitted to the Committee by individuals or groups of individuals claiming to be victims of a violation of any of the rights set forth in the Convention and who are subject to the jurisdiction of a State party bound by a declaration under article 14.

2. The Secretary-General may, if he deems it necessary, request clarification of the author of a communication as to his wish to have his communication submitted to the Committee for consideration under article 14. In case of doubt as to the wish of the author, the Committee shall be seized of the communication.

3. No communication shall be received by the Committee or included in a list under rule 85 below if it concerns a State party which has not made a declaration as provided for in paragraph 1 of article 14.

Information to be contained in a communication

Rule 84   1. The Secretary-General may request clarification from the author of a communication concerning the applicability of article 14 to his communication, in particular:

(a) The name, address, age and occupation of the author and the verification of his identity;

(b) The name(s) of the State party or States parties against which the communication is directed;

(c) The object of the communication;

(d) The provision or provisions of the Convention alleged to have been violated;

(e) The facts of the claim;

(f) Steps taken by the author to exhaust domestic remedies, including pertinent documents;

(g) The extent to which the same matter is being examined under another procedure of international investigation or settlement.

2. When requesting clarification or information, the Secretary-General shall indicate an appropriate time-limit to the author of the communication with a view to avoiding undue delays in the procedure.

3. The Committee may approve a questionnaire for the purpose of requesting the above-mentioned information from the author of the communication.

4. The request for clarification referred to in paragraph 1 of the present rule shall not preclude the inclusion of the communication in the list provided for in rule 85, paragraph 1, below.

5. The Secretary-General shall inform the author of a communication of the procedure that will be followed and that the text of his communica-

tion shall be transmitted confidentially to the State party concerned in accordance with paragraph 6 (a) of article 14.

Transmission of communications to the Committee

Rule 85 1. The Secretary-General shall summarize each communication thus received and shall place the summaries, individually or in composite lists of communications, before the Committee at its next regular session, together with the relevant certified copies of the registers of petitions kept by the national legal body of the country concerned and filed with the Secretary-General in compliance with paragraph 4 of article 14.

2. The Secretary-General shall draw the attention of the Committee to those cases for which certified copies of the registers of petitions have not been received.

3. The contents of replies to requests for clarification and relevant subsequent submissions from either the author of the communication or the State party concerned shall be placed before the Committee in a suitable form.

4. An original case file shall be kept for each summarized communication. The full text of any communication brought to the attention of the Committee shall be made available to any member of the Committee upon request.

B. PROCEDURE FOR DETERMINING ADMISSIBILITY OF COMMUNICATIONS

Method of dealing with communications

Rule 86 1. In accordance with the following rules, the Committee shall decide as soon as possible whether or not a communication is admissible in conformity with article 14 of the Convention.

2. The Committee shall, unless it decides otherwise, deal with communications in the order in which they have been placed before it by the Secretariat. The Committee may, if it deems appropriate, decide to consider jointly two or more communications.

Establishment of a working group

Rule 87 1. The Committee may, in accordance with rule 61, set up a Working Group to meet shortly before its sessions, or at any other convenient time to be decided by the Committee in consultation with the Secretary-General, for the purpose of making recommendations to the Committee regarding the fulfilment of the conditions of admissibility of communications laid down in article 14 of the Convention and assisting the Committee in any manner which the Committee may decide.

2. The Working Group shall not comprise more than five members of the Committee. The Working Group shall elect its own officers, develop its own working methods, and apply as far as possible the rules of procedure of the Committee to its meetings.

Meetings

Rule 88   Meetings of the Committee or its Working Group during which communications under article 14 of the Convention will be examined shall be closed. Meetings during which the Committee may consider general issues such as procedures for the application of article 14 may be public if the Committee so decides.

Inability of a member to take part in the examination of a communication

Rule 89   1. A member of the Committee shall not take part in the examination of a communication by the Committee or its Working Group:

(a) If he has any personal interest in the case; or

(b) If he has participated in any capacity in the making of any decision on the case covered by the communication.

2. Any question which may arise under paragraph 1 above shall be decided by the Committee without the participation of the member concerned.

Withdrawal of a member

Rule 90   If, for any reason, a member considers that he should not take part or continue to take part in the examination of a communication, he shall inform the Chairman of his withdrawal.

Conditions for admissibility of communications

Rule 91   With a view to reaching a decision on the admissibility of a communication, the Committee or its Working Group shall ascertain:

(a) That the communication is not anonymous and that it emanates from an individual or group of individuals subject to the jurisdiction of a State party recognizing the competence of the Committee under article 14 of the Convention;

(b) That the individual claims to be a victim of a violation by the State party concerned of any of the rights set forth in the Convention. As a general rule, the communication should be submitted by the individual himself or by his relatives or designated representatives; the Committee may, however, in exceptional cases accept to consider a communication submitted by others on behalf of an alleged victim when it appears that the victim is unable to submit the communication himself, and the author of the communication justifies his acting on the victim's behalf;

(c) That the communication is compatible with the provisions of the Convention;

(d) That the communication is not an abuse of the right to submit a communication in conformity with article 14;

(e) That the individual has exhausted all available domestic remedies, including, when applicable, those mentioned in paragraph 2 of article 14. However, this shall not be the rule where the application of the remedies is unreasonably prolonged;

(f) That the communication is, except in the case of duly verified exceptional circumstances, submitted within six months after all available domestic remedies have been exhausted, including, when applicable, those indicated in paragraph 2 of article 14.

Additional information, classifications and observations

Rule 92   1. The Committee or the Working Group established under rule 87 may request, through the Secretary-General, the State party concerned or the author of the communication to submit additional written information or clarifications relevant to the question of admissibility of the communication.

2. Such requests shall contain a statement to the effect that the request does not imply that a decision has been reached on the question of admissibility of the communication by the Committee.

3. A communication may not be declared admissible unless the State party concerned has received the text of the communication and has been given an opportunity to furnish information or observations as provided in paragraph 1 of this rule, including information relating to the exhaustion of domestic remedies.

4. The Committee or the Working Group may adopt a questionnaire for requesting such additional information or clarifications.

5. The Committee or the Working Group shall indicate a deadline for the submission of such additional information or clarification.

6. If the deadline is not kept by the State party concerned or the author of a communication, the Committee or the Working Group may decide to consider the admissibility of the communication in the light of available information.

7. If the State party concerned disputes the contention of the author of a communication that all available domestic remedies have been exhausted, the State party is required to give details of the effective remedies available to the alleged victim in the particular circumstances of the case.

Inadmissible communications

Rule 93 1. When the Committee decides that a communication is inadmissible, or its consideration is suspended or discontinued, the Committee shall transmit its decisions as soon as possible, through the Secretary-General, to the petitioner and to the State party concerned.

2. A decision taken by the Committee, in conformity with paragraph 7 (a) of article 14, that a communication is inadmissible, may be reviewed at a later date by the Committee upon a written request by the petitioner concerned. Such written request shall contain documentary evidence to the effect that the reasons for inadmissibility referred to in paragraph 7 (a) of article 14 are no longer applicable.

C. CONSIDERATION OF COMMUNICATIONS ON THEIR MERITS

Method of dealing with admissible communications

Rule 94 1. After it has been decided that a communication is admissible, in conformity with article 14, the Committee shall transmit, confidentially, through the Secretary-General, the text of the communication and other relevant information to the State party concerned without revealing the identity of the individual unless he has given his express consent. The Committee shall also inform, through the Secretary-General, the petitioner of the communication of its decision.

2. The State party concerned shall submit within three months to the Committee written explanations or statements clarifying the case under consideration and the remedy, if any, that may have been taken by that State party. The Committee may indicate, if it deems it necessary, the type of information it wishes to receive from the State party concerned.

3. In the course of its consideration, the Committee may inform the State party of its views on the desirability, because of urgency, of taking interim measures to avoid possible irreparable damage to the person or persons who claim to be victim(s) of the alleged violation. In doing so, the Committee shall inform the State party concerned that such expression of its views on interim measures does not prejudge either its final opinion on the merits of the communication or its eventual suggestions and recommendations.

4. Any explanations or statements submitted by a State party pursuant to this rule may be transmitted, through the Secretary-General, to the petitioner of the communication who may submit any additional written information or observations within such time-limit as the Committee shall decide.

5. The Committee may invite the presence of the petitioner or his representative and the presence of representatives of the State party concerned in order to provide additional information or to answer questions on the merits of the communication.

6. The Committee may revoke its decision that a communication is admissible in the light of any explanations or statements submitted by the State party. However, before the Committee considers revoking that decision, the explanations or statements concerned must be transmitted to the petitioner so that he may submit additional information or observations within the time-limit set by the Committee.

Opinion of the Committee on admissible communications and the Committee's suggestions and recommendations

Rule 95   1. Admissible communications shall be considered by the Committee in the light of all information made available to it by the petitioner and the State party concerned. The Committee may refer the communication to the Working Group in order to be assisted in this task.

2. The Committee or the working group set up by it to consider a communication may at any time, in the course of the examination, obtain through the intermediary of the Secretary-General any documentation that may assist in the disposal of the case from United Nations bodies or the specialized agencies.

3. After consideration of an admissible communication, the Committee shall formulate its opinion thereon. The opinion of the Committee shall be forwarded, through the Secretary-General, to the petitioner and to the State party concerned, together with any suggestions and recommendations the Committee may wish to make.

4. Any member of the Committee may request that a summary of his individual opinion be appended to the opinion of the Committee when it is forwarded to the petitioner and to the State party concerned.

5. The State party concerned shall be invited to inform the Committee in due course of the action it takes in conformity with the Committee's suggestions and recommendations.

Summaries in the Committee's annual report

Rule 96   The Committee shall include in its annual report a summary of the communications examined and, where appropriate, a summary of the explanations and statements of the States parties concerned and of its own suggestions and recommendations.

Press communiqués

Rule 97   The Committee may also issue communiqués, through the Secretary-General, for the use of information media and the general public regarding the activities of the Committee under article 14 of the Convention.

XIX. INTERPRETATION AND AMENDMENTS

Italicized headings

Rule 98   The italicized headings of these rules, which were inserted for reference purposes only, shall be disregarded in the interpretation of the rules.

Amendments

Rule 99   These rules of procedure may be amended by a decision of the Committee.

3. International Covenant on Civil and Political Rights

a) Covenant of December 19, 1966, Part IV

PART IV

Art. 28   1. There shall be established a Human Rights Committee (hereafter referred to in the present Covenant as the Committee). It shall consist of eighteen members and shall carry out the functions hereinafter provided.

2. The Committee shall be composed of nationals of the States Parties to the present Covenant who shall be persons of high moral character and recognized competence in the field of human rights, consideration being given to the usefulness of the participation of some persons having legal experience.

3. The members of the Committee shall be elected and shall serve in their personal capacity.

Art. 29   1. The members of the Committee shall be elected by secret ballot from a list of persons possessing the qualifications prescribed in article 28 and nominated for the purpose by the States Parties to the present Covenant.

2. Each State Party to the present Covenant may nominate not more than two persons. These persons shall be nationals of the nominating State.

3. A person shall be eligible for renomination.

Art. 30   1. The initial election shall be held no later than six months after the date of the entry into force of the present Covenant.

2. At least four months before the date of each election to the Committee, other than an election to fill a vacancy declared in accordance with article 34, the Secretary-General of the United Nations shall address a written invitation to the States Parties to the present Covenant to submit their nominations for membership of the Committee within three months.

3. The Secretary-General of the United Nations shall prepare a list in alphabetical order of all the persons thus nominated, with an indication of the States Parties which have nominated them, and shall submit it to the States Parties to the present Covenant no later than one month before the date of each election.

4. Elections of the members of the Committee shall be held at a meeting of the States Parties to the present Covenant convened by the Secretary-General of the United Nations at the Headquarters of the United Na-

tions. At the meeting, for which two thirds of the States Parties to the present Covenant shall constitute a quorum, the persons elected to the Committee shall be those nominees who obtain the largest number of votes and an absolute majority of the votes of the representatives of States Parties present and voting.

Art. 31   1. The Committee may not include more than one national of the same State.

2. In the election of the Committee, consideration shall be given to equitable geographical distribution of membership and to the representation of the different forms of civilization and of the principal legal systems.

Art. 32   1. The members of the Committee shall be elected for a term of four years. They shall be eligible for re-election if renominated. However, the terms of nine of the members elected at the first election shall expire at the end of two years; immediately after the first election, the names of these nine members shall be chosen by lot by the Chairman of the meeting referred to in article 30, paragraph 4.

2. Elections at the expiry of office shall be held in accordance with the preceding articles of this part of the present Covenant.

Art. 33   1. If, in the unanimous opinion of the other members, a member of the Committee has ceased to carry out his functions for any cause other than absence of a temporary character, the Chairman of the Committee shall notify the Secretary-General of the United Nations, who shall then declare the seat of that member to be vacant.

2. In the event of the death or the resignation of a member of the Committee, the Chairman shall immediately notify the Secretary-General of the United Nations, who shall declare the seat vacant from the date of death or the date on which the resignation takes effect.

Art. 34   1. When a vacancy is declared in accordance with article 33 and if the term of office of the member to be replaced does not expire within six months of the declaration of the vacancy, the Secretary-General of the United Nations shall notify each of the States Parties to the present Covenant, which may within two months submit nominations in accordance with article 29 for the purpose of filling the vacancy.

2. The Secretary-General of the United Nations shall prepare a list in alphabetic order of the persons thus nominated and shall submit it to the States Parties to the present Covenant. The election to fill the vacancy shall then take place in accordance with the relevant provisions of this part of the present Covenant.

3. A member of the Committee elected to fill a vacancy declared in accordance with article 33 shall hold office for the remainder of the term of the member who vacated the seat on the Committee under the provisions of that article.

Art. 35   The members of the Committee shall, with the approval of the General Assembly of the United Nations, receive emoluments from United Nations resources on such terms and conditions as the General Assembly may decide, having regard to the importance of the Committee's responsibilities.

Art. 36   The Secretary-General of the United Nations shall provide the necessary staff and facilities for the effective performance of the functions of the Committee under the present Covenant.

Art. 37   1. The Secretary-General of the United Nations shall convene the initial meeting of the Committee at the Headquarters of the United Nations.

2. After its initial meeting, the Committee shall meet at such times as shall be provided in its rules of procedure.

3. The Committee shall normally meet at the Headquarters of the United Nations or at the United Nations Office at Geneva.

Art. 38   Every member of the Committee shall, before taking up his duties, make a solemn declaration in open committee that he will perform his functions impartially and conscientiously.

Art. 39   1. The Committee shall elect its officers for a term of two years. They may be re-elected.

2. The Committee shall establish its own rules of procedure, but these rules shall provide, *inter alia*, that:

(a) Twelve members shall constitute a quorum;

(b) Decisions of the Committee shall be made by a majority vote of the members present.

Art. 40   1. The States Parties to the present Covenant undertake to submit reports on the measures they have adopted which give effect to the rights recognized herein and on the progress made in the enjoyment of those rights:

(a) Within one year of the entry into force of the present Covenant for the States Parties concerned;

(b) Thereafter whenever the Committee so requests.

2. All reports shall be submitted to the Secretary-General of the United Nations, who shall transmit them to the Committee for consideration. Reports shall indicate the factors and difficulties, if any, affecting the implementation of the present Covenant.

3. The Secretary-General of the United Nations may, after consultation with the Committee, transmit to the specialized agencies concerned copies of such parts of the reports as may fall within their field of competence.

4. The Committee shall study the reports submitted by the States Parties to the present Covenant. It shall transmit its reports, and such general comments as it may consider appropriate, to the States Parties. The Committee may also transmit to the Economic and Social Council these

comments along with the copies of the reports it has received from States Parties to the present Covenant.

5. The States Parties to the present Covenant may submit to the Committee observations on any comments that may be made in accordance with paragraph 4 of this article.

Art. 41 1. A State Party to the present Covenant may at any time declare under this article that it recognizes the competence of the Committee to receive and consider communications to the effect that a State Party claims that another State Party is not fulfilling its obligations under the present Covenant. Communications under this article may be received and considered only if submitted by a State Party which has made a declaration recognizing in regard to itself the competence of the Committee. No communication shall be received by the Committee if it concerns a State Party which has not made such a declaration. Communications received under this article shall be dealt with in accordance with the following procedure:

(a) If a State Party to the present Covenant considers that another State Party is not giving effect to the provisions of the present Covenant, it may, by written communication, bring the matter to the attention of that State Party. Within three months after the receipt of the communication, the receiving State shall afford the State which sent the communication an explanation or any other statement in writing clarifying the matter, which should include, to the extent possible and pertinent, reference to domestic procedures and remedies taken, pending, or available in the matter.

(b) If the matter is not adjusted to the satisfaction of both States Parties concerned within six months after the receipt by the receiving State of the initial communication, either State shall have the right to refer the matter to the Committee, by notice given to the Committee and to the other State.

(c) The Committee shall deal with a matter referred to it only after it has ascertained that all available domestic remedies have been invoked and exhausted in the matter, in conformity with the generally recognized principles of international law. This shall not be the rule where the application of the remedies is unreasonably prolonged.

(d) The Committee shall hold closed meetings when examining communications under this article.

(e) Subject to the provisions of sub-paragraph (c), the Committee shall make available its good offices to the States Parties concerned with a view to a friendly solution of the matter on the basis of respect for human rights and fundamental freedoms as recognized in the present Covenant.

(f) In any matter referred to it, the Committee may call upon the States Parties concerned, referred to in sub-paragraph (b), to supply any relevant information.

(g) The States Parties concerned, referred to in sub-paragraph (b), shall have the right to be represented when the matter is being considered in the Committee and to make submissions orally and/or in writing.

(h) The Committee shall, within twelve months after the date of receipt of notice under sub-paragraph (b), submit a report:

(i) If a solution within the terms of sub-paragraph (e) is reached, the Committee shall confine its report to a brief statement of the facts and of the solution reached;

(ii) If a solution within the terms of sub-paragraph (e) is not reached, the Committee shall confine its report to a brief statement of the facts; the written submissions and record of the oral submissions made by the State Parties concerned shall be attached to the report.

In every matter, the report shall be communicated to the States Parties concerned.

2. The provisions of this article shall come into force when ten States Parties to the present Covenant have made declarations under paragraph 1 of this article. Such declarations shall be deposited by the States Parties with the Secretary-General of the United Nations, who shall transmit copies thereof to the other States Parties. A declaration may be withdrawn at any time by notification to the Secretary-General. Such a withdrawal shall not prejudice the consideration of any matter which is the subject of a communication already transmitted under this article; no further communication by any State Party shall be received after the notification of withdrawal of the declaration has been received by the Secretary-General, unless the State Party concerned had made a new declaration.

Art. 42   1. (a) If a matter referred to the Committee in accordance with article 41 is not resolved to the satisfaction of the States Parties concerned, the Committee may, with the prior consent of the States Parties concerned, appoint an *ad hoc* Conciliation Commission (hereinafter referred to as the Commission). The good offices of the Commission shall be made available to the States Parties concerned with a view to an amicable solution of the matter on the basis of respect for the present Covenant;

(b) The Commission shall consist of five persons acceptable to the States Parties concerned. If the States Parties concerned fail to reach agreement within three months on all or part of the composition of the Commission, the members of the Commission concerning whom no agreement has been reached shall be elected by secret ballot by a two-thirds majority vote of the Committee from among its members.

2. The members of the Commission shall serve in their personal capacity. They shall not be nationals of the States Parties concerned, or of a State not party to the present Covenant, or of a State Party which has not made a declaration under article 41.

3. The Commission shall elect its own Chairman and adopt its own rules of procedure.

4. The meetings of the Commission shall normally be held at the Headquarters of the United Nations or at the United Nations Office at Geneva. However, they may be held at such other convenient places as the Commission may determine in consultation with the Secretary-General of the United Nations and the States Parties concerned.

5. The secretariat provided in accordance with article 36 shall also service the commissions appointed under this article.

6. The information received and collated by the Committee shall be made available to the Commission and the Commission may call upon the States Parties concerned to supply any other relevant information.

7. When the Commission has fully considered the matter, but in any event not later than twelve months after having been seized of the matter, it shall submit to the Chairman of the Committee a report for communication to the States Parties concerned:

(a) If the Commission is unable to complete its consideration of the matter within twelve months, it shall confine its report to a brief statement of the status of its consideration of the matter;

(b) If an amicable solution to the matter on the basis of respect for human rights as recognized in the present Covenant is reached, the Commission shall confine its report to a brief statement of the facts and of the solution reached;

(c) If a solution within the terms of sub-paragraph (b) is not reached, the Commission's report shall embody its findings on all questions of fact relevant to the issues between the States Parties concerned, and its views on the possibilities of an amicable solution of the matter. This report shall also contain the written submissions and a record of the oral submissions made by the States Parties concerned;

(d) If the Commission's report is submitted under sub-paragraph (c), the States Parties concerned shall, within three months of the receipt of the report, notify the Chairman of the Committee whether or not they accept the contents of the report of the Commission.

8. The provisions of this article are without prejudice to the responsibilities of the Committee under article 41.

9. The States Parties concerned shall share equally all the expenses of the members of the Commission in accordance with estimates to be provided by the Secretary-General of the United Nations.

10. The Secretary-General of the United Nations shall be empowered to pay the expenses of the members of the Commission, if necessary, before reimbursement by the States Parties concerned, in accordance with paragraph 9 of this article.

Art. 43   The members of the Committee, and of the *ad hoc* conciliation commissions which may be appointed under article 42, shall be entitled to the facilities, privileges and immunities of experts on mission for the United

Nations as laid down in the relevant sections of the Convention on the Privileges and Immunities of the United Nations.

Art. 44   The provisions for the implementation of the present Covenant shall apply without prejudice to the procedures prescribed in the field of human rights by or under the constituent instruments and the conventions of the United Nations and of the specialized agencies and shall not prevent the States Parties to the present Covenant from having recourse to other procedures for settling a dispute in accordance with general or special international agreements in force between them.

Art. 45   The Committee shall submit to the General Assembly of the United Nations, through the Economic and Social Council, an annual report on its activities.

b) Optional Protocol of December 19, 1966

The States Parties to the Present Protocol,

Considering that in order further to achieve the purposes of the Covenant on Civil and Political Rights (hereinafter referred to as the Covenant) and the implementation of its provisions it would be appropriate to enable the Human Rights Committee set up in part IV of the Covenant (hereinafter referred to as the Committee) to receive and consider, as provided in the present Protocol, communications from individuals claiming to be victims of violations of any of the rights set forth in the Covenant,

Have agreed as follows:

Art. 1   A State Party to the Covenant that becomes a party to the present Protocol recognizes the competence of the Committee to receive and consider communications from individuals subject to its jurisdiction who claim to be victims of a violation by that State Party of any of the rights set forth in the Covenant. No communication shall be received by the Committee if it concerns a State Party to the Covenant which is not a party to the present Protocol.

Art. 2   Subject to the provisions of article 1, individuals who claim that any of their rights enumerated in the Covenant have been violated and who have exhausted all available domestic remedies may submit a written communication to the Committee for consideration.

Art. 3   The Committee shall consider inadmissible any communication under the present Protocol which is anonymous, or which it considers to be an abuse of the rights of submission of such communications or to be incompatible with the provisions of the Covenant.

Art. 4   1. Subject to the provisions of article 3, the Committee shall bring any communication submitted to it under the present Protocol to the attention of the State Party to the present Protocol alleged to be violating any provisions of the Covenant.

2. Within six months, the receiving State shall submit to the Committee written explanations or statements clarifying the matter and the remedy, if any, that may have been taken by that State.

Art. 5   1. The Committee shall consider communications received under the present Protocol in the light of all written information made available to it by the individual and by the State Party concerned.

2. The Committee shall not consider any communication from an individual unless it has ascertained that:

(a) The same matter is not being examined under another procedure of international investigation or settlement;

(b) The individual has exhausted all available domestic remedies. This shall not be the rule where the application of the remedies is unreasonably prolonged.

3. The Committee shall hold closed meetings when examining communications under the present Protocol.

4. The Committee shall forward its views to the State Party concerned and to the individual.

Art. 6   The Committee shall include in its annual report under article 45 of the Covenant a summary of its activities under the present Protocol.

Art. 7   Pending the achievement of the objectives of resolution 1514 (XV) adopted by the General Assembly of the United Nations on 14 December 1960 concerning the Declaration on the Granting of Independence to Colonial Countries and Peoples, the provisions of the present Protocol shall in no way limit the right of petition granted to these peoples by the Charter of the United Nations and other international conventions and instruments under the United Nations and its specialized agencies.

Art. 8   1. The present Protocol is open for signature by any State which has signed the Covenant.

2. The present Protocol is subject to ratification by any State which has ratified or acceded to the Covenant. Instruments of ratification shall be deposited with the Secretary-General of the United Nations.

3. The present Protocol shall be open to accession by any State which has ratified or acceded to the Covenant.

4. Accession shall be effected by the deposit of an instrument of accession with the Secretary-General of the United Nations.

5. The Secretary-General of the United Nations shall inform all States which have signed the present Protocol or acceded to it of the deposit of each instrument of ratification or accession.

Art. 9   1. Subject to the entry into force of the Covenant, the present Protocol shall enter into force three months after the date of the deposit with the

Secretary-General of the United Nations of the tenth instrument of ratification or instrument of accession.

2. For each State ratifying the present Protocol or acceding to it after the deposit of the tenth instrument of ratification or instrument of accession, the present Protocol shall enter into force three months after the date of the deposit of its own instrument of ratification or instrument of accession.

Art. 10 The provisions of the present Protocol shall extend to all parts of federal States without any limitations or exceptions.

Art. 11 1. Any State Party to the present Protocol may propose an amendment and file it with the Secretary-General of the United Nations. The Secretary-General shall there-upon communicate any proposed amendments to the States Parties to the present Protocol with a request that they notify him whether they favour a conference of States Parties for the purpose of considering and voting upon the proposal. In the event that at least one third of the States Parties favours such a conference, the Secretary-General shall convene the conference under the auspices of the United Nations. Any amendment adopted by a majority of the States Parties present and voting at the conference shall be submitted to the General Assembly of the United Nations for approval.

2. Amendments shall come into force when they have been approved by the General Assembly of the United Nations and accepted by a two-thirds majority of the States Parties to the present Protocol in accordance with their respective constitutional processes.

3. When amendments come into force, they shall be binding on those States Parties which have accepted them, other States Parties still being bound by the provisions of the present Protocol and any earlier amendment which they have accepted.

Art. 12 1. Any State Party may denounce the present Protocol at any time by written notification addressed to the Secretary-General of the United Nations. Denunciation shall take effect three months after the date of receipt of the notification by the Secretary-General.

2. Denunciation shall be without prejudice to the continued application of the provisions of the present Protocol to any communication submitted under article 2 before the effective date of denunciation.

Art. 13 Irrespective of the notifications made under article 8, paragraph 5, of the present Protocol, the Secretary-General of the United Nations shall inform all States referred to in article 48, paragraph 1, of the Covenant of the following particulars:

(a) Signatures, ratifications and accessions under article 8;

(b) The date of the entry into force of the present Protocol under article 9 and the date of the entry into force of any amendments under article 11;

(c) Denunciations under article 12.

Art. 14   1. The present Protocol, of which the Chinese, English, French, Russian and Spanish texts are equally authentic, shall be deposited in the archives of the United Nations.

2. The Secretary-General of the United Nations shall transmit certified copies of the present Protocol to all States referred to in article 48 of the Covenant.

c) Rules of Procedure of the Human Rights Committee of May 24, 1994

PART I. GENERAL RULES

I. SESSIONS

Rule 1   The Human Rights Committee (hereinafter referred to as "the Committee") shall hold sessions as may be required for the satisfactory performance of its functions in accordance with the International Covenant on Civil and Political Rights (hereinafter referred to as "the Covenant").

Rule 2   1. The Committee shall normally hold two regular sessions each year.

2. Regular sessions of the Committee shall be convened at dates decided by the Committee in consultation with the Secretary-General of the United Nations (hereinafter referred to as "the Secretary-General"), taking into account the calendar of conferences as approved by the General Assembly.

Rule 3   1. Special sessions of the Committee shall be convened by decision of the Committee. When the Committee is not in session, the Chairman may convene special sessions in consultation with the other officers of the Committee. The Chairman of the Committee shall also convene special sessions:

(a) At the request of a majority of the members of the Committee;

(b) At the request of a State party to the Covenant.

2. Special sessions shall be convened as soon as possible at a date fixed by the Chairman in consultation with the Secretary-General and with the other officers of the Committee, taking into account the calendar of conferences as approved by the General Assembly.

Rule 4   The Secretary-General shall notify the members of the Committee of the date and place of the first meeting of each session. Such notification shall be sent, in the case of a regular session, at least six weeks in advance and, in the case of a special session, at least 18 days in advance.

Rule 5   Sessions of the Committee shall normally be held at the Headquarters of the United Nations or at the United Nations Office at Geneva. Another place for a session may be designated by the Committee in consultation with the Secretary-General.

II. AGENDA

Rule 6   The provisional agenda for each regular session shall be prepared by the Secretary-General in consultation with the Chairman of the Committee, in conformity with the relevant provisions of the Covenant and of the Optional Protocol to the International Covenant on Civil and Political Rights (hereinafter referred to as "the Protocol"), and shall include:

(a) Any item the inclusion of which has been ordered by the Committee at a previous session;

(b) Any item proposed by the Chairman of the Committee;

(c) Any item proposed by a State party to the Covenant;

(d) Any item proposed by a member of the Committee;

(e) Any item proposed by the Secretary-General relating to his functions under the Covenant, the Protocol or these rules.

Rule 7   The provisional agenda for a special session of the Committee shall consist only of those items which are proposed for consideration at that special session.

Rule 8   The first item on the provisional agenda for any session shall be the adoption of the agenda, except for the election of the officers when required under rule 17 of these rules.

Rule 9   During a session, the Committee may revise the agenda and may, as appropriate, defer or delete items; only urgent and important items may be added to the agenda.

Rule 10   The provisional agenda and the basic documents relating to each item appearing thereon shall be transmitted to the members of the Committee by the Secretary-General, who shall endeavour to have the documents transmitted to the members at least six weeks prior to the opening of the session.

III. MEMBERS OF THE COMMITTEE

Rule 11   The members of the Committee shall be the 18 persons appointed in accordance with articles 28 to 34 of the Covenant.

Rule 12   The term of office of the members of the Committee elected at the first election shall begin on 1 January 1977. The term of office of members of the Committee elected at subsequent elections shall begin on the day after the date of expiry of the term of office of the members of the Committee whom they replace.

Rule 13   1. If, in the unanimous opinion of the other members, a member of the Committee has ceased to carry out his functions for any cause other than absence of a temporary character, the Chairman of the Committee shall notify the Secretary-General, who shall then declare the seat of that member to be vacant.

2. In the event of the death or the resignation of a member of the Committee, the Chairman shall immediately notify the Secretary-General, who shall declare the seat vacant from the date of death or the date on which the resignation takes effect. The resignation of a member of the Committee shall be notified by him in writing directly to the Chairman or to the Secretary-General and action shall be taken to declare his seat vacant only after such notification has been received.

Rule 14   A vacancy declared in accordance with rule 13 of these rules shall be dealt with in accordance with article 34 of the Covenant.

Rule 15   Any member of the Committee elected to fill a vacancy declared in accordance with article 33 of the Covenant shall hold office for the remainder of the term of the member who vacated the seat on the Committee under the provisions of that article.

Rule 16   Before assuming his duties, each member of the Committee shall give the following solemn undertaking in open Committee:

"I solemnly undertake to discharge my duties as a member of the Human Rights Committee impartially and conscientiously."

IV. OFFICERS

Rule 17   The Committee shall elect from among its members a Chairman, three Vice-Chairmen and a Rapporteur.

Rule 18   The officers of the Committee shall be elected for a term of two years. They shall be eligible for re-election. None of them, however, may hold office if he ceases to be a member of the Committee.

Rule 19   The Chairman shall perform the functions conferred upon him by the Covenant, the rules of procedure and the decisions of the Committee. In the exercise of his functions, the Chairman shall remain under the authority of the Committee.

Rule 20   If during a session the Chairman is unable to be present at a meeting or any part thereof, he shall designate one of the Vice-Chairmen to act in his place.

Rule 21   A Vice-Chairman acting as Chairman shall have the same rights and duties as the Chairman.

Rule 22   If any of the officers of the Committee ceases to serve or declares his inability to continue serving as a member of the Committee or for any reason is no longer able to act as an officer, a new officer shall be elected for the unexpired term of his predecessor.

V. SECRETARIAT

Rule 23   1. The secretariat of the Committee and of such subsidiary bodies as may be established by the Committee (hereinafter referred to as "the Secretariat") shall be provided by the Secretary-General.

2. The Secretary-General shall provide the necessary staff and facilities for the effective performance of the functions of the Committee under the Covenant.

Rule 24   The Secretary-General or his representative shall attend all meetings of the Committee. Subject to rule 38 of these rules, he or his representative may make oral or written statements at meetings of the Committee or its subsidiary bodies.

Rule 25   The Secretary-General shall be responsible for all the necessary arrangements for meetings of the Committee and its subsidiary bodies.

Rule 26   The Secretary-General shall be responsible for informing the members of the Committee without delay of any questions which may be brought before it for consideration.

Rule 27   Before any proposal which involves expenditure is approved by the Committee or by any of its subsidiary bodies, the Secretary-General shall prepare and circulate to the members of the Committee or subsidiary body, as early as possible, an estimate of the cost involved in the proposal. It shall be the duty of the Chairman to draw the attention of members to this estimate and to invite discussion on it when the proposal is considered by the Committee or subsidiary body.

VI. LANGUAGES

Rule 28   Arabic, Chinese, English, French, Russian and Spanish shall be the official languages, and Arabic, English, French, Russian and Spanish the working languages of the Committee.

Rule 29   Speeches made in any of the working languages shall be interpreted into the other working languages. Speeches made in an official language shall be interpreted into the working languages.

Rule 30   Any speaker addressing the Committee and using a language other than one of the official languages shall normally provide for interpretation into one of the working languages. Interpretation into the other working languages by interpreters of the Secretariat may be based on the interpretation given in the first working language.

Rule 31   Summary records of the meetings of the Committee shall be drawn up in the working languages.

Rule 32   All formal decisions of the Committee shall be made available in the official languages. All other official documents of the Committee shall be issued in the working languages and any of them may, if the Committee so decides, be issued in all the official languages.

VII. PUBLIC AND PRIVATE MEETINGS

Rule 33   The meetings of the Committee and its subsidiary bodies shall be held in public unless the Committee decides otherwise or it appears from the relevant provisions of the Covenant or the Protocol that the meeting should be held in private.

Rule 34   At the close of each private meeting the Committee or its subsidiary body may issue a communiqué through the Secretary-General.

VIII. RECORDS

Rule 35   Summary records of the public and private meetings of the Committee and its subsidiary bodies shall be prepared by the Secretariat. They shall be distributed in provisional form as soon as possible to the members of the Committee and to any others participating in the meeting. All such participants may, within three working days after receipt of the provisional record of the meeting, submit corrections to the Secretariat. Any disagreement concerning such corrections shall be settled by the Chairman of the Committee or the Chairman of the subsidiary body to which the record relates or, in the case of continued disagreement, by decision of the Committee or of the subsidiary body.

Rule 36   1. The summary records of public meetings of the Committee in their final form shall be documents of general distribution unless, in exceptional circumstances, the Committee decides otherwise.

2. The summary records of private meetings shall be distributed to the members of the Committee and to other participants in the meetings. They may be made available to others upon decision of the Committee at such time and under such circumstances as the Committee may decide.

IX. CONDUCT OF BUSINESS

Rule 37   Twelve members of the Committee shall constitute a quorum.

Rule 38   The Chairman shall declare the opening and closing of each meeting of the Committee, direct the discussion, ensure observance of these rules, accord the right to speak, put questions to the vote and announce decisions. The Chairman, subject to these rules, shall have control over the proceedings of the Committee and over the maintenance of order at its meetings. The Chairman may, in the course of the discussion of an item, propose to the Committee the limitation of the time to be allowed to speakers, the limitation of the number of times each speaker may speak on any question and the closure of the list of speakers. He shall rule on points of order. He shall also have the power to propose adjournment or closure of the debate or adjournment or suspension of a meeting. Debate shall be confined to the question before the Committee, and the Chairman may call a speaker to order if his remarks are not relevant to the subject under discussion.

Rule 39   During the discussion of any matter, a member may at any time raise a point of order, and the point of order shall immediately be decided by the Chairman in accordance with the rules of procedure. Any appeal against the ruling of the Chairman shall immediately be put to the vote, and the ruling of the Chairman shall stand unless overruled by a majority of the members present. A member may not, in raising a point of order, speak on the substance of the matter under discussion.

Rule 40   During the discussion of any matter, a member may move the adjournment of the debate on the item under discussion. In addition to the proposer of the motion, one member may speak in favour of and one against the motion, after which the motion shall immediately be put to the vote.

Rule 41   The Committee may limit the time allowed to each speaker on any question. When debate is limited and a speaker exceeds his allotted time, the Chairman shall call him to order without delay.

Rule 42   When the debate on an item is concluded because there are no other speakers, the Chairman shall declare the debate closed. Such closure shall have the same effect as closure by the consent of the Committee.

Rule 43   A member may at any time move the closure of the debate on the item under discussion, whether or not any other member or representative has signified his wish to speak. Permission to speak on the closure of the debate shall be accorded only to two speakers opposing the closure, after which the motion shall immediately be put to the vote.

Rule 44   During the discussion of any matter, a member may move the suspension or the adjournment of the meeting. No discussion on such motions shall be permitted, and they shall immediately be put to the vote.

Rule 45   Subject to rule 39 of these rules, the following motions shall have precedence in the following order over all other proposals or motions before the meeting:

(a) To suspend the meeting;

(b) To adjourn the meeting;

(c) To adjourn the debate on the item under discussion;

(d) For the closure of the debate on the item under discussion.

Rule 46   Unless otherwise decided by the Committee, proposals and substantive amendments or motions submitted by members shall be introduced in writing and handed to the Secretariat, and their consideration shall, if so requested by any member, be deferred until the next meeting on the following day.

Rule 47   Subject to rule 45 of these rules, any motion by a member calling for a decision on the competence of the Committee to adopt a proposal submitted to it shall be put to the vote immediately before a vote is taken on the proposal in question.

Rule 48   A motion may be withdrawn by its proposer at any time before voting on it has commenced, provided that the motion has not been amended. A motion which has thus been withdrawn may be reintroduced by another member.

Rule 49   When a proposal has been adopted or rejected, it may not be reconsidered at the same session unless the Committee so decides. Permission to speak on a motion to reconsider shall be accorded only to two speakers in favour of the motion and two speakers opposing the motion, after which it shall immediately be put to the vote.

X. VOTING

Rule 50   Each member of the Committee shall have one vote.

Rule 51[1]   Except as otherwise provided in the Covenant or elsewhere in these rules, decisions of the Committee shall be made by a majority of the members present.

Rule 52   Subject to rule 58 of these rules, the Committee shall normally vote by show of hands, except that any member may request a roll-call, which shall then be taken in the alphabetical order of the names of the members of the Committee, beginning with the member whose name is drawn by lot by the Chairman.

Rule 53   The vote of each member participating in a roll-call shall be inserted in the record.

Rule 54   After the voting has commenced, it shall not be interrupted unless a member raises a point of order in connection with the actual conduct of

---

[1]   The Committee decided, at its first session, that in a footnote to rule 51 of the provisional rules of procedure attention should be drawn to the following:
1. The members of the Committee generally expressed the view that its method of work normally should allow for attempts to reach decisions by consensus before voting, provided that the Covenant and the rules of procedure were observed and that such attempts did not unduly delay the work of the Committee.
2. Bearing in mind paragraph 1 above, the Chairman at any meeting may, and at the request of any member shall, put the proposal to a vote.

the voting. Brief statements by members consisting solely of explanations of their votes may be permitted by the Chairman before the voting has commenced or after the voting has been completed.

Rule 55   Parts of a proposal shall be voted on separately if a member requests that the proposal be divided. Those parts of the proposal which have been approved shall then be put to the vote as a whole; if all the operative parts of a proposal have been rejected, the proposal shall be considered to have been rejected as a whole.

Rule 56   1. When an amendment to a proposal is moved, the amendment shall be voted on first. When two or more amendments to a proposal are moved, the Committee shall first vote on the amendment furthest removed in substance from the original proposal and then on the amendment next furthest removed therefrom and so on until all the amendments have been put to the vote. If one or more amendments are adopted, the amended proposal shall then be voted upon.

2. A motion is considered an amendment to a proposal if it merely adds to, deletes from or revises part of that proposal.

Rule 57   1. If two or more proposals relate to the same question, the Committee shall, unless it decides otherwise, vote on the proposals in the order in which they have been submitted.

2. The Committee may, after each vote on a proposal, decide whether to vote on the next proposal.

3. Any motions requiring that no decision be taken on the substance of such proposals shall, however, be considered as previous questions and shall be put to the vote before them.

Rule 58   Elections shall be held by secret ballot, unless the Committee decides otherwise in the case of an election to fill a place for which there is only one candidate.

Rule 59   1. When only one person or member is to be elected and no candidate obtains the required majority in the first ballot, a second ballot shall be taken, which shall be restricted to the two candidates who obtained the greatest number of votes.

2. If the second ballot is inconclusive and a majority vote of members present is required, a third ballot shall be taken in which votes may be cast for any eligible candidate. If the third ballot is inconclusive, the next ballot shall be restricted to the two candidates who obtained the greatest number of votes in the third ballot and so on, with unrestricted and restricted ballots alternating, until a person or member is elected.

3. If the second ballot is inconclusive and a two-thirds majority is required, the balloting shall be continued until one candidate secures the necessary two-thirds majority. In the next three ballots, votes may be cast for any eligible candidate. If three such unrestricted ballots are inconclusive, the next three ballots shall be restricted to the two candidates who

obtained the greatest number of votes in the third such unrestricted ballot, and the following three ballots shall be unrestricted, and so on until a person or member is elected.

Rule 60 When two or more elective places are to be filled at one time under the same conditions, those candidates obtaining the required majority in the first ballot shall be elected. If the number of candidates obtaining such majority is less than the number of persons or members to be elected, there shall be additional ballots to fill the remaining places, the voting being restricted to the candidates obtaining the greatest number of votes in the previous ballot, to a number not more than twice the places remaining to be filled; provided that, after the third inconclusive ballot, votes may be cast for any eligible candidate. If three such unrestricted ballots are inconclusive, the next three ballots shall be restricted to the candidates who obtained the greatest number of votes in the third of the unrestricted ballots, to a number not more than twice the places remaining to be filled, and the following three ballots thereafter shall be unrestricted, and so on until all the places have been filled.

Rule 61 If a vote is equally divided on a matter other than an election, the proposal shall be regarded as rejected.

XI. SUBSIDIARY BODIES

Rule 62 1. The Committee may, taking into account the provisions of the Covenant and the Protocol, set up such subcommittees and other *ad hoc* subsidiary bodies as it deems necessary for the performance of its functions, and define their composition and powers.

2. Subject to the provisions of the Covenant and the Protocol and unless the Committee decides otherwise, each subsidiary body shall elect its own officers and may adopt its own rules of procedure. Failing such rules, the present rules of procedure shall apply *mutatis mutandis*.

XII. ANNUAL REPORT OF THE COMMITTEE

Rule 63 As prescribed in article 45 of the Covenant, the Committee shall submit to the General Assembly of the United Nations, through the Economic and Social Council, an annual report on its activities, including a summary of its activities under the Protocol as prescribed in article 6 thereof.

XIII. DISTRIBUTION OF REPORTS AND OTHER OFFICIAL DOCUMENTS OF THE COMMITTEE

Rule 64 1. Without prejudice to the provisions of rule 36 of these rules of procedure and subject to paragraphs 2 and 3 of the present rule, reports, formal decisions and all other official documents of the Committee and its subsidiary bodies shall be documents of general distribution unless the Committee decides otherwise.

2. All reports, formal decisions and other official documents of the Committee and its subsidiary bodies relating to articles 41 and 42 of the Covenant and to the Protocol shall be distributed by the Secretariat to all members of the Committee, to the States parties concerned and, as may be decided by the Committee, to members of its subsidiary bodies and to others concerned.

3. Reports and additional information submitted by States parties pursuant to article 40 of the Covenant shall be documents of general distribution. The same applies to other information provided by a State party unless the State party concerned requests otherwise.

XIV. AMENDMENTS

Rule 65   These rules of procedure may be amended by a decision of the Committee, without prejudice to the relevant provisions of the Covenant and the Protocol.

PART II. RULES RELATING TO THE FUNCTIONS OF THE COMMITTEE

XV. REPORTS FROM STATES PARTIES UNDER ARTICLE 40 OF THE COVENANT

Rule 66   1. The States parties to the Covenant shall submit reports on the measures they have adopted which give effect to the rights recognized in the Covenant and on the progress made in the enjoyment of those rights. Reports shall indicate the factors and difficulties, if any, affecting the implementation of the Covenant.

2. Requests for submission of a report under article 40, paragraph 1 (b), of the Covenant may be made in accordance with the periodicity decided by the Committee or at any other time the Committee may deem appropriate. In the case of an exceptional situation when the Committee is not in session, a request may be made through the Chairman, acting in consultation with the members of the Committee.

3. Whenever the Committee requests States parties to submit reports under article 40, paragraph 1 (b), of the Covenant, it shall determine the dates by which such reports shall be submitted.

4. The Committee may, through the Secretary-General, inform the States parties of its wishes regarding the form and content of the reports to be submitted under article 40 of the Covenant.

Rule 67   1. The Secretary-General may, after consultation with the Committee, transmit to the specialized agencies concerned copies of such parts of the reports from States members of those agencies as may fall within their field of competence.

2. The Committee may invite the specialized agencies to which the Secretary-General has transmitted parts of the reports to submit comments on those parts within such time-limits as it may specify.

Rule 68   The Committee shall, through the Secretary-General, notify the States parties as early as possible of the opening date, duration and place of the session at which their respective reports will be examined. Representatives of the States parties may be present at the meetings of the Committee when their reports are examined. The Committee may also inform a State party from which it decides to seek further information that it may authorize its representative to be present at a specified meeting. Such a representative should be able to answer questions which may be put to him by the Committee and make statements on reports already submitted by his State, and may also submit additional information from his State.

Rule 69   1. At each session the Secretary-General shall notify the Committee of all cases of non-submission of reports or additional information requested under rules 66 and 70 of these rules. In such cases the Committee may transmit to the State party concerned, through the Secretary-General, a reminder concerning the submission of the report or additional information.

2. If, after the reminder referred to in paragraph 1 of this rule, the State party does not submit the report or additional information required under rules 66 and 70 of these rules, the Committee shall so state in the annual report which it submits to the General Assembly of the United Nations through the Economic and Social Council.

Rule 70   1. When considering a report submitted by a State party under article 40 of the Covenant, the Committee shall first satisfy itself that the report provides all the information required under rule 66 of these rules.

2. If a report of a State party to the Covenant, in the opinion of the Committee, does not contain sufficient information, the Committee may request that State to furnish the additional information which is required, indicating by what date the said information should be submitted.

3. On the basis of its examination of the reports and information supplied by a State party, the Committee in accordance with article 40, paragraph 4, of the Covenant, make such comments as it may consider appropriate.

Rule 71   1. The Committee shall, through the Secretary-General, communicate to the States parties for their observations the general comments it has made under article 40, paragraph 4, of the Covenant on the basis of its examination of the reports and information furnished by States parties. The Committee may, where necessary, indicate a time-limit for the receipt of observations from States parties.

2. The Committee may also transmit to the Economic and Social Council the comments referred to in paragraph 1 of this rule, together with copies of the reports it has received from the States parties to the Covenant and the observations, if any, submitted by them.

XVI. PROCEDURE FOR THE CONSIDERATION OF COMMUNICATIONS
RECEIVED UNDER ARTICLE 41 OF THE COVENANT

Rule 72   1. A communication under article 41 of the Covenant may be referred to the Committee by either State party concerned by notice given in accordance with paragraph 1 (b) of that article.

2. The notice referred to in paragraph 1 of this rule shall contain or be accompanied by information regarding:

(a) Steps taken to seek adjustment of the matter in accordance with article 41, paragraphs 1 (a) and (b), of the Covenant, including the text of the initial communication and of any subsequent written explanations or statements by the States parties concerned which are pertinent to the matter;

(b) Steps taken to exhaust domestic remedies;

(c) Any other procedure of international investigation or settlement resorted to by the States parties concerned.

Rule 73   The Secretary-General shall maintain a permanent register of all communications received by the Committee under article 41 of the Covenant.

Rule 74   The Secretary-General shall inform the members of the Committee without delay of any notice given under rule 72 of these rules and shall transmit to them as soon as possible copies of the notice and relevant information.

Rule 75   1. The Committee shall examine communications under article 41 of the Covenant at closed meetings.

2. The Committee may, after consultation with the States parties concerned, issue communiqués, through the Secretary-General, for the use of the information media and the general public regarding the activities of the Committee at its closed meetings.

Rule 76   A communication shall not be considered by the Committee unless:

(a) Both States parties concerned have made declarations under article 41, paragraph 1, of the Covenant which are applicable to the communication;

(b) The time-limit prescribed in article 41, paragraph 1 (b), of the Covenant has expired;

(c) The Committee has ascertained that all available domestic remedies have been invoked and exhausted in the matter in conformity with the generally recognized principles of international law, or that the application of the remedies is unreasonably prolonged.

Rule 77A Subject to the provisions of rule 76 of these rules, the Committee shall proceed to make its good offices available to the States parties concerned with a view to a friendly solution of the matter on the basis of respect for human rights and fundamental freedoms as recognized in the Covenant.

Rule 77B The Committee may, through the Secretary-General, request the States parties concerned or either of them to submit additional information or observations orally or in writing. The Committee shall indicate a time-limit for the submission of such written information or observations.

Rule 77C 1. The States parties concerned shall have the right to be represented when the matter is being considered in the Committee and to make submissions orally and/or in writing.

2. The Committee shall, through the Secretary-General, notify the States parties concerned as early as possible of the opening date, duration and place of the session at which the matter will be examined.

3. The procedure for making oral and/or written submissions shall be decided by the Committee, after consultation with the States parties concerned.

Rule 77D 1. Within 12 months after the date on which the Committee received the notice referred to in rule 72 of these rules, the Committee shall adopt a report in accordance with article 41, paragraph 1 (h), of the Covenant.

2. The provisions of paragraph 1 of rule 77C of these rules shall not apply to the deliberations of the Committee concerning the adoption of the report.

3. The Committee's report shall be communicated, through the Secretary-General, to the States parties concerned.

Rule 77E If a matter referred to the Committee in accordance with article 41 of the Covenant is not resolved to the satisfaction of the States parties concerned, the Committee may, with their prior consent, proceed to apply the procedure prescribed in article 42 of the Covenant.

XVII. PROCEDURE FOR THE CONSIDERATION OF COMMUNICATIONS RECEIVED UNDER THE OPTIONAL PROTOCOL

A. Transmission of communications to the Committee

Rule 78 1. The Secretary-General shall bring to the attention of the Committee, in accordance with the present rules, communications which are or appear to be submitted for consideration by the Committee under article 1 of the Protocol.

2. The Secretary-General, when necessary, may request clarification from the author of a communication as to his wish to have his communication submitted to the Committee for consideration under the Protocol. In case there is still doubt as to the wish of the author, the Committee shall be seized of the communication.

3. No communication shall be received by the Committee or included in a list under rule 79 if it concerns a State which is not a party to the Protocol.

Rule 79 1. The Secretary-General shall prepare lists of the communications submitted to the Committee in accordance with rule 78 above, with a brief summary of their contents, and shall circulate such lists to the members of the Committee at regular intervals. The Secretary-General shall also maintain a permanent register of all such communications.

2. The full text of any communication brought to the attention of the Committee shall be made available to any member of the Committee upon his request.

Rule 80 1. The Secretary-General may request clarification from the author of communication concerning the applicability of the Protocol to his communication, in particular regarding:

(a) The name, address, age and occupation of the author and the verification of his identity;

(b) The name of the State party against which the communication is directed;

(c) The object of the communication;

(d) The provision or provisions of the Covenant alleged to have been violated;

(e) The facts of the claim;

(f) Steps taken by the author to exhaust domestic remedies;

(g) The extent to which the same matter is being examined under another procedure of international investigation or settlement.

2. When requesting clarification or information, the Secretary-General shall indicate an appropriate time-limit to the author of the communication with a view to avoiding undue delays in the procedure under the Protocol.

3. The Committee may approve a questionnaire for the purpose of requesting the above-mentioned information from the author of the communication.

4. The request for clarification referred to in paragraph 1 of the present rule shall not preclude the inclusion of the communication in the list provided for in rule 79, paragraph 1, of these rules.

Rule 81 For each registered communication the Secretary-General shall as soon as possible prepare and circulate to the members of the Committee a summary of the relevant information obtained.

B. General Provisions regarding the consideration of communications by the Committee or its subsidiary bodies

Rule 82 Meetings of the Committee or its subsidiary bodies during which communications under the Protocol will be examined shall be closed. Meetings during which the Committee may consider general issues such as procedures for the application of the Protocol may be public if the Committee so decides.

Rule 83   The Committee may issue communiqués, through the Secretary-General, for the use of the information media and the general public regarding the activities of the Committee at its closed meetings.

Rule 84   1. A member shall not take part in the examination of a communication by the Committee:

(a) If he has any personal interest in the case; or

(b) If he has participated in any capacity in the making of any decision on the case covered by the communication.

2. Any question which may arise under paragraph 1 above shall be decided by the Committee.

Rule 85   If, for any reason, a member considers that he should not take part or continue to take part in the examination of a communication, he shall inform the Chairman of his withdrawal.

Rule 86   The Committee may, prior to forwarding its views on the communication to the State party concerned, inform that State of its views as to whether interim measures may be desirable to avoid irreparable damage to the victim of the alleged violation. In doing so, the Committee shall inform the State party concerned that such expression of its views on interim measures does not imply a determination on the merits of the communication.

C. Procedure to determine admissibility

Rule 87   1. The Committee shall decide as soon as possible and in accordance with the following rules whether the communication is admissible or is inadmissible under the Protocol.

2. A working group established under rule 89, paragraph 1, may also declare a communication admissible when it is composed of five members and all the members so decide.

Rule 88   1. Communications shall be dealt with in the order in which they are received by the Secretariat, unless the Committee or a working group established under rule 89, paragraph 1, decides otherwise.

2. Two or more communications may be dealt with jointly if deemed appropriate by the Committee or a working group established under rule 89, paragraph 1.

Rule 89   1. The Committee may establish one or more working groups of no more than five of its members to make recommendations to the Committee regarding the fulfilment of the conditions of admissibility laid down in articles 1, 2, 3 and 5 (2) of the Protocol.

2. The rules of procedure of the Committee shall apply as far as possible to the meetings of the working group.

3. The Committee may designate special rapporteurs from among its members to assist in the handling of communications.

Rule 90   With a view to reaching a decision on the admissibility of a communication, the Committee, or a working group established under rule 89, paragraph 1, shall ascertain:

(a) That the communication is not anonymous and that it emanates from an individual, or individuals, subject to the jurisdiction of a State party to the Protocol;

(b) That the individual claims, in a manner sufficiently substantiated, to be a victim of a violation by that State party of any of the rights set forth in the Covenant. Normally, the communication should be submitted by the individual himself or by his representative; a communication submitted on behalf of an alleged victim may, however, be accepted when it appears that he is unable to submit the communication himself;

(d) That the communication is not incompatible with the provisions of the Covenant;

(e) That the same matter is not being examined under another procedure of international investigation or settlement;

(f) That the individual has exhausted all available domestic remedies.

Rule 91   1. The Committee or a working group established under rule 89, paragraph 1, or a special rapporteur designated under rule 89, paragraph 3, may request the State party concerned or the author of the communication to submit additional written information or observations relevant to the question of the admissibility of the communication. To avoid undue delays, a time-limit for the submission of such information or observations shall be indicated.

2. A communication may not be declared admissible unless the State party concerned has received the text of the communication and has been given an opportunity to furnish information or observations as provided in paragraph 1 of this rule.

3. A request addressed to a State party under paragraph 1 of this rule shall include a statement of the fact that such a request does not imply that any decision has been reached on the question of admissibility.

4. Within fixed time-limits, each party may be afforded an opportunity to comment on submissions made by the other party pursuant to this rule.

Rule 92   1. Where the Committee decides that a communication is inadmissible under the Protocol it shall as soon as possible communicate its decision, through the Secretary-General, to the author of the communication and, where the communication has been transmitted to a State party concerned, to that State party.

2. If the Committee has declared a communication inadmissible under article 5, paragraph 2, of the Protocol, this decision may be reviewed at a later date by the Committee upon a written request by or on behalf of the individual concerned containing information to the effect that the reasons for inadmissibility referred to in article 5, paragraph 2, no longer apply.

3. Any member of the Committee may request that a summary of his individual opinion shall be appended to the Committee's decision declaring a communication inadmissible under the Protocol.

D. Procedure for the consideration of communications on the merits

Rule 93 1. As soon as possible after the Committee or a working group acting under rule 87, paragraph 2, has taken a decision that a communication is admissible under the Protocol, that decision and the text of the relevant documents shall be submitted, through the Secretary-General, to the State party concerned. The author of the communication shall also be informed, through the Secretary-General, of the decision.

2. Within six months, the State party concerned shall submit to the Committee written explanations or statements clarifying the matter under consideration and the remedy, if any, that may have been taken by that State.

3. Any explanations or statements submitted by a State party pursuant to this rule shall be communicated, through the Secretary-General, to the author of the communication, who may submit any additional written information or observations within fixed time-limits.

4. Upon consideration of the merits, the Committee may review a decision that a communication is admissible in the light of any explanations or statements submitted by the State party pursuant to this rule.

Rule 94 1. If the communication is admissible, the Committee shall consider it in the light of all written information made available to it by the individuals and by the State party concerned and shall formulate its views thereon. For this purpose the Committee may refer the communication to a working group of not more than five of its members or to a special rapporteur to make recommendations to the Committee.

2. The views of the Committee shall be communicated to the individual and to the State party concerned.

3. Any member of the Committee may request that a summary of his individual opinion shall be appended to the views of the Committee.

E. Rules concerning confidentiality

Rule 95 1. All decisions not of a final nature adopted by the Committee in the course of consideration of a communication under the Protocol are confidential. They are transmitted to the parties solely for information or for the purpose of soliciting information, observations or clarifications in respect of (a) questions of admissibility; (b) the merits of the claims; or (c) any remedial action that may have been taken by the State party. No publicity shall be given by the parties to the content of these decisions, which will remain confidential except to the extent that they may be reflected in later decisions of a final nature.

2. Notwithstanding paragraph 1 above, interim measures requested under rule 86 shall not be subject to the rule of confidentiality.

3. Decisions of a final nature are normally made public by the Committee.

(a) Decisions declaring communications inadmissible under the Protocol will normally become public shortly after they have been forwarded to the parties. As a rule, the identity of the authors will be indicated in the text made public, unless the Committee decides otherwise;

(b) The Committee's views on the merits of the claims become public shortly after they have been forwarded to the parties under article 5, paragraph 4, of the Protocol.

4. The text of a decision made public shall carry an indication to that effect.

Rule 96   1. All submissions made by the parties in respect of communications considered under the Protocol shall remain confidential until a final decision has been forwarded to the parties pursuant to rule 95. The parties are under an obligation to observe and respect this rule of confidentiality and shall refrain from giving publicity to any submissions while a communication is under consideration. Thereafter, both parties are free to release their own submissions.

2. If the identity of the author of a communication declared inadmissible has not been disclosed by the Committee, the State party shall refrain from disclosing his identity.

Rule 97   All working documents issued for the Committee by the Secretariat, or placed before a working group established pursuant to rule 89, paragraph 1, or placed before a special rapporteur designated pursuant to rule 89, paragraph 3, are confidential and remain confidential after consideration of a communication is concluded, unless the Committee decides otherwise. This includes the Secretariat summaries of communications, prepared pursuant to rule 79, paragraph 1, which may be made available to States parties at the time when they are requested, under rule 91, paragraph 1, to submit information or observations relevant to the question of admissibility of a communication.

Rule 98   Information furnished by the parties within the framework of follow-up to the Committee's views is not subject to confidentiality, unless the Committee decides otherwise. Decisions of the Committee relating to follow-up activities are equally not subject to confidentiality, unless the Committee decides otherwise.

4. International Covenant on Economic, Social and Cultural Rights

a) Covenant of December 19, 1966, Part IV

Art. 16
1. The States Parties to the present Covenant undertake to submit in conformity with this part of the Covenant reports on the measures which they have adopted and the progress made in achieving the observance of the rights recognized herein.

2. (a) All reports shall be submitted to the Secretary-General of the United Nations, who shall transmit copies to the Economic and Social Council for consideration in accordance with the provisions of the present Covenant:

(b) The Secretary-General of the United Nations shall also transmit to the specialized agencies copies of the reports, or any relevant parts therefrom, from States Parties to the present Covenant which are also members of these specialized agencies in so far as these reports, or parts therefrom, relate to any matters which fall within the responsibilities of the said agencies in accordance with their constitutional instruments.

Art. 17
1. The States Parties to the present Covenant shall furnish their reports in stages, in accordance with a programme to be established by the Economic and Social Council within one year of the entry into force of the present Covenant after consultation with the States Parties and the specialized agencies concerned.

2. Reports may indicate factors and difficulties affecting the degree of fulfilment of obligations under the present Covenant.

3. Where relevant information has previously been furnished to the United Nations or to any specialized agency by any State Party to the present Covenant, it will not be necessary to reproduce that information, but a precise reference to the information so furnished will suffice.

Art. 18
Pursuant to its responsibilities under the Charter of the United Nations in the field of human rights and fundamental freedoms, the Economic and Social Council may make arrangements with the specialized agencies in respect of their reporting to it on the progress made in achieving the observance of the provisions of the present Covenant falling within the scope of their activities. These reports may include particulars of decisions and recommendations on such implementation adopted by their competent organs.

Art. 19   The Economic and Social Council may transmit to the Commission on Human Rights for study and general recommendation or, as appropriate, for information the reports concerning human rights submitted by States in accordance with articles 16 and 17, and those concerning human rights submitted by the specialized agencies in accordance with article 18.

Art. 20   The States Parties to the present Covenant and the specialized agencies concerned may submit comments to the Economic and Social Council on any general recommendation under article 19 or reference to such general recommendation in any report of the Commission on Human Rights or any documentation referred to therein.

Art. 21   The Economic and Social Council may submit from time to time to the General Assembly reports with recommendations of a general nature and a summary of the information received from the States Parties to the present Covenant and the specialized agencies on the measures taken and the progress made in achieving general observance of the rights recognized in the present Covenant.

Art. 22   The Economic and Social Council may bring to the attention of other organs of the United Nations, their subsidiary organs and specialized agencies concerned with furnishing technical assistance any matters arising out of the reports referred to in this part of the present Covenant which may assist such bodies in deciding, each within its field of competence, on the advisability of international measures likely to contribute to the effective progressive implementation of the present Covenant.

Art. 23   The States Parties to the present Covenant agree that international action for the achievement of the rights recognized in the present Covenant includes such methods as the conclusion of conventions, the adoption of recommendations, the furnishing of technical assistance and the holding of regional meetings and technical meetings for the purpose of consultation and study organized in conjunction with the Governments concerned.

Art. 24   Nothing in the present Covenant shall be interpreted as impairing the provisions of the Charter of the United Nations and of the constitutions of the specialized agencies which define the respective responsibilities of the various organs of the United Nations and of the specialized agencies in regard to the matters dealt with in the present Covenant.

Art. 25   Nothing in the present Covenant shall be interpreted as impairing the inherent right of all peoples to enjoy and utilize fully and freely their natural wealth and resources.

b) Provisional Rules of Procedure of February, 21, 1989

PART ONE — GENERAL RULES

I. SESSIONS

Duration and venue of the sessions

Rule 1   The Committee on Economic, Social and Cultural Rights (hereinafter referred to as "the Committee") shall meet annually for a period of up to three weeks, or as may be decided by the Economic and Social Council (hereinafter referred to as "the Council") taking into account the number of reports to be examined by the Committee. Sessions of the Committee shall be held at Geneva or wherever the Council so decides.

Dates of sessions

Rule 2   Sessions of the Committee shall be convened at dates decided by the Council in consultation with the Secretary-General of the United Nations (hereinafter referred to as "the Secretary-General").

Notification of the opening date of sessions

Rule 3   The Secretary-General shall notify the members of the Committee of the date of the first meeting of each session. Such notifications shall be sent at least six weeks in advance of the session.

II. AGENDA

Provisional agenda for the sessions

Rule 4   The provisional agenda of each session shall be prepared by the Secretary-General in consultation with the Chairman of the Committee and shall include:

(a) Any item decided upon by the Committee at a previous session;

(b) Any item proposed by the Council in fulfilment of its responsibilities under the International Covenant on Economic, Social and Cultural Rights (hereinafter referred to as "the Covenant");

(c) Any item proposed by the Chairman of the Committee;

(d) Any item proposed by a State party to the Covenant,

(e) Any item proposed by a member of the Committee;

(f) Any item proposed by the Secretary-General.

Adoption of the agenda

Rule 5   The first item on the provisional agenda of any session shall be the adoption of the agenda, except for the election of the officers when required under rule 14 of these rules.

Revision of the agenda

Rule 6   During a session, the Committee may revise the agenda and may, as appropriate, add, delete or defer items.

Transmission of the provisional agenda and basic documents

Rule 7   The provisional agenda and basic documents relating to items appearing thereon shall be transmitted to the members of the Committee by the Secretary-General as early as possible.

Organization of work

Rule 8   At the beginning of each session the Committee shall consider appropriate organizational matters, including the schedule of its meetings and the possibility of holding a general discussion on the measures adopted and the progress made in achieving the observance of the rights recognized in the Covenant.

III. MEMBERS OF THE COMMITTEE

Members

Rule 9   Members of the Committee shall be the 18 experts elected by the Council in accordance with paragraphs (b) and (c) of its resolution 1985/17.

Term of office

Rule 10   The term of office of members elected to the Committee shall begin on 1 January following their election and expire on the 31 December following the election of members that are to succeed them as members of the Committee.

Declaration of casual vacancies

Rule 11   1. If, in the unanimous opinion of the other members, a member of the Committee has ceased to carry out his functions for any cause other than absence of a temporary character, the Chairman of the Committee shall notify the Secretary-General, who shall then declare the seat of that member to be vacant.

2. In the event of the death or the resignation of a member of the Committee, the Chairman shall immediately notify the Secretary-General, who shall declare the seat vacant from the date of death or the date on which the resignation takes effect. The resignation of a member of the Committee shall be notified by the member in writing directly to the Chairman or the Secretary-General and action shall be taken to declare the seat vacant only after such notification has been received.

Filling of casual vacancies

Rule 12   1. When a vacancy is declared in accordance with rule 11 of these rules and if the term of office of the member to be replaced does not expire within six months of the declaration of the vacancy, the Secretary-General shall notify each of the States parties of the regional group to which the vacant seat in the Committee is allocated in accordance with paragraph (b) of Council resolution 1985/17. Those States parties may within two months submit nominations in accordance with the relevant provisions of paragraphs (b) and (c) of the same resolution.

2. The Secretary-General shall prepare a list in alphabetical order of the persons thus nominated and shall submit it to the Council. The Council shall hold the election to fill the vacancy in the Committee in accordance with the procedure established in paragraph (c) of its resolution 1985/17. The election shall take place at the session of the Council following the deadline for the submission of nominations for the vacant seat.

3. A member of the Committee elected to fill the vacancy declared in accordance with rule 11 of these rules shall hold office for the remainder of the term of the member who vacated the seat on the Committee.

Solemn declaration

Rule 13   Before assuming his duties, each member of the Committee shall make the following solemn declaration in open Committee:

"I solemnly undertake to discharge my duties as a member of the Committee on Economic, Social and Cultural Rights impartially and conscientiously."

IV. OFFICERS

Elections

Rule 14   The Committee shall elect from among its members a Chairman, three Vice-Chairmen and a Rapporteur, with due regard for equitable geographical representation.

Term of office

Rule 15   The officers of the Committee shall be elected for a term of two years. They shall be eligible for re-election. None of them, however, may hold office if he or she ceases to be a member of the Committee.

Position of the Chairman in relation to the Committee

Rule 16   The Chairman shall perform the functions conferred upon him by the rules of procedure and the decisions of the Committee. In the exercise of those functions, the Chairman shall remain under the authority of the Committee.

Acting Chairman

Rule 17   If during a session the Chairman is unable to be present at a meeting or any part thereof, he or she shall designate one of the Vice-Chairmen to act in his or her place.

Powers and duties of the Acting Chairman

Rule 18   A Vice-Chairman acting as Chairman shall have the same powers and duties as the Chairman .

Replacement of officers

Rule 19   If any of the officers of the Committee ceases to serve or declares inability to continue serving as a member of the Committee or for any reason is no longer able to act as an officer, a new officer shall be elected for the unexpired term of his or her predecessor.

V. SECRETARIAT

Duties of the Secretary-General

Rule 20   1. The secretariat of the Committee and of such subsidiary bodies as may be established by the Committee shall be provided by the Secretary-General.

2. The Secretary-General shall provide the Committee with the necessary staff and facilities for the effective performance of its functions, bearing in mind the need to give adequate publicity to its work.

Statements

Rule 21 The Secretary-General or his representative shall attend all meetings of the Committee and, subject to rule 33 of these rules, may make oral or written statements at meetings of the Committee or its subsidiary bodies.

Keeping the members informed

Rule 22 The Secretary-General shall be responsible for informing the members of the Committee without delay of any questions which may be brought before it for consideration.

Financial implications of proposals

Rule 23 Before any proposal which involves expenditure is approved by the Committee or by any of its subsidiary bodies, the Secretary-General shall prepare and circulate to the members of the Committee or subsidiary body, as early as possible, an estimate of the cost involved in the proposal. It shall be the duty of the Chairman to draw the attention of members to this estimate and to invite discussion on it when the proposal is considered by the Committee or subsidiary body.

VI. LANGUAGES

Official and working languages

Rule 24 Arabic, English, French, Russian and Spanish shall be the official languages of the Committee and English, French, Russian and Spanish shall be the working languages of the Committee.

Interpretation

Rule 25 1. Statements made in an official language shall be interpreted into the other official languages.

2. A speaker may make a statement in a language other than an official language if he provides for interpretation into one of the official languages. Interpretation into the other official languages by the interpreters of the Secretariat may be based on the interpretation given in the first such language.

Languages of records

Rule 26 Summary records of the meetings of the Committee shall be drawn up and distributed in English, French and Spanish.

Languages of formal decisions and official documents

Rule 27   All formal decisions of the Committee to be submitted to the Council
           shall be made available in the official languages of the Council. All other
           official documents of the Committee shall be issued in the working lan-
           guages and any of them may, if the Council so decides, be issued in all the
           official languages of the Council.

VII. PUBLIC AND PRIVATE MEETINGS

Public and private meetings

Rule 28   The meetings of the Committee and its subsidiary bodies shall be held in
           public unless the Committee decides otherwise.

Issue of communiqués concerning private meetings

Rule 29   At the close of each private meeting the Committee or its subsidiary body
           may issue a communiqué through the Secretary-General for the use of the
           information media and the general public regarding the activities of the
           Committee at its closed meetings.

VIII. RECORDS

Summary records of the proceedings and corrections to them

Rule 30   1. The Secretary-General shall provide the Committee with summary re-
           cords of its proceedings, which shall be made available to the Council at
           the same time as the report of the Committee.

           2. Summary records are subject to correction to be submitted by partici-
           pants in the meetings to the Secretariat in the language in which the sum-
           mary record is issued. Corrections to the records of the meetings shall be
           consolidated in a single corrigendum to be issued shortly after the end of
           the session concerned.

IX. DISTRIBUTION OF REPORTS AND OTHER OFFICIAL DOCUMENTS OF THE COMMITTEE

Distribution of official documents

Rule 31   Reports, formal decisions and all other official documents of the Com-
           mittee shall be documents of general distribution unless the Committee
           decides otherwise.

X. CONDUCT OF BUSINESS

Quorum

Rule 32   Twelve members of the Committee shall constitute a quorum.

Powers of the Chairman

Rule 33   The Chairman shall declare the opening and closing of each meeting of the Committee, direct the discussion, ensure observance of these rules, accord the right to speak, put questions to the vote and announce decisions. The Chairman, subject to these rules, shall have control over the proceedings of the Committee and over the maintenance of order at its meetings. The Chairman may, in the course of the discussion of an item, propose to the Committee the limitation of the time to be allowed to speakers, the limitation of the number of times each speaker may speak on any question and the closure of the list of speakers. He or she shall rule on points of order and shall also have the power to propose adjournment or closure of the debate or adjournment or suspension of a meeting. Debate shall be confined to the question before the Committee, and the Chairman may call a speaker to order if his or her remarks are not relevant to the subject under discussion.

Time-limit for statements

Rule 34   The Committee may limit the time allowed to each speaker on any question. When debate is limited and a speaker exceeds his allotted time, the Chairman shall call him or her to order without delay.

List of speakers

Rule 35   During the course of a debate, the Chairman may announce the list of speakers and, with the consent of the Committee, declare the list closed. The Chairman may, however, accord the right of reply to any member or representative if a statement delivered after the list is declared closed makes this desirable. When the debate on an item is concluded because there are no other speakers, the Chairman shall declare the debate closed. Such closure shall have the same effect as closure by the consent of the Committee.

Points of order

Rule 36   During the discussion of any matter, a member may at any time raise a point of order, and the point of order shall immediately be decided upon by the Chairman in accordance with the rules of procedure. Any appeal against the ruling of the Chairman shall immediately be put to the vote, and the ruling of the Chairman shall stand unless overruled by a majority of the members present. A member may not, in raising a point of order, speak on the substance of the matter under discussion.

Suspension or adjournment of meetings

Rule 37 During the discussion of any matter, a member may move the suspension or the adjournment of the meeting. No discussion on such motions shall be permitted, and they shall immediately be put to the vote.

Adjournment of debate

Rule 38 During the discussion of any matter, a member may move the adjournment of the debate on the item under discussion. In addition to the proposer of the motion, one member may speak in favour of and one against the motion, after which the motion shall immediately be put to the vote.

Closure of debate

Rule 39 1. When the debate on an item is concluded because there are no other speakers, the Chairman shall declare the debate closed. Such closure shall have the same effect as closure by the consent of the Committee.

2. A member may at any time move the closure of the debate on the item under discussion, whether or not any other member or representative has signified his wish to speak. Permission to speak on the closure of the debate shall be accorded only to two speakers opposing the closure, after which the motion shall immediately be put to the vote.

Order of motions

Rule 40 Subject to rule 36 of these rules, the following motions shall have precedence in the following order over all other proposals or motions before the meeting:

(a) To suspend the meeting;

(b) To adjourn the meeting,

(c) To adjourn the debate on the item under discussion;

(d) To close the debate on the item under discussion.

Submission of proposals

Rule 41 Unless otherwise decided by the Committee, proposals and substantive amendments or motions submitted by members shall be introduced in writing and handed to the Secretariat, and their consideration shall, if so requested by any member, be deferred until the next meeting on a subsequent day.

Decisions on competence

Rule 42 Subject to rule 40 of these rules, any motion by a member calling for a decision on the competence of the Committee to adopt a proposal submitted to it shall be put to the vote immediately before a vote is taken on the proposal in question.

Withdrawal of motions

Rule 43 A motion may be withdrawn by its proposer at any time before voting on it has commenced, provided that the motion has not been amended. A motion which has thus been withdrawn may be reintroduced by any member.

Reconsideration of proposals

Rule 44 When a proposal has been adopted or rejected, it may not be reconsidered at the same session unless the Committee so decides. Permission to speak on a motion to reconsider shall be accorded only to two speakers in favour of the motion and two speakers opposing the motion, after which it shall immediately be put to the vote.

XI. VOTING

Voting rights

Rule 45 Each member of the Committee shall have one vote.

Adoption of decisions

Rule 46 Decisions of the Committee shall be made by a majority of the members present. However, the Committee shall endeavour to work on the basis of the principle of consensus.

Equally divided votes

Rule 47 If a vote is equally divided on a matter other than an election, the proposal shall be regarded as rejected .

lots and to a number not more than twice the places remaining to be filled. The following three ballots thereafter shall be unrestricted, and so on until all the places have been filled.

XIII. SUBSIDIARY BODIES

Ad hoc subsidiary bodies

Rule 56   1. Subject to rule 24, paragraph 2, of the rules of procedure of the Economic and Social Council, the Committee may set up *ad hoc* subsidiary bodies as it deems necessary for the performance of its functions, and define their composition and powers.

2. Each subsidiary body shall elect its own officers and may adopt its own rules of procedure. Failing such rules, the present rules of procedure shall apply *mutatis mutandis* .

XIV. REPORT OF THE COMMITTEE

Annual report

Rule 57   1. The Committee shall submit to the Council an annual report on its activities, including a summary of its consideration of reports submitted by States parties to the Covenant. The report may include general observations by members of the Committee on the basis of their consideration of States parties' reports. A list of States parties to the Covenant shall be annexed to the report of the Committee together with an indication of the status of submission of reports by States parties.

2. The Committee shall also include in its report suggestions and recommendations of a general nature referred to under rule 64 of these rules of procedure.

PART TWO — RULES RELATING TO THE FUNCTIONS OF THE COMMITTEE

XV. REPORTS FROM STATES PARTIES UNDER ARTICLES 16 AND 17 OF THE COVENANT

Submission of reports

Rule 58   1. In accordance with article 16 of the Covenant, the States parties shall submit to the Council for consideration by the Committee reports on the measures which they have adopted and progress made in achieving the observance of the rights recognized in the Covenant.

2. In accordance with article 17 of the Covenant and Council resolution 1988/4, the States parties shall submit their initial reports within two years of the entry into force of the Covenant for the State party concerned and thereafter periodic reports at five-year intervals.

Non-submission of reports

Rule 59   1. At each session, the Secretary-General shall notify the Committee of all cases of non-submission of reports under rule 58 of these rules. In such cases the Committee may recommend to the Council to transmit to the State party concerned, through the Secretary-General, a reminder concerning the submission of such reports.

2. If, after the reminder referred to in paragraph 1 of this rule, the State party does not submit the report required under rule 58 of these rules, the Committee shall so state in the annual report which it submits to the Council.

Form and content of reports

Rule 60   1. Upon approval of the Council, the Committee may inform the States parties, through the Secretary-General, of its wishes regarding the form and contents of the reports to be submitted under article 16 of the Covenant and the programme established by Council resolution 1988/4.

2. The general guidelines for reports by the States parties may, when necessary, be considered by the Committee with a view to making suggestions for their improvement.

Consideration of reports

Rule 61   1. The Committee shall consider the reports submitted by States parties to the Covenant in accordance with the programme established by Council resolution 1988/4.

2. The Committee shall normally consider the reports submitted by States parties under article 16 of the Covenant in the order in which they have been received by the Secretary-General.

3. Reports of the States parties scheduled for consideration by the Committee shall be made available to the members of the Committee at least six weeks before the opening of the session of the Committee. Any reports by States parties received by the Secretary-General for processing less than 12 weeks before the opening of the session shall be made available to the Committee at its session in the following year.

Attendance by States parties at examination of reports

Rule 62   1. Representatives of the reporting States are entitled to be present at the meetings of the Committee when their reports are examined. Such representatives should be able to make statements on the reports submitted by their States and reply to questions which may be put to them by the members of the Committee.

2. The Secretary-General shall notify the States parties as early as possible of the opening date and duration of the session of the Committee at which their respective reports are scheduled for consideration. For the meetings referred to in the preceding paragraph, representatives of the States parties concerned shall be specially invited to attend.

Request for additional information

Rule 63   1. When considering a report submitted by a State party under article 16 of the Covenant, the Committee shall first satisfy itself that the report provides all the information required under existing guidelines.

2. If a report of a State party to the Covenant, in the opinion of the Committee, does not contain sufficient information, the Committee may request the State concerned to furnish the additional information which is required, indicating the manner as well as the time within which the said information should be submitted.

Suggestions and recommendations

Rule 64   The Committee shall make suggestions and recommendations of a general nature on the basis of its consideration of reports submitted by States parties and of the reports submitted by the specialized agencies in order to assist the Council to fulfil, in particular, its responsibilities under articles 21 and 22 of the Covenant. The Committee may also make suggestions for the consideration by the Council with reference to articles 19 and 23 of the Covenant.

General comments

Rule 65   The Committee may prepare general comments based on the various articles and provisions of the Covenant with a view to assisting States parties in fulfilling their reporting obligations.

XVI. REPORTS FROM SPECIALIZED AGENCIES UNDER ARTICLE 18 OF THE COVENANT

Submission of reports

Rule 66   In accordance with the provisions of article 18 of the Covenant and the arrangements made by the Council thereunder, the specialized agencies are called upon to submit reports on the progress made in achieving the observance of the provisions of the Covenant falling within the scope of their activities. These reports may include particulars of decisions and recommendations on such implementation adopted by their competent organs.

Consideration of reports

Rule 67   The Committee is entrusted with the task of considering the reports of the specialized agencies, submitted to the Council in accordance with article 18 of the Covenant and the programme established under Council resolution 1988 (LX).

Participation of specialized agencies

Rule 68   The specialized agencies concerned shall be invited to designate representatives to participate at the meetings of the Committee. Such representatives may make general statements on matters falling within the scope of the activities of their respective organizations at the end of the discussion by the Committee of the report of each State party to the Covenant. The representatives of the States parties presenting reports to the Committee shall be free to respond to, or take into account, the statements made by the specialized agencies.

XVII. OTHER SOURCES OF INFORMATION

Submission of information, documentation and written statements

Rule 69   1. Non-governmental organizations in consultative status with the Council may submit to the Committee written statements that might contribute to full and universal recognition and realization of the rights contained in the Covenant.

2. The Committee may recommend to the Council to invite United Nations bodies concerned and regional intergovernmental organizations to submit to it information, documentation and written statements, as appropriate, relevant to its activities under the Covenant.

PART THREE — INTERPRETATION AND AMENDMENTS

XVIII. INTERPRETATION AND AMENDMENTS

Underlined headings

Rule 70   The underlined headings of these rules, which were inserted for reference purposes only, shall be disregarded in the interpretation of the rules.

Amendments

Rule 71   These rules of procedure may be amended by a decision of the Committee, subject to approval of the Council.

Approval of and modification by the Council

Rule 72   These rules of procedure are subject to the approval by the Council and
shall remain in force in so far as they are not superseded or modified by
decisions of the Council.

c) Draft Optional Protocol to the International Covenant on Economic, Social and Cultural Rights of December 18, 1996 (E/CN.4/1997/105)

PREAMBLE

The States Parties to the present Protocol,

(a) *Emphasizing* that social justice and development, including the realization of economic, social and cultural rights, are essential elements in the construction of a just and equitable national and international order,

(b) *Recalling* that the Vienna Declaration and Programme of Action recognized that "all human rights are universal, indivisible and independent and interrelated";

(c) *Emphasizing* the role of the Economic and Social Council, and through it the Committee on Economic, Social and Cultural Rights (hereinafter referred to as the Committee) in developing a better understanding of the International Covenant on Economic, Social and Cultural Rights (hereinafter referred to as the Covenant) and in promoting the realization of the rights recognized therein,

(d) *Recalling* the provision of article 2 (1) of the Covenant pursuant to which "Each State Party to the present Covenant undertakes to take steps, individually and through international assistance and co-operation, especially economic and technical, to the maximum of its available resources, with a view to achieving progressively the full realization of the rights recognized in the present Covenant by all appropriate means, including particularly the adoption of legislative measures",

(e) *Noting* that the possibility for the subjects of economic, social and cultural rights to submit complaints of alleged violations of those rights is a necessary means of recourse to guarantee the full enjoyment of the rights,

(f) *Considering* that, in order further to achieve the purposes of the Covenant and the implementation of its provisions, it is appropriate to enable the Committee to receive, and examine, in accordance with the provisions of this Protocol, communications alleging violations of the Covenant,

Have agreed as follows:

Art. 1   A State Party to the Covenant that becomes a Party to the present Protocol recognizes the competence of the Committee to receive and examine communications from any individuals or groups subject to its jurisdiction in accordance with the provisions of this Protocol.

Art. 2   1. Any individual or group claiming to be a victim of a violation by the State party concerned of any economic, social or cultural rights recognized in the Covenant, or any individual or group acting on behalf of such claimant(s), may submit a written communication to the Committee for examination.

2. States parties to this Protocol undertake not to hinder in any way the effective exercise of the right to submit a communication and to take all steps necessary to prevent any persecution or sanctioning of any person or group submitting or seeking to submit a communication under this Protocol.

Art. 3   1. No communication shall be received by the Committee if it is anonymous or is directed at a State which is not a party to this Protocol.

2. The Committee shall declare a communication inadmissible if it:

(a) does not contain allegations which, if substantiated, would constitute a violation of rights recognized in the Covenant;

(b) constitutes an abuse of the right to submit a communication, or

(c) relates to acts and omissions which occurred before the entry into force of this Protocol for the State Party concerned, unless those acts or omissions:

(i)   continue to constitute a violation of the Covenant after the entry into force of the Protocol for that State party; or

(ii) have effects which continue beyond the entry into force of this Protocol and those effects themselves appear to constitute a violation of a right recognized in the Covenant,

3. The Committee shall not declare a communication admissible unless it has ascertained:

(a) that all available domestic remedies have been exhausted; or

(b) that a communication submitted by or on behalf of the alleged victim which raises essentially the same issues of fact and law is not being examined under another procedure of international investigation or settlement. The Committee may, however, examine such a communication where the procedure of international investigation or settlement is unreasonably prolonged.

Art. 4   1. The Committee may decline to continue to examine a communication if the author, after being given a reasonable opportunity to do so, fails to provide information which would sufficiently substantiate the allegations contained in the communication.

2. The Committee may, upon the request of the author of the complaint, recommence examination of a communication which it has declared in-

admissible under article 3 if the circumstances which led to its decision, have changed.

Art. 5   If at any time after the receipt of a communication, and before a determination on the merits has been reached, a preliminary study gives rise to a reasonable apprehension that the allegations, if substantiated, could lead to irreparable harm, the Committee may request the State Party concerned to take such interim measures as may be necessary to avoid such irreparable harm.

Art. 6   1. Unless the Committee considers that a communication should be declared inadmissible without reference to the State party concerned, the Committee shall confidentially bring to the attention of the State party any communication referred to it under this Protocol.

2. Within six months, the receiving State shall submit to the Committee explanations or statements and the remedy, if any, that may have been afforded by that State.

3. During its examination of a communication, the Committee shall place itself at the disposal of the parties concerned with a view to facilitating settlement of the matter on the basis of respect for the rights and obligations set forth in the Covenant.

4. If a settlement is reached, the Committee shall prepare a report containing a statement of the facts and of the solution reached.

Art. 7   1. The Committee shall examine communications received under this Protocol in the light of all information made available to it by or on behalf of the author in accordance with paragraph 2, and by the State party concerned. The Committee may also take into account information obtained from other sources, provided that this information is transmitted to the parties concerned for comment.

2. The Committee may adopt such procedures as will enable it to ascertain the facts and to assess the extent to which the State party concerned has fulfilled its obligations under the Covenant.

3. As part of is examination of a communication, the Committee may, with the agreement of the State Party concerned, visit the territory of that State Party.

4. The Committee shall hold closed meetings when examining communications under this Protocol.

5. After examining a communication, the Committee shall adopt its views on the claims made in the communication and shall transmit these to the State party and to the author, together with any recommendations it considers appropriate. The views shall be made public at the same time.

Art. 8   1. Where the Committee is of the view that a State Party has violated its obligations under the Covenant, the Committee may recommend that the State Party take specific measures to remedy the violation and to prevent its recurrence.

2. The State Party concerned, shall, within six months of receiving notice of the decision of the Committee under paragraph 1, or such longer period as may be specified by the Committee, provide the Committee with details of the measures which it has taken in accordance with paragraph 1 above.

Art. 9   1. The Committee may invite a State Party to discuss with it, at a mutually convenient time, the measures which the State Party has taken to give effect to the views or recommendations of the Committee.

2. The Committee may invite the State Party concerned to include in its report under article 17 of the Covenant details of any measures taken in response to the Committee's views and recommendations.

3. The Committee shall include in its annual report an account of the substance of the communication and its examination of the matter, a summary of the explanations and the statements of the State Party concerned, of its own views and recommendations, and the response of the State Party concerned to those views and recommendations.

Art. 10   The Committee may make rules of procedure prescribing the procedure to be followed when it is exercising the functions conferred on it by this Protocol.

Art. 11   1. The Committee shall meet for such period as is necessary to carry out its functions under this Protocol.

2. The Secretary-General of the United Nations shall provide the Committee with the necessary staff, facilities and finances for the performance or its functions under this Protocol, and in particular shall ensure that expert legal service is available to the Committee for this purpose.

Art. 12   1. This Protocol is open for signature by any State Party to the Covenant.

2. This Protocol is subject to ratification or accession by any State Party to the Covenant. Instruments of ratification or accession shall be deposited with the Secretary-General of the United Nations.

Art. 13   1. This Protocol shall enter into force three months after the date of the deposit with the Secretary-General of the United Nations of the fifth instrument of ratification or accession.

2. For each State ratifying this Protocol or acceding to it after its entry into force, this Protocol shall enter into force three months after the date of the deposit of its own instrument of ratification or accession.

Art. 14   1. This Protocol will be binding upon each State Party in respect of all territories subject to its jurisdiction.

2. The Provisions of this Protocol shall extend to all parts of the federal States without any limitations or exceptions.

Art. 15   1. Any State Party to this Protocol may propose an amendment and file it with the Secretary-General of the United Nations. The Secretary-General shall thereupon communicate any proposed amendments to the States

Parties to this Protocol with the request that they notify him or her whether they favour a conference of States Parties for the purpose of considering and voting upon the proposal. If within four months from the date of such communication at least one third of the States Parties favour such a conference, the Secretary-General shall convene such a conference under the auspices of the United Nations. Any amendment adopted by majority of the States parties present and voting at the conference shall be submitted to the General Assembly of the United Nations for approval.

2. Amendments shall come into force when they have been approved by the General Assembly of the United Nations and accepted by a two-thirds majority of the States Parties to this Protocol in accordance with their respective constitutional processes.

3. When amendments come into force, they shall be binding on those States Parties only which have accepted them, other States Parties still being bound by the provisions of this Protocol and any earlier amendment which they have accepted.

Art. 16   1. Any State Party may denounce this Protocol at any time by written notification addressed to the Secretary-General of the United Nations. Denunciation shall take effect one year after the date of receipt of the notification by the Secretary-General.

2. Denunciations shall be without prejudice to the continued application of the provisions of this Protocol to any communication submitted before the effective date of denunciation.

3. Following the date at which the denunciation of a State Party becomes effective, the Committee shall not commence consideration of any new matters regarding that State.

Art. 17   This Protocol, of which the Arabic, Chinese, English, French, Russian and Spanish texts are equally authentic, shall be deposited in the archives of the United Nations.

5. Convention on the Elimination of All Forms of Discrimination against Women

a) Convention of December 18, 1979, Part V

Art. 17   1. For the purpose of considering the progress made in the implementation of the present Convention, there shall be established a Committee on the Elimination of Discrimination against Women (hereinafter referred to as the Committee) consisting, at the time of entry into force of the Convention, of eighteen and, after ratification of or accession to the Convention by the thirty-fifth State Party, of twenty-three experts of high moral standing and competence in the field covered by the Convention. The experts shall be elected by States Parties from among their nationals and shall serve in their personal capacity, consideration being given to equitable geographical distribution and to the representation of the different forms of civilization as well as the principal legal systems.

2. The members of the Committee shall be elected by secret ballot from a list of persons nominated by States Parties. Each State Party may nominate one person from among its own nationals.

3. The initial election shall be held six months after the date of the entry into force of the present Convention. At least three months before the date of each election the Secretary-General of the United Nations shall address a letter to the States Parties inviting them to submit their nominations within two months. The Secretary-General shall prepare a list in alphabetical order of all persons thus nominated, indicating the States Parties which have nominated them, and shall submit it to the States Parties.

4. Elections of the members of the Committee shall be held at a meeting of States Parties convened by the Secretary-General at United Nations Headquarters. At that meeting, for which two thirds of the States Parties shall constitute a quorum, the persons elected to the Committee shall be those nominees who obtain the largest number of votes and an absolute majority of the votes of the representatives of States Parties present and voting.

5. The members of the Committee shall be elected for a term of four years. However, the terms of nine of the members elected at the first election shall expire at the end of two years; immediately after the first election the names of these nine members shall be chosen by lot by the Chairman of the Committee.

6. The election of the five additional members of the Committee shall be held in accordance with the provisions of paragraphs 2, 3 and 4 of this article, following the thirty-fifth ratification or accession. The terms of two of the additional members elected on this occasion shall expire at the end of two years, the names of these two members having been chosen by lot by the Chairman of the Committee.

7. For the filling of casual vacancies, the State Party whose expert has ceased to function as a member of the Committee shall appoint another expert from among its nationals, subject to the approval of the Committee.

8. The members of the Committee shall, with the approval of the General Assembly, receive emoluments from United Nations resources on such terms and conditions as the Assembly may decide, having regard to the importance of the Committee's responsibilities.

9. The Secretary-General of the United Nations shall provide the necessary staff and facilities for the effective performance of the functions of the Committee under the present Convention.

Art. 18   1. States Parties undertake to submit to the Secretary-General of the United Nations, for consideration by the Committee, a report on the legislative, judicial, administrative or other measures which they have adopted to give effect to the provisions of the present Convention and on the progress made in this respect:

(a) Within one year after the entry into force for the State concerned; and

(b) Thereafter at least every four years and further whenever the Committee so requests.

2. Reports may indicate factors and difficulties affecting the degree of fulfilment of obligations under the present Convention.

Art. 19   1. The Committee shall adopt its own rules of procedure.

2. The Committee shall elect its officers for a term of two years.

Art. 20   1. The Committee shall normally meet for a period of not more than two weeks annually in order to consider the reports submitted in accordance with article 18 of the present Convention.

2. The meetings of the Committee shall normally be held at United Nations Headquarters or at any other convenient place as determined by the Committee.

Art. 21   1. The Committee shall, through the Economic and Social Council, report annually to the General Assembly of the United Nations on its activities and may make suggestions and general recommendations based on the examination of reports and information received from the States Parties. Such suggestions and general recommendations shall be included in the report of the Committee together with comments, if any, from States Parties.

2. The Secretary-General shall transmit the reports of the Committee to the Commission on the Status of Women for its information.

Art. 22   The specialized agencies shall be entitled to be represented at the consideration of the implementation of such provisions of the present Convention as fall within the scope of their activities. The Committee may invite the specialized agencies to submit reports on the implementation of the Convention in areas falling within the scope of their activities.

b) Rules of Procedure of the Committee on the Elimination of Discrimination Against Women of October 22, 1982

I. SESSIONS

Rule 1   Annual sessions

The Committee on the Elimination of Discrimination Against Women (hereinafter the "Committee"), established under the Convention on the Elimination of All Forms of Discrimination Against Women (hereinafter the "Convention"), shall normally hold one session annually, for a period of not more than two weeks.

Rule 2   Dates

1. Sessions of the Committee shall be convened on dates decided by the Committee in consultation with the Secretary-General of the United Nations (hereinafter the "Secretary-General"), taking into account the calendar of conferences approved by the General Assembly.

2. The Chairperson, in consultation with the other officers of the Committee, may agree to any necessary changes required to be made in such schedule.

Rule 3   Site

1. The sessions of the Committee shall normally be held at United Nations Headquarters, the Committee can also determine to hold sessions at the United Nations Office at Vienna.

2. Other sites for a session may be determined by the Committee in consultation with the Secretary-General, provided arrangements are made for the actual additional costs directly or indirectly incurred to be reimbursed to the United Nations.

Rule 4   Notification

The Secretary-General shall notify the members of the Committee of the date, duration and place of the session at least six weeks in advance of the opening date.

II. AGENDA

Rule 5   Provisional agenda

1. The provisional agenda for each session shall be prepared by the Secretary-General in consultation with the Chairperson, in conformity with the relevant provisions of articles 17 to 22 of the Convention, giving priority to any item the inclusion of which was decided at a previous session of the Committee.

2. The inclusion of additional items in the provisional agenda can be proposed by:

(a) The Chairperson or any other member of the Committee;

(b) A State party to the Convention;

(c) The Secretary-General relating to his functions under the Convention.

Rule 6   Transmission of provisional agenda

The provisional agenda and the basic documents relating to each item appearing thereon shall be transmitted in all United Nations working languages to the members of the Committee by the Secretary-General, who shall endeavor to do so at least six weeks prior to the opening date of the session.

Rule 7   Adoption of the agenda

1. The agenda shall be adopted by the Committee at the beginning of its meetings.

2. During a session, the Committee may add to the agenda only important items, which cannot be postponed.

III. MEMBERS OF THE COMMITTEE

Rule 8   Beginning of term of office

The term of office of the members of the Committee begins:

(a) On 16 April 1982 (the date of their election) for the members elected at the first election;

(b) No sooner than 16 April of the year of the election for members elected at subsequent elections;

(c) On the date of their approval by the Committee for members appointed to fill a casual vacancy.

Rule 9   Filling casual vacancies

The approval of a member appointed to fill a casual vacancy pursuant to article 17, paragraph 7, of the Convention, shall constitute the first item of business of the Committee after the appointment has been notified to it. Such a member shall hold office for the remainder of the term of the member whose seat on the Committee became vacant.

Rule 10   Solemn declaration

Upon assuming their duties, members of the Committee shall make the following solemn declaration in open Committee:

"I solemnly declare that I shall perform my duties and exercise powers as a member of the Committee on the Elimination of Discrimination against Women honourably, faithfully, impartially and conscientiously."

Rule 11   Inability to attend

1. Members of the Committee may not be represented by alternates.

2. A member unable to attend meetings of the Committee shall inform the Secretary-General as early as possible and, if this inability is likely to be extended, the member should resign.

Rule 12   Advisers

Members of the Committee may be accompanied by advisers of their choice, who may, however, not participate in the proceedings of the Committee.

IV. OFFICERS

Rule 13   Election

The Committee shall elect from among its members a Chairperson, three Vice-Chairpersons and a Rapporteur.

Rule 14   Term of office

The officers of the Committee shall be elected for a term of two years and be eligible for re-election, provided that the principle of rotation is upheld.

Rule 15   Absence of the Chairperson

1. If the Chairperson is absent from a meeting or any part thereof, a Vice-Chairperson designated by the Chairperson shall preside, with the same powers and duties as the latter.

2. If it is not possible for the Chairperson to designate a Vice-Chairperson as provided above, the Vice-Chairperson to preside shall be chosen according to the names of the Vice-Chairpersons as they appear in alphabetical order.

Rule 16   Replacement

If any officer of the Committee resigns or ceases to be a member of the Committee, a new officer shall be elected for the unexpired term.

V. SECRETARIAT

Rule 17   Statements

The Secretary-General or his representatives may make either oral or written statements to the Committee concerning any question under consideration.

Rule 18   Financial implications

Before any proposal that may involve expenditures is approved by the Committee, the Secretary-General shall prepare and circulate a statement of the estimated administrative and financial implications. The Chairperson shall draw the attention of the Committee to this statement and invite discussion on it when the proposal is under consideration.

VI. LANGUAGES

Rule 19   Official and working languages

Arabic, Chinese, English, French, Russian and Spanish shall be the official languages, and Chinese, English, French, Russian and Spanish the working languages of the Committee.

Rule 20   Interpretation

1. Speeches made in any official language shall be interpreted into the other official languages.

2. Any speaker addressing the Committee in a language other than one of the official languages shall provide for interpretation into one of the official languages.

Rule 21   Languages of documents

All formal decisions of the Committee shall be made available in the official languages. All other official documents of the Committee shall be issued in the working languages and any of them shall, if the Committee so decides, also be issued in the other official languages.

VII. CONDUCT OF BUSINESS

Rule 22   Public and closed meetings

The meetings of the Committee shall be held in public, unless the Committee decides that a meeting or a part of a meeting should be closed.

Rule 23   Quorum

Twelve members of the Committee shall constitute a quorum. The presence of two thirds of the members of the Committee is, however, required for a decision to be taken.

Rule 24   General powers of the Chairperson

1. The Chairperson shall declare the opening and closing of each meeting of the Committee, direct the discussions, ensure observance of these rules, accord the right to speak, put questions to the vote and announce decisions. The Chairperson subject to these rules, shall have control over

the proceedings of the Committee and over the maintenance of order at its meetings. The Chairperson may propose to the Committee the limitation of the time to be allowed to speakers, the limitation of the number of times each speaker may speak on any question, the closure of the list of speakers, the adjournment or closure of the debate and the suspension of adjournment of a meeting. Debate shall be confined to the question before the Committee. The Chairperson may call to order a speaker whose remarks are not relevant to the subject under discussion.

2. In the exercise of these functions, the Chairperson remains under the authority of the Committee.

Rule 25   Points of order

During the discussion of any matter, a member may at any time raise a point of order, which shall be immediately decided by the Chairperson in accordance with these rules. Any appeal against the ruling of the Chairperson shall be immediately put to the vote, and the ruling shall stand unless overruled by a majority of the members present. A member may not, in raising a point of order, speak on the substance of the matter under discussion.

Rule 26   Time-limit on speakers

The Committee may limit the time allowed to each speaker on any question. When debate is limited and a speaker exceeds the allotted time, the Chairperson shall call the speaker to order without delay.

Rule 27   Closing list of speakers and right of reply

In the course of a debate, the Chairperson may announce the list of speakers and, with the consent of the Committee, declare the list closed. The chairperson may, however, accord the right of reply to any speaker participating in the proceedings of the Committee as provided by the present rules if a speech delivered after the list was declared closed makes this desirable. Such a right of reply shall be exercised at the end of the same meeting or at the latest at the end of the day. When the debate on an item is concluded because there are no more speakers, the Chairperson shall declare the debate closed; such closure shall have the same effect as closure by the consent of the Committee.

Rule 28   Closure of debate

During the discussion of any matter, a member may move the closure of the debate on the item under discussion, whether or not any other speaker has signified a wish to speak. Permission to speak on the closure of the debate shall be accorded only to two members opposing the closure, after which the motion shall be immediately put to the vote.

Rule 29   Adjournment of debate

During the discussion of any matter, a member may move the adjournment of the debate on the item under discussion. In addition to the proposer of the motion, one member may speak in favour of and one against the motion, after which the motion shall be immediately put to the vote.

Rule 30   Suspension or adjournment of meeting

During the discussion of any matter, a member may move the suspension or the adjournment of the meeting. No discussion on such motions shall be permitted, and they shall be immediately put to the vote.

Rule 31   Order of motions

The following motions shall have precedence in the following order over all other proposals or motions before the meeting:

(a) To suspend the meeting;

(b) To adjourn the meeting;

(c) To adjourn the debate on the item under discussion;

(d) To close the debate on the item under discussion.

Rule 32   Submission of proposals

Unless otherwise decided by the Committee, proposals and substantive amendments shall be introduced in writing and handed to the Secretary of the Committee, and their consideration shall, if so requested by any member, be deferred until the following day.

Rule 33   Decisions on competence

Any motion calling for a decision on the competence of the Committee to adopt a proposal submitted to it shall be put to the vote immediately before a vote is taken on the proposal in question.

Rule 34   Withdrawal of proposals and motions

A proposal or motion may be withdrawn by the member who proposed it at any time before voting on it has commenced, provided that it has not been amended. A proposal or motion thus withdrawn may be reintroduced by any member.

Rule 35   Reconsideration

When a proposal has been adopted or rejected, it may not be reconsidered at the same session unless the Committee, by a two-thirds majority of its members present and voting, so decides. Permission to speak on a motion to reconsider shall be accorded only to two speakers in favour of the motion and to two speakers opposed, after which it shall be immediately put to the vote.

VIII. VOTING

Rule 36   Voting rights

Each member of the Committee shall have one vote.

Rule 37   Adoption of decisions

1. The Committee shall endeavor to reach its decisions by consensus.

2. If and when all efforts to reach consensus have been exhausted, except as otherwise provided in these rules, decisions of the Committee shall be taken by a majority of the members present and voting.

3. For the purpose of these rules, "members present and voting" means members casting an affirmative or negative vote; members who abstain from voting are considered as not voting.

4. If a vote is equally divided on a matter other than an election, the proposal shall be regarded as rejected.

Rule 38   Method of voting

1. Subject to rule 43, the Committee shall normally vote by show of hands, except that any member may request a roll-call, which shall then be taken in the alphabetical order of the names of the members, beginning with the one whose name is drawn by lot by the Chairperson.

2. The vote of each member participating in a roll-call shall be inserted in any report referring to the vote.

Rule 39   Conduct during voting and explanation of votes

After voting has commenced, it shall not be interrupted unless a member raises a point of order in connection with the actual conduct of the voting. Members may make brief statements consisting solely of explanations of their votes before the voting has commenced or after the voting has been completed.

Rule 40   Division of proposals

Parts of a proposal shall be voted on separately if a member requests that the proposal be divided. Those parts of the proposal which have been approved shall then be put to the vote as a whole; if all the operative parts of a proposal have been rejected, the proposal shall be considered to have been rejected as a whole.

Rule 41   Order of voting on amendments

1. When an amendment to a proposal is moved, the amendment shall be voted on first. When two or more amendments to a proposal are moved, the Committee shall first vote on the amendment furthest removed in substance from the original proposal and then on the amendment next furthest removed therefrom and so on until all the amendments have been put to the vote. If one or more amendments are adopted, the amended proposal shall then be voted upon.

2. A motion is considered an amendment to a proposal if it merely adds to, deletes from or revises part of that proposal.

Rule 42   Order of voting on proposals

1. If two or more proposals relate to the same question, the Committee shall, unless it decides otherwise, vote on the proposals in the order in which they have been submitted.

2. The Committee may, after each vote on a proposal, decide whether to vote on the next proposal.

3. A motion requiring that no decision be taken on a proposal shall have priority over that proposal.

Rule 43   Election of officers

1. Elections shall be held by secret ballot, unless the Committee decides otherwise in an election for which the number of candidates does not exceed the number of places to be filled.

2. A single ballot shall be taken in respect of all places to be filled at one time under the same conditions. Those candidates obtaining a simple majority and the greatest number of votes, in a number not exceeding the number of places to be filled, shall be elected. If not all places are filled on the first ballot, additional ballots shall be held, in which, by the elimination of the candidates having received the lowest number of votes on the previous ballot, the number of candidates shall not exceed twice the number of places to be filled. If a tie vote between two or more candidates persists for two successive ballots, a decision shall be taken between them by lot, drawn by the Chairperson.

IX. RECORDS AND REPORTS

Rule 44   Records

1. The Committee shall have summary records.

2. Sound recordings of meetings of the Committee shall be made and kept in accordance with the usual practice of the United Nations.

Rule 45   Annual reports

The Committee shall report annually on its activities, through the Economic and Social Council to the General Assembly of the United Nations, and may make suggestions and general recommendations based on the examination of reports and information received from the States parties. Such suggestions and general recommendations shall be included in the report of the Committee together with any comments from States parties.

X. REPORTS FROM STATES PARTIES UNDER ARTICLE 18 OF THE CONVENTION

Rule 46   Form of reports

1. The Committee may formulate suggestions and general recommendations as to the form, contents and dates of the periodic reports that the States parties are required to submit under article 18 of the Convention.

2. Such suggestions and general recommendations shall take into account the integrated reporting system on the status of women endorsed by the Economic and Social Council in its resolution 1980/38.

Rule 47   Non-receipt of reports

1. At each session the Secretary-General shall notify the Committee of the non-receipt of any report required from a State party under article 18 of the Convention.

2. The Committee may, through the Secretary-General, transmit to the States concerned reminders of any overdue reports.

3. If even after a reminder has been transmitted pursuant to paragraph 2 a State concerned does not submit the report required under the Convention, the Committee shall include a reference to this effect in its annual report to the General Assembly.

Rule 48   Suggestions and general recommendations

1. In case the Committee finds that substantial improvement of its work is likely to be brought about by additional information on the part of a State party, concerning its report, the Committee may invite the State concerned to provide it with such additional information.

2. Suggestions and general recommendations made by the Committee based on the examination of the reports received from States parties under article 18 of the Convention shall be communicated by the Committee, through the Secretary-General, to the States parties for their comments.

3. The Committee may, where necessary, indicate a time-limit within which Comments are to be received.

Rule 49   Attendance by States parties

1. Representatives of States parties shall be present at meetings of the Committee when the State's report is being examined and shall participate in discussions and answer questions concerning the said report.

2. The Committee shall, through the Secretary-General, notify the States parties at least six weeks in advance of the opening date, duration and place of the session at which their respective reports will be examined.

Rule 50   Working methods for examining reports

The Committee may elaborate working methods to assist it in performing most efficiently its task of examining the reports of States parties and to consider the progress made since the entry into force of the Convention for them and since the submission of any previous reports.

XI. PARTICIPATION OF SPECIALIZED AGENCIES

Rule 51   Reports

The Committee may invite the specialized agencies to submit reports on the implementations of the Convention in areas falling within the scope of their activities.

Rule 52   Attendance by specialized agencies

1. The specialized agencies shall be entitled to be represented at meetings of the Committee when the implementation of such provisions of the Convention as fall within the scope of the activities of that agency is being considered.

2. The Secretary-General shall notify each specialized agency as early as possible of the opening date, duration, place and agenda of each session of the Committee.

XII. DISTRIBUTION OF DOCUMENTS

Rule 53   Without prejudice to rule 22 of these rules of procedure, reports, formal decisions and all other official documents of the Committee shall be documents of general distribution unless the Committee decides otherwise.

XIII. RULES OF PROCEDURE

Rule 54   Amendment

These rules may be amended by a decision of the Committee taken by a two-thirds majority of the members present and voting and at least 24 hours after the proposal for the amendment has been circulated, provided that the amendment is not inconsistent with the Convention.

Rule 55   Suspension

Any of these rules may be suspended by a decision of the Committee taken by a two-thirds majority of the members present and voting, provided such suspension is not inconsistent with the Convention and is restricted to the circumstances of the particular situation requiring the suspension.

c) Optional Protocol to the Convention on the Elimination of All Forms of Discrimination against Women of March 12, 1999

The States Parties to the present Protocol,

Noting that the Charter of the United Nations reaffirms faith in fundamental human rights, in the dignity and worth of the human person and in the equal rights of men and women,

Also noting that the Universal Declaration of Human Rights[1] proclaims that all human beings are born free and equal in dignity and rights and that everyone is entitled to all the rights and freedoms set forth therein, without distinction of any kind, including distinction based on sex,

Recalling that the International Covenants on Human Rights[2] and other international human rights instruments prohibit discrimination on the basis of sex,

Also recalling the Convention on the Elimination of All Forms of Discrimination against Women ("the Convention"), in which the States Parties thereto condemn discrimination against women in all its forms and agree to pursue by all appropriate means and without delay a policy of eliminating discrimination against women,

Reaffirming their determination to ensure the full and equal enjoyment by women of all human rights and fundamental freedoms and to take effective action to prevent violations of these rights and freedoms,

Have agreed as follows:

Art. 1   A State Party to the present Protocol ("State Party") recognizes the competence of the Committee on the Elimination of Discrimination against Women ("the Committee") to receive and consider communications submitted in accordance with article 2.

Art. 2   Communications may be submitted by or on behalf of individuals or groups of individuals, under the jurisdiction of a State Party, claiming to be victims of a violation of any of the rights set forth in the Convention by that State Party. Where a communication is submitted on behalf of individuals or groups of individuals, this shall be with their consent unless the author can justify acting on their behalf without such consent.

Art. 3   Communications shall be in writing and shall not be anonymous. No communication shall be received by the Committee if it concerns a State Party to the Convention that is not a party to the present Protocol.

Art. 4   1. The Committee shall not consider a communication unless it has ascertained that all available domestic remedies have been exhausted unless the application of such remedies is unreasonably prolonged or unlikely to bring effective relief.

2. The Committee shall declare a communication inadmissible where:

(a)   The same matter has already been examined by the Committee or has been or is being examined under another procedure of international investigation or settlement;

(b)   It is incompatible with the provisions of the Convention;

(c)   It is manifestly ill-founded or not sufficiently substantiated;

---

[1]   Resolution 217 A (III).

[2]   Resolution 2200 A (XXI), annex.

(d) It is an abuse of the right to submit a communication;

(e) The facts that are the subject of the communication occurred prior to the entry into force of the present Protocol for the State Party concerned unless those facts continued after that date.

Art. 5   1. At any time after the receipt of a communication and before a determination on the merits has been reached, the Committee may transmit to the State Party concerned for its urgent consideration a request that the State Party take such interim measures as may be necessary to avoid possible irreparable damage to the victim or victims of the alleged violation.

2. Where the Committee exercises its discretion under paragraph 1 of the present article, this does not imply a determination on admissibility or on the merits of the communication.

Art. 6   1. Unless the Committee considers a communication inadmissible without reference to the State Party concerned, and provided that the individual or individuals consent to the disclosure of their identity to that State Party, the Committee shall bring any communication submitted to it under the present Protocol confidentially to the attention of the State Party concerned.

2. Within six months, the receiving State Party shall submit to the Committee written explanations or statements clarifying the matter and the remedy, if any, that may have been provided by that State Party.

Art. 7   1. The Committee shall consider communications received under the present Protocol in the light of all information made available to it by or on behalf of individuals or groups of individuals and by the State Party concerned, provided that this information is transmitted to the parties concerned.

2. The Committee shall hold closed meetings when examining communications under the present Protocol.

3. After examining a communication, the Committee shall transmit its views on the communication, together with its recommendations, if any, to the parties concerned.

4. The State Party shall give due consideration to the views of the Committee, together with its recommendations, if any, and shall submit to the Committee, within six months, a written response, including information on any action taken in the light of the views and recommendations of the Committee.

5. The Committee may invite the State Party to submit further information about any measures the State Party has taken in response to its views or recommendations, if any, including as deemed appropriate by the Committee, in the State Party's subsequent reports under article 18 of the Convention.

Art. 8   1. If the Committee receives reliable information indicating grave or systematic violations by a State Party of rights set forth in the Convention, the Committee shall invite that State Party to cooperate in the examination of the information and to this end to submit observations with regard to the information concerned.

2. Taking into account any observations that may have been submitted by the State Party concerned as well as any other reliable information available to it, the Committee may designate one or more of its members to conduct an inquiry and to report urgently to the Committee. Where warranted and with the consent of the State Party, the inquiry may include a visit to its territory.

3. After examining the findings of such an inquiry, the Committee shall transmit these findings to the State Party concerned together with any comments and recommendations.

4. The State Party concerned shall, within six months of receiving the findings, comments and recommendations transmitted by the Committee, submit its observations to the Committee.

5. Such an inquiry shall be conducted confidentially and the cooperation of the State Party shall be sought at all stages of the proceedings.

Art. 9   1. The Committee may invite the State Party concerned to include in its report under article 18 of the Convention details of any measures taken in response to an inquiry conducted under article 8 of the present Protocol.

2. The Committee may, if necessary, after the end of the period of six months referred to in article 8.4, invite the State Party concerned to inform it of the measures taken in response to such an inquiry.

Art. 10   1. Each State Party may, at the time of signature or ratification of the present Protocol or accession thereto, declare that it does not recognize the competence of the Committee provided for in articles 8 and 9.

2. Any State Party having made a declaration in accordance with paragraph 1 of the present article may, at any time, withdraw this declaration by notification to the Secretary-General.

Art. 11   A State Party shall take all appropriate steps to ensure that individuals under its jurisdiction are not subjected to ill treatment or intimidation as a consequence of communicating with the Committee pursuant to the present Protocol.

Art. 12   The Committee shall include in its annual report under article 21 of the Convention a summary of its activities under the present Protocol.

Art. 13   Each State Party undertakes to make widely known and to give publicity to the Convention and the present Protocol and to facilitate access to information about the views and recommendations of the Committee, in particular, on matters involving that State Party.

Art. 14   The Committee shall develop its own rules of procedure to be followed when exercising the functions conferred on it by the present Protocol.

Art. 15 1. The present Protocol shall be open for signature by any State that has signed, ratified or acceded to the Convention.

2. The present Protocol shall be subject to ratification by any State that has ratified or acceded to the Convention. Instruments of ratification shall be deposited with the Secretary-General of the United Nations.

3. The present Protocol shall be open to accession by any State that has ratified or acceded to the Convention.

4. Accession shall be effected by the deposit of an instrument of accession with the Secretary-General of the United Nations.

Art. 16 1. The present Protocol shall enter into force three months after the date of the deposit with the Secretary-General of the United Nations of the tenth instrument of ratification or accession.

2. For each State ratifying the present Protocol or acceding to it after its entry into force, the present Protocol shall enter into force three months after the date of the deposit of its own instrument of ratification or accession.

Art. 17 No reservations to the present Protocol shall be permitted.

Art. 18 1. Any State Party may propose an amendment to the present Protocol and file it with the Secretary-General of the United Nations. The Secretary-General shall thereupon communicate any proposed amendments to the States Parties with a request that they notify her or him whether they favour a conference of States Parties for the purpose of considering and voting on the proposal. In the event that at least one third of the States Parties favour such a conference, the Secretary-General shall convene the conference under the auspices of the United Nations. Any amendment adopted by a majority of the States Parties present and voting at the conference shall be submitted to the General Assembly of the United Nations for approval.

2. Amendments shall come into force when they have been approved by the General Assembly of the United Nations and accepted by a two-thirds majority of the States Parties to the present Protocol in accordance with their respective constitutional processes.

3. When amendments come into force, they shall be binding on those States Parties that have accepted them, other States Parties still being bound by the provisions of the present Protocol and any earlier amendments that they have accepted.

Art. 19 1. Any State Party may denounce the present Protocol at any time by written notification addressed to the Secretary-General of the United Nations. Denunciation shall take effect six months after the date of receipt of the notification by the Secretary-General.

2. Denunciation shall be without prejudice to the continued application of the provisions of the present Protocol to any communication submitted

under article 2 or any inquiry initiated under article 8 before the effective date of denunciation.

Art. 20 The Secretary-General of the United Nations shall inform all States of:

(a) Signatures, ratifications and accessions under the present Protocol;

(b) The date of entry into force of the present Protocol and of any amendment under article 18;

(c) Any denunciation under article 19.

Art. 21 1. The present Protocol, of which the Arabic, Chinese, English, French, Russian and Spanish texts are equally authentic, shall be deposited in the archives of the United Nations.

2. The Secretary-General of the United Nations shall transmit certified copies of the present Protocol to all States referred to in article 25 of the Convention.

6. Convention against Torture and Other Cruel, Inhuman or Degrading Treatment or Punishment

a) Convention of December 10, 1984 as amended in 1985, Part II

Art. 17   1. There shall be established a Committee against Torture (hereinafter referred to as the Committee) which shall carry out the functions hereinafter provided. The Committee shall consist of 10 experts of high moral standing and recognized competence in the field of human rights, who shall serve in their personal capacity. The experts shall be elected by the States Parties, consideration being given to equitable geographical distribution and to the usefulness of the participation of some persons having legal experience.

2. The members of the Committee shall be elected by secret ballot from a list of persons nominated by States Parties. Each State Party may nominate one person from among its own nationals. States Parties shall bear in mind the usefulness of nominating persons who are also members of the Human Rights Committee established under the International Covenant on Civil and Political Rights and are willing to serve on the Committee against Torture.

3. Elections of the members of the Committee shall be held at biennial meetings of States Parties convened by the Secretary-General of the United Nations. At those meetings, for which two thirds of the States Parties shall constitute a quorum, the persons elected to the Committee shall be those who obtain the largest number of votes and an absolute majority of the votes of the representatives of States Parties present and voting.

4. The initial election shall be held no later than six months after the date of the entry into force of this Convention. At least four months before the date of each election, the Secretary-General of the United Nations shall address a letter to the States Parties inviting them to submit their nominations within three months. The Secretary-General shall prepare a list in alphabetical order of all persons thus nominated, indicating the States Parties which have nominated them, and shall submit it to the States Parties.

5. The members of the Committee shall be elected for a term of four years. They shall be eligible for re-election if renominated. However, the term of five members elected at the first election shall expire at the end of two years; immediately after the first election the names of these five

members shall be chosen by lot by the chairman of the meeting referred to in paragraph 3.

6. If a member of the Committee dies or resigns or for any other cause can no longer perform his Committee duties, the State Party which nominated him shall appoint another expert from among its nationals to serve for the remainder of his term, subject to the approval of the majority of the States Parties. The approval shall be considered given unless half or more of the States Parties respond negatively within six weeks after having been informed by the Secretary-General of the United Nations of the proposed appointment.

7. States Parties shall be responsible for the expenses of the members of the Committee while they are in performance of Committee duties.

Art. 18   1. The Committee shall elect its officers for a term of two years. They may be re-elected.

2. The Committee shall establish its own rules of procedure, but these rules shall provide, *inter alia*, that

(a) Six members shall constitute a quorum;

(b) Decisions of the Committee shall be made by a majority vote of the members present.

3. The Secretary-General of the United Nations shall provide the necessary staff and facilities for the effective performance of the functions of the Committee under this Convention.

4. The Secretary-General of the United Nations shall convene the initial meeting of the Committee. After its initial meeting, the Committee shall meet at such times as shall be provided in its rules of procedure.

5. The State Parties shall be responsible for expenses incurred in connection with the holding of meetings of the States Parties and of the Committee, including reimbursement to the United Nations for any expenses, such as the cost of staff and facilities, incurred by the United Nations pursuant to paragraph 3 above.

Art. 19   1. The States Parties shall submit to the Committee, through the Secretary-General of the United Nations, reports on the measures they have taken to give effect to their undertakings under this Convention, within one year after the entry into force of this Convention for the State Party concerned. Thereafter the States Parties shall submit supplementary reports every four years on any new measures taken, and such other reports as the Committee may request.

2. The Secretary-General shall transmit the reports to all States Parties.

3. Each report shall be considered by the Committee which may make such comments or suggestions on the report as it may consider appropriate, and shall forward these to the State Party concerned. That State Party may respond with any observations it chooses to the Committee.

4. The Committee may, at its discretion, decide to include any comments or suggestions made by it in accordance with paragraph 3, together with the observations thereon received from the State Party concerned, in its annual report made in accordance with article 24. If so requested by the State Party concerned, the Committee may also include a copy of the report submitted under paragraph 1.

Art. 20   1. If the Committee receives reliable information which appears to it to contain well-founded indications that torture is being systematically practised in the territory of a State Party, the Committee shall invite that State Party to co-operate in the examination of the information and to this end to submit observations with regard to the information concerned.

2. Taking into account any observations which may have been submitted by the State Party concerned as well as any other relevant information available to it, the Committee may, if it decides that this is warranted, designate one or more of its members to make confidential inquiry and to report to the Committee urgently.

3. If an inquiry is made in accordance with paragraph 2, the Committee shall seek the co-operation of the State Party concerned. In agreement with that State Party, such an inquiry may include a visit to its territory.

4. After examining the findings of its member or members submitted in accordance with paragraph 2, the Committee shall transmit these findings to the State Party concerned together with any comments or suggestions which seem appropriate in view of the situation.

5. All the proceedings of the Committee referred to in paragraphs 1–4 of this article shall be confidential, and at all stages of the proceedings the co-operation of the State Party shall be sought. After such proceedings have been completed with regard to an inquiry made in accordance with paragraph 2, the Committee may, after consultations with the State Party concerned, decide to include a summary account of the results of the proceedings in its annual report made in accordance with article 24.

Art. 21   1. A State Party to this Convention may at any time declare under this article that it recognizes the competence of the Committee to receive and consider communications to the effect that a State Party claims that another State Party is not fulfilling its obligations under this Convention. Such communications may be received and considered according to the procedures laid down in this article only if submitted by a State Party which has made a declaration recognizing in regard to itself the competence of the Committee. No communication shall be dealt with by the Committee under this article if it concerns a State Party which has not made such a declaration. Communications received under this article shall be dealt with in accordance with the following procedure:

(a) If a State Party considers that another State Party is not giving effect to the provisions of this Convention, it may, by written communication, bring the matter to the attention of that State Party. Within three months after the receipt of the communication the receiving State shall afford the State which sent the communication an explanation or any other statement in writing clarifying the matter which should include, to the extent possible and pertinent, reference to domestic procedures and remedies taken pending, or available in the matter.

(b) If the matter is not adjusted to the satisfaction of both States Parties concerned within six months after the receipt by the receiving State of the initial communication, either State shall have the right to refer the matter to the Committee by notice given to the Committee and to the other State.

(c) The Committee shall deal with a matter referred to it under this article only after it has ascertained that all domestic remedies have been invoked and exhausted in the matter, in conformity with the generally recognized principles of international law. This shall not be the rule where the application of the remedies is unreasonably prolonged or is unlikely to bring effective relief to the person who is the victim of the violation of this Convention.

(d) The Committee shall hold closed meetings when examining communications under this article.

(e) Subject to the provisions of subparagraph (c), the Committee shall make available its good offices to the States Parties concerned with a view to a friendly solution of the matter on the basis of respect for the obligations provided for in the present Convention. For this purpose, the Committee may, when appropriate, set up an *ad hoc* conciliation commission.

(f) In any matter referred to it under this article, the Committee may call upon the States Parties concerned, referred to in subparagraph (b), to supply any relevant information.

(g) The States Parties concerned, referred to in subparagraph (b), shall have the right to be represented when the matter is being considered by the Committee and to make submissions orally and/or in writing.

(h) The Committee shall, within 12 months after the date of receipt of notice under subparagraph (b), submit a report.

(i) If a solution within the terms of subparagraph (e) is reached, the Committee shall confine its report to a brief statement of the facts and of the solution reached.

(ii) If a solution within the terms of subparagraph (e) is not reached, the Committee shall confine its report to a brief statement of the facts; the written submissions and record of the oral submissions made by the States Parties concerned shall be attached to the report.

In every matter, the report shall be communicated to the States Parties concerned.

2. The provisions of this article shall come into force when five States Parties to this Convention have made declarations under paragraph 1 of

this article. Such declarations shall be deposited by the States Parties with the Secretary General of the United Nations, who shall transmit copies thereof to the other States Parties. A declaration may be withdrawn at any time by notification to the Secretary-General. Such a withdrawal shall not prejudice the consideration of any matter which is the subject of a communication already transmitted under this article; no further communication by any State Party shall be received under this article after the notification of withdrawal of the declaration has been received by the Secretary-General, unless the State Party concerned has made a new declaration.

Art. 22 1. A State Party to this Convention may at any time declare under this article that it recognizes the competence of the Committee to receive and consider communications from or on behalf of individuals subject to its jurisdiction who claim to be victims of a violation by a State Party of the provisions of the Convention. No communication shall be received by the Committee if it concerns a State Party to the Convention which has not made such a declaration.

2. The Committee shall consider inadmissible any communication under this article which is anonymous, or which it considers to be an abuse of the right of submission of such communications or to be incompatible with the provisions of this Convention.

3. Subject to the provisions of paragraph 2, the Committee shall bring any communications submitted to it under this article to the attention of the State Party to this Convention which has made a declaration under paragraph 1 and is alleged to be violating any provisions of the Convention. Within six months, the receiving State shall submit to the Committee written explanations or statements clarifying the matter and the remedy, if any, that may have been taken by that State.

4. The Committee shall consider communications received under this article in the light of all information made available to it by or on behalf of the individual and by the State Party concerned.

5. The Committee shall not consider any communications from an individual under this article unless it has ascertained that:

(a) The same matter has not been, and is not being, examined under another procedure of international investigation or settlement:

(b) The individual has exhausted all available domestic remedies; this shall not be the rule where the application of the remedies is unreasonably prolonged or is unlikely to bring effective relief to the person who is the victim of the violation of this Convention.

6. The Committee shall hold closed meetings when examining communications under this article.

7. The Committee shall forward its views to the State Party concerned and to the individual.

8. The provisions of this article shall come into force when five States Parties to this Convention have made declarations under paragraph 1 of this article. Such declarations shall be deposited by the States Parties with the Secretary-General of the United Nations, who shall transmit copies thereof to the other States Parties. A declaration may be withdrawn at any time by notification to the Secretary-General. Such a withdrawal shall not prejudice the consideration of any matter which is the subject of a communication already transmitted under this article; no further communication by or on behalf of an individual shall be received under this article after the notification of withdrawal of the declaration has been received by the Secretary-General, unless the State Party concerned has made a new declaration.

Art. 23   The members of the Committee, and of the *ad hoc* conciliation commissions which may be appointed under article 21, paragraph 1 (e), shall be entitled to the facilities, privileges and immunities of experts on mission for the United Nations as laid down in the relevant sections of the Convention on the Privileges and Immunities of the United Nations.

Art. 24   The Committee shall submit an annual report on its activities under this Convention to the States Parties and to the General Assembly of the United Nations.

b) Rules of Procedure of the Committee against Torture of April 20, 1988 and April 25, 1989

PART TWO. RULES RELATING TO THE FUNCTIONS OF THE COMMITTEE

XVI. REPORTS FROM STATES PARTIES UNDER ARTICLE 19 OF THE CONVENTION

Rule 64   Submission of reports.

(1) The States parties shall submit to the Committee, through the Secretary-General, reports on the measures they have taken to give effect to their undertakings under the Convention, within one year after the entry into force of the Convention for the State party concerned. Thereafter the States parties shall submit supplementary reports every four years on any new measures taken and such other reports as the Committee may request.

(2) The Committee may, through the Secretary-General, inform the States parties of its wishes regarding the form and contents of the reports to be submitted under article 19 of the Convention.

Rule 65   Non-submission of reports.

(1) At each session, the Secretary-General shall notify the Committee of all cases of non-submission of reports under rules 64 and 67 of these rules. In such cases the Committee may transmit to the State party concerned, through the Secretary-General, a reminder concerning the submission of such report or reports.

(2) If, after the reminder referred to in paragraph 1 of this rule, the State party does not submit the report required under rules 64 and 67 of these rules, the Committee shall so state in the annual report which it submits to the States parties and to the General Assembly of the United Nations.

Rule 66   Attendance by States parties at examination of reports.

The Committee shall, through the Secretary-General, notify the States parties, as early as possible, of the opening date, duration and place of the session at which their respective reports will be examined. Representatives of the States parties shall be invited to attend the meetings of the Committee when their reports are examined. The Committee may also inform a State party from which it decides to seek further information that it may authorize its representative to be present at a specified meeting. Such a representative should be able to answer questions which may be put to him by the Committee and make statements on reports already submitted by his State, and may also submit additional information from his State.

Rule 67   Request for additional reports.

(1) When considering a report submitted by a State party under article 19 of the Convention, the Committee shall first determine whether the report provides all the information required under rule 64 of these rules.

(2) If a report of a State party to the Convention, in the opinion of the Committee, does not contain sufficient information, the Committee may request that State to furnish an additional report, indicating by what date the said report should be submitted.

Rule 68   General comments by the Committee.

(1) After its consideration of each report, the Committee, in accordance with article 19, paragraph 3, of the Convention, may make such general comments on the report as it may consider appropriate and shall forward these, through the Secretary-General, to the State party concerned, which in reply may submit to the Committee any comment that it considers appropriate. The Committee may, in particular, indicate in its general comments whether, on the basis of its examination of the reports and information supplied by the State party, it appears that some of the obligations of that State under the Convention have not been discharged.

(2) The Committee may, where necessary, indicate a time-limit within which observations from States parties are to be received.

(3) The Committee may, at its discretion, decide to include any comments made by it in accordance with paragraph 1 of this rule, together with any

observations thereon received from the State party concerned in its annual report made in accordance with article 24 of the Convention. If so requested by the State party concerned, the Committee may also include a copy of the report submitted under article 19, paragraph 1, of the Convention.

XVII. PROCEEDINGS UNDER ARTICLE 20 OF THE CONVENTION

Rule 69   Transmission of information to the Committee.

(1) The Secretary-General shall bring to the attention of the Committee, in accordance with the present rules, information which is, or appears to be, submitted for the Committee's consideration under article 20, paragraph 1, of the Convention.

(2) No information shall be received by the Committee if it concerns a State party which, in accordance with article 28, paragraph 1, of the Convention, declared at the time of ratification of or accession to the Convention that it did not recognize the competence of the Committee provided for in article 20, unless that State has subsequently withdrawn its reservation in accordance with article 28, paragraph 2, of the Convention.

Rule 70   Register of information submitted.

The Secretary-General shall maintain a permanent register of information brought to the attention of the Committee in accordance with rule 69 above and shall make the information available to any member of the Committee upon request.

Rule 71   Summary of the information.

The Secretary-General, when necessary, shall prepare and circulate to the members of the Committee a brief summary of the information submitted in accordance with rule 69 above.

Rule 72   Confidentiality of documents and proceedings.

All documents and proceedings of the Committee relating to its functions under article 20 of the Convention shall be confidential, until such time when the Committee decides, in accordance with the provisions of article 20, paragraph 5, of the Convention, to make them public.

Rule 73   Meetings.

(1) Meetings of the Committee concerning its proceedings under article 20 of the Convention shall be closed.

(2) Meetings during which the Committee considers general issues, such as procedures for the application of article 20 of the Convention, shall be public, unless the Committee decides otherwise.

Rule 74   Issue of communiqués concerning closed meetings.

The Committee may decide to issue communiqués, through the Secretary-General, for the use of the information media and the general public regarding its activities under article 20 of the Convention.

Rule 75   Preliminary consideration of information by the Committee.

(1) The Committee, when necessary, may ascertain, through the Secretary-General, the reliability of the information and/or of the sources of the information brought to its attention under article 20 of the Convention or obtain additional relevant information substantiating the facts of the situation.

(2) The Committee shall determine whether it appears to it that the information received contains well-founded indications that torture, as defined in article 1 of the Convention, is being systematically practised in the territory of the State party concerned.

Rule 76   Examination of the information.

(1) If it appears to the Committee that the information received is reliable and contains well-founded indications that torture is being systematically practised in the territory of a State party, the Committee shall invite the State party concerned, through the Secretary-General, to co-operate in its examination of the information and, to this end, to submit observations with regard to that information.

(2) The Committee shall indicate a time-limit for the submission of observations by the State party concerned, with a view to avoiding undue delay in its proceedings.

(3) In examining the information received, the Committee shall take into account any observations which may have been submitted by the State party concerned, as well as any other relevant information available to it.

(4) The Committee may decide, if it deems it appropriate, to obtain from the representatives of the State party concerned, governmental and non-governmental organizations, as well as individuals, additional information or answers to questions relating to the information under examination.

(5) The Committee shall decide, on its initiative and on the basis of its rules of procedure, the form and manner in which such additional information may be obtained.

Rule 77   Documentation from United Nations bodies and specialized agencies.

The Committee may at any time obtain, through the Secretary-General, any relevant documentation from United Nations bodies or specialized agencies that may assist it in the examination of the information received under article 20 of the Convention.

Rule 78   Establishment of an inquiry.

(1) The Committee may, if it decides that this is warranted, designate one or more of its members to make a confidential inquiry and to report to it within a time-limit which may be set by the Committee.

(2) When the Committee decides to make an inquiry in accordance with paragraph 1 of this rule, it shall establish the modalities of the inquiry as it deems it appropriate.

(3) The members designated by the Committee for the confidential inquiry shall determine their own methods of work in conformity with the provisions of the Convention and the rules of procedure of the Committee.

Rule 79   Cooperation of the State party concerned.

The Committee shall invite the State party concerned, through the Secretary-General to co-operate with it in the conduct of the inquiry. To this end, the Committee may request the State party concerned:

a) To designate an accredited representative to meet with the members designated by the Committee;

b) To provide its designated members with any information that they, or the State party, may consider useful for ascertaining the facts relating to the inquiry;

c) To indicate any other form of co-operation that the State may wish to extend to the Committee and to its designated members with a view to facilitating the conduct of the inquiry

Rule 80   Visiting mission.

If the Committee deems it necessary to include in its inquiry a visit of one or more of its members to the territory of the State party concerned, it shall request, through the Secretary-General, the agreement of that State party and shall inform the State party of its wishes regarding the timing of the mission and the facilities required to allow the designated members of the Committee to carry out their task.

Rule 81   Hearings in connection with the inquiry.

(1) The designated members may decide to conduct hearings in connection with the inquiry as they deem it appropriate.

(2) The designated members shall establish, in co-operation with the State party concerned, the conditions and guarantees required for conducting such hearings. They shall request the State party to ensure that no obstacles are placed in the way of witnesses and other individuals wishing to meet with the designated members of the Committee and that no retaliatory measure is taken against those individuals or their families.

(3) Every person appearing before the designated members for the purpose of giving testimony shall be requested to take an oath or make a solemn declaration concerning the veracity of his/her testimony and the respect for confidentiality of the proceedings.

Rule 82   Assistance during the inquiry.

(1) In addition to the staff and facilities to be provided by the Secretary-General in connection with the inquiry and/or the visiting mission to the

territory of the State party concerned, the designated members may invite, through the Secretary-General, persons with special competence in the medical field or in the treatment of prisoners as well as interpreters to provide assistance at all stages of the inquiry.

(2) If the persons providing assistance during the inquiry are not bound by an oath of office to the United Nations, they shall be required to declare solemnly that they will perform their duties honestly, faithfully and impartially, and that they will respect the confidentiality of the proceedings.

(3) The persons referred to in paragraphs 1 and 2 of the present rule shall be entitled to the same facilities, privileges and immunities provided for in respect of the members of the Committee, under article 23 of the Convention.

Rule 83 Transmission of findings, comments or suggestions.

(1) After examining the findings of its designated members submitted to it in accordance with rule 78, paragraph 1, the Committee shall transmit, through the Secretary-General, these findings to the State party concerned, together with any comments or suggestions that it deems appropriate.

(2) The State party concerned shall be invited to inform the Committee within a reasonable delay of the action it takes with regard to the Committee's findings and in response to the Committee's comments or suggestions.

Rule 84 Summary account of the results of the proceedings.

(1) After all the proceedings of the Committee regarding an inquiry made under article 20 of the Convention have been completed, the Committee may decide, after consultations with the State party concerned, to include a summary account of the results of the proceedings in its annual report made in accordance with article 24 of the Convention.

(2) The Committee shall invite the State party concerned, through the Secretary-General, to inform the Committee directly or through its designated representative of its view concerning the question referred to in paragraph 1 of this rule, and may indicate a time-limit within which the view of the State party should be communicated to the Committee.

XVIII. PROCEDURE FOR THE CONSIDERATION OF COMMUNICATIONS RECEIVED UNDER ARTICLE 21 OF THE CONVENTION

Rules concerning article 21 of the Convention

Rule 1/21 Declarations by States parties.

(1) The Secretary-General shall transmit to the other States parties copies of the declarations deposited with him by States parties recognizing the

competence of the Committee, in accordance with article 21 of the Convention.

(2) The withdrawal of a declaration made under article 21 of the Convention shall not prejudice the consideration of any matter that is the subject of a communication already transmitted under that article, no further communication by any State party shall be received under that article after the notification of withdrawal of the declaration has been received by the Secretary-General, unless the State party has made a new declaration.

Rule 2/21 Notification by the State parties concerned.

(1) A communication under article 21 of the Convention may be referred to the Committee by either State party concerned by notice given in accordance with paragraph 1 (b) of that article.

(2) The notice referred to in paragraph 1 of this rule shall contain or be accompanied by information regarding:

a) Steps taken to seek adjustment of the matter in accordance with article 21, paragraphs 1 (a) and (b), of the Convention, including the text of the initial communication and of any subsequent written explanations or statements by the States parties concerned which are pertinent to the matter;

b) Steps taken to exhaust domestic remedies;

c) Any other procedure of international investigation or settlement resorted to by the States parties concerned.

Rule 3/21 Register of communications.

The Secretary-General shall maintain a permanent register of all communications received by the Committee under article 21 of the Convention.

Rule 4/21 Information to the members of the Committee.

The Secretary-General shall inform the members of the Committee without delay of any notice given under rule 2/21 of these rules and shall transmit to them as soon as possible copies of the notice and relevant information.

Rule 5/21 Meetings.

The Committee shall examine communications under article 21 of the Convention at closed meetings.

Rule 6/21 Issue of communiqués concerning closed meetings.

The Committee may, after consultation with the States parties concerned issue communiqués, through the Secretary-General, for the use of the information media and the general public regarding the activities of the Committee under article 21 of the Convention.

Rule 7/21 Requirements for the consideration of communications.

A communication shall not be considered by the Committee unless:

a) Both States parties concerned have made declarations under article 21, paragraph 1, of the Convention;

b) The time-limit prescribed in article 21, paragraph 1 (b), of the Convention has expired;

c) The Committee has ascertained that all available domestic remedies have been invoked and exhausted in the matter, in conformity with the generally recognized principles of international law, or that the application of the remedies is unreasonably prolonged or is unlikely to bring effective relief to the person who is the victim of the violation of the Convention.

Rule 8/21 Good offices.

(1) Subject to the provisions of rule 7/21 of these rules the Committee shall proceed to make its good offices available to the States parties concerned with a view to a friendly solution of the matter on the basis of respect for the obligations provided for in the Convention.

(2) For the purpose indicated in paragraph 1 of this rule, the Committee may, when appropriate, set up an *ad hoc* conciliation commission.

Rule 9/21 Request for information.

The Committee may, through the Secretary-General, request the States parties concerned or either of them to submit additional information or observations orally or in writing. The Committee shall indicate a time-limit for the submission of such written information or observations.

Rule 10/21 Attendance by the States parties concerned.

(1) The States parties concerned shall have the right to be represented when the matter is being considered in the Committee and to make submissions orally and/or in writing.

(2) The Committee shall, through the Secretary-General, notify the States parties concerned as early as possible of the opening date, duration and place of the session at which the matter will be examined.

(3) The procedure for making oral and/or written submissions shall be decided by the Committee, after consultation with the States parties concerned.

Rule 11/21 Report of the Committee.

(1) Within 12 months after the date on which the Committee received the notice referred to in rule 2/21 of these rules, the Committee shall adopt a report in accordance with article 21, paragraph 1 (h), of the Convention.

(2) The provisions of paragraph 1 of rule 10/21 of these rules shall not apply to the deliberations of the Committee concerning the adoption of the report.

(3) The Committee's report shall be communicated, through the Secretary-General, to the States parties concerned.

XIX. PROCEDURE FOR THE CONSIDERATION OF COMMUNICATIONS RECEIVED UNDER ARTICLE 22 OF THE CONVENTION

Rules concerning article 22 of the Convention

A. General provisions

Rule 1/22 Declarations by States parties.

(1) The Secretary-General shall transmit to the other States parties copies of the declarations deposited with him by States parties recognizing the competence of the Committee, in accordance with article 22 of the Convention.

(2) The withdrawal of a declaration made under article 22 of the Convention shall not prejudice the consideration of any matter which is the subject of a communication already transmitted under that article, no further communication by or on behalf of an individual shall be received under that article after the notification of withdrawal of the declaration has been received by the Secretary-General, unless the State party has made a new declaration.

Rule 2/22 Transmission of communications to the Committee.

(1) The Secretary-General shall bring to the attention of the Committee, in accordance with the present rules, communications which are or appear to be submitted for consideration by the Committee under paragraph 1 of article 22 of the Convention.

(2) The Secretary-General, when necessary, may request clarification from the author of a communication as to his wish to have his communication submitted to the Committee for consideration under article 22 of the Convention. In case there is still doubt as to the wish of the author, the Committee shall be seized of the communication.

(3) No communication shall be received by the Committee or included in a list under rule 3/22 if it concerns a State which has not made the declaration provided for in article 22, paragraph 1, of the convention.

Rule 3/22 List and register of communications.

(1) The Secretary-General shall prepare lists of the communications brought to the attention of the Committee in accordance with rule 2/22 above, with a brief summary of their contents, and shall circulate such lists to the members of the Committee at regular intervals. The Secretary-General shall also maintain a permanent register of all such communications.

(2) The full text of any communication brought to the attention of the Committee shall be made available to any member of the Committee upon his request.

Rule 4/22 Request for clarification or additional information.

(1) The Secretary-General may request clarification from the author of a communication concerning the applicability of article 22 of the Convention to his communication, in particular regarding:

a) The name, address, age and occupation of the author and the verification of his identity;

b) The name of the State party against which the communication is directed;

c) The object of the communication;

d) The provision or provisions of the Convention alleged to have been violated;

e) The facts of the claim;

f) Steps taken by the author to exhaust domestic remedies;

g) The extent to which the same matter is being examined under another procedure of international investigation or settlement.

(2) When requesting clarification or information, the Secretary-General shall indicate an appropriate time-limit to the author of the communication with a view to avoiding undue delays in the procedure under article 22 of the Convention.

(3) The Committee may approve a questionnaire for the purpose of requesting the above-mentioned information from the author of the communication.

(4) The request for clarification referred to in paragraph 1 of the present rule shall not preclude the inclusion of the communication in the list provided for in rule 3/22, paragraph 1.

Rule 5/22 Summary of the information.

For each registered communication the Secretary-General shall, as soon as possible, prepare and circulate to the members of the Committee a summary of the relevant information obtained.

Rule 6/22 Meetings.

(1) Meetings of the Committee or its subsidiary bodies during which communications under article 22 of the Convention will be examined shall be closed.

(2) Meetings during which the Committee may consider general issues, such as procedures for the application of article 22 of the Convention, may be public if the Committee so decides.

Rule 7/22 Issue of communiqués concerning closed meetings.

The Committee may issue communiqués, through the Secretary-General, for the use of the information media and the general public regarding the activities of the Committee under article 22 of the Convention.

Rule 8/22 Inability of a member to take part in the examination of a communication.

II. Europe

1. European Convention for the Protection of Human Rights and Fundamental Freedoms

The European Convention on Human Rights created the first regional international system for the protection of human rights. This Convention, established on November 4, 1950 by the member States of the Council of Europe, was intended to grant certain fundamental rights to all people living under their sovereignty. On March 20, 1952 the first Additional Protocol was adopted, adding further rights, such as the right to property, to the rights guaranteed by the Convention and on September 16, 1963 the Protocol No. 4 was signed adding further rights to those already protected such as the freedom of movement, and the interdiction of extradition in certain cases. Protocol No. 6 of April 28, 1983 concerned the abolishment of the death penalty and Protocol No. 7 of November 22, 1984 added some more rights concerning foreigners as well as criminal procedure and the principle of *ne bis in idem*.

The implementation mechanism of the Convention originally provided for three organs charged with the supervision and realization of the granted rights: the European Commission of Human Rights, the European Court of Human Rights and the Committee of Ministers of the Council of Europe.

The European Commission of Human Rights was conceived as a judicial body. It was composed of as many commissioners as there were contracting parties, no State being allowed to have more than one national sitting as commissioner. The commissioners, however, were independent of the country which selected them and sat "in their individual capacity".

A member State could initiate proceedings before the Commission based on a violation of the Convention by another member State if both States had ratified the Convention. The nationality of the victim was irrelevant to a State's standing to have its complaint heard. Furthermore, individuals, groups of individuals and non-governmental organizations were entitled to bring a petition before the Commission on the grounds of a violation of rights guaranteed by the Convention, provided the State which was accused of a violation of such rights had accepted the Commission's jurisdiction over the petitions of individuals (Art. 25).

The principal task of the Commission was to examine whether the petitioner had exhausted local remedies and whether the petition set forth the violation of a right guaranteed by the Convention. Manifestly ill-founded petitions as well as those constituting an abuse of the right of petition had to be rejected. Rejection of a petition by the Commission was final. In the event that a petition was not inadmissible on one of the grounds spelled out in Arts. 26 and 27 and the Commission failed to reach a friendly settlement of the matter, the Commission drew up a report indicating whether violations of the Convention had taken place. This report was then passed on to the Committee of Ministers and the States concerned.

Within three months of the presentation of the Commission's report the Commission, the State whose national had been the victim of a violation of the granted rights, the State against which the claim was brought, as well as — in an interstate application — the State which originally petitioned the Commission could institute proceedings before the Court of Human Rights, provided that the States concerned had recognized the Court's compulsory jurisdiction or accepted its jurisdiction for a specific case (Art. 46). The Court possessed the usual characteristics of an international tribunal; the number of judges on the Court corresponded to the number of States party to the Council of Europe (Art. 38). Judges were elected by the Consultative Assembly, the Parliamentary Assembly of the Council of Europe following nomination by the member States. Said States designated three candidates of whom at least two had to be nationals of the proposing State. The Court decided on the merits of the cases submitted to it. The individuals ultimately concerned were not parties to the proceedings before the Court, although they could be heard for the information of the Court.

By the second Additional Protocol, of May 6, 1963, entered into force on September 21, 1970, the Court acquired the competence to issue advisory opinions.

When proceedings were not instituted before the Court, the matter rested with the Committee of Ministers, the main political body of the Council of Europe. The Committee, then, had to decide by 2/3 majority whether a violation of the Convention had taken place and, if so, what measures should be taken to remedy the violation. If the measures taken were not respected, the Committee decided upon further measures to implement its decision and published them in a report. It should be noted that the Committee had in most cases agreed with the opinion set forth by the Commission.

The growing number of complaints and the increasing number of Member States from Eastern Europe made urgent a revision of the supervisory machinery. On 11 May, 1994, the Council of Europe therefore decided to adopt amending Protocol No. 11 to the Convention to restructure the supervisory machinery. This Protocol provides for the creation of a single Court which replaces the former Court and the Commission. The jurisdiction of the Court covers inter-state complaints as well as individual applications which it may receive from any person, nongovernmental organization or group of individuals claiming to be the victim of a violation of the Convention by one of the States parties. Under the new system, applicants may bring their cases directly before the Court without restrictions.

The new Court is composed of as many judges as there are member States to the Convention. The Court is now conceived as a permanent Court; that means that the judges are full-time judges for their term of office of six years. They may be reelected. In order to guarantee a certain continuity of function one half of the judges elected in the first election will serve for a period of only three years. At the age of 70 the office of the judges expires. In considering cases the Court sits in committees of three judges or in Chambers of seven judges or in a Grand Chamber of seventeen judges. The committees may unanimously declare inadmissible individual applications. The Chambers decide on the admissibility and merits of individual applications or inter-state applications and the Grand Chamber may be seized if a case pending before a Chamber raises a serious question affecting the interpretation of the Convention or the protocols thereto or where the result of the decision differs from a judgment previously delivered by the Court. The Chambers may also relinquish jurisdiction in favour of the Grand Chamber.

The new Court began to function on November 1, 1998, one year after the last ratification of the Protocol by the member States as provided for in Art. 4 of the Protocol.

Texts

For the original texts reference is made to the first edition of Texts and materials, Dispute settlement in Public International Law, 1984
Texts now in force
Protocol No. 11: ILM 34 (1995),1453
Rules of Procedure of the Court:
Council of Europe, Collected Texts 1994, p. 215 et seq.

Bibliographical notes

For bibliographical notes concerning the original implementation system reference is made to Bernhardt (ed.) EPIL, Vol. II (1995): J. A. Frowein, European Convention on Human Rights, 188 et seq.; G. Nolte/S. Oeter, European Commission and Court of Human Rights, Inter-State Applications, 144 et seq.; C. A. Norgaard, European Commission of Human Rights, 154 et seq. and W. J. Ganshof van der Meersch, European Court of Human Rights, 201 et seq.

O. Jacot-Guillarmod (ed.), La fusion de la Commission et de la Cour européenne des droits de l'homme (1987)

J. Meyer-Ladewig, Reform of the Control Machinery, in: Macdonald (ed.) The European System for the Protection of Human Rights (1993), 909 et seq.

J. G. Merrills, The development of international law by the European Court of Human Rights (2. ed. 1993)

J. Polakiewicz, Die Verpflichtungen der Staaten aus den Urteilen des Europäischen Gerichtshofs für Menschenrechte (1993)

J. A. Frowein, a.o., Implementation of the reform of the ECHR control machinery, in: 8th International Colloquy on the ECHR, Budapest (1995)

A. Z. Drzemeczewski, A major overhaul of the Human Rights Convention control mechanism: Protocol No. 11, in: Collected Courses of the Academy of European Law, Florence, 1995, Vol. V, Book 2

J. A. Frowein/W. Peukert, Europäische Menschenrechtskonvention, EMRK-Kommentar (2. ed. 1996)

R. Ryssdal, The enforcement system set up under the European Convention on Human Rights, in: Compliance with judgments of international Courts (1996), 49–69

L. Berg, Bringing cases before the European Commission and Court of Human
    Rights (1997)
A. Z. Drzemczewski, Protocole No. 11 à la Convention européenne des droits de
    l'homme: préparation à l'entrée en vigueur, European Journal of International
    Law 8 (1997), 59–76
L. Hefferman, A comparative view of individual petition proceedings under the
    European Convention on Human Rights and the International Covenant on
    Civil and Political Rights, Human Rights Quarterly 19 (1997), 78–112

Collections of cases

Yearbook of the European Convention on Human Rights/Annuaire de la Conven-
    tion des Droits de l'Homme
Collection of Resolutions adopted by the Committee of Ministers in application of
    Articles 32 and 54 of the European Convention on Human Rights
Digest of the Strasbourg Case-Law relating to the European Convention on Human
    Rights
European Commission of Human Rights, Collection of Decisions, (1960–1974),
    since 1974: Decisions and Reports
Publications of the European Court of Human Rights, Series A: Judgments and De-
    cisions; Series B: Pleadings, Oral Arguments and Documents
P. Kempers, A systematic guide to the case law of the European Court of Human
    Rights, 1960–1994
R. A. Lawson, Leading Cases of the European Court of Human Rights (1997)

a) Section II of the Convention as amended by Protocol No. 11 of May 11, 1994

SECTION II EUROPEAN COURT OF HUMAN RIGHTS

Art. 19   Establishment of the Court

To ensure the observance of the engagements undertaken by the High Contracting Parties in the Convention and the protocols thereto, there shall be set up a European Court of Human Rights, hereinafter referred to as "the Court". It shall function on a permanent basis.

Art. 20   Number of judges

The Court shall consist of a number of judges equal to that of the High Contracting Parties.

Art. 21   Criteria for office

1. The judges shall be of high moral character and must either possess the qualifications required for appointment to high judicial office or be juris-consults of recognised competence.

2. The judges shall sit on the Court in their individual capacity.

3. During their term of office the judges shall not engage in any activity which is incompatible with their independence, impartiality or with the demands of a full-time office; all questions arising from the application of this paragraph shall be decided by the Court.

Art. 22   Election of judges

1. The judges shall be elected by the Parliamentary Assembly with respect to each High Contracting Party by a majority of votes cast from a list of three candidates nominated by the High Contracting Party.

2. The same procedure shall be followed to complete the Court in the event of the accession of new High Contracting Parties and in filling casual vacancies.

Art. 23   Terms of office

1. The judges shall be elected for a period of six years. They may be re-elected. However. the terms of office of one-half of the judges elected at the first election shall expire at the end of three years.

2. The judges whose terms of office are to expire at the end of the initial period of three years shall be chosen by lot by the Secretary General of the Council of Europe immediately after their election.

3. In order to ensure that, as far as possible, the terms of office of one-half of the judges are renewed every three years, the Parliamentary Assembly may decide, before proceeding to any subsequent election, that the term or terms of office of one or more judges to be elected shall be for a period other than six years but not more than nine and not less than three years.

4. In cases where more than one term of office is involved and where the Parliamentary Assembly applies the preceding paragraph, the allocation of the terms of office shall be effected by a drawing of lots by the Secretary General of the Council of Europe immediately after the election.

5. A judge elected to replace a judge whose term of office has not expired shall hold office for the remainder of his predecessor's term.

6. The terms of office of judges shall expire when they reach the age of 70.

7. The judges shall hold office until replaced. They shall, however, continue to deal with such cases as they already have under consideration.

Art. 24   Dismissal

No judge may be dismissed from his office unless the other judges decide by a majority of two-thirds that he has ceased to fulfil the required conditions.

Art. 25   Registry and legal secretaries

The Court shall have a registry, the functions and organisation of which shall be laid down in the rules of the Court. The Court shall be assisted by legal secretaries.

Art. 26   Plenary Court

The plenary Court shall

a. elect its President and one or two Vice-Presidents for a period of three years; they may be re-elected;

b. set up Chambers, constituted for a fixed period of time;

c. elect the Presidents of the Chambers of the Court; they may be re-elected;

d. adopt the rules of the Court; and

e. elect the Registrar and one or more Deputy Registrars.

Art. 27   Committees, Chambers and Grand Chamber

1. To consider cases brought before it, the Court shall sit in committees of three judges, in Chambers of seven judges and in a Grand Chamber of seventeen judges. The Court's Chambers shall set up committees for a fixed period of time.

2. There shall sit as an *ex officio* member of the Chamber and the Grand Chamber the judge elected in respect of the State Party concerned or, if there is none or if he is unable to sit, a person of its choice who shall sit in the capacity of judge.

3. The Grand Chamber shall also include the President of the Court, the Vice-Presidents, the Presidents of the Chambers and other judges chosen in accordance with the rules of the Court. When a case is referred to the Grand Chamber under Article 43, no judge from the Chamber which rendered the judgment shall sit in the Grand Chamber, with the exception of the President of the Chamber and the judge who sat in respect of the State Party concerned.

Art. 28 Declarations of inadmissibility by committees

A committee may, by a unanimous vote, declare inadmissible or strike out of its list of cases an individual application submitted under Article 34 where such a decision can be taken without further examination. The decision shall be final.

Art. 29 Decisions by Chambers on admissibility and merits

1. If no decision is taken under Article 28, a Chamber shall decide on the admissibility and merits of individual applications submitted under Article 34.

2. A Chamber shall decide on the admissibility and merits of inter-State applications submitted under Article 33.

3. The decision on admissibility shall be taken separately unless the Court, in exceptional cases, decides otherwise.

Art. 30 Relinquishment of jurisdiction to the Grand Chamber

Where a case pending before a Chamber raises a serious question affecting the interpretation of the Convention or the protocols thereto or where the resolution of a question before it might have a result inconsistent with a judgment previously delivered by the Court, the Chamber may, at any time before it has rendered its judgment, relinquish jurisdiction in favour of the Grand Chamber unless one of the parties to the case objects.

Art. 31 Powers of the Grand Chamber

The Grand Chamber shall

a. determine applications submitted either under Article 33 or Article 34 when a Chamber has relinquished jurisdiction under Article 30 or when the case has been referred to it under Article 43; and

b. consider requests for advisory opinions submitted under Article 47.

Art. 32 Jurisdiction of the Court

1. The jurisdiction of the Court shall extend to all matters concerning the interpretation and application of the Convention and the protocols thereto which are referred to it as provided in Articles 33. 34 and 47.

2. In the event of dispute as to whether the Court has jurisdiction, the Court shall decide.

Art. 33 Inter-State cases

Any High Contracting Party may refer to the Court any alleged breach of the provisions of the Convention and the protocols thereto by another High Contracting Party.

Art. 34 Individual applications

The Court may receive applications from any person, non-governmental organisation or group of individuals claiming to be the victim of a violation by one of the High Contracting Parties of the rights set forth in the

Convention or the protocols thereto. The High Contracting Parties undertake not to hinder in any way the effective exercise of this right.

Art. 35   Admissibility criteria

1. The Court may only deal with the matter after all domestic remedies have been exhausted, according to the generally recognised rules of international law, and within a period of six months from the date on which the final decision was taken.

2. The Court shall not deal with any individual application submitted under Article 34 that

a. is anonymous; or

b. is substantially the same as a matter that has already been examined by the Court or has already been submitted to another procedure of international investigation or settlement and contains no relevant new information.

3. The Court shall declare inadmissible any individual application submitted under Article 34 which it considers incompatible with the provisions of the Convention or the protocols thereto, manifestly ill-founded, or an abuse of the right of application.

4. The Court shall reject any application which it considers inadmissible under this Article. It may do so at any stage of the proceedings.

Art. 36   Third-party intervention

1. In all cases before a Chamber or the Grand Chamber, a High Contracting Party one of whose nationals is an applicant shall have the right to submit written comments and to take part in hearings.

2. The President of the Court may in the interest of the proper administration of justice, invite any High Contracting Party which is not a party to the proceedings or any person concerned who is not the applicant to submit written comments or take part in hearings.

Art. 37   Striking out applications

1. The Court may at any stage of the proceedings decide to strike an application out of its list of cases where the circumstances lead to the conclusion that

a. the applicant does not intend to pursue his application; or

b. the matter has been resolved; or

c. for any other reason established by the Court, it is no longer justified to continue the examination of the application.

However, the Court shall continue the examination of the application if respect for human rights as defined in the Convention and the protocols thereto so requires.

2. The Court may decide to restore an application to its list of cases if it considers that the circumstances justify such a course.

Art. 38   Examination of the case and friendly settlement proceedings

1. If the Court declares the application admissible, it shall

a. pursue the examination of the case, together with the representatives of the parties, and if need be, undertake an investigation for the effective conduct of which the States concerned shall furnish all necessary facilities;

b. place itself at the disposal of the parties concerned with a view to securing a friendly settlement of the matter on the basis of respect for human rights as defined in the Convention and the protocols thereto.

2. Proceedings conducted under paragraph 1.b shall be confidential.

Art. 39   Finding of a friendly settlement

If a friendly settlement is effected, the Court shall strike the case out of its list by means of a decision which shall be confined to a brief statement of the facts and of the solution reached.

Art. 40   Public hearings and access to documents

1. Hearings shall be public unless the Court in exceptional circumstances decides otherwise.

2. Documents deposited with the Registrar shall be accessible to the public unless the President of the Court decides otherwise.

Art. 41   Just satisfaction

If the Court finds that there has been a violation of the Convention or the protocols thereto, and if the internal law of the High Contracting Party concerned allows only partial reparation to be made, the Court shall, if necessary, afford just satisfaction to the injured party.

Art. 42   Judgments of Chambers

Judgments of Chambers shall become final in accordance with the provisions of Article 44 paragraph 2.

Art. 43   Referral to the Grand Chamber

1. Within a period of three months from the date of the judgment of the Chamber, any party to the case may, in exceptional cases, request that the case be referred to the Grand Chamber.

2. A panel of five judges of the Grand Chamber shall accept the request if the case raises a serious question affecting the interpretation or application of the Convention or the protocols thereto, or a serious issue of general importance.

3. If the panel accepts the request, the Grand Chamber shall decide the case by means of a judgment.

Art. 44   Final judgments

1. The judgment of the Grand Chamber shall be final.

2. The judgment of a Chamber shall become final

a. when the parties declare that they will not request that the case be referred to the Grand Chamber; or

b. three months after the date of the judgment, if reference of the case to the Grand Chamber has not been requested: or

c. when the panel of the Grand Chamber rejects the request to refer under Article 43.

3. The final judgment shall be published.

Art. 45   Reasons for judgments and decisions

1. Reasons shall be given for judgments as well as for decisions declaring applications admissible or inadmissible.

2. If a judgment does not represent, in whole or in part, the unanimous opinion of the judges, any judge shall be entitled to deliver a separate opinion.

Art. 46   Binding force and execution of judgments

1. The High Contracting Parties undertake to abide by the final judgment of the Court in any case to which they are parties.

2. The final judgment of the Court shall be transmitted to the Committee of Ministers, which shall supervise its execution.

Art. 47   Advisory opinions

1. The Court may, at the request of the Committee of Ministers, give advisory opinions on legal questions concerning the interpretation of the Convention and the protocols thereto.

2. Such opinions shall not deal with any question relating to the content or scope of the rights or freedoms defined in Section I of the Convention and the protocols thereto, or with any other question which the Court or the Committee of Ministers might have to consider in consequence of any such proceedings as could be instituted in accordance with the Convention.

3. Decisions of the Committee of Ministers to request an advisory opinion of the Court shall require a majority vote of the representatives entitled to sit on the Committee.

Art. 48   Advisory jurisdiction of the Court

The Court shall decide whether a request for an advisory opinion submitted by the Committee of Ministers is within its competence as defined in Article 47.

Art. 49   Reasons for advisory opinions

1. Reasons shall be given for advisory opinions of the Court.

2. If the advisory opinion does not represent, in whole or in part, the unanimous opinion of the judges, any judge shall be entitled to deliver a separate opinion.

3. Advisory opinions of the Court shall be communicated to the Committee of Ministers.

Art. 50   Expenditure on the Court

The expenditure on the Court shall he borne by the Council of Europe.

Art. 51   Privileges and immunities of judges

The judges shall be entitled, during the exercise of their functions, to the privileges and immunities provided for in Article 40 of the Statute of the Council of Europe and in the agreements made thereunder.

b) Protocol No. 11, Art. 5 and 6

Art. 5   1. Without prejudice to the provisions in paragraphs 3 and 4 below, the terms of office of the judges, members of the Commission, Registrar and Deputy Registrar shall expire at the date of entry into force of this Protocol.

2. Applications pending before the Commission which have not been declared admissible at the date of the entry into force of this Protocol shall be examined by the Court in accordance with the provisions of this Protocol.

3. Applications which have been declared admissible at the date of entry into force of this Protocol shall continue to be dealt with by members of the Commission within a period of one year thereafter. Any applications the examination of which has not been completed within the aforesaid period shall be transmitted to the Court which shall examine them as admissible cases in accordance with the provisions of this Protocol.

4. With respect to applications in which the Commission, after the entry into force of this Protocol, has adopted a report in accordance with former Article 31 of the Convention, the report shall be transmitted to the parties, who shall not be at liberty to publish it. In accordance with the provisions applicable prior to the entry into force of this Protocol, a case may be referred to the Court. The panel of the Grand Chamber shall determine whether one of the Chambers or the Grand Chamber shall decide the case. If the case is decided by a Chamber, the decision of the Chamber shall be final. Cases not referred to the Court shall be dealt with by the Committee of Ministers acting in accordance with the provisions of former Article 32 of the Convention.

5. Cases pending before the Court which have not been decided at the date of entry into force of this Protocol shall be transmitted to the Grand Chamber of the Court, which shall examine them in accordance with the provisions of this Protocol.

6. Cases pending before the Committee of Ministers which have not been decided under former Article 32 of the Convention at the date of entry into force of this Protocol shall be completed by the Committee of Ministers acting in accordance with that Article.

Art. 6   Where a High Contracting Party had made a declaration recognising the competence of the Commission or the jurisdiction of the Court under former Article 25 or 46 of the Convention with respect to matters arising after or based on facts occurring subsequent to any such declaration, this limitation shall remain valid for the jurisdiction of the Court under this Protocol.

c) Rules of the European Court of Human Rights of November 4, 1998

The European Court of Human Rights,

Having regard to the Convention for the Protection of Human Rights and Fundamental Freedoms and the Protocols thereto,

Makes the present Rules:

Rule 1   (Definitions)

For the purposes of these Rules unless the context otherwise requires:

(a) the term "Convention" means the Convention for the Protection of Human Rights and Fundamental Freedoms and the Protocols thereto;

(b) the expression "plenary Court" means the European Court of Human Rights sitting in plenary session;

(c) the term "Grand Chamber" means the Grand Chamber of seventeen judges constituted in pursuance of Article 27 § 1 of the Convention;

(d) the term "Section" means a Chamber set up by the plenary Court for a fixed period in pursuance of Article 26 (b) of the Convention and the expression "President of the Section" means the judge elected by the plenary Court in pursuance of Article 26 (c) of the Convention as President of such a Section;

(e) the term "Chamber" means any Chamber of seven judges constituted in pursuance of Article 27 § 1 of the Convention and the expression "President of the Chamber" means the judge presiding over such a "Chamber";

(f) the term "Committee" means a Committee of three judges set up in pursuance of Article 27 § 1 of the Convention;

(g) the term "Court" means either the plenary Court, the Grand Chamber, a Section, a Chamber, a Committee or the panel of five judges referred to in Article 43 § 2 of the Convention;

(h) the expression "*ad hoc* judge" means any person, other than an elected judge, chosen by a Contracting Party in pursuance of Article 27 § 2 of the Convention to sit as a member of the Grand Chamber or as a member of a Chamber;

(i) the terms "judge" and "judges" mean the judges elected by the Parliamentary Assembly of the Council of Europe or *ad hoc* judges;

(j) the term "Judge Rapporteur" means a judge appointed to carry out the tasks provided for in Rules 48 and 49;

(k) the term "Registrar" denotes the Registrar of the Court or the Registrar of a Section according to the context;

(l) the terms "party" and "parties" mean

– the applicant or respondent Contracting Parties;

– the applicant (the person, non-governmental organisation or group of individuals) that lodged a complaint under Article 34 of the Convention;

(m) the expression "third party" means any Contracting State or any person concerned who, as provided for in Article 36 §§ 1 and 2 of the Convention, has exercised its right or been invited to submit written comments or take part in a hearing;

(n) the expression "Committee of Ministers" means the Committee of Ministers of the Council of Europe;

(o) the terms "former Court" and "Commission" mean respectively the European Court and European Commission of Human Rights set up under former Article 19 of the Convention.

Title I — Organisation and Working of the Court

Chapter I — Judges

Rule 2   (Calculation of term of office)

1. The duration of the term of office of an elected judge shall be calculated as from the date of election. However, when a judge is re-elected on the expiry of the term of office or is elected to replace a judge whose term of office has expired or is about to expire, the duration of the term of office shall, in either case, be calculated as from the date of such expiry.

2. In accordance with Article 23 § 5 of the Convention, a judge elected to replace a judge whose term of office has not expired shall hold office for the remainder of the predecessor's term.

3. In accordance with Article 23 § 7 of the Convention, an elected judge shall hold office until a successor has taken the oath or made the declaration provided for in Rule 3.

Rule 3   (Oath or solemn declaration)

1. Before taking up office, each elected judge shall, at the first sitting of the plenary Court at which the judge is present or, in case of need, before the President of the Court, take the following oath or make the following solemn declaration:

"I swear" – or "I solemnly declare" – "that I will exercise my functions as a judge honourably, independently and impartially and that I will keep secret all deliberations."

2. This act shall be recorded in minutes.

Rule 4   (Incompatible activities)

In accordance with Article 21 § 3 of the Convention, the judges shall not during their term of office engage in any political or administrative activity or any professional activity which is incompatible with their independence or impartiality or with the demands of a full-time office. Each judge shall declare to the President of the Court any additional activity. In the event of a disagreement between the President and the judge concerned, any question arising shall be decided by the plenary Court.

Rule 5   (Precedence)

1. Elected judges shall take precedence after the President and Vice-Presidents of the Court and the Presidents of the Sections, according to the date of their election; in the event of re-election, even if it is not an immediate re-election, the length of time during which the judge concerned previously held office as a judge shall be taken into account.

2. Vice-Presidents of the Court elected to office on the same date shall take precedence according to the length of time they have served as judges. If the length of time they have served as judges is the same, they shall take precedence according to age. The same Rule shall apply to Presidents of Sections.

3. Judges who have served the same length of time as judges shall take precedence according to age.

4. *Ad hoc* judges shall take precedence after the elected judges according to age.

Rule 6   (Resignation)

Resignation of a judge shall be notified to the President of the Court, who shall transmit it to the Secretary General of the Council of Europe. Subject to the provisions of Rules 24 § 3 *in fine* and 26 § 2, resignation shall constitute vacation of office.

Rule 7   (Dismissal from office)

No judge may be dismissed from his or her office unless the other judges, meeting in plenary session, decide by a majority of two-thirds of the elected judges in office that he or she has ceased to fulfil the required conditions. He or she must first be heard by the plenary Court. Any judge may set in motion the procedure for dismissal from office.

CHAPTER II — PRESIDENCY OF THE COURT

Rule 8   (Election of the President and Vice-Presidents of the Court and the Presidents and Vice-Presidents of the Sections)

1. The plenary Court shall elect its President, two Vice-Presidents and the Presidents of the Sections for a period of three years, provided that such period shall not exceed the duration of their terms of office as judges. They may be re-elected.

2. Each Section shall likewise elect for a renewable period of three years a Vice-President, who shall replace the President of the Section if the latter is unable to carry out his or her duties.

3. The Presidents and Vice-Presidents shall continue to hold office until the election of their successors.

4. If a President or a Vice-President ceases to be a member of the Court or resigns from office before its normal expiry, the plenary Court or the relevant Section, as the case may be, shall elect a successor for the remainder of the term of that office.

5. The elections referred to in this Rule shall be by secret ballot; only the elected judges who are present shall take part. If no judge receives an absolute majority of the elected judges present, a ballot shall take place between the two judges who have received most votes. In the event of a tie, preference shall be given to the judge having precedence in accordance with Rule 5.

Rule 9   (Functions of the President of the Court)

1. The President of the Court shall direct the work and administration of the Court. The President shall represent the Court and, in particular, be responsible for its relations with the authorities of the Council of Europe.

2. The President shall preside at plenary meetings of the Court, meetings of the Grand Chamber and meetings of the panel of five judges.

3. The President shall not take part in the consideration of cases being heard by Chambers except where he or she is the judge elected in respect of a Contracting Party concerned.

Rule 10   (Functions of the Vice-Presidents of the Court)

The Vice-Presidents of the Court shall assist the President of the Court. They shall take the place of the President if the latter is unable to carry out his or her duties or the office of President is vacant, or at the request of the President. They shall also act as Presidents of Sections.

Rule 11   (Replacement of the President and the Vice-Presidents)

If the President and the Vice-Presidents of the Court are at the same time unable to carry out their duties or if their offices are at the same time vacant, the office of President of the Court shall be assumed by a President of a Section or, if none is available, by another elected judge, in accordance with the order of precedence provided for in Rule 5.

Rule 12   (Presidency of Sections and Chambers)

The Presidents of the Sections shall preside at the sittings of the Section and Chambers of which they are members. The Vice-Presidents of the

Sections shall take their place if they are unable to carry out their duties or if the office of President of the Section concerned is vacant, or at the request of the President of the Section. Failing that, the judges of the Section and the Chambers shall take their place, in the order of precedence provided for in Rule 5.

Rule 13   (Inability to preside)

Judges of the Court may not preside in cases in which the Contracting Party of which they are nationals or in respect of which they were elected is a party.

Rule 14   (Balanced representation of the sexes)

In relation to the making of appointments governed by this and the following chapter of the present Rules, the Court shall pursue a policy aimed at securing a balanced representation of the sexes.

CHAPTER III — THE REGISTRY

Rule 15   (Election of the Registrar)

1. The plenary Court shall elect its Registrar. The candidates shall be of high moral character and must possess the legal, managerial and linguistic knowledge and experience necessary to carry out the functions attaching to the post.

2. The Registrar shall be elected for a term of five years and may be re-elected. The Registrar may not be dismissed from office, unless the judges, meeting in plenary session, decide by a majority of two-thirds of the elected judges in office that the person concerned has ceased to fulfil the required conditions. He or she must first be heard by the plenary Court. Any judge may set in motion the procedure for dismissal from office.

3. The elections referred to in this Rule shall be by secret ballot; only the elected judges who are present shall take part. If no candidate receives an absolute majority of the elected judges present, a ballot shall take place between the two candidates who have received most votes. In the event of a tie, preference shall be given, firstly, to the female candidate, if any, and, secondly, to the older candidate.

4. Before taking up office, the Registrar shall take the following oath or make the following solemn declaration before the plenary Court or, if need be, before the President of the Court:

"I swear" – or "I solemnly declare" –"that I will exercise loyally, discreetly and conscientiously the functions conferred upon me as Registrar of the European Court of Human Rights."

This act shall be recorded in minutes.

Rule 16   (Election of the Deputy Registrars)

1. The plenary Court shall also elect two Deputy Registrars on the conditions and in the manner and for the term prescribed in the preceding Rule. The procedure for dismissal from office provided for in respect of the Registrar shall likewise apply. The Court shall first consult the Registrar in both these matters.

2. Before taking up office, a Deputy Registrar shall take an oath or make a solemn declaration before the plenary Court or, if need be, before the President of the Court, in terms similar to those prescribed in respect of the Registrar. This act shall be recorded in minutes.

Rule 17   (Functions of the Registrar)

1. The Registrar shall assist the Court in the performance of its functions and shall be responsible for the organisation and activities of the Registry under the authority of the President of the Court.

2. The Registrar shall have the custody of the archives of the Court and shall be the channel for all communications and notifications made by, or addressed to, the Court in connection with the cases brought or to be brought before it.

3. The Registrar shall, subject to the duty of discretion attaching to this office, reply to requests for information concerning the work of the Court, in particular to enquiries from the press.

4. General instructions drawn up by the Registrar, and approved by the President of the Court, shall regulate the working of the Registry.

Rule 18   (Organisation of the Registry)

1. The Registry shall consist of Section Registries equal to the number of Sections set up by the Court and of the departments necessary to provide the legal and administrative services required by the Court.

2. The Section Registrar shall assist the Section in the performance of its functions and may be assisted by a Deputy Section Registrar.

3. The officials of the Registry, including the legal secretaries but not the Registrar and the Deputy Registrars, shall be appointed by the Secretary General of the Council of Europe with the agreement of the President of the Court or of the Registrar acting on the President's instructions.

CHAPTER IV — THE WORKING OF THE COURT

Rule 19   (Seat of the Court)

1. The seat of the Court shall be at the seat of the Council of Europe at Strasbourg. The Court may, however, if it considers it expedient, perform its functions elsewhere in the territories of the member States of the Council of Europe.

2. The Court may decide, at any stage of the examination of an application, that it is necessary that an investigation or any other function be carried out elsewhere by it or one or more of its members.

Rule 20   (Sessions of the plenary Court)

1. The plenary sessions of the Court shall be convened by the President of the Court whenever the performance of its functions under the Convention and under these Rules so requires. The President of the Court shall convene a plenary session if at least one-third of the members of the Court so request, and in any event once a year to consider administrative matters.

2. The quorum of the plenary Court shall be two-thirds of the elected judges in office.

3. If there is no quorum, the President shall adjourn the sitting.

Rule 21   (Other sessions of the Court)

1. The Grand Chamber, the Chambers and the Committees shall sit full time. On a proposal by the President, however, the Court shall fix session periods each year.

2. Outside those periods the Grand Chamber and the Chambers shall be convened by their Presidents in cases of urgency.

Rule 22   (Deliberations)

1. The Court shall deliberate in private. Its deliberations shall remain secret.

2. Only the judges shall take part in the deliberations. The Registrar or the designated substitute, as well as such other officials of the Registry and interpreters whose assistance is deemed necessary, shall be present. No other person may be admitted except by special decision of the Court.

3. Before a vote is taken on any matter in the Court, the President may request the judges to state their opinions on it.

Rule 23   (Votes)

1. The decisions of the Court shall be taken by a majority of the judges present. In the event of a tie, a fresh vote shall be taken and, if there is still a tie, the President shall have a casting vote. This paragraph shall apply unless otherwise provided for in these Rules.

2. The decisions and judgments of the Grand Chamber and the Chambers shall be adopted by a majority of the sitting judges. Abstentions shall not be allowed in final votes on the admissibility and merits of cases.

3. As a general rule, votes shall be taken by a show of hands. The President may take a roll-call vote, in reverse order of precedence.

4. Any matter that is to be voted upon shall be formulated in precise terms.

CHAPTER V — THE CHAMBERS

Rule 24   (Composition of the Grand Chamber)

1. The Grand Chamber shall be composed of seventeen judges and three substitute judges.

2. The Grand Chamber shall be constituted for three years with effect from the election of the presidential office-holders referred to in Rule 8.

3. The Grand Chamber shall include the President and Vice-Presidents of the Court and the Presidents of the Sections. In order to complete the Grand Chamber, the plenary Court shall, on a proposal by its President, divide all the other judges into two groups which shall alternate every nine months and whose membership shall be geographically as balanced as possible and reflect the different legal systems among the Contracting Parties. The judges and substitute judges who are to hear each case referred to the Grand Chamber during each nine-month period shall be designated in rotation within each group; they shall remain members of the Grand Chamber until the proceedings have been completed, even after their terms of office as judges have expired.

4. If he or she does not sit as a member of the Grand Chamber by virtue of paragraph 3 of the present Rule, the judge elected in respect of any Contracting Party concerned shall sit as an *ex officio* member of the Grand Chamber in accordance with Article 27 §§ 2 and 3 of the Convention.

5. (a) Where any President of a Section is unable to sit as a member of the Grand Chamber, he or she shall be replaced by the Vice-President of the Section.

(b) If other judges are prevented from sitting, they shall be replaced by the substitute judges in the order in which the latter were selected under paragraph 3 of the present Rule.

(c) If there are not enough substitute judges in the group concerned to complete the Grand Chamber, the substitute judges lacking shall be designated by a drawing of lots amongst the members of the other group.

6. (a) The panel of five judges of the Grand Chamber called upon to consider requests submitted under Article 43 of the Convention shall be composed of

– the President of the Court,

– the Presidents or, if they are prevented from sitting, the Vice-Presidents of the Sections other than the Section from which was constituted the Chamber that dealt with the case whose referral to the Grand Chamber is being sought,

– one further judge designated in rotation from among the judges other than those who dealt with the case in the Chamber.

(b) No judge elected in respect of, or who is a national of, a Contracting Party concerned may be a member of the panel.

(c) Any member of the panel unable to sit shall be replaced by another judge who did not deal with the case in the Chamber, who shall be designated in rotation.

Rule 25   (Setting up of Sections)

1. The Chambers provided for in Article 26 (b) of the Convention (referred to in these Rules as "Sections") shall be set up by the plenary Court, on a proposal by its President, for a period of three years with effect from the election of the presidential office-holders of the Court under Rule 8. There shall be at least four Sections.

2. Each judge shall be a member of a Section. The composition of the Sections shall be geographically and gender balanced and shall reflect the different legal systems among the Contracting Parties.

3. Where a judge ceases to be a member of the Court before the expiry of the period for which the Section has been constituted, the judge's place in the Section shall be taken by his or her successor as a member of the Court.

4. The President of the Court may exceptionally make modifications to the composition of the Sections if circumstances so require.

5. On a proposal by the President, the plenary Court may constitute an additional Section.

Rule 26   (Constitution of Chambers)

1. The Chambers of seven judges provided for in Article 27 § 1 of the Convention for the consideration of cases brought before the Court shall be constituted from the Sections as follows.

(a) The Chamber shall in each case include the President of the Section and the judge elected in respect of any Contracting Party concerned. If the latter judge is not a member of the Section to which the application has been assigned under Rule 51 or 52, he or she shall sit as an *ex officio* member of the Chamber in accordance with Article 27 § 2 of the Convention. Rule 29 shall apply if that judge is unable to sit or withdraws.

(b) The other members of the Chamber shall be designated by the President of the Section in rotation from among the members of the relevant Section.

(c) The members of the Section who are not so designated shall sit in the case as substitute judges.

2. Even after the end of their terms of office judges shall continue to deal with cases in which they have participated in the consideration of the merits.

Rule 27   (Committees)

1. Committees composed of three judges belonging to the same Section shall be set up under Article 27 § 1 of the Convention. After consulting the Presidents of the Sections, the President of the Court shall decide on the number of Committees to be set up.

2. The Committees shall be constituted for a period of twelve months by rotation among the members of each Section, excepting the President of the Section.

3. The judges of the Section who are not members of a Committee may be called upon to take the place of members who are unable to sit.

4. Each Committee shall be chaired by the member having precedence in the Section.

Rule 28   (Inability to sit, withdrawal or exemption)

1. Any judge who is prevented from taking part in sittings shall, as soon as possible, give notice to the President of the Chamber.

2. A judge may not take part in the consideration of any case in which he or she has a personal interest or has previously acted either as the Agent, advocate or adviser of a party or of a person having an interest in the case, or as a member of a tribunal or commission of inquiry, or in any other capacity.

3. If a judge withdraws for one of the said reasons, or for some special reason, he or she shall inform the President of the Chamber, who shall exempt the judge from sitting.

4. If the President of the Chamber considers that a reason exists for a judge to withdraw, he or she shall consult with the judge concerned; in the event of disagreement, the Chamber shall decide.

Rule 29   (*Ad hoc* judges)

1. If the judge elected in respect of a Contracting Party concerned is unable to sit in the Chamber or withdraws, the President of the Chamber shall invite that Party to indicate within thirty days whether it wishes to appoint to sit as judge either another elected judge or, as an *ad hoc* judge, any other person possessing the qualifications required by Article 21 § 1 of the Convention and, if so, to state at the same time the name of the person appointed. The same rule shall apply if the person so appointed is unable to sit or withdraws.

2. The Contracting Party concerned shall be presumed to have waived its right of appointment if it does not reply within thirty days.

3. An *ad hoc* judge shall, at the opening of the first sitting fixed for the consideration of the case after the judge has been appointed, take the oath or make the solemn declaration provided for in Rule 3. This act shall be recorded in minutes.

Rule 30   (Common interest)

1. If several applicant or respondent Contracting Parties have a common interest, the President of the Court may invite them to agree to appoint a single elected judge or *ad hoc* judge in accordance with Article 27 § 2 of the Convention. If the Parties are unable to agree, the President shall choose by lot, from among the persons proposed as judges by these Parties, the judge called upon to sit *ex officio*.

2. In the event of a dispute as to the existence of a common interest, the plenary Court shall decide.

TITLE II — PROCEDURE

CHAPTER I — GENERAL RULES

Rule 31   (Possibility of particular derogations)

The provisions of this Title shall not prevent the Court from derogating from them for the consideration of a particular case after having consulted the parties where appropriate.

Rule 32   (Practice directions)

The President of the Court may issue practice directions, notably in relation to such matters as appearance at hearings and the filing of pleadings and other documents.

Rule 33   (Public character of proceedings)

1. Hearings shall be public unless, in accordance with paragraph 2 of this Rule, the Chamber in exceptional circumstances decides otherwise, either of its own motion or at the request of a party or any other person concerned.

2. The press and the public may be excluded from all or part of a hearing in the interest of morals, public order or national security in a democratic society, where the interests of juveniles or the protection of the private life of the parties so require, or to the extent strictly necessary in the opinion of the Chamber in special circumstances where publicity would prejudice the interests of justice.

3. Following registration of an application, all documents deposited with the Registry, with the exception of those deposited within the framework of friendly-settlement negotiations as provided for in Rule 62, shall be accessible to the public unless the President of the Chamber, for the reasons set out in paragraph 2 of this Rule, decides otherwise, either of his or her own motion or at the request of a party or any other person concerned.

4. Any request for confidentiality made under paragraphs 1 or 3 above must give reasons and specify whether the hearing or the documents, as the case may be, should be inaccessible to the public in whole or in part.

Rule 34   (Use of languages)

1. The official languages of the Court shall be English and French.

2. Before the decision on the admissibility of an application is taken, all communications with and pleadings by applicants under Article 34 of the Convention or their representatives, if not in one of the Court's official languages, shall be in one of the official languages of the Contracting Parties.

3. (a) All communications with and pleadings by such applicants or their representatives in respect of a hearing, or after a case has been declared admissible, shall be in one of the Court's official languages, unless the President of the Chamber authorises the continued use of the official language of a Contracting Party.

(b) If such leave is granted, the Registrar shall make the necessary arrangements for the oral or written translation of the applicant's observations or statements.

4. (a) All communications with and pleadings by Contracting Parties or third parties shall be in one of the Court's official languages. The President of the Chamber may authorise the use of a non-official language.

(b) If such leave is granted, it shall be the responsibility of the requesting party to provide for and bear the costs of interpreting or translation into English or French of the oral arguments or written statements made.

5. The President of the Chamber may invite the respondent Contracting Party to provide a translation of its written submissions in the or an official language of that Party in order to facilitate the applicant's understanding of those submissions.

6. Any witness, expert or other person appearing before the Court may use his or her own language if he or she does not have sufficient knowledge of either of the two official languages. In that event the Registrar shall make the necessary arrangements for interpreting or translation.

Rule 35   (Representation of Contracting Parties)

The Contracting Parties shall be represented by Agents, who may have the assistance of advocates or advisers.

Rule 36   (Representation of applicants)

1. Persons, non-governmental organisations or groups of individuals may initially present applications under Article 34 of the Convention themselves or through a representative appointed under paragraph 4 of this Rule.

2. Following notification of the application to the respondent Contracting Party under Rule 54 § 3 (b), the President of the Chamber may direct that the applicant should be represented in accordance with paragraph 4 of this Rule.

3. The applicant must be so represented at any hearing decided on by the Chamber or for the purposes of the proceedings following a decision to declare the application admissible, unless the President of the Chamber decides otherwise.

4. (a) The representative of the applicant shall be an advocate authorised to practise in any of the Contracting Parties and resident in the territory of one of them, or any other person approved by the President of the Chamber.

(b) The President of the Chamber may, where representation would otherwise be obligatory, grant leave to the applicant to present his or her own case, subject, if necessary, to being assisted by an advocate or other approved representative.

(c) In exceptional circumstances and at any stage of the procedure, the President of the Chamber may, where he or she considers that the circumstances or the conduct of the advocate or other person appointed under the preceding sub-paragraphs so warrant, direct that the latter may no longer represent or assist the applicant and that the applicant should seek alternative representation.

5. The advocate or other approved representative, or the applicant in person if he or she seeks leave to present his or her own case, must have an adequate knowledge of one of the Court's official languages. However, leave to use a non-official language may be given by the President of the Chamber under Rule 34 § 3.

Rule 37   (Communications, notifications and summonses)

1. Communications or notifications addressed to the Agents or advocates of the parties shall be deemed to have been addressed to the parties.

2. If, for any communication, notification or summons addressed to persons other than the Agents or advocates of the parties, the Court considers it necessary to have the assistance of the Government of the State on whose territory such communication, notification or summons is to have effect, the President of the Court shall apply directly to that Government in order to obtain the necessary facilities.

3. The same rule shall apply when the Court desires to make or arrange for the making of an investigation on the spot in order to establish the facts or to procure evidence or when it orders the appearance of a person who is resident in, or will have to cross, that territory.

Rule 38   (Written pleadings)

1. No written observations or other documents may be filed after the time-limit set by the President of the Chamber or the Judge Rapporteur, as the case may be, in accordance with these Rules. No written observations or other documents filed outside that time-limit or contrary to any practice direction issued under Rule 32 shall be included in the case file unless the President of the Chamber decides otherwise.

2. For the purposes of observing the time-limit referred to in paragraph 1, the material date is the certified date of dispatch of the document or, if there is none, the actual date of receipt at the Registry.

Rule 39   (Interim measures)

1. The Chamber or, where appropriate, its President may, at the request of a party or of any other person concerned, or of its own motion, indicate to the parties any interim measure which it considers should be adopted in the interests of the parties or of the proper conduct of the proceedings before it.

2. Notice of these measures shall be given to the Committee of Ministers.

3. The Chamber may request information from the parties on any matter connected with the implementation of any interim measure it has indicated.

Rule 40   (Urgent notification of an application)

In any case of urgency the Registrar, with the authorisation of the President of the Chamber, may, without prejudice to the taking of any other procedural steps and by any available means, inform a Contracting Party concerned in an application of the introduction of the application and of a summary of its objects.

Rule 41   (Case priority)

The Chamber shall deal with applications in the order in which they become ready for examination. It may, however, decide to give priority to a particular application.

Rule 42   (Measures for taking evidence)

1. The Chamber may, at the request of a party or a third party, or of its own motion, obtain any evidence which it considers capable of providing clarification of the facts of the case. The Chamber may, *inter alia*, request the parties to produce documentary evidence and decide to hear as a witness or expert or in any other capacity any person whose evidence or statements seem likely to assist it in the carrying out of its tasks.

2. The Chamber may, at any time during the proceedings, depute one or more of its members or of the other judges of the Court to conduct an inquiry, carry out an investigation on the spot or take evidence in some other manner. It may appoint independent external experts to assist such a delegation.

3. The Chamber may ask any person or institution of its choice to obtain information, express an opinion or make a report on any specific point.

4. The parties shall assist the Chamber, or its delegation, in implementing any measures for taking evidence.

5. Where a report has been drawn up or some other measure taken in accordance with the preceding paragraphs at the request of an applicant or respondent Contracting Party, the costs entailed shall be borne by that Party unless the Chamber decides otherwise. In other cases the Chamber shall decide whether such costs are to be borne by the Council of Europe or awarded against the applicant or third party at whose request the report was drawn up or the other measure was taken. In all cases the costs shall be taxed by the President of the Chamber.

Rule 43   (Joinder and simultaneous examination of applications)

1. The Chamber may, either at the request of the parties or of its own motion, order the joinder of two or more applications.

2. The President of the Chamber may, after consulting the parties, order that the proceedings in applications assigned to the same Chamber be conducted simultaneously, without prejudice to the decision of the Chamber on the joinder of the applications.

Rule 44   (Striking out and restoration to the list)

1. When an applicant Contracting Party notifies the Registrar of its intention not to proceed with the case, the Chamber may strike the appli-

cation out of the Court's list under Article 37 of the Convention if the other Contracting Party or Parties concerned in the case agree to such discontinuance.

2. The decision to strike out an application which has been declared admissible shall be given in the form of a judgment. The President of the Chamber shall forward that judgment, once it has become final, to the Committee of Ministers in order to allow the latter to supervise, in accordance with Article 46 § 2 of the Convention, the execution of any undertakings which may have been attached to the discontinuance, friendly settlement or solution of the matter.

3. When an application has been struck out, the costs shall be at the discretion of the Court. If an award of costs is made in a decision striking out an application which has not been declared admissible, the President of the Chamber shall forward the decision to the Committee of Ministers

4. The Court may restore an application to its list if it concludes that exceptional circumstances justify such a course.

CHAPTER II — INSTITUTION OF PROCEEDINGS

Rule 45 (Signatures)

1. Any application made under Articles 33 or 34 of the Convention shall be submitted in writing and shall be signed by the applicant or by the applicant's representative.

2. Where an application is made by a non-governmental organisation or by a group of individuals, it shall be signed by those persons competent to represent that organisation or group. The Chamber or Committee concerned shall determine any question as to whether the persons who have signed an application are competent to do so.

3. Where applicants are represented in accordance with Rule 36, a power of attorney or written authority to act shall be supplied by their representative or representatives.

Rule 46 (Contents of an inter-State application)

Any Contracting Party or Parties intending to bring a case before the Court under Article 33 of the Convention shall file with the registry an application setting out

(a) the name of the Contracting Party against which the application is made;

(b) a statement of the facts;

(c) a statement of the alleged violation(s) of the Convention and the relevant arguments;

(d) a statement on compliance with the admissibility criteria (exhaustion of domestic remedies and the six-month rule) laid down in Article 35 § 1 of the Convention;

(e) the object of the application and a general indication of any claims for just satisfaction made under Article 41 of the Convention on behalf of the alleged injured party or parties; and

(f) the name and address of the person(s) appointed as Agent; and accompanied by

(g) copies of any relevant documents and in particular the decisions, whether judicial or not, relating to the object of the application.

Rule 47 (Contents of an individual application)

1. Any application under Article 34 of the Convention shall be made on the application form provided by the registry, unless the President of the Section concerned decides otherwise. It shall set out

(a) the name, date of birth, nationality, sex, occupation and address of the applicant;

(b) the name, occupation and address of the representative, if any;

(c) the name of the Contracting Party or Parties against which the application is made;

(d) a succinct statement of the facts;

(e) a succinct statement of the alleged violation(s) of the Convention and the relevant arguments;

(f) a succinct statement on the applicant's compliance with the admissibility criteria (exhaustion of domestic remedies and the six-month rule) laid down in Article 35 § 1 of the Convention; and

(g) the object of the application as well as a general indication of any claims for just satisfaction which the applicant may wish to make under Article 41 of the Convention; and be accompanied by

(h) copies of any relevant documents and in particular the decisions, whether judicial or not, relating to the object of the application.

2. Applicants shall furthermore

(a) provide information, notably the documents and decisions referred to in paragraph 1 (h) above, enabling it to be shown that the admissibility criteria (exhaustion of domestic remedies and the six-month rule) laid down in Article 35 § 1 of the Convention have been satisfied; and

(b) indicate whether they have submitted their complaints to any other procedure of international investigation or settlement.

3. Applicants who do not wish their identity to be disclosed to the public shall so indicate and shall submit a statement of the reasons justifying such a departure from the normal rule of public access to information in proceedings before the Court. The President of the Chamber may authorise anonymity in exceptional and duly justified cases.

4. Failure to comply with the requirements set out in paragraphs 1 and 2 above may result in the application not being registered and examined by the Court.

5. The date of introduction of the application shall as a general rule be considered to be the date of the first communication from the applicant setting out, even summarily, the object of the application. The Court may for good cause nevertheless decide that a different date shall be considered to be the date of introduction.

6. Applicants shall keep the Court informed of any change of address and of all circumstances relevant to the application.

CHAPTER III — JUDGE RAPPORTEURS

Rule 48   (Inter-State applications)

1. Where an application is made under Article 33 of the Convention, the Chamber constituted to consider the case shall designate one or more of its judges as Judge Rapporteur(s), who shall submit a report on admissibility when the written observations of the Contracting Parties concerned have been received. Rule 49 § 4 shall, in so far as appropriate, be applicable to this report.

2. After an application made under Article 33 of the Convention has been declared admissible, the Judge Rapporteur(s) shall submit such reports, drafts and other documents as may assist the Chamber in the carrying out of its functions.

Rule 49   (Individual applications)

1. Where an application is made under Article 34 of the Convention, the President of the Section to which the case has been assigned shall designate a judge as Judge Rapporteur, who shall examine the application.

2. In their examination of applications Judge Rapporteurs

(a) may request the parties to submit, within a specified time, any factual information, documents or other material which they consider to be relevant;

(b) shall, subject to the President of the Section directing that the case be considered by a Chamber, decide whether the application is to be considered by a Committee or by a Chamber.

3. Where a case is considered by a Committee in accordance with Article 28 of the Convention, the report of the Judge Rapporteur shall contain

(a) a brief statement of the relevant facts;

(b) a brief statement of the reasons underlying the proposal to declare the application inadmissible or to strike it out of the list.

4. Where a case is considered by a Chamber pursuant to Article 29 § 1 of the Convention, the report of the Judge Rapporteur shall contain

(a) a statement of the relevant facts, including any information obtained under paragraph 2 of this Rule;

(b) an indication of the issues arising under the Convention in the application;

(c) a proposal on admissibility and on any other action to be taken, together, if need be, with a provisional opinion on the merits.

5. After an application made under Article 34 of the Convention has been declared admissible, the Judge Rapporteur shall submit such reports, drafts and other documents as may assist the Chamber in the carrying out of its functions.

Rule 50   (Grand Chamber proceedings)

Where a case has been submitted to the Grand Chamber either under Article 30 or under Article 43 of the Convention, the President of the Grand Chamber shall designate as Judge Rapporteur(s) one or, in the case of an inter-State application, one or more of its members.

CHAPTER IV — PROCEEDINGS ON ADMISSIBILITY

Inter-State applications

Rule 51   1. When an application is made under Article 33 of the Convention, the President of the Court shall immediately give notice of the application to the respondent Contracting Party and shall assign the application to one of the Sections.

2. In accordance with Rule 26 § 1 (a), the judges elected in respect of the applicant and respondent Contracting Parties shall sit as *ex officio* members of the Chamber constituted to consider the case. Rule 30 shall apply if the application has been brought by several Contracting Parties or if applications with the same object brought by several Contracting Parties are being examined jointly under Rule 43 § 2.

3. On assignment of the case to a Section, the President of the Section shall constitute the Chamber in accordance with Rule 26 § 1 and shall invite the respondent Contracting Party to submit its observations in writing on the admissibility of the application. The observations so obtained shall be communicated by the Registrar to the applicant Contracting Party, which may submit written observations in reply.

4. Before ruling on the admissibility of the application, the Chamber may decide to invite the parties to submit further observations in writing.

5. A hearing on the admissibility shall be held if one or more of the Contracting Parties concerned so requests or if the Chamber so decides of its own motion.

6. After consulting the Parties, the President of the Chamber shall fix the written and, where appropriate, oral procedure and for that purpose shall lay down the time-limit within which any written observations are to be filed.

7. In its deliberations the Chamber shall take into consideration the report submitted by the Judge Rapporteur(s) under Rule 48 § 1.

Individual applications

Rule 52   (Assignment of applications to the Sections)

1. Any application made under Article 34 of the Convention shall be assigned to a Section by the President of the Court, who in so doing shall endeavour to ensure a fair distribution of cases between the Sections.

2. The Chamber of seven judges provided for in Article 27 § 1 of the Convention shall be constituted by the President of the Section concerned in accordance with Rule 26 § 1 once it has been decided that the application is to be considered by a Chamber.

3. Pending the constitution of a Chamber in accordance with the preceding paragraph, the President of the Section shall exercise any powers conferred on the President of the Chamber by these Rules.

Rule 53   (Procedure before a Committee)

1. In its deliberations the Committee shall take into consideration the report submitted by the Judge Rapporteur under Rule 49 § 3.

2. The Judge Rapporteur, if he or she is not a member of the Committee, may be invited to attend the deliberations of the Committee.

3. In accordance with Article 28 of the Convention, the Committee may, by a unanimous vote, declare inadmissible or strike out of the Court's list of cases an application where such a decision can be taken without further examination. This decision shall be final.

4. If no decision pursuant to paragraph 3 of the present Rule is taken, the application shall be forwarded to the Chamber constituted under Rule 52 § 2 to examine the case.

Rule 54   (Procedure before a Chamber)

1. In its deliberations the Chamber shall take into consideration the report submitted by the Judge Rapporteur under Rule 49 § 4.

2. The Chamber may at once declare the application inadmissible or strike it out of the Court's list of cases.

3. Alternatively, the Chamber may decide to

(a) request the parties to submit any factual information, documents or other material which it considers to be relevant;

(b) give notice of the application to the respondent Contracting Party and invite that Party to submit written observations on the application;

(c) invite the parties to submit further observations in writing.

4. Before taking its decision on admissibility, the Chamber may decide, either at the request of the parties or of its own motion, to hold a hearing. In that event, unless the Chamber shall exceptionally decide otherwise, the parties shall be invited also to address the issues arising in relation to the merits of the application.

5. The President of the Chamber shall fix the procedure, including time-limits, in relation to any decisions taken by the Chamber under paragraphs 3 and 4 of this Rule.

Inter-State and individual applications

Rule 55   (Pleas of inadmissibility)

Any plea of inadmissibility must, in so far as its character and the circumstances permit, be raised by the respondent Contracting Party in its written or oral observations on the admissibility of the application submitted as provided in Rule 51 or 54, as the case may be.

Rule 56   (Decision of a Chamber)

1. The decision of the Chamber shall state whether it was taken unanimously or by a majority and shall be accompanied or followed by reasons.

2. The decision of the Chamber shall be communicated by the Registrar to the applicant and to the Contracting Party or Parties concerned.

Rule 57   (Language of the decision)

1. Unless the Court decides that a decision shall be given in both official languages, all decisions shall be given either in English or in French. Decisions given shall be accessible to the public.

2. Publication of such decisions in the official reports of the Court, as provided for in Rule 78, shall be in both official languages of the Court.

CHAPTER V — PROCEEDINGS AFTER THE ADMISSION OF AN APPLICATION

Rule 58   (Inter-State applications)

1. Once the Chamber has decided to admit an application made under Article 33 of the Convention, the President of the Chamber shall, after consulting the Contracting Parties concerned, lay down the time-limits for the filing of written observations on the merits and for the production of any further evidence. The President may however, with the agreement of the Contracting Parties concerned, direct that a written procedure is to be dispensed with.

2. A hearing on the merits shall be held if one or more of the Contracting Parties concerned so requests or if the Chamber so decides of its own motion. The President of the Chamber shall fix the oral procedure.

3. In its deliberations the Chamber shall take into consideration any reports, drafts and other documents submitted by the Judge Rapporteur(s) under Rule 48 § 2.

Rule 59   (Individual applications)

1. Once the Chamber has decided to admit an application made under Article 34 of the Convention, it may invite the parties to submit further evidence and written observations.

2. A hearing on the merits shall be held if the Chamber so decides of its own motion or, provided that no hearing also addressing the merits has been held at the admissibility stage under Rule 54 § 4, if one of the parties so requests. However, the Chamber may exceptionally decide that the discharging of its functions under Article 38 § 1 (a) of the Convention does not require a hearing to be held.

3. The President of the Chamber shall, where appropriate, fix the written and oral procedure.

4. In its deliberations the Chamber shall take into consideration any reports, drafts and other documents submitted by the Judge Rapporteur under Rule 49 § 5.

Rule 60   (Claims for just satisfaction)

1. Any claim which the applicant Contracting Party or the applicant may wish to make for just satisfaction under Article 41 of the Convention shall, unless the President of the Chamber directs otherwise, be set out in the written observations on the merits or, if no such written observations are filed, in a special document filed no later than two months after the decision declaring the application admissible.

2. Itemised particulars of all claims made, together with the relevant supporting documents or vouchers, shall be submitted, failing which the Chamber may reject the claim in whole or in part.

3. The Chamber may, at any time during the proceedings, invite any party to submit comments on the claim for just satisfaction.

Rule 61   (Third-party intervention)

1. The decision declaring an application admissible shall be notified by the Registrar to any Contracting Party one of whose nationals is an applicant in the case, as well as to the respondent Contracting Party under Rule 56 § 2.

2. Where a Contracting Party seeks to exercise its right to submit written comments or to take part in an oral hearing, pursuant to Article 36 § 1 of the Convention, the President of the Chamber shall fix the procedure to be followed.

3. In accordance with Article 36 § 2 of the Convention, the President of the Chamber may, in the interests of the proper administration of justice, invite or grant leave to any Contracting State which is not a party to the proceedings, or any person concerned who is not the applicant, to submit written comments or, in exceptional cases, to take part in an oral hearing. Requests for leave for this purpose must be duly reasoned and submitted in one of the official languages, within a reasonable time after the fixing of the written procedure.

4. Any invitation or grant of leave referred to in paragraph 3 of this Rule shall be subject to any conditions, including time-limits, set by the President of the Chamber. Where such conditions are not complied with, the President may decide not to include the comments in the case file.

5. Written comments submitted in accordance with this Rule shall be submitted in one of the official languages, save where leave to use another language has been granted under Rule 34 § 4. They shall be transmitted by the Registrar to the parties to the case, who shall be entitled, subject to any conditions, including time-limits, set by the President of the Chamber, to file written observations in reply.

Rule 62   (Friendly settlement)

1. Once an application has been declared admissible, the Registrar, acting on the instructions of the Chamber or its President, shall enter into contact with the parties with a view to securing a friendly settlement of the matter in accordance with Article 38 § 1 (b) of the Convention. The Chamber shall take any steps that appear appropriate to facilitate such a settlement.

2. In accordance with Article 38 § 2 of the Convention, the friendly settlement negotiations shall be confidential and without prejudice to the parties' arguments in the contentious proceedings. No written or oral communication and no offer or concession made in the framework of the attempt to secure a friendly settlement may be referred to or relied on in the contentious proceedings.

3. If the Chamber is informed by the Registrar that the parties have agreed to a friendly settlement, it shall, after verifying that the settlement has been reached on the basis of respect for human rights as defined in the Convention and the protocols thereto, strike the case out of the Court's list in accordance with Rule 44 § 2.

CHAPTER VI — HEARINGS

Rule 63   (Conduct of hearings)

1. The President of the Chamber shall direct hearings and shall prescribe the order in which Agents and advocates or advisers of the parties shall be called upon to speak.

2. Where a fact-finding hearing is being carried out by a delegation of the Chamber under Rule 42, the head of the delegation shall conduct the hearing and the delegation shall exercise any relevant power conferred on the Chamber by the Convention or these Rules.

Rule 64   (Failure to appear at a hearing)

Where, without showing sufficient cause, a party fails to appear, the Chamber may, provided that it is satisfied that such a course is consistent with the proper administration of justice, nonetheless proceed with the hearing.

Rule 65   (Convocation of witnesses, experts and other persons; costs of their appearance)

1. Witnesses, experts and other persons whom the Chamber or the President of the Chamber decides to hear shall be summoned by the Registrar.

2. The summons shall indicate

(a) the case in connection with which it has been issued;

(b) the object of the inquiry, expert opinion or other measure ordered by the Chamber or the President of the Chamber;

(c) any provisions for the payment of the sum due to the person summoned.

3. If the persons concerned appear at the request or on behalf of an applicant or respondent Contracting Party, the costs of their appearance shall be borne by that Party unless the Chamber decides otherwise. In other cases, the Chamber shall decide whether such costs are to be borne by the Council of Europe or awarded against the applicant or third party at whose request the person summoned appeared. In all cases the costs shall be taxed by the President of the Chamber.

Rule 66   (Oath or solemn declaration by witnesses and experts)

1. After the establishment of the identity of the witness and before testifying, every witness shall take the following oath or make the following solemn declaration:

"I swear" – or "I solemnly declare upon my honour and conscience" – "that I shall speak the truth, the whole truth and nothing but the truth."

This act shall be recorded in minutes.

2. After the establishment of the identity of the expert and before carrying out his or her task, every expert shall take the following oath or make the following solemn declaration:

"I swear" – or "I solemnly declare" – "that I will discharge my duty as an expert honourably and conscientiously."

This act shall be recorded in minutes.

3. This oath may be taken or this declaration made before the President of the Chamber, or before a judge or any public authority nominated by the President.

Rule 67   (Objection to a witness or expert; hearing of a person for information purposes)

The Chamber shall decide in the event of any dispute arising from an objection to a witness or expert. It may hear for information purposes a person who cannot be heard as a witness.

Rule 68   (Questions put during hearings)

1. Any judge may put questions to the Agents, advocates or advisers of the parties, to the applicant, witnesses and experts, and to any other persons appearing before the Chamber.

2. The witnesses, experts and other persons referred to in Rule 42 § 1 may, subject to the control of the President of the Chamber, be examined by the Agents and advocates or advisers of the parties. In the event of an objection as to the relevance of a question put, the President of the Chamber shall decide.

Rule 69 (Failure to appear, refusal to give evidence or false evidence)

If, without good reason, a witness or any other person who has been duly summoned fails to appear or refuses to give evidence, the Registrar shall, on being so required by the President of the Chamber, inform the Contracting Party to whose jurisdiction the witness or other person is subject. The same provisions shall apply if a witness or expert has, in the opinion of the Chamber, violated the oath or solemn declaration provided for in Rule 66.

Rule 70 (Verbatim record of hearings)

1. The Registrar shall, if the Chamber so directs, be responsible for the making of a verbatim record of a hearing. The verbatim record shall include

(a) the composition of the Chamber at the hearing;

(b) a list of those appearing before the Court, that is to say Agents, advocates and advisers of the parties and any third party taking part;

(c) the surnames, forenames, description and address of each witness, expert or other person heard;

(d) the text of statements made, questions put and replies given;

(e) the text of any decision delivered during the hearing by the Chamber or the President of the Chamber.

2. If all or part of the verbatim record is in a non-official language, the Registrar shall, if the Chamber so directs, arrange for its translation into one of the official languages.

3. The representatives of the parties shall receive a copy of the verbatim record in order that they may, subject to the control of the Registrar or the President of the Chamber, make corrections, but in no case may such corrections affect the sense and bearing of what was said. The Registrar shall lay down, in accordance with the instructions of the President of the Chamber, the time-limits granted for this purpose.

4. The verbatim record, once so corrected, shall be signed by the President and the Registrar and shall then constitute certified matters of record.

CHAPTER VII — PROCEEDINGS BEFORE THE GRAND CHAMBER

Rule 71 (Applicability of procedural provisions)

Any provisions governing proceedings before the Chambers shall apply, *mutatis mutandis*, to proceedings before the Grand Chamber.

Rule 72   (Relinquishment of jurisdiction by a Chamber in favour of the Grand Chamber)

1. In accordance with Article 30 of the Convention, where a case pending before a Chamber raises a serious question affecting the interpretation of the Convention or the protocols thereto or where the resolution of a question before it might have a result inconsistent with a judgment previously delivered by the Court, the Chamber may, at any time before it has rendered its judgment, relinquish jurisdiction in favour of the Grand Chamber, unless one of the parties to the case has objected in accordance with paragraph 2 of this Rule. Reasons need not be given for the decision to relinquish.

2. The Registrar shall notify the parties of the Chamber's intention to relinquish jurisdiction. The parties shall have one month from the date of that notification within which to file at the Registry a duly reasoned objection. An objection which does not fulfil these conditions shall be considered invalid by the Chamber.

Rule 73   (Request by a party for referral of a case to the Grand Chamber)

1. In accordance with Article 43 of the Convention, any party to a case may exceptionally, within a period of three months from the date of delivery of the judgment of a Chamber, file in writing at the Registry a request that the case be referred to the Grand Chamber. The party shall specify in its request the serious question affecting the interpretation or application of the Convention or the protocols thereto, or the serious issue of general importance, which in its view warrants consideration by the Grand Chamber.

2. A panel of five judges of the Grand Chamber constituted in accordance with Rule 24 § 6 shall examine the request solely on the basis of the existing case file. It shall accept the request only if it considers that the case does raise such a question or issue. Reasons need not be given for a refusal of the request.

3. If the panel accepts the request, the Grand Chamber shall decide the case by means of a judgment.

CHAPTER VIII — JUDGMENTS

Rule 74   (Contents of the judgment)

1. A judgment as referred to in Articles 42 and 44 of the Convention shall contain

(a) the names of the President and the other judges constituting the Chamber concerned, and the name of the Registrar or the Deputy Registrar;

(b) the dates on which it was adopted and delivered;

(c) a description of the parties;

(d) the names of the Agents, advocates or advisers of the parties;

(e) an account of the procedure followed;

(f) the facts of the case;

(g) a summary of the submissions of the parties;

(h) the reasons in point of law;

(i) the operative provisions;

(j) the decision, if any, in respect of costs;

(k) the number of judges constituting the majority;

(l) where appropriate, a statement as to which text is authentic.

2. Any judge who has taken part in the consideration of the case shall be entitled to annex to the judgment either a separate opinion, concurring with or dissenting from that judgment, or a bare statement of dissent.

Rule 75 (Ruling on just satisfaction)

1. Where the Chamber finds that there has been a violation of the Convention, it shall give in the same judgment a ruling on the application of Article 41 of the Convention if that question, after being raised in accordance with Rule 60, is ready for decision; if the question is not ready for decision, the Chamber shall reserve it in whole or in part and shall fix the further procedure.

2. For the purposes of ruling on the application of Article 41 of the Convention, the Chamber shall, as far as possible, be composed of those judges who sat to consider the merits of the case. Where it is not possible to constitute the original Chamber, the President of the Court shall complete or compose the Chamber by drawing lots.

3. The Chamber may, when affording just satisfaction under Article 41 of the Convention, direct that if settlement is not made within a specified time, interest is to be payable on any sums awarded.

4. If the Court is informed that an agreement has been reached between the injured party and the Contracting Party liable, it shall verify the equitable nature of the agreement and, where it finds the agreement to be equitable, strike the case out of the list in accordance with Rule 44 § 2.

Rule 76 (Language of the judgment)

1. Unless the Court decides that a judgment shall be given in both official languages, all judgments shall be given either in English or in French. Judgments given shall be accessible to the public.

2. Publication of such judgments in the official reports of the Court, as provided for in Rule 78, shall be in both official languages of the Court.

Rule 77 (Signature, delivery and notification of the judgment)

1. Judgments shall be signed by the President of the Chamber and the Registrar.

2. The judgment may be read out at a public hearing by the President of the Chamber or by another judge delegated by him or her. The Agents and representatives of the parties shall be informed in due time of the date

of the hearing. Otherwise the notification provided for in paragraph 3 of this Rule shall constitute delivery of the judgment.

3. The judgment shall be transmitted to the Committee of Ministers. The Registrar shall send certified copies to the parties, to the Secretary General of the Council of Europe, to any third party and to any other person directly concerned. The original copy, duly signed and sealed, shall be placed in the archives of the Court.

Rule 78   (Publication of judgments and other documents)

In accordance with Article 44 § 3 of the Convention, final judgments of the Court shall be published, under the responsibility of the Registrar, in an appropriate form. The Registrar shall in addition be responsible for the publication of official reports of selected judgments and decisions and of any document which the President of the Court considers it useful to publish.

Rule 79   (Request for interpretation of a judgment)

1. A party may request the interpretation of a judgment within a period of one year following the delivery of that judgment.

2. The request shall be filed with the Registry. It shall state precisely the point or points in the operative provisions of the judgment on which interpretation is required.

3. The original Chamber may decide of its own motion to refuse the request on the ground that there is no reason to warrant considering it. Where it is not possible to constitute the original Chamber, the President of the Court shall complete or compose the Chamber by drawing lots.

4. If the Chamber does not refuse the request, the Registrar shall communicate it to the other party or parties and shall invite them to submit any written comments within a time-limit laid down by the President of the Chamber. The President of the Chamber shall also fix the date of the hearing should the Chamber decide to hold one. The Chamber shall decide by means of a judgment.

Rule 80   (Request for revision of a judgment)

1. A party may, in the event of the discovery of a fact which might by its nature have a decisive influence and which, when a judgment was delivered, was unknown to the Court and could not reasonably have been known to that party, request the Court, within a period of six months after that party acquired knowledge of the fact, to revise that judgment.

2. The request shall mention the judgment of which revision is requested and shall contain the information necessary to show that the conditions laid down in paragraph 1 have been complied with. It shall be accompanied by a copy of all supporting documents. The request and supporting documents shall be filed with the Registry.

3. The original Chamber may decide of its own motion to refuse the request on the ground that there is no reason to warrant considering it.

Where it is not possible to constitute the original Chamber, the President of the Court shall complete or compose the Chamber by drawing lots.

4. If the Chamber does not refuse the request, the Registrar shall communicate it to the other party or parties and shall invite them to submit any written comments within a time-limit laid down by the President of the Chamber. The President of the Chamber shall also fix the date of the hearing should the Chamber decide to hold one. The Chamber shall decide by means of a judgment.

Rule 81 (Rectification of errors in decisions and judgments)

Without prejudice to the provisions on revision of judgments and on restoration to the list of applications, the Court may, of its own motion or at the request of a party made within one month of the delivery of a decision or a judgment, rectify clerical errors, errors in calculation or obvious mistakes.

CHAPTER IX — ADVISORY OPINIONS

Rule 82 In proceedings relating to advisory opinions the Court shall apply, in addition to the provisions of Articles 47, 48 and 49 of the Convention, the provisions which follow. It shall also apply the other provisions of these Rules to the extent to which it considers this to be appropriate.

Rule 83 The request for an advisory opinion shall be filed with the Registry. It shall state fully and precisely the question on which the opinion of the Court is sought, and also

(a) the date on which the Committee of Ministers adopted the decision referred to in Article 47 § 3 of the Convention;

(b) the names and addresses of the person or persons appointed by the Committee of Ministers to give the Court any explanations which it may require.

The request shall be accompanied by all documents likely to elucidate the question.

Rule 84 1. On receipt of a request, the Registrar shall transmit a copy of it to all members of the Court.

2. The Registrar shall inform the Contracting Parties that the Court is prepared to receive their written comments.

Rule 85 1. The President of the Court shall lay down the time-limits for filing written comments or other documents.

2. Written comments or other documents shall be filed with the Registry. The Registrar shall transmit copies of them to all the members of the Court, to the Committee of Ministers and to each of the Contracting Parties.

Rule 86   After the close of the written procedure, the President of the Court shall decide whether the Contracting Parties which have submitted written comments are to be given an opportunity to develop them at an oral hearing held for the purpose.

Rule 87   If the Court considers that the request for an advisory opinion is not within its consultative competence as defined in Article 47 of the Convention, it shall so declare in a reasoned decision.

Rule 88   1. Advisory opinions shall be given by a majority vote of the Grand Chamber. They shall mention the number of judges constituting the majority.

2. Any judge may, if he or she so desires, attach to the opinion of the Court either a separate opinion, concurring with or dissenting from the advisory opinion, or a bare statement of dissent.

Rule 89   The advisory opinion shall be read out in one of the two official languages by the President of the Court, or by another judge delegated by the President, at a public hearing, prior notice having been given to the Committee of Ministers and to each of the Contracting Parties.

Rule 90   The opinion, or any decision given under Rule 87, shall be signed by the President of the Court and by the Registrar. The original copy, duly signed and sealed, shall be placed in the archives of the Court. The Registrar shall send certified copies to the Committee of Ministers, to the Contracting Parties and to the Secretary General of the Council of Europe.

CHAPTER X — LEGAL AID

Rule 91   1. The President of the Chamber may, either at the request of an applicant lodging an application under Article 34 of the Convention or of his or her own motion, grant free legal aid to the applicant in connection with the presentation of the case from the moment when observations in writing on the admissibility of that application are received from the respondent Contracting Party in accordance with Rule 54 § 3 (b), or where the time-limit for their submission has expired.

2. Subject to Rule 96, where the applicant has been granted legal aid in connection with the presentation of his or her case before the Chamber, that grant shall continue in force for purposes of his or her representation before the Grand Chamber.

Rule 92   Legal aid shall be granted only where the President of the Chamber is satisfied

(a) that it is necessary for the proper conduct of the case before the Chamber;

(b) that the applicant has insufficient means to meet all or part of the costs entailed.

Rule 93   1. In order to determine whether or not applicants have sufficient means to meet all or part of the costs entailed, they shall be required to complete a form of declaration stating their income, capital assets and any financial commitments in respect of dependants, or any other financial obligations. The declaration shall be certified by the appropriate domestic authority or authorities.

2. The Contracting Party concerned shall be requested to submit its comments in writing.

3. After receiving the information mentioned in paragraphs 1 and 2 above, the President of the Chamber shall decide whether or not to grant legal aid. The Registrar shall inform the parties accordingly.

Rule 94   1. Fees shall be payable to the advocates or other persons appointed in accordance with Rule 36 § 4. Fees may, where appropriate, be paid to more than one such representative.

2. Legal aid may be granted to cover not only representatives' fees but also travelling and subsistence expenses and other necessary expenses incurred by the applicant or appointed representative.

Rule 95   On a decision to grant legal aid, the Registrar shall

(a) fix the rate of fees to be paid in accordance with the legal-aid scales in force;

(b) the level of expenses to be paid.

Rule 96   The President of the Chamber may, if satisfied that the conditions stated in Rule 92 are no longer fulfilled, revoke or vary a grant of legal aid at any time.

TITLE III — TRANSITIONAL RULES

Rule 97   (Judges' terms of office)

The duration of the terms of office of the judges who were members of the Court at the date of the entry into force of Protocol No. 11 to the Convention shall be calculated as from that date.

Rule 98   (Presidency of the Sections)

For a period of three years from the entry into force of Protocol No. 11 to the Convention,

(a) the two Presidents of Sections who are not simultaneously Vice-Presidents of the Court and the Vice-Presidents of the Sections shall be elected for a term of office of eighteen months;

(b) the Vice-Presidents of the Sections may not be immediately re-elected.

Rule 99   (Relations between the Court and the Commission)

1. In cases brought before the Court under Article 5 §§ 4 and 5 of Protocol No. 11 to the Convention the Court may invite the Commission to

delegate one or more of its members to take part in the consideration of the case before the Court.

2. In cases referred to in the preceding paragraph the Court shall take into consideration the report of the Commission adopted pursuant to former Article 31 of the Convention.

3. Unless the President of the Chamber decides otherwise, the said report shall be made available to the public through the Registrar as soon as possible after the case has been brought before the Court.

4. The remainder of the case file of the Commission, including all pleadings, in cases brought before the Court under Article 5 §§ 2 to 5 of Protocol No. 11 shall remain confidential unless the President of the Chamber decides otherwise.

5. In cases where the Commission has taken evidence but has been unable to adopt a report in accordance with former Article 31 of the Convention, the Court shall take into consideration the verbatim records, documentation and opinion of the Commission's delegations arising from such investigations.

Rule 100 (Chamber and Grand Chamber proceedings)

1. In cases referred to the Court under Article 5 § 4 of Protocol No. 11 to the Convention, a panel of the Grand Chamber constituted in accordance with Rule 24 § 6 shall determine, solely on the basis of the existing case file, whether a Chamber or the Grand Chamber is to decide the case.

2. If the case is decided by a Chamber, the judgment of the Chamber shall, in accordance with Article 5 § 4 of Protocol No. 11, be final and Rule 73 shall be inapplicable.

3. Cases transmitted to the Court under Article 5 § 5 of Protocol No. 11 shall be forwarded by the President of the Court to the Grand Chamber.

4. For each case transmitted to the Grand Chamber under Article 5 § 5 of the Protocol No 11, the Grand Chamber shall be completed by judges designated by rotation within one of the groups mentioned in Rule 24 § 3, the cases being allocated to the groups on an alternate basis.

Rule 101 (Grant of legal aid)

Subject to Rule 96, in cases brought before the Court under Article 5 §§ 2 to 5 of Protocol No. 11 to the Convention, a grant of legal aid made to an applicant in the proceedings before the Commission or the former Court shall continue in force for the purposes of his or her representation before the Court.

Rule 102 (Request for interpretation or revision of a judgment)

1. Where a party requests interpretation or revision of a judgment delivered by the former Court, the President of the Court shall assign the request to one of the Sections in accordance with the conditions laid down in Rule 51 or 52, as the case may be.

2. The President of the relevant Section shall, notwithstanding Rules 79 § 3 and 80 § 3, constitute a new Chamber to consider the request.

3. The Chamber to be constituted shall include as *ex officio* members

(a) the President of the Section; and, whether or not they are members of the relevant Section,

(b) the judge elected in respect of any Contracting Party concerned or, if he or she is unable to sit, any judge appointed under Rule 29;

(c) any judge of the Court who was a member of the original Chamber that delivered the judgment in the former Court.

4. (a) The other members of the Chamber shall be designated by the President of the Section by means of a drawing of lots from among the members of the relevant Section.

(b) The members of the Section who are not so designated shall sit in the case as substitute judges.

TITLE IV — FINAL CLAUSES

Rule 103 (Amendment or suspension of a Rule)

1. Any Rule may be amended upon a motion made after notice where such a motion is carried at the next session of the plenary Court by a majority of all the members of the Court. Notice of such a motion shall be delivered in writing to the Registrar at least one month before the session at which it is to be discussed. On receipt of such a notice of motion, the Registrar shall inform all members of the Court at the earliest possible moment.

2. A Rule relating to the internal working of the Court may be suspended upon a motion made without notice, provided that this decision is taken unanimously by the Chamber concerned. The suspension of a Rule shall in this case be limited in its operation to the particular purpose for which it was sought.

Rule 104 (Entry into force of the Rules)

The present Rules shall enter into force on 1 November 1998.

2. European Convention for the Prevention of Torture and Inhuman or Degrading Treatment or Punishment

The purpose of the European Convention for the Prevention of Torture is to enable the supervision of persons deprived of their liberty and to prevent ill-treatment or torture of such persons. The Committee established under this Convention is conceived as a proactive non-judicial mechanism besides the existing reactive judicial mechanism under the European Convention on Human Rights. The Committee has a fact-finding and reporting function. It is empowered to carry out visits of a periodic nature and also *ad hoc* visits to places of detention in order to examine the treatment of the persons deprived of their liberty. Periodic visits are undertaken to all contracting parties on a regular basis; *ad hoc* visits only when it appears to the Committee that the circumstances so require. States parties agree to allow visits to any place within their jurisdiction where persons are deprived of their liberty; only in exceptional cases the State concerned may make representations against a visit on grounds of national defence, public safety, serious disorder, the medical conditions of a person. After each visit the Committee draws up a report for transmission to the party concerned; this report is made public only after approval of the State concerned. When a State party refuses co-operation, the Committee may, by a two-thirds majority, issue a public statement. The Committee makes an annual report on its activities to the Committee of Ministers, which is transmitted to the Parliamentary Assembly and made public.

Texts

European Treaty Series No. 126
BGBl. 1989 II, 946

Bibliographical notes

A. Cassese, A New Approach to Human Rights: The European Convention for the Prevention of Torture, AJIL 83 (1989), 128 et seq.

K. Ginther, The European Convention for the Prevention of Torture and Inhuman and Degrading Treatment or Punishment, European Journal of International Law 2 (1991), 123–131

M.Evans/R. Morgan, The European Convention for the Prevention of Torture: Operational Practice, ICLQ 41 (1992), 590 et seq.

J. Murdoch, The Work of the Council of Europe's Torture Committee, EJIL 5 (1994) 220–248

M. Evans/R. Morgan, The European Torture Committee: Membership Issues, EJIL
    5 (1994), 249–258

a) Text of the Convention of November 26, 1989

The member States of the Council of Europe, signatory hereto,

Having regard to the provisions of the Convention for the Protection of Human Rights and Fundamental Freedoms;

Recalling that, under Article 3 of the same Convention, "no one shall be subjected to torture or to inhuman or degrading treatment or punishment";

Noting that the machinery provided for in that Convention operates in relation to persons who allege that they are victims of violations of Article 3;

Convinced that the protection of persons deprived of their liberty against torture and inhuman or degrading treatment or punishment could be strengthened by non-judicial means of a preventive character based on visits,

Have agreed as follows:

CHAPTER I

Art. 1   There shall be established a European Committee for the Prevention of Torture and Inhuman or Degrading Treatment or Punishment (hereinafter referred to as "the Committee"). The Committee shall, by means of visits, examine the treatment of persons deprived of their liberty with a view to strengthening, if necessary, the protection of such persons from torture and from inhuman or degrading treatment or punishment.

Art. 2   Each Party shall permit visits, in accordance with this Convention, to any place within its jurisdiction where persons are deprived of their liberty by a public authority.

Art. 3   In the application of this Convention, the Committee and the competent national authorities of the Party concerned shall co-operate with each other.

CHAPTER II

Art. 4   1. The Committee shall consist of a number of members equal to that of the Parties.

2. The members of the Committee shall be chosen from among persons of high moral character, known for their competence in the field of human rights or having professional experience in the areas covered by this Convention.

3. No two members of the Committee may be nationals of the same State.

4. The members shall serve in their individual capacity, shall be independent and impartial, and shall be available to serve the Committee effectively.

Art. 5   1. The members of the Committee shall be elected by the Committee of Ministers of the Council of Europe by an absolute majority of votes, from a list of names drawn up by the Bureau of the Consultative Assembly of the Council of Europe; each national delegation of the Parties in the Consultative Assembly shall put forward three candidates, of whom two at least shall be its nationals.

2. The same procedure shall be followed in filling casual vacancies.

3. The members of the Committee shall be elected for a period of four years. They may only be re-elected once. However, among the members elected at the first election, the terms of three members shall expire at the end of two years. The members whose terms are to expire at the end of the initial period of two years shall be chosen by lot by the Secretary General of the Council of Europe immediately after the first election has been completed.

Art. 6   1. The Committee shall meet *in camera*. A quorum shall be equal to the majority of its members. The decisions of the Committee shall be taken by a majority of the members present, subject to the provisions of Article 10, paragraph 2.

2. The Committee shall draw up its own rules of procedure.

3. The Secretariat of the Committee shall be provided by the Secretary General of the Council of Europe.

CHAPTER III

Art. 7   1. The Committee shall organise visits to places referred to in Article 2. Apart from periodic visits, the Committee may organise such other visits as appear to it to be required in the circumstances.

2. As a general rule, the visits shall be carried out by at least two members of the Committee. The Committee may, if it considers it necessary, be assisted by experts and interpreters.

Art. 8   1. The Committee shall notify the Government of the Party concerned of its intention to carry out a visit. After such notification, it may at any time visit any place referred to in Article 2.

2. A Party shall provide the Committee with the following facilities to carry out its task:

a. access to its territory and the right to travel without restriction;

b. full information on the places where persons deprived of their liberty are being held;

c. unlimited access to any place where persons are deprived of their liberty, including the right to move inside such places without restriction;

d. other information available to the Party which is necessary for the Committee to carry out its task. In seeking such information, the Committee shall have regard to applicable rules of national law and professional ethics.

3. The Committee may interview in private persons deprived of their liberty.

4. The Committee may communicate freely with any person whom it believes can supply relevant information.

5. If necessary, the Committee may immediately communicate observations to the competent authorities of the Party concerned.

Art. 9   1. In exceptional circumstances, the competent authorities of the Party concerned may make representations to the Committee against a visit at the time or to the particular place proposed by the Committee. Such representations may only be made on grounds of national defence, public safety, serious disorder in places where persons are deprived of their liberty, the medical condition of a person or that an urgent interrogation relating to a serious crime is in progress.

2. Following such representations, the Committee and the Party shall immediately enter into consultations in order to clarify the situation and seek agreement on arrangements to enable the Committee to exercise its functions expeditiously. Such arrangements may include the transfer to another place of any person whom the Committee proposed to visit. Until the visit takes place, the Party shall provide information to the Committee about any person concerned.

Art. 10 1. After each visit, the Committee shall draw up a report on the facts found during the visit, taking account of any observations which may have been submitted by the Party concerned. It shall transmit to the latter its report containing any recommendations it considers necessary. The Committee may consult with the Party with a view to suggesting, if necessary, improvements in the protection of persons deprived of their liberty.

2. If the Party fails to co-operate or refuses to improve the situation in the light of the Committee's recommendations, the Committee may decide, after the Party has had an opportunity to make known its views, by a majority of two-thirds of its members to make a public statement on the matter.

Art. 11 1. The information gathered by the Committee in relation to a visit, its report and its consultations with the Party concerned shall be confidential.

2. The Committee shall publish its report, together with any comments of the Party concerned, whenever requested to do so by that Party.

3. However, no personal data shall be published without the express consent of the person concerned.

Art. 12   Subject to the rules of confidentiality in Article 11, the Committee shall every year submit to the Committee of Ministers a general report on its activities which shall be transmitted to the Consultative Assembly and made public.

Art. 13   The members of the Committee, experts and other persons assisting the Committee are required, during and after their terms of office, to maintain the confidentiality of the facts or information of which they have become aware during the discharge of their functions.

Art. 14   1. The names of persons assisting the Committee shall be specified in the notification under Article 8, paragraph 1.

2. Experts shall act on the instructions and under the authority of the Committee. They shall have particular knowledge and experience in the areas covered by this Convention and shall be bound by the same duties of independence, impartiality and availability as the members of the Committee.

3. A Party may exceptionally declare that an expert or other person assisting the Committee may not be allowed to take part in a visit to a place within its jurisdiction.

CHAPTER IV

Art. 15   Each Party shall inform the Committee of the name and address of the authority competent to receive notifications to its Government, and of any liaison officer it may appoint.

Art. 16   The Committee, its members and experts referred to in Article 7, paragraph 2, shall enjoy the privileges and immunities set out in the annex to this Convention.

Art. 17   1. This Convention shall not prejudice the provisions of domestic law or any international agreement which provide greater protection for persons deprived of their liberty.

2. Nothing in this Convention shall be construed as limiting or derogating from the competence of the organs of the European Convention on Human Rights or from the obligations assumed by the Parties under that Convention.

3. The Committee shall not visit places which representatives or delegates of protecting powers or the International Committee of the Red Cross effectively visit on a regular basis by virtue of the Geneva Conventions of 12 August 1949 and the Additional Protocols of 8 June 1977 thereto.

CHAPTER V

Art. 18   This Convention shall be open for signature by the member States of the Council of Europe. It is subject to ratification, acceptance or approval.

Instruments of ratification, acceptance or approval shall be deposited with the Secretary General of the Council of Europe.

Art. 19 1. This Convention shall enter into force on the first day of the month following the expiration of a period of three months after the date on which seven member States of the Council of Europe have expressed their consent to be bound by the Convention in accordance with the provisions of Article 18.

2. In respect of any member State which subsequently expresses its consent to be bound by it, the Convention shall enter into force on the first day of the month following the expiration of a period of three months after the date of the deposit of the instrument of ratification, acceptance or approval.

Art. 20 1. Any State may at the time of signature or when depositing its instrument of ratification, acceptance or approval, specify the territory or territories to which this Convention shall apply.

2. Any State may at any later date, by a declaration addressed to the Secretary General of the Council of Europe, extend the application of this Convention to any other territory specified in the declaration. In respect of such territory the Convention shall enter into force on the first day of the month following the expiration of a period of three months after the date of receipt of such declaration by the Secretary General.

3. Any declaration made under the two preceding paragraphs may, in respect of any territory specified in such declaration, be withdrawn by a notification addressed to the Secretary General. The withdrawal shall become effective on the first day of the month following the expiration of a period of three months after the date of receipt of such notification by the Secretary General.

Art. 21 No reservation may be made in respect of the provisions of this Convention.

Art. 22 1. Any Party may, at any time, denounce this Convention by means of a notification addressed to the Secretary General of the Council of Europe.

2. Such denunciation shall become effective on the first day of the month following the expiration of a period of twelve months after the date of receipt of the notification by the Secretary General.

Art. 23 The Secretary General of the Council of Europe shall notify the member States of the Council of Europe of:

a. any signature;

b. the deposit of any instrument of ratification, acceptance or approval;

c. any date of entry into force of this Convention in accordance with Articles 19 and 20;

d. any other act, notification or communication relating to this Convention, except for action taken in pursuance of Articles 8 and 10.

b) Rules of Procedure of the European Committee for the Prevention of Torture and Inhuman or Degrading Treatment or Punishment of May 11, 1990

TITLE I: ORGANISATION OF THE COMMITTEE

CHAPTER I: MEMBERS OF THE COMMITTEE

Rule 1   (Calculation of term of office)

(1) The duration of the term of office of a member of the Committee shall be calculated as from his election, unless the Committee of Ministers stipulates otherwise when proceeding to the election. However, when a member is re-elected on the expiry of his term of office or is elected to replace a member whose term of office has expired or is about to expire, the duration of his term of office shall be calculated as from the day following the date of such expiry.

(2) A member elected to replace a member whose term of office has not expired shall be elected for a four year term of office.

Rule 2   (Solemn declaration)

Before taking up his duties, each member of the Committee shall, at the first meeting of the Committee at which he is present after his election, make the following solemn declaration:

"I solemnly declare that I will exercise my functions as a member of this Committee honourably, independently, impartially and conscientiously and that I will keep secret all Committee proceedings".

Rule 3   (Precedence)

(1) Members of the Committee shall take precedence after the President and Vice-Presidents according to the length of time they have been in office.

(2) Members having the same length of time in office shall take precedence according to age.

(3) Re-elected members shall take precedence having regard to the duration of their previous term of office.

Rule 4   (Resignation)

Resignation of a member of the Committee shall be notified to the President, who shall transmit it to the Secretary General of the Council of Europe.

CHAPTER II: PRESIDENCY OF THE COMMITTEE

Rule 5   (Election of the President and Vice-Presidents)

(1) The Committee shall elect from among its members a President and a first and second Vice-President.

(2) The President and Vice-Presidents shall be elected for a term of two years. They may be re-elected. However, the term of office of the President or of a Vice-President shall end if he ceases to be a member of the Committee.

(3) If the President or a Vice-President ceases to be a member of the Committee or resigns his office of President or Vice-President before its normal expiry, the Committee may elect a successor for the remainder of the term of that office.

(4) The elections referred to in this Rule shall be held by secret ballot. Election shall be by a majority of the members present.

(5) If no candidate is elected after the first ballot, a second ballot shall take place between the two candidates who have received most votes; in the case of equal voting, the candidate having precedence under Rule 3 shall take part in the second ballot. If necessary, a third ballot shall take place between the two candidates concerned. The candidate who receives the most votes in such a third ballot or, in the case of equal voting, who has precedence under Rule 3, shall be declared elected.

(6) If there are only two candidates for a vacant office and neither of the candidates is elected after the first ballot, a second ballot shall take place. The candidate who receives the most votes in such a second ballot or, in the case of equal voting, who has precedence under Rule3, shall be declared elected.

Rule 6   (Functions of the President)

(1) The President shall chair the meetings of the Committee and shall perform all other functions conferred upon him by these Rules of Procedure and by the Committee.

(2) In exercising his functions, the President shall remain under the authority of the Committee.

(3) The President may delegate certain of his functions to either Vice-President.

Rule 7   (Functions of the Vice-Presidents)

The first Vice-President shall take the place of the President if the latter is unable to carry out his duties or if the office of President is vacant. The second Vice-President shall replace the first Vice-President if the latter is unable to carry out his duties or if the office of first Vice-President is vacant.

Rule 8   (Replacement of the President and Vice-Presidents)

If the President and Vice-Presidents are at the same time unable to carry out their duties or if their offices are at the same time vacant, the duties of President shall be carried out by another member of the Committee according to the order of precedence laid down in Rule 3.

Rule 9   (Obstacle to the exercise of the functions of President)
          No member of the Committee shall preside when the report on a visit to
          the State Party in respect of which he was elected is being considered.

CHAPTER III: BUREAU OF THE COMMITTEE

Rule 10   (1) The Bureau of the Committee shall consist of the President and Vice-
          Presidents. If one or more members of the Bureau are unable to carry out
          their duties, they shall be replaced by other members of the Committee in
          accordance with the rules of precedence laid down in Rule 3.

          (2) The Bureau shall direct the work of the Committee and shall perform
          all other functions conferred upon it by these Rules of Procedure and by
          the Committee.

CHAPTER IV: SECRETARIAT OF THE COMMITTEE

Rule 11   The Secretariat of the Committee shall consist of a Secretary and other
          staff members appointed by the Secretary General of the Council of
          Europe.

TITLE II: WORKING OF THE COMMITTEE: GENERAL RULES

CHAPTER 1: SEAT OF THE COMMITTEE AND LANGUAGES

Rule 12   (Seat of the Committee)
          The seat of the Committee shall be in Strasbourg.

Rule 13   (Languages)
          The official and working languages of the Committee shall be English and
          French.

CHAPTER II: MEETINGS OF THE COMMITTEE

Rule 14   (Holding of meetings)
          (1) The Committee and its Bureau shall hold such meetings as are re-
          quired for the exercise of their functions.

          (2) Committee meetings shall be convened at dates decided by the Com-
          mittee. The Committee shall meet at other times by decision of the Bu-
          reau, as circumstances may require. It shall also meet if at least one third
          of the members so request.

          (3) The Secretary shall notify the members of the Committee of the date,
          time and place of each Committee meeting. Whenever possible, such no-
          tification shall be given at least six weeks in advance.

Rule 15   (Agenda)

(1) Following consultation with the Bureau, the Secretary shall transmit to the members a draft agenda simultaneously with the notification of the meeting.

(2) The agenda shall be adopted by the Committee at the beginning of the meeting.

Rule 16   (Meeting documentation)

The Secretary shall transmit to the members of the Committee the working documents relating to the different agenda items, whenever possible at least four weeks in advance.

Rule 17   (Quorum)

The quorum of the Committee shall be the majority of its members.

Rule 18   (Privacy of meetings)

(1) The Committee shall meet *in camera*. Its deliberations shall remain confidential.

(2) Apart from members of the Committee, only members of the Committee's Secretariat, interpreters and persons providing technical assistance to the Committee may be present at its meetings, unless the Committee decides otherwise.

Rule 19   (Hearings)

The Committee may hear any person whom it considers to be in a position to assist it in the performance of its functions under the Convention.

CHAPTER III: CONDUCT OF BUSINESS

Rule 20   (Proposals)

A proposal must be submitted in writing if a member of the Committee so requests. In that case it shall not be discussed until it has been circulated.

Rule 21   (Order of voting on proposals and amendments)

(1) Where a number of proposals relate to the same subject, they shall be put to the vote in the order in which they were submitted. In case of doubt, the President shall decide.

(2) Where a proposal is the subject of an amendment, the amendment shall be put to the vote first. Where two or more amendments to the same proposal are presented, the Committee shall vote first on whichever departs furthest in substance from the original proposal. It shall then vote on the next furthest removed from the original proposal, and so on until all the amendments have been put to the vote. However, where the acceptance of one amendment necessarily entails rejection of another, the latter shall not be put to the vote. The final vote shall then be taken on the proposal as amended or not amended. In case of doubt as to the order of priority, the President shall decide.

(3) Parts of a proposal or amendment may be put to the vote separately.

(4) In the case of proposals with financial implications, the most costly shall be put to the vote first.

Rule 22 (Order of procedural motions)

Procedural motions shall take precedence over all other proposals or motions except points of order. They shall be put to the vote in the following order:

a. suspension of the meeting;

b. adjournment of the meeting;

c. adjournment of discussion on the item in hand;

d. closure of discussion on the item in hand.

Rule 23 (Reconsideration of a question)

When a decision has been taken it is only re-examined if a member of the Committee so requests and the Committee accedes to this request.

Rule 24 (Voting)

(1) Subject to the provisions of Rules 44 (paragraph 1), 48 and 49, the decisions of the Committee shall be taken by a majority of the members present.

(2) In matters other than elections, a proposal shall be regarded as rejected if the majority referred to in paragraph 1 is not obtained.

(3) Subject to Rule 5, paragraph 4, the Committee shall normally vote by show of hands. However, any member may request that a vote be taken by roll-call; in this event, the roll shall be called in the alphabetical order of the names of the Committee's members, beginning with the letter 'A'.

(4) After a vote has commenced, there shall be no interruption of the voting except on a point of order by a member in connection with the actual conduct of the voting. Brief statements by members consisting solely of explanations of their votes may be permitted by the President before the voting has commenced or after the voting has been completed.

CHAPTER IV: DECISIONS AND MEETING REPORTS

Rule 25 (Decisions)

At the end of each meeting the Secretary shall submit to the Committee for its approval a list of the decisions adopted during the meeting.

Rule 26 (Meeting reports)

(1) A draft report of the Committee's deliberations at each meeting shall be prepared by the Secretary. The draft report shall be circulated as soon as possible to members of the Committee, who will be given the opportunity to submit corrections within a prescribed time-limit.

(2) If no corrections are submitted, the meeting report shall be deemed to be adopted. If corrections are submitted, they shall be consolidated in a single document and circulated to all members. In this latter case, the adoption of the meeting report shall be taken up at the next meeting of the Committee.

CHAPTER V: WORKING PARTIES

Rule 27   The Committee may set up *ad hoc* working parties comprising a limited number of its members. The terms of reference of such working parties shall be defined by the Committee.

CHAPTER VI: COMMUNICATIONS CONTAINING INFORMATION
SUBMITTED FOR THE COMMITTEE'S CONSIDERATION

Rule 28   (1) The Secretary shall bring to the Committee's attention communications received containing information submitted for the Committee's consideration,[1] unless the information in question relates to matters which manifestly fall outside its field of competence.

(2) Such communications received by individual members of the Committee shall be forwarded to the Secretariat.

(3) The Secretary shall keep a register of all communications received.

(4) The Secretary shall send an acknowledgement of receipt to the authors of such communications.

TITLE III: PROCEDURE CONCERNING VISITS

CHAPTER I: BASIC RULES

Rule 29   (The principle of visits)
Pursuant to Articles 1 and 7 of the Convention, the Committee shall organise visits to places referred to in Article 2 of the Convention to examine the treatment of persons deprived of their liberty, with a view to strengthening, if necessary, the protection of such persons from torture and from inhuman or degrading treatment or punishment.

Rule 30   (Requests for information or explanations)
(1) Before deciding on a particular visit, the Committee or, if appropriate, the Bureau may request information or explanations as regards the general situation in the State concerned, as regards a given place, or as regards an isolated case concerning which it has received reports.

---

[1]   Such communications shall be addressed to: Secrétaire-Général du Conseil de l'Europe, c/o Comité européen pour la prévention de la torture et des peines ou traitements inhumains ou dégradants, F-67006 Strasbourg.

(2) Following receipt of such information or explanations, details of remedial action taken by the national authorities may be requested.

Rule 31 (Periodic visits)

(1) The Committee shall carry out visits of a periodic nature.

(2) By the middle of each calendar year at the latest the Committee shall establish a confidential provisional programme of periodic visits for the following calendar year. In drawing up this programme the Committee shall ensure, as far as possible, that the different States Parties to the Convention are visited on a equitable basis, regard being had to the number of relevant places in each State Party.

(3) The Committee may subsequently decide to modify the above-mentioned programme in the light of circumstances.

(4) The Committee may in due course decide to make public the names of the countries in which periodic visits are envisaged in a given year.

Rule 32 (*Ad hoc* visits)

(1) In addition to periodic visits, the Committee may carry out such *ad hoc* visits as appear to it to be required in the circumstances.

(2) When the Committee is not in session, the Bureau may, in case of urgency, decide on the Committee's behalf on the carrying out of an *ad hoc* visit. The President shall report to the Committee at its next meeting on any action which has been taken under this paragraph.

Rule 33 (Follow-up visits)

The Committee may carry out one or more follow-up visits to any place already visited in the context of a periodic or *ad hoc* visit.

Rule 34 (Responsibility for carrying out visits)

(1) As a general rule, visits shall be carried out by a delegation of the Committee consisting of at least two of its members. Exceptionally, visits may be carried out by the full Committee or by a single member thereof.

(2) The members of the Committee with responsibility for carrying out a visit shall act in the name of the Committee.

Rule 35 (Notification of visits)

(1) The Committee or, if the Committee is not in session at the relevant time, its President shall notify the Government of the Party concerned of the intention to carry out a visit. The notification shall be sent to the authority referred to in Article 15 of the Convention.

(2) The notification shall contain the names of the Committee members responsible for carrying out the visit and of all persons assisting the visiting delegation.

(3) The notification shall indicate the places which the delegation intends to visit. However, this shall not prevent the visiting delegation from deciding to visit also places not indicated in the notification.

(4) The notification of a visit in pursuance of paragraphs 1 to 3 may be given in stages.

Rules 36 (Register of visits)

The Secretary shall maintain a register of all visits carried out by the Committee.

CHAPTER II: VISITING DELEGATIONS

Rule 37 (Choice of members)

(1) The members of the Committee to carry out a visit shall be chosen by the Committee or, in case of urgency when the Committee is not in session, by the Bureau. Due regard shall be had to the nature of the visit in question, and in particular to the type of place or places to be visited, when the composition of the delegation is determined.

(2) The Committee or the Bureau, as appropriate, shall appoint one of the members chosen as Head of the delegation.

Rule 38 (Assistants)

(1) The Committee or, in the case of an *ad hoc* visit under Rule 32, paragraph 2, the Bureau may decide that a visiting delegation shall be assisted by one or more experts or interpreters.

(2) At least one member of the Secretariat of the Committee shall accompany each visiting delegation.

(3) All persons assisting a visiting delegation shall act on the instructions and under the authority of the Head of the delegation.

Rule 39 (Procedure for visits)

(1) Visiting delegations shall carry out visits in accordance with any general or specific instructions or guidelines issued by the Committee or, as the case may be, the Bureau.

(2) A visiting delegation may immediately communicate observations to the authorities of the Party concerned.

Rule 40 (Visiting delegation reports)

On the completion of its visit, a visiting delegation shall as soon as possible submit a report to the Committee. This report shall contain in particular:

–   a description of the different stages of the visit;
–   a detailed account of the facts found during the visit and of all consultations with the authorities of the Party concerned;
–   proposals for any recommendations which the visiting delegation considers should be addressed to the Party.

TITLE IV: POST-VISIT PROCEDURE

CHAPTER I: REPORTS AND RECOMMENDATIONS

Rule 41   (Preparation of the Committee's report)

(1) After each visit the Committee shall draw up, in the light of the visiting delegation's report a report for transmission to the Party concerned. This report shall set out the facts found during the visit and contain any recommendations which the Committee considers necessary with a view to strengthening the protection of persons deprived of their liberty.

(2) When drawing up its report, the Committee shall take account of any observations which the Party concerned might submit to it following a visit. Further, the Committee may on its own initiative seek observations or additional information from the Party.

(3) After its adoption, the report shall be transmitted to the Party concerned by the President.

Rule 42   (Confidential nature of the report)

(1) The report transmitted to a Party following a visit is and, as a rule, shall remain confidential. However, the Committee shall publish its report, together with any comments of the Party concerned, whenever requested to do so by that Party.

(2) If the Party itself makes the report public, but does not do so in its entirety, the Committee may decide to publish the whole report.

(3) Publication of the report by the Committee under paragraphs 1 and 2 of this Rule shall be subject to the provisions of Rule 45, paragraph 2.

Rule 43   (Subsequent consultations)

After transmission of the Committee's report, the Committee and the Party may hold consultations concerning in particular the implementation of any recommendations set out in the report.

CHAPTER II: PUBLIC STATEMENTS

Rule 44   (1) If a Party fails to co-operate with the Committee or refuses to improve the situation in the light of the Committee's recommendations, the Committee may decide, by a majority of two-thirds of its members, to make a public statement on the matter.

(2) Before a decision to make such a statement is taken, the Party concerned shall be given an opportunity to make known its views.

(3) Subject to the provisions of Rule 45, paragraph 2, the Committee shall be released from the obligation of confidentiality set out under Title V when making a public statement.

TITLE V: OBLIGATION OF CONFIDENTIALITY

Rule 45   (1) Subject to Rules 42 and 44, information gathered by the Committee in relation to a visit, its report on that visit, and its consultations with the Party concerned shall be and shall remain confidential. The same shall apply to all Committee meeting reports and working documents.

(2) No personal data shall be published without the express consent of the person concerned.

Rule 46   (1) Members of the Committee, experts and other persons assisting the Committee are required, during and after their terms of office, to maintain the confidentiality of the facts or information of which they have become aware during the discharge of their functions.

(2) A provision to the above effect shall be inserted in the contracts of experts and interpreters recruited to assist the Committee.

TITLE VI: ANNUAL GENERAL REPORT OF THE COMMITTEE

Rule 47   (1) Subject to the obligation of confidentiality set out under Title V, the Committee shall every year submit to the Committee of Ministers a general report on its activities, which shall be transmitted to the Consultative Assembly and made public.

(2) The report shall contain *inter alia* information on the organisation and internal workings of the Committee and on its activities proper, with particular mention of the States visited.

(3) Whenever possible, the report shall be adopted at the first meeting of the Committee in a given calendar year and cover the whole of the preceding calendar year. The Secretary shall submit a draft report to the Committee in good time.

TITLE VII: AMENDMENTS AND SUSPENSION

Rule 48   (Amendment of the Rules)

These Rules of Procedure may be amended by decision taken by a majority of the members of the Committee, subject to the provisions of the Convention.

Rule 49   (Suspension of a Rule)

Upon the proposal of a Committee member, the application of a Rule may be suspended by decision taken by a majority of the members of the Committee, subject to the provisions of the Convention. The suspension of a rule shall be limited in its operation to the particular purpose for which such suspension has been sought.

Bibliographical notes

A. F. Bayefsky, Human Rights: The Helsinki Process, Proceedings of the Annual Meeting of the ASIL, 1990, 113 –130

V. Y. Johnson, International Human Rights – Helsinki Accords – Conference on Security and Cooperation in Europe adopts Copenhagen Document on Human Rights, Georgia Journal of International and Comparative Law 20 (1990), 645–663

Document of the Moscow Meeting of the Conference on the Human Dimension of the CSCE

The representatives of the participating States of the Conference on Security and Co-operation in Europe (CSCE), Albania, Austria, Belgium, Bulgaria, Canada, Cyprus, the Czech and Slovak Federal Republic, Denmark, Estonia, Finland, France, Germany, Greece, the Holy See, Hungary, Iceland, Ireland, Italy, Latvia, Liechtenstein, Lithuania, Luxembourg, Malta, Monaco, the Netherlands, European Community, Norway, Poland, Portugal, Romania, San Marino, Spain, Sweden, Switzerland, Turkey, the USSR, the United Kingdom, the United States of America and Yugoslavia, met in Moscow from 10 September to 4 October 1991, in accordance with the provisions relating to the Conference on the Human Dimension of the CSCE contained in the Concluding Document of the Vienna Follow-up Meeting of the CSCE.

They welcomed the admission as participating States of Estonia, Latvia and Lithuania decided at an additional Meeting at ministerial level of the representatives of the participating States in Moscow on 10 September 1991, convened by the Federal Minister for Foreign Affairs of the Federal Republic of Germany, Chairman-in-Office of the CSCE Council, prior to the opening of the Moscow Meeting.

The first Meeting of the Conference was held in Paris from 30 May to 23 June 1989. The second Meeting of the Conference was held in Copenhagen from 5 to 29 June 1990.

The Moscow Meeting was opened by the Minister for Foreign Affairs of the USSR. An opening address was delivered by the President of the USSR on behalf of the host country.

Opening statements were made by delegates of the participating States, among them Ministers, Deputy Ministers and the Vice-President of the Commission of the European Communities. A contribution to the Meeting was made by the Secretary General of the Council of Europe.

The participating States renew their commitment to implement fully all the principles and provisions of the Final Act of the Conference on Security and Co-operation in Europe, of the Charter of Paris for a New Europe and of the other CSCE documents relating to the human dimension, including, in particular, the Document of the Copenhagen Meeting of the Conference on the Human Dimension of the CSCE, and are determined to achieve still further progress in the implementation of these provisions, as full respect for human rights and fundamental freedoms and the development of societies based on pluralistic democracy and the rule of law, are prerequisites for a lasting order of peace, security, justice and co-operation in Europe.

In this context, the participating States underlined that, in accordance with the Final Act of the Conference on Security and Co-operation in Europe and the Charter of Paris for a New Europe, the equal rights of peoples and their right to self-determination are to be respected in conformity with the Charter of the United Nations and the relevant norms of international law, including those relating to territorial integrity of States.

At the Moscow Meeting views were expressed by the participating States on the implementation of their commitments in the field of the human dimension. They considered that the degree of compliance with the commitments contained in the relevant provisions of the CSCE documents had shown further substantial improvement since the Copenhagen Meeting. They also considered that, in spite of the significant progress made, serious threats to and violations of CSCE principles and provisions continue to exist and have a sobering effect on the assessment of the over all situation in Europe. In particular, they deplored acts of discrimination, hostility and violence against persons or groups on national, ethnic or religious grounds. The participating States therefore expressed the view that, for the full realization of their commitments relating to the human dimension, continued efforts are still required which should benefit substantially from the profound political changes that have occurred.

The participating States emphasize that issues relating to human rights, fundamental freedoms, democracy and the rule of law are of international concern, as respect for these rights and freedoms constitutes one of the foundations of the international order. They categorically and irrevocably declare that the commitments undertaken in the field of the human dimension of the CSCE are matters of direct and legitimate concern to all participating States and do not belong exclusively to the internal affairs of the State concerned. They express their determination to fulfil all of their human dimension commitments and to resolve by peaceful means any related issue, individually and collectively, on the basis of mutual respect and co-operation. In this context they recognize that the active involvement of persons, groups, organizations and institutions is essential to ensure continuing progress in this direction.

The participating States express their collective determination to further safeguard human rights and fundamental freedoms and to consolidate democratic advances in their territories. They also recognize a compelling need to increase the CSCE's effectiveness in addressing human rights concerns that arise in their territories at this time of profound change in Europe.

In order to strengthen and expand the human dimension mechanism described in the section on the human dimension of the CSCE in the Concluding Document of the Vienna Meeting and to build upon and deepen the commitments set forth in the Document of the Copenhagen Meeting of the Conference on the Human Dimension of the CSCE, the participating States adopt the following:

I

(1)   The participating States emphasize that the human dimension mechanism described in paragraphs 1 to 4 of the section on the human dimension of

the CSCE in the Vienna Concluding Document constitutes an essential achievement of the CSCE process, having demonstrated its value as a method of furthering respect for human rights, fundamental freedoms, democracy and the rule of law through dialogue and co-operation and assisting in the resolution of specific relevant questions. In order to improve further the implementation of the CSCE commitments in the human dimension, they decide to enhance the effectiveness of this mechanism and to strengthen and expand it as outlined in the following paragraphs.

(2)   The participating States amend paragraphs 42.1 and 42.2 of the Document of the Copenhagen Meeting to the effect that they will provide in the shortest possible time, but no later than ten days, a written response to requests for information and to representations made to them in writing by other participating States under paragraph 1 of the human dimension mechanism. Bilateral meetings, as referred to in paragraph 2 of the human dimension mechanism, will take place as soon as possible, and as a rule within one week of the date of the request.

(3)   A resource list comprising up to three experts appointed by each participating State will be established without delay at the CSCE Institution[*]. The experts will be eminent persons, preferably experienced in the field of the human dimension, from whom an impartial performance of their functions may be expected.

The experts will be appointed for a period of three to six years at the discretion of the appointing State, no expert serving more than two consecutive terms. Within four weeks after notification by the CSCE Institution of the appointment, any participating State may make reservations regarding no more than two experts to be appointed by another participating State. In such case, the appointing State may, within four weeks of being notified of such reservations, reconsider its decision and appoint another expert or experts; if it confirms the appointment originally intended, the expert concerned cannot take part in any procedure with respect to the State having made the reservation without the latter's express consent.

The resource list will become operational as soon as 45 experts have been appointed.

(4)   A participating State may invite the assistance of a CSCE mission, consisting of up to three experts, to address or contribute to the resolution of questions in its territory relating to the human dimension of the CSCE. In such case, the State will select the person or persons concerned from the resource list. The mission of experts will not include the participating State's own nationals or residents or any of the persons it appointed to the resource list or more than one national or resident of any particular State.

---

[*]   The Council will take the decision on the institution.

The inviting State will inform without delay the CSCE Institution when a mission of experts is established, which in turn will notify all participating States. The CSCE institutions will also, whenever necessary, provide appropriate support to such a mission.

(5)   The purpose of a mission of experts is to facilitate resolution of a particular question or problem relating to the human dimension of the CSCE. Such mission may gather the information necessary for carrying out its tasks and, as appropriate, use its good offices and mediation services to promote dialogue and co-operation among interested parties. The State concerned will agree with the mission on the precise terms of reference and may thus assign any further functions to the mission of experts, *inter alia* fact-finding and advisory services, in order to suggest ways and means of facilitating the observance of CSCE commitments.

(6)   The inviting State will co-operate fully with the mission of experts and facilitate its work. It will grant the mission all the facilities necessary for the independent exercise of its functions. It will, *inter alia*, allow the mission, for the purpose of carrying out its tasks, to enter its territory without delay, to hold discussions and to travel freely therein, to meet freely with officials, non-governmental organizations and any group or person from whom it wishes to receive information. The mission may also receive information in confidence from any individual, group or organization on questions it is addressing The members of such missions will respect the confidential nature of their task.

The participating States will refrain from any action against persons, organizations or institutions on account of their contact with the mission of experts or of any publicly available information transmitted to it. The inviting State will comply with any request from a mission of experts to be accompanied by officials of that State if the mission considers this to be necessary to facilitate its work or guarantee its safety.

(7)   The mission of experts will submit its observations to the inviting State as soon as possible, preferably within three weeks after the mission has been established. The inviting State will transmit the observations of the mission, together with a description of any action it has taken or intends to take upon it, to the other participating States via the CSCE Institution no later than three weeks after the submission of the observations.

These observations and any comments by the inviting State may be discussed by the Committee of Senior Officials, which may consider any possible follow-up action. The observations and comments will remain confidential until brought to the attention of the Senior Officials. Before the circulation of the observations and any comments, no other mission of experts may be appointed for the same issue.

(8)   Furthermore, one or more participating States, having put into effect paragraphs 1 or 2 of the human dimension mechanism, may request that the CSCE Institution inquire of another participating State whether it

would agree to invite a mission of experts to address a particular, clearly defined question on its territory relating to the human dimension of the CSCE. If the other participating State agrees to invite a mission of experts for the purpose indicated, the procedure set forth in paragraphs 4 to 7 will apply.

(9)   If a participating State (a) has directed an enquiry under paragraph 8 to another participating State and that State has not established a mission of experts within a period of ten days after the enquiry has been made, or (b) judges that the issue in question has not been resolved as a result of a mission of experts, it may, with the support of at least five other participating States, initiate the establishment of a mission of up to three CSCE rapporteurs. Such a decision will be addressed to the CSCE Institution, which will notify without delay the State concerned as well as all the other participating States.

(10)   The requesting State or States may appoint one person from the resource list to serve as a CSCE rapporteur. The requested State may, if it so chooses, appoint a further rapporteur from the resource list within six days after notification by the CSCE Institution of the appointment of the rapporteur. In such case the two designated rapporteurs, who will not be nationals or residents of, or persons appointed to the resource list by any of the States concerned, will by common agreement and without delay appoint a third rapporteur from the resource list. In case they fail to reach agreement within eight days, a third rapporteur who will not be a national or resident of, or a person appointed to the resource list by any of the States concerned, will be appointed from the resource list by the ranking official of the CSCE body designated by the Council. The provisions of the second part of paragraph 4 and the whole of paragraph 6 also apply to a mission of rapporteurs.

(11)   The CSCE rapporteur(s) will establish the facts, report on them and may give advice on possible solutions to the question raised. The report of the rapporteur(s), containing observations of facts, proposals or advice, will be submitted to the participating State or States concerned and, unless all the States concerned agree otherwise, to the CSCE-Institution no later than three weeks after the last rapporteur has been appointed. The requested State will submit any observations on the report to the CSCE Institution, unless all the States concerned agree otherwise, no later than three weeks after the submission of the report.

The CSCE Institution will transmit the report, as well as any observations by the requested State or any other participating State, to all participating States without delay. The report may be placed on the agenda of the next regular meeting of the Committee of Senior Officials, which may decide on any possible follow-up action. The report will remain confidential until after that meeting of the Committee. Before the circulation of the report no other rapporteur may be appointed for the same issue.

(12)   If a participating State considers that a particularly serious threat to the fulfilment of the provisions of the CSCE human dimension has arisen in another participating State, it may, with the support of at least nine other participating States, engage the procedure set forth in paragraph 10. The provisions of paragraph 11 will apply.

(13)   Upon the request of any participating State the Committee of Senior Officials may decide to establish a mission of experts or of CSCE rapporteurs. In such case the Committee will also determine whether to apply the appropriate provisions of the preceding paragraphs.

(14)   The participating State or States that have requested the establishment of a mission of experts or rapporteurs will cover the expenses of that mission. In case of the appointment of experts or rapporteurs pursuant to a decision of the Committee of Senior Officials, the expenses will be covered by the participating States in accordance with the usual scale of distribution of expenses. These procedures will be reviewed by the Helsinki Follow-up Meeting of the CSCE.

(15)   Nothing in the foregoing will in any way affect the right of participating States to raise within the CSCE process any issue relating to the implementation of any CSCE commitment, including any commitment relating to the human dimension of the CSCE.

(16)   In considering whether to invoke the procedures in paragraphs 9 and 10 or 19 regarding the case of an individual, participating States should pay due regard to whether that individual's case is already *sub judice* in an international judicial procedure.

III. America

American Convention on Human Rights

Efforts directed toward the protection of human rights have occurred within the framework of the Organization of American States since 1960, when the Council of the OAS adopted the Statute of the Inter-American Commission on Human Rights. In 1969, the OAS established the American Convention on Human Rights under the Pact of San José, Costa Rica. This Convention, which entered into force in July 1978, bears much resemblance to the European one.

In view of the American Convention on Human Rights which announced the creation of a Commission on Human Rights as one of the principal organs of the OAS, the Charter of the OAS was amended in 1967 in order to organize the competence of the Commission created in 1960. Art. 150 of that document provided for the Commission to continue in its functions until the American Convention should enter into force. At that time, the Commission created, or organized by the Convention, would replace the previous one. As, therefore, the Commission created in 1960, is no longer in function, further treatment of the Commission in the present collection is confined to some basic bibliography.

Paralleling the original European Convention on Human Rights, the Pact of San José created a Commission and a Court for the protection of human rights. According to Arts. 34 and 52, para.1, both bodies are to be composed of a fixed number (seven) of members elected following nomination by the member States. Each State may propose three candidates who must be nationals of member States of the OAS. The election of members of the Commission takes place in the General Assembly of the OAS. Commissioners serve for four years. Although the election of judges to serve on the Court also transpires in the General Assembly, it is restricted to member States of the Convention, which vote by secret ballot and choose judges by absolute majority (Art. 53, para. 1). The term of office of the judges is six years. An *ad hoc* judge may be appointed if none of the judges called upon to hear a case is of the nationality of the litigant. Both judges and commissioners are deemed to sit in their "personal capacity" and enjoy diplomatic privileges and immunities in accordance with international law.

The Convention permits applications by States, denoted "communications", as well as by individuals, termed "petitions". The jurisdiction of the Commission to accept and examine petitions is compulsory and cannot be avoided by reservations; moreover, State applications require special acceptance (Arts. 44, 45). Similarities between this Convention and the original European Convention on Human Rights are to be found in the procedural rules of the Commission under which communications and petitions may be heard.

The Commission is entrusted with the examining of the admissibility of applications, ensuring that local remedies are exhausted, that an application is not manifestly groundless or obviously out of order and that it is not substantially the same as a prior one. Once an application is declared admissible, the Commission investigates the facts of the matter and is at the disposal of the parties as a mediator. If no friendly settlement is reached, a report is drawn up and passed on to the States concerned.

Within the following three months, the Commission or the States concerned can appeal to the Court. If a State has not accepted the jurisdiction of the Court, no decision on the case is possible. In this situation the Commission may make recommendations, but cannot impose any legal obligation to remedy the violation of the Convention. Unlike the European system, there exists no mechanism comparable to the Committee of Ministers to further consider resolving the matter on a political basis. If the States concerned, however, have accepted the jurisdiction of the Court, a final judgment can be rendered, which may be preceded by provisional measures of protection, should urgency and imminent irreparable damage so require. In addition, the Court is empowered to issue advisory opinions on the proper interpretation of the Convention or other treaties concerning the protection of human rights in the American States as well as the compatibility of domestic legislation with such international instruments.

The competence of the organs of the American Convention on Human Rights has been extended to the monitoring of the rights granted by the "Additional Protocol to the Convention on Human Rights in the Area of Economic, Social and Cultural Rights" (Protocol of San Salvador of 17 November 1988) as well as to the "Protocol to the American Convention on Human Rights to Abolish the Death Penalty" (June 8, 1990, OAS General Assembly Resolution 1042). Mention should also be made of the fact that the Inter-American Convention to Prevent and Punish Torture of 1985 and the Inter-American Convention on Forced Disappearance of Persons of 1994 do not contain a provision for the implementation of the respective rights through the organs of the Convention. They only make it clear that the powers of these organs are not limited by these conventions so that torture and disappearance may be brought to the inter-American organs for the protection of human rights only under the Inter-American Convention on Human Rights, not under these special conventions. In contrast to these conventions the Inter-American Convention on the Prevention, Punishment and Eradication of Violence Against Women of 1994 provides explicitly for the right of petition to the Inter-American Commission of Human Rights (Art. 12) and according to Article 11 of the Convention States Parties may request advisory opinions of the Inter-American Court of Human Rights concerning the interpretation of the Convention.

Inter-American Commission on Human Rights, 1960 (Spanish, Portuguese. French and English)

Texts

Statute:

Información Jurídica No. 305/1570, pp. 140–174
OAS Handbook of Existing Rules Pertaining to Human Rights, OEA/Ser.L/V/11.23 (1975) (English)
Regulations of the Commission:
OEA/Ser./L/V/11.17, Doc. 26, May 2, 1967

Bibliographical notes

C. G. Fenwick, The Organization of American States (1963)
Ch. Tomuschat, Die Interamerikanische Menschenrechtskommission, ZaöRV Vol. 28 (1968), pp. 531–550
K. Vasak, La Commission interaméricaine des Droits de l'Homme (1968)
M. Ball, OAS in Transition (1969)
A. P. Schreiber, The Inter-American Commission on Human Rights (1970)
T. Buergenthal, The Revised OAS Charter and the Protection of Human Rights, AJIL Vol. 69 (1975), pp. 828–836

American Convention on Human Rights (Spanish, Portuguese, French and English)

Texts

Convention:
OEA/Ser.K/XVI/I.I, Doc. 65, Rev.1, Corr. 2
Handbook of Existing Rules Pertaining to Human Rights, OEA/Ser.L/V/111.50, Doc. 6, July 1, 1980
ILM Vol. 9 (1970), pp. 99–125
Inter-American Yearbook on Human Rights, 1992, vol. I, 164 et seq.
EuGRZ Vol. 7 (1980), pp. 435–443 (German)
Menschenrechte, Ihr internationaler Schutz (Beck-Texte) (1979), pp. 325–345
Statute and Regulations of the Commission:
Handbook of Existing Rules Pertaining to Human Rights, OEA/Ser.L/V/II 60, 1983
Inter-American Yearbook on Human Rights, 1992, vol. I, 256 et seq. (Statute) and 274 et seq. (Regulations)
T. Buergenthal/R. E. Norris/D. Shelton, Human Rights, The Inter-American System, Binders I–VI
F.F. Martin et al., International Human Rights, Law and Practice, Cases, Treaties and Materials, Documentary Supplement, 1997, 446–483
Statute and Rules of the Court:
Inter-American Yearbook on Human Rights, 1992, vol. I, 326 et seq., Statute, and 346 et seq. Rules of Procedure
T. Buergenthal/R.E. Norris/D. Shelton, Human Rights, The Inter-American System, Binders I–VI
F.F. Martin et al., International Human Rights, Law and Practice, Cases, Treaties and Materials, Documentary Supplement, 1997, 484–516

Bibliographical notes

P. D. Camargo, The American Convention on Human Rights, Human Rights Journal/Revue des Droits de l'Homme, Vol. 3 (1970), pp. 332–356

C. Zanghi, La Convenzione Interamericana dei Diritti dell'Uomo, La Comunità Internazionale, Vol. 25 (1970), pp. 266 297

T. Buergenthal, Regional Approaches to Human Rights: The Inter-American Experience, Proceedings of the 72nd Annual Meeting, American Society of International Law 1978, pp. 197–223

H. Gros-Espiell, L'Organisation des Etats américains (OEA), in: K. Vasak (ed.), Les dimensions internationales des Droits de l'Homme (1978), pp. 600 633

La Convención Americana sobre Derechos Humanos OAS, Comisión Interamericana de Derechos Humanos (1980)

C. Garcia Bauer, Symposium: The American Convention on Human Rights, The American University LR Vol. 30 (1980), No. 1 passim

J. A. Frowein, The European and the American Convention on Human Rights, A Comparison, Human Rights Law Journal 1 (1980), 44–65

R. E. Norris, Bringing Individual Petitions before the Inter-American Commission, Santa Clara LR Vol. 20 (1980), pp. 733–772

C. A. Dunshee de Abranches, The Inter-American Court of Human Rights, The American University Law Review, Vol. 30 (1980), pp. 70–127

R. E. Norris, Observations in Loco: Practice and Procedure of the Inter-American Commission on Human Rights, Texas ILJ Vol. 15 (1980), pp. 46–95

T. Buergenthal, The Inter-American Court of Human Rights, AJIL Vol. 76 (1982), pp. 231–245

Interamerican Commission on Human Rights, Ten Years of Activities, 1971–1981 (1982)

J. Kokott, Das Interamerikanische System zum Schutz der Menschenrechte (1986)

T. Buergenthal/C. Grossman/P. Nikken, Manual Internacional de Derechos Humanos (1990)

T. Buergenthal/R. Norris/D. Shelton, Protecting Human Rights in the Americas: Selected Problems (1990)

S. Davidson, The Inter-American Court of Human Rights (1992)

C. M. Cerna, The Structure and Functioning of the Inter-American Court of Human Rights, BYIL 63 (1992), 132–230

J. E. Méndez, La competencia consultativa de la Corte Interamericana de Derechos Humanos, in: Espacios internacionales para la justicia colombiana 1993, 119–1310

A. Aguiar Aranguren, La responsabilidad internacional del estado por violación de Derechos Humanos: Apreciaciones sobre el Pacto de San José, in: Estudios básicos de derechos humanos (1994), 117–153

R. Nieto Navia, La Corte Interamericana de Derechos Humanos, in: Estudios básicos de derechos humanos (1994), 251–273

D. J.Padilla, La Comisión Interamericana de Derechos Humanos, in: Estudios básicos de derechos humanos (1994), 227–249

J. M. Pasqualucci, The inter-American human rights system: establishing precedents and procedure in human rights law, The University of Miami Inter-American Law Review 26 (1994/95), 297–361

T. Buergenthal, Inter-American Court on Human Rights, in: Bernhardt (ed.) EPIL vol. II, 1008–1011

T. J. Farer, Inter-American Commission on Human Rights, in: Bernhardt (ed.) EPIL, vol. II, 1995, 1004–1007

A. P. Ewing, Establishing state responsibility for acts of violence against women under the American Convention on Human Rights, Columbia Human Rights Law Review 26 (1995), 751–800

P. Pirrone, Sui poteri della Corte interamericana in materia di responsabilità per violazione di diritti dell'uomo, Rivista di diritto internazionale 78 (1995), 940–961

A. J. J. Quintana, Los procedimientos incidentales ante la Corte Interamericana de Derechos Humanos, Revista IIDH 21 (1995), 121–148

B. Santoscoy, La Commission interaméricaine des droits de l'homme et le développement de sa compétence par le système des pétitions individuelles, 1995

J. M. Pasqualucci, Victim reparation in the inter-American human rights system: a critical assessment of current practice and procedure, Michigan Journal of International Law 18 (1996), 1–58

V. M. Rodrigez Rescia, Las reparaciones en el sistema interamericano de protección de derechos humanos, Revista IIDH 1996, 129–150

A. J. J. Quintana, Los procedimientos incidentales ante la Corte Interamericana de Derechos Humanos, Revista IIDH 21 (1995), 121–148

Collections of cases

Annual Report of the Commission to the General Assembly of the Organization

T. Buergenthal/R. E. Norris/D. Shelton, Human Rights: The Inter-American System, Binders I–VI, Part 3: Cases and decisions

T. Buergenthal/D. Shelton, Protecting Human Rights in the Americas, Cases and Materials, 4th edition, 1995

F. F. Martin a.o., International Human Rights, Law and Practice, Cases, Treaties and Materials, Documentary Supplement, 1997, 377–516

a) Convention of November 22, 1969, Part II and III

PART II. MEANS OF PROTECTION

CHAPTER VI. COMPETENT ORGANS

Art. 33   The following organs shall have competence with respect to matters relating to the fulfillment of the commitments made by the States Parties to this Convention:

a. the Inter-American Commission on Human Rights, referred to as "The Commission"; and

b. the Inter-American Court of Human Rights, referred to as "The Court".

CHAPTER VII. INTER-AMERICAN COMMISSION ON HUMAN RIGHTS

Section 1. Organization

Art. 34   The Inter-American Commission on Human Rights shall be composed of seven members, who shall be persons of high moral character and recognized competence in the field of human rights.

Art. 35   The Commission shall represent all the member countries of the Organization of American States.

Art. 36   1. The members of the Commission shall be elected in a personal capacity by the General Assembly of the Organization from a list of candidates proposed by the governments of the member states.

2. Each of those governments may propose up to three candidates, who may be nationals of the states proposing them or of any other member state of the Organization of American States. When a slate of three is proposed, at least one of the candidates shall be a national of a state other than the one proposing the slate.

Art. 37   1. The members of the Commission shall be elected for a term of four years and may be re-elected only once, but the terms of three of the members chosen in the first election shall expire at the end of two years. Immediately following that election the General Assembly shall determine the names of those three members by lot.

2. No two nationals of the same state may be members of the Commission.

Art. 38   Vacancies that may occur on the Commission for reasons other than the normal expiration of a term shall be filled by the Permanent Council of the Organization in accordance with the provisions of the Statute of the Commission.

Art. 39   The Commission shall prepare its Statute, which it shall submit to the General Assembly for approval. It shall establish its own Regulations.

Art. 40   Secretariat services for the Commission shall be furnished by the appropriate specialized unit of the General Secretariat of the Organization. This unit shall be provided with the resources required to accomplish the tasks assigned to it by the Commission.

Section 2. Functions

Art. 41   The main functions of the Commission shall be to promote respect for and defense of human rights. In the exercise of its mandate, it shall have the following functions and powers:

a. to develop an awareness of human rights among the peoples of America;

b. to make recommendations to the governments of the member states, when it considers such action advisable, for the adoption of progressive measures in favour of human rights within the framework of their domestic law and constitutional provisions as well as appropriate measures to further the observance of those rights;

c. to prepare such studies or reports as it considers advisable in the performance of its duties,

d. to request the governments of the member states to supply it with information on the measures adopted by them in matters of human rights;

e. to respond, through the General Secretariat of the Organization of American States, to inquiries made by the member states on matters related to human rights and, within the limits of its possibilities, to provide those states with the advisory services they request;

f. to take action on petitions and other communications pursuant to its authority, under the provisions of Articles 44 through 51 of this Convention; and

g. to submit an annual report to the General Assembly of the Organization of American States.

Art. 42   The States Parties shall transmit to the Commission a copy of each of the reports and studies that they submit annually to the Executive Committees of the Inter-American Economic and Social Council and the Inter-American Council for Education, Science, and Culture, in their respective fields, so that the Commission may watch over the promotion of the rights implicit in the economic, social, educational, scientific, and cultural standards set forth in the Charter of the Organization of American States as amended by the Protocol of Buenos Aires.

Art. 43   The States Parties undertake to provide the Commission with such information as it may request of them as to the manner in which their domestic law ensures the effective application of any provisions of this Convention.

Section 3. Competence

Art. 44   Any person or group of persons, or any nongovernmental entity legally recognized in one or more member states of the Organization, may lodge petitions with the Commission containing denunciations or complaints of violation of this Convention by a State Party.

Art. 45   1. Any State Party may, when it deposits its instrument of ratification of or adherence to this Convention, or at any later time, declare that it recognizes the competence of the Commission to receive and examine communications in which a State Party alleges that another State Party has committed a violation of a human right set forth in this Convention.

2. Communications presented by virtue of this article may be admitted and examined only if they are presented by a State Party that has made a declaration recognizing the aforementioned competence of the Commission. The Commission shall not admit any communication against a State Party that has not made such a declaration.

3. A declaration concerning recognition of competence may be made to be valid for an indefinite time, for a specified period, or for a specific case.

4. Declarations shall be deposited with the General Secretariat of the Organization of American States, which shall transmit copies thereof to the member states of that Organization.

Art. 46   1. Admission by the Commission of a petition or communication lodged in accordance with Articles 44 or 45 shall be subject to the following requirements:

a. that the remedies under domestic law have been pursued and exhausted, in accordance with generally recognized principles of international law;

b. that the petition or communication is lodged within a period of six months from the date on which the party alleging violation of his rights was notified of the final judgment;

c. that the subject of the petition or communication is not pending before another international procedure for settlement; and

d. that, in the case of Article 44, the petition contains the name, nationality, profession, domicile, and signature of the person or persons or of the legal representative of the entity lodging the petition.

2. The provisions of paragraphs 1.a and 1.b of this article shall not be applicable when:

a. the domestic legislation of the state concerned does not afford due process of law for the protection of the right or rights that have allegedly been violated;

b. the party alleging violation of his rights has been denied access to the remedies under domestic law or has been prevented from exhausting them; or

c. there has been unwarranted delay in rendering a final judgment under the aforementioned remedies.

Art. 47 The Commission shall consider inadmissible any petition or communication submitted under Articles 44 or 45 if:

a. any of the requirements indicated in Article 46 has not been met;

b. the petition or communication does not state facts that tend to establish a violation of the rights guaranteed by this Convention;

c. the statements of the petitioner or of the state indicate that the petition or communication is manifestly groundless or obviously out of order; or

d. the petition or communication is substantially the same as one previously studied by the Commission or by another international organization.

Section 4. Procedure

Art. 48 1. When the Commission receives a petition or communication alleging violation of any of the rights protected by this Convention, it shall proceed as follows:

a. If it considers the petition or communication admissible, it shall request information from the government of the state indicated as being responsible for the alleged violations and shall furnish that government a transcript of the pertinent portions of the petition or communication. This information shall be submitted within a reasonable period to be determined by the Commission in accordance with the circumstances of each case.

b. After the information has been received, or after the period established has elapsed and the information has not been received, the Commission shall ascertain whether the grounds for the petition or communication still exist. If they do not, the Commission shall order the record to be closed.

c. The Commission may also declare the petition or communication inadmissible or out of order on the basis of information or evidence subsequently received.

d. If the record has not been closed, the Commission shall, with the knowledge of the parties, examine the matter set forth in the petition or communication in order to verify the facts. If necessary and advisable, the Commission shall carry out an investigation, for the effective conduct of which it shall request, and the states concerned shall furnish to it, all necessary facilities.

e. The Commission may request the states concerned to furnish any pertinent information, and, if so requested, shall hear oral statements or receive written statements from the parties concerned.

f. The Commission shall place itself at the disposal of the parties concerned with a view to reaching a friendly settlement of the matter on the basis of respect for the human rights recognized in this Convention.

2. However, in serious and urgent cases, only the presentation of a petition or communication that fulfills all the formal requirements of admissibility shall be necessary in order for the Commission to conduct an investigation with the prior consent of the state in whose territory a violation has allegedly been committed.

Art. 49   If a friendly settlement has been reached in accordance with paragraph 1.f of Article 48, the Commission shall draw up a report, which shall be transmitted to the petitioner and to the States Parties to this Convention, and shall then be communicated to the Secretary General of the Organization of American States for publication. This report shall contain a brief statement of the facts and of the solution reached. If any party in the case so requests, the fullest possible information shall be provided to it.

Art. 50   1. If a settlement is not reached, the Commission shall, within the time limit established by its Statute, draw up a report setting forth the facts and stating its conclusions. If the report, in whole or in part, does nor represent the unanimous agreement of the members of the Commission, any member may attach to it a separate opinion. The written and oral statements made by the parties in accordance with paragraph 1.e of Article 48 shall also be attached to the report.

2. The report shall be transmitted to the states concerned, which shall not be at liberty to publish it.

3. In transmitting the report, the Committee may make such proposals and recommendations as it sees fit.

Art. 51   1. If, within a period of three months from the date of the transmittal of the report of the Commission to the states concerned, the matter has not either been settled or submitted by the Commission or by the state concerned to the Court and its jurisdiction accepted, the Commission may, by the vote of an absolute majority of its members set forth its opinion and conclusions concerning the question submitted for its consideration.

2. Where appropriate, the Commission shall make pertinent recommendations and shall prescribe a period within which the state is to take the measures that are incumbent upon it to remedy the situation examined.

3. When the prescribed period has expired, the Commission shall decide by the vote of an absolute majority of its members whether the state has taken adequate measures and whether to publish its report.

CHAPTER VIII. INTER-AMERICAN COURT OF HUMAN RIGHTS

Section 1. Organization

Art. 52   1. The Court shall consist of seven judges, nationals of the member states of the Organization, elected in an individual capacity from among jurists of the highest moral authority and of recognized competence in the field of human rights, who possess the qualifications required for the exercise of the highest judicial functions in conformity with the law of the State of which they are nationals or of the state that proposes them as candidates.

2. No two judges may be nationals of the same state.

Art. 53   1. The judges of the Court shall be elected by secret ballot by an absolute majority vote of the States Parties to the Convention in the General Assembly of the Organization, from a panel of candidates proposed by those states.

2. Each of the States Parties may propose up to three candidates, nationals of the state that proposes them or of any other member state of the Organization of American States. When a slate of three is proposed, at least one of the candidates shall be a national of a state other than the one proposing the slate.

Art. 54   1. The judges of the Court shall be elected for a term of six years and may be reelected only once. The term of three of the judges chosen in the first election shall expire at the end of three years. Immediately after the election, the names of the three judges shall be determined by lot in the General Assembly.

2. A judge elected to replace a judge whose term has not expired shall complete the term of the latter.

3. The judges shall continue in office until the expiration of their term. However, they shall continue to serve with regard to cases that they have begun to hear and that are still pending, for which purposes they shall not be replaced by the newly elected judges.

Art. 55   1. If a judge is a national of any of the States Parties to a case submitted to the Court, he shall retain his right to hear that case.

2. If one of the judges called upon to hear a case should be a national of one the States Parties to the case, any other State Party in the case may appoint a person of its choice to serve on the Court as an *ad hoc* judge.

3. If among the judges called upon to hear a case none is a national of any of the States Parties to the case, each of the latter may appoint an *ad hoc* judge.

4. An *ad hoc* judge shall possess the qualifications indicated in Article 52.

5. If several States Parties to the Convention should have the same interest in a case, they shall be considered as a single party for purposes of the above provisions. In case of doubt, the Court shall decide.

Art. 56   Five judges shall constitute a quorum for the transaction of business by the Court.

Art. 57   The Commission shall appear in all cases before the Court.

Art. 58   1. The Court shall have its seat at the place determined by the States Parties to the Convention in the General Assembly of the Organization; however, it may convene in the territory of any member state of the Organization of American States when a majority of the Court consider it desirable, and with the prior consent of the state concerned.

The seat of the Court may be changed by the States Parties to the Convention in the General Assembly, by a two thirds vote.

2. The Court shall appoint its own Secretary.

3. The Secretary shall have his office at the place where the Court has its seat and shall attend the meetings that the Court may hold away from its seat.

Art. 59   The Court shall establish its secretariat, which shall function under the direction of the Secretary of the Court, in accordance with the administrative standards of the General Secretariat of the Organization in all respects not incompatible with the independence of the Court. The staff of the Court's secretariat shall be appointed by the Secretary General of the Organization, in consultation with the Secretary of the Court.

Art. 60   The Court shall draw up its statute, which it shall submit to the General Assembly for approval. It shall adopt its own Rules of Procedure.

Section 2. Jurisdiction and Functions

Art. 61   1. Only the States Parties and the Commission shall have the right to submit a case to the Court.

2. In order for the Court to hear a case, it is necessary that the procedures set forth in Articles 48 to 50 shall have been completed.

Art. 62   1. A State Party may, upon depositing its instrument of ratification or adherence to this Convention, or at any subsequent time, declare that it recognizes as binding, *ipso facto*, and not requiring special agreement, the jurisdiction of the Court on all matters relating to the interpretation or application of this Convention.

2. Such declaration may be made unconditionally, on the condition of reciprocity, for a specified period, or for specific cases. It shall be presented to the Secretary General of the Organization, who shall transmit copies thereof to the other member states of the Organization and to the Secretary of the Court.

3. The jurisdiction of the Court shall comprise all cases concerning the interpretation and application of the provisions of this Convention that are submitted to it, provided that the States Parties to the case recognize

or have recognized such jurisdiction, whether by special declaration pursuant to the preceding paragraphs, or by a special agreement.

Art. 63   1. If the Court finds that there has been a violation of a right or freedom protected by this Convention, the Court shall rule that the injured party be ensured the enjoyment of his right or freedom that was violated. It shall also rule, if appropriate, that the consequences of the measure or situation that constituted the breach of such right or freedom be remedied and that fair compensation be paid to the injured party.

2. In cases of extreme gravity and urgency, and when necessary to avoid irreparable damage to persons, the Court shall adopt such provisional measures as it deems pertinent in matters it has under consideration. With respect to a case not yet submitted to the Court, it may act at the request of the Commission.

Art. 64   1. The member states of the Organization may consult the Court regarding the interpretation of this Convention or of other treaties concerning the protection of human rights in the American states. Within their spheres of competence, the organs listed in Chapter X of the Charter of the Organization of American States, as amended by the Protocol of Buenos Aires, may in like manner consult the Court.

2. The Court, at the request of a member state of the Organization, may provide that state with opinions regarding the compatibility of any of its domestic laws with the aforesaid international instruments.

Art. 65   To each regular session of the General Assembly of the Organization of American States the Court shall submit, for the Assembly's consideration, a report on its work during the previous years. It shall specify, in particular, the cases in which a state has not complied with its judgments, making any pertinent recommendations.

Section 3. Procedure

Art. 66   1. Reasons shall be given for the judgment of the Court.

2. If the judgment does not represent in whole or in part the unanimous opinion of the judges, any judge shall be entitled to have his dissenting or separate opinion attached to the judgment.

Art. 67   The judgment of the Court shall be final and not subject to appeal. In case of disagreement as to the meaning or scope of the judgment, the Court shall interpret it at the request of any of the parties, provided the request is made within ninety days from the date of notification of the judgment.

Art. 68   1. The States Parties to the Convention undertake to comply with the judgment of the Court in any case to which they are parties.

2. That part of a judgment that stipulates compensatory damages may be executed in the country concerned in accordance with domestic procedure governing the execution of judgments against the state.

Art. 69   The parties to the case shall be notified of the judgment of the Court and
           it shall be transmitted to the States Parties to the Convention.

CHAPTER IX. COMMON PROVISIONS

Art. 70   1. The judges of the Court and the members of the Commission shall en-
           joy, from the moment of their election and throughout their term of of-
           fice, the immunities extended to diplomatic agents in accordance with in-
           ternational law. During the exercise of their official function they shall, in
           addition, enjoy the diplomatic privileges necessary for the performance of
           their duties

           2. At no time shall the judges of the Court or the members of the Com-
           mission be held liable for any decisions or opinions issued in the exercise
           of their functions.

Art. 71   The position of judge of the Court or member of the Commission is in-
           compatible with any other activity that might affect the independence or
           impartiality of such judge or member, as determined in the respective
           statutes.

Art. 72   The judges of the Court and the members of the Commission shall re-
           ceive emoluments and travel allowances in the form and under the condi-
           tions set forth in their statutes, with due regard for the importance and
           independence of their office. Such emoluments and travel allowances shall
           be determined in the budget of the Organization of American States,
           which shall also include the expenses of the Court and its secretariat. To
           this end, the Court shall draw up its own budget and submit it for ap-
           proval to the General Assembly through the General Secretariat. The lat-
           ter may not introduce any changes in it.

Art. 73   The General Assembly may, only at the request of the Commission or the
           Court, as the case may be, determine sanctions to be applied against
           members of the Commission or judges of the Court when there are justi-
           fiable grounds for such action as set forth in the respective statutes. A
           vote of two-thirds majority of the member states of the Organization
           shall be required for a decision in the case of members of the Commission
           and, in the case of judges of the Court, a two-thirds majority vote of the
           States Parties to the Convention shall also be required.

PART III. GENERAL AND TRANSITORY PROVISIONS

CHAPTER XI. TRANSITORY PROVISIONS

Section 1. Inter-American Commission on Human Rights

Art. 79   Upon the entry into force of this Convention, the Secretary General shall,
           in writing, request each member state of the Organization to present,
           within ninety days, its candidates for membership on the Inter-American

Commission on Human Rights. The Secretary General shall prepare a list in alphabetical order of the candidates presented, and transmit it to the member States of the Organization at least thirty days prior to the next session of the General Assembly.

Art. 80   The members of the Commission shall be elected by secret ballot of the General Assembly from the list of candidates referred to in Article 79. The candidates who obtain the largest number of votes and an absolute majority of the votes of the representatives of the member states shall be declared elected. Should it become necessary to have several ballots in order to elect all the members of the Commission, the candidates who receive the smallest number of votes shall be eliminated successively, in the manner determined by the General Assembly.

Section 2. Inter-American Court of Human Rights

Art. 81   Upon the entry into force of this Convention, the Secretary General shall, in writing, request each State Party to present, within ninety days, its candidates for membership on the Inter-American Court of Human Rights. The Secretary General shall prepare a list in alphabetical order of the candidates presented and transmit it to the States Parties at least thirty days prior to the next session of the General Assembly.

Art. 82   The judges of the Court shall be elected from the list of candidates referred to in Article 81, by secret ballot of the States Parties to the Convention in the General Assembly. The candidates who obtain the largest number of votes and an absolute majority of the votes of the representatives of the States Parties shall be declared elected. Should it become necessary to have several ballots in order to elect all the judges of the Court the candidates who receive the smallest number of votes shall be eliminated successively, in the manner determined by the States Parties.

b) Statute of the Inter-American Commission on Human Rights of October 1979 as amended in 1992

I. NATURE AND PURPOSES

Art. 1   1. The Inter-American Commission on Human Rights is an organ of the Organization of the American States, created to promote the observance and defense of human rights and to serve as consultative organ of the Organization in this matter.

2. For the purpose of the present Statute, human rights are understood to be:

(a) The rights set forth in the American Convention on Human Rights, in relation to the States parties thereto;

(b) The rights set forth in the American Declaration of the Rights and Duties of Man, in relation to the other member states.

II. MEMBERSHIP AND STRUCTURE

Art. 2   1. The Inter-American Commission on Human Rights shall be composed of seven members, who shall be persons of high moral character and recognized competence in the field of human rights.

2. The Commission shall represent all the member states of the Organization.

Art. 3   1. The members of the Commission shall be elected in a personal capacity by the General Assembly of the Organization from a list of candidates proposed by the governments of the member states.

2. Each government may propose up to three candidates, who may be nationals of the state proposing them or of any other member state of the Organization. When a slate of three is proposed, at least one of the candidates shall be a national of a state other than the proposing state.

Art. 4   1. At least six months prior to completion of the terms of office for which the members of the Commission were elected, the Secretary General shall request, in writing, each member state of the Organization to present its candidates within 90 days.

2. The Secretary General shall prepare a list in alphabetical order of the candidates nominated, and shall transmit it to the member states of the Organization at least thirty days prior to the next General Assembly.

Art. 5   The members of the Commission shall be elected by secret ballot of the General Assembly from the list of candidates referred to in Article 3 (2). The candidates who obtain the largest number of votes and an absolute majority of the votes of the member states shall be declared elected. Should it become necessary to hold several ballots to elect all the members of the Commission, the candidates who receive the smallest number of votes shall be eliminated successively, in the manner determined by the General Assembly.

Art. 6   The members of the Commission shall be elected for a term of four years and may be re-elected only once. Their terms of office shall begin on January 1 of the year following the year in which they are elected.

Art. 7   No two nationals of the same state may be members of the Commission.

Art. 8   1. Membership on the Inter-American Commission on Human Rights is incompatible with engaging in other functions that might affect the independence or impartiality of the member or the dignity or prestige of his post on the Commission.

2. The Commission shall consider any case that may arise regarding incompatibility in accordance with the provisions of the first paragraph of this Article, and in accordance with the procedures provided by its Regulations.

If the Commission decides, by an affirmative vote of at least five of its members, that a case of incompatibility exists, it will submit the case, with its background, to the General Assembly for decision.

3. A declaration of incompatibility by the General Assembly shall be adopted by a majority of two thirds of the member states of the Organization and shall occasion the immediate removal of the member of the Commission from his post, but it shall not invalidate any action in which he may have participated.

Art. 9   The duties of the members of the Commission are:

1. Except when justifiably prevented, to attend the regular and special meetings the Commission holds at its permanent headquarters or in any other place to which it may have decided to move temporarily.

2. To serve, except when justifiably prevented, on the special committees which the Commission may form to conduct on-site observations, or to perform any other duties within their ambit.

3. To maintain absolute secrecy about all matters which the Commission deems confidential.

4. To conduct themselves in their public and private life as befits the high moral authority of the office and the importance of the mission entrusted to the Commission.

Art. 10   1. If a member commits a serious violation of any of the duties referred to in Article 9, the Commission, on the affirmative vote of five of its members, shall submit the case to the General Assembly of the Organization, which shall decide whether he should be removed from office.

2. The Commission shall hear the member in question before taking its decision.

Art. 11   1. When a vacancy occurs for reasons other than the normal completion of a member's term of office, the Chairman of the Commission shall immediately notify the Secretary General of the Organization, who shall in turn inform the member states of the Organization.

2. In order to fill vacancies, each government may propose a candidate within a period of 30 days from the date of receipt of the Secretary General's communication that a vacancy has occurred.

3. The Secretary General shall prepare an alphabetical list of the candidates and shall transmit it to the Permanent Council of the Organization, which shall fill the vacancy.

4. When the term of office is due to expire within six months following the date on which a vacancy occurs, the vacancy shall not be filled.

Art. 12   1. In those member states of the Organization that are Parties to the American Convention on Human Rights, the members of the Commission shall enjoy, from the time of their election and throughout their term of office, such immunities as are granted to diplomatic agents under international law. While in office, they shall also enjoy the diplomatic privileges required for the performance of their duties.

2. In those member states of the Organization that are not Parties to the American Convention on Human Rights, the members of the Commission shall enjoy the privileges and immunities pertaining to their posts that are required for them to perform their duties with independence.

3. The system of privileges and immunities of the members of the Commission may be regulated or supplemented by multilateral or bilateral agreements between the Organization and the member states.

Art. 13   The members of the Commission shall receive travel allowances and per diem and fees, as appropriate, for their participation in the meetings of the Commission or in other functions which the Commission, in accordance with its Regulations, entrusts to them, individually or collectively. Such travel and per diem allowances and fees shall be included in the budget of the Organization, and their amounts and conditions shall be determined by the General Assembly.

Art. 14   1. The Commission shall have a Chairman, a First Vice-Chairman and a Second Vice-Chairman, who shall be elected by an absolute majority of its members for a period of one year; they may be re-elected only once in each four-year period.

2. The Chairman and the two Vice-Chairmen shall be the officers of the Commission, and their functions shall be set forth in the Regulations.

Art. 15   The Chairman of the Commission may go to the Commission's headquarters and remain there for such time as may be necessary for the performance of his duties.

III. HEADQUARTERS AND MEETINGS

Art. 16   1. The headquarters of the Commission shall be in Washington, D. C.

2. The Commission may move to and meet in the territory of any American State when it so decides by an absolute majority of votes, and with the consent, or at the invitation of the governments concerned.

3. The Commission shall meet in regular and special sessions, in conformity with provisions of its Regulations.

Art. 17   1. An absolute majority of the members of the Commission shall constitute a quorum.

2. In regard to those states that are Parties to the Convention, decisions shall be taken by an absolute majority vote of the members of the Commission in those cases established by the American Convention on Hu-

man Rights and the present Statute. In other cases, an absolute majority of the members present shall be required.

3. In regard to those states that are not Parties to the Convention, decisions shall be taken by an absolute majority vote of the members of the Commission, except in the case of matters of procedure, in which case, the decisions shall be taken by simple majority.

IV. FUNCTIONS AND POWERS

Art. 18 The Commission shall have the following powers with respect to the member states of the Organization of American States:

a. to develop an awareness of human rights among the people of the Americas;

b. to make recommendations to the governments of the states on the adoption of progressive measures in favor of human rights in the framework of their legislation, constitutional provisions and international commitments, as well as appropriate measures to further observance of those rights;

c. to prepare such studies or reports as it considers advisable for the performance of its duties;

d. to request that the governments of the states provide it with reports on measures they adopt in matters of human rights;

e. to respond to inquiries made by any member state through the General Secretariat of the Organization on matters related to human rights in that state and, within its possibilities, to provide those states with the advisory services they request;

f. to submit an annual report to the General Assembly of the Organization, in which due account shall be taken of the legal regime applicable to those States Parties to the American Convention on Human Rights and of that system applicable to those that are not Parties;

g. to conduct on-site observations in a state, with the consent or at the invitation of the government in question, and

h. to submit the program-budget of the Commission to the Secretary General, so that he may present it to the General Assembly.

Art. 19 With respect to the States Parties to the American Convention on Human Rights, the Commission shall discharge its duties in conformity with the powers granted under the Convention and in the present Statute, and shall have the following powers in addition to those designated in Article 18:

a. to act on petitions and other communications, pursuant to the provisions of Articles 44 to 51 of the Convention;

b. to appear before the Inter-American Court of Human Rights in cases provided for in the Convention;

c. to request the Inter-American Court of Human Rights to take such provisional measures as it considers appropriate in serious and urgent cases which have not yet been submitted to it for consideration, whenever this becomes necessary to prevent irreparable injury to persons;

d. to consult the Court on the interpretation of the American Convention on Human Rights or of others treaties concerning the protection of human rights in the American states;

e. to submit additional draft protocols to the American Convention on Human Rights to the General Assembly, in order progressively to include other rights and freedoms under the system of protection of the Convention, and

f. to submit to the General Assembly, through the Secretary General, proposed amendments to the American Convention on Human Rights, for such action as the General Assembly deems appropriate.

Art. 20   In relation to those member states of the Organization that are not Parties to the American Convention on Human Rights, the Commission shall have the following powers, in addition to those designated in Article 18:

a. to pay particular attention to the observance of the human rights referred to in Articles I, II, III, IV, XVIII, XXV, and XXVI of the American Declaration of the Rights and Duties of Man;

b. to examine communications submitted to it and any other available information, to address the government of any member state not a Party to the Convention for information deemed pertinent by this Commission, and to make recommendations to it, when it finds this appropriate in order to bring about more effective observance of fundamental human rights, and

c. to verify, as a prior condition to the exercise of the powers granted under sub-paragraph b. above, whether the domestic legal procedures and remedies of each member state not a Party to the Convention have been duly applied and exhausted.

V. SECRETARIAT

Art. 21   1. The Secretariat services of the Commission shall be provided by a specialized administrative unit under the direction of an Executive Secretary. This unit shall be provided with the resources and staff required to accomplish the tasks the Commission may assign to it.

2. The Executive Secretary, who shall be a person of high moral character and recognized competence in the field of human rights, shall be responsible for the work of the Secretariat and shall assist the Commission in the performance of its duties in accordance with the Regulations.

3. The Executive Secretary shall be appointed by the Secretary General of the Organization, in consultation with the Commission. Furthermore, for the Secretary General to be able to remove the Executive Secretary, he

shall consult with the Commission and inform its members of the reasons for his decision.

VI. STATUTE AND REGULATIONS

Art. 22   1. The present Statute may be amended by the General Assembly.

2. The Commission shall prepare and adopt its own Regulations, in accordance with the present Statute.

Art. 23   1. In accordance with the provisions of Articles 44 to 51 of the American Convention on Human Rights, the Regulations of the Commission shall determine the procedure to be followed in cases of petitions or communications alleging violation of any of the rights guaranteed by the Convention, and imputing such violation to any State Party to the Convention.

2. If the friendly settlement referred to in Articles 44–51 of the Convention is not reached, the Commission shall draft, within 180 days, the report required by Article 50 of the Convention.

Art. 24   1. The Regulations shall establish the procedure to be followed in cases of communications containing accusations or complaints of violation of human rights imputable to states that are not Parties to the American Convention on Human Rights.

2. The Regulations shall contain, for this purpose, the pertinent rules established in the Statute of the Commission approved by the Council of the Organization in resolutions adopted on May 25 and June 8, 1960, with the modifications and amendments introduced by resolution XXII of the Second Special Inter-American Conference, and by the Council of the Organization at its meeting held on April 24, 1968, taking into account resolutions CP/RES. 253 (343/78), "Transition from the present Inter-American Commission on Human Rights to the Commission provided for in the American Convention on Human Rights", adopted by the Permanent Council of the Organization on September 20,1979.

VII. TRANSITORY PROVISIONS

Art. 25   Until the Commission adopts its new Regulations, the current Regulations (OEA/Ser.L/VII. 17, doc. 26) shall apply to all the member states of the Organization.

Art. 26   1. The present Statute shall enter into effect 30 days after its approval by the General Assembly.

2. The Secretary General shall order immediate publication of the Statute, and shall give it the widest possible distribution.

c) Regulations of the Inter-American Commission on Human Rights

Approved by the Commission on 8 April 1980, and modified on 29 June 1987

TITLE I. ORGANIZATION OF THE COMMISSION

CHAPTER I. NATURE AND COMPOSITION

Art. 1   Nature and Composition

1. The Inter-American Commission on Human Rights is an autonomous entity of the Organization of American States whose principal function is to promote the observance and defense of human rights and to serve as an advisory body to the Organization in this area.

2. The Commission represents all the member states of the Organization.

3. The Commission is composed of seven members elected in their individual capacity by the General Assembly of the Organization who shall be persons of high moral standing and recognized competence in the field of human rights.

CHAPTER II. MEMBERSHIP

Art. 2   Duration of the term of office

1. The members of the Commission shall be elected for four years and may be re-elected only once.

2. In the event that new members of the Commission are not elected to replace those completing their term of office, the latter shall continue to serve until the new members are elected.

Art. 3   Precedence

The members of the Commission shall follow the Chairman and Vice-Chairmen in order of precedence according to their length of service. When there are two or more members with equal seniority, precedence shall be determined according to age.

Art. 4   Incompatibility

1. The position of member of the Inter-American Commission on Human Rights is incompatible with the exercise of activities which could affect the independence, impartiality, dignity or prestige of membership on the Commission.

2. The Commission, with the affirmative vote of at least five of its members, shall decide if a situation of incompatibility exists.

3. The Commission, prior to taking a decision, shall hear the member who is considered to be in a situation of incompatibility.

4. The decision with respect to the incompatibility, together with all the background information, shall be sent to the General Assembly by means of the Secretary General of the Organization for the purposes set forth in Article 8, (3), of the Commission's Statute.

Art. 5   Resignation

In the event that a member resigns, his resignation shall be presented to the Chairman of the Commission who shall notify the Secretary General of the Organization for the appropriate purposes.

CHAPTER III. OFFICERS

Art. 6   Composition and functions

The Commission shall have as its officers a Chairman, a first Vice-Chairman, and a second Vice-Chairman, who shall perform the functions set forth in these regulations.

Art. 7   Elections

1. In the election for each of the posts referred to in the preceding article, only members present shall participate.

2. Elections shall be by secret ballot. However, with the unanimous consent of the members present, the Commission may decide on another procedure.

3. The vote of an absolute majority of the members of the Commission shall be required for election to any of the posts referred to in Article 6.

4. Should it be necessary to hold more than one ballot for election to any of these posts, the names receiving the lowest number of votes shall be eliminated successively.

5. Elections shall be held on the first day of the Commission's first session of the new calendar year.

Art. 8   Duration of Mandate

1. The board of officers shall hold office for a year and may be reelected only once in every four year period.

2. The mandate of the board of officers extends from the date of their election until the elections held the following year for the new board, pursuant to Article 7, paragraph 5.

3. In case the mandate of the Chairman or any of the Vice Chairmen expires, the provisions of Article 9, paragraphs 3 and 4 will apply.

Art. 9   Resignation, Vacancy and Replacements

1. If the Chairman resigns from his post or ceases to be a member of the Commission, the Commission shall elect a successor to fill the post for the remainder of the term of office at the first meeting held after the date on which it is notified of the resignation or vacancy.

2. The same procedure shall be applied in the event of the resignation of either of the Vice-Chairmen, or if a vacancy occurs.

3. The First Vice-Chairman shall serve as Chairman until the Commission elects a new Chairman under the provisions of paragraph 1 of this article.

4. The First Vice-Chairman shall also replace the Chairman if the latter is temporarily unable to perform his duties. The Second Vice-Chairman shall replace the Chairman in the event of the absence or disability of the first Vice-Chairman, or if that post is vacant.

Art. 10   Functions of the Chairman

The Duties of the Chairman shall be:

a. to represent the Commission before all the other organs of the Organization and other institutions;

b. to convoke regular and special meetings of the Commission in accordance with the Statute and these Regulations;

c. to preside over the sessions of the Commission and submit to it, for consideration, all matters appearing on the agenda of the work schedule approved for the corresponding session;

d. to give the floor to members in the order in which they requested it,:

e. to rule on points of order that may arise during the discussions of the Commission. If any member so requests, the Chairman's ruling shall be submitted to the Commission for its decision;

f. to submit to a vote matters within his competence, in accordance with the pertinent provisions of these Regulations;

g. to promote the work of the Commission and see to compliance with its program-budget;

h. to present a written report to the Commission at the beginning of its regular or special sessions on what he has done during its recesses to carry out the functions assigned to him by the Statute and by these Regulations;

i . to see to compliance with the decisions of the Commission;

j. to attend the meetings of the General Assembly of the Organization and, as an observer, those of the United Nations Commission on Human Rights; further, he may participate in the activities of other entities concerned with protecting and promoting respect for human rights;

k. to go to the headquarters of the Commission and remain there for as long as he considers necessary to carry out his functions;

l. to designate special committees, *ad hoc* committees, and subcommittees composed of several members, to carry out any mandate within his area of competence;

m. to perform any other functions that may be conferred upon him in these Regulations.

Art. 11   Delegation of Functions

The Chairman may delegate to one of the Vice-Chairmen or to another member of the Commission the function specified in Article 8(a), (j), and (m).

CHAPTER IV. SECRETARIAT

Art. 12   Composition

The Secretariat of the Commission shall be composed of an Executive Secretary, an Assistant Executive Secretary, and the professional, technical, and administrative staff needed to carry out its activities.

Art. 13   Functions of the Executive Secretary

1. The functions of the Executive Secretary shall be:

a. to direct, plan, and coordinate the work of the Secretariat;

b. to prepare the draft work schedule for each session in consultation with the Chairman;

c. to provide advisory services to the Chairman and members of the Commission in the performance of their duties;

d. to present a written report to the Commission at the beginning of each session, on the activities of the Secretariat since the preceding session, and on any general matters that may be of interest to the Commission;

e. to implement the decisions entrusted to him by the Commission or by the Chairman.

2. The Assistant Executive Secretary shall replace the Executive Secretary in the event of his absence or disability.

3. The Executive Secretary, the Assistant Executive Secretary and the staff of the Secretariat must observe strict discretion in all matters that the Commission considers confidential.

Art. 14   Functions of the Secretariat:

1. The Secretariat shall prepare the draft reports, resolutions, studies and any other papers entrusted to it by the Commission or by the Chairman, and shall see that the summary minutes of the sessions of the Commission and any documents considered by it are distributed among its members.

2. The Secretariat shall receive petitions addressed to the Commission and, when appropriate, shall request the necessary information from the governments concerned and, in general, it shall make the necessary arrangements to initiate any proceedings to which such petitions may give rise.

CHAPTER V. FUNCTIONING OF THE COMMISSION

Art. 15   Sessions

1. The Commission shall meet for a period not to exceed a total of eight weeks a year, divided into however many regular meetings the Commis-

sion may decide, without prejudice to the fact that it may convoke special sessions at the decision of its Chairman, or at the request of an absolute majority of its members.

2. The sessions of the Commission shall be held at its headquarters. However, by an absolute majority vote of its members, the Commission may decide to meet elsewhere, with the consent of or at the invitation of the government concerned.

3. Any member who because of illness or for any other serious reason is unable to attend all or part of any session or meeting of the Commission, or to fulfill any other functions, must notify the Executive Secretary to this effect as soon as possible, and he shall so inform the Chairman.

Art. 16   Meetings

1. During the sessions, the Commission shall hold as many meetings as necessary to carry out its activities.

2. The length of the meetings shall be determined by the Commission subject to any changes that, for justifiable reasons, are decided on by the Chairman after consulting with the members of the Commission.

3. The meetings shall be closed unless the Commission decides otherwise.

4. The date and time for the next meeting shall be set at each meeting.

Art. 17   Working Groups

1. When the Commission considers it advisable, prior to the beginning of every regular session a working group shall convene to prepare the draft resolutions and other decisions on petitions and communications which are dealt with under Title II, Chapters I, II and III of the present Regulations and which are to be considered by the full Commission during the session. Said Working Group will be composed of three members, designated by the Chairman of the Commission, following a rotation policy, when possible.

2. The Commission, with a vote of the absolute majority of its members, shall determine the formation of other working groups the purpose of which shall be the consideration of specific subjects which will then be considered by the full Commission. Each working group will be made up of no more than three members, who will be designated by the Chairman. As far as possible, these working groups will meet immediately before or after each session for the period of time the Commission determines.

Art. 18   Quorum for Meetings

The presence of an absolute majority of the members of the Commission shall be necessary to constitute a quorum.

Art. 19   Discussion and Voting

1. The meetings shall conform primarily to the Regulations and secondarily, to the pertinent provisions of the Regulations of the Permanent Council of the Organization of American States.

2. Members of the Commission may not participate in the discussion, investigation, deliberation or decision of a matter submitted to the Commission in the following cases:

a. if they were nationals or permanent residents of the State which is subject of the Commission's general or specific consideration, or if they were accredited to, or carrying out, a special mission, as diplomatic agents, on behalf of said State.

b. if previously they have participated in any capacity in a decision concerning the same facts on which the matter is based or have acted as an adviser to, or representative of, any of the parties involved in the decision.

3. When any member thinks that he should abstain from participating in the study or decision of a matter, he shall so inform the Commission, which shall decide if the withdrawal is warranted.

4. Any member may raise the issue of the withdrawal of another member provided that it is based upon reasons formulated in paragraph 2 of this article.

5. Any member who has withdrawn from the case shall not participate in the discussion, investigation, deliberation or decision of the matter even though the reason for the withdrawal has been superseded.

6. During the discussion of a given subject, any member may raise a point of order, which shall be ruled upon immediately by the Chairman or, when appropriate, by the majority of the members present. The discussion may be ended at any time, as long as the members have had the opportunity to express their opinion.

7. Once the discussion has been terminated, and if there is no consensus on the subject submitted to the Commission for deliberation, the Chairman shall put the matter to a vote in the reverse order of precedence among the members.

8. The Chairman shall announce the results of the vote and shall declare (as approved) the proposal that has the majority of votes. In the case of a tie, the Chairman shall decide.

9. Any doubt which may arise as regards the application or interpretation of the present article shall be resolved by the Commission.

Art. 20   Special Quorum to take Decisions

1. Decisions shall be taken by an absolute majority vote of the members of the Commission in the following cases:

a. to elect the executive officers of the Commission;

b. for matters where such a majority is required under the provisions of the Convention, the Statute or these Regulations;

c. to adopt a report on the situation of human rights in a specific state;

d. for any amendment or interpretation on the application of these Regulations.

2. To take decisions regarding other matters, a majority vote of members present shall be sufficient.

Art. 21   Explanation of Vote

1. Whether or not members agree with the decisions of the majority, they shall be entitled to present a written explanation of their vote, which shall be included following that decision.

2. If the decision concerns the approval of a report or draft, the explanation of the vote shall be included after that report or draft.

3. When the decision does not appear in a separate document, the explanation of the vote shall be included in the minutes of the meeting, following the decision in question.

Art. 22   Minutes of the Meetings

1. Summary minutes shall be taken of each meeting. They shall state the day and time at which it was held, the names of the members present, the matters dealt with, the decisions taken, the names of those voting for and against each decision, and any statement made by a member especially for inclusion in the minutes.

2. The Secretariat shall distribute copies of the summary minutes of each meeting to the members of the Commission, who may present their observations to the Secretariat prior to the meeting at which they are to be approved.

Art. 23   Compensation for Special Services

The Commission may assign any of its members, with the approval of an absolute majority, the preparation of a special study or other specific papers to be carried out individually outside the sessions. Such work shall be compensated in accordance with funds available in the budget. The amount of the fees shall be set on the basis of the number of days required for preparation and drafting of the paper.

Art. 24   Program-budget

1. The proposed program-budget of the Commission shall be prepared by its Secretariat in consultation with the Chairman and shall be governed by the Organization's current budgetary standards.

2. The Executive Secretary will advise the Commission of said program-budget.

TITLE II. PROCEDURES

CHAPTER I. GENERAL PROVISIONS

Art. 25   Official Languages

1. The official languages of the Commission shall be Spanish, French English and Portuguese. The working languages shall be those decided on

by the Commission every two years, in accordance with the languages spoken by its members.

2. A member of the Commission may allow omission of the interpretation of debates and the preparation of documents in his language.

Art. 26 Presentation of Petitions

1. Any person or group of persons or nongovernmental entity legally recognized in one or more of the member states of the Organization may submit petitions to the Commission, in accordance with these Regulations, on one's own behalf or on behalf of third persons, with regard to alleged violations of a human right recognized, as the case may be, in the American Convention on Human Rights or in the American Declaration of the Rights and Duties of Man.

2. The Commission may also, *motu proprio*, take into consideration any available information that it considers pertinent and which might include the necessary factors to begin processing a case which in its opinion fulfills the requirements for the purpose.

Art. 27 Form

1. The petition shall be lodged in writing.

2. The petitioner may appoint, in the petition itself, or in another written petition, an attorney or other person to represent him before the Commission.

Art. 28 Special Missions

The Commission may designate one or more of its members or staff members of the Secretariat to take specific measures, investigate facts or make the necessary arrangements for the Commission to perform its functions.

Art. 29 Precautionary Measures

1. The Commission may, at its own initiative, or at the request of a party, take any action it considers necessary for the discharge of its functions.

2. In urgent cases, when it becomes necessary to avoid irreparable damage to persons, the Commission may request that provisional measures be taken to avoid irreparable damage in cases where the denounced facts are true.

3. If the Commission is not in session, the Chairman, or in his absence, one of the Vice-Chairmen, shall consult with the other members, through the Secretariat, on implementation of the provisions of paragraphs 1 and 2 above. If it is not possible to consult within a reasonable time, the Chairman shall take the decision on behalf of the Commission and shall so inform its members immediately.

4. The request for such measures and their adoption shall not prejudice the final decision.

Art. 30 Initial Processing

1. The Secretariat of the Commission shall be responsible for the study and initial processing of petitions lodged before the Commission and that fulfill all the requirements set forth in the Statute and in these Regulations.

2. If a petition or communication does not meet the requirements called for in these Regulations, the Secretariat of the Commission may request the petitioner or his representative to complete it.

3. If the Secretariat has any doubt as to the admissibility of a petition, it shall submit it for consideration to the Commission or to the Chairman during recesses of the Commission.

CHAPTER II. PETITIONS AND COMMUNICATIONS REGARDING STATES PARTIES TO THE AMERICAN CONVENTION ON HUMAN RIGHTS

Art. 31   Condition for Considering the Petition

The Commission shall take into account petitions regarding alleged violations by a state party of human rights defined in the American Convention on Human Rights, only when they fulfill the requirements set forth in that Convention, in the Statute and in these Regulations.

Art. 32   Requirements for the Petitions

Petitions addressed to the Commission shall include:

a. the name, nationality, profession or occupation, postal address, or domicile and signature of the person or persons making the denunciation; or in cases where the petitioner is a nongovernmental entity, its legal domicile or postal address, and the name and signature of its legal representative or representatives;

b. an account of the act or situation that is denounced, specifying the place and date of the alleged violations and, if possible, the name of the victims of such violations as well as that of any official that might have been appraised of the act or situation that was denounced;

c. an indication of the state in question which the petitioner considers responsible, by commission or omission, for the violation of a human right recognized in the American Convention on Human Rights in the case of States Parties thereto, even if no specific reference is made to the article alleged to have been violated;

d. information on whether the remedies under domestic law have been exhausted or whether it has been impossible to do so.

Art. 33   Omission of Requirements

Without prejudice to the provisions of Article 26, if the Commission considers that the petition is inadmissible or incomplete, it shall notify the petitioner, whom it shall ask to complete the requirements omitted in petition.

Art. 34   Initial Processing

1. The Commission, acting initially through its Secretariat, shall receive and process petitions lodged with it in accordance with the standards set forth below:

a. it shall enter the petition in a register especially prepared for that purpose, and the date on which it was received shall be marked on the petition or communication itself;

b. it shall acknowledge receipt of the petition to the petitioner, indicating that it will be considered in accordance with the Regulations;

c. if it accepts, in principle, the admissibility of the petition, it shall request information from the government of the State in question and include the pertinent parts of the petitions.

2. In serious or urgent cases or when it is believed that the life, personal integrity or health of a person is in imminent danger, the Commission shall request the promptest reply from the government, using for this purpose the means it considers most expeditious.

3. The request for information shall not constitute a prejudgment with regard to the decision the Commission may finally adopt on the admissibility of the petition.

4. In transmitting the pertinent parts of a communication to the government of the State in question, the identity of the petitioner shall be withheld, as shall any other information that could identify him, except when the petitioner expressly authorizes in writing the disclosure of his identity.

5. The Commission shall request the affected government to provide the information requested within 90 days after the date on which the request is sent.

6. The government of the State in question may, with justifiable cause, request a 30 day extension, but in no case shall extensions be granted for more than 180 days after the date on which the first communication is sent to the government of the State concerned.

7. The pertinent parts of the reply and the documents provided by the government shall be made known to the petitioner or to his representative, who shall be asked to submit his observations and any available evidence to the contrary within 30 days.

8. On receipt of the information or documents requested, the pertinent parts shall be transmitted to the government, which shall be allowed to submit its final observations within 30 days.

Art. 35   Preliminary Questions

The Commission shall proceed to examine the case and decide on the following matters:

a. whether the remedies under domestic law have been exhausted, and it may determine any measures it considers necessary to clarify any remaining doubts;

b. other questions related to the admissibility of the petition or its manifest inadmissibility based upon the record or submission of the parties;

c. whether grounds for the petition exist or subsist, and if not, to order the file closed.

Art. 36   Examination by the Commission

The record shall be submitted by the Secretariat to the Commission for consideration at the first session held after the period referred to in Article 31, paragraph 5, if the government has not provided the information on that occasion, or after the periods indicated in paragraphs 7 and 8 have elapsed if the petitioner has not replied or if the government has not submitted its final observations.

Art. 37   Exhaustion of Domestic Remedies

1. For a petition to be admitted by the Commission, the remedies under domestic jurisdiction must have been invoked and exhausted in accordance with the general principles of international law.

2. The provisions of the preceding paragraph shall not be applicable when:

a. the domestic legislation of the State concerned does not afford due process of law for protection of the right or rights that have allegedly been violated;

b. the party alleging violation of his rights has been denied access to the remedies under domestic law or has been prevented from exhausting them;

c. there has been unwarranted delay in rendering a final judgment under the aforementioned remedies.

3. When the petitioner contends that he is unable to prove exhaustion as indicated in this Article, it shall be up to the government against which this petition has been lodged to demonstrate to the Commission that the remedies under domestic law have not previously been exhausted, unless it is clearly evident from the background information contained in the petition.

Art. 38   Deadline for the Presentation of Petitions

1. The Commission shall refrain from taking up those petitions that are lodged after the six-month period following the date on which the party whose rights have allegedly been violated has been notified of the final ruling in cases where the remedies under domestic law have been exhausted.

2. In the circumstances set forth in Article 34, (2) of these Regulations the deadline for presentation of a petition to the Commission shall be within a reasonable period of time, in the Commission's judgment, as from the date on which the alleged violation of rights has occurred, considering the circumstances of each specific case.

Art. 39   Duplication of Procedures

1. The Commission, shall not consider a petition in cases where the subject of the petition:

a. is pending settlement in another procedure under an international governmental organization of which the State concerned is a member;

b. essentially duplicates a petition pending or already examined and settled by the Commission or by another international governmental organization of which the state concerned is a member.

2. The Commission shall not refrain from taking up and examining a petition in cases provided for in paragraph 1 when:

a. the procedure followed before the other organization or agency is one limited to an examination of the general situation on human rights in the state in question and there has been no decision on the specific facts that are the subject of the petition submitted to the Commission, or is one that will not lead to an effective settlement of the violation denounced;

b. the petitioner before the Commission or a family member is the alleged victim of the violation denounced and the petitioner before the organizations in reference is a third party or a nongovernmental entity having no mandate from the former.

Art. 40   Separation and Combination of Cases

1. Any petition that states different fact that concern more than one person, and that could constitute various violations that are unrelated in time and place shall be separated and processed as separate cases, provided the requirements set forth in Article 32 are met.

2. When two petitions deal with the same facts and persons, they shall be combined and processed in a single file.

Art. 41   Declaration of Inadmissibility

The Commission shall declare inadmissible any petition when:

a. any of the requirements set forth in Article 32 of these Regulations has not been met;

b. when the petition does not state facts that constitute a violation of rights referred to in Article 31 of these Regulations in the case of States Parties to the American Convention on Human Rights;

c. the petition is manifestly groundless or inadmissible on the basis of the statement by the petitioner himself or the government.

Art. 42   Presumption

The facts reported in the petition whose pertinent parts have been transmitted to the government of the State in reference shall be presumed to be true if, during the maximum period set by the Commission under the provisions of Article 34 paragraph 5, the government has not provided the pertinent information, as long as other evidence does not lead to a different conclusion.

Art. 43   Hearing

1. If the file has not been closed and in order to verify the facts, the Commission may conduct a hearing following a summons to the parties and proceed to examine the matter set forth in the petition.

2. At that hearing, the Commission may request any pertinent information from the representative of the State in question and shall receive, if so requested, oral or written statements presented by the parties concerned.

Art. 44   On-site Investigation

1. If necessary and advisable, the Commission shall carry out an on-site investigation, for the effective conduct of which it shall request, and the States concerned shall furnish to it, all necessary facilities.

2. However, in serious and urgent cases, only the presentation of a petition or communication that fulfills all the formal requirements of admissibility shall be necessary in order for the Commission to conduct an on-site investigation with the prior consent of the State in whose territory a violation has allegedly been committed.

3. Once the investigatory stage has been completed, the case shall be brought for consideration before the Commission, which shall prepare its decision in a period of 180 days.

Art. 45   Friendly Settlement

1. At the request of any of the parties, or on its own initiative, the Commission shall place itself at the disposal of the parties concerned, at any stage of the examination of a petition, with a view to reaching a friendly settlement of the matter on the basis of respect for the human rights recognized in the American Convention on Human Rights.

2. In order for the Commission to offer itself as an organ of conciliation for a friendly settlement of the matter it shall be necessary for the positions and allegations of the parties to be sufficiently precise and in the judgment of the Commission, the nature of the matter must be susceptible to the use of the friendly settlement procedure.

3. The Commission shall accept the proposal to act as an organ of conciliation for a friendly settlement presented by one of the parties if the circumstances described in the above paragraph exist and if the other party to the dispute expressly accepts the procedure.

4. The Commission, upon accepting the role of an organ of conciliation for a friendly settlement shall designate a Special Commission or an individual from among its members. The Special Commission or the member so designated shall inform the Commission within the time period set by the Commission.

5. The Commission shall fix a time for the reception and gathering of evidence, it shall set dates for the holding of hearings, if appropriate, it shall plan an on-site observation, which will be carried out following the receipt of consent of the State to be visited and it shall fix a time for the conclusion of the procedure, which the Commission may extend.

6. If a friendly settlement is reached, the Commission shall prepare a report which shall be transmitted to the parties concerned and referred to the Secretary General of the Organization of American States for publication. This report shall contain a brief statement of the facts and of the solution reached. If any party in the case so requests, it shall be provided with the fullest possible information.

7. In a case where the Commission finds, during the course of processing the matter, that the case, by its very nature, is not susceptible to a friendly settlement; or finds that one of the parties does not consent to the application of this procedure; or does not evidence good will in reaching a friendly settlement based on the respect for human rights, the Commission, at any stage of the procedure shall declare its role as organ of conciliation for a friendly settlement to have terminated.

Art. 46   Preparation of the Report

1. If a friendly settlement is not reached, the Commission shall examine the evidence provided by the government in question and the petitioner, evidence taken from witnesses to the facts or that obtained from documents, records, official publications, or through an on-site investigation.

2. After the evidence has been examined, the Commission shall prepare a report stating the facts and conclusions regarding the case submitted to it for its study.

Art. 47   Proposals and Recommendations

1. In transmitting the report, the Commission may make such proposals and recommendations as it sees fit.

2. If, within a period of three months from the date of the transmittal of the report of the Commission to the States concerned, the matter has not been settled or submitted by the Commission, or by the State concerned, to the Court and its jurisdiction accepted, the Commission may, by the vote of an absolute majority of its members, set forth its opinion and conclusions concerning the question submitted for its consideration.

3. The Commission may make the pertinent recommendations and prescribe a period within which the government in question must take the measures that are incumbent upon it to remedy the situation examined.

4. If the report does not represent, in its entirety, or, in part, the unanimous opinion of the members of the Commission, any member may add his opinion separately to that report.

5. Any verbal or written statement made by the parties shall also be included in the report.

6. The report shall be transmitted to the parties concerned, who shall not be authorized to publish it.

Art. 48   Publication of the Report

1. When the prescribed period has expired, the Commission shall decide by the vote of an absolute majority of its members whether the State has taken suitable measures and whether to publish its report.

2. That report may be published by including it in the Annual Report to be presented by the Commission to the General Assembly of the Organization or in any other way the Commission may consider suitable.

Art. 49   Communications from a Government

1. Communications presented by the government of a State Party to the American Convention on Human Rights, which has accepted the competence of the Commission to receive and examine such communications against other States Parties, shall be transmitted to the State Party in question whether or not it has accepted the competence of the Commission. Even if it has not accepted such competence, the communication shall be transmitted so that the State can exercise its option under the provisions of Article 45(3) of the Convention to recognize the Commission's competence in the specific case that is the subject of the communication.

2. Once the State in question has accepted the competence of the Commission to take up the communication of the other State Party, the corresponding procedure shall be governed by the provisions of Chapter II insofar as they may be applicable.

Art. 50   Referral of the Case to the Court

1. If a State Party to the Convention has accepted the Court's jurisdiction in accordance with Article 62 of the Convention, the Commission may refer the case to the Court, subsequent to transmittal of the report referred to in Article 46 of these Regulations to the government of the State in question.

2. When it is ruled that the case is to be referred to the Court, the Executive Secretary of the Commission shall immediately notify the Court, the petitioner and the government of the State in question.

3. If the State Party has not accepted the Court's jurisdiction, the Commission may call upon that State to make use of the option referred to in Article 62, paragraph 2 of the Convention to recognize the Court's jurisdiction in the specific case that is the subject of the report.

CHAPTER III. PETITIONS CONCERNING STATES THAT ARE NOT
PARTIES TO THE AMERICAN CONVENTION ON HUMAN RIGHTS

Art. 51   Receipt of the Petitions

The Commission shall receive and examine any petition that contains a denunciation of alleged violations of the human rights set forth in the American Declaration of the Rights and Duties of Man, concerning the member states of the Organization that are not parties to the American Convention on Human Rights.

Art. 52   Applicable Procedure

The procedure applicable to petitions concerning member states of the Organization that are not parties to the American Convention on Human Rights shall be that provided for in the General Provisions included in Chapter I of Title II, in Articles 32 to 43 of these Regulations, and in the articles indicated below.

Art. 53   Final Decision

1. In addition to the facts and conclusions, the Commission's final decision shall include any recommendations the Commission deems advisable and a deadline for their implementation.

2. That decision shall be transmitted to the State in question or to the petitioner.

3. If the State does not adopt the measures recommended by the Commission within the deadline referred to in paragraphs 1 or 3, the Commission may publish its decision.

4. The decision referred to in the preceding paragraph may be published in the Annual Report to be presented by the Commission to the General Assembly of the Organization or in any other manner the Commission may see fit.

Art. 54   Request for Reconsideration

1. When the State in question or the petitioner, prior to the expiration of the 90 day deadline, invokes new facts or legal arguments which have not been previously considered, it may request a reconsideration of the conclusions or recommendations of the Commission's Report. The Commission shall decide to maintain or modify its decision, fixing a new deadline for compliance, where appropriate.

2. The Commission, if it considers it necessary, may request the State in question or the petitioner, as the case may be, to present any observations for reconsideration.

3. The reconsideration procedure may be utilized only once.

4. The Commission shall consider the request for reconsideration during the first regular session following its presentation.

5. If the State does not adopt the measures recommended by the Commission within the deadline referred to in paragraph 1, the Commission may publish its decision in conformity with Articles 48(2) and 53(43) of the present Regulations.

CHAPTER IV. ON-SITE OBSERVATIONS

Art. 55   Designation of the Special Commission

On-site observations shall be carried out in each case by a Special Commission named for that purpose. The number of members of the Special Commission and the designation of its Chairman shall be determined by the Commission. In cases of great urgency, such decisions may be made by the chairman subject to the approval of the Commission.

Art. 56   Disqualification

A member of the Commission who is a national of or who resides in the territory of the State in which the on-site observation is to be carried out shall be disqualified from participating therein.

Art. 57   Schedule of Activities

The Special Commission shall organize its own activities. To that end, it may appoint its own members and, after hearing the Executive Secretary, any staff members of the Secretariat or personnel necessary to carry out any activities related to its mission.

Art. 58   Necessary Facilities

In extending an invitation for an on-site observation or in giving its consent, the government shall furnish to the Special Commission all necessary facilities for carrying out its mission. In particular, it shall bind itself not to take any reprisals of any kind against any persons or entities cooperating with the Special Commission or providing information or testimony.

Art. 59   Other Applicable Standards

Without prejudice to the provisions in the preceding article, any on-site observation agreed upon by the Commission shall be carried out in accordance with the following standards:

a. The Special Commission or any of its members shall be able to interview freely and in private, any persons, groups, entities or institutions, and the government shall grant the pertinent guarantees to all those who provide the Commission with information, testimony or evidence of any kind;

b. the members of the Special Commission shall be able to travel freely throughout the territory of the country, for which purpose the government shall extend all the corresponding facilities, including the necessary documentation;

c. the government shall ensure the availability of local means of transportation;

d. the members of the Special Commission shall have access to the jails and all other detention and interrogation centers and shall be able to interview in private those persons imprisoned or detained;

e. the government shall provide the Special Commission with any document related to the observance of human rights that it may consider necessary for the presentation of its reports;

f. the Special Commission shall be able to use any method appropriate for collecting, recording or reproducing the information it considers useful;

g. the government shall adopt the security measures necessary to protect the Special Commission;

h. the government shall ensure the availability of appropriate lodging for the members of the Special Commission;

i. the same guarantees and facilities that are set forth here for the members of the Special Commission shall also be extended to the Secretariat staff;

j. any expenses incurred by the Special Committee, any of its members and the Secretariat staff shall be borne by the Organization, subject to the pertinent provisions.

CHAPTER V. GENERAL AND SPECIAL REPORTS

Art. 60   Preparation of Draft Reports

The Commission shall prepare the general or special draft reports that it considers necessary.

Art. 61   Processing and Publication

1. The reports prepared by the Commission shall be transmitted as soon as possible through, the General Secretariat of the Organization to the government or pertinent organs of the Organization.

2. Upon adoption of a report by the Commission, the Secretariat shall publish it in the manner determined by the Commission in each instance, except as provided for in Article 47, paragraph 6, of these Regulations.

Art. 62   Report on Human Rights in a State

The preparation of reports on the status of human rights in a specific state shall meet the following standards:

a. after the draft report has been approved by the Commission, it shall be transmitted to the government of the member state in question so that it may make any observations it deems pertinent;

b. the Commission shall indicate to that government the deadline for presentation of its observations;

c. when the Commission receives the observations from the government, it shall study them and, in light thereof, may uphold its report or change it and decide how it is to be published;

d. if no observation has been submitted on expiration of the deadline by the government, the Commission shall publish the report in the manner it deems suitable.

Art. 63   Annual Report

The Annual Report presented by the Commission to the General Assembly of the Organization shall include the following:

a. a brief account of the origin, legal basis, structure and purposes of the Commission as well as the status of the American Convention;

b. a summary of the mandates and recommendations conferred upon the Commission by the General Assembly and the other competent organs, and of the status of implementation of such mandates and recommendations;

c. a list of the meetings held during the period covered by the report and of other activities carried out by the Commission to achieve its purposes, objectives, and mandates;

d. a summary of the activities of the Commission carried out in cooperation with other organs of the Organization and with regional or world organizations of the same type, and the results achieved through these activities;

e. a statement on the progress made in attaining the objectives set forth in the American Declaration of the Rights and Duties of Man and the American Convention on Human Rights;

f. a report on the areas in which measures should be taken to improve observance of human rights in accordance with the aforementioned Declaration and Convention;

g. any observations that the Commission considers pertinent with respect to petitions it has received, including those processed in accordance with the Statute and the present Regulations which the Commission decides to publish as reports, resolutions, or recommendations;

h. any general or special report that the Commission considers necessary with regard to the situation of human rights in the member states, noting in such reports the progress achieved and difficulties that have arisen in the effective observance of human rights;

i. any other information, observation, or recommendation that the Commission considers advisable to submit to the General Assembly and any new program that implies additional expense.

Art. 64 Economic, Social and Cultural Rights

1. The States Parties shall forward to the Commission copies of the reports and studies referred to in Article 42 of the American Convention on Human Rights on the same date on which they submit them to the pertinent organs.

2. The Commission may request annual reports from the other member states regarding the economic, social, and cultural rights recognized in the American Declaration of the Rights and Duties of Man.

3. Any person, group of persons, or organization may present reports, studies or other information to the Commission on the situation of such rights in all or any of the member states.

4. If the Commission does not receive the information referred to in the preceding paragraphs or considers it inadequate, it may send questionnaires to all or any of the member states, setting a deadline for the reply or it may turn to other available sources of information.

5. Periodically, the Commission may entrust to experts or specialized entities studies on the situation of one or more of the aforementioned rights in a specific country or group of countries.

6. The Commission shall make the pertinent observations and recommendations on the situation of such rights in all or any of the member states and shall include them in the Annual Report to the General Assembly or in a Special Report, as it considers most appropriate.

7. The recommendations may include the need for economic aid or some other form of cooperation to be provided among the member states, as called for in the Charter of the Organization and in other agreements of the American system.

CHAPTER VI. HEARING BEFORE THE COMMISSION

Art. 65   Decision to Hold Hearing

On its own initiative, or at the request of the person concerned, the Commission may decide to hold hearings on matters defined by the Statute as within its jurisdiction.

Art. 66   Purpose of the Hearings

Hearings may be held in connection with a petition or communication alleging a violation of a right set forth in the American Convention on Human Rights or in the American Declaration on the Rights and Duties of Man or in order to receive information of a general or particular nature related to the situation of human rights in one State or in a group of American states.

Art. 67   Hearings on Petitions or Communications

1. Hearings on cases concerning violations of human rights and which the Commission is examining pursuant to the procedures established in Chapters II and III of Title II of these Regulations, will have as their purpose the receipt of testimony oral or written of the parties, relative to the additional information regarding the admissibility of the case, the possibility of applying the friendly settlement procedure, the verification of the facts or the merits of the matter submitted to the Commission for consideration, or as regards any other matter pertinent to the processing of the case.

2. To implement the provisions of the previous article, the Commission may invite the parties to attend a hearing, or one of the parties may request that a hearing be held.

3. If one of the two parties requests a hearing for the purposes indicated above, the Secretariat shall immediately inform the other party of that petition, and when the hearing date is set, shall invite the other party to attend, unless the Commission considers that there are reasons warranting a confidential hearing.

4. The Government shall furnish the appropriate guarantees to all persons attending a hearing or providing the Commission with information, testimony or evidence of any kind during a hearing.

Art. 68   Hearings of a General Nature

1. Persons who are interested in presenting testimony or information of a general nature to the Commission shall indicate, prior to the meeting, to the Executive Secretary that they wish to appear before the next session of the Commission.

2. In their petition, interested persons shall give their reasons for desiring to appear, a summary of the information they will furnish, and the approximate time required for their testimony.

3. The Executive Secretary shall, in consultation with the Chairman of the Commission, accede to the request for a hearing, unless the information presented by the interested person reveals that the hearing bears no relation to matters within the Commission's competence or if the purpose of the hearing and its circumstances are substantially the same as an earlier one.

4. The Executive Secretary shall, in consultation with the Chairperson of the Commission, draw up a schedule and propose the time and date for the general hearings to be held during the session, and shall submit them to the Commission for approval on the first day of the session.

Art. 69   Conduct of Hearings

The Commission shall, in each case, decide which of its members will take part in the hearing.

Art. 70   Attendance at Hearings

1. Hearings shall be private, unless the Commission decides that other persons should attend.

2. Hearings called specifically to review a petition shall be held in private, in the presence of the parties or their representatives, unless they agree that the hearing should be public.

TITLE III. RELATIONS WITH THE INTER-AMERICAN COURT OF HUMAN RIGHTS

CHAPTER I. DELEGATES, ADVISERS, WITNESSES, AND EXPERTS

Art. 71   Delegates and Assistants

1. The Commission shall delegate one or more of its members to represent it and participate as delegates in the consideration of any matter before the Inter-American Court of Human Rights.

2. In appointing such delegates, the Commission shall issue any instruction it considers necessary to guide them in the Court's proceedings.

3. When it designates more than one delegate, the Commission shall assign to one of them the responsibility of settling situations that are not foreseen in the instructions, or of clarifying any doubts raised by a delegate.

4. The delegates may be assisted by any person designated by the Commission. In the discharge of their functions, the advisers shall act in accordance with the instructions of the delegates.

Art. 72   Witnesses and Experts

1. The Commission may also request the Court to summon other persons as witnesses or experts.

2. The summoning of such witnesses or experts shall be in accordance with the Regulations of the Court.

CHAPTER II. PROCEDURE BEFORE THE COURT

Art. 73   Presentation of the Case

1. When, in accordance with Article 61 of the American Convention on Human Rights, the Commission decides to bring a case before the Court, it shall submit a request in accordance with the provisions of the Statute and the Regulations of the Court, and specifying :

a. the parties who will be intervening in the proceedings before the Court;

b. the date on which the Commission approved its report;

c. the names and addresses of its delegates;

d. a summary of the case;

e. the grounds for requesting a ruling by the Court.

2. The Commission's request shall be accompanied by certified copies of the items in the file that the Commission or its delegate considers pertinent.

Art. 74   Transmittal of other Elements

The Commission shall transmit to the Court, at its request, any other petition, evidence, document, or information concerning the case, with the exception of documents concerning futile attempts to reach a friendly settlement. The transmittal of documents shall in each case be subject to the decision of the Commission, which shall withhold the name and identity of the petitioner.

Art. 75   Notification of the Petitioner

When the Commission decides to refer a case to the Court, the Executive Secretary shall immediately notify the petitioner and alleged victim of the Commission's decision and offer him the opportunity of making observations in writing on the request submitted to the Court. The Commission shall decide on the action to be taken with respect to these observations.

Art. 76   Provisional Measures

1. In case of extreme gravity and urgency, and when it becomes necessary to avoid irreparable damage to persons in a matter that has not yet been submitted to the Court for consideration, the Commission may request it to adopt any provisional measures it deems pertinent.

2. When the Commission is not in session, that request may be made by the Chairman, or in his absence by one of the Vice-Chairman, in order of precedence.

TITLE IV. FINAL PROVISIONS

Art. 77   Calendar Computation

All time periods set forth in the present Regulations – in numbers of days — will be understood to be counted as calendar days.

Art. 78   Interpretation

Any doubt that might arise with respect to the interpretation of these Regulations shall be resolved by an absolute majority of the members of the Commission.

Art. 79   Amendment of the Regulations

The Regulations may be amended by an absolute majority of the members of the Commission.

d) Statute of the Inter-American Court of Human Rights of October 31, 1979 as revised in 1992

CHAPTER I. GENERAL PROVISIONS

Art. 1   Nature and legal organization

1. The Inter-American Court of Human Rights is an autonomous judicial institution whose purpose is the application and interpretation of the American Convention on Human Rights. The Court exercises its functions in accordance with the provisions of the afore-mentioned Convention and the present Statute.

Art. 2   Jurisdiction

The Court shall exercise contentious and advisory jurisdiction.

1. Its contentious jurisdiction shall be governed by the provisions of articles 61, 62 and 63 of the Convention, and

2. Its advisory jurisdiction shall be governed by the provisions of Article 64 of the Convention.

Art. 3   Seat

1. The seat of the Court shall be San José, Costa Rica; however, the Court may convene in any member state of the Organization of American States (OAS) when a majority of the Court considers it desirable, and with the prior consent of the state concerned.

2. The seat of the Court may be changed by a vote of two-thirds of the states parties to the Convention, in the OAS General Assembly.

CHAPTER II. COMPOSITION OF THE COURT

Art. 4   Composition

1. The Court shall consist of seven judges, nationals of the member states of the OAS, elected in an individual capacity from among jurists of the highest moral authority and of recognized competence in the field of human rights, who possess the qualifications required for the exercise of the highest judicial functions under the law of the state of which they are nationals or of the state that proposes them as candidates.

2. No two judges may be nationals of the same state.

Art. 5   Judicial Terms

1. The judges of the Court shall be elected for a term of six years and may be reelected only once. A judge elected to replace a judge whose term has not expired shall complete that term.

2. The terms of office of the judges shall run from January 1 of the year following that of their election to December 31 of the year in which their terms expire.

3. The judges shall serve until the end of their terms. Nevertheless, they shall continue to hear the cases they have begun to hear and that are still pending, and shall not be replaced by the newly elected judges in the handling of those cases.

Art. 6   Election of the judges — Date

1. Election of judges shall take place, insofar as possible, during the regular session of the OAS General Assembly immediately prior to the expiration of the term of the outgoing judges.

2. Vacancies on the Court caused by death, permanent disability, resignation or dismissal of the judges shall, insofar as possible, be filled at the next session of the OAS General Assembly. However, an election shall not be necessary when a vacancy occurs within six months of the expiration of a term.

3. If necessary in order to preserve a quorum in the Court, the states parties to the Convention, at a meeting of the OAS Permanent Council, and at the request of the President of the Court, shall appoint one or more interim judges who shall serve until such time as they are replaced by elected judges.

Art. 7   Candidates

1. Judges are elected by the states parties to the Convention, at the OAS General Assembly, from a list of candidates nominated by those states.

2. Each state party may nominate up to three candidates, nationals of the state that proposes them or of any other member state of the OAS.

3. When a slate of three is proposed, at least one of the candidates must be a national of a state other than the nominating state.

Art. 8   Election — Preliminary Procedures

1. Six months prior to the expiration of the terms to which the judges of the Court were elected, the Secretary General of the OAS shall address a written request to each state party to the Convention that it nominate its candidates within the next ninety days.

2. The Secretary General of the OAS shall draw up an alphabetical list of the candidates nominated, and shall forward it to the states parties, if possible, at least thirty days before the session of the OAS General Assembly.

3. In the case of vacancies on the Court, as well as in cases of death or permanent disability of a candidate, the aforementioned time periods shall be shortened to a period that the Secretary General of the OAS deems reasonable.

Art. 9   Voting

1. The judges shall be elected by a secret ballot and by an absolute majority of the states parties to the Convention, from among the candidates referred to in Article 7 of the present Statute.

2. The candidates who obtain the largest number of votes and an absolute majority shall be declared elected. Should several ballots be necessary, those candidates who receive the smallest number of votes shall be eliminated successively, in the manner determined by the states parties.

Art. 10   *Ad hoc* judges

1. If a judge is a national of any of the states parties to a case submitted to the Court, he shall retain his right to hear that case.

2. If one of the judges called upon to hear a case is a national of one of the states parties to the case, any other state party to the case may appoint a person to serve on the Court as an *ad hoc* judge.

3. If among the judges called upon to hear a case none is a national of the states parties to the case, each of the latter may appoint an *ad hoc* judge. Should several states have the same interest in the case, they shall be regarded as a single party for purposes of the above provisions. In case of doubt, the Court shall decide.

4. The right of any state to appoint an *ad hoc* judge shall be considered relinquished if the state should fail to do so within thirty days following the written request from the President of the Court.

5. The provisions of articles 4, 11, 15, 16, 18, 19, and 20 of the present Statute shall apply to *ad hoc* judges.

Art. 11   Oath

1. Upon assuming office, each judge shall take the following oath or make the following solemn declaration "I swear" — or "I solemnly declare" — "that I shall exercise my functions as a judge honorably, independently and impartially and that I shall keep secret all deliberations".

2. The oath shall be administered by the President of the Court and, if possible, in the presence of the other judges.

CHAPTER III. STRUCTURE OF THE COURT

Art. 12   Presidency

1. The Court shall elect from among its members a President and Vice-President who shall serve for a period of two years, and they may be reelected.

2. The President shall direct the work of the Court, represent it, regulate the disposition of matters brought before the Court, and preside over its sessions.

3. The Vice-President shall take the place of the President in the latter's temporary absence, or if the office of the president becomes vacant. In the latter case, the Court shall elect a new Vice-President to serve out the term of the previous Vice-President.

4. In the absence of the President and the Vice-President, their duties shall be assumed by other judges, following the order of precedence established in Article 13 of the present Statute.

Art. 13   Precedence

1. Elected judges shall take precedence after the President and Vice-President according to their seniority in office.

2. Judges having the same seniority in office shall take precedence according to age.

3. *Ad hoc* and interim judges shall take precedence after the elected judges, according to age. However, if an *ad hoc* or interim judge has previously served as an elected judge, he shall have precedence over the other *ad hoc* or interim judge.

Art. 14   Secretariat

1. The Secretariat of the Court shall function under the immediate authority of the Secretary, in accordance with the administrative standards of the OAS General Secretariat, in all matters that are not incompatible with the independence of the Court.

2. The Secretary shall be appointed by the Court. He shall be a full-time employee serving in a position of trust to the Court, shall have his office

at the seat of the Court and shall attend any meetings that the Court holds away from the seat.

3. There shall be an Assistant Secretary who shall assist the Secretary in his duties and shall replace him in his temporary absence.

4. The staff of the Secretariat shall be appointed by the Secretary General of the OAS, in consultation with the Secretary of the Court.

CHAPTER IV. RIGHTS, DUTIES AND RESPONSIBILITIES

Art. 15   Privileges and Immunities

1. The judges of the Court shall enjoy, from the moment of their election and throughout their term of office, the immunities extended to diplomatic agents under international law. During the exercise of their functions, they shall, in addition, enjoy the diplomatic privileges necessary for the performance of their duties.

2. At no time shall the judges of the Court be held liable for any decisions or opinions issued in the exercise of their functions.

3. The Court itself and its staff shall enjoy the privileges and immunities provided for in the Agreement on Privileges and Immunities of the Organization of American States, of May 15, 1949, *mutatis mutandis*, taking into account the importance and independence of the Court.

4. The provisions of paragraphs 1, 2 and 3 of this article shall apply to the states parties to the Convention. They shall also apply to such other member states of the OAS as expressly accept them, either in general or for specific cases.

5. The system of privileges and immunities of the judges of the Court and of its staff may be regulated or supplemented by multilateral or bilateral agreements between the Court, the OAS and its member states.

Art. 16   Service

1. The judges shall remain at the disposal of the Court, and shall travel to the seat of the Court or to the place where the Court is holding its sessions as often and for as long a time as necessary, as established in the Regulations.

2. The President shall render his service on a permanent basis.

Art. 17   Emoluments

1. The emoluments of the President and of the judges of the Court shall be set in accordance with the obligations and incompatibilities imposed on them by Articles 16 and 18, and bearing in mind the importance and independence of their functions.

2. The *ad hoc* judges shall receive the emoluments established by Regulations, within the limits of the Court's budget.

3. The judges shall also receive per diem and travel allowances, when appropriate.

Art. 18   Incompatibilities

1. The position of judge of the Inter-American Court of Human Rights in incompatible with the following positions and activities:

a. Members or high-ranking officials of the executive branch of government, except for those who hold positions that do not place them under the direct control of the executive branch and those of diplomatic agents who are not Chiefs of Missions to the OAS or to any of its member states;

b. Officials of international organizations;

c. Any others that might prevent the judges from discharging their duties, or that might affect their independence or impartiality, or the dignity or prestige of the office.

2. In case of doubt as to incompatibility, the Court shall decide. If the incompatibility is not resolved, the provisions of Article 73 of the Convention and Article 20(2) of the present Statute shall apply.

3. Incompatibilities may lead only to dismissal of the judge and the imposition of applicable liabilities, but shall no invalidate the acts and decisions in which the judge in question participated.

Art. 19   Disqualification

1. Judges may not take part in matters in which, in the opinion of the Court, they or members of their family have a direct interest or in which they have previously taken part as agents, counsel or advocates, or as members of a national or international court or an investigatory committee, or in any other capacity.

2. If a judge is disqualified from hearing a case or for some other appropriate reason considers that he should not take part in a specific matter, he shall advise the President of his disqualification. Should the latter disagree, the Court shall decide.

3. If the President considers that a judge has cause for disqualification or for some other pertinent reason should not take part in a given matter, he shall advise him to that effect. Should the judge in question disagree, the Court shall decide.

4. When one or more judges are disqualified pursuant to this article, the President may request the States parties to the Convention, in a meeting of the OAS Permanent Council, to appoint interim judges to replace them.

Art. 20   Disciplinary Regime

1. In the performance of their duties and at all other times, the judges and staff of the Court shall conduct themselves in a manner that is in keeping with the office of those who perform an international jurisdictional function. They shall be answerable to the Court for their conduct, as well as for any violation, act of negligence or omission committed in the exercise of their functions.

2. The OAS General Assembly shall have disciplinary authority over the judges, but may exercise that authority only at the request of the Court itself, composed for this purpose of the remaining judges. The Court shall inform the General Assembly of the reasons for its request.

3. Disciplinary authority over the Secretary shall lie with the Court, and over the rest of the staff, with the Secretary, who shall exercise that authority with the approval of the President.

4. The Court shall issue disciplinary rules, subject to the administrative regulations of the OAS General Secretariat insofar as they may be applicable in accordance with Article 59 of the Convention.

Art. 21   Resignation — Incapacity

1. Any resignation from the Court shall be submitted in writing to the President of the Court. The resignation shall not become effective until the President has accepted it.

2. The Court shall decide whether a judge is incapable of performing his functions.

3. The President of the Court shall notify the Secretary General of the OAS of the acceptance of a resignation or a determination of incapacity, for appropriate action.

CHAPTER V. THE WORKINGS OF THE COURT

Art. 22   Sessions

1. The Court shall hold regular and special sessions.

2. Regular sessions shall be held as determined by the Regulations of the Court.

3. Special sessions shall be convoked by the President or at the request of a majority of the judges.

Art. 23   Quorum

1. The quorum for deliberations by the Court shall be five judges.

2. The decisions of the Court shall be taken by a majority vote of the judges present.

3. In the event of a tie, the President shall cast the deciding vote.

Art. 24   Hearings, Deliberations, Decisions

1. The hearings shall be public, unless the Court, in exceptional circumstances, decides otherwise.

2. The Court shall deliberate in private. Its deliberations shall remain secret, unless the Court decides otherwise.

3. The decisions, judgments and opinions of the Court shall be delivered in public session, and the parties shall be given written notification thereof. In addition, the decisions, judgments and opinions shall be published, along with judges' individual votes and opinions and with such

other data or background information as the Court may deem appropriate.

Art. 25   Rules and Regulations

1. The Court shall draw up its Rules of Procedure.

2. The Rules of Procedure may delegate to the President or to Committees of the Court authority to carry out certain parts of the legal proceedings, with the exception of issuing final rulings or advisory opinions. Rulings or decisions issued by the President or the Committees of the Court that are not purely procedural in nature may be appealed before the full Court.

3. The Court shall also draw up its own Regulations.

Art. 26   Budget, Financial system

1. The Court shall draw up its own budget and shall submit it for approval to the General Assembly of the OAS, through the General Secretariat. The latter may not introduce any changes in it.

2. The Court shall administer its budget.

CHAPTER VI. RELATIONS WITH GOVERNMENTS AND ORGANIZATIONS

Art. 27   Relations with the Host Country, Governments and Organizations

1. The relations of the Court with the host country shall be governed through a headquarters agreement. The seat of the Court shall be international in nature.

2. The relations of the Court with governments, with the OAS and its organs, agencies and entities and with other international governmental organizations involved in promoting and defending human rights, shall be governed through special agreements.

Art. 28   Relations with the Inter-American Commission on Human Rights

1. The Inter-American Commission on Human Rights shall appear as a party before the Court in all cases within the adjudicatory jurisdiction of the Court, pursuant to Article 2(1) of the present Statute.

Art. 29   Agreements of Cooperation

1. The Court may enter into agreements with such nonprofit institutions as law schools, bar associations, courts, academies and educational or research institutions dealing with related disciplines in order to obtain their cooperation and to strengthen and promote the juridical and institutional principles of the Convention in general and of the Court in particular.

2. The Court shall include an account of such agreements and their results in its Annual Report to the OAS General Assembly.

Art. 30   Report to the OAS General Assembly

The Court shall submit a report on its work of the previous year to each regular session of the OAS General Assembly. It shall indicate those cases in which a state has failed to comply with the Court's ruling. It may also submit to the OAS General Assembly proposals or recommendations on ways to improve the Inter-American system of human rights, insofar as these concern the work of the Court.

CHAPTER VII. FINAL PROVISIONS

Art. 31 Amendments to the Statute

The present Statute may be amended by the OAS General Assembly, at the initiative of any member state or of the Court itself.

Art. 32 Entry into force

The present Statute shall enter into force on January 1, 1980.

e) Rules of Procedure of the Inter-American Court of Human Rights

Adopted by the Court at its Twenty-Third Regular Session held January 9 – 18, 1991 as amended in 1996

Art. 1 Purpose

1. These Rules regulate the organization and establish the procedure of the Inter-American Court of Human Rights.

2. The Court may adopt such other Rules as are necessary to carry out its functions.

3. In the absence of a provision in these Rules or in case of doubt as to their interpretation, the Court shall decide.

Art. 2 Definitions

For the purposes of these Rules:

a. the term "agent" refers to the person designated by a State to represent it before the Court;

b. the expression "General Assembly" refers to the General Assembly of the Organization of American States;

c. the term "Commission" refers to the Inter-American Commission on Human Rights;

d. the expression "Permanent Commission" refers to the Permanent Commission of the Court;

e. the expression "Permanent Council" refers to the Permanent Council of the Organization of American States;

f. the term "Convention" refers to the American Convention on Human Rights (Pact of San José, Costa Rica);

g. the term "Court" refers to the Inter-American Court of Human Rights;

h. the expression "Delegates of the Commission" refers to the persons designated by the Commission to represent it before the Court;

i. the expression "original claimant" refers to the person, group of persons, or nongovernmental entity that instituted the original petition with the Commission pursuant to Article 44 of the Convention;

j. the term "day" shall be understood to be a natural day;

k. the expression "States Parties" refers to the States that have ratified or adhered to the Convention;

l. the expression "Member States" refers to the States that are members of the Organization of American States;

m. the term "Statute" refers to the Statute of the Court, as adopted by the General Assembly of the Organization of American States on October 31, 1979 (AG/RES. 448 [IX-0/791), as amended;

n. the expression "report of the Commission" refers to the report provided for in Article 50 of the Convention;

o. the expression "judge *ad hoc*" refers to any judge appointed in pursuance of Article 55 of the Convention;

p. the expression "interim judge" refers to any judge appointed in pursuance of Articles 6(3) and 19(4) of the Statute;

q. the expression "titular judge" refers to any judge elected in pursuance of Articles 53 and 54 of the Convention;

r. the term "month" shall be understood to be a calendar month;

s. the acronym "OAS" refers to the Organization of American States;

t. the expression "parties to the case" refers to the parties in a case before the Court;

u. the term "Secretariat" refers to the Secretariat of the Court;

v. the term "Secretary" refers to the Secretary of the Court;

w. the expression "Deputy Secretary" refers to the Deputy Secretary of the Court;

x. the expression "Secretary General" refers to the Secretary General of the Organization of American States;

y. the term "victim" refers to the person whose rights under the Convention are alleged to have been violated;

TITLE I. ORGANIZATION AND FUNCTIONING OF THE COURT

CHAPTER I. THE PRESIDENCY AND VICE-PRESIDENCY

Art. 3   Election of the President and Vice-President

1. The President and Vice-President are elected by the Court for a period of two years and may be reelected. Their terms shall begin on July 1 of the corresponding year. The election shall be held during the regular session nearest to that date.

2. The election referred to in this Article shall be by secret ballot of the titular judges present. The judge who wins four or more votes shall be deemed to have been elected. If no candidate receives the required number of votes, a ballot shall take place between the two judges who have received the most votes. In the event of a tie vote, the judge having precedence in accordance with Article 13 of the Statute shall be deemed to have been elected.

Art. 4   Functions of the President

1. The functions of the President are to:

a. represent the Court;

b. preside over the meetings of the Court and to submit for its consideration the topics appearing on the agenda;

c. direct and promote the work of the Court;

d. rule on points of order that may arise during the meetings of the Court. If any judge so requests, the point of order shall be decided by a majority vote;

e. present a biannual report to the Court on the activities he has carried out as President during that period;

f. exercise such other functions as are conferred upon him by the Statute or these Rules, or entrusted to him by the Court.

2. In specific cases, the President may delegate the representation referred to in paragraph 1(a) of this Article to the Vice-President, to any of the judges or, if necessary, to the Secretary or Deputy Secretary.

3. If the President is a national of one of the parties to a case before the Court, or in special situations in which he considers it appropriate, he shall relinquish the Presidency for that particular case. The same rule shall apply to the Vice-President or to any judge called upon to exercise the functions of the President.

Art. 5   Functions of the Vice-President

1. The Vice-President shall replace the President in the latter's temporary absence, and shall assume the Presidency when the absence is permanent. In the latter case, the Court shall elect a Vice-President to serve out that term. The same procedure shall be followed if the absence of the Vice-President is permanent.

2. In the absence of the President and the Vice-President, their functions shall be assumed by the other judges in the order of precedence established in Article 13 of the Statute.

Art. 6   Commissions

1. The Permanent Commission shall be composed of the President, the Vice-President and any other judges the President deems appropriate to appoint, according to the needs of the Court. The Permanent Commission shall assist the President in the exercise of his functions.

2. The Court may appoint other commissions for specific matters. In urgent cases, they may be appointed by the President if the Court is not in session.

3. In the performance of their functions, the commissions shall be governed by the provisions of these Rules, as applicable.

CHAPTER II. THE SECRETARIAT

Art. 7   Election of the Secretary

1. The Court shall elect its Secretary, who must possess the legal qualifications required for the position, a good command of the working languages of the Court, and the experience necessary for discharging his functions.

2. The Secretary shall be elected for a term of five years and may be reelected. He may be freely removed at any time if the Court so decides by the vote of not less than four judges. The vote shall be by secret ballot.

3. The Secretary shall be elected in accordance with the provisions of Article 3(2) of these Rules.

Art. 8   Deputy Secretary

1. The Deputy Secretary shall be appointed on the proposal of the Secretary of the Court, in the manner prescribed in the Statute. He shall assist the Secretary in the performance of his functions and replace him in his temporary absences.

2. If the Secretary and Deputy Secretary are both unable to perform their functions, the President may appoint an Interim Secretary.

Art. 9   Oath

1. The Secretary and Deputy Secretary shall take an oath in the presence of the President.

2. The staff of the Secretariat, including any persons called upon to perform interim or temporary duties, shall, upon assuming their functions, take an oath before the President undertaking to respect the confidential nature of any facts that may come to their attention during their performance of such functions. If the President is not present at the seat of the Court, the Secretary shall administer the oath.

3. All oaths shall be recorded in a document that shall be signed by the person being sworn and by the person administering the oath.

Art. 10   Functions of the Secretary

The functions of the Secretary shall be to:

a. communicate the judgments, advisory opinions, decisions and other rulings of the Court;

b. keep the minutes of the meetings of the Court;

c. attend all meetings of the Court held at the seat or elsewhere;

d. deal with the correspondence of the Court;

e. direct the administration of the Court, pursuant to the instructions of the President;

f. prepare the draft programs, rules and regulations, and budgets of the Court;

g. plan, direct and coordinate the work of the staff of the Court;

h. carry out the tasks assigned to him by the Court or the President;

i. perform any other duties provided for by the Statute and in these Rules.

CHAPTER III. FUNCTIONING OF THE COURT

Art. 11   Regular Sessions

The Court shall meet in two regular sessions each year, one during each semester, on the dates decided upon by the Court at the previous session. In exceptional circumstances, the President may change the dates of these sessions after prior consultation with the Court.

Art. 12   Special Sessions

Special sessions may be convoked by the President on his own initiative or at the request of a majority of the judges.

Art. 13   Quorum

The quorum for the deliberations of the Court shall consist of five judges.

Art. 14   Hearings, Deliberations and Decisions

1. Hearings shall be public and shall be held at the seat of the Court. When exceptional circumstances so warrant, the Court may decide to hold a hearing in private or at a different location. The Court shall decide who may attend such hearings. Even in these exceptional circumstances, however, minutes shall be kept in the manner prescribed in Article 42 of these Rules.

2. The Court shall deliberate in private and its deliberations shall remain secret. Only the judges shall take part in the deliberations, although the Secretary and Deputy Secretary or their substitutes may attend, as well as such other Secretariat staff as may be required. No other persons may be admitted except by special decision of the Court and after taking an oath.

3. Any question that calls for a vote shall be formulated in precise terms in one of the working languages. At the request of any of the judges, the Secretariat shall translate the text thereof into the other working languages and distribute it prior to the vote.

4. The minutes of the deliberations of the Court shall be limited to a statement of the subject of the discussion and the decisions taken. Dissenting and concurring opinions and declarations made for the record shall also be noted.

Art. 15   Decisions and Voting

1. The President shall present, point by point, the matters to be voted upon. Each judge shall vote either in the affirmative or the negative; there shall be no abstentions.

2. The votes shall be cast in inverse order to the order of precedence established in Article 13 of the Statute.

3. The decisions of the Court shall be adopted by a majority of the judges present.

4. In the event of a tie, the President shall have a casting vote.

Art. 16   Continuation in Office by the Judges

1. Judges whose terms have expired shall continue to exercise their functions in cases that they have begun to hear and that are still pending. However, in the event of death, resignation or disqualification, the judge in question shall be replaced by the judge who was elected to take his place, if applicable, or by the judge who has precedence among the new judges elected upon expiration of the term of the judge to be replaced.

2. All matters relating to reparation and indemnities, as well as supervision of the implementation of the judgments of this Court, shall be heard by the judges comprising it at that stage of the proceedings, unless a public hearing has already been held. In that event, they shall be heard by the judges who had attended that hearing.

Art. 17   Interim Judges

Interim judges shall have the same rights and functions as titular judges, except for such limitations as shall have been expressly established.

Art. 18   Judges *Ad Hoc*

1. In a case arising under Articles 55(2) or 55(3) of the Convention and Article 10(2) or 10(3) of the Statute, the President, acting through the Secretariat, shall inform the States referred to in those provisions of their right to appoint an judge *ad hoc* within thirty days of the notification of the petition.

2. When it appears that two or more States have a common interest, the President shall inform them that they may jointly appoint one judge *ad hoc*, pursuant to Article 10 of the Statute. If those States have not communicated any agreement to the Court within thirty-days of the last notification of the petition, each State shall have fifteen days in which to propose a candidate. Thereafter, and if more than one candidate has been nominated, the President shall choose one judge *ad hoc* by lot, and shall communicate the result to the interested parties.

3. Should the interested States fail to exercise their right within the time limits established in the preceding paragraphs, they shall be deemed to have waived that right.

4. The Secretary shall communicate the appointment of judges *ad hoc* to the other parties to the case.

5. A judge *ad hoc* shall take an oath at the first meeting devoted to the consideration of the case for which he has been appointed.

6. Judges *ad hoc* shall receive honoraria on the same terms as titular judges.

Art. 19   Disqualification

1. Disqualification of a judge shall be governed by the provisions of Article 19 of the Statute.

2. Motions for disqualification must be filed prior to the first hearing of the case. However, if the grounds therefor were not known at that time, such motions may be submitted to the Court at the first possible opportunity, so that it can rule on the matter immediately.

3. When, for any reason whatsoever, a judge is not present at one of the hearings or at other stages of the proceedings, the Court may decide to disqualify him from continuing to hear the case, taking all the circumstances it deems relevant into account.

TITLE II. PROCEDURE

CHAPTER I. GENERAL RULES

Art. 20   Official Languages

1. The official languages of the Court shall be those of the OAS.

2. The working languages shall be those agreed upon by the Court each year. However, in a specific case, the language of one of the parties may be adopted as a working language, provided it is one of the official languages.

3. The working languages for each case shall be determined at the start of the proceedings, unless they are the same as those already being employed by the Court.

4. The Court may authorize any person appearing before it to use his own language if he does not have sufficient knowledge of the working languages. In such circumstances, however, the Court shall make the necessary arrangements to ensure that an interpreter is present to translate that testimony into the working languages.

5. The Court shall, in all cases, determine which text is authentic.

Art. 21   Representation of the States

1. The States Parties to a case shall be represented by an Agent, who may, in turn, be assisted by any person of his choice.

2. If a State replaces its Agent, it shall so notify the Court, and the replacement shall only take effect once the notification has been received at the seat of the Court.

3. A Deputy Agent may be designated. His actions shall have the same validity as those of the Agent.

4. When appointing its Agent, the State in question shall indicate the address at which all relevant communications shall be deemed to have been officially received.

Art. 22 Representation of the Commission

1. The Commission shall be represented by the Delegates it has designated for the purpose. The Delegates may be assisted by any person of their choice.

2. If the original claimant or the representatives of the victims or of their next of kin are among the persons selected by the Delegates of the Commission to assist them, in accordance with the preceding paragraph, that fact shall be brought to the attention of the Court, which shall, on the proposal of the Commission, authorize their participation in the discussions.

Art. 23 Representation of the Victims or their Next of Kin

At the reparations stage, the representatives of the victims or of their next of kin may independently submit their own arguments and evidence.

Art. 24 Cooperation of the States

1. The States Parties to a case have the obligation to cooperate so as to ensure that all notices, communications or summonses addressed to persons subject to their jurisdiction are duly executed. They shall also expedite compliance with summonses by persons who either reside or are present within their territory.

2. The same rule shall apply to any proceedings that the Court decides to conduct or order on the territory of a State party to a case.

3. When the performance of any of the measures referred to in the preceding paragraphs requires the cooperation of any other State, the President shall request the government in question to provide the requisite assistance.

Art. 25 Interim Measures

1. At any stage of the proceeding involving cases of extreme gravity and urgency, and when necessary to avoid irreparable damage to persons, the Court may, at the request of a party or on its own motion, order such provisional measures as it deems pertinent, pursuant to Article 63(2) of the Convention.

2. With respect to matters not yet submitted to it, the Court may act at the request of the Commission.

3. The request may be made to the President, to any judge of the Court or to the Secretariat, by any means of communication. The recipient of the request shall immediately bring it to the President's attention.

4. If the Court is not sitting, the President, in consultation with the Permanent Commission and, if possible, with the other judges, shall call upon the government concerned to adopt such urgent measures as may be necessary to ensure the effectiveness of any provisional measures subsequently ordered by the Court at its next session.

5. In its Annual Report to the General Assembly, the Court shall include a statement concerning the provisional measures ordered during the period covered by the report. If those measures have not been duly implemented, the Court shall make such recommendations as it deems appropriate.

Art. 26 Filing of Briefs

1. The application and the reply thereto, and, the communication setting out the preliminary objections and the reply thereto, as well as any other briefs addressed to the Court, may be presented in person, by courier, facsimile, telex, mail or any other method in general use. If they are dispatched by electronic mail, the original documents must be submitted within fifteen days.

2. The President may, in consultation with the Permanent Commission, reject any communication from the parties which he considers patently unreceivable, and shall order that it be returned to the interested party, without further action.

Art. 27 Default Procedure

1. When a party fails to appear in or continue with a case, the Court shall, on its own motion, take such measures as may be necessary to complete the consideration of the case.

2. When a party enters a case at a later stage of the proceedings, it shall take up the proceedings at that stage.

Art. 28 Joinder of Cases and Proceedings

1. The Court may, at any stage of the proceedings, order the joinder of interrelated cases.

2. The Court may also order the joinder of the written or oral proceedings of several cases, including the introduction of witnesses.

3. After consulting the Agents and the Delegates, the President may direct that the proceedings in two or more cases be conducted simultaneously.

Art. 29 Decisions

1. The judgments and interlocutory decisions for discontinuance of a case shall be rendered exclusively by the Court.

2. All other orders shall be rendered by the Court if it is sitting, and by the President, if it is not, unless otherwise provided. Decisions of the

President that are not purely procedural may be appealed before the Court.

3. Judgments and decisions of the Court may not be contested in any way.

Art. 30   Publication of Judgments and Other Decisions

1. The Court shall order the publication of:

a. the judgments and other decisions of the Court; the former shall include only those explanations of votes which fulfill the requirements set forth in Article 55 (2) of these Rules;

b. documents from the dossier, except those considered irrelevant or unsuitable for publication;

c. the records of the hearings;

d. any other document that the Court considers suitable for publication.

2. The judgments shall be published in the working languages used in each case. All other documents shall be published in their original language.

3. Documents relating to cases already adjudicated, and deposited with the Secretariat of the Court, shall be made accessible to the public, unless the Court decides otherwise.

Art. 31   Application of Article 63 (1) of the Convention

Application of this provision may be invoked at any stage of the proceedings.

CHAPTER II. WRITTEN PROCEEDINGS

Art. 32   Institution of Proceedings

For a case to be referred to the Court under Article 61(1) of the Convention, the application shall be filed with the Secretariat of the Court in each of the working languages. Whereas due filing of an application in only one working language shall not suspend the proceeding, the translations into the other language or languages must be submitted within thirty days.

Art. 33   Filing of the Application

The brief containing the application shall indicate:

1. the parties to the case; the purpose of the application; a statement of the facts; the supporting evidence, specifying the facts on which they will bear; the particulars of the witnesses and expert witnesses; the legal arguments , and the conclusions reached.

2. The names of the Agents and Delegates.

If the application is filed by the Commission, it shall be accompanied by the report referred to in Article 50 of the Convention.

Art. 34   Preliminary Review of the Application

When, during a preliminary review of the application, the President finds that the basic requirements have not been met, he shall request the Applicant to correct any deficiencies within twenty days.

Art. 35   Notification of the Application

1. The Secretary of the Court shall give notice of the application to:

a. the President and the judges of the Court;

b. the respondent State;

c. the Commission, when it is not also the Applicant;

d. the original claimant, if known;

e. the victim or his next of kin, if applicable.

2. The Secretary of the Court shall inform the other States Parties and the Secretary General of the filing of the application.

3. When giving the notice, the Secretary shall request that the respondent States designate their Agent and that the Commission appoint its Delegates, within one month. Until the Delegates are duly appointed, the Commission shall be deemed to be properly represented by its Chairman for all purposes of the case.

Art. 36   Preliminary Objections

1. Preliminary objections shall be filed within two months of notification of the application.

2. The document setting out the preliminary objections shall be filed with the Secretariat and shall set out the facts on which the objection is based, the legal arguments, and the conclusions and supporting documents, as well as any evidence which the party filing the objection may wish to produce.

3. The Secretary shall immediately give notice of the preliminary objections to the persons indicated in Article 35 (i) above.

4. The presentation of preliminary objections shall not cause suspension of the proceedings on the merits, nor of the respective time periods or terms.

5. Any parties to the case wishing to submit written briefs on the preliminary objections may do so within thirty days of receipt of the communication.

6. The Court may, if it deems it appropriate, convene a special hearing on the preliminary objections, after which it shall rule on the objections.

Art. 37   Answer to the Application

The respondent shall answer the application in writing within four months of the notification. The requirements indicated in Article 33 of these Rules shall apply. The Secretary shall communicate the answer to the persons referred to in Article 35 (1) above.

Art. 38   Other Steps in the Written Proceedings

Once the application has been answered, and before the start of the oral proceedings, the parties may seek the permission of the President to enter additional written pleadings. In such a case, the President, if he sees fit, shall establish the time limits for presentation of the relevant documents.

CHAPTER III. ORAL PROCEEDINGS

Art. 39 Opening

The President shall announce the date for the opening of the oral proceedings and shall call such hearings as may be necessary.

Art. 40 Conduct of the Hearings

The President shall direct the hearings. He shall prescribe the order in which the persons eligible to take part shall be heard, and determine the measures required for the smooth conduct of the hearings.

Art. 41 Questions Put During the Hearings

1. The judges may ask all persons appearing before the Court any questions they deem proper.

2. The witnesses, expert witnesses and any other persons the Court decides to hear may, subject to the control of the President, be examined by the persons referred to in Articles 21, 22 and 23 of these Rules.

3. The President is empowered to rule on the relevance of the questions posed and to excuse the person to whom the questions are addressed from replying, unless the Court decides otherwise.

Art. 42 Minutes of the Hearings

1. Minutes shall be taken at each hearing and shall contain the following:

a. the names of the judges present;

b. the names of those persons referred to in Articles 21, 22 and 23 of these Rules who are present at the hearing;

c. the names and other relevant information concerning the witnesses, expert witnesses and other persons appearing at the hearing;

d. statements made expressly for the record by the States parties to the case or by the Commission;

e. the statements of the witnesses, expert witnesses and other persons appearing at the hearing, as well as the questions put to them and the replies thereto;

f. the text of the questions put by the judges and the replies thereto;

g. the text of any decisions rendered by the Court during the hearing.

2. The Agents and Delegates, as well as the witnesses, expert witnesses and other persons appearing at the hearing, shall receive a copy of the relevant parts of the transcript of the hearing to enable them, subject to the control of the Secretary, to correct any substantive errors. The Secre-

tary shall set the time limits for this purpose, in accordance with the instructions of the President.

3. The minutes shall be signed by the President and the Secretary, and the latter shall attest to their accuracy.

4. Copies of the minutes shall be transmitted to the Agents and Delegates.

CHAPTER IV. EVIDENCE

Art. 43   Admission of Evidence

Items of evidence tendered by the parties shall be admissible only if previous notification thereof is contained in the application and in the reply thereto and, where appropriate, in the communication setting out the preliminary objections and in the answer thereto. Should any of the parties allege *force majeure*, serious impediment or the emergence of supervening events as grounds for producing an item of evidence, the Court may, in that particular instance, admit such evidence at a time other than those indicated above, provided that the opposing party is guaranteed the right of defense.

Art. 44   Procedure for Taking Evidence

The Court may, at any stage of the proceedings:

1. obtain, on its own motion, any evidence it considers helpful. In particular, it may hear as a witness, expert witness, or in any other capacity, any person whose evidence, statement or opinion it deems to be relevant.

2. Invite the parties to provide any evidence at their disposal or any explanation or statement that, in its opinion, may be useful.

3. Request any entity, office, organ or authority of its choice to obtain information, express an opinion, or deliver a report or pronouncement on any given point. The documents may not be published without the authorization of the Court.

4. Commission one or more of its members to conduct an inquiry, undertake an in situ investigation or obtain evidence in some other manner.

Art. 45   Cost of Evidence

The party requesting the production of evidence shall defray the cost thereof.

Art. 46   Convocation of Witnesses and Expert Witnesses

1. The Court shall determine when the parties are to call their witnesses and expert witnesses whom the Court considers necessary to hear. They shall be summoned in the manner deemed most suitable by the Court.

2. The summons shall indicate:

a. the name of the witness or expert witness;

b. the facts on which the examination will bear or the object of the expert opinion.

Art. 47   Oath or Solemn Declaration by Witnesses and Expert Witnesses

1. After his identity has been established and before giving evidence, every witness shall take an oath or make a solemn declaration as follows:

"I swear" – or "I solemnly declare" – "upon my honour and conscience that I will speak the truth, the whole truth and nothing but the truth."

2. After his identity has been established and before performing his task, every expert witness shall take an oath or make a solemn declaration as follows:

" I swear" – or " I solemnly declare" – " that I will discharge my duty as an expert witness honorably and conscientiously."

3. The oath shall be taken, or the declaration made, before the Court or President or any of the judges so delegated by the Court.

Art. 48   Objections to Witnesses

1. The interested party may object to a witness before he testifies.

2. If the Court considers it necessary, it may nevertheless hear, for purposes of information, a person who is not qualified to be heard as a witness.

3. The Court shall assess the value of the testimony and of the objections by the parties.

Art. 49   Objections to Expert Witness

1. The grounds for disqualification applicable to judges under Article 19 (1) of the Statute shall also apply to expert witnesses.

2. Objections shall be presented within fifteen days of notification of the appointment of the expert witness.

3. If the expert witness who has been challenged contests the ground invoked against him, the Court shall rule on the matter. However, when the Court is not in session, the President may, after consultation with the Permanent Commission, order the evidence to be presented. The Court shall be informed thereof and shall rule on the value of the evidence.

4. Should it become necessary to appoint a new expert witness, the Court shall rule on the matter. Nevertheless, if the evidence needs to be heard as a matter of urgency, the President, after consultation with the Permanent Commission, shall make the appointment and inform the Court accordingly. The Court shall rule on the value of the evidence.

Art. 50   Protection of Witnesses and Expert Witnesses

States may neither nor institute proceedings against witnesses or expert witnesses nor bring illicit pressure to bear on them or on their families on account of declarations or opinions they have delivered before the Court.

Art. 51   Failure to Appear or False Evidence

The Court may request that the States apply the sanctions provided in their domestic legislation against persons who, without good reason, fail to appear or refuse to give evidence or who, in the opinion of the Court, have violated their oath.

CHAPTER V. EARLY TERMINATION OF THE PROCEEDINGS

Art. 52   Discontinuance

1. When the party that has brought the case notifies the Court of its intention not to proceed with it, the Court shall, after hearing the opinions of the other parties thereto and the representatives of the victims or their next of kin, decide whether to discontinue the hearing and, consequently, to strike the case from its list.

2. If the respondent informs the Court of its acquiescence in the claims of the party that has brought the case, the Court shall decide, after hearing the opinion of the latter and the representatives of the victims or their next of kin, whether such acquiescence and its juridical effects are acceptable. In that event, the Court shall determine the appropriate reparations and indemnities.

Art. 53   Friendly Settlement

When the parties to a case before the Court inform it of the existence of a friendly settlement, compromise, or any other occurrence likely to lead to a settlement of the dispute, the Court may, in that case and after hearing the representatives of the victims or their next of kin, decide to discontinue the hearing and strike the case from its list.

Art. 54   Continuation of a Case

The existence of the conditions indicated in the preceding paragraphs notwithstanding, the Court may, bearing in mind its responsibility to protect human rights, decide to continue the consideration of a case.

CHAPTER VI. JUDGMENTS

Art. 55   Contents of the Judgment

1. A judgment shall contain:

a. the names of the President, the judges who rendered it, and the Secretary and Deputy Secretary;

b. the identity of the parties and their representatives and, where appropriate, of the representatives of the victims or their next of kin;

c. a description of the proceedings;

d. the facts of the case;

e. the conclusions of the parties;

f. the legal arguments;

g. the ruling on the case;

h. the decision, if any, in regard to costs;

i. the result of the voting;

j. a statement indicating which text is authentic.

2. Any judge who has taken part in the consideration of a case is entitled to append a concurring opinion to the judgment. These opinions shall be submitted within a time-limit to be fixed by the President, so that the other judges may take cognizance thereof prior to the notification of the judgment.

Art. 56   Judgment on Reparations

1. When no specific ruling on reparations has been made in the judgment on the merits, the Court shall set a time and determine the procedure for the deferred decision thereon.

2. If the Court is informed that the injured party and the party adjudged to be responsible have reached an agreement in regard to the execution of the judgement on the merits, it shall verify the fairness of the agreement and rule accordingly.

Art. 57   Delivery and Communication of the Judgment

1. When a case is ready for a judgment, the Court shall meet in private. A preliminary vote shall be taken, the wording of the judgment approved, and a date fixed for the public hearing at which the parties shall be so notified.

2. The texts, the legal arguments and votes shall all remain secret until the parties have been notified of the judgment.

3. Judgments shall be signed by all the judges who participated in the voting and by the Secretary. However, a judgment signed by only a majority of the judges shall be valid.

4. Dissenting or concurring opinions shall be signed by the judges submitting them and by the Secretary.

5. The judgments shall conclude with an order, signed by the President and the Secretary and sealed by the latter, providing for the communication and execution of the judgment.

6. The originals of the judgments shall be deposited in the archives of the Court. The Secretary shall dispatch certified copies to the States parties to the case, the Commission, the President of the Permanent Council, the Secretary General, the representatives of the victims or their next of kin, and to any interested persons who request them.

7. The Secretary shall transmit the judgment to all the States Parties.

Art. 58   Request for Interpretation

1. The request for interpretation, referred to in Article 67 of the Convention, may be made in connection with judgments on the merits or on reparation and shall be filed with the Secretariat. It shall state with precision the issues relating to the meaning or scope of the judgment on which the interpretation is requested.

2. The Secretary shall transmit the request for interpretation to the States that are parties to the case and to the Commission, as appropriate, and shall invite them to submit any written comments they deem relevant, within a time limit established by the President.

3. When considering a request for interpretation, the Court shall be composed, whenever possible, of the same judges who delivered the judgment of which the interpretation is being sought. However, in the event of death, resignation or disqualification, the judge in question shall be replaced pursuant to Article 16 of these Rules.

4. A request for interpretation shall not suspend the effect of the judgment.

5. The Court shall determine the procedure to be followed and shall render its decision in form of a judgment.

TITLE III. ADVISORY OPINIONS

Art. 59   Interpretation of the Convention

1. Requests for an advisory opinion under Article 64(1) of the Convention shall state with precision the specific questions on which the opinion of the Court is being sought.

2. Requests for an advisory opinion submitted by a Member State or by the Commission shall, in addition, identify the provisions to be interpreted, the considerations giving rise to the request, and the names and addresses of the Agent or of the Delegates.

3. If the advisory opinion is sought by an OAS organ other than the Commission, the request shall also specify, further to the information listed in the preceding paragraph, how it relates to the sphere of competence of the organ in question.

Art. 60   Interpretation of Other Treaties

1. If the interpretation requested refers to other treaties for the protection of human rights in the American states, as provided for in Article 64(1) of the Convention, the request shall indicate the name of, and parties to, the treaty, the specific questions on which the opinion of the Court is being sought, and the considerations giving rise to the request.

2. If the request is submitted by one of the organs of the OAS, it shall also indicate how the subject of the request falls within the sphere of competence of the organ in question.

Art. 61   Interpretation of Domestic Laws

1. A request for advisory opinions presented pursuant to Article 64(2) of the Convention shall indicate the following:

a. the provisions of domestic law and of the Convention or of other treaties concerning the protection of human rights to which the request relates;

b. the specific questions on which the opinion of the Court is being sought;

c. the name and address of the applicant's Agent.

2. Copies of the domestic laws referred to in the request shall accompany the application.

Art. 62   Procedure

1. On receipt of a request for an advisory opinion, the Secretary shall transmit copies thereof to all the Member States, the Commission, the Secretary General, and the OAS organs within whose spheres of competence the subject of the request falls, as appropriate.

2. The President shall establish the time limits for the filing of written comments by interested parties.

3. The President may invite or authorize any interested party to submit a written opinion on the issues covered by the request. If the request is governed by Article 64(2) of the Convention, he may do so after consultation with the Agent.

4. At the conclusion of the written proceedings, the Court shall decide whether there should be oral proceedings and shall fix the date for such a hearing, unless it delegates the latter task to the President. Prior consultation with the Agent is required in cases governed by Article 64(2) of the Convention.

Art. 63   Application by Analogy

The Court shall apply the provisions of Title II of these Rules to advisory proceedings, to the extent that it deems them to be compatible.

Art. 64   Delivery and Content of Advisory Opinions

1. The delivery of advisory opinions shall be governed by Article 57 of these Rules.

2. Advisory opinions shall contain:

a. the name of the President, the judges who rendered the opinion, and the Secretary and Deputy Secretary;

b. the issues presented to the Court;

c. a description of the various steps in the proceedings;

d. the legal arguments;

e. the opinion of the Court,

f. a statement indicating which text is authentic.

3. Any judge who has taken part in the delivery of an advisory opinion is entitled to append a dissenting or concurring opinion to the opinion of the Court. These opinions shall be submitted within a time limit to be fixed by the President, so that the other judges can take cognizance thereof before the advisory opinion is rendered. They shall be published in accordance with Article 30(1)(a) of these Rules.

4. Advisory Opinions may be delivered in public.

TITLE IV. FINAL AND TRANSITORY PROVISIONS

Art. 65   Amendments to the Rules of Procedure

These Rules of Procedure may be amended by the decision of an absolute majority of the titular judges of the Court. Upon entry into force, they shall abrogate the previous Rules of Procedure.

Art. 66   Entry into Force

These Rules of Procedure, the Spanish and English versions of which are equally authentic, shall enter into force on January 1, 1997.

IV. Africa and the Arab Region

1. Arab Charter on Human Rights

In the framework of the Arab League, a Permanent Arab Commission on Human Rights was formed in accordance with UN General Assembly Resolution 2081 (XX) of December 20, 1965 and UN Commission on Human Rights' Resolution 6 (XXIII) of March 23, 1967, both of which Resolutions expressed the desirability of establishing regional commissions on human rights. The decision of the Council of the Arab League to create such a permanent commission can be found in Resolution 2443 of September 3, 1968. Under the terms of Art. 4 of the Pact of the Arab League, the Permanent Arab Commission is technically a committee.

The Commission is composed of representatives from each member State of the Arab League and of the Palestine Liberation Organization which is a full member of the League. Each member State may designate one representative who may be replaced whenever the State deems this useful. The Commission is convened by the Secretary General of the Arab League; its sessions are not public. The only provision concerning the competence of the Commission (Art.12) refers to Art. 4 of the Pact, which contains provisions for instituting particular commissions. Lacking any further powers, the Commission may only issue "draft agreements" which are submitted to the Council of the League. Thus, the Commission clearly does no constitute an international tribunal either in its composition or in its functions. Indeed, on the occasion of its second session on April 26, 1969 the Commission characterized itself as a body concerned with the promotion rather than the protection of human rights.

The Commission decided during its fourth meeting to ask the Secretary-General of the League to elaborate the proposal for an Arab Charter on Human Rights. In September 1970, the task to prepare a proposal was vested in a committee of experts which presented a draft in 1971. The text of the Charter was finally adopted by the Council of the League of Arab States by its resolution 5437 (102nd regular session) on September 15, 1994, but is not yet in force lacking ratification. On the basis of the Charter, a Committee of Experts on Human Rights shall be established whose task will be to consider periodical reports submitted by the States Parties. There is no provision concerning individual complaints, however, the Committee may put questions to the States which may arise when examining the reports. The intention of creating also an Arab Court on Human Rights which was included in the drafts of an Arab Charter on Human Rights has not been included in the text actually adopted which provides only for the Committee with its limited competences already mentioned. Since at the time of terminating this text the Charter was not yet in force and thus the Committee not yet established, we will publish the draft rules of procedure of the permanent Arab Commission on Human Rights which will be replaced by the Committee.

Mention shall be made also of the Declaration on Human Rights in Islam which was adopted in the form of a resolution of the nineteenth Islamic Conference of Foreign Ministers held in Cairo in 1990. This declaration which completes former ones does not specify any organ charged with supervising implementation of the Human Rights granted therein (For the text cf. to F.F. Martin, op. cit. infra p. 608 et seq.)

Texts

K. Vasak (ed.), The International Dimensions of Human Rights, Textbook, UNESCO (1979) (original draft)

Arab Charter on Human Rights, Human Rights Law Journal 18 (1997), 151 et seq. (Translation from the Arab original text) and F.F. Martin et al., International Human Rights, Law and Practice, Cases, Treaties and Materials, Documentary Supplement (1997), 599–607

Bibliographical notes

K. Vasak, Les institutions nationales, régionales et universelles pour la promotion et la protection des Droits de l'Homme, Revue des Droits de l'Homme/Human Rights Journal Vol. 1 (1968), pp. 164–179

S. P. Marks, La Commission permanente arabe des Droits de l'Homme, Revue des Droits de l'Homme/Human Rights Journal Vol. 3 (1970), pp.101 et seq.

B. Boutros-Ghali, La Ligue des Etats arabes, in: K. Vasak (ed.), Les dimensions internationales des Droits de l'Homme (1978), pp. 634–644

R. Daoudi, Human Rights Commission of the Arab League, in: Bernhardt (ed.) EPIL, vol. II (1995), 913 et seq.

a) Arab Charter on Human Rights of September 15, 1994, Part III

PART III

Art. 40 a) The States members of the League's Council which are parties to the Charter shall elect a Committee of Experts on Human Rights by secret ballot.

b) The Committee shall consist of seven members nominated by the member States Parties to the Charter. The initial elections to the Committee shall be held six months after the Charter's entry into force. The Committee shall not include more than one person from the same State.

c) The Secretary-General shall request the member States to submit their candidates two months before the scheduled date of the elections.

d) The candidates, who must be highly experienced and competent in the Committee's field of work, shall serve in their personal capacity with full impartiality and integrity.

e) The Committee's members shall be elected for a three-year term which, in the case of three of them, shall be renewable for one further term, their names being selected by lot. The principle of rotation shall be observed as far as possible.

f) The Committee shall elect its chairman and shall draw up its rules of procedure specifying its method of operation.

g) Meetings of the Committee shall be convened by the Secretary-General at the Headquarters of the League's Secretariat. With the Secretary-General's approval, the Committee may also meet in another Arab country if the exigencies of its work so require.

Art. 41 1. The States Parties shall submit reports to the Committee of Experts on Human Rights in the following manner:

a) An initial report one year after the date of the Charter's entry into force.

b) Periodic reports every three years.

c) Reports containing replies of States to the Committee's questions.

2. The Committee shall consider the reports submitted by the member States Parties to the Charter in accordance with the provisions of paragraph 1 of this article.

3. The Committee shall submit a report, together with the views and comments of the States, to the Standing Committee on Human Rights at the Arab League.

b) Rules of Procedure of the Permanent Arab Commission on Human Rights (Draft)

Art. 1   The Commission's procedures shall be laid down in accordance with the rules given hereunder.

Art. 2   Each Member-State of the League shall be represented, each having a single vote irrespective of the number of its representation. Member-States shall advise the Secretary-General about their appointment.

Art. 3   Representatives shall remain in their representatives capacity in the Commission unless replaced by their States.

Art. 4   The Secretariat-General shall render assistance to the Commission in the discharges of its functions so as to enable the Commission's representatives to be acquainted with the subjects falling in its competence.

Art. 5   The Council of the League of Arab States shall appoint a Chairman for the Commission for a two years term of office that may be renewed on its termination. When the Chairman is absent the Commission shall elect one of its members to sit in the chair in the absence of its Chairman. The Secretariat-General shall send a representative or representatives to the sessions of the Commission.

Art. 6   The Secretary-General shall designate an official of the Secretariat-General, specialized in the field of human rights to be the Secretary of the Commission.

Art. 7   The permanent seat of the Commission is in Cairo; the Commission, however, may resolve to hold a session, subject to the endorsement of the Secretary-General, in any other Member-State of the League if the performance of the Commission's duties so requires.

Art. 8   The Secretariat-General shall call the Commission to meet. The date of the meeting shall be fixed, taking into consideration that a reasonable period shall be provided for the receipt of invitations and the arrival of the delegates.

Art. 9   A meeting shall be valid if attended by the majority of the Member-States. Resolutions are adopted by the majority of the representatives attending the meetings and meetings shall be closed.

Art. 10   A certain matter may be considered by the Permanent Arab Commission on Human Rights and any other commission or commissions of the League. The Senior Chairman will preside over the meeting. This meeting will be valid if attended by the majority of the members in each commission. Resolutions in such meetings are adopted by the majority of the representatives attending the meeting.

Art. 11   Summary records and the full text of the Resolution adopted in each meeting shall be kept.

Art. 12   The Commission's duties as prescribed in the Pact of the League of Arab States are preparatory, being submitted as draft agreements to the League Council. The Commission may submit its researches, recommendations and suggestions to the Council.

Art. 13   The Commission may set up sub-committees, in which any number of its members may participate; each sub-committee shall deal with one of the technical affairs assigned to the Commission.

Art. 14   The Commission may recommend calling for meetings of experts representing the League's Member-States and other countries, if the situation so requires.

           These experts may advise the Commission as to the matters under consideration. The Secretary-General shall contact the League's Member-State to implement this recommendation.

2. African Charter on Human and Peoples' Rights

As in the case of the Permanent Arab Commission on Human Rights, the proposal for an African Commission on Human Rights originated out of the resolution of the UN General Assembly concerning the creation of regional commissions on human rights. The UN Seminar on the Establishment of Regional Commissions on Human Rights with Special Reference to Africa was convened at Monrovia, Liberia, from October 10 to 21, 1979, and led to a "Draft Proposal for a Possible Model of an African Commission on Human Rights" (UN Doc. St./HR/SER A/4). At the same time, the draft of an African Charter on Human Rights was prepared which was unanimously adopted by the Heads of States and Governments of the OAU at their summit meeting in Nairobi in 1981. The Charter entered into force on 21 October 1986, three months after the receipt of ratification of a simple majority of the OAU member States, that is after 26 ratifications.

The Charter set up the African Commission on Human and Peoples' Rights, consisting of eleven members appointed by the Conference of the Heads of State and Government of the OAU, to implement the Charter. Each member of the Commission has to be qualified in the field of human rights and serves in a personal capacity. No more than two commissioners may be designated by each OAU member State and each State is limited in its choice to no more than one of its own nationals. The members of the Commission are elected for a six year term of office in a revolving system which renews a portion of the members every two years (Art. 36). The Commission adopted its rules of procedure in 1988. The mandate of the Commission is similar to the Inter-American Commission on Human Rights. The Commission may hear as of right inter-state complaints (arts. 47–54), although a clear preference for friendly settlement is expressed and no such communications has ever been brought, and other non-state communications (arts. 55–59). The Commission may, however, not take binding decisions, but only adopts a report which is sent to the States concerned and to the Assembly of Heads of State and Government. In addition, there is an obligation on States parties to produce reports every two years upon the measures taken to implement the rights under the Charter. The Commission is to study the reports and to make observations upon them. However, the reporting system has encountered serious problems, not least in that states have failed to submit reports or adequate reports; furthermore the financial difficulties faced by the Commission have been significant.

No provision had been made in the original text of the Charter for a Court. However, on June 9, 1998, the Assembly of Heads of State and Government of the OAU adopted a protocol to the African Charter on Human and People's Rights on the Establishment of an African Court on Human and Peoples' Rights. This Protocol will come into force after fifteen instruments of ratification or accession have been deposited. The Court has jurisdiction to hear contentious cases as well as the authority to deliver advisory opinions. As in the case of the new European Court of Human rights, individuals may directly bring complaints before it. With the creation of the Court the African system on the protection of human rights provides for all preconditions to effectively protect human rights, although the system will probably need some time to develop and overcome the still existing difficulties.

Texts (Amharic, Arabic, English and French)

Charter on Human and Peoples' Rights
  OAU Doc. CAB/LEG/67/3 Rev. 5
  ILM XXI (1982), 58–68
Rules of Procedure of the Commission as amended in 1995
  Human Rights Law Journal 18 (1997), 154–163
  The Review, International Commission of Jurists 40 (1988), 26 et seq.

Bibliographical notes

K. Vasak, Les droits de l'homme et l'Afrique, Revue belge, Vol. 3 (1967), pp. 459–478

A. H. Robertson, A Commission on Human Rights for Africa, Revue des Droits de l'Homme/Human Rights Journal, Vol. 1 (1968), pp. 696–702

Kéba M'Baye, Les Droits de l'Homme en Afrique, in: K. Vasak (ed.), Les dimensions internationales des Droits de l'Homme (1978), pp. 645–664

Birame Ndiaye, La place des Droits de l'Homme dans la Charte, in: K. Vasak (ed.), Les dimensions internationales des Droits de l'Homme (1978), pp. 664–679

E. G. Bello, African Customary Humanitarian Law (1980)

K. Rogge, Eine Menschenrechtskommission für Afrika?, EuGRZ, Vol. 7 (1980), pp. 22 et seq.

R. Gittleman, The African Charter on Human and Peoples' Rights. A Legal Analysis, Virginia Journal of International Law, Vol. 22 (1982), pp. 667–714

M. Hamalengwa/C. Flintermann/E. Dankwa, The International Law of Human Rights in Africa — Basic Documents and Annotated Bibliography (1988)

U.O Umorozike, The Protection of Human Rights under the Banjul (African) Charter on Human and Peoples' Rights, African Journal of International Law 1 (1988), 65 et seq.

K. Mbaye, Les Droits de l'Homme en Afrique (1992)

E. R. Mbaya, African Charter on Human and Peoples' Rights, in: Bernhardt (ed.), EPIL, Vol. I (1992), 54–58 (with bibliographical indications)

W. Benedek, The African Charter and Commission on Human and Peoples' Rights: How to make it more effective, NQHR 1993, 25 et seq.

E. Ankumah, The African Commission on Human and Peoples' Rights (1996)

N. Krisch, The Establishment of an African Court on Human and Peoples' Rights, ZaöRV 58 (1998), 713–732

a) African Charter on Human and Peoples' Rights of January 27, 1981, Part II

PART II. MEASURES OF SAFEGUARD

CHAPTER I. ESTABLISHMENT AND ORGANISATION OF THE AFRICAN COMMISSION ON HUMAN AND PEOPLES' RIGHTS

Art. 30   An African Commission on Human and Peoples' Rights, hereinafter called "the Commission", shall be established within the Organization of African Unity to promote human and peoples' rights and ensure their protection in Africa.

Art. 31   1. The Commission shall consist of eleven members chosen from amongst African personalities of the highest reputation, known for their high morality, integrity, impartiality and competence in matters of human and peoples' rights; particular consideration being given to persons having legal experience.

2. The members of the Commission shall serve in their personal capacity.

Art. 32   The Commission shall not include more than one national of the same State.

Art. 33   The members of the Commission shall be elected by secret ballot by the Assembly of Heads of State and Government, from a list of persons nominated by the States parties to the present Charter.

Art. 34   Each State party to the present Charter may not nominate more than two candidates. The candidates must have the nationality of one of the States parties to the present Charter. When two candidates are nominated by a State, one of them may not be a national of that State.

Art. 35   1. The Secretary General of the Organization of African Unity shall invite States parties to the present Charter at least four months before the elections to nominate candidates;

2. The Secretary General of the Organization of African Unity shall make an alphabetical list of the persons thus nominated and communicate it to the Heads of State and Government at least one month before the elections.

Art. 36   The members of the Commission shall be elected for a six year period and shall be eligible for re-election. However, the term of office of four of the members elected at the first election shall terminate after two years and the term of office of three others, at the end of four years.

Art. 37   Immediately after the first election, the Chairman of the Assembly of Heads of State and Government of the Organization of African Unity shall draw lots to decide the names of those members referred to in Article 36.

Art. 38 After their election, the members of the Commission shall make a solemn declaration to discharge their duties impartially and faithfully.

Art. 39 1. In case of death or resignation of a member of the Commission, the Chairman of the Commission shall immediately inform the Secretary General of the Organization of African Unity, who shall declare the seat vacant from the date of death or from the date on which the resignation takes effect.

2. If, in the unanimous opinion of other members of the Commission, a member has stopped discharging his duties for any reason other than a temporary absence, the Chairman of the Commission shall inform the Secretary General of the Organization of African Unity, who shall then declare the seat vacant.

3. In each of the cases anticipated above, the Assembly of Heads of State and Government shall replace the member whose seat became vacant for the remaining period of his term unless the period is less than six months.

Art. 40 Every member of the Commission shall be in office until the date his successor assumes office.

Art. 41 The Secretary General of the Organization of African Unity shall appoint the Secretary of the Commission. He shall also provide the staff and services necessary for the effective discharge of the duties of the Commission. The Organization of African Unity shall bear the cost of the staff and services.

Art. 42 1. The Commission shall elect its Chairman and Vice Chairman for a two-year period. They shall be eligible for re-election.

2. The Commission shall lay down its rules of procedure.

3. Seven members shall form the quorum.

4. In case of an equality of votes, the Chairman shall have a casting vote.

5. The Secretary-General may attend the meetings of the Commission. He shall neither participate in deliberations nor shall he be entitled to vote. The Chairman of the Commission may, however, invite him to speak.

Art. 43 In discharging their duties, members of the Commission shall enjoy diplomatic privileges and immunities provided for in the General Convention on the privileges and immunities of the Organization of African Unity.

Art. 44 Provision shall be made for the emoluments and allowances of the members of the Commission in the Regular Budget of the Organization of African Unity.

CHAPTER II. MANDATE OF THE COMMISSION

Art. 45   The functions of the Commission shall be:

1. To promote Human and Peoples' Rights and in particular:

a) To collect documents, undertake studies and researches on African problems in the field of human and peoples' rights, organize seminars, symposia and conferences, disseminate information, encourage national and local institutions concerned with human and peoples' rights, and should the case arise, give its views or make recommendations to Governments.

b) To formulate and lay down, principles and rules aimed at solving legal problems relating to human and peoples' rights and fundamental freedoms upon which African Governments may base their legislations.

c) Co-operate with other African and international institutions concerned with the promotion and protection of human and peoples' rights.

2. Ensure the protection of human and peoples' rights under conditions laid down by the present Charter.

3. Interpret all the provisions of the present Charter at the request of a State Party, an institution of the OAU or an African organization recognized by the OAU.

4. Perform any other tasks which may be entrusted to it by the Assembly of Heads of State and Government.

CHAPTER III. PROCEDURE OF THE COMMISSION

Art. 46   The Commission may resort to any appropriate method of investigation; it may hear from the Secretary-General of the Organization of African Unity or any other person capable of enlightening it.

Communication from States

Art. 47   If a State party to the present Charter has good reasons to believe that another State party to this Charter has violated the provisions of the Charter, it may draw, by written communication, the attention of that State to the matter. This communication shall also be addressed to the Secretary-General of the OAU and to the Chairman of the Commission. Within three months of the receipt of the communication, the State to which the communication is addressed shall give the enquiring State, written explanation or statement elucidating the matter. This should include as much as possible relevant information relating to the laws and rules of procedure applied and applicable and the redress already given or course of action available.

Art. 48   If within three months from the date on which the original communication is received by the State to which it is addressed, the issue is not settled to the satisfaction of the two States involved through bilateral negotiation or by any other peaceful procedure either State shall have the right to submit the matter to the Commission through the Chairman and shall notify the other States involved.

Art. 49 Notwithstanding the provisions of Article 47, if a State party to the present Charter considers that another State party has violated the provisions of the Charter, it may refer the matter directly to the Commission by addressing a communication to the Chairman, to the Secretary-General of the Organization of African Unity and the State concerned.

Art. 50 The Commission can only deal with a matter submitted to it after making sure that all local remedies, if they exist, have been exhausted, unless it is obvious to the Commission that the procedure of achieving these remedies would be unduly prolonged.

Art. 51 1. The Commission may ask the States concerned to provide it with all relevant information.

2. When the Commission is considering the matter, States concerned may be represented before it and submit written or oral representations.

Art. 52 After having obtained from the States concerned and from other sources all the information it deems necessary and after having tried all appropriate means to reach an amicable solution based on the respect of Human and Peoples' Rights, the Commission shall prepare, within a reasonable period of time from the notification referred to in Article 48, a report stating the facts and its findings. This report shall be sent to the States concerned and communicated to the Assembly of Heads of State and Government.

Art. 53 While transmitting its report, the Commission may make to the Assembly of Heads of State and Government such recommendations as it deems useful.

Art. 54 The Commission shall submit to each Ordinary Session of the Assembly of Heads of State and Government a report on its activities.

Other Communications

Art. 55 1. Before each Session, the Secretary of the Commission shall make a list of the communications other than those of States parties to the present Charter and transmit them to the Members of the Commission, who shall indicate which communication should be considered by the Commission.

2. A communication shall be considered by the Commission if a simple majority of its members so decide.

Art. 56 Communications relating to human and peoples' rights referred to in Article 55 received by the Commission, shall be considered if they:

1. indicate their authors even if the latter request anonymity,

2. are compatible with the Charter of the Organization of African Unity or with the present Charter,

3. are not written in disparaging or insulting language directed against the State concerned and its institutions or to the Organization of African Unity,

4. are not based exclusively on news disseminated through the mass media,

5. are sent after exhausting local remedies, if any, unless it is obvious that this procedure is unduly prolonged,

6. are submitted within a reasonable period from the time local remedies are exhausted or from the date the Commission is seized of the matter, and

7. do not deal with cases which have been settled by these States involved in accordance with the principles of the Charter of the United Nations, or the Charter of the Organization of African Unity or the provisions of the present Charter.

Art. 57   Prior to any substantive consideration, all communications shall be brought to the knowledge of the State concerned by the Chairman of the Commission.

Art. 58   1. When it appears after deliberations of the Commission that one or more communications apparently relate to special cases which reveal the existence of a series of serious or massive violations of human and peoples' rights, the Commission shall draw the attention of the Assembly of Heads of State and Government to these special cases.

2. The Assembly of Heads of State and Government may then request the Commission to undertake an in-depth study of these cases and make a factual report, accompanied by its finding and recommendations.

3. A case of emergency duly noticed by the Commission shall be submitted by the latter to the Chairman of the Assembly of Heads of State and Government who may request an in-depth study.

Art. 59   1. All measures taken within the provisions of the present Chapter shall remain confidential until such a time as the Assembly of Heads of State and Government shall otherwise decide.

2. However, the report shall be published by the Chairman of the Commission upon the decision of the Assembly of Heads of State and Government.

3. The report on the activities of the Commission shall be published by its Chairman after it has been considered by the Assembly of Heads of State and Government.

CHAPTER IV. APPLICABLE PRINCIPLES

Art. 60   The Commission shall draw inspiration from international law on human and peoples' rights, particularly from the provisions of various African instruments on human and peoples' rights, the Charter of the United Nations, the Charter of the Organization of African Unity, the Universal Declaration of Human Rights, other instruments adopted by the United Nations and by African countries in the field of human and peoples' rights as well as from the provisions of various instruments adopted within the Specialised Agencies of the United Nations of which the parties to the present Charter are members.

Art. 61   The Commission shall also take into consideration, as subsidiary measures to determine the principles of law, other general or special international conventions, laying down rules expressly recognized by member states of the Organization of African Unity, African practices consistent with international norms on human and peoples' rights, customs generally accepted as law, general principles of law recognized by African states as well as legal precedents and doctrine.

Art. 62   Each State party shall undertake to submit every two years, from the date the present Charter comes into force, a report on the legislative or other measures taken with a view to giving effect to the rights and freedoms recognized and guaranteed by the present Charter.

Art. 63   1. The present Charter shall be open to signature, ratification or adherence of the member states of the Organization of African Unity.

2. The instruments of ratification or adherence to the present Charter shall be deposited with the Secretary General of the Organization of African Unity.

3. The present Charter shall come into force three months after the reception by the Secretary General of the instruments of ratification or adherence of a simple majority of the member states of the Organization of African Unity.

PART III. GENERAL PROVISIONS

Art. 64   1. After the coming into force of the present Charter, members of the Commission shall be elected in accordance with the relevant Articles of the present Charter.

2. The Secretary General of the Organization of African Unity shall convene the first meeting of the Commission at the Headquarters of the Organization within three months of the constitution of the Commission. Thereafter, the Commission shall be convened by its Chairman whenever necessary but at least once a year.

Art. 65   For each of the States that will ratify or adhere to the present Charter after its coming into force, the Charter shall take effect three months after the date of the deposit by that State of its instrument of ratification or adherence.

Art. 66   Special protocols of agreements may, if necessary, supplement the provisions of the present Charter.

Art. 67   The Secretary General of the Organization of African Unity shall inform member states of the Organization of the deposit of each instrument of ratification or adherence.

Art. 68   The present Charter may be amended if a State party makes a written request to that effect to the Secretary General of the Organization of African Unity. The Assembly of Heads of State and Government may only consider the draft amendment after all the States parties have been duly informed of it and the Commission has given its opinion on it at the request of the sponsoring State. The amendment shall be approved by a simple majority of the States parties. It shall come into force for each State which has accepted it in accordance with its constitutional procedure three months after the Secretary General has received notice of the acceptance.

b) Rules of Procedure of the African Commission on Human and Peoples' Rights

Adopted on 13 February 1988 as amended on 6 October 1995

PART ONE: GENERAL PROVISIONS
ORGANIZATION OF THE COMMISSION

CHAPTER I — SESSIONS

Rule 1   Number of Sessions

The African Commission on Human and Peoples' Rights (hereinafter referred to as "The Commission") shall hold the sessions which may be necessary to enable it to carry out satisfactorily its functions in conformity with the African Charter on Human and Peoples' Rights (hereinafter referred to as "The Charter").

Rule 2   Opening Date

1. The Commission shall normally hold two ordinary sessions a year each lasting two weeks.

2. The ordinary sessions of the Commission shall be convened on a date fixed by the Commission on the proposal of its Chairman and in consultation with the Secretary-General of the Organization of African Unity (OAU) (hereinafter referred to as "The Secretary-General").

3. The Secretary-General may change, under exceptional circumstances, the opening date of a session, in consultation with the Chairman of the Commission.

Rule 3   Extraordinary Sessions

1. The Commission may decide to hold extraordinary sessions. When the Commission is not in session, the Chairman may convene extraordinary sessions in consultation with the members of the Commission. The Chairman of the Commission shall also convene extraordinary sessions:

a) at the request of the majority of the members of the Commission

b) at the request of the current Chairman of the Organization of African Unity .

2. Extraordinary sessions shall be convened as soon as possible on a date fixed by the Chairman, in consultation with the Secretary-General and the other members of the Commission.

Rule 4   Place of Meetings

The sessions shall normally be held at the Headquarters of the Commission. The Commission may, in consideration with the Secretary-General, decide to hold a session elsewhere.

Rule 5   Notifications of the Opening Date of the Sessions

The Secretary of the Commission (hereinafter referred to as " the Secretary"), shall inform members of the Commission of the date and venue of the first meeting of each session. This notification shall be sent, in the case of an Ordinary Session, at least eight (8) weeks, if possible, before the Session.

CHAPTER II — AGENDA

Rule 6   Drawing up the Provisional Agenda

1. The Provisional Agenda for each Ordinary Session shall be drawn up by the Secretary in consultation with the Chairman of the Commission in accordance with the provisions of the Charter and these Rules.

2. The Provisional Agenda shall include if necessary, items on: "Communications from States", and "Other Communications" in conformity with the provisions of Article 55 of the Charter. It should not contain any information relating to such communications.

3. Except as specified above on the communications, the Provisional Agenda shall include all the items listed by the present Rules of Procedure as well as the items proposed by:

a) the Commission at a previous session;

b) the Chairman of the Commission or another member of the Commission;

c) a State party to the Charter;

d) the Assembly of Heads of State and Government or the Council of Ministers of the Organization of African Unity;

e) the Secretary-General of the Organization of African Unity on any issue relating to the functions assigned to him by the Charter;

f) a national liberation movement recognized by the Organization of African Unity or by a nongovernmental Organization;

g) a specialized institution of which the States parties to the Charter are members.

4. The items to be included in the provisional agenda under subparagraphs b, c, f and g of paragraph 3 must be communicated to the Secretary, accompanied by essential documents, not later than eight (8) weeks before the Opening of the Session.

5. a) All national liberation movements, specialized institutions, intergovernmental or non-governmental Organizations wishing to propose the inclusion of an item in the Provisional Agenda must inform the Secretary at least ten (10) weeks before the opening of the meeting. Before formally proposing the inclusion of an item in the Provisional Agenda, the observations likely to be made by the Secretary must duly be taken into account.

b) All proposals made under the provisions of the present paragraph shall be included only in the Provisional Agenda of the Commission, if at least two thirds (2/3) of the members present and voting so decide.

6. The Provisional Agenda of the Extraordinary session of the Commission shall include only the item proposed to be considered at that Extraordinary session.

Rule 7   Transmission and Distribution of the Provisional Agenda

1. The Provisional Agenda and the essential documents relating to each item shall be distributed to the members of the Commission by the Secretary who shall endeavour to transmit them to members at least six (6) weeks before the opening of the session.

2. The Secretary shall communicate the Provisional Agenda of that session and have the essential documents relating to each Agenda item distributed at least six weeks before the opening of the session of the Commission to the members of the Commission, member States parties to the Charter, to the current Chairman of the Organization of African Unity and observers.

3. The Draft Agenda shall also be sent to the specialized agencies, to nongovernmental organizations and to the national liberation movements concerned with the agenda.

4. In exceptional cases, the Secretary may, while giving his reasons in writing, have the essential documents relating to some items of the Provisional Agenda distributed at least four (4) weeks prior to the opening of the session.

Rule 8   Adoption of the Agenda

At the beginning of each session, the Commission shall if necessary, after the election of officers in conformity with Rule 17, adopt the agenda of the session on the basis of the Provisional Agenda referred to in Rule 6.

Rule 9   Revision of the Agenda

The Commission may, during the session, revise the Agenda if need be, adjourn, cancel or amend items. During the session, only urgent and important issues may be added to the Agenda.

Rule 10   Draft Provisional Agenda for the Next Session

The Secretary shall, at each session of the Commission, submit a Draft Provisional Agenda for the text session of the Commission, indicating, with respect to each item, the documents to be submitted on that item and the decisions of the deliberative organ which authorized their preparation, so as to enable the Commission to consider these documents as regards the contribution they make to its proceedings, as well as their urgency and relevance to the prevailing situation.

CHAPTER III — MEMBERS OF THE COMMISSION

Rule 11   Composition of the Commission

The Commission shall be composed of eleven (11) members elected by the Assembly of Heads of State and Government (hereinafter referred to as "the Assembly"), in conformity with the relevant provisions of the Charter.

Rule 12   Status of the Members

1. The members of the Commission shall be the eleven (11) personalities appointed in conformity with the provisions of Article 31 of the Charter.

2. Each member of the Commission shall sit on the Commission in a personal capacity. No member may be represented by another person.

Rule 13   Term of Office of the Members

1. The term of office of the members of the Commission elected on 29 July 1987 shall begin from that date. The term of office of the members of the Commission elected at subsequent elections shall take effect the day following the expiry date of the term of office of the members of the Commission they shall replace.

2. However, if a member is re-elected at the expiry of his or her term of office, or elected to replace a member whose term of office has expired or will expire, the term of office shall begin from that expiry date.

3. In conformity with Article 39 (3) of the Charter, the member elected to replace a member whose term of office has not expired, shall complete the term of office of his or her predecessor, unless the remaining term of of-

fice is less than six (6) months. In the latter case, there shall be no re-placement.

Rule 14　Cessation of Functions

1. If in the unanimous opinion of the other members of the Commission, a member has stopped discharging his duties for any reason other than a temporary absence, the Chairman of the Commission shall inform the Secretary of the Organization of African Unity, who shall then declare the seat vacant.

2. In case of the death or resignation of a member of the Commission, the Chairman shall immediately inform the Secretary-General who shall de-clare the seat vacant from the date of the death or from that on which the resignation took effect. The member of the Commission who resigns shall address a written notification of his or her resignation directly to the Chairman or to the Secretary-General and steps to declare his or her seat vacant shall only be taken after receiving the said notification. The resig-nation shall make the seat vacant.

Rule 15　Vacant Seat

Every seat declared vacant in conformity with Rule 14 of the present Rules of Procedure shall be filled on the basis of Article 39 of the Charter.

Rule 16　Oath

Before coming into office, every member of the Commission shall make the following solemn commitment at a public sitting:

"I swear to carry out my duties well and faithfully in all impartiality".

CHAPTER IV — OFFICERS

Rule 17　Election of Officers

1. The Commission shall elect among its members a Chairman and a Vice-Chairman.

2. The elections referred to in the present Rule shall be held by secret ballot. Only the members present shall vote, the member who shall obtain the two-thirds majority of the votes of the members present and voting shall be elected.

3. If no member obtains this two-thirds majority in a second, third and fourth ballot, the member having the highest number of votes at the fifth ballot shall be elected.

4. The officers of the Commission shall be elected for a period of two (2) years. They shall be eligible for re-election. None of them, may, however, exercise his or her functions if he or she ceases to be a member of the Commission.

Rule 18　Powers of the Chairman

The Chairman shall carry out the functions assigned to him by the Charter, the Rules of Procedure and the decisions of the Commission. In the exercise of his functions the Chairman shall be under the authority of the Commission.

Rule 19   Absence of the Chairman

1. The Vice-Chairman shall replace the Chairman during a session if the latter is unable to attend a whole or part of a sitting of a session.

2. In the absence of both the Chairman and the Vice-Chairman, members shall elect an acting Chairman.

Rule 20   Functions of the Vice-Chairman

The Vice-Chairman, acting in the capacity of the Chairman, shall have the same rights and the same duties as the Chairman.

Rule 21   Cessation of the Functions of an Officer

If any of the officers ceases to carry out his or her functions or declares that he or she is no longer able to serve as an officer or exercise the functions of a member of the Commission, a new officer shall be elected for the remaining term of office of his or her predecessor.

CHAPTER V — SECRETARIAT

Rule 22   Function of the Secretary-General

1. The Secretary-General or his representative may attend the meetings of the Commission. He shall neither participate in the deliberations, nor in the voting. He may, however, be called upon by the Chairman of the Commission to make written or oral statements at the sittings of the Commission.

2. He shall appoint, in consultation with the Chairman of the Commission the Secretary of the Commission.

3. He shall, in consultation with the Chairman provide the Commission with the necessary staff, means and services for it to carry out effectively the functions and missions assigned to it under the Charter.

4. The Secretary-General acting through the Secretary shall take all the necessary steps for the meetings of the Commission.

Rule 23   Functions of the Secretary to the Commission

The Secretary of the Commission shall be responsible for the activities of the Secretariat under the general supervision of the Chairman, and particularly:

a) He/she shall assist the Commission and its members in the exercise of their functions;

b) He/she shall serve as an intermediary for all the communications concerning the Commission;

c) He/she shall be the custodian of the archives of the Commission;

d) The Secretary shall bring immediately to the knowledge of the members of the Commission all the issues that will be submitted to him/her.

Rule 24   Estimates

Before the Commission shall approve a proposal entailing expenses, the Secretary shall prepare and distribute, as soon as possible, to the members of the Commission, the financial implications of the proposal. It shall be incumbent on the Chairman to draw the attention of the members to those implications, so that they discuss them when the proposal shall be considered by the Commission.

Rule 25   Financial Rules

The Financial Rules adopted pursuant to the provisions of Article 41 and 44 of the Charter, shall be appended to the present Rules of Procedure.

Rule 26   Financial Responsibility

The Organization of African Unity shall bear the expenses of the staff and the facilities and services placed at the disposal of the Commission to carry out its functions.

Rule 27   Records of Cases

A special record, with a reference number and initialed, in which shall be entered the date of registration of each petition and communication and that of the closure of the procedure relating to them before the Commission, shall be kept at the Secretariat.

CHAPTER VI — SUBSIDIARY BODIES

Rule 28   Establishment of Committees and Working Groups

1. The Commission may during a session, taking into account the provisions of the Charter establish, if it deems it necessary for the exercise of its functions, committees or working groups, composed of the members of the Commission and send them any agenda item for consideration and report.

2. These committees or working groups may, in consultation with the Secretary-General, be authorized to sit when the Commission is not in session.

3. The members of the committees or working groups shall be appointed by the Chairman subject to the approval of the absolute majority of the other members of the Commission.

Rule 29   Establishment of Sub-Commissions

1. The Commission may establish sub-Commissions of experts after the prior approval of the Assembly;

2. Unless the Assembly decides otherwise, the Commission shall determine the functions and composition of each sub-Commission.

Rule 30 Officers of the Subsidiary Bodies

Unless the Commission decides otherwise, the subsidiary bodies of the Commission shall elect their own officers.

Rule 31 Rules of Procedure

The Rules of Procedure of the Commission shall apply, as far as possible, to the proceedings of its subsidiary bodies.

CHAPTER VII — PUBLIC SESSIONS AND PRIVATE SESSIONS

Rule 32 General Principle

The sittings of the Commission and of its subsidiary bodies shall be held in public unless the Commission decides otherwise or it appears from the relevant provisions of the Charter that the meeting shall be held in private.

Rule 33 Publication of Proceedings

At the end of each private or public sitting, the Commission or its subsidiary bodies may issue a communiqué.

CHAPTER VIII — LANGUAGES

Rule 34 Working Languages

The working languages of the Commission and of all its institutions shall be those of the Organization of African Unity.

Rule 35 Interpretation

1. The address delivered in one of the working languages shall be interpreted in the other working languages.

2. Any person addressing the Commission in a language other than one of the working languages, shall, in principle, ensure the interpretation in one of the working languages. The interpreters of the Secretariat may take the interpretation of the original language as source language for their interpretation in the other working languages.

Rule 36 Languages to be used for Minutes of Proceedings

The summary minutes of the sittings of the Commission shall be drafted in the working languages.

Rule 37 Languages to be Used for Resolutions and Other Official Decisions

All the official decisions and documents of the Commission will be rendered in the working languages.

CHAPTER IX — MINUTES AND REPORTS

Rule 38 Tape Recordings of the Sessions

The Secretariat shall record and preserve the tapes of the sessions of the Commission. It may also record and conserve the tapes of the sessions of the committees, working groups and sub-commissions if the Commission so decides.

Rule 39   Summary Minutes of the Sessions

The Secretariat shall draft the summary minutes of the public and private sessions of the Commission and of its subsidiary bodies. It shall distribute them as soon as possible in a draft form to the members of the Commission and to all other participants in the session. All those participants may, in the thirty (30) days following the receipt of the draft minutes of the session, submit corrections to the Secretariat. The Chairman may, under special circumstances, in consultation with the Secretary-General, extend the time for the submission of the corrections.

In case the corrections are contested, the Chairman of the Commission or the Chairman of the subsidiary body whose minutes they are, shall resolve the disagreement after having listened to, if necessary, the tape recording of the discussions. If the disagreement persists, the Commission or the subsidiary body shall decide. The corrections shall be published in a distinct volume after the closure of the session.

Rule 40   Distribution of the Minutes of the Private Sessions and Public Sessions

1. The final summary minutes of the public and private sessions shall be documents intended for general distribution unless the Commission decides otherwise.

2. The minutes of the private sessions of the Commission shall be distributed forthwith to all members of the Commission.

Rule 41   Reports to be submitted after each Session

The Commission shall submit to the current Chairman of the Organization of African Unity, a report on the deliberations of each session. This report shall contain a brief summary of the recommendations and statements on issues to which the Commission would like to draw the attention of the current Chairman and member States of the Organization of African Unity.

Rule 42   Submission of official Decisions and Reports

The text of the decisions and reports officially adopted by the Commission shall be distributed to all the members of the Commission as soon as possible.

CHAPTER X — CONDUCT OF THE DEBATES

Rule 43   Quorum

The quorum shall be constituted by seven (7) members of the Commission, as specified in Article 42 (3) of the Charter.

Rule 44   General Powers of the Chairman

1. In addition to the powers entrusted to him/her under other provisions of the present Rules of Procedure, the Chairman shall have the responsibility to open and close each session; he/she shall direct the debates, ensure the application of the present Rules of Procedure, grant the use of the floor, submit to a vote matters under discussion and announce the result of the vote taken.

2. Subject to the provisions of the present Rules of Procedure, the Chairman shall direct the discussions of the Commission and ensure order during meetings. The Chairman may during the discussion of an agenda item, propose to the Commission to limit the time allotted to speakers, as well as the number of interventions of each speaker on the same issue and close the list of speakers.

3. He/she shall rule on the points of order. He/she shall also have the power to propose the adjournment and the closure of debates as well as the adjournment and suspension of a sitting. The debates shall deal solely with the issue submitted to the Commission and the Chairman may call a speaker whose remarks are irrelevant to the matter under discussion, to order.

Rule 45   Points of Order

1. During the debate of any matter a member may, at any time, raise a point of order and the point of order shall be immediately decided by the Chairman, in accordance with the Rules of Procedure. If a member appeals against the decision, the appeal shall immediately be put to the vote and if the Chairman's ruling is not overruled by the majority of the members present, it shall be maintained.

2. A member raising a point of order cannot, in his or her comments, deal with the substance of the matter under discussion.

Rule 46   Adjournment of Debates

During the discussion on any matter, a member may move the adjournment of the debate on the matter under discussion. In addition to the proposer of the motion one member may speak in favour of and one against the motion after which the motion shall be immediately put to the vote.

Rule 47   Limit of the Time accorded to Speakers

The Commission may limit the time accorded to each speaker on any matter, when the time allotted for debates is limited and a speaker spends more than one time accorded, the Chairman shall immediately call him to order.

Rule 48   Closing of the List of Speakers

The Chairman may, during a debate, read out the list of speakers and with the approval of the Commission, declare the list closed. Where there are no more speakers, the Chairman shall, with the approval of the Commission, declare the debate closed.

Rule 49   Closure of Debate

A member may, at any time, move for the closure of the debate on the matter under discussion, even if other members or representatives expressed the desire to take the floor. The authorization to take the floor on the closure of the debate shall be given only to two speakers before the closure, after which the motion shall immediately be put to the vote.

Rule 50   Suspension or Adjournment of the Meeting

During the discussion of any matter, a member may move for the suspension or adjournment of the meeting. No discussion on any such motion shall be permitted and it shall immediately be put to the vote.

Rule 51   Order of the Motions

Subject to the provisions of Rule 45 of the present Rules of Procedure, the following motions shall have precedence in the following order over all the other proposals or motions before the meeting:

a) to suspend the meeting;

b) to adjourn the meeting;

c) to adjourn the debate on the item under discussion;

d) for the closure of the debate on the item under discussion.

Rule 52   Submission of Proposals and Amendments of Substance

Unless the Commission decides otherwise the proposals, amendments or motions of substance made by members shall be submitted in writing to the Secretariat; they shall be considered at the first sitting following their submission.

Rule 53   Decisions on Competence

Subject to the provisions of Rule 45 of the Procedure, any motion tabled by a member for a decision on the competence of the Commission to adopt a proposal submitted to it shall immediately be put to the vote.

Rule 54   Withdrawal of a Proposal or a Motion

The sponsor of a motion or a proposal may still withdraw it before it is put to the vote, provided that it has not been amended. A motion or a proposal thus withdrawn may be submitted again by another member.

Rule 55   New Consideration of a Proposal or Motion

When a proposal is adopted or rejected, it shall not be considered again at the same session, unless the Commission decides otherwise. When a member moves the new consideration of a proposal, only one member may speak in favour of and one against the motion, after which it shall immediately be put to the vote.

Rule 56   Interventions

1. No member may take the floor at a meeting of the Commission without prior authorization of the Chairman. Subject to Rules 45, 48, 49 and 50 the Chairman shall grant the use of the floor to the speakers in the order in which it has been requested.

2. The debates shall deal solely with the matter submitted to the Commission and the Chairman may call to order a speaker whose remarks are irrelevant to the matter under discussion.

3. The Chairman may limit the time accorded to speakers and the number of interventions which each member may make on the same issue, in accordance with Rule 44 of the present Rules.

4. Only two members in favour and two against the motion of fixing such time limits shall be granted the use of the floor after which the motion shall immediately be put to the vote. For questions of procedure the time allotted to each speaker shall not exceed five minutes, unless the Chairman decides otherwise. When the time allotted for discussions is limited and a speaker exceeds the time accorded the Chairman shall immediately call him to order.

Rule 57   Right of Reply

The right of reply shall be granted by the Chairman to any member requesting it. The member must, while exercising this right, be as brief as possible and take the floor preferably at the end of the sitting at which this right has been requested.

Rule 58   Congratulations

The congratulations addressed to the newly elected members to the Commission shall only be presented by the Chairman or a member designated by the latter. Those addressed to the newly elected officers shall only be presented by the outgoing Chairman or a member designated by him.

Rule 59   Condolences

Condolences shall be exclusively presented by the Chairman on behalf of all the members. The Chairman may, with the consent of the Commission, send a message of condolence.

CHAPTER XI — VOTE AND ELECTIONS

Rule 60   Right to Vote

Each member of the Commission shall have one vote. In the case of equal number of votes the Chairman shall have the casting vote.

Rule 61   Asking for a Vote

A proposal or a motion submitted for the decision of the Commission shall be put to the vote if a member so requests. If no member asks for a vote, the Commission may adopt a proposal or a motion without a vote.

Rule 62   Required Majority

1. Except as otherwise provided by the Charter or other Rules of the present Rules of Procedure, decisions of the Commission shall be taken by the simple majority of the members present and voting.

2. For the purpose of the present Rules of Procedure, the expression "members present and voting" shall mean members voting for or against. The members who shall abstain from voting shall be considered as non-voting members.

3. Decisions may be taken by consensus, failing which, the Commission shall resort to voting.

Rule 63   Method of Voting

1. Subject to the provisions of Rule 68, the Commission, unless it otherwise decides, shall normally vote by show of hands, but any member may request the roll-call vote, which shall be taken in the alphabetical order of the names of the members of the Commission beginning with the member whose name is drawn by lot by the Chairman. In all the votes by roll-call each member shall reply "yes", "no", or "abstention". The Commission may decide to hold a secret ballot.

2. In case of vote by roll-call, the vote of each member participating in the ballot shall be recorded in the minutes.

Rule 64   Explanation of Vote

Members may make brief statements for the only purpose of explaining their vote, before the beginning of the vote or once the vote has been taken. The member who is the sponsor of a proposal or a motion cannot explain his vote on that proposal or motion except if it has been amended.

Rule 65   Rules to be Observed while Voting

A ballot shall not be interrupted except if a member raises a point of order relating to the manner in which the ballot is held. The Chairman may allow members to intervene briefly, whether before the ballot beginning or when it is closed, but solely to explain their vote.

Rule 66   Division of Proposals and Amendments

Proposals and amendments may be separated if requested. The parts of the proposals or of the amendments which have been adopted shall later be put to the vote as whole; if all the operative parts of a proposal have been rejected, the proposal shall be considered to have been rejected as a whole.

Rule 67   Amendment

An amendment to a proposal is an addition to, deletion from or revision of part of that proposal.

Rule 68   Order of Vote on Amendments

When an amendment is moved to a proposal, the amendment shall be voted on first. When two or more amendments are moved to a proposal, the Commission shall first vote on the amendment furthest removed in substance from the original proposal and then on the amendment next furthest removed therefrom and so until all the amendments have been put to the vote. Nevertheless when the adoption of an amendment implies the rejection of another amendment, the latter shall not be put to the vote. If one or several amendments are adopted, the amended proposal shall then be put to the vote.

Rule 69   Order of Vote on the Proposals

1. If two or more proposals are made on the same matter, the Commission, unless it decides otherwise, shall vote on these proposals in the order in which they were submitted.

2. After each vote the Commission may decide whether it shall put the next proposal to the vote.

3. However, the motions which are not the substance of the proposals shall be voted upon before the said proposals.

Rule 70   Elections

The elections shall be held by secret ballot, unless the election is for a post for which only one candidate has been proposed and that candidate has been agreed upon by the members of the Commission.

CHAPTER XII — PARTICIPATION OF NON-MEMBERS OF THE COMMISSION

Rule 71   Participation of States in the Deliberations

1. The Commission or its subsidiary bodies may invite any State to participate in the discussion of any issue that shall be of particular interest to that State.

2. A State thus invited shall have no voting right, but may submit proposals which may be put to the vote at the request of any member of the Commission or of the subsidiary body concerned.

Rule 72   Participation of Other Persons or Organizations

The Commission may invite any organization or person capable of enlightening it to participate in its deliberations without voting rights.

Rule 73   Participation of Specialized Institutions and Consultations with the Latter

1. Pursuant to the agreements concluded between the Organization of African Unity and the Specialized Institutions, the latter shall have the right to:

a) be represented in the public sessions of the Commission and its subsidiary bodies,

b) participate, without voting rights, through their representatives in deliberations on issues which shall be of interest to them and to submit, on these issues, proposals which may be put to the vote at the request of any member of the Commission or the interested subsidiary body.

2. Before placing in the provisional agenda an issue submitted by a Specialized Institution, the Secretary-General should initiate such preliminary consultations as may be necessary, with this institution.

3. When an issue proposed for inclusion in the provisional agenda of a session, or which has been added to the agenda of a session pursuant to Rule 5 of the present Rules of Procedure, contains a proposal requesting the Organization of African Unity to undertake additional activities relating to issues concerning directly one or more specialized institutions, the Secretary-General should enter into consultation with the institutions concerned and inform the Commission of the ways and means of ensuring co-ordinated utilization of the resources of the various institutions.

4. When at a meeting of the Commission, a proposal calling upon the Organization of African Unity to undertake additional activities relating to issues directly concerning one or several specialized institutions, the Secretary-General, after consulting as far as possible, the representatives of the interested institutions, should draw the attention of the Commission to the effects of that proposal.

5. Before taking a decision on the proposals mentioned above, the Commission shall make sure that the institutions concerned have been duly consulted.

Rule 74   Participation of other Inter-Governmental Organizations

1.The Secretary shall inform, not later than 4 weeks before a session, non-governmental organizations with observer status of the days and agenda of a forthcoming session.

2. Representatives of Inter-Governmental Organizations to which the Organization of African Unity has granted permanent observer status and other Organizations recognized by the Commission, may participate, without voting rights, in the deliberations of the Commission on issues falling within the framework of the activities of these organizations.

CHAPTER XIII — RELATIONS WITH AND REPRESENTATION OF NON-GOVERNMENTAL ORGANIZATIONS

Rule 75   Representation

Non-governmental organizations, granted observer status by the Commission, may appoint authorized observers to participate in the public sessions of the Commission and of its subsidiary bodies.

Rule 76   Consultation

The Commission may consult the non-governmental organizations either directly or through one or several committees set up for this purpose.

These consultations may be held at the invitation of the Commission or at the request of the organization.

CHAPTER XIV — PUBLICATION AND DISTRIBUTION OF THE REPORTS AND OTHER OFFICIAL DOCUMENTS OF THE COMMISSION

Rule 77   Report of the Commission

Within the framework of the procedure of communication among States parties to the Charter, referred to in Articles 47 and 49 of the Charter, the Commission shall submit to the Assembly a report containing, where possible, recommendations it shall deem necessary. The report shall be confidential. However, it shall be published by the Chairman of the Commission after reporting unless the Assembly directs otherwise.

Rule 78   Periodical reports of Member States

Periodical Reports and other information submitted by States parties to the Charter as requested under Article 62 of the Charter, shall be documents for general distribution. The same thing shall apply to other information supplied by a State party to the Charter, unless the Commission decides otherwise.

Rule 79   Reports on the Activities of the Commission

1. As stipulated in Article 54 of the Charter, the Commission shall each year submit to the Assembly, a report on its deliberations, in which it shall include a summary of its activities.

2. The report shall be published by the Chairman after the Assembly shall have considered it.

Rule 80   Translation of Reports and Other Documents

The Secretary shall endeavour to translate all reports and other documents of the Commission into the working languages.

PART TWO: PROVISIONS RELATING TO THE FUNCTIONS OF THE COMMISSION

CHAPTER XV — PROMOTIONAL ACTIVITIES

Reports submitted by States Parties of the Charter under Article 62 of the Charter

Rule 81   Contents of Reports

1. States parties to the Charter shall submit reports in the form required by the Commission on measures they have taken to give effect to the rights recognized by the Charter and on the progress made with regard to the enjoyment of these rights. The reports should indicate, where possible, the factors and difficulties impeding the implementation of the provisions of the Charter.

2. If a State party fails to comply with Article 62 of the Charter, the Commission shall fix the date for the submission of that State party's report.

3. The Commission may, through the Secretary-General, inform States parties to the Charter of its wishes regarding the form and the contents of the reports to be submitted under Article 62 of the Charter.

Rule 82   Transmission of the Reports

1. The Secretary may, after consultation with the Commission, communicate to the specialized institutions concerned, copies of all parts of the reports which may relate to their areas of competence, produced by member States of these institutions.

2. The Commission may invite the specialized institutions to which the Secretary has communicated parts of the reports, to submit observations relating to these parts within a time limit that it may specify.

Rule 83   Submission of Reports

The Commission shall inform, as early as possible, member States parties to the Charter, through the Secretary, of the opening date, duration and venue of the Session at which their respective reports shall be considered.

Representatives of the States parties to the Charter may participate in the sessions of the Commission at which their reports shall be considered. The Commission may also inform a State party to the Charter from which it wanted complementary information, that it may authorize its representative to participate in a specific session. This representative should be able to reply to questions put to him by the Commission and make statements on reports already submitted by this State. He may also furnish additional information from his State.

Rule 84   Non-submission of Reports

1. The Secretary shall, at each session, inform the Commission of all cases of non-submission of reports or of additional information requested pursuant to Rules 81 and 85 of the Rules of Procedure. In such cases, the Commission may send, through the Secretary, to the State party to the Charter concerned, a report or reminder relating to the submission of the report or additional information.

2. If, after the reminder referred to in paragraph 1 of this Rule, a State party to the Charter does not submit the report or the additional information requested pursuant to Rules 81 and 85 of the Rules of Procedure, the Commission shall point it out in its yearly report to the Assembly.

Rule 85   Examination of Information Contained in Reports

1. When considering a report submitted by a State party to the Charter under Article 62 of the Charter, the Commission should first make sure that the report provides all the necessary information including relevant legislation pursuant to the provisions of Rule 61 of the Rules of Procedure.

2. If, in the opinion of the Commission, a report submitted by a State party to the Charter, does not contain adequate information, the Commission may request this State to furnish the additional information required, by indicating the date on which the information needed should be submitted.

3. If, following the consideration of the reports, and the information submitted by a State party to the Charter, the Commission decides that the State has not discharged some of its obligations under the Charter, it may address all general observations to the State concerned as it may deem necessary.

Rule 86   Adjournment and Transmission of the Reports

1. The Commission shall, through the Secretary, communicate to States parties to the Charter for comments, its general observations made following the consideration of the reports and the information submitted by States parties to the Charter. The Commission may, where necessary, fix a time limit for the submission of the comments by the States parties to the Charter.

2. The Commission may also transmit to the Assembly, the observations mentioned in paragraph 1 of this Rule, accompanied by copies of the reports it has received from the States parties to the Charter as well as the comments supplied by the latter, if possible.

Rule 87   Promotional Activities

1. The Commission shall adopt and carry out a program of action which gives effect to its obligations under the Charter, particularly Article 45 (1).

2. The Commission shall carry out other promotional activities in member states and elsewhere on a continuing basis.

3. Each member of the Commission shall file a written report on his/her activities at each session including countries visited and organizations contacted.

CHAPTER XVI — PROTECTION ACTIVITIES COMMUNICATIONS FROM THE STATES PARTIES TO THE CHARTER

Section I — Procedure for the Consideration of Communications Received in Conformity with Article 47 of the Charter: Procedure for Communications — Negotiations

Rule 88   Procedure

1. A communication submitted under Article 47 of the Charter should be submitted to the Secretary-General, the Chairman of the Commission and the State party concerned.

2. The communication referred to above should be in writing and contain a detailed and comprehensive statement on the actions denounced as well as the provisions of the Charter alleged to have been violated.

3. The notification of the communication to the State party to the Charter, the Secretary-General and the Chairman of the Commission shall be done through the most practicable and reliable means.

Rule 89   Register of Communications

The Secretary shall keep a permanent register for all communications received under Article 47 of the Charter.

Rule 90   Reply and Time Limit

1. The reply of the State party to the Charter to which a communication is addressed should reach the requesting State party to the Charter within 3 months following the receipt of the notification of the communication.

2. It shall be accompanied particularly by:

a) written explanations, declarations or statements relating to the issues raised;

b) possible indications and measures taken to end the situation denounced;

c) indications on the law and rules of procedure applicable or applied;

d) indications on the local procedures for appeal already used, in process or still open.

Rule 91   Non-Settlement of the Issue

1. If within three (3) months from the date the notification of the original communication is received by the addressee State, the issue has not been settled to the satisfaction of the two interested parties, through the selected channel of negotiation or through any other peaceful procedure selected by common consent of the parties, the issue shall be referred to the Commission in accordance with the provisions of Article 48 of the Charter.

2. The issue shall also be referred to the Commission if the addressee State party to the Charter fails to react to the request made under Article 47 of the Charter, within the same 3 months' period of time.

Rule 92   Seizing of the Commission

At the expiration of the 3 months' time limit referred to in Article 47 of the Charter, and in the absence of a satisfactory reply or in case the addressee State party to the Charter fails to react to the request, each State party may submit the communication to the Commission through a notification addressed to its Chairman, to the other interested State party and to the Secretary-General.

Section II — Procedure for the Consideration of the Communications received in Conformity with Articles 48 and 49 of the Charter: Procedure for Communication — Complaint

Rule 93   Seizing of the Commission

1. Any communication submitted under Articles 48 and 49 of the Charter may be submitted to the Commission by anyone of the interested States parties through notification addressed to the Chairman of the Commission, the Secretary-General and the State party concerned.

2. The notification referred to in paragraph 1 of the present Rule shall contain information on the following elements or be accompanied particularly by:

a) measures taken to try to resolve the issue pursuant to Article 47 of the Charter including the text of the initial communication and any future written explanation from the interested States parties to the Charter relating to the issue;

b) measures taken to exhaust local procedures for appeal;

c) any other procedure for the international investigation or international settlement to which the interested States parties have resorted.

Rule 94   Permanent Register of Communications

The Secretary shall keep a permanent register for all communications received by the Commission under Articles 48 and 49 of the Charter.

Rule 95   Seizing of the Members of the Commission

The Secretary shall immediately inform members of the Commission of any notification received pursuant to Rule 91 of these Rules of Procedure and shall send to them, as early as possible, a copy of the notification as well as the relevant information.

Rule 96   Private Session and Press Releases

1. The Commission shall consider the communications referred to in Article 48 and 49 of the Charter in closed session.

2. After consulting the interested States parties to the Charter, the Commission may issue through the Secretary, release on its private sessions for the attention of the media and the public.

Rule 97   Consideration of the Communication

The Commission shall consider a communication only when:

a) the procedure offered to the States parties by Articles 47 of the Charter has been exhausted;

b) the time limit set in Article 48 of the Charter has expired;

c) the Commission is certain that all the available local remedies have been utilized and exhausted, in accordance with the generally recognized principles of international law, or that the application of these remedies is unreasonably prolonged or that there are no effective remedies.

Rule 98   Amicable settlement

Except for the provisions of the present Rules of Procedure, the Commission shall place its good offices at the disposal of the interested States parties to the Charter so as to reach an amicable solution on the issue based on the respect of human rights and fundamental liberties, as recognised by the Charter.

Rule 99   Additional Information

The Commission may through the Secretary, request the States parties or one of them to communicate additional information or observations orally or in writing. The Commission shall fix a time limit for the submission of the written information or observations.

Rule 100   Representation of States Parties

1. The States parties to the Charter concerned shall have the right to be represented during the consideration of the issue by the Commission and to submit observations orally and in writing or in either form.

2. The Commission shall notify, as soon as possible, the States parties concerned, through the Secretary, of the opening day, the duration and the venue of the session at which the issue will be examined.

3. The procedure to be followed for the presentation of oral or written observations shall be determined by the Commission.

Rule 101   Report of the Commission

1. The Commission shall adopt a report pursuant to Article 52 of the Charter within 12 months, following the notification referred to in Article 48 of the Charter and Rule 90 of the present Rules of Procedure.

2. The provisions of paragraph 1 of Rule 99 of these Rules of Procedure shall not apply to the deliberations of the Commission relating to the adoption of the report.

3. The report referred to above shall concern the decisions and conclusions that the Commission will reach.

4. The report of the Commission shall be communicated to the States parties concerned through the Secretary.

5. The report of the Commission shall be sent to the Assembly through the Secretary-General, together with the recommendations it shall deem useful.

CHAPTER XVII — OTHER COMMUNICATIONS
PROCEDURE FOR THE CONSIDERATION OF THE COMMUNICATIONS
RECEIVED IN CONFORMITY WITH ARTICLE 55 OF THE CHARTER

Section I — Transmission of Communications to the Commission

Rule 102   Seizing of the Commission

1. Pursuant to these Rules of Procedure, the Secretary shall transmit to the Commission the communications submitted to him for consideration by the Commission in accordance with the Charter.

2. No communication concerning a State which is not a party to the Charter shall be received by the Commission or placed in a list under Rule 103 of the present Rules.

Rule 103   List of Communications

1. The Secretary of the Commission shall prepare lists of communications submitted to the Commission pursuant to Rule 101 above, to which he shall attach a brief summary of their contents and regularly cause these lists to be distributed to members of the Commission. Besides, the Secretary shall keep a permanent register of all these Communications which shall be made public.

2. The full text of each communication referred to the Commission shall be communicated to each member of the Commission on request.

Rule 104   Request for Clarifications

1. The Commission, through the Secretary, may request the author of a communication to furnish clarifications on the applicability of the Charter to his communication, and to specify in particular:

a) his name, address, age and profession by justifying his very identity, if ever he /she is requesting the Commission to be kept anonymous;

b) name of the State party referred to in the communication;

c) purpose of the communication;

d) provision(s) of the Charter allegedly violated;

e) the facts of the claim;

f) measures taken by the author to exhaust local remedies, or explanation why local remedies will be futile;

g) the extent to which the same issue has been settled by another international investigation or settlement body.

2. When asking for clarification or information, the Commission shall fix an appropriate time limit for the author to submit the communication so as to avoid undue delay in the procedure provided for by the Charter.

3. The Commission may adopt a questionnaire for use by the author of the communication in providing the above mentioned information.

4. The request for clarification referred to in paragraph 1 of this Rule shall not prevent the inclusion of the communication on the lists mentioned in paragraph 1 of Rule 102 above.

Rule 105   Distribution of Communications

For each communication recorded, the Secretary shall prepare as soon as possible, a summary of the relevant information received, which shall be distributed to the members of the Commission.

Section II — General Provisions Governing the Consideration of the Communications by the Commission or its Subsidiary Bodies

Rule 106 Private Session

The sessions of the Commission or its subsidiary bodies during which the communications are examined as provided for in the Charter shall be private.

Rule 107 Public Sessions

The sessions during which the Commission may consider other general issues. such as the application procedure of the Charter, shall be public.

Rule 108 Press Releases

The Commission may issue, through the Secretary and for the attention of the media and the public, releases on the activities of the Commission in its private session.

Rule 109 Incompatibility

1. No member shall take part in the consideration of a communication by the Commission:

a) if he/she has any personal interest in the case, or

b) if he/she has participated, in any capacity, in the adoption of any decision relating to the case which is the subject of the communication.

2. Any issue relating to the application of paragraph 1 above shall be resolved by the Commission.

Rule 110 Withdrawal of a Member

If, for any reason, a member considers that he/she should not take part or continue to take part in the consideration of a communication, he/she shall inform the Chairman of his/her decision to withdrawal.

Rule 111 Provisional Measures

1. Before making its final views known to the Assembly on the communication, the Commission may inform the State party concerned of its views on the appropriateness of taking provisional measures to avoid irreparable damage being caused to the victim of the alleged violation. In so doing, the Commission shall inform the State party that the expression of its views on the adoption of those provisional measures does not imply a decision on the substance of the communication.

2. The Commission, or when it is not in session, the Chairman, in consultation with other members of the Commission, may indicate to the parties any interim measure, the adoption of which seems desirable in the interest of the parties or the proper conduct of the proceedings before it.

3. In case of urgency when the Commission is not in session, the Chairman in consultation with other members of the Commission, may take any necessary action on behalf of the Commission. As soon as the Com-

mission is again in session, the Chairman shall report to it on any action taken.

Rule 112 Information to the State Party to the Charter

Prior to any substantive consideration, every communication should be made known to the State concerned through the Chairman of the Commission pursuant to Article 57 of the Charter.

Section III — Procedures to Determine Admissibility

Rule 113 Time Limits for Consideration of the Admissibility

The Commission shall decide, as early as possible and pursuant to the following provisions, whether or not the communication shall be admissible under the Charter.

Rule 114 Order of Consideration of Communications

1. Unless otherwise decided, the Commission shall consider the communications in the order they have been received by the Secretariat.

2. The Commission may decide, if it deems it good, to consider jointly two or more communications.

Rule 115 Working Groups

1. The Commission may set up one or more working groups, each composed of three of its members at most, to submit recommendations on admissibility as stipulated in Article 56 of the Charter.

Rule 116 Admissibility of the Communications

The Commission shall determine questions of admissibility pursuant to Article 56 of the Charter.

Rule 117 Additional Information

1. The Commission or a working group set up under Rule 113, may request the State party concerned or the author of the communication to submit in writing additional information or observations relating to the issue of admissibility of the communication. The Commission or the working group shall fix a time limit for the submission of the information or observations to avoid the issue dragging on too long.

2. A communication may be declared admissible if the State party concerned has been given the opportunity to submit the information and observations pursuant to paragraph 1 of this Rule.

3. A request made under paragraph 1 of this Rule should indicate clearly that the request does not mean that any decision whatsoever has been taken on the issue of admissibility.

4. However, the Commission shall decide on the issue of admissibility if the State party fails to send a written response within three (3) months from the date of notification of the text of the communication.

Rule 118 Decision of the Commission on Admissibility

1. If the Commission decides that a communication is inadmissible under the Charter, it shall make its decision known as early as possible, through the Secretary to the author of the communication and, if the communication has been transmitted to a State party concerned, to that State.

2. If the Commission has declared a communication inadmissible under the Charter, it may re-consider this decision at a later date if it receives a request for reconsideration.

Section IV — Procedures for the Consideration of Communications

Rule 119 Proceedings

1. If the Commission decides that a communication is admissible under the Charter, its decision and the text of the relevant documents shall as soon as possible, be submitted to the State party concerned, through the Secretary. The author of the communication shall also be informed of the Commission's decision through the Secretary.

2. The State party to the Charter concerned shall, within the 3 ensuing months, submit in writing to the Commission explanations or statements elucidating the issue under consideration and indicating, if possible, measures it was able to take to remedy the situation.

3. All explanations or statements submitted by a State party pursuant to the present Rule shall be communicated, through the Secretary, to the author of the communication who may submit in writing additional information and observations within a time limit fixed by the Commission.

4. State parties from whom explanations or statements are sought within specified times shall be informed that if they fail to comply within those times the Commission will act on the evidence before it.

Rule 120 Final Decision of the Commission

1. If the communication is admissible, the Commission shall consider it in the light of all the information that the individual and the State party concerned has submitted in writing; it shall make known its observations on this issue. To this end, the Commission may refer the communication to a working group, composed of 3 of its members at most, which shall submit recommendations to it.

2. The observations of the Commission shall be communicated to the Assembly through the Secretary-General and to the State concerned.

3. The Assembly or its Chairman may request the Commission to conduct an in-depth study on these cases and to submit a factual report accompanied by its findings and recommendations, in accordance with the provisions of the Charter. The Commission may entrust this function to a Special Rapporteur or a working group.

FINAL CHAPTER — AMENDMENT AND SUSPENSION OF THE RULES OF PROCEDURE

Rule 121   Method of Amendment

Only the Commission may modify the present Rules of Procedure.

Rule 122   Method of Suspension

The Commission may suspend temporarily the application of any Rule of the present Rules of Procedure, on condition that such a suspension shall not be incompatible with any applicable decision of the Commission or the Assembly or with any relevant provision of the Charter and that the proposal shall have been submitted 24 hours in advance. This condition may be set aside if no member opposes it. Such a suspension may take place only with a specific and precise object in view and should be limited to the duration necessary to achieve that aim.

c) Protocol to the African Charter on Human and Peoples' Rights on the Establishment of an African Court on Human and Peoples' Rights

Adopted by the 34th Ordinary Session of the Assembly of Heads of State and Government of the OAU from 8–10 June, 1998

The Member States of the Organization of African Unity hereinafter referred to as the OAU, States Parties to the African Charter on Human and Peoples' Rights:

Considering that the Charter of the Organization of African Unity recognizes that freedom, equality, justice, peace and dignity are essential objectives for the achievement of the legitimate aspirations of the African peoples;

Noting that the African Charter on Human and Peoples' Rights reaffirms adherence to the principles of human and peoples' rights, freedoms and duties contained in the declarations, conventions and other instruments adopted by the Organization of African Unity, and other international organizations;

Recognizing that the twofold objective of the African Charter on Human and peoples' Rights is to ensure on the one hand promotion and on the other protection of human and peoples' rights, freedoms and duties;

Recognizing further, the efforts of the African Commission on Human and Peoples' Rights in the promotion and protection of human and peoples' rights since its inception in 1987,

Recalling resolution AHG/Res. 230 (XXX) adopted by the Assembly of Heads of State and Government in June 1994 in Tunis, Tunisia, requesting the Secretary-General to convene a Government experts' meeting to ponder, in conjunction with the African Commission, over the means to enhance the efficiency of the African Commission and to consider in particular the establishment of an African Court on Human and Peoples' Rights;

Noting the first and second Government legal experts' meetings held respectively in Cape Town, South Africa (September, 1995) and Nouakchott, Mauritania (April, 1997), and the third Government Legal Experts meeting held in Addis Ababa, Ethiopia (December, 1997), which was enlarged to include Diplomats;

Firmly convinced that the attainment of the objectives of the African Charter on Human and Peoples' Rights requires the establishment of an African Court on Human and Peoples' Rights to complement and reinforce the functions of the African Commission on Human and Peoples' Rights.

Have agreed as follows:

Art. 1   Establishment of the Court.

There shall be established within the Organization of African Unity an African Court on Human and Peoples' Rights hereinafter referred to as "the Court", the organization, jurisdiction and functioning of which shall be governed by the present Protocol.

Art. 2   Relationship between the Court and the Commission.

The Court shall, bearing in mind the provisions of this Protocol, complement the protective mandate of the African Commission on Human and Peoples' Rights hereinafter referred to as "the Commission", conferred upon it by the African Charter on Human and Peoples' Rights, hereinafter referred to as "the Charter".

Art. 3   Jurisdiction.

(1) The jurisdiction of the Court shall extend to all cases and disputes submitted to it concerning the interpretation and application of the Charter, this Protocol and any other Human Rights instrument ratified by the States concerned.

(2) In the event of a dispute as to whether the Court has jurisdiction, the Court shall decide.

Art. 4   Advisory Opinions.

(1) At the request of a Member State of the OAU, the OAU, any of its organs, or any African organization recognized by the OAU, the Court may provide an opinion on any legal matter relating to the Charter or any other relevant human rights instruments, provided that the subject matter of the opinion is not related to a matter being examined by the Commission.

(2) The Court shall give reasons for its advisory opinions provided that every judge shall be entitled to deliver a separate or dissenting decision.

Art. 5   Access to the Court.

(1) The following are entitled to submit cases to the Court

a. The Commission

b. The State Party which has lodged a complaint to the Commission;

c. The State Party against which the complaint has been lodged at the Commission;

d. The State Party whose citizen is a victim of human rights violations;

e. The African Intergovernmental Organizations.

(2) When a State Party has an interest in a case, it may submit a request to the Court to be permitted to join.

(3) The Court may entitle the relevant Non Governmental Organizations (NGOs) with observer status before the Commission, and individuals to institute cases directly before it, in accordance with Article 34 (6) of this Protocol.

Art. 6   Admissibility of Cases.

(1) The Court, when deciding on the admissibility of a case instituted under article 5 (3) of this Protocol, may request the opinion of the Commission which shall give it as soon as possible.

(2) The Court shall rule on the admissibility of cases taking into account the provisions of article 56 of the Charter.

(3) The Court may consider cases or transfer them to the Commission.

Art. 7   Sources of Law.

The Court shall apply the provisions of the Charter and any other relevant human rights instruments ratified by the States concerned.

Art. 8   Consideration of Cases.

The Rules of Procedure of the Court shall lay down the detailed conditions under which the Court shall consider cases brought before it, bearing in mind the complementarity between the Commission and the Court.

Art. 9   Amicable Settlement.

The Court may try to reach an amicable settlement in case pending before it in accordance with the provisions of the Charter.

Art. 10   Hearings and Representation.

(1) The Court shall conduct its proceedings in public. The Court may, however, conduct proceedings *in camera* as may be provided for in the Rules of Procedure.

(2) Any party to a case shall be entitled to be represented by a legal representative of the party's choice. Free legal representation may be provided where the interests of justice so require.

(3) Any person, witness or representative of the parties, who appears before the Court, shall enjoy protection and all facilities, in accordance with

international law, necessary for the discharging of their functions, tasks and duties in relation to the Court.

Art. 11   Composition.

(1) The Court shall consist of eleven judges, nationals of Member States of the OAU, elected in an individual capacity from among jurists of high moral character and of recognized practical, judicial or academic competence and experience in the field of human and peoples' rights.

(2) No two judges shall be nationals of the same State.

Art. 12   Nominations.

(1) States Parties to the Protocol may each propose up to three candidates, at least two of whom shall be nationals of that State.

(2) Due consideration shall be given to adequate gender representation in the nomination process.

Art. 13   List of Candidates.

(1) Upon entry into force of this Protocol, the Secretary-General of the OAU shall request each State Party to the Protocol to present, within ninety (90) days of such a request, its nominees for the office of judge of the Court.

(2) The Secretary-General of the OAU shall prepare a list in alphabetical order of the candidates nominated and transmit it to the Member States of the OAU at least thirty days prior to the next session of the Assembly of Heads of State and Government of the OAU hereinafter referred to as "the Assembly".

Art. 14   Elections.

(1) The judges of the Court shall be elected by secret ballot by the Assembly from the list referred to in Article 13 (2) of the present Protocol.

(2) The Assembly shall ensure that in the Court as a whole there is a representation of the main regions of Africa and of their principal legal traditions.

(3) In the election of judges, the Assembly shall ensure that there is adequate gender representation.

Art. 15   Terms of Office.

(1) The judges of the Court shall be elected for a period of six years and may be re-elected only once. The terms of four judges elected at the first election shall expire at the end of two years, and the terms of four more judges shall expire at the end of four years.

(2) The judges whose terms are to expire at the end of the initial periods of two and four years shall be chosen by lot to be drawn by the Secretary-General of the OAU immediately after the first election has been completed.

(3) A judge elected to replace a judge whose term of office has not expired shall hold office for the remainder of the predecessor's term.

(4) All judges except the President shall perform their functions on part-time basis. However, the Assembly may change this arrangement as it deems appropriate.

Art. 16   Oath of Office.

After their election, the judges of the Court shall make a solemn declaration to discharge their duties impartially and faithfully.

Art. 17   Independence.

(1) The independence of the judges shall be fully ensured in accordance with international law.

(2) No judge may hear any case in which the same judge has previously taken part as agent, counsel or advocate for one of the parties or as a member of a national or international court or commission of enquiry or in any other capacity. Any doubt on this point shall be settled by decision of the Court.

(3) The judges of the Court shall enjoy, from the moment of their election and throughout their term of office, the immunities extended to diplomatic agents in accordance with international law.

(4) At no time shall the judges of the Court be held liable for any decision or opinion issued in the exercise of their functions.

Art. 18   Incompatibility.

The position of judge of the Court is incompatible with any activity that might interfere with the independence or impartiality of such a judge or the demands of the office, as determined in the Rules of Procedure of the Court.

Art. 19   Cessation of Office.

(1) A judge shall not be suspended or removed from office unless, by the unanimous decision of the other judges of the Court, the judge concerned has been found to no longer fulfilling the required conditions to be a judge of the Court.

(2) Such a decision of the Court shall become final unless it is set aside by the Assembly at its next session.

Art. 20   Vacancies.

(1) In case of death or resignation of a judge of the Court, the President of the Court shall immediately inform the Secretary-General of the Organization of African Unity, who shall declare the seat vacant from the date of death or from the date on which the resignation takes effect.

(2) The Assembly shall replace the judge whose office became vacant unless the remaining period of the term is less than one hundred and eighty (180) days.

(3) The same procedure and considerations as set out in Articles 12, 13 and 14 shall be followed for the filling of vacancies.

Art. 21   Presidency of the Court.

(1) The Court shall elect its President and one Vice-President for a period of two years. They may be re-elected only once.

(2) The President shall perform judicial functions on a full-time basis and shall reside at the seat of the Court.

(3) The functions of the President and the Vice-President shall be set out in the Rules of Procedure of the Court.

Art. 22   Exclusion.

If a judge is a national of any State which is a party to a case submitted to the Court, that judge shall not hear the case.

Art. 23   Quorum.

The Court shall examine the cases brought before it, if it has a quorum of seven judges.

Art. 24   Registry of the Court.

(1) The Court shall appoint its own Registrar and other staff of the registry from among nationals of Member States of the OAU according to the Rules of Procedure.

(2) The office and residence of the Registrar shall be at the place where the Court has its seat.

Art.25   Seat of the Court.

(1) The Court shall have its seat at the place determined by the Assembly from, among States Parties to this Protocol. However, it may convene in the territory of any Member State of the OAU when the majority of the Court considers it desirable, and with the prior consent of the State concerned.

(2) The seat of the Court may be changed by the Assembly after due consultation with the Court.

Art. 26   Evidence.

(1) The Court shall hear submission by all parties and if deemed necessary, hold an enquiry. The States concerned shall assist by providing relevant facilities for the efficient handling of the case.

(2) The Court may receive written and oral evidence including expert testimony and shall make its decision on the basis of such evidence.

Art. 27   Findings.

(1) If the Court finds that there has been a violation of a human or peoples' right, it shall make appropriate orders to remedy the violation, including the payment of fair compensation or reparation.

(2) In cases of extreme gravity and urgency, and when necessary to avoid irreparable harm to persons, the Court shall adopt such provisional measures as it deems necessary.

Art. 28   Judgment.

(1) The Court shall render its judgment within ninety (90) days of having completed its deliberations.

(2) The judgement of the Court decided by majority shall be final and not subject to appeal.

(3) Without prejudice to sub-article 2 above, the Court may review its decision in the light of new evidence under conditions to be set out in the Rules of Procedure.

(4) The Court may interpret its own decision.

(5) The judgment of the Court shall be read in open court, due notice having been given to the parties.

(6) Reasons shall be given for the judgment of the Court.

(7) If the judgment of the Court does not represent, in whole or in part, the unanimous decision of the judges, any judge shall be entitled to deliver a separate or dissenting opinion.

Art. 29   Notification of Judgment.

(1) The parties to the case shall be notified of the judgment of the Court and it shall be transmitted to the Member States of the OAU and the Commission.

(2) The Council of Ministers shall also be notified of the judgment and shall monitor its execution on behalf of the Assembly.

Art. 30   Execution of Judgment.

The States Parties to the present Protocol undertake to comply with the judgment in any case to which they are parties within the time stipulated by the Court and to guarantee its execution.

Art. 31   Report.

The Court shall submit to each regular session of the Assembly, a report on its work during the previous year. The report shall specify, in particular, the cases in which a State has not complied with the Court's judgment.

Art. 32   Budget.

Expenses of the Court, emoluments and allowances for judges and the budget of its registry, shall be determined and borne by the OAU, in accordance with criteria laid down by the OAU in consultation with the Court.

Art. 33   Rules of Procedure.

The Court shall draw up its Rules and determine its own procedures. The Court shall consult the Commission as appropriate.

Art. 34   Ratification.

(1) This Protocol shall be open for signature and ratification or accession by any State Party to the Charter.

(2) The instrument of ratification or accession to the present Protocol shall be deposited with the Secretary-General of the OAU.

(3) The Protocol shall come into force thirty days after fifteen instruments of ratification or accession have been deposited.

(4) For any State Party ratifying or acceding subsequently, the present Protocol shall come into force in respect of that State on the date of the deposit of its instrument of ratification or accession.

(5) The Secretary-General of the OAU shall inform all Member States of the entry into force of the present Protocol.

(6) At the time of the ratification of this Protocol or any time thereafter, the State shall make a declaration accepting the competence of the Court to receive cases under article 5 (3) of this Protocol. The Court shall not receive any petition under article 5 (3) involving a State Party which has not made such a declaration.

(7) Declarations made under sub-article 6 above shall be deposited with the Secretary-General, who shall transmit copies thereof to the State parties.

Art. 35   Amendments.

(1) The present Protocol may be amended if a State Party to the Protocol makes a written request to that effect to the Secretary-General of the OAU. The Assembly may adopt, by simple majority, the draft amendment after all the States Parties to the present Protocol have been duly informed of it and the Court has given its opinion on the amendment.

(2) The Court shall also be entitled to propose such amendments to the present Protocol as it may deem necessary, through the Secretary-General of the OAU.

(3) The amendment shall come into force for each State Party which has accepted it thirty days after the Secretary-General of the OAU has received notice of the acceptance.

Third Part:
Treaties Concerning Economic Cooperation

I. Universal Treaties

World Trade Organization of April 15, 1994

The post-war economic system was designed to create efficient mechanisms to cope with international economic crises. Such efforts were particularly undertaken within the United Nations by creating the Economic and Social Council as a principal organ of the Unites Nations, which engaged in creating an international trade order. The first result of these efforts was the adoption of the Charter for an International Trade Organization, the Havana Charter, in 1948. At the same time measures were taken to lower tariff barriers which led to the drafting of a General Agreement on Tariffs and Trade on the basis of parts of the Havana Charter. In 1947 a Protocol on the provisional application of this Agreement was concluded giving life to the GATT. While the Havana Charter finally failed, the GATT remained. GATT engaged in further reducing tariffs by convoking the so-called GATT rounds, one of the more important rounds being held at Tokyo in 1979 leading to the conclusion of additional and separate agreements, the codes, which had different membership. In order to reach a systematic organization of the numerous trade agreements, the Uruguay-Round (1986–1994) was convoked which finally ended by strengthening the institutional structures and rules of GATT and by establishing the World Trade Organization (WTO). The WTO provides for a consolidated institutional basis for world trade relations, relying largely on GATT structures and the GATT Agreement of 1947 which was incorporated into the new WTO by a specific agreement called "GATT 1994". The new order requires all Members — with a few exceptions only — to accept all agreements. New concerns were included such as trade related aspects of intellectual property and trade in services.

A significant development has also been reached for the dispute settlement system by the new Dispute Settlement Understanding (DSU) replacing the former system and strengthening the rule of law; it bars circumvention manoeuvres, which had been rather frequent under GATT. The DSU is based on Art. XXII and XXIII GATT and further elaborates and modifies those provisions. The DSU covers all Agreements of the WTO, but excludes the Trade Policy Review Mechanism (TPRM). A number of Agreements have some special provisions on dispute settlement, which are listed in Appendix 2. The causes for action are laid down in Art. XXIII GATT. Contrary to the former GATT dispute settlement system, the reports adopted by the panel have binding force between the parties.

The WTO system provides for a series of dispute settlement institutions which are the following: a) The Dispute Settlement Body (DSB), which assures the administration of the dispute settlement system and is entrusted to the General Council, which, however, may elect a different chairperson and acts under specific rules of procedure; b) the panels, which are established *ad hoc* for each dispute on the request by a complaining Party; c) the Appellate Body, which is a standing body of 7 persons and has to review panel reports on request of the parties. The appeal is limited to issues of law and legal interpretation covered in the panel report.

As had been the case under Art. XXII of GATT, the dispute settlement procedures start with consultations between the members concerned according to provisions laid down in the DSU concerning particularly time-limits. Only after the failure of consultations, the complaining party has the right to request the establishment of a panel. After the adoption of the report of the panel or eventually the appellate body the members concerned have to inform the DSB about their intentions in respect of the implementation of the report. The DSB remains seized of the matter until the issue is finally resolved. In case of disagreement about due compliance with the report, recourse to the dispute settlement procedures is open, if possible to the original panel. If the report is not implemented within a reasonable time, compensation and suspension of concessions or other obligations are possible as a temporary measure awaiting full implementation. A detailed procedure is provided for to reach agreement on implementation failing which further retaliation measures may be taken by the DSB. If the member concerned objects to the retaliation measures, the matter shall be referred to arbitration which shall be preferably carried out by the original panel. The surveillance of the DSU remains in effect until the report has been finally implemented.

Texts

WTO, The Results of the Uruguay Round of Multilateral Trade Negotiations: The Legal Texts, Geneva, 1994

WTO, Legal Instruments embodying the Results of the Uruguay Round, 34 vols., Geneva, 1994

Multilateral Trade Negotiations Final Act Embodying the Results of the Uruguay Round of Trade Negotiations, ILM 33 (1994), 1125 ff.

Bibliographical notes

Y. Iwasawa, The Dispute Settlement of the World Trade Organization (1995)

P. Pescatore/W. J. Davey/A.F. Lowenfeld, Handbook of WTO, GATT dispute settlement, loose leaf collection (basic edition 1992)

E. U. Petersmann (ed.), International Trade Law and the GATT/WTO dispute settlement system (1997)

E. U. Petersmann et al., WTO Dispute Settlement System, Journal of International Economic Law, Special Issue 1 (1998), 175 ff.

T. Cottier, Die Durchsetzung der Prinzipien und Beschlüsse der WTO: das Streitbeilegungsverfahren und seine Auswirkungen, in: Die Bedeutung der WTO für die europäische Wirtschaft (1997), 121–137

E.U. Petersmann, The GATT/WTO dispute settlement system: international Law, international organizations and dispute settlement (1997)

J. Cameron/K. Campbell (eds.), Dispute Resolution in the World Trade Organisation (1998)

J. H. Jackson, Dispute Settlement and the WTO: emerging problems, Journal of International Economic Law 1 (1998), 329–351

J. Wiers, The WTO's Rules of Conduct for Dispute Settlement, Leiden Journal of International Law 11 (1998), 265–274

T. Stoll, WTO, in: R. Bernhardt (ed.), EPIL, vol. IV

T. Stoll, WTO and Dispute settlement, in: R. Bernhardt (ed.), EPIL, vol. IV

Activity

Cases of panels and of the appellate body are to be found on the WTO homepage under http://www.wto.org/wto.dispute/dispute.htm

a) Basic Text of October 30, 1947

Art.   Consultation

XXII   1. Each contracting party shall accord sympathetic consideration to and
shall afford adequate opportunity for consultation regarding such representations as may be made by another contracting party with respect to
any matter affecting the operation of this Agreement.

2. The CONTRACTING PARTIES may, at the request of a contracting
party, consult with any contracting party or parties in respect of any
matter for which it has not been possible to find a satisfactory solution
through consultation under paragraph 1.

Art   Nullification or Impairment

XXIII   1. If any contracting party should consider that any benefit accruing to it
directly or indirectly under this Agreement is being nullified or impaired
or that the attainment of any objective of the Agreement is being impeded
as a result of

(a) the failure of another Contracting party to carry out its obligations
under this Agreement, or

(b) the application by another contracting party of any measure, whether
or not it conflicts with the provisions of this Agreement, or

(c) the existence of any other situation,

the contracting party may, with a view to the satisfactory adjustment of
the matter, make written representations or proposals to the other contracting party or parties which it considers to be concerned. Any contracting party thus approached shall give sympathetic consideration to the
representations or proposals made to it.

2. If no satisfactory adjustment is effected between the contracting parties
concerned within a reasonable time, or if the difficulty is of the type described in paragraph 1 (c) of this Article, the matter may be referred to
the CONTRACTING PARTIES. The CONTRACTING PARTIES
shall promptly investigate any matter so referred to them and shall make
appropriate recommendations to the contracting parties which they consider to be concerned, or give a ruling on the matter, as appropriate. The
CONTRACTING PARTIES may consult with contracting parties, with
the Economic and Social Council of the United Nations and with any appropriate inter-governmental organization in cases where they consider
such consultation necessary. If the CONTRACTING PARTIES consider
that the circumstances are serious enough to justify such action, they may
authorize a contracting party or parties to suspend the application to any
other contracting party or parries of such concessions or other obligations
under this Agreement as they determine to be appropriate in the circumstances. If the application to any contracting party of any concession or
other obligation is in fact suspended that contracting party shall be free,
not later than sixty days after such action is taken, to give written notice

to the Executive Secretary to the CONTRACTING PARTIES of its intention to withdraw from this Agreement and such withdrawal shall take effect upon the sixtieth day following the day on which such notice is received by him.

b) Agreement Establishing the World Trade Organization of April 15, 1994

Art. IV   Structure of the WTO

1. There shall be a Ministerial Conference composed of representatives of all the Members, which shall meet at least once every two years. The Ministerial Conference shall carry out the functions of the WTO and take actions necessary to this effect. The Ministerial Conference shall have the authority to take decisions on all matters under any of the Multilateral Trade Agreements, if so requested by a Member, in accordance with the specific requirements for decision-making in this Agreement and in the relevant Multilateral trade Agreement.

2. There shall be a General Council composed of representatives of all the Members, which shall meet as appropriate. In the intervals between meetings of the Ministerial Conference, is functions shall be conducted by the General Council. The General Council shall also carry out the functions assigned to it by this Agreement. The General Council shall establish its rules of procedure and approve the rules of procedure for the Committees provided for in paragraph 7.

3. The General Council shall convene as appropriate to discharge the responsibilities of the Dispute Settlement Body provided for in the Dispute Settlement Understanding. The Dispute Settlement Body may have its own chairman and shall establish such rules of procedure as it deems necessary for the fulfilment of those responsibilities.

4. The General Council shall convene as appropriate to discharge the responsibilities of the trade Policy Review Body provided for in the TPRM. The Trade Policy Review Body may have its own chairman and shall establish such rules of procedure as it deems necessary for the fulfilment of those responsibilities.

5. .....

c) Annex 2 to the Agreement

Understanding on Rules and Procedures Governing the Settlement of Disputes

Members hereby *agree* as follows:

Art. 1   Coverage and Application

1. The rules and procedures of this Understanding shall apply to disputes brought pursuant to the consultation and dispute settlement provisions of the agreements listed in Appendix 1 to this Understanding (referred to in this Understanding as the "covered agreements"). The rules and procedures of this Understanding shall also apply to consultations and the settlement of disputes between Members concerning their rights and obligations under the provisions of the Agreement Establishing the World Trade Organization (referred to in this Understanding as the "WTO Agreement") and of this Understanding taken in isolation or in combination with any other covered agreement.

2. The rules and procedures of this Understanding shall apply subject to such special or additional rules and procedures on dispute settlement contained in the covered agreements as are identified in Appendix 2 to this Understanding. To the extent that there is a difference between the rules and procedures of this Understanding and the special or additional rules and procedures set forth in Appendix 2, the special or additional rules and procedures in Appendix 2 shall prevail. In disputes involving rules and procedures under more than one covered agreement, if there is a conflict between special or additional rules and procedures of such agreements under review, and where the parties to the dispute cannot agree on rules and procedures within 20 days of the establishment of the panel, the Chairman of the Dispute Settlement Body provided for in paragraph 1 of Article 2 (referred to in this Understanding as the "DSB"), in consultation with the parties to the dispute, shall determine the rules and procedures to be followed within 10 days after a request by either Member. The Chairman shall be guided by the principle that special or additional rules and procedures should be used where possible, and the rules and procedures set out in this Understanding should be used to the extent necessary to avoid conflict.

Art. 2   Administration

1. The Dispute Settlement Body is hereby established to administer these rules and procedures and, except as otherwise provided in a covered agreement, the consultation and dispute settlement provisions of the covered agreements. Accordingly, the DSB shall have the authority to establish panels, adopt panel and Appellate Body reports, maintain surveillance of implementation of rulings and recommendations, and authorize suspension of concessions and other obligations under the covered agree-

ments. With respect to disputes arising under a covered agreement which is a Plurilateral Trade Agreement, the term "Member" as used herein shall refer only to those Members that are parties to the relevant Plurilateral Trade Agreement. Where the DSB administers the dispute settlement provisions of a Plurilateral Trade Agreement, only those Members that are parties to that Agreement may participate in decisions or actions taken by the DSB with respect to that dispute.

2. The DSB shall inform the relevant WTO Councils and Committees of any developments in disputes related to provisions of the respective covered agreements.

3. The DSB shall meet as often as necessary to carry out its functions within the time-frames provided in this Understanding.

4. Where the rules and procedures of this Understanding provide for the DSB to take a decision, it shall do so by consensus.[1]

Art. 3   General Provisions

1. Members affirm their adherence to the principles for the management of disputes heretofore applied under Articles XXII and XXIII of GATT 1947, and the rules and procedures as further elaborated and modified herein.

2. The dispute settlement system of the WTO is a central element in providing security and predictability to the multilateral trading system. The Members recognize that it serves to preserve the rights and obligations of Members under the covered agreements, and to clarify the existing provisions of those agreements in accordance with customary rules of interpretation of public international law. Recommendations and rulings of the DSB cannot add to or diminish the rights and obligations provided in the covered agreements.

3. The prompt settlement of situations in which a Member considers that any benefits accruing to it directly or indirectly under the covered agreements are being impaired by measures taken by another Member is essential to the effective functioning of the WTO and the maintenance of a proper balance between the rights and obligations of Members.

4. Recommendations or rulings made by the DSB shall be aimed at achieving a satisfactory settlement of the matter in accordance with the rights and obligations under this Understanding and under the covered agreements.

5. All solutions to matters formally raised under the consultation and dispute settlement provisions of the covered agreements, including arbitration awards, shall be consistent with those agreements and shall not nul-

---

[1] The DSB shall be deemed to have decided by consensus on a matter submitted for its consideration, if no Member, present at the meeting of the DSB when the decision is taken, formally objects to the proposed decision.

lify or impair benefits accruing to any Member under those agreements, nor impede the attainment of any objective of those agreements.

6. Mutually agreed solutions to matters formally raised under the consultation and dispute settlement provisions of the covered agreements shall be notified to the DSB and the relevant Councils and Committees, where any Member may raise any point relating thereto.

7. Before bringing a case, a Member shall exercise its judgement as to whether action under these procedures would be fruitful. The aim of the dispute settlement mechanism is to secure a positive solution to a dispute. A solution mutually acceptable to the parties to a dispute and consistent with the covered agreements is clearly to be preferred. In the absence of a mutually agreed solution, the first objective of the dispute settlement mechanism is usually to secure the withdrawal of the measures concerned if these are found to be inconsistent with the provisions of any of the covered agreements. The provision of compensation should be resorted to only if the immediate withdrawal of the measure is impracticable and as a temporary measure pending the withdrawal of the measure which is inconsistent with a covered agreement. The last resort which this Understanding provides to the Member invoking the dispute settlement procedures is the possibility of suspending the application of concessions or other obligations under the covered agreements on a discriminatory basis vis-à-vis the other Member, subject to authorization by the DSB of such measures.

8. In cases where there is an infringement of the obligations assumed under a covered agreement, the action is considered prima facie to constitute a case of nullification or impairment This means that there is normally a presumption that a breach of the rules has an adverse impact on other Members parties to that covered agreement, and in such cases, it shall be up to the Member against whom the complaint has been brought to rebut the charge.

9. The provisions of this Understanding are without prejudice to the rights of Members to seek authoritative interpretation of provisions of a covered agreement through decision-making under the WTO Agreement or a covered agreement which is a Plurilateral Trade Agreement.

10. It is understood that requests for conciliation and the use of the dispute settlement procedures should not be intended or considered as contentious acts and that, if a dispute arises, all Members will engage in these procedures in good faith in an effort to resolve the dispute. It is also understood that complaints and counter-complaints in regard to distinct matters should not be linked.

11. This Understanding shall be applied only with respect to new requests for consultations under the consultation provisions of the covered agreements made on or after the date of entry into force of the WTO Agreement. With respect to disputes for which the request for consultations was made under GATT 1947 or under any other predecessor agreement

to the covered agreements before the date of entry into force of the WTO Agreement, the relevant dispute settlement rules and procedures in effect immediately prior to the date of entry into force of the WTO Agreement shall continue to apply.[1]

12. Notwithstanding paragraph 11, if a complaint based on any of the covered agreements is brought by a developing country Member against a developed country Member, the complaining party shall have the right to invoke, as an alternative to the provisions contained in Articles 4, 5, 6 and 12 of this Understanding, the corresponding provisions of the Decision of 5 April 1966 (BISD 14S/18), except that where the Panel considers that the time-frame provided for in paragraph 7 of that Decision is insufficient to provide its report and with the agreement of the complaining party, that time-frame may be extended. To the extent that there is a difference between the rules and procedures of Articles 4, 5, 6 and 12 and the corresponding rules and procedures of the Decision, the latter shall prevail.

Art. 4   Consultations

1. Members affirm their resolve to strengthen and improve the effectiveness of the consultation procedures employed by Members.

2. Each Member undertakes to accord sympathetic consideration to and afford adequate opportunity for consultation regarding any representations made by another Member concerning measures affecting the operation of any covered agreement taken within the territory of the former.[2]

3. If a request for consultations is made pursuant to a covered agreement, the Member to which the request is made shall, unless otherwise mutually agreed, reply to the request within 10 days after the date of its receipt and shall enter into consultations in good faith within a period of no more than 30 days after the date of receipt of the request, with a view to reaching a mutually satisfactory solution. If the Member does not respond within 10 days after the date of receipt of the request, or does not enter into consultations within a period of no more than 30 days, or a period otherwise mutually agreed, after the date of receipt of the request, then the Member that requested the holding of consultations may proceed directly to request the establishment of a panel.

4. All such requests for consultations shall be notified to the DSB and the relevant Councils and Committees by the Member which requests consultations. Any request for consultations shall be submitted in writing and shall give the reasons for the request, including identification of the measures at issue and an indication of the legal basis for the complaint.

---

[1] This paragraph shall also be applied to disputes on which panel reports have not been adopted or fully implemented.

[2] Where the provisions of any other covered agreement concerning measures taken by regional or local governments or authorities within the territory of a Member contain provisions different from the provisions of this paragraph, the provisions of such other covered agreement shall prevail.

5. In the course of consultations in accordance with the provisions of a covered agreement, before resorting to further action under this Understanding, Members should attempt to obtain satisfactory adjustment of the matter.

6. Consultations shall be confidential, and without prejudice to the rights of any Member in any further proceedings.

7. If the consultations fail to settle a dispute within 60 days after the date of receipt of the request for consultations, the complaining party may request the establishment of a panel. The complaining party may request a panel during the 60-day period if the consulting parties jointly consider that consultations have failed to settle the dispute.

8. In cases of urgency, including those which concern perishable goods, Members shall enter into consultations within a period of no more than 10 days after the date of receipt of the request. If the consultations have failed to settle the dispute within a period of 20 days after the date of receipt of the request, the complaining party may request the establishment of a panel.

9. In cases of urgency, including those which concern perishable goods, the parties to the dispute, panels and the Appellate Body shall make every effort to accelerate the proceedings to the greatest extent possible.

10. During consultations Members should give special attention to the particular problems and interests of developing country Members.

11. Whenever a Member other than the consulting Members considers that it has a substantial trade interest in consultations being held pursuant to paragraph 1 of Article XXII of GATT 1994, paragraph 1 of Article XXII of GATS, or the corresponding provisions in other covered agreements[1], such Member may notify the consulting Members and the DSB, within 10 days after the date of the circulation of the request for consultations under said Article, of its desire to be joined in the consultations. Such Member shall be joined in the consultations, provided that the Member to which the request for consultations was addressed agrees that

---

[1]   The corresponding consultation provisions in the covered agreements are listed hereunder: Agreement on Agriculture, Article 19; Agreement on the Application of Sanitary and Phytosanitary Measures, paragraph 1 of Article 11; Agreement on Textiles and Clothing, paragraph 4 of Article 8; Agreement on Technical Barriers to Trade, paragraph 1 of Article 14; Agreement on Trade-Related Investment Measures, Article 8; Agreement on Implementation of Article VI of GATT 1994, paragraph 2 of Article 17; Agreement on Implementation of Article VII of GATT 1994, paragraph 2 of Article 19; Agreement on Preshipment Inspection, Article 7; Agreement on Rules of Origin, Article 7; Agreement on Import Licensing Procedures, Article 6; Agreement on Subsidies and Countervailing Measures, Article 30; Agreement on Safeguards, Article 14; Agreement on Trade-Related Aspects of Intellectual Property Rights, Article 64.1; and any corresponding consultation provisions in Plurilateral Trade Agreements as determined by the competent bodies of each Agreement and as notified to the DSB.

the claim of substantial interest is well-founded. In that event they shall so inform the DSB. If the request to be joined in the consultations is not accepted, the applicant Member shall be free to request consultations under paragraph 1 of Article XXII or paragraph 1 of Article XXIII of GATT 1994, paragraph 1 of Article XXII or paragraph 1 of Article XXIII of GATS, or the corresponding provisions in other covered agreements.

Art. 5   Good Offices, Conciliation and Mediation

1. Good offices, conciliation and mediation are procedures that are undertaken voluntarily if the parties to the dispute so agree.

2. Proceedings involving good offices, conciliation and mediation, and in particular positions taken by the parties to the dispute during these proceedings, shall be confidential, and without prejudice to the rights of either party in any further proceedings under these procedures.

3. Good offices, conciliation or mediation may be requested at any time by any party to a dispute. They may begin at any time and be terminated at any time. Once procedures for good offices, conciliation or mediation are terminated, a complaining party may then proceed with a request for the establishment of a panel.

4. When good offices, conciliation or mediation are entered into within 60 days after the date of receipt of a request for consultations, the complaining party must allow a period of 60 days after the date of receipt of the request for consultations before requesting the establishment of a panel. The complaining party may request the establishment of a panel during the 60-day period if the parties to the dispute jointly consider that the good offices, conciliation or mediation process has failed to settle the dispute.

5. If the parties to a dispute agree, procedures for good offices, conciliation or mediation may continue while the panel process proceeds.

6. The Director-General may, acting in an *ex officio* capacity, offer good offices, conciliation or mediation with the view to assisting Members to settle a dispute.

Art. 6   Establishment of Panels

1. If the complaining party so requests, a panel shall be established at the latest at the DSB meeting following that at which the request first appears as an item on the DSB's agenda, unless at that meeting the DSB decides by consensus not to establish a panel.[1]

2. The request for the establishment of a panel shall be made in writing. It shall indicate whether consultations were held, identify the specific measures at issue and provide a brief summary of the legal basis of the complaint sufficient to present the problem clearly. In case the applicant re-

---

[1] If the complaining party so requests, a meeting of the DSB shall be convened for this purpose within 15 days of the request, provided that at least 10 days' advance notice of the meeting is given.

quests the establishment of a panel with other than standard terms of reference, the written request shall include the proposed text of special terms of reference.

Art. 7   Terms of Reference of Panels

1. Panels shall have the following terms of reference unless the parties to the dispute agree otherwise within 20 days from the establishment of the panel:

"To examine, in the light of the relevant provisions in (name of the covered agreement(s) cited by the parties to the dispute), the matter referred to the DSB by (name of party) in document ... and to make such findings as will assist the DSB in making the recommendations or in giving the rulings provided for in that/those agreement(s)."

2. Panels shall address the relevant provisions in any covered agreement or agreements cited by the parties to the dispute.

3. In establishing a panel, the DSB may authorize its Chairman to draw up the terms of reference of the panel in consultation with the parties to the dispute, subject to the provisions of paragraph 1. The terms of reference thus drawn up shall be circulated to all Members. If other than standard terms of reference are agreed upon, any Member may raise any point relating thereto in the DSB.

Art. 8   Composition of Panels

1. Panels shall be composed of well-qualified governmental and/or non-governmental individuals, including persons who have served on or presented a case to a panel, served as a representative of a Member or of a contracting party to GATT 1947 or as a representative to the Council or Committee of any covered agreement or its predecessor agreement, or in the Secretariat, taught or published on international trade law or policy, or served as a senior trade policy official of a Member.

2. Panel members should be selected with a view to ensuring the independence of the members, a sufficiently diverse background and a wide spectrum of experience.

3. Citizens of Members whose governments[1] are parties to the dispute or third parties as defined in paragraph 2 of Article 10 shall not serve on a panel concerned with that dispute, unless the parties to the dispute agree otherwise.

4. To assist in the selection of panelists, the Secretariat shall maintain an indicative list of governmental and non-governmental individuals possessing the qualifications outlined in paragraph 1, from which panelists may be drawn as appropriate. That list shall include the roster of non-governmental panelists established on 30 November 1984 (BISD 31 S/9),

---

[1]   In the case where customs unions or common markets are parties to a dispute, this provision applies to citizens of all member countries of the customs unions or common markets.

and other rosters and indicative lists established under any of the covered agreements, and shall retain the names of persons on those rosters and indicative lists at the time of entry into force of the WTO Agreement. Members may periodically suggest names of governmental and nongovernmental individuals for inclusion on the indicative list, providing relevant information on their knowledge of international trade and of the sectors or subject matter of the covered agreements, and those names shall be added to the list upon approval by the DSB. For each of the individuals on the list, the list shall indicate specific areas of experience or expertise of the individuals in the sectors or subject matter of the covered agreements.

5. Panels shall be composed of three panelists unless the parties to the dispute agree, within 10 days from the establishment of the panel, to a panel composed of five panelists. Members shall be informed promptly of the composition of the panel.

6. The Secretariat shall propose nominations for the panel to the parties to the dispute. The parties to the dispute shall not oppose nominations except for compelling reasons.

7. If there is no agreement on the panelists within 20 days after the date of the establishment of a panel, at the request of either party, the Director-General, in consultation with the Chairman of the DSB and the Chairman of the relevant Council or Committee, shall determine the composition of the panel by appointing the panelists whom the Director-General considers most appropriate in accordance with any relevant special or additional rules or procedures of the covered agreement or covered agreements which are at issue in the dispute, after consulting with the parties to the dispute. The Chairman of the DSB shall inform the Members of the composition of the panel thus formed no later than 10 days after the date the Chairman receives such a request.

8. Members shall undertake, as a general rule, to permit their officials to serve as panelists.

9. Panelists shall serve in their individual capacities and not as government representatives, nor as representatives of any organization. Members shall therefore not give them instructions nor seek to influence them as individuals with regard to matters before a panel.

10. When a dispute is between a developing country Member and a developed country Member the panel shall, if the developing country Member so requests, include at least one panelist from a developing country Member.

11. Panelists' expenses, including travel and subsistence allowance, shall be met from the WTO budget in accordance with criteria to be adopted by the General Council, based on recommendations of the Committee on Budget, Finance and Administration.

Art. 9   Procedures for Multiple Complainants

1. Where more than one Member requests the establishment of a panel related to the same matter, a single panel may be established to examine these complaints taking into account the rights of all Members concerned. A single panel should be established to examine such complaints whenever feasible.

2. The single panel shall organize its examination and present its findings to the DSB in such a manner that the rights which the parties to the dispute would have enjoyed had separate panels examined the complaints are in no way impaired. If one of the parties to the dispute so requests, the panel shall submit separate reports on the dispute concerned. The written submissions by each of the complainants shall be made available to the other complainants, and each complainant shall have the right to be present when any one of the other complainants presents its views to the panel.

3. If more than one panel is established to examine the complaints related to the same matter, to the greatest extent possible the same persons shall serve as panelists on each of the separate panels and the timetable for the panel process in such disputes shall be harmonized.

Art. 10 Third Parties

1. The interests of the parties to a dispute and those of other Members under a covered agreement at issue in the dispute shall be fully taken into account during the panel process.

2. Any Member having a substantial interest in a matter before a panel and having notified its interest to the DSB (referred to in this Understanding as a "third party") shall have an opportunity to be heard by the panel and to make written submissions to the panel. These submissions shall also be given to the parties to the dispute and shall be reflected in the panel report.

3. Third parties shall receive the submissions of the parties to the dispute to the first meeting of the panel.

4. If a third party considers that a measure already the subject of a panel proceeding nullifies or impairs benefits accruing to it under any covered agreement, that Member may have recourse to normal dispute settlement procedures under this Understanding. Such a dispute shall be referred to the original panel wherever possible.

Art. 11 Function of Panels

The function of panels is to assist the DSB in discharging its responsibilities under this Understanding and the covered agreements. Accordingly, a panel should make an objective assessment of the matter before it, including an objective assessment of the facts of the case and the applicability of and conformity with the relevant covered agreements, and make such other findings as will assist the DSB in making the recommendations or in giving the rulings provided for in the covered agreements. Panels should consult regularly with the parties to the dispute and give them adequate opportunity to develop a mutually satisfactory solution.

Art. 12   Panel Procedures

1. Panels shall follow the Working Procedures in Appendix 3 unless the panel decides otherwise after consulting the parties to the dispute.

2. Panel procedures should provide sufficient flexibility so as to ensure high-quality panel reports, while not unduly delaying the panel process.

3. After consulting the parties to the dispute, the panelists shall, as soon as practicable and whenever possible within one week after the composition and terms of reference of the panel have been agreed upon, fix the timetable for the panel process, taking into account the provisions of paragraph 9 of Article 4, if relevant.

4. In determining the timetable for the panel process, the panel shall provide sufficient time for the parties to the dispute to prepare their submissions.

5. Panels should set precise deadlines for written submissions by the parties and the parties should respect those deadlines.

6. Each party to the dispute shall deposit its written submissions with the Secretariat for immediate transmission to the panel and to the other party or parties to the dispute. The complaining party shall submit its first submission in advance of the responding party's first submission unless the panel decides, in fixing the timetable referred to in paragraph 3 and after consultations with the parties to the dispute, that the parties should submit their first submissions simultaneously. When there are sequential arrangements for the deposit of first submissions, the panel shall establish a firm time-period for receipt of the responding party's submission. Any subsequent written submissions shall be submitted simultaneously.

7. Where the parties to the dispute have failed to develop a mutually satisfactory solution, the panel shall submit its findings in the form of a written report to the DSB. In such cases, the report of a panel shall set out the findings of fact, the applicability of relevant provisions and the basic rationale behind any findings and recommendations that it makes. Where a settlement of the matter among the parties to the dispute has been found, the report of the panel shall be confined to a brief description of the case and to reporting that a solution has been reached.

8. In order to make the procedures more efficient, the period in which the panel shall conduct its examination, from the date that the composition and terms of reference of the panel have been agreed upon until the date the final report is issued to the parties to the dispute, shall, as a general rule, not exceed six months. In cases of urgency, including those relating to perishable goods, the panel shall aim to issue its report to the parties to the dispute within three months.

9. When the panel considers that it cannot issue its report within six months, or within three months in cases of urgency, it shall inform the

DSB in writing of the reasons for the delay together with an estimate of the period within which it will issue its report. In no case should the period from the establishment of the panel to the circulation of the report to the Members exceed nine months.

10. In the context of consultations involving a measure taken by a developing country Member, the parties may agree to extend the periods established in paragraphs 7 and 8 of Article 4. If, after the relevant period has elapsed, the consulting parties cannot agree that the consultations have concluded, the Chairman of the DSB shall decide, after consultation with the parties, whether to extend the relevant period and, if so, for how long. In addition, in examining a complaint against a developing country Member, the panel shall accord sufficient time for the developing country Member to prepare and present its argumentation. The provisions of paragraph 1 of Article 20 and paragraph 4 of Article 21 are not affected by any action pursuant to this paragraph.

11. Where one or more of the parties is a developing country Member, the panel's report shall explicitly indicate the form in which account has been taken of relevant provisions on differential and more favourable treatment for developing country Members that form part of the covered agreements which have been raised by the developing country Member in the course of the dispute settlement procedures.

12. The panel may suspend its work at any time at the request of the complaining party for a period not to exceed 12 months. In the event of such a suspension, the time-frames set out in paragraphs 8 and 9 of this Article, paragraph 1 of Article 20, and paragraph 4 of Article 21 shall be extended by the amount of time that the work was suspended. If the work of the panel has been suspended for more than 12 months, the authority for establishment of the panel shall lapse.

Art. 13   Right to Seek Information

1. Each panel shall have the right to seek information and technical advice from any individual or body which it deems appropriate. However, before a panel seeks such information or advice from any individual or body within the jurisdiction of a Member it shall inform the authorities of that Member. A Member should respond promptly and fully to any request by a panel for such information as the panel considers necessary and appropriate. Confidential information which is provided shall not be revealed without formal authorization from the individual, body, or authorities of the Member providing the information.

2. Panels may seek information from any relevant source and may consult experts to obtain their opinion on certain aspects of the matter. With respect to a factual issue concerning a scientific or other technical matter raised by a party to a dispute, a panel may request an advisory report in writing from an expert review group. Rules for the establishment of such a group and its procedures are set forth in Appendix 4.

Art. 14   Confidentiality

1. Panel deliberations shall be confidential.

2. The reports of panels shall be drafted without the presence of the parties to the dispute in the light of the information provided and the statements made.

3. Opinions expressed in the panel report by individual panelists shall be anonymous.

Art. 15   Interim Review Stage

1. Following the consideration of rebuttal submissions and oral arguments, the panel shall issue the descriptive (factual and argument) sections of its draft report to the parties to the dispute. Within a period of time set by the panel, the parties shall submit their comments in writing.

2. Following the expiration of the set period of time for receipt of comments from the parties to the dispute, the panel shall issue an interim report to the parties, including both the descriptive sections and the panel's findings and conclusions. Within a period of time set by the panel, a party may submit a written request for the panel to review precise aspects of the interim report prior to circulation of the final report to the Members. At the request of a party, the panel shall hold a further meeting with the parties on the issues identified in the written comments. If no comments are received from any party within the comment period, the interim report shall be considered the final panel report and circulated promptly to the Members.

3. The findings of the final panel report shall include a discussion of the arguments made at the interim review stage. The interim review stage shall be conducted within the time-period set out in paragraph 8 of Article 12.

Art. 16   Adoption of Panel Reports

1. In order to provide sufficient time for the Members to consider panel reports, the reports shall not be considered for adoption by the DSB until 20 days after the date they have been circulated to the Members.

2. Members having objections to a panel report shall give written reasons to explain their objections for circulation at least 10 days prior to the DSB meeting at which the panel report will be considered.

3. The parties to a dispute shall have the right to participate fully in the consideration of the panel report by the DSB, and their views shall be fully recorded.

4. Within 60 days after the date of circulation of a panel report to the Members, the report shall be adopted at a DSB meeting[1] unless a party to

---

[1]   If a meeting of the DSB is not scheduled within this period at a time that enables the requirements of paragraphs 1 and 4 of Article 16 to be met, a meeting of the DSB shall be held for this purpose.

the dispute formally notifies the DSB of its decision to appeal or the DSB decides by consensus not to adopt the report. If a party has notified its decision to appeal, the report by the panel shall not be considered for adoption by the DSB until after completion of the appeal. This adoption procedure is without prejudice to the right of Members to express their views on a panel report.

Art. 17   Appellate Review

Standing Appellate Body

1. A standing Appellate Body shall be established by the DSB. The Appellate Body shall hear appeals from panel cases. It shall be composed of seven persons, three of whom shall serve on any one case. Persons serving on the Appellate Body shall serve in rotation. Such rotation shall be determined in the working procedures of the Appellate Body.

2. The DSB shall appoint persons to serve on the Appellate Body for a four-year term, and each person may be reappointed once. However, the terms of three of the seven persons appointed immediately after the entry into force of the WTO Agreement shall expire at the end of two years, to be determined by lot. Vacancies shall be filled as they arise. A person appointed to replace a person whose term of office has not expired shall hold office for the remainder of the predecessor's term.

3 The Appellate Body shall comprise persons of recognized authority, with demonstrated expertise in law, international trade and the subject matter of the covered agreements generally. They shall be unaffiliated with any government. The Appellate Body membership shall be broadly representative of membership in the WTO. All persons serving on the Appellate Body shall be available at all times and on short notice, and shall stay abreast of dispute settlement activities and other relevant activities of the WTO. They shall not participate in the consideration of any disputes that would create a direct or indirect conflict of interest.

4. Only parties to the dispute, not third parties, may appeal a panel report. Third parties which have notified the DSB of a substantial interest in the matter pursuant to paragraph 2 of Article 10 may make written submissions to, and be given an opportunity to be heard by, the Appellate Body.

5. As a general rule, the proceedings shall not exceed 60 days from the date a party to the dispute formally notifies its decision to appeal to the date the Appellate Body circulates its report. In fixing its timetable the Appellate Body shall take into account the provisions of paragraph 9 of Article 4, if relevant. When the Appellate Body considers that it cannot provide its report within 60 days, it shall inform the DSB in writing of the reasons for the delay together with an estimate of the period within which it will submit its report. In no case shall the proceedings exceed 90 days.

6. An appeal shall be limited to issues of law covered in the panel report and legal interpretations developed by the panel.

7. The Appellate Body shall be provided with appropriate administrative and legal support as it requires.

8. The expenses of persons serving on the Appellate Body, including travel and subsistence allowance, shall be met from the WTO budget in accordance with criteria to be adopted by the General Council, based on recommendations of the Committee on Budget, Finance and Administration.

Procedures for Appellate Review

9. Working procedures shall be drawn up by the Appellate Body in consultation with the Chairman of the DSB and the Director-General, and communicated to the Members for their information.

10. The proceedings of the Appellate Body shall be confidential. The reports of the Appellate Body shall be drafted without the presence of the parties to the dispute and in the light of the information provided and the statements made.

11. Opinions expressed in the Appellate Body report by individuals serving on the Appellate Body shall be anonymous.

12. The Appellate Body shall address each of the issues raised in accordance with paragraph 6 during the appellate proceeding.

13. The Appellate Body may uphold, modify or reverse the legal findings and conclusions of the panel.

Adoption of Appellate Body Reports

14. An Appellate Body report shall be adopted by the DSB and unconditionally accepted by the parties to the dispute unless the DSB decides by consensus not to adopt the Appellate Body report within 30 days following its circulation to the Members.[1] This adoption procedure is without prejudice to the right of Members to express their views on an Appellate Body report.

Art. 18   Communications with the Panel or Appellate Body

1. There shall be no *ex parte* communications with the panel or Appellate Body concerning matters under consideration by the panel or Appellate Body.

2. Written submissions to the panel or the Appellate Body shall be treated as confidential, but shall be made available to the parties to the dispute. Nothing in this Understanding shall preclude a party to a dispute from disclosing statements of its own positions to the public. Members shall treat as confidential information submitted by another Member to the panel or the Appellate Body which that Member has designated as confidential. A party to a dispute shall also, upon request of a Member, provide a non-confidential summary of the information contained in its written submissions that could be disclosed to the public.

---

[1] If a meeting of the DSB is not scheduled during this period, such a meeting of the DSB shall be held for this purpose.

Art. 19   Panel and Appellate Body Recommendations

1. Where a panel or the Appellate Body concludes that a measure is inconsistent with a covered agreement, it shall recommend that the Member concerned[1] bring the measure into conformity with that agreement.[2] In addition to its recommendations, the panel or Appellate Body may suggest ways in which the Member concerned could implement the recommendations.

2. In accordance with paragraph 2 of Article 3, in their findings and recommendations, the panel and Appellate Body cannot add to or diminish the rights and obligations provided in the covered agreements.

Art. 20   Time-frame for DSB Decisions

Unless otherwise agreed to by the parties to the dispute, the period from the date of establishment of the panel by the DSB until the date the DSB considers the panel or appellate report for adoption shall as a general rule not exceed nine months where the panel report is not appealed or 12 months where the report is appealed. Where either the panel or the Appellate Body has acted, pursuant to paragraph 9 of Article 12 or paragraph 5 of Article 17, to extend the time for providing its report, the additional time taken shall be added to the above periods.

Art. 21   Surveillance of Implementation of Recommendations and Rulings

1. Prompt compliance with recommendations or rulings of the DSB is essential in order to ensure effective resolution of disputes to the benefit of all Members.

2. Particular attention should be paid to matters affecting the interests of developing country Members with respect to measures which have been subject to dispute settlement.

3. At a DSB meeting held within 30 days[3] after the date of adoption of the panel or Appellate Body report, the Member concerned shall inform the DSB of its intentions in respect of implementation of the recommendations and rulings of the DSB. If it is impracticable to comply immediately with the recommendations and rulings, the Member concerned shall have a reasonable period of time in which to do so. The reasonable period of time shall be:

(a)   the period of time proposed by the Member concerned, provided that such period is approved by the DSB; or, in the absence of such approval,

---

[1]   The 'Member concerned' is the party to the dispute to which the panel or Appellate Body recommendations are directed.

[2]   With respect to recommendations in cases not involving a violation of GATT 1994 or any other covered agreement, see Article 26.

[3]   If a meeting of the DSB is not scheduled during this period, such a meeting of the DSB shall be held for this purpose.

(b) a period of time mutually agreed by the parties to the dispute within 45 days after the date of adoption of the recommendations and rulings; or, in the absence of such agreement,

(c) a period of time determined through binding arbitration within 90 days after the date of adoption of the recommendations and rulings.[1] In such arbitration, a guideline for the arbitrator[2] should be that the reasonable period of time to implement panel or Appellate Body recommendations should not exceed 15 months from the date of adoption of a panel or Appellate Body report. However, that time may be shorter or longer, depending upon the particular circumstances.

4. Except where the panel or the Appellate Body has extended, pursuant to paragraph 9 of Article 12 or paragraph 5 of Article 17, the time of providing its report, the period from the date of establishment of the panel by the DSB until the date of determination of the reasonable period of time shall not exceed 15 months unless the parties to the dispute agree otherwise. Where either the panel or the Appellate Body has acted to extend the time of providing its report, the additional time taken shall be added to the 15-month period; provided that unless the parties to the dispute agree that there are exceptional circumstances, the total time shall not exceed 18 months.

5. Where there is disagreement as to the existence or consistency with a covered agreement of measures taken to comply with the recommendations and rulings such dispute shall be decided through recourse to these dispute settlement procedures, including wherever possible resort to the original panel. The panel shall circulate its report within 90 days after the date of referral of the matter to it. When the panel considers that it cannot provide its report within this time frame, it shall inform the DSB in writing of the reasons for the delay together with an estimate of the period within which it will submit its report.

6. The DSB shall keep under surveillance the implementation of adopted recommendations or rulings. The issue of implementation of the recommendations or rulings may be raised at the DSB by any Member at any time following their adoption. Unless the DSB decides otherwise, the issue of implementation of the recommendations or rulings shall be placed on the agenda of the DSB meeting after six months following the date of establishment of the reasonable period of time pursuant to paragraph 3 and shall remain on the DSB's agenda until the issue is resolved. At least 10 days prior to each such DSB meeting, the Member concerned shall

---

[1] If the parties cannot agree on an arbitrator within ten days after referring the matter to arbitration, the arbitrator shall be appointed by the Director-General within ten days, after consulting the parties.

[2] The expression "arbitrator" shall be interpreted as referring either to an individual or a group.

provide the DSB with a status report in writing of its progress in the implementation of the recommendations or rulings.

7. If the matter is one which has been raised by a developing country Member, the DSB shall consider what further action it might take which would be appropriate to the circumstances.

8. If the case is one brought by a developing country Member, in considering what appropriate action might be taken, the DSB shall take into account not only the trade coverage of measures complained of, but also their impact on the economy of developing country Members concerned.

Art. 22   Compensation and the Suspension of Concessions

1. Compensation and the suspension of concessions or other obligations are temporary measures available in the event that the recommendations and rulings are not implemented within a reasonable period of time. However, neither compensation nor the suspension of concessions or other obligations is preferred to full implementation of a recommendation to bring a measure into conformity with the covered agreements. Compensation is voluntary and, if granted, shall be consistent with the covered agreements.

2. If the Member concerned fails to bring the measure found to be inconsistent with a covered agreement into compliance therewith or otherwise comply with the recommendations and rulings within the reasonable period of time determined pursuant to paragraph 3 of Article 21, such Member shall, if so requested, and no later than the expiry of the reasonable period of time, enter into negotiations with any party having invoked the dispute settlement procedures, with a view to developing mutually acceptable compensation. If no satisfactory compensation has been agreed within 20 days after the date of expiry of the reasonable period of time, any party having invoked the dispute settlement procedures may request authorization from the DSB to suspend the application to the Member concerned of concessions or other obligations under the covered agreements.

3. In considering what concessions or other obligations to suspend, the complaining party shall apply the following principles and procedures:

(a) the general principle is that the complaining party should first seek to suspend concessions or other obligations with respect to the same sector(s) as that in which the panel or Appellate Body has found a violation or other nullification or impairment;

(b) if that party considers that it is not practicable or effective to suspend concessions or other obligations with respect to the same sector(s), it may seek to suspend concessions or other obligations in other sectors under the same agreement;

(c) if that party considers that it is not practicable or effective to suspend concessions or other obligations with respect to other sectors under the same agreement, and that the circumstances are serious enough, it may seek to suspend concessions or other obligations under another covered agreement;

(d) in applying the above principles, that party shall take into account:

(i)   the trade in the sector or under the agreement under which the panel or Appellate Body has found a violation or other nullification or impairment, and the importance of such trade to that party;

(ii) the broader economic elements related to the nullification or impairment and the broader economic consequences of the suspension of concessions or other obligations;

(e) if that party decides to request authorization to suspend concessions or other obligations pursuant to subparagraphs (b) or (c), it shall state the reasons therefor in its request. At the same time as the request is forwarded to the DSB, it also shall be forwarded to the relevant Councils and also, in the case of a request pursuant to subparagraph (b), the relevant sectoral bodies;

(f) for purposes of this paragraph, "sector" means:

(i)   with respect to goods, all goods;

(ii) with respect to services, a principal sector as identified in the current "Services Sectoral Classification List" which identifies such sectors;[1]

(iii) with respect to trade-related intellectual property rights, each of the categories of intellectual property rights covered in Section 1, or Section 2, or Section 3, or Section 4, or Section 5, or Section 6, or Section 7 of Part II, or the obligations under Part III or Part IV of the Agreement on TRIPS;

(g) for purposes of this paragraph, "agreement" means:

(i)   with respect to goods, the agreements listed in Annex 1A of the WTO Agreement, taken as a whole as well as the Plurilateral Trade Agreements in so far as the relevant parties to the dispute are parties to these agreements;

(ii) with respect to services, the GATS;

(iii) with respect to intellectual property rights, the Agreement on TRIPS.

4. The level of the suspension of concessions or other obligations authorized by the DSB shall be equivalent to the level of the nullification or impairment.

5. The DSB shall not authorize suspension of concessions or other obligations if a covered agreement prohibits such suspension.

6. When the situation described in paragraph 2 occurs, the DSB, upon request, shall grant authorization to suspend concessions or other obliga-

---

[1]   The list in document MTN.GNS/W/120 identifies eleven sectors.

tions within 30 days of the expiry of the reasonable period of time unless the DSB decides by consensus to reject the request. However, if the Member concerned objects to the level of suspension proposed, or claims that the principles and procedures set forth in paragraph 3 have not been followed where a complaining party has requested authorization to suspend concessions or other obligations pursuant to paragraph 3(b) or (c), the matter shall be referred to arbitration. Such arbitration shall be carried out by the original panel, if members are available, or by an arbitrator[1] appointed by the Director-General and shall be completed within 60 days after the date of expiry of the reasonable period of time. Concessions or other obligations shall not be suspended during the course of the arbitration.

7. The arbitrator[2] acting pursuant to paragraph 6 shall not examine the nature of the concessions or other obligations to be suspended but shall determine whether the level of such suspension is equivalent to the level of nullification or impairment. The arbitrator may also determine if the proposed suspension of concessions or other obligations is allowed under the covered agreement. However, if the matter referred to arbitration includes a claim that the principles and procedures set forth in paragraph 3 have not been followed, the arbitrator shall examine that claim. In the event the arbitrator determines that those principles and procedures have not been followed, the complaining party shall apply them consistent with paragraph 3. The parties shall accept the arbitrator's decision as final and the parties concerned shall not seek a second arbitration. The DSB shall be informed promptly of the decision of the arbitrator and shall upon request, grant authorization to suspend concessions or other obligations where the request is consistent with the decision of the arbitrator, unless the DSB decides by consensus to reject the request.

8. The suspension of concessions or other obligations shall be temporary and shall only be applied until such time as the measure found to be inconsistent with a covered agreement has been removed, or the Member that must implement recommendations or rulings provides a solution to the nullification or impairment of benefits, or a mutually satisfactory solution is reached. In accordance with paragraph 6 of Article 21, the DSB shall continue to keep under surveillance the implementation of adopted recommendations or rulings, including those cases where compensation has been provided or concessions or other obligations have been suspended but the recommendations to bring a measure into conformity with the covered agreements have not been implemented.

---

[1] The expression "arbitrator" shall be interpreted as referring either to an individual or a group.

[2] The expression "arbitrator" shall be interpreted as referring either to an individual or a group or to the members of the original panel when serving in the capacity of arbitrator.

9. The dispute settlement provisions of the covered agreements may be invoked in respect of measures affecting their observance taken by regional or local governments or authorities within the territory of a Member. When the DSB has ruled that a provision of a covered agreement has not been observed, the responsible Member shall take such reasonable measures as may be available to it to ensure its observance. The provisions of the covered agreements and this Understanding relating to compensation and suspension of concessions or other obligations apply in cases where it has not been possible to secure such observance.[1]

Art. 23   Strengthening of the Multilateral System

1 . When Members seek the redress of a violation of obligations or other nullification or impairment of benefits under the covered agreements or an impediment to the attainment of any objective of the covered agreements, they shall have recourse to, and abide by, the rules and procedures of this Understanding.

2. In such cases, Members shall:

(a) not make a determination to the effect that a violation has occurred, that benefits have been nullified or impaired or that the attainment of any objective of the covered agreements has been impeded, except through recourse to dispute settlement in accordance with the rules and procedures of this Understanding, and shall make any such determination consistent with the findings contained in the panel or Appellate Body report adopted by the DSB or an arbitration award rendered under this Understanding;

(b) follow the procedures set forth in Article 21 to determine the reasonable period of time for the Member concerned to implement the recommendations and rulings; and

(c) follow the procedures set forth in Article 22 to determine the level of suspension of concessions or other obligations and obtain DSB authorization in accordance with those procedures before suspending concessions or other obligations under the covered agreements in response to the failure of the Member concerned to implement the recommendations and rulings within that reasonable period of time.

Art. 24   Special Procedures Involving Least-Developed Country Members

1. At all stages of the determination of the causes of a dispute and of dispute settlement procedures involving a least-developed country Member, particular consideration shall be given to the special situation of least-developed country Members. In this regard, Members shall exercise due restraint in raising matters under these procedures involving a least-

---

[1]   Where the provisions of any covered agreement concerning measures taken by regional or local governments or authorities within the territory of a Member contain provisions different from the provisions of this paragraph, the provisions of such covered agreement shall prevail.

developed country Member. If nullification or impairment is found to result from a measure taken by a least-developed country Member, complaining parties shall exercise due restraint in asking for compensation or seeking authorization to suspend the application of concessions or other obligations pursuant to these procedures.

2. In dispute settlement cases involving a least-developed country Member, where a satisfactory solution has not been found in the course of consultations the Director-General or the Chairman of the DSB shall, upon request by a least-developed country Member offer their good offices, conciliation and mediation with a view to assisting the parties to settle the dispute, before a request for a panel is made. The Director-General or the Chairman of the DSB, in providing the above assistance, may consult any source which either deems appropriate.

Art. 25   Arbitration

1. Expeditious arbitration within the WTO as an alternative means of dispute settlement can facilitate the solution of certain disputes that concern issues that are clearly defined by both parties.

2. Except as otherwise provided in this Understanding, resort to arbitration shall be subject to mutual agreement of the parties which shall agree on the procedures to be followed. Agreements to resort to arbitration shall be notified to all Members sufficiently in advance of the actual commencement of the arbitration process.

3. Other Members may become party to an arbitration proceeding only upon the agreement of the parties which have agreed to have recourse to arbitration. The parties to the proceeding shall agree to abide by the arbitration award. Arbitration awards shall be notified to the DSB and the Council or Committee of any relevant agreement where any Member may raise any point relating thereto.

4. Articles 21 and 22 of this Understanding shall apply *mutatis mutandis* to arbitration awards.

Art. 26   1. Non-Violation Complaints of the Type Described in Paragraph 1(b) of Article XXIII of GATT 1994

Where the provisions of paragraph 1(b) of Article XXIII of GATT 1994 are applicable to a covered agreement, a panel or the Appellate Body may only make rulings and recommendations where a party to the dispute considers that any benefit accruing to it directly or indirectly under the relevant covered agreement is being nullified or impaired or the attainment of any objective of that Agreement is being impeded as a result of the application by a Member of any measure, whether or not it conflicts with the provisions of that Agreement. Where and to the extent that such party considers and a panel or the Appellate Body determines that a case concerns a measure that does not conflict with the provisions of a covered agreement to which the provisions of paragraph 1(b) of Article XXIII of

GATT 1994 are applicable, the procedures in this Understanding shall apply, subject to the following:

(a) the complaining party shall present a detailed justification in support of any complaint relating to a measure which does not conflict with the relevant covered agreement;

(b) where a measure has been found to nullify or impair benefits under, or impede the attainment of objectives, of the relevant covered agreement without violation thereof, there is no obligation to withdraw the measure. However, in such cases, the panel or the Appellate Body shall recommend that the Member concerned make a mutually satisfactory adjustment;

(c) notwithstanding the provisions of Article 21, the arbitration provided for in paragraph 3 of Article 21, upon request of either party, may include a determination of the level of benefits which have been nullified or impaired, and may also suggest ways and means of reaching a mutually satisfactory adjustment; such suggestions shall not be binding upon the parties to the dispute;

(d) notwithstanding the provisions of paragraph 1 of Article 22, compensation may be part of a mutually satisfactory adjustment as final settlement of the dispute.

2. Complaints of the Type Described in Paragraph 1 (c) of Article XXIII of GATT 1994

Where the provisions of paragraph 1(c) of Article XXIII of GATT 1994 are applicable to a covered agreement, a panel may only make rulings and recommendations where a party considers that any benefit accruing to it directly or indirectly under the relevant covered agreement is being nullified or impaired or the attainment of any objective of that Agreement is being impeded as a result of the existence of any situation other than those to which the provisions of paragraphs 1(a) and 1(b) of Article XXIII of GATT 1994 are applicable. Where and to the extent that such party considers and a panel determines that the matter is covered by this paragraph, the procedures of this Understanding shall apply only up to and including the point in the proceedings where the panel report has been circulated to the Members. The dispute settlement rules and procedures contained in the Decision of 12 April 1989 (BISD 36S/61-67) shall apply to consideration for adoption, and implementation of recommendations and rulings. The following shall also apply:

(a) the complaining party shall present a detailed justification in support of any argument made with respect to issues covered under this paragraph;

(b) in cases involving matters covered by this paragraph, if a panel finds that cases also involve dispute settlement matters other than those covered by this paragraph, the panel shall circulate a report to the DSB addressing any such matters and a separate report on matters falling under this paragraph.

Art. 27   Responsibilities of the Secretariat

1. The Secretariat shall have the responsibility of assisting panels, especially on the legal, historical and procedural aspects of the matters dealt with, and of providing secretarial and technical support.

2. While the Secretariat assists Members in respect of dispute settlement at their request, there may also be a need to provide additional legal advice and assistance in respect of dispute settlement to developing country Members. To this end, the Secretariat shall make available a qualified legal expert from the WTO technical cooperation services to any developing country Member which so requests. This expert shall assist the developing country Member in a manner ensuring the continued impartiality of the Secretariat.

3. The Secretariat shall conduct special training courses for interested Members concerning these dispute settlement procedures and practices so as to enable Members' experts to be better informed in this regard.

APPENDIX 1: AGREEMENTS COVERED BY THE UNDERSTANDING

(A)   Agreement Establishing the World Trade Organization

(B)   Multilateral Trade Agreements

    Annex 1A: Multilateral Agreements on Trade in Goods

    Annex 1B: General Agreement on Trade in Services

    Annex 1C: Agreement on Trade-Related Aspects of Intellectual Property Rights

    Annex 2:   Understanding on Rules and Procedures Governing the Settlement of Disputes

(C)   Plurilateral Trade Agreements

    Annex 4:   Agreement on Trade in Civil Aircraft

                     Agreement on Government Procurement

                      International Dairy Agreement

                      International Bovine Meat Agreement

The applicability of this Understanding to the Plurilateral Trade Agreements shall be subject to the adoption of a decision by the parties to each agreement setting out the terms for the application of the Understanding to the individual agreement, including any special or additional rules or procedures for inclusion in Appendix 2, as notified to the DSB.

APPENDIX 2: SPECIAL OR ADDITIONAL RULES AND PROCEDURES CONTAINED IN THE COVERED AGREEMENTS

Agreements	*Rules and Procedures*
Agreement on the Application of Sanitary and Phytosanitary Measures	11.2

Agreement on Textiles and Clothing	2.14, 2.21, 4.4, 5.2, 5.6, 6.9, 6.10, 6.11, 8.1 through 8.12
Agreement on Technical Barriers to Trade	14.2 through 14.4, Annex 2
Agreement on Implementation of Article VI of GATT 1994	17.4 through 17.7
Agreement on Implementation of Article VII of GATT 1994	19.3 through 19.5, Annex II.2(f), 3, 9, 21
Agreement on Subsidies and Countervailing Measures	4.2. through 4.12, 6.6, 7.2 through 7.10, 8.5, footnote 35, 24,4, 27,7, Annex V
General Agreement on Trade in Services	XXII:3; XXIII:3
Annex on Financial Services	4
Annex on Air Transport Services	4
Decision on Certain Dispute Settlement Procedures for the GATS	1 through 5

The list of rules and procedures in this Appendix includes provisions where only a part of the provision may be relevant in this context.

Any special or additional rules or procedures in the Plurilateral Trade Agreements as determined by the competent bodies of each agreement and as notified to the DSB.

APPENDIX 3: WORKING PROCEDURES

1. In its proceedings the panel shall follow the relevant provisions of this Understanding. In addition, the following working procedures shall apply.

2. The panel shall meet in closed session. The parties to the dispute, and interested parties, shall be present at the meetings only when invited by the panel to appear before it.

3. The deliberations of the panel and the documents submitted to it shall be kept confidential. Nothing in this Understanding shall preclude a party to a dispute from disclosing statements of its own position to the public. Members shall treat as confidential information submitted by another Member to the panel which that Member has designated as confidential. Where a party to a dispute submits a confidential version of its written submissions to the panel, it shall also, upon request of a Member, provide a non-confidential summary of the information contained in its submissions that could be disclosed to the public.

4. Before the first substantive meeting of the panel with the parties, the parties to the dispute shall transmit to the panel written submissions in which they present the facts of the case and their arguments.

5. At its first substantive meeting with the parties, the panel shall ask the party which has brought the complaint to present its case. Subsequently, and still at the same meeting, the party against which the complaint has been brought shall be asked to present its point of view.

6. All third parties which have notified their interest in the dispute to the DSB shall be invited in writing to present their views during a session of the first substantive meting of the panel set aside for that purpose. All such third parties may be present during the entirety of this session.

7. Formal rebuttals shall be made at a second substantive meeting of the panel. The party complained against shall have the right to take the floor first to be followed by the complaining party. The parties shall submit, prior to that meeting, written rebuttals to the panel.

8. The Panel may at any time put questions to the parties and ask them for explanations either in the course of a meeting with the parties or in writing.

9. The parties to the dispute and any third party invited to present its views in accordance with Article 10 shall make available to the panel a written version of their oral statements.

10. In the interest of full transparency, the presentation, rebuttals and statements referred to in paragraphs 5 to 9 shall be made in the presence of the parties. Moreover, each party's written submissions, including any comments on the descriptive part of the report and responses to questions put by the panel, shall be made available to the other party or parties.

11. Any additional procedures specific to the panel.

12. Proposed timetable for panel work:

a)	Receipt of first written submissions of the parties:	
(1)	complaining Party:	3-6 weeks
(2)	Party complained against:	2-3 weeks
b)	Date, time and place of first substantive meeting With the parties; third party session:	1-2 weeks
c)	Receipt of written rebuttals of the parties:	2-3 weeks
d)	Date, time and place of second substantive Meeting with the parties:	1-2 weeks
e)	Issuance of descriptive part of the report to the parties:	2-4 weeks
f)	Receipt of comments by the parties on the Descriptive part of the report:	2 weeks
g)	Issuance of the interim report, including the Findings and conclusions, to the parties:	2-4 weeks

h) Deadline for party to request review of
   Part(s) of report: 1 week
i) Period of review by panel, including possible
   additional meeting with parties: 2 weeks
j) Issuance of final report to parties to dispute: 2 weeks
k) Circulation of the final report to the Members: 3 weeks

The above calendar may be changed in the light of unforeseen developments. Additional meetings with the parties shall be scheduled if required.

APPENDIX 4: EXPERT REVIEW GROUPS

The following rules and procedures shall apply to expert review groups established in accordance with the provisions of paragraph 2 of Article 13.

1. Expert review groups are under the panel's authority. Their terms of reference and detailed working procedures shall be decided by the panel, and they shall report to the panel.

2. Participation in expert review groups shall be restricted to persons of professional standing and experience in the field in question.

3. Citizens of parties to the dispute shall not serve on an expert review group without the joint agreement of the parties to the dispute, except in exceptional circumstances when the panel considers that the need for specialized scientific expertise cannot be fulfilled otherwise. Government officials of parties to the dispute shall not serve on an expert review group. Members of expert review groups shall serve in their individual capacities and not as government representatives, nor as representatives of any organizations. Governments and organizations shall therefore not give them instructions with regard to matters before an expert review group.

4. Expert review groups may consult and seek information and technical advice from any source they deem appropriate. Before an expert review group seeks such information or advice from a source within the jurisdiction of a Member, it shall inform the government of that Member. Any Member shall respond promptly and fully to any request by an expert review group for such information as the expert review group considers necessary and appropriate.

5. The parties to a dispute shall have access to all relevant information provided to an expert review group, unless it is of a confidential nature. Confidential information provided to an expert review group shall not be released without formal authorization from the government, organization or person providing the information. Where such information is requested from the expert review group but release of such information by the expert review group is not authorized, a non-confidential summary of the information will be provided by the government, organization or person supplying the information.

6. The expert review group shall submit a draft report to the parties to the dispute with a view to obtaining their comments, and taking them into account, as appropriate, in the final report, which shall also be issued to the parties to the dispute when it is submitted to the panel. The final report of the expert review group shall be advisory only.

d) Decision on the Application and Review of the Understanding on Rules and Procedures Governing the Settlement of Disputes

Ministers,

Recalling the Decision of 22 February 1994 that existing rules and procedures of GATT 1947 in the field of dispute settlement shall remain in effect until the date of entry into force of the Agreement Establishing the World Trade Organization,

Invite the relevant Councils and Committees to decide that they shall remain in operation for the purpose of dealing with any dispute for which the request for consultation was made before that date.

Invite the Ministerial Conference to complete a full review of dispute settlement rules and procedures under the World Trade Organization within four years after the entry into force of the Agreement Establishing the World Trade Organization, and to take a decision on the occasion of its first meeting after the completion of the review, whether to continue, modify or terminate such dispute settlement rules and procedures.

e) Trade Policy Review Mechanism

Members hereby *agree* as follows:

A. OBJECTIVES

(i) The purpose of the Trade Policy Review Mechanism ("TPRM") is to contribute to improved adherence by all Members to rules, disciplines and commitments made under the Multilateral Trade Agreements and, where applicable, the Plurilateral Trade Agreements, and hence to the smoother functioning of the multilateral trading system. by achieving greater transparency in, and understanding of. the trade policies and practices of Members. Accordingly, the review mechanism enables the regular collective appreciation and evaluation of the full range of individual Members' trade policies and practices and their impact on the functioning of the multilateral trading system. It is not, however, intended to serve as a basis for the enforcement of specific obligations under the

Agreements or for dispute settlement procedures, or to impose new policy commitments on Members.

(ii) The assessment carried out under the review mechanism takes place, to the extent relevant, against the background of the wider economic and developmental needs, policies and objectives of the Member concerned, as well as of its external environment. However, the function of the review mechanism is to examine the impact of a Member's trade policies and practices on the multilateral trading system.

B. DOMESTIC TRANSPARENCY

Members recognize the inherent value of domestic transparency of government decision-making on trade policy matters for both Members' economies and the multilateral trading system, and agree to encourage and promote greater transparency within their own systems, acknowledging that the implementation of domestic transparency must be on a voluntary basis and take account of each Member's legal and political systems.

C. PROCEDURES FOR REVIEW

(i) The Trade Policy Review Body (referred to herein as the "TPRB") is hereby established to carry out trade policy reviews.

(ii) The trade policies and practices of all Members shall be subject to periodic review. The impact of individual Members on the functioning of the multilateral trading system, defined in terms of their share of world trade in a recent representative period, will be the determining factor in deciding on the frequency of reviews. The first four trading entities so identified (counting the European Communities as one) shall be subject to review every two years. The next 16 shall be reviewed every four years. Other Members shall be reviewed every six years, except that a longer period may be fixed for least-developed country Members. It is understood that the review of entities having a common external policy covering more than one Member shall cover all components of policy affecting trade including relevant policies and practices of the individual Members. Exceptionally, in the event of changes in a Member's trade policies or practices that may have a significant impact on its trading partners, the Member concerned may be requested by the TPRB, after consultation, to bring forward its next review.

(iii) Discussions in the meetings of the TPRB shall be governed by the objectives set forth in paragraph A. The focus of these discussions shall be on the Member's trade policies and practices, which are the subject of the assessment under the review mechanism.

(iv) The TPRB shall establish a basic plan for the conduct of the reviews. It may also discuss and take note of updated reports from Members. The

TPRB shall establish a programme of reviews for each year in consultation with the Members directly concerned. In consultation with the Member or Members under review, the Chairman may choose discussants who, acting in their personal capacity, shall introduce the discussions in the TPRB.

(v) The TPRB shall base its work on the following documentation:

(a) a full report, referred to in paragraph D, supplied by the Member or Members under review;

(b) a report, to be drawn up by the Secretariat on its own responsibility, based on the information available to it and that provided by the Member or Members concerned. The Secretariat should seek clarification from the Member or Members concerned of their trade policies and practices.

(vi) The reports by the Member under review and by the Secretariat, together with the minutes of the respective meeting of the TPRB, shall be published promptly after the review.

(vii) These documents will be forwarded to the Ministerial Conference, which shall take note of them.

D. REPORTING

In order to achieve the fullest possible degree of transparency, each Member shall report regularly to the TPRB. Full reports shall describe the trade policies and practices pursued by the Member or Members concerned, based on an agreed format to be decided upon by the TPRB. This format shall initially be based on the Outline Format for Country Reports established by the Decision of 19 July 1989 (BISD 36S/406-409), amended as necessary to extend the coverage of reports to all aspects of trade policies covered by the Multilateral Trade Agreements in Annex I and, where applicable, the Plurilateral Trade Agreements. This format may be revised by the TPRB in the light of experience. Between reviews, Members shall provide brief reports when there are any significant changes in their trade policies; an annual update of statistical information will be provided according to the agreed format. Particular account shall be taken of difficulties presented to least-developed country Members in compiling their reports. The Secretariat shall make available technical assistance on request to developing country Members, and in particular to the least-developed country Members. Information contained in reports should to the greatest extent possible be coordinated with notifications made under provisions of the Multilateral Trade Agreements and, where applicable, the Plurilateral Trade Agreements.

E. Relationship with the Balance-of-Payments Provisions of GATT 1994 and GATS

Members recognize the need to minimize the burden for governments also subject to full consultations under the balance-of-payments provisions of GATT 1994 or GATS. To this end, the Chairman of the TPRB shall, in consultation with the Member or Members concerned, and with the Chairman of the Committee on Balance-of-Payments Restrictions, devise administrative arrangements that harmonize the normal rhythm of the trade policy reviews with the timetable for balance-of-payments consultations but do not postpone the trade policy review by more than 12 months.

F. Appraisal of the Mechanism

The TPRB shall undertake an appraisal of the operation of the TPRM not more than five years after the entry into force of the Agreement Establishing the WTO. The results of the appraisal will be presented to the Ministerial Conference. It may subsequently undertake appraisals of the TPRM at intervals to be determined by it or as requested by the Ministerial Conference.

G. Overview of the Developments in the International Trading Environment

An annual overview of developments in the international trading environment which are having an impact on the multilateral trading system shall also be undertaken by the TPRB. The overview is to be assisted by an annual report by the Director-General setting out major activities of the WTO and highlighting significant policy issues affecting the trading system.

f) Working Procedures for Appellate Review of February 15, 1996 as amended on February 28, 1997

Definitions

1. In these *Working Procedures for Appellate Review*,

"appellant" means any party to the dispute that has filed a Notice of Appeal pursuant to Rule 20 or has filed a submission pursuant to paragraph 1 of Rule 23;

"appellate report" means an Appellate Body report as described in Article 17 of the *DSU*;

"appellee" means any party to the dispute that has filed a submission pursuant to Rule 22 or paragraph 3 of Rule 23;

"consensus": a decision is deemed to be made by consensus if no Member formally objects to it;

"covered agreements" has the same meaning as "covered agreements" in paragraph 1 of Article 1 of the *DSU*;

"division" means the three Members who are selected to serve on any one appeal in accordance with paragraph 1 of Article 17 of the *DSU* and paragraph 2 of Rule 6;

"documents" means the Notice of Appeal and the submissions and other written statements presented by the participants;

"DSB" means the Dispute Settlement Body established under Article 2 of the *DSU*;

"*DSU*" means the *Understanding on Rules and Procedures Governing the Settlement of Disputes* which is Annex 2 to the *WTO Agreement*;

"Member" means a Member of the Appellate Body who has been appointed by the DSB in accordance with Article 17 of the *DSU*;

"participant" means any party to the dispute that has filed a Notice of Appeal pursuant to Rule 20 or a submission pursuant to Rule 22 or paragraphs 1 or 3 of Rule 23;

"party to the dispute" means any WTO Member who was a complaining or defending party in the panel dispute, but does not include a third party;

"proof of service" means a letter or other written acknowledgement that a document has been delivered, as required, to the parties to the dispute, participants, third parties or third participants, as the case may be;

"Rules" means these *Working Procedures for Appellate Review*;

"*Rules of Conduct*" means the *Rules of Conduct for the Understanding on Rules and Procedures Governing the Settlement of Disputes* as attached in Annex II to these Rules;

"*SCM Agreement*" means the *Agreement on Subsidies and Countervailing Measures* which is in Annex 1A to the *WTO Agreement*;

"Secretariat" means the Appellate Body Secretariat;

"service address" means the address of the party to the dispute, participant, third party or third participant as generally used in WTO dispute settlement proceedings, unless the party to the dispute, participant, third party or third participant has clearly indicated another address;

"third participant" means any third party that has filed a submission pursuant to Rule 24;

"third party" means any WTO Member who has notified the DSB of its substantial interest in the matter before the panel pursuant to paragraph 2 of Article 10 of the *DSU*;

"WTO" means the World Trade Organization;

"*WTO Agreement*" means the *Marrakesh Agreement Establishing the World Trade Organization*, done at Marrakesh, Morocco on 15 April 1994;

"WTO Member" means any State or separate customs territory possessing full autonomy in the conduct of its external commercial relations that has accepted or acceded to the WTO in accordance with Articles XI, XII or XIV of the *WTO Agreement*; and

"WTO Secretariat" means the Secretariat of the World Trade Organization.

PART I.

MEMBERS

Duties and Responsibilities

2. (1) A Member shall abide by the terms and conditions of the *DSU*, these Rules and any decisions of the DSB affecting the Appellate Body.

(2) During his/her term, a Member shall not accept any employment nor pursue any professional activity that is inconsistent with his/her duties and responsibilities.

(3) A Member shall exercise his/her office without accepting or seeking instructions from any international, governmental, or non-governmental organization or any private source.

(4) A Member shall be available at all times and on short notice and, to this end, shall keep the Secretariat informed of his/her whereabouts at all times.

Decision-Making

3. (1) In accordance with paragraph 1 of Article 17 of the *DSU*, decisions relating to an appeal shall be taken solely by the division assigned to that appeal. Other decisions shall be taken by the Appellate Body as a whole.

(2) The Appellate Body and its divisions shall make every effort to take their decisions by consensus. Where, nevertheless, a decision cannot be arrived at by consensus, the matter at issue shall be decided by a majority vote.

Collegiality

4. (1) To ensure consistency and coherence in decision-making, and to draw on the individual and collective expertise of the Members, the

Members shall convene on a regular basis to discuss matters of policy, practice and procedure.

(2) The Members shall stay abreast of dispute settlement activities and other relevant activities of the WTO and, in particular, each Member shall receive all documents filed in an appeal.

(3) In accordance with the objectives set out in paragraph 1, the division responsible for deciding each appeal shall exchange views with the other Members before the division finalizes the appellate report for circulation to the WTO Members. This paragraph is subject to paragraphs 2 and 3 of Rule 11.

(4) Nothing in these Rules shall be interpreted as interfering with a division's full authority and freedom to hear and decide an appeal assigned to it in accordance with paragraph 1 of Article 17 of the *DSU*.

Chairman

5. (1) There shall be a Chairman of the Appellate Body who shall be elected by the Members.

(2) The first Chairman of the Appellate Body shall have a term of office of two years. Thereafter, the term of office of the Chairman shall be one year. In order to ensure rotation of the Chairmanship, no Member shall serve as Chairman for more than one term consecutively.

(3) The Chairman shall be responsible for the overall direction of the Appellate Body business, and in particular, his/her responsibilities shall include:

  (a) the supervision of the internal functioning of the Appellate Body; and

  (b) any such other duties as the Members may agree to entrust to him/her.

(4) Where the office of the Chairman becomes vacant due to permanent incapacity as a result of illness or death or by resignation or expiration of his/her term, the Members shall elect a new Chairman who shall serve a full term in accordance with paragraph 2.

(5) In the event of a temporary absence or incapacity of the Chairman, the Appellate Body shall authorize another Member to act as Chairman *ad interim*, and the Member so authorized shall temporarily exercise all the powers, duties and functions of the Chairman until the Chairman is capable of resuming his/her functions.

Divisions

6. (1) In accordance with paragraph 1 of Article 17 of the *DSU*, a division consisting of three Members shall be established to hear and decide an appeal.

(2) The Members constituting a division shall be selected on the basis of rotation, while taking into account the principles of random selection, unpredictability and opportunity for all Members to serve regardless of their national origin.

(3) A Member selected pursuant to paragraph 2 to serve on a division shall serve on that division, unless:

    (i) he/she is excused from that division pursuant to Rules 9 or 10;

    (ii) he/she has notified the Chairman and the Presiding Member that he/she is prevented from serving on the division because of illness or other serious reasons pursuant to Rule 12; or

    (iii) he/she has notified his/her intentions to resign pursuant to Rule 14.

Presiding Member of the Division

7. (1) Each division shall have a Presiding Member, who shall be elected by the Members of that division.

(2) The responsibilities of the Presiding Member shall include:

    (a) coordinating the overall conduct of the appeal proceeding;

    (b) chairing all oral hearings and meetings related to that appeal; and

    (c) coordinating the drafting of the appellate report.

(3) In the event that a Presiding Member becomes incapable of performing his/her duties, the other Members serving on that division and the Member selected as a replacement pursuant to Rule 13 shall elect one of their number to act as the Presiding Member.

Rules of Conduct

8. (1) On a provisional basis, the Appellate Body adopts those provisions of the *Rules of Conduct for the Understanding on Rules and Procedures Governing the Settlement of Disputes*, attached in Annex II to these Rules, which are applicable to it, until *Rules of Conduct* are approved by the DSB.

(2) Upon approval of *Rules of Conduct* by the DSB, such *Rules of Conduct* shall be directly incorporated and become part of these Rules and shall supersede Annex II.

9. (1) Upon the filing of a Notice of Appeal, each Member shall take the steps set out in Article VI:4(b)(i) of Annex II, and a Member may consult with the other Members prior to completing the disclosure form.

(2) Upon the filing of a Notice of Appeal, the professional staff of the Secretariat assigned to that appeal shall take the steps set out in Article VI:4(b)(ii) of Annex II.

(3) Where information has been submitted pursuant to Article VI:4(b)(i) or (ii) of Annex II, the Appellate Body shall consider whether further action is necessary.

(4) As a result of the Appellate Body's consideration of the matter pursuant to paragraph 3, the Member or the professional staff member concerned may continue to be assigned to the division or may be excused from the division.

10. (1) Where evidence of a material violation is filed by a participant pursuant to Article VIII of Annex II, such evidence shall be confidential and shall be supported by affidavits made by persons having actual knowledge or a reasonable belief as to the truth of the facts stated.

(2) Any evidence filed pursuant to Article VIII:1 of Annex II shall be filed at the earliest practicable time: that is, forthwith after the participant submitting it knew or reasonably could have known of the facts supporting it. In no case shall such evidence be filed after the appellate report is circulated to the WTO Members.

(3) Where a participant fails to submit such evidence at the earliest practicable time, it shall file an explanation in writing of the reasons why it did not do so earlier, and the Appellate Body may decide to consider or not to consider such evidence, as appropriate.

(4) While taking fully into account paragraph 5 of Article 17 of the *DSU*, where evidence has been filed pursuant to Article VIII of Annex II, an appeal shall be suspended for fifteen days or until the procedure referred to in Article VIII:14-16 of Annex II is completed, whichever is earlier.

(5) As a result of the procedure referred to in Article VIII:14-16 of Annex II, the Appellate Body may decide to dismiss the allegation, to excuse the Member or professional staff member concerned from being assigned to the division or make such other order as it deems necessary in accordance with Article VIII of Annex II.

11. (1) A Member who has submitted a disclosure form with information attached pursuant to Article VI:4(b)(i) or is the subject of evidence of a material violation pursuant to Article VIII:1 of Annex II, shall not participate in any decision taken pursuant to paragraph 4 of Rule 9 or paragraph 5 of Rule 10.

(2) A Member who is excused from a division pursuant to paragraph 4 of Rule 9 or paragraph 5 of Rule 10 shall not take part in the exchange of views conducted in that appeal pursuant to paragraph 3 of Rule 4.

(3) A Member who, had he/she been a Member of a division, would have been excused from that division pursuant to paragraph 4 of Rule 9, shall not take part in the exchange of views conducted in that appeal pursuant to paragraph 3 of Rule 4.

Incapacity

12. (1) A Member who is prevented from serving on a division by illness or for other serious reasons shall give notice and duly explain such reasons to the Chairman and to the Presiding Member.

(2) Upon receiving such notice, the Chairman and the Presiding Member shall forthwith inform the Appellate Body.

Replacement

13. Where a Member is unable to serve on a division for a reason set out in paragraph 3 of Rule 6, another Member shall be selected forthwith pursuant to paragraph 2 of Rule 6 to replace the Member originally selected for that division.

Resignation

14. (1) A Member who intends to resign from his/her office shall notify his/her intentions in writing to the Chairman of the Appellate Body who shall immediately inform the Chairman of the DSB, the Director-General and the other Members of the Appellate Body.

(2) The resignation shall take effect 90 days after the notification has been made pursuant to paragraph 1, unless the DSB, in consultation with the Appellate Body, decides otherwise.

Transition

15. A person who ceases to be a Member of the Appellate Body may, with the authorization of the Appellate Body and upon notification to the DSB, complete the disposition of any appeal to which that person was assigned while a Member, and that person shall, for that purpose only, be deemed to continue to be a Member of the Appellate Body.

PART II

PROCESS

General Provisions

16. (1) In the interests of fairness and orderly procedure in the conduct of an appeal, where a procedural question arises that is not covered by these Rules, a division may adopt an appropriate procedure for the purposes of that appeal only, provided that it is not inconsistent with the *DSU*, the other covered agreements and these Rules. Where such a procedure is adopted, the Division shall immediately notify the participants and third participants in the appeal as well as the other Members of the Appellate Body.

(2) In exceptional circumstances, where strict adherence to a time period set out in these Rules would result in a manifest unfairness, a party to the dispute, a participant, a third party or a third participant may request that a division modify a time period set out in these Rules for the filing of documents or the date set out in the working schedule for the oral hearing. Where such a request is granted by a division, any modification of time shall be notified to the parties to the dispute, participants, third parties and third participants in a revised working schedule.

17. (1) Unless the DSB decides otherwise, in computing any time period stipulated in the *DSU* or in the special or additional provisions of the covered agreements, or in these Rules, within which a communication must be made or an action taken by a WTO Member to exercise or preserve its rights, the day from which the time period begins to run shall be excluded and, subject to paragraph 2, the last day of the time-period shall be included.

(2) The DSB Decision on "Expiration of Time-Periods in the *DSU*", WT/DSB/M/7, shall apply to appeals heard by divisions of the Appellate Body.

Documents

18. (1) No document is considered filed with the Appellate Body unless the document is received by the Secretariat within the time period set out for filing in accordance with these Rules.

(2) Except as otherwise provided in these Rules, every document filed by a party to the dispute, a participant, a third party or a third participant shall be served on each of the other parties to the dispute, participants, third parties and third participants in the appeal.

(3) A proof of service on the other parties to the dispute, participants, third parties and third participants shall appear on, or be affixed to, each document filed with the Secretariat under paragraph 1 above.

(4) A document shall be served by the most expeditious means of delivery or communication available, including by:

  (a) delivering a copy of the document to the service address of the party to the dispute, participant, third party or third participant; or

  (b) sending a copy of the document to the service address of the party to the dispute, participant, third party or third participant by facsimile transmission, expedited delivery courier or expedited mail service.

(5) Upon authorization by the division, a participant or a third participant may correct clerical errors in any of its submissions. Such correction shall be made within 3 days of the filing of the original sub-

mission and a copy of the revised version shall be filed with the Secretariat and served upon the other participants and third participants.

Ex Parte Communications

19. (1) Neither a division nor any of its Members shall meet with or contact one participant or third participant in the absence of the other participants and third participants.

(2) No Member of the division may discuss any aspect of the subject matter of an appeal with any participant or third participant in the absence of the other Members of the division.

(3) A Member who is not assigned to the division hearing the appeal shall not discuss any aspect of the subject matter of the appeal with any participant or third participant.

Commencement of Appeal

20. (1) An appeal shall be commenced by notification in writing to the DSB in accordance with paragraph 4 of Article 16 of the *DSU* and simultaneous filing of a Notice of Appeal with the Secretariat.

(2) A Notice of Appeal shall include the following information:

(a) the title of the panel report under appeal;

(b) the name of the party to the dispute filing the Notice of Appeal;

(c) the service address, telephone and facsimile numbers of the party to the dispute; and

(d) a brief statement of the nature of the appeal, including the allegations of errors in the issues of law covered in the panel report and legal interpretations developed by the panel.

Appellant's Submission

21. (1) The appellant shall, within 10 days after the date of the filing of the Notice of Appeal, file with the Secretariat a written submission prepared in accordance with paragraph 2 and serve a copy of the submission on the other parties to the dispute and third parties.

(2) A written submission referred to in paragraph 1 shall

(a) be dated and signed by the appellant; and

(b) set out

(i) a precise statement of the grounds for the appeal, including the specific allegations of errors in the issues of law covered in the panel report and legal interpretations developed by the panel, and the legal arguments in support thereof;

(ii) a precise statement of the provisions of the covered agreements and other legal sources relied on; and

(iii) the nature of the decision or ruling sought.

Appellee's Submission

22. (1) Any party to the dispute that wishes to respond to allegations raised in an appellant's submission filed pursuant to Rule 21 may, within 25 days after the date of the filing of the Notice of Appeal, file with the Secretariat a written submission prepared in accordance with paragraph 2 and serve a copy of the submission on the appellant, other parties to the dispute and third parties.

(2) A written submission referred to in paragraph 1 shall

    (a) be dated and signed by the appellee; and

    (b) set out

    (i) a precise statement of the grounds for opposing the specific allegations of errors in the issues of law covered in the panel report and legal interpretations developed by the panel raised in the appellant's submission, and the legal arguments in support thereof;

    (ii) an acceptance of, or opposition to, each ground set out in the appellant's submission;

    (iii) a precise statement of the provisions of the covered agreements and other legal sources relied on; and

    (iv) the nature of the decision or ruling sought.

Multiple Appeals

23. (1) Within 15 days after the date of the filing of the Notice of Appeal, a party to the dispute other than the original appellant may join in that appeal or appeal on the basis of other alleged errors in the issues of law covered in the panel report and legal interpretations developed by the panel.

(2) Any written submission made pursuant to paragraph 1 shall be in the format required by paragraph 2 of Rule 21.

(3) The appellant, any appellee and any other party to the dispute that wishes to respond to a submission filed pursuant to paragraph 1 may file a written submission within 25 days after the date of the filing of the Notice of Appeal, and any such submission shall be in the format required by paragraph 2 of Rule 22.

(4) This Rule does not preclude a party to the dispute which has not filed a submission under Rule 21 or paragraph 1 of this Rule from exercising its right of appeal pursuant to paragraph 4 of Article 16 of the *DSU*.

(5) Where a party to the dispute which has not filed a submission under Rule 21 or paragraph 1 of this Rule exercises its right to appeal as set out in paragraph 4, a single division shall examine the appeals.

Third Participants

24. Any third party may file a written submission, stating its intention to participate as a third participant in the appeal and containing the grounds and legal arguments in support of its position, within 25 days after the date of the filing of the Notice of Appeal.

Transmittal of Record

25. (1) Upon the filing of a Notice of Appeal, the Director-General of the WTO shall transmit forthwith to the Appellate Body the complete record of the panel proceeding.

(2) The complete record of the panel proceeding includes, but is not limited to:

   (i) written submissions, rebuttal submissions, and supporting evidence attached thereto by the parties to the dispute and the third parties;

   (ii) written arguments submitted at the panel meetings with the parties to the dispute and the third parties, the recordings of such panel meetings, and any written answers to questions posed at such panel meetings;

   (iii) the correspondence relating to the panel dispute between the panel or the WTO Secretariat and the parties to the dispute or the third parties; and

   (iv) any other documentation submitted to the panel.

Working Schedule

26. (1) Forthwith after the commencement of an appeal, the division shall draw up an appropriate working schedule for that appeal in accordance with the time periods stipulated in these Rules.

(2) The working schedule shall set forth precise dates for the filing of documents and a timetable for the division's work, including where possible, the date for the oral hearing.

(3) In accordance with paragraph 9 of Article 4 of the *DSU*, in appeals of urgency, including those which concern perishable goods, the Appellate Body shall make every effort to accelerate the appellate proceedings to the greatest extent possible. A division shall take this into account in drawing up its working schedule for that appeal.

(4) The Secretariat shall serve forthwith a copy of the working schedule on the appellant, the parties to the dispute and any third parties.

Oral Hearing

27. (1) A division shall hold an oral hearing, which shall be held, as a general rule, 30 days after the date of the filing of the Notice of Appeal.

(2) Where possible in the working schedule or otherwise at the earliest possible date, the Secretariat shall notify all parties to the dispute, participants, third parties and third participants of the date for the oral hearing.

(3) Any third participant who has filed a submission pursuant to Rule 24 may appear to make oral arguments or presentations at the oral hearing.

(4) The Presiding Member may, as necessary, set time-limits for oral arguments and presentations.

Written Responses

28. (1) At any time during the appellate proceeding, including, in particular, during the oral hearing, the division may address questions orally or in writing to, or request additional memoranda from, any participant or third participant, and specify the time periods by which written responses or memoranda shall be received.

(2) Any such questions, responses or memoranda shall be made available to the other participants and third participants in the appeal, who shall be given an opportunity to respond.

Failure to Appear

29. Where a participant fails to file a submission within the required time periods or fails to appear at the oral hearing, the division shall, after hearing the views of the participants, issue such order, including dismissal of the appeal, as it deems appropriate.

Withdrawal of Appeal

30. (1) At any time during an appeal, the appellant may withdraw its appeal by notifying the Appellate Body, which shall forthwith notify the DSB.

(2) Where a mutually agreed solution to a dispute which is the subject of an appeal has been notified to the DSB pursuant to paragraph 6 of Article 3 of the *DSU*, it shall be notified to the Appellate Body.

Prohibited Subsidies

31. (1) Subject to Article 4 of the *SCM Agreement*, the general provisions of these Rules shall apply to appeals relating to panel reports concerning prohibited subsidies under Part II of that *Agreement*.

(2) The working schedule for an appeal involving prohibited subsidies under Part II of the *SCM Agreement* shall be as set out in Annex I to these Rules.

Entry into Force and Amendment

32. (1) These Rules shall enter into force on 15 February 1996.

(2) The Appellate Body may amend these Rules in compliance with the procedures set forth in paragraph 9 of Article 17 of the *DSU*.

(3) Whenever there is an amendment to the *DSU* or to the special or additional rules and procedures of the covered agreements, the Appellate Body shall examine whether amendments to these Rules are necessary.

ANNEX I — TIMETABLE FOR APPEALS

	General Appeals Day	Prohibited Subsidies Appeals Day
Notice of Appeal[1]	0	0
Appellant's Submission[2]	10	5
Other Appellant(s) Submission(s)[3]	15	7
Appellee(s) Submission(s)[4]	25	12
Third Participant(s) Submission(s)[5]	25	12
Oral Hearing[6]	30	15
Circulation of Appellate Report	60 - 90[7]	30 - 60[8]
DSB Meeting for Adoption	90 - 120[9]	50 - 80[10]

---

[1] Rule 20.

[2] Rule 21.

[3] Rule 23(1).

[4] Rules 22 and 23(3).

[5] Rule 24.

[6] Rule 27.

[7] Article 17:5, *DSU*.

[8] Article 4:9, *SCM Agreement*.

[9] Article 17:14, *DSU*.

[10] Article 4:9, *SCM Agreement*.

ANNEX II — RULES OF CONDUCT FOR THE UNDERSTANDING ON RULES AND PROCEDURES GOVERNING THE SETTLEMENT OF DISPUTES

I. PREAMBLE

Members,

Recalling that on 15 April 1994 in Marrakesh, Ministers welcomed the stronger and clearer legal framework they had adopted for the conduct of international trade, including a more effective and reliable dispute settlement mechanism;

Recognizing the importance of full adherence to the Understanding on Rules and Procedures Governing the Settlement of Disputes ("DSU") and the principles for the management of disputes applied under Articles XXII and XXIII of GATT 1947, as further elaborated and modified by the DSU;

Affirming that the operation of the DSU would be strengthened by rules of conduct designed to maintain the integrity, impartiality and confidentiality of proceedings conducted under the DSU thereby enhancing confidence in the new dispute settlement mechanism;

Hereby establish the following Rules of Conduct.

II. GOVERNING PRINCIPLE

1. Each person covered by these Rules (as defined in paragraph 1 of Section IV below and hereinafter called "covered person") shall be independent and impartial, shall avoid direct or indirect conflicts of interest and shall respect the confidentiality of proceedings of bodies pursuant to the dispute settlement mechanism, so that through the observance of such standards of conduct the integrity and impartiality of that mechanism are preserved. These Rules shall in no way modify the rights and obligations of Members under the DSU nor the rules and procedures therein.

III. OBSERVANCE OF THE GOVERNING PRINCIPLE

1. To ensure the observance of the Governing Principle of these Rules, each covered person is expected (1) to adhere strictly to the provisions of the DSU; (2) to disclose the existence or development of any interest, relationship or matter that that person could reasonably be expected to know and that is likely to affect, or give rise to justifiable doubts as to, that person's independence or impartiality; and (3) to take due care in the performance of their duties to fulfil these expectations, including through avoidance of any direct or indirect conflicts of interest in respect of the subject matter of the proceedings.

2. Pursuant to the Governing Principle, each covered person, shall be independent and impartial, and shall maintain confidentiality. Moreover, such persons shall consider only issues raised in, and necessary to fulfil their responsibilities within, the dispute settlement proceeding and shall not delegate this responsibility to any other person. Such person shall not incur any obligation or accept any benefit that would in anyway interfere with, or which could give rise to, justifiable doubts as to the proper performance of that person's dispute settlement duties.

IV. Scope

1. These Rules shall apply, as specified in the text, to each person serving: (a) on a panel; (b) on the Standing Appellate Body; (c) as an arbitrator pursuant to the provisions mentioned in Annex "1a"; or (d) as an expert participating in the dispute settlement mechanism pursuant to the provisions mentioned in Annex "1b". These Rules shall also apply, as specified in this text and the relevant provisions of the Staff Regulations, to those members of the Secretariat called upon to assist the panel in accordance with Article 27.1 of the DSU or to assist in formal arbitration proceedings pursuant to Annex "1a"; to the Chairman of the Textiles Monitoring Body (hereinafter called "TMB") and other members of the TMB Secretariat called upon to assist the TMB in formulating recommendations, findings or observations pursuant to the WTO Agreement on Textiles and Clothing; and to Standing Appellate Body support staff called upon to provide the Standing Appellate Body with administrative or legal support in accordance with Article 17.7 of the DSU (hereinafter "Member of the Secretariat or Standing Appellate Body support staff"), reflecting their acceptance of established norms regulating the conduct of such persons as international civil servants and the Governing Principle of these Rules.

2. The application of these Rules shall not in any way impede the Secretariat's discharge of its responsibility to continue to respond to Members' requests for assistance and information.

3. These Rules shall apply to the members of the TMB to the extent prescribed in Section V.

V. Textiles Monitoring Body

1. Members of the TMB shall discharge their functions on an ad personam basis, in accordance with the requirement of Article 8.1 of the Agreement on Textiles and Clothing, as further elaborated in the working procedures of the TMB, so as to preserve the integrity and impartiality of its proceedings.[1]

---

[1] These working procedures, as adopted by the TMB on 26 July 1995 (G/TMB/R/1), currently include, *inter alia*, the following language in paragraph 1.4: "In discharging their functions in accordance with paragraph 1.1 above, the TMB members and al-

VI. SELF-DISCLOSURE REQUIREMENTS BY COVERED PERSONS

1. (a) Each person requested to serve on a panel, on the Standing Appellate Body, as an arbitrator, or as an expert shall, at the time of the request, receive from the Secretariat these Rules, which include an Illustrative List (Annex 2) of examples of the matters subject to disclosure.

(b) Any member of the Secretariat described in paragraph IV:1, who may expect to be called upon to assist in a dispute, and Standing Appellate Body support staff, shall be familiar with these Rules.

2. As set out in paragraph VI:4 below, all covered persons described in paragraph VI.1(a) and VI.1(b) shall disclose any information that could reasonably be expected to be known to them at the time which, coming within the scope of the Governing Principle of these Rules, is likely to affect or give rise to justifiable doubts as to their independence or impartiality. These disclosures include the type of information described in the Illustrative List, if relevant.

3. These disclosure requirements shall not extend to the identification of matters whose relevance to the issues to be considered in the proceedings would be insignificant. They shall take into account the need to respect the personal privacy of those to whom these Rules apply and shall not be so administratively burdensome as to make it impracticable for otherwise qualified persons to serve on panels, the Standing Appellate Body, or in other dispute settlement roles.

4. (a) All panelists, arbitrators and experts, prior to confirmation of their appointment, shall complete the form at Annex 3 of these Rules. Such information would be disclosed to the Chair of the Dispute Settlement Body ("DSB") for consideration by the parties to the dispute.

(b) (i) Persons serving on the Standing Appellate Body who, through rotation, are selected to hear the appeal of a particular panel case, shall review the factual portion of the Panel report and complete the form at Annex 3. Such information would be disclosed to the Standing Appellate Body for its consideration whether the member concerned should hear a particular appeal.

(ii) Standing Appellate Body support staff shall disclose any relevant matter to the Standing Appellate Body, for its consideration in

---

ternates shall undertake not to solicit, accept or act upon instructions from governments, nor to be influenced by any other organisations or undue extraneous factors. They shall disclose to the Chairman any information that they may consider likely to impede their capacity to discharge their functions on an ad personam basis. Should serious doubts arise during the deliberations of the TMB regarding the ability of a TMB member to act on an ad personam basis, they shall be communicated to the Chairman. The Chairman shall deal with the particular matter as necessary".

deciding on the assignment of staff to assist in a particular appeal.

(c) When considered to assist in a dispute, members of the Secretariat shall disclose to the Director-General of the WTO the information required under paragraph VI:2 of these Rules and any other relevant information required under the Staff Regulations, including the information described in the footnote[1].

5. During a dispute, each covered person shall also disclose any new information relevant to paragraph VI:2 above at the earliest time they become aware of it.

6. The Chair of the DSB, the Secretariat, parties to the dispute, and other individuals involved in the dispute settlement mechanism shall maintain the confidentiality of any information revealed through this disclosure process, even after the panel process and its enforcement procedures, if any, are completed.

VII. CONFIDENTIALITY

1. Each covered person shall at all times maintain the confidentiality of dispute settlement deliberations and proceedings together with any information identified by a party as confidential. No covered person shall at any time use such information acquired during such deliberations and proceedings to gain personal advantage or advantage for others.

2. During the proceedings, no covered person shall engage in *ex parte* contacts concerning matters under consideration. Subject to paragraph VII:1, no covered person shall make any statements on such proceedings

---

[1] Pending adoption of the Staff Regulations, members of the Secretariat shall make disclosures to the Director-General in accordance with the following draft provision to be included in the Staff Regulations:

" When paragraph VI:4(c) of the Rules of Conduct for the DSU is applicable, members of the Secretariat would disclose to the Director-General of the WTO the information required in paragraph VI:2 of those Rules, as well as any information regarding their participation in earlier formal consideration of the specific measure at issue in a dispute under any provisions of the WTO Agreement, including through formal legal advice under Article 27.2 of the DSU, as well as any involvement with the dispute as an official of a WTO Member government or otherwise professionally, before having joined the Secretariat.

The Director-General shall consider any such disclosures in deciding on the assignment of members of the Secretariat to assist in a dispute.

When the Director-General, in the light of his consideration, including of available Secretariat resources, decides that a potential conflict of interest is not sufficiently material to warrant non-assignment of a particular member of the Secretariat to assist in a dispute, the Director-General shall inform the panel of his decision and of the relevant supporting information. "

or the issues in dispute in which that person is participating, until the report of the panel or the Standing Appellate Body has been derestricted.

VIII. PROCEDURES CONCERNING SUBSEQUENT DISCLOSURE AND POSSIBLE MATERIAL VIOLATIONS

1. Any party to a dispute, conducted pursuant to the WTO Agreement, who possesses or comes into possession of evidence of a material violation of the obligations of independence, impartiality or confidentiality or the avoidance of direct or indirect conflicts of interest by covered persons which may impair the integrity, impartiality or confidentiality of the dispute settlement mechanism, shall at the earliest possible time and on a confidential basis, submit such evidence to the Chair of the DSB, the Director-General or the Standing Appellate Body, as appropriate according to the respective procedures detailed in paragraphs VIII:5 to VIII:17 below, in a written statement specifying the relevant facts and circumstances. Other Members who possess or come into possession of such evidence, may provide such evidence to the parties to the dispute in the interest of maintaining the integrity and impartiality of the dispute settlement mechanism.

2. When evidence as described in paragraph VIII:1 is based on an alleged failure of a covered person to disclose a relevant interest, relationship or matter, that failure to disclose, as such, shall not be a sufficient ground for disqualification unless there is also evidence of a material violation of the obligations of independence, impartiality, confidentiality or the avoidance of direct or indirect conflicts of interests and that the integrity, impartiality or confidentiality of the dispute settlement mechanism would be impaired thereby.

3. When such evidence is not provided at the earliest practicable time, the party submitting the evidence shall explain why it did not do so earlier and this explanation shall be taken into account in the procedures initiated in paragraph VIII:1.

4. Following the submission of such evidence to the Chair of the DSB, the Director-General of the WTO or the Standing Appellate Body, as specified below, the procedures outlined in paragraphs VIII:5 to VIII:17 below shall be completed within fifteen working days.

Panelists, Arbitrators, Experts

5. If the covered person who is the subject of the evidence is a panelist, an arbitrator or an expert, the party shall provide such evidence to the Chair of the DSB.

6. Upon receipt of the evidence referred to in paragraphs VIII:1 and VIII:2, the Chair of the DSB shall forthwith provide the evidence to the person who is the subject of such evidence, for consideration by the latter.

7. If, after having consulted with the person concerned, the matter is not resolved, the Chair of the DSB shall forthwith provide all the evidence, and any additional information from the person concerned, to the parties to the dispute. If the person concerned resigns, the Chair of the DSB shall inform the parties to the dispute and, as the case may be, the panelists, the arbitrator(s) or experts.

8. In all cases, the Chair of the DSB, in consultation with the Director-General and a sufficient number of Chairs of the relevant Council or Councils to provide an odd number, and after having provided a reasonable opportunity for the views of the person concerned and the parties to the dispute to be heard, would decide whether a material violation of these Rules as referred to in paragraphs VIII:1 and VIII:2 above has occurred. Where the parties agree that a material violation of these Rules has occurred, it would be expected that, consistent with maintaining the integrity of the dispute settlement mechanism, the disqualification of the person concerned would be confirmed.

9. The person who is the subject of the evidence shall continue to participate in the consideration of the dispute unless it is decided that a material violation of these Rules has occurred.

10. The Chair of the DSB shall thereafter take the necessary steps for the appointment of the person who is the subject of the evidence to be formally revoked, or excused from the dispute as the case may be, as of that time.

Secretariat

11. If the covered person who is the subject of the evidence is a member of the Secretariat, the party shall only provide the evidence to the Director-General of the WTO, who shall forthwith provide the evidence to the person who is the subject of such evidence and shall further inform the other party or parties to the dispute and the panel.

12. It shall be for the Director-General to take any appropriate action in accordance with the Staff Regulations.[1]

13. The Director-General shall inform the parties to the dispute, the panel and the Chair of the DSB of his decision, together with relevant supporting information.

---

[1] Pending adoption of the Staff Regulations, the Director-General would act in accordance with the following draft provision for the Staff Regulations: "If paragraph VIII:11 of the Rules of Conduct for the DSU governing the settlement of disputes is invoked, the Director-General shall consult with the person who is the subject of the evidence and the panel and shall, if necessary, take appropriate disciplinary action".

Standing Appellate Body

14. If the covered person who is the subject of the evidence is a member of the Standing Appellate Body or of the Standing Appellate Body support staff, the party shall provide the evidence to the other party to the dispute and the evidence shall thereafter be provided to the Standing Appellate Body.

15. Upon receipt of the evidence referred to in paragraphs VIII:1 and VIII:2 above, the Standing Appellate Body shall forthwith provide it to the person who is the subject of such evidence, for consideration by the latter.

16. It shall be for the Standing Appellate Body to take any appropriate action after having provided a reasonable opportunity for the views of the person concerned and the parties to the dispute to be heard.

17. The Standing Appellate Body shall inform the parties to the dispute and the Chair of the DSB of its decision, together with relevant supporting information.

18. Following completion of the procedures in paragraphs VIII:5 to VIII:17, if the appointment of a covered person, other than a member of the Standing Appellate Body, is revoked or that person is excused or resigns, the procedures specified in the DSU for initial appointment shall be followed for appointment of a replacement, but the time periods shall be half those specified in the DSU.[1] The member of the Standing Appellate Body who, under that Body's rules, would next be selected through rotation to consider the dispute, would automatically be assigned to the appeal. The panel, members of the Standing Appellate Body hearing the appeal, or the arbitrator, as the case may be, may then decide after consulting with the parties to the dispute, on any necessary modifications to their working procedures or proposed timetable.

19. All covered persons and Members concerned shall resolve matters involving possible material violations of these Rules as expeditiously as possible so as not to delay the completion of proceedings, as provided in the DSU.

20. Except to the extent strictly necessary to carry out this decision, all information concerning possible or actual material violations of these Rules shall be kept confidential.

IX. REVIEW

1. These Rules of Conduct shall be reviewed within two years of their adoption and a decision shall be taken by the DSB as to whether to continue, modify or terminate these Rules.

---

[1] Appropriate adjustments would be made in the case of appointments pursuant to the Agreement on Subsidies and Countervailing Measures.

Annex 1A

Arbitrators acting pursuant to the following provisions:

– Articles 21.3(c); 22.6 and 22.7; 26.1(c) and 25 of the DSU;

– Article 8.5 of the Agreement on Subsidies and Countervailing Measures;

– Articles XXI.3 and XXII.3 of the General Agreement on Trade in Services.

Annex 1B

Experts advising or providing information pursuant to the following provisions:

– Article 13.1; 13.2 of the DSU;

– Article 4.5 of the Agreement on Subsidies and Countervailing Measures;

– Article 11.2 of the Agreement on the Application of Sanitary and Phytosanitary Measures;

– Article 14.2; 14.3 of the Agreement on Technical Barriers to Trade.

Annex 2 — Illustrative List of Information to be Disclosed

This list contains examples of information of the type that a person called upon to serve in a dispute should disclose pursuant to the Rules of Conduct for the Understanding on Rules and Procedures Governing the Settlement of Disputes.

Each covered person, as defined in Section IV:1 of these Rules of Conduct has a continuing duty to disclose the information described in Section VI:2 of these Rules which may include the following:

(a) financial interests (e.g. investments, loans, shares, interests, other debts); business interests (e.g. directorship or other contractual interests); and property interests relevant to the dispute in question;

(b) professional interests (e.g. a past or present relationship with private clients, or any interests the person may have in domestic or international proceedings, and their implications, where these involve issues similar to those addressed in the dispute in question);

(c) other active interests (e.g. active participation in public interest groups or other organisations which may have a declared agenda relevant to the dispute in question);

(d) considered statements of personal opinion on issues relevant to the dispute in question (e.g. publications, public statements);

(e) employment or family interests (e.g. the possibility of any indirect advantage or any likelihood of pressure which could arise from their employer, business associates or immediate family members).

ANNEX 3

Dispute Number: _____

WORLD TRADE ORGANIZATION

DISCLOSURE FORM

I have read the Understanding on Rules and Procedures Governing the Settlement of Disputes (DSU) and the Rules of Conduct for the DSU. I understand my continuing duty, while participating in the dispute settlement mechanism, and until such time as the Dispute Settlement Body (DSB) makes a decision on adoption of a report relating to the proceeding or notes its settlement, to disclose herewith and in future any information likely to affect my independence or impartiality, or which could give rise to justifiable doubts as to the integrity and impartiality of the dispute settlement mechanism; and to respect my obligations regarding the confidentiality of dispute settlement proceedings.

Signed: Dated:

II. Regional Treaties

1. Europe

a) Court of Justice of the European Communities

The 1951 Treaty which established the European Coal and Steel Community (ECSC) provided for a judicial body to supervise the conduct of the Community's institutions as well as of the member States. The subsequently founded Euratom Community and European Economic Community (EEC) (renamed European Community (EC) in 1992) merely adopted the existing institutional system. By the Convention of March 25, 1957 relating to certain institutions common to the European Communities (UNTS vol. 298, p. 269), a single Court was created to exercise jurisdiction over matters concerning the ECSC, the EEC/EC and Euratom, reference to which is now made in Art. 9, para. 2 of the Treaty of Amsterdam.

In addition, the most recent amendments to the treaty founding the European Union now also provide for a limited jurisdiction over normative acts adopted within the framework of the European Union (cf. Art. 35 TEU).

In 1992, a Court of First Instance was established besides the Court of Justice which exercises jurisdiction over complaints by officials of the Communities as well as over complaints by individuals against the community, mainly in the field of competition law (cf. Art. 225 EC-Treaty).

As of today, the Court consists of 15 judges who are appointed for six years "by common accord of the Governments of the Member States". In addition, currently nine Advocates-General are appointed in order to assist the Court. The Advocate-General is an institution previously unknown in international adjudication. It is derived from the French *Commissaire du Gouvernement* who participates in administrative proceedings in an impartial capacity. The Advocate-General must act with complete impartiality and independence and is expected to formulate an extensively reasoned opinion on the case. By this means, he exerts a considerable influence on the decision-making of the Court. A partial replacement of the judicial panel as well as of the Advocates-General is to be effected every three years.

Both State applications and applications brought before the Court by organs of the three Communities fall within the Court's competence.

Direct inter-State disputes are however rather rare because of the effectiveness of the European Commission in ensuring adherence to the provisions of the Treaty and measures taken under those provisions. In the case, however, where a government considers that another member State has failed to fulfil its Treaty obligations, allegations must first be brought before the Commission, which has to submit a reasoned opinion within three months, after having heard the respondent State. Only then, or when the Commission does not act within the period prescribed, may the matter be brought before the Court.

Under Art. 88 of the ECSC treaty, the Commission is empowered to render decisions in regard to a State based on an application which does allege a Treaty violation; this decision may be then challenged before the Court. Under the EC Treaty, on the other hand, the Commission is not empowered to make such binding decisions, but only to give a reasoned opinion (Art 226 EC Treaty) and bring a suit before the Court if the State concerned does not comply with the proposals in its opinion. In practice, this type of application has been more frequently used than the direct inter-State applications, which have nearly lost the *raison d'être* since the Community exercises legal control over the member States. It can be said that claims under Art. 88 of the ECSC Treaty and under Art. 226 of the EC Treaty have, in fact, an inter-State character.

The most important possibility for an individual to bring a claim before the Court is found in both EC Treaty, Arts. 234 and 68 as well as in the Treaty on European Union, Art. 35, which sets forth a procedure on preliminary rulings.

Under Art. 234 EC Treaty national tribunals may or, if the matter is before a national court of last appeal, must refer to the Court of the Communities questions which concern interpretation of the Treaty, the validity and interpretation of acts of the institutions of the Community, and, through the Court's practice, the jurisdiction of the Court has expanded to include the question as to whether a provision of the Treaty is self-executing. Thus, Art. 234 EC Treaty has resulted in an additional level of judicial review of national legislation with respect to its conformity to the terms of the Treaty.

Under Art. 35 EU Treaty, member States may make declarations empowering either all of their national courts and tribunals or at least courts and tribunals of last resort to request the Court to give preliminary rulings on the validity and interpretation of normative acts adopted within the framework of the European Union. So far Austria, Belgium, Finland, Germany, Greece, Italy, Luxembourg, the Netherlands, Portugal and Sweden have made such declarations. Besides, several member States have reserved their right to provide in their national legislation for an *obligation* of courts and tribunals of last resort to request a preliminary ruling.

Texts

Treaty of Amsterdam amending the Treaty on European Union, the Treaties establishing the European Communities and certain related acts (1997)
Treaties Establishing the European Communities (ECSC, EEC, EAEC), Single European Act, other basic instruments (1987)

Bibliographical notes

D. Ehle, Klage- und Prozeßrecht des EWG-Vertrages mit Entscheidungssammlung (1964)
L. J. Brinkhorst/H. G Schermers. Judicial Remedies in the European Communities. A Case Book (1969)
D. Schumacher, Rechtsschutz in den Europäischen Gemeinschaften (1974)

L. Plouvier, Les décisions de la Cour de justice des Communautés européennes et leurs effets juridiques (1975)

G Vandersanden/A. Barav, Contentieux communautaire (1977)

G. Myles, The Court of Justice of the European Communities (1978)

M. Hilf, Europäische Gemeinschaften und internationale Streitbeilegung, in: Völkerrecht als Rechtsordnung. Internationale Gerichtsbarkeit, Menschenrechte, Festschrift für Hermann Mosler (Beiträge zum ausländischen öffentlichen Recht und Völkerrecht, vol 81) (1983), pp. 337–428

H. Rasmussen, On Law and Policy in the European Court of Justice — A comparative study in Judicial Policymaking (1986)

U. Klinke, Der Gerichtshof der Europäischen Gemeinschaften, Aufbau und Arbeitsweise (1989)

J. Dine/S. Douglas-Scott/I. Persaud, Procedure and the European Court (1991)

H. Schermers/D. Waelbroeck, Judicial protection in the European Communities (5th ed., 1992)

L. Brown/T. Kennedy, The Court of Justice of the European Communities (4th ed., 1994)

K. Lasok, The European Court of Justice: Practice and Procedure, (2nd ed., 1994)

v. d. Groeben/Thiesing/Ehlermann, Kommentar zum EU/EG-Vertrag, Artikel 164–188 (5th ed., 1999) with further bibliographical notes

Collections of cases

European Court Reports (in all official languages)

aa) Treaty on European Union as amended by the Treaty of Amsterdam of October 2, 1997

TITLE VI

PROVISIONS ON POLICE AND JUDICIAL COOPERATION IN CRIMINAL MATTERS

Art. 35 1. The Court of Justice of the European Communities shall have jurisdiction, subject to the conditions laid down in this Article, to give preliminary rulings on the validity and interpretation of framework decisions and decisions, on the interpretation of conventions established under this Title and on the validity and interpretation of the measures implementing them.

2. By a declaration made at the time of signature of the Treaty of Amsterdam or at any time thereafter, any Member State shall be able to accept the jurisdiction of the Court of Justice to give preliminary rulings as specified in paragraph 1.

3. A Member State making a declaration pursuant to paragraph 2 shall specify that either:

(a) any court or tribunal of that State against whose decisions there is no judicial remedy under national law may request the Court of Justice to give a preliminary ruling on a question raised in a case pending before it and concerning the validity or interpretation of an act referred to in paragraph 1 if that court or tribunal considers that a decision on the question is necessary to enable it to give judgment, or

(b) any court or tribunal of that State may request the Court of Justice to give a preliminary ruling on a question raised in a case pending before it and concerning the validity or interpretation of an act referred to in paragraph 1 if that court or tribunal considers that a decision on the question is necessary to enable it to give judgment.

4. Any Member State, whether or not it has made a declaration pursuant to paragraph 2, shall be entitled to submit statements of case or written observations to the Court in cases which arise under paragraph 1.

5. The Court of Justice shall have no jurisdiction to review the validity or proportionality of operations carried out by the police or other law enforcement services of a Member State or the exercise of the responsibilities incumbent upon Member States with regard to the maintenance of law and order and the safeguarding of internal security.

6. The Court of Justice shall have jurisdiction to review the legality of framework decisions and decisions in actions brought by a Member State or the Commission on grounds of lack of competence, infringement of an essential procedural requirement, infringement of this Treaty or of any rule of law relating to its application, or misuse of powers. The proceedings provided for in this paragraph shall be instituted within two months of the publication of the measure.

7. The Court of Justice shall have jurisdiction to rule on any dispute between Member States regarding the interpretation or the application of acts adopted under Article 34(2) whenever such dispute cannot be settled by the Council within six months of its being referred to the Council by one of its members. The Court shall also have jurisdiction to rule on any dispute between Member States and the Commission regarding the interpretation or the application of conventions established under Article 34(2)(d).

Art. 40   1. Member States which intend to establish closer cooperation between themselves may be authorised, subject to Articles 43 and 44, to make use of the institutions, procedures and mechanisms laid down by the Treaties provided that the cooperation proposed:

(a) respects the powers of the European Community, and the objectives laid down by this Title;

(b) has the aim of enabling the Union to develop more rapidly into an area of freedom, security and justice.

2. The authorisation referred to in paragraph 1 shall be granted by the Council, acting by a qualified majority at the request of the Member States concerned and after inviting the Commission to present its opinion; the request shall also be forwarded to the European Parliament.

If a member of the Council declares that, for important and stated reasons of national policy, it intends to oppose the granting of an authorisation by qualified majority, a vote shall not be taken. The Council may, acting by a qualified majority, request that the matter be referred to the European Council for decision by unanimity.

The votes of the members of the Council shall be weighted in accordance with Article 205(2) of the Treaty establishing the European Community. For their adoption, decisions shall require at least 62 votes in favour, cast by at least 10 members.

3. Any Member State which wishes to become a party to cooperation set up in accordance with this Article shall notify its intention to the Council and to the Commission, which shall give an opinion to the Council within three months of receipt of that notification, possibly accompanied by a recommendation for such specific arrangements as it may deem necessary for that Member State to become a party to the cooperation in question. Within four months of the date of that notification, the Council shall decide on the request and on such specific arrangements as it may deem necessary. The decision shall be deemed to be taken unless the Council, acting by a qualified majority, decides to hold it in abeyance; in this case, the Council shall state the reasons for its decision and set a deadline for reexamining it. For the purposes of this paragraph, the Council shall act under the conditions set out in Article 44.

4. The provisions of Articles 29 to 41 shall apply to the closer cooperation provided for by this Article, save as otherwise provided for in this Article and in Articles 43 and 44.

The provisions of the Treaty establishing the European Community concerning the powers of the Court of Justice of the European Communities and the exercise of those powers shall apply to paragraphs 1, 2 and 3.

5. This Article is without prejudice to the provisions of the Protocol integrating the Schengen acquis into the framework of the European Union.

TITLE VIII

FINAL PROVISIONS

Art. 46   The provisions of the Treaty establishing the European Community, the Treaty establishing the European Coal and Steel Community and the Treaty establishing the European Atomic Energy Community concerning the powers of the Court of Justice of the European Communities and the exercise of those powers shall apply only to the following provisions of this Treaty:

(a) provisions amending the Treaty establishing the European Economic Community with a view to establishing the European Community, the Treaty establishing the European Coal and Steel Community and the Treaty establishing the European Atomic Energy Community;

(b) provisions of Title VI, under the conditions provided for by Article 35;

(c) provisions of Title VII, under the conditions provided for by Article 11 of the Treaty establishing the European Community and Article 40 of this Treaty;

(d) Article 6(2) with regard to action of the institutions, insofar as the Court has jurisdiction under the Treaties establishing the European Communities and under this Treaty;

(e) Articles 46 to 53.

bb) Treaty Establishing the European Coal and Steel Community as amended by the Treaty of Amsterdam of October 2, 1997

CHAPTER 4 – THE COURT OF JUSTICE

Art. 31   The Court shall ensure that in the interpretation and application of this Treaty, and of rules laid down for the implementation thereof, the law is observed.

Art. 32   The Court of Justice shall consist of 15 Judges.

The Court of Justice shall sit in plenary session. It may, however, form chambers, each consisting of three, five or seven Judges, either to undertake certain preparatory inquiries or to adjudicate on particular categories of cases in accordance with the rules laid down for these purposes. The Court of Justice shall sit in plenary session when a Member State or a Community institution that is a party to the proceedings so requests.

Should the Court of Justice so request, the Council may, acting unanimously, increase the number of Judges and make the necessary adjustments to the second and third paragraphs of this Article and to the second paragraph of Article 32b.

Art. 32a The Court of Justice shall be assisted by eight Advocates General. However, a ninth Advocate General shall be appointed as from 1 January 1995 until 6 October 2000.

It shall be the duty of the Advocate General acting with complete impartiality and independence, to make, in open court, reasoned submissions on cases brought before the Court, in order to assist the Court in the performance of the task assigned to it in Article 31.

Should the Court so request, the Council may, acting unanimously, increase the number of Advocates General and make the necessary adjustments to the third paragraph of Article 32b.

Art. 32b The Judges and Advocates General shall be chosen from persons whose independence is beyond doubt and who possess the qualifications required for appointment to the highest judicial offices in their respective countries or who are jurisconsults of recognized competence; they shall be appointed by common accord of the governments of the Member States for a term of six years.

Every three years there shall be a partial replacement of the Judges. Eight and seven Judges shall be replaced alternately.

Every three years there shall be a partial replacement of the Advocates General. Four Advocates General shall be replaced on each occasion.

Retiring Judges and Advocates General shall be eligible for reappointment.

The Judges shall elect the President of the Court from among their number for a term of three years. He may be re elected.

Art. 32c The Court shall appoint its Registrar and lay down the rules governing his service.

Art. 32d 1. A Court of First Instance shall be attached to the Court of Justice with jurisdiction to hear and determine at first instance, subject to a right of appeal to the Court of Justice on points of law only and in accordance with the conditions laid down by the Statute, certain classes of action or proceeding defined in accordance with the conditions laid down in paragraph 2. The Court of First Instance shall not be competent to hear and determine questions referred for a preliminary ruling under Article 41.

2. At the request of the Court of Justice and after consulting the European Parliament and the Commission, the Council, acting unanimously, shall determine the classes of action or proceeding referred to in paragraph 1, and the composition of the Court of First Instance and shall adopt the

necessary adjustments and additional provisions to the Statute of the Court of Justice. Unless the Council decides otherwise, the provisions of this Treaty relating to the Court of Justice, in particular the provisions of the Protocol on the Statute of the Court of Justice, shall apply to the Court of First Instance.

3. The members of the Court of First Instance shall be chosen from persons whose independence is beyond doubt and who possess the ability required for appointment to judicial office; they shall be appointed by common accord of the governments of the Member States for a term of six years. The membership shall be partially renewed every three years. Retiring members shall be eligible for reappointment.

4. The Court of First Instance shall establish its Rules of Procedure in agreement with the Court of Justice. Those rules shall require the unanimous approval of the Council.

Art. 33   The Court of Justice shall have jurisdiction in actions brought by a Member State or by the Council to have decisions or recommendations of the Commission declared void on grounds of lack of competence, infringement of an essential procedural requirement, infringement of this Treaty or of any rule of law relating to its application, or misuse of powers. The Court of Justice may not, however, examine the evaluation of the situation, resulting from economic facts or circumstances, in the light of which the Commission took its decisions or made its recommendations, save where the Commission is alleged to have misused its powers or to have manifestly failed to observe the provisions of this Treaty or any rule of law relating to its application.

Undertakings or associations referred to in Article 48 may, under the same conditions, institute proceedings against decisions or recommendations concerning them which are individual in character or against general decisions or recommendations which they consider to involve a misuse of powers affecting them.

The proceedings provided for in the first two paragraphs of this Article shall be instituted within one month of the notification or publication, as the case may be, of the decision or recommendation. The Court of Justice shall have jurisdiction under the same conditions in actions brought by the European Parliament for the purpose of protecting its prerogatives.

Art. 34   If the Court declares a decision or recommendation void, it shall refer the matter back to the Commission. The Commission shall take the necessary steps to comply with the judgment. If direct and special harm is suffered by an undertaking or group of undertakings by reason of a decision or recommendation held by the Court to involve a fault of such a nature as to render the Community liable, the Commission shall, using the powers conferred upon it by this Treaty, take steps to ensure equitable redress for the harm resulting directly from the decision or recommendation declared void and, where necessary, pay appropriate damages.

If the Commission fails to take within a reasonable time the necessary steps to comply with the judgment, proceedings for damages may be instituted before the Court.

Art. 35   Wherever the Commission is required by this Treaty, or by rules laid down for the implementation thereof, to take a decision or make a recommendation and fails to fulfil this obligation, it shall be for States, the Council, undertakings or associations, as the case may be, to raise the matter with the Commission.

The same shall apply if the Commission, where empowered by this Treaty, or by rules laid down for the implementation thereof, to take a decision or make a recommendation, abstains from doing so and such abstention constitutes a misuse of powers.

If at the end of two months the Commission has not taken any decision or made any recommendation, proceedings may be instituted before the Court within one month against the implied decision of refusal which is to be inferred from the silence of the Commission on the matter.

Art. 36   Before imposing a pecuniary sanction or ordering a periodic penalty payment as provided for in this Treaty, the Commission must give the party concerned the opportunity to submit its comments.

The Court shall have unlimited jurisdiction in appeals against pecuniary sanctions and periodic penalty payments imposed under this Treaty.

In support of its appeal, a party may, under the same conditions as in the first paragraph of Article 33 of this Treaty, contest the legality of the decision or recommendation which that party is alleged not to have observed.

Art. 37   If a Member State considers that in a given case action or failure to act on the part of the Commission is of such a nature as to provoke fundamental and persistent disturbances in its economy, it may raise the matter with the Commission.

The Commission, after consulting the Council, shall, if there are grounds for so doing, recognize the existence of such a situation and decide on the measures to be taken to end it, in accordance with the provisions of this Treaty, while at the same time safeguarding the essential interests of the Community.

When proceedings are instituted in the Court under this Article against such a decision or against an express or implied decision refusing to recognize the existence of the situation referred to above, it shall be for the Court to determine whether it is well founded.

If the Court declares the decision void, the Commission shall, within the terms of the judgment of the Court, decide on the measures to be taken for the purposes indicated in the second paragraph of this Article.

Art. 38   The Court may, on application by a Member State or the Commission, declare an act of the European Parliament or of the Council to be void.

Application shall be made within one month of the publication of the act of the European Parliament or the notification of the act of the Council to the Member States or to the Commission.

The only grounds for such application shall be lack of competence or infringement of an essential procedural requirement.

Art. 39   Actions brought before the Court shall not have suspensory effect.

The Court may, however, if it considers that circumstances so require, order that application of the contested decision or recommendation be suspended.

The Court may prescribe any other necessary interim measures.

Art. 40   Without prejudice to the first paragraph of Article 34, the Court shall have jurisdiction to order pecuniary reparation from the Community, on application by the injured party, to make good any injury caused in carrying out this Treaty by a wrongful act or omission on the part of the Community in the performance of its functions.

The Court shall also have jurisdiction to order the Community to make good any injury caused by a personal wrong by a servant of the Community in the performance of his duties. The personal liability of its servants towards the Community shall be governed by the provisions laid down in their Staff Regulations or the Conditions of Employment applicable to them.

All other disputes between the Community and persons other than its servants to which the provisions of this Treaty or the rules laid down for the implementation thereof do not apply shall be brought before national courts or tribunals.

Art. 41   The Court shall have sole jurisdiction to give preliminary rulings on the validity of acts of the Commission and of the Council where such validity is in issue in proceedings brought before a national court or tribunal.

Art. 42   The Court shall have jurisdiction to give judgment pursuant to any arbitration clause contained in a contract concluded by or on behalf of the Community, whether that contract be governed by public or private law.

Art. 43   The Court shall have jurisdiction in any other case provided for by a provision supplementing this Treaty.

It may also rule in all cases which relate to the subject matter of this Treaty where jurisdiction is conferred upon it by the law of a Member State.

Art. 44   The judgments of the Court shall be enforceable in the territory of Member States under the conditions laid down in Article 92.

Art. 45   The Statute of the Court is laid down in a Protocol annexed to this Treaty.

The Council may, acting unanimously at the request of the Court of Justice and after consulting the Commission and the European Parliament, amend the provisions of Title III of the Statute.

TITLE IV — GENERAL PROVISIONS

Art. 87   The High Contracting Parties undertake not to avail themselves of any treaties, conventions or declarations made between them for the purpose of submitting a dispute concerning the interpretation or application of this Treaty to any method of settlement other than those provided for therein.

Art. 88   If the Commission considers that a State has failed to fulfil an obligation under this Treaty, it shall record this failure in a reasoned decision after giving the State concerned the opportunity to submit its comments. It shall set the State a time limit for the fulfilment of its obligation.

The State may institute proceedings before the Court within two months of notification of the decision; the Court shall have unlimited jurisdiction in such cases.

If the State has not fulfilled its obligation by the time limit set by the Commission, or if it brings an action which is dismissed, the Commission may, with the assent of the Council acting by a two thirds majority:

a)   suspend the payment of any sums which it may be liable to pay to the State in question under this Treaty;

b)   take measures, or authorize the other Member States to take measures, by way of derogation from the provisions of Article 4, in order to correct the effects of the infringement of the obligation.

Proceedings may be instituted before the Court against decisions taken under subparagraphs (a) and (b) within two months of their notification; the Court shall have unlimited jurisdiction in such cases.

If these measures prove ineffective, the Commission shall bring the matter before the Council.

Art. 89   Any dispute between Member States concerning the application of this Treaty which cannot be settled by another procedure provided for in this Treaty may be submitted to the Court on application by one of the States which are parties to the dispute.

The Court shall also have jurisdiction in any dispute between Member States which relates to the subject matter of this Treaty, if the dispute is submitted to it under a special agreement between the parties.

cc) Treaty Establishing the European Community as amended by the Treaty of Amsterdam of October 2, 1997

PART THREE — COMMUNITY POLICIES

TITLE IV — VISAS, ASYLUM, IMMIGRATION AND OTHER POLICIES RELATED TO FREE MOVEMENT OF PERSONS

Art. 68   1. Article 234 shall apply to this Title under the following circumstances and conditions: where a question on the interpretation of this Title or on the validity or interpretation of acts of the institutions of the Community based on this Title is raised in a case pending before a court or a tribunal of a Member State against whose decisions there is no judicial remedy under national law, that court or tribunal shall, if it considers that a decision on the question is necessary to enable it to give judgment, request the Court of Justice to give a ruling thereon.

2. In any event, the Court of Justice shall not have jurisdiction to rule on any measure or decision taken pursuant to Article 62(1) relating to the maintenance of law and order and the safeguarding of internal security.

3. The Council, the Commission or a Member State may request the Court of Justice to give a ruling on a question of interpretation of this Title or of acts of the institutions of the Community based on this Title. The ruling given by the Court of Justice in response to such a request shall not apply to judgments of courts or tribunals of the Member States which have become *res judicata*.

PART FIVE — INSTITUTIONS OF THE COMMUNITY

TITLE I — PROVISIONS GOVERNING THE INSTITUTIONS

Chapter 1 — The institutions

Section 4 — The Court of Justice

Art. 220   The Court of Justice shall ensure that in the interpretation and application of this Treaty the law is observed.

Art. 221   The Court of Justice shall consist of 15 Judges.

The Court of Justice shall sit in plenary session. It may, however, form chambers, each consisting of three, five or seven Judges, either to undertake certain preparatory inquiries or to adjudicate on particular categories of cases in accordance with rules laid down for these purposes.

The Court of Justice shall sit in plenary session when a Member State or a Community institution that is a party to the proceedings so requests.

Should the Court of Justice so request, the Council may, acting unanimously, increase the number of Judges and make the necessary adjustments to the second and third paragraphs of this Article and to the second paragraph of Article 223.

Art. 222   The Court of Justice shall be assisted by eight Advocates-General. However, a ninth Advocate-General shall be appointed as from 1 January 1995 until 6 October 2000.

It shall be the duty of the Advocate-General, acting with complete impartiality and independence, to make, in open court, reasoned submissions on cases brought before the Court of Justice, in order to assist the Court in the performance of the task assigned to it in Article 220.

Should the Court of Justice so request, the Council may, acting unanimously, increase the number of Advocates-General and make the necessary adjustments to the third paragraph of Article 223.

Art. 223   The Judges and Advocates-General shall be chosen from persons whose independence is beyond doubt and who possess the qualifications required for appointment to the highest judicial offices in their respective countries or who are jurisconsults of recognised competence; they shall be appointed by common accord of the governments of the Member States for a term of six years.

Every three years there shall be a partial replacement of the Judges. Eight and seven Judges shall be replaced alternately.

Every three years there shall be a partial replacement of the Advocates-General. Four Advocates-General shall be replaced on each occasion.

Retiring Judges and Advocates-General shall be eligible for reappointment.

The Judges shall elect the President of the Court of Justice from among their number for a term of three years. He may be re-elected.

Art. 224   The Court of Justice shall appoint its Registrar and lay down the rules governing his service.

Art. 225   1. A Court of First Instance shall be attached to the Court of Justice with jurisdiction to hear and determine at first instance, subject to a right of appeal to the Court of Justice on points of law only and in accordance with the conditions laid down by the Statute, certain classes of action or proceeding defined in accordance with the conditions laid down in paragraph 2. The Court of First Instance shall not be competent to hear and determine questions referred for a preliminary ruling under Article 234.

2. At the request of the Court of Justice and after consulting the European Parliament and the Commission, the Council, acting unanimously, shall determine the classes of action or proceeding referred to in paragraph 1 and the composition of the Court of First Instance and shall adopt the necessary adjustments and additional provisions to the Statute of the Court of Justice. Unless the Council decides otherwise, the provisions of this Treaty relating to the Court of Justice, in particular the provisions of the Protocol on the Statute of the Court of Justice, shall apply to the Court of First Instance.

3. The members of the Court of First Instance shall be chosen from persons whose independence is beyond doubt and who possess the ability required for appointment to judicial office; they shall be appointed by common accord of the governments of the Member States for a term of six years. The membership shall be partially renewed every three years. Retiring members shall be eligible for reappointment.

4. The Court of First Instance shall establish its Rules of Procedure in agreement with the Court of Justice. Those rules shall require the unanimous approval of the Council.

Art. 226   If the Commission considers that a Member State has failed to fulfil an obligation under this Treaty, it shall deliver a reasoned opinion on the matter after giving the State concerned the opportunity to submit its observations.

If the State concerned does not comply with the opinion within the period laid down by the Commission, the latter may bring the matter before the Court of Justice.

Art. 227   A Member State which considers that another Member State has failed to fulfil an obligation under this Treaty may bring the matter before the Court of Justice.

Before a Member State brings an action against another Member State for an alleged infringement of an obligation under this Treaty, it shall bring the matter before the Commission.

The Commission shall deliver a reasoned opinion after each of the States concerned has been given the opportunity to submit its own case and its observations on the other party's case both orally and in writing.

If the Commission has not delivered an opinion within three months of the date on which the matter was brought before it, the absence of such opinion shall not prevent the matter from being brought before the Court of Justice.

Art. 228   1. If the Court of Justice finds that a Member State has failed to fulfil an obligation under this Treaty, the State shall be required to take the necessary measures to comply with the judgment of the Court of Justice.

2. If the Commission considers that the Member State concerned has not taken such measures it shall, after giving that State the opportunity to submit its observations, issue a reasoned opinion specifying the points on which the Member State concerned has not complied with the judgment of the Court of Justice.

If the Member State concerned fails to take the necessary measures to comply with the Court's judgment within the time-limit laid down by the Commission, the latter may bring the case before the Court of Justice. In so doing it shall specify the amount of the lump sum or penalty payment to be paid by the Member State concerned which it considers appropriate in the circumstances.

If the Court of Justice finds that the Member State concerned has not complied with its judgment it may impose a lump sum or penalty payment on it.

This procedure shall be without prejudice to Article 227.

Art. 229 Regulations adopted jointly by the European Parliament and the Council, and by the Council, pursuant to the provisions of this Treaty, may give the Court of Justice unlimited jurisdiction with regard to the penalties provided for in such regulations.

Art. 230 The Court of Justice shall review the legality of acts adopted jointly by the European Parliament and the Council, of acts of the Council, of the Commission and of the ECB, other than recommendations and opinions, and of acts of the European Parliament intended to produce legal effects vis-à-vis third parties.

It shall for this purpose have jurisdiction in actions brought by a Member State, the Council or the Commission on grounds of lack of competence, infringement of an essential procedural requirement, infringement of this Treaty or of any rule of law relating to its application, or misuse of powers.

The Court of Justice shall have jurisdiction under the same conditions in actions brought by the European Parliament, by the Court of Auditors and by the ECB for the purpose of protecting their prerogatives.

Any natural or legal person may, under the same conditions, institute proceedings against a decision addressed to that person or against a decision which, although in the form of a regulation or a decision addressed to another person, is of direct and individual concern to the former.

The proceedings provided for in this Article shall be instituted within two months of the publication of the measure, or of its notification to the plaintiff, or, in the absence thereof, of the day on which it came to the knowledge of the latter, as the case may be.

Art. 231 If the action is well founded, the Court of Justice shall declare the act concerned to be void.

In the case of a regulation, however, the Court of Justice shall, if it considers this necessary, state which of the effects of the regulation which it has declared void shall be considered as definitive.

Art. 232 Should the European Parliament, the Council or the Commission, in infringement of this Treaty, fail to act, the Member States and the other institutions of the Community may bring an action before the Court of Justice to have the infringement established.

The action shall be admissible only if the institution concerned has first been called upon to act. If, within two months of being so called upon, the institution concerned has not defined its position, the action may be brought within a further period of two months.

Any natural or legal person may, under the conditions laid down in the preceding paragraphs, complain to the Court of Justice that an institution of the Community has failed to address to that person any act other than a recommendation or an opinion.

The Court of Justice shall have jurisdiction, under the same conditions, in actions or proceedings brought by the ECB in the areas falling within the latter's field of competence and in actions or proceedings brought against the latter.

Art. 233   The institution or institutions whose act has been declared void or whose failure to act has been declared contrary to this Treaty shall be required to take the necessary measures to comply with the judgment of the Court of Justice.

This obligation shall not affect any obligation which may result from the application of the second paragraph of Article 288.

This Article shall also apply to the ECB.

Art. 234   The Court of Justice shall have jurisdiction to give preliminary rulings concerning:

(a)   the interpretation of this Treaty;

(b)   the validity and interpretation of acts of the institutions of the Community and of the ECB;

(c)   the interpretation of the statutes of bodies established by an act of the Council, where those statutes so provide.

Where such a question is raised before any court or tribunal of a Member State, that court or tribunal may, if it considers that a decision on the question is necessary to enable it to give judgment, request the Court of Justice to give a ruling thereon.

Where any such question is raised in a case pending before a court or tribunal of a Member State against whose decisions there is no judicial remedy under national law, that court or tribunal shall bring the matter before the Court of Justice.

Art. 235   The Court of Justice shall have jurisdiction in disputes relating to compensation for damage provided for in the second paragraph of Article 288.

Art. 236   The Court of Justice shall have jurisdiction in any dispute between the Community and its servants within the limits and under the conditions laid down in the Staff Regulations or the Conditions of Employment.

Art. 237   The Court of Justice shall, within the limits hereinafter laid down, have jurisdiction in disputes concerning:

(a)   the fulfilment by Member States of obligations under the Statute of the European Investment Bank. In this connection, the Board of Directors of the Bank shall enjoy the powers conferred upon the Commission by Article 226;

(b)   measures adopted by the Board of Governors of the European Investment Bank. In this connection, any Member State, the Commission or the Board of Directors of the Bank may institute proceedings under the conditions laid down in Article 230;

    (c) measures adopted by the Board of Directors of the European Investment Bank. Proceedings against such measures may be instituted only by Member States or by the Commission, under the conditions laid down in Article 230, and solely on the grounds of non-compliance with the procedure provided for in Article 21(2), (5), (6) and (7) of the Statute of the Bank;

    (d) the fulfilment by national central banks of obligations under this Treaty and the Statute of the ESCB. In this connection the powers of the Council of the ECB in respect of national central banks shall be the same as those conferred upon the Commission in respect of Member States by Article 226. If the Court of Justice finds that a national central bank has failed to fulfil an obligation under this Treaty, that bank shall be required to take the necessary measures to comply with the judgment of the Court of Justice.

Art. 238 The Court of Justice shall have jurisdiction to give judgment pursuant to any arbitration clause contained in a contract concluded by or on behalf of the Community, whether that contract be governed by public or private law.

Art. 239 The Court of Justice shall have jurisdiction in any dispute between Member States which relates to the subject matter of this Treaty if the dispute is submitted to it under a special agreement between the parties.

Art. 240 Save where jurisdiction is conferred on the Court of Justice by this Treaty, disputes to which the Community is a party shall not on that ground be excluded from the jurisdiction of the courts or tribunals of the Member States.

Art. 241 Notwithstanding the expiry of the period laid down in the fifth paragraph of Article 230, any party may, in proceedings in which a regulation adopted jointly by the European Parliament and the Council, or a regulation of the Council, of the Commission, or of the ECB is at issue, plead the grounds specified in the second paragraph of Article 230 in order to invoke before the Court of Justice the inapplicability of that regulation.

Art. 242 Actions brought before the Court of Justice shall not have suspensory effect. The Court of Justice may, however, if it considers that circumstances so require, order that application of the contested act be suspended.

Art. 243 The Court of Justice may in any cases before it prescribe any necessary interim measures.

Art. 244 The judgments of the Court of Justice shall be enforceable under the conditions laid down in Article 256.

Art. 245 The Statute of the Court of Justice is laid down in a separate Protocol.

          The Council may, acting unanimously at the request of the Court of Justice and after consulting the Commission and the European Parliament, amend the provisions of Title III of the Statute.

The Court of Justice shall adopt its Rules of Procedure. These shall require the unanimous approval of the Council.

dd) Treaty Establishing the European Atomic Energy Community as amended by the Treaty of Amsterdam of October 2, 1997

Art. 136 The Court of Justice shall ensure that in the interpretation and application of this Treaty the law is observed.

Art. 137 The Court of Justice shall consist of 15 Judges.

The Court of Justice shall sit in plenary session. It may, however, form chambers, each consisting of three, five or seven Judges, either to undertake certain preparatory inquiries or to adjudicate on particular categories of cases in accordance with the rules laid down for these purposes.

The Court of Justice shall sit in plenary session when a Member State or a Community institution that is party to the proceedings so requests.

Should the Court of Justice so request, the Council may, acting unanimously, increase the number of Judges and make the necessary adjustments to the second and third paragraphs of this Article and to the second paragraph of Article 139.

Art. 138 The Court of Justice shall be assisted by eight Advocates-General. However, a ninth Advocate-General shall be appointed as from 1 January 1999 until 6 October 2000.

It shall be the duty of the Advocate-General, acting with complete impartiality and independence, to make, in open court, reasoned submissions on cases brought before the Court of Justice, in order to assist the Court in the performance of the task assigned to it in Article 136.

Should the Court of Justice so request, the Council may, acting unanimously, increase the number of Advocates-General and make the necessary adjustments to the third paragraph of Article 139.

Art. 139 The Judges and Advocates-General shall be chosen from persons whose independence is beyond doubt and who possess the qualifications required for appointment to the highest judicial offices in their respective countries or who are jurisconsults of recognised competence; they shall be appointed by common accord of the governments of the Member States for a term of six years.

Every three years there shall be a partial replacement of the Judges. Eight and seven Judges shall be replaced alternately.

Every three years there shall be a partial replacement of the Advocates-General. Four Advocates-General shall be replaced on each occasion.

Retiring Judges and Advocates-General shall be eligible for reappointment.

The Judges shall elect the President of the Court of Justice from among their number for a term of three years. He may be re-elected.

Art. 140 The Court of Justice shall appoint its Registrar and lay down the rules governing his service.

Art. 140a 1. A Court of First Instance shall be attached to the Court of Justice with jurisdiction to hear and determine at first instance, subject to a right of appeal to the Court of Justice on points of law only and in accordance with the conditions laid down by the Statute, certain classes of action or proceeding defined in accordance with the conditions laid down in paragraph 2. The Court of First Instance shall not be competent to hear and determine questions referred for a preliminary ruling under Article 150.

2. At the request of the Court of Justice and after consulting the European Parliament and the Commission, the Council, acting unanimously, shall determine the classes of action or proceeding referred to in paragraph 1 and the composition of the Court of First Instance and shall adopt the necessary adjustments and additional provisions to the Statute of the Court of Justice. Unless the Council decides otherwise, the provisions of this Treaty relating to the Court of Justice, in particular the provisions of the Protocol on the Statute of the Court of Justice, shall apply to the Court of First Instance.

3. The Members of the Court of First Instance shall be chosen from persons whose independence is beyond doubt and who possess the ability required for appointment to judicial office; they shall be appointed by common accord of the governments of the Member States for a term of six years. The membership shall be partially renewed every three years. Retiring Members shall be eligible for re-appointment.

4. The Court of First Instance shall establish its Rules of Procedure in agreement with the Court of Justice. Those rules shall require the unanimous approval of the Council.

Art. 141 If the Commission considers that a Member State has failed to fulfil an obligation under this Treaty, it shall deliver a reasoned opinion on the matter after giving the State concerned the opportunity to submit its observations.

If the State concerned does not comply with the opinion within the period laid down by the Commission, the latter may bring the matter before the Court of Justice.

Art. 142 A Member State which considers that another Member State has failed to fulfil an obligation under this Treaty may bring the matter before the Court of Justice.

Before a Member State brings an action against another Member State for an alleged infringement of an obligation under this Treaty, it shall bring the matter before the Commission.

The Commission shall deliver a reasoned opinion after each of the States concerned has been given the opportunity to submit its own case and its observations on the other party's case both orally and in writing.

If the Commission has not delivered an opinion within three months of the date on which the matter was brought before it, the absence of such opinion shall not prevent the matter from being brought before the Court of Justice.

Art. 143 1. If the Court of Justice finds that a Member State has failed to fulfil an obligation under this Treaty, the State shall be required to take the necessary measures to comply with the judgment of the Court of Justice.

2. If the Commission considers that the Member State concerned has not taken such measures it shall, after giving that State the opportunity to submit its observations, issue a reasoned opinion specifying the points on which the Member State concerned has not complied with the judgment of the Court of Justice.

If the Member State concerned fails to take the necessary measures to comply with the Court's judgment within the time-limit laid down by the Commission, the latter may bring the case before the Court of Justice. In so doing it shall specify the amount of the lump sum or penalty payment to be paid by the Member State concerned which it considers appropriate in the circumstances.

If the Court of Justice finds that the Member State concerned has not complied with its judgment it may impose a lump sum or penalty payment on it.

This procedure shall be without prejudice to Article 142.

Art. 144 The Court of Justice shall have unlimited jurisdiction in:

(a) proceedings instituted under Article 12 to have the appropriate terms fixed for the granting by the Commission of licences or sublicences;

(b) proceedings instituted by persons or undertakings against sanctions imposed on them by the Commission under Article 83.

Art. 145 If the Commission considers that a person or undertaking has committed an infringement of this Treaty to which the provisions of Article 83 do not apply, it shall call upon the Member State having jurisdiction over that person or undertaking to cause sanctions to be imposed in respect of the infringement in accordance with its national law.

If the State concerned does not comply with such a request within the period laid down by the Commission, the latter may bring an action before the Court of Justice to have the infringement of which the person or undertaking is accused established.

Art. 146 The Court of Justice shall review the legality of acts of the Council and of the Commission, other than recommendations or opinions, and of acts of the European Parliament intended to produce legal effects *vis-à-vis* third parties.

It shall for this purpose have jurisdiction in actions brought by a Member State, the Council or the Commission on grounds of lack of competence, infringement of an essential procedural requirement, infringement of this Treaty or of any rule of law relating to its application, or misuse of powers.

The Court shall have jurisdiction under the same conditions in actions brought by the European Parliament for the purpose of protecting its prerogatives.

Any natural or legal person may, under the same conditions, institute proceedings against a decision addressed to that person or against a decision which, although in the form of a regulation or a decision addressed to another person, is of direct and individual concern to the former.

The proceedings provided for in this Article shall be instituted within two months of the publication of the measure, or of its notification to the plaintiff, or, in the absence thereof, of the day on which it came to the knowledge of the latter, as the case may be.

Art. 147   If the action is well founded, the Court shall declare the act concerned to be void.

In the case of a regulation, however, the Court of Justice shall, if it considers this necessary, state which of the effects of the regulation which it has declared void shall be considered as definitive.

Art. 148   Should the Council or the Commission, in infringement of this Treaty, fail to act, the Member States and the other institutions of the Community may bring an action before the Court of Justice to have the infringement established.

The action shall be admissible only if the institution concerned has first been called upon to act. If, within two months of being so called upon, the institution concerned has not defined its position, the action may be brought within a further period of two months.

Any natural or legal person may, under the conditions laid down in the preceding paragraphs, complain to the Court of Justice that an institution of the Community has failed to address to that person any act other than a recommendation or an opinion.

Art. 149   The institution whose act has been declared void or whose failure to act has been declared contrary to this Treaty shall be required to take the necessary measures to comply with the judgment of the Court of Justice.

This obligation shall not affect any obligation which may result from the application of the second paragraph of Article 188.

Art. 150   The Court of Justice shall have jurisdiction to give preliminary rulings concerning:

(a)   the interpretation of this Treaty;

(b)   the validity and interpretation of acts of the institutions of the Community;

(c) the interpretation of the statutes of bodies established by an act of the Council, save where those statutes provide otherwise.

Where such a question is raised before any court or tribunal of a Member State, that court or tribunal may, if it considers that a decision on the question is necessary to enable it to give judgment, request the Court of Justice to give a ruling thereon.

Where any such question is raised in a case pending before a court or tribunal of a Member State, against whose decisions there is no judicial remedy under national law, that court or tribunal shall bring the matter before the Court of Justice.

Art. 151 The Court of Justice shall have jurisdiction in disputes relating to the compensation for damage provided for in the second paragraph of Article 188.

Art. 152 The Court of Justice shall have jurisdiction in any dispute between the Community and its servants within the limits and under the conditions laid down in the Staff Regulations or the Conditions of Employment.

Art. 153 The Court of Justice shall have jurisdiction to give judgment pursuant to any arbitration clause contained in a contract concluded by or on behalf of the Community, whether that contract be governed by public or private law.

Art. 154 The Court of Justice shall have jurisdiction in any dispute between Member States which relates to the subject-matter of this Treaty if the dispute is submitted to it under a special agreement between the parties.

Art. 155 Save where jurisdiction is conferred on the Court of Justice by this Treaty, disputes to which the Community is a party shall not on that ground be excluded from the jurisdiction of the courts or tribunals of the Member States.

Art. 156 Notwithstanding the expiry of the period laid down in the fifth paragraph of Article 146, any party may, in proceedings in which a regulation of the Council or of the Commission is in issue, plead the grounds specified in the second paragraph of Article 146, in order to invoke before the Court of Justice the inapplicability of that regulation.

Art. 157 Save as otherwise provided in this Treaty, actions brought before the Court of Justice shall not have suspensory effect. The Court of Justice may, however, if it considers that circumstances so require, order that application of the contested act be suspended.

Art. 158 The Court of Justice may in any cases before it prescribe any necessary interim measures.

Art. 159 The judgments of the Court of Justice shall be enforceable under the conditions laid down in Article 164.

Art. 160 The Statute of the Court of Justice is laid down in a separate Protocol.

The Council may, acting unanimously at the request of the Court of Justice and after consulting the Commission and the European Parliament, amend the provisions of Title III of the Statute.

The Court of Justice shall adopt its rules of procedure. These shall require the unanimous approval of the Council.

Art. 164 Enforcement shall be governed by the rules of civil procedure in force in the State in the territory of which it is carried out. The order for its enforcement shall be appended to the decision, without other formality than verification of the authenticity of the decision, by the national authority which the government of each Member State shall designate for this purpose and shall make known to the Commission, to the Court of Justice and to the Arbitration Committee set up by Article 18.

When these formalities have been completed on application by the party concerned, the latter may proceed to enforcement in accordance with the national law, by bringing the matter directly before the competent authority.

Enforcement may be suspended only by a decision of the Court of Justice. However, the courts of the country concerned shall have jurisdiction over complaints that enforcement is being carried out in an irregular manner.

Art. 188 The contractual liability of the Community shall be governed by the law applicable to the contract in question.

In the case of non-contractual liability, the Community shall, in accordance with the general principles common to the laws of the Member States, make good any damage caused by its institutions or by its servants in the performance of their duties.

The personal liability of its servants towards the Community shall be governed by the provisions laid down in the Staff Regulations or in the Conditions of Employment applicable to them.

Art. 193 Member States undertake not to submit a dispute concerning the interpretation or application of this Treaty to any method of settlement other than those provided for therein.

ee) Treaty of Amsterdam amending the Treaty on European Union, the Treaties Establishing the European Communities and Certain Related Acts of October 2, 1997

Art. 9 1. Without prejudice to the paragraphs following hereinafter, which have as their purpose to retain the essential elements of their provisions, the Convention of 25 March 1957 on certain institutions common to the European Communities and the Treaty of 8 April 1965 establishing a Single Council and a Single Commission of the European Communities, but with the exception of the Protocol referred to in paragraph 5, shall be repealed.

2. The powers conferred on the European Parliament, the Council, the Commission, the Court of Justice and the Court of Auditors by the Treaty establishing the European Community, the Treaty establishing the European Coal and Steel Community and the Treaty establishing the European Atomic Energy Community shall be exercised by the single institutions under the conditions laid down respectively by the said Treaties and this Article.

ff) Protocol on the Statute of the Court of Justice of the European Community as amended by the Treaty of Amsterdam of October 2, 1997

THE HIGH CONTRACTING PARTIES TO THE TREATY ESTABLISHING THE EUROPEAN COMMUNITY.

DESIRING to lay down the Statute of the Court provided for in Article 188 of this Treaty,

HAVE AGREED upon the following provisions, which shall be annexed to the Treaty establishing the European Community.

Art. 1 The Court established by Article 7 [ex-Article 7] of this Treaty shall be constituted and shall function in accordance with the provisions of this Treaty and of this Statute.

TITLE I — JUDGES AND ADVOCATES GENERAL

Art. 2 Before taking up his duties each Judge shall, in open court, take an oath to perform his duties impartially and conscientiously and to preserve the secrecy of the deliberations of the Court.

Art. 3 The Judges shall be immune from legal proceedings. After they have ceased to hold office, they shall continue to enjoy immunity in respect of acts performed by them in their official capacity including words spoken or written.

The Court, sitting in plenary session, may waive the immunity.

Where immunity has been waived and criminal proceedings are instituted against a Judge, he shall be tried, in any of the Member States, only by the Court competent to judge the members of the highest national judiciary.

Articles 12 to 15 and 18 of the Protocol on the privileges and immunities of the European Communities shall apply to the Judges, Advocates-General, Registrar and Assistant Rapporteurs of the Court of Justice, without prejudice to the provisions relating to immunity from legal proceedings of Judges which are set out in the preceding paragraphs.

Art. 4 The Judges may not hold any political or administrative office.

They may not engage in any occupation, whether gainful or not, unless exemption is exceptionally granted by the Council.

When taking up their duties, they shall give a solemn undertaking that, both during and after their term of office, they will respect the obligations arising therefrom, in particular the duty to behave with integrity and discretion as regards the acceptance, after they have ceased to hold office, of certain appointments or benefits.

Any doubt on this point shall be settled by decision of the Court.

Art. 5   Apart from normal replacement, or death, the duties of a Judge shall end when he resigns.

Where a Judge resigns, his letter of resignation shall be addressed to the President of the Court for transmission to the President of the Council. Upon this notification a vacancy shall arise on the bench.

Save where Article 6 applies, a Judge shall continue to hold office until his successor takes up his duties.

Art. 6   A Judge may be deprived of his office or of his right to a pension or other benefits in its stead only if, in the unanimous opinion of the Judges and Advocates General of the Court, he no longer fulfils the requisite conditions or meets the obligations arising from his office. The Judge concerned shall not take part in any such deliberations.

The Registrar of the Court shall communicate the decision of the Court to the President of the European Parliament and to the President of the Commission and shall notify it to the President of the Council.

In the case of a decision depriving a Judge of his office, a vacancy shall arise on the bench upon this latter notification.

Art. 7   A Judge who is to replace a member of the Court whose term of office has not expired shall be appointed for the remainder of his predecessor's term.

Art. 8   The provisions of Articles 2 to 7 shall apply to the Advocates General.

TITLE II — ORGANIZATION

Art. 9   The Registrar shall take an oath before the Court to perform his duties impartially and conscientiously and to preserve the secrecy of the deliberations of the Court.

Art. 10   The Court shall arrange for replacement of the Registrar on occasions when he is prevented from attending the Court.

Art. 11   Officials and other servants shall be attached to the Court to enable it to function. They shall be responsible to the Registrar under the authority of the President.

Art. 12   On a proposal from the Court, the Council may, acting unanimously, provide for the appointment of Assistant Rapporteurs and lay down the rules governing their service. The Assistant Rapporteurs may be required, under conditions laid down in the Rules of Procedure, to participate in preparatory inquiries in cases pending before the Court and to cooperate with the Judge who acts as Rapporteur.

The Assistant Rapporteurs shall be chosen from persons whose independence is beyond doubt and who possess the necessary legal qualifications; they shall be appointed by the Council. They shall take an oath before the Court to perform their duties impartially and conscientiously and to preserve the secrecy of the deliberations of the Court.

Art. 13   The Judges, the Advocates General and the Registrar shall be required to reside at the place where the Court has its seat.

Art. 14   The Court shall remain permanently in session. The duration of the judicial vacations shall be determined by the Court with due regard to the needs of its business.

Art. 15* Decisions of the Court shall be valid only when an uneven number of its members is sitting in the deliberations. Decisions of the full Court shall be valid if nine members are sitting. Decisions of the Chambers consisting of three or five Judges shall be valid only if three Judges are sitting. Decisions of the Chambers consisting of seven Judges shall be valid only if five Judges are sitting. In the event of one of the Judges of a Chamber being prevented from attending, a Judge of another Chamber may be called upon to sit in accordance with conditions laid down in the Rules of Procedure.

Art. 16   No Judge or Advocate General may take part in the disposal of any case in which he has previously taken part as agent or adviser or has acted for one of the parties, or in which he has been called upon to pronounce as a member of a court or tribunal, of a commission of inquiry or in any other capacity.

If, for some special reason, any Judge or Advocate General considers that he should not take part in the judgment or examination of a particular case, he shall so inform the President. If, for some special reason, the President considers that any Judge or Advocate General should not sit or make submissions in a particular case, he shall notify him accordingly.

Any difficulty arising as to the application of this Article shall be settled by decision of the Court.

A party may not apply for a change in the composition of the Court or of one of its Chambers on the grounds of either the nationality of a Judge or the absence from the Court or from the Chamber of a Judge of the nationality of that party.

---

*   Text as amended by Article 19 AA A/FIN/SWE.

TITLE III — PROCEDURE

Art. 17   The States and the institutions of the Community shall be represented
before the Court by an agent appointed for each case; the agent may be assisted by an adviser or by a lawyer entitled to practise before a court of a
Member State.

Other parties must be represented by a lawyer entitled to practise before a
court of a Member State.

Such agents, advisers and lawyers shall, when they appear before the
Court, enjoy the rights and immunities necessary to the independent exercise of their duties, under conditions laid down in the Rules of Procedure.

As regards such advisers and lawyers who appear before it, the Court shall
have the powers normally accorded to courts of law, under conditions laid
down in the Rules of Procedure.

University teachers being nationals of a Member State whose law accords
them a right of audience shall have the same rights before the Court as are
accorded by this Article to lawyers entitled to practise before a court of a
Member State.

Art. 18   The procedure before the Court shall consist of two parts: written and
oral.

The written procedure shall consist of the communication to the parties
and to the institutions of the Community whose decisions are in dispute,
of applications, statements of case, defences and observations, and of replies, if any, as well as of all papers and documents in support or of certified copies of them.

Communications shall be made by the Registrar in the order and within
the time laid down in the Rules of Procedure.

The oral procedure shall consist of the reading of the report presented by
a Judge acting as Rapporteur, the hearing by the Court of agents, advisers
and lawyers entitled to practise before a court of a Member State and of
the submissions of the Advocate General, as well as the hearing, if any, of
witnesses and experts.

Art. 19   A case shall be brought before the Court by a written application addressed to the Registrar. The application shall contain the applicant's
name and permanent address and the description of the signatory, the
name of the party against whom the application is made, the subject matter of the dispute, the submissions and a brief statement of the grounds on
which the application is based.

The application shall be accompanied, where appropriate, by the measure
the annulment of which is sought or, in the circumstances referred to in
Article 232 [ex-Article 175] of this Treaty, by documentary evidence of
the date on which an institution was, in accordance with that Article, requested to act. If the documents are not submitted with the application,
the Registrar shall ask the party concerned to produce them within a reasonable period, but in that event the rights of the party shall not lapse

even if such documents are produced after the time limit for bringing proceedings.

Art. 20 In the cases governed by Article 234 [ex-Article 177] of this Treaty, the decision of the court or tribunal of a Member State which suspends its proceedings and refers a case to the Court shall be notified to the Court by the court or tribunal concerned. The decision shall then be notified by the Registrar of the Court to the parties, to the Member States and to the Commission, and also to the Council if the act the validity or interpretation of which is in dispute originates from the Council.

Within two months of this notification, the parties, the Member State, the Commission and, where appropriate, the Council, shall be entitled to submit statements of case or written observations to the Court.

Art. 21 The Court may require the parties to produce all documents and to supply all information which the Court considers desirable. Formal note shall be taken of any refusal.

The Court may also require the Member States and institutions not being parties to the case to supply all information which the Court considers necessary for the proceedings.

Art. 22 The Court may at any time entrust any individual, body, authority, committee or other organization it chooses with the task of giving an expert opinion.

Art. 23 Witnesses may be heard under conditions laid down in the Rules of Procedure.

Art. 24 With respect to defaulting witnesses the Court shall have the powers generally granted to courts and tribunals and may impose pecuniary penalties under conditions laid down in the Rules of Procedure.

Art. 25 Witnesses and experts may be heard on oath taken in the form laid down in the Rules of Procedure or in the manner laid down by the law of the country of the witness or expert.

Art. 26 The Court may order that a witness or expert be heard by the judicial authority of his place of permanent residence.

The order shall be sent for implementation to the competent judicial authority under conditions laid down in the Rules of Procedure. The documents drawn up in compliance with the letters rogatory shall be returned to the Court under the same conditions.

The Court shall defray the expenses, without prejudice to the right to charge them, where appropriate, to the parties.

Art. 27 A Member State shall treat any violation of an oath by a witness or expert in the same manner as if the offence had been committed before one of its courts with jurisdiction in civil proceedings. At the instance of the Court, the Member State concerned shall prosecute the offender before its competent court.

Art. 28   The hearing in court shall be public, unless the Court, of its own motion or on application by the parties, decides otherwise for serious reasons.

Art. 29   During the hearings the Court may examine the experts, the witnesses and the parties themselves. The latter, however, may address the Court only through their representatives.

Art. 30   Minutes shall be made of each hearing and signed by the President and the Registrar.

Art. 31   The case list shall be established by the President.

Art. 32   The deliberations of the Court shall be and shall remain secret.

Art. 33   Judgments shall state the reasons on which they are based. They shall contain the names of the Judges who took part in the deliberations.

Art. 34   Judgments shall be signed by the President and the Registrar. They shall be read in open court.

Art. 35   The Court shall adjudicate upon costs.

Art. 36   The President of the Court may, by way of summary procedure, which may, in so far as necessary, differ from some of the rules contained in this Statute and which shall be laid down in the Rules of Procedure, adjudicate upon applications to suspend execution, as provided for in Article 242 [ex-article 185] of this Treaty, or to prescribe interim measures in pursuance of Article 243 [ex-Article 186], or to suspend enforcement in accordance with the last paragraph of Article 256 [ex-Article 192].

Should the President be prevented from attending, his place shall be taken by another Judge under conditions laid down in the Rules of Procedure.

The ruling of the President or of the Judge replacing him shall be provisional and shall in no way prejudice the decision of the Court on the substance of the case.

Art. 37   Member States and institutions of the Community may intervene in cases before the Court.

The same right shall be open to any other person establishing an interest in the result of any case submitted to the Court, save in cases between Member States, between institutions of the Community or between Member States and institutions of the Community.

Submissions made in an application to intervene shall be limited to supporting the submissions of one of the parties.

Art. 38   Where the defending party, after having been duly summoned, fails to file written submissions in defence, judgment shall be given against that party by default. An objection may be lodged against the judgment within one month of it being notified. The objection shall not have the effect of staying enforcement of the judgment by default unless the Court decides otherwise.

Art. 39   Member States, institutions of the Community and any other natural or legal persons may, in cases and under conditions to be determined by the Rules of Procedure, institute third party proceedings to contest a judgment rendered without their being heard, where the judgment is prejudicial to their rights.

Art. 40   If the meaning or scope of a judgment is in doubt, the Court shall construe it on application by any party or any institution of the Community establishing an interest therein.

Art. 41   An application for revision of a judgment may be made to the Court only on discovery of a fact which is of such a nature as to be a decisive factor, and which, when the judgment was given, was unknown to the Court and to the party claiming the revision.

The revision shall be opened by a judgment of the Court expressly recording the existence of a new fact, recognizing that it is of such a character as to lay the case open to revision and declaring the application admissible on this ground.

No application for revision may be made after the lapse of 10 years from the date of the judgment.

Art. 42   Periods of grace based on considerations of distance shall be determined by the Rules of Procedure.

No right shall be prejudiced in consequence of the expiry of a time limit if the party concerned proves the existence of unforeseeable circumstances or of force majeure.

Art. 43   Proceedings against the Community in matters arising from non contractual liability shall be barred after a period of five years from the occurrence of the event giving rise thereto. The period of limitation shall be interrupted if proceedings are instituted before the Court or if prior to such proceedings an application is made by the aggrieved party to the relevant institution of the Community. In the latter event the proceedings must be instituted within the period of two months provided for in Article 230 [ex-Article 173]; the provisions of the second paragraph of Article 232 [ex-Article 175] shall apply where appropriate.

TITLE IV* — THE COURT OF FIRST INSTANCE OF THE EUROPEAN COMMUNITIES

Art. 44   Articles 2 to 8 and 13 to 16 of this Statute shall apply to the Court of First Instance and its members. The oath referred to in Article 2 shall be taken before the Court of Justice and the decisions referred to in Articles 3, 4 and 6 shall be adopted by that Court after hearing the Court of First Instance.

---

* Inserted by Article 7 of the Council Decision of 24 October 1988 establishing a Court of First Instance of the European Communities (OJ L 319, 25. 11. 1988, p. 1).

Art. 45   The Court of First Instance shall appoint its Registrar and lay down the rules governing his service. Articles 9, 10 and 13 of this Statute shall apply to the Registrar of the Court of First Instance mutatis mutandis.

The President of the Court of Justice and the President of the Court of First Instance shall determine, by common accord, the conditions under which officials and other servants attached to the Court of Justice shall render their services to the Court of First Instance to enable it to function. Certain officials or other servants shall be responsible to the Registrar of the Court of First Instance under the authority of the President of the Court of First Instance.

Art. 46   The procedure before the Court of First Instance shall be governed by Title III of this Statute, with the exception of Article 20.

Such further and more detailed provisions as may be necessary shall be laid down in the Rules of Procedure established in accordance with Article 225 (4) [ex-Article 168a(4)] of this Treaty.

Notwithstanding the fourth paragraph of Article 18 of this Statute, the Advocate General may make his reasoned submissions in writing.

Art. 47   Where an application or other procedural document addressed to the Court of First Instance is lodged by mistake with the Registrar of the Court of Justice, it shall be transmitted immediately by that Registrar to the Registrar of the Court of First Instance; likewise, where an application or other procedural document addressed to the Court of Justice is lodged by mistake with the Registrar of the Court of First Instance, it shall be transmitted immediately by that Registrar to the Registrar of the Court of Justice.

Where the Court of First Instance finds that it does not have jurisdiction to hear and determine an action in respect of which the Court of Justice has jurisdiction, it shall refer that action to the Court of Justice; likewise, where the Court of Justice finds that an action falls within the jurisdiction of the Court of First Instance, it shall refer that action to the Court of First Instance, whereupon that Court may not decline jurisdiction.

Where the Court of Justice and the Court of First Instance are seised of cases in which the same relief is sought, the same issue of interpretation is raised or the validity of the same act is called in question, the Court of First Instance may, after hearing the parties, stay the proceedings before it until such time as the Court of Justice shall have delivered judgment. Where applications are made for the same act to be declared void, the Court of First Instance may also decline jurisdiction in order that the Court of Justice may rule on such applications. In the cases referred to in this subparagraph, the Court of Justice may also decide to stay the proceedings before it; in that event, the proceedings before the Court of First Instance shall continue.

Art. 48   Final decisions of the Court of First Instance, decisions disposing of the substantive issues in part only or disposing of a procedural issue concerning a plea of lack of competence or inadmissibility, shall be notified by the Registrar of the Court of First Instance to all parties as well as all Member States and the Community institutions even if they did not intervene in the case before the Court of First Instance.

Art. 49   An appeal may be brought before the Court of Justice, within two months of the notification of the decision appealed against, against final decisions of the Court of First Instance and decisions of that Court disposing of the substantive issues in part only or disposing of a procedural issue concerning a plea of lack of competence or inadmissibility.

Such an appeal may be brought by any party which has been unsuccessful, in whole or in part, in its submissions. However, interveners other than the Member States and the Community institutions may bring such an appeal only where the decision of the Court of First Instance directly affects them.

With the exception of cases relating to disputes between the Community and its servants, an appeal may also be brought by Member States and Community institutions which did not intervene in the proceedings before the Court of First Instance. Such Member States and institutions shall be in the same position as Member States or institutions which intervened at first instance.

Art. 50   Any person whose application to intervene has been dismissed by the Court of First Instance may appeal to the Court of Justice within two weeks of the notification of the decision dismissing the application.

The parties to the proceedings may appeal to the Court of Justice against any decision of the Court of First Instance made pursuant to Articles 242 [ex-Article 185] or 243 [ex-Article 186] or the fourth paragraph of Article 256 [ex-Article 192] of this Treaty within two months from their notification.

The appeal referred to in the first two paragraphs of this Article shall be heard and determined under the procedure referred to in Article 36 of this Statute.

Art. 51   An appeal to the Court of Justice shall be limited to points of law. It shall lie on the grounds of lack of competence of the Court of First Instance, a breach of procedure before it which adversely affects the interests of the appellant as well as the infringement of Community law by the Court of First Instance.

No appeal shall lie regarding only the amount of the costs or the party ordered to pay them.

Art. 52   Where an appeal is brought against a decision of the Court of First Instance, the procedure before the Court of Justice shall consist of a written part and an oral part. In accordance with conditions laid down in the Rules of Procedure the Court of Justice, having heard the Advocate General and the parties, may dispense with the oral procedure.

Art. 53   Without prejudice to Articles 242 [ex-Article 185] and 243 [ex-Article 186] of this Treaty, an appeal shall not have suspensory effect.

By way of derogation from Article 244 [ex-Article 187] of this Treaty, decisions of the Court of First Instance declaring a regulation to be void shall take effect only as from the date of expiry of the period referred to in the first paragraph of Article 49 of this Statute or, if an appeal shall have been brought within that period, as from the date of dismissal of the appeal, without prejudice, however, to the right of a party to apply to the Court of Justice, pursuant to Articles 242 [ex-Article 185] and 243 [ex-Article 186] of this Treaty, for the suspension of the effects of the regulation which has been declared void or for the prescription of any other interim measure.

Art. 54 If the appeal is well founded, the Court of Justice shall quash the decision of the Court of First Instance. It may itself give final judgment in the matter, where the state of the proceedings so permits, or refer the case back to the Court of First Instance for judgment.

Where a case is referred back to the Court of First Instance, that Court shall be bound by the decision of the Court of Justice on points of law.

When an appeal brought by a Member State or a Community institution, which did not intervene in the proceedings before the Court of First Instance, is well founded the Court of Justice may, if it considers this necessary, state which of the effects of the decision of the Court of First Instance which has been quashed shall be considered as definitive in respect of the parties to the litigation.

Art. 55 The Rules of Procedure of the Court provided for in Article 188 of this Treaty shall contain, apart from the provisions contemplated by this Statute, any other provisions necessary for applying and, where required, supplementing it.

Art. 56 The Council may, acting unanimously, make such further adjustments to the provisions of this Statute as may be required by reason of measures taken by the Council in accordance with the last paragraph of Article 221 [ex-Article 165] of this Treaty.

gg) Rules of Procedure of the Court of Justice of the European Communities of June 19, 1991 as amended[1]

INTERPRETATION

Art. 1 In these Rules:

'EC Treaty' means the Treaty establishing the European Community;

'EC Statute' means the Protocol on the Statute of the Court of Justice of the European Community;

---

[1] C 65/1 EN Official Journal of the European Communities 6.3.1999.

'ECSC Treaty' means the Treaty establishing the European Coal and Steel Community;

'ECSC Statute' means the Protocol on the Statute of the Court of Justice of the European Coal and Steel Community;

'EAEC Treaty' means the Treaty establishing the European Atomic Energy Community;

'EAEC Statute' means the Protocol on the Statute of the Court of Justice of the European Atomic Energy Community;

'EEA Agreement' means the Agreement on the European Economic Area.

For the purposes of these Rules:

— 'institutions' means the institutions of the Communities and bodies which are established by the Treaties, or by an act adopted in implementation thereof, and which may be parties before the Court,

— 'EFTA Surveillance Authority' means the surveillance authority referred to in the EEA Agreement.

TITLE I — ORGANISATION OF THE COURT

CHAPTER 1 — JUDGES AND ADVOCATES-GENERAL

Art. 2 The term of office of a Judge shall begin on the date laid down in his instrument of appointment. In the absence of any provisions regarding the date, the term shall begin on the date of the instrument.

Art. 3 1. Before taking up his duties, a Judge shall at the first public sitting of the Court which he attends after his appointment take the following oath:

'I swear that I will perform my duties impartially and conscientiously; I swear that I will preserve the secrecy of the deliberations of the Court'.

2. Immediately after taking the oath, a Judge shall sign a declaration by which he solemnly undertakes that, both during and after his term of office, he will respect the obligations arising therefrom, and in particular the duty to behave with integrity and discretion as regards the acceptance, after he has ceased to hold office, of certain appointments and benefits.

Art. 4 When the Court is called upon to decide whether a Judge no longer fulfils the requisite conditions or no longer meets the obligations arising from his office, the President shall invite the Judge concerned to make representations to the Court, in closed session and in the absence of the Registrar.

Art. 5 Articles 2, 3 and 4 of these Rules shall apply in a corresponding manner to Advocates-General.

Art. 6 Judges and Advocates-General shall rank equally in precedence according to their seniority in office.

Where there is equal seniority in office, precedence shall be determined by age.

Retiring Judges and Advocates-General who are reappointed shall retain their former precedence.

CHAPTER 2 — PRESIDENCY OF THE COURT AND CONSTITUTION OF THE CHAMBERS

Art. 7 1. The Judges shall, immediately after the partial replacement provided for in Article 167 of the EC Treaty, Article 32b of the ECSC Treaty and Article 139 of the EAEC Treaty, elect one of their number as President of the Court for a term of three years.

2. If the office of the President of the Court falls vacant before the normal date of expiry thereof, the Court shall elect a successor for the remainder of the term.

3. The elections provided for in this Article shall be by secret ballot. If a Judge obtains an absolute majority he shall be elected. If no Judge obtains an absolute majority, a second ballot shall be held and the Judge obtaining the most votes shall be elected. Where two or more Judges obtain an equal number of votes the oldest of them shall be deemed elected.

Art. 8 The President shall direct the judicial business and the administration of the Court; he shall preside at hearings and deliberations.

Art. 9 1. The Court shall set up Chambers in accordance with the provisions of the second paragraph of Article 165 of the EC Treaty, the second paragraph of Article 32 of the ECSC Treaty and the second paragraph of Article 137 of the EAEC Treaty and shall decide which Judges shall be attached to them.

The composition of the Chambers shall be published in the *Official Journal of the European Communities.*

2. As soon as an application initiating proceedings has been lodged, the President shall assign the case to one of the Chambers for any preparatory inquiries and shall designate a Judge from that Chamber to act as Rapporteur.

3. The Court shall lay down criteria by which, as a rule, cases are to be assigned to Chambers.

4. These Rules shall apply to proceedings before the Chambers.

In cases assigned to a Chamber the powers of the President of the Court shall be exercised by the President of the Chamber.

Art. 10 1. The Court shall appoint for a period of one year the Presidents of the Chambers and the First Advocate-General.

The provisions of Article 7(2) and (3) shall apply.

Appointments made in pursuance of this paragraph shall be published in the *Official Journal of the European Communities.*

2. The First Advocate-General shall assign each case to an Advocate-General as soon as the Judge-Rapporteur has been designated by the

President. He shall take the necessary steps if an Advocate-General is absent or prevented from acting.

Art. 11   When the President of the Court is absent or prevented from attending or when the office of President is vacant, the functions of President shall be exercised by a President of a Chamber according to the order of precedence laid down in Article 6 of these Rules.

If the President of the Court and the President of the Chambers are all prevented from attending at the same time, or their posts are vacant at the same time, the functions of President shall be exercised by one of the other Judges according to the order of precedence laid down in Article 6 of these Rules.

CHAPTER 3 — REGISTRY

Section 1 — The Registrar and Assistant Registrars

Art. 12   1. The Court shall appoint the Registrar. Two weeks before the date fixed for making the appointment, the President shall inform the Members of the Court of the applications which have been made for the post.

2. An application shall be accompanied by full details of the candidate's age, nationality, university degrees, knowledge of any languages, present and past occupations and experience, if any, in judicial and international fields.

3. The appointment shall be made following the procedure laid down in Article 7(3) of these Rules.

4. The Registrar shall be appointed for a term of six years. He may be reappointed.

5. The Registrar shall take the oath in accordance with Article 3 of these Rules.

6. The Registrar may be deprived of his office only if he no longer fulfils the requisite conditions or no longer meets the obligations arising from his office; the Court shall take its decision after giving the Registrar an opportunity to make representations.

7. If the office of Registrar falls vacant before the normal date of expiry of the term thereof, the Court shall appoint a new Registrar for a term of six years.

Art. 13   The Court may, following the procedure laid down in respect of the Registrar, appoint one or more Assistant Registrars to assist the Registrar and to take his place in so far as the Instructions to the Registrar referred to in Article 15 of these Rules allow.

Art. 14   Where the Registrar and the Assistant Registrars are absent or prevented from attending or their posts are vacant, the President shall designate an official to carry out temporarily the duties of Registrar.

Art. 15   Instructions to the Registrar shall be adopted by the Court acting on a proposal from the President.

Art. 16   1. There shall be kept in the Registry, under the control of the Registrar, a register initialled by the President, in which all pleadings and supporting documents shall be entered in the order in which they are lodged.

2. When a document has been registered, the Registrar shall make a note to that effect on the original and, if a party so requests, on any copy submitted for the purpose.

3. Entries in the register and the notes provided for in the preceding paragraph shall be authentic.

4. Rules for keeping the register shall be prescribed by the Instructions to the Registrar referred to in Article 15 of these Rules.

5. Persons having an interest may consult the register at the Registry and may obtain copies or extracts on payment of a charge on a scale fixed by the Court on a proposal from the Registrar.

The parties to a case may on payment of the appropriate charge also obtain copies of pleadings and authenticated copies of judgments and orders.

6. Notice shall be given in the *Official Journal of the European Communities* of the date of registration of an application initiating proceedings, the names and addresses of the parties, the subject-matter of the proceedings, the form of order sought by the applicant and a summary of the pleas in law and of the main supporting arguments.

7. Where the Council or the Commission is not a party to a case, the Court shall send to it copies of the application and of the defence, without the annexes thereto, to enable it to assess whether the inapplicability of one of its acts is being invoked under Article 184 of the EC Treaty, the third paragraph of Article 36 of the ECSC Treaty or Article 156 of the EAEC Treaty.

Art. 17   1. The Registrar shall be responsible, under the authority of the President, for the acceptance, transmission and custody of documents and for effecting service as provided for by these Rules.

2. The Registrar shall assist the Court, the Chambers, the President and the Judges in all their official functions.

Art. 18   The Registrar shall have custody of the seals. He shall be responsible for the records and be in charge of the publications of the Court.

Art. 19   Subject to Articles 4 and 27 of these Rules, the Registrar shall attend the sittings of the Court and of the Chambers.

Section 2 — Other departments

Art. 20   1. The official and other servants of the Court shall be appointed in accordance with the provisions of the Staff Regulations.

2. Before taking up his duties, an official shall take the following oath before the President, in the presence of the Registrar:

'I swear that I will perform loyally, discreetly and conscientiously the duties assigned to me by the Court of Justice of the European Communities'.

Art. 21 The organisation of the departments of the Court shall be laid down, and may be modified, by the Court on a proposal from the Registrar.

Art. 22 The Court shall set up a translating service staffed by experts with adequate legal training and a thorough knowledge of several official languages of the Court.

Art. 23 The Registrar shall be responsible, under the authority of the President, for the administration of the Court, its financial management and its accounts; he shall be assisted in this by an administrator.

CHAPTER 4 — ASSISTANT RAPPORTEURS

Art. 24 1. Where the Court is of the opinion that the consideration of and preparatory inquiries in cases before it so require, it shall, pursuant to Article 12 of the EC Statute, Article 16 of the ECSC Statute and Article 12 of the EAEC Statute, propose the appointment of Assistant Rapporteurs.

2. Assistant Rapporteurs shall in particular:

— assist the President in connection with applications for the adoption of interim measures

— assist the Judge-Rapporteurs in their work.

3. In the performance of their duties the Assistant Rapporteurs shall be responsible to the President of the Court, the President of a Chamber or a Judge-Rapporteur, as the case may be.

4. Before taking up his duties, an Assistant Rapporteur shall take before the Court the oath set out in Article 3 of these Rules.

CHAPTER 5 — THE WORKING OF THE COURT

Art. 25 1. The dates and times of the sittings of the Court shall be fixed by the President.

2. The dates and times of the sittings of the Chambers shall be fixed by their respective Presidents.

3. The Court and the Chambers may choose to hold one or more sittings in a place other than that in which the Court has its seat.

Art. 26 1. Where, by reason of a Judge being absent or prevented from attending, there is an even number of Judges, the most junior Judge within the meaning of Article 6 of these Rules shall abstain from taking part in the deliberations unless he is the Judge-Rapporteur. In that case the Judge immediately senior to him shall abstain from taking part in the deliberations.

2. If after the Court has been convened it is found that the quorum of seven Judges referred to in Article 15 of the EC Statute, Article 18 of the ECSC Statute and Article 15 of the EAEC Statute has not been attained, the President shall adjourn the sitting until there is a quorum.

3. If in any Chamber the quorum of three Judges referred to in Article 15 of the EC Statute, Article 18 of the ECSC Statute and Article 15 of the EAEC Statute has not been attained, the President of that Chamber shall so inform the President of the Court who shall designate another Judge to complete the Chamber.

Art. 27   1. The Court and Chambers shall deliberate in closed session.

2. Only those Judges who were present at the oral proceedings and the Assistant Rapporteur, if any, entrusted with the consideration of the case may take part in the deliberations.

3. Every Judge taking part in the deliberations shall state his opinion and the reasons for it.

4. Any Judge may require that any questions be formulated in the language of his choice and communicated in writing to the Court or Chamber before being put to the vote.

5. The conclusions reached by the majority of the Judges after final discussion shall determine the decision of the Court. Votes shall be cast in reverse order to the order of precedence laid down in Article 6 of these Rules.

6. Differences of view on the substance, wording or order of questions, or on the interpretation of the voting shall be settled by decision of the Court or Chamber.

7. Where the deliberations of the Court concern questions of its own administration, the Advocates-General shall take part and have a vote. The Registrar shall be present, unless the Court decides to the contrary.

8. Where the Court sits without the Registrar being present it shall, if necessary, instruct the most junior Judge within the meaning of Article 6 of these Rules to draw up minutes. The minutes shall be signed by that Judge and by the President.

Art. 28   1. Subject to any special decision of the Court, its vacations shall be as follows:

— from 18 December to 10 January,
— from the Sunday before Easter to the second Sunday after Easter,
— from 15 July to 15 September.

During the vacations, the functions of President shall be exercised at the place where the Court has its seat either by the President himself, keeping in touch with the Registrar, or by a President of Chamber or other Judge invited by the President to take his place.

2. In a case of urgency, the President may convene the Judges and the Advocates-General during the vacations.

3. The Court shall observe the official holidays of the place where it has its seat.

4. The Court may, in proper circumstances, grant leave of absence to any Judge or Advocate-General.

CHAPTER 6 — LANGUAGES

Art. 29 1. The language of a case shall be Danish, Dutch, English, Finnish, French, German, Greek, Irish, Italian, Portuguese, Spanish or Swedish.

2. The language of a case shall be chosen by the applicant, except that:

(a) where the defendant is a Member State or a natural or legal person having the nationality of a Member State, the language of the case shall be the official language of that State; where that State has more than one official language, the applicant may choose between them;

(b) at the joint request of the parties the use of another of the languages mentioned in paragraph 1 for all or part of the proceedings may be authorised;

(c) at the request of one of the parties, and after the opposite party and the Advocate-General have been heard, the use of another of the languages mentioned in paragraph 1 as the language of the case for all or part of the proceedings may be authorised by way of derogation from subparagraphs (a) and (b); such a request may not be submitted by an institution of the European Communities.

In cases to which Article 103 of these Rules applies, the language of the case shall be the language of the national court or tribunal which refers the matter to the Court. At the duly substantiated request of one of the parties to the main proceedings, and after the opposite party and the Advocate-General have been heard, the use of another of the languages mentioned in paragraph 1 may be authorised for the oral procedure.

Requests as above may be decided on by the President; the latter may and, where he wishes to accede to a request without the agreement of all the parties, must refer the request to the Court.

3. The language of the case shall in particular be used in the written and oral pleadings of the parties and in supporting documents, and also in the minutes and decisions of the Court.

Any supporting documents expressed in another language must be accompanied by a translation into the language of the case.

In the case of lengthy documents, translations may be confined to extracts. However, the Court or Chamber may, of its own motion or at the request of a party, at any time call for a complete or fuller translation.

Notwithstanding the foregoing provisions, a Member State shall be entitled to use its official language when intervening in a case before the Court or when taking part in any reference of a kind mentioned in Article 103. This provision shall apply both to written statements and to oral addresses. The Registrar shall cause any such statement or address to be translated into the language of the case.

The States, other than the Member States, which are parties to the EEA Agreement, and also the EFTA Surveillance Authority, may be authorised to use one of the languages mentioned in paragraph 1, other than the language of the case, when they intervene in a case before the Court or participate in preliminary ruling proceedings envisaged by Article 20 of the EC Statute. This provision shall apply both to written statements and oral addresses. The Registrar shall cause any such statement or address to be translated into the language of the case.

4. Where a witness or expert states that he is unable adequately to express himself in one of the languages referred to in paragraph (1) of this Article, the Court or Chamber may authorise him to give his evidence in another language. The Registrar shall arrange for translation into the language of the case.

5. The President of the Court and the Presidents of Chambers in conducting oral proceedings, the Judge-Rapporteur both in his preliminary report and in his report for the hearing, Judges and Advocates-General in putting questions and Advocates-General in delivering their opinions may use one of the languages referred to in paragraph 1 of this Article other than the language of the case. The Registrar shall arrange for translation into the language of the case.

Art. 30   1. The Registrar shall, at the request of any Judge, of the Advocate-General or of a party, arrange for anything said or written in the course of the proceedings before the Court or a Chamber to be translated into the languages he chooses from those referred to in Article 29(1).

2. Publications of the Court shall be issued in the languages referred to in Article 1 of Council Regulation No 1.

Art. 31   The texts of documents drawn up in the language of the case or in any other language authorised by the Court pursuant to Article 29 of these Rules shall be authentic.

CHAPTER 7 — RIGHTS AND OBLIGATIONS OF AGENTS, ADVISERS AND LAWYERS

Art. 32   1. Agents, advisers and lawyers appearing before the Court or before any judicial authority to which the Court has addressed letters rogatory, shall enjoy immunity in respect of words spoken or written by them concerning the case or the parties.

2. Agents, advisers and lawyers shall enjoy the following further privileges and facilities:

   (a) papers and documents relating to the proceedings shall be exempt from both search and seizure; in the event of a dispute the customs officials or police may seal those papers and documents; they shall then be immediately forwarded to the Court for inspection in the presence of the Registrar and of the person concerned;

(b) agents, advisers and lawyers shall be entitled to such allocation of foreign currency as may be necessary for the performance of their duties;

(c) agents, advisers and lawyers shall be entitled to travel in the course of duty without hindrance.

Art. 33   In order to qualify for the privileges, immunities and facilities specified in Article 32, persons entitled to them shall furnish proof of their status as follows:

(a) agents shall produce an official document issued by the party for whom they act, and shall forward without delay a copy thereof to the Registrar;

(b) advisers and lawyers shall produce a certificate signed by the Registrar. The validity of this certificate shall be limited to a specified period, which may be extended or curtailed according to the length of the proceedings.

Art. 34   The privileges, immunities and facilities specified in Article 32 of these Rules are granted exclusively in the interests of the proper conduct of proceedings.

The Court may waive the immunity where it considers that the proper conduct of proceedings will not be hindered thereby.

Art. 35   1. Any adviser or lawyer whose conduct towards the Court, a Chamber, a Judge, an Advocate-General or the Registrar is incompatible with the dignity of the Court, or who uses his rights for purposes other than those for which they were granted, may at any time be excluded from the proceedings by an order of the Court or Chamber, after the Advocate-General has been heard; the person concerned shall be given an opportunity to defend himself.

The order shall have immediate effect.

2. Where an adviser or lawyer is excluded from the proceedings, the proceedings shall be suspended for a period fixed by the President in order to allow the party concerned to appoint another adviser or lawyer.

3. Decisions taken under this Article may be rescinded.

Art. 36   The provisions of this Chapter shall apply to university teachers who have a right of audience before the Court in accordance with Article 17 of the EC Statute, Article 20 of the ECSC Statute and Article 17 of the EAEC Statute.

TITLE II — PROCEDURE

CHAPTER 1 — WRITTEN PROCEDURE

Art. 37   1. The original of every pleading must be signed by the party's agent or lawyer.

The original, accompanied by all annexes referred to therein, shall be lodged together with five copies for the Court and a copy for every other party to the proceedings. Copies shall be certified by the party lodging them.

2. Institutions shall in addition produce, within time-limits laid down by the Court, translations of all pleadings into the other languages provided for by Article 1 of Council Regulation No 1. The second subparagraph of paragraph 1 of this Article shall apply.

3. All pleadings shall bear a date. In the reckoning of time-limits for taking steps in proceedings, only the date of lodgment at the Registry shall be taken into account.

4. To every pleading there shall be annexed a file containing the documents relied on in support of it, together with a schedule listing them.

5. Where in view of the length of a document only extracts from it are annexed to the pleading, the whole document or a full copy of it shall be lodged at the Registry.

Art. 38   1. An application of the kind referred to in Article 19 of the EC Statute, Article 22 of the ECSC Statute and Article 19 of the EAEC Statute shall state:

(a)   the name and address of the applicant;

(b)   the designation of the party against whom the application is made;

(c)   the subject-matter of the proceedings and a summary of the pleas in law on which the application is based;

(d)   the form of order sought by the applicant;

(e)   where appropriate, the nature of any evidence offered in support.

2. For the purpose of the proceedings, the application shall state an address for service in the place where the Court has its seat and the name of the person who is authorised and has expressed willingness to accept service.

If the application does not comply with these requirements, all service on the party concerned for the purpose of the proceedings shall be effected, for so long as the defect has not been cured, by registered letter addressed to the agent or lawyer of that party. By way of derogation from Article 79, service shall then be deemed to be duly effected by the lodging of the registered letter at the post office of the place where the Court has its seat.

3. The lawyer acting for a party must lodge at the Registry a certificate that he is authorised to practise before a court of a Member State or of another State which is a party to the EEA Agreement.

4. The application shall be accompanied, where appropriate, by the documents specified in the second paragraph of Article 19 of the EC Statute, the second paragraph of Article 22 of the ECSC Statute and the second paragraph of Article 19 of the EAEC Statute.

5. An application made by a legal person governed by private law shall be accompanied by:

(a) the instrument or instruments constituting or regulating that legal person or a recent extract from the register of companies, firms or associations or any other proof of its existence in law;

(b) proof that the authority granted to the applicant's lawyer has been properly conferred on him by someone authorised for the purpose.

6. An application submitted under Articles 181 and 182 of the EC Treaty, Articles 42 and 89 of the ECSC Treaty and Articles 153 and 154 of the EAEC Treaty shall be accompanied by a copy of the arbitration clause contained in the contract governed by private or public law entered into by the Communities or on their behalf, or, as the case may be, by a copy of the special agreement concluded between the Member States concerned.

7. If an application does not comply with the requirements set out in paragraphs 3 to 6 of this Article, the Registrar shall prescribe a reasonable period within which the applicant is to comply with them whether by putting the application itself in order or by producing any of the abovementioned documents. If the applicant fails to put the application in order or to produce the required documents within the time prescribed, the Court shall, after hearing the Advocate-General, decide whether the noncompliance with these conditions renders the application formally inadmissible.

Art. 39   The application shall be served on the defendant. In a case where Article 38(7) applies, service shall be effected as soon as the application has been put in order or the Court has declared it admissible notwithstanding the failure to observe the formal requirements set out in that Article.

Art. 40   1. Within one month after service on him of the application, the defendant shall lodge a defence, stating:

(a) the name and address of the defendant;

(b) the arguments of fact and law relied on;

(c) the form of order sought by the defendant;

(d) the nature of any evidence offered by him.

The provisions of Article 38(2) to (5) of these Rules shall apply to the defence.

2. The time-limit laid down in paragraph 1 of this Article may be extended by the President on a reasoned application by the defendant.

Art. 41   1. The application initiating the proceedings and the defence may be supplemented by a reply from the applicant and by a rejoinder from the defendant.

2. The President shall fix the time-limits within which these pleadings are to be lodged.

Art. 42   1. In reply or rejoinder a party may offer further evidence. The party must, however, give reasons for the delay in offering it.

2. No new plea in law may be introduced in the course of proceedings unless it is based on matters of law or of fact which come to light in the course of the procedure.

If in the course of the procedure one of the parties puts forward a new plea in law which is so based, the President may, even after the expiry of the normal procedural time-limits, acting on a report of the Judge-Rapporteur and after hearing the Advocate-General, allow the other party time to answer on that plea.

The decision on the admissibility of the plea shall be reserved for the final judgment.

Art. 43   The Court may, at any time, after hearing the parties and the Advocate-General, if the assignment referred to in Article 10(2) has taken place, order that two or more cases concerning the same subject-matter shall, on account of the connection between them, be joined for the purposes of the written or oral procedure or of the final judgment. The cases may subsequently be disjoined. The President may refer these matters to the Court.

Art. 44   1. After the rejoinder provided for in Article 41(1) of these Rules has been lodged, the President shall fix a date on which the Judge-Rapporteur is to present his preliminary report to the Court. The report shall contain recommendations as to whether a preparatory inquiry or any other preparatory step should be undertaken and whether the case should be referred to the Chamber to which it has been assigned under Article 9(2).

The Court shall decide, after hearing the Advocate-General, what action to take upon the recommendations of the Judge-Rapporteur.

The same procedure shall apply:

(a) where no reply or no rejoinder has been lodged within the time-limit fixed in accordance with Article 41(2) of these Rules;

(b) where the party concerned waives his right to lodge a reply or rejoinder.

2. Where the Court orders a preparatory inquiry and does not undertake it itself, it shall assign the inquiry to the Chamber.

Where the Court decides to open the oral procedure without an inquiry, the President shall fix the opening date.

Art. 44a   Without prejudice to any special provisions laid down in these Rules, and except in the specific cases in which, after the pleadings referred to in Article 40(1) and, as the case may be, in Article 41(1) have been lodged, the Court, acting on a report from the Judge-Rapporteur, after hearing the Advocate-General and with the express consent of the parties, decides otherwise, the procedure before the Court shall also include an oral part.

CHAPTER 2 — PREPARATORY INQUIRIES

Section 1 — Measures of inquiry

Art. 45   1. The Court, after hearing the Advocate-General, shall prescribe the measures of inquiry that it considers appropriate by means of an order setting out the facts to be proved. Before the Court decides on the measures of inquiry referred to in paragraph 2(c), (d) and (e) the parties shall be heard. The order shall be served on the parties.

2. Without prejudice to Articles 21 and 22 of the EC Statute, Articles 24 and 25 of the ECSC Statute and Articles 22 and 23 of the EAEC Statute, the following measures of inquiry may be adopted:

(a)   the personal appearance of the parties;

(b)   a request for information and production of documents;

(c)   oral testimony;

(d)   the commissioning of an expert's report;

(e)   an inspection of the place or thing in question.

3. The measures of inquiry which the Court has ordered may be conducted by the Court itself, or be assigned to the Judge-Rapporteur.

The Advocate-General shall take part in the measures of inquiry.

4. Evidence may be submitted in rebuttal and previous evidence may be amplified.

Art. 46   1. A Chamber to which a preparatory inquiry has been assigned may exercise the powers vested in the Court by Articles 45 and 47 to 53 of these Rules; the powers vested in the President of the Court may be exercised by the President of the Chamber.

2. Articles 56 and 57 of these Rules shall apply to proceedings before the Chamber.

3. The parties shall be entitled to attend the measures of inquiry.

Section 2 — The summoning and examination of witnesses and experts

Art. 47   1. The Court may, either of its own motion or on application by a party, and after hearing the Advocate-General, order that certain facts be proved by witnesses. The order of the Court shall set out the facts to be established.

The Court may summon a witness of its own motion or on application by a party or at the instance of the Advocate-General.

An application by a party for the examination of a witness shall state precisely about what facts and for what reasons the witness should be examined.

2. The witness shall be summoned by an order of the Court containing the following information:

(a)   the surname, forenames, description and address of the witness;

(b) an indication of the facts about which the witness is to be examined;

(c) where appropriate, particulars of the arrangements made by the Court for reimbursement of expenses incurred by the witness, and of the penalties which may be imposed on defaulting witnesses.

The order shall be served on the parties and the witnesses.

3. The Court may make the summoning of a witness for whose examination a party has applied conditional upon the deposit with the cashier of the Court of a sum sufficient to cover the taxed costs thereof; the Court shall fix the amount of the payment.

The cashier shall advance the funds necessary in connection with the examination of any witness summoned by the Court of its own motion.

4. After the identity of the witness has been established, the President shall inform him that he will be required to vouch the truth of his evidence in the manner laid down in these Rules.

The witness shall give his evidence to the Court, the parties having been given notice to attend. After the witness has given his main evidence the President may, at the request of a party or of his own motion, put questions to him.

The other Judges and the Advocate-General may do likewise.

Subject to the control of the President, questions may be put to witnesses by the representatives of the parties.

5. After giving his evidence, the witness shall take the following oath:

'I swear that I have spoken the truth, the whole truth and nothing but the truth.'

The Court may, after hearing the parties, exempt a witness from taking the oath.

6. The Registrar shall draw up minutes in which the evidence of each witness is reproduced.

The minutes shall be signed by the President or by the Judge-Rapporteur responsible for conducting the examination of the witness, and by the Registrar. Before the minutes are thus signed, witnesses must be given an opportunity to check the content of the minutes and to sign them.

The minutes shall constitute an official record.

Art. 48   1. Witnesses who have been duly summoned shall obey the summons and attend for examination.

2. If a witness who has been duly summoned fails to appear before the Court, the Court may impose upon him a pecuniary penalty not exceeding ECU 5 000 and may order that a further summons be served on the witness at his own expense.

The same penalty may be imposed upon a witness who, without good reason, refuses to give evidence or to take the oath or where appropriate to make a solemn affirmation equivalent thereto.

3. If the witness proffers a valid excuse to the Court, the pecuniary penalty imposed on him may be cancelled. The pecuniary penalty imposed may be

reduced at the request of the witness where he establishes that it is disproportionate to his income.

4. Penalties imposed and other measures ordered under this Article shall be enforced in accordance with Articles 187 and 192 of the EC Treaty, Articles 44 and 92 of the ECSC Treaty and Articles 159 and 164 of the EAEC Treaty.

Art. 49　　1. The Court may order that an expert's report be obtained. The order appointing the expert shall define his task and set a time-limit within which he is to make his report.

2. The expert shall receive a copy of the order, together with all the documents necessary for carrying out his task. He shall be under the supervision of the Judge-Rapporteur, who may be present during his investigation and who shall be kept informed of his progress in carrying out his task.

The Court may request the parties or one of them to lodge security for the costs of the expert's report.

3. At the request of the expert, the Court may order the examination of witnesses. Their examination shall be carried out in accordance with Article 47 of these Rules.

4. The expert may give his opinion only on points which have been expressly referred to him.

5. After the expert has made his report, the Court may order that he be examined, the parties having been given notice to attend.

Subject to the control of the President, questions may be put to the expert by the representatives of the parties.

6. After making his report, the expert shall take the following oath before the Court:

'I swear that I have conscientiously and impartially carried out my task.'

The Court may, after hearing the parties, exempt the expert from taking the oath.

Art. 50　　1. If one of the parties objects to a witness or to an expert on the ground that he is not a competent or proper person to act as witness or expert or for any other reason, or if a witness or expert refuses to give evidence, to take the oath or to make a solemn affirmation equivalent thereto, the matter shall be resolved by the Court.

2. An objection to a witness or to an expert shall be raised within two weeks after service of the order summoning the witness or appointing the expert; the statement of objection must set out the grounds of objection and indicate the nature of any evidence offered.

Art. 51　　1. Witnesses and experts shall be entitled to reimbursement of their travel and subsistence expenses. The cashier of the Court may make a payment to them towards these expenses in advance.

2. Witnesses shall be entitled to compensation for loss of earnings, and experts to fees for their services. The cashier of the Court shall pay witnesses

and experts their compensation or fees after they have carried out their respective duties or tasks.

Art. 52   The Court may, on application by a party or of its own motion, issue letters rogatory for the examination of witnesses or experts, as provided for in the supplementary rules mentioned in Article 125 of these Rules.

Art. 53   1. The Registrar shall draw up minutes of every hearing. The minutes shall be signed by the President and by the Registrar and shall constitute an official record.

2. The parties may inspect the minutes and any expert's report at the Registry and obtain copies at their own expense.

Section 3 — Closure of the preparatory inquiry

Art. 54   Unless the Court prescribes a period within which the parties may lodge written observations, the President shall fix the date for the opening of the oral procedure after the preparatory inquiry has been completed.

Where a period had been prescribed for the lodging of written observations, the President shall fix the date for the opening of the oral procedure after that period has expired.

CHAPTER 3 — ORAL PROCEDURE

Art. 55   1. Subject to the priority of decisions provided for in Article 85 of these Rules, the Court shall deal with the cases before it in the order in which the preparatory inquiries in them have been completed. Where the preparatory inquiries in several cases are completed simultaneously, the order in which they are to be dealt with shall be determined by the dates of entry in the register of the applications initiating them respectively.

2. The President may in special circumstances order that a case be given priority over others.

The President may in special circumstances, after hearing the parties and the Advocate-General, either on his own initiative or at the request of one of the parties, defer a case to be dealt with at a later date. On a joint application by the parties the President may order that a case be deferred.

Art. 56   1. The proceedings shall be opened and directed by the President, who shall be responsible for the proper conduct of the hearing.

2. The oral proceedings in cases heard in camera shall not be published.

Art. 57   The President may in the course of the hearing put questions to the agents, advisers or lawyers of the parties.

The other Judges and the Advocate-General may do likewise.

Art. 58   A party may address the Court only through his agent, adviser or lawyer.

Art. 59   1. The Advocate-General shall deliver his opinion orally at the end of the oral procedure.

2. After the Advocate-General has delivered his opinion, the President shall declare the oral procedure closed.

Art. 60   The Court may at any time, in accordance with Article 45(1), after hearing the Advocate-General, order any measure of inquiry to be taken or that a previous inquiry be repeated or expanded. The Court may direct the Chamber or the Judge-Rapporteur to carry out the measures so ordered.

Art. 61   The Court may after hearing the Advocate-General order the reopening of the oral procedure.

Art. 62   1. The Registrar shall draw up minutes of every hearing. The minutes shall be signed by the President and by the Registrar and shall constitute an official record.

2. The parties may inspect the minutes at the Registry and obtain copies at their own expense.

CHAPTER 4 — JUDGMENTS

Art. 63   The judgment shall contain:
  — a statement that it is the judgment of the Court,
  — the date of its delivery,
  — the names of the President and of the Judges taking part in it,
  — the name of the Advocate-General,
  — the name of the Registrar,
  — the description of the parties,
  — the names of the agents, advisers and lawyers of the parties,
  — a statement of the forms of order sought by the parties,
  — a statement that the Advocate-General has been heard,
  — a summary of the facts,
  — the grounds for the decision,
  — the operative part of the judgment, including the decision as to costs.

Art. 64   1. The judgment shall be delivered in open court; the parties shall be given notice to attend to hear it.

2. The original of the judgment, signed by the President, by the Judges who took part in the deliberations and by the Registrar, shall be sealed and deposited at the Registry; the parties shall be served with certified copies of the judgment.

3. The Registrar shall record on the original of the judgment the date on which it was delivered.

Art. 65   The judgment shall be binding from the date of its delivery.

Art. 66   1. Without prejudice to the provisions relating to the interpretation of judgments the Court may, of its own motion or on application by a party made within two weeks after the delivery of a judgment, rectify clerical mistakes, errors in calculation and obvious slips in it.

2. The parties, whom the Registrar shall duly notify, may lodge written observations within a period prescribed by the President.

3. The Court shall take its decision in closed session after hearing the Advocate-General.

4. The original of the rectification order shall be annexed to the original of the rectified judgment. A note of this order shall be made in the margin of the original of the rectified judgment.

Art. 67   If the Court should omit to give a decision on a specific head of claim or on costs, any party may within a month after service of the judgment apply to the Court to supplement its judgment.

The application shall be served on the opposite party and the President shall prescribe a period within which that party may lodge written observations.

After these observations have been lodged, the Court shall, after hearing the Advocate-General, decide both on the admissibility and on the substance of the application.

Art. 68   The Registrar shall arrange for the publication of reports of cases before the Court.

CHAPTER 5 — COSTS

Art. 69   1. A decision as to costs shall be given in the final judgment or in the order which closes the proceedings.

2. The unsuccessful party shall be ordered to pay the costs if they have been applied for in the successful party's pleadings.

Where there are several unsuccessful parties the Court shall decide how the costs are to be shared.

3. Where each party succeeds on some and fails on other heads, or where the circumstances are exceptional, the Court may order that the costs be shared or that the parties bear their own costs.

The Court may order a party, even if successful, to pay costs which the Court considers that party to have unreasonably or vexatiously caused the opposite party to incur.

4. The Member States and institutions which intervene in the proceedings shall bear their own costs.

The States, other than the Member States, which are parties to the EEA Agreement, and also the EFTA Surveillance Authority, shall bear their own costs if they intervene in the proceedings.

The Court may order an intervener other than those mentioned in the preceding subparagraphs to bear his own costs.

5. A party who discontinues or withdraws from proceedings shall be ordered to pay the costs if they have been applied for in the other party's

observations on the discontinuance. However, upon application by the party who discontinues or withdraws from proceedings, the costs shall be borne by the other party if this appears justified by the conduct of that party.

Where the parties have come to an agreement on costs, the decision as to costs shall be in accordance with that agreement.

If costs are not claimed, the parties shall bear their own costs.

6. Where a case does not proceed to judgment the costs shall be in the discretion of the Court.

Art. 70   Without prejudice to the second subparagraph of Article 69(3) of these Rules, in proceedings between the Communities and their servants the institutions shall bear their own costs.

Art. 71   Costs necessarily incurred by a party in enforcing a judgment or order of the Court shall be refunded by the opposite party on the scale in force in the State where the enforcement takes place.

Art. 72   Proceedings before the Court shall be free of charge, except that:

(a)   where a party has caused the Court to incur avoidable costs the Court may, after hearing the Advocate-General, order that party to refund them;

(b)   where copying or translation work is carried out at the request of a party, the cost shall, in so far as the Registrar considers it excessive, be paid for by that party on the scale of charges referred to in Article 16(5) of these Rules.

Art. 73   Without prejudice to the preceding Article, the following shall be regarded as recoverable costs:

(a)   sums payable to witnesses and experts under Article 51 of these Rules;

(b)   expenses necessarily incurred by the parties for the purpose of the proceedings, in particular the travel and subsistence expenses and the remuneration of agents, advisers or lawyers.

Art. 74   1. If there is a dispute concerning the costs to be recovered, the Chamber to which the case has been assigned shall, on application by the party concerned and after hearing the opposite party and the Advocate-General, make an order, from which no appeal shall lie.

2. The parties may, for the purposes of enforcement, apply for an authenticated copy of the order.

Art. 75   1. Sums due from the cashier of the Court shall be paid in the currency of the country where the Court has its seat.

At the request of the person entitled to any sum, it shall be paid in the currency of the country where the expenses to be refunded were incurred or where the steps in respect of which payment is due were taken.

2. Other debtors shall make payment in the currency of their country of origin.

3. Conversions of currency shall be made at the official rates of exchange ruling on the day of payment in the country where the Court has its seat.

CHAPTER 6 — LEGAL AID

Art. 76   1. A party who is wholly or in part unable to meet the costs of the proceedings may at any time apply for legal aid.

The application shall be accompanied by evidence of the applicant's need of assistance, and in particular by a document from the competent authority certifying his lack of means.

2. If the application is made prior to proceedings which the applicant wishes to commence, it shall briefly state the subject of such proceedings.

The application need not be made through a lawyer.

3. The President shall designate a Judge to act as Rapporteur. The Chamber to which the latter belongs shall, after considering the written observations of the opposite party and after hearing the Advocate-General, decide whether legal aid should be granted in full or in part, or whether it should be refused. The Chamber shall consider whether there is manifestly no cause of action.

The Chamber shall make an order without giving reasons, and no appeal shall lie therefrom.

4. The Chamber may at any time, either of its own motion or on application, withdraw legal aid if the circumstances which led to its being granted alter during the proceedings.

5. Where legal aid is granted, the cashier of the Court shall advance the funds necessary to meet the expenses.

In its decision as to costs the Court may order the payment to the cashier of the Court of the whole or any part of amounts advanced as legal aid.

The Registrar shall take steps to obtain the recovery of these sums from the party ordered to pay them.

CHAPTER 7 — DISCONTINUANCE

Art. 77   If, before the Court has given its decision, the parties reach a settlement of their dispute and intimate to the Court the abandonment of their claims, the President shall order the case to be removed from the register and shall give a decision as to costs in accordance with Article 69(5), having regard to any proposals made by the parties on the matter.

This provision shall not apply to proceedings under Articles 173 and 175 of the EC Treaty, Articles 33 and 35 of the ECSC Treaty and Articles 146 and 148 of the EAEC Treaty.

Art. 78 If the applicant informs the Court in writing that he wishes to discontinue the proceedings, the President shall order the case to be removed from the register and shall give a decision as to costs in accordance with Article 69(5).

CHAPTER 8 — SERVICE

Art. 79 Where these Rules require that a document be served on a person, the Registrar shall ensure that service is effected at that person's address for service either by the dispatch of a copy of the document by registered post with a form for acknowledgement of receipt or by personal delivery of the copy against a receipt.

The Registrar shall prepare and certify the copies of documents to be served, save where the parties themselves supply the copies in accordance with Article 37(1) of these Rules.

CHAPTER 9 — TIME-LIMITS

Art. 80 1. Any period of time prescribed by the EC, ECSC and EAEC Treaties, the Statutes of the Court or these Rules for the taking of any procedural step shall be reckoned as follows:

(a) where a period expressed in days, weeks, months or years is to be calculated from the moment at which an event occurs or an action takes place, the day during which that event occurs or that action takes place shall not be counted as falling within the period in question;

(b) a period expressed in weeks, months or in years shall end with the expiry of whichever day in the last week, month or year is the same day of the week, or falls on the same date, as the day during which the event or action from which the period is to be calculated occurred or took place. If, in a period expressed in months or in years, the day on which it should expire does not occur in the last month, the period shall end with the expiry of the last day of that month;

(c) where a period is expressed in months and days, it shall first be reckoned in whole months, then in days;

(d) periods shall include official holidays, Sundays and Saturdays;

(e) periods shall not be suspended during the judicial vacations.

2. If the period would otherwise end on a Saturday, Sunday or an official holiday, it shall be extended until the end of the first following working day.

A list of official holidays drawn up by the Court shall be published in the *Official Journal of the European Communities*.

Art. 81 1. Where the period of time allowed for initiating proceedings against a measure adopted by an institution runs from the publication of that measure, that period shall be calculated, for the purposes of Article 80(1)(a), from the end of the 14th day after publication thereof in the *Official Journal of the European Communities*.

2. The extensions, on account of distance, of prescribed time-limits shall be provided for in a decision of the Court which shall be published in the *Official Journal of the European Communities*.

Art. 82   Any time-limit prescribed pursuant to these Rules may be extended by whoever prescribed it.

The President and the Presidents of Chambers may delegate to the Registrar power of signature for the purpose of fixing time-limits which, pursuant to these Rules, it falls to them to prescribe or of extending such time-limits.

CHAPTER 10 — STAY OF PROCEEDINGS

Art. 82a   1. The proceedings may be stayed:

(a)   in the circumstances specified in the third paragraph of Article 47 of the EC Statute, the third paragraph of Article 47 of the ECSC Statute and the third paragraph of Article 48 of the EAEC Statute, by order of the Court or of the Chamber to which the case has been assigned, made after hearing the Advocate-General;

(b)   in all other cases, by decision of the President adopted after hearing the Advocate-General and, save in the case of references for a preliminary ruling as referred to in Article 103, the parties.

The proceedings may be resumed by order or decision, following the same procedure.

The orders or decisions referred to in this paragraph shall be served on the parties.

2. The stay of proceedings shall take effect on the date indicated in the order or decision of stay or, in the absence of such indication, on the date of that order or decision.

While proceedings are stayed time shall cease to run for the purposes of prescribed time-limits for all parties.

3. Where the order or decision of stay does not fix the length of stay, it shall end on the date indicated in the order or decision of resumption or, in the absence of such indication, on the date of the order or decision of resumption.

From the date of resumption time shall begin to run afresh for the purposes of the time-limits.

TITLE III — SPECIAL FORMS OF PROCEDURE

CHAPTER 1 — SUSPENSION OF OPERATION OR ENFORCEMENT AND OTHER INTERIM MEASURES

Art. 83   1. An application to suspend the operation of any measure adopted by an institution, made pursuant to Article 185 of the EC Treaty, the second paragraph of Article 39 of the ECSC Treaty and Article 157 of the EAEC Treaty, shall be admissible only if the applicant is challenging that measure in proceedings before the Court.

An application for the adoption of any other interim measure referred to in Article 186 of the EC Treaty the third paragraph of Article 39 of the ECSC Treaty and Article 158 of the EAEC Treaty, shall be admissible only if it is made by a party to a case before the Court and relates to that case.

2. An application of a kind referred to in paragraph 1 of this Article shall state the subject-matter of the proceedings, the circumstances giving rise to urgency and the pleas of fact and law establishing a prima facie case for the interim measures applied for.

3. The application shall be made by a separate document and in accordance with the provisions of Articles 37 and 38 of these Rules.

Art. 84   1. The application shall be served on the opposite party, and the President shall prescribe a short period within which that party may submit written or oral observations.

2. The President may order a preparatory inquiry.

The President may grant the application even before the observations of the opposite party have been submitted. This decision may be varied or cancelled even without any application being made by any party.

Art. 85   The President shall either decide on the application himself or refer it to the Court.

If the President is absent or prevented from attending, Article 11 of these Rules shall apply.

Where the application is referred to it, the Court shall postpone all other cases, and shall give a decision after hearing the Advocate-General. Article 84 shall apply.

Art. 86   1. The decision on the application shall take the form of a reasoned order, from which no appeal shall lie. The order shall be served on the parties forthwith.

2. The enforcement of the order may be made conditional on the lodging by the applicant of security, of an amount and nature to be fixed in the light of the circumstances.

3. Unless the order fixes the date on which the interim measure is to lapse, the measure shall lapse when final judgment is delivered.

4. The order shall have only an interim effect, and shall be without prejudice to the decision of the Court on the substance of the case.

Art. 87   On application by a party, the order may at any time be varied or cancelled on account of a change in circumstances.

Art. 88   Rejection of an application for an interim measure shall not bar the party who made it from making a further application on the basis of new facts.

Art. 89   The provisions of this Chapter shall apply to applications to suspend the enforcement of a decision of the Court or of any measure adopted by another institution, submitted pursuant to Articles 187 and 192 of the EC Treaty, Articles 44 and 92 of the ECSC Treaty and Articles 159 and 164 of the EAEC Treaty.

The order granting the application shall fix, where appropriate, a date on which the interim measure is to lapse.

Art. 90   1. An application of a kind referred to in the third and fourth paragraphs of Article 81 of the EAEC Treaty shall contain:

(a) the names and addresses of the persons or undertakings to be inspected;

(b) an indication of what is to be inspected and of the purpose of the inspection.

2. The President shall give his decision in the form of an order. Article 86 of these Rules shall apply.

If the President is absent or prevented from attending, Article 11 of these Rules shall apply.

CHAPTER 2 — PRELIMINARY ISSUES

Art. 91   1. A party applying to the Court for a decision on a preliminary objection or other preliminary plea not going to the substance of the case shall make the application by a separate document.

The application must state the pleas of fact and law relied on and the form of order sought by the applicant; any supporting documents must be annexed to it.

2. As soon as the application has been lodged, the President shall prescribe a period within which the opposite party may lodge a document containing a statement of the form of order sought by that party and its pleas in law.

3. Unless the Court decides otherwise, the remainder of the proceedings shall be oral.

4. The Court shall, after hearing the Advocate-General, decide on the application or reserve its decision for the final judgment.

If the Court refuses the application or reserves its decision, the President shall prescribe new time-limits for the further steps in the proceedings.

Art. 92   1. Where it is clear that the Court has no jurisdiction to take cognisance of an action or where the action is manifestly inadmissible, the Court may, by reasoned order, after hearing the Advocate-General and without taking further steps in the proceedings, give a decision on the action.

2. The Court may at any time of its own motion consider whether there exists any absolute bar to proceeding with a case or declare, after hearing the parties, that the action has become devoid of purpose and that there is no need to adjudicate on it; it shall give its decision in accordance with Article 91(3) and (4) of these Rules.

CHAPTER 3 — INTERVENTION

Art. 93   1. An application to intervene must be made within three months of the publication of the notice referred to in Article 16(6) of these Rules.

The application shall contain:

(a)   the description of the case;

(b)   the description of the parties;

(c)   the name and address of the intervener;

(d)   the intervener's address for service at the place where the Court has its seat;

(e)   the form of order sought, by one or more of the parties, in support of which the intervener is applying for leave to intervene;

(f)   a statement of the circumstances establishing the right to intervene, where the application is submitted pursuant to the second or third paragraph of Article 37 of the EC Statute, Article 34 of the ECSC Statute or the second paragraph of Article 38 of the EAEC Statute.

The intervener shall be represented in accordance with Article 17 of the EC Statute, Article 20 of the ECSC Statute and Article 17 of the EAEC Statute.

Articles 37 and 38 of these Rules shall apply.

2. The application shall be served on the parties.

The President shall give the parties an opportunity to submit their written or oral observations before deciding on the application.

The President shall decide on the application by order or shall refer the application to the Court.

3. If the President allows the intervention, the intervener shall receive a copy of every document served on the parties. The President may, however, on application by one of the parties, omit secret or confidential documents.

4. The intervener must accept the case as he finds it at the time of his intervention.

5. The President shall prescribe a period within which the intervener may submit a statement in intervention.

The statement in intervention shall contain:

(a) a statement of the form of order sought by the intervener in support of or opposing, in whole or in part, the form of order sought by one of the parties;

(b) the pleas in law and arguments relied on by the intervener;

(c) where appropriate, the nature of any evidence offered.

6. After the statement in intervention has been lodged, the President shall, where necessary, prescribe a time-limit within which the parties may reply to that statement.

CHAPTER 4 — JUDGMENTS BY DEFAULT AND APPLICATIONS TO SET THEM ASIDE

Art. 94 1. If a defendant on whom an application initiating proceedings has been duly served fails to lodge a defence to the application in the proper form within the time prescribed, the applicant may apply for judgment by default.

The application shall be served on the defendant. The Court may decide to open the oral procedure on the application.

2. Before giving judgment by default the Court shall, after hearing the Advocate-General, consider whether the application initiating proceedings is admissible, whether the appropriate formalities have been complied with, and whether the application appears well founded. The Court may order a preparatory inquiry.

3. A judgment by default shall be enforceable. The Court may, however, grant a stay of execution until the Court has given its decision on any application under paragraph 4 to set aside the judgment, or it may make execution subject to the provision of security of an amount and nature to be fixed in the light of the circumstances; this security shall be released if no such application is made or if the application fails.

4. Application may be made to set aside a judgment by default.

The application to set aside the judgment must be made within one month from the date of service of the judgment and must be lodged in the form prescribed by Articles 37 and 38 of these Rules.

5. After the application has been served, the President shall prescribe a period within which the other party may submit his written observations.

The proceedings shall be conducted in accordance with Article 44 et seq. of these Rules.

6. The Court shall decide by way of a judgment which may not be set aside. The original of this judgment shall be annexed to the original of the judgment by default. A note of the judgment on the application to set aside shall be made in the margin of the original of the judgment by default.

CHAPTER 5 — CASES ASSIGNED TO CHAMBERS

Art. 95   1. The Court may assign any case brought before it to a Chamber in so far as the difficulty or importance of the case or particular cicumstances are not such as to require that the Court decide it in plenary session.

2. The decision so to assign a case shall be taken by the Court at the end of the written procedure upon consideration of the preliminary report presented by the Judge-Rapporteur and after the Advocate-General has been heard.

However, a case may not be so assigned if a Member State or an institution of the Communities, being a party to the proceedings, has requested that the case be decided in plenary session. In this subparagraph the expression 'party to the proceedings' means any Member State or any institution which is a party to or an intervener in the proceedings or which has submitted written observations in any reference of a kind mentioned in Article 103 of these Rules.

The request referred to in the preceding subparagraph may not be made in proceedings between the Communities and their servants.

3. A Chamber may at any stage refer a case back to the Court.

Art. 96   (repealed)

CHAPTER 6 — EXCEPTIONAL REVIEW PROCEDURES

Section 1 — Third-party proceedings

Art. 97   1. Articles 37 and 38 of these Rules shall apply to an application initiating third-party proceedings. In addition such an application shall:

(a) specify the judgment contested;

(b) state how that judgment is prejudicial to the rights of the third party;

(c) indicate the reasons for which the third party was unable to take part in the original case.

The application must be made against all the parties to the original case.

Where the judgment has been published in the *Official Journal of the European Communities*, the application must be lodged within two months of the publication.

2. The Court may, on application by the third party, order a stay of execution of the judgment. The provisions of Title III, Chapter I, of these Rules shall apply.

3. The contested judgment shall be varied on the points on which the submissions of the third party are upheld.

The original of the judgment in the third-party proceedings shall be annexed to the original of the contested judgment. A note of the judgment in the third-party proceedings shall be made in the margin of the original of the contested judgment.

Section 2 — Revision

Art. 98   An application for revision of a judgment shall be made within three months of the date on which the facts on which the application is based came to the applicant's knowledge.

Art. 99   1. Articles 37 and 38 of these Rules shall apply to an application for revision. In addition such an application shall:

(a) specify the judgment contested;

(b) indicate the points on which the judgment is contested;

(c) set out the facts on which the application is based;

(d) indicate the nature of the evidence to show that there are facts justifying revision of the judgment, and that the time-limit laid down in Article 98 has been observed.

2. The application must be made against all parties to the case in which the contested judgment was given.

Art. 100   1. Without prejudice to its decision on the substance, the Court, in closed session, shall, after hearing the Advocate-General and having regard to the written observations of the parties, give in the form of a judgment its decision on the admissibility of the application.

2. If the Court finds the application admissible, it shall proceed to consider the substance of the application and shall give its decision in the form of a judgment in accordance with these Rules.

3. The original of the revising judgment shall be annexed to the original of the judgment revised. A note of the revising judgment shall be made in the margin of the original of the judgment revised.

CHAPTER 7 — APPEALS AGAINST DECISIONS OF THE ARBITRATION COMMITTEE

Art. 101   1. An application initiating an appeal under the second paragraph of Article 18 of the EAEC Treaty shall state:

(a) the name and address of the applicant;

(b) the description of the signatory;

(c) a reference to the arbitration committee's decision against which the appeal is made;

(d) the description of the parties;

(e) a summary of the facts;

(f) the pleas in law of and the form of order sought by the applicant.

2. Articles 37(3) and (4) and 38(2), (3) and (5) of these Rules shall apply.

A certified copy of the contested decision shall be annexed to the application.

3. As soon as the application has been lodged, the Registrar of the Court shall request the arbitration committee registry to transmit to the Court the papers in the case.

4. Articles 39, 40 and 55 et seq. of these Rules shall apply to these proceedings.

5. The Court shall give its decision in the form of a judgment. Where the Court sets aside the decision of the arbitration committee it may refer the case back to the committee.

CHAPTER 8 — INTERPRETATION OF JUDGMENTS

Art. 102   1. An application for interpretation of a judgment shall be made in accordance with Articles 37 and 38 of these Rules. In addition it shall specify:

(a)   the judgment in question;

(b)   the passages of which interpretation is sought.

The application must be made against all the parties to the case in which the judgment was given.

2. The Court shall give its decision in the form of a judgment after having given the parties an opportunity to submit their observations and after hearing the Advocate-General.

The original of the interpreting judgment shall be annexed to the original of the judgment interpreted. A note of the interpreting judgment shall be made in the margin of the original of the judgment interpreted.

CHAPTER 9 — PRELIMINARY RULINGS AND OTHER REFERENCES FOR INTERPRETATION

Art. 103   1. In cases governed by Article 20 of the EC Statute and Article 21 of the EAEC Statute, the procedure shall be governed by the provisions of these Rules, subject to adaptations necessitated by the nature of the reference for a preliminary ruling.

2. The provisions of paragraph 1 shall apply to the references for a preliminary ruling provided for in the Protocol concerning the interpretation by the Court of Justice of the Convention of 29 February 1968 on the mutual recognition of companies and legal persons and the Protocol concerning the interpretation by the Court of Justice of the Convention of 27 September 1968 on jurisdiction and the enforcement of judgments in civil and commercial matters, signed at Luxembourg on 3 June 1971, and to the references provided for by Article 4 of the latter Protocol.

The provisions of paragraph 1 shall apply also to references for interpretation provided for by other existing or future agreements.

3. In cases provided for in Article 41 of the ECSC Treaty, the text of the decision to refer the matter shall be served on the parties in the case, the Member States, the Commission and the Council.

These parties, States and institutions may, within two months from the date of such service, lodge written statements of case or written observations.

The provisions of paragraph 1 shall apply.

Art. 104 1. The decisions of national courts or tribunals referred to in Article 103 shall be communicated to the Member States in the original version, accompanied by a translation into the official language of the State to which they are addressed.

In the cases governed by Article 20 of the EC Statute, the decisions of national courts or tribunals shall be notified to the States, other than the Member States, which are parties to the EEA Agreement, and also to the EFTA Surveillance Authority, in the original version, accompanied by a translation into one of the languages mentioned in Article 29(1), to be chosen by the addressee of the notification.

2. As regards the representation and attendance of the parties to the main proceedings in the preliminary ruling procedure the Court shall take account of the rules of procedure of the national court or tribunal which made the reference.

3. Where a question referred to the Court for a preliminary ruling is manifestly identical to a question on which the Court has already ruled, the Court may, after informing the court or tribunal which referred the question to it, hearing any observations submitted by the persons referred to in Article 20 of the EC Statute, Article 21 of the EAEC Statute and Article 103(3) of these Rules and hearing the Advocate-General, give its decision by reasoned order in which reference is made to its previous judgment.

4. Without prejudice to paragraph 3 of this Article, the procedure before the Court in the case of a reference for a preliminary ruling shall also include an oral part. However, after the statements of case or written observations referred to in Article 20 of the EC Statute, Article 21 of the EAEC Statute and Article 103(3) of these Rules have been submitted, the Court, acting on a report from the Judge-Rapporteur, after informing the persons who under the aforementioned provisions are entitled to submit such statements or observations, may, after hearing the Advocate-General, decide otherwise, provided that none of those persons has asked to present oral argument.

5. It shall be for the national court or tribunal to decide as to the costs of the reference.

In special circumstances the Court may grant, by way of legal aid, assistance for the purpose of facilitating the representation or attendance of a party.

CHAPTER 10 — SPECIAL PROCEDURES UNDER ARTICLES 103 TO 105 OF
THE EAEC TREATY

Art. 105   1. Four certified copies shall be lodged of an application under the third
paragraph of Article 103 of the EAEC Treaty. The Commission shall be
served with a copy.

2. The application shall be accompanied by the draft of the agreement or
contract in question, by the observations of the Commission addressed to
the State concerned and by all other supporting documents.

The Commission shall submit its observations to the Court within a period of 10 days, which may be extended by the President after the State
concerned has been heard.

A certified copy of the observations shall be served on that State.

3. As soon as the application has been lodged the President shall designate
a Judge to act as Rapporteur. The First Advocate-General shall assign the
case to an Advocate-General as soon as the Judge-Rapporteur has been
designated.

4. The decision shall be taken in closed session after the Advocate-General
has been heard.

The agents and advisers of the State concerned and of the Commission
shall be heard if they so request.

Art. 106   1. In cases provided for in the last paragraph of Article 104 and the last
paragraph of Article 105 of the EAEC Treaty, the provisions of Article 37
et seq. of these Rules shall apply.

2. The application shall be served on the State to which the respondent
person or undertaking belongs.

CHAPTER 11 — OPINIONS

Art. 107   1. A request by the Council for an Opinion pursuant to Article 228 of the
EC Treaty shall be served on the Commission and on the European Parliament. Such a request by the Commission shall be served on the Council, on the European Parliament and on the Member States. Such a request
by a Member State shall be served on the Council, on the Commission, on
the European Parliament and the other Member States.

The President shall prescribe a period within which the institutions and
Member States which have been served with a request may submit their
written observations.

2. The Opinion may deal not only with the question whether the envisaged agreement is compatible with the provisions of the EC Treaty but
also with the question whether the Community or any Community institution has the power to enter into that agreement.

Art. 108   1. As soon as the request for an Opinion has been lodged, the President
shall designate a Judge to act as Rapporteur.

2. The Court sitting in closed session shall, after hearing the Advocates-General, deliver a reasoned Opinion.

3. The Opinion, signed by the President, by the Judges who took part in the deliberations and by the Registrar, shall be served on the Council, the Commission, the European Parliament and the Member States.

Art. 109   Requests for the Opinion of the Court under the fourth paragraph of Article 95 of the ECSC Treaty shall be submitted jointly by the Commission and the Council.

The Opinion shall be delivered in accordance with the provisions of the preceding Article. It shall be communicated to the Commission, the Council and the European Parliament.

TITLE IV — APPEALS AGAINST DECISIONS OF THE COURT OF FIRST INSTANCE

Art. 110   Without prejudice to the arrangements laid down in Article 29(2)(b) and (c) and the fourth subparagraph of Article 29(3) of these Rules, in appeals against decisions of the Court of First Instance as referred to in Articles 49 and 50 of the EC Statute, Articles 49 and 50 of the ECSC Statute and Articles 50 and 51 of the EAEC Statute, the language of the case shall be the language of the decision of the Court of First Instance against which the appeal is brought.

Art. 111   1. An appeal shall be brought by lodging an application at the Registry of the Court of Justice or of the Court of First Instance.

2. The Registry of the Court of First Instance shall immediately transmit to the Registry of the Court of Justice the papers in the case at first instance and, where necessary, the appeal.

Art. 112   1. An appeal shall contain:

(a)   the name and address of the appellant;

(b)   the names of the other parties to the proceedings before the Court of First Instance;

(c)   the pleas in law and legal arguments relied on;

(d)   the form or order sought by the appellant.

Article 37 and Article 38(2) and (3) of these Rules shall apply to appeals.

2. The decision of the Court of First Instance appealed against shall be attached to the appeal. The appeal shall state the date on which the decision appealed against was notified to the appellant.

3. If an appeal does not comply with Article 38(3) or with paragraph 2 of this Article, Article 38(7) of these Rules shall apply.

Art. 113   1. An appeal may seek:

—   to set aside, in whole or in part, the decision of the Court of First Instance;

— the same form of order, in whole or in part, as that sought at first instance and shall not seek a different form of order.

2. The subject-matter of the proceedings before the Court of First Instance may not be changed in the appeal.

Art. 114   Notice of the appeal shall be served on all the parties to the proceedings before the Court of First Instance. Article 39 of these Rules shall apply.

Art. 115   1. Any party to the proceedings before the Court of First Instance may lodge a response within two months after service on him of notice of the appeal. The time-limit for lodging a response shall not be extended.

2. A response shall contain:

(a)   the name and address of the party lodging it;

(b)   the date on which notice of the appeal was served on him;

(c)   the pleas in law and legal arguments relied on;

(d)   the form of order sought by the respondent.

Article 38(2) and (3) of these Rules shall apply.

Art. 116   1. A response may seek:

— to dismiss, in whole or in part, the appeal or to set aside, in whole or in part, the decision of the Court of First Instance;

— the same form of order, in whole or in part, as that sought at first instance and shall not seek a different form of order.

2. The subject-matter of the proceedings before the Court of First Instance may not be changed in the response.

Art. 117   1. The appeal and the response may be supplemented by a reply and a rejoinder or any other pleading, where the President, on application made within seven days of service of the response or of the reply, considers such further pleading necessary and expressly allows it in order to enable the party concerned to put forward its point of view or in order to provide a basis for the decision on the appeal.

2. Where the response seeks to set aside, in whole or in part, the decision of the Court of First Instance on a plea in law which was not raised in the appeal, the appellant or any other party may submit a reply on that plea alone within two months of the service of the response in question. Paragraph 1 shall apply to any further pleading following such a reply.

3. Where the President allows the lodging of a reply and a rejoinder, or any other pleading, he shall prescribe the period within which they are to be submitted.

Art. 118   Subject to the following provisions, Articles 42(2), 43, 44, 55 to 90, 93, 95 to 100 and 102 of these Rules shall apply to the procedure before the Court of Justice on appeal from a decision of the Court of First Instance.

Art. 119   Where the appeal is, in whole or in part, clearly inadmissible or clearly unfounded, the Court may at any time, acting on a report from the Judge-

Rapporteur and after hearing the Advocate-General, by reasoned order dismiss the appeal in whole or in part.

Ar. 120   After the submission of pleadings as provided for in Articles 115(1) and, if any, Article 117(1) and (2) of these Rules, the Court may, acting on a report from the Judge-Rapporteur and after hearing the Advocate-General and the parties, decide to dispense with the oral part of the procedure unless one of the parties objects on the ground that the written procedure did not enable him fully to defend his point of view.

Art. 121   The report referred to in Article 44(1) shall be presented to the Court after the pleadings provided for in Article 115(1) and Article 117(1) and (2) of these Rules have been lodged. The report shall contain, in addition to the recommendations provided for in Article 44(1), a recommendation as to whether Article 120 of these Rules should be applied. Where no such pleadings are lodged, the same procedure shall apply after the expiry of the period prescribed for lodging them.

Art. 122   Where the appeal is unfounded or where the appeal is well founded and the Court itself gives final judgment in the case, the Court shall make a decision as to costs.

In proceedings between the Communities and their servants:

—   Article 70 of these Rules shall apply only to appeals brought by institutions;

—   by way of derogation from Article 69(2) of these Rules, the Court may, in appeals brought by officials or other servants of an institution, order the parties to share the costs where equity so requires.

If the appeal is withdrawn Article 69(5) shall apply.

When an appeal brought by a Member State or an institution which did not intervene in the proceedings before the Court of First Instance is well founded, the Court of Justice may order that the parties share the costs or that the successful appellant pay the costs which the appeal has caused an unsuccessful party to incur.

Art. 123   An application to intervene made to the Court in appeal proceedings shall be lodged before the expiry of a period of one month running from the publication referred to in Article 16(6).

TITLE V — PROCEDURES PROVIDED FOR BY THE EEA AGREEMENT

Art. 123a 1. In the case governed by Article 111(3) of the EEA Agreement[1], the matter shall be brought before the Court by a request submitted by the Contracting Parties to the dispute. The request shall be served on the other Contracting Parties, on the Commission, on the EFTA Surveillance Authority and, where appropriate, on the other persons to whom a refer-

---

[1]   OJ L 1 of 3.1.1994, p. 27.

ence for a preliminary ruling raising the same question of interpretation of Community legislation would be notified.

The President shall prescribe a period within which the Contracting Parties and the other persons on whom the request has been served may submit written observations.

The request shall be made in one of the languages mentioned in Article 29(1). Paragraphs 3 and 5 of that Article shall apply. The provisions of Article 104(1) shall apply *mutatis mutandis*.

2. As soon as the request referred to in paragraph 1 of this Article has been submitted, the President shall appoint a Judge-Rapporteur. The First Advocate-General shall, immediately afterwards, assign the request to an Advocate-General.

The Court shall, after hearing the Advocate-General, give a reasoned decision on the request in closed session.

3. The decision of the Court, signed by the President, by the Judges who took part in the deliberations and by the Registrar, shall be served on the Contracting Parties and on the other persons referred to in paragraph 1.

Art. 123b In the case governed by Article 1 of Protocol 34 to the EEA Agreement, the request of a court or tribunal of an EFTA State shall be served on the parties to the case, on the Contracting Parties, on the Commission, on the EFTA Surveillance Authority and, where appropriate, on the other persons to whom a reference for a preliminary ruling raising the same question of interpretation of Community legislation would be notified.

If the request is not submitted in one of the languages mentioned in Article 29(1), it shall be accompanied by a translation into one of those languages.

Within two months of this notification, the parties to the case, the Contracting Parties and the other persons referred to in the first paragraph shall be entitled to submit statements of case or written observations.

The procedure shall be governed by the provisions of these Rules, subject to the adaptations called for by the nature of the request.

Miscellaneous Provisions

Art. 124 1. The President shall instruct any person who is required to take an oath before the Court, as witness or expert, to tell the truth or to carry out his task conscientiously and impartially, as the case may be, and shall warn him of the criminal liability provided for in his national law in the event of any breach of this duty.

2. The witness shall take the oath either in accordance with the first subparagraph of Article 47(5) of these Rules or in the manner laid down by his national law.

Where his national law provides the opportunity to make, in judicial proceedings, a solemn affirmation equivalent to an oath as well as or instead of taking an oath, the witness may make such an affirmation under the conditions and in the form prescribed in his national law.

Where his national law provides neither for taking an oath nor for making a solemn affirmation, the procedure described in paragraph 1 shall be followed.

3. Paragraph 2 shall apply *mutatis mutandis* to experts, a reference to the first subparagraph of Article 49(6) replacing in this case the reference to the first subparagraph of Article 47(5) of these Rules.

Art. 125   Subject to the provisions of Article 188 of the EC Treaty and Article 160 of the EAEC Treaty and after consultation with the Governments concerned, the Court shall adopt supplementary rules concerning its practice in relation to:

(a) letters rogatory;

(b) applications for legal aid;

(c) reports of perjury by witnesses or experts, delivered pursuant to Article 27 of the EC Statute and Article 28 of the ECSC and EAEC Statutes.

Art. 126   These Rules replace the Rules of Procedure of the Court of Justice of the European Communities adopted on 4 December 1974 (*Official Journal of the European Communities* L 350 of 28 December 1974, p. 1), as last amended on 15 May 1991.

Art. 127   These Rules, which are authentic in the languages mentioned in Article 29(1) of these Rules, shall be published in the *Official Journal of the European Communities* and shall enter into force on the first day of the second month following their publication.

hh) Rules of Procedure of the Court of First Instance of the European Communities of May 2, 1991

INTERPRETATION

Art. 1   In these Rules:

–   'EC Treaty' means the Treaty establishing the European Community,

–   'EC Statute' means the Protocol on the Statute of the Court of Justice of the European Community,

–   'ECSC Treaty' means the Treaty establishing the European Coal and Steel Community,

–   'ECSC Statute' means the Protocol on the Statute of the Court of Justice of the European Coal and Steel Community

- 'EAEC Treaty' means the Treaty establishing the European Atomic Energy Community (Euratom);
- 'EAEC Statute' means the Protocol on the Statute of the Court of Justice of the European Atomic Energy Community.
- 'EEA Agreement' means the Agreement on the European Economic Area.

For the purposes of these Rules:

- 'institutions' means the institutions of the Communities and bodies which are established by the Treaties, or by an act adopted in implementation thereof, and which may be parties before the Court of First Instance.
- 'EFTA Surveillance Authority' means the surveillance authority referred to in the EEA Agreement.

TITLE 1 — ORGANISATION OF THE COURT OF FIRST INSTANCE

CHAPTER 1 — PRESIDENT AND MEMBERS OF THE COURT OF FIRST INSTANCE

Art. 2 1. Every Member of the Court of First Instance shall, as a rule, perform the function of Judge.

Members of the Court of First Instance are hereinafter referred to as 'Judges'.

2. Every Judge, with the exception of the President, may, in the circumstances specified in Articles 17 to 19, perform the function of Advocate-General in a particular case.

References to the Advocate-General in these Rules shall apply only where a Judge has been designated as Advocate-General.

Art. 3 The term of office of a Judge shall begin on the date laid down in his instrument of appointment. In the absence of any provision regarding the date, the term shall begin on the date of the instrument.

Art. 4 1. Before taking up his duties, a Judge shall take the following oath before the Court of Justice of the European Communities:

'I swear that I will perform my duties impartially and conscientiously; I swear that I will preserve the secrecy of the deliberations of the Court.'

2. Immediately after taking the oath, a Judge shall sign a declaration by which he solemnly undertakes that, both during and after his term of office, he will respect the obligations arising therefrom, and in particular the duty to behave with integrity and discretion as regards the acceptance, after he has ceased to hold office, of certain appointments and benefits.

Art. 5 When the Court of Justice is called upon to decide, after consulting the Court of First Instance, whether a Judge of the Court of First Instance no longer fulfils the requisite conditions or no longer meets the obligations arising from his office, the President of the Court of First Instance shall invite the Judge concerned to make representations to the Court of First Instance, in closed session and in the absence of the Registrar.

The Court of First Instance shall state the reasons for its opinion.

An opinion to the effect that a Judge of the Court of First Instance no longer fulfils the requisite conditions or no longer meets the obligations arising from his office must receive the votes of at least seven Judges of the Court of First Instance. In that event, particulars of the voting shall be communicated to the Court of Justice.

Voting shall be by secret ballot; the Judge concerned shall not take part in the deliberations.

Art. 6   With the exception of the President of the Court of First Instance and of the Presidents of the Chambers, the Judges shall rank equally in precedence according to their seniority in office.

Where there is equal seniority in office, precedence shall be determined by age.

Retiring Judges who are reappointed shall retain their former precedence.

Art. 7   1. The Judges shall, immediately after the partial replacement provided for in Article 168a of the EC Treaty, Article 32d of the ECSC Treaty and Article 140a of the EAEC Treaty, elect one of their number as President of the Court of First Instance for a term of three years.

2. If the office of President of the Court of First Instance falls vacant before the normal date of expiry thereof, the Court of First Instance shall elect a successor for the remainder of the term.

3. The elections provided for in this Article shall be by secret ballot. If a Judge obtains an absolute majority he shall be elected. If no Judge obtains an absolute majority, a second ballot shall be held and the Judge obtaining the most votes shall be elected. Where two or more Judges obtain an equal number of votes the oldest of them shall be deemed elected.

Art. 8   The President of the Court of First Instance shall direct the judicial business and the administration of the Court of First Instance. He shall preside at plenary sittings and deliberations.

Art. 9   When the President of the Court of First Instance is absent or prevented from attending or when the office of President is vacant, the functions of President shall be exercised by a President of a Chamber according to the order of precedence laid down in Article 6.

If the President of the Court of First Instance and the Presidents of the Chambers are all prevented from attending at the same time, or their posts are vacant at the same time, the functions of President shall be exercised by one of the other Judges according to the order of precedence laid down in Article 6.

CHAPTER 2 — CONSTITUTION OF THE CHAMBERS AND DESIGNATION
OF JUDGE-RAPPORTEURS AND ADVOCATES-GENERAL

Art. 10   1. The Court of First Instance shall set up Chambers composed of three or
           five Judges and shall decide which Judges shall be attached to them.

           2. The composition of the Chambers shall be published in the *Official
           Journal of the European Communities.*

Art. 11   1. Cases before the Court of First Instance shall be heard by Chambers
           composed in accordance with Article 10.

           Cases may be heard by the Court of First Instance sitting in plenary ses-
           sion under the conditions laid down in Articles 14, 51, 106, 118, 124, 127
           and 129.

           2. In cases coming before a Chamber, the term 'Court of First Instance' in
           these Rules shall designate that Chamber.

Art. 12   1. The Court of First Instance shall lay down criteria by which cases are to
           be allocated among the Chambers.

           The decision shall be published in the *Official Journal of the European
           Communities.*[1]

Art. 13   1. As soon as the application initiating proceedings has been lodged, the
           President of the Court of First Instance shall assign the case to one of the
           Chambers.

           2. The President of the Chamber shall propose to the President of the
           Court of First Instance, in respect of each case assigned to the Chamber,
           the designation of a Judge to act as Rapporteur; the President of the Court
           of First Instance shall decide on the proposal.

Art. 14   Whenever the legal difficulty or the importance of the case or special cir-
           cumstances so justify, a case may be referred to the Court of First Instance
           sitting in plenary session or to a Chamber composed of a different number
           of Judges.

           Any decision to refer a case shall be taken under the conditions laid down
           in Article 51.

Art. 15   The Court of First Instance shall appoint for a period of one year the
           Presidents of the Chambers.

           The provisions of Article 7(2) and (3) shall apply.

           The appointments made in pursuance of this Article shall be published in
           the *Official Journal of the European Communities.*

Art. 16   In cases coming before a Chamber the powers of the President shall be ex-
           ercised by the President of the Chamber.

---

[1]   The decision in force at the time of publication of the present edition is published in
       OJ C 271 of 6.9.1997.

Art. 17 When the Court of First Instance sits in plenary session, it shall be assisted by an Advocate-General designated by the President of the Court of First Instance.

Art. 18 A Chamber of the Court of First Instance may be assisted by an Advocate-General if it is considered that the legal difficulty or the factual complexity of the case so requires.

Art. 19 The decision to designate an Advocate-General in a particular case shall be taken by the Court of First Instance sitting in plenary session at the request of the Chamber before which the case comes.

The President of the Court of First Instance shall designate the Judge called upon to perform the function of Advocate-General in that case.

CHAPTER 3 — REGISTRY

Section 1 – The Registrar

Art. 20 1. The Court of First Instance shall appoint the Registrar.

Two weeks before the date fixed for making the appointment, the President of the Court of First Instance shall inform the Judges of the applications which have been submitted for the post.

2. An application shall be accompanied by full details of the candidate's age, nationality, university degrees, knowledge of any languages, present and past occupations and experience, if any, in judicial and international fields.

3. The appointment shall be made following the procedure laid down in Article 7(3).

4. The Registrar shall be appointed for a term of six years. He may be reappointed.

5. Before he takes up his duties the Registrar shall take the oath before the Court of First Instance in accordance with Article 4.

6. The Registrar may be deprived of his office only if he no longer fulfils the requisite conditions or no longer meets the obligations arising from his office; the Court of First Instance shall take its decision after giving the Registrar an opportunity to make representations.

7. If the office of Registrar falls vacant before the usual date of expiry of the term thereof, the Court of First Instance shall appoint a new Registrar for a term of six years.

Art. 21 The Court of First Instance may, following the procedure laid down in respect of the Registrar, appoint one or more Assistant Registrars to assist the Registrar and to take his place in so far as the Instructions to the Registrar referred to in Article 23 allow.

Art. 22 Where the Registrar is absent or prevented from attending and, if necessary, where the Assistant Registrar is absent or so prevented, or where their posts are vacant, the President of the Court of First Instance shall designate an official or servant to carry out the duties of Registrar.

Art. 23   Instructions to the Registrar shall be adopted by the Court of First Instance acting on a proposal from the President of the Court of First Instance.

Art. 24   1. There shall be kept in the Registry, under the control of the Registrar, a register initialled by the President of the Court of First Instance, in which all pleadings and supporting documents shall be entered in the order in which they are lodged.

2. When a document has been registered, the Registrar shall make a note to that effect on the original and, if a party so requests, on any copy submitted for the purpose.

3. Entries in the register and the notes provided for in the preceding paragraph shall be authentic.

4. Rules for keeping the register shall be prescribed by the Instructions to the Registrar referred to in Article 23.

5. Persons having an interest may consult the register at the Registry and may obtain copies or extracts on payment of a charge on a scale fixed by the Court of First Instance on a proposal from the Registrar.

The parties to a case may on payment of the appropriate charge also obtain copies of pleadings and authenticated copies of orders and judgments.

6. Notice shall be given in the *Official Journal of the European Communities* of the date of registration of an application initiating proceedings, the names and addresses of the parties, the subject-matter of the proceedings, the form of order sought by the applicant and a summary of the pleas in law and of the main supporting arguments.

7. Where the Council or the Commission is not a party to a case, the Court of First Instance shall send to it copies of the application and of the defence, without the annexes thereto, to enable it to assess whether the inapplicability of one of its acts is being invoked under Article 184 of the EC Treaty, the third paragraph of Article 36 of the ECSC Treaty or Article 156 of the EAEC Treaty.

Art. 25   1. The Registrar shall be responsible, under the authority of the President, for the acceptance, transmission and custody of documents and for effecting service as provided for by these Rules.

2. The Registrar shall assist the Court of First Instance, the President and the Judges in all their official functions.

Art. 26   The Registrar shall have custody of the seals. He shall be responsible for the records and be in charge of the publications of the Court of First Instance.

Art. 27   Subject to Articles 5 and 33, the Registrar shall attend the sittings of the Court of First Instance.

Section 2 – Other Departments

Art. 28   The officials and other servants whose task is to assist directly the President, the Judges and the Registrar shall be appointed in accordance with the Staff Regulations. They shall be responsible to the Registrar, under the authority of the President of the Court of First Instance.

Art. 29   The officials and other servants referred to in Article 28 shall take the oath provided for in Article 20(2) of the Rules of Procedure of the Court of Justice before the President of the Court of First Instance in the presence of the Registrar.

Art. 30   The Registrar shall be responsible, under the authority of the President of the Court of First Instance, for the administration of the Court of First Instance, its financial management and its accounts; he shall be assisted in this by the departments of the Court of Justice.

CHAPTER 4 — THE WORKING OF THE COURT OF FIRST INSTANCE

Art. 31   1. The dates and times of the sittings of the Court of First Instance shall be fixed by the President.

2. The Court of First Instance may choose to hold one or more sittings in a place other than that in which the Court of First Instance has its seat.

Art. 32   1. Where, by reason of a Judge being absent or prevented from attending, there is an even number of Judges, the most junior Judge within the meaning of Article 6 shall abstain from taking part in the deliberations unless he is the Judge-Rapporteur. In this case, the Judge immediately senior to him shall abstain from taking part in the deliberations.

Where, following the designation of an Advocate-General pursuant to Article 17, there is an even number of Judges in the Court of First Instance sitting in plenary session, the President of the Court shall designate, before the hearing and in accordance with a rota established in advance by the Court of First Instance and published in the *Official Journal of the European Communities*, the Judge who will not take part in the judgment of the case.

2. If after the Court of First Instance has been convened in plenary session, it is found that the quorum of nine Judges has not been attained, the President of the Court of First Instance shall adjourn the sitting until there is a quorum.

3. If in any Chamber the quorum of three Judges has not been attained, the President of that Chamber shall so inform the President of the Court of First Instance who shall designate another Judge to complete the Chamber.

4. If in any Chamber of three or five Judges the number of Judges assigned to that Chamber is higher than three or five respectively, the President of the Chamber shall decide which of the Judges will be called upon to take part in the judgment of the case.

Art. 33   1. The Court of First Instance shall deliberate in closed session.

2. Only those Judges who were present at the oral proceedings may take part in the deliberations.

3. Every Judge taking part in the deliberations shall state his opinion and the reasons for it.

4. Any Judge may require that any question be formulated in the language of his choice and communicated in writing to the other Judges before being put to the vote.

5. The conclusions reached by the majority of the Judges after final discussion shall determine the decision of the Court of First Instance. Votes shall be cast in reverse order to the order of precedence laid down in Article 6.

6. Differences of view on the substance, wording or order of questions, or on the interpretation of a vote shall be settled by decision of the Court of First Instance.

7. Where the deliberations of the Court of First Instance concern questions of its own administration, the Registrar shall be present, unless the Court of First Instance decides to the contrary.

8. Where the Court of First Instance sits without the Registrar being present it shall, if necessary, instruct the most junior Judge within the meaning of Article 6 to draw up minutes. The minutes shall be signed by this Judge and by the President.

Art. 34   1. Subject to any special decision of the Court of First Instance, its vacations shall be as follows:

–   from 18 December to 10 January,
–   from the Sunday before Easter to the second Sunday after Easter,
–   from 15 July to 15 September.

During the vacations, the functions of President shall be exercised at the place where the Court of First Instance has its seat either by the President himself, keeping in touch with the Registrar, or by a President of Chamber or other Judge invited by the President to take his place.

2. In a case of urgency, the President may convene the Judges during the vacations.

3. The Court of First Instance shall observe the official holidays of the place where it has its seat.

4. The Court of First Instance may, in proper circumstances, grant leave of absence to any Judge.

CHAPTER 5 — LANGUAGES

Art. 35   1. The language of a case shall be Danish, Dutch, English, Finnish, French, German, Greek, Irish, Italian, Portuguese, Spanish or Swedish.

2. The language of the case shall be chosen by the applicant, except that:

(a) at the joint request of the parties, the use of another of the languages mentioned in paragraph 1 for all or part of the proceedings may be authorised;

(b) at the request of one of the parties, and after the opposite party and the Advocate-General have been heard, the use of another of the languages mentioned in paragraph 1 as the language of the case for all or part of the proceedings may be authorised by way of derogation from subparagraph (a); such a request may not be submitted by an institution.

Requests as above may be decided on by the President; the latter may and, where he proposes to accede to a request without the agreement of all the parties, must refer the request to the Court of First Instance.

3. The language of the case shall be used in the written and oral pleadings of the parties and in supporting documents, and also in the minutes and decisions of the Court of First Instance.

Any supporting documents expressed in another language must be accompanied by a translation into the language of the case.

In the case of lengthy documents, translations may be confined to extracts. However, the Court of First Instance may, of its own motion or at the request of a party, at any time call for a complete or fuller translation.

Notwithstanding the foregoing provisions, a Member State shall be entitled to use its official language when intervening in a case before the Court of First Instance. This provision shall apply both to written statements and to oral addresses. The Registrar shall cause any such statement or address to be translated into the language of the case.

The States, other than the Member States, which are parties to the EEA Agreement, and also the EFTA Surveillance Authority, may be authorised to use one of the languages mentioned in paragraph 1, other than the language of the case, when they intervene in a case before the Court of First Instance. This provision shall apply both to written statements and oral addresses. The Registrar shall cause any such statement or address to be translated into the language of the case.

4. Where a witness or expert states that he is unable adequately to express himself in one of the languages referred to in paragraph 1 of this Article, the Court of First Instance may authorise him to give his evidence in another language. The Registrar shall arrange for translation into the language of the case.

5. The President in conducting oral proceedings, the Judge-Rapporteur both in his preliminary report and in his report for the hearing, Judges and the Advocate-General in putting questions and the Advocate-General in delivering his opinion may use one of the languages referred to in paragraph 1 of this Article other than the language of the case. The Registrar shall arrange for translation into the language of the case.

Art. 36   1. The Registrar shall, at the request of any Judge, of the Advocate-General or of a party, arrange for anything said or written in the course of the proceedings before the Court of First Instance to be translated into the languages he chooses from those referred to in Article 35(1).

2. Publications of the Court of First Instance shall be issued in the languages referred to in Article 1 of Council Regulation No 1.

Art. 37   The texts of documents drawn up in the language of the case or in any other language authorised by the Court of First Instance pursuant to Article 35 shall be authentic.

CHAPTER 6 — RIGHTS AND OBLIGATIONS OF AGENTS, ADVISERS AND LAWYERS

Art. 38   1. Agents, advisers and lawyers, appearing before the Court of First Instance or before any judicial authority to which it has addressed letters rogatory, shall enjoy immunity in respect of words spoken or written by them concerning the case or the parties.

2. Agents, advisers and lawyers shall enjoy the following further privileges and facilities:

(a) papers and documents relating to the proceedings shall be exempt from both search and seizure; in the event of a dispute the customs officials or police may seal those papers and documents; they shall then be immediately forwarded to the Court of First Instance for inspection in the presence of the Registrar and of the person concerned;

(b) agents, advisers and lawyers shall be entitled to such allocation of foreign currency as may be necessary for the performance of their duties;

(c) agents, advisers and lawyers shall be entitled to travel in the course of duty without hindrance.

Art. 39   In order to qualify for the privileges, immunities and facilities specified in Article 38, persons entitled to them shall furnish proof of their status as follows:

(a) agents shall produce an official document issued by the party for whom they act and shall forward without delay a copy thereof to the Registrar;

(b) advisers and lawyers shall produce a certificate signed by the Registrar. The validity of this certificate shall be limited to a specified period, which may be extended or curtailed according to the length of the proceedings.

Art. 40   The privileges, immunities and facilities specified in Article 38 are granted exclusively in the interests of the proper conduct of proceedings.

The Court of First Instance may waive the immunity where it considers that the proper conduct of proceedings will not be hindered thereby.

Art. 41   1. Any adviser or lawyer whose conduct towards the Court of First Instance, the President, a Judge or the Registrar is incompatible with the dignity of the Court of First Instance, or who uses his rights for purposes other than those for which they were granted, may at any time be excluded from the proceedings by an order of the Court of First Instance; the person concerned shall be given an opportunity to defend himself.

The order shall have immediate effect.

2. Where an adviser or lawyer is excluded from the proceedings, the proceedings shall be suspended for a period fixed by the President in order to allow the party concerned to appoint another adviser or lawyer.

3. Decisions taken under this Article may be rescinded.

Art. 42   The provisions of this Chapter shall apply to university teachers who have a right of audience before the Court of First Instance in accordance with Article 17 of the EC Statute, Article 20 of the ECSC Statute and Article 17 of the EAEC Statute.

TITLE 2 — PROCEDURE

CHAPTER 1 — WRITTEN PROCEDURE

Art. 43   1. The original of every pleading must be signed by the party's agent or lawyer.

The original, accompanied by all annexes referred to therein, shall be lodged together with five copies for the Court of First Instance and a copy for every other party to the proceedings. Copies shall be certified by the party lodging them.

2. Institutions shall in addition produce, within time-limits laid down by the Court of First Instance, translations of all pleadings into the other languages provided for by Article 1 of Council Regulation No 1. The second subparagraph of paragraph 1 of this Article shall apply.

3. All pleadings shall bear a date. In the reckoning of time-limits for taking steps in proceedings only the date of lodgment at the Registry shall be taken into account.

4. To every pleading there shall be annexed a file containing the documents relied on in support of it, together with a schedule listing them.

5. Where in view of the length of a document only extracts from it are annexed to the pleading, the whole document or a full copy of it shall be lodged at the Registry.

Art. 44   1. An application of the kind referred to in Article 19 of the EC Statute, Article 22 of the ECSC Statute and Article 19 of the EAEC Statute shall state:

(a) the name and address of the applicant;

(b) the designation of the party against whom the application is made;

(c) the subject-matter of the proceedings and a summary of the pleas in law on which the application is based;

(d) the form of order sought by the applicant;

(e) where appropriate, the nature of any evidence offered in support.

2. For the purposes of the proceedings, the application shall state an address for service in the place where the Court of First Instance has its seat and the name of the person who is authorised and has expressed willingness to accept service.

If the application does not comply with these requirements, all service on the party concerned for the purposes of the proceedings shall be effected, for so long as the defect has not been cured, by registered letter addressed to the agent or lawyer of that party. By way of derogation from Article 100, service shall then be deemed to have been duly effected by the lodging of the registered letter at the post office of the place where the Court of First Instance has its seat.

3. The lawyer acting for a party must lodge at the Registry a certificate that he is authorised to practise before a Court of a Member State or of another State which is a party to the EEA Agreement.

4. The application shall be accompanied, where appropriate, by the documents specified in the second paragraph of Article 19 of the EC Statute, in the second paragraph of Article 22 of the ECSC Statute and in the second paragraph of Article 19 of the EAEC Statute.

5. An application made by a legal person governed by private law shall be accompanied by:

(a) the instrument or instruments constituting and regulating that legal person or a recent extract from the register of companies, firms or associations or any other proof of its existence in law;

(b) proof that the authority granted to the applicant's lawyer has been properly conferred on him by someone authorised for the purpose.

5a. An application submitted under Article 181 of the EC Treaty, Article 42 of the ECSC Treaty or Article 153 of the EAEC Treaty pursuant to an arbitration clause contained in a contract governed by public or private law, entered into by the Community or on its behalf, shall be accompanied by a copy of the contract which contains that clause.

6. If an application does not comply with the requirements set out in paragraphs 3 to 5 of this Article, the Registrar shall prescribe a reasonable period within which the applicant is to comply with them whether by putting the application itself in order or by producing any of the above-mentioned documents. If the applicant fails to put the application in order or to produce the required documents within the time prescribed, the Court of First Instance shall decide whether the non-compliance with these conditions renders the application formally inadmissible.

Art. 45 The application shall be served on the defendant. In a case where Article 44(6) applies, service shall be effected as soon as the application has been put in order or the Court of First Instance has declared it admissible notwithstanding the failure to observe the formal requirements set out in that Article.

Art. 46 Within one month after service on him of the application, the defendant shall lodge a defence, stating:

(a) the name and address of the defendant;

(b) the arguments of fact and law relied on;

(c) the form of order sought by the defendant;

(d) the nature of any evidence offered by him.

The provisions of Article 44(2) to (5) shall apply to the defence.

2. In proceedings between the Communities and their servants the defence shall be accompanied by the complaint within the meaning of Article 90(2) of the Staff Regulations of Officials and by the decision rejecting the complaint together with the dates on which the complaint was submitted and the decision notified.

3. The time-limit laid down in paragraph 1 of this Article may be extended by the President on a reasoned application by the defendant.

Art. 47   1. The application initiating the proceedings and the defence may be supplemented by a reply from the applicant and by a rejoinder from the defendant.

2. The President shall fix the time-limits within which these pleadings are to be lodged.

Art. 48   1. In reply or rejoinder a party may offer further evidence. The party must, however, give reasons for the delay in offering it.

2. No new plea in law may be introduced in the course of proceedings unless it is based on matters of law or of fact which come to light in the course of the procedure.

If in the course of the procedure one of the parties puts forward a new plea in law which is so based, the President may, even after the expiry of the normal procedural time-limits, acting on a report of the Judge-Rapporteur and after hearing the Advocate-General, allow the other party time to answer on that plea.

Consideration of the admissibility of the plea shall be reserved for the final judgment.

Art. 49   At any stage of the proceedings the Court of First Instance may, after hearing the Advocate-General, prescribe any measure of organisation of procedure or any measure of inquiry referred to in Articles 64 and 65 or order that a previous inquiry be repeated or expanded.

Art. 50   The President may, at any time, after hearing the parties and the Advocate-General, order that two or more cases concerning the same subject-matter shall, on account of the connection between them, be joined for the purposes of the written or oral procedure or of the final judgment. The cases may subsequently be disjoined. The President may refer these matters to the Court of First Instance.

Art. 51   1. In the cases specified in Article 14, and at any stage in the proceedings, the Chamber hearing the case may, either on its own initiative or at the request of one of the parties, propose to the Court of First Instance sitting in plenary session that the case be referred to the Court of First Instance sitting in plenary session or to a Chamber composed of a different number of Judges. The Court of First Instance sitting in plenary session shall, after hearing the parties and the Advocate-General, decide whether or not to refer a case.

2. The case shall be maintained before or referred to a Chamber composed of five Judges where a Member State or an institution of the European Communities which is a party to the proceedings so requests.

Art. 52   1. Without prejudice to the application of Article 49, the President shall, after the rejoinder has been lodged, fix a date on which the Judge-Rapporteur is to present his preliminary report to the Court of First Instance. The report shall contain recommendations as to whether measures of organisation of procedure or measures of inquiry should be undertaken and whether the case should be referred to the Court of First Instance sitting in plenary session or to a Chamber composed of a different number of Judges.

2. The Court of First Instance shall decide, after hearing the Advocate-General, what action to take upon the recommendations of the Judge-Rapporteur.

The same procedure shall apply:

(a)   where no reply or no rejoinder has been lodged within the time-limit fixed in accordance with Article 47(2);

(b)   where the party concerned waives his right to lodge a reply or rejoinder.

Art. 53   Where the Court of First Instance decides to open the oral procedure without undertaking measures of organisation of procedure or ordering a preparatory inquiry, the President of the Court of First Instance shall fix the opening date.

Art. 54   Without prejudice to any measures of organisation of procedure or measures of inquiry which may be arranged at the stage of the oral procedure, where, during the written procedure, measures of organisation of procedure or measures of inquiry have been instituted and completed, the President shall fix the date for the opening of the oral procedure.

CHAPTER 2 — ORAL PROCEDURE

Art. 55   1. Subject to the priority of decisions provided for in Article 106, the Court of First Instance shall deal with the cases before it in the order in which the preparatory inquiries in them have been completed. Where the preparatory inquiries in several cases are completed simultaneously, the order in which they are to be dealt with shall be determined by the dates of entry in the register of the applications initiating them respectively.

2. The President may in special circumstances order that a case be given priority over others.

The President may in special circumstances, after hearing the parties and the Advocate-General, either on his own initiative or at the request of one of the parties, defer a case to be dealt with at a later date. On a joint application by the parties the President may order that a case be deferred.

Art. 56   The proceedings shall be opened and directed by the President, who shall be responsible for the proper conduct of the hearing.

Art. 57   The oral proceedings in cases heard *in camera* shall not be published.

Art. 58   The President may in the course of the hearing put questions to the agents, advisers or lawyers of the parties.

The other Judges and the Advocate-General may do likewise.

Art. 59   A party may address the Court of First Instance only through his agent, adviser or lawyer.

Art. 60   Where an Advocate-General has not been designated in a case, the President shall declare the oral procedure closed at the end of the hearing.

Art. 61   1. Where the Advocate-General delivers his opinion in writing, he shall lodge it at the Registry, which shall communicate it to the parties.

2. After the delivery, orally or in writing, of the opinion of the Advocate-General the President shall declare the oral procedure closed.

Art. 62   The Court of First Instance may, after hearing the Advocate-General, order the reopening of the oral procedure.

Art. 63   1. The Registrar shall draw up minutes of every hearing. The minutes shall be signed by the President and by the Registrar and shall constitute an official record.

2. The parties may inspect the minutes at the Registry and obtain copies at their own expense.

CHAPTER 3 — MEASURES OF ORGANISATION OF PROCEDURE AND MEASURES OF INQUIRY

Section 1 – Measures of organisation of procedure

Art. 64   1. The purpose of measures of organisation of procedure shall be to ensure that cases are prepared for hearing, procedures carried out and disputes resolved under the best possible conditions. They shall be prescribed by the Court of First Instance, after hearing the Advocate-General.

2. Measures of organisation of procedure shall, in particular, have as their purpose:

(a)   to ensure efficient conduct of the written and oral procedure and to facilitate the taking of evidence;

(b)   to determine the points on which the parties must present further argument or which call for measures of inquiry;

(c) to clarify the forms of order sought by the parties, their pleas in law and arguments and the points at issue between them;

(d) to facilitate the amicable settlement of proceedings.

3. Measures of organisation of procedure may, in particular, consist of:

(a) putting questions to the parties;

(b) inviting the parties to make written or oral submissions on certain aspects of the proceedings;

(c) asking the parties or third parties for information or particulars;

(d) asking for documents or any papers relating to the case to be produced;

(e) summoning the parties' agents or the parties in person to meetings.

4. Each party may, at any stage of the procedure, propose the adoption or modification of measures of organisation of procedure. In that case, the other parties shall be heard before those measures are prescribed.

Where the procedural circumstances so require, the Registrar shall inform the parties of the measures envisaged by the Court of First Instance and shall give them an opportunity to submit comments orally or in writing.

5. If the Court of First Instance sitting in plenary session decides to prescribe measures of organisation of procedure and does not undertake such measures itself, it shall entrust the task of so doing to the Chamber to which the case was originally assigned or to the Judge-Rapporteur.

If a Chamber prescribes measures of organisation of procedure and does not undertake such measures itself, it shall entrust the task to the Judge-Rapporteur.

The Advocate-General shall take part in measures of organisation of procedure.

Section 2 – Measures of inquiry

Art. 65   Without prejudice to Articles 21 and 22 of the EC Statute, Articles 24 and 25 of the ECSC Statute and Articles 22 and 23 of the EAEC Statute, the following measures of inquiry may be adopted:

(a) the personal appearance of the parties;

(b) a request for information and production of documents;

(c) oral testimony;

(d) the commissioning of an expert's report;

(e) an inspection of the place or thing in question.

Art. 66   1. The Court of First Instance, after hearing the Advocate-General, shall prescribe the measures of inquiry that it considers appropriate by means of an order setting out the facts to be proved. Before the Court of First Instance decides on the measures of inquiry referred to in Article 65(c), (d) and (e) the parties shall be heard.

The order shall be served on the parties.

2. Evidence may be submitted in rebuttal and previous evidence may be amplified.

Art. 67   1. Where the Court of First Instance sitting in plenary session orders a preparatory inquiry and does not undertake such an inquiry itself, it shall entrust the task of so doing to the Chamber to which the case was originally assigned or to the Judge-Rapporteur.

Where a Chamber orders a preparatory inquiry and does not undertake such an inquiry itself, it shall entrust the task of so doing to the Judge-Rapporteur.

The Advocate-General shall take part in the measures of inquiry.

2. The parties may be present at the measures of inquiry.

Section 3 – The summoning and examination of witnesses and experts

Art. 68   1. The Court of First Instance may, either of its own motion or on application by a party, and after hearing the Advocate-General and the parties, order that certain facts be proved by witnesses. The order shall set out the facts to be established.

The Court of First Instance may summon a witness of its own motion or on application by a party or at the instance of the Advocate-General.

An application by a party for the examination of a witness shall state precisely about what facts and for what reasons the witness should be examined.

2. The witness shall be summoned by an order containing the following information:

(a) the surname, forenames, description and address of the witness;

(b) an indication of the facts about which the witness is to be examined;

(c) where appropriate, particulars of the arrangements made by the Court of First Instance for reimbursement of expenses incurred by the witness, and of the penalties which may be imposed on defaulting witnesses.

The order shall be served on the parties and the witnesses.

3. The Court of First Instance may make the summoning of a witness for whose examination a party has applied conditional upon the deposit with the cashier of the Court of First Instance of a sum sufficient to cover the taxed costs thereof, the Court of First Instance shall fix the amount of the payment.

The cashier of the Court of First Instance shall advance the funds necessary in connection with the examination of any witness summoned by the Court of First Instance of its own motion.

4. After the identity of the witness has been established, the President shall inform him that he will be required to vouch the truth of his evidence in the manner laid down in paragraph 5 of this Article and in Article 71.

The witness shall give his evidence to the Court of First Instance, the parties having been given notice to attend. After the witness has given his main evidence the President may, at the request of a party or of his own motion, put questions to him.

The other Judges and the Advocate-General may do likewise.

Subject to the control of the President, questions may be put to witnesses by the representatives of the parties.

5. Subject to the provisions of Article 71, the witness shall, after giving his evidence, take the following oath:

'I swear that I have spoken the truth, the whole truth and nothing but the truth.'

The Court of First Instance may, after hearing the parties, exempt a witness from taking the oath.

6. The Registrar shall draw up minutes in which the evidence of each witness is reproduced.

The minutes shall be signed by the President or by the Judge-Rapporteur responsible for conducting the examination of the witness, and by the Registrar. Before the minutes are thus signed, witnesses must be given an opportunity to check the content of the minutes and to sign them.

The minutes shall constitute an official record.

Art. 69   1. Witnesses who have been duly summoned shall obey the summons and attend for examination.

2. If a witness who has been duly summoned fails to appear before the Court of First Instance, the latter may impose upon him a pecuniary penalty not exceeding ECU 5 000 and may order that a further summons be served on the witness at his own expense.

The same penalty may be imposed upon a witness who, without good reason, refuses to give evidence or to take the oath or where appropriate to make a solemn affirmation equivalent thereto.

3. If the witness proffers a valid excuse to the Court of First Instance, the pecuniary penalty imposed on him may be cancelled. The pecuniary penalty imposed may be reduced at the request of the witness where he establishes that it is disproportionate to his income.

4. Penalties imposed and other measures ordered under this Article shall be enforced in accordance with Articles 187 and 192 of the EC Treaty, Articles 44 and 92 of the ECSC Treaty and Articles 159 and 164 of the EAEC Treaty.

Art. 70   1. The Court of First Instance may order that an expert's report be obtained. The order appointing the expert shall define his task and set a time-limit within which he is to make his report.

2. The expert shall receive a copy of the order, together with all the documents necessary for carrying out his task. He shall be under the supervision of the Judge-Rapporteur, who may be present during his investiga-

tion and who shall be kept informed of his progress in carrying out his task.

The Court of First Instance may request the parties or one of them to lodge security for the costs of the expert's report.

3. At the request of the expert, the Court of First Instance may order the examination of witnesses. Their examination shall be carried out in accordance with Article 68.

4. The expert may give his opinion only on points which have been expressly referred to him.

5. After the expert has made his report, the Court of First Instance may order that he be examined, the parties having been given notice to attend.

Subject to the control of the President, questions may be put to the expert by the representatives of the parties.

6. Subject to the provisions of Article 71, the expert shall, after making his report, take the following oath before the Court of First Instance:

'I swear that I have conscientiously and impartially carried out my task.'

The Court of First Instance may, after hearing the parties, exempt the expert from taking the oath.

Art. 71   1. The President shall instruct any person who is required to take an oath before the Court of First Instance, as witness or expert, to tell the truth or to carry out his task conscientiously and impartially, as the case may be, and shall warn him of the criminal liability provided for in his national law in the event of any breach of this duty.

2. Witnesses and experts shall take the oath either in accordance with the first subparagraph of Article 68(5) and the first subparagraph of Article 70(6) or in the manner laid down by their national law.

3. Where the national law provides the opportunity to make, in judicial proceedings, a solemn affirmation equivalent to an oath as well as or instead of taking an oath, the witnesses and experts may make such an affirmation under the conditions and in the form prescribed in their national law.

Where their national law provides neither for taking an oath nor for making a solemn affirmation, the procedure described in the first paragraph of this Article shall be followed.

Art. 72   1. The Court of First Instance may, after hearing the Advocate-General, decide to report to the competent authority referred to in Annex III to the Rules supplementing the Rules of Procedure of the Court of Justice of the Member State whose courts have penal jurisdiction in any case of perjury on the part of a witness or expert before the Court of First Instance, account being taken of the provisions of Article 71.

2. The Registrar shall be responsible for communicating the decision of the Court of First Instance. The decision shall set out the facts and circumstances on which the report is based.

Art. 73   1. If one of the parties objects to a witness or to an expert on the ground that he is not a competent or proper person to act as witness or expert or for any other reason, or if a witness or expert refuses to give evidence, to take the oath or to make a solemn affirmation equivalent thereto, the matter shall be resolved by the Court of First Instance.

2. An objection to a witness or to an expert shall be raised within two weeks after service of the order summoning the witness or appointing the expert; the statement of objection must set out the grounds of objection and indicate the nature of any evidence offered.

Art. 74   1. Witnesses and experts shall be entitled to reimbursement of their travel and subsistence expenses. The cashier of the Court of First Instance may make a payment to them towards these expenses in advance.

2. Witnesses shall be entitled to compensation for loss of earnings, and experts to fees for their services. The cashier of the Court of First Instance shall pay witnesses and experts their compensation or fees after they have carried out their respective duties or tasks.

Art. 75   1. The Court of First Instance may, on application by a party or of its own motion, issue letters rogatory for the examination of witnesses or experts.

2. Letters rogatory shall be issued in the form of an order which shall contain the name, forenames, description and address of the witness or expert, set out the facts on which the witness or expert is to be examined, name the parties, their agents, lawyers or advisers, indicate their addresses for service and briefly describe the subject-matter of the proceedings.

Notice of the order shall be served on the parties by the Registrar.

3. The Registrar shall send the order to the competent authority named in Annex I to the Rules supplementing the Rules of Procedure of the Court of Justice of the Member State in whose territory the witness or expert is to be examined. Where necessary, the order shall be accompanied by a translation into the official language or languages of the Member State to which it is addressed.

The authority named pursuant to the first subparagraph shall pass on the order to the judicial authority which is competent according to its national law.

The competent judicial authority shall give effect to the letters rogatory in accordance with its national law. After implementation the competent judicial authority shall transmit to the authority named pursuant to the first subparagraph the order embodying the letters rogatory, any documents arising from the implementation and a detailed statement of costs. These documents shall be sent to the Registrar.

The Registrar shall be responsible for the translation of the documents into the language of the case.

4. The Court of First Instance shall defray the expenses occasioned by the letters rogatory without prejudice to the right to charge them, where appropriate, to the parties.

Art. 76 1. The Registrar shall draw up minutes of every hearing. The minutes shall be signed by the President and by the Registrar and shall constitute an official record.

2. The parties may inspect the minutes and any expert's report at the Registry and obtain copies at their own expense.

CHAPTER 4 — STAY OF PROCEEDINGS AND DECLINING OF JURISDICTION BY THE COURT OF FIRST INSTANCE

Art. 77 Without prejudice to Article 123(4), Article 128 and Article 129(4), proceedings may be stayed:

(a) in the circumstances specified in the third paragraph of Article 47 of the EC Statute, the third paragraph of Article 47 of the ECSC Statute and the third paragraph of Article 48 of the EAEC Statute;

(b) where an appeal is brought before the Court of Justice against a decision of the Court of First Instance disposing of the substantive issues in part only, disposing of a procedural issue concerning a plea of lack of competence or inadmissibility or dismissing an application to intervene;

(c) at the joint request of the parties.

Art. 78 The decision to stay the proceedings shall be made by order of the President after hearing the parties and the Advocate-General; the President may refer the matter to the Court of First Instance. A decision ordering that the proceedings be resumed shall be adopted in accordance with the same procedure. The orders referred to in this Article shall be served on the parties.

Art. 79 1. The stay of proceedings shall take effect on the date indicated in the order of stay or, in the absence of such an indication, on the date of that order.

While proceedings are stayed time shall, except for the purposes of the time-limit prescribed in Article 115(1) for an application to intervene, cease to run for the purposes of prescribed time-limits for all parties.

2. Where the order of stay does not fix the length of the stay, it shall end on the date indicated in the order of resumption or, in the absence of such indication, on the date of the order of resumption.

From the date of resumption time shall begin to run afresh for the purposes of the time-limits.

Art. 80 Decisions declining jurisdiction in the circumstances specified in the third paragraph of Article 47 of the EC Statute, the third paragraph of Article 47 of the ECSC Statute and the third paragraph of Article 48 of the EAEC Statute shall be made by the Court of First Instance by way of an order which shall be served on the parties.

CHAPTER 5 — JUDGMENTS

Art. 81   The judgment shall contain:

– a statement that it is the judgment of the Court of First Instance,
– the date of its delivery,
– the names of the President and of the Judges taking part in it,
– the name of the Advocate-General, if designated,
– the name of the Registrar,
– the description of the parties,
– the names of the agents, advisers and lawyers of the parties,
– a statement of the forms of order sought by the parties,
– a statement, where appropriate, that the Advocate-General delivered his opinion,
– a summary of the facts,
– the grounds for the decision,
– the operative part of the judgment, including the decision as to costs.

Art. 82   1. The judgment shall be delivered in open court; the parties shall be given notice to attend to hear it.

2. The original of the judgment, signed by the President, by the Judges who took part in the deliberations and by the Registrar, shall be sealed and deposited at the Registry; the parties shall be served with certified copies of the judgment.

3. The Registrar shall record on the original of the judgment the date on which it was delivered.

Art. 83   Subject to the provisions of the second paragraph of Article 53 of the EC Statute, the second paragraph of Article 53 of the ECSC Statute and the second paragraph of Article 54 of the EAEC Statute, the judgment shall be binding from the date of its delivery.

Art. 84   1. Without prejudice to the provisions relating to the interpretation of judgments, the Court of First Instance may, of its own motion or on application by a party made within two weeks after the delivery of a judgment, rectify clerical mistakes, errors in calculation and obvious slips in it.

2. The parties, whom the Registrar shall duly notify, may lodge written observations within a period prescribed by the President.

3. The Court of First Instance shall take its decision in closed session.

4. The original of the rectification order shall be annexed to the original of the rectified judgment. A note of this order shall be made in the margin of the original of the rectified judgment.

Art. 85   If the Court of First Instance should omit to give a decision on costs, any party may within a month after service of the judgment apply to the Court of First Instance to supplement its judgment.

The application shall be served on the opposite party and the President shall prescribe a period within which that party may lodge written observations.

After these observations have been lodged, the Court of First Instance shall decide both on the admissibility and on the substance of the application.

Art. 86   The Registrar shall arrange for the publication of cases before the Court of First Instance.

CHAPTER 6 — COSTS

Art. 87   1. A decision as to costs shall be given in the final judgment or in the order which closes the proceedings.

2. The unsuccessful party shall be ordered to pay the costs if they have been applied for in the successful party's pleadings.

Where there are several unsuccessful parties the Court of First Instance shall decide how the costs are to be shared.

3. Where each party succeeds on some and fails on other heads, or where the circumstances are exceptional, the Court of First Instance may order that the costs be shared or that each party bear its own costs.

The Court of First Instance may order a party, even if successful, to pay costs which it considers that party to have unreasonably or vexatiously caused the opposite party to incur.

4. The Member States and institutions which intervened in the proceedings shall bear their own costs.

The States, other than the Member States, which are parties to the EEA Agreement, and also the EFTA Surveillance Authority, shall bear their own costs if they intervene in the proceedings.

The Court of First Instance may order an intervener other than those mentioned in the preceding subparagraph to bear his own costs.

5. A party who discontinues or withdraws from proceedings shall be ordered to pay the costs if they have been applied for in the observations of the other party on the discontinuance. However, upon application by the party who discontinues or withdraws from proceedings, the costs shall be borne by the other party if this appears justified by the conduct of that party.

Where the parties have come to an agreement on costs, the decision as to costs shall be in accordance with that agreement.

If costs are not claimed in the written pleadings, the parties shall bear their own costs.

6. Where a case does not proceed to judgment, the costs shall be in the discretion of the Court of First Instance.

Art. 88 Without prejudice to the second subparagraph of Article 87(3), in proceedings between the Communities and their servants the institutions shall bear their own costs.

Art. 89 Costs necessarily incurred by a party in enforcing a judgment or order of the Court of First Instance shall be refunded by the opposite party on the scale in force in the State where the enforcement takes place.

Art. 90 Proceedings before the Court of First Instance shall be free of charge, except that:

(a) where a party has caused the Court of First Instance to incur avoidable costs, the Court of First Instance may order that party to refund them;

(b) where copying or translation work is carried out at the request of a party, the cost shall, in so far as the Registrar considers it excessive, be paid for by that party on the scale of charges referred to in Article 24(5).

Art. 91 Without prejudice to the preceding Article, the following shall be regarded as recoverable costs:

(a) sums payable to witnesses and experts under Article 74;

(b) expenses necessarily incurred by the parties for the purpose of the proceedings, in particular the travel and subsistence expenses and the remuneration of agents, advisers or lawyers.

Art. 92 1. If there is a dispute concerning the costs to be recovered, the Court of First Instance hearing the case shall, on application by the party concerned and after hearing the opposite party, make an order, from which no appeal shall lie.

2. The parties may, for the purposes of enforcement, apply for an authenticated copy of the order.

Art. 93 1. Sums due from the cashier of the Court of First Instance shall be paid in the currency of the country where the Court of First Instance has its seat.

At the request of the person entitled to any sum, it shall be paid in the currency of the country where the expenses to be refunded were incurred or where the steps in respect of which payment is due were taken.

2. Other debtors shall make payment in the currency of their country of origin.

3. Conversions of currency shall be made at the official rates of exchange ruling on the day of payment in the country where the Court of First Instance has its seat.

CHAPTER 7 — LEGAL AID

Art. 94 1. A party who is wholly or in part unable to meet the costs of the proceedings may at any time apply for legal aid.

The application shall be accompanied by evidence of the applicant's need of assistance, and in particular by a document from the competent authority certifying his lack of means.

2. If the application is made prior to proceedings which the applicant wishes to commence, it shall briefly state the subject of such proceedings.

The application need not be made through a lawyer.

The President shall, after considering the written observations of the opposite party, decide whether legal aid should be granted in full or in part, or whether it should be refused. He shall consider whether there is manifestly no cause of action. He may refer the matter to the Court of First Instance.

The decision shall be taken by way of an order without giving reasons, and no appeal shall lie therefrom.

Art. 95   1. The Court of First Instance, by any order by which it decides that a person is entitled to receive legal aid, shall order that a lawyer be appointed to act for him.

2. If the person does not indicate his choice of lawyer, or if the Court of First Instance considers that his choice is unacceptable, the Registrar shall send a copy of the order and of the application for legal aid to the authority named in Annex II to the Rules supplementing the Rules of Procedure of the Court of Justice, being the competent authority of the State concerned.

3. The Court of First Instance, in the light of the suggestions made by that authority, shall of its own motion appoint a lawyer to act for the person concerned.

4. An order granting legal aid may specify an amount to be paid to the lawyer appointed to act for the person concerned or fix a limit which the lawyer's disbursements and fees may not, in principle, exceed.

Art. 96   The Court of First Instance may at any time, either of its own motion or on application, withdraw legal aid if the circumstances which led to its being granted alter during the proceedings.

Art. 97   1. Where legal aid is granted, the cashier of the Court of First Instance shall advance the funds necessary to meet the expenses.

2. The President, who may refer the matter to the Court of First Instance, shall adjudicate on the lawyer's disbursements and fees; he may, on application by the lawyer, order that he receive an advance.

3. In its decision as to costs the Court of First Instance may order the payment to the cashier of the Court of First Instance of the whole or any part of amounts advanced as legal aid.

The Registrar shall take steps to obtain the recovery of these sums from the party ordered to pay them.

CHAPTER 8 — DISCONTINUANCE

Art. 98   If, before the Court of First Instance has given its decision, the parties reach a settlement of their dispute and intimate to the Court of First Instance the abandonment of their claims, the President shall order the case to be removed from the register and shall give a decision as to costs in accordance with Article 87(5) having regard to any proposals made by the parties on the matter.

This provision shall not apply to proceedings under Articles 173 and 175 of the EC Treaty, Articles 33 and 35 of the ECSC Treaty and Articles 146 and 148 of the EAEC Treaty.

Art. 99   If the applicant informs the Court of First Instance in writing that he wishes to discontinue the proceedings, the President shall order the case to be removed from the register and shall give a decision as to costs in accordance with Article 87(5).

CHAPTER 9 — SERVICE

Art. 100   Where these Rules require that a document be served on a person, the Registrar shall ensure that service is effected at that person's address for service either by the dispatch of a copy of the document by registered post with a form for acknowledgement of receipt or by personal delivery of the copy against a receipt.

The Registrar shall prepare and certify the copies of documents to be served, save where the parties themselves supply the copies in accordance with Article 43(1).

CHAPTER 10 — TIME-LIMITS

Art. 101   1. Any period of time prescribed by the EC, ECSC and EAEC Treaties, the Statutes of the Court of Justice or these Rules for the taking of any procedural step shall be reckoned as follows:

(a)   Where a period expressed in days, weeks, months or years is to be calculated from the moment at which an event occurs or an action takes place, the day during which that event occurs or that action takes place shall not be counted as falling within the period in question;

(b)   A period expressed in weeks, months or in years shall end with the expiry of whichever day in the last week, month or year is the same day of the week, or falls on the same date, as the day during which the event or action from which the period is to be calculated occurred or took place. If, in a period expressed in months or in years, the day on which it should expire does not occur in the last month, the period shall end with the expiry of the last day of that month;

(c)   Where a period is expressed in months and days, it shall first be reckoned in whole months, then in days;

(d)   Periods shall include official holidays, Sundays and Saturdays;

(e)   Periods shall not be suspended during the judicial vacations.

2. If the period would otherwise end on a Saturday, Sunday or official holiday, it shall be extended until the end of the first following working day.

The list of official holidays drawn up by the Court of Justice and published in the *Official Journal of the European Communities* shall apply to the Court of First Instance.

Art. 102   1. Where the period of time allowed for commencing proceedings against a measure adopted by an institution runs from the publication of that measure, that period shall be calculated, for the purposes of Article 101 (1), from the end of the 14th day after publication thereof in the *Official Journal of the European Communities*.

2. The extensions, on account of distance, of prescribed time-limits provided for in a decision of the Court of Justice and published in the *Official Journal of the European Communities* shall apply to the Court of First Instance.

Art. 103   1. Any time-limit prescribed pursuant to these Rules may be extended by whoever prescribed it.

2. The President may delegate power of signature to the Registrar for the purpose of fixing time-limits which, pursuant to these Rules, it falls to the President to prescribe, or of extending such time-limits.

TITLE 3 — SPECIAL FORMS OF PROCEDURE

CHAPTER 1 — SUSPENSION OF OPERATION OR ENFORCEMENT AND OTHER INTERIM MEASURES

Art. 104   1. An application to suspend the operation of any measure adopted by an institution, made pursuant to the second paragraph of Article 185 of the EC Treaty, the second paragraph of Article 39 of the ECSC Treaty and Article 157 of the EAEC Treaty, shall be admissible only if the applicant is challenging that measure in proceedings before the Court of First Instance.

An application for the adoption of any other interim measure referred to in the third paragraph of Article 186 of the EC Treaty, the third paragraph of Article 39 of the ECSC Treaty and Article 158 of the EAEC Treaty shall be admissible only if it is made by a party to a case before the Court of First Instance and relates to that case.

2. An application of a kind referred to in paragraph 1 of this Article shall state the subject-matter of the proceedings, the circumstances giving rise to urgency and the pleas of fact and law establishing a prima facie case for the interim measures applied for.

3. The application shall be made by a separate document and in accordance with the provisions of Articles 43 and 44.

Art. 105   1. The application shall be served on the opposite party, and the President of the Court of First Instance shall prescribe a short period within which that party may submit written or oral observations.

2. The President of the Court of First Instance may order a preparatory inquiry.

The President of the Court of First Instance may grant the application even before the observations of the opposite party have been submitted. This decision may be varied or cancelled even without any application being made by any party.

Art. 106   The President of the Court of First Instance shall either decide on the application himself or refer it to the Chamber to which the case has been assigned in the main proceedings or to the Court of First Instance sitting in plenary session if the case has been assigned to it.

If the President of the Court of First Instance is absent or prevented from attending, he shall be replaced by the President or the most senior Judge, within the meaning of Article 6, of the bench of the Court of First Instance to which the case has been assigned.

Where the application is referred to a bench of the Court of First Instance, that bench shall postpone all other cases and shall give a decision. Article 105 shall apply.

Art. 107   1. The decision on the application shall take the form of a reasoned order. The order shall be served on the parties forthwith.

2. The enforcement of the order may be made conditional on the lodging by the applicant of security, of an amount and nature to be fixed in the light of the circumstances.

3. Unless the order fixes the date on which the interim measure is to lapse, the measure shall lapse when final judgment is delivered.

4. The order shall have only an interim effect, and shall be without prejudice to the decision on the substance of the case by the Court of First Instance.

Art. 108   On application by a party, the order may at any time be varied or cancelled on account of a change in circumstances.

Art. 109   Rejection of an application for an interim measure shall not bar the party who made it from making a further application on the basis of new facts.

Art. 110   The provisions of this Chapter shall apply to applications to suspend the enforcement of a decision of the Court of First Instance or of any measure adopted by another institution, submitted pursuant to Articles 187 and 192 of the EC Treaty, Articles 44 and 92 of the ECSC Treaty and Articles 159 and 164 of the EAEC Treaty.

The order granting the application shall fix, where appropriate, a date on which the interim measure is to lapse.

Chapter 2 — Preliminary Issues

Art. 111 Where it is clear that the Court of First Instance has no jurisdiction to take cognisance of an action or where the action is manifestly inadmissible or manifestly lacking any foundation in law, the Court of First Instance may, by reasoned order, after hearing the Advocate-General and without taking further steps in the proceedings, give a decision on the action.

Art. 112 The decision to refer an action to the Court of Justice, pursuant to the second paragraph of Article 47 of the EC Statute, the second paragraph of Article 47 of the ECSC Statute and the second paragraph of Article 48 of the EAEC Statute, shall, in the case of manifest lack of competence, be made by reasoned order and without taking any further steps in the proceedings.

Art. 113 The Court of First Instance may at any time, of its own motion, consider whether there exists any absolute bar to proceeding with an action or declare, after hearing the parties, that the action has become devoid of purpose and that there is no need to adjudicate on it; it shall give its decision in accordance with Article 114(3) and (4).

Art. 114 1. A party applying to the Court of First Instance for a decision on admissibility, on lack of competence or other preliminary plea not going to the substance of the case shall make the application by a separate document.

The application must contain the pleas of fact and law relied on and the form of order sought by the applicant; any supporting documents must be annexed to it.

2. As soon as the application has been lodged, the President shall prescribe a period within which the opposite party may lodge a document containing a statement of the form of order sought by that party and its pleas in law.

3. Unless the Court of First Instance otherwise decides, the remainder of the proceedings shall be oral.

4. The Court of First Instance shall, after hearing the Advocate-General, decide on the application or reserve its decision for the final judgment. It shall refer the case to the Court of Justice if the case falls within the jurisdiction of that Court.

If the Court of First Instance refuses the application or reserves its decision, the President shall prescribe new time-limits for further steps in the proceedings.

Chapter 3 — Intervention

Art. 115 1. An application to intervene must be made within three months of the publication of the notice referred to in Article 24(6).

2. The application shall contain:

(a) the description of the case;

(b) the description of the parties;

(c) the name and address of the intervener;

(d) the intervener's address for service at the place where the Court of First Instance has its seat;

(e) the form of order sought, by one or more of the parties, in support of which the intervener is applying for leave to intervene;

(f) a statement of the circumstances establishing the right to intervene, where the application is submitted pursuant to the second or third paragraph of Article 37 of the EC Statute, Article 34 of the ECSC Statute or the second paragraph of Article 38 of the EAEC Statute.

Articles 43 and 44 shall apply.

3. The intervener shall be represented in accordance with Article 17 of the EC Statute, the first and second paragraphs of Article 20 of the ECSC Statute and Article 17 of the EAEC Statute.

Art. 116 1. The application shall be served on the parties.

The President shall give the parties an opportunity to submit their written or oral observations before deciding on the application.

The President shall decide on the application by order or shall refer the decision to the Court of First Instance. The order must be reasoned if the application is dismissed.

2. If the President allows the intervention, the intervener shall receive a copy of every document served on the parties. The President may, however, on application by one of the parties, omit secret or confidential documents.

3. The intervener must accept the case as he finds it at the time of his intervention.

4. The President shall prescribe a period within which the intervener may submit a statement in intervention.

The statement in intervention shall contain:

(a) a statement of the form of order sought by the intervener in support of or opposing, in whole or in part, the form of order sought by one of the parties;

(b) the pleas in law and arguments relied on by the intervener;

(c) where appropriate, the nature of any evidence offered.

5. After the statement in intervention has been lodged, the President shall, where necessary, prescribe a time-limit within which the parties may reply to that statement.

CHAPTER 4 — JUDGMENTS OF THE COURT OF FIRST INSTANCE
DELIVERED AFTER ITS DECISION HAS BEEN SET ASIDE AND THE CASE
REFERRED BACK TO IT

Art. 117   Where the Court of Justice sets aside a judgment or an order of the Court
of First Instance and refers the case back to that Court, the latter shall be
seised of the case by the judgment so referring it.

Art. 118   1. Where the Court of Justice sets aside a judgment or an order of a
Chamber, the President of the Court of First Instance may assign the case
to another Chamber composed of the same number of Judges.

2. Where the Court of Justice sets aside a judgment delivered or an order
made by the Court of First Instance sitting in plenary session, the case
shall be assigned to that Court as so constituted.

3. In the cases provided for in paragraphs 1 and 2 of this Article, Articles
13(2), 14 and 51 shall apply.

Art. 119   1. Where the written procedure before the Court of First Instance has
been completed when the judgment referring the case back to it is delivered, the course of the procedure shall be as follows:

(a) Within two months from the service upon him of the judgment of the
     Court of Justice the applicant may lodge a statement of written ob-
     servations;

(b) In the month following the communication to him of that statement,
     the defendant may lodge a statement of written observations. The
     time allowed to the defendant for lodging it may in no case be less
     than two months from the service upon him of the judgment of the
     Court of Justice;

(c) In the month following the simultaneous communication to the in-
     tervener of the observations of the applicant and the defendant, the
     intervener may lodge a statement of written observations. The time
     allowed to the intervener for lodging it may in no case be less than
     two months from the service upon him of the judgment of the Court
     of Justice.

2. Where the written procedure before the Court of First Instance had not
been completed when the judgment referring the case back to the Court of
First Instance was delivered, it shall be resumed, at the stage which it had
reached, by means of measures of organisation of procedure adopted by
the Court of First Instance.

3. The Court of First Instance may, if the circumstances so justify, allow
supplementary statements of written observations to be lodged.

Art. 120   The procedure shall be conducted in accordance with the provisions of
Title II of these Rules.

Art. 121   The Court of First Instance shall decide on the costs relating to the proceedings instituted before it and to the proceedings on the appeal before
the Court of Justice.

CHAPTER 5 — JUDGMENTS BY DEFAULT AND APPLICATIONS TO SET
THEM ASIDE

Art. 122   1. If a defendant on whom an application initiating proceedings has been
duly served fails to lodge a defence to the application in the proper form
within the time prescribed, the applicant may apply to the Court of First
Instance for judgment by default.

The application shall be served on the defendant. The Court of First Instance may decide to open the oral procedure on the application.

2. Before giving judgment by default the Court of First Instance shall consider whether the application initiating proceedings is admissible, whether
the appropriate formalities have been complied with, and whether the application appears well founded. It may order a preparatory inquiry.

3. A judgment by default shall be enforceable. The Court of First Instance
may, however, grant a stay of execution until it has given its decision on
any application under paragraph 4 of this Article to set aside the judgment, or it may make execution subject to the provision of security of an
amount and nature to be fixed in the light of the circumstances; this security shall be released if no such application is made or if the application
fails.

4. Application may be made to set aside a judgment by default.

The application to set aside the judgment must be made within one month
from the date of service of the judgment and must be lodged in the form
prescribed by Articles 43 and 44.

5. After the application has been served, the President shall prescribe a period within which the other party may submit his written observations.

The proceedings shall be conducted in accordance with the provisions of
Title II of these Rules.

6. The Court of First Instance shall decide by way of a judgment which
may not be set aside. The original of this judgment shall be annexed to the
original of the judgment by default. A note of the judgment on the application to set aside shall be made in the margin of the original of the judgment by default.

CHAPTER 6 — EXCEPTIONAL REVIEW PROCEDURES

Section 1 – Third-party proceedings

Art. 123   1. Articles 43 and 44 shall apply to an application initiating third-party
proceedings. In addition such an application shall:

(a)   specify the judgment contested;

(b)   state how that judgment is prejudicial to the rights of the third party;

(c)   indicate the reasons for which the third party was unable to take part
in the original case before the Court of First Instance.

The application must be made against all the parties to the original case.

Where the judgment has been published in the *Official Journal of the European Communities*, the application must be lodged within two months of the publication.

2. The Court of First Instance may, on application by the third party, order a stay of execution of the judgment. The provisions of Title III Chapter 1, shall apply.

3. The contested judgment shall be varied on the points on which the submissions of the third party are upheld.

The original of the judgment in the third-party proceedings shall be annexed to the original of the contested judgment. A note of the judgment in the third-party proceedings shall be made in the margin of the original of the contested judgment.

4. Where an appeal before the Court of Justice and an application initiating third-party proceedings before the Court of First Instance contest the same judgment of the Court of First Instance, the Court of First Instance may, after hearing the parties, stay the proceedings until the Court of Justice has delivered its judgment.

Art. 124 The application initiating third-party proceedings shall be assigned to the Chamber which delivered the judgment which is the subject of the application; if the Court of First Instance sitting in plenary session delivered the judgment, the application shall be assigned to it.

Section 2 – Revision

Art. 125 Without prejudice to the period of ten years prescribed in the third paragraph of Article 41 of the EC Statute, the third paragraph of Article 38 of the ECSC Statute and the third paragraph of Article 42 of the EAEC Statute, an application for revision of a judgment shall be made within three months of the date on which the facts on which the application is based came to the applicant's knowledge.

Art. 126 1. Articles 43 and 44 shall apply to an application for revision. In addition such an application shall:

(a) specify the judgment contested;

(b) indicate the points on which the application is based;

(c) set out the facts on which the application is based;

(d) indicate the nature of the evidence to show that there are facts justifying revision of the judgment, and that the time-limits laid down in Article 125 have been observed.

2. The application must be made against all parties to the case in which the contested judgment was given.

Art. 127 1. The application for revision shall be assigned to the Chamber which delivered the judgment which is the subject of the application; if the Court of First Instance sitting in plenary session delivered the judgment, the application shall be assigned to it.

2. Without prejudice to its decision on the substance, the Court of First Instance shall, after hearing the Advocate-General, having regard to the written observations of the parties, give its decision on the admissibility of the application.

3. If the Court of First Instance finds the application admissible, it shall proceed to consider the substance of the application and shall give its decision in the form of a judgment in accordance with these Rules.

4. The original of the revising judgment shall be annexed to the original of the judgment revised. A note of the revising judgment shall be made in the margin of the original of the judgment revised.

Art. 128   Where an appeal before the Court of Justice and an application for revision before the Court of First Instance concern the same judgment of the Court of First Instance, the Court of First Instance may, after hearing the parties, stay the proceedings until the Court of Justice has delivered its judgment.

Section 3 – Interpretation of judgments

Art. 129   1. An application for interpretation of a judgment shall be made in accordance with Articles 43 and 44. In addition it shall specify:

(a)   the judgment in question;

(b)   the passages of which interpretation is sought.

The application must be made against all the parties to the case in which the judgment was given.

2. The application for interpretation shall be assigned to the Chamber which delivered the judgment which is the subject of the application; if the Court of First Instance sitting in plenary session delivered the judgment, the application shall be assigned to it.

3. The Court of First Instance shall give its decision in the form of a judgment after having given the parties an opportunity to submit their observations and after hearing the Advocate-General.

The original of the interpreting judgment shall be annexed to the original of the judgment interpreted. A note of the interpreting judgment shall be made in the margin of the original of the judgment interpreted.

4. Where an appeal before the Court of Justice and an application for interpretation before the Court of First Instance concern the same judgment of the Court of First Instance, the Court of First Instance may, after hearing the parties, stay the proceedings until the Court of Justice has delivered its judgment.

TITLE IV — PROCEEDINGS RELATING TO INTELLECTUAL PROPERTY RIGHTS

Art. 130   1. Subject to the special provisions of this Title, the provisions of these Rules of Procedure shall apply to proceedings brought against the Office for Harmonisation in the Internal Market (Trade Marks and Designs) and against the Community Plant Variety Office, (both hereinafter referred to as 'the Office'), and concerning the application of the rules relating to an intellectual property regime.

2. The provisions of this Title shall not apply to actions brought directly against the Office without prior proceedings before a Board of Appeal.

Art. 131   1. The application shall be drafted in one of the languages described in Article 35(1), according to the applicant's choice.

2. The language in which the application is drafted shall become the language of the case if the applicant was the only party to the proceedings before the Board of Appeal or if another party to those proceedings does not object to this within a period laid down for that purpose by the Registrar after the application has been lodged.

If, within that period, the parties to the proceedings before the Board of Appeal inform the Registrar of their agreement on the choice, as the language of the case, of one of the languages referred to in Article 35(1), that language shall become the language of the case before the Court of First Instance.

In the event of an objection to the choice of the language of the case made by the applicant within the period referred to above and in the absence of an agreement on the matter between the parties to the proceedings before the Board of Appeal, the language in which the application for registration in question was filed at the Office shall become the language of the case. If, however, on a reasoned request by any party and after hearing the other parties, the President finds that the use of that language would not enable all parties to the proceedings before the Board of Appeal to follow the proceedings and defend their interests and that only the use of another language from among those mentioned in Article 35(1) makes it possible to remedy that situation, he may designate that other language as the language of the case; the President may refer the matter to the Court of First Instance.

3. In the pleadings and other documents addressed to the Court of First Instance and during the oral procedure, the applicant may use the language chosen by him in accordance with paragraph 1 and each of the other parties may use a language chosen by that party from those mentioned in Article 35(1).

4. If, by virtue of paragraph 2, a language other than that in which the application is drafted becomes the language of the case, the Registrar shall cause the application to be translated into the language of the case.

Each party shall be required, within a reasonable period to be prescribed for that purpose by the Registrar, to produce a translation into the language of the case of the pleadings or documents other than the application that are lodged by that party in a language other than the language of the case pursuant to paragraph 3. The party producing the translation, which shall be authentic within the meaning of Article 37, shall certify its accuracy. If the translation is not produced within the period prescribed, the pleading or the procedural document in question shall be removed from the file.

The Registrar shall cause everything said during the oral procedure to be translated into the language of the case and, at the request of any party, into the language used by that party in accordance with paragraph 3.

Art. 132　1. Without prejudice to Article 44, the application shall contain the names of all the parties to the proceedings before the Board of Appeal and the addresses which they had given for the purposes of the notifications to be effected in the course of those proceedings.

The contested decision of the Board of Appeal shall be appended to the application. The date on which the applicant was notified of that decision must be indicated.

2. If the application does not comply with paragraph 1, Article 44(6) shall apply.

Art. 133　1. The Registrar shall inform the Office and all the parties to the proceedings before the Board of Appeal of the lodging of the application. He shall arrange for service of the application after determining the language of the case in accordance with Article 131(2).

2. The application shall be served on the Office, as defendant, and on the parties to the proceedings before the Board of Appeal other than the applicant. Service shall be effected in the language of the case.

Service of the application on a party to the proceedings before the Board of Appeal shall be effected by registered post with a form of acknowledgment of receipt at the address given by the party concerned for the purposes of the notifications to be effected in the course of the proceedings before the Board of Appeal.

3. Once the application has been served, the Office shall forward to the Court of First Instance the File relating to the proceedings before the Board of Appeal.

Art. 134　1. The parties to the proceedings before the Board of Appeal other than the applicant may participate, as interveners, in the proceedings before the Court of First Instance.

2. The interveners referred to in paragraph 1 shall have the same procedural rights as the main parties.

They may support the form of order sought by a main party and they may apply for a form of order and put forward pleas in law independently of those applied for and put forward by the main parties.

3. An intervener, as referred to in paragraph 1, may, in his response lodged in accordance with Article 135(1), seek an order annulling or altering the

decision of the Board of Appeal on a point not raised in the application and put forward pleas in law not raised in the application.

Such submissions seeking orders or putting forward pleas in law in the intervener's response shall cease to have effect should the applicant discontinue the proceedings.

4. In derogation from Article 122, the default procedure shall not apply where an intervener, as referred to in paragraph 1 of this Article, has responded to the application in the manner and within the period prescribed.

Art. 135 1. The Office and the interveners referred to in Article 134(1) may submit responses to the application within a period of two months from the service of the application.

Article 46 shall apply to the responses.

2. The application and the responses may be supplemented by replies and rejoinders by the parties, including the interveners referred to in Article 134(1), where the President, on a reasoned application made within two weeks of service of the responses or replies, considers such further pleading necessary and allows it in order to enable the party concerned to put forward its point of view.

The President shall prescribe the period within which such pleadings are to be submitted.

3. Without prejudice to the foregoing, in the cases referred to in Article 134(3), the other parties may, within a period of two months of service upon them of the response, submit a pleading confined to responding to the form of order sought and the pleas in law submitted for the first time in the response of an intervener. That period may be extended by the President on a reasoned application from the party concerned.

4. The parties' pleadings may not change the subject-matter of the proceedings before the Board of Appeal.

Art. 136 1. Where an action against a decision of a Board of Appeal is successful, the Court of First Instance may order the Office to bear only its own costs.

2. Costs necessarily incurred by the parties for the purposes of the proceedings before the Board of Appeal and costs incurred for the purposes of the production, prescribed by the second subparagraph of Article 131(4), of translations of pleadings or other documents into the language of the case shall be regarded as recoverable costs.

In the event of inaccurate translations being produced, the second subparagraph of Article 87(3) shall apply.

FINAL PROVISIONS

Art. 137 These Rules, which are authentic in the languages mentioned in Article 35(1), shall be published in the *Official Journal of the European Commu-*

nities. They shall enter into force on the first day of the second month from the date of their publication.

ii) Amendments to the Rules of Procedure of the Court of First Instance to enable it to give decisions in cases when constituted by a single judge[1]

1) Article 11 shall be amended as follows:

(a) in paragraph (1) the following subparagraph shall be added:

'Cases may be heard by a single Judge where they are delegated to him under the conditions specified in Articles 14 and 51 or assigned to him pursuant to Article 124, Article 127(1) or Article 129(2).';

(b) in paragraph (2) the following sentence shall be added:

'In cases delegated or assigned to a single Judge the term "Court of First Instance" used in these Rules shall also designate that Judge.';

2) Article 14 shall be amended as follows:

(a) the first paragraph shall become paragraph (1) and the second paragraph shall be deleted;

(b) the following paragraphs shall be added:

'2. (1) The following cases, assigned to a Chamber composed of three Judges, may be heard and determined by the Judge-Rapporteur sitting as a single Judge where, having regard to the lack of difficulty of the questions of law or fact raised, to the limited importance of the case and to the absence of other special circumstances, they are suitable for being so heard and determined and have been delegated under the conditions laid down in Article 51:

a) cases brought pursuant to Article 179 of the EC Treaty or Article 152 of the EAEC Treaty;

(b) cases brought pursuant to the fourth paragraph of Article 173, the third paragraph of Article 175 and Article 178 of the EC Treaty, to the second paragraph of Article 33, Article 35 and the first and second paragraphs of Article 40 of the ECSC Treaty and to the fourth paragraph of Article 146, the third paragraph of Article 148 and Article 151 of the EAEC Treaty that raise only questions already clarified by established case-[hyphen]law or that form part of a series of cases in which the same relief is sought and of which one has already been finally decided;

(c) cases brought pursuant to Article 181 of the EC Treaty, Article 42 of the ECSC Treaty and Article 153 of the EAEC Treaty.

(2) Delegation to a single judge shall not be possible:

(a) in cases which raise issues as to the legality of an act of general application;

(b) in cases concerning the implementation of the rules:

---

[1] OJ L 135 of 29.5.1999.

–   on competition and on control of concentrations,

–   relating to aid granted by States,

–   relating to measures to protect trade,

–   relating to the common organisation of the agricultural markets, with the exception of cases that form part of a series of cases in which the same relief is sought and where one of those cases has already been finally decided;

(c) in the cases referred to in Article 130(1).

(3) The single judge shall refer the case back to the Chamber if he finds that the conditions justifying delegation of the case are no longer satisfied.

3. The decisions to refer or to delegate a case which are provided for in paragraphs (1) and (2) shall be taken under the conditions laid down in Article 51.';

3) in Article 16 the following subparagraph shall be added:

'In cases assigned or delegated to a single Judge the powers of the President, with the exception of those referred to in Articles 105 and 106, shall be exercised by that Judge.';

4) in Article 32 the following paragraph shall be added:

5. 'If the single Judge to whom the case has been delegated or assigned is absent or prevented from attending, the President of the Court of First Instance shall designate another Judge to replace that Judge.';

5) Article 51 shall be replaced by the following:

'Art. 51   1. In the cases specified in Article 14(1), and at any stage in the proceedings, the Chamber hearing the case may, either on its own initiative or at the request of one of the parties, propose to the Court of First Instance sitting in plenary session that the case be referred to the Court of First Instance sitting in plenary session or to a Chamber composed of a different number of Judges. The Court of First Instance sitting in plenary session shall, after hearing the parties and the Advocate General, decide whether or not to refer a case.

The case shall be maintained before or referred to a Chamber composed of five Judges where a Member State or an institution of the European Communities which is a party to the proceedings so requests.

2. The decision to delegate a case to a single Judge in the situations set out in Article 14(2) shall be taken, after the parties have been heard, unanimously by the Chamber composed of three Judges before which the case is pending.

Where a Member State or an institution of the European Communities which is a party to the proceedings objects to the case being heard by a single judge the case shall be maintained before or referred to the Chamber to which the Judge-[hyphen]-Rapporteur belongs.';

6) Article 118 shall be amended as follows:

(a) the following paragraph shall be inserted:

'2a. Where the Court of Justice sets aside a judgement delivered or an order made by a single Judge, the President of the Court of First Instance shall assign the case to a Chamber composed of three Judges of which that Judge is not a member.';

(b) in paragraph (3) the words 'paragraphs (1) and (2) of this Article, Articles 13(2), 14' shall be replaced by the words 'paragraphs (1), (2) and (2a) of this Article, Articles 13(2), 14(1)';

7) in Article 124 the following sentence shall be added:

'If the judgment has been delivered by a single Judge, the application initiating third-[hyphen]-party proceedings shall be assigned to that Judge.';

8) in Article 127(1) the following sentence shall be added:

'If the judgment has been delivered by a single Judge, the application for revision shall be assigned to that Judge.';

9) in Article 129(2) the following sentence shall be added:

'If the judgment has been delivered by a single Judge, the application for interpretation shall be assigned to that Judge.'.

b) Court of Justice of the European Free Trade Association (EFTA Court)

The European Economic Area (EEA) was created by the European Community on the one side and the remaining member States of the European Free Trade Association with the exception of Switzerland, i.e. Iceland, Liechtenstein and Norway. The aim of the EEA Agreement is to guarantee the free movement of persons, goods, services and capital; to provide equal conditions of competition and to abolish discrimination on grounds of nationality in all 18 EEA States.

In order to guarantee the implementation and application of the common rules of the EEA States which are not members of the European Union and which are therefore not subject to the jurisdiction of the European Court of Justice, an EFTA Surveillance Authority (ESA) and an EFTA Court were created. While the ESA has been given powers corresponding to those of the Commission in the exercise of its surveillance role, the EFTA Court operates in parallel to the Court of Justice of the European.

The EFTA Court has jurisdiction with regard to EFTA States which are parties to the EEA Agreement (at present Iceland, Liechtenstein and Norway) and is competent to deal with infringement actions brought by the EFTA Surveillance Authority against an EFTA State with regard to the implementation, application or interpretation of an EEA rule (Art. 31 Agreement on the Establishment of a Surveillance Authority and a Court of Justice), for the settlement of disputes between two or more EFTA States (Art. 32 Agreement on the Establishment of a Surveillance Authority and a Court of Justice), for appeals concerning decisions taken by the EFTA Surveillance Authority (Art. 31 Agreement on the Establishment of a Surveillance Authority and a Court of Justice), and for giving advisory opinions to courts in EFTA States on the interpretation of EEA rules (Art. 34 Agreement on the Establishment of a Surveillance Authority and a Court of Justice). Thus the jurisdiction of the EFTA Court mainly corresponds to the jurisdiction of the Court of Justice of the European Communities over EC States.

The EFTA Court consists of three Judges, one nominated by each of the EFTA States party to the EEA Agreement. The Judges are appointed by common accord of the Governments for a period of six years and elect their President for a term of three years.

The procedure followed by the Court is laid down in the Statute of the EFTA Court and in its Rules of Procedure.

Texts

EFTA Court Texts (1996) (English)

Bibliographical notes

C. Hausen, Das grundsätzliche Verhältnis der Rechtsprechung von EuGH und EFTA-Gerichtshof: Ein Überblick am Beispiel der Vereinbarkeit des norwegischen Einzelhandelsmonopols für Alkohol mit dem EWR-Abkommen, RIW 1998, pp. 842-849

O. Jacot-Guillarmod (éd.), Accord EEE: commentaires et réflexions (1992)

V. Kronenberger, Does the EFTA Court interpret the EEA Agreement as if it were the EC Treaty? Some questions raised by the Restamark judgment, ICLQ 1996, pp. 198-212

R. Zäch (ed.), Das Abkommen über den Europäischen Wirtschaftsraum: eine Orientierung (1992)

Collections of cases

Annual Report of the EFTA Court (includes the Reports of Cases decided by the Court) (English)

aa) Agreement on the European Economic Area of May 2, 1992

CHAPTER 3 — HOMOGENEITY, SURVEILLANCE PROCEDURE AND
SETTLEMENT OF DISPUTES

Section 1 — Homogeneity

Art. 105   1. In order to achieve the objective of the Contracting Parties to arrive at
as uniform an interpretation as possible of the provisions of the Agreement and those provisions of Community legislation which are substantially reproduced in the Agreement, the EEA Joint Committee shall act in
accordance with this Article.

2. The EEA Joint Committee shall keep under constant review the development of the case law of the Court of Justice of the European Communities and the EFTA Court. To this end judgments of these Courts shall
be transmitted to the EEA Joint Committee which shall act so as to preserve the homogeneous interpretation of the Agreement.

3. If the EEA Joint Committee within two months after a difference in the
case law of the two Courts has been brought before it, has not succeeded
to preserve the homogeneous interpretation of the Agreement, the procedures laid down in Article 111 may be applied.

Art. 106   In order to ensure as uniform an interpretation as possible of this Agreement, in full deference to the independence of courts, a system of exchange of information concerning judgments by the EFTA Court, the
Court of Justice of the European Communities and the Court of First Instance of the European Communities and the Courts of last instance of
the EFTA States shall be set up by the EEA Joint Committee. This system
shall comprise:

(a) transmission to the Registrar of the Court of Justice of the European
Communities of judgments delivered by such courts on the interpretation and application of, on the one hand, this Agreement or, on the
other hand, the Treaty establishing the European Economic Community and the Treaty establishing the European Coal and Steel
Community, as amended or supplemented, as well as the acts adopted
in pursuance thereof in so far as they concern provisions which are
identical in substance to those of this Agreement;

(b) classification of these judgments by the Registrar of the Court of Justice of the European Communities including, as far as necessary, the
drawing up and publication of translations and abstracts;

(c) communications by the Registrar of the Court of Justice of the European Communities of the relevant documents to the competent national authorities, to be designated by each Contracting Party.

Art. 107   Provisions on the possibility for an EFTA State to allow a court or tribunal to ask the Court of Justice of the European Communities to decide on
the interpretation of an EEA rule are laid down in Protocol 34.

Section 2 — Surveillance procedure

Art. 108   1. The EFTA States shall establish an independent surveillance authority (EFTA Surveillance Authority) as well as procedures similar to those existing in the Community including procedures for ensuring the fulfilment of obligations under this Agreement and for control of the legality of acts of the EFTA Surveillance Authority regarding competition.

2. The EFTA States shall establish a court of justice (EFTA Court).

The EFTA Court shall, in accordance with a separate agreement between the EFTA States, with regard to the application of this Agreement be competent, in particular, for:

(a)   actions concerning the surveillance procedure regarding the EFTA States;

(b)   appeals concerning decisions in the field of competition taken by the EFTA Surveillance Authority;

(c)   the settlement of disputes between two or more EFTA States.

Art. 109   1. The fulfilment of the obligations under this Agreement shall be monitored by, on the one hand, the EFTA Surveillance Authority and, on the other, the EC Commission acting in conformity with the Treaty establishing the European Economic Community, the Treaty establishing the European Coal and Steel Community and this Agreement.

2. In order to ensure a uniform surveillance throughout the EEA, the EFTA Surveillance Authority and the EC Commission shall cooperate, exchange information and consult each other on surveillance policy issues and individual cases.

3. The EC Commission and the EFTA Surveillance Authority shall receive any complaints concerning the application of this Agreement. They shall inform each other of complaints received.

4. Each of these bodies shall examine all complaints falling within its competence and shall pass to the other body any complaints which fall within the competence of that body.

5. In case of disagreement between these two bodies with regard to the action to be taken in relation to a complaint or with regard to the result of the examination, either of the bodies may refer the matter to the EEA Joint Committee which shall deal with it in accordance with Article 111.

Art. 110   Decisions under this Agreement by the EFTA Surveillance Authority and the EC Commission which impose a pecuniary obligation on persons other than States, shall be enforceable. The same shall apply to such judgments under this Agreement by the Court of Justice of the European Communities, the Court of First Instance of the European Communities and the EFTA Court.

Enforcement shall be governed by the rules of civil procedure in force in the State in the territory of which it is carried out. The order for its enforcement shall be appended to the decision, without other formality than verification of the authenticity of the decision, by the authority which each Contracting Party shall designate for this purpose and shall make known to the other Contracting Parties, the EFTA Surveillance Authority, the EC Commission, the Court of Justice of the European Communities, the Court of First Instance of the European Communities and the EFTA Court.

When these formalities have been completed on application by the party concerned, the latter may proceed to enforcement, in accordance with the law of the State in the territory of which enforcement is to be carried out, by bringing the matter directly before the competent authority.

Enforcement may be suspended only by a decision of the Court of Justice of the European Communities, as far as decisions by the EC Commission, the Court of First Instance of the European Communities or the Court of Justice of the European Communities are concerned, or by a decision of the EFTA Court as far as decisions by the EFTA Surveillance Authority or the EFTA Court are concerned. However, the courts of the States concerned shall have jurisdiction over complaints that enforcement is being carried out in an irregular manner.

Section 3 — Settlement of disputes

Art. 111   1. The Community or an EFTA State may bring a matter under dispute which concerns the interpretation or application of this Agreement before the EEA Joint Committee in accordance with the following provisions.

2. The EEA Joint Committee may settle the dispute. It shall be provided with all information which might be of use in making possible an indepth examination of the situation, with a view to finding an acceptable solution. To this end, the EEA Joint Committee shall examine all possibilities to maintain the good functioning of the Agreement.

3. If a dispute concerns the interpretation of provisions of this Agreement, which are identical in substance to corresponding rules of the Treaty establishing the European Economic Community and the Treaty establishing the European Coal and Steel Community and to acts adopted in application of these two Treaties and if the dispute has not been settled within three months after it has been brought before the EEA Joint Committee, the Contracting Parties to the dispute may agree to request the Court of Justice of the European Communities to give a ruling on the interpretation of the relevant rules.

If the EEA Joint Committee in such a dispute has not reached an agreement on a solution within six months from the date on which this procedure was initiated or if, by then, the Contracting Parties to the dispute have not decided to ask for a ruling by the Court of Justice of the European Communities, a Contracting Party may, in order to remedy possible imbalances,

–   either take a safeguard measure in accordance with Article 112(2) and following the procedure of Article 113;

–   or apply Article 102 *mutatis mutandis.*

4. If a dispute concerns the scope or duration of safeguard measures taken in accordance with Article 111(3) or Article 112, or the proportionality of rebalancing measures taken in accordance with Article 114, and if the EEA Joint Committee after three months from the date when the matter has been brought before it has not succeeded to resolve the dispute, any Contracting Party may refer the dispute to arbitration under the procedures laid down in Protocol 33. No question of interpretation of the provisions of this Agreement referred to in paragraph 3 may be dealt with in such procedures. The arbitration award shall be binding on the parties to the dispute.

bb) Agreement between the EFTA States on the Establishment of a Surveillance Authority and a Court of Justice (ESA/Court Agreement)

The Republic of Iceland,

The Principality of Liechtenstein and

The Kingdom of Norway

Having Regard to the EEA Agreement;

Considering that, in accordance with Article 108(1) of the EEA Agreement, the EFTA States shall establish an independent surveillance authority (EFTA Surveillance Authority) as well as create procedures similar to those existing in the European Community including procedures for ensuring the fulfilment of the obligations under the EEA Agreement and for control of the legality of acts of the EFTA Surveillance Authority regarding competition;

Further Considering that, in accordance with Article 108(2) of the EEA Agreement, the EFTA States shall establish a court of justice of the EFTA States;

Recalling the objective of the Contracting Parties to the EEA Agreement, in full deference to the independence of the courts, to arrive at and maintain a uniform interpretation and application of the EEA Agreement and those provisions of the Community legislation which are substantially reproduced in that Agreement and to arrive at an equal treatment of individuals and economic operators as regards the four freedoms and the conditions of competition;

Reiterating that the EFTA Surveillance Authority and the Commission of the European Communities shall cooperate, exchange information and consult each other on surveillance policy issues and individual cases;

Considering that the preambles to acts adopted in application of the Treaties establishing the European Economic Community and the European Coal and Steel Community shall, in so far as those acts correspond to the provisions of Protocols 1 to 4 and to the provisions of the acts corresponding to those listed in Annexes I and II to this Agreement, be relevant to the extent necessary for the proper interpretation and application of the provisions of these Protocols and Annexes;

Whereas in the application of Protocols 1 to 4 to this Agreement due account shall be paid to the legal and administrative practices of the Commission of the European Communities prior to the entry into force of this Agreement;

Have Decided to conclude the following Agreement:

PART I

Art. 1   For the purposes of this Agreement:

(a) the term 'EEA Agreement' means the main part of the EEA Agreement, its Protocols and Annexes as well as the acts referred to therein;

(b) the term 'EFTA States' means the Republic of Iceland and the Kingdom of Norway and, under the conditions laid down by Article 1(2) of the Protocol Adjusting the Agreement between the EFTA States on the Establishment of a Surveillance Authority and a Court of Justice, the Principality of Liechtenstein.

Art. 2   The EFTA States shall take all appropriate measures, whether general or particular, to ensure fulfilment of the obligations arising out of this Agreement.

They shall abstain from any measure which could jeopardize the attainment of the objectives of this Agreement.

Art. 3   1. Without prejudice to future developments of case law, the provisions of Protocols 1 to 4 and the provisions of the acts corresponding to those listed in Annexes I and II to this Agreement, in so far as they are identical in substance to corresponding rules of the Treaty establishing the European Economic Community and the Treaty establishing the European Coal and Steel Community and to acts adopted in application of these two Treaties, shall in their implementation and application be interpreted in conformity with the relevant rulings of the Court of Justice of the European Communities given prior to the date of signature of the EEA Agreement.

2. In the interpretation and application of the EEA Agreement and this Agreement, the EFTA Surveillance Authority and the EFTA Court shall pay due account to the principles laid down by the relevant rulings by the Court of Justice of the European Communities given after the date of signature of the EEA Agreement and which concern the interpretation of that Agreement or of such rules of the Treaty establishing the European Economic Community and the Treaty establishing the European Coal and Steel Community in so far as they are identical in substance to the provisions of the EEA Agreement or to the provisions of Protocols 1 to 4 and the provisions of the acts corresponding to those listed in Annexes I and II to the present Agreement.

PART IV — THE EFTA COURT

Art. 27   A court of justice of the EFTA States, hereinafter referred to as the EFTA Court, is hereby established. It shall function in accordance with the provisions of this Agreement and of the EEA Agreement.

Art. 28   The EFTA Court shall consist of three judges.

Art. 29   Decisions of the Court shall be valid only when all its members are sitting in the deliberations.

Art. 30   The Judges shall be chosen from persons whose independence is beyond doubt and who possess the qualifications required for appointment to the highest judicial offices in their respective countries or who are jurisconsults of recognized competence. They shall be appointed by common accord of the Governments of the EFTA States for a term of six years.

Retiring Judges shall be eligible for reappointment.

The Judges shall elect the President of the EFTA Court from among their number for a term of three years. He may be re-elected.

In case one of the Judges, in the opinion of the two other Judges, is disqualified from acting in a particular case, the two other Judges shall agree on a person to replace him chosen from a list established by common accord by the Governments of the EFTA States. If they cannot agree that person shall be chosen from the list by lot by the President. With regard to a Judge chosen in this way the rules applicable to regular Judges shall apply mutatis mutandis. In any case Article 4, second paragraph, and Article 13, of Protocol 5 shall not apply.

Art. 31   If the EFTA Surveillance Authority considers that an EFTA State has failed to fulfil an obligation under the EEA Agreement or of this Agreement, it shall, unless otherwise provided for in this Agreement, deliver a reasoned opinion on the matter after giving the State concerned the opportunity to submit its observations.

If the State concerned does not comply with the opinion within the period laid down by the EFTA Surveillance Authority, the latter may bring the matter before the EFTA Court.

Art. 32   The EFTA Court shall have jurisdiction in actions concerning the settlement of disputes between two or more EFTA States regarding the interpretation or application of the EEA Agreement, the Agreement on a Standing Committee of the EFTA States or the present Agreement.

Art. 33   The EFTA States concerned shall take the necessary measures to comply with the judgments of the EFTA Court.

Art. 34   The EFTA Court shall have jurisdiction to give advisory opinions on the interpretation of the EEA Agreement.

Where such a question is raised before any court or tribunal in an EFTA State, that court or tribunal may, if it considers it necessary to enable it to give judgment, request the EFTA Court to give such an opinion.

An EFTA State may in its internal legislation limit the right to request such an advisory opinion to courts and tribunals against whose decisions there is no judicial remedy under national law.

Art. 35 The EFTA Court shall have unlimited jurisdiction in regard to penalties imposed by the EFTA Surveillance Authority.

Art. 36 The EFTA Court shall have jurisdiction in actions brought by an EFTA State against a decision of the EFTA Surveillance Authority on grounds of lack of competence, infringement of an essential procedural requirement, or infringement of this Agreement, of the EEA Agreement or of any rule of law relating to their application, or misuse of powers.

Any natural or legal person may, under the same conditions, institute proceedings before the EFTA Court against a decision of the EFTA Surveillance Authority addressed to that person or against a decision addressed to another person, if it is of direct and individual concern to the former.

The proceedings provided for in this Article shall be instituted within two months of the publication of the measure, or of its notification to the plaintiff, or, in the absence thereof, of the day on which it came to the knowledge of the latter, as the case may be.

If the action is well founded the decision of the EFTA Surveillance Authority shall be declared void.

Art. 37 Should the EFTA Surveillance Authority, in infringement of this Agreement or the provisions of the EEA Agreement, fail to act, an EFTA State may bring an action before the EFTA Court to have the infringement established.

The action shall be admissible only if the EFTA Surveillance Authority has first been called upon to act. If, within two months of being so called upon, the EFTA Surveillance Authority has not defined its position, the action may be brought within a further period of two months.

Any natural or legal person may, under the conditions laid down in the preceding paragraphs, complain to the EFTA Court that the EFTA Surveillance Authority has failed to address to that person any decision.

Art. 38 If a decision of the EFTA Surveillance Authority has been declared void or if it has been established that the EFTA Surveillance Authority, in infringement of this Agreement or of the provisions of the EEA Agreement, has failed to act, the EFTA Surveillance Authority shall take the necessary measures to comply with the judgment.

This obligation shall not affect any obligation which may result from the application of Article 46, second paragraph.

Art. 39 Save as otherwise provided for in Protocol 7 to this Agreement, the EFTA Court shall have jurisdiction in actions against the EFTA Surveillance Authority relating to compensation for damage provided for in Article 46, second paragraph.

Art. 40   Actions brought before the EFTA Court shall not have suspensory effect. The EFTA Court may, however, if it considers that circumstances so require, order that application of the contested act be suspended.

Art. 41   The EFTA Court may in any case before it prescribe any necessary interim measures.

PART V — GENERAL AND FINAL PROVISIONS

Art. 42   The Protocols and Annexes to this Agreement shall form an integral part thereof.

Art. 43   1. The Statute of the EFTA Court is laid down in Protocol 5 to this Agreement.

2. The EFTA Court shall adopt its rules of procedure to be approved by the Governments of the EFTA States by common accord.

Art. 44   1. The legal capacity, privileges and immunities to be recognized and granted by the EFTA States in connection with the EFTA Surveillance Authority and the EFTA Court are laid down in Protocols 6 and 7 to this Agreement, respectively.

2. The EFTA Surveillance Authority and the EFTA Court, respectively, may conclude with the Government of the States in whose territory their seats are situated an agreement relating to the privileges and immunities to be recognized and granted in connection with it.

Art. 45   The seat of the EFTA Surveillance Authority and the EFTA Court, respectively, shall be determined by common accord of the Governments of the EFTA States.

Art. 46   The contractual liability of the EFTA Surveillance Authority shall be governed by the law applicable to the contract in question.

In the case of non-contractual liability, the EFTA Surveillance Authority shall, in accordance with the general principles of law, make good any damage caused by it, or by its servants, in the performance of its duties.

Art. 47   The Governments of the EFTA States shall, on a proposal from the EFTA Surveillance Authority and after consulting a committee consisting of the members of Parliament of the EFTA States who are members of the EEA Joint Parliamentary Committee, each year before 1 January by common accord establish a budget for the coming year and the apportionment of those expenses between the EFTA States.

The EFTA Surveillance Authority shall be consulted before a decision modifying or amending its proposal for a budget is adopted.

Art. 48   The Governments of the EFTA States shall, on a proposal from the EFTA Court, each year before 1 January by common accord establish a budget for the EFTA Court for the coming year and the apportionment of those expenses between them.

Art. 49   The Governments of the EFTA States may, unless otherwise provided in this Agreement, on a proposal from or after hearing the EFTA Surveillance Authority, by common accord amend the main Agreement as well as Protocols 1 to 4 and 6 and 7. Such an amendment shall be submitted to the EFTA States for acceptance and shall enter into force provided it is approved by all EFTA States. Instruments of acceptance shall be deposited with the Government of Sweden which shall notify all other EFTA States.

Art. 50   1. Any EFTA State which withdraws from the EEA Agreement shall ipso facto cease to be a Party to the present Agreement on the same day as that withdrawal takes effect.

2. Any EFTA State which accedes to the European Community shall ipso facto cease to be a Party to the present Agreement on the same day as that accession takes effect.

3. The Governments of the remaining EFTA States shall, by common accord, decide on the necessary amendments to be made to the present Agreement.

Art. 51   Any EFTA State acceding to the EEA Agreement shall accede to the present Agreement on such terms and conditions as may be laid down by common accord by the EFTA States. The instrument of accession shall be deposited with the Government of Sweden which shall notify the other EFTA States.

Art. 52   The EFTA States shall communicate to the EFTA Surveillance Authority the measures taken for the implementation of this Agreement.

Art. 53   1. This Agreement, drawn up in a single copy and authentic in the English language, shall be ratified by the Contracting Parties in accordance with their respective constitutional requirements.

Before the entry into force of this Agreement, it shall also be drawn up and authenticated in Finnish, French, German, Icelandic, Italian, Norwegian and Swedish.

2. This Agreement shall be deposited with the Government of Sweden which shall transmit a certified copy to each EFTA State.

The instruments of ratification shall be deposited with the Government of Sweden which shall notify all other EFTA States.

3. This Agreement shall enter into force on the date and under the conditions provided for in the Protocol Adjusting the Agreement between the EFTA States on the Establishment of a Surveillance Authority and a Court of Justice.

In Witness Whereof the undersigned plenipotentiaries, being duly authorized thereto, have signed the present Agreement.

Done at Oporto, this 2nd day of May 1992, in a single authentic copy in the English language which shall be deposited with the Government of Sweden. The Depositary shall transmit certified copies to all Signatory States and States acceding to this Agreement.

cc) Protocol 5 to the ESA/Court Agreement on the Statute of the EFTA Court

Art. 1   The EFTA Court established by Article 27 of this Agreement shall be constituted and function in accordance with the provisions of this Agreement and of this Statute.

PART I – JUDGES

Art. 2   Before taking up his duties each Judge shall, in open court, take an oath to perform his duties impartially and conscientiously and to preserve the secrecy of the deliberations of the Court.

Art. 3[1]

Art. 4   The Judges may not hold any political or administrative office.

They may not engage in any occupation, whether gainful or not, unless exemption is granted by the Governments of the EFTA States acting by common accord.

When taking up their duties, they shall give a solemn undertaking that, both during and after their term of office, they will respect the obligations arising therefrom, in particular the duty to behave with integrity and discretion as regards the acceptance, after they have ceased to hold office, of certain appointments or benefits.

Any doubt on this point shall be settled by decision of the Court.

Art. 5   Apart from normal replacement, or death, the duties of a Judge shall end when he resigns.

Where a Judge resigns, his letter of resignation shall be addressed to the President of the Court for transmission to the Governments of the EFTA States. Upon this notification a vacancy shall arise on the bench.

Save where Article 6 applies, a Judge shall continue to hold office until his successor takes up his duties.

Art. 6   A Judge may be deprived of his office or of his right to a pension or other benefits in its stead only if, in the unanimous opinion of the Court in plenary, he no longer fulfils the requisite conditions or meets the obligations arising from his office. The Judge concerned shall not take part in any such deliberations.

The Registrar of the Court shall notify such a decision to the Governments of the EFTA States.

Art. 7   A Judge who is to replace a member of the Court whose term of office has not expired shall be appointed for the remainder of his predecessor's term.

---

[1]   Article 3 deleted on 29 December 1994.

Part II — Organization

Art. 8   Decisions of the Court shall be taken by a majority of the Judges sitting in the deliberations and in accordance with conditions laid down in the rules of procedure.

Art. 9   The Court shall appoint its Registrar and lay down the rules governing his service.

Art. 10   The Registrar shall take an oath before the Court to perform his duties impartially and conscientiously and to preserve the secrecy of the deliberations of the Court.

Art. 11[1]   The Court determines the extent to which the Registrar shall attend the Court, and shall arrange for replacement of the Registrar on occasions when he is prevented from attending the Court.

Art. 12   Officials and other servants shall be attached to the Court to enable it to function. They shall be responsible to the Registrar under the authority of the President.

Art. 13   The Judges and the Registrar shall be required to reside at the place where the Court has its seat.

Art. 14   The Court shall remain permanently in session. The duration of the judicial vacations shall be determined by the Court with due regard to the needs of its business.

Art. 15[2]   No Judge may take part in the disposal of a case in which he has previously taken part as agent or adviser or has acted for one of the parties, or in which he has been called upon to pronounce as a member of a court or tribunal, of a commission of inquiry or in any other capacity.

    If, for some special reason, any Judge considers that he should not take part in the judgment or examination of a particular case, he shall so inform the President of the Court. If, for some reason, the President considers that any Judge should not sit in a particular case, he shall notify him accordingly.

    Any difficulty arising as to the application of this Article shall be settled according to the fourth paragraph of Article 30 of this Agreement.

    If according to this Article a Judge shall not take part in a particular case, a person to replace him shall be chosen in accordance with Article 30, fourth paragraph, of the Agreement, among those persons on the list who have been nominated by the Government which has nominated the regular Judge who is to be replaced.

    A party may not apply for a change in the composition of the Court on the grounds of either nationality of a Judge or the absence from the Court of a Judge of the nationality of that party.

---

[1]   As amended.

[2]   As amended.

Art. 16   Rules governing the languages of the Court shall be laid down in the rules of procedure of the Court.

PART III – PROCEDURE

Art. 17[1]   The EFTA States, the EFTA Surveillance Authority, the Community and the EC Commission shall be represented before the Court by an agent appointed for each case; the agent may be assisted by an adviser or by a lawyer.

Other parties must be represented by a lawyer.

Only a lawyer authorized to practice before a court of a Contracting Party to the EEA Agreement may represent or assist a party before the Court.

Such agents, advisers and lawyers shall, when they appear before the Court, enjoy the rights and immunities necessary to the independent exercise of their duties, under conditions laid down in the rules of procedure of the Court.

As regards such advisers and lawyers who appear before it, the Court shall have the powers normally accorded to courts of law, in accordance with the rules of procedure of the Court.

Art. 18   The procedure before the Court shall consist of two parts: written and oral.

The written procedure shall consist of the communication to the parties of applications, statements of case, defences and observations, and of replies, if any, as well as of all papers and documents in support or of certified copies of them.

Communications shall be made by the Registrar in the order and within the time laid down in the rules of procedure of the Court.

The oral procedure shall consist of the reading of the report presented by a Judge acting as Rapporteur, the hearing by the Court of agents, advisers and lawyers, as well as the hearing, if any, of witnesses and experts.

Art. 19[2]   A case shall be brought before the Court by a written application addressed to the Registrar. The application shall contain the applicant's name and permanent address and the description of the signatory, the name of the party or names of the parties against whom the application is made, the subject matter of the dispute, the form of order sought and a brief statement of the pleas in law on which the application is based.

The application shall be accompanied, where appropriate, by the measure the annulment of which is sought or by any other relevant documents. If the documents are not submitted with the application, the Registrar shall ask the party concerned to produce them within a reasonable period, but

---

[1]   As amended.

[2]   As amended.

in that event the rights of the party shall not lapse even if such documents are produced after the time-limit for bringing proceedings.

Art. 20 As soon as a case is pending before the Court, the Registrar shall notify the Governments of the EFTA States, the EFTA Surveillance Authority, the Community and the EC Commission. Within two months of this notification, the EFTA States, the EFTA Surveillance Authority, the Community and the EC Commission shall be entitled to submit statements of case or written observations to the Court.

Art. 21 The Court may require the parties to produce all documents and to supply all information which the Court considers desirable. Formal note shall be taken of any refusal.

The Court may also require the EFTA States not being parties to the case to supply all information which the Court considers necessary for the proceedings.

Art. 22 The Court may at any time entrust any individual, body, authority, committee or other organization it chooses with the task of giving an expert opinion.

Art. 23 Witnesses may be heard in accordance with the rules of procedure of the Court.

Art. 24 Witnesses and experts may be heard on oath taken in accordance with the rules of procedure of the Court or in the manner laid down by the law of the country of the witness or expert.

Art. 25 The Court may order that a witness or expert be heard by the judicial authority of his place of permanent residence.

The order shall be sent for implementation to the competent judicial authority under conditions laid down in the rules of procedure of the Court. The documents drawn up in compliance with the letters rogatory shall be returned to the Court under the same conditions.

The Court shall defray the expenses, without prejudice to the right to charge them, where appropriate, to the parties.

Art. 26 An EFTA State shall treat any defaulting witness or any violation of an oath by a witness or expert in the same manner as if the offence had been committed before one of its courts with jurisdiction in civil proceedings. At the instance of the Court, the EFTA State concerned shall prosecute the offender before its competent court.

Art. 27 The hearing in court shall be public, unless the Court, of its own motion or on application by the parties, decides otherwise for serious reasons.

Art. 28 During the hearings the Court may examine the experts, the witnesses and the parties themselves. The latter, however, may address the Court only through their representatives.

Art. 29[1]   Minutes shall be made of each hearing and signed by the President and the Registrar or a Judge designated to provide for the minutes.

Art. 30   The case list shall be established by the President.

Art. 31   The deliberations of the Court shall be and shall remain secret.

Art. 32   Judgments shall state the reasons on which they are based. They shall contain the names of the Judges who took part in the deliberations.

Art. 33   Judgments shall be signed by the President and the Registrar. They shall be read in open court.

Art. 34   The Court shall adjudicate upon costs.

Art. 35   The President of the Court may, by way of summary procedure, which may, in so far as necessary, differ from some of the rules contained in this Agreement and which shall be laid down in the rules of procedure, adjudicate upon applications to suspend execution as provided for in Article 40 of this Agreement, or to prescribe interim measures in pursuance of Article 41 of this Agreement, or to suspend enforcement in accordance with Article 110, fourth paragraph, of the EEA Agreement.

Should the President be prevented from attending, his place shall be taken by another Judge in accordance with the rules of procedure.

The ruling of the President or of the Judge replacing him shall be provisional and shall in no way prejudice the decision of the Court on the substance of the case.

Art. 36[2]   Any EFTA State, the EFTA Surveillance Authority, the Community and the EC Commission may intervene in cases before the Court.

The same right shall be open to any person establishing an interest in the result of any case submitted to the Court, save in cases between EFTA States or between EFTA States and the EFTA Surveillance Authority.

An application to intervene shall be limited to supporting the form of order sought by one of the parties.

Art. 37   Where the defending party, after having been duly summoned, fails to file written submissions in defence, judgment shall be given against that party by default. An objection may be lodged against the judgment within one month of it being notified. The objection shall not have the effect of staying enforcement of the judgment by default unless the Court decides otherwise.

Art. 38   EFTA States, and any other natural or legal persons may, in cases and under conditions to be determined by the rules of procedure, institute third-party proceedings to contest a judgment rendered without their being heard, where the judgment is prejudicial to their rights.

---

[1]   As amended.

[2]   As amended.

Art. 39   If the meaning or scope of a judgment is in doubt, the Court shall con-
           strue it on application by any party establishing an interest therein or by
           the EFTA Surveillance Authority.

Art. 40   An application for revision of a judgment may be made to the Court only
           on discovery of a fact which is of such nature as to be a decisive factor,
           and which, when the judgment was given, was unknown to the Court and
           to the party claiming the revision.

           The revision shall be opened by a judgment of the Court expressly re-
           cording the existence of a new fact, recognizing that it is of such a charac-
           ter as to lay the case open to revision and declaring the application admis-
           sible on this ground.

           No application for revision may be made after the lapse of ten years from
           the date of the judgment.

Art. 41   Periods of grace based on considerations of distance shall be determined
           by the rules of procedure of the Court.

           No right shall be prejudiced in consequence of the expiry of a time-limit if
           the party concerned proves the existence of unforeseeable circumstances
           or of force majeure.

Art. 42   Proceedings against the EFTA Surveillance Authority in matters arising
           from non-contractual liability shall be barred after a period of five years
           from the occurrence of the event giving rise thereto. The period of limita-
           tion shall be interrupted if proceedings are instituted before the Court or
           if prior to such proceedings an application is made by the aggrieved party
           to the EFTA Surveillance Authority. In the latter event the proceedings
           must be instituted within two months of the publication of the measure,
           or of its notification to the plaintiff, or, in the absence thereof, of the day
           on which it came to the knowledge of the latter, as the case may be.

PART IV — GENERAL PROVISIONS

Art. 43   The rules of procedure of the Court shall contain, apart from the provi-
           sions contemplated by this Statute, any other provisions necessary for ap-
           plying and, where required, supplementing it.

Art. 44   The Governments of the EFTA States may, on a proposal from or after
           hearing the Court, by common accord amend this Statute.

dd) Rules of Procedures of the EFTA Court as amended

           Having regard to the Agreement on the European Economic Area,

           Having regard to the competences conferred on the Court by the Agree-
           ment between the EFTA States on the Establishment of a Surveillance
           Authority and a Court of Justice,

Having regard to the approval given by the Governments of the EFTA States,

Adopts the Following Rules of Procedure:

INTERPRETATION

Art. 1   In these Rules:

(a) 'Agreement' means the Agreement between the EFTA States on the Establishment of a Surveillance Authority and a Court of Justice, its Protocols and Annexes;

(b) 'EFTA State' means a Member of the European Free Trade Association which is a Party to the Agreement and to the Agreement on the European Economic Area;

(c) 'Statute' means Protocol 5 to the Agreement, on the Statute of the EFTA Court.

TITLE I — ORGANIZATION OF THE COURT

CHAPTER 1 — JUDGES

Art. 2   The term of office of a Judge shall begin on the date laid down in his instrument of appointment. In the absence of any provisions regarding the date, the term shall begin on the date of the instrument.

Art. 3   1. Before taking up his duties, a Judge shall, in accordance with Article 2 of the Statute, at the first public sitting of the Court which he attends after his appointment, take the following oath:

"I swear that I will perform my duties impartially and conscientiously; I swear that I will preserve the secrecy of the deliberations of the EFTA Court."

2. Immediately after taking the oath, a Judge shall, in accordance with Article 4 of the Statute, sign a declaration by which he solemnly undertakes that, both during and after his term of office, he will respect the obligations arising therefrom, and in particular the duty to behave with integrity and discretion as regards the acceptance, after he has ceased to hold office, of certain appointments or benefits.

Art. 4   When the Court is called upon to decide whether a Judge no longer fulfils the requisite conditions or no longer meets the obligations arising from his office, the President shall invite the Judge concerned to make representations to the Court, in closed session and in the absence of the Registrar.

Art. 5   Judges shall rank equally in precedence according to their seniority in office.

Where there is equal seniority in office, precedence shall be determined by age.

Retiring Judges who are reappointed shall retain their former precedence.

Judges chosen from the list provided for in Article 30, fourth paragraph, of the Agreement shall rank after the regular Judges. If two or more such Judges are acting in the same case, their internal rank shall be determined by age.

CHAPTER 2 — PRESIDENCY OF THE COURT

Art. 6   1. The Judges shall, in accordance with Article 30 of the Agreement, elect one of their number as President of the Court for a term of three years.

2. If the office of the President of the Court falls vacant before the normal date of expiry thereof, the Court shall elect a successor for the remainder of the term.

3. The elections provided for in this Article shall be by secret ballot. If a Judge obtains an absolute majority he shall be elected. If no Judge obtains an absolute majority, a second ballot shall be held and the Judge obtaining the most votes shall be elected. Where two or more Judges obtain an equal number of votes the oldest of them shall be deemed elected.

Art. 7   The President shall direct the judicial business and the administration of the Court; he shall preside at hearings and deliberations.

Art. 8   1. As soon as an application initiating proceedings has been lodged, the President shall designate a Judge to act as Rapporteur.

2. The Court shall lay down criteria by which, as a rule, cases are to be assigned to Judges.

Art. 9   When the President of the Court is absent or prevented from attending or when the office of President is vacant, the functions of President shall be exercised by a Judge according to the order of precedence laid down in Article 5.

CHAPTER 3 — REGISTRY

Section 1 – The Registrar and Assistant Registrars

Art. 10   1. The Court shall appoint the Registrar.

2. An application shall be accompanied by full details of the candidate's age, nationality, university degrees, knowledge of any languages, present and past occupations and experience, if any, in judicial and international fields.

3. The appointment shall be made following the procedure laid down in Article 6(3).

4. The Registrar shall be appointed for a term of three years. He may be reappointed.

5. The Registrar shall take the oath in accordance with Article 3.

6. The Registrar may be deprived of his office only if he no longer fulfils the requisite conditions or no longer meets the obligations arising from his office; the Court shall take its decision after giving the Registrar an opportunity to make representations.

7. If the office of Registrar falls vacant before the normal date of expiry of the term thereof, the Court shall appoint a new Registrar for a term of three years.

Art. 11   The Court may, following the procedure laid down in respect of the Registrar, appoint one or more Assistant Registrars.

Art. 12   Where the Registrar is absent or prevented from attending or his post is vacant, the President shall designate an official or other servant to carry out temporarily the duties of Registrar.

Art. 13   Instructions to the Registrar shall be adopted by the Court acting on a proposal from the President.

Art. 14   1. There shall be kept in the Registry, under the control of the Registrar, a register initialled by the President, in which all pleadings and supporting documents shall be entered in the order in which they are lodged.

2. When a document has been registered, the Registrar shall make a note to that effect on the original and, if a party so requests, on any copy submitted for the purpose.

3. Entries in the register and the notes provided for in the preceding paragraph shall be authentic.

4. Rules for keeping the register shall be prescribed by the Instructions to the Registrar referred to in Article 13.

5. Persons having an interest may consult the register at the Registry and may obtain copies or extracts on payment of a charge on a scale fixed by the Court.

The parties to a case may on payment of the appropriate charge also obtain copies of pleadings and authenticated copies of judgments, advisory opinions and orders.

6. Notice shall be given in the EEA Section of and the EEA Supplement to the Official Journal of the European Communities of the date of registration of an application initiating proceedings, the names and addresses of the parties, the subject-matter of the proceedings, the form of order sought by the applicant and a summary of the pleas in law and of the main supporting arguments. Notice shall also be given in respect of a request for an advisory opinion.

Art. 15   1. The Registrar shall be responsible, under the authority of the President, for the acceptance, transmission and custody of documents and for effecting service as provided for by these Rules.

2. Where called for, the Registrar shall assist the Court, the President and the Judges in their official functions.

Art. 16   The Registrar shall have custody of the seals. He shall be responsible for
           the records and be in charge of the publications of the Court.

Art. 17   The Court may, subject to Articles 4 and 23, call upon the Registrar to
           attend the sittings of the Court.

Section 2 – Officials and other Servants of the Court

Art. 18   1. The officials and other servants of the Court shall be appointed in ac-
           cordance with the provisions of the Staff Regulations for the EFTA
           Court.

           2. Before taking up his duties, an official shall take the following oath be-
           fore the President, in the presence of the Registrar:

           "I swear that I will perform loyally, discreetly and conscientiously the
           duties assigned to me by the EFTA Court."

Art. 19   The organization of the Court shall be laid down, and may be modified,
           by the Court.

Art. 20   Subject to further decisions by the Court, the Registrar shall be responsi-
           ble, under the authority of the President, for the administration of the
           Court, its financial management and its accounts.

CHAPTER 4 — THE WORKING OF THE COURT

Art. 21   1. The dates and times of the sittings of the Court shall be fixed by the
           President.

           2. The Court may choose to hold one or more sittings in a place other
           than that in which the Court has its seat.

Art. 22   1. Decisions of the Court shall be valid only when all its members are sit-
           ting in the deliberations. However, decisions of the Court on administra-
           tive matters may be adopted with two Judges present. In the latter case the
           President shall have a casting vote.

           2. If after the Court has been convened it is found that the quorum has not
           been attained, the President shall adjourn the sitting until there is a quo-
           rum.

Art. 23   1. The Court shall deliberate in closed session.

           2. Only those Judges who were present at the oral proceedings may take
           part in the deliberations.

           3. Every Judge taking part in the deliberations shall state his opinion and
           the reasons for it.

           4. The conclusions reached by the majority of the Judges after final discus-
           sion shall determine the decision of the Court. Votes shall be cast in re-
           verse order to the order of precedence laid down in Article 5.

5. Differences of view on the substance, wording or order of questions, or on the interpretation of the voting shall be settled by decision of the Court.

6. Where the deliberations of the Court concern questions of its own administration, the Registrar shall be present, unless the Court decides to the contrary.

7. Where the Court sits without the Registrar being present it shall, if necessary, instruct a Judge to draw up minutes. The minutes shall be signed by this Judge and by the President.

Art. 24   1. Subject to any special decision of the Court, its vacations shall be as follows:

–　　from 18 December to 10 January,

–　　from the Sunday before Easter to the second Sunday after Easter,

–　　from 15 July to 15 September.

During the vacations, the functions of President shall be exercised at the place where the Court has its seat either by the President himself or by a Judge invited by the President to take his place.

2. In a case of urgency, the President may convene the Judges during the vacations.

3. The Court shall observe the official holidays of the place where it has its seat.

4. The Court may, in proper circumstances, grant leave of absence to any Judge.

CHAPTER 5 – LANGUAGES

Art. 25   1. The language of the Court shall be English. This shall cover the whole procedure including deliberations, minutes and decisions of the Court.

2. English shall be used in the written and oral part of the procedure by the parties, the interveners and the EFTA States, the EFTA Surveillance Authority, the Community and the EC Commission, unless otherwise provided in these Rules.

3. Without prejudice to the provisions of Article 27, all supporting documents submitted to the Court shall be in English or be accompanied by a translation into English, unless the Court decides otherwise.

In the case of lengthy documents, translations may be confined to extracts. However, the Court may, of its own motion or at the request of a party, at any time call for a complete or fuller translation.

4. The Court may, if deemed necessary, at the request of a party or intervener other than an EFTA State, the EFTA Surveillance Authority, the Community or the EC Commission, allow this party or intervener to address and be addressed by the Court in an official language of an EFTA State or of the European Communities in the oral part of the procedure. The Court shall arrange for interpretation to and from English. Such a re-

quest shall be submitted at least two weeks in advance of the oral part of the procedure.

Art. 26   Where a witness or expert states that he is unable adequately to express himself in English the Court may authorize him to give his evidence in another language. The Court shall arrange for interpretation to and from English. Such a request shall normally be submitted at least two weeks in advance of the oral part of the procedure.

Art. 27   1. Where a request for an advisory opinion is referred to the Court in accordance with Article 34 of the Agreement, the requesting court or tribunal is entitled to make its request in the language in which the case is dealt with before that court or tribunal. The Court shall arrange for translation into English.

2. The requesting court or tribunal and the parties to the dispute before it may submit documents to the Court in the language in which the case is dealt with before that court or tribunal. Such documents shall be translated into English to the extent that it is found necessary by the Court. The Court shall arrange for the translation.

3. The Court shall arrange for translation of the report of the Judge-Rapporteur in order to make it available in English and in the language in which the case is dealt with before the requesting court or tribunal.

4. Parties to the dispute before the requesting court or tribunal are entitled orally to address and be addressed by the Court in the language in which the case is dealt with before that court or tribunal. The Court shall arrange for interpretation to and from English. A party wishing to use such a language shall inform the Registrar at least two weeks in advance of the oral part of the procedure.

5. The opinion of the Court shall be given in the language in which the request was made and in English. The opinion shall be authentic in these languages.

CHAPTER 6 — RIGHTS AND OBLIGATIONS OF AGENTS, ADVISERS AND LAWYERS

Art. 28   1. Agents, advisers and lawyers appearing before the Court or before any judicial authority to which the Court has addressed letters rogatory, shall enjoy immunity in respect of words spoken or written by them concerning the case or the parties.

2. Agents, advisers and lawyers shall enjoy the following further privileges and facilities:

(a)   papers and documents relating to the proceedings shall be exempt from both search and seizure; in the event of a dispute the customs officials or police may seal those papers and documents; they shall then be immediately forwarded to the Court for inspection in the presence of the Registrar and of the person concerned;

(b) agents, advisers and lawyers shall be entitled to such allocation of foreign currency as may be necessary for the performance of their duties;

(c) agents, advisers and lawyers shall be entitled to travel in the course of duty without hindrance.

Art. 29   In order to qualify for the privileges, immunities and facilities specified in Article 28, persons entitled to them shall furnish proof of their status as follows:

(a) agents shall produce an official document issued by the party for whom they act, and shall forward without delay a copy thereof to the Registrar;

(b) advisers and lawyers shall produce a certificate signed by the Registrar. The validity of this certificate shall be limited to a specified period, which may be extended or curtailed according to the length of the proceedings.

Art. 30   The privileges, immunities and facilities specified in Article 28 are granted exclusively in the interests of the proper conduct of proceedings.

The Court may waive the immunity where it considers that the proper conduct of proceedings will not be hindered thereby.

Art. 31   1. Any adviser or lawyer whose conduct towards the Court, a Judge or the Registrar is incompatible with the dignity of the Court, or who uses his rights for purposes other than those for which they were granted, may at any time be excluded from the proceedings by an order of the Court; the person concerned shall be given an opportunity to defend himself.

The order shall have immediate effect.

2. Where an adviser or lawyer is excluded from the proceedings, the proceedings shall be suspended for a period fixed by the President in order to allow the party concerned to appoint another adviser or lawyer.

3. Decisions taken under this Article may be rescinded.

Title II — Procedure

Chapter 1 — Written Procedure

Art. 32   1. The original of every pleading must be signed by the party's agent or lawyer.

The original, accompanied by all annexes referred to therein, shall be lodged together with five copies for the Court and a copy for every other party to the proceedings. Copies shall be certified by the party lodging them.

2. All pleadings shall bear a date. In the reckoning of time-limits for taking steps in proceedings, only the date of lodgment at the Registry shall be taken into account.

3. To every pleading there shall be annexed a file containing the documents relied on in support of it, together with a schedule listing them.

4. Where in view of the length of a document only extracts from it are annexed to the pleading, the whole document or a full copy of it shall be lodged at the Registry.

5. Pleadings and other documents shall be lodged at the Registry within the official opening hours.

6. Without prejudice to the provisions in the preceding paragraphs of this Article, pleadings and other documents may, in urgent cases, be lodged at the Registry by telefax. In the reckoning of time-limits for taking steps in proceedings, a telefax shall be deemed as validly lodged provided its reception is fully completed within the official opening hours on the last day of the time-limit and to the extent that the original document and the copies referred to in paragraph 1 are delivered to the Registry within 7 days thereafter.

Art. 33   1. An application of the kind referred to in Article 19 of the Statute shall state:

(a)   the name and address of the applicant;

(b)   the designation of the party or the parties against whom the application is made;

(c)   the subject-matter of the proceedings and a summary of the pleas in law on which the application is based;

(d)   the form of order sought by the applicant;

(e)   where appropriate, the nature of any evidence offered in support.

2. For the purpose of the proceedings, the application shall state an address for service in the place where the Court has its seat and the name of the person who is authorized and has expressed willingness to accept service.

If the application does not comply with these requirements, all service on the party concerned for the purpose of the proceedings shall be effected, for so long as the defect has not been cured, by registered letter addressed to the agent or lawyer of that party. By way of derogation from Article 75, service shall then be deemed to be duly effected by the lodging of the registered letter at a post office of the place where the Court has its seat.

3. The lawyer acting for a party must lodge at the Registry a certificate that he is authorized to practice before a court of a Contracting Party to the Agreement on the European Economic Area.

4. The application shall be accompanied, where appropriate, by the documents specified in Article 19 of the Statute.

5. An application made by a legal person governed by private law shall be accompanied by:

(a)   the instrument or instruments constituting or regulating that legal person or a recent extract from the register of companies, firms or associations or any other proof of its existence in law;

    (b)   proof that the authority granted to the applicant's lawyer has been properly conferred on him by someone authorized for the purpose.

6. If an application does not comply with the requirements set out in paragraphs 3 to 5 of this Article, the Registrar shall prescribe a reasonable period within which the applicant is to comply with them whether by putting the application itself in order or by producing any of the above-mentioned documents. If the applicant fails to put the application in order or to produce the required documents within the time prescribed, the Court shall decide whether the non-compliance with these conditions renders the application formally inadmissible.

Art. 34   The application shall be served on the defendant. In a case where Article 33(6) applies, service shall be effected as soon as the application has been put in order or the Court has declared it admissible notwithstanding the failure to observe the formal requirements set out in that Article.

Art. 35   1. Within one month after service on him of the application, the defendant shall lodge a defence, stating:

    (a)   the name and address of the defendant;

    (b)   the arguments of fact and law relied on;

    (c)   the form of order sought by the defendant;

    (d)   the nature of any evidence offered by him.

The provisions of Article 33(2) to (6) shall apply to the defence.

2. The time-limit laid down in paragraph (1) of this Article may in exceptional circumstances be extended by the President on a reasoned application by the defendant.

Art. 36   1. The application initiating the proceedings and the defence may be supplemented by a reply from the applicant and by a rejoinder from the defendant.

2. The President shall fix the time-limits within which these pleadings are to be lodged.

Art. 37   1. In reply or rejoinder a party may offer further evidence. The party must, however, give reasons for the delay in offering it.

2. No new plea in law may be introduced in the course of proceedings unless it is based on matters of law or of fact which come to light in the course of the procedure.

If in the course of the procedure one of the parties puts forward a new plea in law which is so based, the President may, even after the expiry of the normal procedural time-limits, acting on a report of the Judge-Rapporteur, allow the other party time to answer on that plea.

The decision on the admissibility of the plea shall be reserved for the final judgment.

Art. 38   At any stage of the proceedings the Court may prescribe any measure of organization of procedure or any measure of inquiry referred to in Articles 49 and 50 or order that a previous inquiry be repeated or expanded.

Art. 39   The Court may, at any time, after giving the parties an opportunity to express their views, order that two or more cases concerning the same subject-matter shall, on account of the connection between them, be joined for the purposes of the written or oral procedure or of the final judgment. The cases may subsequently be disjoined.

Art. 40   1. Without prejudice to the application of Article 38, after the rejoinder has been lodged the President shall fix a date on which the Judge-Rapporteur is to present his preliminary report to the Court. The report shall contain recommendations as to whether measures of organization of procedure or measures of inquiry should be undertaken.

The Court shall decide what action to take upon the recommendations of the Judge-Rapporteur.

The same procedure shall apply:

(a)   where no reply or no rejoinder has been lodged within the time-limit fixed in accordance with Article 36(2);

(b)   where the party concerned waives his right to lodge a reply or rejoinder.

2. Where the Court decides to open the oral procedure without undertaking measures of organization of procedure or ordering measures of inquiry, the President shall fix the opening date.

Art. 41   1. Without prejudice to any measures of organization of procedure or measures of inquiry which may be prescribed at the stage of the oral procedure, where, during the written procedure, measures of organization of procedure or measures of inquiry have been instituted and completed, the President shall, subject to the provisions in paragraph 2 of this Article, fix the date for the opening of the oral procedure.

2. The Court may, acting on a report from the Judge-Rapporteur, with the express consent of the parties, decide to dispense with the oral procedure.

CHAPTER 2 — ORAL PROCEDURE

Art. 42   1. Subject to the priority of decisions provided for in Article 82, the Court shall deal with the cases before it in the order in which the preparatory inquiries in them have been completed. Where the preparatory inquiries in several cases are completed simultaneously, the order in which they are to be dealt with shall be determined by the dates of entry in the register of the applications initiating them respectively.

2. The President may in special circumstances order that a case be given priority over others.

The President may in special circumstances, after hearing the parties, either on his own initiative or at the request of one of the parties, defer a case to be dealt with at a later date. On a joint application by the parties the President may order that a case be deferred.

Art. 43   1. The proceedings shall be opened and directed by the President, who shall be responsible for the proper conduct of the hearing.

2. The oral proceedings in cases heard in camera shall not be made public.

Art. 44   The President may in the course of the hearing put questions to the agents, advisers or lawyers of the parties.

The other Judges may do likewise.

Art. 45   A party may address the Court only through his agent, adviser or lawyer.

Art. 46   The President shall declare the oral procedure closed at the end of the hearing.

Art. 47   The Court may order the reopening of the oral procedure.

Art. 48   1. The Registrar or a Judge designated by the President shall draw up minutes of every hearing.

2. The minutes shall contain the date and place of the hearing, the names of the Judges and the Registrar present, the reference to the case, the names of the parties, the names and descriptions of the parties' agents, advisers and lawyers, an indication of the documents lodged by the parties in the course of the hearing and the decisions of the Court or the President, given at the hearing.

3. The minutes shall be signed by the President and by the Registrar or the Judge designated to draw up the minutes and shall constitute an official record.

4. The parties may inspect the minutes at the Registry and obtain copies at their own expense.

CHAPTER 3 — MEASURES OF ORGANIZATION OF PROCEDURE AND MEASURES OF INQUIRY

Section 1 – Measures of organization of procedure

Art. 49   1. The purpose of measures of organization of procedure shall be to ensure that cases are prepared for hearing, procedures carried out and disputes resolved under the best possible conditions. They shall be prescribed by the Court.

2. Measures of organization of procedure shall, in particular, have as their purpose:

(a)   ensuring efficient conduct of the written and oral procedure and facilitating the taking of evidence;

(b)   determining the points on which the parties must present further argument or which call for measures of inquiry;

(c)   clarifying the forms of order sought by the parties, their pleas in law and arguments and the points at issue between them;

(d)   facilitating the amicable settlement of disputes.

3. Measures of organization of procedure may, in particular, consist of:

(a) putting questions to the parties;

(b) inviting the parties to make written or oral submissions on certain aspects of the proceedings;

(c) asking the parties or third parties for information or particulars;

(d) asking for documents or any papers relating to the case to be produced;

(e) summoning the parties' agents, advisers, lawyers or the parties in person to meetings.

4. Each party may, at any stage of the procedure, propose the adoption or modification of measures of organization of procedure. In that case, the other parties shall be heard before those measures are prescribed.

Where the procedural circumstances so require, the Registrar shall inform the parties of the measures envisaged by the Court and shall give them an opportunity to submit comments orally or in writing.

Section 2 – Measures of inquiry

Art. 50 1. Without prejudice to Articles 21 and 22 of the Statute the following measures of inquiry may be adopted:

(a) the personal appearance of the parties;

(b) a request for information and production of documents;

(c) oral testimony;

(d) the commissioning of an expert's report;

(e) an inspection of the place or thing in question.

2. The measures of inquiry which the Court has ordered may be conducted by the Court itself, or be assigned to the Judge-Rapporteur.

3. The Court shall prescribe the measures of inquiry that it considers appropriate by means of an order setting out the facts to be proved. Before the Court decides on the measures of inquiry referred to in paragraph (1)(c), (d) and (e) the parties shall be heard.

The order shall be served on the parties.

4. Evidence may be submitted in rebuttal and previous evidence may be amplified.

Art. 51 The parties shall be entitled to attend the measures of inquiry.

Section 3 – The summoning and examination of witnesses and experts

Art. 52 1. The Court may, either of its own motion or on application by a party, order that certain facts be proved by witnesses. The order of the Court shall set out the facts to be established.

The Court may summon a witness of its own motion or on application by a party.

An application by a party for the examination of a witness shall state precisely about what facts and for what reasons the witness should be examined.

2. The witness shall be summoned by an order of the Court containing the following information:

(a) the surname, forenames, description and address of the witness;

(b) an indication of the facts about which the witness is to be examined;

(c) where appropriate, particulars of the arrangements made by the Court for reimbursement of expenses incurred by the witness, and of the penalties which may be imposed on defaulting witnesses.

The order shall be served on the parties and the witnesses.

3. The Court may make the summoning of a witness for whose examination a party has applied conditional upon the deposit with the cashier of the Court of a sum sufficient to cover the taxed costs thereof; the Court shall fix the amount of the payment.

The cashier shall advance the funds necessary in connection with the examination of any witness summoned by the Court of its own motion.

A witness who has been duly summoned shall obey the summons and attend for examination, unless he proffers a valid excuse to the Court.

4. After the identity of the witness has been established, the President shall inform him that he will be required to vouch the truth of his evidence in the manner laid down in these Rules and that any violation by him constitutes an offence under Article 26 of the Statute.

5. Subject to the provisions of Article 54 the witness shall, before giving his evidence, take the following oath:

'I swear that I will tell the truth, the whole truth and nothing but the truth'.

The Court may, after hearing the parties, exempt a witness from taking the oath.

6. The witness shall give his evidence to the Court, the parties having been given notice to attend. After the witness has given his main evidence the President may, at the request of a party or of his own motion, put questions to him.

The other Judges may do likewise.

Subject to the control of the President, questions may be put to witnesses by the representatives of the parties.

7. The Registrar or a Judge designated by the President shall draw up minutes of every hearing of a witness, which shall contain, in addition to the information mentioned in Article 48(2), the name, forenames, description and permanent address of each witness, and in which the evidence of each witness is reproduced.

The minutes shall be signed by the President or by the Judge-Rapporteur responsible for conducting the examination of the witness, and by the Registrar or the Judge designated to draw up the minutes. Before the minutes are thus signed, witnesses shall be given an opportunity to check the content of the minutes and to sign them.

The minutes shall constitute an official record.

Art. 53   1. The Court may order that an expert's report be obtained. The order appointing the expert shall define his task and set a time-limit within which he is to make his report.

2. The expert shall receive a copy of the order, together with all the documents necessary for carrying out his task. He shall be under the supervision of the Judge-Rapporteur, who may be present during his investigation and who shall be kept informed of his progress in carrying out his task.

The Court may request the parties or one of them to lodge security for the taxed costs of the expert's report.

3. At the request of the expert, the Court may order the examination of witnesses. Their examination shall be carried out in accordance with Article 52.

4. The expert may give his opinion only on points which have been expressly referred to him.

5. After the expert has made his report, the Court may order that he be examined, the parties having been given notice to attend.

Subject to the control of the President, questions may be put to the expert by the representatives of the parties.

6. Subject to the provisions of Article 54, the expert shall, after making his report, take the following oath before the Court:

'I swear that I have conscientiously and impartially carried out my task.'

The Court may, after hearing the parties, exempt the expert from taking the oath.

Art. 54   1. The President shall instruct any person who is required to take an oath before the Court as witness or expert, to tell the truth or to carry out his task conscientiously and impartially, as the case may be, and shall warn him of the criminal liability provided for in his national law in the event of any breach of this duty.

2. Witnesses and experts shall take the oath either in accordance with the first subparagraph of Article 52(5) and the first subparagraph of Article 53(6) or in the manner laid down by their national law.

3. Where their national law provides the opportunity to make, in judicial proceedings, a solemn affirmation equivalent to an oath as well as or instead of taking an oath, the witnesses and experts may make such an affirmation under the conditions and in the form prescribed in their national law.

Where their national law provides neither for taking an oath nor for making a solemn affirmation, the procedure described in the first paragraph of this Article shall be followed.

Art. 55   The Court may, in accordance with Article 26 of the Statute, decide to report to the competent authority of the EFTA State referred to in Annex I any defaulting witness or any violation of an oath by a witness or expert.

The Registrar shall be responsible for communicating the decision of the Court. The decision shall set out the facts and circumstances on which the report is based.

Art. 56   1. If one of the parties objects to a witness or to an expert on the ground that he is not a competent or proper person to act as witness or expert or for any other reason, or if a witness or expert refuses to give evidence, to take the oath or to make a solemn affirmation equivalent thereto, the matter shall be resolved by the Court.

2. An objection to a witness or to an expert shall be raised within two weeks after service of the order summoning the witness or appointing the expert; the statement of objection must set out the grounds of objection and indicate the nature of any evidence offered.

Art. 57   1. Witnesses and experts shall be entitled to reimbursement of their travel and subsistence expenses. The cashier of the Court may make a payment to them towards these expenses in advance.

2. Witnesses shall be entitled to compensation for loss of earnings, and experts to fees for their services. The cashier of the Court shall pay witnesses and experts their compensation or fees after they have carried out their respective duties or tasks.

Art. 58   1. The Court may, on application by a party or of its own motion, issue letters rogatory for the examination of witnesses or experts.

2. Letters rogatory shall be issued in the form of an order which shall contain the name, forenames, description and address of the witness or expert, set out the facts on which the witness or expert is to be examined, name the parties, their agents, lawyers or advisers, indicate their addresses for service and briefly describe the subject-matter of the proceedings.

Notice of the order shall be served on the parties by the Registrar.

3. The Registrar shall send the order to the competent authority of the EFTA State referred to in Annex II in whose territory the witness or expert is to be examined. Where necessary, the order shall be accompanied by a translation into the official language or languages of the State to which it is addressed.

The authority named pursuant to the first subparagraph shall pass on the order to the judicial authority which is competent according to its national law.

The competent judicial authority shall give effect to the letters rogatory in accordance with its national law. After implementation the competent judicial authority shall transmit to the authority named pursuant to the first subparagraph the order embodying the letters rogatory, any documents arising from the implementation and a detailed statement of costs. These documents shall be sent to the Registrar.

The Registrar shall be responsible for the translation of the documents into English.

4. The Court shall defray the expenses occasioned by the letters rogatory without prejudice to the right to charge them, where appropriate, to the parties.

Art. 59 1. The Registrar or a Judge designated by the President shall draw up minutes of every hearing.

2. The minutes of a hearing of an expert shall contain, in addition to the information mentioned in Article 48(2), the name, forenames, descriptions and permanent address of the expert examined.

3. The minutes shall be signed by the President and by the Registrar or the Judge designated to draw up the minutes and shall constitute an official record.

4. The parties may inspect the minutes and any expert's report at the Registry and obtain copies at their own expense.

CHAPTER 4 — JUDGMENTS

Art. 60 The judgment shall contain:
- a statement that it is the judgment of the Court,
- the date of its delivery,
- the names of the President and of the Judges taking part in it,
- the name of the Registrar,
- the description of the parties,
- the names of the agents, advisers and lawyers of the parties,
- a statement of the forms of order sought by the parties,
- a summary of the facts,
- the grounds for the decision,
- the operative part of the judgment, including the decision as to costs.

Art. 61 1. The judgment shall be delivered in open court; the parties shall be given notice to attend to hear it.

2. The original of the judgment, signed by the President, by the Judges who took part in the deliberations and by the Registrar, shall be sealed and deposited at the Registry; the parties shall be served with certified copies of the judgment.

3. The Registrar shall record on the original of the judgment the date on which it was delivered.

Art. 62 The judgment shall be binding from the date of its delivery.

Art. 63 1. Without prejudice to the provisions relating to the interpretation of judgments the Court may, of its own motion or on application by a party made within two weeks after the delivery of a judgment, rectify clerical mistakes, errors in calculation and obvious slips in it.

2. The parties, whom the Registrar shall duly notify, may lodge written observations within a period prescribed by the President.

3. The Court shall take its decision in closed session.

4. The original of the rectification order shall be annexed to the original of the rectified judgment. A note of this order shall be made in the margin of the original of the rectified judgment.

Art. 64   If the Court should omit to give a decision on a specific head of claim or on costs, any party may within a month after service of the judgment apply to the Court to supplement its judgment.

The application shall be served on the opposite party and the President shall prescribe a period within which that party may lodge written observations.

After these observations have been lodged, the Court shall decide both on the admissibility and on the substance of the application.

Art. 65   The Registrar shall arrange for the publication of reports of cases before the Court.

CHAPTER 5 — COSTS

Art. 66   1. A decision as to costs shall be given in the final judgment or in the order which closes the proceedings.

2. The unsuccessful party shall be ordered to pay the costs if they have been applied for in the successful party's pleadings.

Where there are several unsuccessful parties the Court shall decide how the costs are to be shared.

3. Where each party succeeds on some and fails on other heads, or where the circumstances are exceptional, the Court may order that the costs be shared or that the parties bear their own costs.

The Court may order a party, even if successful, to pay costs which the Court considers that party to have unreasonably or vexatiously caused the opposite party to incur.

4. The EFTA States, the EFTA Surveillance Authority, the Community and the EC Commission which intervene in the proceedings shall bear their own costs.

The Court may order an intervener other than those mentioned in the preceding subparagraph to bear his own costs.

5. A party who discontinues or withdraws from proceedings shall be ordered to pay the costs if they have been applied for in the other party's pleadings. However, upon application by the party who discontinues or withdraws from proceedings, the costs shall be borne by the other party if this appears justified by the conduct of that party.

Where the parties have come to an agreement on costs, the decision as to costs shall be in accordance with that agreement.

If costs are not claimed, the parties shall bear their own costs.

6. Where a case does not proceed to judgment the costs shall be in the discretion of the Court.

Art. 67   Costs necessarily incurred by a party in enforcing a judgment or an order of the Court shall be refunded by the opposite party on the scale in force in the State where the enforcement takes place.

Art. 68   Proceedings before the Court shall be free of charge, except that:

(a)   where a party has caused the Court to incur avoidable costs the Court may order that party to refund them;

(b)   where copying or translation work is carried out at the request of a party, the cost shall, in so far as the Registrar considers it excessive, be paid for by that party on the scale of charges referred to in Article 14(5).

Art. 69   Without prejudice to the preceding Article, the following shall be regarded as recoverable costs:

(a)   sums payable to witnesses and experts under Article 57;

(b)   expenses necessarily incurred by the parties for the purpose of the proceedings, in particular the travel and subsistence expenses and the remuneration of agents, advisers or lawyers.

Art. 70   1. If there is a dispute concerning the costs to be recovered, the Court shall, on application by the party concerned and after hearing the opposite party, make an order.

2. The parties may, for the purposes of enforcement, apply for an authenticated copy of the order.

Art. 71   1. Sums due from the cashier of the Court shall be paid in the currency of the country where the Court has its seat.

At the request of the person entitled to any sum, it shall be paid in the currency of the country where the expenses to be refunded were incurred or where the steps in respect of which payment is due were taken.

2. Other debtors shall make payment in the currency of their country of origin.

3. Conversions of currency shall be made at the official rates of exchange ruling on the day of payment in the country where the Court has its seat.

CHAPTER 6 — LEGAL AID

Art. 72   1. A party who is wholly or in part unable to meet the costs of the proceedings may at any time apply for legal aid.

The application shall be accompanied by evidence of the applicant's need of assistance, and in particular by a document from the competent authority certifying his lack of means.

2. If the application is made prior to proceedings which the applicant wishes to commence, it shall briefly state the subject of such proceedings.

The application need not be made through a lawyer.

3. The President shall designate a Judge to act as Rapporteur. The Court shall, after considering the written observations of the opposite party, decide whether legal aid should be granted in full or in part, or whether it should be refused. The Court shall consider whether there is manifestly no cause of action.

The Court shall make an order without giving reasons.

4. The Court, by any order by which it decides that a person is entitled to receive legal aid, shall order that a lawyer be appointed to act for him.

5. If the person does not indicate his choice of lawyer, or if the Court considers that his choice is unacceptable, the Registrar shall send a copy of the order and of the application for legal aid to the authority named in Annex III being the competent authority of the EFTA State concerned.

6. The Court, in the light of the suggestions made by that authority, shall of its own motion appoint a lawyer to act for the person concerned.

7. The Court may at any time, either of its own motion or on application, withdraw legal aid if the circumstances which led to its being granted alter during the proceedings.

8. Where legal aid is granted, the cashier of the Court shall advance the funds necessary to meet the expenses.

The Court shall adjudicate on the lawyer's disbursements and fees; the President may, on application by the lawyer, order that he receives an advance.

In its decision as to costs the Court may order the payment to the cashier of the Court of the whole or any part of amounts advanced as legal aid.

The Registrar shall take steps to obtain the recovery of these sums from the party ordered to pay them.

CHAPTER 7 — DISCONTINUANCE

Art. 73   If, before the Court has given its decision, the parties reach a settlement of their dispute and intimate to the Court the abandonment of their claims, the President shall order the case to be removed from the register and shall give a decision as to costs in accordance with Article 66(5), having regard to any proposals made by the parties on the matter.

             This provision shall not apply to proceedings under Articles 36 and 37 of the Agreement.

Art. 74   If the applicant informs the Court in writing that he wishes to discontinue the proceedings, the President shall order the case to be removed from the register and shall give a decision as to costs in accordance with Article 66(5).

CHAPTER 8 — SERVICE

Art. 75   1. Where a document is to be served on an EFTA State, the EFTA Surveillance Authority, the Community or the EC Commission, service is effected on the day on which, at the seat of the Court, the Permanent Delegation of the State concerned, or the Permanent Delegation of the EC Commission or the Council of the European Union, or the EFTA Surveillance Authority has been notified by post or by telefax that the document is available at the Court.

2. Where these Rules require that a document be served on any other person, the Registrar shall ensure that service is effected at that person's address for service either by the dispatch of a copy of the document by registered post with a form for acknowledgement of receipt or by personal delivery of the copy against a receipt.

3. The Registrar shall prepare and certify the copies of documents to be served, save where the parties themselves supply the copies in accordance with Article 32(1).

CHAPTER 9 — TIME-LIMITS

Art. 76   1. Any period of time prescribed by the Agreement, the Statute or these Rules for the taking of any procedural step shall be reckoned as follows:

(a)   where a period expressed in days, weeks, months or years is to be calculated from the moment at which an event occurs or an action takes place, the day during which that event occurs or that action takes place shall not be counted as falling within the period in question;

(b)   a period expressed in weeks, months or in years shall end with the expiry of whichever day in the last week, month or year is the same day of the week, or falls on the same date, as the day during which the event or action from which the period is to be calculated occurred or took place. If, in a period expressed in months or in years, the day on which it should expire does not occur in the last month, the period shall end with the expiry of the last day of that month;

(c)   where a period is expressed in months and days, it shall first be reckoned in whole months, then in days;

(d)   periods shall include official holidays, Saturdays and Sundays;

(e)   periods shall not be suspended during the judicial vacations.

2. If the period would otherwise end on a Saturday, Sunday or an official holiday, it shall be extended until the end of the first following working day.

A list of official holidays drawn up by the Court shall be published in the EEA Section of and the EEA Supplement to the Official Journal of the European Communities.

Art. 77   The period of time allowed for commencing proceedings against a measure adopted by the EFTA Surveillance Authority shall run from the day following the receipt by the person concerned of notification of the measure or, where the measure is published, from the 15th day after publication thereof in the EEA Section of and the EEA Supplement to the Official Journal of the European Communities.

Art. 78   Any time-limit prescribed pursuant to these Rules may be extended by whomever prescribed it.

Any period of time prescribed by the Agreement, the Statute or these Rules may not be extended on considerations of distance alone.

The President may delegate to the Registrar power of signature for the purpose of fixing time-limits which, pursuant to these Rules, it falls to him to prescribe or of extending such time-limits.

CHAPTER 10 — STAY OF PROCEEDINGS

Art. 79   1. The proceedings may be stayed by decision of the President, after hearing the Judge-Rapporteur, and, save in the case of references for an advisory opinion as referred to in Article 96, the parties.

The proceedings may be resumed by decision of the President, following the same procedure.

The decisions referred to in this paragraph shall be served on the parties.

2. The stay of proceedings shall take effect on the date indicated in the decision of stay or, in the absence of such indication, on the date of that decision.

While proceedings are stayed time shall cease to run for the purposes of prescribed time-limits for all parties.

3. Where the decision of stay does not fix the length of stay, it shall end on the date indicated in the decision of resumption or, in the absence of such indication, on the date of the decision of resumption.

From the date of resumption time shall begin to run afresh for the purposes of the time-limits.

TITLE III — SPECIAL FORMS OF PROCEDURE

CHAPTER 1 — SUSPENSION OF OPERATION OR ENFORCEMENT AND OTHER INTERIM MEASURES

Art. 80   1. An application to suspend the operation of any measure adopted by the EFTA Surveillance Authority, made pursuant to Article 40 of the Agreement shall be admissible only if the applicant is challenging that measure in proceedings before the Court.

An application for the adoption of any other interim measure referred to in Article 41 of the Agreement shall be admissible only if it is made by a party to a case before the Court and relates to that case.

2. An application of a kind referred to in paragraph (1) of this Article shall state the subject-matter of the proceedings, the circumstances giving rise

to urgency and the pleas of fact and law establishing a prima facie case for the interim measures applied for.

3. The application shall be made by a separate document and in accordance with the provisions of Articles 32 and 33.

Art. 81 1. The application shall be served on the opposite party, and the President shall prescribe a short period within which that party may submit written or oral observations.

2. The President may order a preparatory inquiry.

The President may grant the application even before the observations of the opposite party have been submitted. This decision may be varied or cancelled even without any application being made by any party.

Art. 82 The President shall either decide on the application himself or refer it to the Court.

If the President is absent or prevented from attending, Article 9 shall apply.

Where the application is referred to it, the Court shall postpone all other cases, and shall give a decision. Article 81 shall apply.

Art. 83 1. The decision on the application shall take the form of a reasoned order. The order shall be served on the parties forthwith.

2. The enforcement of the order may be made conditional on the lodging by the applicant of security, of an amount and nature to be fixed in the light of the circumstances.

3. Unless the order fixes the date on which the interim measure is to lapse, the measure shall lapse when final judgment is delivered.

4. The order shall have only an interim effect, and shall be without prejudice to the decision of the Court on the substance of the case.

Art. 84 On application by a party, the order may at any time be varied or cancelled on account of a change in circumstances.

Art. 85 Rejection of an application for an interim measure shall not bar the party who made it from making a further application on the basis of new facts.

Art. 86 The provisions of this Chapter shall apply to applications to suspend the enforcement of a decision of the Court or of any measure adopted by the EFTA Surveillance Authority, submitted pursuant to Article 19 of the Agreement.

The order granting the application shall fix, where appropriate, a date on which the interim measure is to lapse.

CHAPTER 2 — PRELIMINARY ISSUES

Art. 87 1. A party applying to the Court for a decision on a preliminary objection or other preliminary plea not going to the substance of the case shall make the application by a separate document.

The application must state the pleas of fact and law relied on and the form of order sought by the applicant; any supporting documents must be annexed to it.

2. As soon as the application has been lodged, the President shall prescribe a period within which the opposite party may lodge a document containing a statement of the form of order sought by that party and its pleas in law.

3. Unless the Court decides otherwise, the remainder of the proceedings shall be oral.

4. The Court shall decide on the application or reserve its decision for the final judgment.

If the Court refuses the application or reserves its decision, the President shall prescribe new time-limits for the further steps in the proceedings.

Art. 88   1. Where it is clear that the Court has no jurisdiction to take cognizance of an action or where the action is manifestly inadmissible, the Court may, by reasoned order, and without taking further steps in the proceedings, give a decision on the action.

2. The Court may at any time of its own motion consider whether there exists any absolute bar to proceeding with a case, and shall give its decision in accordance with Article 87(3) and (4).

CHAPTER 3 — INTERVENTION

Art. 89   1. An application to intervene must be made within three months of the publication of the notice referred to in Article 14(6).

The application shall contain:

(a) the description of the case;

(b) the description of the parties;

(c) the name and address of the intervener;

(d) the intervener's address for service at the place where the Court has its seat;

(e) the form of order sought, by one or more of the parties, in support of which the intervener is applying for leave to intervene;

(f) a statement of the circumstances establishing the right to intervene, where the application is submitted pursuant to the second paragraph of Article 36 of the Statute.

The intervener shall be represented in accordance with Article 17 of the Statute.

Articles 32 and 33 shall apply.

2. The application shall be served on the parties.

The President shall give the parties an opportunity to submit their written or oral observations before deciding on the application.

The President shall decide on the application by order or shall refer the application to the Court.

3. If the President allows the intervention, the intervener shall receive a copy of every document served on the parties. The President may, however, on application by one of the parties, omit secret or confidential documents.

4. The intervener must accept the case as he finds it at the time of his intervention.

5. The President shall prescribe a period within which the intervener may submit a statement in intervention.

The statement in intervention shall contain:

(a) a statement of the form of order sought by the intervener in support of or opposing, in whole or in part, the form of order sought by one of the parties;

(b) the pleas in law and arguments relied on by the intervener;

(c) where appropriate, the nature of any evidence offered.

6. After the statement in intervention has been lodged, the President shall, where necessary, prescribe a time-limit within which the parties may reply to that statement.

CHAPTER 4 — JUDGMENTS BY DEFAULT AND APPLICATIONS TO SET THEM ASIDE

Art. 90   1. If a defendant on whom an application initiating proceedings has been duly served fails to lodge a defence to the application in the proper form within the time prescribed, the applicant may apply for judgment by default.

The application shall be served on the defendant. The President shall fix a date for the opening of the oral procedure.

2. Before giving judgment by default the Court shall consider whether the application initiating proceedings is admissible, whether the appropriate formalities have been complied with, and whether the application appears well founded. The Court may order a preparatory inquiry.

3. A judgment by default shall be enforceable. The Court may, however, grant a stay of execution until the Court has given its decision on any application under paragraph 4 to set aside the judgment, or it may make execution subject to the provision of security of an amount and nature to be fixed in the light of the circumstances; this security shall be released if no such application is made or if the application fails.

4. Application may be made to set aside a judgment by default.

The application to set aside the judgment must be made within one month from the date of service of the judgment and must be lodged in the form prescribed by Articles 32 and 33.

5. After the application has been served, the President shall prescribe a period within which the other party may submit his written observations.

The proceedings shall be conducted in accordance with Articles 40 et seq.

6. The Court shall decide by way of a judgment which may not be set aside. The original of this judgment shall be annexed to the original of the judgment by default. A note of the judgment on the application to set aside shall be made in the margin of the original of the judgment by default.

CHAPTER 5 — EXCEPTIONAL REVIEW PROCEDURES

Section 1 – Third-party proceedings

Art. 91   1. Articles 32 and 33 shall apply to an application initiating third-party proceedings. In addition such an application shall:

(a) specify the judgment contested;

(b) state how that judgment is prejudicial to the rights of the third party;

(c) indicate the reasons for which the third party was unable to take part in the original case.

The application must be made against all the parties to the original case.

Where the judgment has been published in the EEA Section of and the EEA Supplement to the Official Journal of the European Communities, the application must be lodged within two months of the publication.

2. The Court may, on application by the third party, order a stay of execution of the judgment. The provisions of Title III, Chapter 1, shall apply.

3. The contested judgment shall be varied on the points on which the submissions of the third party are upheld.

The original of the judgment in the third-party proceedings shall be annexed to the original of the contested judgment. A note of the judgment in the third-party proceedings shall be made in the margin of the original of the contested judgment.

Section 2 – Revision

Art. 92   An application for revision of a judgment shall be made within three months of the date on which the facts on which the application is based, came to the applicant's knowledge.

Art. 93   1. Articles 32 and 33 shall apply to an application for revision. In addition such an application shall:

(a) specify the judgment contested;

(b) indicate the points on which the judgment is contested;

(c) set out the facts on which the application is based;

(d) indicate the nature of the evidence to show that there are facts justi-
      fying revision of the judgment, and that the time-limit laid down in
      Article 92 has been observed.

2. The application must be made against all parties to the case in which the
contested judgment was given.

Art. 94   1. Without prejudice to its decision on the substance, the Court in closed
session, shall, having regard to the written observations of the parties, give
in the form of a judgment its decision on the admissibility of the application.

2. If the Court finds the application admissible, it shall proceed to consider the substance of the application and shall give its decision in the
form of a judgment in accordance with these Rules.

3. The original of the revising judgment shall be annexed to the original of
the judgment revised. A note of the revising judgment shall be made in the
margin of the original of the judgment revised.

CHAPTER 6 — INTERPRETATION OF JUDGMENTS

Art. 95   1. An application for interpretation of a judgment shall be made in accordance with Articles 32 and 33. In addition it shall specify:

(a) the judgment in question;

(b) the passages of which interpretation is sought.

The application must be made against all the parties to the case in which
the judgment was given.

2. The Court shall give its decision in the form of a judgment after having
given the parties an opportunity to submit their observations.

The original of the interpreting judgment shall be annexed to the original
of the judgment interpreted. A note of the interpreting judgment shall be
made in the margin of the original of the judgment interpreted.

CHAPTER 7 — ADVISORY OPINIONS

Art. 96   1. An EFTA State which, in application of Article 34 of the Agreement,
has limited in its internal legislation the right to request an advisory opinion to courts and tribunals against whose decisions there is no judicial
remedy under national law, should without delay inform the Court of
such legislation and subsequent amendments to it. The notification shall
be accompanied by the text of the relevant legislation.

2. In cases governed by Article 34 of the Agreement the procedure shall be
governed by the provisions of these Rules, subject to adaptations necessitated by the nature of the reference for an advisory opinion.

3. The request for an advisory opinion shall be accompanied by a summary of the case before the national court including a description of the
facts of the case as well as a presentation of the provision in issue in rela-

tion to the national legal order, necessary to enable the Court to assess the question to which a reply is sought.

4. The Court may ask the national court for clarification which shall be put in the language in which the request for an advisory opinion was made.

Art. 97   1. The requests of national courts or tribunals referred to in Article 96 shall be communicated to the Governments of the EFTA States, the EFTA Surveillance Authority, the Community, the EC Commission and the parties to the dispute in the original version, accompanied by a translation into English of the request. The provisions on statements of case and written observations in Article 20 of the Statute shall apply also to the parties to the dispute.

2. As regards the representation and attendance of the parties to the main proceedings in the advisory opinion procedure the Court shall take account of the rules of procedure of the national court or tribunal which made the reference.

3. Where a question referred to the Court for an advisory opinion is manifestly identical to a question on which the Court has already ruled or given an opinion, the Court may, after informing the court or tribunal which referred the question to it and hearing any observations submitted by the Governments of the EFTA States, the EFTA Surveillance Authority, the Community, the EC Commission and the parties to the dispute, give its decision by reasoned order in which reference is made to its previous judgment or opinion.

4. Without prejudice to paragraph 3 of this Article, the procedure before the Court in the case of a reference for an advisory opinion shall also include an oral part.

However, after the submission of the statements or observations, as provided for in Article 20 of the Statute and paragraph 1 of this Article, the Court, acting on a report from the Judge-Rapporteur, after informing those who are thus entitled to submit such statements or observations, may decide otherwise, provided that none of those has asked to present oral argument.

Before the oral part of the procedure, a report from the Judge-Rapporteur shall be communicated to the Governments of the EFTA States, the EFTA Surveillance Authority, the Community, the EC Commission and the parties to the dispute. The report shall be accompanied by a translation as provided for in Article 27(3).

5. It shall be for the national court or tribunal to decide as to the costs of the reference.

In special circumstances the Court may grant, by way of legal aid, assistance for the purpose of facilitating the representation or attendance of a party. The provisions of Article 72 shall apply mutatis mutandis.

TITLE IV — MISCELLANEOUS PROVISIONS

Art. 98   These Rules, which are authentic in the English language, shall be published in the EEA Section of and the EEA Supplement to the Official Journal of the European Communities.

These Rules shall be officially translated by the Court into the German, Icelandic and Norwegian languages.

c) Association Agreements of the European Community and its Member States with third States

The association agreements concluded by the European Community under Art. 310 of the EC-treaty (ex. Art. 238) provide that in case of a dispute as to the interpretation or application of the respective agreement the Association Council/the ACP-EC Council of Ministers will settle the matter. Where no settlement can be reached, the matter might as the case may be, either brought before an ad hoc arbitral tribunal (see e.g. Art. 52 of the Association agreement concluded with Marocco, the Europe Agreements concluded with several Central and Eastern European Countries and Art. 352 Lomé IV) or be referred to the Court of Justice of the European communities (Art. 25 para. 2 of the Association Agreement with Turkey).

The texts reproduced demonstrate the different possibilities of dispute settlement mechanisms agreed upon in the different association agreements.

Bibliographical notes

E. Antalovsky (ed.), Assoziierungsabkommen der EU mit Drittstaaten (1998)

T. Bachl, Streitschlichtungsmechanismen im Rahmen von Assoziierungsverträgen zwischen den Europäischen Gemeinschaften und Drittstaaten (1996)

J. Gomula, Dispute settlement under association agreements with Central and Eastern European states, Polish Yearbook of International Law 1995/96, pp. 107 et seq.

S. Richter, Die Assoziierung osteuropäischer Staaten durch die Europäischen Gemeinschaften: eine Untersuchung der rechtlichen Grundlagen der Vertragsgestaltung zwischen den Europäischen Gemeinschaften und Polen, Ungarn und der Tschechoslowakei (1993)

v. d. Groeben/Thiesing/Ehlermann, Kommentar zum EU/EG-Vertrag. Artikel 238, marginal note 39 (5th ed., 1999) with further bibliographical notes

aa) Association Agreement between the European Community and Turkey of September 12, 1963[1]

Art. 25   1. The Contracting Parties may submit to the Council of Association any dispute relating to the application or interpretation of this Agreement which concerns the Community, a Member State of the Community, or Turkey.

2. The Council of Association may settle the dispute by decision; it may also decide to submit the dispute to the Court of Justice of the European Communities or to any other existing court or tribunal.

3. Each Party shall be required to take the measures necessary to comply with such decisions.

4. Where the dispute cannot be settled in accordance with paragraph (2) of this article, the Council of Association shall determine, in accordance with Article 8 of this Agreement, the detailed rules for arbitration or for any other judicial procedure to which the Contracting Parties may resort during the transitional and final stages of this Agreement.

bb) Fourth ACP-EC Convention (Lomé IV) as amended on November 4, 1995

Art. 352   1. Any dispute which arises between one or more Member States or the Community, on the one hand, and one or more ACP States, on the other, concerning the interpretation or the application of this Convention shall be referred to the Council of Ministers.

2. Between meetings of the Council of Ministers, such disputes shall be referred to the Committee of Ambassadors for settlement.

3. If the Committee of Ambassadors fails to settle the dispute, it shall refer the matter to the Council of Ministers at its next meeting.

4. If the Council of Ministers fails to settle the dispute at that meeting it may, at the request of either Contracting Party, initiate a good offices procedure, the result of which shall be transmitted to the Council in the form of a report at its next meeting.

5. (a) If a settlement of the dispute is not reached, the Council of Ministers shall initiate an arbitration procedure at the request of either Contracting Party. Two arbitrators shall be appointed by the parties to the dispute within thirty days, one by either side as set out in paragraph 1. The two arbitrators in question shall then appoint a third arbitrator within two months. Should the latter not be appointed within the time limit set, he shall be appointed by the co-President of

---

[1]   Official Journal L 217, 29.12.1964.

the Council of Ministers from among eminent persons providing every guarantee of independence.

(b) The decision of the arbitrators shall be taken by majority vote, as a general rule within five months.

(c) Each party to the dispute must take the measures required for the implementation of the arbitrators' decision.

cc) Europe Agreement between the European Communities and their Member States and the Republic of Hungary[1]

Art. 107 1. Each of the two Parties may refer to the Association Council any dispute relating to the application or interpretation of this Agreement.

2. The Association council may settle the dispute by means of a decision.

3. Each Party shall be bound to take the measures involved in carrying out the decision referred to in paragraph 2.

4. In the event of it not being possible to settle the dispute in accordance with paragraph 2, either Party may notify the other of the appointment of an arbitrator within two months. For the application of this procedure, the Community and the Member States shall be deemed to be one Party to the dispute.

The Association Council shall appoint a third arbitrator.

The arbitrators' decisions shall be taken by majority vote.

Each party to the dispute must take the steps required to implement the decision of the arbitrators.

[1] OJ No L/347/1.

d) Benelux Economic Union

In 1944, the Governments of Belgium, Luxembourg and the Netherlands signed a Customs Convention which provided for the abolition of customs duties between those three States and for further development of a common economic policy. After numerous agreements on economic cooperation were signed the three countries finally, on February 3, 1958, adopted the Agreement Establishing the Benelux Economic Union envisaged already in the 1944 Customs Convention. According to the treaties establishing the European Economic Community and the European Atomic Energy Community an economic union between the Benelux-countries was not precluded. The Union Treaty codified the earlier arrangements and provided for measures to be taken in order to complete the process of unification. The main purposes of the Union were the free movement of persons, goods, capital and services throughout the three countries, the coordination of economic, financial and social policies and the pursuit of a joint policy in economic relations with third countries.

Two judicial organs comprise the dispute settlement mechanism of the Union: the Arbitral College was created as an integral part of the Union with the task to settle disputes between any of the three Benelux countries; the Benelux Court of Justice is an independent institution whose function is mainly interpretative.

The Arbitral College for the settlement of disputes between the contracting parties concerning "the application of the Treaty and of the Treaty provisions concerning its object" (Arts. 41 ff.) is composed of four sections, representing the major types of disputes which may arise, i.e. economic, financial, social and agricultural (Art. 1, para. 2, of the Statute). Each party to the Treaty appoints an arbitrator and a substitute to each of the four sections. Both serve three year terms of office which are implicitly extended if no new appointment has been made. Once a dispute arises the tribunal is established consisting of the arbitrators previously appointed by both parties to one of the Arbitral College sections as well as a President. However, the President need not necessarily be a neutral person: the office is filled on a rotation basis by one of six arbitrators out of a panel set up by the Committee of Ministers of the Benelux Treaty (Art. 42. para. 3, of the Treaty; Art. 3, para. 1. of the Statute). The candidates for this panel are nominated by the Presidents of the Belgium Cour de cassation, the Luxembourg Cour supérieure de justice and the Dutch Hoge Raad der Nederlanden from judges serving on these Courts or from judges on the respective Courts of Appeal. Each State may propose four candidates and the Committee of Ministers selects two from each country The rotation of panel members serving as President is determined by nationality. Therefore, it is possible that in a specific case two of the three Arbitral College judges may be of the same nationality and may form the absolute majority required for a decision. Such a composition is incompatible with the traditional rules of international arbitration and adjudication, which generally preclude the appointment of two judges of the same nationality. Therefore, some authorities are reluctant to accept the official designation of the institution as an "Arbitral" College.

If the Committee of Ministers is unable to settle a dispute, the College acquires compulsory jurisdiction. The parties may bring unilateral applications or refer matters jointly to the College. The College is entitled to render advisory opinions on request of the Committee of Ministers.

In accordance with the Treaty of March 31, 1965 the Benelux Court of Justice was created in order to promote uniform application of the legal norms common to Belgium, Luxembourg and the Netherlands as manifested either in conventions or the decisions of the Committee of Ministers. Under the Protocols of April 29, 1969 and May 11, 1974, the contracting parties specifically designated the conventions and rules common to the three States according to Art. 1, para. 2, of the Treaty instituting the Court.

The Court is composed of nine judges, one President, two Vice-Presidents and six substitutes, and is assisted by three Advocates-General (Art 3). The judges and substitute judges are selected from the judges of the Supreme Court of each State. In the case of Luxembourg, a special provision allows for such a selection from the members of the Comité du contentieux du Conseil d'Etat. An equal number of judges and Advocates-General for each member State is appointed by the Committee of Ministers. Once appointed, the judges and substitute judges remain in office as long as they actually exercise their office in the national courts. Holders of the offices of President and Vice-President are rotated every three years. While the Court is composed normally of nine judges, its rules provide for cases in which it may be constituted by only three judges, each of whom represents a member State.

Art. 6 generally establishes the jurisdiction of the Court over questions of interpretation, regarding the legal norms valid in the Benelux Union which arise during proceedings before national tribunals in the member States or before the Arbitral College. Furthermore, the Court is empowered to render advisory opinions upon request of each of the three governments.

Thus, the Court performs a strictly indirect task by way of preliminary review and may not deliver judgments directly binding upon the parties. It functions more as an advisory organ which may deliver binding interpretations of points of law than as a true court.

Besides these international functions, the Court was instituted by Protocol of April 29, 1969 as an administrative tribunal for the settlement of disputes between the organization and its officers. However, the Court may decide such cases only after having heard the opinion of a consultative commission, which is not a judicial body although it exercises functions akin to one and operates under its own rules of procedure.

While the Arbitral College's activity is still rather limited, the Court of Justice has been addressed more often.

Texts

Benelux, Affaires Juridiques - Cour Benelux, Textes de Base. Vol. 4 (French and Dutch)
Benelux Treaty:
    Moniteur belge 1960 No. 258, pp. 8402 ff.
    Tractatenblad van het Koninkrijk der Nederlanden 1958 No. 18
Court of Justice:
    Moniteur belge 1973 No. 237

Tractatenblad van het Koninkrijk der Nederlanden 1965 No 71 (French and Dutch)

Mémorial du Grand-Duché de Luxembourg, Recueil de Législation 1973 II A, p. 984

Mémorial du Grand-Duché de Luxembourg 1960 Nr. 50

European Yearbook 13 (1965), 259-266 (French)

Bibliographical notes

J G. Sauceplanne, Die Schiedsgerichtsbarkeit in den Benelux, JIR Vol. 7 (1957), pp. 86-96

W.-J. Ganshof van der Meersch, La juridiction internationale dans l'union économique Benelux, AFDI Vol 15 (1969), pp. 245 - 265

E. Mewissen, Het Beneluxgerechtshof: een beknopt overzicht van zijn statuut, Rechtskundig Weekblad Vol. 35 (1972), pp. 1330-1338

J. W Schneider, The Benelux Court, Netherlands Yearbook of International Law 4 (1973), pp. 193 - 235

S. Swartenbroux-Vandenhaegen, De rechtsprekende bevoegdheid van het Benelux-Gerechtshof, Rechtskundig Weekblad Vol. 37 (1974), pp. 1681-1716

G. Demez, La Cour de justice Benelux, Cahiers de droit européen 12 (1976), pp. 149-178

A. de Caluwé, Cour de justice Benelux – Chronique, Cahiers de droit européen 16 (1980), pp. 240-296

F. Dumon, La Cour de justice Benelux (1980)

A. de Vreese, Het Benelux-Gerechtshof, Sociaal-Ekonomische Wetgeving 30 (1982), 563-582

E.D.J. Kruijtbosch, Benelux Economic Union, College of Arbitrators and Court of Justice, in: R. Bernhardt (ed.), EPIL, Vol. I (1992), 377-380

Collection of cases

Benelux, Affaires Juridiques - Cour Benelux, Textes de Base, Vol. 4 I, pp. 500 ff.

Cour de Justice Benelux/Benelux Gerechtshof, Jurisprudence/Jurisprudentie 1975-1979 (1979), 1981-1992 (1993)

aa) Treaty Instituting the Benelux Economic Union of February 3, 1958

CHAPITRE 7. DU COLLEGE ARBITRAL

Art. 41   Le Collège arbitral a pour mission de régler les différends qui pourraient s'élever entre les Hautes Parties Contractantes en ce qui concerne l'application du présent Traité et des dispositions conventionnelles relatives à son objet.

Art. 42   1. Le Collège arbitral est constitué en sections d'après les catégories de différends.

2. Pour chaque section, chacune des Hautes Parties Contractantes désigne un arbitre national titulaire et un arbitre national suppléant.

3. Pour chaque litige, la section est composée de l'arbitre national de chacune des deux parties au litige ainsi que d'une personne désignée par roulement sur une liste arrêtée à cet effet par le Comité de Ministres. Cette personne assume la présidence de la section.

Art. 43   Si le Président estime que l'importance des questions de droit soulevées dans le litige le rend opportun, il peut, soit d'office, soit à la demande d'une des parties, décider que la section sera complétée par l'adjonction de deux arbitres inscrits sur la liste prévue à l'article 42, alinéa 3 du présent Traité. Ces arbitres doivent avoir la même nationalité que les parties au litige.

Art. 44   Lorsqu'un différend n'a pas pu être aplani au sein du Comité de Ministres, le Collège arbitral est saisi, soit par requête conjointe des parties au différend, soit par requête unilatérale de l'une d'elles.

Art. 45   1. Le Collège arbitral statue sur la base du respect du droit. Avant de rendre sa sentence, il peut, dans tout état du litige, proposer à l'agrément des parties un règlement à l'amiable du différend.

2. Si les parties sont d'accord, le Collège arbitral statue ex aequo et bono.

Art. 46   1. Les sentences et les propositions de règlement à l'amiable sont adoptées par le Collège arbitral à la majorité des voix. Les sentences sont définitives et sans recours. Les règlements à l'amiable acceptés par les parties ont le même effet que les sentences.

2. A moins de stipulations contraires, le Collège arbitral peur prescrire, lorsqu'il a réuni les éléments d'information suffisants, les mesures conservatoires qu'il estime nécessaires.

Art. 47   1. Chacune des Hautes Parties Contractantes peut intervenir dans un litige entre les deux autres Parties Contractantes si elle justifie d'un intérêt à la solution de celui-ci; l'intervention ne peut avoir d'autre objet que le soutien des prétentions d'une des parties.

2. L'intervention ne modifie pas la composition initiale de la section saisie du litige.

Art. 48   Par une sentence, le Collège arbitral peut déclarer qu'une décision prise par une autorité judiciaire ou qu'une mesure émanant de toute autre autorité de l'une des Hautes Parties Contractantes est entièrement ou partiellement en opposition avec des stipulations du présent Traité ou avec des dispositions conventionnelles relatives à son objet. Si le droit interne de ladite Partie Contractante ne permet pas d'effacer les conséquences de cette décision ou de cette mesure, l'Etat lésé a droit à une réparation équitable. A défaut d'accord des parties au différend, le Collège arbitral, sur requête de la partie intéressée, fixe la nature et l'étendue de la réparation.

Art. 49   Lorsque le Collège arbitral est saisi d'un différend, les parties s'abstiennent de toute acte susceptible d'en compromettre le règlement ou d'aggraver le différend.

Art. 50   Au cas où l'une des parties n'aurait pas exécuté une sentence du Collège arbitral ou une mesure conservatoire prescrite par celui-ci, l'autre partie est en droit de saisir la Cour Internationale de Justice en application de l'article 36, alinéa 2 du Statut de celle-ci, à moins que les parties au différend n'aient recours de commun accord à un autre mode de règlement.

Art. 51   1.Les Hautes Parties Contractantes s'engagent à ne pas soumettre les différends visés par l'article 41 à des modes de règlement autres que ceux prévus dans le présent Traité.

2. Toutefois, les Hautes Parties Contractantes conviennent de soumettre les différends mettant également en cause l'interprétation ou l'application du Traité instituant la Communauté Economique Européenne ou du Traité instituant la Communauté Européenne de l'Energie Atomique, à la Cour de Justice instituée par lesdits Traités. Dans la mesure où la Cour de Justice se déclare incompétente pour trancher le différend, le Collège arbitral prévu à l'article 15 du présent Traité, est compétent.

Art. 52   1. Le Comité de Ministres peut demander au Collège arbitral des avis consultatifs sur des questions de droit relatives aux stipulations du présent Traité et aux dispositions conventionnelles relatives à son objet.

2. Les avis sont émis à la majorité des voix par les Présidents de section siégeant ensemble.

Art. 53   Le statut du Collège arbitral est détermine par décision du Comité de Ministres.

bb) Decision of the Committee of Ministers of the Benelux Economic Union Determining the Statute of the Arbitral College of November 3, 1960

Art. 1   Le Statut du Collège arbitral est déterminé dans le texte annexé à la présente décision.

Art. 2   La présente décision entre en vigueur le jour de sa signature.

Fait à Bruxelles, le 3 novembre 1960.

Le Président du Comité de Ministres.

STATUT DU COLLEGE ARBITRAL

COMPOSITION

Art. 1   1. Le Collège arbitral exerce ses fonctions conformément aux dispositions du Traité d'Union.

2. Il est composé des sections suivantes:

Section économique;

Section financière;

Section sociale;

Section agricole.

3. Le Comité de Ministres peut instituer d'autres sections.

4. Le Secrétaire général de l'Union économique assume les fonctions de greffier du Collège arbitral. Il conserve les archives et assure le service administratif.

DESIGNATION DES MEMBRES DES SECTIONS

Art. 2   1. Pour chaque section, chacune des Hautes Parties Contractantes au Traité d'Union désigne un arbitre effectif en un arbitre suppléant de sa nationalité. Une personne peut être désignée dans plusieurs sections à la fois.

2. Ces arbitres sont nommés parmi des personnalités offrant toutes garanties d'indépendance et de compétence.

3. Le mandat des arbitres a une durée de trois ans. Si à l'expiration de ce terme, ils n'ont pas été remplacés, leur mandat est tacitement reconduit pour une nouvelle période de trois ans.

Art. 3   1. En vue d'assurer la présidence des sections, le Comité de Ministres établit une liste de six arbitres, dont deux de la nationalité de chaque Haute Partie Contractante.

2. Ces arbitres sont désignés parmi les Premiers Présidents, Présidents, Vice-Présidents et Conseillers des Cours de cassation ou des Cours d'appel des trois Hautes Parties Contractantes.

3. A cette fin, le Premier Président de la Cour de cassation de Belgique, le Président de la Cour supérieure de justice du Luxembourg et le Président du «Hoge Raad der Nederlanden» sont invités à communiquer au Comité de Ministres une liste de quatre personnes choisies parmi les magistrats précités de la Cour de cassation et des Cours d'appel de leur pays.

Art. 4   1. La désignation des arbitres mentionnés aux articles 2 et 3 se fait dès l'entrée en vigueur du présent Statut.

2. En cas décès, de démission ou d'empêchement permanent d'un arbitre, il est pourvu à son remplacement. Le nouvel arbitre achève le terme de son prédécesseur.

En cas d'empêchement temporaire d'un arbitre mentionné à l'article 2, son suppléant prend sa place.

En cas d'empêchement temporaire d'un arbitre mentionné à l'article 3, il appartient au Comité de Présidence visé à l'article 6 d'arrêter les mesures nécessaires.

3. Le remplacement des arbitres s'effectue suivant la procédure prévue pour leur désignation. Toutefois, dans le cas du remplacement d'un des arbitres mentionnés à l'article 3, la liste communiquée au Comité de Ministres ne comprend que deux personnes.

COMPOSITION DES SECTIONS

Art. 5   1. Chaque section saisie d'un différend est composée de la façon suivante:

a) La présidence est exercée par un arbitre de la liste mentionnée à l'article 3, alinéa 1, et désigné suivant un système de roulement fixé par le Comité de Ministres. Une personne peut présider plusieurs sections.

b) L'arbitre national de chacune des deux parties en litige siège à la section.

2. La composition d'une section saisie d'un différend reste invariable sauf dans les cas prévus à l'article 4, alinéa 2.

COMITE DE PRESIDENCE

Art. 6   1. Les arbitres mentionnés à l'article 3 constituent le Comité de Présidence du Collège arbitral. Le Comité élit parmi ses membres un président qui reste en fonction pour une année et qui est rééligible. Son mandat est reconduit tacitement s'il n'y a pas de nouvelle élection avant l'expiration de son terme.

2. Les délibérations du Comité de Présidence sont acquises à la majorité des voix.

3. Le Comité de Présidence arrête le règlement d'ordre intérieur du Collège arbitral. En arrêtant ce règlement, le Comité de Présidence tient compte, dans la mesure du possible, du Modèle des Règles sur la Procédure arbitrale élaboré par la Commission de Droit international des Nations Unies (Document A/3859), étant entendu que la procédure doit être contradictoire.

4. Le Comité de Présidence peut, à l'initiative d'un de ses membres, décider à l'unanimité que, pour un motif grave, un arbitre ne doit pas concourir à la décision d'un litige déterminé. Si cet arbitre est membre du Comité de Présidence, il ne prend pas part au vote afférent.

DECLARATION DES ARBITRES

Art. 7   Les arbitres ne peuvent assumer leurs fonctions qu'après avoir déposé au greffe du Collège arbitral une déclaration écrite libellée comme suit:

«Je déclare solennellement que j'exercerai tous mes devoirs et attributions d'arbitre en tout honneur et dévouement, en pleine et parfaite impartialité et en toute conscience.»

FIN DU MANDAT DES ARBITRES

Art. 8   1. Lorsqu'un arbitre demande à être déchargé de ses fonctions, le Comité de Présidence décide à la majorité des voix si la démission sera accordée.

2. Le Comité de Présidence peut décider que la démission ne prendra effet qu'après l'achèvement de toutes ou certaines affaires en cours auxquelles l'arbitre participe.

3. Le Comité de Présidence avise immédiatement le Comité de Ministres de toute démission accordée. Ce dernier peut désigner un nouvel arbitre même si la démission est accordée dans le cas prévu à l'alinéa 2 du présent article.

4. Un arbitre ne peut être relevé de ses fonctions avant le terme pour lequel il a été nommé que si, au jugement unanime du Comité de Présidence, il ne remplit plus les conditions requises pour l'exécution de ses fonctions.

5. Dans les cas prévus au présent article, l'arbitre qui est membre du Comité de Présidence ne prend pas part aux votes qui le concernent.

PROCEDURE

Art. 9   1. Lorsqu'une Haute Partie Contractante fait appel à l'arbitrage, elle dépose une requête au greffe du Collège arbitral et en transmet une copie au Gouvernement de la Haute Partie Contractante mise en cause.

2. Lorsque deux Hautes Parties Contractantes font conjointement appel à l'arbitrage pour résoudre le différend qui les oppose, elles déposent une requête conjointe au greffe du Collège arbitral.

3. Le greffier transmet une copie certifiée conforme des requêtes aux membres du Comité de Présidence ainsi qu'à la troisième Partie Contractante.

4. Le président du Comité de Présidence défère chaque requête à la section que l'affaire concerne.

5. Le greffier communique dans le plus bref délai le dossier relatif au différend aux membres de la section saisie.

6. La section se réunit dans les huit jours qui suivent la communication du dossier.

Art. 10   1. Les délibérations des sections sont acquises à la majorité des voix.

2. A défaut d'autres dispositions prises de commun accord par les parties en litige, la section suit les règles de procédure arrêtées par le Comité de présidence conformément à l'article 6, alinéa 3.

3. Chaque partie en litige se fait représenter devant la section saisie par un agent. Celui-ci peut se faire assister de conseils et d'experts.

INTERVENTION

Art. 11   1. Le Gouvernement d'une Haute Partie Contractante demanderesse en intervention dépose sa demande au greffe du Collège arbitral et en transmet une copie aux parties en litige.

2. La section saisie admet la demande en intervention si celle-ci répond aux conditions prévues par l'article 47 du Traité d'Union.

PREUVES ET RENSEIGNEMENTS

Art. 12   1. La section juge de l'admissibilité et de la valeur des preuves invoquées par les parties.

2. Les parties communiquent à la section les renseignements que celle-ci leur demande. Si une partie manque à cette obligation, la section en prend acte.

3. La section peut demander les renseignements prévus à l'alinéa 2 du présent article jusqu'à la clôture des débats.

Art. 13   Toute pièce produite par l'une des parties doit être communiquée en copie certifiée conforme, par l'intermédiaire du greffier, à la partie adverse et, le cas échéant, à la partie intervenante.

PUBLICITE DES SEANCES ET DELIBERATIONS

Art. 14   1. Les séances des sections ne sont pas publiques, à moins que les parties n'en aient décidé autrement. Les délibérations sont tenues secrètes.

2. Les arbitres doivent garder le secret sur tout ce qui est porté à leur connaissance dans l'exercice de leur fonction.

DEFAUT

Art. 15   1. Lorsqu'une des parties ne se présente pas ou s'abstient de faire valoir ses moyens, l'autre partie peut demander à la section saisie de lui adjuger ses conclusions.

2. La section, avant d'y faire droit, doit s'assurer que le Collège arbitral est compétent et que les conclusions sont fondées en fait et en droit.

DESISTEMENT

Art. 16   1. Moyennant l'accord de la partie adverse, la partie demanderesse peut se désister jusqu'au prononcé de la sentence.

2. En cas de dessaisissement de la section par accord des deux parties, la section en prend acte.

3. La section peut prendre acte d'une transaction intervenue entre les parties et lui donner, à leur requête, la forme d'une sentence.

SENTENCE ARBITRALE

Art. 17   1. La sentence est adoptée à la majorité des voix par la section saisie du différend. Elle doit être rendue dans les trois mois qui suivent la date de communication du dossier aux membres de la section, à moins que les parties en litige ne soient d'accord pour prolonger ce délai. Une demande en intervention n'exerce aucune influence sur ce délai.

2. La sentence est motivée. Elle indique le nom des arbitres; elle est signée par le président de la section et par le greffier.

3. La sentence est prononcée en séance publique. Le greffier veille à ce que les Ministres des Affaires étrangères des parties reçoivent communication de la sentence dans les huit jours qui suivent le prononcé de celle-ci; il en assure la communication dans le même délai au Ministre des Affaires étrangères du Gouvernement resté en dehors du litige.

Art. 18   La sentence est obligatoire dès le huitième jour qui suit le prononcé. Elle doit être exécutée de bonne foi et immédiatement, à moins qu'elle ne prévoie des délais pour tout ou partie de cette exécution.

Art. 19   En cas de contestation sur le sens et la portée d'une sentence, il appartient à la section qui l'a rendue de l'interpréter. La demande d'interprétation doit être formulée par les parties ou par l'une d'elles, dans le délai d'un mois après que la contestation s'est manifestée et au plus tard dans les six mois qui suivent le prononcé de la sentence.

Art. 20   1. La révision d'une sentence ne peut être demandée qu'à la section qui l'a rendue et en raison de la découverte d'un fait qui eût été de nature à exercer une influence décisive sur la sentence et qui, avant le prononcé de celle-ci, n'était connu ni par la section, ni par la partie qui demande la révision sans qu'il y ait de sa part faute grave à l'ignorer.

2. La demande en révision ne peut être formulée par les parties ou par l'une d'entre elles, que dans le délai de six mois après la découverte du fait visé à l'alinéa 1er du présent article et au plus tard dans les trois années qui suivent le prononcé de la sentence.

3. Avant tout examen du fond, la section saisie se prononce par une décision motivée sur la recevabilité de la demande en révision.

4. Sauf décision contraire de la section, l'exécution de la sentence est suspendue, dès que la demande en révision est déclarée recevable.

MESURES CONSERVATOIRES

Art. 21   1. Les mesures conservatoires prévues à l'article 46, alinéa 2, du Traité d'Union sont prescrites par la section saisie du différend.

2. Les mesures conservatoires ne préjugent pas le fond de l'affaire.

3. La section peut, en tout état du litige, modifier ou révoquer les mesures conservatoires qu'elle a prescrites ou confirmées.

DEMANDE D'AVIS CONSULTATIF

Art. 22   1. Si le Comité de Ministres demande un avis consultatif en vertu de l'article 52 du Traité d'Union, le greffier communique dans le plus bref délai le dossier y relatif aux membres du Comité de Présidence.

2. Le Comité se réunit dans les vingt et un jours qui suivent la communication du dossier.

3. L'avis consultatif doit être rendu dans les deux mois qui suivent la communication du dossier. L'avis ne peut être publié qu'avec le consentement du Comité de Ministres.

EMPLOI DES LANGUES

Art. 23   1. Les parties sont libres de choisir une des langues officielles des institutions de l'Union, tant pour les actes de procédure et leurs annexes que lors des débats oraux. En cas de besoin, à la demande d'une partie ou d'un arbitre, le greffier assure la traduction dans l'autre langue.

2. Les pièces et documents produits ou annexés qui sont rédigés dans une langue autre que le français ou le néerlandais doivent, à la demande d'une partie ou d'un arbitre, être accompagnés d'une traduction dans l'une ou l'autre de ces langues. Dans le cas de pièces et documents volumineux, des traductions en extrait peuvent être présentées. A tout moment, la section peut exiger une traduction plus complète ou intégrale, soit d'office, soit à la demande d'une des parties.

3. Lorsqu'un témoin ou un expert déclare qu'il ne peut s'exprimer convenablement dans une des langues officielles, la section l'autorise à faire sa déclaration dans une autre langue et décide, s'il y a lieu, des dispositions à prendre pour assurer la traduction dans les langues officielles.

Art. 24   Le Collège arbitral a son siège à Bruxelles. Les sections peuvent toutefois se réunir en dehors du siège.

Art. 25   Les dispositions du présent Statut peuvent être modifiées ou complétées par décision du Comité de Ministres sur avis du Comité de Présidence.

cc) Treaty Concerning the Creation and the Statute of a Benelux Court of Justice of March 31, 1965

PREAMBULE

Sa Majesté le Roi des Belges,

Son Altesse Royale le Grand-Duc de Luxembourg,

Sa Majesté la Reine des Pays-Bas,

Considérant qu'il convient de promouvoir l'uniformité dans l'application des règles juridiques communes à la Belgique, au Luxembourg et aux Pays-Bas,

Ont décidé, dans ce but, de conclure un Traité instituant une Cour de Justice Benelux et ont nommé Leurs Plénipotentiaires, savoir:

Sa Majesté le Roi des Belges:

Son Excellence Monsieur H. Fayat, Ministre-Adjoint aux Affaires étrangères,

Son Altesse Royale le Grand-Duc de Luxembourg:

Son Excellence Monsieur P. Werner, Ministre d'Etat, Ministre des Affaires étrangères;

Sa Majesté la Reine des Pays-Bas:

Son Excellence Monsieur J.M.A.H. Luns, Ministre des Affaires étrangères;

lesquels, après s'être communiqué leurs pleins pouvoirs trouvés en bonne et due forme, sont convenus des dispositions suivantes:

CHAPITRE 1. INSTITUTION, BUT ET SIEGE DE LA COUR

Art. 1   1. Il est institué une Cour de Justice Benelux.

2. La Cour est chargée de promouvoir l'uniformité dans l'application des règles juridiques qui sont communes:

a)   aux trois pays du Benelux, et qui sont désignées:

–   soit par une convention;

–   soit par une décision du Comité de Ministres prévu par le Traité du 3 février 1958 instituant l'Union économique Benelux;

b)   à deux pays du Benelux et qui sont désignées par une convention en vigueur entre ces deux pays et signée par les trois pays du Benelux.

3. La décision du Comité de Ministres visée à l'alinéa 2 peut exclure l'application d'un des chapitres III, IV ou V du présent Traité, ou de deux de ces chapitres.

4. Le Comité de Ministres peut, également par décision, exclure de l'application du présent Traité ou d'un ou de deux des chapitres III, IV et V de celui-ci, des dispositions désignées par lui comme règles juridiques communes.

5. Les décisions visées aux alinéas 3 et 4 sont prises après avis du Conseil interparlementaire consultatif de Benelux. Elles sont publiées, avant la date de leur entrée en vigueur, dans chacun des trois Etats dans les formes qui y sont prévues pour la publication des traités.

Art. 2 1. Le siège permanent de la Cour est au lieu où se trouve fixé le Secrétariat général de l'Union économique Benelux. Le greffe est établi au siège de ce secrétariat.

2. La Cour peut aussi tenir audience dans un autre lieu situé dans l'un des trois pays.

CHAPITRE II. ORGANISATION

Art. 3 1. La Cour est composée de neuf juges dont un président, un premier et un second vice-président et de six juges suppléants. Son organisation comporte un Parquet de trois avocats généraux dont un chef de Parquet. La Cour est assistée de trois greffiers dont un greffier en chef. Les juges et les juges suppléants sont choisis parmi les membres du siège de la Cour suprême de chacun des trois pays. Pour le Grand-Duché de Luxembourg, les juges et les juges suppléants peuvent également être choisis parmi les membres du Comité du Contentieux du Conseil d'Etat. Les avocats généraux sont choisis parmi les magistrats du Parquet près la Cour suprême de chacun des trois pays. Les greffiers sont choisis sur proposition du Secrétaire général parmi les membres du Secrétariat général de l'Union économique Benelux.

2. Les juges, les juges suppléants, les avocats généraux et les greffiers sont nommés en nombre égal pour chacun des trois pays, par décision du Comité de Ministres. Les juges, les juges suppléants et les avocats généraux font partie de la Cour Benelux tant qu'ils sont en fonction effective dans leur pays. Néanmoins, les juges, les juges suppléants et avocats généraux luxembourgeois, mis à la retraite pour limite d'âge peuvent rester en fonction à la Cour Benelux jusqu'à l'âge de 70 ans. Cette limite d'âge s'applique également aux juges et juges suppléants choisis parmi les membres du Conseil d'Etat luxembourgeois.

3. Au cas où un juge, un juge suppléant ou un avocat général ne remplit plus les conditions pour exercer ses fonctions à la Cour Benelux, celle-ci le constate. Si un juge, un juge suppléant ou un avocat général présente sa démission, celle-ci est remise au Président de la Cour et s'il s'agit de lui-même, au Chef du Parquet. Dans ces cas, le Président de la Cour ou le Chef du Parquet en donne notification au Comité de Ministres qui en donne acte. Ce donné acte emporte vacance de siège. Il est mis fin aux fonctions des greffiers par le Comité de Ministres.

4. Les magistrats qui restent membres de la Cour et du Parquet bien qu'ils aient cessé pour cause de retraite d'appartenir à la magistrature de leur pays sont assujettis aux incompatibilités applicables aux magistrats de la Cour suprême dans leur pays. Ils restent soumis au pouvoir disciplinaire de leur pays.

5. L'attribution des fonctions de Président, de premier et de second vice-président au sein de la Cour Benelux est organisée par roulement entre les trois pays et par période de trois ans. Chaque mandat de trois ans commencé et interrompu doit être achevé par un juge de la même nationalité. Le Président, un premier et un second vice-président de nationalité différente sont élus à la majorité absolue des membres présents, par la Cour réunie en assemblée générale. Toutefois, la première élection du Président de la Cour est faite à la majorité absolue des magistrats désignés par le Comité de Ministres comme membres de la Cour et présents à l'assemblée générale. L'ordre de succession des nationalités à la présidence et aux vice-présidences établi au suffrage pendant les neuf premières années du fonctionnement de la Cour, sera répété par roulement dans la suite.

6. L'attribution de la fonction de Chef du Parquet près la Cour Benelux est organisée par roulement entre les trois pays et par période de trois ans. Chaque mandat de trois ans commencé et interrompu doit être achevé par un avocat général de la même nationalité. L'ordre de succession des nationalité à la fonction de Chef du Parquet est pendant les neuf premières années déterminé par l'âge. Cet ordre de succession sera répété par roulement dans la suite.

Art. 4   1. Les membres de la Cour et du Parquet exercent leurs fonctions en toute impartialité et en toute indépendance.

2. Devant l'assemblée générale, réunie en séance plénière, le Président prête le serment de remplir ses fonctions avec intégrité, exactitude et impartialité et de garder le secret des délibérations. Les membres de la Cour et du Parquet prêtent le même serment entre les mains du Président.

3. Les greffiers prêtent, entre les mains du Président, le serment de remplir leurs fonctions avec intégrité et exactitude et de garder le secret des délibérations.

4. Le serment est prêté, ou, le cas échéant, remplacé par une promesse suivant les modalités prévues par la législation nationale du magistrat ou du greffier.

5. Les membres de la Cour et du Parquet et les greffiers ne sont pas rémunérés. Les frais de déplacement et de séjour sont à charge du budget du Secrétariat général de l'Union économique Benelux.

Art. 5   1. La Cour siège en principe au nombre de neuf juges, trois de chaque pays. Elle peut cependant, dans les cas prévus par son Règlement d'ordre intérieur, siéger au nombre de trois juges, un de chaque pays. L'avocat général appartient de préférence au pays où l'affaire est pendante au fond.

2. Un Règlement d'ordre intérieur, délibéré en assemblée générale de la Cour, détermine notamment la composition du siège, la dévolution éventuelle des affaires à des chambres composées de trois juges, les préséances, les congés, les assemblées générales, l'intervention du Parquet, le mode de votation, l'établissement du rôle, la fixation des audiences et le fonctionnement du greffe.

3. Se récusent les membres de la Cour et du Parquet qui auraient, à quelque degré que ce soit, concouru comme membres d'une juridiction nationale à une décision rendue dans l'affaire portée devant la Cour. Ne doit pas être considérée telle la décision par laquelle la juridiction nationale s'est bornée à surseoir de statuer conformément aux dispositions de l'article 6 du présent Traité.

4. Le Ministre de la Justice de chacun des trois pays correspond directement avec le Parquet près la Cour. Il peut, par cette voie, communiquer à la Cour un exposé contenant sa façon de voir sur une question en litige, à charge d'en transmettre copie aux Ministres de la Justice des deux autres pays. Les membres du Parquet ne sont pas tenus de défendre l'opinion exprimée par le Ministre.

5. Les avocats généraux se suppléent réciproquement à quelque pays qu'ils appartiennent. En cas d'empêchement de tous les titulaires, la Cour désigne un de ses membres ou membres suppléants pour en remplir momentanément les fonctions.

CHAPITRE III. ATTRIBUTIONS JURIDICTIONNELLES

Art. 6 1. Dans les cas spécifiés ci-après, la Cour Benelux connaît des questions d'interprétation des règles juridiques désignées en vertu de l'article premier, qui se pose à l'occasion de litiges pendants soit devant les juridictions de l'un des trois pays, siégeant dans leur territoire en Europe, soit devant le Collège arbitral prévu par le Traité d'Union économique Benelux.

2. Lorsqu'il apparaît qu'une décision dans une affaire pendante devant une juridiction nationale implique la solution d'une difficulté d'interprétation d'une règle juridique désignée en vertu de l'article premier, cette juridiction peut, si elle estime qu'une décision sur ce point est nécessaire pour rendre son jugement, surseoir même d'office à toute décision définitive afin que la Cour Benelux se prononce sur la question d'interprétation.

3. Dans les conditions déterminées dans l'alinéa précédent, une juridiction nationale dont les décisions ne sont pas susceptibles d'un recours juridictionnel de droit interne, est tenue de saisir la Cour Benelux.

4. Néanmoins, la juridiction visée aux alinéas 2 et 3 passe outre:

1° si elle estime que la question qui se pose n'est pas de nature à faire naître un doute raisonnable.

2° si l'affaire revêt un caractère de particulière urgence.

Elle peut passer outre si elle se rallie à la solution précédemment donnée par la Cour Benelux à l'occasion d'un autre litige ou dans un avis consultatif.

5. La décision de demande d'interprétation énonce les faits à propos desquels l'interprétation à donner par la Cour Benelux doit être appliquée. Elle n'est ni levée, ni notifiée, mais envoyée d'office, dans le plus bref délai, par le greffier et en copie certifiée conforme, à la Cour Benelux.

Celle-ci en fait parvenir copie aux ministres de la Justice des trois pays. La Cour peut demander la communication des dossiers.

6. La juridiction qui, sans statuer en même temps sur le fond statue conformément à l'alinéa 2 du présent article sur l'opportunité de demander une interprétation à la Cour Benelux, peut décider que le recours ouvert contre sa décision peut être exercé dès la prononciation de cette décision ou conjointement avec le recours contre la décision à intervenir ultérieurement sur le fond.

Art. 7   1. En statuant sur la demande d'interprétation, la Cour ne décide que de la réponse à donner à la question qui lui est soumise. Il en est justifié par l'expédition délivrée par le greffier de cette juridiction. Cette expédition est, dans le plus bref délai, envoyée par le greffier de la Cour à la juridiction devant laquelle l'affaire est pendante au fond, ainsi qu'aux parties ou à leurs mandataires.

2. Les juridictions nationales qui statuent ensuite dans la cause sont liées par l'interprétation résultant de la décision rendue par la Cour Benelux.

3. Les délais de procédure à observer devant la juridiction nationale ainsi que les délais de prescription sont suspendus de plein droit pendant la durée de l'instance suivie devant la Cour Benelux, à savoir depuis le jour de la surséance prononcée par l'application de l'article 6, jusqu'au jour de l'entrée au greffe de la décision conformément aux dispositions de l'alinéa 1er du présent article.

Art. 8   La Cour Benelux peut connaître d'une demande d'interprétation même si la décision du juge national portant demande d'interprétation n'a pas acquis force de chose jugée d'après les dispositions de son droit national.

Art. 9   1. Lorsque, pour l'interprétation d'une règle juridique désignée en vertu de l'article premier, il est nécessaire de qualifier une institution juridique ou les rapports qui en découlent et que cette qualification n'est pas déterminée par une telle règle juridique, la Cour Benelux procède à cette qualification conformément à la loi du pays où a été rendue la décision portant demande d'interprétation.

2. La Cour Benelux n'est pas compétente pour apprécier si l'application d'une règle juridique à laquelle renvoie une règle juridique désignée en vertu de l'article premier est contraire à l'ordre public.

Chapitre IV. Attributions consultatives

Art. 10   1. Chacun des trois Gouvernements peut requérir la Cour Benelux de se prononcer par un avis consultatif sur l'interprétation d'une règle juridique désignée en vertu de l'article premier.

2. La requête est communiquée par le greffe de la Cour aux deux autres Gouvernements qui peuvent adresser leurs observations à la Cour. Celle-ci fait, à bref délai, insérer au journal officiel de chacun des trois pays un avis énonçant sommairement l'objet de la requête.

3. Les parties qui seraient engagées dans une instance judiciaire ou arbitrale où la même question est débattue peuvent également adresser leurs observations à la Cour, laquelle peut surseoir à prononcer jusqu'à la décision de la juridiction saisie du litige.

4. Dans l'exercice de ses attributions consultatives, la Cour s'inspire des dispositions du présent Traité qui s'appliquent en matière juridictionnelle, dans la mesure où elle les reconnaît applicables.

CHAPITRE V. COLLEGE ARBITRAL

Art. 11   1. Lorsqu'il apparaît qu'une décision dans une affaire pendante devant le Collège arbitral prévu par le Traité d'Union économique Benelux implique la solution d'une difficulté d'interprétation d'une règle juridique désignée en vertu de l'article premier, le Collège arbitral, s'il estime qu'une décision sur ce point est nécessaire pour rendre sa sentence, doit surseoir, même d'office, à toute décision définitive afin que la Cour Benelux se prononce sur la question d'interprétation.

2. Néanmoins, le Collège arbitral passe outre:

1° s'il estime que la question qui se pose n'est pas de nature à faire naître un doute raisonnable;

2° si l'affaire revêt un caractère de particulière urgence.

3. Il peut passer outre s'il se rallie à la solution précédemment donnée par la Cour Benelux à l'occasion d'un autre litige ou dans un avis consultatif.

4. Il est lié par l'interprétation résultant de la décision rendue par la Cour Benelux.

CHAPITRE VI. PROCEDURE ET FRAIS DE JUSTICE

Art. 12   1. L'exercice des attributions juridictionnelles de la Cour est, en principe, soumis aux règles traditionnellement observées par les tribunaux de l'ordre judiciaire.

2. La Cour arrête son règlement de procédure et le soumet à l'approbation du Comité de Ministres.

3. La procédure à suivre devant la Cour est essentiellement écrite. La Cour peut décider des débats oraux et publics aux lieu, jour et heure à fixer par elle.

4. Chaque partie a le droit de déposer un mémoire communiquant ses arguments et ses conclusions, dans le délai qui sera fixé par le Président. Un délai peut, selon les nécessités de la cause, être accordé aux parties pour déposer un mémoire de réponse. Ces délais peuvent être prorogés.

5. Sont admis à plaider devant la Cour les membres des barreaux des trois pays, ainsi que toutes autres personnes agréées par la Cour dans chaque cause.

6. Les délibérations de la Cour sont secrètes. La décision est motivée; elle porte le nom des juges qui l'ont prise et elle est prononcée en audience publique. La décision n'est susceptible d'aucune voie de recours.

7. Les langues employées par et devant la Cour sont le français et le néerlandais. Les actes de procédure doivent toujours être accompagnés d'une traduction dans l'autre langue. La procédure, les plaidoiries et la décision ont lieu dans la langue employé pour la procédure devant la juridiction où l'affaire est pendante au fond. La Cour peut admettre des dérogations à cette dernière règle en ce qui concerne les plaidoiries. Si des débats oraux ont eu lieu, une note de plaidoirie et sa traduction doivent être déposées.

8. Un service de traduction est annexé au greffe de la Cour. Il délivre gratuitement toutes les traductions prévues ci-dessus.

Art. 13   1. En matière juridictionnelle, la Cour fixe le montant des frais exposés devant elle. Ces frais comprennent les honoraires promérités par les conseils des parties pour autant que cela soit conforme à la législation du pays où le procès est pendant.

2. Les frais ainsi déterminés font partie des dépens sur lesquels il sera statué par la juridiction nationale.

3. Dans les trois pays, les actes de la procédure suivie devant la Cour Benelux et les décisions ou avis de celle-ci sont exempts des formalités et droits de timbre et d'enregistrement ainsi que de tous autres droits fiscaux.

CHAPITRE VII. CLAUSE FINANCIERE

Art. 14   Les frais de fonctionnement de la Cour, du greffe et du service de traduction sont portés au budget du Secrétariat général de l'Union économique Benelux.

CHAPITRE VIII. DISPOSITIONS FINALES

Art. 15   1. En ce qui concerne le Royaume des Pays-Bas, le présent Traité ne s'appliquera qu'au territoire situé en Europe.

2. Le Gouvernement du Royaume des Pays-Bas pourra étendre l'application du présent Traité au Surinam et aux Antilles néerlandaises par une déclaration à cet effet à adresser au Secrétariat général de l'Union économique Benelux.

Art. 16   1. Le présent Traité sera ratifié et les instruments de ratification seront déposés auprès du Secrétariat général de l'Union économique Benelux.

2. Il entrera en vigueur le premier jour du mois qui suivra la date du dépôt du troisième instrument de ratification.

3. Il prendra fin en même temps que le Traité instituant l'Union économique Benelux.

En foi de quoi, les Plénipotentiaires ont signé le présent Traité et l'ont revêtu de leur sceau.

dd) Additional Protocol to the Treaty Creating a Benelux Court of Justice of October 25, 1966

> Le Gouvernement du Royaume de Belgique,
>
> Le Gouvernement du Grand-Duché de Luxembourg,
>
> Le Gouvernement du Royaume des Pays-Bas,
>
> Se référant à l article 12, paragraphe 7 du Traité relatif à l'institution et au statut d'une Cour de Justice Benelux, signé à Bruxelles le 31 mars 1965;
>
> Considérant qu'il s'indique de déterminer l'emploi des langues devant la Cour de Justice Benelux, lorsque la décision de demande d'interprétation a été rendue en langue allemande;
>
> Ont décidé de conclure à cet effet un Protocole additionnel au dit Traité, et sont convenus des dispositions suivantes:

Art. 1   L'article 12, paragraphe 7 du Traité relatif à l'institution et au statut d'une Cour de Justice Benelux est complété par la disposition suivante qui en formera le second alinéa:

«Lorsque la décision de demande d'interprétation a été rendue en langue allemande, la Cour peut ordonner que la procédure et la décision aient lieu, soit en français, soit en néerlandais. Les actes de procédure doivent toujours être accompagnés d'une traduction dans les deux autres langues. Les plaidoiries peuvent avoir lieu dans l'une des trois langues; une note de plaidoirie et sa traduction dans les deux autres langues doivent être déposées".

Art. 2   1. Le présent Protocole sera ratifié et les instruments de ratification seront déposés auprès du Secrétariat général de l'Union économique Benelux.

2. Il entrera en vigueur le premier jour du mois qui suivra la date du dépôt du troisième instrument de ratification.

3. Il fera partie intégrante du Traité relatif à l'institution et au statut d'une Cour de Justice Benelux, signé à Bruxelles, le 31 mars 1965.

ee) Internal Rules of the Benelux Court of Justice of October 25, 1974 as amended on April 18, 1988

DISPOSITION PRELIMINAIRE

Dans le présent Règlement:

– Est dénommé «Traité», le Traité relatif à l'institution et au statut d'une Cour de Justice Benelux, signé à Bruxelles le 31 mars 1965, tel qu'il a été modifié par le Protocole du 10 juin 1981 modifiant l'article 1er dudit Traité et par le Protocole du 23 novembre 1984 modifiant et complétant ledit Traité;

- Est dénommé «Protocole concernant la protection juridictionnelle», le Protocole additionnel au Traité relatif à l'institution et au statut d'une Cour de Justice Benelux concernant la protection juridictionnelle des personnes au service de l'Union économique Benelux, signé à La Haye le 29 avril 1969, tel qu'il a été complété par le Protocole du 11 mai 1974 concernant la protection juridictionnelle des personnes au service du Bureau Benelux des marques et du Bureau Benelux des dessins ou modèles.

CHAPITRE 1ER. DES JUGES, DES JUGES SUPPLEANTS, DES AVOCATS GENERAUX, DES AVOCATS GENERAUX SUPPLEANTS ET DES GREFFIERS

Art. 1   La fonction d'un magistrat prend cours dès sa prestation de serment.

Art. 2   Les magistrats prennent rang d'après leur ancienneté à la Cour de Justice Benelux. Cette ancienneté résulte de la date de leur nomination. S'ils ont la même ancienneté, ils prennent rang d'après celle qu'ils ont dans leur juridiction nationale. En ce qui concerne les magistrats luxembourgeois, cette ancienneté est déterminée par leur première nomination dans l'une des deux juridictions nationales mentionnées dans l'article 3 du Traité.

Art. 3   1. La Cour prend rang avant le Parquet et le Parquet avant le Greffe.

2. Le rang des membres de la Cour est le suivant: le président, le premier vice-président, le second vice-président, les juges selon leur ancienneté et les juges suppléants selon leur ancienneté.

3. Celui des membres du Parquet: le chef du Parquet, les avocats généraux selon leur ancienneté et les avocats généraux suppléants selon leur ancienneté.

4. Celui des membres du Greffe: le greffier en chef et ensuite les greffiers selon leur ancienneté; s'il ont la même ancienneté, selon l'ordre de nomination.

5. L'ordre des préséances individuelles est le suivant: le président, le chef du Parquet, le premier vice-président, le second vice-président, les juges et avocats généraux selon leur ancienneté, les juges suppléants et les avocats généraux suppléants selon leur ancienneté et ensuite le greffier en chef et les greffiers selon leur ancienneté.

Art. 4   1. Les membres de la Cour, du Parquet et du Greffe prêtent serment ou, si leur législation nationale le permet, font éventuellement une promesse: ceux de nationalité belge en français ou en néerlandais en se conformant à leur législation nationale; ceux de nationalité luxembourgeoise en français; ceux de nationalité néerlandaise en néerlandais.

2. Devant l'assemblée générale, réunie en séance plénière, le président prête le serment ou fait la promesse dans les termes suivants: « Je jure (promets) de remplir mes fonctions avec intégrité, exactitude et impartialité et de garder le secret des délibérations ».

3. Après que le président a donné lecture de la formule du serment ou de la promesse telle qu'elle résulte, pour les membres de la Cour et du Parquet de l'article 4, alinéa 2 du Traité et pour les greffiers de l'article 4, alinéa 3 du Traité, les membres de la Cour, du Parquet et du Greffe prêtent ce serment ou formulent cette promesse.

4. Le greffier en chef remet aux membres de la Cour, du Parquet et du Greffe une pièce d'identité dont le président et le chef du Parquet déterminent la forme et le contenu. Lesdits membres sont tenus de présenter cette pièce à toute réquisition d'une autorité compétente.

Art. 5   Lorsque la Cour est appelée, par application de l'article 3, alinéa 3 du Traité, à constater si un juge effectif ou suppléant ou un avocat général effectif ou suppléant qui n'a pas présenté sa démission, ne remplit plus les conditions requises pour exercer ses fonctions à la Cour, le président — ou s'il s'agit d'un membre du Parquet, le chef du Parquet — invite l'intéressé à comparaître en chambre du conseil pour présenter ses observations ou, s'il le désire, à formuler celles-ci par écrit. La Cour siège au nombre de neuf juges, trois de chacune des nationalités. Elle statue après conclusions d'un avocat général.

Art. 6   1. Le président, les vice-présidents et les juges sont de plein droit affectés au service de la Cour siégeant au nombre de neuf juges. Les juges suppléants sont affectés à ce service selon les besoins de remplacement des juges.

2. Le président désigne annuellement les vice-présidents, juges et juges suppléants qui seront affectés au service des chambres visées par l'article 5, alinéas 1er et 2 du Traité.

3. La Chambre de la Cour qui exerce les attributions visées par le Protocole concernant la protection juridictionnelle est composée comme le prescrit l'article 2 dudit Protocole.

4. Les avocats généraux et les avocats généraux suppléants occupent le siège à l'une ou l'autre des chambres selon les besoins du service déterminés par le chef du Parquet après consultation de ses collègues. Ils participent aux audiences de la Cour, formée par neuf juges, selon les causes qui leur ont été distribuées. L'avocat général ou l'avocat général suppléant appartient de préférence au pays où l'affaire est pendante au fond.

CHAPITRE 2. DU PRESIDENT ET DES VICE-PRESIDENTS

Art. 7   1. La première période de trois ans durant laquelle sont, par application de l'article 3, alinéa 5 du Traité, exercées les fonctions de président et de vice-président prend cours le 22 mars 1974, date de la première assemblée générale de la Cour.

2. Conformément à la décision prise par la Cour en vertu de l'article 3, alinéa 5, dernière phrase du Traité, lors de l'assemblée générale du 22 mars 1974, l'ordre des nationalités pour lesdites fonctions est le suivant:

quant à la présidence: première période de trois ans: Pays-Bas; deuxième période de trois ans: Belgique; troisième période de trois ans: Luxembourg;

quant à la première vice-présidence: première période de trois ans: Luxembourg; deuxième période de trois ans: Pays-Bas; troisième période de trois ans: Belgique;

quant à la seconde vice-présidence: première période de trois ans: Belgique; deuxième période de trois ans: Luxembourg; troisième période de trois ans: Pays-Bas. Cet ordre de succession est répété par la suite.

3. Sans préjudice des dispositions de l'article 3, alinéa 2 du Traité, les président et vice-présidents continuent à exercer leurs fonctions aussi longtemps qu'il n'a pas été pourvu par élection à leur remplacement.

Art. 8   L'élection du président et des vice-présidents a lieu au scrutin secret.

Art. 9   1. Le président dirige les travaux de la Cour; il préside les assemblées générales, les audiences et les délibérations en chambre du conseil.

2. En cas d'absence ou d'empêchement du président ou en cas de vacance de la présidence, celle-ci est assurée par le premier vice-président.

3. En cas d'empêchement simultané du président et du premier vice-président, la présidence est assurée par le second vice-président ou à défaut, par un des autres juges selon l'ordre établi à l'article 3 du présent règlement.

CHAPITRE 3. DES AVOCATS GENERAUX ET DES AVOCATS GENERAUX SUPPLEANTS

Art. 10   1. La première période de trois ans durant laquelle un avocat général remplit les fonctions de chef du Parquet prend cours à la date indiquée à l'article 7, alinéa 1er.

2. En cas d'absence ou d'empêchement du chef du Parquet, cette fonction est exercée par l'avocat général le plus ancien et en cas d'absence ou d'empêchement de celui-ci par le suivant.

3. Conformément à l'article 3, alinéa 6 du Traité, la Cour réunie lors de l'assemblée générale du 22 mars 1974 a constaté que l'ordre des nationalités pour remplir les fonctions de chef du Parquet est le suivant:

pour la première période de trois ans: Belgique;

pour la deuxième période de trois ans: Luxembourg;

pour la troisième période de trois ans: Pays-Bas.

Cet ordre de succession est répété par la suite.

Art. 11   Sans préjudice des autres interventions précisées par le Règlement de procédure, les avocats généraux et les avocats généraux suppléants ont spécialement pour mission de présenter en toute indépendance des conclusions motivées sur toutes les affaires soumises à la Cour en vue d'assister celle-ci dans l'accomplissement de sa mission. Ces conclusions sont, selon ce que prescrit le Règlement de procédure, soit présentées oralement en audience publique, soit communiquées par écrit aux membres de la Cour et selon le cas, aux ministres de la justice, aux gouvernements et aux parties.

CHAPITRE 4. DU SIEGE DE LA COUR ET DU LIEU DE SES AUDIENCES — COMPOSITION — AUDIENCES

Art. 12   La Cour a son siège permanent à Bruxelles. Sur décision du président après avis ou requête du chef du Parquet, elle peut aussi tenir ses audiences dans un autre lieu situé dans l'un des trois pays.

Art. 13   1. La Cour siège en principe au nombre de neuf juges, trois de chaque pays. Le président peut décider qu'un ou plusieurs juges suppléants assisteront aux débats en vue de remplacer le ou les juges empêchés.

2. Sans préjudice de l'article 2, alinéa 2 du Protocole concernant la protection juridictionnelle, il est institué une Chambre dite de procédure composée de trois juges, un de chaque pays, qui peut prendre les décisions relatives à la procédure qui, aux termes du Règlement de procédure, sont prises par la Cour.

Art. 14   1. La Cour siège aux dates qui, selon les nécessités du service, sont fixées par le président après avis du chef du Parquet.

2. Toutefois, sauf urgence, la Cour ne siège point huit jours avant et huit jours après le premier janvier, huit jours avant et huit jours après Pâques ni pendant les mois de juillet et août.

Art. 15   La Cour observe les jours fériés légaux du lieu où elle a son siège permanent de même que les fêtes nationales luxembourgeoise et néerlandaise.

Art. 16   1. Pendant les périodes de vacances judiciaires fixées ci-dessus, la présidence est assurée par le président ou par le juge qu'il délègue et les fonctions de chef du Parquet sont assurées par le chef du Parquet ou l'avocat général qu'il désigne.

2. Le président et le chef du Parquet prennent les mesures nécessaires pour assurer en cas d'urgence les besoins du service.

3. Pendant les périodes de vacances judiciaires fixées ci-dessus, la direction du Greffe est assurée par le greffier en chef ou par le greffier qu'il désigne.

CHAPITRE 5. DES DELIBERATIONS DE LA COUR

Art. 17   1. La Cour ainsi que les chambres délibèrent en chambre du conseil. Seuls prennent part aux délibérations respectivement neuf ou trois juges ou juges suppléants qui ont assisté aux débats.

2. Chaque juge ou juge suppléant lors des délibérations émet son opinion motivée dans un ordre inverse à celui du rang.

3. La décision est prise à la majorité des voix.

4. Le délibéré de la Chambre de procédure peut se faire par écrit ou par téléphone. Dans ce dernier cas, la décision est confirmée par écrit. La décision est réputée rendue en chambre du conseil à la date précisée dans l'ordonnance.

CHAPITRE 6. DE L'ASSEMBLEE GENERALE DE LA COUR

Art. 18   1. L'assemblée générale est convoquée par le président soit d'office soit à la demande de trois membres de la Cour soit à la demande du chef du Parquet.

2. Elle est convoquée afin de délibérer et de décider dans les cas prévus par le Traité ainsi que sur tout autre objet intéressant le statut et le fonctionnement de la Cour.

Art. 19   L'assemblée générale se compose du président, des vice-présidents, des juges, des juges suppléants, des avocats généraux et des avocats généraux suppléants. Chaque membre a voix délibérative.

Art. 20   L'assemblée générale ne délibère valablement que si au moins les deux tiers de ses membres sont présents.

Art. 21   Le greffier en chef et les greffiers assistent à l'assemblée générale. Ils sont consultés sur toutes les questions relatives au Greffe. Le greffier en chef ou un greffier désigné par lui est chargé de dresser le procès-verbal des délibérations de l'assemblée générale qu'il signe avec le président.

CHAPITRE 7. DU GREFFE ET DU SERVICE DE TRADUCTION

Art. 22   1. Le Greffe est ouvert du lundi au vendredi de 9 à 12 et de 14 à 16 heures, sauf les jours fériés selon la législation belge, et les fêtes nationales luxembourgeoise et néerlandaise.

2. En dehors des heures d'ouverture du Greffe, toutes pièces et notamment les pièces de procédure peuvent être déposées dans la boîte aux lettres du Greffe. Cette boîte est levée chaque jour à l'ouverture du Greffe et le greffier de service appose sur la pièce un cachet mentionnant la date de cette levée.

Art. 23   Le greffier en chef est responsable de la tenue des dossiers des affaires pendantes et de leur mise à jour constante.

Art. 24   Les minutes des arrêts, ordonnances et autres décisions sont soumises par le greffier à la signature des magistrats compétents.

Art. 25   Il est délivré sur demande un accusé de réception de toute pièce de procédure déposée au Greffe.

Art. 26   1. Le greffier assiste les juges et les avocats généraux dans l'exercice de leur mission.

2. Le Greffe assure la garde des minutes, registres et actes.

3. Le greffier constate de manière authentique le dépôt des actes, pièces ou documents visés par le Traité, les Protocoles et les Règlements de la Cour, de même que leur date.

4. Le greffier assure la transmission des actes, pièces et autres documents aux gouvernements, aux ministres de la justice et aux parties et est chargé de faire les communications que prescrit notamment le Règlement de procédure.

Art. 27   1. Les greffiers et le personnel du Greffe agréé par le greffier en chef sont placés sous la direction et la surveillance de ce dernier.

2. Le greffier en chef répartit le service entre les greffiers et détermine les attributions du personnel de Greffe.

3. Le président et le chef du Parquet exercent une surveillance générale sur les activités du Greffe et peuvent donner des directives au greffier en chef.

Art. 28   1. Les membres du service de traduction annexé au Greffe sont placés sous la direction du greffier en chef.

2. Font partie de ce service ceux qui ont été agréés à cette fin par une commission de trois membres dont un magistrat du siège, un avocat général et le greffier en chef.

3. En cas de besoin, le greffier en chef est autorisé à avoir recours en vue des traductions à des personnes ou services étrangers au Greffe. Sauf cas d'urgence, le greffier en chef demande toutefois l'accord préalable du président ou du chef du Parquet.

Art. 29   Le greffier délivre les expéditions, copies ou extraits des arrêts, ordonnances ou avis et dresse acte des diverses formalités dont l'accomplissement doit être constaté.

Art. 30   1. Le Greffe tient deux registres: l'un relatif aux demandes et requêtes tendant à interprétation par voie d'arrêt ou d'avis, l'autre relatif aux recours des personnes visées par l'article 3 du Protocole concernant la protection juridictionnelle.

2. Chaque demande, requête et recours donne lieu à la constitution du dossier prévu à l'article 23. Ce dossier reçoit le numéro d'ordre repris au registre.

3. Le greffier inscrit ou mentionne dans le registre l'identité de l'auteur de la demande, de la requête ou du recours, la date de ceux-ci, ainsi que celle de leur entrée ou de leur dépôt au Parquet ou au Greffe de la Cour, les communications du Greffe, le dépôt des pièces de procédure, les autres actes de procédure ainsi que les ordonnances, arrêts et avis de la Cour.

Art. 31   Le greffier établit, dans la langue de la procédure, un procès-verbal de chaque audience publique. Ce procès-verbal mentionne:
   – la date et l'heure de l'audience;
   – le numéro de la cause ou des causes et sommairement leur objet;
   – les noms du président, des vice-présidents, des juges, de l'avocat général et du greffier présents;

- les noms des avocats et personnes autorisées à plaider devant la Cour;
- une indication sommaire de la décision ou de l'avis.

CHAPITRE 8. DES PUBLICATIONS DE LA COUR

Art. 32   1. A la requête du greffier en chef, des avis sont publiés dans le mois au Bulletin Benelux; ils indiquent d'une part la date de l'inscription au Greffe d'une demande ou d'une requête introduite par application des chapitres III, IV et V du Traité, d'autre part le gouvernement, la juridiction ou le Collège arbitral qui est l'auteur de la requête ou de la demande ainsi que l'objet de celle-ci. La même règle s'applique en ce qui concerne les arrêts rendus et les avis émis par application des dispositions visées ci-dessus.

2. Le président et le chef du Parquet veillent à ce que les arrêts et avis ou certains de ceux-ci soient publiés dans des revues juridiques des trois pays.

Art. 33   Le greffier en chef veille à la publication au Bulletin Benelux et donne communication aux ministres de la justice des trois pays en vue d'une publication dans les journaux officiels:

a)   des nominations, élections, désignations et démissions des magistrats et greffiers de la Cour;

b)   du Règlement d'ordre intérieur et du Règlement de procédure ainsi que des modifications y apportées;

c)   du modèle de la pièce d'identité arrêté conformément à l'article 4, alinéa 4.

Arrêté en assemblée générale, tenue à Senningen, le 18 avril 1988, en langues française et néerlandaise, les deux textes faisant également foi.

ff) Rules of Procedure of the Benelux Court of Justice of December 20, 1978

DISPOSITIONS PRELIMINAIRES

Dans le présent Règlement

- le Traité relatif à l'institution et au statut d'une Cour de Justice Benelux signé à Bruxelles le 31 mars 1965 est dénommé «Traité»;

- le Protocole additionnel au Traité relatif à l'institution et au statut d'une Cour de Justice Benelux signé à Bruxelles le 25 octobre 1966 est dénommé «Protocole additionnel»;

- le Protocole additionnel au Traité relatif à l'institution et au statut d'une Cour de Justice Benelux concernant la protection juridictionnelle des personnes au service de l'Union économique Benelux, signé à La Haye le 29 avril 1969 est dénommé «Protocole concernant la protection juridictionnelle»[1].

Titre I. Interprétation des regles juridiques communes

Chapitre 1er. Des demandes d'interprétation de regles juridiques introduites par les juridictions nationales

Art. 1   La décision de la juridiction nationale demandant à la Cour l'interprétation de règles juridiques est notifiée en copie par le greffier aux parties en cause ainsi qu'aux ministres de la justice des trois pays, en autant d'exemplaires qu'il est nécessaire pour la communication aux ministres concernés.

Art. 2   1. La Cour, le président ou le juge délégué par lui peuvent en tout état de cause demander communication du dossier de la procédure à la juridiction nationale qui l'a saisie d'une demande d'interprétation.

2. Ils peuvent aussi demander aux parties de produire toutes les pièces et de fournir toutes les informations qu'ils jugent nécessaires.

Art. 3   1. Dans un délai à fixer par le président ou par le juge délégué par lui, les parties peuvent déposer un mémoire au greffe.

2. Dans le même délai les ministres de la justice peuvent communiquer à la Cour un exposé écrit contenant leur façon de voir sur une question en litige. Cet exposé peut soit être adressé au chef du parquet qui le dépose au greffe, soit être déposé directement au greffe.

3. Le greffier notifie en copie ces mémoires et exposés aux autres parties ainsi qu'aux autres ministres de la justice.

4. Dans les dix jours de l'envoi de ces copies les parties et les ministres de la justice peuvent demander à la Cour de les autoriser à déposer un mémoire en réponse.

5. Si la Cour décide d'accueillir une telle demande, le président ou le juge délégué par lui fixe le délai dans lequel les mémoires en réponse doivent être déposés.

6. Le greffier fait parvenir en copie les mémoires en réponse aux autres parties et aux autres ministres de la justice.

7. La partie qui n'est pas domiciliée ou établie dans un des pays du Benelux et qui désire déposer un mémoire ou un mémoire en réponse doit faire élection de domicile dans un de ces pays et y désigner un mandataire qui s'est engagé à recevoir les pièces qui lui sont destinées de même que celles destinées à la personne agréée par la Cour pour les plaidoiries.

---

[1]   Le protocole additionnel concernant la protection juridictionnelle des personnes au service de l'Union économique Benelux du 29 avril 1969 n'est pas reproduit dû à son caractère plutôt administratif qu'international.

Art. 4   1. Les parties et les ministres de la justice qui ont participé à la procédure écrite peuvent aussi demander, soit en déposant leur mémoire ou exposé écrit, soit dans le délai de dix jours de l'envoi à eux fait des copies des mémoires, exposés écrits et mémoires en réponse, à être autorisés à faire un exposé oral à l'audience.

2. La Cour décide selon la nature de la cause et le déroulement de la procédure d'accueillir ou de rejeter cette demande.

3. La procédure orale peut aussi être ordonnée d'office par la Cour.

4. Le président fixe, après avoir pris l'avis de l'avocat général, les lieu, jour et heure de l'audience.

5. Sont seuls autorisés à faire plaider, ceux qui ont déposé un mémoire, exposé écrit ou mémoire en réponse; ils sont avisés par le greffier au moins un mois d'avance des lieu, jour et heure de l'audience.

6. Sont seuls admis à plaider, les membres des barreaux des trois pays et les autres personnes qui ont été agréées dans chaque cause par la Cour. La partie ou les ministres de la justice qui souhaitent faire plaider une telle personne doivent au plus tard dix jours avant la date fixée pour l'audience déposer une requête afin d'obtenir son agrément.

Art. 5   1. Les décisions fixant le délai dans lequel un mémoire, un exposé écrit ou un mémoire en réponse doit être déposé, déterminent la date à laquelle il expire. Le président ou le juge délégué par lui peuvent proroger ce délai à la demande motivée de la partie intéressée ou du ministre de la justice intéressé.

2. Ces décisions sont portées par le greffier à la connaissance des parties et des ministres de la justice qu'elles concernent.

3. Le greffier communique aux parties et aux ministres de la justice qu'elles concernent les décisions de la Cour refusant le droit de déposer un mémoire en réponse, accueillant ou rejetant une requête tendant à prescrire la procédure orale ou ordonnant d'office une telle procédure.

Art. 6   1. Le président dirige les débats et exerce la police de l'audience.

2. Le président peut demander aux avocats et personnes agréées de se dispenser d'exposer des points au sujet desquels la Cour s'estimerait suffisamment informée. Il peut aussi leur demander de s'expliquer spécialement sur certains points.

Art. 7   1. Après l'échange des mémoires, ou, en cas de procédure orale, après les plaidoiries, le président fixe, en accord avec l'avocat général, la date à laquelle celui-ci donnera ses conclusions.

2. Celles-ci sont motivées et, en cas de procédure orale, données à l'audience à moins que la Cour décide, en accord avec l'avocat général, qu'elles feront l'objet d'une communication écrite aux membres de la Cour, aux parties et aux ministres de la justice ayant déposé, selon le cas, un mémoire, un mémoire en réponse ou un exposé écrit.

Art. 8   Après que l'avocat général a donné ses conclusions, la Court rend son arrêt qui contient:

a. la date du prononcé;

b. les noms du président et des juges qui ont statué, ainsi que celui de l'avocat général qui a donné ses conclusions;

c. la demande d'interprétation;

d. la désignation des parties et des ministres de la justice visés à l'article 7, alinéa 2 in fine;

e. les noms des avocats et des autres personnes agréées par la Cour;

f. la décision motivée;

g. la décision relative aux frais conformément à l'article 13 du Traité;

h. les noms des magistrats et du greffier présents au prononcé.

Art. 9   1. L'arrêt est prononcé en audience publique au jour, heure et lieu que le greffier porte à la connaissance des parties et des ministres de la justice visés à l'article 7, alinéa 2 in fine, au moins huit jours avant ladite audience.

2. L'arrêt est prononcé par le président ou par un des juges qu'il délègue et qui a participé au délibéré. Un avocat général et un greffier assistent au prononcé. La présence des autres juges n'est pas requise.

3. La minute de l'arrêt est signée sur le champ par le juge qui a prononcé l'arrêt et par le greffier. Elle est ensuite déposée au greffe.

Art. 10 Des copies de l'arrêt sont communiquées par le greffier à la juridiction qui a demandé l'interprétation, aux parties et aux ministres de la justice.

Art. 11 Le greffier établit un procès-verbal de chaque audience; ce procès-verbal est signé par le président et le greffier.

Art. 12 1. Toutes les notifications et communications confiées à la diligence du greffier sont effectuées soit par envoi recommandé à la poste soit par remise contre reçu.

2. Les copies sont certifiées conformes par le greffier.

Art. 13 1. Le délai se compte de minuit à minuit. Il est calculé depuis le lendemain du jour de l'acte, du fait ou de l'événement qui y donne cours et comprend tous les jours même le samedi, le dimanche et les jours fériés légaux.

2. Lorsque le point de départ d'un délai est déterminé par une notification ou communication, ce délai prend cours le quatrième jour suivant celui de l'envoi ou le jour de la remise contre reçu.

3. Le jour de l'échéance est compris dans le délai. Toutefois lorsque ce jour est un samedi, un dimanche ou un jour férié légal, le jour de l'échéance est reporté au plus prochain jour ouvrable.

4. Les jours fériés légaux sont ceux considérés comme tels par le Règlement d'ordre intérieur.

5. Une pièce ou un acte déposé dans la boîte aux lettres du greffe est réputé y déposé la veille du jour de la levée de ladite boîte faite dans les conditions précisées par le Règlement d'ordre intérieur.

6. Le délai établi en mois se compte de quantième à veille de quantième.

Art. 14   Les dispositions des articles précédents sont applicables à la procédure visée par l'article 39 du Protocole concernant la protection juridictionnelle.

CHAPITRE 2. DES DEMANDES D'INTERPRÉTATION DE RÈGLES JURIDIQUES INTRODUITES PAR LE COLLÈGE ARBITRAL

Art. 15   1. La décision du Collège arbitral demandant interprétation à la Cour est notifiée en copie par le greffier au ministre des affaires étrangères des pays parties au différend soumis au Collège, et le cas échéant au ministre des affaires étrangères du pays qui est intervenu dans la procédure suivie devant ce Collège et, dans le cas visé par l'article 52 du Traité instituant l'Union économique Benelux, au Comité de Ministres de l'Union économique Benelux.

La décision du Collège arbitral est aussi notifiée en copie par le greffier au ministre des affaires étrangères du troisième pays qui n'est pas partie au différend soumis au Collège et qui n'est pas encore intervenu dans le litige.

2. Les ministres des affaires étrangères des pays auxquels la décision du Collège arbitral doit être notifiée ainsi que le Comité de Ministres de l'Union économique Benelux dans le cas visé par le susdit article 52 peuvent, conformément aux dispositions des articles 3 et 4 du présent Règlement, déposer un exposé écrit ou un mémoire en réponse et adresser une requête tendant à obtenir une procédure orale.

Lorsque le pays visé à l'article 15 alinéa 1er, deuxième phrase, est intervenu dans le litige, son ministre des affaires étrangères peut, conformément aux articles 3 et 4 du présent règlement, communiquer un exposé écrit, déposer un mémoire en réponse et adresser une requête tendant à obtenir une procédure orale, dans les délais à fixer par la Cour ou par son président.

3. Les dispositions des articles 2 à 13 inclus du Chapitre 1er du présent Titre s'appliquent à la procédure que concerne le présent Chapitre.

4. Les dispositions des alinéas précédents sont applicables à la procédure visée par l'article 39 du Protocole concernant la protection juridictionnelle.

CHAPITRE 3. DES ATTRIBUTIONS CONSULTATIVES DE LA COUR

Art. 16   1. Lorsque l'un ou plusieurs des trois gouvernements demandent à la Cour de se prononcer, par un avis consultatif, sur l'interprétation d'une règle juridique, le greffier, en même temps qu'il communique la requête aux autres gouvernements, fait connaître à ceux-ci qu'ils disposent du délai qui a été fixé par le président ou par le juge délégué par lui pour adresser leur observations à la Cour par le dépôt d'un mémoire au greffe.

2. A la demande écrite et motivée d'un gouvernement, le président ou le juge délégué par lui peut accorder une prolongation du délai. La décision du président ou du juge est portée, par le greffier, à la connaissance de ce gouvernement.

3. Les notifications et communications qui, aux termes des dispositions du présent Chapitre, doivent être faites à un gouvernement sont adressées à son ministre des affaires étrangères.

Art. 17   1. Dans le délai d'un mois à compter du dépôt de la requête, le greffier fait insérer directement au journal officiel[1] de chacun des trois pays un avis énonçant sommairement l'objet de ladite requête.

2. Les parties engagées dans une instance judiciaire ou arbitrale où la même question est débattue, peuvent déposer au greffe un mémoire contenant leurs observations dans le délai d'un mois à compter du jour de la publication de l'avis visé à l'alinéa précédent, dans le journal officiel du pays dans lequel siège la juridiction, l'arbitre ou le Collège arbitral devant lequel la question serait débattue.

3. Les gouvernements et les parties peuvent prendre connaissance au greffe de la requête qui a saisi la Cour ainsi que des mémoires. Ils peuvent aussi en demander copie.

Art. 18   1. Les dispositions des articles 4 à 13 inclus du Chapitre 1er du présent Titre, sauf en tant qu'elles concernent les mémoires en réponse, s'appliquent à la procédure et à l'avis que vise le présent Chapitre.

2. La décision de surséance visée par l'article 10, alinéa 3 du Traité peut être prise par la Chambre de procédure visée à l'article 13 du Règlement d'ordre intérieur.

CHAPITRE 4. DE L'EMPLOI DES LANGUES

Art. 19   Sans préjudice des dispositions du Protocole additionnel, les langues employées par et devant la Cour sont le français et le néerlandais.

Art. 20   1. La langue de la procédure, des plaidoiries et des décisions de la Cour relatives aux attributions juridictionnelles visées par les chapitres III et V du Traité, est celle de la procédure devant la juridiction nationale ou le Collège arbitral qui a saisi la Cour.

2. Lorsque la décision qui saisit la Cour est rédigée en français, sa notification au ministre néerlandais de la justice est accompagnée d'une traduction en néerlandais; lorsqu'une telle décision est rédigée en néerlandais, sa notification au ministre luxembourgeois de la justice est accompagnée d'une traduction en français.

3. Lorsque, par application de l'article 2, la juridiction nationale ou des parties ont communiqué le dossier ou certaines pièces de la procédure, le président ou le juge désigné par lui indique au service de traduction annexé au greffe, soit d'office, soit à la demande d'un autre juge ou de l'avocat général, les pièces qui seront traduites.

---

[1]   Pour la Belgique: le Moniteur belge; pour le Luxembourg: le Mémorial B; pour les Pays-Bas: le « Staatscourant ».

4. Lorsque la décision de demande d'interprétation a été rendue en langue allemande, la Cour peut, sur conclusions de l'avocat général, décider que la procédure, les plaidoiries et la décision auront lieu soit en français soit en néerlandais. Cette décision est notifiée par le greffier aux parties et aux ministres de la justice.

Art. 21   1. La langue de la procédure, des plaidoiries et de l'avis de la Cour relatifs aux attributions consultatives visées par le Chapitre IV du Traité, est celle de la requête qui a saisi la Cour.

2. Si cette requête est rédigée en français, sa notification au gouvernement néerlandais est accompagnée d'une traduction en néerlandais. Si elle est rédigée en néerlandais, sa notification au gouvernement luxembourgeois est accompagnée d'une traduction en français.

3. Les parties visées par l'article 17, alinéa 2 adressent leurs observations à la Cour soit dans la langue de la requête du gouvernement, soit dans celle de la procédure de la juridiction ou de la procédure arbitrale dans laquelle elles sont engagées.

Art. 22   1. Le service de traduction annexé au greffe assure la traduction dans l'autre langue de toutes les pièces de la procédure, en ce compris les décisions et avis de la Cour.

2. Une décision de demande d'interprétation rendue en langue allemande est traduite en français et en néerlandais.

3. Lorsque la procédure se déroule en langue allemande, toutes les décisions et toutes les pièces de la procédure rédigées dans cette langue sont traduites dans les deux autres langues. D'autre part, la Cour décide quelles pièces de la procédure rédigées en langue française ou néerlandaise doivent être traduites en allemand.

Art. 23   1. La Cour peut autoriser les avocats et les autres personnes admises à plaider devant elle à se servir de la langue officielle autre que celle de la procédure.

2. Lorsque la décision de demande d'interprétation ou le mémoire d'une partie visée par l'article 17, alinéa 2 est, conformément aux dispositions de l'article 22, alinéa 3, rédigée en langue allemande, la Cour peut aussi autoriser l'avocat ou la personne admise à plaider devant elle, à plaider soit en allemand, soit en français, soit en néerlandais.

3. La note de plaidoirie, qui doit être accompagnée de sa traduction dans l'autre langue officielle, est déposée au greffe. Si la plaidoirie a eu lieu en langue allemande, la traduction est établie dans les deux langues officielles.

Art. 24   1. Au cours de la procédure orale, le président, les juges et l'avocat général peuvent faire usage de la langue officielle autre que celle de la procédure.

2. De même, lorsque la procédure a lieu en langue allemande ou lorsqu'il est fait usage, pour la plaidoirie, de cette langue, le président, les juges et l'avocat général peuvent s'exprimer dans une des langues officielles.

Art. 25   1. Le service de traduction annexé au greffe assure, au cours de la procédure orale, la traduction consécutive ou simultanée en français des interventions des magistrats et des plaidoiries faites en néerlandais, et la traduction en néerlandais de ces interventions et plaidoiries faites en français.

2. Lorsque la procédure a lieu en allemand, les interventions faites dans cette langue sont traduites dans les deux langues officielles et les interventions faites dans ces dernières langues sont traduites en allemand.

3. Lorsque, dans une procédure se déroulant en français ou en néerlandais, il est fait usage de la langue allemande, la traduction est faite dans les deux langues officielles.

4. Le président décide si la traduction sera consécutive ou simultanée.

Art. 26   Les publications de la Cour sont faites dans les deux langues officielles et, lorsque la langue de la procédure est l'allemand, aussi dans cette langue.

CHAPITRE 5. DE L'ASSISTANCE JUDICIAIRE GRATUITE

Art. 26   1. Si une partie se trouve dans l'impossibilité de faire face en totalité ou en
bis   partie aux frais de l'instance, elle peut à tout moment demander le bénéfice de l'assistance judiciaire gratuite. Elle fournit à l'appui de sa demande les renseignements et les pièces qui la justifient.

2. La Cour statue, l'avocat général entendu, sur l'admission totale ou partielle au bénéfice de l'assistance judiciaire gratuite ou sur son rejet.

3. En cas d'admission au bénéfice de l'assistance judiciaire gratuite, la caisse de la Cour avance le montant des frais déterminé par la Cour, y compris les honoraires et frais de représentation et d'assistance.

4. Si le juge du fond met tout ou partie desdits frais à charge de la partie adverse, la partie admise au bénéfice de l'assistance judiciaire gratuite est tenue de verser au greffier de la Cour les sommes reçues à ce titre de la partie adverse. Si ces frais ne sont pas mis à charge de la partie adverse ou si la partie admise au bénéfice de l'assistance judiciaire gratuite n'obtient pas gain de cause devant le juge du fond, le greffier de la Cour peut, le cas échéant, recouvrer les frais auprès de cette dernière partie.

TITRE II. PROTECTION JURIDICTIONNELLE DES PERSONNES AU SERVICE DE L'UNION ECONOMIQUE BENELUX

CHAPITRE 1ER. DE LA PROCEDURE ECRITE

Art. 27   1. La requête visée à l'article 17 du Protocole concernant la protection juridictionnelle contient:

a)   le nom et le domicile du requérant;

b)   l'objet du litige et l'exposé sommaire des moyens invoqués;

c)   les conclusions du requérant;

d)   les offres de preuve s'il y a lieu;

e)   l'élection de domicile au lieu où la Cour a son siège permanent, si le requérant n'est pas domicilié dans un des pays du Benelux.

Elle est signée par le requérant ou par un membre du barreau de l'un des trois pays.

2. La requête est, le cas échéant, accompagnée:

a)   d'une copie de la décision attaquée;

b)   de l'original ou d'une copie des pièces invoquées à l'appui de la requête;

c)   d'une pièce justifiant de la date de la décision prévue à l'article 12 du Protocole concernant la protection juridictionnelle.

Art. 28   1. Les personnes visées par l'article 3, sous a, du Protocole concernant la protection juridictionnelle introduisent leurs recours dans les deux mois qui suivent la date à laquelle elles ont eu connaissance de la décision qu'elles attaquent ou celle à laquelle une décision de rejet est censée avoir été prise comme le prévoit le Chapitre III du Protocole.

2. Les recours des personnes visées par les articles 3, sous b et c, et 5 du Protocole ne sont recevables qu'après qu'ait été rendue la décision visée à l'article 9, alinéa 2 dudit Protocole ensuite du recours préalable interne que prescrit l'article 7 du même Protocole.

3. Les recours, en raison du silence de l'administration, visés au Chapitre III du Protocole, introduits par les mêmes personnes, ne sont, de même, recevables qu'après qu'ait été rendue ou considérée être rendue la décision visée à l'article 9, alinéa 2 du Protocole ensuite du recours préalable interne que prescrit l'article 7 du même Protocole.

4. Le délai de deux mois visé à l'article 17 du Protocole prend cours, en ce qui concerne les recours visés aux alinéas 2 et 3 du présent article, à la date de la notification au requérant de la décision rendue par l'autorité sur le recours interne.

5. Lorsque l'autorité n'a point statué sur le recours interne, trois mois après que la Commission consultative lui ait communiqué son avis, le délai de deux mois visé à l'article 17 du Protocole prend cours à l'expiration dudit délai de trois mois éventuellement prolongé de deux mois comme il est dit à l'article 12 du Protocole.

Art. 29   Si la requête n'est pas conforme aux conditions prescrites à l'article 27, le greffier invite le requérant à régulariser sa requête dans le délai d'un mois.

Art. 30   1. La requête est notifiée en copie par le greffier au représentant de l'Union visé à l'article 14 du Protocole concernant la protection juridictionnelle. Dans le cas prévu à l'article 29, la notification est faite dès la régularisation de la procédure ou dès l'expiration du délai qui y est prévu.

2. En vue de l'application éventuelle de l'article 25 du Protocole concernant la protection juridictionnelle, l'avocat général peut communiquer la requête à des personnes visées par les articles 3 et 5 dudit Protocole.

Art. 31   1. Le mémoire en réponse déposé par le défendeur, dans le délai fixé par le président de la Chambre, dénommé ci-après le président, contient outre les documents visés à l'article 18, alinéas 1 et 2 du Protocole concernant la protection juridictionnelle:

a. les réponses aux moyens invoqués dans la requête et les éléments de fait et de droit sur lesquels elles se fondent;

b. les conclusions du défendeur;

c. éventuellement les offres de preuves.

2. Le greffier fait parvenir en copie à l'autre partie le mémoire en réponse ainsi que les notes complémentaires visées par l'article 20 du Protocole concernant la protection juridictionnelle.

Art. 32   1. Les décisions fixant le délai dans lequel un mémoire en réponse ou une note complémentaire doivent être déposés, déterminent la date à laquelle il expire. Le président peut proroger ce délai à la demande motivée de la partie intéressée.

2. Ces décisions sont portées par le greffier à la connaissance des parties qu'elles concernent.

3. Lorsqu'un mémoire en réponse ou une note complémentaire ont été déposés après le délai visé à l'alinéa premier, la Chambre peut, selon les circonstances de la cause, décider qu'ils seront néanmoins pris en considération.

Art. 33   1. Après l'expiration des délais fixés pour le dépôt des mémoires en réponse et notes complémentaires, la Chambre, l'avocat général entendu, décide s'il est nécessaire de procéder à des mesures d'instruction.

2. Elle fixe par voie d'ordonnance soit d'office, soit à la demande d'une partie, les mesures d'instruction qu'elle juge convenir, la date à laquelle et éventuellement le lieu où elles seront exécutées. La Chambre peut décider que les mesures d'instruction et les débats oraux auront lieu à la même audience.

3. Si elle ordonne une expertise, l'ordonnance précise la mission de l'expert et lui fixe, le cas échéant, un délai pour le dépôt de son rapport.

4. Le délibéré de la Chambre sur les ordonnances visées aux alinéas précédents peut se faire par écrit ou par téléphone. Dans ce dernier cas la décision est confirmée par écrit. La décision est réputée rendue en chambre du conseil à la date précisée dans l'ordonnance.

5. L'ordonnance est notifiée en copie par le greffier aux parties.

CHAPITRE 2. DE L'INSTRUCTION

Art. 34   1. Les mesures d'instruction comprennent:

a. la comparution personnelle des parties;

b. la preuve par témoins;

c. la descente sur les lieux;

d. l'expertise;

e. toute autre mesure ordonnée par la Chambre.

2. Sans préjudice des dispositions de l'article 21 du Protocole concernant la protection juridictionnelle, la Chambre procède à l'audience aux mesures d'instruction.

3. La preuve contraire et l'ampliation des offres de preuve restent réservées.

Art. 35   1. Les personnes dont la Chambre a ordonné la comparution personnelle et les témoins dont elle a décidé l'audition sont convoqués au moins dix jours d'avance par le greffier.

2. La convocation indique:

a.   le nom de la personne convoquée;

b.   le nom des parties;

c.   l'objet du litige;

d.   la mention que le président fixe en équité les indemnités des témoins.

Art. 36   Lorsque la comparution personnelle du requérant et d'un représentant de l'Union est ordonnée, ceux-ci peuvent se faire assister à l'audience comme le prescrivent les articles 15 et 16 du Protocole concernant la protection juridictionnelle. Le président dirige l'audition des parties. Avec l'autorisation du président, les parties peuvent se poser mutuellement des questions. Le greffier établit sous la direction du président un procès-verbal de l'audience; après qu'il en a été donné lecture, ce procès-verbal est signé par les parties, le président et le greffier. Si une des parties refuse de signer, il en est fait mention dans le procèsverbal.

Art. 37   1. Le président vérifie l'identité des témoins. Ceux-ci, conformément aux dispositions de l'article 23 du Protocole concernant la protection juridictionnelle, prêtent le serment ou font la promesse de dire la vérité, toute la vérité et rien que la vérité.

2. Les témoins sont entendus par la Chambre. Après leur déposition, le président peut soit d'office, soit à la demande des parties, poser des questions aux témoins. Chaque juge et l'avocat général ont aussi la faculté de poser des questions aux témoins.

3. Sous la direction du président, le greffier établit un procès-verbal de chaque déposition qui, après lecture, est signé par le témoin. Si un témoin refuse de signer, il en est fait mention dans le procès-verbal. Le président et le greffier signent ce procès-verbal à la clôture de l'audience.

Art. 38   Les témoins régulièrement cités sont tenus de se présenter à l'audience, de prêter le serment ou la promesse prévus à l'article 37 et de déposer.

Art. 39   1. Le greffier notifie à l'expert la copie de l'ordonnance de sa désignation et l'invite à adresser au président dans les huit jours un écrit contenant acceptation de sa mission. Dans le cas où un rapport écrit est demandé, l'expert prête le serment ou fait la promesse conformément aux dispositions de l'article 23 du Protocole concernant la protection juridictionnelle, en envoyant au président un écrit contenant le serment ou la promesse, suivi de sa signature, de remplir sa mission en conscience et en toute impartialité.

Lorsqu'un rapport écrit n'a pas été demandé, l'expert prête le serment ou fait la promesse à l'audience.

2. Dans le même délai de huit jours, l'expert avise par pli recommandé à la poste le président et les parties des lieu, jour et heure où il commencera ses opérations.

3. Les pièces nécessaires sont remises à l'expert; les parties peuvent faire tels dires et réquisitions qu'elles jugent convenables; il en est fait mention dans le rapport.

4. Si l'expert n'accepte pas ou n'exécute pas sa mission, il est remplacé par la Chambre soit d'office, soit à la demande d'une des parties.

5. A la demande de l'expert, la Chambre peut décider, l'avocat général entendu, de procéder à l'audition de témoins qui sont entendus suivant les dispositions prévues à l'article 37.

6. L'expert ne peut donner son avis que sur les points qui lui sont expressément soumis.

7. Si l'expert n'est pas en mesure de déposer son rapport dans le délai fixé par la Chambre, il pourra demander un nouveau délai; la Chambre, l'avocat général entendu, décide par voie d'ordonnance.

Si le rapport n'est pas déposé au greffe dans le délai fixé par la Chambre et si l'expert n'a pas demandé une prorogation du délai, le président le mettra en demeure de terminer sa mission. Le cas échéant, la Chambre ordonnera son remplacement. Les dispositions de l'article 33, alinéa 4 sont applicables.

8. Les parties peuvent prendre connaissance au greffe du rapport de l'expert et en obtenir copie.

9. Après le dépôt du rapport au greffe, la Chambre peut ordonner que l'expert soit entendu à l'audience, les parties convoquées. Dans ce cas, il est entendu sous la foi du serment qu'il a prêté ou de la promesse qu'il a faite antérieurement. Procès-verbal est dressé de cette audition selon les modalités prévues à l'article 37, alinéa 3.

Art. 40   1. Si une des parties récuse un témoin ou un expert pour incapacité, indignité ou toute autre cause, la Chambre statue, l'avocat général entendu.

2. La récusation d'un témoin ou d'un expert pour incapacité, indignité ou toute autre cause est opposée dans le délai de huit jours à compter de la notification de l'ordonnance qui décide d'entendre le témoin ou nommer l'expert, par acte déposé au greffe contenant les causes de récusation et contenant les offres de preuve.

Cet acte est notifié en copie par le greffier à la partie adverse.

3. Si la récusation de l'expert est admise, il sera d'office, par le même arrêt, nommé un nouvel expert.

Art. 41   1. Si un témoin ou un expert est soupçonné de s'être rendu coupable de faux témoignage ou de fausse déclaration alors qu'il était sous la foi du serment ou de la promesse, un procès-verbal distinct du témoignage ou de la déclaration peut être dressé à l'audience. Il est donné lecture de ce procès-verbal qui est signé par le Président et le témoin ou l'expert. Si le témoin ou l'expert refuse de signer, il en est fait mention dans ledit procès-verbal.

2. La Chambre, l'avocat général entendu, décide si le fait sera ou non dénoncé aux fins de poursuites répressives. Cette dénonciation est faite au ministre de la justice au Pays du Benelux dont les juridictions ont, selon la Chambre, le meilleur titre de compétence. La décision de la Chambre est transmise par les soins du greffier; elle expose les faits et circonstances sur lesquels la dénonciation est fondée.

3. La Chambre peut inviter le ministre concerné à faire connaître à la Cour la décision qu'il a prise au sujet de la dénonciation ainsi que l'aboutissement des poursuites éventuelles.

4. La Chambre peut décider qu'en raison de cette dénonciation, il sera sursis à l'examen de la cause.

CHAPITRE 3. DE LA PROCEDURE ORALE

Art. 42   1. Si la date de l'audience à laquelle la procédure orale aura lieu n'a pas été déjà fixée par application de l'article 33, les lieu, jour et heure en sont fixés par le président, l'avocat général entendu.

2. Les parties sont avisées par le greffier au moins vingt jours d'avance des lieu, jour et heure de l'audience.

3. La partie qui désire faire plaider une personne autre qu'un membre des barreaux des trois pays doit se conformer aux dispositions de l'article 4, alinéa 6.

Art. 43   1. Le président dirige les débats et exerce la police de l'audience.

2. Le président peut demander aux parties, avocats et personnes agréées de se dispenser d'exposer des points au sujet desquels la Chambre s'estimerait suffisamment informée. Il peut aussi leur demander de s'expliquer spécialement sur certains points.

Art. 44   1. Après la plaidoirie, le président fixe, en accord avec l'avocat général, la date à laquelle celui-ci donnera ses conclusions.

2. Celles-ci sont motivées et données à l'audience à moins que la Chambre ne décide, en accord avec l'avocat général, qu'elles seront communiquées par écrit aux membres de la Chambre et aux parties.

Art. 45   1. La Chambre peut, à tout moment, ordonner une mesure d'instruction ou prescrire le renouvellement et l'ampliation de tout acte d'instruction.

2. La Chambre peut ordonner la réouverture de la procédure orale.

Art. 46   Après que l'avocat général a donné ses conclusions, la Chambre rend son arrêt qui contient:

a.   la date du prononcé;

    b.   les noms du président et des juges qui ont statué, ainsi que celui de l'avocat général qui a donné ses conclusions;

    c.   la désignation des parties;

    d.   l'objet du litige;

    e.   les noms des avocats et des autres personnes agréées par la Chambre;

    f.   la décision motivée;

    g.   la décision relative aux dépens, prise conformément à l'article 32 du Protocole concernant la protection juridictionnelle;

    h.   les noms des magistrats et du greffier présents au prononcé.

Art. 47   1. L'arrêt est rendu en audience publique aux jour, heure et lieu que le greffier porte à la connaissance des parties au moins huit jours avant ladite audience.

2. L'arrêt est prononcé par le président ou par un des juges qu'il délègue et qui a participé au délibéré. Un avocat général et un greffier assistent au prononcé. La présence des autres juges n'est pas requise.

3. La minute de l'arrêt est signée sur le champ par le juge qui a prononcé l'arrêt et par le greffier. Elle est ensuite déposée au greffe.

Art. 48   Des copies de l'arrêt sont notifiées par le greffier aux parties.

Art. 49   Le greffier établit un procès-verbal de chaque audience; ce procès-verbal est signé par le président et le greffier.

CHAPITRE 4. DE L'EFFET SUSPENSIF DU RECOURS

Art. 50   1. La requête tendant à obtenir un effet suspensif d'un recours est adressée par acte séparé au président. Elle spécifie l'objet du litige, les circonstances établissant l'urgence, ainsi que les moyens de fait et de droit paraissant justifier à première vue l'octroi de la mesure à laquelle elle conclut.

2. La requête peut aussi être formée dès l'introduction du recours interne visé au Chapitre II du Protocole concernant la protection juridictionnelle.

Art. 51   1. La requête est notifiée en copie par le greffier à l'autre partie; le président fixe à cette dernière un bref délai pour la présentation de ses observations écrites ou orales.

2. Le président décide s'il y a lieu d'ordonner l'ouverture d'une instruction.

3. Le président peut faire droit à la requête avant même que l'autre partie ait présenté ses observations. Cette mesure peut être ultérieurement modifiée ou rapportée, même d'office.

Art. 52   1. Il est statué par le président sur la requête par voie d'ordonnance motivée, l'avocat général entendu. Dans le cas visé par l'article 50, alinéa 2, le président statue après avoir recueilli l'avis du président de la Commission consultative. L'ordonnance est immédiatement notifiée aux parties.

2. L'exécution de l'ordonnance peut être subordonnée à la constitution d'une caution à déposer à la caisse de la Cour.

3. L'ordonnance peut fixer une date à partir de laquelle la suspension prend fin. Dans tous les cas la suspension prend fin dès que l'arrêt qui met fin à l'instance est rendu.

4. L'ordonnance n'a qu'un caractère provisoire et ne préjuge en rien de la décision de la Chambre statuant sur le principal.

Art. 53   A la demande d'une partie, l'ordonnance accordant ou refusant le sursis peut à tout moment être modifiée ou rapportée sur le fondement de circonstances ou faits nouveaux.

CHAPITRE 5. DE L'INTERVENTION

Art. 54   La requête en intervention des personnes visées à l'article 25 du Protocole concernant la protection juridictionnelle est déposée au greffe au plus tard huit jours avant l'ouverture de la procédure orale.

Art. 55   1. La requête contient:

   a.   l'indication des parties et le numéro d'ordre de l'affaire;

   b.   le nom et le domicile de l'intervenant;

   c.   l'exposé des raisons justifiant l'intérêt de l'intervenant à l'issue du litige;

   d.   les conclusions de l'intervenant;

   e.   les offres de preuve et en annexe les pièces à l'appui;

   f.   l'élection de domicile au lieu où la Cour a son siège permanent, si l'intervenant n'est pas domicilié dans un des pays du Benelux.

La requête est signée par l'intervenant ou par un membre du barreau de l'un des trois pays.

2. Si la requête n'est pas conforme aux conditions prescrites à l'alinéa 1er, le président peut inviter le requérant à régulariser sa requête dans le délai qu'il fixe.

Art. 56   La requête est notifiée en copie par le greffier aux parties au litige principal. Après les avoir mises en demeure de présenter leurs observations écrites, dans le délai déterminé par le président, la Chambre, l'avocat général entendu, décide par voie d'ordonnance si l'intervention est admise. Les dispositions de l'article 33, alinéa 4 sont applicables.

Art. 57   1. Si l'intervention est admise, copie de toutes les pièces de la procédure est donnée à l'intervenant, à la diligence du greffier, à moins que la Chambre, l'avocat général entendu, n'en décide autrement.

2. L'instance se poursuit dans l'état où elle se trouve à moins que la Chambre, l'avocat général entendu, n'en décide autrement.

3. Le président fixe le délai dans lequel l'intervenant expose par écrit ses moyens à l'appui de ses conclusions, le délai dans lequel les parties au li-

tige principal peuvent répondre et, le cas échéant, remet les débats oraux à une date ultérieure.

4. Les dispositions de l'article 16 du Protocole concernant la protection juridictionnelle et de l'article 42, alinéa 3 du présent Règlement sont applicables.

CHAPITRE 6. DE LA TIERCE OPPOSITION

Art. 58   1. Peut former tierce opposition quiconque veut s'opposer à un arrêt qui préjudicie à ses droits et auquel ni lui ni ceux qu'il représente n'ont été partie.

2. N'est pas recevable à former tierce opposition celui qui s'est abstenu d'intervenir dans la cause alors qu'il en avait connaissance.

Art. 59   La tierce opposition doit être formée dans les deux mois qui suivent la date à laquelle le tiers opposant a eu connaissance de l'arrêt attaqué et au plus tard dans le délai d'un an à compter de son prononcé.

Art. 60   1. La tierce opposition est formée par requête déposée au greffe.

2. La requête contient:

a.   le nom et le domicile du tiers opposant;

b.   si le tiers opposant n'a pas son domicile dans un des pays du Benelux: l'élection de domicile au lieu où la Cour a son siège permanent;

c.   la spécification de l'arrêt attaqué;

d.   l'exposé des raisons pour lesquelles le tiers opposant n'a pu participer au litige principal;

e.   l'indication des droits du tiers opposant auxquels l'arrêt attaqué aurait préjudicié;

f.   les moyens à l'appui de la requête et les conclusions du tiers opposant;

g.   les offres de preuve et en annexe les pièces à l'appui.

La requête est signée par le tiers opposant ou par un membre du barreau de l'un des trois pays.

3. La demande est formée contre toutes les parties au litige principal.

4. Les dispositions de l'article 16 du Protocole concernant la protection juridictionnelle et des articles 42, alinéa 3 et 55, alinéa 2 du présent Règlement sont applicables.

Art. 61   Le sursis à l'exécution de l'arrêt attaqué peut être ordonné à la demande du tiers opposant. Les dispositions du Chapitre 14 du présent Titre sont applicables.

Art. 62   1. La requête est notifiée en copie par le greffier aux parties au litige principal.

2. Copie de toutes les pièces de la procédure est donnée au tiers opposant à la diligence du greffier, à moins que la Chambre, l'avocat général entendu, n'en décide autrement.

3. Le président fixe le délai dans lequel les parties au litige principal peuvent répondre.

4. Les articles 31 à 49 inclus du présent Règlement sont applicables.

Art. 63   1. L'arrêt attaqué est modifié dans la mesure où il est fait droit à la tierce opposition.

2. La minute de l'arrêt rendu sur tierce opposition est annexé à la minute de l'arrêt attaqué. Mention de l'arrêt rendu sur tierce opposition est faite en marge de la minute de l'arrêt attaqué.

CHAPITRE 7. DE LA REVISION

Art. 64   1. La révision de l'arrêt ne peut être demandée à la Chambre qu'en raison de la découverte d'un fait qui aurait été de nature à exercer une influence décisive et qui, avant le prononcé de l'arrêt, était inconnu de la partie qui demande la révision.

2. La demande en révision doit être présentée au greffe au plus tard dans les deux mois suivant le jour auquel le requérant a eu connaissance du fait qui fonde la demande en révision.

3. La demande comprend:

a.   le nom et le domicile du requérant;

b.   si le requérant n'a pas son domicile dans un des pays du Benelux: l'élection de domicile au lieu où la Cour a son siège permanent;

c.   la spécification de l'arrêt attaqué;

d.   les points sur lesquels l'arrêt est attaqué;

e.   l'articulation des faits sur lesquels la demande est basée;

f.   l'indication des moyens de preuve tendant à démontrer qu'il existe des faits justifiant la révision et à établir que le délai prévu à l'alinéa 2 a été respecté.

La demande est signée par le requérant ou par un membre du barreau de l'un des trois pays.

4. La disposition de l'article 55, alinéa 2 est applicable.

5. La demande en révision est formée contre toutes les parties à l'arrêt dont la révision est demandée.

Le greffier notifie une copie de la demande à ces parties et les informe qu'elles disposent d'un mois pour déposer au greffe leurs observations écrites.

Art. 65   1. La Chambre statue en chambre du conseil, l'avocat général entendu, sur la recevabilité de la demande.

2. Si la Chambre déclare la demande recevable, elle poursuit l'examen au fond conformément aux dispositions du présent Titre.

3. La minute de l'arrêt portant révision est annexée à la minute de l'arrêt révisé. Mention de l'arrêt portant révision est faite en marge de la minute de l'arrêt.

CHAPITRE 8. DE L'INTERPRETATION DES ARRETS

Art. 66   1. Si l'arrêt rendu est obscur ou ambigu ou en cas d'erreur matérielle ou de calcul contenue dans l'arrêt, la Chambre le précisera ou le rectifiera à la demande de la partie qui justifie d'un intérêt à cette fin.

2. La demande à cet effet est introduite au greffe dans le délai d'un mois à compter de la notification de la copie de l'arrêt. Le greffier fait parvenir une copie de la demande aux parties et les informe qu'elles disposent d'un mois pour déposer au greffe leurs observations écrites.

3. La Chambre statue sur pièces.

CHAPITRE 9. DES NOTIFICATIONS ET DES DELAIS

Art. 67   Les articles 12 et 13 sont applicables à la procédure visée au présent Titre.

CHAPITRE 10. DE L'ASSISTANCE JUDICIAIRE GRATUITE

Art. 68   1. Si le requérant ou l'intervenant se trouve dans l'impossibilité de faire face en totalité ou en partie aux frais de l'instance, il peut à tout moment demander le bénéfice de l'assistance judiciaire gratuite. Il fournit à l'appui de sa demande les renseignements et les pièces qui la justifient.

2. Si la demande est présentée antérieurement au recours que le demandeur se propose d'intenter, elle expose sommairement l'objet de ce recours.

3. La Chambre statue, après avoir pris connaissance des observations éventuelles de l'autre partie et l'avocat général entendu, sur l'admission totale ou partielle au bénéfice de l'assistance judiciaire gratuite ou de son rejet. Elle est rejetée si le recours est manifestement mal fondé.

4. En cas d'admission au bénéfice de l'assistance judiciaire gratuite, la caisse de la Cour avance les frais, en ce compris les frais de représentation et d'assistance.

CHAPITRE 11. DE LA REPRISE DE L'INSTANCE

Art. 69   1. Si, avant la clôture des débats, le décès d'un requérant est porté à la connaissance de la Chambre, l'instance est suspendue durant le délai fixé par le président.

2. Avant l'expiration de ce délai, la procédure peut être reprise par les héritiers et successeurs, par acte déposé au greffe.

CHAPITRE 12. DU DESISTEMENT

Art. 70   Tout requérant peut en tout état de cause renoncer à son recours par acte déposé au greffe et signé par lui. Copie de cet acte est notifiée par le greffier à l'autre partie ou aux autres parties. La Chambre décrète le désistement et statue sur les dépens, à moins qu'elle ne décide que la procédure sera poursuivie.

CHAPITRE 13. DE L'INSCRIPTION DE FAUX

Art. 71   1. Dans le cas où une partie s'inscrit en faux contre une pièce produite, la partie qui a produit celle-ci est invitée à déclarer sans délai si elle persiste dans son intention de s'en servir.

2. Si la partie ne satisfait pas à cette demande ou si elle déclare qu'elle n'entend pas se servir de la pièce, celle-ci sera rejetée.

3. Si elle déclare vouloir s'en servir, la Chambre détermine si la pièce arguée de faux est essentielle pour la solution du litige. Dans la négative, il est passé outre. Dans l'affirmative, la Chambre peut soit statuer elle-même soit surseoir à statuer jusqu'après le jugement sur le faux par la juridiction compétente.

CHAPITRE 14. DU SURSIS A L'EXECUTION

Art. 72   1. La demande tendant à obtenir le sursis de l'exécution est adressée à la Chambre.

Elle indique l'arrêt dont l'exécution forcée est imminente ou en cours, les moyens justifiant la demande et, le cas échéant, les mesures d'exécution.

2. La Chambre décide, l'avocat général entendu, après avoir mis l'autre partie en mesure de prendre attitude soit oralement soit par écrit.

3. L'arrêt qui fait droit à la demande fixe la date à laquelle la suspension cesse ses effets et éventuellement les conditions auxquelles elle est subordonnée.

CHAPITRE 15. DE LA PUBLICITE DES AUDIENCES

Art. 73   1. Les audiences au cours desquelles un arrêt est prononcé sont publiques.

2. Les autres audiences sont publiques à moins que la Chambre n'en décide autrement, soit pour des raisons touchant à l'ordre public ou aux bonnes mœurs, soit à la requête expresse d'une partie pour la protection de sa vie privée conformément à l'article 6 de la Convention européenne de sauvegarde des droits de l'homme et des libertés fondamentales.

CHAPITRE 16. DE L'EMPLOI DES LANGUES

Art. 74   1. Le requérant et les experts utilisent la langue qu'ils auraient utilisée devant la juridiction administrative de leur pays. La procédure se poursuit dans la langue ainsi utilisée par le requérant.

2. Les témoins utilisent la langue de leur choix.

3. Lorsque les personnes visées par les articles 3, sous c, et 5 du Protocole concernant la protection juridictionnelle comparaissent personnellement, elles utilisent la langue de leur choix. Un interprète sera le cas échéant désigné par la Chambre. L'indemnité qui lui revient est fixée par le président et reste à charge de l'Union.

Art. 75   Les dispositions des articles 20, alinéa 3 et 22 à 26 inclus sont applicables.

CHAPITRE 17. DISPOSITION FINALE

Art. 76   Sans préjudice des dispositions des Chapitres 6, 7 et 8 du présent Titre, les décisions de la Chambre ne sont susceptibles d'aucune voie de recours.

TITRE III. PROTECTION JURIDICTIONNELLE DES PERSONNES AU SERVICE DU BUREAU BENELUX DES MARQUES ET DU BUREAU BENELUX DES DESSINS OU MODELES

Art. 77   1. Les dispositions du Titre II s'appliquent à la procédure visée dans le Protocole concernant la protection juridictionnelle des personnes au service du Bureau Benelux des marques et du Bureau Benelux des dessins ou modèles, signé à Bruxelles le 11 mai 1974.

2. Pour l'application des articles 30 et 36 du présent Règlement les mots « de l'Union » sont remplacés par « du Bureau ».

Arrêté en assemblée générale, tenue à Bruxelles le 1er mars 1975, en langues française et néerlandaise, les deux textes faisant également foi.

e) Commonwealth of Independent States

The Commonwealth of Independent States was established by an agreement between Russia, Belarus and Ukraine in Minsk on 8 December 1991, to which eight other former Republics of the USSR adhered at Alma Ata on 21 December that year; Georgia joined in 1993 so that all former Soviet Republics except the three Baltic States are members of the Commonwealth. The Organization is based on the respect for territorial integrity and cooperation particularly in safeguarding international peace and security and reduction of armaments. The CIS adopted a "Charter of Cooperation" in Minsk on 22 January 1993 according to which the Commonwealth is based on the sovereign equality of its members who are independent subjects of international law.

Part IV of the Charter deals with problems of conflict prevention and dispute settlement, without, however, making provisions for binding dispute settlement. According to Art. 17 disputes have to be settled by peaceful means; otherwise, they may be brought to the attention of the Council of Heads of State (CHS), the supreme organ of the Commonwealth. It is, however, not clear what kind of measures the CHS is able to take in such a situation. According to Art. 18 the CHS may recommend methods for settling the dispute, if the dispute could threaten the maintenance of peace and security within the Commonwealth, measures to be taken in other cases have not been defined.

Besides this general competence of dispute settlement vested in the CHS, the Charter provides for a really judicial organ of the Commonwealth which is the Economic Court. According to Art. 32 of the Charter this court "shall act with a view to ensuring the implementation of economic obligations within the Commonwealth". The Court was established in Article 5 of the Agreement of 15 May 1992 on measures facilitating transfers between economic structures of states participating in the CIS. Its organization was considered on 6 July 1992 and 9 October 1992 when further agreements and decisions on the Court's functions and its organization were made. On 24 September 1993 the structure and the division of the expenses of the Court were approved.

On September 24, 1993, the Treaty on Creation of an Economic Union was adopted between the CIS members Russia, Belarus, Armenia, Moldova, Kazakhstan, Kyrgyzstan, Uzbekistan, Tajikistan and Azerbaijan. Ukraine and Turkmenistan became associated members and Georgia joined the Treaty in October 1993. This Treaty, which is not self-executing, provides only legal guidelines for the formation of the common economic space based on market principles through a free trade area, a common market of goods, services, capital and labor, payments and customs unions, monetary union and new joint executive and coordinating organs. According to Art. 31, the member states agreed to settle their disputes regarding the interpretation and implementation of the treaty by negotiations or through the CIS Economic Court. They decided to conclude a special agreement on the procedures for examination of disputed issues regarding relations between their enterprises. If by the means provided for the dispute is not settled, other international judicial bodies may be employed.

Texts

Agreement Establishing the Commonwealth of Independent States of December 8, 1991: ILM 31 (1992), 138

Charter of the Commonwealth of Independent States of June 22, 1993: ILM 34 (1995), 1279; The Finnish Yearbook of International Law IV (1993), 263

Treaty on Creation of Economic Union of September 24, 1993: ILM 34 (1995), 1298

Bibliographical notes

V. N. Fissenko/I. V. Fissenko, The Charter of Cooperation, The Finnish Yearbook of International Law IV (1993), 229-262

aa) Charter of the Commonwealth of Independent States, Part IV, Part VI, Art. 32

PART IV — CONFLICT PREVENTION AND DISPUTE SETTLEMENT

Art. 16   The Member States shall take all possible measures to prevent conflicts, primarily those arising on an interethnic and interconfessional basis, which might entail violation of human rights.

On a basis of mutual consent, they shall render each other aid in resolving such conflicts, *inter alia* within the framework of international organizations.

Art. 17   The Member States of the Commonwealth shall refrain from actions liable to injure other Member States or lead to aggravation of latent disputes.

The Member States shall make efforts, in a spirit of good faith and cooperation, towards the just and peaceful resolution of their disagreements by means of negotiations, or the reaching of an understanding on a proper alternative procedure for dispute settlement.

Should the Member States fail to resolve a dispute through the means mentioned in the second paragraph of this Article, they may refer the matter to the Council of Heads of State.

Art. 18   The Council of Heads of State shall be empowered to recommend to the parties an appropriate procedure or methods for settling, at any stage of its evolution, a dispute whose continuation could threaten the maintenance of peace and security within the Commonwealth.

PART VI — ECONOMIC COURT

Art. 32   The Economic Court shall act with a view to ensuring the implementation of economic obligations within the Commonwealth.

Disputes arising with regard to the implementation of economic obligations shall be within the jurisdiction of the Economic Court. The Court may also resolve other disputes referred to its jurisdiction by agreement between Member States.

The Economic Court may interpret the provisions of agreements and other acts of the Commonwealth on economic issues.

The Economic Court shall act in accordance with the Agreement on the Status of the Economic Court and the Regulation on it to be adopted by the Council of Heads of State.

The seat of the Court shall be the city of Minsk.

bb) Treaty on Creation of Economic Union, Article 31

Art. 31   The Contracting Parties pledge to resolve their disputes in respect to interpretation and implementation of the present treaty by means of negotiations or through the Economic Court of the Commonwealth of Independent States.

If the Economic Court finds that a State Member of the Economic Union has failed to fulfill an obligation under the present Treaty, the State shall be required to take necessary measures to comply with the judgment of the Economic Court.

The Contracting Parties shall work out and conclude a special agreement on the procedures for deliberation of disputed issues in respect to economic relations to the entities of the Member States of the Economic Union, as well as on a system of sanctions for non-fulfillment of the assumed obligations,

If the Contracting Parties fail to resolve their disputes by means of negotiations or through the Economic Court of the Commonwealth of Independent States, they have agreed to resolve them in other international judicial bodies in accordance with their respective rules of procedure.

cc) Agreement on Status of Economic Court of the Commonwealth of Independent States[1]

Member-states of the present Agreement, later called member-states,

for the purpose of determining of the status of Economic Court of the Commonwealth of Independent States, which is formed in accordance with article 5 of Agreement between the Council of the heads of the states of the Commonwealth of Independent States on measures of providing of calculation improvement between industrial organizations of member-states of the Commonwealth of Independent States dated on May 15, 1992,

agreed on the following:

Art. 1   To confirm the appendix Statute on Economic Court of the Commonwealth of Independent States as inseparable part of the present Agreement.

Art. 2   To determine quota of the amount of judges from member-states, elected (appointed) to the staff of the Economic Court of the Commonwealth of Independent States, in quantity of two persons.

---

[1]   The only available English translation of the Statute of the Court is legally unsatisfactory; a reliable German version is reproduced together with the English text.

896 Economic Cooperation – Regional Treaties – Europe

Art. 3   The finance support of the Economic Court of the Commonwealth of Independent States is realized in equal portions of Rubles equivalent by member-states. The location of the Economic Court of the Commonwealth of Independent States is the city Minsk.

The expenses for keeping of the Economic Court of the Commonwealth of Independent States and the amount of its staff are determined by the Council of the heads of the states with suggestion of the governments of member-states of the Commonwealth with participation of the representatives of economic and arbitration high courts.

Art. 4   The present Agreement is open for other states to sign. It is in effect from the date of signing and for the member-states, the legislation of which need ratification, from the date of passing the ratification papers to the deposit state.

Made in Moscow, on 6 July 1992, in one real copy in Russian language. The real copy is in Archive of the government of Republic of Belarussia, which will send to states, who signed the Agreement, its conformed copy.

*The Agreement has been signed by Republic of Moldova with the exception of the 3rd paragraph of point 3 of Statute and with taking into consideration the fact of passing the quarrels by the agreement of States.

** The Agreement has not been signed by Turkmenistan and Ukraine.

Confirmed by Agreement of Council of the heads of the states of the Commonwealth of Independent States dated on July 6, 1992.

Statute on Economic Court of the Commonwealth of Independent States

1. The Economic Court of the Commonwealth of Independent States (later called Economic Court) is formed for the purpose of uniform realization of agreements of member-states of the Commonwealth of Independent States and obligations based on them and contracts by the way of resolution of disputes, coming out from economic relations.

2. Organization, form of activity, competence of Economic Court are determined by international agreements and by the present Statute. The procedure of resolution of disputes is determined by Regulation, confirmed by Plenary Session of Economic Court of the Commonwealth.

3. The Economic Court make resolutions on the economic disputes between states:

–   raised during the realization of economic obligations, which are specified by agreements, decisions of the Council of heads of states, of the Council of heads of governments of the Commonwealth (later called acts of Commonwealth) and of its other institutions;

- about correspondence of normative and other acts of the Commonwealth of Independent States, adopted on economic issues, agreements and other acts of the Commonwealth.

By the agreements of member-states of the Commonwealth the Economic Court can also trial other disputes connected with realization of agreements and other acts of the Commonwealth adopted on their base.

The disputes are trialed by Economic Court by the requests of authorized organs on behalf of the interested states, institutions of Commonwealth.

Economic Court can not refuse to solve the dispute because of the absence or not clearness of the law norm, which should be realized.

4. With the results of trialing the disputes the Economic Court make a judgment in which the fact of violation of the agreements, of the other acts of the Commonwealth or its institution by the member-state exists (or the absence of violation) and measures are determined, which are recommended to the appropriate state for the purpose of elimination of violations and their consequences. The state, toward which the judgment is directed, provide its realization.

The judgment should be in accordance with the provisions of the agreements and other acts of the Commonwealth, and also of the realized normative acts.

5. Economic Court comments:

- realization of provisions of the agreements, other acts of the Commonwealth and its institutions;
- legislative acts of former USSR for the period of mutually agreed realization of them, the possibilities of realization of those acts and also and opposing to the agreements, adopted on the base of the other acts of the Commonwealth.

Commenting is done while making decision for concrete case, and also by request of high bodies of state governing, institutions of the Commonwealth, high economic and arbitration courts and other high bodies who solve economic disputes in the states.

6. Economic Court is formed by the equal number of judges from every member-state.

7. The judges of Economic Court are elected (appointed) by the laws of member-states for electing (appointing) of judges of high economic and arbitration courts of member-states of the Commonwealth, for the period of 10 years, on the very professional grounds, from the judges of economic and arbitration courts and other people, who are high qualified specialists in the sphere of economic legal relations, having high law education.

The Chairman of the Economic Court and Deputy Chairmen are elected by the judges of that Court with the majority and are confirmed by the Council of the heads of the states of the Commonwealth for 5 years.

The Chairman of the Economic Court, Deputy Chairmen and judges can not be retired before the determined period, and also be kept away by any other means, besides when the elected (appointed) body in the case of overuse of the position, committing a crime or because of illness.

For the judges of Economic Court after the end of their acting period in the case of retirement and illness have the guarantees which are specified by the legislation of the member-states for the judges of that states.

8. The judges of Economic Court are independent and inviolable, are out of jurisdiction of the states where they work, they cannot be accused in criminal or administrative cases, arrested without the agreement of the Economic Court.

The Chairman of the Economic Court, Deputy Chairmen and judges can't represent the interests of any state or interstate body or organization, commercial structure, political party and movement as well as territory, nationality, ethnic group, social and religion group and single person. They have no right to have any activity, connected with getting profits, besides scientific or pedagogic.

9. Economic Court has the right to request necessary for the case materials from the bodies of member-states, subjects of industry and officials. The demands of Economic Court, which are in its competence, are compulsory.

10. The highest collegial body of the Economic Court is Plenary Session.

The Plenary Session consists of the Chairman of the Economic Court, Deputy Chairmen, and the judges of that Court, and also the representatives of highest economic, arbitration courts and other high state bodies, who solve the economic disputes in member-states.

The Plenary Session:

– trials the protests on the resolution of Economic Court by present order of Regulation. Plenary Session keeps its meetings not less than once in quartile. The decisions of Plenary Session are made by majority of participants and are definite;

– takes recommendations for providing one way practice for implementing the agreements, other acts of the Commonwealth and its institutions while solving economic disputes;

– cultivates and carries in for the member-states, institutions of the Commonwealth suggestions for overcoming collisions in legislation of member-states.

11. Procedure in Economic Court is realized on the language of between states communication, accepted within the Commonwealth.

12. Appealing to the Economic Court is not under the tax. Judicial expenses, fixed by court, are on the party who is accused in violation or who start the dispute without grounds.

13. The quantity of the staff of the Economic Court, the amount of assignation on its keeping and the ways of covering the work expenses of judges are determined by the Council of the heads of the states of the Commonwealth.

14. The chairman of the Economic Court organizes the work of the staff of the Court, confirms the structure and crew, put on the position and fire the members of the staff, determines the conditions of payment of their work, realizes other authorities within his competence.

The finance support, domestic and other insurance of the Economic Court are realized by the means, apportioned by the agreed decision of member-states. Providing the judges with the habitable square in the place where the Economic Court is located is realized by the order of co-workers of diplomatic corpuses in foreign countries.

15. Economic Court is juridical person, has a stamp by its name.

16. The judgments of Economic Court and resolutions of its Plenary Session should be compulsory printed in publishing of the Commonwealth and in mass media of the member-states.

dd) Abkommen über den Status des Wirtschaftsgerichts der Gemeinschaft Unabhängiger Staaten

Die Mitgliedstaaten des vorliegenden Abkommens, fortan "Mitgliedstaaten" genannt,

Zum Zweck der Bestimmung des Status des Wirtschaftsgerichts der Gemeinschaft Unabhängiger Staaten, welches gemäß Art. 5 des Abkommens des Rates der Staatsoberhäupter der Gemeinschaft Unabhängiger Staaten über die Maßnahmen zur Gewährleistung der Verbesserung der Rechnungsführung zwischen den Wirtschaftsorganisationen der Mitgliedstaaten der Gemeinschaft Unabhängiger Staaten vom 15. Mai 1992,

haben folgendes *vereinbart*:

Art. 1   Das vorgeschlagene Statut des Wirtschaftsgerichts der Gemeinschaft Unabhängiger Staaten als untrennbaren Bestandteil des vorliegenden Abkommens zu bestätigen.

Art. 2   Die Anzahl der Richter aus den Mitgliedstaaten, welche in das Wirtschaftsgericht gewählt (oder ernannt) werden, auf zwei Richter pro Staat festzulegen.

Art. 3   Die Finanzierung des Wirtschaftsgerichts der Gemeinschaft Unabhängiger Staaten wird zu gleichen Teilen durch die Mitgliedstaaten in einem Rubeläquivalent sichergestellt. Sitz des Wirtschaftsgerichts der Gemeinschaft Unabhängiger Staaten ist die Stadt Minsk.

Die Gebühren für das Tätigwerden des Wirtschaftsgerichts der Gemeinschaft Unabhängiger Staaten und die Größe seines Apparates werden vom Rat der Regierungschefs der Mitgliedstaaten der Gemeinschaft Unabhängiger Staaten unter Beteiligung der Vorsitzenden der Obersten Wirtschafts- bzw. Arbitragegerichte bestätigt.

Art. 4   Das vorliegende Abkommen steht zur Unterzeichnung durch andere
Staaten offen. Es tritt am Tag seiner Unterzeichnung in kraft, jedoch für
die Staaten, deren Gesetzgebung die Ratifikation solcher Abkommen er-
fordert, am Tage, an dem sie die Ratifikationsurkunde bei dem Depositar-
staat hinterlegen.

So vereinbart in Moskau am 06. Juli 1992 in einem verbindlichen Exemplar in russischer Sprache. Das verbindliche Exemplar wird im Archiv der
Regierung der Republik Weißrußland aufbewahrt, welche den Unter-
zeichnerstaaten des vorliegenden Abkommens eine beglaubigte Kopie zu-
kommen läßt.

Republik Armenien, Republik Belarus, Republik Kazachstan, Republik
Kyrgyzstan, Republik Moldova (mit Ausnahme von Pkt 3 Abs 3 des Statuts und unter Berücksichtigung der Streitübertragung aufgrund von Par-
teivereinbarung), Rußländische Föderation, Republik Tadzikistan, Republik Uzbekistan.

Statut des Wirtschaftsgerichts der Gemeinschaft Unabhängiger Staaten

1. Das Wirtschaftsgericht der Gemeinschaft Unabhängiger Staaten, fortan
"Wirtschaftsgericht", wird zum Zweck der Gewährleistung der einheitli-
chen Anwendung der Vereinbarungen der Mitgliedstaaten der Gemeinschaft Unabhängiger Staaten und der aus diesen folgenden wirtschaftli-
chen Pflichten und Verträgen im Wege der Entscheidung von Streitigkeiten, welche aus Wirtschaftsbeziehungen entstehen, gegründet.

2. Die Organisation, das Verfahren der Tätigkeit und die Kompetenz des
Wirtschaftsgerichts werden durch zwischenstaatliche Vereinbarungen und
das vorliegende Statut bestimmt. Das Verfahren der Streitentscheidung
wird durch das Reglement festgelegt, welches vom Plenum des Wirtschaftsgerichts der Gemeinschaft zu bestätigen ist.

3. In die Zuständigkeit des Wirtschaftsgericht fällt die Entscheidung von
zwischenstaatlichen Wirtschaftsstreitigkeiten:

- die bei der Erfüllung wirtschaftlicher Verpflichtungen entstehen, welche von Vereinbarungen und Entscheidungen des Rates der Staatsoberhäupter, des Rates der Regierungschefs (fortan "Akte der Gemeinschaft") der GUS-Mitgliedstaaten und anderer ihrer Institutionen vorgesehen werden;

- über die Übereinstimmung der Normativ- und anderen Akte der
Mitgliedstaaten der Gemeinschaft, welche im Zusammenhang mit
Wirtschaftsstreitigkeiten oder mit Vereinbarungen und anderen Ak-
ten der Gemeinschaft erlassen wurden.

Auf Vereinbarungen der Mitgliedstaaten der Gemeinschaft hin können
auch andere Streitigkeiten in die Zuständigkeit des Wirtschaftsgerichts
gelangen, welche mit der Erfüllung von Abkommen und der auf ihrer
Grundlage erlassenen anderen Akte der Gemeinschaft verbunden sind.

Streitigkeiten werden vom Wirtschaftsgericht auf Antrag der interessierten Staaten durch die von ihnen bevollmächtigten Organe oder die Institutionen der Gemeinschaft erörtert.

Das Wirtschaftsgericht kann die Entscheidung von Streitigkeiten nicht aufgrund des Fehlens oder der Unklarheit von zur Anwendung kommender Rechtsnormen versagen.

4. Entsprechend dem Ergebnis der Erörterung einer Streitigkeit trifft das Wirtschaftsgericht eine Entscheidung, in welcher der Gegenstand der Verletzung der Vereinbarung oder anderer Akte der Gemeinschaft oder ihrer Institutionen durch den Mitgliedstaat festgestellt oder aber keine Rechtsverletzung festgestellt wird und bestimmt die Maßnahmen, welche dem Staat anempfohlen werden, um die Verletzung und deren Folgen zu beseitigen. Der Staat, auf welchen die Entscheidung des Gerichts bezogen ist, gewährleistet deren Erfüllung.

Die Entscheidung des Gerichts muß mit den Bestimmungen des Abkommens und anderen Akten der Gemeinschaft sowie den angewandten Normativakten übereinstimmen.

5. Das Wirtschaftsgericht nimmt Auslegungen vor:

– zur Anwendung der Bestimmungen des Abkommens und anderer Akte der Gemeinschaft und ihrer Institutionen;

– von Gesetzgebungsakten der früheren UdSSR für die Periode ihrer gegenseitig vereinbarten Anwendung, darunter auch über die Zulässigkeit der Anwendung dieser Akte, soweit sie den Abkommen und den auf ihrer Grundlage angenommenen anderen Akten der Gemeinschaft nicht widersprechen.

Die Auslegung wird vorgenommen, wenn eine Entscheidung über eine konkrete Sache gefällt wird sowie auf Anfragen der obersten Organe der Staatsgewalt und der Regierungen der Staaten hin, der Institutionen der Gemeinschaft, der Obersten Wirtschafts- und Arbitragegerichte und andere oberster Organe, welche in den Staaten über Wirtschaftsstreitigkeiten befinden.

6. Das Wirtschaftsgericht wird aus der gleichen Anzahl von Richtern aus jedem Mitgliedstaat gebildet.

7. Die Richter des Wirtschaftsgerichts werden in dem Verfahren, das in den Mitgliedstaaten für die Wahl (Ernennung) von Richtern der Obersten Wirtschafts- und Arbitragegerichte der Mitgliedstaaten der Gemeinschaft gilt, auf zehn Jahre auf streng professioneller Grundlage aus der Anzahl der Richter der Wirtschafts- und Arbitragegerichte sowie anderer Personen, welche auf dem Gebiet der Wirtschaftsrechtsbeziehungen Spezialisten hoher Qualifikation sind und über eine Juristische Hochschulbildung verfügen, gewählt (ernannt).

Der Vorsitzende des Wirtschaftsgerichts und seine Stellvertreter werden von den Richtern dieses Gerichts mit Stimmenmehrheit gewählt und vom Rat der Staatsoberhäupter auf fünf Jahre bestätigt.

Der Vorsitzende des Wirtschaftsgerichts, seine Stellvertreter und die Richter können nicht vorzeitig abberufen werden oder aus irgendeinem Grunde ihres Amtes enthoben werden, mit Ausnahme der Abberufung durch die Organe, welche sie gewählt (ernannt) haben im Falle des Miß-brauchs der Dienstvorschriften, der Begehung einer Straftat und von Krankheit.

Für die Richter des Wirtschaftsgerichts gelten bei Ablauf ihres Mandats oder im Falle ihres Rücktritts — auch im Krankheitsfalle — dieselben Ga-rantien, welche von dem Recht der Mitgliedstaaten für Richter in diesen Staaten vorgesehen sind.

8. Die Richter des Wirtschaftsgerichts sind unabhängig und unverletzlich und unterfallen nicht der Gerichtsbarkeit ihres Aufenthaltsstaates, sie können weder zur strafrechtlichen noch zu einer verwaltungsrechtlichen Verantwortung in einem gerichtlichen Verfahren gezogen werden und können weder festgenommen noch einer Untersuchung ohne die Zustim-mung des Wirtschaftsgerichts unterzogen werden.

Der Vorsitzende des Wirtschaftsgerichts, seine Stellvertreter und die Richter dürfen keine Interessen irgendwelcher staatlicher oder zwischen-staatlicher Organe und Organisationen, wirtschaftlicher Strukturen, poli-tischer Parteien und Bewegungen sowie von Territorien, Nationen, Völ-kern, sozialen oder religiösen Gruppen und einzelnen Personen vertreten. Sie sind nicht berechtigt, irgendeine entgeltliche Tätigkeit, außer einer wissenschaftlichen oder einer Lehrtätigkeit auszuüben.

9. Das Wirtschaftsgericht ist berechtigt, von den Organen der Mitglied-staaten, den Wirtschaftssubjekten und den Amtspersonen, die für die Er-örterung der Sache unerläßlichen Materialien anzufordern. Die vom Wirt-schaftsgericht im Rahmen seiner Kompetenzen erhobenen Forderungen sind verbindlich.

10. Das Plenum ist das höchste Kollektivorgan des Wirtschaftsgerichts.

Das Plenum besteht aus dem Vorsitzenden des Wirtschaftsgerichts, seinen Stellvertretern und den Richtern dieses Gerichts sowie den Vorsitzenden der Obersten Wirtschafts- und Arbitragegerichte und anderer oberster Gerichtsorgane, die in den Mitgliedstaaten Wirtschaftsstreitigkeiten ent-scheiden.

Das Plenum

– erörtert Beschwerden gegen Entscheidungen des Wirtschaftsgerichts in dem Verfahren, das im Statut festgelegt ist. Das Plenum tritt min-destens einmal pro Quartal zusammen. Die Entscheidungen des Ple-nums werden mit Stimmenmehrheit seiner Mitglieder getroffen und sind abschließend,

– verabschiedet Empfehlungen, um die einheitliche Anwendungspraxis von Abkommen und anderer Akte der Gemeinschaft und ihrer In-stitutionen bei der Entscheidung von Wirtschaftsstreitigkeiten sicher-zustellen;

- erarbeitet Vorschläge zur Beseitigung von Kollisionen in der Gesetz-gebung der Mitgliedstaaten und legt diese den Mitgliedstaaten und Institutionen der Gemeinschaft zur Erörterung vor.

11. Ein Gerichtsverfahren vor dem Wirtschaftsgericht wird in der Sprache des zwischenstaatlichen Verkehrs durchgeführt, welche in der Gemein-schaft angewandt wird.

12. Die Anrufung des Wirtschaftsgerichts erfolgt ohne Gebühr. Die Ge-richtskosten, welche vom Gericht bestimmt werden, werden der Partei auferlegt, die einer Rechtsverletzung für schuldig befunden wird oder welche die Streitigkeit grundlos eingebracht hat.

13. Die Größe des Apparates des Wirtschaftsgerichts, die Anzahl der bei ihm assignierten Einrichtungen und die Bedingungen der Entlohnung der Richter sind vom Rat der Staatsoberhäupter der Gemeinschaft festzule-gen.

14. Der Vorsitzende des Wirtschaftsgerichts organisiert die Arbeit des Ge-richtsapparates, bestätigt dessen Struktur und Personalbestand, ernennt und entläßt die Angestellten des Apparates, bestimmt deren Vergütungs- und Arbeitsbedingungen und erfüllt andere Aufgaben im Rahmen seiner Kompetenzen.

Die Finanzierung, die Unterhaltung und die übrige Versorgung des Wirt-schaftsgerichts wird mit den Mitteln bestritten, welche auf einvernehmli-che Entscheidung der Mitgliedstaaten hierfür bereitgestellt werden. Die Richter werden am Sitz des Wirtschaftsgerichts in der Weise mit Wohn-raum versorgt, die für die Mitarbeiter diplomatischer Vertretungen aus-ländischer Staaten festgelegt wurde.

15. Das Wirtschaftsgericht ist eine juristische Person und besitzt ein Siegel mit dem eigenen Namen.

16. Die Entscheidungen des Wirtschaftsgerichts und die Verordnungen des Plenums unterliegen der unbedingten Veröffentlichung in den Publi-kationen der Gemeinschaft und den Masseninformationsmitteln der Mit-gliedstaaten.

2. America

a) Central American Common Market (CACM)

On December 13, 1960 the General Treaty on Central American Economic Integration was signed at Managua between Guatemala, Salvador, Honduras and Nicaragua, providing for ad hoc arbitration of legal disputes which could not be settled amicably through the Executive Council or the Central American Economic Council of the CACM.

In contrast to the usual ad hoc arbitration procedure in which only the States parties to the dispute are permitted to appoint the judges, the Treaty of Managua involves all member States in the selection of judges. The competence of the arbitral tribunal is limited to disputes concerning interpretation or application of the Treaty. Despite the ambiguous wording of Art. XXVI, it appears that a unilateral request for arbitration is admissible without the prior conclusion of a compromis between the disputing parties The relevant rules of procedure contemplate settlement of disputes only by the political organs of the CACM and not by the Court. Thus, until now, nearly all disputes have been settled by the Executive Council with the active participation of the Permanent Secretariat of the organization (SIECA). Those which were not settled by this means never came before the Arbitration Tribunal The Rules adopted in 1963 set forth a three phase procedure for the settlement of disputes: first, a solution is sought by negotiation (Arts 15-30); failing settlement at this stage, the Executive Council is seized with the matter (Arts. 31 - 45), and finally, an appeal from the Executive Council's decision may be filed with the Economic Council on the ground that there has been a violation of legal norms (Arts. 46-52). Under the Rules, the Permanent Secretariat (SIECA) has the right to participate in proceedings before the Executive Council and, if the parties so desire, even in the direct negotiations between the parties (Art. 10).

Until now the proposals to reinforce the dispute settlement concerning interpretation of the General Treaty by means of an international tribunal have not been successful.

Text

General Treaty on Central American Economic Integration:
   UNTS Vol. 455, pp. 4 ff. (Spanish, English and French)
Regulation on Procedure:
   Derecho de la Integración 1968 No. 3, pp. 148 ff.
   ILM Vol. 8 (1969), pp. 629-646 (English translation)

Bibliographical notes

F. Villagrán-Kramer, Teoría general del derecho de integración económica (1969)

Instituto Interamericano de Estudios Jurídicos Internacionales: Derecho Comunitario Centroamericano (1968)

F.V. García-Amador, The Developing Law of Latin American Integration, Rutgers Camden LJ Vol. 1 (1969), pp. 202 – 228

C. Prieto-Aceres, Perspective d'une Communauté Latinoaméricaine: l'exemple de l'intégration économique centre-américaine, Perspectivas de Derecho Público Segunda Metad Siglo XX, 2 (1969), pp. 619-744

A. Barbante, Estructura institucional del Mercado Común Centroamericano, Lecciones y Ensayos 1970 No 42, pp. 133-170

S. García-Granadas/R. A. Sato-Jiménez, A Bibliography on the Central American Common Market, Bulletin for International Fiscal Documentation Vol. 24 (1970), pp. 214-224

G. Fonseca/D. Ramirez, Los órganos del Tratado General de Integración Económica Centroamericana, Derecho de la Integración 1970 No. 6, pp. 66 ff.

Bulmer-Thomas, The Political Economy of Central America since 1920 (1987)

K. R. Simmonds, Central American Common Market, Arbitration Tribunal, in R. Bernhardt (ed.) EPIL; Vol. I (1992), 550 f.

W. Niehaus-Bonilla, International economic integration and mechanisms for dispute settlement: the case for a permanent tribunal for the central American Common Market, 1993

aa) General Treaty on Central American Economic Integration between Guatemala, El Salvador, Honduras and Nicaragua, Signed at Managua, on December 13, 1960

Art.   The Signatory States agree to settle amicably, in the spirit of this Treaty,
XXVI   and through the Executive Council or the Central American Economic
            Council, as the case may be, any differences which may arise regarding
            the interpretation or application of any of its provisions. If agreement
            cannot be reached, they shall submit the matter to arbitration. For the
            purpose of constituting the arbitration tribunal, each Contracting Party
            shall propose to the General Secretariat of the Organization of Central
            American States the names of three magistrates from its Supreme Court
            of Justice. From the complete list of candidates, the Secretary-General of
            the Organization of Central American States and the Government repre-
            sentatives in the Organization shall select, by drawing lots, one arbitrator
            for each Contracting Party, no two of whom may be nationals of the
            same State. The award of the arbitration tribunal shall require the concur-
            ring votes of not less than three members, and shall have the effect of *res
            judicata* for all the Contracting Parties so far as it contains any ruling
            concerning the interpretation or application of the provisions of this
            Treaty.

bb) Regulation on Procedures for Settlement of Disputes of April 7, 1968

Art. 1   When the expressions or terms mentioned below are used in the text of
            this Regulation, they shall have the following definition:

            General Treaty: The General Treaty of Central American Integration;

            Instruments of Central American Economic Integration: The treaties,
            conventions, protocols or agreements signed and binding on the Central
            American States, the administration of which is entrusted to the Executive
            Council of the General Treaty;

            Economic Council: The Central American Economic Council, created by
            the General Treaty;

            Executive Council: The Executive Council created by the General Treaty;

            Permanent Secretariat, Secretariat, or *SIECA*: The Permanent Secretariat
            of the General Treaty;

            General Secretariat: The General Secretariat of SIECA;

            Arbitration Tribunal: The Arbitration Tribunal provided for in Article
            XXVI of the General Treaty;

            Central American Organs: Institutions or organs, such as the Central
            American Institute of Industrial Research and Technology (ICAITI); the

Central American Institute of Public Administration (ICAP); the Central American Bank of Economic Integration, etc.;

Ministry of Economy: That organ which each nation has at this level in charge of matters of its Economic Integration;

Party, or Parties: The States between whom a controversy has arisen and who seek a solution pursuant to the procedures established in the present document;

Action (instancia): Conventional form to indicate the body of proceedings that take place when the Executive Council or the Economic Council, as the case may be, take cognizance of a dispute;

Session: The period of a meeting of the Executive or Economic Councils at which they hear the controversy for the purpose of solving it.

CHAPTER II — GENERAL PROVISIONS

Art. 2   Pursuant to Articles XXII and XXVI of the General Treaty, [Article] XIII of the Convention on Equalization of Import Duties, and other analogous provisions incorporated in the Central American conventions on economic integration, any disputes which arise based on application or interpretation of the clauses incorporated in these instruments, when the administration of same is entrusted to the Economic Council, shall be decided by following the procedures stipulated in the present Regulation.

Notwithstanding the preceding, such procedure shall not be applicable if a different procedure is indicated in one of the economic integration instruments.

Art. 3   The parties to a controversy may in no case refuse to seek a solution thereto, nor may the Executive or Economic Councils refuse to hear the same when submitted to them pursuant to this Regulation.

Art. 4   The solution to every dispute should first be sought through direct settlement between the parties, and if this is not successful, or if impossible due to provisions of some of the economic integration instruments, they shall be brought to the Executive Council and the Economic Council, as the subject matter may indicate.

If the latter Council fails to settle the dispute, the parties to it may submit it to arbitration, pursuant to Article XXVI of the General Treaty.

The procedure established by the present Regulation shall not be applicable when the controversy is one that must be resolved through arbitration.

Art. 5   Direct settlements and the other forms for solution of conflicts provided in the preceding article shall be characterized as successive and compulsory. Consequently, the parties to a controversy may not evade any one by a direct approach to the one which is immediately superior thereto.

Art. 6　　At any stage of the dispute the parties, by mutual agreement, may discontinue a Council hearing to which the dispute had been submitted, for the purpose of finding a solution by direct settlement.

The Executive Council, or the Economic Council, as the case may be, shall grant such a petition provided that, by its nature, the problem is one which it is possible to settle by direct action.

Art. 7　　The disputes submitted to the Council must be decided with absolute impartiality and objectivity, without relating them to other pending problems or to compliance with previous obligations.

The decision, therefore, must be based solely on the points submitted by the parties to the dispute and shall be binding only in the case which gave rise to it. The latter, nevertheless, shall not bar the Councils from basing their decisions on former ones rendered by them.

Art. 8　　When the Councils of the General Treaty take cognizance over a controversy, their members must act independently of any consideration derived from their own nationality, in view of the Central American character of said organs.

Art. 9　　No decree or resolution adopted, whether by means of a direct settlement or through the actions provided in this Regulation, may be contradictory to the rule of law or to the principles on which the Program of Central American Economic Integration is founded.

Art. 10　　The Secretariat shall be present at all sessions in which the Executive or Economic Councils are hearing a dispute and, whenever possible, at the meetings for direct settlement. Other organs of economic integration may attend when so requested by the parties to the direct settlement or at the meeting of the said Councils.

No provision of this Regulation shall be understood to affect the provisions of the preceding paragraph.

CHAPTER III – APPEARANCE

Art. 11　　Only those persons designated by the Delegation Heads representing the parties may appear before the Executive or Economic Councils at the hearings held by them to settle disputes.

Physical persons may make an appearance in person or by proxy, Corporate persons (legal entities) may do so through their representatives or attorneys.

The authority of the representative, in any case, shall be sufficiently evidenced by the sole fact that the Chief of the Delegation officially testifies as to his status.

The provisions of this article shall not prohibit attendance at the hearings by representatives of public or private associations, provided this is agreed to by the Councils.

Art. 12   The members of the Executive or Economic Councils, as long as they participate therein, may not act as representatives or attorneys for the parties.

Art. 13   Physical or corporate persons interested in having a dispute settled by means of direct agreement, or, as the case may be, through the actions provided for in this Regulation, must give notice of their interest to the Ministry of Economy of the corresponding Central American nation, and request its intervention in order that a solution may be found to their problem.

The Ministry of Economy shall not initiate any action until it has verified, with the greatest possible precision, the existence of the acts on which it is to be based.

If the results of the investigation so merit it, the said Ministry shall file the matter in the form determined in the present Regulation, and include on its Delegation those persons who are to represent the interests of the private persons, in order that they may make an appearance pursuant to the provisions of the preceding article.

In the event that the Ministry declares such petition to be without basis, it shall be proper to invoke the appeals available under the domestic law of the country against the corresponding decision.

Art. 14   The Member States of the General Treaty, without need for summons by the interested party, may appear of course through their Ministry of Economy.

CHAPTER IV — PROCEDURE

SECTION ONE — DIRECT SETTLEMENT

Art. 15   Attempts shall first be made to settle by direct agreement between the parties every dispute arising by reason of application or interpretation of provisions incorporated in the General Treaty, or in any other Central American economic integration instrument, with the exception of those cases for which these same instruments provide some other procedure.

Art. 16   Direct settlement may be called for by the parties to the dispute, by another Central American state, or by the Permanent Secretariat.

Art. 17   Direct settlement may be initiated through: 1) telephone, telegraphic, written or any other analogous communication; or b) meetings which the parties have agreed to hold.

In the former case, the party to whom the problem has been presented, must reply as to its merits without any delay whatever, or within the five calendar days following the date of the communication. Simultaneously, or within the course of the above mentioned term, the party who has taken the initiative to settle the dispute shall notify the Permanent Secretariat of its existence and may request that it offer its good offices to secure a prompt settlement of the conflict.

If the said term mentioned in the preceding paragraph has lapsed without producing a reply, or if this were negative, the parties shall proceed in conformity with the provisions of Section 2 of the present Chapter, unless there has been agreement to hold a meeting to attempt a solution to the dispute.

The fact that the dispute has been resolved through telephonic, telegraphic, written or any other analogous communication shall not exempt the parties from the obligation to communicate to the other Governments, through the Secretariat, the agreements which have been reached.

Art. 18   When the parties agree to hold a meeting to solve a dispute and believe it appropriate to have the Permanent Secretariat participate therein, they shall give it notice as far in advance as possible.

This communication shall be accompanied by pertinent documents. If the parties do not have such documents at their disposal, they shall so indicate to the Secretariat, and should present these at the latest at the opening of the meeting.

Art. 19   The Permanent Secretariat, by its own initiative or at the request of the parties, shall undertake the necessary studies and tasks to clarify and solve the controversy.

For the better compliance with its functions, the Permanent Secretariat may seek counsel from Central American or international technical organs that it may be necessary to consult.

Art. 20   If the studies or works, as the case may be, that have been undertaken by the Permanent Secretariat, or the evidence presented by the parties, are sufficient in their own opinion to put an end to the dispute, they shall so indicate to this office in order that, without delay, it shall notify all of the Central American governments.

In such event, the differences shall be considered as resolved as of the date on which this last mentioned communication has been released by the Secretariat.

Art. 21   If the opinion mentioned in the first paragraph of the preceding article is that of only one of the parties, this fact shall be communicated to the Secretariat in order that it may be transmitted to the other interested Government party. If the reply from the latter concurs with the already expressed opinion, the conflict shall be considered as terminated as of the date mentioned in the last paragraph of the preceding article. If the contrary is the case, the other procedures indicated in the present Regulation shall then be observed

Notwithstanding the provisions of this article and the preceding one, when any of the parties has manifested his satisfaction with the evidence presented, or with the point of view of the Secretariat, and the latter has not received a response from any of the others within the fifteen days following the date of its communication released to them, it shall be understood that the latter have agreed as to the evidence or the views, and that the conflict has been decided with finality.

In the event that the situation described in the preceding paragraph is produced, the Secretariat shall, in due time, send out notices of the case.

Art. 22 Without prejudice to the provisions of the preceding article, on the same date on which SIECA gives its views to the parties in the dispute, it shall likewise transmit by cable a summary of the conclusions it has reached.

If, by the tenth day of the period fixed in the second paragraph of the preceding article, the Secretariat has not received a reply from any of the parties, it should remind these, by the same channels, of the effects which this Regulation attributes to their silence.

Art. 23 If, after learning the views of the Secretariat or on the evidence presented, the parties consider that a meeting should be held, and this, for any reason, is not held on the date agreed upon, the said Office, on its own initiative or at the request of any of the interested Governments, shall undertake to fix a new place and date. If the parties do not reach an agreement on this point, or if a meeting has been held without reaching a solution to the dispute, it shall be submitted to the Executive Council pursuant to the present Regulation.

If the Executive or Economic Councils must meet in advance of the date agreed upon by the parties to effect a direct settlement, they shall, on their own initiative or as recommended by the Permanent Secretariat, do whatever is in their power to have the meeting for a direct settlement coincide with a date on which one of the two organs is scheduled to convene.

Art. 24 The meetings for a direct settlement may be developed within the time period desired by the parties. Nevertheless, they have the right to request and obtain concrete answers on each and every one of their petitions, at the very latest within three days following the date on which the meetings were convened.

Art. 25 During the meetings for direct settlement, the parties may commission the Permanent Secretariat or any other organ of economic integration to broaden its investigation or issue additional rulings necessary to obtain a better solution to the dispute.

Art. 26 The agreements that result as a consequence of direct settlement, the discrepancies which remain outstanding, if any, and the points of view of each party must be recorded in writing.

Art. 27 The Permanent Secretariat, if this is the case, shall be the organ charged with performance of the administrative functions originating from the said meetings. In regard to this function, it shall record the minutes of the meetings, which, once signed by the respective Delegation Heads, it must certify and forward, within the following forty-eight hours, to all of the Central American governments.

If the Secretariat is not represented at the direct settlement meetings, it shall be the duty of the parties to draw up and forward to said office, within the following two work days, the documents referred to in the preceding article, in order that they may be transmitted to the other Governments.

Art. 28   The agreements reached through direct settlement shall be binding on the parties agreeing thereto, from the date indicated on the document in which these are incorporated, and if none is indicated on the matter, then on the date of the signature of said document.

The fact that a dispute is settled directly shall not relieve the Secretariat of the obligation imposed on it by the first paragraph of Article XXIV of the General Treaty. Consequently, this office shall verify that all agreements reached fall within the legal framework of the economic integration régime. If in compliance with this duty it has any observations to make on any point, it must notify the Governments of these in order that they may, if deemed appropriate, submit them to the Executive Council.

The compliance with the said duty on the part of the Secretariat shall not cause any suspension concerning the agreements reached.

Art. 29   The States that have not participated in the direct settlement may, within the fifteen days following the date of the document containing the certified proceedings, or that on which the solution to the dispute was communicated to them, as provided in Articles 20 and 21, manifest to the Secretariat their intention to object, before the Executive Council, to all or any part of the agreements reached.

If none of the said States manifests such intention within the indicated term, the agreements reached in direct settlements shall be final, insofar as these may concern them.

The exercise of the power contemplated in this article shall not cause the suspension of the agreements reached, and must be presented to the next session of the said Council.

Art. 30   If, after a dispute has been settled through direct negotiation, one of the parties should learn of facts which, had he been informed of them during the meeting, would have affected the terms of the agreement, he may bring these to the notice of the other parties, through the Permanent Secretariat, in order to have a new meeting convened, if justified.

The right acknowledged by this article prescribes within sixty days from the date on which the agreement became final, if it has not been exercised within that period.

The learning of the facts referred to in this provision will not exempt the party having knowledge from his duty to comply with the agreements reached through direct settlement.

SECTION TWO — FIRST INSTANCE [TRIAL STAGE OF SUIT]

Art. 31 Every dispute must be submitted to the Executive Council which it has not been possible to settle totally or partially through direct negotiation of the parties, or which is not susceptible to negotiation according to the instruments of economic integration.

This organ shall also take cognizance over all matters which violate the legal order of Central American economic integration or the principles upon which it is based in the opinion of the States that have not intervened in the direct negotiations, or in that of the Permanent Secretariat, as the case may be.

These matters and the actions originating therefrom shall constitute the first instance hearing (trial stage).

Art. 32 In the cases covered by the preceding article, any State wishing to submit a dispute to the decision of the Executive Council must, through its Ministry of Economy, notify the Permanent Secretariat as far in advance as possible, in order that the matter may be included on the preliminary agenda for the next closest meeting of that organ.

For the purposes of Article 28, the Permanent Secretariat may, on its own initiative, include on the preliminary agenda those matters it deems necessary for discussion.

The Executive Council may not fail to include on the final agenda for the respective meeting the controversies which had appeared on the preliminary agenda, nor may it fail to hear these.

The provisions of this article shall not prevent that the final agenda include controversies concerning the existence of which the Secretariat has not been informed in advance.

Art. 33 The Permanent Secretariat, with due advance notice, must send the corresponding documents to all members of the Executive Council.

Art. 34 Only the members and the parties may be present at the sessions during which the Executive Council will hear a controverted matter.

The above shall be understood to be without prejudice to the provisions of the last paragraph of Article 11.

Art. 35 The Council shall open the hearings on the dispute with a reading by the Secretariat of the documents related thereto.

The above having been completed, the floor will be given to the party who has submitted the dispute for hearing, and to other parties, in order that they may state what they deem proper in defense of their viewpoints.

The Council members may request from the parties any explanations or clarifications they deem necessary, but should abstain from expressing any opinions on the merits of the problem.

The steps described in the preceding paragraphs having been exhausted, the presentation phase of the case shall be taken as concluded.

Art. 36   The proceedings described in the preceding article having been completed, the members of the Executive Committee shall meet in closed session to discuss and agree on a solution to the dispute.

Art. 37   The Executive Council, prior to rendering a decision, may agree:

1) To have any document brought in that it believes necessary to clarify the rights of the disputing parties, or request from them any clarification or enlargement of their contentions;

2) To carry out any investigation, inspection, analysis, evaluation, or any analogous act deemed necessary, or which will amplify those already undertaken;

3) To entrust to the Permanent Secretariat, or to any other economic integration organ, investigations or rendering of opinions which, in its discretion, it believes necessary for the better solution of the dispute.

Art. 38   The resolutions adopted by the Executive Council to terminate a dispute shall be based on the following, among others:

a) The Central American economic integration instruments;

b) The rules adopted to facilitate the application of said instruments;

c) The rulings of the Councils created by the General Treaty of Economic Integration, and the arbitration judgments or awards;

d) The opinions and recommendations of economic integration organs;

e) The general principles of law and economic science; and

f) The learned opinion of the most expert textwriters.

Art. 39   The decrees of the Executive Council which terminate a controversy must contain the following, with all possible clarity and precision:

1) As a caption, the term "Ruling No...," followed by the designation of the Council,

2) In the findings of fact in the decision (*resultandos*), a succinct digest of the facts:

3) In the "whereas clauses" (*considerandos*), the conclusion on the points of law presented by the parties;

4) In the "therefore" clause, the legal bases which are considered applicable to the decision which is to be rendered;

5) As the final part, the corresponding decree or rulings.

Art. 40   The rulings shall be considered to be signed by the mere fact of the signature on the records in which they are incorporated, and the place and date of same shall be considered to be those where and on which the corresponding record is signed.

Art. 41   The rulings adopted by the Executive Council to terminate a controversy, or the statement that no agreement has been reached on the merits of same, must be incorporated in the proceedings.

In the event that any member dissents from the decision, he may state the reasons on which his dissent is based by means of a vote with a justification [*voto razonado*] which shall be incorporated in the proceedings, immediately following the respective decision.

A record should also be made in the proceedings of the more important allegations made by the parties in turn, as well as any other outstanding matter in the consideration of the dispute.

Art. 42   When the Executive Council has not been able to reach an agreement as to the solution of the dispute, the Permanent Secretariat shall include it on the preliminary agenda for the next meeting of the Economic Council, and this organ may not refuse to hear it.

Art. 43   The Permanent Secretariat of the General Treaty of Economic Integration shall be the organ entrusted with certification and notification to the States of the Council rulings rendered.

Those decisions shall be considered as certified and notified by the mere fact that the Permanent Secretariat complies with these requirements with respect to the records in which the rulings are incorporated.

Art. 44   The decisions referred to in the present Regulation shall be effective in the manner and on the date indicated thereon or, if nothing is stated on this point, eight days after the date of the document which the Permanent Secretariat transmits to the States with the certified records incorporating the rulings.

The term referred to in the preceding paragraph shall be understood to be consecutive days.

Notwithstanding the above, the members of the corresponding Council have a duty not to await the expiration of the term mentioned in this article before taking those measures which will be necessary to make the rulings effective in their respective countries, upon expiration of the designated term.

Art. 45   The Permanent Secretariat shall be the organ entrusted to comply with the administrative functions at the meetings of the Executive Council held to resolve disputes. In this rôle, it shall keep the minutes of same, which, once signed, it should then certify and forward to all the Central American Governments within the ten days following the close of the corresponding meeting.

SECTION THREE — SECOND INSTANCE (APPELLATE)

Art. 46   The Economic Council may review the rulings rendered by the Executive Council in order to end a controversy in any of the following cases:

a)   When the ruling violates express provisions of any economic integration instrument;

b)   When it deals with matters on which a regional policy has not yet been formulated;

c)   When the Executive Council, by means of its decision, would have interpreted for the first time a provision of one of the economic integration instruments and there are grounds to believe such interpretation to be erroneous;

d)   When the decision contradicts others previously adopted by said organ, or by the Economic Council.

The Economic Council shall take cognizance also of all controversies which the Executive Council has not been able to resolve.

Art. 47   The review should be requested by the party or parties considering themselves wronged, at any time from the moment of rendering of the decision up to the tenth day following the date of its enforcement. In the first case, the request may be made orally, but a statement of same should be incorporated in the corresponding records. In the second case, it must be in written form, forwarded through the corresponding Ministry of Economy.

Petitions for review should clearly express the ground or grounds on which they are based.

Art. 48   When review is petitioned in writing, the Ministry of Economy must notify the Permanent Secretariat for the purposes provided in Articles 32 and 33 of the present Regulation.

If the petition was made orally, the said Secretariat shall forward, together with the certified records, those documents consulted by the Executive Council in resolving the issue.

Art. 49   A petition for review shall not suspend the execution of the questioned ruling, but the Economic Council may not fail to hear the matter referred to at its very next meeting.

Art. 50   The Economic Council, upon hearing the case, shall receive the documentary evidence presented to it by the parties, and may hear the latter in the manner prescribed in Article 35.

Once compliance has been made with the above, it shall proceed in the manner provided in Article 36.

Art. 51   The decision rendered by the Economic Council shall be limited to those points expressly submitted to it.

This decision or ruling shall be formulated in the form established in Articles 38 and 39.

Art. 52   With respect to remaining issues, it shall proceed pursuant to the provisions of Articles 34, 37, 40, 41, 43, 44 and 45 of the present Regulation.

CHAPTER V — FINAL PROVISIONS

Art. 53   The present Regulation shall become enforceable eight days following the date on which the Permanent Secretariat transmits to the States the certified record containing its approval.

The same Council may propose therein any amendments deemed necessary, which shall become enforceable pursuant to the provisions of the preceding paragraph.[1]

---

[1]   The present Regulation was approved by Resolution 50 adopted at the Fifteenth Extraordinary Session of the Central American Economic Council held in San Salvador, El Salvador, on March 27, 1968. The corresponding Record of Minutes was certified and distributed to the Member States on March 30, 1968. The Regulation became enforceable as of April 7, 1968.

b) Latin American Integration Association (LAIA) and Agreement of Subregional Integration of the Andean Group

The efforts concerning the furtherance of economic development in Latin American countries originated in the Economic Commission for Latin America and finally led to the creation of the Latin American Free Trade Association (LAFTA). The Treaty establishing the LAFTA was signed at Montevideo, Uruguay, on February 18, 1960. As its immediate objective it called for a Free Trade Area through the gradual reciprocal reduction of all duties within a twelve year period. LAFTA could not live up to the ambitious objectives and finally failed due to the considerable differences in the levels of development among member countries. In 1980 LAFTA was replaced by the Latin American Integration Association (LAIA) created by the treaty signed at Montevideo on August 12, 1980 by all LAFTA countries.

The Treaty of Montevideo of 1960 creating LAFTA did not itself provide for dispute settlement mechanisms, however, a Protocol for the Settlement of Disputes based on the Montevideo Treaty was adopted on September 2, 1967, at Asuncion, Paraguay. This Protocol provided for an Arbitration Court consisting of a panel of arbitrators designated by each member State similar to the Permanent Court of Arbitration formed under the Hague Convention of 1907. It further supplied the means for establishing a tribunal if the parties failed to fulfil their obligations in a specific case. The Treaty of Montevideo of 1980, concluded between the identical parties, and replacing the LAFTA by the LAIA, was also silent with regard to the settlement of disputes. Moreover, the resolutions adopted on August 12, 1980 and incorporated into the Treaty according to Art. 69 do not even mention the 1967 Protocol for the Settlement of Disputes. Since this Protocol established one of the organs of the LAFTA, i.e. the Standing Executive Committee, as the entity to facilitate the settlement of disputes and, according to Art. 66 of the 1980 Treaty, the organs of the LAFTA cease to exist with the entry into force of the 1980 Treaty, the Protocol has to be regarded as no longer in effect. For the text of the Protocol, reference therefore may be made to the first edition of the Dispute Settlement in Public International Law, of 1984, p. 453 ff.

When the difficulties for reaching the objectives of LAFTA due to the differences in the economic development of the member countries became apparent some of the less developed countries, namely Bolivia, Chile, Ecuador and Peru, later joined also by Venezuela, created a subregional agreement within the framework of LAFTA, the Andean Pact based on the Cartagena Agreement of 1969. The creation of the Andean Pact was based on Resolution 222 of the LAFTA Conference, which provided for the promulgation of subregional integration agreements " ... through which the LAFTA countries which sign them promote the process of economic integration in a balanced and more accelerated form than the one which derives from the commitments undertaken in the framework of the Treaty of Montevideo ...". The Cartagena Agreement aims at promoting the balanced and harmonious development of its member countries, accelerating growth through economic integration, facilitating participation in the process of integration provided by the Montevideo

Treaty and establishing favourable conditions for the conversion of LAFTA, later LAIA, into a common market.

The subregional agreement of the Andean Group provides for the pacific settlement of disputes by direct negotiations, by resorting to the good offices of the Commission, the supreme organ of the Agreement (Art. 6), or to a procedure of conciliation or mediation. If the dispute was not settled by these means, or if the parties so agreed, compulsory arbitration was required as provided for in the Protocol for the Settlement of Disputes under the LAFTA.

On May 28, 1979 the Andean Group concluded a "Treaty Creating the Court of Justice of the Cartagena Agreement". This Court, a principal organ of the Andean Group, is a permanent institution empowered to decide upon the claims of member States, the Commission or the Junta (or Board, the technical organ of the Agreement, Art. 13), and natural or juridical persons concerning nullification of Decisions of the Commission or Resolutions of the Junta. The Junta may also bring an action against a member State because of non-compliance with its obligations and the Court has the power to render advisory opinions by which national courts are bound in their interpretation of the Cartagena Agreement.

By means of this Treaty the Cartagena Agreement took on an existence independent of the Treaty of Montevideo. In Art. 33 of the Treaty creating the Court the procedures laid out in Art. 23 of the Cartagena Agreement are restricted to disputes concerning a contracting party to the Treaty of Montevideo (1960). Art. 38, para. II, spells out explicitly that "both, this Treaty and the Cartagena Agreement shall remain in effect independently of the continuation in effect of the Treaty of Montevideo". Thus, the termination of the LAFTA Treaty of Montevideo in 1980 did not imply the end of the Andean Court of Justice. Moreover, the new Treaty of Montevideo, 1980, lends additional support to subregional integration agreements such as that which provided for the Court of Justice.

Texts

Treaty of Montevideo establishing the Latin American Integration Association:
    ILM Vol. 20 (1981), pp.672-688
    Spanish Text in Integración Latinoamericana Vol. 5 (1980), pp. 78 ff.
Agreement of Subregional Integration of the Andean Group:
    Revista de Política Internacional 1969, Nos 105-106, 1970; Nos 107- 112 (Spanish)
    ILM Vol. 8 (1969), pp. 910 ff. (English)
    Instruments of Economic Integration in Latin America and the Caribbean Vol.1 (1975), pp. 175 ff. (English)
Protocol for the Settlement of Disputes:
    Instrumentos relativos a la integración económica de America Latina (2nd ed. 1968), pp. 411 - 417 (Spanish)
    Instruments of Economic Integration in Latin America and the Caribbean Vol.1 (1975), pp. 127 ff. (English)
Provisional Mechanism for the Settlement of Disputes:

Instrumentos relativos a la integración económica de America Latina (2nd ed. 1968), pp. 418 ff. (Spanish)

Derecho de la Integración 1957, pp. 188-191 and 1968, p. 160

Instruments of Economic Integration in Latin America and the Caribbean Vol. 1 (1975) pp. 136 ff. (English)

ILM Vol. 7 (1968), pp. 747 ff.

Rules of Procedure of a Provisional Mechanism for the Settlement of Disputes:

Instruments of Economic Integration in Latin America and the Caribbean Vol. 1 (1975), pp. 139 ff. (English)

Derecho de la Integración 1967, pp. 186-187 (Spanish)

Treaty Creating the Court of Justice of the Cartagena Agreement:

ILM Vol. 18 (1979), pp. 1203-1210 (English)

Integración Latinoamericana 1979, pp. 66-68 (Spanish)

Statute of the Court of Justice, ILM Vol. 23 (1984), 425-441

Internal Regulations of the Court of Justice, Gaceta Oficial del Acuerdo de Cartagena, No. 8, July 6, 1984

Bibliographical notes

R. Barros, Análisis comparativo de los Tratados de Montevideo 1960 y 1980. Integración Latinoamericana, No. 50 (1980), 30-48

O. Chaparro Alfonzo, ALADI o un nuevo orden de integración regional (1980)

V. Hummer, Die "Lateinamerikanische Integrationsassoziation" (ALADI) als Rechtsnachfolger der "Lateinamerikanischen Freihandelsassoziation" (ANALC), Verfassung und Recht in Übersee 13 (1980), 361 –370

H. A. Grigera Naón, Latin American Integration Association, in R. Bernhardt (ed.), EPIL, vol. III (1997), 144-147

D. Morawetz, The Andean Group (Cambridge Mass. London 1974) (with bibliography)

I. Cohen Orantes, Regional Integration in Central America (1972)

F. Orrego Vicuña, La creación de un Tribunal de Justícia en el Grupo Andino, Revista de derecho de la integración, No. 15 (1974), 31-45

D. B. Furnish, Establishment of Mechanisms for the Settlement of Economic Disputes, Georgia JICL Vol. 5 (1975), pp. 145 ff.

F. J. Vendrell, La organización del Acuerdo de Cartagena, Derecho de la Integración, Vol. 8 (1975) Nos 18/19, pp. 59-79

F. Salazar, Solución de conflictos en organizaciones interestatales para la integración económica y otras formas de cooperación económica, Derecho de la Integración, Vol. 11 (1978) Nos 28/29, pp. 19-34

A. Weber, Neuere Tendenzen im Integrationsrecht Lateinamerikas, VRÜ Vol. 11 (1978), pp. 89 ff.

D. J. Padilla, The Judicial Resolution of Legal Disputes in the Integration Movement of the Hemisphere, Lawyer of the Americas, Vol. 11 (1979), pp. 75-95

W. Hammer, Neueste Entwicklungen im fortschreitenden Integrationsprozeß in Latein-Amerika, JöR, Vol. 29 (1980), pp. 527-563

E. P. Lochridge, The Role of the Andean Court in Consolidating Regional Integration Efforts, Georgia Journal of International Law and Comparative Law, Vol. 10 (1980), 351-383

G. Poppe Entrambasaguas, Disposiciones jurídicas vigentes en el Tribunal de Justícia del Acuerdo de Cartagena, Publicaciones del tribunal/Estudios, Vol. 1 (1985)

E. B. Keener, The Andean Common Market Court of Justice: Its Purpose, Structure, and Future, Emory Journal of International Dispute Resolution, Vol. 2 (1987), 39-71

N. De Pierola, The Andean Court of Justice, Emory Journal of International Dispute Resolution, Vol. 2 (1987), 11-37

R. Meisel Lanner, El Tribunal Andino de Justícia (1988)

P. Nikken/J. Polakiewicz, Andean Common Market, Court of Justice, in R. Bernhardt (ed.), EPIL Vol. I (1992), 159-164

aa) Agreement of Subregional Integration of the Andean Group of May 26, 1969 as amended by the Protocol of Quito of May 12, 1987, Section E

SECTION E — RESOLUTION OF CONTROVERSIES

Art. 23   The resolution of controversies that arise due to the application of the legal order of this Agreement shall be subject to the norms of the treaty creating the Court of Justice of the Cartagena Agreement.

bb) Treaty Creating the Court of Justice of the Cartagena Agreement of May 28, 1979

The Governments of Bolivia, Colombia, Ecuador, Peru and Venezuela,

Persuaded that Latin American economic integration, and particularly the integration process consecrated in the Cartagena Agreement, constitute a common purpose of economic and social development; and taking into account the Declaration of the Presidents of the Andean countries formulated at Bogota on August 8, 1978;

Aware that it is essential to guarantee the strict fulfillment of the commitments directly and indirectly deriving from the Cartagena Agreement, in order that the integration process may achieve the objectives which the peoples of the member countries expect from it;

Convinced that some of the difficulties encountered in the execution of the Cartagena Agreement, and of the actions agreed upon in fulfillment of it, are due, among other factors, to the complexity of its juridical structure;

Certain that both the stability of the Cartagena Agreement and the rights and obligations deriving from it must be safeguarded by a juridical entity at the highest level, independent of the governments of the member countries and from the other bodies of the Cartagena Agreement, with the authority to define communitarian law, resolve the controversies which arise under it, and to interpret it uniformly;

Agree, through their duly authorized plenipotentiary representatives, to subscribe, for this purpose,

the following

CHAPTER I — JURIDICAL STRUCTURE OF THE CARTAGENA AGREEMENT

Art. 1   The juridical structure of the Cartagena Agreement comprises the following:

a)   Cartagena Agreement, its Protocols and Additional Instruments,

b)   this Treaty,

c)   Decisions of the Commission, and

d)   Resolutions of the Junta.

Art. 2   Decisions are obligatory for the member countries as of the date they are approved by the Commission.

Art. 3   Decisions of the Commission are directly applicable in the member countries from the date of their publication in the Official Gazette of the Cartagena Agreement, unless the Decision provides for a later date.

In the event that the text of a Decision so provides, such Decision must be adopted as internal law by means of an express act indicating the date of entry into force in each member country.

Art. 4   Resolutions of the Junta enter into force on the date and under the conditions established in the regulations of the Junta.

Art. 5   The member countries are committed to adopt the measures necessary to assure the fulfillment of the norms which comprise the juridical structure of the Cartagena Agreement.

Likewise, they are committed not to adopt or apply any measure which may be contrary to such norms, or which may, in any way, prejudice their application.

CHAPTER II — CREATION AND ORGANIZATION OF THE COURT

Art. 6   The Court of Justice of the Cartagena Agreement is hereby created as one of the principal institutions of the Cartagena Agreement endowed with the organization and functions established in this Treaty.

The site of the Court shall be in the city of Quito, Ecuador.

Art. 7   The Court shall be composed of five justices who shall be nationals of the member countries, be of high moral reputation and fulfill the standards required in their countries of origin for undertaking the highest judicial functions, or be jurisconsults of recognized competence.

The justices shall be fully independent in the exercise of their functions, they may not undertake any other professional activities, whether or not remunerated, except those of a professorial nature, and they shall abstain from any activity incompatible with the nature of their office.

Upon the unanimous proposal of the Court, the Commission of the Cartagena Agreement may modify the number of justices and create the position of Attorney General; the number and functions of this official shall be established, in this case, in the statute referred to in Article 14.

Art. 8   The justices shall be designated from lists presented by each member country and selected by the unanimous vote of the plenipotentiaries accredited for this purpose. The government of the situs country shall convoke the plenipotentiaries.

Art. 9   The justices shall be designated for a term of six years; they shall he partially replaced every three years, and they may be reelected once.

Art. 10   Each justice shall have a first and second alternate who shall replace him, in turn, in the event of definitive or temporary absence, or in the event of impediment or challenge, in accordance with the provisions established in the statute of the Court.

            The alternates must possess the same qualifications as the principals. They shall be designated on the same date, in the same manner and for a term equal to that of the justices.

Art. 11   A justice may be removed upon the complaint of the government of a member country solely if, in the exercise of his functions, he has committed a grievous fault stipulated in the statute of the Court, and in accordance with the procedure established therein. For this purpose, the governments of the member countries shall designate plenipotentiaries who, when convoked by the government of the situs country, shall decide on the complaint in a special meeting by unanimous vote.

Art. 12   Upon the termination of his term, the respective justice shall continue to fulfill his functions until the date on which his successor takes office.

Art. 13   The member countries are obligated to grant the Court all of the facilities necessary for the adequate fulfillment of its functions. The Court and the justices shall be entitled in the territories of the member countries to the immunities recognized by international practice and, in particular, by the Vienna Convention with respect to diplomatic relations, including the inviolability of its archives and official correspondence and with respect to all matters under civil and criminal jurisdiction, except as otherwise provided in Article 31 of the Vienna Convention.

            The justices, the Secretary of the Court and the functionaries designated as international employees shall be entitled to the immunities and privileges corresponding to their respective office in the territory of the situs country. For this purpose, the justices shall have the rank equivalent to that of chief of a diplomatic mission, and the other functionaries to that which is provided by common agreement between the Court and the government of the situs country.

Art. 14   Upon the proposal of the Junta and within three months following the date on which this Treaty enters into force, the Commission shall approve the statute which will govern both the functioning of the Court and the judicial procedures to which the causes of action contemplated in this Treaty shall be subject.

            Modifications to this statute shall be decided by the Commission, upon the proposal of the Court.

> The Decisions of the Commission in regard to this matter shall require a two-thirds affirmative vote, and provided there is no negative vote.
>
> The Court shall issue its internal regulations.

Art. 15   The Court shall appoint its Secretary and such personnel as are essential for the fulfillment of its functions.

Art. 16   The Commission shall approve annually the budget of the Court. For this purpose, the President of the Court shall opportunely send every year the corresponding proposed budget.

CHAPTER III — JURISDICTION OF THE COURT

FIRST SECTION — ACTIONS OF NULLIFICATION

Art. 17   It shall correspond to the Court to decide the nullification of Decisions of the Commission and Resolutions of the Junta adopted in violation of the norms which comprise the juridical structure of the Cartagena Agreement, including ultra vires acts, when these are impugned by any member country, by the Commission, by the Junta, or by natural or juridical persons as provided in Article 19 of this Treaty.

Art. 18   The member countries may only bring an action of nullification against the Decisions approved without their affirmative vote.

Art. 19   Natural and juridical persons may bring actions of nullification against Decisions of the Commission or Resolutions of the Junta which are applicable to them and cause them harm.

Art. 20   An action of nullification must be presented to the Court within one year following the date of entry into force of the Decision of the Commission or the Resolution of the Junta.

Art. 21   The bringing of an action of nullification shall not affect the applicability or enforceability of the norm impugned.

Art. 22   In the event that the Court rules the total or partial nullification of a Decision or Resolution, it shall indicate the effects of its ruling over such period of time as may be deemed appropriate under the circumstances.

> The body of the Cartagena Agreement whose act has been nullified must adopt the measures required to assure the effective fulfillment of the decision of the Court.

SECOND SECTION — ACTIONS OF NONCOMPLIANCE

Art. 23   Whenever the Junta considers that a member country is not complying with its obligations under the norms which comprise the juridical structure of the Cartagena Agreement, it shall present its written observations to said country. The member country must respond to them within a period compatible with the urgency of the matter, which in no case may exceed two months. Upon the receipt of the response, or once the referred to period has terminated, the Junta shall issue its considered opinion.

If the Junta finds that there is noncompliance, and the member country persists in the action which was the object of the observations, then the Junta may present the matter to the Court for its decision.

Art. 24   Whenever a member country considers that another member country is not complying with its obligations under the norms which comprise the juridical structure of the Cartagena Agreement, it may present its complaint, together with the facts on which the complaint is based, to the Junta which shall issue its considered opinion, after completing the procedure referred to in the first paragraph of Article 23.

If the Junta finds that there is noncompliance and the accused member country persists in the action which was the object of the complaint, the Junta must present the matter to the Court. In the event that the Junta has not brought the action within the period of two months following the date of its opinion, the complainant country may present the matter directly to the Court.

In the event that the Junta has not issued its opinion within three months following the date on which the complaint is presented, or the finding is that there has not been noncompliance, then the complainant country may present the matter directly to the Court.

Art. 25   In the event that the ruling of the Court is of noncompliance, the member country whose action is the object of the complaint is obligated to adopt the measures necessary for complying with the decision within three months following notification.

In the event that said member country does not comply with the obligation referred to in the preceding paragraph, the Court, summarily and after hearing the opinion of the Junta, shall determine the limits within which the complainant country, or any other member country, may restrict or suspend, totally or partially, the advantages deriving from the Cartagena Agreement which benefit the noncomplying member country. The Court, through the Junta, shall notify the member countries of its decision.

Art. 26   The rulings issued in actions of noncompliance may be reviewed by the Court, upon the petition of an interested party, if such petition is based on a fact which could have decisively influenced the outcome of the proceeding, provided that such fact was unknown to the party petitioning for review as of the date on which the ruling was handed down.

The petition for review must be presented within two months from the date of discovery of the fact and, in all cases, within one year following the date of the ruling.

Art. 27   Natural and juridical persons shall have the right to bring causes of action in the competent national courts, in accordance with the provisions of domestic law, when the member countries do not comply with that provided in Article 5 of this Treaty and the rights of such persons are affected by this noncompliance.

THIRD SECTION — ADVISORY OPINIONS

Art. 28   It shall correspond to the Court to interpret, through prior advisory opinions, the norms which comprise the juridical structure of the Cartagena Agreement, in order to assure uniform application in the territories of the member countries.

Art. 29   National judges who have before them a case in which any of the norms which comprise the juridical structure of the Cartagena Agreement must be applied may petition the Court for its interpretation of such norms, but provided that the ruling is subject to appeal within the national judicial system. In the event that it is necessary for the national court to issue its ruling before receiving the interpretation of the Court, the judge must proceed to decide the case.

In the event that the ruling is not subject to appeal within the national judicial system, the judge shall suspend the proceeding and petition the interpretation of the Court, ex officio in all cases, or upon the petition of an interested party, if so required by law.

Art. 30   The Court shall restrict its interpretation to defining the content and scope of the norms of the juridical structure of the Cartagena Agreement. The Court may not interpret the content and scope of domestic law nor judge the substantive facts of the case.

Art. 31   The judge hearing the case must adopt the interpretation of the Court.

CHAPTER IV — GENERAL PROVISIONS

Art. 32   To be enforceable, the rulings of the Court shall not require homologation or exequatur in any of the member countries.

Art. 33   The member countries shall not submit any controversy which may arise from the application of the norms which comprise the juridical structure of the Cartagena Agreement to any court, arbitration system or any other procedure not contemplated by this Treaty.

The member countries agree to recur to the procedure established in Article 23 of the Cartagena Agreement only in the event of controversies which arise between any of them and another contracting party of the Treaty of Montevideo which is not a member of the Cartagena Agreement.

Art. 34   The Junta shall publish the Official Gazette of the Cartagena Agreement in which the Decisions of the Commission, the Resolutions of the Junta and the rulings of the Court shall be published.

Art. 35   In the event that it is considered necessary for the fulfillment of its functions, the Court may directly communicate with the authorities of the member countries.

CHAPTER V — ACCESSION, ENTRY INTO FORCE AND DENUNCIATION

Art. 36   This Treaty may not be subscribed with reservations. The states which accede to the Cartagena Agreement must accede to this Treaty.

Art. 37   This Treaty shall enter into force when all the subscribing member countries have deposited their respective instruments of ratification with the Secretary of the Commission of the Cartagena Agreement.

Art. 38   This Treaty shall remain in effect for as long as the Cartagena Agreement is in force, and it may not be denounced independently of the latter. The denunciation of the Cartagena Agreement shall simultaneously signify the denunciation of this Treaty.

           Both this Treaty and the Cartagena Agreement shall remain in effect independently of the continuation in effect of the Treaty of Montevideo.

CHAPTER VI — TRANSITORY PROVISIONS

First. The action of nullification referred to in the First Section of Chapter III of this Treaty may be brought against the Decisions of the Commission and the Resolutions of the Junta which have been approved prior to the date of entry into force of this Treaty, provided they are commenced within one year of the referred to date.

Second. The government of the situs country must convoke the plenipotentiaries referred to in Article 8 for the first designation of justices within three months following the date of entry into force of this Treaty.

Third. On the occasion of the first designation, two of the justices shall be appointed for three years and three for six years, decided by lot immediately following their designation.

In Witness Whereof, the accredited plenipotentiaries, having deposited their full powers which were found in due and proper form, subscribe this Treaty in the name of their respective governments.

Subscribed in the city of Cartagena, on the 28th day of May, 1979.

cc) Statute of the Court of Justice of the Cartagena Agreement

The COMMISSION of the CARTAGENA AGREEMENT,

IN VIEW OF Article 14 of the Treaty which creates the Court of Justice of the Cartagena Agreement and Proposal 141 of the Junta, and finding said Treaty to be in effect by virtue of its having been ratified by all the Member Countries,

DECIDES to approve the following:

STATUTE OF THE COURT OF JUSTICE OF THE CARTAGENA AGREEMENT

PRELIMINARY PROVISION

Art. 1   In the provisions of this Statute the following definitions mean:

– Agreement: the Cartagena Agreement;

– Treaty: the Treaty which creates the Court of Justice of the Cartagena Agreement;

– Commission, Junta, Court: the Commission, the Junta, and the Court of Justice of the Cartagena Agreement;

– Member Country, Member Countries: a Member Country, the Member Countries of the Cartagena Agreement;

– Internal Regulations: the Internal Regulations of the Court of Justice of the Cartagena Agreement.

TITLE I — THE COURT: GENERAL PROVISION

Art. 2   The Court, the jurisdictional body created to assure respect for law in the application and interpretation of the juridical order of the Agreement, is governed by the Treaty, the present Statute and the Internal Regulations.

CHAPTER I — THE JUSTICES AND THEIR ALTERNATES

Art. 3   The terms of the justices and their alternates are fixed and shall begin from the date following the termination of the terms of their predecessors.

Art. 4   On the first day of the term, or no later than thirty days thereafter, the designated justice shall, at a session of the Court and at its chambers, take the oath that he shall fulfill the responsibilities of his office conscientiously and with absolute impartiality, shall preserve the secrecy of the Court's deliberations and shall fulfill the duties inherent to his functions.

Immediately thereafter, the President of the Court shall declare the justice to have taken office, and he shall then immediately begin to fulfill his official functions.

Of this session an act shall be prepared, which shall be signed by the President, the justice and the Secretary.

Art. 5   The Court, at the request of the corresponding person and in plenary session, may grant the immunity established for the justices by virtue of Article 13 of the Treaty. For this purpose, the Court shall issue a deliberated resolution, upon due consideration of the antecedents.

If, once immunity has been granted, the justice were to be subjected to a trial, this must occur before the competent jurisdiction to try the highest justices of the Member Country where the case is presented.

In such event, if there were to be a verdict of guilty in a criminal proceeding, the justice shall be deemed to have vacated his office.

Art. 6   For purposes of Article 11 of the Treaty, the following shall be considered grave offenses by a justice:

a)   Notoriously bad conduct;

b)   Any comportment incompatible with the nature of his office;

c)   Repeated failure to fulfill the duties inherent to his responsibilities;

d)   The undertaking of professional activities, whether or not remunerated, except for those of a professional or academic nature; and

e)   The violation of the oath referred to in Article 4.

Letter d) of this Article is not applicable to the alternates who occasionally sit on the bench.

Art. 7   When in fulfillment of his duties a justice commits any of the offenses contemplated in the preceding Article, the Government of a Member Country may present, through the Government of Ecuador, a deliberated request for removal.

The Government of Ecuador, the headquarters country, shall communicate the request to the Governments of the other Member Countries and to the accused justice, and shall convoke the plenipotentiaries referred to in Article 11 of the Treaty to a meeting, to be convened in not more than thirty days.

At said meeting the plenipotentiaries shall hear the accused justice and shall, unanimously and after due consideration, decide if there is cause for removal.

Art. 8   The first and second alternates, in order, shall be called by the President and shall replace the justice:

a)   In cases in which the designated justice, without sufficient justification in the opinion of the Court in plenary session, does not take the oath of office within thirty days following the commencement of his term, for the time remaining in his term;

b)   In cases of death, resignation, removal or vacancy of office, for the time remaining in the respective term;

c)   In cases of leave of absence, for the duration thereof; and

d)   In cases of impediment or challenge accepted by the Court, solely with respect to the corresponding hearing and opinion of that case.

The alternate so convoked shall take the oath referred to in Article 4 and shall immediately begin to fulfill his functions.

Art. 9   The justices and their alternates shall be designated no later than two months prior to the termination of the terms of their predecessors.

For this purpose, the Government of the headquarters' country shall require the presentation of the respective nominees and shall convoke the plenipotentiaries no later than three months prior to the termination of said term.

CHAPTER II — THE PRESIDENT

Art. 10   The Court shall have a President who shall hold office for one year. This office shall be held successively by each one of the justices, according to the order agreed upon by them or by lot.

Art. 11   The President shall represent the Court, direct its work and services, and convoke and preside over its sessions and hearings.

In addition to the attributes and functions conferred by this Statute and the Internal Regulations, the President shall also have those attributes and functions, in general, that are inherent to his office.

CHAPTER III — THE SECRETARY

Art. 12   The Court shall name its Secretary in plenary session.

Art. 13   The Secretary must be a national of one of the Member Countries, possess high moral esteem and be a jurist of notorious competence.

Art. 14   The Secretary shall be named for a period of five years and may not be reelected.

Art. 15   Upon taking office, the Secretary shall take, before the Court, the oath contemplated in Article 4.

Art. 16   The Secretary shall:

a)   Direct, under the authority of the President, the Secretariat of the Court;

b)   Undertake, according to the instructions of the President, the judicial labors of the Court, the reception, handling and custody of all documents, case files and notices required by the present Statute, as well as the organization and maintenance of the general registry of matters submitted to the Court;

    c)   Attest and issue certifications, copies and, according to the instructions and under the authority of the President, testimonies relative to the matters which are within the jurisdiction of the Court; and

    d)   Fulfill the other obligations and attributes contemplated by the present Statute and the Internal Regulations.

Art. 17   If the Secretary commits any of the offenses referred to in Article 6, the Tribunal will examine the case, hear testimony by the person involved and adopt a resolution.

Art. 18   In the case of definite absence, vacancy or abandonment of office, the Tribunal shall name a new Secretary for a period of five years.

In the event of the temporary absence of the Secretary, the President shall designate an official who shall serve as Secretary ad interim.

Chapter IV — Organization, Personnel and Administration

Art. 19   The Court, in plenary session, shall define the structure of the Secretariat and the Administration.

Art. 20   In hiring the personnel which are indispensable for the fulfillment of its functions, the Court shall solely take into account the suitability, competence and honor of the candidates and shall endeavor to the extent not incompatible with the foregoing criteria, to assure, for such offices, the widest possible geographic distribution among the subregion.

Art. 21   The Court shall establish in the Internal Regulations the selection procedures, hiring conditions, categories and terms, as well as the rights and obligations of officers and employees.

Art. 22   Before taking office, employees shall swear before the President of the Court in the presence of the Secretary, that they shall preserve secrecy and fulfill with absolute loyalty, impartiality, discretion and conscientiousness the functions entrusted to them by the Court.

Art. 23   The Court shall prepare an annual budget proposal and the President shall send it to the Commission no later than thirty days prior to the last Period of Ordinary Sessions of each year.

Chapter V — Sessions

Art. 24   The Court shall be in permanent session at its seat, the city of Quito.

Art. 25   On the dates and at the hours established in the Internal Regulations, the Court shall meet in full session, with a quorum of five justices, and shall adopt its resolutions by an affirmative vote of at least three of its members.

Art. 26   The Court shall render judgment in plenary session. Likewise, it shall hear and resolve in plenary session such matters as are so expressly required by this Statute.

Art. 27   For those matters with respect to which this Statute does not require a plenary session, the Court may meet with a quorum of three justices.

In such case, it shall adopt its resolutions with an affirmative vote of at least three justices, if there are four or five members voting, or of at least two justices, if there are three members voting.

Art. 28   The Secretary shall attend all sessions, except as established to the contrary by this Statute or the Court.

When the Tribunal meets without the Secretary being present, the justice designated as Secretary ad hoc shall prepare the corresponding record, if required, which shall be signed by the President and said justice.

Art. 29   The deliberations of the Court shall be secret and shall so remain.

Art. 30   In the final deliberation of a proceeding, the justices shall express their reasoned opinion.

Judgments of the Court must be signed by the President, the other justices and the Secretary, and shall not indicate abstentions or dissenting opinions.

After judgments are executed, the Secretary shall communicate them to the Junta for their publication in the Official Gazette of the Cartagena Agreement.

Art. 31   The Court, in plenary session and by means of a resolution to be published in the Official Gazette of the Cartagena Agreement, shall determine the regulations and period for the annual judicial recess, which may not exceed thirty days.

CHAPTER VI — REPRESENTATIVES, ATTORNEYS AND ADVISERS

Art. 32   The Parties shall bring matters before the Court themselves or through a representative or agent to whom has been granted a power of attorney in accordance with the legislation of the Member Country or of the corresponding jurisdiction, who, if not an attorney, necessarily must be assisted by an attorney entitled to practice in a Member Country. The parties may utilize such advisers as they deem appropriate.

Art. 33   The representatives, attorneys and advisers in a proceeding shall enjoy all the guarantees and facilities necessary for the unrestricted pursuit of their activities within the Court.

For its part, the Court shall have, with respect to the representatives, attorneys and advisers, such disciplinary powers as may be necessary for the normal conduct of the proceeding.

TITLE II — PROCEDURE

Art. 34　　The object of the procedures contemplated in the present Statute are the effectiveness of rights, safeguarding of the spirit of integration, maintaining equality between the parties, and the guarantee of due process.

CHAPTER I — ACTIONS OF NULLITY AND NONCOMPLIANCE

Section 1 — The Complaint

Art. 35　　All proceedings with respect to actions of nullity and noncompliance contemplated in the Treaty shall be initiated by means of a complaint signed by the party and its attorney, directed to the President of the Court and presented to the Secretary in one original and three copies.

Art. 36　　The complaint must contain:

　　　　a)　The names and domiciles of the plaintiff and the defendant;

　　　　b)　The purpose of the complaint;

　　　　c)　A statement of the facts and of the legal basis; and

　　　　d)　The presentation of evidence, if any.

　　　　For purposes of the proceeding, the complaint shall also indicate the domicile of the plaintiff at the situs of the Court and the name of the person authorized to receive notifications.

　　　　If the plaintiff has to proceed through a representative or agent, said person must be accredited with the corresponding legal document.

Art. 37　　The complaint of nullity must include, annexed thereto:

　　　　a)　If the plaintiff is a Member Country, the certification of the Junta that the Decision in dispute was not approved with its affirmative vote;

　　　　b)　If the plaintiff is a juridical entity, an authentic copy of its statutes and of the power of attorney granted to its attorney by a representative qualified to so grant;

　　　　c)　Necessarily, if the plaintiff is a juridical entity or a natural person, the presentation of evidence that the Decision or Resolution in dispute applies to it and causes harm; and

　　　　d)　A copy of the Decision or Resolution that is being disputed.

Art. 38　　The complaint of noncompliance must include, annexed thereto:

　　　　a)　A copy, certified by the Junta, of its reasoned opinion; or

　　　　b)　The demonstration that three months have passed without the Junta having issued its opinion.

Art. 39　　The complaint of noncompliance may refer, among others, to the promulgation of norms contrary to legal order, to the failure to promulgate norms which fulfill the legal order, or to acts or conduct in opposition to the legal order, despite there having been adopted provisions ordering fulfillment.

Art. 40   The Secretary shall seal the original and the copies of the complaint and shall attest to the date of presentation. One copy shall be returned to the plaintiff.

Art. 41   If the complaint does not comply with any of the requisites indicated in Articles 36, and 37 or 38, the Court, within five days following presentation of the complaint, shall establish a reasonable time within which the plaintiff may perfect the complaint or present the pertinent documents. If this period terminates without the plaintiff having perfected the complaint or presented the documents, the Court shall return the complaint.

Art. 42   Once admitted, the defendant party shall be notified.

Section 2 — The Answer

Art. 43   Within thirty days from the date of notification of the complaint, the defendant party must answer the complaint. The answer to the complaint must contain:
   a)   The name and domicile of the defendant;
   b)   The factual and legal arguments; and
   c)   The presentation of evidence, if any.
   Paragraphs two and three of Article 36 are applicable to the answer.

Art. 44   If the defendant, duly notified of the complaint, does not present the answer within the term stipulated in the preceding article, it shall be presumed that the basis of the complaint, both as to fact and as to law, has been denied. The Court shall attest to this fact in the record.

Section 3 — The Evidence

Art. 45   Within eight days following the presentation of the answer to the complaint, the Court, solely or on a motion by a party, shall decide whether evidence is required.
   If the Court decides that there is no cause for the evidentiary stage, the President shall set the day and hour for the hearing, and shall arrange for the convocation of the parties.
   If the Court decides to open the evidentiary stage, it shall indicate the facts involved and the period within which they should be proven. The parties shall be notified of the decision and they shall be ordered to act correspondingly.

Art. 46   Evidence may be presented by:
   a)   The declaration of the parties;
   b)   The request for reports and the presentation of documents;

c)   Testimony;

d)   Expert reports; and

e)   Physical inspection.

The Court shall determine the evidence to be presented, in accordance with which the parties shall defray the expenses caused thereby.

The Court shall consider the evidence submitted as a whole in accordance with the principles of sound judgment.

Art. 47   Upon the termination of the evidentiary stage, the President shall set the day and hour for the hearing and shall arrange for the convocation of the parties.

Section 4 — The Hearing

Art. 48   Hearings shall be public unless for serious motives the Court, of its own accord or at the request of a party, decides to hold them in private.

The President shall open and direct the proceedings.

The absence of one or both of the parties does not annul the proceeding.

Art. 49   The Court shall consider the cases which have been submitted to it in the order which they were set for hearing. Among various cases which were simultaneously set for hearing, the order shall be determined according to the date on which the complaint was presented.

The Court, in consideration of special circumstances and by a reasoned resolution, may grant priority to a case to be heard.

Art. 50   The hearing shall be initiated by the narration of the proceeding by the Secretary, who shall solely objectively summarize the history of the case.

Art. 51   Under the authority and instructions of the President, the plaintiff and the defendant, in turn, may intervene, with replication and rejoinder also being permitted.

Art. 52   Once the oral arguments have been terminated, the parties may present their written conclusions during the hearing or within three days thereafter.

Art. 53   When the Court considers that based on the oral arguments of the parties it is necessary to seek additional evidence or to augment the evidence already presented, it shall suspend the hearing for one time only, grant a prudential time for presenting the evidence and indicate the day and hour for reinitiating the hearing.

Art. 54   The Secretary shall make a record of each hearing, which shall be signed by the President and the Secretary.

Section 5 — The Judgment

Art. 55   Within fifteen days following the completion of the hearing, the Court shall hand down its judgment in full session.

Art. 56   The judgment must contain:

a)   A statement that it has been handed down by the Court;

b)   The date on which it is handed down;

c)   The names of the parties;

d)   A summary exposition of the facts;

e)   A summary of the conclusions of the parties;

f)   The considerations or elements on which the judgment is based; and

g)   The decision.

If the judgment declares the total or partial nullity of a Decision or Resolution, it must further indicate the date on which it becomes effective.

The judgment shall include the decision of the Court concerning the payment or exoneration of costs.

In a judgment of noncompliance, the Court shall instruct the corresponding Member Country as to the measures it must adopt for the execution thereof.

Art. 57   The judgment shall be read in a public hearing, after the convocation of the parties. A record shall be made of such act.

The judgment, signed by the President, the other justices and the Secretary, shall be sealed and deposited in the Secretariat.

Art. 58   The judgment shall have obligatory effect from the day after it is read in public hearing.

Section 6 — The Amendment, Extension and Clarification of a Judgment

Art. 59   The Court, on its own accord or at the request of a party presented within a period of five days following the reading of the judgment, may amend or extend it.

Amendment may occur if the judgment contains manifest errors of drafting, or of calculations, or evident inaccuracies, or if there is any pronouncement concerning a matter not presented in the complaint, and extension, when any of the points contested was not resolved.

The other party shall be informed of the request for amendment or extension, in order to make the proceeding unnecessary, if deemed suitable.

The Court, in full session and within ten days following the termination of the period referred to in the first paragraph, shall adopt a resolution on the amendment or extension, shall notify the parties and shall annex it to the judgment. In this event, the execution of the judgment shall occur upon the last notification to the parties.

Art. 60   Within the period of ten days following the reading of the judgment, a party, a Member Country, the Commission or the Junta may request the clarification of the points of the judgment which it deems to be ambiguous.

The parties shall be informed of the request for clarification, in order that they may avoid the proceeding, if deemed suitable.

The fourth paragraph of the preceding Article is applicable to a clarification.

CHAPTER II — PRE-JUDICIAL INTERPRETATION

Art. 61   The request for interpretation that judges or national tribunals address to the Court in accordance with Article 29 of the Treaty must contain:

a) The name and hierarchy of the judge or national tribunal;

b) A listing of the norms of the legal order of the Cartagena Agreement of which an interpretation is requested;

c) The identification of the case originating the request and a succint report of the facts that the petitioner considers relevant for the interpretation; and

d) The place and address at which the judge or tribunal will receive the corresponding notification.

Art. 62   Upon receiving the request, the Secretary shall affix the seal, record the date of presentation and remit it to the President for consideration by the Court.

Art. 63   Within a period of thirty days following receipt of the request, the Court shall hand down its judgment in full session.

Art. 64   The judgment of the Court, signed by the President, the other justices and the Secretary, shall be sealed and deposited in the Secretariat.

The judge or national tribunal shall be notified of the judgment by a sealed and certified copy thereof.

CHAPTER III — REVIEW OF JUDGMENTS

Art. 65   Only judgments in suits of noncompliance are susceptible to review in accordance with Article 26 of the Treaty. The appeal shall be by the parties in the previous proceeding.

Art. 66   An appeal for review must be presented within two months of the date on which the appellants discovered the fact upon which it is based, and, in any case, within one year following the date of the judgment of noncompliance.

Art. 67   An appeal for review must contain, in addition to that contemplated in
           Article 36, as applicable:

    a)   Identification of the judgment being challenged;

    b)   Specification of the points of the judgment being challenged;

    c)   Description of the facts upon which the appeal is based; and

    d)   Explanation of the alleged evidence to demonstrate the existence of
          such facts and the moment in which they were discovered or became
          known.

Art. 68   Once an appeal is admitted, the procedure shall be in accordance with the
           present Statute, and a judgment will be rendered in plenary session.

CHAPTER IV — SANCTIONS FOR NONFULFILLMENT OF A JUDGMENT

Art. 69   If the judgment is of noncompliance and the corresponding Member
           Country does not adopt the necessary measures for compliance with it
           within the term established in the first paragraph of Article 25 of the
           Treaty, the Court, upon the expiration of said term and in accordance
           with the provisions of the second paragraph of said Article, shall request
           the opinion of the Junta and the Junta shall express its opinion within
           thirty days following the communication of said request.

Art. 70   Having received the opinion of the Junta, the Court, if appropriate, shall
           determine the day and hour for a hearing.

Art. 71   Within either ten days following receipt of the opinion of the Junta or of
           five days following the final day of the hearing, the Court, in plenary ses-
           sion, shall deliberate and determine the limits within which the Member
           Countries may restrict or suspend, totally or partially, the advantages of
           the Agreement that benefit the Member Country in violation. Said limits
           must be in relation to the gravity of the noncompliance.

           Immediately and through the Junta, the Court shall communicate its deci-
           sion to the Member Countries.

           The application of the measures of restriction or suspension referred to in
           the first paragraph of this Article shall not require the promulgation of
           any decisions whatsoever by the Commission or the Junta.

CHAPTER V — IMPEDIMENT AND CHALLENGE

Art. 72   The impediment or challenge of the justices may occur at any stage of the
           proceeding.

Art. 73   Reasons for impediment or challenge of the justices, in relation to the
           parties or their representatives or agents, include:

    a)   Kinship of the justice or his spouse within the fourth degree of con-
          sanguinity or the second degree of affinity;

b) Interest of the justice or his spouse in the matter submitted to the Court or in another of a similar nature;

c) Previous involvement in the matter; and

d) Intimate friendship or manifest enmity of the justice or his spouse.

Art. 74 Without waiting to be challenged, a justice who is aware of the existence of any of the reasons indicated in the preceding Article, with respect to himself, is obligated to so declare to the Court.

The President, having received the declaration, shall suspend the case until the Court resolves the situation.

Art. 75 A challenge shall be presented to the Court, by written document which shall state the reasons on which it is based.

Once the challenge has been proposed, the President shall suspend the case until the Court decides the situation and, if deemed appropriate, shall order that any relevant evidence be presented within the period of eight days.

Once this period has passed, the Court shall definitively render its decision.

Art. 76 Neither impediment nor challenge have any effect on the proceeding prior to that time.

TITLE III — FINAL AND TRANSITORY PROVISIONS

CHAPTER I — FINAL PROVISIONS

Art. 77 On their own initiative or at the request of the Court, at any stage of the proceeding but prior to judgment, the Member Countries, the Commission or the Junta, although not parties, may present to the Court information or legal arguments that are considered necessary for a more perfect solution of the case.

Art. 78 The procedural periods established by this Statute shall be calendar or continuous days and shall be calculated excluding the initial date of such period.

If the period ends on a non-working day, the expiration of the period is extended until the end of the following business day.

The length of periods, as well as the non-working days referred to in the preceding paragraph, shall be established by the Court, in plenary session, by a resolution which shall be published in the Official Gazette of the Agreement.

Art. 79 The Court, in plenary session and by a resolution which shall be published in the Official Gazette of the Agreement, shall determine the norms which shall govern the notices contemplated in Title II of this Statute.

Art. 80   Individuals or juridical entities whose rights are affected by the noncompliance of a Member Country shall have the right to resort to the competent tribunals of said State, according to its internal law, to request that the provisions of Article 5 of the Treaty be fulfilled.

CHAPTER II — TRANSITORY PROVISIONS

Art. 81   The terms of the justices designated in accordance with the second and third Transitory Provisions of the Treaty, shall be deemed to have been initiated on January 2, 1984, the date on which they shall take their oaths before the Ministry of Foreign Affairs of the headquarters country, who shall declare them to have taken office and shall install the Court, by delegation of the Member Countries.

Art. 82   The Court shall subscribe with the Member Countries, as soon as possible, the necessary agreements for the recognition of the rights of the alternates to the justices, representatives or agents, attorneys and advisers of the parties and the persons who intervene in the regular course of proceedings, in order to assure that their actions in a proceeding are fully independent.

Art. 83   Prior to the thirty-first day of January of 1984, the Member Countries shall designate and communicate to the Court the national authorities who shall represent them in all actions and proceedings, as contemplated in the Treaty and this Statute.

Done at the city of Quito on the nineteenth of August 1983.

dd) Internal Rules of the Court of Justice of the Cartagena Agreement of May 9, 1984 and June 19, 1985

REGLAMENTO INTERNO DEL TRIBUNAL

El Tribunal de Justícia del Acuerdo de Cartagena, en uso de la facultad que le atribuye el artículo 14 del Tratado que lo creó y en sesión plenaria, dicta el siguiente:

REGLAMENTO INTERNO DEL TRIBUNAL

TÍTULO I — DISPOSICIÓN GENERAL

Art. 1   (Reglamento Interno: contenido)

El presente Reglamento desarrolla las normas del Estatuto relativas a la organización y funcionamiento del Tribunal y a los procedimientos judiciales que se sigan ante este órgano jurisdiccional.

CAPÍTULO I — DE LOS MAGISTRADOS Y SUS SUPLENTES

Art. 2   (Magistrados: iniciación de funciones)

El período de los magistrados comenzará a correr el día 2 de enero del año que finalice el período de sus predecesores.

Art. 3   (Magistrados: juramento y posesión)

La juramentación y toma de posesión de los magistrados y sus suplentes se registrará en un libro de actas que será llevado por el Secretario.

Art. 4   (Magistrados: procedimiento para levantar su inmunidad)

Para levantar la inmunidad a un magistrado, según lo dispuesto en el artículo 50 del Estatuto, se seguirá el siguiente procedimiento: Recibida la solicitud, se correrá traslado al magistrado y se le darán cinco días para ser oído. El Tribunal podrá abrir un término para recibir la información que corresponda y resolverá la solicitud en sesión plenaria.

El procedimiento para el levantamiento de la inmunidad tendrá carácter de reservado.

Art. 5   (Magistrados suplentes: su elección)

A los suplentes les será comunicada su elección en la misma forma que a los magistrados principales y se les solicitará que manifiesten su aprobación o negativa. En caso de no aceptación se procederá conforme a lo dispuesto en el artículo 10 del Tratado.

Art. 6   (Suplentes: casos en que reemplazan a los magistrados)

Los suplentes, en su orden, reemplazarán a los magistrados principales: transitoriamente en los casos de impedimento, recusación o licencia, y hasta la terminación del período por remoción, renuncia, incapacidad permanente, muerte, caducidad del nombramiento en el caso del literal a) del artículo 8°del Estatuto o vacancia en el caso del inciso 3°del artículo 5°del Estatuto.

Art. 7   (Suplentes: remuneración)

Los suplentes, durante el tiempo que reemplacen al magistrado, devengarán igual remuneración que el principal.

Art. 8   (Magistrados y suplentes: oportunidad de su elección)

El Presidente del Tribunal dará aviso al gobierno del país sede de la finalización de los períodos de los magistrados con treinta días de anticipación a la iniciación del término señalado en el artículo 9°del Estatuto, para que se proceda en la forma prevista en esta norma.

En la misma forma procederá el Presidente del Tribunal cuando convocados los dos suplentes expresen su renuncia, se excusen o no concurran para suplir al magistrado principal.

Art. 9   (Licencia para magistrados)

Los magistrados podrán obtener licencia sin remuneración hasta por un año, siempre que no sea para el ejercicio de actividades incompatibles con las de magistrado del Tribunal.

También podrán obtener licencia por enfermedad hasta por seis meses, de acuerdo con la reglamentación sobre personal.

CAPÍTULO II — DEL PRESIDENTE

Art. 10   (Presidente del Tribunal: designación)

En la primera semana posterior a las vacaciones anuales, se designará Presidente del Tribunal mediante sorteo. No participarán en el sorteo los magistrados de reciente designación mientras los más antiguos no hubieren ejercido la Presidencia. Tampoco podrán ser designados los magistrados suplentes, a menos que asuman la magistratura con carácter de titular. Efectuado el sorteo, el Presidente asumirá el cargo de inmediato, previo el juramento.

Art. 11   (Presidente del Tribunal: su reemplazante)

En los casos de falta del Presidente por licencia, ausencia u otro motivo, será reemplazado por el magistrado que ejerció la presidencia en el período inmediatamente anterior.

En los casos de impedimento o recusación del Presidente, se procederá de la misma manera.

Si la falta fuere definitiva, el Tribunal designará Presidente para el resto del período por el mismo procedimiento previsto en el artículo anterior.

Art. 12   (Presidente del Tribunal: atribuciones)

Son atribuciones del Presidente:

a)   Representar oficialmente al Tribunal

b)   Suscribir los actos y contratos del Tribunal;

c)   Ordenar el otorgamiento de copias y certificaciones, previa notificación a las partes;

d)   Conceder licencia a los magistrados y demás funcionarios hasta por cuatro días;

e)   Suscribir la correspondencia e informar al Tribunal de la recibida;

f)   Convocar extraordinariamente al Tribunal y anticipar o prorrogar las horas de despacho, cuando la urgencia de algún asunto así lo exija;

g)   Mantener la disciplina e imponer sanciones al personal administrativo del Tribunal:

h)   Cuidar de que se expidan, cumplan y ejecuten los reglamentos, acuerdos, resoluciones y demás disposiciones del Tribunal;

i)   Preparar oportunamente el proyecto de presupuesto anual y someterlo a consideración del Tribunal y la Comisión;

j)   Las demás que le confieren el Estatuto y otras normas reglamentarias.

CAPÍTULO III – DEL SECRETARIO

Art. 13   (Secretario: su elección)

La elección del Secretario se hará en sesión plenaria con dos meses de anticipación al vencimiento del período. El cargo de Secretario se rotará entre los Países Miembros.

Art. 14   (Secretario: sus deberes)

Son deberes del Secretario:

a)   Preparar, con la debida antelación, la documentación necesaria para las sesiones y las audiencias;

b)   Concurrir a las sesiones, salvo disposición contraria del Estatuto, del Reglamento o del Tribunal;

c)   Recibir las demandas, representaciones y cualesquiera otra clase de escritos o comunicaciones que le sean presentadas, anotar al pie de los documentos el día y hora de su presentación y pasarlos al conocimiento del Presidente a más tardar el día siguiente;

d)   Redactar las actas de las sesiones del Tribunal y suscribirlas juntamente con el Presidente, después de haber sido aprobadas;

e)   Efectuar estudios, elaborar documentos y realizar los trabajos que le señalen el Tribunal o el Presidente;

f)   Presentar al Presidente, el primer día hábil de cada semana, una lista cronológica de los casos que se hallen en estado de resolver, con indicación de la fecha en que se hubieren iniciado;

g)   Registrar, sellar y firmar las providencias y despachos que libre el Tribunal;

h)   Hacer las notificaciones con la demanda, prueba, sentencias y autos definitivos. Las demás notificaciones podrá hacerlas por sí o mediante el funcionario a quien designe, bajo su responsabilidad;

i)   Certificar la autenticidad de las copias, compulsas o reproducciones por cualquier sistema de piezas procesales que confiera, previo decreto del Presidente;

j)   Guardar secreto en el despacho de las causas y en sus actuaciones judiciales;

k)   Dar recibo a los interesados cuando lo exigieren de las solicitudes, títulos y demás documentos que presentaren, y

l)   Los demás que le confieren el Estatuto y los Reglamentos.

Art. 15   (Libros y registros: debe llevar el Secretario)

El Secretario llevará los siguientes libros y registros:

a)   de presentaciones de demanda;

b)   de representantes, apoderados y asesores de las partes;

c)   de citaciones a los magistrados a sesiones y audiencias;

d)   de actas de las sesiones del Tribunal;

e)   de resoluciones y acuerdos;

f)   de nombramientos y posesiones;

g)   de despacho diario;

h)   de autos definitivos y sentencias.

Art. 16   (Secretario: responsabilidades)

El Secretario tendrá bajo su custodia los expedientes y, bajo su responsabilidad, dará las informaciones y permitirá la consulta personal de los procesos a los representantes de las partes, sus abogados y asesores.

Art. 17   (Secretario: actos que le están prohibidos)

Es Prohibido al Secretario:

a)   Expedir copias que no se limiten a transcribir literalmente el texto de los documentos que consten en el respectivo expediente;

b)   Aconsejar o absolver consultas que se le hagan sobre los asuntos que cursen en el Tribunal, y

c)   Dar a conocer el contenido de los cuestionarios presentados en sobre cerrado.

Art. 18   (Archivo del Tribunal)

El archivo del Tribunal estará a cargo del Secretario, quien deberá recibirlo bajo inventario.

Art. 19   (Secretario ad hoc)

En caso de impedimento o recusación del Secretario, el Tribunal designará uno ad hoc dentro del personal de funcionarios permanentes.

CAPÍTULO IV — DE LA ORGANIZACIÓN, DEL PERSONAL Y DE LA ADMINISTRACIÓN

Art. 20   (Tribunal: su organización)

Son dependencias del Tribunal: la Secretaría y la Dirección de Administración y Servicios. La planta de personal de estas dependencias, el sistema de selección y las funciones correspondientes a los cargos se determinarán en el Reglamento respectivo.

Art. 21   (Cargos administrativos: período)

Los cargos de Director Administrativo, Bibliotecario y Contador pagador se proveerán por períodos de tres años y preferentemente por concurso.

CAPÍTULO V — DEL FUNCIONAMIENTO

Art. 22   (Sesiones plenarias)

El Tribunal tendrá dos clases de sesiones: las judiciales y las administrativas. Las sesiones judiciales serán plenarias en los casos señalados en los artículos 26, 55, 59, 60, 63, 68 y 71 y las sesiones administrativas serán plenarias en los casos de los artículos 5, 12, 19, 31 y 79 del Estatuto.

Las sesiones serán convocadas por el Presidente. Las sesiones administrativas se efectuarán ordinariamente los días martes, extraordinariamente cualquier otro día y las judiciales cuando corresponda.

La convocatoria será hecha por conducto del Secretario, con 24 horas de antelación, por lo menos, y en aquella constará el orden del día, así como la fecha y hora de la sesión. No obstante, podrá celebrarse una sesión en cualquier momento, sin necesidad de convocatoria previa, si encontrándose presentes los cinco Magistrados aceptan por unanimidad la celebración de la sesión y los asuntos a tratar.

Art. 23   (Sesiones: quorum)

Las sesiones plenarias solo podrán efectuarse con la asistencia de los cinco Magistrados y las decisiones se adoptarán con la mayoría establecida en el artículo 25 del Estatuto. Las sesiones no plenarias podrán efectuarse con la asistencia de, al menos, tres Magistrados y las decisiones se adoptarán conforme a lo establecido en el inciso 2 del artículo 27 del Estatuto.

El Tribunal podrá resolver que la votación sea secreta.

CAPÍTULO VI — DE LOS REPRESENTANTES, ABOGADOS Y ASESORES

Art. 24   (Personas naturales: identificación)

Las personas naturales que concurran a cumplir alguna actuación judicial se identificarán con su cédula de identidad o con su pasaporte.

Art. 25   (Representantes de Países Miembros, Comisión y Junta)

Los Países Miembros estarán representados por las autoridades nacionales que hayan sido acreditadas ante el Tribunal de conformidad con el artículo 83 del Estatuto. La Comisión lo estará por su Presidente y la Junta por su Coordinador, de conformidad con sus reglamentos.

Art. 26   (Representantes de personas jurídicas)

Las personas jurídicas actuarán por medio de sus representantes, cuya calidad se acreditará de acuerdo con lo que dispone la legislación de cada País Miembro.

Art. 27   (Mandatarios, forma de acreditarlos)

Los Países Miembros, la Comisión y la Junta constituirán sus mandatarios mediante oficio dirigido al Presidente del Tribunal. Las personas naturales y jurídicas lo harán con poder o mandato otorgado ante Notario o Juez competente, de acuerdo con las formalidades vigentes en el respectivo País Miembro.

Art. 28   (Abogados: su acreditación)

Los abogados acreditarán su calidad con el correspondiente carnet profesional.

Art. 29   (Credencial para representantes, abogados y asesores)

El Tribunal otorgará a los representantes, abogados y asesores una credencial que los identifique y les permita obtener el reconocimiento de las facilidades y garantías a que tengan derecho.

Art. 30   (Sanciones puede aplicar el Tribunal)

El Tribunal podrá aplicar a los representantes, mandatarios, abogados o asesores las siguientes sanciones disciplinarias:

a)   amonestación verbal o escrita;

b)   suspensión del derecho de palabra en audiencia cuando fuere desatendida una amonestación, y

c)   comunicación al Colegio de Abogados del respectivo País Miembro y al mandante de las sanciones impuestas.

El Tribunal también podrá ordenar que se tachen las exposiciones injuriosas u otras similares contenidas en los escritos o que se devuelva el escrito injurioso. Si este contuviese alguna petición, se dejará en el expediente copia certificada de la misma.

TÍTULO II — DEL PROCEDIMIENTO

CAPÍTULO I — DISPOSICIONES GENERALES

Art. 31   (Procedimiento para tramitar acciones)

Las acciones de nulidad e incumplimiento, previstas en el Tratado, se tramitarán de acuerdo con el procedimiento establecido en el Estatuto y en el presente Reglamento.

Art. 32   (Trámites son gratuitos)

Las actuaciones ante el Tribunal se harán en papel común y no causarán derecho alguno, excepto los gastos por cualquier trabajo de copia, reproducción o similares según arancel que aprobará el Tribunal.

Art. 33   (Autos en trámites y decisión de causas)

El Tribunal, en el trámite de las causas, dictará autos interlocutorios para resolver cuestiones secundarias, previas o incidentales; autos definitivos que sin decidir la cuestión principal ponen fin al juicio y sentencias para decidir la cuestión principal.

Art. 34   (Acuerdos y Resoluciones administrativas)

Además de las providencias judiciales, el Tribunal dictará las reglamentaciones generales que le corresponda bajo la forma de Acuerdos y las decisiones administrativas de carácter particular mediante actos denominados Resoluciones.

Art. 35   (Magistrado sustanciador)

Las cuestiones de simple sustanciación de los procesos serán atendidas por un magistrado sustanciador, designado por el Presidente para cada causa.

Art. 36   (Dinámica procesal)

El Tribunal conducirá el proceso de acuerdo con lo dispuesto en el Estatuto y para tal efecto, podrá, de oficio, adoptar todas las medidas necesarias para ordenar y agilizar el juicio, así como rechazar de plano aquellas peticiones que manifiestamente tiendan a dilatar o desviar la causa. Las peticiones que sean admitidas podrán ser resueltas antes de la sentencia o en ésta, según la naturaleza y efectos de la cuestión planteada.

CAPÍTULO II – DE LAS NOTIFICACIONES

Art. 37   (Notificaciones: forma de practicarlas)

La notificación con la demanda a los Países Miembros se hará mediante télex, a la autoridad nacional acreditada ante el Tribunal para representarlos en las acciones y procedimientos previstos en el Tratado y en el Estatuto. Una copia de la demanda y de la providencia judicial que hubiere recaído será entregada por el Secretario al Jefe de la misión diplomática permanente del País Miembro en Quito para su remisión a la autoridad nacional competente.

En el caso de la notificación a la República del Ecuador, la copia de la demanda y de la providencia judicial se entregará en el despacho de la autoridad competente.

Art. 38   (Notificaciones en Quito)

Cuando un País Miembro hubiese acreditado en Quito representante, mandatario o delegado con facultades para recibir notificaciones con la demanda, la notificación se hará mediante oficio a la persona del representante, mandatario o delegado, al que se acompañará copia de la demanda y de la providencia judicial.

Art. 39   (Notificaciones a Comisión y Junta)

La notificación con la demanda a la Comisión y a la Junta se hará mediante télex a su Presidente o a su Coordinador, según el caso. Una copia de la demanda y de la providencia judicial se remitirá por correo o por valija diplomática.

Art. 40   (Término para contestar a la demanda: cómputo)

El término para dar contestación a la demanda se contará a partir de la fecha de remisión del télex a la autoridad nacional competente, al Presidente de la Comisión o al Coordinador de la Junta, según el caso.

Art. 41   (Notificaciones en Quito: constancia)

Las notificaciones ordenadas por los artículos 41, 45, 47, 57, 59 y 60 del Estatuto se harán en Quito en la persona y en el lugar designados a ese fin por las partes.

De estas diligencias se extenderá acta que será suscrita por el Secretario y el notificado, Si éste se negare a firmar, el Secretario dejará constancia de este hecho y se tendrá por cumplida la notificación.

Art. 42   (Notificaciones a jueces y tribunales nacionales)

La notificación a los jueces o tribunales nacionales a que se refiere el artículo 64 del Estatuto se hará por correo.

Art. 43   (Notificaciones para regularizar demanda)

Cuando el Tribunal ordene al demandante la regularización de la demanda porque no señaló domicilio en Quito, la notificación de esta providencia se hará por correo.

Art. 44   (Notificaciones: sólo se harán las previstas en el Estatuto)

Fuera de las notificaciones previstas en el Estatuto no se hará ninguna otra, debiendo las partes concurrir al Tribunal para informarse de las providencias que se dicten en los procesos.

Art. 45   (Notificaciones: se harán sólo en días hábiles)

Las notificaciones se harán en días hábiles desde las ocho hasta las dieciocho horas. El Tribunal, en casos especiales y mediante providencia expresa, podrá habilitar otros días para que se efectúe alguna notificación.

CAPÍTULO III — DE LOS TÉRMINOS

Art. 46   (Días hábiles y feriados)

Son hábiles o de despacho, todos los días, excepto los feriados, desde las nueve hasta las doce y desde las quince hasta las dieciocho horas.

Se tendrán por feriados los sábados y los domingos, los de vacaciones anuales del Tribunal, el Jueves Santo y los siguientes días de fiesta según la legislación ecuatoriana: 10 de enero, 10 de mayo, 24 de mayo, 24 de julio, 10 de agosto, 9 de octubre, 12 de octubre, 2 de noviembre, 3 de noviembre, 6 de diciembre, 25 de diciembre y viernes santo.

Art. 47   (Vacaciones colectivas)

Las vacaciones anuales del Tribunal serán colectivas, comenzarán el 16 de diciembre y terminarán el 15 de enero del año siguiente. Durante estas vacaciones se suspenderán los términos.

Art. 48   (Habilitación de días para diligencias judiciales)

Fuera de los días y horas hábiles no se podrán practicar diligencias judiciales sin la habilitación expresa del Tribunal, de oficio o a petición de parte.

Art. 49   (Términos: forma de computarlos)

Los términos se computarán por días continuos y se calcularán excluyendo el día de la fecha que constituye el punto de partida.

Si el término finaliza un día no laborable la expiración del término se postergará hasta las 18 horas del día hábil siguiente.

A los términos principales se añadirán, en razón de la distancia, los siguientes: para Bolivia 15 días, para Colombia 8 días, y para Perú y Venezuela 10 días cada uno.

El Término de la distancia se computará en la misma forma que el término principal.

Art. 50   (Términos se computan desde última notificación)

Cuando en el Estatuto o en este Reglamento se ordene notificar a las partes, los términos comenzarán a contarse a partir de la última notificación.

Capítulo IV — De las acciones de nulidad e incumplimiento

Sección Primera — De la demanda

Art. 51   (Demanda: requisitos)

La demanda será dirigida al Presidente del Tribunal, deberá estar suscrita por la parte y su abogado y será presentada personalmente al Secretario en original y tres copias. También podrá enviarse la demanda y la documentación que la acompañe, por correo. En este caso, cuando el demandante sea una persona natural o jurídica, las firmas de la parte o de su representante y las del abogado deberán estar debidamente reconocidas ante el Notario o Juez competente.

Art. 52   (Demanda: debe señalar domicilio del actor)

Además de los requisitos exigidos por el artículo 36 del Estatuto, la demanda contendrá la indicación del lugar en Quito donde deban hacerse las notificaciones del actor.

Art. 53   (Copia fehaciente)

A los efectos previstos en el literal b) del artículo 37 del Estatuto, se entiende por copia fehaciente aquella que es expedida por la autoridad competente del respectivo País Miembro.

Art. 54   (Certificación de la Junta para acción de incumplimiento)

La demostración a que se refiere el literal b) del artículo 38 del Estatuto se hará con una certificación de la Junta en la que conste la fecha de presentación del reclamo previsto en el artículo 24 del Tratado.

Art. 55   (Demanda: trámites de su presentación en secretaría)

Al recibir la demanda, el Secretario sellará el original y sus copias, dejará constancia en ellos de la hora y fecha de presentación con expresión de si la demanda fue presentada personalmente o por correo, El Secretario devolverá una de las copias al demandante con inserción de las constancias exigidas por este artículo, numerará el expediente, le dará ingreso en el libro respectivo y lo pasará de inmediato al Presidente, quien lo pondrá en conocimiento del Tribunal.

Art. 56 (Regularización de la demanda: término)

Cuando corresponda y para que el demandante regularice la demanda o presente los documentos pertinentes, el Tribunal concederá un término que no podrá exceder de quince días. Vencido este término sin que el demandante haya cumplido con lo ordenado por el Tribunal, se le devolverá la demanda con los documentos que hubiere acompañado a ella. Quedará en el Tribunal copia certificada de la demanda.

Art. 57 (Demanda: término para admitirla)

El Tribunal decidirá acerca de la admisibilidad de la demanda dentro de los cinco días siguientes a la fecha en que tuvo conocimiento de la causa.

Art. 58 (Demanda no admite modificaciones después de admitida)

La demanda no podrá ser reformada o complementada una vez admitida por el Tribunal.

Sección Segunda — De la contestación

Art. 59 (Contestación a la demanda: su regularización)

Si la contestación de la demanda no reuniere los requisitos señalados en el artículo 43 del Estatuto, el Tribunal ordenará que el demandante la regularice precisando los puntos que deba completar o aclarar. Si el demandado no la subsanare en el plazo que el Tribunal le haya concedido, se procederá conforme a lo previsto en el artículo 44 del Estatuto. El Secretario dejará constancia de este hecho en el expediente.

Art. 60 (Contestación a la demanda debe señalar domicilio del demandado en Quito)

El demandado señalará en la contestación a la demanda el lugar en Quito donde se le harán las notificaciones. La omisión de esta exigencia facultará al Tribunal para ordenar que las notificaciones a la parte demandada se cumplan mediante la fijación de un cartel en las puertas de la Secretaría. El Secretario dejará constancia de este hecho en el expediente.

Este sistema de notificación cesará cuando el demandado indique un lugar en el que se le deba notificar.

Sección Tercera — De la Prueba

Art. 61 (Prueba: apertura del término para probar)

El Tribunal, de oficio o a petición de parte, decidirá si se debe abrir la etapa de prueba. Si decidiese abrirla señalará los hechos a probar, la forma y el término para practicar las pruebas decretadas, y ordenará a las partes lo que fuere pertinente, de todo lo cual éstas serán notificadas. En caso contrario, el Presidente del Tribunal fijará día y hora para la audiencia y dispondrá a tal fin la convocatoria a las partes.

Art. 62   (Prueba: término para ordenarla)

La apertura de la etapa de prueba deberá decretarse dentro de los ocho días siguientes a la contestación de la demanda, a su regularización o a la constancia puesta por el Secretario de que la demanda no fue contestada.

Art. 63   (Prueba: puede ordenar el Tribunal en cualquier momento antes de sentencia)

El Tribunal de oficio y en cualquier estado de la causa, antes de la sentencia, podrá ordenar las pruebas que juzgue necesarias para el esclarecimiento de los hechos.

Art. 64   (Carga de la prueba)

Cada parte está obligada a probar los hechos que alegue y a sufragar los gastos que esas pruebas ocasionen.

Art. 65   (Prueba: se practica previa notificación de partes)

El Tribunal ordenará que las pruebas se practiquen previa notificación de las partes. Para la recepción de las pruebas, en los casos que corresponda, el Tribunal fijará día y hora.

Art. 66   (Práctica de pruebas y diligencias por jueces nacionales)

Si el Tribunal considerase conveniente podrá solicitar directamente a los jueces nacionales de los Países Miembros la práctica de diligencias para la recepción de pruebas y el cumplimiento de otras obligaciones judiciales.

Art. 67   (Audiencia: preparación)

Antes de la audiencia, el Tribunal se reunirá con el fin de iniciar el estudio conjunto de la causa y preparar el desarrollo de la audiencia.

Sección Cuarta — De la audiencia

Art. 68   (Audiencia: convocatoria a las partes y prioridad de causas)

Concluída la etapa de prueba, el Presidente del Tribunal fijará día y hora para la audiencia y convocará a las partes.

Cuando la etapa de prueba hubiere terminado simultáneamente para varias causas, el orden para convocar la audiencia se determinará por la fecha de presentación de las demandas.

Art. 79   (Sentencia: secretario concurrirá a sesión final aprobatoria)

El Secretario asistirá a la sesión de la deliberación final a que se refiere el artículo anterior.

Art. 80   (Sentencia: su contenido)

La sentencia contendrá decisión expresa sobre los puntos objeto de la controversia y sobre aquellos que, durante el proceso, el Tribunal hubiese reservado para decidirlos en la sentencia definitiva.

Art. 81   (Costas deben estar contenidas en sentencia)

En la sentencia se condenará al demandante al pago de las costas cuando la acción por él intentada se declare infundada y se condenará al demandado cuando la sentencia declare la acción fundada.

No habrá lugar a condenar en costas cuando la sentencia declare que la acción es parcialmente fundada o cuando el Tribunal estime que existieron motivos razonables para litigar.

Art. 82   (Costas: monto)

En los casos de condena en costas el Tribunal determinará, por auto separado, la cantidad que debe pagar el deudor por los gastos del proceso y por honorarios de abogado. A tal fin, la parte acreedora deberá presentar al Tribunal comprobantes de los gastos hechos en el proceso y una estimación de los honorarios de abogado.

La parte deudora podrá objetar el monto de los gastos y de los honorarios. El Tribunal, vistas las exposiciones de las partes y teniendo como referencia, entre otras, los reglamentos de honorarios profesionales de los Países Miembros, determinará el monto de las costas.

TÍTULO III — DE LAS DISPOSICIONES FINALES Y TRANSITORIAS

Art. 83   (Reglamento Interno: vigencia)

El presente Reglamento entrará en vigencia a partir de la fecha de su publicación en la Gaceta Oficial del Acuerdo de Cartagena.

Art. 84   (Presidencia del Tribunal en 1984 y 1985)

Durante los años 1984 y 1985, la presidencia del Tribunal será ejercida sucesivamente por los magistrados nombrados por el período de tres años. Después se cumplirá con lo dispuesto en el artículo 10 de este reglamento.

Art. 85   (Reglamento Interno codificado)

Este Reglamento contiene las reformas aprobadas por el Tribunal mediante Resoluciones de fecha 9 de mayo de 1984 y 19 de junio de 1985.

Dado en la sede del Tribunal de Justicia del Acuerdo de Cartagena el día diecinueve de junio de mil novecientos ochenta y cinco.

c) Treaty Establishing a Common Market (MERCOSUR) Between Argentina, Brazil, Paraguay and Uruguay of March 26, 1991

The longlasting efforts to create a common market between the States of Latin America resulted first in the Latin American Free Trade Association (LAFTA) which was replaced by the Latin American Integration Association (LAIA) which, however, conceived the integration process mainly as a series of bilateral treaties. Therefore, Brazil and Argentina decided to approach a mutual integration process by means of a series of sectoral protocols, subsequent to the "Declaration of Buenos Aires" of 1986 and the Agreement on Argentine-Brazilian Integration of 1988. In 1991 they signed the Treaty for the establishment of a Common Market (Mercado Común del Sur (MERCOSUR) incorporating Uruguay and Paraguay. This Treaty provided for the establishment of a common market until December 31, 1994. It contained rules for this transition period concerning i.e. general rules of origin, safeguard clauses to prevent significant fluctuations in certain market areas and a system for the settlement of disputes. Art. 18 of the Treaty provided that, prior to the establishment of the common market on 31 December 1994, the Parties "shall convene a special meeting to determine the final institutional structure of the administrative organs of the common market". Accordingly, on December 17, 1994 they adopted the "Additional Protocol to the Treaty of Asuncion on the Institutional Structure of MERCOSUR" ("Protocol of Ouro Preto"). The Protocol provides for the institution of a Common Market Council, a Common Market Group and a MERCOSUR Trade Commission with powers of decision; furthermore, the institutional organization comprises a Joint Parliamentary Commission, an Economic and Social Consultative Forum and the Mercosur Administrative Secretariat. This structure characterises Mercosur as an intergovernmental organization without supranational powers, resembling more to the Benelux Union than to the European Union.

In order to avoid previous problems due to the lack of an adequate dispute settlement system, the treaty of Asuncion stipulated that the parties "shall adopt ... a system for the settlement of disputes" as contained in Annex III to the Treaty. This Annex also provided that within 120 days from the entry into force of the Treaty, the Common Market Group should draft a Dispute Resolution System for the period of transition and that, before December 31, 1994, a permanent system should be adopted by the States parties to the treaty. According to these provisions the Parties adopted, on December 17, 1991, the Protocol of Brasilia for the Settlement of Disputes, which forms an integral part of the Treaty of Asuncion and provides first, for direct negotiations between the parties to a dispute and, failing this, empowers the Common Market Group to find a solution, if necessary by consulting panels of experts in order to obtain technical advice or, finally, to resort to an arbitral tribunal. As this Protocol, also the Protocol of Ouro Preto is an integral part of the treaty of Asuncion. The Protocol of Ouro Preto refers to dispute resolution in Article 21, which defines the functions of the Mercosur Trade Commission, in Article 43, which reproduces Article 1 of the Protocol of Brasilia and in an Annex on the general procedure for complaints to the Mercosur Trade Commission. The dispute settlement mechanism through negotiations and by the Trade Commission seems to work sufficiently effective; the settlement by the Common Market Group has only rarely been resorted to. On August 5, 1994 the Parties to the Treaty of Asuncion adopted the Protocol of Buenos Aires on International Jurisdiction in Disputes relating to Contracts. This Protocol provides for the settlement of disputes affecting private parties within the framework of Mercosur concerning claims initiated by juridical or physical persons because of damage suffered as a result of restrictive or discriminatory measures or unfair competition, as provided for in Chapter V, articles 25 to 32 of the Protocol of Brasilia. For the text of this Protocol, which only concerns private claims and which therefore is not reproduced here, see ILM 36 (1994), 1263.

Texts

Treaty of Asuncion: ILM 30 (1991), 1041

Protocol of Brasilia: ILM 36 (1997), 691

Protocol of Ouro Preto: ILM 34 (1994), 1244

All texts in Spanish in: M. E. Uzal, El Mercosur en el Camino de la Integración (1998)

Bibliographical notes

M. Halperin, El Mercado Común del Sur y un nuevo sistema regional de relaciones económicas multilaterales, Intergración Latinoamericana 167 (1991), 46-56

J. B. Mesquita Machado, Integración Económica y arancel aduanero común en el cono sur, Integración Latinoamericana 167 (1991), 36-45

F. González, Solución de conflictos en un sistema de integración: los casos MERCOSUR y la CEE, in: Integración Latinoamericana 17 (1992), 33 ff.

J. P. Otermin, Solución de Controversias en el Mercosur (1992)

H. Arbuet Vignali, La solución de controversias en el Mercosur: un aspecto esencial aún por resolver, in: M. Rama-Montalso, El derecho internacional en un mundo en transformación (1994), 2, 1229-1261

L. O. Baptista, As instituciones do Mercosul comparacoes e perspectiva, Deisy de Fretas Vebntura, Lima o mercosul en movimiento (1995), 54-74

V. G. Arnaud, MERCOSUR, Unión Europea, NAFTA y los procesos de integración regional (1996)

S. M. Williamas, Integration in South America: the Mercosur experience, International Relations 13 (1996), 51-61

E. J. Rey Caro, La solución de controversias en el Mercosur, Annuario Argentino de Derecho Internacional 7 (1996/97), 279-299

H. Wanderlei Rodrigues (ed.), Soluçao de controvérsias no MERCOSUL (1997)

M. E. Uzal, El Mercosur en el camino de la integración (1998)

aa) Treaty of Asunción, Article 3 and Annex III

Art. 3 During the transition period, which shall last from the entry into force of this treaty until 31 December 1994, and in order to facilitate the formation of the common market, the States Parties shall adopt general rules of origin, a system for the settlement of disputes and safeguard clauses, as contained in annexes I, III and IV respectively to this Treaty.

ANNEX III – SETTLEMENT OF DISPUTES

1. Any disputes arising between the States Parties as a result of the application of the Treaty shall be settled by means of direct negotiation.

If no solution can be found, the States Parties shall refer the dispute to the Common Market Group which, after evaluating the situation, shall within a period of 60 days make the relevant recommendations to the Parties for settling the dispute. To that end, the Common Market Group may establish or convene panels of experts or groups of specialists in order to obtain the necessary technical advice.

If the Common Market Group also fails to find a solution, the dispute shall be referred to the Council of the common market to adopt the relevant recommendations.

2. Within 120 days of the entry into force of the Treaty, the Common Market Group shall propose to the Government of States Parties a system for the settlement of disputes which shall apply during the transition period.

3. Before 31 December 1994, the States Parties shall adopt a permanent disputes settlement system for the common market.

bb) Protocol of Brasilia for the Settlement of Disputes

The Argentine Republic, the Federative Republic of Brasil, the Republic of Paraguay and the Eastern Republic of Uruguay, hereinafter referred to as the "States Parties",

In compliance with the provisions of Article 3, and Annex III of the Treaty of Asuncion, signed on March 26, 1991, stipulating that State Parties shall adopt a Dispute Settlement System for the period of transition,

Aware of the importance of an adequate instrument to ensure compliance with the aforementioned Treaty and provisions deriving therefrom,

Convinced that the Dispute Settlement System of the present Protocol will strengthen relations among the Parties on the basis of Justice and Equity,

Have agreed to the following:

CHAPTER 1 — SCOPE

Art. 1   Disputes arising among State Parties concerning the interpretation, application or non-fulfillment of the provisions of the Treaty of Asunción, or agreements entered into within the framework of the aforementioned Treaty, as well as decisions of the Council of the Common Market, and resolutions of the Common Market Group shall be submitted to the settlement procedures outlined in this Protocol.

CHAPTER II — DIRECT NEGOTIATIONS

Art. 2   States Parties to a Dispute shall attempt to settle, first, by means of direct negotiations.

Art. 3   1) States Parties to a Dispute shall keep the Common Market Group informed, through the Administrative Secretariat, of action taken during the aforementioned negotiations and the result thereof.

2) Unless the Parties to a Dispute agree to the contrary, direct negotiations shall not exceed a period of fifteen (15) days after the date on which a complaint was initiated.

CHAPTER III — INTERVENTION OF THE COMMON MARKET GROUP

Art. 4   1) If there is no agreement, or only partial agreement after direct negotiations, any of the States Parties to a Dispute may submit it to the Common Market Group.

2) The Common Market Group shall evaluate the situation, giving the Parties to the Dispute an opportunity to express their respective positions and, when needed, requesting the advice of experts selected from the list referred to in Article 30 of this Protocol.

3) The expenses incurred by this procedure shall be borne, either equally by the States Parties to the Dispute, or in proportions determined by the Common Market Group.

Art. 5   At the end of this stage, the Common Market Group shall make recommendations to the States Parties to the Dispute, with a view to resolving the controversy.

Art. 6   The procedure outlined in this Chapter may not extend beyond a period of thirty (30) days from the date on which the Dispute was put to the consideration of the Common Market Group.

CHAPTER IV — ARBITRATION

Art. 7   1) If the Dispute has not been solved by the procedures referred to in Chapters II and III, any State Party to the Dispute may give notice to the

Administrative Secretariat of its intention to make use of the Arbitral Proceedings laid down in this Protocol.

2) The Administrative Secretariat shall transmit this notice immediately to the other State Party or Parties involved in the Dispute, as well as to the Common Market Group. It shall be responsible for all the formalities concerning the proceedings.

Art. 8   The States Parties state that they recognize, *ipso facto*, the jurisdiction of the Arbitral Tribunal, without need for a special agreement. The Tribunal shall be established, in each case, to examine and resolve any controversy within the framework of this Protocol.

Art. 9   1) Arbitral Proceedings shall be substantiated by an ad hoc Tribunal composed of three (3) arbitrators selected from the list referred to in Article 10.

2) The Arbitrators shall be selected in the following manner:

I: Each State Party to the Dispute shall select one (1) Arbitrator. The third Arbitrator, who shall preside at the Tribunal, may not be a national of any of the States Parties to the Dispute and shall be selected by mutual agreement among them. Arbitrators are appointed for a period of fifteen days from the date on which the Administrative Secretariat has given notice to the other States Parties to the Dispute that one of them has decided to submit the Dispute to Arbitration.

II: Each of the States Parties to the Dispute shall also appoint an alternative arbitrator, under the same requirements, for the event of incapacity, or excusal from sitting on the Arbitral Tribunal, of the designated Arbitrator(s) either at the time of designation of the Tribunal or during the course of the proceedings.

Art. 10 Each State Party shall designate ten (10) arbitrators comprising a list, to be filed with the Administrative Secretariat. This list, and all subsequent amendments, shall be notified to the States Parties.

Art. 11 When a State Party to a Dispute has failed to appoint an Arbitrator within the terms provided for in Article 9, the Administrative Secretariat shall designate this Arbitrator from the list presented by that State Party, in the order established therein.

Art. 12 1) If, within the delay provided for by Article 9, the States Parties to a Dispute have failed to appoint a third arbitrator, any one of them may request that the Administrative Secretariat do so, by means of a random selection from the list of sixteen (16) arbitrators drawn up by the Common Market Group.

2) This list, also to be filed with the Administrative Secretariat, shall comprise nationals of the States Parties and Nationals of third States in equal parts.

Art. 13   Arbitrators referred to in Articles 10 and 12 must be jurisconsults of rec-
          ognized competence in the subject matter over which the controversy has
          arisen.

Art. 14   When two or more States Parties hold the same position in the Dispute,
          they shall be jointly represented before the Arbitral Tribunal and shall
          elect an Arbitrator by mutual agreement within the delay provided in Ar-
          ticle 9 (2) I.

Art. 15   The Arbitral Tribunal shall establish its offices, for each case, within the
          territory of one of the States Parties. It shall adopt its own rules of proce-
          dure. Such rules shall ensure that each of the parties to the Dispute has a
          fair hearing and the opportunity to present evidence and arguments and
          that proceedings are expeditious.

Art. 16   States Parties to a Dispute shall notify the Arbitral Tribunal of action
          taken prior to the Arbitral Proceedings and shall state, briefly, the facts
          and applicable law concerning their respective positions.

Art. 17   States Parties to a Dispute shall be represented by agents and may desig-
          nate counsel or advocates for the defense of their rights.

Art. 18   1) Upon request from the party concerned, and if there is good cause to
          believe that a continuation of the existing situation will produce serious
          and irreparable damage to one of the parties, the Arbitral Tribunal may
          order such interim measures as it deems necessary or desirable, to prevent
          an aggravation of the situation.

          2) The parties shall comply immediately, or within the delay established
          by the Arbitral Tribunal, with all interim measures, until an Award is en-
          tered in conformity with Article 20.

Art. 19   1) The Arbitral Tribunal shall settle the Dispute by applying: the provi-
          sions of the Treaty of Asunción, agreements concluded within the frame-
          work thereof, the decisions of the Council of the Common Market, the
          resolutions of the Common Market Group, and applicable principles and
          rules of international law.

          2) This provision shall not prejudice the power of the Arbitral Tribunal to
          decide a Dispute *ex aequo et bono* if the parties agree thereto.

Art. 20   1) The Arbitral Tribunal shall enter an Award, in writing, within sixty
          (60) days, renewable, at most, for another thirty (30) days after the desig-
          nation of its President.

          2) The Award shall be decided by a majority of Arbitrators. It shall state
          the reasons on which it is based and shall be signed by the President and
          other Arbitrators. Dissenting Arbitrators are not entitled to a separate
          opinion and must maintain the confidentiality of the vote.

Art. 21   1) The Awards of Arbitral Tribunals are final and without appeal. They
          shall have binding force for the States Parties to the Dispute from the
          moment of notification thereof.

2) Awards shall be complied with within fifteen (15) days, unless the Arbitral Tribunal decides otherwise.

Art. 22 1) Within fifteen (15) days of having received notice of the Award, any of the States Parties to the Dispute may request a clarification of the meaning thereof or an interpretation regarding the manner in which it is to be carried out.

2) The Arbitral Tribunal shall enter a decision within the subsequent fifteen (15) days.

Art. 23 In the event of non-compliance by a State Party of the Award of the Arbitral Tribunal, within a period of thirty (30) days, the remaining States Parties to the Dispute may adopt temporary compensatory measures, such as the suspension of concessions, or other equivalent measures, with a view to achieving compliance.

Art. 24 1) Each State Party to the Dispute shall bear the expenses incurred by its designated Arbitrator.

2) The President of the Arbitral Tribunal shall receive a pecuniary compensation which, together with the remaining expenses of the Arbitral Tribunal, shall be borne in equal parts by the States Parties to the Dispute, unless the Tribunal should decide on a different form of distribution.

CHAPTER V — CLAIMS BY PRIVATE PARTIES

Art. 25 The procedure laid down in this chapter applies to claims initiated by private parties (natural or legal persons), by reason of the adoption or application, by a State Party, of legal or administrative measures of a restrictive or discriminatory nature or leading to unfair competition, in violation of the Treaty of Asunción, the agreements concluded within the framework thereof, decisions of the Council of the Common Market or resolutions of the Common Market Group.

Art. 26 1) Individual claimants shall submit their complaints to the National Section of the Common Market Group corresponding either to their place of residence or their corporate headquarters.

2) They shall provide the necessary elements for the National Section to determine the plausibility of the violation and the existence or threat of prejudice.

Art. 27 Unless the claim concerns a matter already having motivated the initiation of a Dispute settlement procedure under Chapters II, III, or IV of this Protocol, the National Section of the Common Market Group that has accepted the claim in conformity with Article 26 of this Chapter, in consultation with the affected party, may:

a)   Enter into direct contact with the National Section of the Common Market Group of the State Party allegedly responsible for the violation, in order to seek an immediate solution to the controversy; or

b)   Submit the claim to the Common Market Group without prior formalities.

Art. 28   If, within fifteen (15) days after the date of notification of the claim, the controversy has not been solved, in conformity with Article 27 (a), the National Section having served the notice may, upon request from the affected party, submit it, forthwith, to the Common Market Group.

Art. 29   1) At its first meeting after notification of the claim, the Common Market Group shall evaluate the reasons for its acceptance by the National Section. If it decides that the requirements needed to hear the claim have not been met, it shall reject the claim outright.

2) If the Common Market Group does not reject the claim, it shall convene, immediately, a group of experts to submit an opinion on the matter within a peremptory period of thirty (30) days after their designation.

3) Within this delay, the Group of Experts shall give the claimant and the State Party against which the claim was presented an opportunity to be heard and to present arguments.

Art. 30   1) The Group of Experts referred to in Article 29 shall comprise three (3) members, appointed by the Common Market Group. Failing agreement on one or more experts, these shall be elected by ballot, with a vote taken on a list of twenty four (24) experts. The Administrative Secretariat shall notify the Common Market Group of the experts having received the greatest number of votes. In the latter case and unless the Common Market Group decides otherwise, one of the experts shall not be either a national of the State against which the claim has been made or of the State in which the claimant has formalized the complaint, under Article 26.

2) In drawing up the list of experts, each State Party shall designate six (6) persons of recognized competence in the subject matter over which the claim was made. This list shall be filed with the Administrative Secretariat.

Art. 31   The expenses incurred by the Group of Experts shall be distributed in the proportions to be determined by the Common Market Group. Failing agreement, they shall be borne in equal parts by the parties directly involved.

Art. 32   The Group of Experts shall submit its opinion to the Common Market Group. If this opinion considers the claim against a State Party to be justified, any other State Party may request the adoption of corrective measures or the annulment of the challenged provision. If this request is not granted within fifteen (15) days, the requesting State Party may immediately initiate Arbitral Proceedings, under the conditions provided in Chapter IV of this Protocol.

CHAPTER VI — CONCLUDING PROVISIONS

Art. 33   This Protocol forms an integral part of the Treaty of Asuncion. It shall enter into force once the four States Parties have deposited their instruments of ratification. These instruments shall be deposited with the Government of the Republic of Paraguay, which shall communicate the date of deposit to the Governments of the remaining States Parties.

Art. 34   This Protocol shall remain in force until the entry into force of the Permanent System of Dispute Settlement for the Common Market provided for in paragraph 3 of Annex III of the Treaty of Asunción.

Art. 35   Any State acceding to the Treaty of Asunción accedes, *ipso iure*, to this Protocol.

Art. 36   The official languages for all proceedings under this Protocol are Spanish and Portuguese, as needed.

           Done in the city of Brasilia on December 17, 1991 in one original in the Spanish and Portuguese languages, both texts being equally authentic. The government of the Republic of Paraguay shall be the depositary of this Protocol and shall send a duly authenticated copy to the other States Parties.

cc) Additional Protocol to the Treaty of Asunción on the Institutional Structure of Mercosur (Protocol of Ouro Preto) of December 17, 1994

CHAPTER I, SECTION III AND CHAPTER VI

SECTION III — THE MERCOSUR TRADE COMMISSION

Art. 16   It shall be the task of the Mercosur Trade Commission, a body responsible for assisting the Common Market Group, to monitor the application of the common trade policy instruments agreed by the States Parties in connection with the operation of the customs union, as well as to follow up and review questions and issues relating to common trade policies, intra-Mercosur trade and third countries.

Art. 17   The Mercosur Trade Commission shall consist of four members and four alternates for each State Party and shall be coordinated by the Ministries of Foreign Affairs.

Art. 18   The Mercosur Trade Commission shall meet at least once a month, or whenever requested to do so by the Common Market Group or any of the States Parties.

Art. 19   The following are duties and functions of the Mercosur Trade Commission:

I. To monitor the application of the common trade policy instruments both within Mercosur and with respect to third countries, international organizations and trade agreements;

II. To consider and rule upon the requests submitted by the States Parties in connection with the application of and compliance with the common external tariff and other instruments of common trade policy;

III. To follow up the application of the common trade policy instruments in the States Parties;

IV. To analyse the development of the common trade policy instruments relating to the operation of the customs union and to submit Proposals in this respect to the Common Market Group;

V. To take decisions connected with the administration and application of the common external tariff and the common trade policy instruments agreed by the States Parties;

VI. To report to the Common Market Group on the development and application of the common trade policy instruments, on the consideration of requests received and on the decisions taken with respect to such requests;

VII. To propose to the Common Market Group new Mercosur trade and customs regulations or changes in the existing regulations;

VIII. To propose the revision of the tariff rates for specific items of the common external tariff, *inter alia*, in order to deal with cases relating to new production activities within Mercosur;

IX. To set up the technical committees needed for it to perform its duties properly, and to direct and supervise their activities;

X. To perform tasks connected with the common trade policy requested by the Common Market Group;

XI. To adopt rules of procedure to be submitted to the Common Market Group for approval.

Art. 20   The decisions of the Mercosur Trade Commission shall take the form of Directives or Proposals. The Directives shall be binding upon the States Parties.

Art. 21   In addition to the duties and functions described in Articles 16 and 19 of this Protocol, the Mercosur Trade Commission shall be responsible for considering complaints referred to it by the National Sections of the Mercosur Trade Commission and originated by States Parties or individuals, whether natural or legal persons, relating to the situations provided for in Article 1 or 25 of the Brasilia Protocol, when they fall within its sphere of competence.

Paragraph 1. The examination of the aforesaid complaints within the Mercosur Trade Commission shall not prevent the complainant State Party taking action under the Brasilia Protocol for the Settlement of Disputes.

Paragraph 2. Complaints arising in the circumstances described in this Article shall be dealt with in accordance with the procedure laid down in the Annex to this Protocol.

CHAPTER VI — DISPUTE SETTLEMENT SYSTEM

Art. 43 Disputes which arise between the States Parties concerning the interpretation, application or non-fulfilment of the provisions of the Treaty of Asuncion and the agreements concluded within its framework or of Decisions of the Council of the Common Market, Resolutions of the Common Market Group and Directives of the Mercosur Trade Commission shall be subject to the settlement procedures laid down in the Brasilia Protocol of 17 December 1991.

Sole paragraph. The Directives of the Mercosur Trade Commission are also incorporated in Articles 19 and 25 of the Brasilia Protocol.

Art. 44 Before the Common External Tariff convergence process is complete, the States Parties shall review the present Mercosur dispute settlement system with a view to adopting the permanent system referred to in paragraph 3 of Annex III to the Treaty of Asuncion and Article 34 of the Brasilia Protocol.

ANNEX TO THE PROTOCOL OF OURO PRETO

GENERAL PROCEDURE FOR COMPLAINTS TO THE MERCOSUR TRADE COMMISSION

Art. 1 Complaints submitted by the National Sections of the Mercosur Trade Commission and originated, by States Parties or individuals, whether natural or legal persons, in accordance with the provisions of Article 21 of the Protocol of Ouro Preto shall be subject to the procedure laid down in this Annex.

Art. 2 The complainant State Party shall submit its complaint to the Pro-Tempore Chairman of the Mercosur Trade Commission who shall take the necessary steps to include the question on the Agenda of the next meeting of the Mercosur Trade Commission at least one week beforehand. If no decision is taken at that meeting, the Mercosur Trade Commission shall, without taking further action, pass on the dossier to a Technical Committee.

Art. 3 Within a maximum of thirty (30) calendar days, the Technical Committee shall prepare and submit to the Mercosur Trade Commission a joint opinion on the question. This opinion or the conclusions of the experts making up the Technical Committee, if there is no joint opinion, shall be taken into consideration by the Mercosur Trade Commission when it rules on the complaint.

Art. 4   The Mercosur Trade Commission shall rule on the complaint at its first ordinary meeting following receipt of the joint opinion or, should there be none, the conclusions of the experts, although an extraordinary meeting may also be convened for the purpose.

Art. 5   If a consensus cannot be reached at the first meeting mentioned in Article 4, the Mercosur Trade Commission shall submit to the Common Market Group the various alternatives proposed, together with the joint opinion or the conclusions of the experts on the Technical Committee, in order that an appropriate decision may be taken. The Common Market Group shall give a ruling within thirty (30) calendar days of the receipt by the Pro-Tempore Chairman of the proposals submitted by the Mercosur Trade Commission.

Art. 6   If there is agreement that the complaint is justified, the State Party against which it is made shall adopt the measures approved in the Mercosur Trade Commission or the Common Market Group. In each case, the Mercosur Trade Commission or, subsequently, the Common Market Group shall fix a reasonable period for the implementation of these measures. If this period expires without the State against which the complaint is made having complied with the provisions of the decision adopted, whether by the Mercosur Trade Commission or the Common Market Group, the complainant State may resort directly to the procedure provided for in Chapter IV of the Brasilia Protocol.

Art. 7   If a consensus cannot be reached in the Mercosur Trade Commission, or subsequently, in the Common Market Group or if the State against which the complaint is made does not comply within the period provided for in Article 6 with the provisions of the decision adopted, the complainant State may resort directly to the procedure established in Chapter IV of the Brasilia Protocol and shall inform the Mercosur Administrative Secretariat accordingly.

Before giving a ruling, within fifteen (15) days of its being set up, the Arbitration Tribunal must announce the interim measures it considers appropriate under the conditions laid down in Article 18 of the Brasilia Protocol.

d) North American Free Trade Agreement of December 8 and 17, 1992

In 1988 the United States of America and Canada concluded a Free Trade Agreement (CFTA) which created the most comprehensive bilateral free trade régime in the world. The scope of the Agreement was to eliminate barriers to trade in goods and services and to facilitate conditions of fair competition within the free trade area, to liberalize investment conditions, to establish effective procedures for administering the Agreement and the resolution of disputes and to lay the basis for further bilateral and multilateral cooperation in trade matters. This Agreement was the basis of the North American Free Trade Agreement (NAFTA) which was concluded in 1992 between the United States of America, Canada and Mexico. The Agreement aims at the creation of a large free trade area, which may be extended further to southern countries, and which is conceived as a counterpart to the European Communities and Japan. The Agreement follows closely the model of the CFTA. Of particular interest are the provisions concerning the settlement of disputes, which improve those of the CFTA and GATT. The general dispute regulation provisions are laid down in Chapter 20 and cover "all disputes between the Parties regarding the interpretation or application" of the Agreement or situations where "a Party considers that an actual or proposed measure of another Party is or would be inconsistent with the obligations of the agreement or cause nullification or impairment" of the Agreement (Art. 2004). The range of subjects covered by the NAFTA dispute resolution provisions is broader than the one of the CFTA and GATT and includes such nontraditional and complex subjects as the environment, health, sanitary and phytosanitary standards, intellectual property and financial standards.

Chapter 20 of the NAFTA establishes a three-step dispute settlement mechanism: 1. Consultations between the disputing Parties; 2. A meeting with the Free Trade Commission if consultations fail; 3. As a last resort the convening of an arbitral panel. The NAFTA also creates a series of detailed rules governing dispute settlement, which build on prior agreements. The Parties of NAFTA are required to establish Model Rules of Procedure, which will be shaped to accommodate the wide array of disputes subject to Chapter 20.

As the CFTA also the NAFTA provides in Chapter 19 for special dispute settlement by binational panels in antidumping and countervailing duty cases brought in any one of the three contracting countries. These panels consist of members composed of panelists from the two countries involved in the dispute and act in the place of a domestic reviewing court that would otherwise decide the case. Therefore panels must apply the same domestic substantive law that the administering agency applies and the same standard of review and the general legal principles that would be applied by the reviewing court of the importing Party. Since those panels act as trade courts of last resort of the respective countries, Chapter 19 will not be reproduced here.

Furthermore, a special dispute settlement mechanism has been instituted for disputes between a Party and an Investor of another Party which, however, is without prejudice to the rights and obligations of the Parties under Chapter 20. According to Chapter 11, Section B, such disputes may be submitted to international arbitration. This provision constitutes one of the key achievements of the investment chapter since it is the first time that Mexico has entered into an international agreement providing for investor-state arbitration. Section B contains detailed regulations concerning investment arbitration.

Finally, mention has to be made of the NAFTA Side Agreements on environment and labor. These Side Agreements, which are not part of NAFTA itself, do not provide additional mechanisms for the settlement of disputes concerning NAFTA rights as such; the panels established under the Side Agreements are not empowered to consider the same disputes as the Chapter 20 panels, but may be seized only with allegations that there has been "a persistent pattern of failure" by a Party to effectively enforce its labor or environmental laws.

Texts

North American Free Trade Agreement: ILM 32 (1993), 289 ff.
North American Free Trade Agreements; Treaty Materials compiled by J. R. Holbein/D. J. Musch, 2 Binders;
NAFTA, Documents and Materials, 30 Binders, compiled by B. D. Reams/J. S. Schultz
Dispute Settlement, compiled by J. R. Holbein/D. J. Musch, 2 Binders

Bibliographical notes

J.H. Bello/A.F. Holmer/J.J. Norton (eds.), A New Frontier in International Trade and Investments in the Americas (1994)

M. Barber, NAFTA dispute resolution provisions: leaving room for abusive tactics by airlines looking southward, The Journal of Air Law and Commerce 61 (1996), 991-1016

Metz, A NAFTA Bibliography (1996)

W.A. Orme jr., Understanding NAFTA (1996)

G.W. Carman, Resolution of Trade Disputes by Chapter 19 Panels: a Procedure of Dubious Constitutionality, Fordham International Law Journal 21 (1997), 1-11

R. Cruz Miramantes, El TLC: Controversias, soluciones y otros temas conexos (1997)

D. Lopez, Dispute Resolution under a free trade area of the Americas: the shape of things to come, The University of Miami interAmerican Law Review 28 (1997), 597-627

S. Picker, The NAFTA Chapter 20 dispute resolution process: a view from the inside, Canada United States Law Journal 23 (1997), 525-540

J.C. Thomure, Star chamber accountability: appellate review of NAFTA chapter 20 Panel Decisions, The University of Miami interAmerican Law Review 28 (1997), 629-659

D.A. Gantz, Resolution of Trade Disputes under NAFTA's Chapter 19: The lessons of extending the binational panel process to Mexico, Law and Policy in International Business 29 (1998), 297-363

M.S. Valihora, NAFTA chapter 19 or the WTO's dispute settlement body: a Hobson's choice for Canada? Case Western Reserve Journal of International Law 30 (1998), 447-487

aa) Part Seven: Administrative and Institutional Provisions

CHAPTER TWENTY — INSTITUTIONAL ARRANGEMENTS AND DISPUTE SETTLEMENT PROCEDURES

SECTION A — INSTITUTIONS

Art. 2001 The Free Trade Commission

1. The Parties hereby establish the Free Trade Commission, comprising cabinet-level representatives of the Parties or their designees.

2. The Commission shall:

(a) supervise the implementation of this Agreement;

(b) oversee its further elaboration;

(c) resolve disputes that may arise regarding its interpretation or application;

(d) supervise the work of all committees and working groups established under this Agreement, referred to in Annex 2001.2; and

(e) consider any other matter that may affect the operation of this Agreement.

3. The Commission may:

(a) establish, and delegate responsibilities to, ad hoc or standing committees, working groups or expert groups;

(b) seek the advice of non-governmental persons or groups; and

(c) take such other action in the exercise of its functions as the Parties may agree.

4. The Commission shall establish its rules and procedures. All decisions of the Commission shall be taken by consensus, except as the Commission may otherwise agree.

5. The Commission shall convene at least once a year in regular session. Regular sessions of the Commission shall be chaired successively by each Party.

Art. 2002 The Secretariat

1. The Commission shall establish and oversee a Secretariat comprising national Sections.

2. Each Party shall:

(a) establish a permanent office of its Section;

(b) be responsible for

(i) the operation and costs of its Section, and

(ii) the remuneration and payment of expenses of panelists and members of committees and scientific review boards established under this Agreement, as set out in Annex 2002.2;

(c) designate an individual to serve as Secretary for its Section, who shall be responsible for its administration and management; and

(d) notify the Commission of the location of its Section's office.

3. The Secretariat shall:

(a) provide assistance to the Commission;

(b) provide administrative assistance to

(i) panels and committees established under Chapter Nineteen (Review and Dispute Settlement in Antidumping and Countervailing Duty Matters), in accordance with the procedures established pursuant to Article 1908, and

(ii) panels established under this Chapter, in accordance with procedures established pursuant to Article 2012; and

(c) as the Commission may direct

(i) support the work of other committees and groups established under this Agreement, and

(ii) otherwise facilitate the operation of this Agreement.

SECTION B — DISPUTE SETTLEMENT

Art. 2003 Cooperation

The Parties shall at all times endeavor to agree on the interpretation and application of this Agreement, and shall make every attempt through cooperation and consultations to arrive at a mutually satisfactory resolution of any matter that might affect its operation.

Art. 2004 Recourse to Dispute Settlement Procedures

Except for the matters covered in Chapter Nineteen (Review and Dispute Settlement in Antidumping and Countervailing Duty Matters) and as otherwise provided in this Agreement, the dispute settlement provisions of this Chapter shall apply with respect to the avoidance or settlement of all disputes between the Parties regarding the interpretation or application of this Agreement or wherever a Party considers that an actual or proposed measure of another Party is or would he inconsistent with the obligations of this Agreement or cause nullification or impairment in the sense of Annex 2004.

Art. 2005 GATT Dispute Settlement

1. Subject to paragraphs 2, 3 and 4, disputes regarding any matter arising under both this Agreement and the General Agreement on Tariffs and Trade, any agreement negotiated thereunder, or any successor agreement (GATT), may be settled in either forum at the discretion of the complaining Party.

2. Before a Party initiates a dispute settlement proceeding in the GATT against another Party on grounds that are substantially equivalent to those available to that Party under this Agreement, that Party shall notify

any third Party of its intention. If a third Party wishes to have recourse to dispute settlement procedures under this Agreement regarding the matter, it shall inform promptly the notifying Party and those Parties shall consult with a view to agreement on a single forum. If those Parties cannot agree, the dispute normally shall be settled under this Agreement.

3. In any dispute referred to in paragraph 1 where the responding Party claims that its action is subject to Article 104 (Relation to Environmental and Conservation Agreements) and requests in writing that the matter be considered under this Agreement, the complaining Party may, in respect of that matter, thereafter have recourse to dispute settlement procedures solely under this Agreement.

4. In any dispute referred to in paragraph 1 that arises under Section B of Chapter Seven (Sanitary and Phytosanitary Measures) or Chapter Nine (Standards-Related Measures):

(a) concerning a measure adopted or maintained by a Party to protect its human, animal or plant life or health, or to protect its environment, and

b) that raises factual issues concerning the environment, health, safety or conservation, including directly related scientific matters,

where the responding Party requests in writing that the matter be considered under this Agreement, the complaining Party may, in respect of that matter, thereafter have recourse to dispute settlement procedures solely under this Agreement.

5. The responding Party shall deliver a copy of a request made pursuant to paragraph 3 or 4 to the other Parties and to its Section of the Secretariat. Where the complaining Party has initiated dispute settlement proceedings regarding any matter subject to paragraph 3 or 4, the responding Party shall deliver its request no later than 15 days thereafter. On receipt of such request, the complaining Party shall promptly withdraw from participation in those proceedings and may initiate dispute settlement procedures under Article 2007.

6. Once dispute settlement procedures have been initiated under Article 2007 or dispute settlement proceedings have been initiated under the GATT, the forum selected shall be used to the exclusion of the other, unless a Party makes a request pursuant to paragraph 3 or 4.

7. For purposes of this Article, dispute settlement proceedings under the GATT are deemed to be initiated by a Party's request for a panel, such as under Article XXIII:2 of the *General Agreement on Tariffs and Trade 1947*, or for a committee investigation, such as under Article 20.1 of the Customs Valuation Code.

Consultations

Art. 2006 Consultations

1. Any Party may request in writing consultations with any other Party regarding any actual or proposed measure or any other matter that it considers might affect the operation of this Agreement.

2. The requesting Party shall deliver the request to the other Parties and to its Section of the Secretariat.

3. Unless the Commission otherwise provides in its rules and procedures established under Article 2001(4), a third Party that considers it has a substantial interest in the matter shall be entitled to participate in the consultations on delivery of written notice to the other Parties and to its Section of the Secretariat.

4. Consultations on matters regarding perishable agricultural goods shall commence within 15 days of the date of delivery of the request.

5. The consulting Parties shall make every attempt to arrive at a mutually satisfactory resolution of any matter through consultations under this Article or other consultative provisions of this Agreement. To this end, the consulting Parties shall:

(a) provide sufficient information to enable a full examination of how the actual or proposed measure or other matter might affect the operation of this Agreement;

(b) treat any confidential or proprietary information exchanged in the course of consultations on the same basis as the Party providing the information; and

(c) seek to avoid any resolution that adversely affects the interests under this Agreement of any other Party.

Art. 2007 Commission — Good Offices, Conciliation and Mediation

1. If the consulting Parties fail to resolve a matter pursuant to Article 2006 within:

(a) 30 days of delivery of a request for consultations,

(b) 45 days of delivery of such request if any other Party has subsequently requested or has participated in consultations regarding the same matter,

(c) 15 days of delivery of a request for consultations in matters regarding perishable agricultural goods, or

(d) such other period as they may agree,

any such Party may request in writing a meeting of the Commission.

2. A Party may also request in writing a meeting of the Commission where:

(a) it has initiated dispute settlement proceedings under the GATT regarding any matter subject to Article 2005(3) or (4), and has received a request pursuant to Article 2005(5) for recourse to dispute settlement procedures under this Chapter; or

(b) consultations have been held pursuant to Article 513 (Working Group on Rules of Origin), Article 723 (Sanitary and Phytosanitary

Measures – Technical Consultations) and Article 914 (Standards-Related Measures – Technical Consultations).

3. The requesting Party shall state in the request the measure or other matter complained of and indicate the provisions of this Agreement that it considers relevant, and shall deliver the request to the other Parties and to its Section of the Secretariat.

4. Unless it decides otherwise, the Commission shall convene within 10 days of delivery of the request and shall endeavor to resolve the dispute promptly.

5. The commission may:

(a) call on such technical advisers or create such working groups or expert groups as it deems necessary,

(b) have recourse to good offices, conciliation, mediation or such other dispute resolution procedures, or

(c) make recommendations,

as may assist the consulting Parties to reach a mutually satisfactory resolution of the dispute.

6. Unless it decides otherwise, the Commission shall consolidate two or more proceedings before it pursuant to this Article regarding the same measure. The Commission may consolidate two or more proceedings regarding other matters before it pursuant to this Article that it determines are appropriate to be considered jointly.

Panel Proceedings

Art. 2008 Request for an Arbitral Panel

1. If the Commission has convened pursuant to Article 2007(4), and the matter has not been resolved within

(a) 30 days thereafter,

(b) 30 days after the Commission has convened in respect of the matter most recently referred to it, where proceedings have been consolidated pursuant to Article 2007(6), or

(c) such other period as the consulting Parties may agree,

any consulting Party may request by writing the establishment of an arbitral panel. The requesting Party shall deliver the request to the other Parties and to its Section of the Secretariat.

2. On delivery of the request, the Commission shall establish an arbitral panel.

3. A third Party that considers it has a substantial interest in the matter shall be entitled to join as a complaining Party on delivery of written notice of its intention to participate to the disputing Parties and its Section of the Secretariat. The notice shall be delivered at the earliest possible

time, and in any event not later than seven days after the date of delivery of a request by a Party for the establishment of a panel.

4. If a third Party does not join as a complaining Party in accordance with paragraph 3, it normally shall refrain, thereafter from initiating or continuing:

(a) a dispute settlement procedure under this Agreement, or

(b) a dispute settlement proceeding in the GATT on grounds that are substantially equivalent to those available to that Party under this Agreement.

regarding the same matter in the absence of a significant change in economic or commercial circumstances.

5. Unless otherwise agreed by the disputing Parties, the panel shall be established and perform its functions in a manner consistent with the provisions of this Chapter.

Art. 2009 Roster

1. The Parties shall establish by January 1, 1994 and maintain a roster of up to 30 individuals who are willing and able to serve as panelists. The roster members shall be appointed by consensus for terms of three years, and may be reappointed.

2. Roster members shall:

(a) have expertise or experience in law, international trade, other matters covered by this Agreement or the resolution of disputes arising under international trade agreements, and shall be chosen strictly on the basis of objectivity, reliability and sound judgment;

(b) be independent of, and not be affiliated with or take instructions from, any Party; and

(c) comply with a code of conduct to be established by the Commission.

Art. 2010 Qualifications of Panelists

1. All panelists shall meet the qualifications set out in Article 2009(2).

2. Individuals may not serve as panelists for a dispute in which they have participated pursuant to Article 2007(5).

Art. 2011 Panel Selection

1. Where there are two disputing Parties, the following procedures shall apply:

(a) The panel shall comprise five members.

(b) The disputing Parties shall endeavor to agree on the chair of the panel within 15 days of the delivery of the request for the establishment of the panel. If the disputing Parties are unable to agree on the chair within this period, the disputing Party chosen by lot shall select within five days as chair an individual who is not a citizen of that Party.

(c) Within 15 days of selection of the chair, each disputing Party shall select two panelists who are citizens of the other disputing Party.

(d) If a disputing Party fails to select its panelists within such period, such panelists shall be selected by lot from among the roster members who are citizens of the other disputing Party.

2. Where there are more than two disputing Parties, the following procedures shall apply:

(a) The panel shall comprise five members.

(b) The disputing Parties shall endeavor to agree on the chair of the panel within 15 days of the delivery of the request for the establishment of the panel. If the disputing Parties are unable to agree on the chair within this period, the Party or Parties on the side of the dispute chosen by lot shall select within 10 days a chair who is not a citizen of such Party or Parties.

(c) Within 15 days of selection of the chair, the Party complained against shall select two panelists, one of whom is a citizen of a complaining Party, and the other of whom is a citizen of another complaining Party. The complaining Parties shall select two panelists who are citizens of the Party complained against.

(d) If any disputing Party fails to select a panelist within such period, such panelist shall be selected by lot in accordance with the citizenship criteria of subparagraph (c).

3. Panelists shall normally be selected from the roster. Any disputing Party may exercise a peremptory challenge against any individual not on the roster who is proposed as a panelist by a disputing Party within 15 days after the individual has been proposed.

4. If a disputing Party believes that a panelist is in violation of the code of conduct, the disputing Parties shall consult and if they agree, the panelist shall be removed and a new panelist shall be selected in accordance with this Article.

Art. 2012 Rules of Procedure

1. The Commission shall establish by January 1, 1994 Model Rules of Procedure, in accordance with the following principles:

(a) the procedures shall assure a right to at least one hearing before the panel as well as the opportunity to provide initial and rebuttal written submissions; and

(b) the panel's hearings, deliberations and initial report, and all written submissions to and communications with the panel shall be confidential.

2. Unless the disputing Parties otherwise agree, the panel shall conduct its proceedings in accordance with the Model Rules of Procedure.

3. Unless the disputing Parties otherwise agree within 20 days from the date of the delivery of the request for the establishment of the panel, the terms of reference shall be:

"To examine, in the light of the relevant provisions of the Agreement, the matter referred to the Commission (as set out in the request for a Commission meeting) and to make findings, determinations and recommendations as provided in Article 2016(2)."

4. If a complaining Party wishes to argue that a matter has nullified or impaired benefits, the terms of reference shall so indicate.

5. If a disputing Party wishes the panel to make findings as to the degree of adverse trade effects on any Party of any measure found not to conform with the obligations of the Agreement or to have caused nullification or impairment in the sense of Annex 2004, the terms of reference shall so indicate.

Art. 2013 Third Party Participation

A Party that is not a disputing Party, on delivery of a written notice to the disputing Parties and to its Section of the Secretariat, shall be entitled to attend all hearings, to make written and oral submissions to the panel and to receive written submissions of the disputing Parties.

Art. 2014 Role of Experts

On request of a disputing Party, or on its own initiative, the panel may seek information and technical advice from any person or body that it deems appropriate, provided that the disputing Parties so agree and subject to such terms and conditions as such Parties may agree.

Art. 2015 Scientific Review Boards

1. On request of a disputing Party or, unless the disputing Parties disapprove, on its own initiative, the panel may request a written report of a scientific review board on any factual issue concerning environmental, health, safety or other scientific matters raised by a disputing Party in a proceeding, subject to such terms and conditions as such Parties may agree.

2. The board shall be selected by the panel from among highly qualified, independent experts in the scientific matters, after consultations with the disputing Parties and the scientific bodies set out in the Model Rules of Procedure established pursuant to Article 2012(1).

3. The participating Parties shall be provided:

(a) advance notice of, and an opportunity to provide comments to the panel on the proposed factual issues to be referred to the board; and

(b) a copy of the board's report and an opportunity to provide comments on the report to the panel.

4. The panel shall take the board's report and any comments by the Parties on the report into account in the preparation of its report.

Art. 2016 Initial Report

1. Unless the disputing Parties otherwise agree, the panel shall base its report on the submissions and arguments of the Parties and on any information before it pursuant to Article 2014 or 2015.

2. Unless the disputing Parties otherwise agree, the panel shall, within 90 days after the last panelist is selected or such other period as the Model Rules of Procedure established pursuant to Article 2012(1) may provide, present to the disputing Parties an initial report containing:

(a) findings of fact, including any findings pursuant to a request under Article 2012(5);

(b) its determination as to whether the measure at issue is or would be inconsistent with the obligations of this Agreement or cause nullification or impairment in the sense of Annex 2004, or any other determination requested in the terms of reference, and

(c) its recommendations, if any, for resolution of the dispute.

3. Panelists may furnish separate opinions on matters not unanimously agreed.

4. A disputing Party may submit written comments to the panel on its initial report within 14 days of presentation of the report.

5. In such an event, and after considering such written comments, the panel, on its own initiative or on the request of any disputing Party, may:

(a) request the views of any participating Party;

(b) reconsider its report; and

(c) make any further examination that it considers appropriate.

Art. 2017 Final Report

1. The panel shall present to the disputing Parties a final report, including any separate opinions on matters not unanimously agreed, within 30 days of presentation of the initial report, unless the disputing Parties otherwise agree.

2. No panel may, either in its initial report or its final report, disclose which panelists are associated with the majority or minority opinions.

3. The disputing Parties shall transmit to the Commission the final report of the panel, including any report of a scientific review board established under Article 2015, as well as any written views that a disputing Party desires to be appended, on a confidential basis within a reasonable period of time after it is presented to them.

4. Unless the Commission decides otherwise, the final report of the panel shall be published 15 days after it is transmitted to the Commission.

Implementation of Panel Reports

Art. 2018 Implementation of Final Report

1. On receipt of the final report of a panel, the disputing Parties shall agree on the resolution of the dispute, which normally shall conform with the determinations and recommendations of the panel, and shall notify their Sections of the Secretariat of any agreed resolution of any dispute.

2. Wherever possible, the resolution shall be non-implementation or removal of a measure not conforming with this Agreement or causing nullification or impairment in the sense of Annex 2004 or, failing such a resolution, compensation.

Art. 2019 Non-Implementation — Suspension of Benefits

1. If in its Final report a panel has determined that a measure is inconsistent with the obligations of this Agreement or causes nullification or impairment in the sense of Annex 2004 and the Party complained against has not reached agreement with any complaining Party on a mutually satisfactory resolution pursuant to Article 2018(1) within 30 days of receiving the final report, such complaining Party may suspend the application to the Party complained against of benefits of equivalent effect until such time as they have reached agreement on a resolution of the dispute.

2. In considering what benefits to suspend pursuant to paragraph 1:

(a) a complaining Party should first seek to suspend benefits in the same sector or sectors as that affected by the measure or other matter that the panel has found to be inconsistent with the obligations of this Agreement or to have caused nullification or impairment in the sense of Annex 2004; and

(b) a complaining Party that considers it is not practicable or effective to suspend benefits in the same sector or sectors may suspend benefits in other sectors.

3. On the written request of any disputing Party delivered to the other Parties and its Section of the Secretariat, the Commission shall establish a panel to determine whether the level of benefits suspended by a Party pursuant to paragraph 1 is manifestly excessive.

4. The panel proceedings shall be conducted in accordance with the Model Rules of Procedure. The panel shall present its determination within 60 days after the last panelist is selected or such other period as the disputing Parties may agree.

SECTION C — DOMESTIC PROCEEDINGS AND PRIVATE COMMERCIAL DISPUTE SETTLEMENT

Art. 2020 Referrals of Matters from Judicial or Administrative Proceedings

1. If an issue of interpretation or application of this Agreement arises in any domestic judicial or administrative proceeding of a Party that any Party considers would merit its intervention, or if a court or administrative body solicits the views of a Party, that Party shall notify the other

Parties and its Section of the Secretariat. The Commission shall endeavor to agree on an appropriate response as expeditiously as possible.

2. The Party in whose territory the court or administrative body is located shall submit any agreed interpretation of the Commission to the court or administrative body in accordance with the rules of that forum.

3. If the Commission is unable to agree, any Party may submit its own views to the court or administrative body in accordance with the rules of that forum.

Art. 2021 Private Rights

No Party may provide for a right of action under its domestic law against any other Party on the ground that a measure of another Party is inconsistent with this Agreement.

Art. 2022 Alternative Dispute Resolution

1. Each Party shall, to the maximum extent possible, encourage and facilitate the use of arbitration and other means of alternative dispute resolution for the settlement of international commercial disputes between private parties in the free trade area.

2. To this end, each Party shall provide appropriate procedures to ensure observance of agreements to arbitrate and for the recognition and enforcement of arbitral awards in such disputes.

3. A Party shall be deemed to be in compliance with paragraph 2 if it is a party to and is in compliance with the 1958 United Nations Convention on the Recognition and Enforcement of Foreign Arbitral Awards or the 1975 Inter-American Convention on International Commercial Arbitration.

4. The Commission shall establish an Advisory Committee on Private Commercial Disputes comprising persons with expertise or experience in the resolution of private international commercial disputes. The Committee shall report and provide recommendations to the Commission on general issues referred to it by the Commission respecting the availability, use and effectiveness of arbitration and other procedures for the resolution of such disputes in the free trade area.

ANNEX 2001.2 — COMMITTEES AND WORKING GROUPS

A.   Committees:

1. Committee on Trade in Goods (Article 316)

2. Committee on Trade in Worn Clothing (Annex 300-B, Section 9.1)

3. Committee on Agricultural Trade (Article 706)

–   Advisory Committee on Private Commercial Disputes Regarding Agricultural Goods (Article 707)

4. Committee on Sanitary and Phytosanitary Measures (Article 722)

5. Committee on Standards-Related Measures (Article 913)

–   Land Transportation Standards Subcommittee (Article 913(5))

–   Telecommunications Standards Subcommittee (Article 913(5))

–   Automotive Standards Council (Article 913(5))

–   Subcommittee on Labelling of Textile and Apparel Goods (Article 913(5))

6. Committee on Small Business (Article 1021)

7. Financial Services Committee (Article 1412)

8. Advisory Committee on Private Commercial Disputes (Article 2022(4))

B.   Working Groups:

1. Working Group on Rules of Origin (Article 513)

–   Customs Subgroup (Article 513(6))

2. Working Group on Agricultural Subsidies (Article 705(6))

3. Bilateral Working Group (Mexico – United States) (Annex 703.2(A)(25))

4. Bilateral Working Group (Canada – Mexico) (Annex 703.2(B)(13))

5. Working Group on Trade and Competition (Article 1504)

6. Temporary Entry Working Group (Article 1605)

C.   Other Committees and Working Groups Established under this Agreement

ANNEX 2002.2 – REMUNERATION AND PAYMENT OF EXPENSES

1. The Commission shall establish the amounts of remuneration and expenses that will be paid to the panelists, committee members and members of scientific review boards.

2. The remuneration of panelists or committee members and their assistants, members of scientific review boards, their travel and lodging expenses, and all general expenses of panels, committees or scientific review boards shall be borne equally by:

(a) in the case of panels or committees established under Chapter Nineteen (Review and Dispute Settlement in Antidumping and Countervailing Duty Matters), the involved Parties, as they are defined in Article 1911; or

(b) in the case of panels and scientific review boards established under this Chapter, the disputing Parties.

3. Each panelist or committee member shall keep a record and render a final account of the person's time and expenses, and the panel, committee or scientific review board shall keep a record and render a final account of all general expenses. The Commission shall establish amounts of remu-

neration and expenses that will be paid to panelists and committee members.

ANNEX 2004 — NULLIFICATION AND IMPAIRMENT

1. If any Party considers that any benefit it could reasonably have expected to accrue to it under any provision of:

(a) Part Two (Trade in Goods), except for those provisions of Annex 300-A (Automotive Sector) or Chapter Six (Energy) relating to investment,

(b) Part Three (Technical Barriers to Trade),

(c) Chapter Twelve (Cross-Border Trade in Services), or

(d) Part Six (Intellectual Property),

is being nullified or impaired as a result of the application of any measure that is not inconsistent with this Agreement, the Party may have recourse to dispute settlement under this Chapter.

2. A Party may not invoke:

(a) paragraph 1(a) or (b), to the extent that the benefit arises from any cross-border trade in services provision of Part Two,

(b) paragraph 1(c) or (d),

with respect to any measure subject to an exception under Article 2101 (General Exceptions).

bb) Model Rules of Procedure for Chapter Twenty of the North American Free Trade Agreement

APPLICATION

1. These rules are established under Article 2012(1) and shall apply to dispute settlement proceedings under Chapter Twenty unless the disputing Parties otherwise agree.

DEFINITIONS

2. In these rules:

adviser means a person retained by a Party to advise or assist the Party in connection with the panel proceeding;

Agreement means the North American Free Trade Agreement;

complaining Party means any Party that requests the establishment of an arbitral panel under Article 2008(1) or any Party that joins a panel proceeding under Article 2008(3);

disputing Parties means the complaining Party or Parties, and the Party complained against;

legal holiday, with respect to a Party's section of the Secretariat, means every Saturday and Sunday and any other day designated by that Party as a holiday for the purposes of these rules and notified by that Party to its section of the Secretariat and by that section to the other sections of the Secretariat and the other Parties;

panel means a panel established under Article 2008(2);

participating Parties means the disputing Parties and a third Party;

Party means a Party to the Agreement;

representative of a participating Party means an employee of a government department or agency or of any other government entity of a participating Party;

responsible section of the Secretariat means the section of the Secretariat of the Party complained against:

Secretariat means the Secretariat established under Article 2002(1); and

third Party means a Party, other than a disputing Party, that delivers a written notice in accordance with Article 2013.

3. Any reference made in these rules to an Article, Annex or Chapter is a reference to the appropriate Article, Annex or Chapter of the Agreement.

TERMS OF REFERENCE

4. The disputing Parties shall promptly deliver any agreed terms of reference to the responsible section of the Secretariat which, in turn, shall provide for their delivery to any third Party, to the other sections of the Secretariat and to the panel on selection of the last panelist, by the most expeditious means practicable.

5. If the disputing Parties have not agreed on terms of reference after 20 days of the request for the establishment of the panel, the complaining Party may so notify the responsible section of the Secretariat. On receipt of such notification, that section shall deliver the terms of reference set out in Article 2012(3) to the participating Parties, to the other sections of the Secretariat, and to the panel on selection of the last panelist by the most expeditious means practicable.

WRITTEN SUBMISSIONS AND OTHER DOCUMENTS

6. A participating Party shall deliver the original and nine copies of each of its written submissions to its section of the Secretariat and shall make a

copy of each of its written submissions available to the Embassy of each other participating Party at the time it delivers the written submission to its section.

7. A complaining Party shall deliver the original and nine copies of its initial written submission to its section of the Secretariat no later than 10 days after the date on which the last panelist is selected. The Party complained against shall deliver the original and nine copies of its written counter-submission to its section of the Secretariat no later than 20 days after the date of delivery of the initial written submission. A third Party shall deliver the original and nine copies of its initial written submission to its section of the Secretariat no later than the date on which the counter-submission is due.

8. A section of the Secretariat that receives a written submission shall forward it by the most expeditious means practicable to the responsible section of the Secretariat which, in turn, shall provide for delivery of that submission by the most expeditious means practicable to the other sections of the Secretariat, the other participating Parties and the panel.

9. In the case of any request, notice or other document related to the panel proceeding that is not covered by rule 6, 7 or 8, the participating Party shall deliver the original and nine copies of the document to its section of the Secretariat and, on the same day, it shall deliver a copy to the other participating Parties by facsimile or other means of electronic transmission.

10. Minor errors of a clerical nature in any request, notice, written submission or other document related to the panel proceeding may be corrected by delivery of a new document clearly indicating the changes.

11. A participating Party that delivers any request, notice, written submission or other document to its section of the Secretariat shall, to the extent practicable, deliver a copy of the document in electronic form to that section.

12. Any delivery to a section of the Secretariat under these rules shall be made during the normal business hours of that section.

13. If the last day for delivery of a document to a section of the Secretariat falls on a legal holiday observed by that section or on any other day on which the offices of that section are closed by order of the government or by *force majeure*, the document may be delivered to that section on the next business day.

OPERATION OF PANELS

14. The chair of the panel shall preside at all of its meetings. A panel may delegate to the chair authority to make administrative and procedural decisions.

15. Except as otherwise provided in these rules, the panel may conduct its business by any means, including by telephone, facsimile transmission or computer links.

16. Only panelists may take part in the deliberations of the panel but the panel may permit assistants, Secretariat personnel, interpreters or translators to be present during such deliberations.

17. Where a procedural question arises that is not covered by these rules, a panel may adopt an appropriate procedure that is not inconsistent with the Agreement.

18. If a panelist dies, withdraws or is removed, a replacement shall be selected as expeditiously as possible in accordance with the selection procedure followed to select the panelist.

19. Any time period applicable to the panel proceeding shall be suspended for a period beginning on the date the panelist dies, withdraws or is removed and ending on the date the replacement is selected.

20. A panel may, in consultation with the disputing Parties, modify any time period applicable in the panel proceeding and make such other procedural or administrative adjustments as may be required in the proceeding, such as where a panelist is replaced or where the Parties are required to reply in writing to the questions of a panel.

HEARINGS

21. The chair shall fix the date and time of the hearing in consultation with the participating Parties, the other members of the panel and the responsible section of the Secretariat. The responsible section of the Secretariat shall notify in writing the participating Parties of the date, time and location of the hearing.

22. The hearing shall be held in the capital of the Party complained against.

23. The panel may convene additional hearings if the disputing Parties so agree.

24. All panelists shall be present at hearings.

25. The following persons may attend a hearing:

(a) representatives of a participating Party;

(b) advisers to a participating Party provided that they do not address the panel and provided further that neither they nor their employers, partners, business associates or family members have a financial or personal interest in the proceeding;

(c) Secretariat personnel, interpreters, translators and court reporters; and

(d) panelists' assistants.

26. No later than five days before the date of a hearing, each participating Party shall deliver to the other participating Parties and the responsible section of the Secretariat a list of the names of those persons who will make oral arguments or presentations at the hearing on behalf of that Party and of other representatives or advisers who will be attending the hearing.

27. The hearing shall be conducted by the panel in the following manner. ensuring that the complaining Party or Parties and the Party complained against are afforded equal time:

Argument -

(i)   Argument of the complaining Party or Parties.

(ii) Argument of the Party complained against.

(iii) Presentation of a third Party.

Rebuttal Argument -

(iv) Reply of the complaining Party or Parties.

(v)   Counter-reply of the Party complained against.

28. The panel may direct questions to any participating Party at any time during a hearing.

29. The responsible section of the Secretariat shall arrange for a transcript of each hearing to be prepared and shall, as soon as possible after it is prepared, deliver a copy of the transcript to the participating Parties, the other sections of the Secretariat and the panel.

SUPPLEMENTARY WRITTEN SUBMISSIONS

30. The panel may at any time during a proceeding address questions in writing to one or more of the participating Parties. The panel shall deliver the written questions to the Party or Parties to whom the questions are addressed through the responsible section of the Secretariat which, in turn, shall provide for the delivery of copies of the questions by the most expeditious means practicable to the other sections of the Secretariat and any other participating Party.

31. A participating Party to whom the panel addresses written questions shall deliver a copy of any written reply to its section of the Secretariat which, in turn, shall forward it by the most expeditious means practicable to the responsible section of the Secretariat. The responsible section of the Secretariat shall provide for the delivery of copies of the reply by the most expeditious means practicable to the other sections of the Secretariat and any other participating Party. Each other participating Party shall be given the opportunity to provide written comments on the reply within five days after the date of delivery.

32. Within 10 days after the date of the hearing, each participating Party may deliver to its section of the Secretariat a supplementary written submission responding to any matter that arose during the hearing.

Burden of Proof Regarding Inconsistent Measures and Exceptions

33. A Party asserting that a measure of another Party is inconsistent with the provisions of the Agreement shall have the burden of establishing such inconsistency.

34. A Party, asserting that a measure is subject to an exception under the Agreement shall have the burden of establishing that the exception applies.

Availability of Information

35. The Parties shall maintain the confidentiality of the panel's hearings, deliberations and initial report, and all written submissions to and, communications with the panel. in accordance with such procedures as may be agreed from to time to time between representatives of the Parties.

Ex Parte Contacts

36. The panel shall not meet or contact one participating Party in the absence of the other participating Parties.

37. No panelist may discuss any aspect of the subject matter of the proceeding with a participating Party or Parties in the absence of the other panelists.

Scientific Review Boards

38. No panel may decide to request a written report of a scientific review board any later than 15 days after the date of the hearing, whether on its own initiative or at the request of a disputing Party.

39. Within five days after the date on which the panel decides to request a written report of a scientific review board, the panel shall request that the scientific bodies designated by each Party from time to time and set out in Appendix 1 provide, within 15 days after the date of the delivery of the request, a list of the names of possible members of the scientific review board, in such numbers as the panel requests and having expertise in the scientific matters that the panel identifies.

40. The panel shall deliver the request for the list of names of possible members of the scientific review board to the responsible section of the Secretariat which, in turn, shall provide for the delivery of copies of the request by the most expeditious means practicable to the other sections of the Secretariat and the participating Parties.

41. Within 25 days after its decision to request a written report of a scientific review board and after consulting the disputing Parties, the panel

North American Free Trade Agreement

shall select up to three members to constitute the scientific review board. The panel shall make its selection from the lists provided by the scientific bodies wherever possible.

42. The panel shall not select as a member of a scientific review board an individual who has, or whose employers, partners, business associates or family members have, a financial or personal interest in the proceeding.

43. A participating Party may, before the date on which the last member of the scientific review board is selected, submit written comments to the panel on the factual issues to be referred to the board.

44. Within five days after the date on which the last member of the scientific review board is selected, the panel shall finalize the factual issues to be referred to the board, and may consult with members of the board in this regard.

45. The panel shall deliver a copy of its referral to the responsible section of the Secretariat which, in turn, shall provide for the delivery of copies of the referral by the most expeditious means practicable to the other sections of the Secretariat, the participating Parties and the board.

46. A scientific review board shall deliver its report to the responsible section of the Secretariat within 30 days after the date on which the factual issues are referred to the board.

47. The responsible section of the Secretariat shall deliver the board's report to the participating Parties and their respective sections of the Secretariat. Any participating Party may provide comments on the report to its section of the Secretariat within 14 days after the date of delivery of the report. The appropriate section of the Secretariat shall promptly deliver any such comments to the responsible section of the Secretariat which, in turn, shall no later than the next business day deliver such comments to the other participating Parties and their respective sections of the Secretariat, and shall deliver the report and all such comments to the panel.

48. Where a request is made for a written report of a scientific review board, any time period applicable to the panel proceeding shall be suspended for a period beginning on the date of delivery of the request and ending on the date the report is delivered to the panel.

TRANSLATION AND INTERPRETATION

49. A participating Party shall, within a reasonable period of time before it delivers its initial written submission in a panel proceeding, advise its section of the Secretariat in writing of the language in which its written submissions will be made and in which it wishes to receive the written submissions of the other participating Parties. A section of the Secretariat that is so advised shall promptly notify the responsible section of the Sec-

retariat which, in turn, shall promptly notify the other sections of the Secretariat, the other participating Parties and the panel.

50. A participating Party shall, within a reasonable period of time before the date of a hearing, advise its section of the Secretariat in writing of the language in which it will make oral arguments or presentations at the hearing and in which it wishes to hear oral arguments and presentations. A section of the Secretariat that is so advised shall promptly notify the responsible section of the Secretariat which, in turn, shall promptly notify the other sections of the Secretariat, the other participating Parties and the panel.

51. In lieu of the procedure set out in rule 49 or 50, a Party may advise its section of the Secretariat of:

(a) the language in which it will make, and in which it wishes to receive, written submissions in all panel proceedings; or

(b) the language in which it will make, and in which it wishes to hear, oral arguments and presentations at hearings in all panel proceedings.

A section of the Secretariat that is so advised shall promptly notify the other sections of the Secretariat and the other Parties.

52. Where in accordance with the advice provided by each Party under rules 49 through 51, written submissions or oral arguments and presentations in a panel proceeding will be made in more than one language, or if a panelist requests, the responsible section of the Secretariat shall arrange for the translation of the written submissions and the panel reports or for the interpretation of arguments at any hearing, as the case may be.

53. Where the responsible section of the Secretariat is required to arrange for the translation of a written submission or report in one or more languages, it shall not provide for the delivery of that written submission as required by rule 8 or for the delivery of that report until all translated versions of that written submission or report have been prepared.

54. Any time period applicable to a panel proceeding shall be suspended for the period necessary to complete the translation of any written submissions.

55. The costs incurred to prepare a translation of a written submission shall be borne by the Party making the submission. The costs incurred to prepare a translation of a final report shall be borne equally by each section of the Secretariat. The costs of all other translation and interpretation requirements in a panel proceeding shall be borne equally by the participating Parties in that proceeding.

56. Any Party may provide comments on a translated version of a document that is prepared in accordance with these rules.

COMPUTATION OF TIME

57. Where anything under the Agreement or these rules is to be done, or the panel requires anything to be done, within a number of days after, before or of a specified date or event, the specified date or the date on which the specified event occurs shall not be included in calculating that number of days.

58. Where, by reason of the operation of rule 13, a participating Party

(a) receives a document on a date other than the date on which the same document is received by any other participating Party, or

(b) receives a document from a second participating Party on a date that is either before or after the date on which it receives the corresponding document from a third participating Party,

any period of time the calculation of which is dependent on such receipt shall be calculated from the date of receipt of the last such document.

SUSPENSION OF BENEFITS PANELS

59. These rules shall apply to a panel established under Article 2019(3) except that:

(a) the Party that requests the establishment of the panel shall deliver its initial written submission to its section of the Secretariat within 10 days after the date on which the last panelist is selected;

(b) the responding Party shall deliver its written counter-submission to its section of the Secretariat within 15 days after the date of delivery of the initial written submission;

(c) the panel shall fix the time limit for delivering any further written submissions, including rebuttal written submissions, so as to provide each disputing Party with the opportunity to make an equal number of written submissions subject to the time limits for panel proceedings set out in the Agreement and these Rules; and

(d) unless the disputing Parties disagree, the panel may decide not to convene a hearing.

PANELS REGARDING INVESTMENT DISPUTES IN FINANCIAL SERVICES

60. These rules shall apply to a panel convened under Article 1415(3) except that the terms of reference shall be as set out in Article 1415(2).

RESPONSIBLE SECTION OF THE SECRETARIAT

61. The responsible section of the Secretariat shall:

(a) provide administrative assistance to the panel and any scientific review board;

(b) compensate, and provide administrative assistance to, experts, panelists and their assistants, members of scientific review boards, interpreters, translators, court reporters or other individuals that it retains in a panel proceeding;

(c) make available to the panelists, on confirmation of their appointment, copies of the Agreement and other documents relevant to the proceedings, such as the Uniform Regulations and these Rules; and

(d) retain indefinitely a copy of the complete record of the panel proceeding.

MAINTENANCE OF ROSTERS

62. The Parties shall inform each section of the Secretariat of the composition of the roster established under Article 1414(3) and the roster established under Article 2009(1). The Parties shall promptly inform each section of the Secretariat of any changes made to the roster.

cc) Part Five, Chapter 11 (Investment), Section B — Settlement of Disputes between a Party and an Investor of Another Party

Art. 1115 Purpose

Without prejudice to the rights and obligations of the Parties under Chapter Twenty (Institutional Arrangements and Dispute Settlement Procedures), this Section establishes a mechanism for the settlement of investment disputes that assures both equal treatment among investors of the Parties in accordance with the principle of international reciprocity and due process before an impartial tribunal.

Art. 1116 Claim by an Investor of a Party on Its Own Behalf

1. An investor of a Party may submit to arbitration under this Section a claim that another Party has breached an obligation under:

(a) Section A or Article 1503(2) (State Enterprises), or

(b) Article 1502(3)(a) (Monopolies and State Enterprises) where the monopoly has acted in a manner inconsistent with the Party's obligations under Section A,

and that the investor has incurred loss or damage by reason of, or arising out of, that breach.

2. An investor may not make a claim if more than three years have elapsed from the date on which the investor first acquired, or should have first acquired, knowledge of the alleged breach and knowledge that the investor has incurred loss or damage.

Art. 1117 Claim by an Investor of a Party on Behalf of an Enterprise

1. An investor of a Party, on behalf of an enterprise of another Party that is a juridical person that the investor owns or controls directly or indirectly, may submit to arbitration under this Section a claim that the other Party has breached an obligation under:

(a) Section A or Article 1503(2) (State Enterprises), or

(b) Article 1502(3)(a) (Monopolies and State Enterprises) where the monopoly has acted in a manner inconsistent with the Party's obligations under Section A,

and that the enterprise has incurred loss or damage by reason of or arising out of, that breach.

2. An investor may not make a claim on behalf of an enterprise described in paragraph 1 if more than three years have elapsed from the date on which the enterprise first acquired, or should have first acquired, knowledge of the alleged breach and knowledge that the enterprise has incurred loss or damage.

3. Where an investor makes a claim under this Article and the investor or a non-controlling investor in the enterprise makes a claim under Article 1116 arising out of the same events that gave rise to the claim under this Article, and two or more of the claims are submitted to arbitration under Article 1120, the claims should be heard together by a Tribunal established under Article 1126, unless the Tribunal finds that the interests of a disputing party would be prejudiced thereby.

4. An investment may not make a claim under this Section.

Art. 1118 Settlement of a Claim through Consultation and Negotiation

The disputing parties should first attempt to settle a claim through consultation or negotiation.

Art. 1119 Notice of Intent to Submit a Claim to Arbitration

The disputing investor shall deliver to the disputing Party written notice of its intention to submit a claim to arbitration at least 90 days before the claim is submitted, which notice shall specify:

(a) the name and address of the disputing investor and, where a claim is made under Article 1117, the name and address of the enterprise;

(b) the provisions of this Agreement alleged to have been breached and any other relevant provisions;

(c) the issues and the factual basis for the claim; and

(d) the relief sought and the approximate amount of damages claimed.

Art. 1120 Submission of a Claim to Arbitration

1. Except as provided in Annex 1120.1, and provided that six months have elapsed since the events giving rise to a claim, a disputing investor may submit the claim to arbitration under:

(a) the ICSID Convention, provided that both the disputing Party and the Party of the investor are parties to the Convention;

(b) the Additional Facility Rules of ICSID, provided that either the disputing Party or the Party of the investor, but not both, is a party to the ICSID Convention; or

(c) the UNCITRAL Arbitration Rules

2. The applicable arbitration rules shall govern the arbitration except to the extent modified by this Section.

Art. 1121 Conditions Precedent to Submission of a Claim to Arbitration

1. A disputing investor may submit a claim under Article 1116 to arbitration only if:

(a) the investor consents to arbitration in accordance with the procedures set out in this Agreement; and

(b) the investor and, where the claim is for loss or damage to an interest in an enterprise of another Party that is a juridical person that the investor owns or controls directly or indirectly, the enterprise, waive their right to initiate or continue before any administrative tribunal or court under the law of any Party, or other dispute settlement procedures, any proceedings with respect to the measure of the disputing Party that is alleged to be a breach referred to in Article 1116, except for proceedings for injunctive, declaratory or other extraordinary relief, not involving the payment of damages, before an administrative tribunal or court under the law of the disputing Party.

2. A disputing investor may submit a claim under Article 1117 to arbitration only if both the investor and the enterprise:

(a) consent to arbitration in accordance with the procedures set out in this Agreement; and

(b) waive their right to initiate or continue before any administrative tribunal or court under the law of any Party, or other dispute settlement procedures, any proceedings with respect to the measure of the disputing Party that is alleged to be a breach referred to in Article 1117, except for proceedings for injunctive, declaratory or other extraordinary relief, not involving the payment of damages, before an administrative tribunal or court under the law of the disputing Party.

3. A consent and waiver required by this Article shall be in writing, shall be delivered to the disputing Party and shall be included in the submission of a claim to arbitration.

4. Only where a disputing Party has deprived a disputing investor of control of an enterprise:

(a) a waiver from the enterprise under paragraph 1(b) or 2(b) shall not be required; and

(b) Annex 1120.1(A)(b) shall not apply.

Art. 1122 Consent to Arbitration

1. Each Party consents to the submission of a claim to arbitration in accordance with the procedures set out in this Agreement.

2. The consent given by paragraph 1 and the submission by a disputing investor of a claim to arbitration shall satisfy the requirement of:

(a) Chapter 11 of the ICSID Convention (Jurisdiction of the Centre) and the Additional Facility Rules for written consent of the parties;

(b) Article II of the New York Convention for an agreement in writing; and

(c) Article I of the Inter-American Convention for an agreement.

Art. 1123 Number of Arbitrators and Method of Appointment

Except in respect of a Tribunal established under Article 1126, and unless the disputing parties otherwise agree, the Tribunal shall comprise three arbitrators, one arbitrator appointed by each of the disputing parties and the third, who shall be the presiding arbitrator, appointed by agreement of the disputing parties.

Art. 1124 Constitution of a Tribunal When a Party Fails to Appoint an Arbitrator or the Disputing Parties Are Unable to Agree on a Presiding Arbitrator

1. The Secretary-General shall serve as appointing authority for an arbitration under this Section.

2. If a Tribunal, other than a Tribunal established under Article 1126, has not been constituted within 90 days from the date that a claim is submitted to arbitration, the Secretary-General, on the request of either disputing party, shall appoint, in his discretion, the arbitrator or arbitrators not yet appointed, except that the presiding arbitrator shall be appointed in accordance with paragraph 3.

3. The Secretary-General shall appoint the presiding arbitrator from the roster of presiding arbitrators referred to in paragraph 4, provided that the presiding arbitrator shall not be a national of the disputing Party or a national of the Party of the disputing investor. In the event that no such presiding arbitrator is available to serve, the Secretary-General shall appoint, from the ICSID Panel of Arbitrators, a presiding arbitrator who is not a national of any of the Parties.

4. On the date of entry into force of this Agreement, the Parties shall establish, and thereafter maintain, a roster of 45 presiding arbitrators meeting the qualifications of the Convention and rules referred to in Article 1120 and experienced in international law and investment matters. The roster members shall be appointed by consensus and without regard to nationality

Art. 1125 Agreement to Appointment of Arbitrators

For purposes of Article 39 of the ICSID Convention and Article 7 of Schedule C to the ICSID Additional Facility Rules, and without prejudice to an objection to an arbitrator based on Article 1124(3) or on a ground other than nationality:

(a) the disputing Party agrees to the appointment of each individual member of a Tribunal established under the ICSID Convention or the ICSID Additional Facility Rules:

(b) a disputing investor referred to in Article 1116 may submit a claim to arbitration, or continue a claim, under the ICSID Convention or the ICSID Additional Facility Rules, only on condition that the disputing investor agrees by writing to the appointment of each individual member of the Tribunal; and

c) a disputing investor referred to in Article 1117(1) may submit a claim to arbitration, or continue a claim, under the ICSID Convention or the ICSID Additional Facility Rules, only on condition that the disputing investor and the enterprise agree in writing to the appointment of each individual member of the Tribunal.

Art. 1126 Consolidation

1. A Tribunal established under this Article shall be established under the UNCITRAL Arbitration Rules and shall conduct its proceedings in accordance with those Rules, except as modified by this Section.

2. Where a Tribunal established under this Article is satisfied that claims have been submitted to arbitration under Article 1120 that have a question of law or fact in common, the Tribunal may, in the interests of fair and efficient resolution of the claims, and after hearing the disputing parties, by order:

(a) assume jurisdiction over, and hear and determine together, all or part of the claims; or

(b) assume jurisdiction over, and hear and determine one or more of the claims, the determination of which it believes would assist in the resolution of the others.

3. A disputing party that seeks an order under paragraph 2 shall request the Secretary-General to establish a Tribunal and shall specify in the request:

(a) the name of the disputing Party or disputing investors against which the order is sought;

(b) the nature of the order sought; and

(c) the grounds on which the order is sought.

4. The disputing party shall deliver to the disputing Party or disputing investors against which the order is sought a copy of the request.

5. Within 60 days of receipt of the request, the Secretary-General shall establish a Tribunal comprising three arbitrators. The Secretary-General shall appoint the presiding arbitrator from the roster referred to in Article 1124(4). In the event that no such presiding arbitrator is available to serve, the Secretary-General shall appoint, from the ICSID Panel of Arbitrators, a presiding arbitrator who is not a national of any of the Parties. The Secretary-General shall appoint the two other members from the roster re-

ferred to by Article 1124(4), and to the extent not available from that roster, from the ICSID Panel of Arbitrators, and to the extent not available from that Panel, in the discretion of the Secretary-General. One member shall be a national of the disputing Party and one member shall be a national of a Party of the disputing investors.

6. Where a Tribunal has been established under this Article, a disputing investor that has submitted a claim to arbitration under Article 1116 or 1117 and that has not been named in a request made under paragraph 3 may make a written request to the Tribunal that it be included in an order made under paragraph 2, and shall specify in the request:

(a)   the name and address of the disputing investor;

(b)   the nature of the order sought; and

(c)   the grounds on which the order is sought.

7. A disputing investor referred to in paragraph 6 shall deliver a copy of its request to the disputing parties named in a request made under paragraph 3.

8. A Tribunal established under Article 1120 shall not have jurisdiction to decide a claim, or a part of a claim, over which a Tribunal established under this Article has assumed jurisdiction.

9. On application of a disputing party, a Tribunal established under this Article, pending its decision under paragraph 2, may order that the proceedings of a Tribunal established under Article 1120 be stayed, unless the latter Tribunal has already adjourned its proceedings.

10. A disputing Party shall deliver to the Secretariat, within 15 days of receipt by the disputing Party, a copy of:

(a)   a request for arbitration made under paragraph (1) of Article 36 of the ICSID Convention;

(b)   a notice of arbitration made under Article 2 of Schedule C of the ICSID Additional Facility Rules; or

(c)   a notice of arbitration given under the UNCITRAL Arbitration Rules.

11. A disputing Party shall deliver to the Secretariat a copy of a request made under paragraph 3:

(a)   within 15 days of receipt of the request, in the case of a request made by a disputing investor;

(b)   within 15 days of making the request, in the case of a request made by the disputing Party.

12. A disputing Party shall deliver to the Secretariat a copy of a request made under paragraph 6 within 15 days of receipt of the request.

13. The Secretariat shall maintain a public register of the documents referred to in paragraphs 10, 11 and 12.

Art. 1127 Notice

A disputing Party shall deliver to the other Parties:

(a)   written notice of a claim that has been submitted to arbitration no later than 30 days after the date that the claim is submitted; and

(b)   copies of all pleadings filed in the arbitration.

Art. 1128 Participation by a Party

On written notice to the disputing parties, a Party may make submissions to a Tribunal on a question of interpretation of this Agreement.

Art. 1129 Documents

1. A Party shall be entitled to receive from the disputing Party, at the cost of the requesting Party a copy of:

(a)   the evidence that has been tendered to the Tribunal; and

(b)   the written argument of the disputing parties.

2. A Party receiving information pursuant to paragraph 1 shall treat the information as if it were a disputing Party.

Art. 1130 Place of Arbitration

Unless the disputing parties agree otherwise, a Tribunal shall hold an arbitration in the territory of a Party that is a party to the New York Convention, selected in accordance with:

(a)   the ICSID Additional Facility Rules if the arbitration is under those Rules or the ICSID Convention; or

(b)   the UNCITRAL Arbitration Rules if the arbitration is under those Rules.

Art. 1131 Governing Law

1. A Tribunal established under this Section shall decide the issues in dispute in accordance with this Agreement and applicable rules of international law.

2. An interpretation by the Commission of a provision of this Agreement shall be binding on a Tribunal established under this Section.

Art. 1132 Interpretation of Annexes

1. Where a disputing Party asserts as a defense that the measure alleged to be a breach is within the scope of a reservation or exception set out in Annex I, Annex II, Annex III or Annex IV, on request of the disputing Party, the Tribunal shall request the interpretation of the Commission on the issue. The Commission, within 60 days of delivery of the request, shall submit in writing its interpretation to the Tribunal.

2. Further to Article 1131(2), a Commission interpretation submitted under paragraph 1 shall be binding on the Tribunal. If the Commission fails to submit an interpretation within 60 days, the Tribunal shall decide the issue.

Art. 1133 Expert Reports

Without prejudice to the appointment of other kinds of experts where authorized by the applicable arbitration rules, a Tribunal, at the request of a disputing party or, unless the disputing parties disapprove, on its own initiative, may appoint one or more experts to report to it in writing on any factual issue concerning environmental, health, safety or other scientific matters raised by a disputing party in a proceeding, subject to such terms and conditions as the disputing parties may agree.

Art. 1134 Interim Measures of Protection

A Tribunal may order an interim measure of protection to preserve the rights of a disputing party, or to ensure that the Tribunal's jurisdiction is made fully effective, including an order to preserve evidence in the possession or control of a disputing party or to protect the Tribunal's jurisdiction. A Tribunal may not order attachment or enjoin the application of the measure alleged to constitute a breach referred to in Article 1116 or 1117. For purposes of this paragraph, an order includes a recommendation.

Art. 1135 Final Award

1. Where a Tribunal makes a final award against a Party, the Tribunal may award, separately or in combination, only:

(a) monetary damages and any applicable interest;

(b) restitution of property, in which case the award shall provide that the disputing Party may pay monetary damages and any applicable interest in lieu of restitution,

A tribunal may also award costs in accordance with the applicable arbitration rules.

2. Subject to paragraph 1, where a claim is made under Article 1117(1):

(a) an award of restitution of property shall provide that restitution be made to the enterprise;

(b) an award of monetary damages and any applicable interest shall provide that the sum be paid to the enterprise; and

(c) the award shall provide that it is made without prejudice to any right that any person may have in the relief under applicable domestic law.

3. A Tribunal may not order a Party to pay punitive damages.

Art. 1136 Finality and Enforcement of an Award

1. An award made by a Tribunal shall have no binding force except between the disputing parties and in respect of the particular case.

2. Subject to paragraph 3 and the applicable review procedure for an interim award, a disputing party shall abide by and comply with an award without delay.

3. A disputing party may not seek enforcement of a final award until:

(a) in the case of a final award made under the ICSID Convention

    (i)   120 days have elapsed from the date the award was rendered and no disputing party has requested revision or annulment of the award, or

   (ii)   revision or annulment proceedings have been completed; and

   (b)   in the case of a final award under the ICSID Additional Facility Rules or the UNCITRAL Arbitration Rules

    (i)   three months have elapsed from the date the award was rendered and no disputing party has commenced a proceeding to revise, set aside or annul the award, or

   (ii)   a court has dismissed or allowed an application to revise, set aside or annul the award and there is no further appeal.

4. Each Party shall provide for the enforcement of an award in its territory.

5. If a disputing Party fails to abide by or comply with a final award, the Commission, on delivery of a request by a Party whose investor was a party to the arbitration, shall establish a panel under Article 2008 (Request for an Arbitral Panel). The requesting Party may seek in such proceedings:

   (a)   a determination that the failure to abide by or comply with the final award is inconsistent with the obligations of this Agreement; and

   (b)   a recommendation that the Party abide by or comply with the final award.

6. A disputing investor may seek enforcement of an arbitration award under the ICSID Convention, the New York Convention or the Inter-American Convention regardless of whether proceedings have been taken under paragraph 5.

7. A claim that is submitted to arbitration under this Section shall be considered to arise out of a commercial relationship or transaction for purposes of Article I of the New York Convention and Article I of the Inter-American Convention.

Art. 1137 General

Time when a Claim is Submitted to Arbitration

1. A claim is submitted to arbitration under this Section when:

   (a)   the request for arbitration under paragraph (1) of Article 36 of the ICSID Convention has been received by the Secretary-General;

   (b)   the notice of arbitration under Article 2 of Schedule C of the ICSID Additional Facility Rules has been received by the Secretary-General; or

   (c)   the notice of arbitration given under the UNCITRAL Arbitration Rules is received by the disputing Party.

Service of Documents

2. Delivery of notice and other documents on a Party shall be made to the place named for that Party in Annex 1137.2.

Receipts under Insurance or Guarantee Contracts

3. In an arbitration under this Section, a Party shall not assert, as a defense, counterclaim, right of setoff or otherwise, that the disputing investor has received or will receive, pursuant to an insurance or guarantee contract, indemnification or other compensation for all or part of its alleged damages.

Publication of an Award

4. Annex 1137.4 applies to the Parties specified in that Annex with respect to, publication of an award.

Art. 1138 Exclusions

1. Without prejudice to the applicability or non-applicability of the dispute settlement provisions of this Section or of Chapter Twenty (Institutional Arrangements and Dispute Settlement Procedures) to other actions taken by a Party pursuant to Article 2102 (National Security), a decision by a Party to prohibit or restrict the acquisition of an investment in its territory by an investor of another Party, or its investment, pursuant to that Article shall not be subject to such provisions.

2. The dispute settlement provisions of this Section and of Chapter Twenty shall not apply to the matters referred to in Annex 1138.2.

SECTION C — DEFINITIONS

Art. 1139 Definitions

For purposes of this Chapter:

disputing investor means an investor that makes a claim under Section B;

disputing parties means the disputing investor and the disputing Party;

disputing party means the disputing investor or the disputing Party;

disputing Party means a Party against which a claim is made under Section B;

enterprise means an "enterprise" as defined in Article 201 (Definitions of General Application), and a branch of an enterprise;

enterprise of a Party means an enterprise constituted or organized under the law of a Party, and a branch located in the territory of a Party and carrying out business activities there.

equity or debt securities includes voting and non-voting shares, bonds, convertible debentures, stock options and warrants;

G7 Currency means the currency of Canada, France, Germany, Italy, Japan, the United Kingdom of Great Britain and Northern Ireland or the United States;

ICSID means the International Centre for Settlement of Investment Disputes;

ICSID Convention means the Convention on the Settlement of Investment Disputes between States and Nationals of other States, done at Washington, March 18, 1965;

Inter-American Convention means the *Inter-American Convention on International Commercial Arbitration*, done at Panama, January 30, 1975;

investment means:

(a) an enterprise;

(b) an equity security of an enterprise;

(c) a debt security of an enterprise

(i)   where the enterprise is an affiliate of the investor, or

(ii) where the original maturity of the debt security is at least three years, but does not include a debt security, regardless of original maturity, of a state enterprise;

(d) loan to an enterprise

(i)   where the enterprise is an affiliate of the investor, or

(ii) where the original maturity of the loan is at least three years, but does not include a loan, regardless of original maturity, to a state enterprise;

(e) an interest in an enterprise that entitles the owner to share in income or profits of the enterprise;

(f) an interest in an enterprise that entitles the owner to share in the assets of that enterprise on dissolution, other than a debt security or a loan excluded from subparagraph (c) or (d);

(g) real estate or other property, tangible or intangible, acquired in the expectation or used for the purpose of economic benefit or other business purposes; and

(h) interests arising from the commitment of capital or other resources in the territory of a Party to economic activity in such territory, such as under

(i)   contracts involving the presence of an investor's property in the territory of the Party, including turnkey or construction contracts, or concessions, or

(ii) contracts where remuneration depends substantially on the production, revenues or profits of an enterprise;

but investment does not mean,

(i)   claims to money that arise solely from

(i)   commercial contracts for the sale of goods or services by a national or enterprise in the territory of a Party to an enterprise in the territory of another Party, or

(ii) the extension of credit in connection with a commercial transaction such as trade financing, other than a loan covered by subparagraph (d);

(j)   any other claims to money, that do not involve the kinds of interests set out in subparagraphs (a) through (h);

investment of an investor of a Party means an investment owned or controlled directly or indirectly by an investor of such Party;

investor of a Party means a Party or state enterprise thereof, or a national or an enterprise of such Party, that seeks to make, is making or has made an investment;

investor of a non-Party means an investor other than an investor of a Party, that seeks to make, is making or has made an investment;

New York Convention means the *United Nations Convention on the Recognition and Enforcement of Foreign Arbitral Awards*, done at New York, June 10, 1958;

Secretary-General means the Secretary-General of ICSID;

transfers means transfers and international payments;

Tribunal means an arbitration tribunal established under Article 1120 or 1126; and

UNCITRAL Arbitration Rules means the arbitration rules of the United Nations Commission on International Trade Law, approved by the United Nations General Assembly on December 15, 1976.

ANNEX 1120.1 — SUBMISSION OF A CLAIM TO ARBITRATION

MEXICO

With respect to the submission of a claim to arbitration:

(a)   an investor of another Party may not allege that Mexico has breached an obligation under

(i)   Section A or Article 1503(2) (State Enterprises), or

(ii)   Article 1502(3)(a) (Monopolies and State Enterprises) where the monopoly has acted in a manner inconsistent with the Party's obligations under Section A,

both in an arbitration under this Section and in proceedings before a Mexican court or administrative tribunal; and

(b)   where an enterprise of Mexico that is a juridical person that an investor of another Party owns or controls directly or indirectly alleges in proceedings before a Mexican court or administrative tribunal that Mexico has breached an obligation under:

(i)   Section A or Article 1503(2) (State Enterprises), or

(ii)   Article 1502(3)(a) (Monopolies and State Enterprises) where the monopoly has acted in a manner inconsistent with the Party's obligations under Section A,

the investor may not allege the breach by an arbitration under this Section.

ANNEX 1137.2 — SERVICE OF DOCUMENTS ON A PARTY UNDER SECTION B

Each Party shall set out in this Annex and publish in its official journal by January 1, 1994, the place for delivery of notice and other documents under this Section.

ANNEX 1137.4 — PUBLICATION OF AN AWARD

CANADA

Where Canada is the disputing Party, either Canada or a disputing investor that is a party to the arbitration may make an award public.

MEXICO

Where Mexico is the disputing Party, the applicable arbitration rules apply to the publication of an award.

UNITED STATES

Where the United States is the disputing Party, either the United States or a disputing investor that is a party to the arbitration may make an award public.

ANNEX 1138.2 — EXCLUSIONS FROM DISPUTE SETTLEMENT

CANADA

A decision by Canada following a review under the Investment Canada Act, with respect to whether or not to permit an acquisition that is subject to review, shall not be subject to the dispute settlement provisions of Section B or of Chapter Twenty (Institutional Arrangements and Dispute Settlement Procedures).

MEXICO

A decision by the National Commission on Foreign Investment ("Comisión Nacional de Inversiones Extranjeras") following a review pursuant to Annex I, page I-M-4, with respect to whether or not to permit an acquisition that is subject to review, shall not be subject to the dispute settlement provisions of Section B or of Chapter Twenty (Institutional Arrangements and Dispute Settlement Procedures).

dd) Part Five, Chapter 14, Financial Services, Articles 1414 and 1415

Art. 1414 Dispute Settlement

1. Section B of Chapter Twenty (Institutional Arrangements and Dispute Settlement Procedures) applies as modified by this Article to the settlement of disputes arising under this Chapter.

2. The Parties shall establish by January 1, 1994 and maintain a roster of up to 15 individuals who are willing and able to serve as financial services panelists. Financial services roster members shall be appointed by consensus for terms of three years, and may be reappointed.

3. Financial services roster members shall:

(a) have expertise or experience in financial services law or practice, which may include the regulation of financial institutions;

(b) be chosen strictly on the basis of objectivity, reliability and sound judgment; and

(c) meet the qualifications set out in Article 2009(2)(b) and (c) (Roster).

4. Where a Party claims that a dispute arises under this Chapter, Article 2011 (Panel Selection) shall apply, except that:

(a) where the disputing Parties so agree, the panel shall be composed entirely of panelists meeting the qualifications in paragraph 3; and

(b) in any other case,

(i) each disputing Party may select panelists meeting the qualifications set out in paragraph 3 or in Article 2010(1) (Qualifications of Panelists), and

(ii) if the Party complained against invokes Article 1410, the chair of the panel shall meet the qualifications set out in paragraph 3.

5. In any dispute where a panel finds a measure to be inconsistent with the obligations of this Agreement and the measure affects:

(a) only the financial services sector, the complaining Party may suspend benefits only in the financial services sector;

(b) the financial services sector and any other sector, the complaining Party may suspend benefits in the financial services sector that have an effect equivalent to the effect of the measure in the Party's financial services sector; or

(c) only a sector other than the financial services sector, the complaining Party may not suspend benefits in the financial services sector.

Art. 1415 Investment Disputes in Financial Services

1. Where an investor of another Party submits a claim under Article 1116 or 1117 to arbitration under Section B of Chapter Eleven (Investment — Settlement of Disputes between a Party and an Investor of Another Party) against a Party and the disputing Party invokes Article 1410, on request of the disputing Party, the Tribunal shall refer the matter in writ-

ing to the Committee for a decision. The Tribunal may not proceed pending receipt of a decision or report under this Article.

2. In a referral pursuant to paragraph 1, the Committee shall decide the issue of whether and to what extent Article 1410 is a valid defense to the claim of the investor. The Committee shall transmit a copy of its decision to the Tribunal and to the Commission. The decision shall be binding on the Tribunal.

3. Where the Committee has not decided the issue within 60 days of the receipt of the referral under paragraph 1, the disputing Party or the Party of the disputing investor may request the establishment of an arbitral panel under Article 2008 (Request for an Arbitral Panel). The panel shall be constituted in accordance with Article 1414. Further to Article 2017 (Final Report), the panel shall transmit its final report to the Committee and to the Tribunal. The report shall be binding on the Tribunal.

4. Where no request for the establishment of a panel pursuant to paragraph 3 has been made within 10 days of the expiration of the 60-day period referred to in paragraph 3, the Tribunal may proceed to decide the matter.

ee) Part Two: Trade in Goods, Chapter 8: Emergency Action

Art. 804 Dispute Settlement in Emergency Action Matters

No Party may request the establishment of an arbitral panel under Art. 2008 (Request for an Arbitral Panel) regarding any proposed emergency action.

e) North American Agreement on Labour Cooperation of 1993

PART FIVE — RESOLUTION OF DISPUTES

Art. 27 Consultations

1. Following presentation to the Council under Article 26(1) of an ECE final report that addresses the enforcement of a Party's occupational safety and health, child labor or minimum wage technical labor standards, any Party may request in writing consultations with any other Party regarding whether there has been a persistent pattern of failure by that other Party to effectively enforce such standards in respect of the general subject matter addressed in the report.

2. The requesting Party shall deliver the request to the other Parties and to the Secretariat.

3. Unless the Council otherwise provides in its rules and procedures established under Article 9(2), a third Party that considers it has a substantial interest in the matter shall be entitled to participate in the consultations on delivery of written notice to the other Parties and to the Secretariat.

4. The consulting Parties shall make every attempt to arrive at a mutually satisfactory resolution of the matter through consultations under this Article.

Art. 28 Initiation of Procedures

1. If the consulting Parties fail to resolve the matter pursuant to Article 27 within 60 days of delivery of a request for consultations, or such other period as the consulting Parties may agree, any such Party may request in writing a special session of the Council.

2. The requesting Party shall state in the request the matter complained of and shall deliver the request to the other Parties and to the Secretariat.

3. Unless it decides otherwise, the Council shall convene within 20 days of delivery of the request and shall endeavor to resolve the dispute promptly.

4. The Council may:

(a) call on such technical advisers or create such working groups or expert groups as it deems necessary,

(b) have recourse to good offices, conciliation, mediation or such other dispute resolution procedures, or

(c) make recommendations,

as may assist the consulting Parties to reach a mutually satisfactory resolution of the dispute. Any such recommendations shall be made public if the Council, by a two-thirds vote, so decides.

5. Where the Council decides that a matter is more properly covered by another agreement or arrangement to which the consulting Parties are party, it shall refer the matter to those Parties for appropriate action in accordance with such other agreement or arrangement.

Art. 29   Request for an Arbitral Panel

1. If the matter has not been resolved within 60 days after the Council has convened pursuant to Article 28, the Council shall, on the written request of any consulting Party and by a two-thirds vote convene an arbitral panel to consider the matter where the alleged persistent pattern of failure by the Party complained against to effectively enforce its occupational safety and health, child labor or minimum wage technical labor standards is:

(a)   trade-related; and

(b)   covered by mutually recognized labor laws.

2. A third Party that considers it has a substantial interest in the matter shall be entitled to join as a complaining Party on delivery of written notice of its intention to participate to the disputing Parties and the Secretariat. The notice shall be delivered at the earliest possible time, and in any event no later than seven days after the date of the vote of the Council to convene a panel.

3. Unless otherwise agreed by the disputing Parties, the panel shall be established and perform its functions in a manner consistent with the provisions of this Part.

Art. 30   Roster

1. The Council shall establish and maintain a roster of up to 45 individuals who are willing and able to serve as panelists. The roster members shall be appointed by consensus for terms of three years, and may be reappointed.

2. Roster members shall:

(a)   have expertise or experience in labor law or its enforcement, or in the resolution of disputes arising under international agreements, or other relevant scientific, technical or professional expertise or experience;

(b)   be chosen strictly on the basis of objectivity, reliability and sound judgment;

(c)   be independent of, and not be affiliated with or take instructions from, any Party or the Secretariat; and

(d)   comply with a code of conduct to be established by the Council.

Art. 31   Qualifications of Panelists

1. All panelists shall meet the qualifications set out in Article 30.

2. Individuals may not serve as panelists for a dispute where:

(a) they have participated pursuant to Article 28(4) or participated as members of an ECE that addressed the matter; or

b) they have, or a person or organization, with which they are affiliated has, an interest in the matter, as set out in the code of conduct established under Article 30(2)(d).

Art. 32   Panel Selection

1. Where there are two disputing Parties, the following procedures shall apply:

(a) The panel shall comprise five members.

(b) The disputing Parties shall endeavor to agree on the chair of the panel within 15 days after the Council votes to convene the panel. If the disputing Parties are unable to agree on the chair within this period, the disputing Party chosen by lot shall select within five days a chair who is not a citizen of that Party.

(c) Within 15 days of selection of the chair, each disputing Party shall select two panelists who are citizens of the other disputing Party.

(d) If a disputing Party fails to select its panelists within such period, such panelists shall be selected by lot from among the roster members who are citizens of the other disputing Party.

2. Where there are more than two disputing Parties, the following procedures shall apply:

(a) The panel shall comprise five members.

(b) The disputing Parties shall endeavor to agree on the chair of the panel within 15 days after the Council votes to convene the panel. If the disputing Parties are unable to agree on the chair within this period, the Party or Parties on the side of the dispute chosen by lot shall select within 10 days a chair who is not a citizen of such Party or Parties.

(c) Within 30 days of selection of the chair, the Party complained against shall select two panelists, one of whom is a citizen of a complaining Party, and the other of whom is a citizen of another complaining Party. The complaining Parties shall select two panelists who are citizens of the Party complained against.

(d) If any disputing Party fails to select a panelist within such period, such panelist shall be selected by lot in accordance with the citizenship criteria of subparagraph (c).

3. Panelists shall normally be selected from the roster. Any disputing Party may exercise a peremptory challenge against any individual not on the roster who is proposed as a panelist by a disputing Party within 30 days after the individual has been proposed.

4. If a disputing Party believes that a panelist is in violation of the code of conduct, the disputing Parties shall consult and if they agree, the panelist

shall be removed and a new panelist shall be selected in accordance with this Article.

Art. 33   Rules of Procedure

1. The Council shall establish Model Rules of Procedure. The procedures shall provide:

(a) a right to at least one hearing before the panel;

(b) the opportunity to make initial and rebuttal written submissions; and

(c) that no panel may disclose which panelists are associated with majority or minority opinions.

2. Unless the disputing Parties otherwise agree, panels convened under this Part shall be established and conduct their proceedings in accordance with the Model Rules of Procedure.

3. Unless the disputing Parties otherwise agree within 20 days after the Council votes to convene the panel, the terms of reference shall be:

"To examine, in light of the relevant provisions of the Agreement, including those contained in Part Five, whether there has been a persistent pattern of failure by the Party complained against to effectively enforce its occupational safety and health, child labor or minimum wage technical labor standards, and to make findings, determinations and recommendations in accordance with Article 36(2)."

Art. 34   Third Party Participation

A Party that is not a disputing Party, on delivery of a written notice to the disputing Parties and the Secretarial, shall be entitled to attend all hearings, to make written and oral submissions to the panel and to receive written submissions of the disputing Parties.

Art. 35   Role of Experts

On request of a disputing Party, or on its own initiative, the panel may seek information and technical advice from any person or body that it deems appropriate, provided that the disputing Parties so agree and subject to such terms and conditions as such Parties may agree.

Art. 36   Initial Report

1. Unless the disputing Parties otherwise agree, the panel shall base its report on the submissions and arguments of the disputing Parties and on any information before it pursuant to Article 35.

2. Unless the disputing Parties otherwise agree, the panel shall, within 180 days after the last panelist is selected, present to the disputing Parties an initial report containing:

(a) findings of fact;

(b) its determination as to whether there has been a persistent pattern of failure by the Party complained against to effectively enforce its occupational safety and health, child labor or minimum wage technical labor standards in a matter that is trade-related and covered by mutually recognized labor laws, or any other determination requested in the terms of reference; and

(c) in the event the panel makes an affirmative determination under subparagraph (b), its recommendations, if any, for the resolution of the dispute, which normally shall be that the Party complained against adopt and implement an action plan sufficient to remedy the patters of non-enforcement.

3. Panelists may furnish separate opinions on matters not unanimously agreed.

4. A disputing Party may submit written comments to the panel on its initial report within 30 days of presentation of the report.

5. In such an event, and after considering such written comments, the panel, on its own initiative or on the request of any disputing Party, may:

(a) request the views of any participating Party:

(b) reconsider its report; and

(c) make any further examination that it considers appropriate.

Art. 37   Final Report

1. The panel shall present to the disputing Parties a final report, including any separate opinions on matters not unanimously agreed, within 60 days of presentation of the initial report, unless the disputing Parties otherwise agree.

2. The disputing Parties shall transmit to the Council the final report of the panel, as well as any written views that a disputing Party desires to be appended, on a confidential basis within 15 days after it is presented to them.

3. The final report of the panel shall be published five days after it is transmitted to the Council.

Art. 38   Implementation of Final Report

If, in its final report, a panel determines that there has been a persistent pattern of failure by the Party complained against to effectively enforce its occupational safety and health, child labor or minimum wage technical labor standards, the disputing Parties may agree on a mutually satisfactory action plan, which normally shall conform with the determinations and recommendations of the panel. The disputing Parties shall promptly notify the Secretariat and the Council of any agreed resolution of the dispute.

Art. 39   Review of Implementation

1. If, in its final report, a panel determines that there has been a persistent pattern of failure by the Party complained against to effectively enforce its occupational safety and health, child labor or minimum wage technical labor standards, and:

(a) the disputing Parties have not agreed on an action plan under Article 38 within 60 days of the date of the final report, or

(b) the disputing Parties cannot agree on whether the Party complained against is fully implementing

(i) an action plan agreed under Article 38,

(ii) an action plan deemed to have been established by a panel under paragraph 2, or

(iii) an action plan approved or established by a panel under paragraph 4,

any disputing Party may request that the panel be reconvened. The requesting Party shall deliver the request in writing to the other Parties and to the Secretariat. The Council shall reconvene the panel on delivery of the request to the Secretariat.

2. No Party may make a request under paragraph 1(a) earlier than 60 days or later than 120 days after the date of the final report. If the disputing Parties have not agreed to an action plan and if no request was made under paragraph 1(a) the last action plan, if any, submitted by the Party complained against to the complaining Party or Parties within 60 days of the date of the final report, or such other period as the disputing Parties may agree, shall be deemed to have been established by the panel 120 days after the date of the final report.

3. A request under paragraph 1(b) may be made no earlier than 180 days after an action plan has been:

(a) agreed under Article 38,

(b) deemed to have been established by a panel under paragraph 2, or

(c) approved or established by a panel under paragraph 4,

and only during the term of any such action plan.

4. Where a panel has been reconvened under paragraph 1(a), it:

(a) shall determine whether any action plan proposed by the Party complained against is sufficient to remedy the pattern of non-enforcement and

(i) if so, shall approve the plan, or

(ii) if not, shall establish such a plan consistent with the law of the Party complained against, and

(b) may, where warranted, impose a monetary enforcement assessment in accordance with Annex 39,

within 90 days after the panel has been reconvened or such other period as the disputing Parties may agree.

5. Where a panel has been reconvened under paragraph 1(b), it shall determine either that:

(a) the Party complained against is fully implementing the action plan, in which case the panel may not impose a monetary enforcement assessment, or

(b) the Party complained against is not fully implementing the action plan in which case the panel shall impose a monetary enforcement assessment in accordance with Annex 39,

within 60 days after it has been reconvened or such other period as the disputing Parties may agree.

6. A panel reconvened under this Article shall provide that the Party complained against shall fully implement any action plan referred to in paragraph 4(a)(ii) or 5(b) and pay any monetary enforcement assessment imposed under paragraph 4(b) or 5(b) and any such provision shall be final.

Art. 40 Further Proceeding

A complaining Party may, at any time beginning 180 days after a panel determination under Article 39(5)(b), request in writing that a panel be reconvened to determine whether the Party complained against is fully implementing the action plan. On delivery of the request to the other Parties and the Secretariat, the Council shall reconvene the panel. The panel shall make the determination within 60 days after it has been reconvened or such other period as the disputing Parties may agree.

Art. 41 Suspension of Benefits

1. Subject to Annex 41A where a Party fails to pay a monetary enforcement assessment within 180 days after it is imposed by a panel:

(a) under Article 39(4)(b), or

(b) under Article 39(5)(b) except, where benefits may be suspended under paragraph 2(a),

any complaining Party or Parties may suspend, in accordance with Annex 41B, the application to the Party complained against of NAFTA benefits in an amount no greater than that sufficient to collect the monetary enforcement assessment.

2. Subject to Annex 41A, where a panel has made a determination under Article 39 (5)(b) and the panel

(a) has previously imposed a monetary enforcement assessment under Article 39(4)(b) or established an action plan under Article 39(4)(a)(ii) or

(b) has subsequently determined under Article 40 that a Party is not fully implementing an action plan,

the complaining Party or Parties may, in accordance with Annex 41B, suspend annually the application to the Party complained against of NAFTA benefits in an amount not greater than the monetary enforcement assessment imposed by the panel under Article 39(5)(b).

Where more than one complaining Party suspends benefits under paragraph 1 or 2, the combined suspension shall be not greater than the amount of the monetary enforcement assessment.

4. Where a Party has suspended benefits under paragraph 1 or 2, the Council shall, on the delivery of a written request by the Party complained against to the other Parties and the Secretariat, reconvene the panel to determine whether the monetary enforcement assessment has been paid or collected, or whether the Party complained against is fully implementing the action plan, as the case may be. The panel shall submit its report within 45 days after it has been reconvened. If the panel determines that the assessment has been paid or collected, or that the Party complained against is fully implementing the action plan, the suspension of benefits under paragraph 1 or 2, as the case may be, shall be terminated.

5. On the written request of the Party complained against, delivered to the other Parties and the Secretariat, the Council shall reconvene the panel to determine whether the suspension of benefits by the complaining Party or Parties pursuant to paragraph 1 or 2 is manifestly excessive. Within 45 days of the request, the panel shall present a report to the disputing Parties containing its determination.

3. Africa and the Arab Region

Africa is the region of the world with the greatest number of economic integration agreements. The economic cooperation experience started already under the colonial period and intensified after the decolonization process. In the 80s, Africa had the most economic integration communities in the world; however, the experiences were not very fruitful. Therefore, the OAU took initiatives to improve the situation which led in 1979 to a Declaration calling for the creation of an African Common Market and taking the engagement to promote economic integration on the African continent. The second step was taken one year later when the Lagos Plan of Action was adopted which emphasizes the necessity of building up an economic structure at continental level which was to take place in two phases:

During the 80s the existing economic integration communities should be strengthened and new ones created and during the 90s the preparation of the setting up of an African Common Market and of the realization of the objective of the African Economic Community was on the agenda.

With regard to provisions on dispute settlement it may be stated that a growing number of economic communities provided for a jurisdictional organ, mostly in rather general terms and leaving the regulation of details, particularly the elaboration of a statute, to the adoption of additional Protocols which have, however, as far as information is available, not been elaborated. This is the case for the ECCAS (Economic Community of Central African States), created on 19 October 1983 at Libreville, Gabon; articles 16 and 17 of the Treaty provide for the creation of a Court of Justice. The same is true for the SADC (South African Development Community), created at Windhoek, Namibia, on 17 August 1992, which provides in article 16 for a Tribunal as well as for the CEMAC (Communauté Economique de Monétaire de l'Afrique Centrale) created on 16 March 1994, which provides in article 2 for a Community Court of Justice. As there is no information concerning the statutes of those tribunals, the rather general articles of the treaties of those communities will not be reproduced here.

Only for four of the African economic communities have the necessary details been adopted concerning the functioning of the judicial organ, which therefore will be treated below in more detail.

a) West African Economic Community (CEAO)

On June 3, 1972 the West African Economic Community was founded, replacing the former Union Douanière des Etats de l'Afrique de l'Ouest (UDEAO). The CEAO seeks to achieve the economic integration of its members through the development of common policies with regard to transport and communication, agriculture, industry, external trade, tourism, etc. It emphasizes the need for expanded trade among the members, particularly with regard to agricultural and industrial products.

The Treaty instituting the CEAO has created four principal organs: the Conference of Chiefs of States, the Council of Ministers, the General Secretariat of the Community and the Court of Arbitration. Protocol "J" sets forth details governing the functioning of the Court. According to this Protocol, the Court is competent to settle disputes between "States of the Community or between one or more Member States of the Community with respect to the interpretation or application of the Treaty and of the Protocols appended thereto" (Protocol J, Art. 2). The right to bring a claim is granted to the member States and the Chairman of the Conference of Chiefs of States, the main administrative organ of the organization. Decisions of the Court are binding upon the parties.

The Court is to be composed of three permanent members and four alternate members, each of whom serve two year terms. The President of the Court, the two permanent members and the alternates are appointed by the Conference of Chiefs of States upon motion of the Council of Ministers. A quorum of three is required for rendering a judgment; decisions are taken by majority vote.

The Court is to set up its own rules of procedure at its first meeting.

The member States of the CEAO are Benin, Burkina Faso (ex Upper Volta), Ivory Coast, Mali, Mauritania, Niger and Senegal. Since each of these States is also a member State of the ECOWAS (see infra under point (b)), questions have arisen as to the relation between ECOWAS and CEAO. According to prevailing opinion, the relation is comparable to that between Benelux and the European Economic Community. However, it is unclear as to whether the more economically developed member States of CEAO are to be governed by the lower economic standard of the other ECOWAS member States.

Texts

C.E.A.O., Communauté Economique de l'Afrique de l'Ouest, Traité et Protocoles, Bamako 3 juin 1972/Abidjan 17avril 1973 (French)

African Law Digest Vol. 10 No.1 (1974) (only text of the Treaty) (French)

S. Belaouane-Gherari, Les organisations régionales africaines, Recueil de textes et documents, 1988, 138 ff.(French)

Bibliographical notes

K. von der Ropp, Die westafrikanische Wirtschaftsgemeinschaft, AP Vol. 24 (1973), pp. 467-475

L. K. Mytelka, A Genealogy of Francophone West and Equatorial African Regional Organization, The Journal of Modern African Studies (London) Vol. 12 (1976), pp. 297-320

M. A. Ajomo, Regional Economic Organisations: the African Experience, ICLQ Vol. 25 (1976), pp. 58-101

T. O. Elias, The Economic Community of West Africa, Journal of World Affairs
    Vol. 32 (1978), pp. 93 - 116
M. Hedrich/ K. von der Ropp, Chancen regionaler Integration in Westafrika, AP
    Vol. 29 (1978), pp. 84-97
R. Kühn/F. Seelow, Regionale Wirtschaftsintegration in Westafrika. CEAO und
    ECOWAS, Afrika Spectrum Vol. 14 (1979), pp. 135-149
K. Ouali, Intégration africaine, le cas de la CEAO (1982)
R. P. Lavergne, Regional Integration and Cooperation in West Africa (1997)

aa) Treaty of June 3, 1972

Art. 38   La composition, la compétence de la Cour Arbitrale et la procédure devant cette Cour sont précisées dans le protocole «J» annexé au présent
Traité et qui en fait parti intégrante.

bb) Protocol "J" with Respect to the Court of Arbitration of the West African Community

Art. 1   Le fonctionnement de la Cour Arbitrale de la Communauté instituée par
l'article 38 du Traité et sa composition sont définis par les articles
ci-après.

CHAPITRE PREMIER. DU FONCTIONNEMENT DE LA COUR

Art. 2   Les différends entre Etats de la Communauté ou entre un ou plusieurs
Etats membres de la Communauté relatifs à l'interprétation ou à
l'application du Traité et des protocoles qui lui sont annexés peuvent être
portés par les Etats membres parties au litige ou par le Président en exercice de la Conférence des Chefs d'Etat devant la Cour arbitrale de la
Communauté.

Art. 3   La Cour est saisie en la personne de son Président par une requête à lui
adressée concernant:

– Un exposé de l'objet du différend;

– Des conclusions de la partie requérante;

– Un exposé sommaire des moyens évoqués.

Art. 4   La Cour se réunit sur convocation de son Président.

Pour siéger et délibérer valablement, la Cour doit être composé du président et de deux juges.

Art. 5   Les parties sont représentées par un ou plusieurs agents mandatés à cet
effet. L'agent peut être assisté d'un ou plusieurs avocats inscrits à un barreau d'un Etat membre, ou d'un ou plusieurs Professeurs Conseils res-
sortissants d'un Etat membre dont la législation leur reconnaît le droit de
plaider.

Art. 6   Les agents, avocats et conseils devant la Cour jouissent, pendant la durée
de leurs missions, y compris le temps passé en voyage pour
l'accomplissement de celles-ci, des privilèges et immunités d'usage.

A ce titre, ils jouissent notamment de l'immunité de juridiction pour les
actes commis verbalement ou par écrit à l'occasion ou dans l'exécution de
leur mandat.

Art. 7 La procédure est contradictoire. Ses modalités sont fixées par la Cour Arbitrale qui, à l'occasion de sa première réunion, arrête son règlement de procédure.

Art. 8 La Cour peut procéder ou faire procéder à des mesures d'instruction. Les témoins régulièrement cités sont tenus de déférer et de se présenter à l'audience.

La Cour peut dénoncer aux autorités nationales le faux témoignage, la défaillance des témoins ou leur subordination.

Art. 9 La Cour peut demander aux parties de produire tous documents et de fournir toutes informations qu'elle estime nécessaires.

La Cour peut également demander aux Etats membres non parties au différend tous renseignements nécessaires à sa solution.

Art. 10 Les délibérations de la Cour sont et restent secrètes.

Art. 11 La Cour statue à la majorité.

Art. 12 Les sentences arbitrales de la Cour sont motivées.

Elles sont lues en audience publique.

Les décisions de la Cour sont obligatoires pour les parties au différend qui sont tenues de prendre les mesures que comporte leur exécution.

CHAPITRE II. DE LA COMPOSITION DE LA COUR

Art. 13 La Cour est composée de trois membres titulaires et de quatre membres suppléants désignés pour deux ans dans les conditions ci-après.

Art. 14 Le Président, les deux Juges titulaires et leurs suppléants sont nommés par la Conférence des Chefs d'Etat sur proposition du Conseil des Ministres quatre mois au plus tard à compter de la date d'entrée en vigueur du Traité.

Ils appartiennent obligatoirement à l'ordre judiciaire d'un Etat membre.

Art. 15 Les membres de la Cour prêtent serment d'exercer leurs fonctions impartialement et en toute conscience et de ne rien divulguer du secret des délibérations. Ce serment est prêté dans les formes prévues par la législation nationale de l'Etat du siège de la Communauté.

Art. 16 En cas de décès ou de démission d'un Juge titulaire ou d'un Juge suppléant, le Président de la Cour en informe la Conférence des Chefs d'Etat qui procède à la désignation du nouveau Juge titulaire ou suppléant.

En cas de démission les Juges titulaires et les Juges suppléants restent en fonction jusqu'à la nomination de leur successeur.

Art. 17 En cas de décès ou de démission du Président de la Cour, la Cour en informe la Conférence des Chefs d'Etat qui procède à la nomination d'un nouveau Président.

En cas de démission, le Président reste en fonction jusqu'à la nomination de son successeur.

Art. 18   Si l'un des membres de la Cour estime devoir ne pas participer au jugement d'une affaire déterminée, il en fait part à la Cour qui statue.

Si le Président estime qu'un des Juges ne doit pas participer au jugement d'une affaire déterminée il en saisit la Cour qui statue.

Art. 19   En cas d'empêchement d'un Juge titulaire son suppléant le remplace à titre temporaire; si, à son tour, celui-ci est empêché, un autre suppléant le remplace.

Le Juge suppléant appelé à participer au règlement d'une affaire siège dans cette affaire jusqu'à sa solution.

En cas d'empêchement du Président, la Conférence des Chefs d'Etat désigne un nouveau Président par la procédure d'urgence prévue à l'article 31 du Traité.

Art. 20   Les membres de la Cour jouissent, dans l'intérêt de l'accomplissement de la mission de la Cour, des privilèges, immunités et facilités normalement reconnus aux membres de juridictions internationales et des tribunaux arbitraux internationaux.

A ce titre, ils ne peuvent notamment être poursuivis ni recherchés pour les actes accomplis par eux en leur qualité officielle; ils continuent à bénéficier de cette immunité après la cessation de leurs fonctions.

A l'exception de celle protégeant les actes visés au deuxième paragraphe ci-dessus, les immunités prévues au présent article peuvent être levées par la Cour.

CHAPITRE III. DE L'ORGANISATION ET DES SERVICES DE LA COUR

Art. 21   La Cour siège au lieu du siège du Secrétariat Général de la Communauté.

Art. 22   Le fonctionnement des services de la Cour et, notamment, de son greffe, est assuré par les services de la Cour Suprême de l'Etat membre dans lequel est situé le siège du Secrétariat Général de la Communauté.

CHAPITRE IV. DES FRAIS DE FONCTIONNEMENT DE LA COUR

Art. 23   Les fonctions des membres de la Cour Arbitrale sont gratuites.

Les frais de séjour et de voyages à l'occasion des réunions de la Cour sont pris en charge par le budget du Secrétariat Général de la Communauté.

Les dépenses afférentes au Greffe de la Cour Arbitrale, à l'instruction des différends et à l'organisation matérielle des audiences sont également supportées par le budget du Secrétariat Général de la Communauté.

Lorsque la Cour décide, soit à la demande d'une des parties, soit d'office, d'avoir recours à des mesures extraordinaires d'instruction, elle ordonne aux parties ou à l'une d'entre elles, de consigner à un compte spécial, le montant des avances qu'elle estime nécessaires pour faire face à ces mesures d'instruction.

Ces avances font l'objet, le cas échéant, d'un remboursement par la Communauté.

b) Economic Community of West African States of May 28, 1975 as amended on July 24, 1993 (ECOWAS)

By the Treaty of Lagos of May 28, 1975 the West African States established the Economic Community of West African States (ECOWAS, English speaking/ CEDEAO, French speaking). This Treaty originated in 1963, when the Lagos Conference on Industrial Cooperation in West Africa was held under the auspices of the United Nations Economic Commission for Africa. The aim of the Community is the promotion of cooperation and development in all fields of economic activity. Among the organs of the Community, according to Art. 4 of the Treaty, is the Tribunal of the Community, which "shall ensure the observance of law and justice in the interpretation of the provisions of this Treaty" (Art. 11) and settle disputes arising "among Member States regarding the interpretation or application of this Treaty" which cannot be settled by direct agreement (Art. 56). In the case of such a dispute, each party may unilaterally lodge an application with the Tribunal whose decision is final.

The composition, competence, statute as well as all other matters relating to the Tribunal are to be prescribed by the principal Community organ: the Authority of Heads of State and Government.

Currently, the members of the Economic Community are: Benin, Burkina Faso (ex Upper Volta), Cape Verde, the Gambia, Ghana, Guinea, Guinea-Bissau, Ivory Coast, Liberia, Mali, Mauritania, Niger, Nigeria, Senegal, Sierra Leone and Togo.

Text

ILM Vol. 14 (1975), p. 1200 ff. (English and French)
S. Belaoune-Gherari, Les organisations régionales africaines (1988), 152 ff.
Revised Treaty
ILM 35 (1996), 663-692
African Journal of International and Comparative Law 8 (1996), 187-227

Bibliographical notes

H. M. A. Onitiri, Towards a West African Economic Community, The Nigerian Journal of Economic and Social Studies, Vol. 5 (1963), pp. 27-53

A. Y. Yansane, Westafrican Economic Integration: Is ECOWAS the Answer?, Africa Today, Vol. 24 (1977), pp. 43-59

B. Zagaris, The Economic Community of West African States ECOWAS: An Analysis and Prospects, Case Western Reserve JIL Vol. 10 (1978), pp. 93-128

R. Kühn/F. Seelow, Regionale Wirtschaftsintegration in Westafrika. CEAO und ECOWAS, Afrika Spectrum 14 (1979), pp. 135-149

S. Ajulo, Economic Community of West African States, in R. Bernhardt (ed.), EPIL, vol. II (1995), 16 ff. with bibliographical notes

D. van den Boom, Regionale Kooperation in Westafrika: Politik und Probleme der ECOWAS (1996)

K. O. Kufuor, Securing Compliance with the judgments of the ECOWAS Court of Justice, African Journal of International and Comparative Law 8 (1996), 1-11

M. Kamto, Les cours de justice des communautés et des organisations d'intégration économique africaines, African Yearbook of International Law 6 (1998), 107-150

aa) Article 15, 16 and 76 of the Treaty of 1993

Art. 15   The Court of Justice, Establishment and Function

[Formerly Art. 11, to which the Protocol on the Community Court, which has not yet been adapted to the amended Treaty, is still referring]

1. There is hereby established a Court of Justice of the Community.

2. The status, composition, powers, procedure and other issues concerning the Court of Justice shall be as set out in a Protocol relative thereto.

3. The Court of Justice shall carry out the functions assigned to it independently of the Member States and the institutions of the Community.

4. Judgements of the Court of Justice shall be binding on the Member States and the Institutions of the Community and on individuals and corporate bodies.

Art. 16   Arbitration Tribunal, Establishment and Functions

1. There is hereby established an Arbitration Tribunal of the Community.

2. The status, composition, powers, procedure and other issues concerning the Arbitration Tribunal shall be as set out in a Protocol relating thereto.

CHAPTER XV – DISPUTES

Art. 76   Settlement of Disputes

1. Any dispute regarding the interpretation or the application of the provisions of this Treaty shall be amicably settled through direct agreement without prejudice to the provisions of this Treaty and relevant Protocols.

2. Failing this, either party or any other Member States or the Authority may refer the matter to the Court of the Community whose decision shall be final and shall not be subject to appeal.

bb) Protocol A/P.1/7/91 on the Community Court of Justice of July 6, 1991

The High Contracting Parties

Mindful of Article 5 of the Treaty of the Economic Community of West African States, establishing the Authority of Heads of State and Government and defining its composition and functions;

Mindful of the provisions of Article 4 paragraph (e) and Article 11 of the Treaty relating respectively to the Institutions of the Community and the establishment of a Community Court of Justice;

Aware that the essential role of the Community Court of Justice is to ensure the observance of law and justice in the interpretation and application of the Treaty and the Protocols and Conventions annexed thereto, and to be seized with responsibility for settling such disputes as may be referred to it in accordance with the provisions of Article 56 of the Treaty and disputes between States and the Institutions of the Community;

Desirous of concluding a Protocol defining the composition, competence, statutes and other matters relating to the Community Court of Justice;

Hereby agree as follows

Art. 1   Definitions

In this Protocol, the following expressions shall have the meanings assigned to them hereunder:

"Treaty" means the Treaty of the Economic Community of West African States and includes Protocols and Conventions annexed thereto;

"Community" means the Economic Community of West African States established by Article I of the Treaty;

"Member State" or "Member States" means a Member State or Member States of the Community;

"Authority" means Authority of Heads of State and Government of the Community established by Article 5 of the Treaty;

"Chairman of the Authority" means the current Chairman of the Authority of Heads of State and Government of the Economic Community of West African States;

"Council" means the Council of Ministers of the Community established by Article 6 of the Treaty;

"Executive Secretariat" means the Executive Secretariat established in accordance with Article 8 (1) of the Treaty;

"Executive Secretary" means the Executive Secretary of the Community appointed under Article 8 (2) of the Treaty;

"Court" means the Community Court of Justice established by Article 11 of the Treaty;

"Member of the Court" or "Members of the Court" means a person or persons appointed as judge or judges in accordance with the provisions of Article 3.2 of the Protocol.

Art. 2   Establishment of the Court

1. The Community Court of Justice established under Article 11 of the Treaty as the principal legal organ of the Community shall be constituted and execute its functions in accordance with the provisions of this Protocol.

Art. 3   Composition

1. The Court shall be composed of independent judges selected and appointed by the Authority from nationals of the Member States who are persons of high moral character, and possess the qualification required in

their respective countries for appointment to the highest judicial officers, or are jurisconsults of recognised competence in international law.

2. The Court shall consist of seven (7) members, no two of whom may be nationals of the same State. The members of the Court shall elect a President and Vice-President from among their number who shall serve in that capacity for a term of three (3) years.

3. A person who for the purposes of membership of the Court could be regarded as a national of more than one Member State shall be deemed to be a national of the one in which he ordinarily exercises civil and political rights.

4. The Members of the Court shall be appointed by the Authority and selected from a list of persons nominated by Member States. No Member State shall nominate more than two persons.

5. The Executive Secretary shall prepare a list in alphabetical order of all the persons thus nominated which he shall forward to the Council.

6. The Authority shall appoint the Members of the Court from a shortlist of fourteen persons proposed by the Council.

7. No person below the age of 40 years and above the age of 60 years shall be eligible for appointment as a member of the Court. A member of the Court shall not be eligible for reappointment after the age of 65 years.

Art. 4   Terms of Office of Members of the Court

1. Members of the Court shall be appointed to serve in such office for a period of five years and may be eligible for reappointment for another term of five years only; provided, however, that of the members of the Court appointed for the first time, the terms of office of four members shall expire at the end of three years and the terms of the other three members shall expire at the end of five years.

2. The members of the Court whose terms are to expire at the end of the above-mentioned initial periods of three and five years shall be chosen by lot to be drawn by the Chairman of the Authority immediately after the first appointments have been made.

3. At the expiration of the term of a member of the Court, the said member shall remain in office until the appointment and assumption of office of his successor. Though replaced, he shall finish any cases which he may have begun.

4. In the absence of the President, or where it becomes impossible for the President to continue to carry out his duties and functions, the Vice-President shall assume these assignments of the President.

5. In the temporary absence of a member of the Court, another member shall be nominated to replace him in accordance with the provisions of the Rules of Procedure.

6. Where a member of the Court can no longer perform his duties, the Executive Secretary shall inform Council thereof. Council shall then propose to the Authority that a new member be appointed to replace him.

7. In the event of gross misconduct, inability to exercise his functions or physical or mental disability on the part of one of its members, the Court shall meet in plenary session to take cognisance of the fact. The Court shall then draw up a report which will be promptly transmitted to the Authority which may decide to relieve the member in question of his post.

8. Where the President of the Court cannot participate in the proceedings of a given case, he shall be replaced by the Vice-President or where the latter is absent he shall be replaced by another member of the Court appointed in accordance with the Rules of Procedure of the Court.

9. Where a member of the Court cannot participate in the proceedings of a given case, he shall inform the President of the Court who shall replace him with another member of the Court for the purposes of that case.

10. Whenever the Vice-President or any member of the Court replaces the President in accordance with the provisions of paragraph 8 of this Article, he shall exercise all the authority and powers vested in the office of the President of the Court.

11. No member of the Court may exercise any political or administrative function or engage in any other occupation of a professional nature.

Art. 5   Oath of Office or Solemn Declaration

1. Before assuming office, members of the Court shall take an oath of office or make a solemn declaration before the Chairman of the Authority.

2. The oath or declaration shall be as follows:

"I ... solemnly swear (declare) that I will perform my duties and exercise my powers as Member of the Court honorably, faithfully, impartially and conscienciously. "

Art. 6   Privileges and Immunities

1. The Court, and its members shall during the period of their tenure, enjoy privileges and immunities identical to those enjoyed by diplomatic missions and diplomatic agents in the territory of Member States, as well as those normally accorded to international courts and the members of such courts.

2. In this capacity, members of the Court shall not be liable to prosecution or arrest for acts carried out or statements made in the exercise of their functions.

Art. 7   Resignation

1. Members of the Court may resign at any time by addressing a letter of resignation to the Executive Secretary, who shall forward the letter to the Authority.

2. In case of resignation of a member of the Court, his duties shall end. However, such a member shall continue to hold office until the appointment and assumption of office of his successor.

3. In case of resignation of any member of the Court, the Executive Secretary shall inform Council which shall propose two persons to the Authority who shall appoint one to fill the vacant post.

Art. 8   Replacement of Any Member of the Court

A person nominated to replace a member of the Court, whose term of office has not expired shall be appointed under the same conditions as his predecessor and shall hold office for the remainder of his predecessor's term.

Art. 9   Competence of the Court

1. The Court shall ensure the observance of law and of the principles of equity in the interpretation and application of the provisions of the Treaty.

2. The Court shall also be competent to deal with disputes referred to it, in accordance with the provisions of Article 56 of the Treaty, by Member States or the Authority, when such disputes arise between the Member States or between one or more Member States and the Institutions of the Community on the interpretation or application of the provisions of the Treaty.

3. A Member State may, on behalf of its nationals, institute proceedings against another Member State or Institution of the Community, relating to the interpretation and application of the provisions of the Treaty, after attempts to settle the dispute amicably have failed.

4. The Court shall have any powers conferred upon it, specifically by the provisions of this Protocol.

Art. 10   Advisory Opinion

1. The Court may, at the request of the Authority, Council, one or more Member States, or the Executive Secretary, and any other institution of the Community, express, in an advisory capacity, a legal opinion on questions of the Treaty.

2. Requests for advisory opinion as contained in paragraph 1 of this Article shall be made in writing and shall contain a statement of the questions upon which advisory opinion is required. They must be accompanied by all relevant documents likely to throw light upon the question.

3. Upon receipt of the request referred to in paragraph 2 of this Article, the Chief Registrar shall immediately inform member States, notify them of the time limit fixed by the President for receipt of their written observations or for hearing their oral declarations.

4. The Court shall give the advisory opinion in public.

5. In the exercise of its advisory functions, the Court shall be governed by the provisions of this Protocol which apply in contentions cases, where the Court recognises them to be applicable.

Art. 11   Applications to the Tribunal

1. Cases may be brought before the Court by an application addressed to the Court Registry. This application shall set out the subject matter of the dispute and the parties involved and shall contain a summary of the argument put forward as well as the plea of the plaintiff.

2. The Chief Registrar of the Court shall immediately serve notice of the application and of all documents relating to the subject matter of the dispute to the other party, who shall make known his grounds for defence, within the time limit stipulated by the rules of procedure of the Court.

Art. 12   Representation Before the Court

Each party to a dispute shall be represented before the Court by one or more agents nominated by the party concerned for this purpose. The agents may, where necessary, request the assistance of one or more Advocates or Counsels who are recognised by the laws and regulations of the Member States as being empowered to appear in Court in their area of jurisdiction.

Art. 13   Proceedings Before the Court

1. Proceedings before the Court shall consist of two parts; written and oral.

2. Written proceedings shall consist of the application entered in the Court, notification of the application, the defence, the reply or counter-statement, the rejoinder and any other briefs or documents in support.

3. Documents comprising the written proceedings shall be addressed to the Chief Registrar of the Court in the order and within the time limit fixed by the Rules of Procedure of the Court. A copy of each document produced by one party shall be communicated to the other party.

4. The oral proceedings shall consist of the hearing of parties, agents witnesses, experts, advocates or counsels.

Art. 14   Sittings of the Court

1. The President shall issue summons to the parties to appear before the court. He shall determine the roll of the Court and preside over its sittings.

2. Sittings and deliberations of the Court shall be valid when the President and at least two judges are present, but such that any sitting of the Court shall comprise of an uneven number of its members.

3. Sittings of the Court shall be public. The Court may however sit in camera at the request of one of the parties or for reasons which only the Court may determine.

Art. 15   Production of Documents

1. At any time, the Court may request the parties to produce any documents and provide any information or explanation which it may deem useful. Formal note shall be taken of any refusal.

2. The Court may also request a Member State which is not involved in the dispute or any Community Institution to make available any information which it deems necessary for the settlement of the dispute.

Art. 16   Enquiries and Expert Opinion

The Court may, in any circumstances, and, in accordance with its Rules of Procedure, order any manner of judicial enquiry, summon any person, organisation or institution to make available any information which it deems necessary for the settlement of the dispute.

Art. 17   Examination of Witnesses

1. Witnesses upon whom a summon has been served must appear before the Court. They shall be heard under conditions specified in the Rules of Procedure of the Court.

2. Experts may testify as witnesses under oath, in accordance with the provisions of the Rules of Procedure of the Court.

3. All hearings shall be recorded and signed by the President and the Chief Registrar of the Court.

Art. 18   Deposition Upon Request

1. The Court may request the judicial authority of his place of residence to hear the evidence of a witness or an expert.

2. Such a request shall be made to the judicial authority in accordance with the conditions stipulated in the Rules of Procedure of the Court. Documents emanating from such hearing shall be transmitted to the Court under the same conditions.

3. Expenses incurred by this procedure shall be borne by the parties to the dispute.

Art. 19   Decisions of the Court

1. The Court shall examine the dispute before it in accordance with the provisions of the Treaty and its Rules of Procedure. It shall also apply, as necessary, the body of laws as contained in Article 38 of the Statutes of the International Court of Justice.

2. Decisions of the Court shall be read in open court and shall state the reasons on which they are based. Subject to the provisions on review contained in this Protocol, such decisions shall be final and immediately enforceable.

3. The Court shall give only one decision in respect of each dispute brought before it. Its deliberations shall be secret and its decisions shall be taken by a majority of the members.

Art. 20   Provisional Measures and Instructions

The Court, each time a case is brought before it, may order any provisional measures or issue any provisional instructions which it may consider necessary or desirable.

Art. 21   Application for Intervention

Should a Member State consider that it has an interest that may be affected by the subject matter of a dispute before the Court, it may submit by way of a written application a request to be permitted to intervene.

Art. 22   Exclusivity of Competence and Recognition of the Decisions of the Court.

1. No dispute regarding interpretation or application of the provisions of the Treaty may be referred to any other form of settlement except that which is provided for by the Treaty or this Protocol.

2. When a dispute is brought before the Court, Member States or Institutions of the Community shall refrain from any action likely to aggravate or militate against its settlement.

3. Member States and Institutions of the Community shall take immediately all necessary measures to ensure execution of the decision of the Court.

Art. 23   Interpretation of Decisions

If the meaning or scope of a decision or advisory opinion is in doubt, the Court shall construe it on application by any party or any Institution of the Community establishing an interest therein.

Art. 24   Legal Costs

Unless the Court shall decide otherwise, each party to the dispute shall bear its own legal expenses.

Art. 25   Application for Revision

1. An application for revision for a decision may be made only when it is based upon the discovery of some fact of such a nature as to be a decisive factor, which fact was, when the decision was given, unknown to the Court and also to the party claiming revision, provided always that such ignorance was not due to negligence.

2. The proceedings for revision shall be opened by a decision of the Court expressly recording the existence of the new fact, recognising that it has such a character as to lay the case open to revision and declaring the application admissible on this ground.

3. The Court may require prior compliance with the terms of the decision before it admits proceedings in revision.

4. No application for revision may be made after five (5) years from the date of decision.

5. The decision of the Court has no binding force except between the parties and in respect of that particular case.

Art. 26   Seat of the Court

1. The seat of the Court shall be fixed by the Authority.

2. However, where circumstances or facts of the case so demand, the Court may decide to sit in the territory of another Member State.

Art. 27   Session of the Court

1. Sessions of the Court shall be convened by its President.

2. The dates and duration of the sessions shall be fixed by the President and shall be determined by the roll of the Court.

3. The President and other members of the Court shall be bound to attend all sessions of the Court unless they are prevented from attending by any reasons duly explained to the Authority or the President of the Court, as the case may be.

4a. Subject to the provisions of this Protocol and its Rules of Procedure, the Court shall meet in plenary session when it is composed as stated in Article 3, paragraph 2 of this Protocol.

4b. Where, however, the Court being thus constituted and one of its members cannot continue to participate in the proceedings, the Court may, nevertheless, continue its hearing provided that the parties to the dispute so agree.

5. The Court may form one or more Chambers, composed of three or more members when, in its opinion, the nature of the business of the Court so requires.

Art. 28   Remuneration and Fringe Benefits

Subject to the provisions of this Protocol, the remuneration, allowances and all other benefits of the President and other members of the Court shall be determined by the Authority.

Art. 29   Registrars and Other Staff of the Court

1. The Court Register shall be kept by a Chief Registrar and Registrars. Subject to the provisions of this Protocol, the number of Registrars, the conditions of their appointments and their duties shall be determined by the Rules of Procedure of the Court.

2. Before taking office, the Chief Registrar and Registrars shall take an oath, or swear to a written declaration before the President of the Court as prescribed by the Rules of Procedure of the Court.

3. The Community shall appoint and provide the Court with the necessary officers and officials to enable it to carry out its functions.

Art. 30   Expenses of the Court

All the operational expenses of the Court shall be charged to the budget of the Executive Secretariat of the Community.

Art. 31   Official Languages

The official languages of the Court shall be English and French.

Art. 32   Rules of Procedure

The Court shall establish its own Rules of Procedure to be approved by the Council. Amendments thereto shall likewise be approved by Council.

Art. 33   Amendments

1. Any Member State or the President of the Court, may after consultation with the other members, submit proposals for amendments of this Protocol.

2. All proposals shall be transmitted to the Executive Secretariat which shall forward them to Member States within thirty days of receipt. Such amendments shall be examined by the Authority on the expiration of the thirty days notice to Member States.

Art. 34   Entry into Force

1. This Protocol shall enter into force, provisionally, upon signature by the Heads of State and Government of Member States and, definitively, upon ratification by at least seven (7) signatory States in accordance with the constitutional regulations in force in each Member State.

2. This Protocol and all instruments of ratification shall be deposited with the Executive Secretariat of the Community which shall transmit certified true copies of the Protocol to all Member States, notify them of the date of deposit of the instruments of ratification and register the Protocol with the Organisation of African Unity, the United Nations and any other Organisations which may be determined by Council.

3. This Protocol is annexed to the Treaty and shall form an integral part thereof.

c) Arab Maghreb Union of February 17, 1989

The Arab Maghreb Union was created on February 17, 1989 at Marrakech, Morocco, between Morocco, Tunisia, Algeria, Libya and Mauritania. The aims of the Union are to intensify the regional integration by establishing close cooperation and by enhancing mutual commercial exchanges in order to play an active role in world equilibrium through the consolidation of peaceful relations and the strengthening of security and stability in the world. The Arab Maghreb Union is understood as a necessary precursor for a more complete Arab Union regrouping other Arab and African countries. The organs of the Union are a Presidential Council comprising the Heads of member States which is the only body authorized to make decisions which are taken unanimously. Furthermore, there is a Council of Ministers of Foreign Affairs which prepares the sessions of the Presidential Council and a Secretariat as well as a Consultative Assembly which advises on draft resolutions of the Presidential Council and may make recommendations. Finally the treaty provides for a Court of Justice with competence to take binding decisions on all litigations concerning the interpretation and application of the Treaty and agreements concluded within the Union. The statutes of the Court were prepared by the Court and submitted to the approval of the Presidential Council. The Statute was adopted on March 10/11th, 1991.

Texts

Text of the Treaty

UN Doc. A/44/594, 2nd October 1989

Etudes internationales 1991, p. 198 ff. (French), 227 ff. (English)

Text of the Statute

Documents fondamentaux de l'Union de Maghreb Arabe, Secrétariat général, Rabat Ed Maarif El Djaddid-Rabat 1994

Bibliographical notes

S. Belaid, Le traité de Marrakech et la construction de l'Union du Maghreb Arabe in: Mélanges Virally (1991), 125 ff.

L. Bouony, La Cour maghrébienne de Justice, Revue Belge de Droit International 26 (1993), 351-373

H. Kistenfeger, Maghreb-Union und Golfrat (1994)

A. Benhamou, L'apport de la Cour de Justice maghrébine à la construction d'un ordre juridique communautaire, African Journal of International and Comparative Law 7 (1995), 349-359

aa) Art. 13 of the Treaty

Art. 13   The Union has also a judicial body of 2 judges nominated by each member State for 6 years, half of its members will be renewed every 3 years. A president will be elected from amongst the members for one year. This body is to examine all litigations about the interpretation and application of the Treaty and agreements concluded within the framework of the Union and which might be submitted by the presidential council or one of the States. Its decisions will be binding and final. It may advise on legal questions submitted by the presidential Council. It must prepare its statutes and submit them to the presidential Council for approval. These statutes are an integral part of the Treaty. The presidential Council is to determine its headquarters and budget.

bb) Statute of the Court of Justice

COUR DE JUSTICE DE L'UNION DU MAGHREB ARABE[1] — STATUT

Art. 1   Il faut entendre par les expressions contenues dans le présent statut les significations correspondantes :

L'Union: L'Union du Maghreb Arabe.

Le traité: Le traité constituant l'Union du Maghreb Arabe.

Le conseil de la présidence: Le conseil de la présidence de l'Union du Maghreb Arabe.

La cour: La cour de justice de l'Union du Maghreb Arabe.

Le statut: Le statut de la cour de justice.

Les magistrats: Les membres de la cour de justice.

Le mandataire: Le représentant des justiciables dans les contentieux.

CHAPITRE PREMIER — ORGANISATION DE LA COUR

Art. 2   1- La cour de justice créée par l'article 13 du traité, constitue l'appareil judiciaire de l'Union et fonctionne conformément aux dispositions dudit traité et du présent statut.

2- Le siège de la cour est établi en République Islamique de Mauritanie.

3- La cour tient ses audiences en son siège ; Le cas échéant, elle peut décider de siéger dans l'un quelconque des Etats de l'Union.

Art. 3   Sont parties au présent statut, tous les Etats membre de l'Union.

---

[1] Traduction non officielle procurée du Secrétariat Général de l'UMA

Art. 4   Chaque Etat membre de l'Union nomme deux magistrats conformément à l'article 13 du traité.

Art. 5   Les magistrats sont nommés pour une période de six années, sous réserve de leur renouvellement pour moitié à l'expiration de la troisième année du premier mandat, et dans ce cas, chaque Etat procède à la nomination du second membre. La durée du mandat court à dater de la prestation de serment.

Art. 6   Avant d'entrer en fonction, le magistrat prête, par-devant la cour le serment suivant: «Je jure devant Dieu, de juger en toute équité et d'exercer mes fonctions en toute intégrité et impartialité» ; les magistrats de la première formation de la Cour prêtent serment en audience publique, devant le président du conseil de la présidence.

Art. 7   1- Dans les Etats membres, la cour bénéficie des immunités et des privilèges nécessaires à la réalisation de ses objectifs et à l'accomplissement de ses fonctions ; de même, ses fonctionnaires, ses experts, ses témoins ainsi que les représentants des Etats justiciables jouissent des immunités et privilèges nécessaires à la garantie de leur indépendance et de leur liberté dans l'accomplissement de leur mission.

2- Les magistrats jouissent au sein des Etats membres, durant ou à l'occasion de l'accomplissement de leur tache, de l'immunité judiciaire et des autres immunités et privilèges diplomatiques, et ce, dans le cadre d'une convention passée entre la cour et l'État du siège.

Art. 8   Les Etats membres s'engagent, au respect de l'impartialité et de l'indépendance des magistrats, à ne pas influencer, de quelque manière que ce soit, l'un quelconque d'entre eux durant leur mandat, et à l'expiration de celui ci, de ne pas leur demander de rendre compte de leur exercice.

Art. 9   Il appartient au membre de la cour désirant démissionner, de porter sa demande au président qui la notifie au président du conseil de la présidence et au chef de l'Etat concerné.

Dès notification, le poste est réputé vacant.

Art. 10   En cas de vacance de siège, l'Etat concerné pourvoit à son remplacement pour la période restante.

Le magistrat en fin de mandat achève de statuer dans les affaires en état.

Art. 11   Durant son mandat, le magistrat ne peut remplir aucune fonction ou mission incompatible avec son statut.

Le règlement intérieur, prévu par l'article 22 du présent statut, détermine les fonctions et tâches incompatibles.

Art. 12   Le magistrat ne peut statuer dans une affaire dans laquelle il a été mandataire ou avocat de l'une des parties, membre d'une juridiction nationale ou internationale ou d'une commission d'enquête, ou dans laquelle il a donné un avis, ou enfin, dans laquelle il est intervenu en quelque qualité que ce soit.

Art. 13   Si, pour un motif personnel, un magistrat estime nécessaire sa récusation, il en avise la cour, et est réputé récusé à compter de cet avis.

Si un membre de la cour estime que, pour un motif personnel, un magistrat ne peut participer au jugement d'une affaire déterminée, il doit en informer la cour qui en décidera.

Art. 14   Le conseil de la présidence décide de la fixation des rémunérations, indemnités et avantages financiers des magistrats.

Art. 15   Les membres de la cour élisent, pour une année, le président et son vice-président.

Art. 16   La cour se réunit en assemblée générale au moins une fois par an pour examiner les questions d'ordre administratif et financier.

Art. 17   Il appartient à la cour de designer des chambres ad-hoc pour la prise de certaines mesures d'instruction ou de référé.

Art. 18   La cour est permanente; le règlement intérieur détermine les vacances judiciaires en conformité avec les nécessites de service.

Art. 19   La cour est régulièrement réunie lorsque le quorum minimum de huit magistrats est atteint, dont au moins un magistrat par Etat de l'Union; les jugements sont rendus par consensus de sept des membres présents.

Art. 20   L'arabe est la langue officielle de la cour; Cette dernière peut, à la condition de les traduire en langue arabe, autoriser la production de pièces et documents établis en langue étrangère.

Art. 21   La cour a un budget autonome qu'elle prépare et soumet au conseil de la présidence pour approbation.

Art. 22   La cour établit le règlement intérieur relatif à son fonctionnement, aux procédures suivies devant elle et aux questions d'ordre administratif et financier la concernant.

Art. 23   1- La cour a un secrétaire, assisté d'un nombre suffisant de fonctionnaires qu'elle nomme.

2- Avant son entrée en fonction, le secrétaire prête par-devant la cour le serment suivant: «Je jure devant Dieu d'accomplir les actes de ma fonction en toute loyauté et intégrité et de préserver les secrets des travaux et des documents de la cour».

3- Le secrétaire assiste aux audiences, et si la cour le lui demande, aux délibérations.

CHAPITRE DEUXIEME — COMPETENCE JURIDICTIONNELLE DE LA COUR

Art. 24   La cour est compétente à raison des conflits, liés à l'interprétation et à l'application du traité et des conventions conclues dans le cadre de l'Union, dont elle est saisie par le conseil de la présidence ou par l'un des Etats partie au litige.

Art. 25   La cour examine les litiges survenant entre les organes de l'Union et leurs fonctionnaires, conformément à leur statut particulier.

Art. 26   La cour statue sur les litiges dont elle est saisie.

     a) - A titre principal en conformité avec:

     – Le traite.

     – Les conventions liant les Etats membres dans le cadre de l'Union.

     – Les décisions d'exécution émanant des organes de l'Union.

     b) - A titre subsidiaire en conformité avec:

     – Les principes généraux du droit commun aux différents systèmes législatifs des Etats membres de l'Union.

     – Les principes généraux du droit international en accord avec le traité.

Art. 27   La cour peut s'inspirer de la jurisprudence ainsi que de la doctrine de juristes émérites de différentes nations, si elles ne sont pas contraires aux dispositions du traité.

CHAPITRE TROISIEME — PROCEDURE

Art. 28   Le conseil de la présidence saisit le président de la cour, par écrit, de l'action.

Art. 29   1- Les autres actions sont introduites, par écrit, auprès du secrétaire de la cour.

     2- L'action doit contenir détermination de l'objet et des parties au litige.

     3- Les parties à l'action désignent leurs mandataires, et peuvent être assistés devant la cour par des conseillers et des avocats.

Art. 30   Le secrétaire de la cour notifie expédition de la requête aux parties, et en informe les Etats membres.

Art. 31   1- Si l'un des Etats membres estime avoir un intérêt juridique sur lequel le jugement serait susceptible d'influer, il peut, avant la clôture des débats, se faire autoriser par la cour à intervenir dans l'action introduite.

     2- La cour statue sur la demande d'intervention.

     3- Si la cour déclare l'intervention recevable, l'intervenant est réputé être partie à l'action.

Art. 32   A tout moment, et avant le prononcé du jugement, le demandeur peut se désister de son action; à moins que l'une des parties ne s'y oppose, la cour statue sur la recevabilité du désistement.

Art. 33   1- Dès sa première réplique à l'action principale, le défendeur est admis à introduire à l'encontre du demandeur une demande reconventionnelle.

2- Cette demande n'est recevable qu'autant qu'elle présente un lien direct avec l'action principale, et qu'elle relève de la compétence de la cour.

Art. 34   Si l'une des parties fait défaut ou s'abstient de soutenir son action, l'autre partie peut demander à la cour de lui faire droit de ses demandes; il ne pourra y être fait droit qu'après qu'il sera établi que l'action est fondée sur les plans du fait et du droit.

Art. 35   Il appartient à la cour, le cas échéant, de prendre toute mesure provisoire qu'elle jugera utile à la protection des droits de toute partie ; cette décision est notifiée sur-le-champ, suivant les circonstances, soit au conseil de la présidence par la voie du président de la cour, soit aux parties par la voie du secrétaire de la cour en vue de prendre les mesures nécessaires.

Art. 36   La cour peut, soit spontanément, soit à la demande de l'une des parties à l'action, décider de l'audition des témoins; le témoin doit prêter serment suivant la formule suivante : «Je jure devant Dieu de dire la vérité et rien que la vérité».

Art. 37   1- Si la cour estime une mesure d'instruction nécessaire, elle l'accomplit soit par elle-même, soit par l'une de ses chambres.

2- A tout moment, la cour peut assigner, à un ou plusieurs experts, d'effectuer une enquête ou de produire un avis sur une question déterminée.

Art. 38   La cour peut, par la voie du secrétariat général de l'Union, demander aux Etats membres, aux conseils, aux commissions et aux organes qui en dépendent, communication de renseignements et documents relatifs aux affaires qui lui sont soumises.

Art. 39   La procédure diligentée devant la cour peut être de nature, soit écrite, soit orale.

1- La procédure écrite recouvre tout autant les mémoires, les réponses et les répliques présentés à la cour et aux parties, que les pièces et les documents leur servant de fondement.

2- Les mémoires, les réponses et les répliques sont présentées au secrétaire de la cour conformément aux conditions et délais que celle-ci fixe.

3- La procédure orale concerne l'audition des témoins, les dires des experts, des mandataires, des conseillers et des avocats.

Art. 40   1- A moins que la cour n'en décide autrement, spontanément ou sur la demande de l'une des parties, ses audiences sont publiques.

2- Dès achèvement de l'examen de l'affaire, le président clôt les débats.

3- Les délibérations sont secrètes ; n'y participent que les magistrats qui ont pris part à l'examen de l'affaire.

Art. 41   1- Dans tous les cas, et après en avoir régulièrement avisé les parties et leurs mandataires, la décision est rendue en audience publique.

2- Le jugement doit être motivé et doit mentionner les magistrats qui y ont pris part.

3- Si le jugement n'est pas, en tout ou partie, rendu à l'unanimité, tout magistrat ne partageant pas cette unanimité a le droit de rendre un avis séparé qui sera joint à la décision.

4- Le jugement est signé conjointement par le président et le secrétaire de la cour.

Art. 42   Les jugements de la cour sont obligatoires, définitifs et ont autorité à l'égard des parties à l'action.

Art. 43   La cour, soit spontanément, soit à la demande de l'une des parties, et sans qu'il soit besoin de plaidoirie, se charge de rendre un arrêt rétablissant les erreurs matérielles glissées dans le dispositif du jugement.

Art. 44   Toute partie à l'action peut solliciter de la cour l'interprétation de ce qui est susceptible de lui paraître, dans le dispositif du jugement, obscur ou imprécis.

Art. 45   1- La rétractation n'est recevable que dans l'un des deux cas suivants

– Si la cour a statué ultra petita

– S'il y a découverte d'un élément déterminant à la solution du litige, qu'ignoraient, jusqu'au prononcé du jugement, la cour et la partie demanderesse à la rétractation, à moins que ce ne soit le résultat d'une négligence de cette dernière.

2- A moins que la cour n'en décide autrement, la demande en rétractation ne peut avoir d'effet suspensif à l'exécution du jugement.

Art. 46   La demande en rétractation est, dans le premier cas, introduite dans un délai de six mois à dater du prononcé du jugement, et, dans le second cas, à compter de l'époque de la découverte du fait donnant lieu à ouverture de la rétractation ; la demande en rétractation n'est, en aucun cas, recevable à l'expiration de dix années après le prononcé du jugement.

Art. 47   La cour statue sur la demande en rétractation dans un délai de trois mois à compter de la date de son introduction, et le jugement à intervenir est notifié aux parties.

Art. 48   Toute partie à l'action supporte ses propres dépens, à moins que la cour n'en décide autrement.

CHAPITRE QUATRIEME — COMPETENCE CONSULTATIVE DE LA COUR

Art. 49   1- La cour rend des avis consultatifs sur toutes les questions qui lui sont soumises par le conseil de la présidence.

2- Le président adresse au conseil de la présidence l'avis consultatif de la cour.

Art. 50   Les dispositions des articles 11, 12 et 13 du présent statut s'appliquent aux avis consultatifs.

CHAPITRE CINQUIEME — MODIFICATION DES STATUTS

Art. 51   1- L'initiative de la modification du présent statut appartient au conseil de la présidence et à la cour.

2- Dans les deux cas, la cour prépare un projet à cet effet et le soumet, pour approbation, au conseil de la présidence.

Art. 52   La modification prend effet à compter de son approbation par le conseil de la présidence.

d) African Economic Community of June 3, 1991

The objective of creating an organization for the economic integration of the whole continent, which had been pursued within the OAU since the 1970s, finally resulted in the conclusion of the Treaty establishing the African Economic Community in 1991, which entered into force in 1994. This treaty provides for a gradual economic integration which shall be reached in six stages within a period of at least 34 years. The Community "shall be established mainly through the coordination, harmonization and progressive integration of the activities of regional economic communities". This means that the Community itself will play only a marginal role until the harmonization of the regional customs unions will have led to a continental customs union which is provided for as the fifth stage of implementation. The African Economic Community forms an integral part of the OAU (art. 98) and the Treaty and the Protocols form an integral part of the OAU Charter (art. 99); likewise the principal organs are common to both organizations, the OUA and the AEC.

One of the organs of the Community is the Court of Justice. The Treaty itself contains only rather general provisions and leaves the details, such as the statute, membership, procedure and other matters, to the emanation of a special Protocol which has not yet been adopted. Although the most important provisions concerning the Court of Justice are still lacking it may be said that the institution of a Court as such constitutes an important innovation because it allows judicial control on the activities of States and Governments.

Text

ILM 30 (1991), 1241 ff.

Bibliographical notes

M. A. Ajomo (ed.), African Economic Treaty: issues, prospects and problems (1993)
A. Mahiou, La Communauté économique africaine, Etudes Internationales (Tunis) (1994), 5 ff.
K. Danso, The African Economic Community: Problems and Prospects, Africa Today 42 (1995), 31-55
B. Thompson, Prerequisites for Economic Integration in Africa: An Analysis of the Abuja Treaty, Africa Today 42 (1995), 56 ff.
P. Pennetta, Le Organizzazioni Internazionali dei Paesi in via di Sviluppo (1998), 346 ff.

Art. 18, 19, 20 and 87 of the Treaty

Art. 18   Court of Justice — Constitution and Functions

1. A Court of Justice of the Community is hereby established.

2. The Court of Justice shall ensure the adherence to law in the interpretation and application of this Treaty and shall decide on disputes submitted thereto pursuant to this Treaty.

3. to this end, it shall:

a)   decide on actions brought by a Member State or the Assembly on grounds of the violation of the provisions of this Treaty, or of a decision or regulation or on grounds of lack of competence or abuse of powers by an organ, an authority or a Member State; and

b)   at the request of the Assembly or Council, give advisory opinion.

4. The Assembly may confer on the Court of Justice the power to assume jurisdiction by virtue of this Treaty over any dispute other than those referred to in paragraph 3 (a) of this Article.

5. The Court of Justice shall carry out the functions assigned to it independent of the Member States and the other organs of the Community.

Art. 19   Decisions of the Court

The Decisions of the Court of Justice shall be binding on Member States and organs of the Community.

Art. 20   Organization

The statutes, membership, procedures, and other matters relating to the Court of Justice shall be determined by the Assembly in a protocol relating to the Court of Justice.

CHAPTER XVIII — SETTLEMENT OF DISPUTES

Art. 87   Procedure for the Settlement of Disputes

1. Any dispute regarding the interpretation and application of the provisions of the Treaty shall be amicably settled through direct agreement by the parties to the dispute. If the parties concerned fail to settle such dispute, either party may, within a period of twelve (12) months, refer the matter to the Court of Justice.

2. The Decisions of the Court of Justice shall be final and shall not be subject to appeal.

e) Common Market for Eastern and Southern Africa (COMESA) of November 5, 1993

The Common Market for Eastern and Southern Africa was established on 5 November 1993. The membership is open for 22 States listed up in the preamble to the treaty. Nearly all of them are actually parties to the Treaty including also those three States, Kenya, Uganda and Tanzania, which had formed the East African Community which was the most advanced integration process that ever existed in the developing world (as this community no longer exists, reference is made to the 1984 edition of Dispute Settlement in Public International Law, p. 463 ff.).

As its predecessor, the Preferential Trade Area (PTA), which has been replaced by COMESA, COMESA is aimed at the regional economic integration and economic cooperation "through the implementation of common policies and programmes aimed at achieving sustainable growth and development" (Art. 2). By the creation of the Common Market the regional integration in Eastern and Southern Africa has progressed from a preferential trade area to a common market which shall be reached in three phases: the first phase relates to the establishment of a preferential trade area; the second phase to the conversion of the trade area into a common market and the third phase to the development of the common market to an economic community. However, the COMESA Treaty does not draw any clear distinctions in relation to the three phases of the COMESA regional integration scheme. What is clear, however, is that the scheme is now moving from its first phase into the second one.

The organs of COMESA are provided for in Art. 7 and include a Court of Justice, which has a general competence in order to "ensure the adherence to law and interpretation and application of this Treaty" (Art. 19). How effective this Court will be depends largely on the supreme political organs of the Member States of COMESA, namely whether they will accept that successful integration is only possible if the regional organs are given real power in order to implement the integration process.

Text

ILM 33 (1994), 1067 ff.

Bibliographical notes

P. K. Kiplagat, Dispute recognition and dispute settlement in integration processes: the COMESA experience, Northwestern Journal of International Law and Business 15 (1995), 437-490

P. K. Kiplagat, Legal studies of integration treaties and the enforcement of treaty obligations: a look at the COMESA process, The Denver Journal of International Law and Policy 23 (1995), 259-286

A. P. Mutharika, Creating an attractive investment climate in the Common Market for Eastern and Southern Africa (COMESA) Region, International Centre for Settlement of Investment Disputes Review 12 (1997), 237-286

K. K. Mwenda, Legal aspects of regional integration: COMESA and SADC on the regulation of foreign investment in Southern and Eastern Africa, African Journal of International and Comparative Law 9 (1997), 324-348

M. Gondwe, From PTA to COMESA: The Quest for Sub-Regional Economic Integration in Eastern and Southern Africa, African Yearbook of International Law 6 (1998), 3-22

Chapter Five — The Court of Justice

Art. 19   Establishment of the Court

The Court of Justice established under Article 7 of this Treaty shall ensure the adherence to law in the interpretation and application of this Treaty.

Art. 20   Composition of the Court

1. Subject to paragraph 2 of this Article, the Court shall be composed of seven Judges who shall be appointed by the Authority and one of whom shall be appointed by the Authority as the President of the Court.

2. The Judges of the Court shall be chosen from among persons of impartiality and independence who fulfill the conditions required for the holding of high judicial office in their respective countries of domicile or who are jurists of recognised competence:

Provided that no two or more Judges shall at any time be nationals of the same Member State.

3. Not withstanding the provisions of paragraph 1 of this Article, the Authority may, upon the request of the court, appoint additional Judges.

Art. 21   Tenure of Office and Resignation

1. The President and Judges shall hold office for a period of five years and shall be eligible for reappointment for a further period of five years.

2. The President and the Judges shall hold office throughout the term of their respective appointments unless they resign or die or are removed from office in accordance with the provisions of this Treaty.

3. Where the term of office of a Judge comes to an end by effluxion of time or on resignation before a decision or opinion of the court with respect to a matter which has been argued before the Court of which he was a member is delivered, such Judge shall, only for the purpose of completing that particular matter, continue to sit as a Judge

4. The President may, at any time, resign his office by giving one year's written notice to the Chairman of the Authority, but his resignation shall not take effect until his successor has been appointed by the Authority and has taken office.

5. A Judge may, at any time, resign his office by letter delivered to the President for transmission to the Chairman of the Authority, and his resignation shall take effect on the date it has been accepted by the Authority.

Art. 22   Removal from Office and temporary Membership of the Court

1. The President or a Judge shall not be removed from office except by the Authority for stated misbehaviour or for inability to perform the functions of his office due to infirmity of mind or body or due to any other specified cause.

2. If a Judge is appointed by the Authority to replace the President or another Judge before the term of office of the President or a Judge expires, the Judge so appointed shall serve in that office for the remainder of the term of the replaced President or Judge.

3. If a Judge is temporarily absent or otherwise unable to carry out his functions, the Authority shall, if such absence or inability to act appears to the Authority to be likely to be of such duration as to cause a significant delay in the work of the Court, appoint a temporary Judge to act in place of the said Judge.

4. If a Judge is directly or indirectly interested in a case before the Court, he shall immediately report the nature of his interest to the President, and, if in his opinion the President considers the Judge's interest in the case prejudicial, he shall make a report to the Authority, and the Authority shall appoint a temporary Judge to act for that case only in place of the interested Judge.

5. If the President is directly or indirectly interested in a case before the Court he shall, if he considers that the nature of his interest is such that it would be prejudicial for him to take part in that case, make a report to the Authority and the Authority shall appoint a temporary President, chosen in the same manner as the substantive President, to act as President for that case only in place of the substantive President.

Art. 23   General Jurisdiction of the Court

The Court shall have jurisdiction to adjudicate upon all matters which may be referred to it pursuant to this Treaty.

Art. 24   Reference by Member States

1. A Member State which considers that another Member State or the Council has failed to fulfill an obligation under this Treaty or has infringed a provision of this Treaty, may refer the matter to the Court.

2. A Member State may refer for determination by the Court, the legality of any act, regulation, directive or decision of the Council on the grounds that such act, regulation, directive or decision is ultra vires or unlawful or an infringement of the provisions of this Treaty or any rule of law relating to its application or amounts to a misuse or abuse of power.

Art. 25   Reference by the Secretary-General

1. Where the Secretary-General considers that a Member State has failed to fulfill an obligation under this Treaty or has infringed a provision of this Treaty, he shall submit his findings to the Member State concerned to enable that Member State to submit its observations on the findings.

2. If the Member State concerned does not submit its observations to the Secretary-General within two months, or if the observations submitted are unsatisfactory, the Secretary-General shall refer the matter to the Bureau of the Council which shall decide whether the matter shall be re-

ferred by the Secretary-General to the Court immediately or be referred to the Council.

3. Where a matter has been referred to the Council under the provisions of paragraph 2 of this Article and the Council fails to resolve the matter, the Council shall direct the Secretary-General to refer the matter to the Court.

Art. 26   Reference by Legal and Natural Persons

Any person who is resident in a Member State may refer for determination by the Court the legality of any act, regulation, directive, or decision of the Council or of a Member State on the grounds that such act, directive, decision or regulation is unlawful or an infringement of the provisions of this Treaty:

Provided that where the matter for determination relates to any act, regulation, directive or decision by a Member State, such person shall not refer the matter for determination under this Article unless he has first exhausted local remedies in the national courts or tribunals of the Member State.

Art. 27   Jurisdiction Over Claims by Common Market Employees and Third Parties Against the Common Market or its Institutions

1. The Court shall have jurisdiction to hear disputes between the Common Market and its employees that arise out of the application and interpretation of the Staff Rules and Regulations of the Secretariat or the terms and conditions of employment of the employees of the Common Market.

2. The Court shall have jurisdiction to determine claims by any person against the Common Market or its institutions for acts of their servants or employees in the performance of their duties.

Art. 28   Jurisdiction Under Arbitration Clauses and Special Agreements

The Court shall have jurisdiction to hear and determine any matter:

(a) arising from an arbitration clause contained in a contract which confers such jurisdiction to which the Common Market or any of its institutions is a party, and

(b) arising from a dispute between the Member States regarding this Treaty if the dispute is submitted to it under a special agreement between the Member States concerned.

Art. 29   Jurisdiction of National Courts

1. Except where the jurisdiction is conferred on the court by or under this Treaty, disputes to which the Common Market is a party shall not on that ground alone, be excluded from the jurisdiction of national courts.

2. Decisions of the Court on the interpretation of the provisions of this Treaty shall have precedence over decisions of national courts.

Art. 30   National Courts and Preliminary Rulings

1. Where a question is raised before any court or tribunal of a Member State concerning the application or interpretation of this Treaty or the validity of the regulations, directives and decisions of the Common Market, such court or tribunal shall, if it considers that a ruling on the question is necessary to enable it to give judgment, request the Court to give a preliminary ruling thereon.

2. Where any question as that referred to in paragraph 1 of this Article is raised in a case pending before a court or tribunal of a Member State against whose judgment there is no judicial remedy under the national law of that Member State, that court or tribunal shall refer the matter to the Court.

Art. 31   Judgment of the Court

1. The Court shall consider and determine every reference made to it pursuant to this Treaty in accordance with the Rules of Court, and shall deliver in public session a reasoned judgment which, subject to the provisions of the said Rules as to review, shall be final and conclusive and not open to appeal:

Provided that, if the Court considers that in the special circumstances of the case it is undesirable that its judgment be delivered in open Court, the Court may make an order to that effect and deliver its judgment before the parties privately.

2. The Court shall deliver one judgment only in respect of every reference to it, which shall be the judgment of the Court reached in private by majority verdict.

3. An application for revision of a judgment may be made to the Court only if it is based upon the discovery of some fact which by its nature might have had a decisive influence on the judgment if it had been known to the Court at the time the judgment was given, but which fact, at that time, was unknown to both the Court and the party making the application, and which could not, with reasonable diligence, have been discovered by that party before the judgment was made, or on account of some mistake or error on the face of the record.

Art. 32   Advisory Opinions of the Court

1. The Authority, the Council or a Member State may request the Court to give an advisory opinion regarding questions of law arising from the provisions of this Treaty affecting the Common Market, and the Member States shall in the case of every such request have the right to be represented and take part in the proceedings.

2. A request for an advisory opinion under paragraph 1 of this Article shall be made in writing and shall contain an exact statement of the question upon which an opinion is required and shall be accompanied by all relevant documents likely to be of assistance to the Court.

3. Upon the receipt of the request under paragraph 1 of this Article, the Registrar shall forthwith give notice thereof, to all the Member States, and

shall notify them that the Court shall be prepared to accept, within a time fixed by the President, written submissions, or to hear oral submissions relating to the question.

4. In the exercise of its advisory function, the Court shall be governed by the provisions of this Treaty and the Rules of Court relating to references of disputes to the extent that the Court considers appropriate.

Art. 33   Representation before the Court

Every party to a reference before the Court shall be represented by Counsel appointed by that party.

Art. 34   Acceptance of Court Judgments

1. Any dispute concerning the interpretation or application of this Treaty or any of the matters referred to the Court pursuant to this Chapter shall not be subjected to any method of settlement other than those provided for in this Treaty.

2. Where a dispute has been referred to the Council or the Court, the Member States shall refrain from any action which might be detrimental to the resolution of the dispute or might aggravate the dispute.

3. A Member State or the Council shall take without delay the measures required to implement a judgment of the Court.

4. The Court may prescribe such sanctions as it shall consider necessary to be imposed against a party who defaults in implementing the decisions of the Court.

Art. 35   Interim Orders

The Court may in any case referred to it make any interim order or issue any directions which it considers necessary or desirable. Interim orders and other directions issued by the Court shall have the same effect ad interim as decisions of the Court.

Art. 36   Intervention

A Member State, the Secretary-General or a resident of a Member State who is not a party to a case before the Court may with leave of the Court intervene in that case but the submissions of the intervening party shall be limited to evidence supporting or opposing the arguments of a party to the case.

Art. 37   Proceedings

1. The proceedings before the Court shall be either written or oral.

2. Records of each hearing shall be signed by the President and shall be kept and maintained by the Registrar.

Art. 38   Rules of Court

The Court shall make Rules of Court which shall, subject to the provisions of this Treaty regulate the detailed conduct of business of the Court.

Art. 39   Immunity of the President and Judges

The President and the Judges shall be immune from legal action for any act or omission committed in the discharge of their functions under this Treaty.

Art. 40 Execution of Judgment

The execution of a judgment of the Court which imposes a pecuniary obligation on a person shall be governed by the rules of civil procedure in force in the Member State in which execution is to take place. The order for execution shall be appended to the judgment of the Court which shall require only the verification of the authenticity of the judgment by the Registrar whereupon the party in whose favour execution is to take place may proceed to execution in accordance with the rules of civil procedure in force in that Member State.

Art. 41 Registrar and Other Staff

1 The Council shall appoint a Registrar from among nationals of the Member States qualified to hold high judicial office in their respective States.

2. The Court shall employ such other staff as may be required to enable it to perform its functions and who shall hold office in the service of the Court.

3. The terms and conditions of service of the Registrar and other staff shall subject to this Treaty be determined by the Council on the recommendation of the Court.

4. Subject to the overall supervision of the President the Registrar shall be responsible for the day to day administration of the business of the Court. The Registrar shall also carry out the duties imposed upon him by this Treaty and the Rules of Court.

Art. 42 Budget

1. The budget of the Court shall be borne by the Member States.

2. The formula for contributions to the budget for the Court shall be the formula applicable to the determination of contributions by the Member States to the budget of the Secretariat.

3. The President shall present the budget of the Court to the Council for approval through the Intergovernmental Committee.

4. The Council shall determine the payment and currencies of contributions by the Member State to the budget of the Court.

Art. 43 Official Languages of the Court

The official languages of the Court shall be English, French and Portuguese.

Art. 44 Seat of the Court

The Seat of the Court shall be determined by the Authority.

f) Union Economique et Monétaire Ouest Africaine (UEMOA) of January 10, 1994

The UEMOA was created by the francophone States of Africa. The UEMOA Treaty is largely inspired by the European Community Treaties and therefore may be characterised as a supranational integration organization similar to the European Communities with rather far reaching competences. It has replaced the UMOA (l'Union monétaire ouest-africaine, which had been created in 1973, as well as the CEAO (Communauté Economique de l'Afrique de l'Ouest). The UEMOA aims at a reinforcement of economic activities in a prospect of open regionalism and the coordination of the economic and monetary policies. Furthermore the UEMOA provides for a harmonization of special economic sectors as well as fiscal legislation. In order to reach this aim the Treaty provides for the immediate applicability of the Union acts within the member States comparable to the effect of regulations within the framework of the European Communities. Besides the usual organs, i.e. the Conference of the Heads of State and Government and the Council of Ministers, UEMOA was the first African organization to institute, according to the model of the European Communities, a Commission which exercises all the powers transferred to it by the Treaty in the general interest of the Union. Like some other African organizations, i.e. ECOWAS, also UEMOA has instituted a Parliament which is to strengthen the economic integration by bringing together the Member States on the political field. And finally, UEMOA provides for two judicial organs, the Court of Justice which also resembles largely to the Court of Justice of the European Communities and the Court of Accounts. These Courts have been set up by Protocol No. 1 which is an integral part of the Treaty and in January 1995 the judges were appointed, so that the Court is in place and able to decide cases which may be brought before it.

Texts

Traité de l'UEMOA: Banque centrale des Etats de l'Afrique de l'Ouest, No. 440, Août–Septembre 1994
Protocol on the Court of Justice: Banque centrale des Etats de l'Afrique de l'Ouest, No.443, Décembre 1994

Bibliographical notes

L. Verbraken, Les interprétatins de la Cour de Justice de Luxembourg en matière de droits de douane et de contingentements peuvent-elles utilement inspirer la Cour de Justice de l'UEMOA? Revue Burkinabé de Droit 30 (1996), 217-233
L. M. Ibriga, L'UEMOA: une nouvelle approche de l'intégration économique régionale en Afrique de l'Ouest, African Yearbook of International Law 6 (1998), 23-64

aa) Treaty of UEMOA, Section III

Section III: des organes de controle juridictionnel

Art. 38 Il est créé au niveau de l'union deux organes de contrôle juridictionnel dénommés Cour de Justice et Cour des Comptes.

Le statut, la composition, les compétences ainsi que les règles de procédures et de fonctionnement de la Cour de Justice et de la Cour des Comptes sont énoncés dans le protocole additionnel no 1.

Art. 39 Le protocole additionnel no 1 fait partie intégrante du présent traité.

bb) Protocole Additionnel No 1 relatif aux organes de contrôle de l'UEMOA

Preambule

Les Gouvernements des Etats signataires du Traité de l'UEMOA,

– Convaincus que la bonne marche de l'Union exige la mise en place d'organes de contrôle appropriés,

– Persuadés de la nécessité d'instituer un mécanisme chargé du contrôle des engagements des Etats membres de l'Union,

– Conscients de la nécessité de mettre en place un système destiné à rendre plus transparente la gestion financière de l'Union,

Sont convenus de la création, au sein de l'Union, d'une Cour de Justice et d'une Cour des Comptes.

Chapitre I: de la Cour de Justice

Art. 1 La Cour de Justice veille au respect du droit quant à l'interprétation et à l'application du Traité de l'Union.

Art. 2 La Cour de Justice est composée de sept (7) membres nommés pour un mandat de six (6) ans, renouvelable, par la Conférence des Chefs d'Etat et de Gouvernement. Les membres de la Cour de Justice sont choisis parmi des personnalités offrant toutes les garanties d'indépendance et de compétence juridique, nécessaires à l'exercice des plus hautes fonctions juridictionnelles.

Les membres de la Cour désignent en leur sein pour trois (3) ans le Président de la Cour de Justice.

Ils répartissent entre eux les fonctions de juges et d'avocats généraux.

Art. 3   La Cour de Justice se réunit en tant que de besoin sur convocation de son Président. Elle siège en séance plénière. Ses audiences sont publiques.

Art. 4   La Cour de justice nomme un greffier. Le statut de celui-ci sera déterminé conformément aux dispositions de l'article 21.

Art. 5   La Cour de Justice connaît, sur recours de la Commission ou de tout Etat membre des manquements des Etats membres aux obligations qui leur incombent en vertu du Traité de l'Union.

Art. 6   Si la Cour de Justice constate qu'un Etat membre a manqué à une des obligations, qui lui incombent en vertu du Traité de l'Union, cet Etat est tenu de prendre les mesures qui comporte l'exécution des arrêts de la Cour. En cas d'abstention de l'Etat membre dont le manquement a été constaté, la Commission a la faculté de saisir la Conférence des Chefs d'Etat et de Gouvernement afin qu'elle invite l'Etat membre défaillant à l'exécuter.

Art. 7   Lorsque le recours en manquement est formé par un Etat membre, la Cour, avant de statuer, invite la Commission à lui communiquer ses observations.

Art. 8   Sur recours formé par un Etat membre, par le Conseil ou par la Commission, la Cour de Justice apprécie la légalité des règlements, directives et décisions.

          Le recours en appréciation de la légalité est ouvert, en outre, à toute personne physique ou morale, contre tout acte d'un organe de l'Union lui faisant grief.

          Les recours prévus au présent article doivent être formés dans un délai de deux (2) mois à compter de la publication de l'acte, de sa notification au requérant ou, à défaut, du jour où celui-ci en a eu connaissance.

          Une amende de folle action peut être prononcée par la Cour à l'encontre de toute personne de droit privé, physique ou morale, en cas de recours manifestement abusif ou dilatoire.

Art. 9   Lorsqu'elle est saisie d'un recours en appréciation de légalité, la Cour de Justice prononce la nullité totale ou partielle des actes entachés de vice de forme, d'incompétence, de détournement de pouvoir, de violation du Traité de l'Union ou des actes pris en application de celui-ci.

Art. 10   L'organe de l'Union dont émane l'acte annulé est tenu de prendre les mesures que comporte l'exécution de l'arrêt de la Cour de Justice. Celle-ci a la faculté d'indiquer les effets des actes annulés qui doivent être considérés comme définitifs.

Art. 11   Toute partie peut, à l'occasion d'un litige, soulever l'exception d'illégalité à l'encontre d'un acte du Conseil ou de la Commission, nonobstant l'expiration du délai mentionné à l'article 8 alinéa 3.

Art. 12   La Cour de Justice statue à titre préjudiciel sur l'interprétation du Traité de l'Union, sur la légalité et l'interprétation des actes pris par les organes de l'Union, sur la légalité et l'interprétation des statuts des organismes créés par un acte du Conseil, quand une juridiction nationale ou une autorité à fonction juridictionnelle est appelée à en connaître à l'occasion d'un litige.

Les juridictions nationales statuant en dernier ressort sont tenues de saisir la Cour de Justice. La saisine de la Cour de Justice par les autres juridictions nationales ou les autorités à fonction juridictionnelle est facultative.

Art. 13   Les interprétations formulées par la Cour de Justice dans le cadre de la procédure de recours préjudiciel s'imposent à toutes les autorités administratives et juridictionnelles dans l'ensemble des Etats membres. L'inobservation de ces interprétations peut donner lieu à un recours en manquement.

Art. 14   Si, à la requête de la Commission, la Cour de Justice constate que, dans un Etat membre, le fonctionnement insuffisant de la procédure de recours préjudicielle permet la mise en œuvre d'interprétations erronées du Traité de l'Union, des actes pris par les organes de l'Union ou des statuts des organismes créés par un acte du Conseil, elle notifie à la juridiction supérieure de l'Etat membre un arrêt établissant les interprétations exactes. Ces interprétations s'imposent à toutes les autorités administratives et juridictionnelles dans l'Etat concerné.

Art. 15   Sans préjudice des dispositions prévues à l'article 9 du Traité de l'Union, la Cour de Justice connaît des litiges relatifs à la réparation des dommages causés par les organes de l'Union ou par les agents de celle-ci dans l'exercice de leurs fonctions.

Art. 16   La Cour de Justice connaît des litiges entre l'Union et ses agents.

Art. 17   La Cour de Justice connaît des différends entre Etats membres relatifs au Traité de l'Union si ces différends lui sont soumis en vertu d'un compromis.

Art. 18   Les recours formés devant la Cour de Justice n'ont pas d'effet suspensif. Toutefois, la Cour de Justice peut ordonner le sursis à exécution des actes contestés devant elle.

Art. 19   Dans les affaires dont elle est saisie, la Cour de Justice peut prescrire les mesures conservatoires nécessaires.

Art. 20   Les arrêts de la Cour de Justice ont force exécutoire, conformément aux dispositions de son règlement de procédures. Ils sont publiés au Bulletin Officiel de l'Union.

Art. 21   Les Statuts de la Cour de Justice sont établis par un acte additionnel de la Conférence des Chefs d'Etat et de Gouvernement.

La Cour de Justice établit son règlement de procédures. Ce règlement est soumis à l'approbation du Conseil, statuant à l'unanimité. Il est publié au Bulletin Officiel de l'Union.

Art. 22   Les traitements, indemnités et pensions des membres de la Cour sont fixés par le Conseil, statuant à la majorité des deux tiers (2/3) de ses membres.

CHAPITRE II: DE LA COUR DES COMPTES

Art. 23   La Cour des Comptes assure le contrôle de l'ensemble des comptes des organes de l'Union. Ce contrôle porte notamment sur la régularité et l'efficacité de l'utilisation de leurs ressources.

Art. 24   La Cour des Comptes est composée de trois (3) Conseillers. Les Conseillers sont nommés pour un mandat de six (6) ans, renouvelable une (1) seule fois, par la Conférence des Chefs d'Etat et de Gouvernement, parmi des personnalités proposées par le Conseil et offrant toutes les garanties de compétence et d'indépendance requises.

Art. 25   Les Conseillers peuvent se faire assister par des collaborateurs. Ils peuvent recourir dans l'exercice de leurs fonctions à un système d'audit externe.

Art. 26   Les modalités du contrôle devant être exercé par la Cour des Comptes sont arrêtées par le Conseil, statuant à la majorité des deux tiers (2/3) de ses membres sur recommandation des Conseillers.

g) Gulf Cooperation Council (GCC) of May 25, 1981 and November 11, 1982

After longlasting discussions about cooperation and association among Gulf Arab States, the Gulf Cooperation Council was finally established in 1982. Important external security events, in particular the Iranian revolution, the Soviet invasion of Afghanistan and the launching of the Iran-Iraq war may be considered as the decisive factors for the adoption of the Charter of the Cooperation Council. The GCC countries share a common background based on language (Arabic), religion (Islam), system of government (conservative monarchy) and standard of economic development. The Gulf Cooperation Council may be described as a closed organization since the Charter does not contain any provision relating to the admission of new members, nor the withdrawal or expulsion of existing members. The GCC is composed of three principal organs: the Supreme Council, the Ministerial Council and the Secretariat. Attached to the Supreme Council, the highest authority, which is composed of the Heads of the Member States, is the Commission for Settlement of disputes which has only advisory functions. The GCC has been rather successful in its economic efforts: it adopted a Unified Economic Agreement which provides for cooperation and coordination in economic activities and has led to the free movement of goods, the elimination of customs duties on domestically produced goods, the creation of new institutions such as the Gulf Investment Corporation. But also in the field of security and defence the GCC has taken steps for close cooperation, particularly by creating a rapid deployment force in 1984. The GCC has played so far a role of moderation and conciliation in the Arab region and has succeeded in reducing tension between the Sultanate of Oman and the People's Republic of Yemen. With regard to the Iran-Iraq conflict the GCC took the initiative for a Security Council Resolution in 1984 calling on "all States to respect the right of free navigation in the Gulf and to refrain from any act which may lead to further escalation and widening of the conflict". With a view to these latter activities, it may be stated that the significance of the GCC is not limited to economic cooperation but that its growing role in conflict prevention in the region make it a factor of regional stability in addition to its economic achievements.

Texts

Charter of the GCC: ILM 26 (1997), 1131 ff.
Rules of Procedures for the Commission for Settlement of Disputes: ILM 26 (1987), 1157 ff.

Bibliographical notes

J. A. Sandwick (ed.), The Gulf Cooperation Council: Moderation and Stability in an Interdependent World (1987)

Bouachba, Le Conseil de Coopération des Etats Arabes du Golfe, RGDI 89 (1985), 29 ff.

U. Braun, Der Kooperationsrat arabischer Staaten am Golf: Eine neue Kraft? (1986)

E. R. Peterson, The Gulf Cooperation Council: search for unity in a dynamic region (1988)

R. K. Ramazani, The Gulf Cooperation Council: record and analysis (1988)

S. N. A. Rizvi, The Gulf Cooperation Council: united thoughts and legal hopes, India Quarterly 53 (1997), 125-146

aa) Article 10 of the Charter

Art. 10   Commission for Settlement of Disputes

1. The Cooperation Council shall have a commission called "Commission for Settlement of Disputes" and shall be attached to the Supreme Council.

2. The Supreme Council shall form the Commission for every case separately based on the nature of the dispute.

3. If a dispute arises over interpretation or implementation of the Charter and such dispute is not resolved within the Ministerial Council or the Supreme Council the Supreme Council may refer such dispute to the Commission for Settlement of Disputes.

4. The Commission shall submit its recommendations or opinion, as applicable, to the Supreme Council for appropriate action.

bb) Rules of Procedures for the Commission for Settlement of Disputes

PREAMBLE

In accordance with the provisions of Article Six of the Charter of the Gulf Arab States Cooperation Council; and

In execution of the provision of Article Ten of the Cooperation Council Charter,

A Commission for Settlement of Disputes, hereinafter referred to as The Commission, shall be set up and its jurisdiction and rules for its proceedings shall be as follows:

Art. 1   Terminology

Terms used in these Rules of Procedures shall have the same meanings established in the Charter of the Gulf Arab States Cooperation Council.

Art. 2   Commission's Seat and Meetings

The Commission shall have its headquarters at Riyadh, Saudi Arabia, and shall hold its meetings on the territory of the state where its headquarters is located, but may hold its meetings elsewhere, when necessary.

Art. 3   Jurisdiction

The Commission shall, once installed, have jurisdiction to consider the following matters referred to it by the Supreme Council:

a.   Disputes between member states.

b.   Differences of opinion as to the interpretation or execution of the Cooperation Council Charter.

Art. 4   Commission's Membership

a.   The Commission shall be formed of an appropriate number of citizen of member states not involved in the dispute as the Council selects in every case separately depending on the nature of the dispute, provided that the number shall not be less than three members.

b.   The Commission may seek the advice of any such experts as it may deem necessary.

c.   Unless the Supreme Council decides otherwise, the Commission's task shall end with the submission of its recommendations or opinion to the Supreme Council which, after the conclusion of the Commission's task, may summon it at any time to explain or elaborate on its recommendations or opinions.

Art. 5   Meetings and Internal Procedures

a.   The Commission's meeting shall be valid if attended by all members.

b.   The Secretariat General of the Cooperation Council shall prepare procedures required to conduct the Commission's affairs and such procedures shall go into effect as of the date of approval by the Ministerial Council.

c.   Each party to the dispute shall send representatives to the Commission who shall be entitled to follow proceedings and present their defense.

Art. 6   Chairmanship

The Commission shall select a chairman from among its members.

Art. 7   Voting

Every member of the Commission shall have one vote, and shall issue its recommendations or opinions on matters referred to it by majority of the members. In case of a tie, the party with chairman vote shall prevail.

Art. 8   Commission's Secretariat

a.   The Secretary-General shall appoint a recorder for the Commission, and a sufficient number of employees to carry out the secretarial work.

b.   The Supreme Council may create an independent organization to carry out the Commission's secretarial work when the need arises.

Art. 9   Recommendations & Opinions

a.   The Commission shall issue its recommendations or opinions in accordance with the Cooperation Council's Charter, international laws and practices, and the principles of Islamic Shari'ah. The Commission shall submit its findings on the case on hand to the Supreme Council for appropriate action.

b.   The Commission may, while considering any dispute referred to it and pending the issue of its final recommendations thereon, ask the Supreme Council to take interim action called for by necessity or circumstances.

    c.   The Commission's recommendations or opinions shall spell out the reasons on which they were based and shall be signed by the chairman and recorder.

    d.   If an opinion is passed wholly or partially by unanimous vote of the members, the dissenting members shall be entitled to document their dissenting opinion.

Art. 10   Immunities and Privileges

The Commission and its members shall enjoy such immunities and privileges in the territories of the member states as are required to realize its objectives and in accordance with Article Seventeen of the Cooperation Council Charter.

Art. 11   Commission's Budget

The Commission's budget shall be considered part of the Secretariat General's budget. Remunerations of the Commission's members shall be established by the Supreme Council.

Art. 12   Amendments

    a.   Any member state may request for amendments of these Rules of Procedures.

    b.   Requests for amendments shall be submitted to the Secretary-General who shall relay them to the member states by at least four months before submission to the Ministerial Council.

    c.   An amendment shall be effective if approved unanimously by the Supreme Council.

Art. 13   Effective Date

These rules of procedures shall go into effect as of the date of approval by the Supreme Council.

These Rules of Procedures were signed at Abu Dhabi City, United Arab Emirates on 21 Rajab 1401 AH corresponding to 25 May 1981 AD.

4. Asia

Association of Southeast Asian Nations (ASEAN)

The Association of Southeast Asian Nations (ASEAN) was founded in 1967 by five States (Indonesia, Malaysia, the Philippines, Singapore and Thailand, Brunei joining in 1985 and Vietnam in 1995) in order to develop intra-regional cooperation and to "accelerate the economic growth, social progress and cultural development in the region through joint endeavors in spirit of equality and partnership". It was, however, not conceived as an economic cooperation agreement with an institutionalized organization, but developed and institutionalized through a series of Declarations. Formal economic integration was not a main topic of ASEAN until the Third Summit in 1987, when an Agreement for the Promotion and Protection of Investments containing a dispute settlement clause was adopted; serious steps toward a real economic integration were, however, not taken until the Fourth Summit at Singapore in 1992, when ASEAN committed itself to creating a free-trade area (AFTA). At this Summit the ASEAN member States signed three documents: the Singapore Declaration of 1992, the Framework Agreement for Enhancing the ASEAN Economic Cooperation and the Agreement on the Common Effective Preferential Tariff (CEPT) Scheme for the ASEAN Free Trade Area (AFTA). The ASEAN member states recognised and agreed to accomplish the full establishment and functioning of AFTA within 15 years (by 2008) and agreed that the main mechanism for improving trade amongst the member states was the Common Effective Preferential Tariff (CEPT). AFTA may be considered as a direct response to the formation of other territorial organisations such as i.e. NAFTA and the European Union. AFTA was therefore conceived to protect the collective economic interest of ASEAN. The instruments adopted within the framework of ASEAN provided only in general for dispute settlement without creating a detailed system (Art. 9 of the AFTA Framework Agreement and Art. 8 of the CEPT Agreement) envisioning AFTA disputes as government-to-government disputes which were expected to be resolved by consultation amongst themselves. If an amicable solution was not reached by the parties, the AFTA Council was to help the parties to resolve the dispute. This structure of dispute settlement was recognized as not being satisfactory, however, a formal dispute settlement system seemed "unthinkable" with a view to the ASEAN'S abhorrence of legalistic approaches. Nevertheless, finally the ASEAN Economic Ministers agreed on the creation of an AFTA dispute settlement system in 1996. In 1996, the Protocol on Dispute Settlement Mechanism was signed, which is applicable to the CEPT Agreement as well as other agreements on economic cooperation in ASEAN. This mechanism took the WTO Dispute Settlement

System as a model, however according to ASEAN tradition it leaves the way open for an amicable settlement until the panel is established.

Texts

Treaty of Amity and Cooperation: ILM 27 (1988), 610

Agreement for Promotion and Protection of Investments of 1987: ILM 27 (1988), 612

Framework Agreement on Enhancing ASEAN Economic Cooperation of 1992: ILM 31 (1992), 506

Agreement on the Common Effective Preferential Tariff (CEPT) of 1992: ILM 31 (1992), 514

Protocol on Dispute Settlement Mechanism: http://www.aseansec.org/economic/dsm.html

Bibliographical notes

J. A. Kaplan, ASEAN's Rubicon: a dispute settlement mechanism for AFTA, UCLA Pacific Basin Law Journal 14 (1996), 147-195

M. S. Goeltom, Asia's economic prospects in the 21st century and the role of AFTA, The Indonesian Quarterly 25 (1997), 276-301

J. I. Garvey, AFTA after NAFTA: regional trade blocs and the propagation of environmental and labor standards, Berkeley Journal of International Law 15 (1997), 245-274

V. K. Aggarwai/C. E. Morrison, Asia-Pacific Crossroads, Regime Creation and the Future of Apec (1998)

M. Dutta, Economic Regionalization in the Asia-Pacific (1998)

F. Fletcher, The ASEAN Free Trade Area and the necessity for the creation of a legal mechanism for resolving private disputes of an international nature, The Journal of Business Law, 1998, March, 213-216

a) Agreements and Statements from the Third Summit of December 14-15, 1987

aa) Treaty of Amity and Cooperation of July 15, 1976 as amended in 1987

CHAPTER IV — PACIFIC SETTLEMENT OF DISPUTES

Art. 13   The High Contracting Parties shall have the determination and good faith to prevent disputes from arising. In case disputes on matters directly affecting them should arise, especially disputes likely to disturb regional peace and harmony, they shall refrain from the threat or use of force and shall at all times settle such disputes among themselves through friendly negotiations.

Art. 14   To settle disputes through regional processes, the High Contracting Parties shall constitute, as a continuing body, a High Council comprising a Representative at ministerial level from each of the High Contracting Parties to take cognizance of the existence of disputes or situations likely to disturb regional peace and harmony.

Art. 15   In the event no solution is reached through direct negotiations, the High Council shall take cognizance of the dispute or the situation and shall recommend to the parties in dispute appropriate means of settlement such as good offices, mediation, inquiry or conciliation. The High Council may however offer its good offices, or upon agreement of the parties in dispute, constitute itself into a committee of mediation, inquiry or conciliation. When deemed necessary, the High Council shall recommend appropriate measures for the prevention of a deterioration of the dispute or the situation.

Art. 16   The foregoing provisions of this Chapter shall not apply to a dispute unless all the parties to the dispute agree to their application to that dispute. However, this shall not preclude the other High Contracting Parties not party to the dispute from offering all possible assistance to settle the said dispute. Parties to the dispute should be well disposed towards such offer of assistance.

Art. 17   Nothing in this Treaty shall preclude recourse to the modes of peaceful settlement contained in Article 33 (1) of the Charter of the United Nations. The High Contracting Parties which are parties to a dispute should be encouraged to take initiatives to solve it by friendly negotiations before resorting to the other procedures provided for in the Charter of the United Nations.

bb) Agreement for the Promotion and Protection of Investments; Arts. IX, X and XI

Art. IX   Disputes between the Contracting Parties

1) Any dispute between and among the Contracting Parties concerning the interpretation of this Agreement shall, as far as possible, be settled amicably between the parties to the dispute. Such settlement shall be reported to the ASEAN Economic Ministers (AEM)

2) If such a dispute cannot thus be settled it shall be submitted to the AEM for resolution.

Art. X   Arbitration

1) Any legal dispute arising directly out of an investment between any Contracting Party and a national or company of any of the other Contracting Parties shall, as far as possible, be settled amicably between the parties to the dispute.

2) If such a dispute cannot thus be settled within six months of its being raised, then either party can elect to submit the dispute for conciliation or arbitration and such election shall be binding on the other party. The dispute may be brought before the International Centre for Settlement of Investment Disputes (ICSID), the United Nations Commission on International Trade Law (UNCITRAL), the Regional Centre for Arbitration at Kuala Lumpur or any other regional centre for arbitration in ASEAN whichever body the parties to the dispute mutually agree to appoint for the purposes of conducting the arbitration.

3) In the event that the parties cannot agree within a period of three months on a suitable body for arbitration, an arbitral tribunal consisting of three members shall be formed. The parties to the dispute shall appoint one member each, and these two members shall then select a national of a third Contracting Party to be the chairman of the Tribunal, subject to the approval of the parties to the dispute. The appointment of the members and the chairman shall be made within two months and three months respectively, from the date a decision to form such an arbitral tribunal is made

4) If the arbitral tribunal is not formed in the periods specified in paragraph 3 above, then either party to the dispute may, in the absence of any other relevant arrangement, request the President of the International Court of Justice to make the required appointments.

5) The arbitral tribunal shall reach its decision by a majority of votes and its decisions shall be binding. The Parties involved in the dispute shall bear the cost of their respective members to the arbitral tribunal and share equally the cost of the chairman and other relevant costs. In all other respects, the arbitral tribunal shall determine its own procedures.

Art. XI   Consultation

The Contracting Parties agree to consult each other at the request of any Party on any matter relating to investments covered by this Agreement, or otherwise affecting the implementation of this Agreement.

b) Agreements from the Fourth Summit of January 28, 1992

aa) Framework Agreement on Enhancing ASEAN Economic Cooperation, Article 9

Art. 9   Settlement of Disputes

Any differences between the Member States concerning the interpretation or application of this Agreement or any arrangements arising therefrom shall, as far as possible, be settled amicably between the parties. Whenever necessary, an appropriate body shall be designated for the settlement of disputes.

bb) Agreement on the Common Preferential Tariff, Article 8

Art. 8   Consultations

1. Member States shall accord adequate opportunity for consultations regarding any representations made by other Member States with respect to any matter affecting the implementation of this Agreement. The Council referred to in Article 7 of this Agreement, may seek guidance from the AEM [ASEAN Economic Ministers] in respect of any matter for which it has not been possible to find a satisfactory solution during previous consultations.

2. Member States, which consider that any other Member State has not carried out its obligations under this Agreement, resulting in the nullification or impairment of any benefit accruing to them, may, with a view to achieving satisfactory adjustment of the matter, make representations or proposals to the other Member States concerned, which shall give due consideration to the representations or proposals made to it.

3. Any differences between Member States concerning the interpretation or application of this Agreement shall, as far as possible, be settled amicably between the parties. If such differences cannot be settled amicably, it shall be submitted to the Council referred to in Article 7 of this Agreement, and, if necessary, to the AEM.

cc) Protocol on Dispute Settlement Mechanism

The Governments of Brunei Darussalam, the Republic of Indonesia, Malaysia, the Republic of the Philippines, the Republic of Singapore, the Kingdom of Thailand and the Socialist Republic of Vietnam, Member States of the Association of South East Asian Nations (ASEAN);

Recalling the Framework Agreement on Enhancing ASEAN Economic Cooperation signed in Singapore on 28 January 1992, as amended by the Protocol to Amend the Framework Agreement on Enhancing ASEAN Economic Cooperation signed in Bangkok on 15 December 1995 (the "Agreement");

Recognizing the need to expand Article 9 of the Agreement to strengthen the mechanism for the settlement of disputes in the area of ASEAN economic cooperation;

Have agreed as follows :

Art. 1   Coverage and Application

1. The rules and procedures of this Protocol shall apply to disputes brought pursuant to the consultation and dispute settlement provisions of the Agreement as well as the agreements listed in Appendix 1 and future ASEAN economic agreements (the "covered agreements").

2. The rules and procedures of this Protocol shall apply subject to such special or additional rules and procedures on dispute settlement contained in the covered agreements. To the extent that there is a difference between the rules and procedures of this Protocol and the special or additional rules and procedures in the covered agreements, the special or additional rules and procedures shall prevail.

3. The provisions of this Protocol are without prejudice to the rights of Member States to seek recourse to other fora for the settlement of disputes involving other Member States. A Member State involved in a dispute can resort to other fora at any stage before the Senior Economic Officials Meeting ("SEOM") has made a ruling on the panel report.

Art. 2   Consultations

1. Member States shall accord adequate opportunity for consultations regarding any representations made by other Member States with respect to any matter affecting the implementation, interpretation or application of the Agreement or any covered agreement. Any differences shall, as far as possible, be settled amicably between the Member States.

2. Member States which consider that any benefit accruing to them directly or indirectly, under the Agreement or any covered agreement is being nullified or impaired, or that the attainment of any objective of the Agreement or any covered agreement is being impeded as a result of failure of another Member State to carry out its obligations under the Agreement or any covered agreement, or the existence of any other situa-

tion may, with a view to achieving satisfactory settlement of the matter, make representations or proposals to the other Member State concerned, which shall give due consideration to the representations or proposals made to it.

3. If a request for consultations is made, the Member State to which the request is made shall reply to the request within ten (10) days after the date of its receipt and shall enter into consultations within a period of no more than thirty (30) days after the date of receipt of the request, with a view to reaching a mutually satisfactory solution.

Art. 3   Good Offices, Conciliation or Mediation

1. Member States which are parties to a dispute may at any time agree to good offices, conciliation or mediation. They may begin at any time and be terminated at any time. Once procedures for good offices, conciliation or mediation are terminated, a complaining party may then proceed to raise the matter to SEOM.

2. If the parties to a dispute agree, procedures for good offices, conciliation or mediation may continue while the dispute proceeds.

Art. 4   Senior Economic Officials Meeting

1. If the consultations fail to settle a dispute within sixty (60) days after the date of receipt of the request for consultations, the matter shall be raised to the SEOM.

2. The SEOM shall:

a)   establish a panel; or

b)   where applicable, raise the matter to the special body in charge of the special or additional rules and procedures for its consideration.

3. Notwithstanding Article 4 paragraph 2, if the SEOM considers it desirable to do so in a particular case, it may decide to deal with the dispute to achieve an amicable settlement without appointing a panel. This step shall be taken without any extension of the thirty (30)-day period in Article 5 paragraph 2.

Art. 5   Establishment of Panel

1. The function of the panel is to make an objective assessment of the dispute before it, including an examination of the facts of the case and the applicability of and conformity with the sections of the Agreement or any covered agreement, and make such other findings as will assist the SEOM in making the rulings provided for under the Agreement or any covered agreement.

2. The SEOM shall establish a panel no later than thirty (30) days after the date on which the dispute has been raised to it.

3. The SEOM shall make the final determination of the size, composition and terms of reference of the panel.

Art. 6   Function of the Panel

1. The panel shall, apart from the matters covered in Appendix 2, regulate its own procedures in relation to the rights of parties to be heard and its deliberations.

2. The panel shall submit its findings to the SEOM within sixty (60) days of its formation. In exceptional cases, the panel may take an additional ten (10) days to submit its findings to SEOM. Within this time period, the panel shall accord adequate opportunity to the parties to the dispute to review the report before submission.

3. The panel shall have the right to seek information and technical advice from any individual or body which it deems appropriate. A Member State should respond promptly and fully to any request by a panel for such information as the panel considers necessary and appropriate.

4. Panel deliberations shall be confidential. The reports of panels shall be drafted without the presence of the parties to the dispute in the light of the information provided and the statements made.

Art. 7   Treatment of Panel Result

The SEOM shall consider the report of the panel in its deliberations and make a ruling on the dispute within thirty (30) days from the submission of the report by the panel. In exceptional cases, SEOM may take an additional ten (10) days to make a ruling on the dispute. SEOM representatives from Member States which are parties to a dispute can be present during the process of deliberation but shall not participate in the ruling of SEOM. SEOM shall make a ruling based on simple majority.

Art. 8   Appeal

1. Member States, who are parties to the dispute, may appeal the ruling by the SEOM to the ASEAN Economic Ministers ("AEM") within thirty (30) days of the ruling.

2. The AEM shall make a decision within thirty (30) days of the appeal. In exceptional cases, AEM may take an additional ten (10) days to make a decision on the dispute. Economic Ministers from Member States which are parties to a dispute can be present during the process of deliberation but shall not participate in the decision of AEM. AEM shall make a decision based on simple majority. The decision of the AEM on the appeal shall be final and binding on all parties to the dispute.

3. Since prompt compliance with the rulings of the SEOM or decisions of the AEM is essential in order to ensure effective resolution of disputes, Member States who are parties to the dispute shall comply with the ruling or decision, as the case may be, within a reasonable time period. The reasonable period of time shall be a period of time mutually agreed to by the parties to the dispute but under no circumstances should it exceed thirty (30) days from the SEOM's ruling or in the event of an appeal thirty (30) days from the AEM's decision. The Member States concerned shall provide the SEOM or the AEM, as the case may be, with a status report in writing of their progress in the implementation of the ruling or decision.

Art. 9   Compensation and the Suspension of Concessions

1. If the Member State concerned fails to bring the measure found to be inconsistent with the Agreement or any covered agreement into compliance therewith or otherwise comply with SEOM's rulings or AEM's decisions within the reasonable period of time, such Member State shall, if so requested, and no later than the expiry of the reasonable period of time, enter into negotiations with any party having invoked the dispute settlement procedures, with a view to developing mutually acceptable compensation. If no satisfactory compensation has been agreed within 20 (twenty) days after the date of expiry of the reasonable period of time, any party having invoked the dispute settlement procedures may request authorization from the AEM to suspend the application to the Member State concerned of concessions or other obligations under the Agreement or any covered agreements.

2. However, neither compensation nor the suspension of concessions or other obligations is preferred to full implementation of a recommendation to bring a measure into conformity with the Agreement or any covered agreements.

Art. 10   Maximum Time-Frame

Member States agree that the total period for the disposal of a dispute pursuant to Articles 2, 4, 5, 6, 7, 8 and 9 of this Protocol shall not exceed two hundred and ninety (290) days.

Art. 11   Responsibilities of the Secretariat

1. The ASEAN Secretariat shall have the responsibility of assisting the panels, especially on the historical and procedural aspects of the matters dealt with, and of providing secretarial and technical support.

2. The ASEAN Secretariat shall have the responsibility of monitoring and maintaining under surveillance the implementation of the SEOM's ruling and AEM's decision as the case may be.

3. The ASEAN Secretariat may offer good offices, conciliation or mediation with the view to assisting Members to settle a dispute.

Art. 12   Final Provisions

1. This Protocol shall be deposited with the Secretary-General of ASEAN who shall promptly furnish a certified copy thereof to each Member State.

2. This Protocol shall enter into force upon the deposit of instruments of ratification or acceptance by all signatory governments with the Secretary-General of ASEAN.

In Witness Whereof, the undersigned, being duly authorized thereto by their respective Governments, have signed the Protocol on Dispute Settlement Mechanism.

Done at Manila, this 20th day of November 1996 in a single copy in the English Language.

APPENDIX 1 — COVERED AGREEMENTS

1. Multilateral Agreement on Commercial Rights of Non-Scheduled Services among ASEAN, Manila, 13 March 1971.

2. Agreement on ASEAN Preferential Trading Arrangements, Manila, 24 February 1977.

3. Memorandum of Understanding on the ASEAN Swap Arrangements, Kuala Lumpur, 5 August 1977.

4. Supplementary Agreement to the Memorandum of Understanding on the ASEAN Swap Arrangement, Washington D.C., 26 September 1978.

5. Second Supplementary Agreement to the Memorandum of Understanding on the ASEAN Swap Arrangement, Denpasar, Bali, 9 September 1979.

6. Agreement on the ASEAN Food Security Reserve, New York, 4 October 1979.

7. Basic Agreement on ASEAN Industrial Projects, Kuala Lumpur, 6 March 1980.

8. Supplementary Agreement of the Basic Agreement on ASEAN Industrial Projects ASEAN Urea Project (Indonesia), Kuala Lumpur, 6 March 1980.

9. Supplementary Agreement of the Basic Agreement on ASEAN Industrial Projects ASEAN Urea Project (Malaysia), Kuala Lumpur, 6 March 1980.

10. Amendments to the Memorandum of Understanding on the ASEAN Swap Arrangement Colombo, Sri Lanka, 16 January 1981.

11. Basic Agreement on ASEAN Industrial Complementation, Manila, 18 June 1981.

12. Third Supplementary Agreement to the Memorandum of Understanding on the ASEAN Swap Arrangement, Bangkok, 4 February 1982.

13. ASEAN Ministerial Understanding on Plant Quarantine Ring, Kuala Lumpur, 8-9 October 1982.

14. ASEAN Ministerial Understanding on the Standardization of Import and Quarantine Regulation on Animal and Animal Products, Kuala Lumpur, 8-9 October 1982.

15. Protocol to Amend the Agreement on the ASEAN Food Security Reserve, Bangkok, 22 October 1982.

16. ASEAN Customs Code of Conduct, Jakarta, 18 March 1983.

17. ASEAN Ministerial Understanding on Fisheries Cooperation, Singapore, 20-22 October 1983.

18. Basic Agreement on ASEAN Industrial Joint Ventures, Jakarta, 7 November 1983.

19. ASEAN Ministerial Understanding on ASEAN Cooperation in Agricultural Cooperatives, Manila, 4-5 October 1984.

20. ASEAN Ministerial Understanding on Plant Pest Free Zone, Manila, 4-5 October 1984.

21. Agreement on ASEAN Energy Cooperation, Manila, 24 June 1986.

22. ASEAN Petroleum Security Agreement, Manila, 24 June 1986.

23. Agreement on the Preferential Shortlisting of ASEAN Contractors, Jakarta, 20 October 1986.

24. Supplementary Agreement to the Basic Agreement on ASEAN Industrial Joint Ventures, Singapore, 16 June 1987.

25. Fourth Supplementary Agreement to the Memorandum of Understanding on the ASEAN Swap Arrangement, Kathmandu, Nepal, 21 January 1987.

26. Protocol on Improvements on Extensions of Tariff Preferences under the ASEAN Preferential Trading Arrangement, Manila, 15 December 1987.

27. Memorandum of Understanding on Standstill and Rollback on Non-Tariff Barriers among ASEAN Countries, Manila, 15 December 1987.

28. Revised Basic Agreement on ASEAN Industrial Joint Ventures, Manila, 15 December 1987.

29. Agreement Among the Government of Brunei Darussalam, the Republic of Indonesia, Malaysia, the Republic of the Philippines, the Republic of Singapore, and the Kingdom of Thailand for the Promotion and Protection of Investments, Manila, 15 December 1987.

30. Protocol on Improvements on Extension of Tariff Preferences under the ASEAN Preferential Trading Arrangement, Manila, 15 December 1987.

31. Agreement on the Establishment of the ASEAN Tourism Information Centre, Kuala Lumpur, 26 September 1988.

32. Financial Regulations of the ASEAN Tourism Information Centre, Kuala Lumpur, 26 September 1988.

33. Memorandum of Understanding Brand-to-Brand Complementation on the Automotive Industry Under the Basic Agreement on ASEAN Industrial Complementation (BAAIC), Pattaya, Thailand, 18 October 1988.

34. Protocol to Amend the Revised Basic Agreement on ASEAN Industrial Joint Ventures, 1 January 1991.

35. Supplementary Agreement to the Basic Agreement on ASEAN industrial Projects - ASEAN Potash Mining Projects (Thailand), Kuala Lumpur, 20 July 1991.

36. Agreement on the Common Effective Preferential Tariff Scheme for the ASEAN Free Trade Area, Singapore, 28 January 1992.

37. Second Protocol to Amend the Revised Basic Agreement on ASEAN Industrial Joint Ventures, Manila, 23 October 1992.

38. Ministerial Understanding on ASEAN Cooperation in Food, Agriculture and Forestry, Bandar Seri Begawan, 28-30 October 1993.

39. Memorandum of Understanding on ASEAN Cooperation and Joint Approaches in Agriculture and Forest Products Promotion Scheme, Langkawi, Malaysia, 1994.

40. Third Protocol to Amend the Revised Basic Agreement on ASEAN Industrial Joint Ventures, 2 March 1995.

41. Protocol to Amend the Agreement on the Common Effective Preferential Tariff (CEPT) Scheme for the ASEAN Free Trade Area (AFTA), Bangkok, 15 December 1995.

42. Protocol to Amend the Agreement on ASEAN Preferential Trading Arrangements, Bangkok, 15 December 1995.

43. ASEAN Framework Agreement on Services, Bangkok, 15 December 1995.

44. ASEAN Framework Agreement on Intellectual Property Cooperation, Bangkok, 15 December 1995.

45. Protocol Amending the Agreement on ASEAN Energy Cooperation, Bangkok, 15 December 1995.

46. Basic Agreement on ASEAN Industrial Cooperation, Singapore, 26 April 1996.

47. Protocol to Amend the Agreement Among the Government of Brunei Darussalam, the Republic of Indonesia, Malaysia, the Republic of the Philippines, the Republic of Singapore, and the Kingdom of Thailand for the Promotion and Protection of Investments, Jakarta, 12 September 1996.

APPENDIX 2 — WORKING PROCEDURES OF THE PANEL

I. COMPOSITION OF PANELS

1. Panels shall be composed of well-qualified governmental and/or nongovernmental individuals, including persons who have served on or presented a case to a panel, served in the Secretariat, taught or published on international trade law or policy, or served as a senior trade policy official of a Member State. In the nomination to the panels, preference shall be given to individuals who are nationals of ASEAN Member States.

2. Panel members should be selected with a view to ensuring the independence of the members, a sufficiently diverse background and a wide spectrum of experience.

3. Nationals of Member States whose governments are parties to the dispute shall not serve on a panel concerned with that dispute, unless the parties to the dispute agree otherwise.

4. To assist in the selection of panelists, the Secretariat shall maintain an indicative list of governmental and non-governmental individuals possessing the qualifications outlined in paragraph 1, from which panelists may be drawn as appropriate. Members may periodically suggest names

of governmental and non-governmental individuals for inclusion on the indicative list, providing relevant information on their knowledge of international trade and of the sectors or subject matter of the covered agreements, and those names shall be added to the list upon approval by the SEOM. For each of the individuals on the list, the list shall indicate specific areas of experience or expertise of the individuals in the sectors or subject matter of the covered agreements.

5. Panels shall be composed of three panelists unless the parties to the dispute agree, within 10 days from the establishment of the panel, to a panel composed of five panelists. Members shall be informed promptly of the composition of the panel.

6. The Secretariat shall propose nominations for the panel to the parties to the dispute. The parties to the dispute shall not oppose nominations except for compelling reasons.

7. If there is no agreement on the panelists within 20 days after the date of the establishment of a panel, at the request of either party, the Secretary-General, in consultation with the SEOM Chairman, shall determine the composition of the panel by appointing the panelists whom the Secretary-General considers most appropriate in accordance with any relevant special or additional rules or procedures of the covered agreement or covered agreements which are at issue in the dispute, after consulting with the parties to the dispute. The SEOM Chairman shall inform the Members of the composition of the panel thus formed no later than 10 days after the date the Chairman receives such a request.

8. Member States shall undertake, as a general rule, to permit their officials to serve as panelists.

9. Panelists shall serve in their individual capacities and not as government representatives, nor as representatives of any organization. Member States shall therefore not give them instructions nor seek to influence them as individuals with regard to matters before a panel.

II. PANEL PROCEEDINGS

1. In its proceedings the panel shall follow the relevant provisions of this Protocol. In addition, the following working procedures shall apply.

2. The panel shall meet in closed session. The parties to the dispute, and interested parties, shall be present at the meetings only when invited by the panel to appear before it.

3. The deliberations of the panel and the documents submitted to it shall be kept confidential. Nothing in this Protocol shall preclude a party to a dispute from disclosing statements of its own positions to the public. Member States shall treat as confidential information submitted by another Member State to the panel which that Member State has designated as confidential. Where a party to a dispute submits a confidential version of its written submissions to the panel, it shall also, upon request of a

Member State, provide a non-confidential summary of the information contained in its submissions that could be disclosed to the public.

4. Before the first substantive meeting of the panel with the parties, the parties to the dispute shall transmit to the panel written submissions in which they present the facts of the case and their arguments.

5. At its first substantive meeting with the parties, the panel shall ask the party which has brought the complaint to present its case. Subsequently, and still at the same meeting, the party against which the complaint has been brought shall be asked to present its point of view.

6. Formal rebuttals shall be made at a second substantive meeting of the panel. The party complained against shall have the right to take the floor first to be followed by the complaining party. The parties shall submit, prior to that meeting, written rebuttals to the panel.

7. The panel may at any time put questions to the parties and ask them for explanations either in the course of a meeting with the parties or in writing.

8. The parties to the dispute shall make available to the panel a written version of their oral statements.

9. In the interest of full transparency, the presentations, rebuttals and statements referred to in paragraphs 5 to 9 shall be made in the presence of the parties. Moreover, each party's written submissions, including any comments on the descriptive part of the report and responses to questions put by the panel, shall be made available to the other party or parties.

10. Any additional procedures specific to the panel.

Printing: Weihert-Druck GmbH, Darmstadt
Binding: Buchbinderei Schäffer, Grünstadt